ELEVENTH EDITION

Programming iOS 14
Dive Deep into Views, View Controllers, and Frameworks

Matt Neuburg

Beijing · Boston · Farnham · Sebastopol · Tokyo

Programming iOS 14, Eleventh Edition

by Matt Neuburg

Copyright © 2021 Matt Neuburg. All rights reserved.

Printed in Canada.

Published by O'Reilly Media, Inc., 1005 Gravenstein Highway North, Sebastopol, CA 95472.

O'Reilly books may be purchased for educational, business, or sales promotional use. Online editions are also available for most titles (*http://oreilly.com*). For more information, contact our corporate/institutional sales department: 800-998-9938 or *corporate@oreilly.com*.

Editors: Rachel Roumeliotis and Suzanne McQuade	**Indexer:** Matt Neuburg
Production Editor: Kristen Brown	**Cover Designer:** Karen Montgomery
Proofreader: O'Reilly Production Services	**Interior Designer:** David Futato
Illustrator: Matt Neuburg	

November 2015:	Sixth Edition
November 2016:	Seventh Edition
December 2017:	Eighth Edition
October 2018:	Ninth Edition
October 2019:	Tenth Edition
October 2020:	Eleventh Edition

Revision History for the Eleventh Edition:

2020-10-08:   First release

See *http://oreilly.com/catalog/errata.csp?isbn=9781492092179* for release details.

The O'Reilly logo is a registered trademark of O'Reilly Media, Inc. *Programming iOS 14*, the cover image of a kingbird, and related trade dress are trademarks of O'Reilly Media, Inc.

Many of the designations used by manufacturers and sellers to distinguish their products are claimed as trademarks. Where those designations appear in this book, and O'Reilly Media, Inc., was aware of a trademark claim, the designations have been printed in caps or initial caps.

While the publisher and the author have used good faith efforts to ensure that the information and instructions contained in this work are accurate, the publisher and the author disclaim all responsibility for errors or omissions, including without limitation responsibility for damages resulting from the use of or reliance on this work. Use of the information and instructions contained in this work is at your own risk. If any code samples or other technology this work contains or describes is subject to open source licenses or the intellectual property rights of others, it is your responsibility to ensure that your use thereof complies with such licenses and/or rights.

978-1-492-09217-9

[MBP]

Table of Contents

Part II.   Interface

Part III. Some Frameworks

Part IV.   Final Topics

Preface

Aut lego vel scribo; doceo scrutorve sophian.
—Sedulius Scottus

Back in 2005, when Apple started to contemplate making the iPhone programmable, there was already a well-established mature application programming interface (API) for programming the Mac — Cocoa. Therefore, as the iPhone grew to fruition, the core Cocoa frameworks were adapted for it, forming Cocoa Touch. The Foundation framework, containing basic classes like NSString and NSArray, was migrated to the phone more or less unchanged; AppKit, containing interface classes like NSWindow and NSView, was simplified and rationalized to form UIKit, with classes such as UIViewController and UIView. Cocoa Touch was made available to developers in 2008, and has been the main way to program Apple's mobile devices ever since.

The language that developers used for Cocoa Touch programming was originally Objective-C. But in July of 2010, Chris Lattner created a folder on his computer called *Shiny,* and a new computer language was born. Four years later, in 2014, that language, renamed Swift, was offered to developers as an alternative way of programming iOS. Since then, the Swift language has attained a high degree of maturity. Among other things, it has achieved ABI stability, which means that it has become part of the system. Swift apps are smaller and faster than ever. It is fair to assume that, for the vast majority of iOS programmers, Swift is the language of choice.

This book, then, is about programming iOS, the system that powers the iPhone and iPad, using the Swift programming language to interface with Cocoa Touch and UIKit.

Even when you're writing in Swift, some awareness of Objective-C (including C) can still be useful. The Foundation and Cocoa APIs are still written in Objective-C and C. So when you're programming Cocoa, a major part of Swift's job is to interact with those languages. In order to do that, you might need to know something about what those languages would expect. So I do refer to Objective-C and C from time to time, even though the book contains no actual Objective-C code.

This book does not discuss SwiftUI. SwiftUI is a relatively new framework, first released in 2019, that makes it possible to program iOS without reference to Cocoa Touch and the UIKit framework. In SwiftUI, there are no UIViews and no UIView-Controllers. Data flow helps to ensure that the interface coherently reflects the state of the app. And the same code, for the most part, works on multiple platforms, not just the iPhone and iPad, but also the Apple Watch and the Mac desktop. Nevertheless, in the real world, UIKit is by no means superseded; programming Cocoa Touch and UIKit remains the primary subject of this book.

The Scope of This Book

Programming iOS 14 is the second of a pair with my other book, *iOS 14 Programming Fundamentals with Swift*; it picks up where the other book leaves off. If writing an iOS program is like building a house of bricks, *iOS 14 Programming Fundamentals with Swift* teaches you what a brick is and how to handle it, while *Programming iOS 14* hands you some actual bricks and tells you how to assemble them.

So this book, like Homer's *Iliad*, begins in the middle of the story. The reader is expected to jump with all four feet into views and view controllers. Topics such as the Swift programming language, the Xcode IDE, including the nature of nibs, outlets, and actions, and the mechanics of nib loading, and the fundamental conventions, classes, and architectures of the Cocoa Touch framework, including delegation, the responder chain, key–value coding, key–value observing, memory management, and so on, were all taught in *iOS 14 Programming Fundamentals with Swift*.

So if something appears to be missing from this book, that's why! If you start reading *Programming iOS 14* and wonder about such unexplained matters as Swift language basics, Xcode usage, the UIApplicationMain function, the nib-loading mechanism, Cocoa patterns of delegation and notification, and retain cycles, wonder no longer! I don't explain them here because I have already explained them in *iOS 14 Programming Fundamentals with Swift*. If you're not conversant with those topics, you might want to read that book first; you will then be completely ready for this one.

Here's a summary of the major sections of *Programming iOS 14:*

- Part I describes views, the fundamental units of an iOS app's interface. Views are what the user can see and touch in an iOS app. To make something appear before the user's eyes, you need a view. To let the user interact with your app, you need a view. This part of the book explains how views are created, arranged, drawn, layered, animated, and touched.

- Part II starts by discussing view controllers. Perhaps the most important aspect of Cocoa programming, view controllers enable views to come and go coherently within the interface, allowing a single-windowed app running on what may be a tiny screen to contain multiple screens of material. View controllers are used to manage interface and to respond to user actions; most of your app's code will be in a view controller. This part of the book talks about how view controllers work, and the major built-in types of view controller that Cocoa gives you. It also describes every kind of view provided by the UIKit framework — the primary building blocks with which you'll construct an app's interface.

- Part III surveys the most commonly used frameworks provided by iOS. These are clumps of code, sometimes with built-in interface, that are not part of your app by default, but are there for the asking if you need them, allowing you to work with such things as sound, video, user libraries, maps, and the device's sensors.

- Part IV wraps up the book with some miscellaneous but significant topics: files, networking, threading, and how to implement undo.

- Appendix A summarizes the basic lifetime event messages sent to your app.

- Appendix B catalogs some useful utility functions that I've written. My example code takes advantage of these functions, so you should keep an eye on this appendix, consulting it whenever a mysterious method name appears.

- Appendix C is an excursus discussing an often misunderstood aspect of iOS programming: asynchronous code.

Someone who has read this book and is conversant with the material in *iOS 14 Programming Fundamentals with Swift* should be capable of writing a real-life iOS app with a clear understanding of the underlying fundamentals and techniques and a good sense of where the app is going as it grows and develops. The book itself doesn't show how to write any particularly interesting iOS apps, but it is backed by dozens of example projects that you can download from my GitHub site, *http://github.com/mattneub/Programming-iOS-Book-Examples*, and it uses my own real apps and real programming situations to illustrate and motivate its explanations.

What's Not in This Book

iOS programming is a vast subject. I can't possibly cover it all, so this book is intended to prepare you for your own further explorations. Certain chapters, especially in Parts III and IV, introduce a topic, providing an initial basic survey of its concepts, its capabilities, and its documentation, along with some code examples; but the topic itself may be far more extensive. My goal is to set your feet firmly on the path; after reading the discussion here, you'll be equipped to proceed on your own whenever the need or interest arises.

In addition, many entire areas of iOS have had to be excluded from this book entirely:

SpriteKit

SpriteKit provides a built-in framework for designing 2D animated games.

SceneKit

Ported from macOS, the SceneKit framework makes it much easier to create 3D games and interactive graphics.

GameplayKit

This framework provides the architectural underpinnings for writing a game app.

Metal

Metal performs intensive computation, especially for 3D graphics It supersedes OpenGL and GLKit.

GameKit

The GameKit framework covers areas that can enhance your user's multiplayer game experience, such as peer-to-peer device communication (including voice communication) and Game Center.

Printing

See the "Printing" chapter of Apple's *Drawing and Printing Guide for iOS.*

Security

This book does not discuss security topics such as keychains, certificates, and encryption. See Apple's *Security Overview* and the Security framework.

Accessibility

VoiceOver assists visually impaired users by describing the interface aloud. To participate, views must be configured to describe themselves usefully. Built-in views already do this to a large extent, and you can extend this functionality. See Apple's *Accessibility Programming Guide for iOS.*

Telephone

The Core Telephony framework lets your app get information about a particular cellular carrier and call. CallKit allows VoIP apps to integrate with the built-in Phone app.

PassKit

The PassKit framework allows creation of downloadable passes to go into the user's Wallet app.

HealthKit

The HealthKit framework lets your app obtain, store, share, and present data and statistics related to body activity and exercise.

Externalities

The user can attach an external accessory to the device, either directly via USB or wirelessly via Bluetooth. Your app can communicate with such an accessory. See Apple's *External Accessory Programming Topics*. The HomeKit framework lets the user communicate with devices in the physical world, such as light switches and door locks. This book also doesn't discuss iBeacon or near field communication (the Core NFC framework).

Handoff

Handoff permits your app to communicate a record of what the user is doing, so that the user can switch to another copy of your app on another device and resume doing the same thing. See Apple's *Handoff Programming Guide*.

Spotlight

The user's Spotlight search results can include data supplied by your app. See Apple's *App Search Programming Guide*.

SiriKit

The SiriKit framework lets you configure your app so that the user can talk to the device to tell it what to do.

Augmented Reality

Certain devices can impose drawn objects into the world viewed live through the device's camera by means of the ARKit framework.

Machine Learning

The Core ML framework embraces image analysis (the Vision framework) as well as decision trees (GameplayKit). Language analysis classes (such as Foundation NSLinguisticTagger) are now part of the Natural Language framework.

Low-Level Networking

The Network framework lets you implement low-level networking protocols such as TLS, TCP, and UDP without resorting to BSD sockets.

PencilKit

Introduced in iOS 13, PencilKit provides tools for implementing drawing and graphical annotations.

SwiftUI

SwiftUI is a domain-specific language wrapped around Swift, along with a framework that lets you program for iOS and other platforms without direct use of UIKit.

WidgetKit

New in iOS 14, Today extensions are replaced by Widget extensions; widget interfaces are created using SwiftUI.

From the Preface to the First Edition (Programming iOS 4)

A programming framework has a kind of personality, an overall flavor that provides an insight into the goals and mindset of those who created it. When I first encountered Cocoa Touch, my assessment of its personality was: "Wow, the people who wrote this are really clever!" On the one hand, the number of built-in interface objects was severely and deliberately limited; on the other hand, the power and flexibility of some of those objects, especially such things as UITableView, was greatly enhanced over their OS X counterparts. Even more important, Apple created a particularly brilliant way (UIViewController) to help the programmer make entire blocks of interface come and go and supplant one another in a controlled, hierarchical manner, thus allowing that tiny iPhone display to unfold virtually into multiple interface worlds within a single app without the user becoming lost or confused.

The popularity of the iPhone, with its largely free or very inexpensive apps, and the subsequent popularity of the iPad, have brought and will continue to bring into the fold many new programmers who see programming for these devices as worthwhile and doable, even though they may not have felt the same way about OS X. Apple's own annual WWDC developer conventions have reflected this trend, with their emphasis shifted from OS X to iOS instruction.

The widespread eagerness to program iOS, however, though delightful on the one hand, has also fostered a certain tendency to try to run without first learning to walk. iOS gives the programmer mighty powers that can seem as limitless as imagination itself, but it also has fundamentals. I often see questions online from programmers who are evidently deep into the creation of some interesting app, but who are stymied in a way that reveals quite clearly that they are unfamiliar with the basics of the very world in which they are so happily cavorting.

It is this state of affairs that has motivated me to write this book, which is intended to ground the reader in the fundamentals of iOS. I love Cocoa and have long wished to write about it, but it is iOS and its popularity that has given me a proximate excuse to do so. Here I have attempted to marshal and expound, in what I hope is a pedagogically helpful and instructive yet ruthlessly Euclidean and logical order, the principles and elements on which sound iOS programming rests. My hope, as with my previous books, is that you will both read this book cover to cover (learning something new often enough to keep you turning the pages) and keep it by you as a handy reference.

This book is not intended to disparage Apple's own documentation and example projects. They are wonderful resources and have become more wonderful as time goes on. I have depended heavily on them in the preparation of this book. But I also find that they don't fulfill the same function as a reasoned, ordered presentation of the facts. The online documentation must make assumptions as to how much you already know; it can't guarantee that you'll approach it in a given order. And online documentation is more suitable to reference than to instruction. A fully written example, no matter how well commented, is difficult to follow; it demonstrates, but it does not teach.

A book, on the other hand, has numbered chapters and sequential pages; I can assume you know views before you know view controllers for the simple reason that Part I precedes Part II. And along with facts, I also bring to the table a degree of experience, which I try to communicate to you. Throughout this book you'll find me referring to "common beginner mistakes"; in most cases, these are mistakes that I have made myself, in addition to seeing others make them. I try to tell you what the pitfalls are because I assume that, in the course of things, you will otherwise fall into them just as naturally as I did as I was learning. You'll also see me construct many examples piece by piece or extract and explain just one tiny portion of a larger app. It is not a massive finished program that teaches programming, but an exposition of the thought process that developed that program. It is this thought process, more than anything else, that I hope you will gain from reading this book.

Versions

This book is geared to Swift 5.3, iOS 14, and Xcode 12.

In general, only very minimal attention is given to earlier versions of iOS and Xcode. Earlier versions can be very different from the current version, and it would be impossible to go into detail about all that has changed over the years. Besides, that information is readily and compendiously available in my earlier books. Recent innovations are called out clearly. The book does contain some advice about backward compatibility, especially with regard to scene support.

I generally give method names in Swift, in the style of a function reference — the base name plus parentheses containing the parameter labels followed by colon. Now and then, if a method is already under discussion and there is no ambiguity, I'll use the bare base name. In a few places, where the Objective-C language is explicitly under discussion, I use Objective-C method names.

I have tried to keep my code up-to-date right up to the moment when the manuscript left my hands; but if, at some future time, a new version of Xcode is released along with a new version of Swift or with revisions to the Cocoa APIs, some of the code in this book might be slightly incorrect. Please make allowances, and be prepared to compensate.

Screenshots of Xcode were taken using Xcode 12 under macOS 11 Big Sur. I have waited until the last moment before publication to take these screenshots; I don't expect the interface to have changed significantly by the time you read this, and if it does, the difference shouldn't cause any confusion.

Acknowledgments

This book was written with the aid of some wonderful software:

- Git (*http://git-scm.com*)
- Sourcetree (*http://www.sourcetreeapp.com*)
- TextMate (*http://macromates.com*)
- AsciiDoc (*http://www.methods.co.nz/asciidoc*)
- Asciidoctor (*http://asciidoctor.org*)
- BBEdit (*http://barebones.com/products/bbedit*)
- EasyFind (*https://www.devontechnologies.com/support/download*)
- Snapz Pro X (*http://www.ambrosiasw.com*)
- GraphicConverter (*http://www.lemkesoft.com*)
- OmniGraffle (*http://www.omnigroup.com*)

At O'Reilly Media, many people have made writing this book fun and easy; particular thanks go to Kristen Brown, Rachel Roumeliotis, Dan Fauxsmith, Adam Witwer, Nick Adams, Heather Scherer, Melanie Yarbrough, Sarah Schneider, and Sanders Kleinfeld. My first editor was Brian Jepson; his influence is present throughout.

Finally, a special thanks to my beloved wife, Charlotte Wilson, for her sharp eye, her critical ear, and her unflagging encouragement. This book could not have been written without her.

Conventions Used in This Book

The following typographical conventions are used in this book:

Italic
> Indicates new terms, URLs, email addresses, filenames, and file extensions.

`Constant width`
> Used for program listings, as well as within paragraphs to refer to program elements such as variable or function names, databases, data types, environment variables, statements, and keywords.

`Constant width bold`
> Shows commands or other text that should be typed literally by the user.

`Constant width italic`
> Shows text that should be replaced with user-supplied values or by values determined by context.

This element signifies a tip or suggestion.

 This element signifies a general note.

 This element indicates a warning or caution.

Using Code Examples

Supplemental material (code examples, exercises, etc.) is available for download at *https://github.com/mattneub/Programming-iOS-Book-Examples*.

If you have a technical question or a problem using the code examples, please send email to *bookquestions@oreilly.com*.

This book is here to help you get your job done. In general, if example code is offered with this book, you may use it in your programs and documentation. You do not need to contact us for permission unless you're reproducing a significant portion of the code. For example, writing a program that uses several chunks of code from this book does not require permission. Selling or distributing examples from O'Reilly books does require permission. Answering a question by citing this book and quoting example code does not require permission. Incorporating a significant amount of example code from this book into your product's documentation does require permission.

We appreciate, but do not require, attribution. An attribution usually includes the title, author, publisher, and ISBN. For example: "*Programming iOS 14* by Matt Neuburg (O'Reilly). Copyright 2021 Matt Neuburg, 978-1-492-09217-9."

If you feel your use of code examples falls outside fair use or the permission given above, feel free to contact us at *permissions@oreilly.com*.

O'Reilly Online Learning

 For more than 40 years, *O'Reilly Media* has provided technology and business training, knowledge, and insight to help companies succeed.

Our unique network of experts and innovators share their knowledge and expertise through books, articles, and our online learning platform. O'Reilly's online learning platform gives you on-demand access to live training courses, in-depth learning paths, interactive coding environments, and a vast collection of text and video from O'Reilly and 200+ other publishers. For more information, please visit *http:// oreilly.com*.

How to Contact Us

Please address comments and questions concerning this book to the publisher:

O'Reilly Media, Inc.
1005 Gravenstein Highway North
Sebastopol, CA 95472
800-998-9938 (in the United States or Canada)
707-829-0515 (international or local)
707-829-0104 (fax)

We have a web page for this book, where we list errata, examples, and any additional information. You can access this page at *https://oreil.ly/programming_iOS14*.

Email *bookquestions@oreilly.com* to comment or ask technical questions about this book.

For news and more information about our books and courses, see our website at *http://www.oreilly.com*.

Find us on Facebook: *http://facebook.com/oreilly*

Follow us on Twitter: *http://twitter.com/oreillymedia*

Watch us on YouTube: *http://www.youtube.com/oreillymedia*

Views

Views are what your user sees on the screen and interacts with by touching the screen. The book begins by explaining how they work:

- Chapter 1 discusses views in their most general aspect — their hierarchy, visibility, position, and layout.

- Chapter 2 is about drawing. A view knows how to draw itself; this chapter explains how to tell a view what you want it to draw.

- Chapter 3 explains about layers. The drawing power of a view comes ultimately from its layer.

- Chapter 4 talks about animation, which you'll use to enliven your app's interface.

- Chapter 5 explains how your app senses and responds to the user touching the screen.

Views

A *view* (an object whose class is UIView or a subclass of UIView) knows how to draw itself into a rectangular area of the interface. Your app has a visible interface thanks to views; everything the user sees is ultimately because of a view. Creating and configuring a view can be extremely simple: "Set it and forget it." You can configure a UIButton in the nib editor; when the app runs, the button appears, and works properly. But you can also manipulate views in powerful ways, in real time. Your code can do some or all of the view's drawing of itself (Chapter 2); it can make the view appear and disappear, move, resize itself, and display many other physical changes, possibly with animation (Chapter 4).

A view is also a responder (UIView is a subclass of UIResponder). This means that a view is subject to user interactions, such as taps and swipes. Views are the basis not only of the interface that the user sees, but also of the interface that the user touches (Chapter 5). Organizing your views so that the correct view reacts to a given touch allows you to allocate your code neatly and efficiently.

The *view hierarchy* is the chief mode of view organization. A view can have subviews; a subview has exactly one immediate superview. We may say there is a *tree* of views. This hierarchy allows views to come and go together. If a view is removed from the interface, its subviews are removed; if a view is hidden (made invisible), its subviews are hidden; if a view is moved, its subviews move with it; and other changes in a view are likewise shared with its subviews. The view hierarchy is also the basis of, though it is not identical to, the responder chain.

A view may come from a nib, or you can create it in code. On balance, neither approach is to be preferred over the other; it depends on your needs and inclinations and on the overall architecture of your app.

Window and Root View

The top of the view hierarchy is a window. It is an instance of UIWindow (or your own subclass thereof), which is a UIView subclass. At launch time, a window is created and displayed; otherwise, the screen would be black. Starting in iOS 13, your app might support multiple windows on an iPad (Chapter 10); if it doesn't, or if we're running on an iPhone, your app will have exactly one window (the *main* window). A visible window forms the background to, and is the ultimate superview of, all your other visible views. Conversely, all visible views are visible by virtue of being subviews, at some depth, of a visible window.

In Cocoa programming, you do not manually or directly populate a window with subviews. Rather, the link between your window and the interface that it contains is the window's *root view controller*. A view controller is instantiated, and that instance is assigned to the window's rootViewController property. That view controller's *main view* — its view — henceforth occupies the entirety of the window. It is the window's sole subview; all other visible views are subviews (at some depth) of the root view controller's view. (The root view controller itself will be the top of the *view controller hierarchy,* of which I'll have much more to say in Chapter 6.)

Window Scene Architecture

Starting in iOS 13, an app's window is backed by a window scene (UIWindowScene). This is a major architectural change from iOS 12 and before, where window scenes didn't exist:

Window architecture
> The old architecture, in iOS 12 and before, is window-based. The window is a property of the *app delegate.* If your app was created in Xcode 10 or before, it uses the old architecture by default.

Scene architecture
> The new architecture, in iOS 13 and later, is scene-based. The window is a property of the *scene delegate.* If your app was created in Xcode 11 or later, it uses the new architecture by default.

An old-architecture app running on iOS 13 or later is given a window scene, but it is unaware of that fact and its behavior is not affected; it still runs under the old architecture. A new-architecture app, on the other hand, cannot run on, or even compile for, iOS 12 or earlier, without alterations to the code.

What determines the architecture? To find out, just create a new app! In Xcode 12 (and Xcode 11), the app template configures the app for the new architecture. Here are the marks of a new-architecture app:

Scene delegate

The app has a scene delegate, which contains the `window` property:

```
class SceneDelegate: UIResponder, UIWindowSceneDelegate {
    var window: UIWindow?
    // ...
}
```

Scene-related app delegate methods

The app delegate contains two methods that refer to scenes:

```
class AppDelegate: UIResponder, UIApplicationDelegate {
    // ...
    func application(_ application: UIApplication,
        configurationForConnecting connectingSceneSession: UISceneSession,
        options: UIScene.ConnectionOptions) -> UISceneConfiguration {
            // ...
    }
    func application(_ application: UIApplication,
        didDiscardSceneSessions sceneSessions: Set<UISceneSession>) {
            // ...
    }
}
```

Application Scene Manifest

The *Info.plist* contains an "Application Scene Manifest" entry:

```
<key>Application Scene Manifest</key>
<dict>
    <!-- ... -->
</dict>
```

If you want your new-architecture app to be also backward compatible to iOS 12 and before:

1. Copy and paste the `window` property declaration into the AppDelegate class. Now both the AppDelegate and the SceneDelegate have `window` properties.

2. In the AppDelegate class, mark any *methods* that refer to UISceneSession as `@available(iOS 13.0, *)`.

3. In the SceneDelegate class, mark the *entire class* as `@available(iOS 13.0, *)`.

The result is that when this app runs in iOS 13 or later, it uses the new architecture and the scene delegate's `window` property holds the window, but when it runs in iOS 12 or before, it uses the old architecture and the app delegate's `window` property holds the window — and your other code may then need to take account of *that* in order to be backward compatible. Lifetime delegate messages and notifications (see Appendix A) will be routed differently; for instance, on iOS 12 and before, you'll get the `applicationDidBecomeActive(_:)` message in the app delegate, but on iOS 13 and after, you'll get the `sceneDidBecomeActive(_:)` message in the scene delegate.

If all of that is too overwhelming and you want your new app to run with the old architecture even on iOS 13 and later, then theoretically you can: delete all code that refers to UISceneSession or SceneDelegate, and delete the "Application Scene Manifest" entry in the *Info.plist*. You have now reduced your code to look as if it was created in Xcode 10. (But I'm not actually recommending that you do that!)

How an App Launches

How does your app, at launch time, come to have its window in the first place, and how does that window come to be populated and displayed? If your app uses a main storyboard, it all happens automatically. But "automatically" does *not* mean "by magic!" The procedure at launch is straightforward and deterministic, and your code can take a hand in it. It is useful to know how an app launches, not least so that if you misconfigure something and app launch goes wrong, you'll be able to figure out why.

Your app consists, ultimately, of a single call to the UIApplicationMain function. (Unlike an Objective-C project, a typical Swift project doesn't make this call explicitly, in code; it is called for you, behind the scenes.) This call creates some of your app's most important initial instances; if your app uses a main storyboard, those instances include the window and its root view controller.

Exactly how UIApplicationMain proceeds depends on whether your app uses the old or new architecture. They are two quite different launch trajectories. I will describe just the launch trajectory for the new architecture.

Here's how UIApplicationMain bootstraps your app with window scene support as it launches on iOS 13 and later:

1. UIApplicationMain instantiates UIApplication and retains this instance, to serve as the shared application instance, which your code can later refer to as UIApplication.shared. It then instantiates the app delegate class; it knows which class that is because it is marked @main. (Before Swift 5.3, this attribute was @UIApplicationMain). It retains the app delegate instance, ensuring that it will persist for the lifetime of the app, and assigns it as the application instance's delegate.

2. UIApplicationMain calls the app delegate's application(_:didFinish-LaunchingWithOptions:), giving your code an opportunity run.

3. UIApplicationMain creates a UISceneSession, a UIWindowScene, and an instance that will serve as the window scene's delegate. The *Info.plist* specifies, as a string, what the class of the window scene delegate instance should be ("Delegate Class Name" inside the "Application Scene Manifest" dictionary's "Scene Configuration"). In the built-in app templates, it is the SceneDelegate class; this is written in the *Info.plist* as $(PRODUCT_MODULE_NAME).SceneDelegate to take account of Swift "name mangling."

4. `UIApplicationMain` looks to see whether your initial scene uses a storyboard. The *Info.plist* specifies, as a string, the name of its storyboard ("Storyboard Name" inside the "Application Scene Manifest" dictionary's "Scene Configuration"). If so, it instantiates that storyboard's initial view controller.

5. If the scene uses a storyboard, `UIApplicationMain` instantiates UIWindow and assigns the window instance to the scene delegate's `window` property, which retains it.

6. If the scene uses a storyboard, `UIApplicationMain` assigns the initial view controller instance to the window instance's `rootViewController` property, which retains it. The view controller's view becomes the window's sole subview.

7. `UIApplicationMain` causes your app's interface to appear, by calling the UIWindow instance method `makeKeyAndVisible`.

8. The scene delegate's `scene(_:willConnectTo:options:)` is called, giving more of your code an opportunity to run.

App Without a Storyboard

The previous section described how the app launches when it has a main storyboard. It is also possible to write an app that lacks a main storyboard:

- Under the old architecture, this means that the *Info.plist* contains no "Main storyboard file base name" entry.

- Under the new architecture, it means that there is no "Storyboard Name" entry under "Application Scene Configuration" in the "Application Scene Manifest" dictionary.

Such an app must do in code everything that `UIApplicationMain` does automatically if the app has a main storyboard. Under the old architecture, you would do those things in the app delegate's `application(_:didFinishLaunchingWithOptions:)`. Under the new architecture, you do them in the scene delegate's `scene(_:willConnectTo:options:)`:

```
func scene(_ scene: UIScene,
    willConnectTo session: UISceneSession,
    options connectionOptions: UIScene.ConnectionOptions) {
        if let windowScene = scene as? UIWindowScene {
            self.window = UIWindow(windowScene: windowScene) ❶
            let vc = // ...                                  ❷
            self.window!.rootViewController = vc             ❸
            self.window!.makeKeyAndVisible()                 ❹
        }
}
```

❶ Instantiate UIWindow and assign it as the scene delegate's `window` property. It is crucial to make the connection between the window scene and the window by calling `init(windowScene:)`.

❷ Instantiate a view controller and configure it as needed.

❸ Assign the view controller as the window's `rootViewController` property.

❹ Call `makeKeyAndVisible` on the window, to show it.

A variant that is sometimes useful is an app that has a storyboard but doesn't let UIApplicationMain see it at launch. That way, we can dictate at launch time which view controller from within that storyboard should be the window's root view controller. A typical scenario is that our app has something like a login or registration screen that appears at launch if the user has not logged in, but doesn't appear on subsequent launches once the user *has* logged in:

```
func scene(_ scene: UIScene,
    willConnectTo session: UISceneSession,
    options connectionOptions: UIScene.ConnectionOptions) {
        if let windowScene = scene as? UIWindowScene {
            self.window = UIWindow(windowScene: windowScene)
            let userHasLoggedIn : Bool = // ...
            let vc = UIStoryboard(name: "Main", bundle: nil)
                .instantiateViewController(identifier: userHasLoggedIn ?
                    "UserHasLoggedIn" : "LoginScreen") // *
            self.window!.rootViewController = vc
            self.window!.makeKeyAndVisible()
        }
}
```

Referring to the Window

Once the app is running, there are various ways for your code to refer to the window:

From a view

If a UIView is in the interface, it automatically has a reference to the window that contains it, through its own `window` property. Your code will probably be running in a view controller with a main view, so `self.view.window` is usually the best way to refer to the window.

You can also use a UIView's `window` property as a way of asking whether it is ultimately embedded in the window; if it isn't, its `window` property is `nil`. A UIView whose `window` property is `nil` cannot be visible to the user.

From the scene delegate

The scene delegate instance maintains a reference to the window through its `window` property.

From the application

The shared application maintains a reference to the window through its `windows` property:

```
let w = UIApplication.shared.windows.first!
```

 Do not expect that the window you know about is the app's only window. The runtime can create additional mysterious windows, such as the UITextEffects-Window and the UIRemoteKeyboardWindow.

Experimenting with Views

In the course of this and subsequent chapters, you may want to experiment with views in a project of your own. If you start your project with the basic App template, it gives you the simplest possible app — a main storyboard containing one scene consisting of one view controller instance along with its main view. As I described in the preceding section, when the app runs, that view controller will become the window's `rootViewController`, and its main view will become the window's root view. If you can get *your* views to become subviews of that view controller's main view, they will be present in the app's interface when it launches.

In the nib editor, you can drag a view from the Library into the main view as a subview, and it will be instantiated in the interface when the app runs. However, my initial examples will all create views and add them to the interface *in code*. So where should that code go? The simplest place is the view controller's `viewDidLoad` method, which is provided as a stub by the project template code; it runs once, before the view appears in the interface for the first time.

The `viewDidLoad` method can refer to the view controller's main view by saying `self.view`. In my code examples, whenever I say `self.view`, you can assume we're in a view controller and that `self.view` is this view controller's main view:

```
override func viewDidLoad() {
    super.viewDidLoad() // this is template code
    let v = UIView(frame:CGRect(x:100, y:100, width:50, height:50))
    v.backgroundColor = .red // small red square
    self.view.addSubview(v) // add it to main view
}
```

Try it! Make a new project from the App template, and make the ViewController class's `viewDidLoad` look like that. Run the app. You will actually *see* the small red square in the running app's interface.

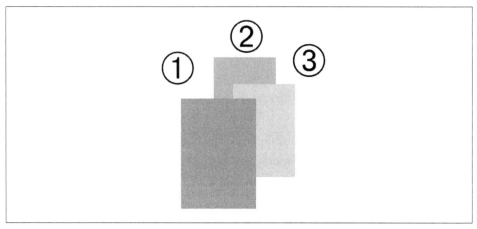

Figure 1-1. Overlapping views

Subview and Superview

Once upon a time, and not so very long ago, a view owned precisely its own rectangular area. No part of any view that was not a subview of this view could appear inside it, because when this view redrew its rectangle, it would erase the overlapping portion of the other view. No part of any subview of this view could appear outside it, because the view took responsibility for its own rectangle and no more.

Those rules were gradually relaxed, and starting in OS X 10.5, Apple introduced an entirely new architecture for view drawing that lifted those restrictions completely. iOS view drawing is based on this revised architecture. In iOS, some or all of a subview can appear outside its superview, and a view can overlap another view and can be drawn partially or totally in front of it without being its subview.

Figure 1-1 shows three overlapping views. All three views have a background color, so each is completely represented by a colored rectangle. You have no way of knowing, from this visual representation, exactly how the views are related within the view hierarchy. In actual fact, View 1 is a sibling view of View 2 (they are both direct subviews of the root view), and View 3 is a subview of View 2.

When views are created in the nib, you can examine the view hierarchy in the nib editor's document outline to learn their actual relationship (Figure 1-2). When views are created in code, you know their hierarchical relationship because you created that hierarchy. But the visible interface doesn't tell you, because view overlapping is so flexible.

Nevertheless, a view's position within the view hierarchy is extremely significant. For one thing, the view hierarchy dictates the *order* in which views are drawn. Sibling subviews of the same superview have a definite order; an earlier sibling is drawn

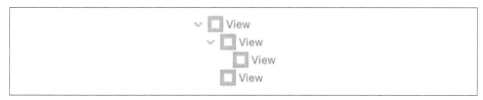

Figure 1-2. A view hierarchy as displayed in the nib editor

before a later sibling, so if they overlap, the earlier one will appear to be behind the later one. Similarly, a superview is drawn before its subviews, so if the subviews overlap their superview, the superview will appear to be behind them.

You can see this illustrated in Figure 1-1. View 3 is a subview of View 2 and is drawn on top of it. View 1 is a sibling of View 2, but it is a later sibling, so it is drawn on top of View 2 and on top of View 3. View 1 *cannot* appear behind View 3 but in front of View 2, because Views 2 and 3 are subview and superview and are drawn together — both are drawn either before or after View 1, depending on the ordering of the siblings.

This layering order can be governed in the nib editor by arranging the views in the document outline. (If you click in the canvas, you may be able to use the menu items of the Editor → Arrange menu instead — Send to Front, Send to Back, Send Forward, Send Backward.) In code, there are methods for arranging the sibling order of views, which we'll come to in a moment.

Here are some other effects of the view hierarchy:

- If a view is removed from or moved within its superview, its subviews go with it.
- A view's degree of transparency is inherited by its subviews.
- A view can optionally limit the drawing of its subviews so that any parts of them outside the view are not shown. This is called *clipping* and is set with the view's `clipsToBounds` property.
- A superview *owns* its subviews, in the memory-management sense, much as an array owns its elements; it retains its subviews, and is responsible for releasing a subview when that subview is removed from the collection of this view's subviews, or when the superview itself goes out of existence.
- If a view's size is changed, its subviews can be resized automatically (and I'll have much more to say about that later in this chapter).

A UIView has a `superview` property (a UIView) and a `subviews` property (an array of UIView objects, in back-to-front order), allowing you to trace the view hierarchy in code. There is also a method `isDescendant(of:)` letting you check whether one view is a subview of another at any depth.

If you need a reference to a particular view, you will probably arrange it beforehand as a property, perhaps through an outlet. Alternatively, a view can have a numeric tag (its `tag` property), and can then be referred to by sending any view higher up the view hierarchy the `viewWithTag(_:)` message. Seeing that all tags of interest are unique within their region of the hierarchy is up to you.

Manipulating the view hierarchy in code is easy. This is part of what gives iOS apps their dynamic quality. It is perfectly reasonable for your code to rip an entire hierarchy of views out of the superview and substitute another, right before the user's very eyes! You can do this directly; you can combine it with animation (Chapter 4); you can govern it through view controllers (Chapter 6).

The method `addSubview(_:)` makes one view a subview of another; `removeFromSuperview` takes a subview out of its superview's view hierarchy. In both cases, if the superview is part of the visible interface, the subview will appear or disappear respectively at that moment; and of course the subview may have subviews of its own that accompany it. Removing a subview from its superview releases it; if you intend to reuse that subview later on, you will need to retain it first by assigning it to a variable.

Events inform a view of these dynamic changes. To respond to these events requires subclassing. Then you'll be able to override any of these methods:

- `willRemoveSubview(_:)`, `didAddSubview(_:)`
- `willMove(toSuperview:)`, `didMoveToSuperview`
- `willMove(toWindow:)`, `didMoveToWindow`

When `addSubview(_:)` is called, the view is placed last among its superview's subviews, so it is drawn last, meaning that it appears frontmost. That might not be what you want. A view's subviews are indexed, starting at 0 which is rearmost, and there are methods for inserting a subview at a given index or below (behind) or above (in front of) a specific view; for swapping two sibling views by index; and for moving a subview all the way to the front or back among its siblings:

- `insertSubview(_:at:)`
- `insertSubview(_:belowSubview:)`, `insertSubview(_:aboveSubview:)`
- `exchangeSubview(at:withSubviewAt:)`
- `bringSubviewToFront(_:)`, `sendSubviewToBack(_:)`

Oddly, there is no command for removing all of a view's subviews at once. However, a view's `subviews` array is an immutable copy of the internal list of subviews, so it is legal to cycle through it and remove each subview one at a time:

```
myView.subviews.forEach {$0.removeFromSuperview()}
```

Color

A view can be assigned a background color through its `backgroundColor` property. A view distinguished by nothing but its background color is a colored rectangle, and is an excellent medium for experimentation, as in Figure 1-1.

A view whose background color is `nil` (the default) has a transparent background. If this view does no additional drawing of its own, it will be invisible! Such a view is perfectly reasonable; a view with a transparent background might act as a convenient superview to other views, making them behave together.

A color is a UIColor, which will typically be specified using `.red`, `.blue`, `.green`, and `.alpha` components, which are CGFloat values between 0 and 1:

```
v.backgroundColor = UIColor(red: 0, green: 0.1, blue: 0.1, alpha: 1)
```

There are also numerous named colors, vended as static properties of the UIColor class:

```
v.backgroundColor = .red
```

Starting in iOS 13, you may need to be rather more circumspect about the colors you assign to things. The problem is that the user can switch the device between light and dark modes. This can cause a cascade of color changes that can make hard-coded colors look bad. Suppose we give the view controller's main view a subview with a dark color:

```
override func viewDidLoad() {
    super.viewDidLoad()
    let v = UIView(frame:CGRect(x:100, y:100, width:50, height:50))
    v.backgroundColor = UIColor(red: 0, green: 0.1, blue: 0.1, alpha: 1)
    self.view.addSubview(v)
}
```

If we run the project in the simulator, we see a small very dark square against a white background. But now suppose we switch to dark mode. Now the background becomes black, and we don't see our dark square any longer. The reason is that the view controller's main view has a *dynamic* color, which is white in light mode but black in dark mode, and now our dark square is black on black.

One solution is to make our UIColor dynamic. We can do this with the initializer `init(dynamicProvider:)`, giving it as parameter a function that takes a trait collection and returns a color. I'll explain more about what a trait collection is later in this chapter; right now, all you need to know is that its `userInterfaceStyle` may or may not be `.dark`:

```
v.backgroundColor = UIColor { tc in
    switch tc.userInterfaceStyle {
    case .dark:
        return UIColor(red: 0.3, green: 0.4, blue: 0.4, alpha: 1)
    default:
        return UIColor(red: 0, green: 0.1, blue: 0.1, alpha: 1)
    }
}
```

We have created our own custom dynamic color, which is different depending what mode we're in. In dark mode, our view's color is now a dark gray that is visible against a black background.

 To switch to dark mode in the simulator, choose Features → Toggle Appearance (new in Xcode 12). Alternatively, in Xcode, while running your app in the debugger, click the Environment Overrides button in the debug bar; in the pop-over that appears, click the first switch, at the upper right.

A more compact way to get a dynamic color is to use one of the many dynamic colors vended as static properties by UIColor starting in iOS 13. Most of these have names that start with .system, such as .systemYellow; others have semantic names describing their role, such as .label. For details, see Apple's *Human Interface Guidelines.*

You can also design a custom named color in the asset catalog. When you create a new color set, the Appearances pop-up menu in the Attributes inspector says Any, Dark, and there are two color swatches, one for dark mode and the other for everything else; select each swatch in turn and design the color in the Attributes inspector.

The result is a custom named color that is also dynamic. Let's say our color set in the asset catalog is called myDarkColor. Then you could say:

```
v.backgroundColor = UIColor(named: "myDarkColor")
```

Custom named colors from the asset catalog also appear in the Library and in the color pop-up menus in the Attributes inspector when you select a view.

Visibility and Opacity

Three properties relate to the visibility and opacity of a view:

isHidden

A view can be made invisible by setting its isHidden property to true, and visible again by setting it to false. Hiding a view takes it (and its subviews, of course) out of the visible interface without actually removing it from the view hierarchy. A hidden view does not (normally) receive touch events, so to the user it really is as if the view weren't there. But it is there, so it can still be manipulated in code.

alpha

A view can be made partially or completely transparent through its `alpha` property: `1.0` means opaque, `0.0` means transparent, and a value may be anywhere between them, inclusive. This property affects both the apparent transparency of the view's background color and the apparent transparency of its contents. If a view displays an image and has a background color and its `alpha` is less than 1, the background color will seep through the image (and whatever is behind the view will seep through both). Moreover, it affects the apparent transparency of the view's subviews! If a superview has an `alpha` of `0.5`, none of its subviews can have an *apparent* opacity of more than `0.5`, because whatever `alpha` value they have will be drawn relative to `0.5`. A view that is completely transparent (or very close to it) is like a view whose `isHidden` is `true`: it is invisible, along with its subviews, and cannot (normally) be touched.

(Just to make matters more complicated, colors have an alpha value as well. A view can have an `alpha` of `1.0` but still have a transparent background because its `backgroundColor` has an alpha less than `1.0`.)

isOpaque

This property is a horse of a different color; changing it has no effect on the view's appearance. Rather, it is a hint to the drawing system. If a view is completely filled with opaque material and its `alpha` is `1.0`, so that the view has no effective transparency, then it can be drawn more efficiently (with less drag on performance) if you inform the drawing system of this fact by setting its `isOpaque` to `true`. Otherwise, you should set its `isOpaque` to `false`. The `isOpaque` value is *not* changed for you when you set a view's `backgroundColor` or `alpha`! Setting it correctly is entirely up to you; the default, perhaps surprisingly, is `true`.

Frame

A view's `frame` property, a CGRect, is the position of its rectangle within its superview, *in the superview's coordinate system*. By default, the superview's coordinate system will have the origin at its top left, with the x-coordinate growing positively rightward and the y-coordinate growing positively downward.

Setting a view's frame to a different CGRect value repositions the view, or resizes it, or both. If the view is visible, this change will be visibly reflected in the interface. On the other hand, you can also set a view's frame when the view is not visible, such as when you create the view in code. In that case, the frame describes where the view *will* be positioned within its superview when it is given a superview.

UIView's designated initializer is `init(frame:)`, and you'll often assign a frame this way, especially because the default frame might otherwise be `CGRect.zero`, which is rarely what you want. A view with a zero-size frame is effectively invisible (though you might still see its subviews). Forgetting to assign a view a frame when creating it in code, and then wondering why it isn't appearing when added to a superview, is a common beginner mistake. If a view has a standard size that you want it to adopt, especially in relation to its contents (like a UIButton in relation to its title), an alternative is to call its `sizeToFit` method.

We are now in a position to generate programmatically the interface displayed in Figure 1-1; we determine the layering order of `v1` and `v3` (the middle and left views, which are siblings) by the order in which we insert them into the view hierarchy:

```
let v1 = UIView(frame:CGRect(113, 111, 132, 194))
v1.backgroundColor = UIColor(red: 1, green: 0.4, blue: 1, alpha: 1)
let v2 = UIView(frame:CGRect(41, 56, 132, 194))
v2.backgroundColor = UIColor(red: 0.5, green: 1, blue: 0, alpha: 1)
let v3 = UIView(frame:CGRect(43, 197, 160, 230))
v3.backgroundColor = UIColor(red: 1, green: 0, blue: 0, alpha: 1)
self.view.addSubview(v1)
v1.addSubview(v2)
self.view.addSubview(v3)
```

 That code, and all subsequent code in this book, uses a custom CGRect initializer with no argument labels. Please read the sidebar "Core Graphics Initializers" right now!

Figure 1-3. A subview inset from its superview

When a UIView is instantiated from a nib, its `init(frame:)` is *not called* — `init(coder:)` is called instead. Implementing `init(frame:)` in a UIView subclass, and then wondering why your code isn't called when the view is instantiated from a nib (such as the storyboard), is a common beginner mistake.

Bounds and Center

Suppose we have a superview and a subview, and the subview is to appear inset by 10 points, as in Figure 1-3. So we want to set the subview's frame. But to what value? CGRect methods like `insetBy(dx:dy:)` make it easy to derive one rectangle as an inset from another. But *what* rectangle should we inset from? Not from the superview's frame; the frame represents a view's position within *its* superview, and in that superview's coordinates. What we're after is a CGRect describing our superview's rectangle in its *own* coordinates, because those are the coordinates in which the subview's frame is to be expressed. The CGRect that describes a view's rectangle in its own coordinates is the view's bounds property.

So, the code to generate Figure 1-3 looks like this:

```
let v1 = UIView(frame:CGRect(113, 111, 132, 194))
v1.backgroundColor = UIColor(red: 1, green: 0.4, blue: 1, alpha: 1)
let v2 = UIView(frame:v1.bounds.insetBy(dx: 10, dy: 10))
v2.backgroundColor = UIColor(red: 0.5, green: 1, blue: 0, alpha: 1)
self.view.addSubview(v1)
v1.addSubview(v2)
```

You'll very often use a view's bounds in this way. When you need coordinates for positioning content inside a view, whether drawing manually or placing a subview, you'll refer to the view's bounds.

If you change a view's bounds *size*, you change its *frame*. The change in the view's frame takes place around its *center*, which remains unchanged:

Figure 1-4. A subview exactly covering its superview

```
let v1 = UIView(frame:CGRect(113, 111, 132, 194))
v1.backgroundColor = UIColor(red: 1, green: 0.4, blue: 1, alpha: 1)
let v2 = UIView(frame:v1.bounds.insetBy(dx: 10, dy: 10))
v2.backgroundColor = UIColor(red: 0.5, green: 1, blue: 0, alpha: 1)
self.view.addSubview(v1)
v1.addSubview(v2)
v2.bounds.size.height += 20
v2.bounds.size.width += 20
```

What appears is a single rectangle; the subview completely and exactly covers its superview, its frame being the same as the superview's bounds. The call to insetBy started with the superview's bounds and shaved 10 points off the left, right, top, and bottom to set the subview's frame (Figure 1-3). But then we added 20 points to the subview's bounds height and width, which added 20 points to the subview's frame height and width as well (Figure 1-4). The subview's center didn't move, so we effectively put the 10 points back onto the left, right, top, and bottom of the subview's frame.

If you change a view's bounds *origin*, you move the *origin of its internal coordinate system*. When you create a UIView, its bounds coordinate system's zero point (0.0,0.0) is at its top left. Because a subview is positioned in its superview with respect to its superview's coordinate system, a change in the bounds origin of the superview will change the apparent position of a subview. To illustrate, we start once again with our subview inset evenly within its superview, and then change the bounds origin of the superview:

```
let v1 = UIView(frame:CGRect(113, 111, 132, 194))
v1.backgroundColor = UIColor(red: 1, green: 0.4, blue: 1, alpha: 1)
let v2 = UIView(frame:v1.bounds.insetBy(dx: 10, dy: 10))
v2.backgroundColor = UIColor(red: 0.5, green: 1, blue: 0, alpha: 1)
self.view.addSubview(v1)
v1.addSubview(v2)
v1.bounds.origin.x += 10
v1.bounds.origin.y += 10
```

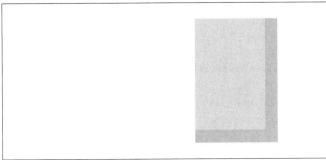

Figure 1-5. The superview's bounds origin has been shifted

Nothing happens to the superview's size or position. But the subview has moved up and to the left so that it is flush with its superview's top-left corner (Figure 1-5). Basically, what we've done is to say to the superview, "Instead of calling the point at your upper left (0.0,0.0), call that point (10.0,10.0)." Because the subview's frame origin is itself at (10.0,10.0), the subview now touches the superview's top-left corner. The effect of changing a view's bounds origin may seem directionally backward — we increased the superview's origin in the positive direction, but the subview moved in the negative direction — but think of it this way: a view's bounds origin point coincides with its frame's top left.

We have seen that changing a view's bounds size affects its frame size. The converse is also true: changing a view's frame size affects its bounds size. What is *not* affected by changing a view's bounds size is the view's center.

A view's center is a single point establishing the positional relationship between the view's bounds and its superview's bounds. It represents a subview's position within its superview, in the superview's coordinates; in particular, it is the position *within the superview* of the subview's own *bounds center*, the point derived from the bounds like this:

```
let c = CGPoint(theView.bounds.midX, theView.bounds.midY)
```

Changing a view's bounds does not change its center; changing a view's center does not change its bounds. A view's bounds and center are orthogonal (independent), and completely describe the view's size and its position within its superview. The view's frame is therefore superfluous! In fact, the frame property is merely a convenient expression of the center and bounds values. In most cases, this won't matter to you; you'll use the frame property anyway. When you first create a view from scratch, the designated initializer is init(frame:). You can change the frame, and the bounds size and center will change to match. You can change the bounds size or the center, and the frame will change to match. Nevertheless, the proper and most reliable way to position and size a view within its superview is to use its bounds and center, not its frame; there are some situations in which the frame is meaningless (or will at least behave very oddly), but the bounds and center will always work.

We have seen that every view has its own coordinate system, expressed by its bounds, and that a view's coordinate system has a clear relationship to its superview's coordinate system, expressed by its center. This is true of every view in a window, so it is possible to convert between the coordinates of any two views in the same window. Convenience methods are supplied to perform this conversion both for a CGPoint and for a CGRect:

- `convert(_:to:)`
- `convert(_:from:)`

The first parameter is either a CGPoint or a CGRect. The second parameter is a UIView; if the second parameter is nil, it is taken to be the window. The recipient is another UIView; the CGPoint or CGRect is being converted between its coordinates and the second view's coordinates. If v1 is the superview of v2, then to center v2 within v1 you could say:

```
v2.center = v1.convert(v1.center, from:v1.superview)
```

A more common approach is to place the subview's center at the superview's *bounds* center, like this:

```
v2.center = CGPoint(v1.bounds.midX, v1.bounds.midY)
```

That's such a common thing to do that I've written an extension that provides the center of a CGRect as its center property (see Appendix B), allowing me to talk like this:

```
v2.center = v1.bounds.center
```

Observe that the following is *not* the way to center a subview v2 in a superview v1:

```
v2.center = v1.center // that won't work!
```

Trying to center one view within another like that is a common beginner mistake. It can't succeed, and will have unpredictable results, because the two center values are in different coordinate systems.

When setting a view's position by setting its center, if the height or width of the view is not an integer (or, on a single-resolution screen, not an even integer), the view can end up *misaligned*: its point values in one or both dimensions are located between the screen pixels. This can cause the view to be displayed incorrectly; if the view contains text, the text may be blurry. You can detect this situation in the Simulator by checking Debug → Color Misaligned Images. A simple solution is to set the view's frame to its own integral.

Transform

A view's `transform` property alters how the view is drawn, changing the view's *apparent* size, location, or orientation, without affecting its *actual* bounds and center. A transformed view continues to behave correctly: a rotated button is still a button, and can be tapped in its apparent location and orientation. Transforms are useful particularly as temporary visual indicators. You might call attention to a view by applying a transform that scales it up slightly, and then reversing that transform to restore it to its original size, and animating those changes (Chapter 4).

A transform value is a CGAffineTransform, which is a struct representing six of the nine values of a 3×3 transformation matrix (the other three values are constants, so there's no need to represent them in the struct). You may have forgotten your high-school linear algebra, so you may not recall what a transformation matrix is. For the details, which are quite simple really, see the "Transforms" chapter of Apple's *Quartz 2D Programming Guide* in the documentation archive, especially the section called "The Math Behind the Matrices." But you don't really need to know those details, because initializers are provided for creating three of the basic types of transform: rotation, scale (size), and translation (location). A fourth basic transform type, skewing or shearing, has no initializer and is rarely used.

By default, a view's transformation matrix is `CGAffineTransform.identity`, the identity transform. It has no visible effect, so you're unaware of it. Any transform that you do apply takes place around the view's center, which is held constant.

Here's some code to illustrate use of a transform:

```
let v1 = UIView(frame:CGRect(113, 111, 132, 194))
v1.backgroundColor = UIColor(red: 1, green: 0.4, blue: 1, alpha: 1)
let v2 = UIView(frame:v1.bounds.insetBy(dx: 10, dy: 10))
v2.backgroundColor = UIColor(red: 0.5, green: 1, blue: 0, alpha: 1)
self.view.addSubview(v1)
v1.addSubview(v2)
v1.transform = CGAffineTransform(rotationAngle: 45 * .pi/180)
print(v1.frame)
```

The `transform` property of the view v1 is set to a rotation transform. The result (Figure 1-6) is that the view appears to be rocked 45 degrees clockwise. (I think in degrees, but Core Graphics thinks in radians, so my code has to convert.) Observe that the view's `center` property is unaffected, so that the rotation seems to have occurred around the view's center. Moreover, the view's `bounds` property is unaffected; the internal coordinate system is unchanged, so the subview is drawn in the same place relative to its superview.

The view's `frame` is now useless, as no mere rectangle can describe the region of the superview apparently occupied by the view; the frame's actual value, roughly (63.7,92.7,230.5,230.5), describes the minimal bounding rectangle surrounding

Figure 1-6. A rotation transform

Figure 1-7. A scale transform

the view's apparent position. The rule is that if a view's transform is not the identity transform, you should not set its frame; also, automatic resizing of a subview, discussed later in this chapter, requires that the superview's transform be the identity transform.

Suppose, instead of a rotation transform, we apply a scale transform, like this:

```
v1.transform = CGAffineTransform(scaleX:1.8, y:1)
```

The bounds property of the view v1 is still unaffected, so the subview is still drawn in the same place relative to its superview; this means that the two views seem to have stretched horizontally together (Figure 1-7). No bounds or centers were harmed by the application of this transform!

Methods are provided for transforming an existing transform. This operation is not commutative; order matters. (That high school math is starting to come back to you now, isn't it?) If you start with a transform that translates a view to the right and then apply a rotation of 45 degrees, the rotated view appears to the right of its original position; on the other hand, if you start with a transform that rotates a view 45 degrees and then apply a translation to the right, the meaning of "right" has changed,

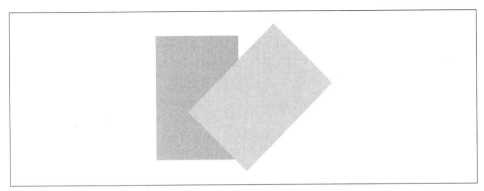

Figure 1-8. Translation, then rotation

so the rotated view appears 45 degrees down from its original position. To demonstrate the difference, I'll start with a subview that exactly overlaps its superview:

```
let v1 = UIView(frame:CGRect(20, 111, 132, 194))
v1.backgroundColor = UIColor(red: 1, green: 0.4, blue: 1, alpha: 1)
let v2 = UIView(frame:v1.bounds)
v2.backgroundColor = UIColor(red: 0.5, green: 1, blue: 0, alpha: 1)
self.view.addSubview(v1)
v1.addSubview(v2)
```

Then I'll apply two transforms to the subview, leaving the superview to show where the subview was originally. In this example, I rotate a translation transform (Figure 1-8):

```
v2.transform =
    CGAffineTransform(translationX:100, y:0).rotated(by: 45 * .pi/180)
```

In this example, I translate a rotation transform (Figure 1-9):

```
v2.transform =
    CGAffineTransform(rotationAngle: 45 * .pi/180).translatedBy(x: 100, y: 0)
```

The concatenating method concatenates two transform matrices using matrix multiplication. Again, this operation is not commutative. The order is the *opposite* of the order when transforming a transform. This code gives the same result as the previous example (Figure 1-9):

```
let r = CGAffineTransform(rotationAngle: 45 * .pi/180)
let t = CGAffineTransform(translationX:100, y:0)
v2.transform = t.concatenating(r) // not r.concatenating(t)
```

To remove a transform from a combination of transforms, apply its inverse. The inverted method lets you obtain the inverse of a given affine transform. Again, order matters. In this example, I rotate the subview and shift it to its "right," and then remove the rotation, demonstrating how to translate a view at an angle (Figure 1-10):

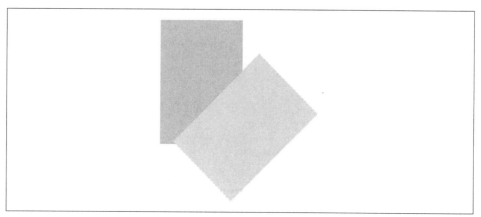

Figure 1-9. Rotation, then translation

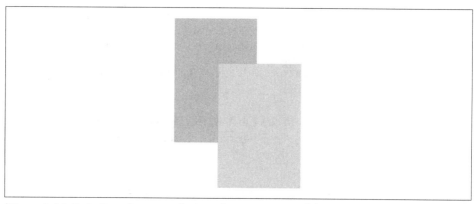

Figure 1-10. Rotation, then translation, then inversion of the rotation

```
let r = CGAffineTransform(rotationAngle: 45 * .pi/180)
let t = CGAffineTransform(translationX:100, y:0)
v2.transform = t.concatenating(r)
v2.transform = r.inverted().concatenating(v2.transform)
```

CGPoint, CGSize, and CGRect all have an applying(_:) method that permits you to apply an affine transform to them. With it, you can calculate what the result *would* be if you were to apply the transform to a view. However, the transform is centered at the origin, so if that isn't what you want, you have to translate the rotation point to the origin, apply the real transform, and then invert the translation transform. Earlier we rotated a view and printed its frame, like this:

```
let v1 = UIView(frame:CGRect(113, 111, 132, 194))
v1.transform = CGAffineTransform(rotationAngle: 45 * .pi/180)
print(v1.frame) // 63.7,92.7,230.5,230.5
```

Here's how to learn what the rotation transform *would* do to the frame of that view, without actually rotating the view:

```
let rect = CGRect(113, 111, 132, 194)
let shift = CGAffineTransform(translationX: -rect.midX, y: -rect.midY)
let rotate = v1.transform
let transform = shift.concatenating(rotate).concatenating(shift.inverted())
let rect2 = rect.applying(transform)
print(rect2) // 63.7,92.7,230.5,230.5
```

Transform3D

Starting in iOS 13, a UIView has a transform3D property. This is actually the underlying layer's transform property (Chapter 3), but since it is also now exposed through the view, I'll explain it here.

As the name implies, a transform3D takes place in three-dimensional space; its description includes a z-axis, perpendicular to both the x-axis and y-axis. (By default, the positive z-axis points out of the screen, toward the viewer's face.) The result of such a transformation does not necessarily *look* three-dimensional; but it *operates* in three dimensions, quite sufficiently to give a cartoonish but effective sense of reality, especially when performing an animation. We've all seen the screen image flip like turning over a piece of paper to reveal what's on the back; that's a rotation in three dimensions.

Like a view's transform, a transform3D takes place by default around the view's center, which is unaffected. (You can get finer control by dropping down to the level of the layer.) The transform itself is described mathematically by a struct called a CATransform3D. The Core Animation *Transforms* documentation lists the functions for working with these transforms. They are a lot like the CGAffineTransform functions, except they've got a third dimension. A 2D scale transform depends upon two values, the scale on the x-axis and the y-axis; for a 3D scale transform, there's also a z-axis so you have to supply a third parameter.

The rotation 3D transform is a little more complicated. In addition to the angle, you also have to supply three coordinates describing the *vector* around which the rotation is to take place. Perhaps you've forgotten from your high-school math what a vector is, or perhaps trying to visualize three dimensions boggles your mind, so here's another way to think of it.

For purposes of discussion, imagine a coordinate system in which the center of the rotation (by default, the view's center) is at the origin (0.0,0.0,0.0). Now imagine an arrow emanating from that origin; its other end, the pointy end, is described by the three coordinates you provide in that coordinate system. Now imagine a plane that intersects the origin, perpendicular to the arrow. That is the plane in which the rotation will take place; a positive angle is a clockwise rotation, as seen from the side

Figure 1-11. An anchor point plus a vector defines a rotation plane

blɿow ,olləH

Figure 1-12. A backward label

of the plane with the arrow (Figure 1-11). In effect, the three coordinates you supply describe (relative to the origin) where your eye would have to be to see this rotation as an old-fashioned two-dimensional rotation.

A vector specifies a direction, not a point. It makes no difference on what scale you give the coordinates: (1.0,1.0,1.0) means the same thing as (10.0,10.0,10.0), so you might as well say (1.0,1.0,1.0), sticking to the unit scale; when you do, the vector is said to be *normalized.*

If the three normalized values are (0.0,0.0,1.0), with all other things being equal, the case is collapsed to a simple CGAffineTransform, because the rotational plane is the screen. If the three normalized values are (0.0,0.0,-1.0), it's a backward CGAffineTransform, so that a positive angle looks counterclockwise (because we are looking at the "back side" of the rotational plane).

In this example, I'll flip a UIView around its vertical axis. If this view is a UILabel whose text is "Hello, world", the result is that we see the words "Hello, world" written *backward* (Figure 1-12):

```
v.transform3D = CATransform3DMakeRotation(.pi, 0, 1, 0)
```

Window Coordinates and Screen Coordinates

The device screen has no frame, but it has bounds. The window has no superview, but its frame is set automatically to match the screen's bounds. The window starts out life filling the screen, and generally continues to fill the screen, and so, for the most part, *window coordinates are screen coordinates.* (I'll discuss the possible exceptions on an iPad in Chapter 10.)

In iOS 7 and before, the screen's coordinates were invariant. The `transform` property lay at the heart of an iOS app's ability to rotate its interface: the window's frame and bounds were locked to the screen, and an app's interface rotated to compensate for a change in device orientation by applying a rotation transform to the root view, so that its origin moved to what the user now saw as the top left of the view.

But iOS 8 introduced a major change: when the app rotates to compensate for the rotation of the device, the screen (and with it, the window) is what rotates. None of the views in the story — neither the window, nor the root view, nor any of its subviews — receives a rotation transform when the app's interface rotates. Instead, there is a transposition of the dimensions of the screen's bounds (and a corresponding transposition of the dimensions of the window's bounds and its root view's bounds): in portrait orientation, the size is taller than wide, but in landscape orientation, the size is wider than tall.

Therefore, there are actually *two* sets of screen coordinates. Each is reported through a UICoordinateSpace, a protocol (also adopted by UIView) that provides a `bounds` property:

UIScreen's `coordinateSpace` *property*
> This coordinate space *rotates.* Its `bounds` height and width are transposed when the app rotates to compensate for a change in the orientation of the device; its bounds origin is at the top left of the *app.*

UIScreen's `fixedCoordinateSpace` *property*
> This coordinate space is *invariant.* Its `bounds` origin stays at the top left of the *physical device,* remaining always in the same relationship to the device's hardware buttons regardless of how the device itself is held.

To help you convert between coordinate spaces, UICoordinateSpace provides methods parallel to the coordinate-conversion methods I listed earlier:

- `convert(_:from:)`
- `convert(_:to:)`

The first parameter is either a CGPoint or a CGRect. The second parameter is a UICoordinateSpace, which might be a UIView or the UIScreen; so is the recipient.

Suppose we have a UIView v in our interface, and we wish to learn its position in fixed device coordinates. We could do it like this:

```
let screen = UIScreen.main.fixedCoordinateSpace
let r = v.superview!.convert(v.frame, to: screen)
```

Imagine that we have a subview of our main view, at the exact top left corner of the main view. When the device and the app are in portrait orientation, the subview's top left is at (0.0,0.0) both in window coordinates and in screen fixedCoordinate-Space coordinates. When the device is rotated left into landscape orientation, and if the app rotates to compensate, the window rotates, so the subview is *still* at the top left from the user's point of view, and is *still* at the top left in window coordinates. But in screen fixedCoordinateSpace coordinates, the subview's top left x-coordinate will have a large positive value, because the origin is now at the lower left and its x grows positively upward.

Occasions where you need such information will be rare. Indeed, my experience is that it is rare even to worry about window coordinates. All of your app's visible action takes place within your root view controller's main view, and the bounds of that view, which are adjusted for you automatically when the app rotates to compensate for a change in device orientation, are probably the highest coordinate system that will interest you.

Trait Collections

Because of the dynamic nature of the larger environment in which views live, it is useful to have an object describing that environment that propagates down through the hierarchy of view controllers and views, along with a way of alerting each element of that hierarchy that the environment has changed. This is managed through the *trait collection*.

The trait collection originates in the screen (UIScreen) and works its way down through the window and any view controllers whose view is part of the interface all the way down to every individual subview. All the relevant classes (UIScreen, UIViewController and UIPresentationController, and UIView) implement the UITraitEnvironment protocol, which supplies the traitCollection property and the traitCollectionDidChange method.

The traitCollection is a UITraitCollection, a value class. It is freighted with a considerable number of properties describing the environment. Its displayScale tells you the screen resolution; its userInterfaceIdiom states the general device type, iPhone or iPad; it reports such things as the device's force touch capability and display gamut; and so on.

If any property of the trait collection changes while the app is running, the trait-CollectionDidChange(_:) message is propagated down the hierarchy of UITraitEn-vironments; the old trait collection (if any) is provided as the parameter, and the new trait collection can be retrieved as self.traitCollection.

 If you implement traitCollectionDidChange(_:), always call super in the first line. Forgetting to do this is a common beginner mistake.

It is also possible to construct a trait collection yourself. Oddly, you can't set any trait collection properties directly; instead, you form a trait collection through an initial-izer that determines just *one* property, and if you want to add further property set-tings, you have to combine trait collections by calling init(traitsFrom:) with an array of trait collections:

```
let tcdisp = UITraitCollection(displayScale: UIScreen.main.scale)
let tcphone = UITraitCollection(userInterfaceIdiom: .phone)
let tc1 = UITraitCollection(traitsFrom: [tcdisp, tcphone])
```

The init(traitsFrom:) array works like inheritance: an *ordered intersection* is per-formed. If two trait collections are combined, and they both set the same property, the winner is the trait collection that appears later in the array or further down the inheritance hierarchy. If one sets a property and the other doesn't, the one that sets the property wins. If you create a trait collection, the value for any unspecified prop-erty will be inherited if the trait collection finds itself in the inheritance hierarchy.

To compare trait collections, call containsTraits(in:). This returns true if the value of every *specified* property of the parameter trait collection matches that of this trait collection.

The trait collection properties that are of chief concern with regard to UIViews in general are the interface style and the size classes, so I'll talk about those now.

Interface Style

The trait collection's userInterfaceStyle (a UIUserInterfaceStyle) reports whether the environment is in light mode (.light) or dark mode (.dark). For the significance of these for your app, see the discussion of colors earlier in this chapter. If your colors are dynamic colors, then for the most part everything will happen automatically; the user switches modes, and your colors change in response. However, there are circum-stances under which you may be managing some colors manually, and you'll want to know when the interface style changes so that *you* can change a color in response.

Let's say we're applying a custom named dynamic color from the asset catalog to the border of a view. This is actually done at the level of the view's layer (Chapter 3), and requires that we take the color's cgColor property:

```
self.otherView.layer.borderWidth = 4
self.otherView.layer.borderColor =
    UIColor(named: "myDarkColor")?.cgColor
```

The problem is that neither a layer nor a color's cgColor knows anything about the trait collection. So it is up to us to listen for trait collection changes and apply our dynamic color *again*. We can save ourselves from doing unnecessary work, thanks to the trait collection hasDifferentColorAppearance method:

```
override func traitCollectionDidChange(_ prevtc: UITraitCollection?) {
    super.traitCollectionDidChange(prevtc)
    if prevtc?.hasDifferentColorAppearance(
        comparedTo: self.traitCollection) ?? true {
            self.otherView.layer.borderColor =
                UIColor(named: "myDarkColor")?.cgColor
    }
}
```

Observe that we don't have to know what the userInterfaceStyle actually is; we simply take our dynamic color's cgColor and apply it, exactly as we did before. How can this be? It's because the act of accessing the named color from the asset catalog — UIColor(named: "myDarkColor") — takes place in the presence of a global value, UITraitCollection.current. In traitCollectionDidChange and various other places where the runtime is drawing or performing layout, this value is set for us, and so our dynamic color arrives in the correct interface style variant and our derived cgColor is the correct color. In contexts where UITraitCollection.current is *not* set automatically, you are free to set it manually, ensuring that subsequent operations involving dynamic colors will take place in the correct environment.

The trait collection is also the key to understanding what color a named dynamic color really is. What color is .systemYellow? Well, it depends on the trait collection. So to find out, you have to *supply* a trait collection. That's easy, because you can *make* a trait collection. Now you can call resolvedColor:

```
let yellow = UIColor.systemYellow
let light = UITraitCollection(userInterfaceStyle: .light)
let dark = UITraitCollection(userInterfaceStyle: .dark)
let yellowLight = yellow.resolvedColor(with: light)
// 1 0.8 0 1
let yellowDark = yellow.resolvedColor(with: dark)
// 1 0.839216 0.0392157 1
```

In addition to the userInterfaceStyle, the trait collection also has a userInterfaceLevel, which is .base or .elevated. This affects dynamic background colors. Only confined regions in front of the main interface are normally affected. An alert (Chapter 14) has an .elevated interface level, even if the main interface behind the alert does not.

Size Classes

The salient fact about app rotation and the like is not the rotation *per se* but the change in the app's dimensional proportions. Consider a subview of the root view, located at the bottom right of the screen when the device is in portrait orientation. If the root view's bounds width and bounds height are effectively transposed, then that poor old subview will now be outside the bounds height, and therefore off the screen — unless your app responds in some way to this change to reposition it. (Such a response is called *layout*, a subject that will occupy most of the rest of this chapter.)

The dimensional characteristics of the environment are embodied in a pair of *size classes* which are vended as trait collection properties:

horizontalSizeClass
verticalSizeClass
> A UIUserInterfaceSizeClass value, either .regular or .compact.

In combination, the size classes have the following meanings when, as will usually be the case, your app's window occupies the entire screen:

Both the horizontal and vertical size classes are .regular
> We're running on an iPad.

The horizontal size class is .compact *and the vertical size class is* .regular
> We're running on an iPhone with the app in portrait orientation.

The horizontal size class is .regular *and the vertical size class is* .compact
> We're running on a "big" iPhone with the app in landscape orientation.

Both the horizontal and vertical size classes are .compact
> We're running on an iPhone (other than a "big" iPhone) with the app in landscape orientation.

 The "big" iPhones are currently the iPhone 6/7/8 Plus, iPhone XR, iPhone XS Max, iPhone 11, and iPhone 11 Pro Max.

Clearly, a change in the size classes detected through traitCollectionDidChange is *not* the way to learn simply that the interface has rotated. Size classes don't distinguish between an iPad in portrait orientation and an iPad in landscape orientation. They distinguish between the most important extreme situations: if the horizontal size class goes from .regular to .compact, the app is suddenly tall and narrow, and you might want to compensate by changing the interface in some way. In my experience, however, you won't typically implement traitCollectionDidChange in order to hear about a change in size classes; rather, the size classes are something you'll *consult* in response to some *other* event. (I'll talk more in Chapter 6 about how to detect actual rotation at the level of the view controller.)

Overriding Trait Collections

Under certain circumstances, it can be useful to isolate part of the UITraitEnvironment hierarchy and lie to it about what the trait collection is. You might like part of the hierarchy to believe that we are on an iPhone in landscape when in fact we are on an iPhone in portrait. (I'll give an example in Chapter 6.) Or there might be some area of your app that should not respond to a change between light and dark mode.

You cannot insert a trait collection directly into the inheritance hierarchy simply by setting a view's trait collection; traitCollection isn't a settable property. However, in a UIViewController you can inject your own trait collection by way of the overrideTraitCollection property (and UIPresentationController has a method that is similar).

For the user interface style, there is a simpler facility available both for a UIViewController and for a UIView: the overrideUserInterfaceStyle property. It isn't a trait collection; it's a UIUserInterfaceStyle. The default value is .unspecified, which means that the interface style of the trait collection should just pass on down the hierarchy. But if you set it to .light or .dark, you block inheritance of just the userInterfaceStyle property of the trait collection starting at that point in the hierarchy, substituting your own custom setting.

Layout

We have seen that a subview moves when its superview's bounds *origin* is changed. But what happens to a subview when its superview's *size* is changed?

Of its own accord, *nothing* happens. The subview's bounds and center haven't changed, and the superview's bounds origin hasn't moved, so the subview stays in the same position relative to the top left of its superview. In real life, that usually won't be what you want. You'll want subviews to be resized and repositioned when their superview's size is changed. This is called *layout*.

Here are some ways in which a superview might be resized dynamically:

- Your app might compensate for the user rotating the device 90 degrees by rotating itself so that its top moves to the new top of the screen, matching its new orientation — and, as a consequence, transposing the width and height values of its bounds.

- An iPhone app might launch on screens with different aspect ratios: for instance, the screen of the iPhone SE is relatively shorter than the screen of later iPhone models, and the app's interface may need to adapt to this difference.

- A universal app might launch on an iPad or on an iPhone. The app's interface may need to adapt to the size of the screen on which it finds itself running.

- A view instantiated from a nib, such as a view controller's main view or a table view cell, might be resized to fit the interface into which it is placed.

- A view might respond to a change in its surrounding views. For instance, when a navigation bar is shown or hidden dynamically, the remaining interface might shrink or grow to compensate, filling the available space.

- The user might alter the width of your app's window on an iPad, as part of the iPad multitasking interface.

In any of those situations, and others, layout will probably be needed. Subviews of the view whose size has changed will need to shift, change size, redistribute themselves, or compensate in other ways so that the interface still looks good and remains usable.

Layout is performed in three primary ways:

Manual layout
> The superview is sent the `layoutSubviews` message whenever it is resized; so, to lay out subviews manually, provide your own subclass and override `layout-Subviews`. Clearly this could turn out to be a lot of work, but it means you can do anything you like.

Autoresizing
> Autoresizing is the oldest way of performing layout automatically. When its superview is resized, a subview will respond in accordance with the rules prescribed by its own `autoresizingMask` property value, which describes the resizing relationship between the subview and its superview.

Autolayout
> Autolayout depends on the *constraints* of views. A constraint is a full-fledged object with numeric values describing some aspect of the size or position of a view, often in terms of some other view; it is much more sophisticated, descriptive, and powerful than the `autoresizingMask`. Multiple constraints can apply to an individual view, and they can describe a relationship between *any* two views (not just a subview and its superview). Autolayout is implemented behind the scenes in `layoutSubviews`; in effect, constraints allow you to write sophisticated `layoutSubviews` functionality without code.

Your layout strategy can involve any combination of those. The need for manual layout is rare, but you can implement it if you need it. Autoresizing is the default. Autolayout is an opt-in alternative to autoresizing. But in real life, it is quite likely that *all* your views will opt in to autolayout, because it's so powerful and best suited to help your interface adapt to a great range of screen sizes.

The default layout behavior for a view depends on how it was created:

In code
> A view that your code creates and adds to the interface, by default, uses autoresizing, not autolayout. If you want such a view to use autolayout, you must deliberately suppress its use of autoresizing.

In a nib file
> All new *.storyboard* and *.xib* files opt in to autolayout. Their views are ready for autolayout. But a view in the nib editor can still use autoresizing if you prefer.

Autoresizing

Autoresizing is a matter of conceptually assigning a subview "springs and struts." A spring can expand and contract; a strut can't. Springs and struts can be assigned internally or externally, horizontally or vertically. With two internal springs or struts, you specify whether and how the view can be resized; with four external springs or struts, you specify whether and how the view can be repositioned:

- Imagine a subview that is centered in its superview and is to stay centered, but is to resize itself as the superview is resized. It would have four struts externally and two springs internally.

- Imagine a subview that is centered in its superview and is to stay centered, and is *not* to resize itself as the superview is resized. It would have four springs externally and two struts internally.

- Imagine an OK button that is to stay in the lower right of its superview. It would have two struts internally, two struts externally from its right and bottom, and two springs externally from its top and left.

- Imagine a text field that is to stay at the top of its superview. It is to widen as the superview widens. It would have three struts externally and a spring from its bottom; internally it would have a vertical strut and a horizontal spring.

In code, a combination of springs and struts is set through a view's `autoresizing-Mask` property, which is a bitmask (UIView.AutoresizingMask) so that you can combine options. The options represent springs; whatever isn't specified is a strut. The default is the empty set, apparently meaning all struts — but of course it can't really be *all* struts, because if the superview is resized, *something* needs to change, so in reality an empty `autoresizingMask` is the same as `.flexibleRightMargin` together with `.flexibleBottomMargin`, meaning the view is pinned by struts to the top left.

In debugging, when you log a UIView to the console, its `autoresizingMask` is reported using the word `autoresize` and a list of the springs. The external springs are LM, RM, TM, and BM; the internal springs are W and H. `autoresize = LM+TM` means there

Figure 1-13. Before autoresizing

Figure 1-14. After autoresizing

are external springs from the left and top; `autoresize` = `W+BM` means there's an internal horizontal spring and a spring from the bottom.

To demonstrate autoresizing, I'll start with a view and two subviews, one stretched across the top, the other confined to the lower right (Figure 1-13):

```
let v1 = UIView(frame:CGRect(100, 111, 132, 194))
v1.backgroundColor = UIColor(red: 1, green: 0.4, blue: 1, alpha: 1)
let v2 = UIView(frame:CGRect(0, 0, 132, 10))
v2.backgroundColor = UIColor(red: 0.5, green: 1, blue: 0, alpha: 1)
let v1b = v1.bounds
let v3 = UIView(frame:CGRect(v1b.width-20, v1b.height-20, 20, 20))
v3.backgroundColor = UIColor(red: 1, green: 0, blue: 0, alpha: 1)
self.view.addSubview(v1)
v1.addSubview(v2)
v1.addSubview(v3)
```

To that example, I'll add code applying springs and struts to the two subviews to make them behave like the text field and the OK button I was hypothesizing earlier:

```
v2.autoresizingMask = .flexibleWidth
v3.autoresizingMask = [.flexibleTopMargin, .flexibleLeftMargin]
```

Now I'll resize the superview, bringing autoresizing into play; as you can see (Figure 1-14), the subviews remain pinned in their correct relative positions:

```
v1.bounds.size.width += 40
v1.bounds.size.height -= 50
```

If autoresizing isn't sophisticated enough to achieve what you want, you have two choices:

- Combine it with manual layout in `layoutSubviews`. Autoresizing happens before `layoutSubviews` is called, so your `layoutSubviews` code is free to come marching in and tidy up whatever autoresizing didn't get quite right.

- Use autolayout. This is actually the same solution, because autolayout is in fact a way of injecting functionality into `layoutSubviews`. But using autolayout is a lot easier than writing your own `layoutSubviews` code!

Autolayout and Constraints

Autolayout is an opt-in technology, at the level of each individual view. You can use autoresizing and autolayout in different areas of the same interface; one sibling view can use autolayout while another sibling view does not, and a superview can use autolayout while some or all of its subviews do not. However, autolayout is implemented through the superview chain, so if a view uses autolayout, then automatically so do all its superviews; and if (as will almost certainly be the case) one of those views is the main view of a view controller, that view controller receives autolayout-related events.

But *how* does a view opt in to using autolayout? Simply by becoming involved with a constraint. Constraints are your way of telling the autolayout engine that you want it to perform layout on this view, as well as how you want the view laid out.

An autolayout constraint, or simply *constraint*, is an NSLayoutConstraint instance, and describes either the absolute width or height of a view, or else a *relationship* between an attribute of one view and an attribute of another view. In the latter case, the attributes don't have to be the same attribute, and the two views don't have to be siblings (subviews of the same superview) or parent and child (superview and subview) — the only requirement is that they share a common ancestor (a superview somewhere up the view hierarchy).

Here are the chief properties of an NSLayoutConstraint:

`firstItem`, `firstAttribute`, `secondItem`, `secondAttribute`
: The two views and their respective attributes (NSLayoutConstraint.Attribute) involved in this constraint. The possible attribute values are:

- `.width`, `.height`
- `.top`, `.bottom`
- `.left`, `.right`, `.leading`, `.trailing`
- `.centerX`, `.centerY`
- `.firstBaseline`, `.lastBaseline`

If the constraint is describing a view's absolute height or width, the `secondItem` will be `nil` and the `secondAttribute` will be `.notAnAttribute`.

`.firstBaseline` applies primarily to multiline labels, and is some distance down from the top of the label (Chapter 11); `.lastBaseline` is some distance up from the bottom of the label.

The meanings of the other attributes are intuitively obvious, except that you might wonder what `.leading` and `.trailing` mean: they are the international equivalent of `.left` and `.right`, automatically reversing their meaning on systems for which your app is localized and whose language is written right-to-left. The *entire* interface is automatically reversed on such systems — but that will work properly only if you've used `.leading` and `.trailing` constraints throughout the interface.

`multiplier, constant`
These numbers will be applied to the second attribute's value to determine the first attribute's value. The second attribute's value is multiplied by the `multiplier`; the `constant` is added to that product; and the first attribute is set to the result. Basically, you're writing an equation $a_1 = ma_2 + c$, where a_1 and a_2 are the two attributes, and m and c are the multiplier and the constant. In the degenerate case where the first attribute's value is to equal the second attribute's value, the multiplier will be 1 and the constant will be 0. If you're describing a view's width or height absolutely, the multiplier will be 1 and the constant will be the width or height value.

`relation`
How the two attribute values are to be related to one another, as modified by the `multiplier` and the `constant`. This is the operator that goes in the spot where I put the equal sign in the equation in the preceding paragraph. Possible values are (NSLayoutConstraint.Relation):

- `.equal`
- `.lessThanOrEqual`
- `.greaterThanOrEqual`

`priority`
Priority values range from 1000 (required) down to 1, and certain standard behaviors have standard priorities. Constraints can have different priorities, determining the order in which they are applied. Starting in iOS 11, a priority is not a number but a UILayoutPriority struct wrapping the numeric value as its `rawValue`.

A constraint belongs to a view. A view can have many constraints: a UIView has a `constraints` property, along with these instance methods:

- `addConstraint(_:)`, `addConstraints(_:)`
- `removeConstraint(_:)`, `removeConstraints(_:)`

The question then is *which* view a given constraint should belong to. The answer is: the view that is closest up the view hierarchy from both views involved in the constraint. If possible, it should *be* one of those views. If the constraint dictates a view's absolute width, it belongs to that view; if it sets the top of a view in relation to the top of its superview, it belongs to that superview; if it aligns the tops of two sibling views, it belongs to their common superview.

However, you'll probably never worry about that! Instead of adding a constraint to a particular view explicitly, you can *activate* the constraint. An activated constraint is *added to the correct view automatically*, relieving you from having to determine what view that would be. A constraint has an `isActive` property; you can set it to activate or deactivate a single constraint, plus it tells you whether a given constraint is part of the interface at this moment. There is also an NSLayoutConstraint class method `activate(_:)`, which takes an array of constraints, along with `deactivate(_:)`. Deactivating a constraint is like removing a subview: the constraint is removed from its view, and will go out of existence if you haven't retained it.

NSLayoutConstraint properties are read-only, except for `priority`, `constant`, and `isActive`. If you want to change anything else about an existing constraint, you must remove the constraint and replace it with a new one.

An NSLayoutConstraint also has a writable string `identifier` property. It can be set to any value you like, and can be useful for debugging or for finding a constraint later — so useful, in fact, that it might be good to have on hand an extension that lets you activate a constraint and set its identifier at the same time:

```
extension NSLayoutConstraint {
    func activate(withIdentifier id: String) {
        (self.identifier, self.isActive) = (id, true)
    }
}
```

(I owe that idea to Stack Overflow user Exquisitian; see *https://stackoverflow.com/a/57102973/341994*.)

 Once you are using explicit constraints to position and size a view, *do not set its frame* (or bounds and center); use constraints alone. Otherwise, when `layoutSubviews` is called, the view will jump back to where its constraints position it. (However, you may set a view's frame from *within* an implementation of `layoutSubviews`, and it is perfectly normal to do so.)

Implicit Autoresizing Constraints

The mechanism whereby individual views can opt in to autolayout can suddenly involve other views in autolayout, even though those other views were not using autolayout previously. Therefore, there needs to be a way, when such a view becomes involved in autolayout, to generate constraints for it — constraints that will determine that view's position and size identically to how its frame and autoresizingMask were determining them. The autolayout engine takes care of this for you: it reads the view's frame and autoresizingMask settings and translates them into *implicit* constraints (of class NSAutoresizingMaskLayoutConstraint). The autolayout engine treats a view in this special way only if the view has its translatesAutoresizingMask-IntoConstraints property set to true — which happens to be the default.

To demonstrate, I'll construct an example in two stages. In the first stage, I add to my interface, in code, a UILabel ("Hello") that *doesn't* use autolayout. I'll decide that this view's position is to be somewhere near the top right of the screen. To keep it in position near the top right, its autoresizingMask will be [.flexibleLeft-Margin, .flexibleBottomMargin]:

```
let lab1 = UILabel(frame:CGRect(270,20,42,22))
lab1.autoresizingMask = [.flexibleLeftMargin, .flexibleBottomMargin]
lab1.text = "Hello"
self.view.addSubview(lab1)
```

If we now rotate the device (or Simulator window), and the app rotates to compensate, the label stays correctly positioned near the top right corner by autoresizing.

Now I'll add a second label ("Howdy") that *does* use autolayout — and in particular, I'll attach it by a constraint to the first label (the meaning of this code will be made clear in subsequent sections; just accept it for now):

```
let lab2 = UILabel()
lab2.translatesAutoresizingMaskIntoConstraints = false
lab2.text = "Howdy"
self.view.addSubview(lab2)
NSLayoutConstraint.activate([
    lab2.topAnchor.constraint(
        equalTo: lab1.bottomAnchor, constant: 20),
    lab2.trailingAnchor.constraint(
        equalTo: self.view.trailingAnchor, constant: -20)
])
```

This causes the first label ("Hello") to be involved in autolayout. Therefore, the first label magically acquires four automatically generated implicit constraints of class NSAutoresizingMaskLayoutConstraint, such as to give the label the same size and position, and the same *behavior* when its superview is resized, that it had when it was configured by its frame and autoresizingMask:

```
<NSAutoresizingMaskLayoutConstraint H:[UILabel:'Hello']-(63)-|>
<NSAutoresizingMaskLayoutConstraint UILabel:'Hello'.minY == 20>
<NSAutoresizingMaskLayoutConstraint UILabel:'Hello'.width == 42>
<NSAutoresizingMaskLayoutConstraint UILabel:'Hello'.height == 22>
```

Recall that the original frame was (270,20,42,22). I'm on an iPhone 8 simulator, so the main view width is 375. I've simplified and rearranged the output, but what it says is that the label's right edge is 63 points from the main view's right (the label's original x value of 270 plus its width of 42 is 312, and the main view's width of 375 minus 312 is 63), its top is 20 points from the main view's top, and it is 42×22 in size.

But within this helpful automatic behavior lurks a trap. Suppose a view has acquired automatically generated implicit constraints, and suppose you then proceed to attach *further constraints* to this view, explicitly setting its position or size. There will then almost certainly be a *conflict* between your explicit constraints and the implicit constraints. The solution is to set the view's `translatesAutoresizingMaskInto-Constraints` property to `false`, so that the implicit constraints are *not* generated, and the view's *only* constraints are your explicit constraints.

The trouble is most likely to arise when you create a view *in code* and then position or size that view with constraints, *forgetting* that you also need to set its `translates-AutoresizingMaskIntoConstraints` property to `false`. If that happens, you'll get a conflict between constraints. (To be honest, I usually *do* forget, and am reminded only when I *do* get a conflict between constraints.)

Creating Constraints in Code

We are now ready to write some code that creates constraints! I'll start by using the NSLayoutConstraint initializer:

- `init(item:attribute:relatedBy:toItem:attribute:multiplier:constant:)`

This initializer sets every property of the constraint, as I described them a moment ago — except the `priority`, which defaults to `.required` (1000), and the `identifier`, both of which can be set later if desired.

I'll generate the same views and subviews and layout behavior as in Figures 1-13 and 1-14, but using constraints. First, I'll create the views and add them to the interface. Observe that I don't bother to assign the subviews `v2` and `v3` explicit frames as I create them, because constraints will take care of positioning them. Also, I remember (for once) to set their `translatesAutoresizingMaskIntoConstraints` properties to `false`, so that they won't sprout additional implicit NSAutoresizingMaskLayout-Constraints:

```
let v1 = UIView(frame:CGRect(100, 111, 132, 194))
v1.backgroundColor = UIColor(red: 1, green: 0.4, blue: 1, alpha: 1)
let v2 = UIView()
v2.backgroundColor = UIColor(red: 0.5, green: 1, blue: 0, alpha: 1)
let v3 = UIView()
v3.backgroundColor = UIColor(red: 1, green: 0, blue: 0, alpha: 1)
self.view.addSubview(v1)
v1.addSubview(v2)
v1.addSubview(v3)
v2.translatesAutoresizingMaskIntoConstraints = false
v3.translatesAutoresizingMaskIntoConstraints = false
```

And here come the constraints; I'll add them to their views manually, just to show how it's done:

```
v1.addConstraint(
    NSLayoutConstraint(item: v2,
        attribute: .leading,
        relatedBy: .equal,
        toItem: v1,
        attribute: .leading,
        multiplier: 1, constant: 0)
)
v1.addConstraint(
    NSLayoutConstraint(item: v2,
        attribute: .trailing,
        relatedBy: .equal,
        toItem: v1,
        attribute: .trailing,
        multiplier: 1, constant: 0)
)
v1.addConstraint(
    NSLayoutConstraint(item: v2,
        attribute: .top,
        relatedBy: .equal,
        toItem: v1,
        attribute: .top,
        multiplier: 1, constant: 0)
)
v2.addConstraint(
    NSLayoutConstraint(item: v2,
        attribute: .height,
        relatedBy: .equal,
        toItem: nil,
        attribute: .notAnAttribute,
        multiplier: 1, constant: 10)
)
v3.addConstraint(
    NSLayoutConstraint(item: v3,
        attribute: .width,
        relatedBy: .equal,
        toItem: nil,
        attribute: .notAnAttribute,
```

```
                multiplier: 1, constant: 20)
    )
    v3.addConstraint(
        NSLayoutConstraint(item: v3,
            attribute: .height,
            relatedBy: .equal,
            toItem: nil,
            attribute: .notAnAttribute,
            multiplier: 1, constant: 20)
    )
    v1.addConstraint(
        NSLayoutConstraint(item: v3,
            attribute: .trailing,
            relatedBy: .equal,
            toItem: v1,
            attribute: .trailing,
            multiplier: 1, constant: 0)
    )
    v1.addConstraint(
        NSLayoutConstraint(item: v3,
            attribute: .bottom,
            relatedBy: .equal,
            toItem: v1,
            attribute: .bottom,
            multiplier: 1, constant: 0)
    )
```

Now, I know what you're thinking. You're thinking: "What are you, nuts? That is a boatload of code!" (Except that you probably used another four-letter word instead of "boat.") But that's something of an illusion. I'd argue that what we're doing here is actually *simpler* than the code with which we created Figure 1-13 using explicit frames and autoresizing.

After all, we merely create eight constraints in eight simple commands. (I've broken each command into multiple *lines*, but that's mere formatting.) They're verbose, but they are the same command repeated with different parameters, so creating them is simple. Moreover, our eight constraints determine the *position, size, and layout behavior* of our two subviews, so we're getting a lot of bang for our buck. Even more telling, these constraints are a far clearer expression of what's supposed to happen than setting a frame and `autoresizingMask`. The position of our subviews is described once and for all, both as they will initially appear and as they will appear if their superview is resized. And we don't have to use arbitrary math. Recall what we had to say before:

```
let v1b = v1.bounds
let v3 = UIView(frame:CGRect(v1b.width-20, v1b.height-20, 20, 20))
```

That business of subtracting the view's height and width from its superview's bounds height and width in order to position the view is confusing and error-prone. With constraints, we can speak the truth directly; our constraints say, plainly and simply, "v3 is 20 points wide and 20 points high and *flush with the bottom-right corner* of v1."

In addition, constraints can express things that autoresizing can't. Instead of applying an absolute height to v2, we could require that its height be exactly one-tenth of v1's height, regardless of how v1 is resized. To do that without autolayout, you'd have to implement `layoutSubviews` and enforce it manually, in code.

Anchor notation

The `NSLayoutConstraint(item:...)` initializer is rather verbose, though it has the virtue of singularity: one method can create any constraint. There's another way to do everything I just did, making exactly the same eight constraints and adding them to the same views, using a much more compact notation that takes the opposite approach: it concentrates on brevity but sacrifices singularity. Instead of focusing on the constraint, the compact notation focuses on the *attributes* to which the constraint relates. These attributes are expressed as *anchor* properties of a UIView:

- `widthAnchor, heightAnchor`
- `topAnchor, bottomAnchor`
- `leftAnchor, rightAnchor, leadingAnchor, trailingAnchor`
- `centerXAnchor, centerYAnchor`
- `firstBaselineAnchor, lastBaselineAnchor`

The anchor values are instances of NSLayoutAnchor subclasses. The constraint-forming methods are anchor instance methods. There are three possible relations — equal to, greater than or equal to, and less than or equal to — and the relationship might be with a constant or another anchor, yielding six combinations:

A constant alone
> These methods are for an absolute width or height constraint:
>
> - `constraint(equalToConstant:)`
> - `constraint(greaterThanOrEqualToConstant:)`
> - `constraint(lessThanOrEqualToConstant:)`

Another anchor
> In a relationship with another anchor, we need a constant and a multiplier:
>
> - `constraint(equalTo:multiplier:constant:)`
> - `constraint(greaterThanOrEqualTo:multiplier:constant:)`
> - `constraint(lessThanOrEqualTo:multiplier:constant:)`

For brevity, you can omit the `multiplier:`, the `constant:`, or both. If the constant is omitted, it is 0; if the multiplier is omitted, it is 1.

In iOS 10, a method was added that generates, not a constraint, but a new width or height anchor expressing the distance between two anchors; you can then set a view's width or height anchor in relation to that distance:

- `anchorWithOffset(to:)`

Starting in iOS 11, additional methods create a constraint based on a `constant` value provided by the runtime. This is helpful for getting the standard spacing between views, and is especially valuable when connecting text baselines vertically, because the system spacing will change according to the text size:

- `constraint(equalToSystemSpacingAfter:multiplier:)`
- `constraint(greaterThanOrEqualToSystemSpacingAfter:multiplier:)`
- `constraint(lessThanOrEqualToSystemSpacingAfter:multiplier:)`
- `constraint(equalToSystemSpacingBelow:multiplier:)`
- `constraint(greaterThanOrEqualToSystemSpacingBelow:multiplier:)`
- `constraint(lessThanOrEqualToSystemSpacingBelow:multiplier:)`

All of that may sound very elaborate when I describe it, but when you see it in action, you will appreciate immediately the benefit of this compact notation: it's easy to write (especially thanks to Xcode's code completion), easy to read, and easy to maintain. Here we generate exactly the same constraints as in the preceding example; I'll call `activate` instead of adding each constraint to its view manually:

```
NSLayoutConstraint.activate([
    v2.leadingAnchor.constraint(equalTo:v1.leadingAnchor),
    v2.trailingAnchor.constraint(equalTo:v1.trailingAnchor),
    v2.topAnchor.constraint(equalTo:v1.topAnchor),
    v2.heightAnchor.constraint(equalToConstant:10),
    v3.widthAnchor.constraint(equalToConstant:20),
    v3.heightAnchor.constraint(equalToConstant:20),
    v3.trailingAnchor.constraint(equalTo:v1.trailingAnchor),
    v3.bottomAnchor.constraint(equalTo:v1.bottomAnchor)
])
```

That's eight constraints in eight lines of code.

Visual format notation

Another way to abbreviate your creation of constraints is to use a text-based shorthand called a *visual format*. This has the advantage of allowing you to describe multiple constraints simultaneously, and is appropriate particularly when you're arranging a series of views horizontally or vertically. I'll start with a simple example:

```
"V:|[v2(10)]"
```

In that expression, V: means that the vertical dimension is under discussion; the alternative is H:, which is also the default (so you can omit it). A view's name appears in square brackets, and a pipe (|) signifies the superview, so we're portraying v2's top edge as butting up against its superview's top edge. Numeric dimensions appear in parentheses, and a numeric dimension accompanying a view's name sets that dimension of that view, so we're also setting v2's height to 10.

To use a visual format, you have to provide a dictionary that maps the string name of each view mentioned by the visual format string to the actual view. The dictionary accompanying the preceding expression might be ["v2":v2].

Here, then, is yet another way of expressing the preceding examples, generating exactly the same eight constraints using four commands instead of eight, thanks to the visual format shorthand:

```
let d = ["v2":v2,"v3":v3]
NSLayoutConstraint.activate([
    NSLayoutConstraint.constraints(withVisualFormat:
        "H:|[v2]|", metrics: nil, views: d),
    NSLayoutConstraint.constraints(withVisualFormat:
        "V:|[v2(10)]", metrics: nil, views: d),
    NSLayoutConstraint.constraints(withVisualFormat:
        "H:[v3(20)]|", metrics: nil, views: d),
    NSLayoutConstraint.constraints(withVisualFormat:
        "V:[v3(20)]|", metrics: nil, views: d)
].flatMap {$0})
```

(The constraints(withVisualFormat:...) class method yields an array of constraints, so my overall array is an array of arrays of constraints. But activate(_:) expects an array of constraints, so I flatten my overall array.)

Here are some further things to know when generating constraints with the visual format syntax:

- The metrics: parameter is a dictionary with numeric values. This lets you use a name in the visual format string where a numeric value needs to go.

- The options: parameter, omitted in the preceding example, is a bitmask (NSLayoutConstraint.FormatOptions) chiefly allowing you to specify alignments to be applied to all the views mentioned in the visual format string.

- To specify the distance between two successive views, use hyphens surrounding the numeric value, like this: "[v1]-20-[v2]". The numeric value may optionally be surrounded by parentheses.

- A numeric value in parentheses may be preceded by an equality or inequality operator, and may be followed by an at sign with a priority. Multiple numeric values, separated by comma, may appear in parentheses together, as in "[v1(>=20@400,<=30)]".

For formal details of the visual format syntax, see the "Visual Format Syntax" appendix of Apple's *Auto Layout Guide* in the documentation archive.

The visual format syntax shows itself to best advantage when multiple views are laid out in relation to one another along the same dimension; in that situation, you can get many constraints generated by a single compact visual format string. However, it hasn't been updated for recent iOS versions, so there are some important types of constraint that visual format syntax can't express (such as pinning a view to the safe area, discussed later in this chapter).

Constraints as Objects

The examples so far have involved creating constraints and adding them directly to the interface — and then forgetting about them. But it is frequently useful to form constraints and keep them on hand for future use, typically in a property. A common use case is where you intend, at some future time, to change the interface in some radical way, such as by inserting or removing a view; you'll probably find it convenient to keep multiple sets of constraints on hand, each set being appropriate to a particular configuration of the interface. It is then trivial to swap constraints out of and into the interface along with the views that they affect.

In this example, we create within our main view (self.view) three views, v1, v2, and v3, which are red, yellow, and blue rectangles respectively. For some reason, we will later want to remove the yellow view (v2) dynamically as the app runs, moving the blue view to where the yellow view was; and then, still later, we will want to insert the yellow view once again (Figure 1-15). So we have two alternating view configurations.

To prepare for this, we create *two* sets of constraints, one describing the positions of v1, v2, and v3 when all three are present, the other describing the positions of v1 and v3 when v2 is absent. For purposes of maintaining these sets of constraints, we have already prepared two properties, constraintsWith and constraintsWithout, initialized as empty arrays of NSLayoutConstraint. We will also need a strong reference to v2, so that it doesn't vanish when we remove it from the interface:

```
var v2 : UIView!
var constraintsWith = [NSLayoutConstraint]()
var constraintsWithout = [NSLayoutConstraint]()
```

Here's the code for creating the views:

```
let v1 = UIView()
v1.backgroundColor = .red
v1.translatesAutoresizingMaskIntoConstraints = false
let v2 = UIView()
v2.backgroundColor = .yellow
```

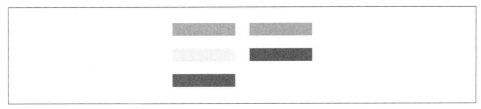

Figure 1-15. Alternate sets of views and constraints

```
v2.translatesAutoresizingMaskIntoConstraints = false
let v3 = UIView()
v3.backgroundColor = .blue
v3.translatesAutoresizingMaskIntoConstraints = false
self.view.addSubview(v1)
self.view.addSubview(v2)
self.view.addSubview(v3)
self.v2 = v2 // retain
```

Now we create the constraints. In what follows, c1, c3, and c4 are in common to both situations (v2 is present or v2 is absent), so we simply activate them once and for all. The remaining constraints we store in two groups, one for each of the two situations:

```
// construct constraints
let c1 = NSLayoutConstraint.constraints(withVisualFormat:
    "H:|-(20)-[v(100)]", metrics: nil, views: ["v":v1])
let c2 = NSLayoutConstraint.constraints(withVisualFormat:
    "H:|-(20)-[v(100)]", metrics: nil, views: ["v":v2])
let c3 = NSLayoutConstraint.constraints(withVisualFormat:
    "H:|-(20)-[v(100)]", metrics: nil, views: ["v":v3])
let c4 = NSLayoutConstraint.constraints(withVisualFormat:
    "V:|-(100)-[v(20)]", metrics: nil, views: ["v":v1])
let c5with = NSLayoutConstraint.constraints(withVisualFormat:
    "V:[v1]-(20)-[v2(20)]-(20)-[v3(20)]", metrics: nil,
    views: ["v1":v1, "v2":v2, "v3":v3])
let c5without = NSLayoutConstraint.constraints(withVisualFormat:
    "V:[v1]-(20)-[v3(20)]", metrics: nil, views: ["v1":v1, "v3":v3])
// apply common constraints
NSLayoutConstraint.activate([c1, c3, c4].flatMap {$0})
// first set of constraints (for when v2 is present)
self.constraintsWith.append(contentsOf:c2)
self.constraintsWith.append(contentsOf:c5with)
// second set of constraints (for when v2 is absent)
self.constraintsWithout.append(contentsOf:c5without)
```

Now we're ready to start alternating between constraintsWith and constraints-Without. We start with v2 present, so it is constraintsWith that we initially make active:

```
// apply first set
NSLayoutConstraint.activate(self.constraintsWith)
```

All that preparation may seem extraordinarily elaborate, but the result is that when the time comes to swap v2 out of or into the interface, it's trivial to swap the appropriate constraints at the same time:

```
func doSwap() {
    if self.v2.superview != nil {
        self.v2.removeFromSuperview()
        NSLayoutConstraint.deactivate(self.constraintsWith)
        NSLayoutConstraint.activate(self.constraintsWithout)
    } else {
        self.view.addSubview(v2)
        NSLayoutConstraint.deactivate(self.constraintsWithout)
        NSLayoutConstraint.activate(self.constraintsWith)
    }
}
```

In that code, I deactivate the old constraints before activating the new ones. Always proceed in that order; activating the new constraints with the old constraints still in force will cause a conflict (as I'll explain later in this chapter).

Margins and Guides

So far, I've been assuming that the anchor points of your constraints represent the literal edges and centers of views. Sometimes, however, you want a view to vend a set of secondary edges, with respect to which other views can be positioned. You might want subviews to keep a minimum distance from the edge of their superview, and the superview should be able to dictate what that minimum distance is. This notion of secondary edges is expressed in two different ways:

Edge insets
    A view vends secondary edges as a UIEdgeInsets, a struct consisting of four floats representing inset values starting at the top and proceeding counterclockwise — top, left, bottom, right. This is useful when you need to interface with the secondary edges as numeric values — perhaps to set them or to perform manual layout based on them.

Layout guides
    The UILayoutGuide class represents secondary edges as a kind of pseudoview. It has a frame (its `layoutFrame`) with respect to the view that vends it, but its important properties are its anchors, which are the same as for a view. This, obviously, is useful for autolayout.

Safe area

An important set of secondary edges (introduced in iOS 11) is the *safe area*. This is a feature of a UIView, but it is imposed by the UIViewController that manages this view. One reason the safe area is needed is that the top and bottom of the interface are often occupied by a bar (status bar, navigation bar, toolbar, tab bar — see Chapter 13). Your layout of subviews will typically occupy the region *between* these bars. But that's not easy, because:

- A view controller's main view will typically extend vertically to the edges of the window *behind* those bars.
- The bars can come and go dynamically, and can change their heights. By default, in an iPhone app, the status bar will be present when the app is in portrait orientation, but will vanish when the app is in landscape orientation; similarly, a navigation bar is taller when the app is in portrait orientation than when the app is in landscape orientation.

Therefore, you need something else, other than the *literal* top and bottom of a view controller's main view, to which to anchor the vertical constraints that position its subviews — something that will *move* dynamically to reflect the current location of the bars. Otherwise, an interface that looks right under some circumstances will look wrong in others. Consider a view whose top is literally constrained to the top of the view controller's main view, which is its superview:

```
let arr = NSLayoutConstraint.constraints(withVisualFormat:
    "V:|-0-[v]", metrics: nil, views: ["v":v])
```

When the app is in landscape orientation, with the status bar removed by default, this view will be right up against the top of the screen, which is fine. But when the app is in portrait orientation, this view will *still* be right up against the top of the screen — which might look bad, because the status bar reappears and overlaps it.

To solve this problem, a UIViewController imposes the safe area on its main view, describing the region of the main view that is overlapped by the status bar and other bars:

- The top of the safe area matches the bottom of the lowest top bar, or the top of the main view if there is no top bar.
- The bottom of the safe area matches the top of the bottom bar, or the bottom of the main view if there is no bottom bar.

The safe area changes as the situation changes — when the top or bottom bar changes its height, or vanishes entirely. On a device without a bezel, such as the iPhone X, the safe area is of even greater importance; its boundaries help keep your views away from the rounded corners of the screen, and prevent them from being interfered with by the sensors and the home indicator, both in portrait and in landscape.

In real life, therefore, you'll be particularly concerned to position subviews of a view controller's main view with respect to the main view's safe area. Your views constrained to the main view's safe area will avoid being overlapped by bars, and will move to track the edges of the main view's visible area. But *any* view — not just the view controller's main view — can participate in the safe area. When a view performs layout, it imposes the safe area on its own subviews, describing the region of each subview that is overlapped by its own safe area; so *every* view "knows" where the bars are. (There are some additional complexities that I'm omitting, because for practical purposes you probably won't encounter them.)

To retrieve a view's safe area as edge insets, fetch its `safeAreaInsets`. To retrieve a view's safe area as a layout guide, fetch its `safeAreaLayoutGuide`. You can learn that a subclassed view's safe area has changed by overriding `safeAreaInsetsDidChange`, or that a view controller's main view's safe area has changed by overriding the view controller's `viewSafeAreaInsetsDidChange`.

In real life, however, using autolayout, you probably won't need that information — you'll just allow views pinned to a safe area layout guide to move as the safe area changes. In this example, v is a view controller's main view, and v1 is its subview; we construct a constraint between the top of v1 and the top of the main view's safe area:

```
let c = v1.topAnchor.constraint(equalTo: v.safeAreaLayoutGuide.topAnchor)
```

A view controller can inset even further the safe area it imposes on its main view: set its `additionalSafeAreaInsets`. This, as the name implies, is added to the automatic safe area. It is a UIEdgeInsets. If you set a view controller's `additionalSafeArea-Insets` to a UIEdgeInsets with a top of 50, and if the status bar is showing and there is no other top bar, the default safe area top would be 20, so now it's 70. The `additionalSafeAreaInsets` is helpful if your main view has material at its edge that must always remain visible.

Margins

A view also has margins of its own. Unlike the safe area, which propagates down the view hierarchy from the view controller, you are free to set an individual view's margins. The idea is that a subview might be positioned with respect to its superview's margins, especially through an autolayout constraint. By default, a view has a margin of 8 on all four edges.

A view's margins are available as a UILayoutGuide through the UIView `layout-MarginsGuide` property. Here's a constraint between a subview's leading edge and its superview's leading margin:

```
let c = v.leadingAnchor.constraint(equalTo:
    self.view.layoutMarginsGuide.leadingAnchor)
```

In visual format syntax, a view pinned to its superview's edge using a single hyphen, with no explicit distance value, is interpreted as a constraint to the superview's margin:

```
let arr = NSLayoutConstraint.constraints(withVisualFormat:
    "H:|-[v]", metrics: nil, views: ["v":v])
```

The `layoutMarginsGuide` property is read-only. To allow you to set a view's margins, a UIView has a `layoutMargins` property, a writable UIEdgeInsets. Starting in iOS 11, Apple would prefer that you set the `directionalLayoutMargins` property instead; this has the feature that when your interface is reversed in a right-to-left system language for which your app is localized, its leading and trailing values behave correctly. It is expressed as an NSDirectionalEdgeInsets struct, whose properties are `top`, `leading`, `bottom`, and `trailing`.

Optionally, a view's layout margins can propagate down to its subview, in the following sense: a subview that overlaps its superview's margin may acquire the amount of overlap as a minimum margin of its own. To switch on this option, set the subview's `preservesSuperviewLayoutMargins` to `true`. Suppose we set the superview's `directionalLayoutMargins` to an NSDirectionalEdgeInsets with a `leading` value of 40. And suppose the subview is pinned 10 points from the superview's leading edge, so that it overlaps the superview's leading margin by 30 points. Then, if the subview's `preservesSuperviewLayoutMargins` is `true`, the subview's leading margin is 30.

By default, a view's margin values are treated as insets *from the safe area*. Suppose a view's top margin is 8. And suppose this view underlaps the entire status bar, acquiring a safe area top of 20. Then its *effective* top margin value is 28 — meaning that a subview whose top is pinned exactly to this view's top margin will appear 28 points below this view's top. If you don't like that behavior (perhaps because you have code that predates the existence of the safe area), you can switch it off by setting the view's `insetsLayoutMarginsFromSafeArea` property to `false`; now a top margin value of 8 means an effective top margin value of 8.

A view controller also has a `systemMinimumLayoutMargins` property; it imposes these margins on its main view as a minimum, meaning that you can increase the main view's margins beyond these limits, but an attempt to decrease a margin below them will fail silently. You can evade that restriction, however, by setting the view controller's `viewRespectsSystemMinimumLayoutMargins` property to `false`. The system-MinimumLayoutMargins default value is a top and bottom margin of 0 and side margins of 16 on a smaller device, with side margins of 20 on a larger device.

A second set of margins, a UIView's `readableContentGuide` (a UILayoutGuide), which you cannot change, enforces the idea that a subview consisting of text should not be allowed to grow as wide as an iPad in landscape, because that's too wide to read easily, especially if the text is small. By constraining such a subview horizontally to its superview's `readableContentGuide`, you ensure that that won't happen.

Custom layout guides

You can add your own custom UILayoutGuide objects to a view, for whatever purpose you like. They constitute a view's `layoutGuides` array, and are managed by calling addLayoutGuide(_:) or removeLayoutGuide(_:). Each custom layout guide object must be configured entirely using constraints.

Why would you want to do that? Well, you can constrain a view to a UILayoutGuide, by means of its anchors. Since a UILayoutGuide is configured by constraints, and since other views can be constrained to it, it can participate in autolayout exactly as if it were a subview — but it is *not* a subview, and therefore it avoids all the overhead and complexity that a UIView would have.

Consider the question of how to *distribute views equally* within their superview. This is easy to arrange initially, but it is not obvious how to design evenly spaced views that will remain evenly spaced when their superview is resized. The problem is that constraints describe relationships between *views*, not between *constraints*; there is no way to constrain the spacing constraints between views to remain *equal to one another* automatically as the superview is resized.

You can, on the other hand, constrain the heights or widths of *views* to remain equal to one another. The traditional solution, therefore, is to resort to spacer views with their isHidden set to true. Suppose I have four views of equal heights that are to remain equally distributed vertically. Between them, I interpose three spacer views, also of equal heights. If we pin every view to the view below it, and the first and last views to the top and bottom of the superview, and *hide* the spacer views, they become the equal *spaces* between the visible views.

But spacer views are views; hidden or not, they add overhead with respect to drawing, memory, touch detection, and more. Custom UILayoutGuides solve the problem; they can serve the same purpose as spacer views, but they are *not* views.

I'll demonstrate. We have four views that are to remain equally distributed vertically. I constrain the left and right edges of the four views, their heights, and the top of the first view and the bottom of the last view. Now we want to set the vertical position of the two middle views such that they are always equidistant from their vertical neighbors (Figure 1-16).

To solve the problem, I introduce three UILayoutGuide objects between my real views. A custom UILayoutGuide object is added to a UIView, so I'll add mine to the view controller's main view. I then involve my three layout guides in the layout. Remember, they must be configured entirely using constraints! The four views are referenced through an array, views:

```
var guides = [UILayoutGuide]()
// one fewer guides than views ❶
for _ in views.dropLast() {
    let g = UILayoutGuide()
    self.view.addLayoutGuide(g)
    guides.append(g)
}
```

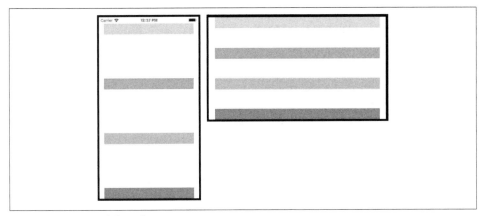

Figure 1-16. Equal distribution

```
// guides leading and width are arbitrary ❷
let anc = self.view.leadingAnchor
for g in guides {
    g.leadingAnchor.constraint(equalTo:anc).isActive = true
    g.widthAnchor.constraint(equalToConstant:10).isActive = true
}
// guides top to previous view ❸
for (v,g) in zip(views.dropLast(), guides) {
    v.bottomAnchor.constraint(equalTo:g.topAnchor).isActive = true
}
// guides bottom to next view ❹
for (v,g) in zip(views.dropFirst(), guides) {
    v.topAnchor.constraint(equalTo:g.bottomAnchor).isActive = true
}
// guide heights equal to each other! ❺
let h = guides[0].heightAnchor
for g in guides.dropFirst() {
    g.heightAnchor.constraint(equalTo:h).isActive = true
}
```

❶ I create the layout guides and add them to the interface.

❷ I constrain the leading edges of the layout guides (arbitrarily, to the leading edge of the main view) and their widths (arbitrarily).

❸ I constrain each layout guide to the bottom of the view above it.

❹ I constrain each layout guide to the top of the view below it.

❺ Finally, our whole purpose is to distribute our views *equally*, so the heights of our layout guides must be *equal to one another*.

In real life, if the problem is equal distribution, you are unlikely to use this technique directly, because you will use a UIStackView instead, and let the UIStackView generate all of that code for you — as I will explain a little later.

Constraint alignment

You can also change the location of your view's anchors themselves. Constraints are measured by default from a view's edges, but consider a view that draws, internally, a rectangle with a shadow; you probably want to pin other views to that drawn rectangle, not to the outside of the shadow.

To effect this, you can override your view's `alignmentRectInsets` property (or, more elaborately, its `alignmentRect(forFrame:)` and `frame(forAlignmentRect:)` methods). When you change a view's `alignmentRectInsets`, you are effectively changing where the view's edges are for purposes of *all* constraints involving those edges. If a view's alignment rect has a left inset of 30, then all constraints involving that view's `.leading` attribute or `leadingAnchor` are reckoned from that inset.

By the same token, you may want to be able to align your custom UIView with another view by their baselines. The assumption here is that your view has a subview containing text that itself has a baseline. Your custom view will return that subview in its implementation of `forFirstBaselineLayout` or `forLastBaselineLayout`.

Intrinsic Content Size

Certain built-in interface objects, when using autolayout, have an *inherent size* in one or both dimensions, dependent upon the object type and its content. Here are some examples:

- A UIButton has a standard height, and its width is determined by the length of its title.
- A UIImageView adopts the size of the image that it is displaying.
- A UILabel consisting of a single line of text adopts the size of the text that it is displaying.

This inherent size is the object's *intrinsic content size*. The intrinsic content size is used to generate constraints implicitly (of class NSContentSizeLayoutConstraint).

A change in the characteristics or content of a built-in interface object — a button's title, an image view's image, a label's text or font, and so forth — may cause its intrinsic content size to change. This, in turn, may alter your layout. You will want to configure your autolayout constraints so that your interface responds gracefully to such changes.

You do not have to supply explicit constraints configuring a dimension of a view whose intrinsic content size configures that dimension. But you might! And when you do, the tendency of an interface object to size itself to its intrinsic content size must not be allowed to conflict with its obedience to your explicit constraints. Therefore, the constraints generated from a view's intrinsic content size have a *lowered priority*, and come into force only if no constraint of a higher priority prevents them. The following methods allow you to access these priorities (the parameter is an NSLayoutConstraint.Axis, either `.horizontal` or `.vertical`):

contentHuggingPriority(for:)
> A view's resistance to growing larger than its intrinsic size in this dimension. In effect, there is an inequality constraint saying that the view's size in this dimension should be less than or equal to its intrinsic size. The default priority is usually `.defaultLow` (250), though some interface classes will default to a higher value if created in a nib.

contentCompressionResistancePriority(for:)
> A view's resistance to shrinking smaller than its intrinsic size in this dimension. In effect, there is an inequality constraint saying that the view's size in this dimension should be greater than or equal to its intrinsic size. The default priority is usually `.defaultHigh` (750).

Those methods are getters; there are corresponding setters, because you might need to change the priorities. Here are visual formats configuring two horizontally adjacent labels (`lab1` and `lab2`) to be pinned to the superview and to one another:

```
"V:|-20-[lab1]"
"V:|-20-[lab2]"
"H:|-20-[lab1]"
"H:[lab2]-20-|"
"H:[lab1(>=100)]-(>=20)-[lab2(>=100)]"
```

The inequalities ensure that as the superview becomes narrower or the text of the labels becomes longer, a reasonable amount of text will remain visible in both labels. At the same time, one label will be squeezed down to 100 points width, while the other label will be allowed to grow to fill the remaining horizontal space. The question is: which label is which? You need to answer that question. To do so, it suffices to give the two labels different compression resistance priorities; even a tiny difference will do:

```
let p = lab2.contentCompressionResistancePriority(for: .horizontal)
lab1.setContentCompressionResistancePriority(p+1, for: .horizontal)
```

You can supply an intrinsic size in your own custom UIView subclass by overriding `intrinsicContentSize`. Obviously you should do this only if your view's size somehow depends on its content. If you need the runtime to ask for your `intrinsicContentSize` again, because the contents have changed and the view needs to be laid out afresh, it's up to you to call your view's `invalidateIntrinsicContentSize` method.

Figure 1-17. A self-sizing view

Self-Sizing Views

So far, I have talked about layout (and autolayout in particular) as a way of solving the problem of what should happen to a superview's subviews when the superview is resized. However, autolayout also works in the opposite direction. If a superview's subviews determine their own size, they can also determine the size of the superview.

Consider this simple example. We have a plain vanilla UIView, which has as its sole subview a UIButton. And suppose this UIButton is pinned by constraints from all four edges to its superview, the plain vanilla UIView. Well, as I've already said, a UIButton under autolayout has an intrinsic size: its height is standard, and its width is dependent upon its title. So, all other things being equal, the size of the button is *determined*. Then, all other things being equal, the size of the plain vanilla view is *also* determined, *from the inside out,* by the size of the button, its subview. (See Figure 1-17; the inner rectangle with the black border is the button, and the outer rectangle is the plain vanilla UIView.)

What I mean by "all other things being equal" is simply that you don't determine the size of the plain vanilla superview in any *other* way. Let's say you pin the leading and top edges of the superview to *its* superview. Now we know the *position* of the super-view. But we do not pin its trailing or bottom edges, and we don't give it a width or height constraint. You might say: Then the width and height of the superview are unknown! But not so. In this situation, the autolayout engine simply gets the width and height of the superview from the width and height of its subview, the button — because the width and height of the button *are* known, and there is a complete constraint relationship between the width and height of the button and the width and height of the superview.

I call a view such as our plain vanilla superview a *self-sizing view*. In effect, it has an intrinsic content size — not literally (we have not configured its `instrinsicContentSize`), but in the sense that it is, in fact, sized by its content. A self-sizing view's size does not have to be determined *solely* by its content; it is fine to give a self-sizing view a width constraint (or pin it on both sides) but allow its height to be determined by its content. If the superview is also pinned to its subview(s) horizontally to determine its width, that could result in a conflict between constraints — but in many cases it won't. Our plain vanilla superview can have its width determined by a hard-coded width constraint without causing a conflict; its subview is pinned to it horizontally, but its subview is a button whose width is determined by its intrinsic content size *at a lower priority* than the superview's width constraint, so the superview's width wins without a struggle (and the button subview is widened to match).

When a view is self-sizing based on the constraints of its subviews, you can ask it in code to size itself immediately in order to discover what its size *would* be if the auto-layout engine were to perform layout at this moment: send the view the `system-LayoutSizeFitting(_:)` message. The system will attempt to reach or at least approach the size you specify, at a very low priority. This call is relatively slow and expensive, because a temporary autolayout engine has to be created, set to work, and discarded. But sometimes that's the best way to get the information you need. Mostly likely you'll specify either `UIView.layoutFittingCompressedSize` or `UIView.layout-FittingExpandedSize`, depending on whether what you're after is the smallest or largest size the view can legally attain. There are a few situations where the iOS runtime actually does size a view that way (most notably with regard to UITableView-Cells and UIBarButtonItems). I'll show an example in Chapter 7.

Stack Views

A stack view (UIStackView) is a kind of pseudoview whose job is to *generate constraints* for some or all of its subviews. These are its *arranged subviews*. In particular, a stack view solves the problem of providing constraints when subviews are to be configured linearly in a horizontal row or a vertical column. In practice, it turns out that many layouts can be expressed as an arrangement, possibly nested, of simple rows and columns of subviews. You are likely to resort to stack views to make your layout easier to construct and maintain.

You can supply a stack view with arranged subviews by calling its initializer `init(arrangedSubviews:)`. The arranged subviews become the stack view's `arrangedSubviews` read-only property. You can also manage the arranged subviews with these methods:

- `addArrangedSubview(_:)`
- `insertArrangedSubview(_:at:)`
- `removeArrangedSubview(_:)`

The `arrangedSubviews` array is different from, but is a subset of, the stack view's `subviews`. It's fine for the stack view to have subviews that are *not* arranged (for which you'll have to provide constraints yourself); on the other hand, if you set a view as an arranged subview and it is not already a subview, the stack view will adopt it as a subview at that moment.

The *order* of the `arrangedSubviews` is independent of the order of the `subviews`; the `subviews` order, you remember, determines the order in which the subviews are *drawn*, but the `arrangedSubviews` order determines how the stack view will *position* those subviews.

Using its properties, you configure the stack view to tell it *how* it should arrange its arranged subviews:

`axis`

 Which way should the arranged subviews be arranged? Your choices are (NSLayoutConstraint.Axis):

- `.horizontal`
- `.vertical`

`alignment`

 This describes how the arranged subviews should be laid out with respect to the *other* dimension. Your choices are (UIStackView.Alignment):

- `.fill`
- `.leading` (or `.top`)
- `.center`
- `.trailing` (or `.bottom`)
- `.firstBaseline` or `.lastBaseline` (if the `axis` is `.horizontal`)

 If the `axis` is `.vertical`, you can still involve the subviews' baselines in their spacing by setting the stack view's `isBaselineRelativeArrangement` to `true`.

`distribution`

 How should the arranged subviews be positioned along the `axis`? This is why you are here! You're using a stack view because you want this positioning performed for you. Your choices are (UIStackView.Distribution):

 `.fill`

  The arranged subviews can have real size constraints or intrinsic content sizes along the arranged dimension. Using those sizes, the arranged subviews will fill the stack view from end to end. But there must be at least *one* view *without* a real size constraint, so that it can be resized to fill the space not taken up by the other views. If more than one view lacks a real size constraint, one of them must have a lowered priority for its content hugging (if stretching) or compression resistance (if squeezing) so that the stack view knows which view to resize.

`.fillEqually`

No view may have a real size constraint along the arranged dimension. The arranged subviews will be made the same size in the arranged dimension, so as to fill the stack view.

`.fillProportionally`

All arranged subviews *must* have an intrinsic content size and *no* real size constraint along the arranged dimension. The views will then fill the stack view, sized according to the *ratio* of their intrinsic content sizes.

`.equalSpacing`

The arranged subviews can have real size constraints or intrinsic content sizes along the arranged dimension. Using those sizes, the arranged subviews will fill the stack view from end to end with equal space between each adjacent pair.

`.equalCentering`

The arranged subviews can have real size constraints or intrinsic content sizes along the arranged dimension. Using those sizes, the arranged subviews will fill the stack view from end to end with equal distance between the centers of each adjacent pair.

The stack view's `spacing` property determines the spacing (or minimum spacing) between *all* the views. Starting in iOS 11, you can set the spacing for *individual* views by calling `setCustomSpacing(_:after:)`; if you need to turn individual spacing back off for a view, reverting to the overall `spacing` property value, set the custom spacing to `UIStackView.spacingUseDefault`. To impose the spacing that the system would normally impose, set the spacing to `UIStackView.spacingUseSystem`.

`isLayoutMarginsRelativeArrangement`

If `true`, the stack view's internal `layoutMargins` are involved in the positioning of its arranged subviews. If `false` (the default), the stack view's literal edges are used.

 Do *not* manually add constraints positioning an arranged subview! Adding those constraints is precisely the job of the stack view. Your constraints will conflict with the constraints created by the stack view. On the other hand, you *must* constrain the stack view *itself*; otherwise, the layout engine has no idea what to do. Trying to use a stack view without constraining it is a common beginner mistake.

To illustrate, I'll rewrite the equal distribution code from earlier in this chapter (Figure 1-16). I have four views, with height constraints. I want to distribute them vertically in my main view. This time, I'll have a stack view do all the work for me:

```
// give the stack view arranged subviews
let sv = UIStackView(arrangedSubviews: views)
// configure the stack view
sv.axis = .vertical
sv.alignment = .fill
sv.distribution = .equalSpacing
// constrain the stack view
sv.translatesAutoresizingMaskIntoConstraints = false
self.view.addSubview(sv)
let marg = self.view.layoutMarginsGuide
let safe = self.view.safeAreaLayoutGuide
NSLayoutConstraint.activate([
    sv.topAnchor.constraint(equalTo:safe.topAnchor),
    sv.leadingAnchor.constraint(equalTo:marg.leadingAnchor),
    sv.trailingAnchor.constraint(equalTo:marg.trailingAnchor),
    sv.bottomAnchor.constraint(equalTo:self.view.bottomAnchor),
])
```

Inspecting the resulting constraints, you can see that the stack view is doing for us effectively just what we did earlier (generating UILayoutGuide objects and using them as spacers). But letting the stack view do it is a lot easier!

Another nice feature of UIStackView is that it responds intelligently to changes. Having configured things with the preceding code, if we were subsequently to make one of our arranged subviews invisible (by setting its isHidden to true), the stack view would respond by distributing the remaining subviews evenly, as if the hidden subview didn't exist. Similarly, we can change properties of the stack view itself in real time. Such flexibility can be very useful for making whole areas of your interface come and go and rearrange themselves at will.

A stack view, in certain configurations, can behave as a self-sizing view: its size, if not determined in any other way, in one or both dimensions, can be based on its subviews.

Internationalization

Your app's entire interface and its behavior are reversed when the app runs on a system for which the app is localized and whose language is right-to-left. Wherever you use leading and trailing constraints instead of left and right constraints, or if your constraints are generated by stack views or are constructed using the visual format language, your app's layout will participate in this reversal more or less automatically.

There may, however, be exceptions. Apple gives the example of a horizontal row of transport controls that mimic the buttons on a CD player: you wouldn't want the Rewind button and the Fast Forward button to be reversed just because the user's language reads right-to-left. Therefore, a UIView is endowed with a semanticContentAttribute property stating whether it should be flipped; the default is .unspecified, but a value of .playback or .spatial will prevent flipping, and you can also force an absolute direction with `.forceLeftToRight` or `.forceRightToLeft`. This property can also be set in the nib editor (using the Semantic pop-up menu in the Attributes inspector).

Interface directionality is a trait, a trait collection's `layoutDirection`; and a UIView has an `effectiveUserInterfaceLayoutDirection` property that reports the direction that it will use to lay out its contents. You can consult this property if you are constructing a view's subviews in code.

 You can test your app's right-to-left behavior easily by changing the scheme's Run option Application Language to "Right to Left Pseudolanguage."

Mistakes with Constraints

Creating constraints manually, as I've been doing so far in this chapter, is an invitation to make a mistake. Your totality of constraints constitute instructions for view layout, and it is all too easy, as soon as more than one or two views are involved, to generate faulty instructions. You can (and will) make two major kinds of mistake with constraints:

Conflict
> You have applied constraints that can't be satisfied simultaneously. This will be reported in the console (at great length).

Underdetermination (ambiguity)
> A view uses autolayout, but you haven't supplied sufficient information to determine its size and position. This is a far more insidious problem, because nothing bad may seem to happen. If you're lucky, the view will at least fail to appear, or will appear in an undesirable place, alerting you to the problem.

Only `.required` constraints (priority 1000) can contribute to a conflict, as the runtime is free to ignore lower-priority constraints that it can't satisfy. Constraints with different priorities do not conflict with one another. Nonrequired constraints with the same priority can contribute to ambiguity.

Under normal circumstances, layout isn't performed until your code finishes running — and even then only if needed. Ambiguous layout isn't ambiguous until layout actually takes place; it is perfectly reasonable to cause an ambiguous layout temporarily, provided you resolve the ambiguity before `layoutSubviews` is called. On the other hand, a conflicting constraint conflicts the instant it is added. That's why, when replacing constraints in code, you should deactivate first and activate second, and not the other way round.

To illustrate, let's start by generating a conflict. In this example, we return to our small red square in the lower right corner of a big magenta square (Figure 1-13) and append a contradictory constraint:

```
let d = ["v2":v2,"v3":v3]
NSLayoutConstraint.activate([
    NSLayoutConstraint.constraints(withVisualFormat:
        "H:|[v2]|", metrics: nil, views: d),
    NSLayoutConstraint.constraints(withVisualFormat:
        "V:|[v2(10)]", metrics: nil, views: d),
    NSLayoutConstraint.constraints(withVisualFormat:
        "H:[v3(20)]|", metrics: nil, views: d),
    NSLayoutConstraint.constraints(withVisualFormat:
        "V:[v3(20)]|", metrics: nil, views: d),
    NSLayoutConstraint.constraints(withVisualFormat:
        "V:[v3(10)]|", metrics: nil, views: d) // *
].flatMap {$0})
```

The height of v3 can't be both 10 and 20. The runtime reports the conflict, and tells you which constraints are causing it:

```
Unable to simultaneously satisfy constraints. Probably at least one of the
constraints in the following list is one you don't want...

<NSLayoutConstraint:0x60008b6d0 UIView:0x7ff45e803.height == 20 (active)>,
<NSLayoutConstraint:0x60008bae0 UIView:0x7ff45e803.height == 10 (active)>
```

 Assigning a constraint (or a UILayoutGuide) an `identifier` string, as I described earlier, can make it easier to determine which constraint is which in a conflict report.

Now we'll generate an ambiguity. Here, we neglect to give our small red square a height:

```
let d = ["v2":v2,"v3":v3]
NSLayoutConstraint.activate([
    NSLayoutConstraint.constraints(withVisualFormat:
        "H:|[v2]|", metrics: nil, views: d),
    NSLayoutConstraint.constraints(withVisualFormat:
        "V:|[v2(10)]", metrics: nil, views: d),
    NSLayoutConstraint.constraints(withVisualFormat:
        "H:[v3(20)]|", metrics: nil, views: d)
].flatMap {$0})
```

No console message alerts us to our mistake. Fortunately, v3 fails to appear in the interface, so we know something's wrong. *If your views fail to appear, suspect ambiguity.* In a less fortunate case, the view might appear, but (if we're lucky) in the wrong place. In a truly unfortunate case, the view might appear in the right place, but not consistently.

Figure 1-18. The view debugger reports an ambiguity

Suspecting ambiguity is one thing; tracking it down and proving it is another. Fortunately, the *view debugger* will report ambiguity instantly (Figure 1-18). With the app running, choose Debug → View Debugging → Capture View Hierarchy, or click the Debug View Hierarchy button in the debug bar. The exclamation mark in the Debug navigator, at the left, is telling us that this view (which does not appear in the canvas) has ambiguous layout; moreover, the Issue navigator, in the Runtime pane, tells us more explicitly, in words: "Height and vertical position are ambiguous for UIView."

Another useful trick is to pause in the debugger and conduct the following mystical conversation in the console:

```
(lldb) e -l objc -- [[UIApplication sharedApplication] windows][0]
(UIWindow *) $1 = ...
(lldb) e -l objc -O -- [$1 _autolayoutTrace]
```

The result is a graphical tree describing the view hierarchy and calling out any ambiguously laid out views:

```
•UIView:0x7f9fa36045c0
|   +UIView:0x7f9fa3604930
|   |   *UIView:0x7f9fa3604a90
|   |   *UIView:0x7f9fa3604e20- AMBIGUOUS LAYOUT
            for UIView:.minY{id: 33}, UIView:.Height{id: 34}
```

UIView also has a hasAmbiguousLayout property. I find it useful to set up a utility method that lets me check a view and all its subviews at any depth for ambiguity; see Appendix B.

To get a full list of the constraints responsible for positioning a particular view within its superview, log the results of calling the UIView instance method constraints-AffectingLayout(for:). The parameter is an axis (NSLayoutConstraint.Axis), either .horizontal or .vertical. These constraints do not necessarily belong to this view (and the output doesn't tell you what view they do belong to). If a view doesn't participate in autolayout, the result will be an empty array. Again, a utility method can come in handy; see Appendix B.

Given the notions of conflict and ambiguity, it is easier to understand what priorities are for. Imagine that all constraints have been placed in boxes, where each box is a priority value, in descending order. Now pretend that we are the runtime, performing layout in obedience to these constraints. How do we proceed?

The first box (.required, 1000) contains all the required constraints, so we obey them first. (If they conflict, that's bad, and we report this in the log.) If there still isn't enough information to perform unambiguous layout given the required priorities alone, we pull the constraints out of the next box and try to obey them. If we can, consistently with what we've already done, fine; if we can't, or if ambiguity remains, we look in the *next* box — and so on.

For a box after the first, we don't care about obeying exactly the constraints it contains; if an ambiguity remains, we can use a lower-priority constraint value to give us something to aim at, resolving the ambiguity, without fully obeying the lower-priority constraint's desires. An inequality is an ambiguity, because an infinite number of values will satisfy it; a lower-priority equality can tell us what value to prefer, resolving the ambiguity, but there's no conflict even if we can't fully achieve that preferred value.

Configuring Layout in the Nib

The focus of the discussion so far has been on configuring layout in code. But that will often be unnecessary; instead, you'll set up your layout in the nib, using the nib editor. It would not be strictly true to say that you can do absolutely anything in the nib that you could do in code, but the nib editor is certainly a remarkably powerful way of configuring layout (and where it falls short, you can supplement it with code).

In the File inspector when a *.storyboard* or *.xib* file is selected, you can make two major choices related to layout, by way of checkboxes. The default is that these checkboxes are *checked*, and I recommend that you leave them that way:

Use Trait Variations
> If checked, various settings in the nib editor, such as the value of a constraint's constant, can be made to depend upon the environment's size classes at runtime; moreover, the modern repertoire of segues, such as popover and detail segues, springs to life.

Use Safe Area Layout Guides
> If checked, the safe area is present, and you can construct constraints pinned to it. By default, only a view controller's *main view's* safe area can have constraints pinned to it, but you can change that.

What you actually *see* in the nib editor canvas depends also on the checked menu items in the Editor → Canvas hierarchical menu (or use the Editor Options pop-up menu at the top right of the editor pane). If Layout Rectangles is unchecked, you won't see the outline of the safe area, though you can still construct constraints to it. If Constraints is unchecked, you won't see any constraints, though you can still construct them.

Autoresizing in the Nib

When you drag a view from the Library into the canvas, it uses autoresizing by default, and will continue to do so unless you involve it in autolayout by adding a constraint that affects it.

When editing a view that uses autoresizing, you can assign it springs and struts in the Size inspector. A solid line externally represents a strut; a solid line internally represents a spring. A helpful animation shows you the effect on your view's position and size as its superview is resized.

Starting in Xcode 11, in the nib editor an individual view has a Layout pop-up menu in the Size inspector allowing you specify its behavior with regard to constraints:

Inferred

The default. The view's `translatesAutoresizingMaskIntoConstraints` is `true`, and you can position the view with autoresizing, until the view becomes involved in constraints, at which point its `translatesAutoresizingMaskIntoConstraints` becomes `false` and you will have to position and size this view entirely with constraints. New in Xcode 12, the title of this pop-up menu changes to help you; if `translatesAutoresizingMaskIntoConstraints` is `true`, the title is Inferred (Autoresizing Mask), but if it is `false` (because you've involved the view in constraints), the title is Inferred (Constraints).

Autoresizing Mask

The view's `translatesAutoresizingMaskIntoConstraints` is `true`, and it will stay `true`. This view will resist becoming involved in constraints within the nib; it wants to use autoresizing only. You can't give it a width constraint or a constraint to its superview. You can involve the view in constraints from other views, as long as these would not cause a problem.

You can cause problems yourself by behaving irrationally; if a view starts out as Inferred and you give it constraints, and then you switch it to Autoresizing Mask, you can readily create a conflict at runtime. Don't do that.

Creating a Constraint

The nib editor provides two primary ways to create a constraint:

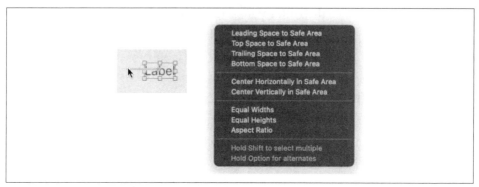

Figure 1-19. Creating a constraint by Control-dragging

Control-drag

> Control-drag from one view to another. A HUD (heads-up display) appears, listing constraints that you can create (Figure 1-19). Either view can be in the canvas or in the document outline. To create an internal width or height constraint, Control-drag from a view to itself.

> When you Control-drag within the canvas, the direction of the drag might be used to winnow the options presented in the HUD: if you Control-drag horizontally within a view in the canvas, the HUD lists Width but not Height.

> While viewing the HUD, you might want to toggle the Option key to see some alternatives; this might make the difference between an edge or safe area constraint and a margin-based constraint. Holding the Shift key lets you create multiple constraints simultaneously.

Layout bar buttons

> Click the Align or Add New Constraints button at the right end of the layout bar below the canvas. These buttons summon little popover dialogs where you can choose multiple constraints to create (possibly for multiple views, if that's what you've selected beforehand) and provide them with numeric values (Figure 1-20). Constraints are not actually added until you click Add Constraints at the bottom!

 A constraint that you create in the nib does not have to be perfect immediately upon creation. You will subsequently be able to edit the constraint and configure it further, as I'll explain in the next section.

If you create constraints and then move or resize a view affected by those constraints, the constraints are *not* automatically changed. This means that the constraints no longer match the way the view is portrayed; if the constraints were now to position the view, they wouldn't put it where you've put it. The nib editor will alert you to this

Figure 1-20. Creating constraints from the layout bar

situation (a Misplaced Views issue), and can readily resolve it for you, but it won't change anything unless you explicitly ask it to.

There are additional view settings in the Size inspector:

- To set a view's layout margins explicitly, change the Layout Margins pop-up menu to Fixed (or better, to Language Directional).

- To make a view's layout margins behave as `readableContentGuide` margins, check Follow Readable Width.

- To allow construction of a constraint to the safe area of a view that isn't a view controller's main view, check its Safe Area Layout Guide.

Viewing and Editing Constraints

Constraints in the nib are full-fledged objects. They can be selected, edited, and deleted. Moreover, you can create an outlet to a constraint (and there are reasons why you might want to do so).

Constraints in the nib are visible in three places (Figure 1-21):

In the document outline
Constraints are listed in a special category, "Constraints," under the view to which they belong. (You'll have a much easier time distinguishing these constraints if you give your views meaningful labels!)

In the canvas
Constraints appear graphically as dimension lines when you select a view that they affect (unless you uncheck Editor → Canvas → Constraints).

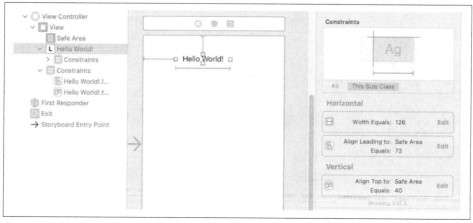

Figure 1-21. A view's constraints displayed in the nib

In the Size inspector

> When a view affected by constraints is selected, the Size inspector lists those constraints, along with a grid that displays the view's constraints graphically. Clicking a constraint in the grid filters the constraints listed below it.

When you select a constraint in the document outline or the canvas, or when you double-click a constraint in a view's Size inspector, you can view and edit that constraint's values in the Attributes or Size inspector. The inspector gives you access to almost all of a constraint's features: the anchors involved in the constraint (the First Item and Second Item pop-up menus), the relation between them, the constant and multiplier, and the priority. You can also set the identifier here (useful when debugging, as I mentioned earlier).

The First Item and Second Item pop-up menus may list alternative constraint types; a width constraint may be changed to a height constraint, for example. These pop-up menus may also list alternative *objects* to constrain to, such as other sibling views, the superview, and the safe area. Also, these pop-up menus may have a "Relative to margin" option, which you can check or uncheck to toggle between an edge-based and a margin-based constraint.

So if you accidentally created the wrong constraint, or if you weren't quite able to specify the desired constraint at creation time, editing will usually permit you to fix things. When you constrain a subview to the view controller's main view, the HUD offers no way to constrain to the main view's edge; your choices are to constrain to the main view's safe area (the default) or to its margin (if you hold Option). But having constrained the subview to the main view's safe area, you can then change Safe Area to Superview in the pop-up menu.

For simple editing of a constraint's constant, relation, priority, and multiplier, double-click the constraint in the canvas to summon a little popover dialog. When a constraint is listed in a view's Size inspector, double-click it to edit it in its own inspector, or click its Edit button to summon the little popover dialog.

A view's Size inspector also provides access to its content hugging and content compression resistance priority settings. Beneath these, there's an Intrinsic Size pop-up menu. The idea here is that your custom view might have an intrinsic size, but the nib editor doesn't know this, so it will report an ambiguity when you fail to provide (say) a width constraint that you know isn't actually needed; choose Placeholder to supply an intrinsic size and relieve the nib editor's worries.

In a constraint's Attributes or Size inspector, there is a Placeholder checkbox ("Remove at build time"). If you check this checkbox, the constraint you're editing *won't* be instantiated when the nib is loaded: in effect, you are deliberately generating ambiguous layout when the views and constraints are instantiated from the nib. You might do this because you want to simulate your layout in the nib editor, but you intend to provide a different constraint in code; perhaps you weren't quite able to describe this constraint in the nib, or the constraint depends upon circumstances that won't be known until runtime.

 Unfortunately, a custom UILayoutGuide can be created and configured only in code. If you want to configure a layout entirely in the nib editor, and if this configuration requires the use of spacer views and cannot be constructed by a UIStackView, you'll have to use spacer views — you cannot replace them with UILayoutGuide objects, because there are no UILayoutGuide objects in the nib editor.

Problems with Nib Constraints

I've already said that generating constraints manually, in code, is error-prone. But it isn't error-prone in the nib editor! The nib editor *knows* whether it contains problematic constraints. If a view is affected by any constraints, the Xcode nib editor will permit them to be ambiguous or conflicting, but it will also complain helpfully. You should pay attention to such complaints! The nib editor will bring the situation to your attention in various places:

In the canvas
> Constraints drawn in the canvas when you select a view that they affect use color coding to express their status:

> *Satisfactory constraints*
>> Drawn in blue.

> *Problematic constraints*
>> Drawn in red.

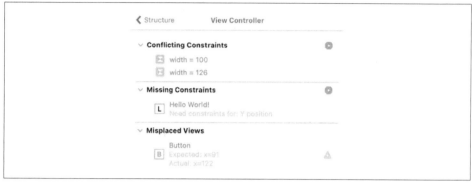

Figure 1-22. Layout Issues In the document outline

Misplacement constraints
> Drawn in orange; these constraints are valid, but they are inconsistent with the frame you have imposed upon the view. I'll discuss misplaced views in the next paragraph.

In the document outline
> If there are layout issues, the document outline displays a right arrow in a red or orange circle. Click it to see a detailed list of the issues (Figure 1-22). Hover the mouse over a title to see an Info button which you can click to learn more about the nature of this issue. The icons at the right are buttons: click one for a list of things the nib editor is offering to do to fix the issue for you. The chief issues are:

Conflicting Constraints
> A conflict between constraints.

Missing Constraints
> Ambiguous layout. You can turn off ambiguity checking for a particular view; use the Ambiguity pop-up menu in the view's Size inspector. This means you can omit a needed constraint and *not* be notified by the nib editor that there's a problem. You will need to generate the missing constraint in code, obviously, or you'll have ambiguous layout in the running app.

Misplaced Views
> If you manually change the frame of a view that is affected by constraints (including its intrinsic size), then the canvas may be displaying that view differently from how it would really appear if the current constraints were obeyed. A Misplaced Views situation is also described in the canvas:
>
> - The constraints in the canvas, drawn in orange, display the numeric *difference* between their values and the view's frame.
>
> - A dotted outline in the canvas may show where the view *would* be drawn if the existing constraints were obeyed.

Having warned you of problems with your layout, the nib editor also provides tools to fix them.

The Update Frames button in the layout bar (or Editor → Update Frames) changes the way the selected views or all views are drawn in the canvas, to show how things would really appear in the running app under the constraints as they stand. Alternatively, if you have resized a view with intrinsic size constraints, such as a button or a label, and you want it to resume the size it would have according to those intrinsic size constraints, select the view and choose Editor → Size to Fit Content.

 Be careful with Update Frames: if constraints are ambiguous, *this can cause a view to disappear.*

The Resolve Auto Layout Issues button in the layout bar (or the Editor → Resolve Auto Layout Issues hierarchical menu) proposes large-scale moves involving all the constraints affecting either selected views or all views:

Update Constraint Constants
Choose this menu item to change numerically all the existing constraints affecting a view to match the way the canvas is currently drawing the view's frame.

Add Missing Constraints
Create new constraints so that the view has sufficient constraints to describe its frame unambiguously. The added constraints correspond to the way the canvas is currently drawing the view's frame. This command may not do what you ultimately want; you should regard it as a starting point. After all, the nib editor can't read your mind! It doesn't know whether you think a certain view's width should be determined by an internal width constraint or by pinning it to the left and right of its superview; and it may generate alignment constraints with other views that you never intended.

Reset to Suggested Constraints
This is as if you chose Clear Constraints followed by Add Missing Constraints: it removes all constraints affecting the view, and replaces them with a complete set of automatically generated constraints describing the way the canvas is currently drawing the view's frame.

Clear Constraints
Removes all constraints affecting the view.

Varying the Screen Size

The purpose of constraints will usually be to design a layout that responds to the possibility of the app launching on devices of different sizes, and perhaps subsequently being rotated. Imagining how this is going to work in real life is not always easy, and you may doubt that you are getting the constraints right as you configure them in the nib editor. Have no fear: Xcode is here to help.

There's a View As button at the lower left of the canvas. Click it to reveal (if they are not already showing) menus or buttons representing a variety of device types and orientations. Choose one, and the canvas's main views are resized accordingly. When that happens, the layout dictated by your constraints is obeyed immediately. So you can try out the effect of your constraints under different screen sizes right there in the canvas.

(This feature works only if the view controller's Simulated Size pop-up menu in the Size inspector says Fixed. If it says Freeform, the view won't be resized when you click a device type or orientation button.)

Conditional Interface Design

The View As button at the lower left of the canvas states the size classes for the currently chosen device and orientation, using a notation like this: wC hR. The w and h stand for "width" and "height," corresponding to the trait collection's `.horizontalSizeClass` and `.verticalSizeClass` respectively; the R and C stand for `.regular` and `.compact`.

The reason you're being given this information is that you might want the configuration of your constraints and views in the nib editor to be *conditional* upon the size classes that are in effect *at runtime*. You can arrange in the nib editor for your app's interface to detect the `traitCollectionDidChange` notification and respond to it:

- You can design your interface to rearrange itself when an iPhone app rotates to compensate for a change in device orientation.
- A single *.storyboard* or *.xib* file can be used to design the interface of a universal app, even if the iPad interface and the iPhone interface are quite different from one another.

The idea when constructing a conditional interface is that you design first for the most general case. When you've done that, and when you want to do something *different* for a *particular* size class situation, you'll describe that difference in the Attributes or Size inspector, or design that difference in the canvas:

In the Attributes or Size inspector
Look for a Plus symbol to the left of a value in the Attributes or Size inspector. This is a value that you can vary conditionally, depending on the environment's size class at runtime. The Plus symbol is a button! Click it to see a popover from which you can choose a specialized size class combination. When you do, that value now appears *twice*: once for the general case, and once for the specialized

case which is marked using wC hR notation. You can now provide different values for those two cases.

In the canvas

Click the Vary for Traits button, to the right of the device types buttons (click View As if you don't see the Vary for Traits button). Two checkboxes appear, allowing you to specify that you want to match the width or height size class (or both) of the current size class. Any designing you now do in the canvas will be applied only to that width or height size class (or both), and the Attributes or Size inspector will be modified as needed.

I'll illustrate these approaches with a little tutorial. You'll need to have an example project on hand; make sure it's a universal app.

Size classes in the inspectors

Suppose we have a button in the canvas, and we want this button to have a yellow background *on iPad only*. (This is improbable but dramatic.) You can configure this directly in the Attributes inspector:

1. Select the button in the interface.

2. Switch to the Attributes inspector, and locate the Background pop-up menu in the View section of the inspector.

3. Click the Plus button to bring up a popover with pop-up menus for specifying size classes. An iPad has width (horizontal) size class Regular and height (vertical) size class Regular, so change the first two pop-up menus so that they both say Regular. Click Add Variation.

4. A second Background pop-up menu has appeared! It is marked wR hR. Change it to yellow (or any desired color).

The button now has a colored background on iPad but not on iPhone. To see that this is true, without running the app on different device types, use the View As button and the device buttons at the lower left of the canvas to switch between different screen sizes. When you click an iPad button, the button in the canvas has a yellow background. When you click an iPhone button, the button in the canvas has its default clear background.

Now that you know what the Plus button means, look over the Attributes and Size inspectors. Anything with a Plus button can be varied in accordance with the size class environment. A button's text can be a different font and size; this makes sense because you might want the text to be larger on an iPad. A button's Hidden checkbox can be different for different size classes, making the button invisible on some device types. And at the bottom of the Attributes inspector is the Installed checkbox; unchecking this for a particular size class combination causes the button to be entirely absent from the interface.

Size classes in the canvas

Suppose your interface has a button pinned to the top *left* of its superview. And suppose that, on iPad devices only, you want this button to be pinned to the top *right* of its superview. (Again, this is improbable but dramatic.) That means the button's leading constraint will exist only on iPhone devices, to be replaced by a trailing constraint on iPad devices. The constraints are different objects. The way to configure different objects for different size classes is to use the Vary for Traits button:

1. Among the device type buttons, click one of the iPhone buttons (furthest to the right). Configure the button so that it's pinned by its top and left to the top left of the main view.

2. Among the device type buttons, click one of the iPad buttons (furthest to the left). The size classes are now listed as wR hR.

3. Click Vary for Traits. In the little popover that appears, check *both* boxes: we want the change we are about to make to apply only when *both* the width size class *and* the height size class match our *current* size class (they should *both* be .regular). The entire layout bar becomes blue, to signify that we are operating in a special conditional design mode.

4. Make the desired change: Select the button in the interface; select the left constraint; delete the left constraint; slide the button to the right of the interface; Control-drag from the button to the right and create a new trailing constraint. If necessary, click the Update Frames button to make the orange Misplaced Views warning symbol go away.

5. Click Done Varying. The layout bar ceases to be blue.

We've created a conditional constraint. To see that this is true, click an iPhone device button and then click an iPad device button. As you do, the button in the interface jumps between the left and right sides of the interface. Its position depends upon the device type!

The inspectors for this button accord with the change we've just made. To see that this is true, click the button, select the trailing or leading constraint (depending on the device type), and look in the Attributes or Size inspector. The constraint has two Installed checkboxes, one for the general case and one for wR hR. Only one of these checkboxes is checked; the constraint is present in one case but not the other.

 In the document outline, a constraint or view that is not installed for the current set of size classes is listed with a faded icon.

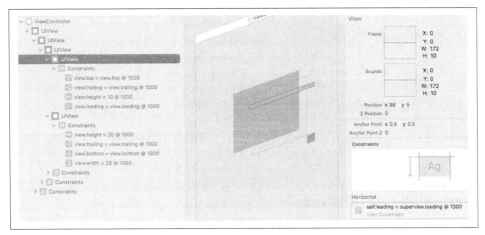

Figure 1-23. View debugging (again)

Xcode View Features

This section summarizes some miscellaneous view-related features of Xcode that are worth knowing about.

View Debugger

To enter the view debugger, choose Debug → View Debugging → Capture View Hierarchy, or click the Debug View Hierarchy button in the debug bar. The result is that your app's current view hierarchy is analyzed and displayed (Figure 1-23):

- On the left, in the Debug navigator, the views and their constraints are listed hierarchically. (View controllers are also listed as part of the hierarchy.)
- In the center, in the canvas, the views and their constraints are displayed graphically. The window starts out facing front, much as if you were looking at the screen with the app running; but if you swipe sideways a little in the canvas (or click the Orient to 3D button at the bottom of the canvas, or choose Editor → Orient to 3D), the window rotates and its subviews are displayed in front of it, in layers. You can adjust your perspective in various ways:
  - The slider at the lower left changes the distance between the layers.
  - The double-slider at the lower right lets you eliminate the display of views from the front or back of the layering order (or both).
  - You can Option-double-click a view to focus on it, eliminating its superviews from the display. Double-click outside the view to exit focus mode.
  - You can switch to wireframe mode.
  - You can display constraints for the currently selected view.

- On the right, the Object inspector and the Size inspector tell you details about the currently selected object (view or constraint).

When a view is selected in the Debug navigator or in the canvas, the Size inspector lists its bounds and the constraints that determine those bounds. This, along with the layered graphical display of your views and constraints in the canvas, can help you ferret out the cause of any constraint-related difficulties.

 New in Xcode 12, the view hierarchy displayed in the view debugger can be exported for later examination. Choose File → Export View Hierarchy. Open the resulting file to view it in its own view debugger window in Xcode.

Previewing Your Interface

When you're displaying the nib editor in Xcode, you're already seeing the results of your constraints in the current device size. You can change device size using the buttons or menu that appears when you click View As at the lower left. The same interface lets you toggle orientation and switch between light and dark mode.

For an even more realistic display, choose Editor → Preview (or choose Preview from the Editor Options pop-up menu). You'll see a preview of the currently selected view controller's view (or, in a *.xib* file, the top-level view).

At the bottom of each preview, a label tells you what device you're seeing, and a rotate button lets you toggle its orientation. At the lower left, a Plus button lets you add previews for different devices and device sizes, so you can view your interface on different devices *simultaneously*. The previews take account of constraints and conditional interface. At the lower right, a language pop-up menu lets you switch your app's text (buttons and labels) to another language for which you have localized your app, or to an artificial "double-length" language. To remove a previewed device, click to select it and press Delete.

Designable Views and Inspectable Properties

Your custom view can be drawn in the nib editor canvas and preview *even if it is configured in code*. To take advantage of this feature, you need a UIView subclass declared @IBDesignable. If an instance of this UIView subclass appears in the nib editor, then its self-configuration methods, such as willMove(toSuperview:), will be compiled and run as the nib editor prepares to portray your view. In addition, your view can implement the special method prepareForInterfaceBuilder to perform visual configurations aimed specifically at how it will be portrayed in the nib editor; in this way, you can portray in the nib editor a feature that your view will adopt *later* in the life of the app. If your view contains a UILabel that is created and configured empty but will eventually contain text, you could implement prepareForInterface-Builder to give the label some sample text to be displayed in the nib editor.

Figure 1-24. A designable view

 New in Xcode 12, a notification appears at the top of your @IBDesignable view's Attributes inspector when its nib-related code has compiled (or failed to compile).

In Figure 1-24, I refactor a familiar example. Our view subclass gives itself a magenta background, along with two subviews, one across the top and the other at the lower right — all designed in code. The nib contains an instance of this view subclass. When the app runs, willMove(toSuperview:) will be called, the code will run, and the subviews will be present. But because willMove(toSuperview:) is also called by the nib editor, the subviews are displayed in the nib editor as well:

```
@IBDesignable class MyView: UIView {
    func configure() {
        self.backgroundColor = UIColor(red: 1, green: 0.4, blue: 1, alpha: 1)
        let v2 = UIView()
        v2.backgroundColor = UIColor(red: 0.5, green: 1, blue: 0, alpha: 1)
        let v3 = UIView()
        v3.backgroundColor = UIColor(red: 1, green: 0, blue: 0, alpha: 1)
        v2.translatesAutoresizingMaskIntoConstraints = false
        v3.translatesAutoresizingMaskIntoConstraints = false
        self.addSubview(v2)
        self.addSubview(v3)
        NSLayoutConstraint.activate([
            v2.leftAnchor.constraint(equalTo:self.leftAnchor),
            v2.rightAnchor.constraint(equalTo:self.rightAnchor),
            v2.topAnchor.constraint(equalTo:self.topAnchor),
            v2.heightAnchor.constraint(equalToConstant:20),
            v3.widthAnchor.constraint(equalToConstant:20),
            v3.heightAnchor.constraint(equalTo:v3.widthAnchor),
            v3.rightAnchor.constraint(equalTo:self.rightAnchor),
```

```
                v3.bottomAnchor.constraint(equalTo:self.bottomAnchor),
        ])
    }
    override func willMove(toSuperview newSuperview: UIView?) {
        self.configure()
    }
}
```

In addition, you can configure a custom view property directly in the nib editor. To do that, your UIView subclass needs a property that's declared @IBInspectable, and this property's type needs to be one of a limited list of inspectable property types (I'll tell you what they are in a moment). If there's an instance of this UIView subclass in the nib, that property will get a field of its own at the top of the view's Attributes inspector, where you can set the initial value of that property in the nib editor rather than its having to be set in code. (This feature is actually a convenient equivalent of setting a nib object's User Defined Runtime Attributes in the Identity inspector.)

The inspectable property types are: Bool, number, String, CGRect, CGPoint, CGSize, NSRange, UIColor, or UIImage. The property won't be displayed in the Attributes inspector unless its type is declared explicitly. You can assign a default value in code; the Attributes inspector won't portray this value as the default, but you can tell it to use the default by leaving the field empty (or, if you've entered a value, by deleting that value).

 An IBInspectable property's value, as set in the nib editor, is not applied until *after* init(coder:) and willMove(toSuperview:) have run. The earliest your code can retrieve this value at runtime is in awakeFromNib.

@IBDesignable and @IBInspectable are unrelated, but the former is aware of the latter. An inspectable property can change the nib editor's display of your interface! In this example, we use @IBDesignable and @IBInspectable to work around an annoying limitation of the nib editor. A UIView can draw its own border automatically, by setting its layer's borderWidth (Chapter 3). But this can be configured only in code. There's nothing in a view's Attributes inspector that lets you set a layer's border-Width, and special layer configurations are not normally portrayed in the canvas. @IBDesignable and @IBInspectable to the rescue:

```
@IBDesignable class MyButton : UIButton {
    @IBInspectable var borderWidth : Int {
        set {
            self.layer.borderWidth = CGFloat(newValue)
        }
        get {
            return Int(self.layer.borderWidth)
        }
    }
}
```

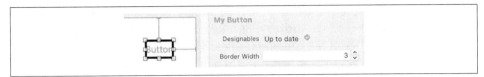

Figure 1-25. A designable view with an inspectable property

The result is that, in the nib editor, our button's Attributes inspector has a Border Width custom property, and when we change the Border Width property setting, the button is redrawn with that border width (Figure 1-25). Moreover, we are setting this property in the nib, so when the app runs and the nib loads, the button really does have that border width in the running app.

Layout Events

This section summarizes three chief UIView events related to layout. These are events that you can receive and respond to by overriding them in your UIView subclass. You might want to do this in situations where layout is complex — when you need to supplement autoresizing or autolayout with manual layout in code, or when your layout configuration needs to change in response to changing conditions. (Closely related to these UIView events are some layout-related events you can receive and respond to in a UIViewController; I'll discuss them in Chapter 6.)

updateConstraints

If your interface involves autolayout and constraints, then updateConstraints is propagated *up* the hierarchy, starting at the deepest subview, when the runtime thinks your code might need an opportunity to configure constraints. You might override updateConstraints because you have a UIView subclass capable of altering its own constraints. If you do, you must finish up by calling super or the app will crash (with a helpful error message).

updateConstraints is called at launch time, but rarely after that unless you *cause* it to be called. You should never call updateConstraints directly. To trigger an immediate call to updateConstraints, send a view the updateConstraintsIf-Needed message. To force updateConstraints to be sent to a particular view, send it the setNeedsUpdateConstraints message.

traitCollectionDidChange(_:)

If the environment's trait collection changes, the traitCollectionDid-Change(_:) message is propagated *down* the hierarchy of UITraitEnvironments. The incoming parameter is the *old* trait collection; to get the new trait collection, ask for self.traitCollection.

Earlier in this chapter I showed some code for swapping a view into or out of the interface together with the entire set of constraints laying out that interface. But I left open the matter of the conditions under which we wanted such swapping to occur; traitCollectionDidChange might be an appropriate moment, if the idea is to change the interface when the app rotates on an iPhone.

layoutSubviews

The layoutSubviews message is the moment when layout actually takes place. It is propagated *down* the hierarchy, starting at the top (typically the root view) and working down to the deepest subview. Layout can be triggered even if the trait collection didn't change; perhaps a constraint was changed, or the text of a label was changed, or a superview's size changed.

You can override layoutSubviews in a UIView subclass in order to take a hand in the layout process. If you're not using autolayout, layoutSubviews does nothing by default; layoutSubviews is your opportunity to perform manual layout after autoresizing has taken place. If you are using autolayout, you must call super or the app will crash (with a helpful error message).

You should never call layoutSubviews directly; to trigger an immediate call to layoutSubviews, send a view the layoutIfNeeded message (which may cause layout of the entire view tree, not only below but also above this view), or send setNeedsLayout to trigger a call to layoutSubviews later on, after your code finishes running, when layout would normally take place.

When you're using autolayout, what happens in layoutSubviews? The runtime, having examined and resolved all the constraints affecting this view's subviews, and having worked out values for their center and bounds, now simply assigns center and bounds values to them. In other words, layoutSubviews performs manual layout!

Knowing this, you might override layoutSubviews when you're using autolayout, in order to tweak the outcome. A typical structure is: first you call super, causing all the subviews to adopt their new frames; then you examine those frames; if you don't like the outcome, you can change things; and finally you call super *again*, to get a new layout outcome. As I mentioned earlier, setting a view's frame (or bounds or center) explicitly in layoutSubviews is perfectly fine, even if this view uses autolayout; that, after all, is what the autolayout engine itself is doing. Keep in mind, however, that you must *cooperate* with the autolayout engine. Do not call setNeedsUpdateConstraints — that moment has passed — and do not stray beyond the subviews *of this view*. (Disobeying those strictures can cause your app to hang.)

Drawing

The views illustrated in Chapter 1 were mostly colored rectangles; they had a backgroundColor and no more. But that's not what a real iOS program looks like. Everything the user sees is a UIView, and what the user sees is a lot more than a bunch of colored rectangles. That's because the views that the user sees have *content*. They contain *drawing*.

Many UIView subclasses, such as a UIButton or a UILabel, know how to draw themselves. Sooner or later, you're also going to want to do some drawing of your own. You can prepare your drawing as an image file beforehand. You can draw an image as your app runs, in code. You can display an image in a UIView subclass that knows how to show an image, such as a UIImageView or a UIButton. A pure UIView is all about drawing, and it leaves that drawing largely up to you; your code determines what the view draws, and hence what it looks like in your interface.

This chapter discusses the mechanics of drawing. Don't be afraid to write drawing code of your own! It isn't difficult, and it's often the best way to make your app look the way you want it to. (I'll discuss how to draw text in Chapter 11.)

Images and Image Views

The basic general UIKit image class is UIImage. UIImage knows how to deal with many standard image types, such as HEIC, TIFF, JPEG, GIF, and PNG. A UIImage can be used wherever an image is to be displayed; it knows how to provide the image data, and may be thought of loosely as wrapping the image data. It also provides supplementary information about its image, and lets you tweak certain aspects of the image's behavior.

Where will the image data inside a UIImage come from? There are three main sources:

- An image file previously stored on disk.
- An image that your app constructs in code.
- Image data that your app downloads from the network.

The first two are what this chapter is about. Downloading image data is discussed in Chapter 24.

Image Files

UIImage can read a stored file, so if an image does not need to be created dynamically, but has already been created before your app runs, then drawing may be as simple as providing an image file as a resource inside your app itself. When an image file is to be included inside your app, iOS has a special affinity for PNG files, and you should prefer them whenever possible. (The converse operation, saving image data as an image file, is discussed in Chapter 23.)

A pre-existing image file in your app's bundle is most commonly obtained in code through the UIImage initializer init(named:), which takes a string and returns a UIImage wrapped in an Optional, in case the image doesn't exist. This method looks in two places for the image:

Asset catalog
　　We look in the asset catalog for an image set with the supplied name. The name is case-sensitive.

Top level of app bundle
　　We look at the top level of the app's bundle for an image file with the supplied name. The name is case-sensitive and should include the file extension; if it doesn't, *.png* is assumed.

When calling init(named:), an asset catalog is searched before the top level of the app's bundle. If there are multiple asset catalogs, they are all searched, but the search order is indeterminate, so avoid multiple image sets with the same name.

 The Image library lists images both in the asset catalog and at the app bundle's top level. Instead of calling init(named:), which takes a literal string that you might type incorrectly, you can drag or double-click an image in the Image library to enter an *image literal* directly into your code. The resulting token represents a call to the UIImage initializer init(imageLiteralResourceName:), and produces a UIImage, not an Optional.

With init(named:), the image data may be cached in memory, and if you ask for the same image by calling init(named:) again later, the cached data may be supplied immediately. Caching is usually good, because decoding the image on disk into usable bitmap data is expensive.

Nevertheless, sometimes caching may not be what you want; if you know you're just going to fetch the image once and put it into the interface immediately, caching might represent an unnecessary strain on your app's memory. If so, there's another way: you can read an image file from your app bundle (not the asset catalog) directly and without caching, by calling `init(contentsOfFile:)`, which expects a pathname string. To obtain that pathname string, you can get a reference to your app's bundle with `Bundle.main`, and Bundle then provides instance methods for getting the pathname of a file within the bundle, such as `path(forResource:ofType:)`.

Hardware-related image variants

An image file can come in multiple variants for use on different hardware. When the image file is stored in the app bundle, these variants are distinguished through the use of special name suffixes:

High-resolution variants
> On a device with a double-resolution screen, when an image is obtained by name from the app bundle, a file with the same name extended by `@2x`, if there is one, will be used automatically, with the resulting UIImage marked as double-resolution by assigning it a `scale` property value of `2.0`. Similarly, if there is a file with the same name extended by `@3x`, it will be used on a device with a triple-resolution screen, with a `scale` property value of `3.0`.
>
> Double- and triple-resolution variants of an image file should have dimensions double and triple those of the base file. But thanks to the UIImage `scale` property, a high-resolution variant of an image has the same CGSize as the single-resolution image. On a high-resolution screen, your code and your interface continue to work without change, but your images look sharper.
>
> This works for UIImage `init(named:)` and `init(contentsOfFile:)`. If there is a file called *pic.png* and a file called *pic@2x.png*, then on a device with a double-resolution screen, these methods will access *pic@2x.png* as a UIImage with a scale of `2.0`:
>
> ```
> let im = UIImage(named:"pic") // uses pic@2x.png
> if let path = Bundle.main.path(forResource: "pic", ofType: "png") {
>     let im2 = UIImage(contentsOfFile:path) // uses pic@2x.png
> }
> ```

Device type variants
> A file with the same name extended by `~ipad` will automatically be used if the app is running natively on an iPad. You can use this in a universal app to supply different images automatically depending on whether the app runs on an iPhone (or iPod touch), on the one hand, or on an iPad, on the other. (This is true not

just for images but for *any* resource obtained by name from the bundle. See Apple's *Resource Programming Guide* in the documentation archive.)

This works for UIImage `init(named:)` and Bundle `path(forResource:of-Type:)`. If there is a file called *pic.png* and a file called *pic~ipad.png*, then on an iPad, these methods will access *pic~ipad.png*:

```
let im = UIImage(named:"pic") // uses pic~ipad.png
let path = Bundle.main.path(
    forResource: "pic", ofType: "png") // uses pic~ipad.png
```

If possible, however, you will probably prefer to supply your image in an asset catalog rather than in the app bundle. This has the advantage, among other things, that you can forget all about those name suffixes! An asset catalog knows when to use an alternate image within an image set, not from its *name*, but from its *place* in the catalog:

- Put the single-, double-, and triple-resolution alternatives into the slots marked "1x," "2x," and "3x" respectively.

- For a distinct iPad variant of an image, check iPhone and iPad in the Attributes inspector for the image set; separate slots for those device types will appear in the asset catalog.

Moreover, an image set in an asset catalog can make numerous further distinctions based on a device's processor type, wide color capabilities, and more. Many of these distinctions are used not only by the runtime when the app runs, but also by the App Store when thinning your app for a specific target device.

Vector images

An image file in the asset catalog can be a vector-based PDF or (new in Xcode 12) an SVG. By default, a vector-based image will be resized automatically for double or triple resolution, and because it's a vector image, the resizing will be sharp. If you check Preserve Vector Data, the image will be resized sharply for *any* size, either when scaled automatically (by a UIImageView or other interface item), or when your code scales the image by redrawing it (as I'll describe later in this chapter).

Starting in Xcode 11 and iOS 13, the system also supplies a large collection of standard named SVG *symbol images* intended for use both as icons and in conjunction with text. In iOS 14 there are about 2400 of them. To obtain one as a UIImage in code, call the UIImage initializer `init(systemName:)`. In the nib editor, an interface object that accepts an image, such as a UIImageView or a UIButton, lets you specify a symbol image by name using a pop-up menu. The symbol images are displayed along with their names in the SF Symbols application, available for download from Apple.

(A few symbol images are also vended directly as UIImage class properties: `.add`, `.remove`, `.close`, `.actions`, `.checkmark`, and `.strokedCheckmark`.)

Certain details of how a symbol image is drawn may be dictated through its `symbol-Configuration` (UIImage.SymbolConfiguration). You can supply this when you create the image, or you can change it by calling the UIImage instance methods `.withConfiguration(_:)` or `.applyingSymbolConfiguration(_:)`. Alternatively, you can attach a symbol configuration to the image view that displays the symbol image. Configurations can involve one of nine weights, one of three scales, a font or text style, and a point size, in various combinations; this is to facilitate association with text. I'll talk about that in detail in Chapter 11.

 If your app is backward compatible to iOS 13, pay attention to the availability information about symbol images. Some symbol images are new in iOS 14, and trying to obtain one of these under iOS 13 will fail (and possibly crash). Also, some symbol images that are present in iOS 13 have a different name in iOS 14.

Asset catalogs and trait collections

An asset catalog can distinguish between variants of an asset intended for different trait collections ("Trait Collections" on page 28). The chief distinctions you might want to draw will involve size classes or user interface style (light and dark mode).

Consider an image that is to appear in different variants depending on the size class situation. In the Attributes inspector for your image set, use the Width Class and Height Class pop-up menus to specify which size class possibilities you want slots for. If we're on an iPhone with the app rotated to landscape orientation, and if there's both an Any Height and a Compact Height alternative in the image set, the Compact Height variant is used. These features are live as the app runs; if the app rotates from landscape to portrait, the Compact Height variant is *replaced* with the Any Height variant in your interface, there and then, *automatically*.

Similarly, an image can vary depending on whether the environment is in light mode or dark mode. To display the necessary slots, in the Attributes inspector, use the Appearance pop-up menu. If you choose Any, Dark, you'll get a slot for light or unspecified mode and a slot for dark mode. A UIImage obtained from the asset catalog will switch *automatically* to the appropriate variant when the interface style changes. A named color defined in the asset catalog can make the same distinction, making it a dynamic color (as I described in Chapter 1).

If you need a specific trait collection variant of an image or named color in an asset catalog, and you know its name, you can call `init(named:in:compatibleWith:)`; the third parameter is the trait collection. But what if you *already* have this UIImage or UIColor in your interface? How does the interface in your running app, which *already* contains a UIImage or a UIColor, automatically change when the trait collection changes? This magic is baked into UIImage and UIColor.

Let's start with UIImage. When an image is obtained from an asset catalog through UIImage init(named:), its imageAsset property is a UIImageAsset that effectively points back into the asset catalog at the image set that it came from. Each image in the image set has a trait collection associated with it (its traitCollection). By calling the UIImageAsset method image(with:), passing a trait collection, you can ask an image's imageAsset for the image from the same image set appropriate to that trait collection.

A built-in interface object that displays an image, such as a UIImageView, is automatically trait collection–aware; it receives the traitCollectionDidChange(_:) message and responds accordingly. To demonstrate how this works under the hood, we can build a custom UIView with an image property that behaves the same way:

```
class MyView: UIView {
    var image : UIImage!
    override func traitCollectionDidChange(_ prevtc: UITraitCollection?) {
        super.traitCollectionDidChange(prevtc)
        self.setNeedsDisplay() // causes draw(_:) to be called
    }
    override func draw(_ rect: CGRect) {
        if var im = self.image {
            if let asset = self.image.imageAsset {
                im = asset.image(with:self.traitCollection)
            }
            im.draw(at:.zero)
        }
    }
}
```

The really interesting part is that no actual asset catalog is needed. You can treat images as trait-based alternatives for one another *without* using an asset catalog. You might do this because your code has constructed the images from scratch or has obtained them over the network while the app is running. The technique is to instantiate a UIImageAsset and then associate each image with a different trait collection by *registering* it with this same UIImageAsset. Here's an example:

```
let tcreg = UITraitCollection(verticalSizeClass: .regular)
let tccom = UITraitCollection(verticalSizeClass: .compact)
let moods = UIImageAsset()
let frowney = UIImage(named:"frowney")!
let smiley = UIImage(named:"smiley")!
moods.register(frowney, with: tcreg)
moods.register(smiley, with: tccom)
```

If we now display either frowney or smiley in a UIImageView, we see the image associated with the environment's current vertical size class, and, amazingly, it automatically switches to the other image when the app changes orientation on an iPhone. Moreover, this works even though I didn't keep any persistent reference to frowney, smiley, or the UIImageAsset! (The reason is that the images are cached by the system and they maintain a strong reference to the UIImageAsset with which they are registered.)

UIColor works in a simpler way. The knowledge of the color corresponding to a trait collection is baked directly into a dynamic color, and you can extract it by calling `resolvedColor(with:)`, passing a trait collection. This works not only with a dynamic color declared in code by calling `init(dynamicProvider:)`, as we saw in Chapter 1, but also with a named color from the asset catalog.

Namespacing image files

When image files are numerous or need to be clumped into groups, the question arises of how to divide them into namespaces. Here are some possibilities:

Folder reference
> Instead of keeping images at the top level of your app bundle, you can keep them in a *folder* in the app bundle. This is easiest to maintain if you put a *folder reference* into your project; the folder itself is then copied into the app bundle at build time, along with all its contents. There are various ways to retrieve an image in such a folder:
>
> - Call UIImage `init(named:)` with the folder name and a forward slash in front of the image's name in the name string. If the folder is called *pix* and the image file is called *pic.png*, then the "name" of the image is `"pix/pic.png"`.
>
> - Call Bundle `path(forResource:ofType:inDirectory:)` to get the image file's path, followed by UIImage `init(contentsOfFile:)`.
>
> - Obtain the bundle path (`Bundle.main.bundlePath`) and use NSString pathname and FileManager methods to drill down to the desired file.

Asset catalog folder
> An asset catalog can provide virtual folders that function as namespaces. Suppose that an image set *myImage* is inside an asset catalog folder called *pix*; if you check Provides Namespace in the Attributes inspector for that folder, then the image can be accessed through UIImage `init(name:)` by the name `"pix/myImage"`.

Bundle
> A fuller form of `init(named:)` is `init(named:in:)`, where the second parameter is a bundle. This means you can keep images in a secondary bundle, such as a framework, and specify that bundle as a way of namespacing the image. This approach works regardless of whether the image comes from an asset catalog or sits at the top level of the bundle.

Image files in the nib editor

Many built-in Cocoa interface objects will accept a UIImage as part of how they draw themselves; a UIButton can display an image, a UINavigationBar or a UITabBar can have a background image (Chapter 13), and so on. The image you want to supply will often come from an image file.

The nib editor stands ready to help you. The Attributes inspector of an interface object that can have an image will have a pop-up menu from which you can choose an image in your project, or a built-in symbol image. Your project's images, as well as the built-in symbol images, are also listed in the Image library; from here, you can drag an image onto an interface object in the canvas, such as a button.

Image Views

When you want an image to appear in your interface, not inside a button or other interface object but purely as an image, you'll probably hand it to an image view — a UIImageView — which has the most knowledge and flexibility with regard to displaying images and is intended for this purpose. An image view is the displayer of images *par excellence*. In code, just set the image as the image view's `image`. In the nib editor, drag the image from the Image library onto an image view or set its image through the Image pop-up menu, or drag an image from the Image library directly into a plain UIView to get a UIImageView whose image is that image.

 An image view (or a UIButton, because its image is contained in an image view) can be configured to display a particular variant of any symbol image assigned to it by setting its `preferredSymbolConfiguration`; you can do that in code or in the nib editor.

A UIImageView can actually have *two* images, one assigned to its `image` property and the other assigned to its `highlightedImage` property; the value of the UIImageView's `isHighlighted` property dictates which of the two is displayed at any given moment. A UIImageView does not automatically highlight itself merely because the user taps it, the way a button does. However, there are certain situations where a UIImageView will respond to the highlighting of its surroundings; within a table view cell, for instance, a UIImageView will show its highlighted image when the cell is highlighted (Chapter 8).

A UIImageView is a UIView, so it can have a background color in addition to its image, it can have an alpha (transparency) value, and so forth (see Chapter 1). An image may have areas that are transparent, and a UIImageView will respect this, so an image of any shape can appear. A UIImageView without a background color is invisible except for its image, so the image simply appears in the interface, without the user being aware that it resides in a rectangular host. A UIImageView without an image and without a background color is invisible, so you could start with an empty

Figure 2-1. Mars appears in my interface

UIImageView in the place where you will later need an image and subsequently assign the image in code. You can assign a new image to substitute one image for another, or set the image view's image property to nil to remove its image.

How a UIImageView draws its image depends upon the setting of its contentMode property (UIView.ContentMode); this property is actually inherited from UIView, and I'll discuss its more general purpose later in this chapter. .scaleToFill means the image's width and height are set to the width and height of the view, filling the view completely even if this alters the image's aspect ratio; .center means the image is drawn centered in the view without altering its size; and so on. Most commonly you'll use .scaleAspectFit or .scaleAspectFill; they both keep the image's aspect ratio while filling the image view. The difference is that .scaleAspectFill fills the image view in both dimensions, permitting some of the image to fall outside the image view. The best way to get a feel for the meanings of the various contentMode settings is to experiment with an image view in the nib editor: in the image view's Attributes inspector, change the Content Mode pop-up menu to see where and how the image draws itself.

You should also pay attention to a UIImageView's clipsToBounds property; if it is false, its image, even if it is larger than the image view and even if it is not scaled down by the contentMode, may be displayed in its entirety, extending beyond the image view itself.

When creating a UIImageView in code, you can take advantage of a convenience initializer, init(image:). The default contentMode is .scaleToFill, but the image is not initially scaled; rather, *the image view itself is sized to match its image.* You will still probably need to position the UIImageView correctly in its superview. In this example, I'll put a picture of the planet Mars in the center of the app's interface (Figure 2-1; for the CGRect center property, see Appendix B):

```
let iv = UIImageView(image:UIImage(named:"Mars"))
self.view.addSubview(iv)
iv.center = iv.superview!.bounds.center
iv.frame = iv.frame.integral
```

What happens to the size of an existing UIImageView when you assign a new image to it depends on whether the image view is using autolayout. Under autolayout, the size of the image becomes the image view's `intrinsicContentSize`, so the image view *adopts the image's size* unless other constraints prevent.

An image view automatically acquires its `alignmentRectInsets` (see Chapter 1) from its image's `alignmentRectInsets`. If you're going to be aligning the image view to some other object using autolayout, you can attach appropriate `alignmentRect-Insets` to the image that the image view will display, and the image view will do the right thing. To do so in code, derive a new image by calling the original image's `withAlignmentRectInsets(_:)` method; alternatively, you can set an image's `alignmentRectInsets` in the asset catalog (using the four Alignment fields).

Resizable Images

Certain interface contexts require an image that can be coherently resized to any desired proportions. For instance, a custom image that serves as the track of a slider or progress view (Chapter 13) must be able to fill a space of any length. Such an image is called a *resizable image*.

To make a resizable image in code, start with a normal image and call its `resizableImage(withCapInsets:resizingMode:)` method. The `capInsets:` argument is a UIEdgeInsets, whose components represent distances inward from the edges of the image. In a context larger than the image, a resizable image can behave in one of two ways, depending on the `resizingMode:` value (UIImage.ResizingMode):

`.tile`
> The interior rectangle of the inset area is tiled (repeated) in the interior; each edge is formed by tiling the corresponding edge rectangle outside the inset area. The four corner rectangles outside the inset area are drawn unchanged.

`.stretch`
> The interior rectangle of the inset area is stretched *once* to fill the interior; each edge is formed by stretching the corresponding edge rectangle outside the inset area *once*. The four corner rectangles outside the inset area are drawn unchanged.

In these examples, assume that `self.iv` is a UIImageView with absolute height and width (so that it won't adopt the size of its image) and with a `contentMode` of `.scaleToFill` (so that the image will exhibit resizing behavior). First, I'll illustrate tiling an entire image (Figure 2-2); note that the `capInsets:` is `.zero`, meaning no insets at all:

```
let mars = UIImage(named:"Mars")!
let marsTiled =
    mars.resizableImage(withCapInsets:.zero, resizingMode: .tile)
self.iv.image = marsTiled
```

Figure 2-2. Tiling the entire image of Mars

Figure 2-3. Tiling the interior of Mars

Figure 2-4. Stretching the interior of Mars

Now we'll tile the interior of the image, changing the `capInsets:` argument from the previous code (Figure 2-3):

```
let marsTiled = mars.resizableImage(withCapInsets:
    UIEdgeInsets(
        top: mars.size.height / 4.0,
        left: mars.size.width / 4.0,
        bottom: mars.size.height / 4.0,
        right: mars.size.width / 4.0
    ), resizingMode: .tile)
```

Next, I'll illustrate stretching. We'll start by changing just the `resizingMode:` from the previous code (Figure 2-4):

```
let marsTiled = mars.resizableImage(withCapInsets:
    UIEdgeInsets(
        top: mars.size.height / 4.0,
        left: mars.size.width / 4.0,
        bottom: mars.size.height / 4.0,
        right: mars.size.width / 4.0
    ), resizingMode: .stretch)
```

A common stretching strategy is to make almost half the original image serve as a cap inset, leaving just a tiny rectangle in the center that must stretch to fill the entire interior of the resulting image (Figure 2-5):

Figure 2-5. Stretching a few pixels at the interior of Mars

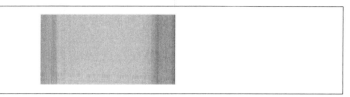

Figure 2-6. Mars, stretched and clipped

```
let marsTiled = mars.resizableImage(withCapInsets:
    UIEdgeInsets(
        top: mars.size.height / 2.0 - 1,
        left: mars.size.width / 2.0 - 1,
        bottom: mars.size.height / 2.0 - 1,
        right: mars.size.width / 2.0 - 1
    ), resizingMode: .stretch)
```

In the preceding example, if the image view's contentMode is .scaleAspectFill, and if the image view's clipsToBounds is true, we get a sort of gradient effect, because the top and bottom of the stretched image are outside the image view and aren't drawn (Figure 2-6).

Alternatively, you can configure a resizable image in the asset catalog. It is often the case that a particular image will be used in your app chiefly as a resizable image, and always with the same capInsets: and resizingMode:, so it makes sense to configure this image once rather than having to repeat the same code.

To configure an image in an asset catalog as a resizable image, select the image and, in the Slicing section of the Attributes inspector, change the Slices pop-up menu to Horizontal, Vertical, or Horizontal and Vertical. When you do this, additional interface appears. You can specify the resizingMode with the Center pop-up menu. You can work numerically, or click Show Slicing at the lower right of the canvas and work graphically.

This feature is even more powerful than resizableImage(withCapInsets:resizing-Mode:). It lets you specify the end caps *separately* from the tiled or stretched region, with the rest of the image being sliced out. In Figure 2-7, the dark areas at the top left, top right, bottom left, and bottom right will be drawn as is; the narrow bands will be stretched, and the small rectangle at the top center will be stretched to fill most of the

Figure 2-7. Mars, sliced in the asset catalog

Figure 2-8. Mars, sliced and stretched

interior; but the rest of the image, the large central area covered by a sort of gauze curtain, will be omitted entirely. The result is shown in Figure 2-8.

Transparency Masks

Certain interface contexts, such as buttons and button-like interface objects, want to treat an image as a *transparency mask*, also known as a *template*. This means that the image color values are ignored, and only the transparency (alpha) values of each pixel matter. The image shown on the screen is formed by combining the image's transparency values with a single tint color.

The way an image will be treated is a property of the image, its `renderingMode`. This property is read-only; to change it in code, start with an image and generate a new image with a different rendering mode, by calling its `withRenderingMode(_:)` method.

The rendering mode values (UIImage.RenderingMode) are:

- `.automatic`
- `.alwaysOriginal`
- `.alwaysTemplate`

The default is `.automatic`, which means that the image is drawn normally except in those particular contexts that want to treat it as a transparency mask. With the other two rendering mode values, you can *force* an image to be drawn normally, even in a

Figure 2-9. One image in two rendering modes

context that would usually treat it as a transparency mask, or you can *force* an image to be treated as a transparency mask, even in a context that would otherwise treat it normally.

To accompany this feature, iOS gives every UIView a `tintColor`, which will be used to tint any template images it contains. Moreover, this `tintColor` by default is inherited down the view hierarchy, and indeed throughout the entire app, starting with the window (Chapter 1). Assigning your app's main window a tint color is probably one of the few changes you'll make to the window; otherwise, your app adopts the system's blue tint color. (Alternatively, if you're using a main storyboard, set the Global Tint color in the File inspector.) Individual views can be assigned their own tint color, which is inherited by their subviews. Figure 2-9 shows two buttons displaying the same background image, one in normal rendering mode, the other in template rendering mode, in an app whose window tint color is red. (I'll say more about template images and `tintColor` in Chapter 13.)

You can assign an image a rendering mode in the asset catalog. Select the image set in the asset catalog, and use the Render As pop-up menu in the Attributes inspector to set the rendering mode to Default (`.automatic`), Original Image (`.alwaysOriginal`), or Template Image (`.alwaysTemplate`). This is an excellent approach whenever you have an image that you will use primarily in a specific rendering mode, because it saves you from having to remember to set that rendering mode in code every time you fetch the image. Instead, any time you call `init(named:)`, this image arrives with the rendering mode already set.

The symbol images, in general, have no color of their own, so in effect they are *always* template images. New in iOS 14, however, about 150 of the symbol images are *multicolor* images. (The other symbol images are called *monochrome*.) Multicolor symbol images possess inherent colors of their own. Some have a single color; most of them have two. In a template environment, such as a button, if you apply the `.alwaysOriginal` rendering mode to a multicolor symbol image, its inherent colors will appear.

Starting in iOS 13, a tint color can be applied to a UIImage directly; call `withTintColor(_:)` or `withTintColor(_:renderingMode:)`. This is useful particularly when you want to draw a symbol image or a template image in a context where there is no inherited tint color (such as a graphics context). Nonetheless, I find the behavior of these methods rather weird:

Original images become template images

If you apply `withTintColor` to an ordinary image, it is then treated as a template image — even if you also set the rendering mode to `.alwaysOriginal`.

Template images may ignore the assigned tint color

If you apply `withTintColor(_:)` to a template image — because it's a symbol image, or because you said `.alwaysTemplate`, or because we're in a context that treats an image as a transparency mask — then if you assign it into a view with a `tintColor` of its own, the tint color you specify is ignored! The view's tint color wins. If you want the tint color you specify to be obeyed, you must also set the rendering mode to `.alwaysOriginal`.

For example, the following code specifically sets a symbol image's tint color to red; nevertheless, what appears on the screen is a blue symbol image (because the default image view `tintColor` is blue):

```
let im = UIImage(systemName:"circle.fill")?.withTintColor(.red)
let iv = UIImageView(image:im)
self.view.addSubview(iv)
```

To get a red symbol image, you have to say this:

```
let im = UIImage(systemName:"circle.fill")?.withTintColor(.red,
    renderingMode: .alwaysOriginal) // *
let iv = UIImageView(image:im)
self.view.addSubview(iv)
```

(Applying a tint color directly to a multicolor symbol image turns it monochrome, even if you also apply the `.alwaysOriginal` rendering mode.)

 New in Xcode 12, in the nib editor, when you have assigned a symbol image to an image view (or a button), pop-up menus appear that let you assign it a rendering mode, as well as a scale.

Reversible Images

The entire interface is automatically reversed when your app runs on a system for which your app is localized if the system language is right-to-left. In general, this probably won't affect your images. The runtime assumes that you *don't* want images to be reversed when the interface is reversed, so its default behavior is to leave them alone.

Nevertheless, you *might* want an image to be reversed when the interface is reversed. Suppose you've drawn an arrow pointing in the direction from which new interface will arrive when the user taps a button. If the button pushes a view controller onto a navigation interface, that direction is from the right on a left-to-right system, but from the left on a right-to-left system. This image has directional meaning within the app's own interface; it needs to flip horizontally when the interface is reversed.

To make this possible in code, call the image's `imageFlippedForRightToLeftLayout-Direction` method and use the resulting image in your interface. On a left-to-right system, the normal image will be used; on a right-to-left system, a reversed variant of the image will be created and used automatically. You can override this behavior, even if the image is reversible, for a particular UIView displaying the image, such as a UIImageView, by setting that view's `semanticContentAttribute` to prevent mirroring.

You can make the same determination for an image in the asset catalog using the Direction pop-up menu (choose one of the Mirrors options). Moreover, the layout direction (as I mentioned in Chapter 1) is a trait, so you can have image variants to be used under left-to-right or right-to-left layout. The easy way to configure this is to choose Both in the asset catalog's Direction pop-up menu; now there are left-to-right and right-to-left image slots where you can place your images. Alternatively, you can register the image variants with a UIImageAsset in code, as I demonstrated earlier in this chapter.

You can also force an image to be flipped horizontally without regard to layout direction or semantic content attribute by calling its `withHorizontallyFlipped-Orientation` method.

Graphics Contexts

Instead of plopping an image from an existing image file directly into your interface, you may want to create some drawing yourself, in code. To do so, you will need a *graphics context*. This is where the fun really begins!

A graphics context is basically a place you can draw. Conversely, you can't draw in code unless you've got a graphics context. There are several ways in which you might obtain a graphics context; these are the most common:

Cocoa creates the graphics context
> You subclass UIView and override `draw(_:)`. At the time your `draw(_:)` implementation is called, Cocoa has already created a graphics context and is asking you to draw into it, right now; whatever you draw is what the UIView will display.

Cocoa passes you a graphics context
> You subclass CALayer and override `draw(in:)`, or else you give a CALayer a delegate and implement the delegate's `draw(_:in:)`. The `in:` parameter is a graphics context. (Layers are discussed in Chapter 3.)

You create an image context
> The preceding two ways of getting a graphics context amount to drawing *on demand:* you slot your drawing code into the right place, and it is called

whenever drawing needs to happen. The other major way to draw is just to make a UIImage yourself, once and for all. To create the graphics context that generates the image, you use a UIGraphicsImageRenderer.

Moreover, at any given moment there either is or is not a *current* graphics context:

- When UIView's `draw(_:)` is called, the UIView's drawing context is already the current graphics context.

- When CALayer's `draw(in:)` or its delegate's `draw(_:in:)` is called, the `in:` parameter is a graphics context, but it is *not* the current context. It's up to you to make it current if you need to.

- When you create an image context, that image context automatically becomes the current graphics context.

What beginners find most confusing about drawing is that there are two sets of tools for drawing, which take different attitudes toward the context in which they will draw. One set needs a current context; the other just needs a context:

UIKit

Various Cocoa classes know how to draw themselves; these include UIImage, NSString (for drawing text), UIBezierPath (for drawing shapes), and UIColor. Some of these classes provide convenience methods with limited abilities; others are extremely powerful. In many cases, UIKit will be all you'll need.

With UIKit, you can draw *only into the current context*. If there's already a current context, you just draw. But with CALayer, where you are handed a context as a parameter, if you want to use the UIKit convenience methods, you'll have to make that context the current context; you do this by calling `UIGraphicsPushContext(_:)` (and be sure to restore things with `UIGraphicsPopContext` later).

Core Graphics

This is the full drawing API. Core Graphics, often referred to as Quartz, or Quartz 2D, is the drawing system that underlies all iOS drawing; UIKit drawing is built on top of it. It is low-level and consists of C functions (though in Swift these are mostly "renamified" to look like method calls). There are a lot of them! This chapter will familiarize you with the fundamentals; for complete information, you'll want to study Apple's *Quartz 2D Programming Guide* in the documentation archive.

With Core Graphics, you must *specify a graphics context* (a CGContext) to draw into, explicitly, for each bit of your drawing. With CALayer, you are handed the context as a parameter, and that's the graphics context you want to draw into. But if there is already a current context, you have no reference to it until you call `UIGraphicsGetCurrentContext` to obtain it.

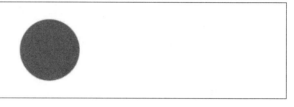

Figure 2-10. A blue circle

You don't have to use UIKit or Core Graphics *exclusively*. On the contrary, you can intermingle UIKit calls and Core Graphics calls in the same chunk of code to operate on the same graphics context. They merely represent two different ways of telling a graphics context what to do.

We have two sets of tools and three ways in which a context might be supplied; that makes six ways of drawing. I'll now demonstrate all six of them! To do so, I'll draw a blue circle (Figure 2-10). Without worrying just yet about the actual drawing commands, focus your attention on how the context is specified and on whether we're using UIKit or Core Graphics.

Drawing on Demand

There are four ways of drawing on demand, and I'll start with those. First, I'll implement a UIView subclass's draw(_:), using UIKit to draw into the current context, which Cocoa has already prepared for me:

```
override func draw(_ rect: CGRect) {
    let p = UIBezierPath(ovalIn: CGRect(0,0,100,100))
    UIColor.blue.setFill()
    p.fill()
}
```

Now I'll do the same thing with Core Graphics; this will require that I first get a reference to the current context:

```
override func draw(_ rect: CGRect) {
    let con = UIGraphicsGetCurrentContext()!
    con.addEllipse(in:CGRect(0,0,100,100))
    con.setFillColor(UIColor.blue.cgColor)
    con.fillPath()
}
```

Next, I'll implement a CALayer delegate's draw(_:in:). In this case, we're handed a reference to a context, but it isn't the current context. So I have to make it the current context in order to use UIKit (and I must remember to stop making it the current context when I'm done drawing):

```
override func draw(_ layer: CALayer, in con: CGContext) {
    UIGraphicsPushContext(con)
    let p = UIBezierPath(ovalIn: CGRect(0,0,100,100))
    UIColor.blue.setFill()
    p.fill()
    UIGraphicsPopContext()
}
```

To use Core Graphics in a CALayer delegate's `draw(_:in:)`, I simply keep referring to the context I was handed:

```
override func draw(_ layer: CALayer, in con: CGContext) {
    con.addEllipse(in:CGRect(0,0,100,100))
    con.setFillColor(UIColor.blue.cgColor)
    con.fillPath()
}
```

Drawing a UIImage

Now I'll make a UIImage of a blue circle. We can do this at any time (we don't need to wait for some particular method to be called) and in any class (we don't need to be in a UIView subclass).

To construct a UIImage in code, use a UIGraphicsImageRenderer. The basic technique is to create the renderer and call its `image` method to obtain the UIImage, handing it a function containing your drawing instructions.

In this example, I draw my image using UIKit:

```
let r = UIGraphicsImageRenderer(size:CGSize(100,100))
let im = r.image { _ in
    let p = UIBezierPath(ovalIn: CGRect(0,0,100,100))
    UIColor.blue.setFill()
    p.fill()
}
// im is the blue circle image, do something with it here ...
```

And here's the same thing using Core Graphics:

```
let r = UIGraphicsImageRenderer(size:CGSize(100,100))
let im = r.image { _ in
    let con = UIGraphicsGetCurrentContext()!
    con.addEllipse(in:CGRect(0,0,100,100))
    con.setFillColor(UIColor.blue.cgColor)
    con.fillPath()
}
// im is the blue circle image, do something with it here ...
```

In those examples, we're calling UIGraphicsImageRenderer's `init(size:)` and accepting its default configuration, which is usually what's wanted. To configure the image context further, call the UIGraphicsImageRendererFormat class method default, configure the format through its properties, and pass it to UIGraphicsImage-Renderer's init(size:format:). Those properties are:

opaque
> By default, false; the image context is transparent. If true, the image context is opaque and has a black background, and the resulting image has no transparency.

scale
> By default, the same as the scale of the main screen, UIScreen.main.scale. This means that the resolution of the resulting image will be correct for the device we're running on

preferredRange
> The color gamut. Your choices are (UIGraphicsImageRendererFormat.Range):
>
> - .standard
> - .extended
> - .automatic (same as .extended if we're running on a device that supports "wide color")

A single parameter (ignored in the preceding examples) arrives into the UIGraphics-ImageRenderer's image function. It's a UIGraphicsImageRendererContext. This provides access to the configuring UIGraphicsImageRendererFormat (its format). It also lets you obtain the graphics context (its cgContext); you can alternatively get this by calling UIGraphicsGetCurrentContext, and the preceding code does so, for consistency with the other ways of drawing. In addition, the UIGraphicsImageRenderer-Context can hand you a copy of the image as drawn up to this point (its currentImage); also, it implements a few basic drawing commands of its own.

UIImage Drawing

A UIImage provides methods for drawing itself into the current context. We already know how to obtain a UIImage, and we already know how to obtain a graphics context and make it the current context, so we are ready to experiment! Here, I'll make a UIImage consisting of two pictures of Mars side by side (Figure 2-11):

```
let mars = UIImage(named:"Mars")!
let sz = mars.size
let r = UIGraphicsImageRenderer(size:CGSize(sz.width*2, sz.height),
    format:mars.imageRendererFormat)
let im = r.image { _ in
    mars.draw(at:CGPoint(0,0))
    mars.draw(at:CGPoint(sz.width,0))
}
```

Figure 2-11. Two images of Mars combined side by side

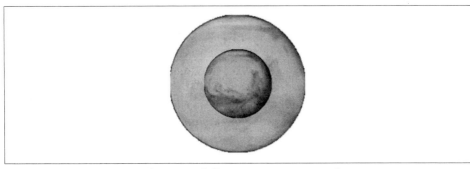

Figure 2-12. Two images of Mars in different sizes, composited

If we have multiple resolution variants of our original Mars image, the correct one for the current device is used, and is assigned the correct scale value. The image context that we are drawing into also has the correct scale by default. And the resulting image im has the correct scale as well. Our code produces an image that looks correct on the current device, whatever its screen resolution may be.

 If your purpose in creating an image graphics context is to draw an existing UIImage into it, you can gain some efficiency by initializing the image renderer's format to the image's imageRendererFormat.

Additional UIImage methods let you scale an image into a desired rectangle as you draw (effectively resizing the image), and specify the compositing (blend) mode whereby the image should combine with whatever is already present. To illustrate, I'll create an image showing Mars centered in another image of Mars that's twice as large, using the .multiply blend mode (Figure 2-12):

```
let mars = UIImage(named:"Mars")!
let sz = mars.size
let r = UIGraphicsImageRenderer(size:CGSize(sz.width*2, sz.height*2),
    format:mars.imageRendererFormat)
let im = r.image { _ in
    mars.draw(in:CGRect(0,0,sz.width*2,sz.height*2))
    mars.draw(in:CGRect(sz.width/2.0, sz.height/2.0, sz.width, sz.height),
        blendMode: .multiply, alpha: 1.0)
}
```

Figure 2-13. Half the original image of Mars

Redrawing an image at a smaller size is of particular importance in iOS programming, because it is a waste of valuable memory to hand a UIImageView a large image and ask the image view to display it smaller. Some frameworks such as Image I/O (Chapter 23) and PhotoKit (Chapter 18) allow you to load a downsized image thumbnail directly, but sometimes you'll need to downscale an image to fit within a given size yourself. For a general utility method that downsizes a UIImage to fit within a given CGSize, see Appendix B. (For a better downscaling algorithm, use the Core Image CILanczosScaleTransform filter; I'll discuss Core Image a little later.)

Sometimes, you may want to extract a smaller region of the original image — effectively cropping the image as you draw it. Unfortunately, there is no UIImage drawing method for specifying the source rectangle. You can work around this by creating a smaller graphics context and positioning the image drawing so that the desired region falls into it. There is no harm in doing this, and it's a perfectly standard strategy; what falls outside the graphics context simply isn't drawn. For instance, to obtain an image of the right half of Mars, you can make a graphics context half the width of the mars image, and then draw mars shifted left, so that only its right half intersects the graphics context (Figure 2-13):

```
let mars = UIImage(named:"Mars")!
let sz = mars.size
let r = UIGraphicsImageRenderer(size:CGSize(sz.width/2.0, sz.height),
    format:mars.imageRendererFormat)
let im = r.image { _ in
    mars.draw(at:CGPoint(-sz.width/2.0,0))
}
```

A nice feature of UIGraphicsImageRenderer is that we can initialize it with a bounds instead of a size. Instead of drawing mars shifted left, we can achieve the same effect by drawing mars at .zero into a bounds that is shifted right:

```
let mars = UIImage(named:"Mars")!
let sz = mars.size
let r = UIGraphicsImageRenderer(
    bounds:CGRect(sz.width/2.0, 0, sz.width/2.0, sz.height),
    format:mars.imageRendererFormat)
let im = r.image { _ in
    mars.draw(at:.zero)
}
```

Vector images work like normal images. When you call `draw(in:)`, a PDF vector image in the asset catalog for which you have checked Preserve Vector Data will scale sharply; an SVG image in the asset catalog, or a symbol image, always scales sharply:

```
let symbol = UIImage(systemName:"rhombus")!
let sz = CGSize(100,100)
let r = UIGraphicsImageRenderer(size:sz)
let im = r.image { _ in
    symbol.withTintColor(.purple).draw(in:CGRect(origin:.zero, size:sz))
}
```

The resulting rhombus is purple, because we gave the image a tint color before drawing it, and is smoothly drawn at 100×100, because it's a vector image. But of course, once you've drawn the vector image into a UIImage like our `im`, *that* image does *not* scale sharply; it isn't a vector image.

(Instead of calling `draw(in:)` on a symbol image, however, it is probably better to generate a UIImage with a custom symbol configuration, specifying a point size, and call `draw(at:)`, letting the symbol image size itself according to the point size you provided.)

CGImage Drawing

The Core Graphics analog to UIImage is CGImage. In essence, a UIImage is (usually) a wrapper for a CGImage: the UIImage is bitmap image data plus scale, orientation, and other information, whereas the CGImage is the bare bitmap image data alone. The two are easily converted to one another: a UIImage has a `cgImage` property that accesses its Quartz image data, and you can make a UIImage from a CGImage using `init(cgImage:)` or `init(cgImage:scale:orientation:)`.

A CGImage lets you create a new image cropped from a rectangular region of the original image, which you can't do with UIImage. (A CGImage has other powers a UIImage doesn't have; for instance, you can apply an image mask to a CGImage.) I'll demonstrate by splitting the image of Mars in half and drawing the two halves separately (Figure 2-14):

```
let mars = UIImage(named:"Mars")!
// extract each half as CGImage
let marsCG = mars.cgImage!
let sz = mars.size
let marsLeft = marsCG.cropping(to:
    CGRect(0,0,sz.width/2.0,sz.height))!
let marsRight = marsCG.cropping(to:
    CGRect(sz.width/2.0,0,sz.width/2.0,sz.height))!
let r = UIGraphicsImageRenderer(size: CGSize(sz.width*1.5, sz.height),
    format:mars.imageRendererFormat)
let im = r.image { ctx in
    let con = ctx.cgContext
```

Figure 2-14. Image of Mars split in half (badly)

```
        con.draw(marsLeft, in:
            CGRect(0,0,sz.width/2.0,sz.height))
        con.draw(marsRight, in:
            CGRect(sz.width,0,sz.width/2,0,sz.height))
    }
```

Well, *that* was a train wreck! In the first place, the drawing is upside-down. It isn't rotated; it's mirrored top to bottom, or, to use the technical term, *flipped*. This phenomenon can arise when you create a CGImage and then draw it, and is due to a mismatch in the native coordinate systems of the source and target contexts.

In the second place, we didn't split the image of Mars in half; we seem to have split it into quarters instead. The reason is that we're using a high-resolution device, and there is a high-resolution variant of our image file. When we call UIImage's init(named:), we get a UIImage that compensates for the increased size of a high-resolution image by setting its own scale property to match. But a CGImage doesn't have a scale property, and knows nothing of the fact that the image dimensions are increased! Therefore, on a high-resolution device, the CGImage that we extract from our Mars UIImage as mars.cgImage is larger (in each dimension) than mars.size, and all our calculations after that are wrong.

The simplest solution, when you drop down to the CGImage world to perform some transmutation, is to wrap the resulting CGImage in a UIImage and draw the UIImage *instead* of the CGImage. The UIImage can be formed in such a way as to compensate for scale — call init(cgImage:scale:orientation:) — and by drawing a UIImage instead of a CGImage, we avoid the flipping problem:

```
    let mars = UIImage(named:"Mars")!
    let sz = mars.size
    let marsCG = mars.cgImage!
    let szCG = CGSize(CGFloat(marsCG.width), CGFloat(marsCG.height))
    let marsLeft =
        marsCG.cropping(to:
            CGRect(0,0,szCG.width/2.0,szCG.height))
    let marsRight =
        marsCG.cropping(to:
            CGRect(szCG.width/2.0,0,szCG.width/2.0,szCG.height))
    let r = UIGraphicsImageRenderer(size:CGSize(sz.width*1.5, sz.height),
        format:mars.imageRendererFormat)
    let im = r.image { _ in
```

```
        UIImage(cgImage: marsLeft!,
            scale: mars.scale,
            orientation: mars.imageOrientation).draw(at:CGPoint(0,0))
        UIImage(cgImage: marsRight!,
            scale: mars.scale,
            orientation: mars.imageOrientation).draw(at:CGPoint(sz.width,0))
    }
```

Snapshots

An entire view — anything from a single button to your whole interface, complete
with its contained hierarchy of views — can be drawn into the current graphics context by calling the UIView instance method drawHierarchy(in:afterScreen-
Updates:). The result is a *snapshot* of the original view: it looks like the original view,
but it's basically just a bitmap image of it, a lightweight visual duplicate.

 drawHierarchy(in:afterScreenUpdates:) is much faster than the CALayer
method render(in:); nevertheless, the latter does still come in handy, as I'll
show in Chapter 5.

An even faster way to obtain a snapshot of a view is to use the UIView (or UIScreen)
instance method snapshotView(afterScreenUpdates:). The result is a UIView, not
a UIImage; it's rather like a UIImageView that knows how to draw only one image,
namely the snapshot. Such a snapshot view will typically be used as is, but you can
enlarge its bounds and the snapshot image will stretch. If you want the stretched
snapshot to behave like a resizable image, call resizableSnapshotView(from:after-
ScreenUpdates:withCapInsets:) instead. It is perfectly reasonable to make a snapshot view from a snapshot view.

Snapshots are useful because of the dynamic nature of the iOS interface. You might
place a snapshot of a view in your interface in front of the real view to hide what's
happening, or use it during an animation to present the illusion of a view moving
when in fact it's just a snapshot.

Here's an example from one of my apps. It's a card game, and its views portray cards.
I want to animate the removal of all those cards from the board, flying away to an
offscreen point. But I don't want to animate the views themselves! They need to stay
put, to portray future cards. So I make a snapshot view of each of the card views; I
then make the card views invisible, put the snapshot views in their place, and animate
the snapshot views. This code will mean more to you after you've read Chapter 4, but
the strategy is evident:

```
for v in views {
    let snapshot = v.snapshotView(afterScreenUpdates: false)!
    let snap = MySnapBehavior(item:snapshot, snapto:CGPoint(
        x: self.anim.referenceView!.bounds.midX,
        y: -self.anim.referenceView!.bounds.height)
```

```
        )
        self.snaps.append(snapshot) // keep a list so we can remove them later
        snapshot.frame = v.frame
        v.isHidden = true
        self.anim.referenceView!.addSubview(snapshot)
        self.anim.addBehavior(snap)
    }
```

CIFilter and CIImage

The "CI" in CIFilter and CIImage stands for Core Image, a technology for transforming images through mathematical filters. Core Image started life on the desktop (macOS), and when it was originally migrated into iOS 5, some of the filters available on the desktop were not available in iOS, presumably because they were then too intensive mathematically for a mobile device. Over the years, more and more macOS filters were added to the iOS repertoire, and now the two have complete parity: *all* macOS filters are available in iOS, and the two platforms have nearly identical APIs.

A filter is a CIFilter. There are more than 200 available filters; they fall naturally into several broad categories:

Patterns and gradients
> These filters create CIImages that can then be combined with other CIImages, such as a single color, a checkerboard, stripes, or a gradient.

Compositing
> These filters combine one image with another, using compositing blend modes familiar from image processing programs.

Color
> These filters adjust or otherwise modify the colors of an image. You can alter an image's saturation, hue, brightness, contrast, gamma and white point, exposure, shadows and highlights, and so on.

Geometric
> These filters perform basic geometric transformations on an image, such as scaling, rotation, and cropping.

Transformation
> These filters distort, blur, or stylize an image.

Transition
> These filters provide a frame of a transition between one image and another; by asking for frames in sequence, you can animate the transition (I'll demonstrate in Chapter 4).

Special purpose

These filters perform highly specialized operations such as face detection and generation of barcodes.

A CIFilter is a set of instructions for generating a CIImage — the filter's *output image*. Moreover, most CIFilters operate on a CIImage — the filter's *input image*. So the output image of one filter can be the input image of another filter. In this way, filters can be *chained*. As you build a chain of filters, nothing actually happens; you're just configuring a sequence of instructions.

If the first CIFilter in the sequence needs an input image, you can get a CIImage from a CGImage with `init(cgImage:)`, or from a UIImage with `init(image:)`. When the last CIFilter in the sequence produces a CIImage, you can transform it into a bitmap drawing — a CGImage or a UIImage. In this way, you've transformed an image into another image, using CIImages and CIFilters as intermediaries. The final step, when you generate the bitmap drawing, is called *rendering* the image. When you render the image, the entire calculation described by the chain of filters is actually performed. Rendering the last CIImage in the sequence is the *only* calculation-intensive move.

 A common beginner mistake is trying to obtain a CIImage directly from a UIImage through the UIImage's `ciImage` property. In general, that's not going to work. That property does not transform a UIImage into a CIImage; it is applicable only to a UIImage that *already* wraps a CIImage, and most UIImages don't (they wrap a CGImage).

The basic use of a CIFilter is quite simple:

Obtain a CIFilter object

You can specify a CIFilter by its string name, by calling `init(name:)`; to learn the names, consult Apple's *Core Image Filter Reference* in the documentation archive, or call the CIFilter class method `filterNames(inCategories:)` with a `nil` argument. Starting in iOS 13, you can obtain a CIFilter object by calling a CIFilter convenience class method named after the string name; to learn about the convenience names, look in the *CIFilterBuiltins* header:

```
let filter = CIFilter(name: "CICheckerboardGenerator")!
// or:
let filter = CIFilter.checkerboardGenerator()
```

Configure the filter

A filter has keys and values that determine its behavior. These are its *parameters*. You set them as desired. You can learn about a filter's parameters entirely in code, but typically you'll consult the documentation. To set a parameter, call `setValue(_:forKey:)`, or use the corresponding *CIFilterBuiltins* convenience property:

```
filter.setValue(30, forKey: "inputWidth")
// or:
filter.width = 30
```

There are several variations on those steps:

- Instead of calling `setValue(_:forKey:)` repeatedly, you can call `setValuesFor-Keys(_:)` with a dictionary to set multiple parameters at once.

- Instead of obtaining the filter and then setting parameters, you can do both in a single move by calling `init(name:parameters:)`.

- If a CIFilter requires that you provide a CIImage as its input, you can call `applyingFilter(_:parameters:)` on the CIImage to obtain the filter, set its parameters, and receive the output image, in a single move.

Now let's talk about how to render a CIImage. This, as I've said, is the only calculation-intensive move; it can be slow and expensive. There are three main ways:

With a CIContext

Create a CIContext by calling `init()` or `init(options:)`; this itself is expensive, so try to make just one CIContext and retain and reuse it. Then call the CIContext's `createCGImage(_:from:)`. The first parameter is the CIImage. The second parameter is a CGRect specifying the region of the CIImage to be rendered. A CIImage does not have a frame or bounds; its CGRect is its `extent`. The output is a CGImage.

With a UIImage

Create a UIImage wrapping the CIImage by calling `init(ciImage:)` or `init(ci-Image:scale:orientation:)`. You then *draw* the UIImage into some graphics context; that is what causes the image to be rendered.

With a UIImageView

This is a shortcut for the preceding approach. Create a UIImage wrapping the CIImage and use it to set a UIImageView's `image`. The display of the image view causes the image to be rendered. In general, this approach works only on a device, though it might work in the simulator in Xcode 12.

 There are other ways of rendering a CIImage that have the advantage of being very fast and suitable for animated or rapid rendering. In particular, you could use Metal. But that's outside the scope of this book.

We're ready for an example! I'll start with an ordinary photo of myself (it's true I'm wearing a motorcycle helmet, but it's still ordinary) and create a circular vignette effect (Figure 2-15). I'll take advantage of the convenience methods and properties; to bring these to life, we must `import CoreImage.CIFilterBuiltins`:

Figure 2-15. A photo of me, vignetted

```
let moi = UIImage(named:"Moi")!
let moici = CIImage(image:moi)! ❶
let moiextent = moici.extent
let smaller = min(moiextent.width, moiextent.height)
let larger = max(moiextent.width, moiextent.height)
// first filter
let grad = CIFilter.radialGradient() ❷
grad.center = moiextent.center
grad.radius0 = Float(smaller)/2.0 * 0.7
grad.radius1 = Float(larger)/2.0
let gradimage = grad.outputImage!
// second filter
let blend = CIFilter.blendWithMask() ❸
blend.inputImage = moici
blend.maskImage = gradimage
let blendimage = blend.outputImage!
```

❶ From the image of me (moi), we derive a CIImage (moici).

❷ We use a CIFilter (grad) to form a radial gradient between the default colors of white and black.

❸ We use a second CIFilter (blend) to treat the radial gradient as a mask for blending between the photo of me and a default clear background: where the radial gradient is white (everything inside the gradient's inner radius) we see just me, and where the radial gradient is black (everything outside the gradient's outer radius) we see just the clear color, with a gradation in between, so that the image fades away in the circular band between the gradient's radii.

We have obtained the final CIImage in the chain (blendimage), but nothing has actually happened yet; the processor has not yet performed any rendering. Now we want to generate the final bitmap and display it. Let's say we're going to display it as the image of a UIImageView self.iv. I'll demonstrate two of the ways of doing that.

First, the CIContext approach. `self.context` is a property initialized to a CIContext. The starred line is the actual rendering:

```
let moicg = self.context.createCGImage(blendimage, from: moiextent)! // *
self.iv.image = UIImage(cgImage: moicg)
```

Second, the UIImage drawing approach; the starred line is the actual rendering:

```
let r = UIGraphicsImageRenderer(size:moiextent.size)
self.iv.image = r.image { _ in
    UIImage(ciImage: blendimage).draw(in:moiextent) // *
}
```

A filter chain can be encapsulated into a single custom filter by subclassing CIFilter. Your subclass just needs to override the outputImage property (and possibly other methods such as `setDefaults`), with additional properties to make it key–value coding compliant for any input keys. Here's our vignette filter as a simple CIFilter subclass with two input keys; `inputImage` is the image to be vignetted, and `input-Percentage` is a percentage (between 0 and 1) adjusting the gradient's inner radius:

```
class MyVignetteFilter : CIFilter {
    @objc var inputImage : CIImage?
    @objc var inputPercentage : NSNumber? = 1.0
    override var outputImage : CIImage? {
        return self.makeOutputImage()
    }
    private func makeOutputImage () -> CIImage? {
        guard let inputImage = self.inputImage else {return nil}
        guard let inputPercentage = self.inputPercentage else {return nil}
        let extent = inputImage.extent
        let smaller = min(extent.width, extent.height)
        let larger = max(extent.width, extent.height)
        let grad = CIFilter.radialGradient()
        grad.center = extent.center
        grad.radius0 = Float(smaller)/2.0 * inputPercentage.floatValue
        grad.radius1 = Float(larger)/2.0
        let gradimage = grad.outputImage!
        let blend = CIFilter.blendWithMask()
        blend.inputImage = self.inputImage
        blend.maskImage = gradimage
        return blend.outputImage
    }
}
```

And here's how to use our CIFilter subclass and display its output in a UIImageView:

```
let vig = MyVignetteFilter()
let moici = CIImage(image: UIImage(named:"Moi")!)!
vig.setValuesForKeys([
    "inputImage":moici,
    "inputPercentage":0.7
```

```
])
let outim = vig.outputImage!
let outimcg = self.context.createCGImage(outim, from: outim.extent)!
self.iv.image = UIImage(cgImage: outimcg)
```

CIImage is a powerful class in its own right, with many valuable convenience methods. You can apply a transform to a CIImage, crop it, and even apply a Gaussian blur directly to it. Also, CIImage understands EXIF orientations and can use them to reorient itself.

Blur and Vibrancy Views

Certain views on iOS, such as navigation bars and the control center, are translucent and display a blurred rendition of what's behind them. You can create similar effects using the UIVisualEffectView class.

A UIVisualEffectView is initialized by calling `init(effect:)`; the parameter is a UIVisualEffect. UIVisualEffect is an abstract superclass; the concrete subclasses are UIBlurEffect and UIVibrancyEffect:

1. Start with a visual effect view with a *blur* effect to blur what's behind it.

2. If you like, you can add a visual effect view with a *vibrancy* effect, along with subviews to be displayed with vibrancy. Never give a UIVisualEffectView a *direct* subview! Instead:

    -   The vibrancy effect view goes inside the blur effect view's `contentView`.

    -   Any subviews of the vibrancy effect view go inside *its* `contentView`, and they will be treated as templates: all that matters is their opacity or transparency, as their color is replaced.

UIBlurEffect is initialized by calling `init(style:)`. The styles are adaptive to light and dark user interface style, and are called *materials*. There are five of them (plus each material has two nonadaptive variants with `Light` or `Dark` appended to the name):

-   `.systemUltraThinMaterial`

-   `.systemThinMaterial`

-   `.systemMaterial`

-   `.systemThickMaterial`

-   `.systemChromeMaterial`

UIVibrancyEffect is initialized by calling `init(blurEffect:style:)`. The first parameter will be the blur effect of the underlying UIVisualEffectView. The `style:` will be one of these:

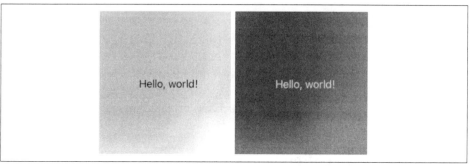

Figure 2-16. A blurred background and a vibrant label

- `.label`

- `.secondaryLabel`

- `.tertiaryLabel`

- `.quaternaryLabel`

- `.fill`

- `.secondaryFill`

- `.tertiaryFill`

- `.separator`

Here's an example of a blur effect view covering and blurring the interface (`self.view`), and containing a UILabel wrapped in a vibrancy effect view:

```
let blurEffect = UIBlurEffect(style: .systemThinMaterial)
let blurView = UIVisualEffectView(effect: blurEffect)
blurView.frame = self.view.bounds
blurView.autoresizingMask = [.flexibleWidth, .flexibleHeight]
self.view.addSubview(blurView)
let vibEffect = UIVibrancyEffect(
    blurEffect: blurEffect, style: .label)
let vibView = UIVisualEffectView(effect:vibEffect)
let lab = UILabel()
lab.text = "Hello, world"
lab.sizeToFit()
vibView.bounds = lab.bounds
vibView.center = self.view.bounds.center
vibView.autoresizingMask =
    [.flexibleTopMargin, .flexibleBottomMargin,
    .flexibleLeftMargin, .flexibleRightMargin]
blurView.contentView.addSubview(vibView)
vibView.contentView.addSubview(lab)
```

Figure 2-16 shows the result in light and dark mode.

Both a blur effect view and a vibrancy effect view embedded in a blur effect view are available as Library objects in the nib editor.

Drawing a UIView

Most of the examples of drawing so far in this chapter have produced UIImage objects. But, as I've already explained, a UIView itself provides a graphics context; whatever you draw into that graphics context will appear directly in that view. The technique here is to subclass UIView and implement the subclass's draw(_:) method. The result is that, from time to time, or whenever you send it the setNeedsDisplay message, your view's draw(_:) will be called. This is your subclass and your code, so you get to say how this view draws itself at that moment. Whatever drawing you do in draw(_:), that's what the interface will display.

When you override draw(_:), there will usually be no need to call super, since UIView's own implementation of draw(_:) does nothing. At the time that draw(_:) is called, the current graphics context has already been set to the view's own graphics context. You can use Core Graphics functions or UIKit convenience methods to draw into that context. I gave some basic examples earlier in this chapter ("Graphics Contexts" on page 96).

The need to draw in real time, on demand, surprises some beginners, who worry that drawing may be a time-consuming operation. This can indeed be a reasonable consideration, and where the same drawing will be used in many places in your interface, it may make sense to construct a UIImage instead, once, and then reuse that UIImage by drawing it in a view's draw(_:).

In general, though, you should not optimize prematurely. The code for a drawing operation may appear verbose and yet be extremely fast. Moreover, the iOS drawing system is efficient; it doesn't call draw(_:) unless it has to (or is told to, through a call to setNeedsDisplay), and once a view has drawn itself, the result is cached so that the cached drawing can be reused instead of repeating the drawing operation from scratch. (Apple refers to this cached drawing as the view's *bitmap backing store*.) You can readily satisfy yourself of this fact with some caveman debugging, logging in your draw(_:) implementation; you may be amazed to discover that your custom UIView's draw(_:) code is called only once in the entire lifetime of the app!

In fact, moving code to draw(_:) is commonly a way to *increase* efficiency. This is because it is more efficient for the drawing engine to render directly onto the screen than for it to render offscreen and then copy those pixels onto the screen.

Here are three important caveats with regard to UIView's draw(_:) method:

- Don't call draw(_:) yourself. If a view needs updating and you want its draw(_:) called, send the view the setNeedsDisplay message. This will cause draw(_:) to be called at the next proper moment.

- Don't override draw(_:) unless you are assured that this is legal. It is not legal to override draw(_:) in a subclass of UIImageView, for instance; you cannot combine your drawing with that of the UIImageView.

- Don't do anything in draw(_:) except draw. That sort of thing is a common beginner mistake. Other configurations, such as setting the view's background color, or adding subviews or sublayers, should be performed elsewhere, such as the initializer or layoutSubviews.

Where drawing is extensive and can be compartmentalized into sections, you may be able to gain some additional efficiency by paying attention to the parameter passed into draw(_:). This parameter is a CGRect designating the region of the view's bounds that needs refreshing. Normally, this is the view's entire bounds; but if you call setNeedsDisplay(_:), which takes a CGRect parameter, it will be the CGRect that you passed in as argument. You could respond by drawing only what goes into those bounds; but even if you don't, your drawing will be clipped to those bounds, so, while you may not spend less time drawing, the system will draw more efficiently.

When a custom UIView subclass has a draw(_:) implementation and you create an instance of this subclass in code, you may be surprised (and annoyed) to find that the view has a black background! This is a source of considerable confusion among beginners. The black background arises particularly when two things are true:

- The view's backgroundColor is nil.

- The view's isOpaque is true.

When a UIView is created in code with init(frame:), by default both those things *are* true. If this issue arises for you and you want to get rid of the black background, override init(frame:) and have the view set its own isOpaque to false:

```
class MyView : UIView {
    override init(frame: CGRect) {
        super.init(frame:frame)
        self.isOpaque = false
    }
    required init?(coder: NSCoder) {
        fatalError("init(coder:) has not been implemented")
    }
}
```

With a UIView created in the nib, on the other hand, the black background problem doesn't arise. This is because the UIView's backgroundColor is not nil. The nib assigns it *some* actual background color, even if that color is UIColor.clear.

Graphics Context Commands

Whenever you draw, you are giving commands to the graphics context into which you are drawing. This is true regardless of whether you use UIKit methods or Core Graphics functions. Learning to draw is really a matter of understanding how a graphics context works. That's what this section is about.

Under the hood, Core Graphics commands to a graphics context are global C functions with names like `CGContextSetFillColor`; but Swift "renamification" recasts them as if a CGContext were a genuine object representing the graphics context, with the Core Graphics functions appearing as methods of the CGContext. Moreover, thanks to Swift overloading, multiple functions are collapsed into a single command; for example, `CGContextSetFillColor` and `CGContextSetFillColorWithColor` and `CGContextSetRGBFillColor` and `CGContextSetGrayFillColor` all become the same command, `setFillColor`.

Graphics Context Settings

As you draw in a graphics context, the drawing obeys the context's current settings. For this reason, the procedure is always to configure the context's settings first, and then draw. To draw a red line and then a blue line, you would first set the context's line color to red, and draw the first line; then you'd set the context's line color to blue, and draw the second line. To the eye, it appears that the redness and blueness are properties of the individual lines, but in fact, at the time you draw each line, line color is a feature of the entire graphics context.

A graphics context has, at every moment, a *state*, which is the sum total of all its current settings; the way a piece of drawing looks is the result of what the graphics context's state was at the moment that piece of drawing was performed. To help you manipulate entire states, the graphics context provides a *stack* for holding states. Every time you call `saveGState`, the context pushes the current state onto the stack; every time you call `restoreGState`, the context retrieves the state from the top of the stack (the state that was most recently pushed) and sets itself to that state. A common pattern is:

1. Call `saveGState`.
2. Manipulate the context's settings, changing its state.
3. Draw.
4. Call `restoreGState` to restore the state and the settings to what they were before you manipulated them.

You do not have to do this before *every* manipulation of a context's settings, because settings don't necessarily conflict with one another or with past settings. You can set the context's line color to red and then later to blue without any difficulty. But in certain situations you do want your manipulation of settings to be undoable, and I'll point out several such situations later in the discussion.

Many of the settings that constitute a graphics context's state, and that determine the behavior and appearance of drawing performed at that moment, are similar to those of any drawing application. Here are some of them, along with some of the commands that determine them (and some UIKit properties and methods that call them):

Line thickness and dash style
> setLineWidth(_:), setLineDash(phase:lengths:)
> UIBezierPath lineWidth, setLineDash(_:count:phase:)

Line end cap style and join style
> setLineCap(_:), setLineJoin(_:), setMiterLimit(_:)
> UIBezierPath lineCapStyle, lineJoinStyle, miterLimit

Line color or pattern
> setStrokeColor(_:), setStrokePattern(_:colorComponents:)
> UIColor setStroke

Fill color or pattern
> setFillColor(_:), setFillPattern(_:colorComponents:)
> UIColor setFill

Shadow
> setShadow(offset:blur:color:)

Overall transparency and compositing
> setAlpha(_:), setBlendMode(_:)

Anti-aliasing
> setShouldAntialias(_:)

Additional settings include:

Clipping area
> Drawing outside the clipping area is not physically drawn.

Transform (or "CTM," for "current transform matrix")
> Changes how points that you specify in subsequent drawing commands are mapped onto the physical space of the canvas.

Many of these settings will be illustrated by examples later in this chapter.

Paths and Shapes

By issuing a series of instructions for moving an imaginary pen, you construct a *path*, tracing it out from point to point. You must first tell the pen where to position itself, setting the current point; after that, you issue commands telling the pen how to trace out each subsequent piece of the path, one by one. Each new piece of the path starts by default at the current point; its end becomes the new current point.

A path can be compound, meaning that it consists of multiple independent pieces. A single path might consist of two separate closed shapes: say, a rectangle and a circle. When you call move(to:) in the *middle* of constructing a path, you pick up the imaginary pen and move it to a new location without tracing a segment, preparing to start an independent piece of the same path.

If you're worried, as you begin to trace out a path, that there might be an existing path and that your new path might be seen as a compound part of that existing path, you can call beginPath to specify that this is a different path; many of Apple's examples do this, but in practice I usually do not find it necessary.

Here are some path-drawing commands you're likely to give:

Position the current point
>   move(to:)

Trace a line
>   addLine(to:), addLines(between:)

Trace a rectangle
>   addRect(_:), addRects(_:)

Trace an ellipse or circle
>   addEllipse(in:)

Trace an arc
>   addArc(tangent1End:tangent2End:radius:)

Trace a Bezier curve with one or two control points
>   addQuadCurve(to:control:), addCurveTo(to:control1:control2:)

Close the current path
>   closePath. This appends a line from the last point of the path to the first point. There's no need to do this if you're about to fill the path, since it's done for you.

Note that a path, in and of itself, does *not* constitute drawing! First you provide a path; *then* you draw. Drawing can mean stroking the path or filling the path, or both. Again, this should be a familiar notion from certain drawing applications. The important thing is that stroking or filling a path *clears the path*. That path is now gone and we're ready to begin constructing a new path if desired:

Stroke or fill the current path (and clear the path)

strokePath, fillPath(using:), drawPath. Use drawPath if you want both to fill and to stroke the path in a single command, because if you merely stroke it first with strokePath, the path is cleared and you can no longer fill it. There are also some convenience functions that create a path from a CGRect or similar and stroke or fill it, in a single move:

- stroke(_:), strokeLineSegments(between:)
- fill(_:)
- strokeEllipse(in:)
- fillEllipse(in:)

If a path needs to be reused or shared, you can encapsulate it as a CGPath. Like CGContext, CGPath and its mutable partner CGMutablePath are treated as class types under "renamification," and the global C functions that manipulate them are treated as methods. You can copy the graphics context's current path using the CGContext path method, or you can create a new CGMutablePath and construct the path using various functions, such as move(to:transform:) and add-Line(to:transform:), that parallel the CGContext path-construction functions. Also, there are ways to create a path based on simple geometry or on an existing path:

- init(rect:transform:)
- init(ellipseIn:transform:)
- init(roundedRect:cornerWidth:cornerHeight:transform:)
- copy(strokingWithWidth:lineCap:lineJoin:miterLimit:transform:)
- copy(dashingWithPhase:lengths:transform:)
- copy(using:) (takes a pointer to a CGAffineTransform)

To illustrate the typical use of path-drawing commands, I'll generate the up-pointing arrow shown in Figure 2-17. This might not be the best way to create the arrow, and I'm deliberately avoiding use of the convenience functions, but it's clear and shows a nice basic variety of typical commands:

```
// obtain the current graphics context
let con = UIGraphicsGetCurrentContext()!
// draw a black (by default) vertical line, the shaft of the arrow
con.move(to:CGPoint(100, 100))
con.addLine(to:CGPoint(100, 19))
con.setLineWidth(20)
con.strokePath()
// draw a red triangle, the point of the arrow
con.setFillColor(UIColor.red.cgColor)
con.move(to:CGPoint(80, 25))
con.addLine(to:CGPoint(100, 0))
```

Figure 2-17. A simple path drawing

```
con.addLine(to:CGPoint(120, 25))
con.fillPath()
// snip a triangle out of the shaft by drawing in Clear blend mode
con.move(to:CGPoint(90, 101))
con.addLine(to:CGPoint(100, 90))
con.addLine(to:CGPoint(110, 101))
con.setBlendMode(.clear)
con.fillPath()
```

The UIKit class UIBezierPath is actually a wrapper for CGPath; the wrapped path is its cgPath property. It provides methods parallel to the CGContext and CGPath functions for constructing a path, such as:

- init(rect:)
- init(ovalIn:)
- init(roundedRect:cornerRadius:)
- move(to:)
- addLine(to:)
- addArc(withCenter:radius:startAngle:endAngle:clockwise:)
- addQuadCurve(to:controlPoint:)
- addCurve(to:controlPoint1:controlPoint2:)
- close

When you call the UIBezierPath instance methods fill or stroke or fill(with:alpha:) or stroke(with:alpha:), the current graphics context settings are saved, the wrapped CGPath is made the current graphics context's path and stroked or filled, and the current graphics context settings are restored.

Using UIBezierPath together with UIColor, we could rewrite our arrow-drawing routine entirely with UIKit methods:

```
let p = UIBezierPath()
// shaft
p.move(to:CGPoint(100,100))
p.addLine(to:CGPoint(100, 19))
p.lineWidth = 20
```

```
p.stroke()
// point
UIColor.red.set()
p.removeAllPoints()
p.move(to:CGPoint(80,25))
p.addLine(to:CGPoint(100, 0))
p.addLine(to:CGPoint(120, 25))
p.fill()
// snip
p.removeAllPoints()
p.move(to:CGPoint(90,101))
p.addLine(to:CGPoint(100, 90))
p.addLine(to:CGPoint(110, 101))
p.fill(with:.clear, alpha:1.0)
```

There's no savings of code here over calling Core Graphics functions, so your choice of Core Graphics or UIKit is a matter of taste.

Clipping

A path can be used to mask out areas, protecting them from future drawing. This is called *clipping*. By default, a graphics context's clipping region is the entire graphics context, meaning that you can draw anywhere within the context.

The clipping area is a feature of the context as a whole, and any new clipping area is applied by intersecting it with the existing clipping area. To restore your clipping area to the default, call `resetClip`.

To illustrate, I'll rewrite the code that generated our original arrow (Figure 2-17) to use clipping instead of a blend mode to "punch out" the triangular notch in the tail of the arrow. This is a little tricky, because what we want to clip to is not the region inside the triangle but the region outside it. To express this, we'll use a compound path consisting of more than one closed area — the triangle, and the drawing area as a whole (which we can obtain as the context's `boundingBoxOfClipPath`).

Both when filling a compound path and when using it to express a clipping region, the system follows one of two rules:

Winding rule
> The fill or clipping area is denoted by an alternation in the direction (clockwise or counterclockwise) of the path demarcating each region.

Even-odd rule (EO)
> The fill or clipping area is denoted by a simple count of the paths demarcating each region.

Our situation is extremely simple, so it's easier to use the even-odd rule:

```
// obtain the current graphics context
let con = UIGraphicsGetCurrentContext()!
// punch triangular hole in context clipping region
con.move(to:CGPoint(90, 100))
con.addLine(to:CGPoint(100, 90))
con.addLine(to:CGPoint(110, 100))
con.closePath()
con.addRect(con.boundingBoxOfClipPath)
con.clip(using:.evenOdd) // *
// draw the vertical line
con.move(to:CGPoint(100, 100))
con.addLine(to:CGPoint(100, 19))
con.setLineWidth(20)
con.strokePath()
// draw the red triangle, the point of the arrow
con.setFillColor(UIColor.red.cgColor)
con.move(to:CGPoint(80, 25))
con.addLine(to:CGPoint(100, 0))
con.addLine(to:CGPoint(120, 25))
con.fillPath()
```

(The UIBezierPath clipping commands are usesEvenOddFillRule and addClip.)

Gradients

Gradients can range from the simple to the complex. A simple gradient (which is all I'll describe here) is determined by a color at one endpoint along with a color at the other endpoint, plus (optionally) colors at intermediate points; the gradient is then painted either linearly between two points or radially between two circles. You can't use a gradient as a path's fill color, but you can restrict a gradient to a path's shape by clipping, which will sometimes be good enough.

To illustrate, I'll redraw our arrow, using a linear gradient as the "shaft" of the arrow (Figure 2-18):

```
// obtain the current graphics context
let con = UIGraphicsGetCurrentContext()!
// punch triangular hole in context clipping region
con.move(to:CGPoint(10, 100))
con.addLine(to:CGPoint(20, 90))
```

Figure 2-18. Drawing with a gradient

```
con.addLine(to:CGPoint(30, 100))
con.closePath()
con.addRect(con.boundingBoxOfClipPath)
con.clip(using: .evenOdd)
// draw the vertical line, add its shape to the clipping region
con.move(to:CGPoint(20, 100))
con.addLine(to:CGPoint(20, 19))
con.setLineWidth(20)
con.replacePathWithStrokedPath()
con.clip()
// draw the gradient
let locs : [CGFloat] = [ 0.0, 0.5, 1.0 ]
let colors : [CGFloat] = [
    0.8, 0.4, // starting color, transparent light gray
    0.1, 0.5, // intermediate color, darker less transparent gray
    0.8, 0.4, // ending color, transparent light gray
]
let sp = CGColorSpaceCreateDeviceGray()
let grad = CGGradient(
    colorSpace:sp, colorComponents: colors, locations: locs, count: 3)!
con.drawLinearGradient(grad,
    start: CGPoint(89,0), end: CGPoint(111,0), options:[])
con.resetClip() // done clipping
// draw the red triangle, the point of the arrow
con.setFillColor(UIColor.red.cgColor)
con.move(to:CGPoint(80, 25))
con.addLine(to:CGPoint(100, 0))
con.addLine(to:CGPoint(120, 25))
con.fillPath()
```

The call to `replacePathWithStrokedPath` pretends to stroke the current path, using the current line width and other line-related context state settings, but then creates a new path representing the outside of that stroked path. Instead of a thick line we now have a rectangular region that we can use as the clip region.

We then create the gradient and paint it. The procedure is verbose but simple; everything is boilerplate. We describe the gradient as an array of locations on the continuum between one endpoint (0.0) and the other endpoint (1.0), along with the color components of the colors corresponding to each location; in this case, I want the gradient to be lighter at the edges and darker in the middle, so I use three locations, with the dark one at 0.5. We must also supply a color space; this will tell the gradient how to interpret our color components. Finally, we create the gradient and paint it into place.

(See also the discussion of gradient CIFilters earlier in this chapter. For yet another way to create a simple gradient, see the discussion of CAGradientLayer in the next chapter.)

Colors and Patterns

A color is a CGColor. CGColor is not difficult to work with, and can be converted to and from a UIColor through UIColor's `init(cgColor:)` and its `cgColor` property.

When the user interface style (light or dark mode) changes, your `draw(_:)` override is called and `UITraitCollection.current` is set for you, so any dynamic UIColors you use while drawing will be correct for the current interface style. But there's no such thing as a dynamic CGColor, so if you're using CGColor in some other situation, you might need to trigger a redraw manually. For an example, see "Interface Style" on page 29.

A pattern is also a kind of color. You can create a pattern color and stroke or fill with it. The simplest way is to draw a minimal tile of the pattern into a UIImage and create the color by calling UIColor's `init(patternImage:)`. To illustrate, I'll create a pattern of horizontal stripes and use it to paint the point of the arrow instead of a solid red color (Figure 2-19):

```
// create the pattern image tile
let r = UIGraphicsImageRenderer(size:CGSize(4,4))
let stripes = r.image { ctx in
    let imcon = ctx.cgContext
    imcon.setFillColor(UIColor.red.cgColor)
    imcon.fill(CGRect(0,0,4,4))
    imcon.setFillColor(UIColor.blue.cgColor)
    imcon.fill(CGRect(0,0,4,2))
}
// paint the point of the arrow with it
let stripesPattern = UIColor(patternImage:stripes)
stripesPattern.setFill()
let p = UIBezierPath()
p.move(to:CGPoint(80,25))
p.addLine(to:CGPoint(100,0))
p.addLine(to:CGPoint(120,25))
p.fill()
```

The Core Graphics equivalent, CGPattern, is considerably more powerful, but also much more elaborate:

```
con.saveGState()
let sp2 = CGColorSpace(patternBaseSpace:nil)!
con.setFillColorSpace(sp2)
let drawStripes : CGPatternDrawPatternCallback = { _, con in
```

Figure 2-19. A patterned fill

```
        con.setFillColor(UIColor.red.cgColor)
        con.fill(CGRect(0,0,4,4))
        con.setFillColor(UIColor.blue.cgColor)
        con.fill(CGRect(0,0,4,2))
    }
    var callbacks = CGPatternCallbacks(
        version: 0, drawPattern: drawStripes, releaseInfo: nil)
    let patt = CGPattern(info:nil, bounds: CGRect(0,0,4,4),
        matrix: .identity,
        xStep: 4, yStep: 4,
        tiling: .constantSpacingMinimalDistortion,
        isColored: true, callbacks: &callbacks)!
    var alph : CGFloat = 1.0
    con.setFillPattern(patt, colorComponents: &alph)
    con.move(to:CGPoint(80, 25))
    con.addLine(to:CGPoint(100, 0))
    con.addLine(to:CGPoint(120, 25))
    con.fillPath()
    con.restoreGState()
```

To understand that code, it helps to read it backward. Everything revolves around the creation of patt using the CGPattern initializer. A pattern is a drawing in a rectangular "cell"; we have to state both the size of the cell (bounds:) and the spacing between origin points of cells (xStep:, yStep:). In this case, the cell is 4×4, and every cell exactly touches its neighbors both horizontally and vertically. We have to supply a transform to be applied to the cell (matrix:); in this case, we're not doing anything with this transform, so we supply the identity transform. We supply a tiling rule (tiling:). We have to state whether this is a color pattern or a stencil pattern; it's a color pattern, so isColored: is true. And we have to supply a pointer to a callback function that actually draws the pattern into its cell (callbacks:).

Except that that's *not* what we have to supply as the callbacks: argument. What we actually have to supply here is a pointer to a CGPatternCallbacks struct. This struct consists of a version: whose value is fixed at 0, along with pointers to *two* functions, the drawPattern: to draw the pattern into its cell, and the releaseInfo: called when the pattern is released. We're not specifying the second function here; it is for memory management, and we don't need it in this simple example.

As you can see, the actual pattern-drawing function (drawStripes) is very simple. The only tricky issue is that it must agree with the CGPattern as to the size of a cell, or the pattern won't come out the way you expect. We know in this case that the cell is 4×4. So we fill it with red, and then fill its lower half with blue. When these cells are tiled touching each other horizontally and vertically, we get the stripes that you see in Figure 2-19.

Having generated the CGPattern, we call the context's setFillPattern; instead of setting a fill color, we're setting a fill pattern, to be used the next time we fill a path (in this case, the triangular arrowhead). The colorComponents: parameter is a pointer to a CGFloat, so we have to set up the CGFloat itself beforehand.

The only thing left to explain is the first three lines of our code. It turns out that before you can call setFillPattern with a colored pattern, you have to set the context's fill color space to a pattern color space. If you neglect to do this, you'll get an error when you call setFillPattern. This means that the code as presented has left the graphics context in an undesirable state, with its fill color space set to a pattern color space. This would cause trouble if we were later to try to set the fill color to a normal color. The solution is to wrap the code in calls to saveGState and restore-GState.

You may have observed in Figure 2-19 that the stripes do not fit neatly inside the triangle of the arrowhead: the bottommost stripe is something like half a blue stripe. This is because a pattern is positioned not with respect to the shape you are filling (or stroking), but with respect to the graphics context as a whole. We could shift the pattern position by calling setPatternPhase before drawing.

Graphics Context Transforms

Just as a UIView can have a transform, so can a graphics context. Applying a transform to a graphics context has no effect on the drawing that's already in it; like other graphics context settings, it affects only the drawing that takes place after it is applied, altering the way the coordinates you provide are mapped onto the graphics context's area. A graphics context's transform is called its *CTM*, for "current transform matrix."

It is quite usual to take full advantage of a graphics context's CTM to save yourself from performing even simple calculations. You can multiply the current transform by any CGAffineTransform using concatCTM; there are also convenience functions for applying a translate, scale, or rotate transform to the current transform.

The base transform for a graphics context is already set for you when you obtain the context; that's how the system is able to map context drawing coordinates onto screen coordinates. Whatever transforms you apply are applied to the current transform, so the base transform remains in effect and drawing continues to work. You can return to the base transform after applying your own transforms by wrapping your code in calls to `saveGState` and `restoreGState`.

Here's an example. We have hitherto been drawing our upward-pointing arrow with code that knows how to place that arrow at only one location: the top left of its rectangle is hard-coded at (80,0). This is silly. It makes the code hard to understand, as well as inflexible and difficult to reuse. Surely the sensible thing would be to draw the arrow at (0,0), by subtracting 80 from all the x-values in our existing code. Now it is easy to draw the arrow at *any* position, simply by applying a translate transform beforehand, mapping (0,0) to the desired top-left corner of the arrow. To draw it at (80,0), we would say·

```
con.translateBy(x:80, y:0)
// now draw the arrow at (0,0)
```

A rotate transform is particularly useful, allowing you to draw in a rotated orientation without any nasty trigonometry. It's a bit tricky because the point around which the rotation takes place is the origin. This is rarely what you want, so you have to apply a translate transform first, to map the origin to the point around which you really want to rotate. But then, after rotating, in order to figure out where to draw, you will probably have to reverse your translate transform.

To illustrate, here's code to draw our arrow repeatedly at several angles, pivoting around the end of its tail (Figure 2-20). Since the arrow will be drawn multiple times, I'll start by encapsulating the drawing of the arrow as a UIImage. This is not merely to reduce repetition and make drawing more efficient; it's also because we want the entire arrow to pivot, including the pattern stripes, and this is the simplest way to achieve that:

```
lazy var arrow : UIImage = {
    let r = UIGraphicsImageRenderer(size:CGSize(40,100))
    return r.image { _ in
        self.arrowImage()
    }
}()
func arrowImage () {
    // obtain the current graphics context
    let con = UIGraphicsGetCurrentContext()!
    // draw the arrow into the graphics context
    // draw it at (0,0)! adjust all x-values by subtracting 80
    // ... actual code omitted ...
}
```

In our `draw(_:)` implementation, we draw the arrow image multiple times:

```
override func draw(_ rect: CGRect) {
    let con = UIGraphicsGetCurrentContext()!
    self.arrow.draw(at:CGPoint(0,0))
    for _ in 0..<3 {
```

Figure 2-20. Drawing rotated

Figure 2-21. Drawing with a shadow

```
            con.translateBy(x: 20, y: 100)
            con.rotate(by: 30 * .pi/180.0)
            con.translateBy(x: -20, y: -100)
            self.arrow.draw(at:CGPoint(0,0))
        }
    }
```

Shadows

To add a shadow to a drawing, give the context a shadow value before drawing. The shadow position is expressed as a CGSize, where the positive direction for both values indicates down and to the right. The blur value is an open-ended positive number; Apple doesn't explain how the scale works, but experimentation shows that 12 is nice and blurry, 99 is so blurry as to be shapeless, and higher values become problematic.

Figure 2-21 shows the result of the same code that generated Figure 2-20, except that before we start drawing the arrow repeatedly, we give the context a shadow:

```
let con = UIGraphicsGetCurrentContext()!
con.setShadow(offset: CGSize(7, 7), blur: 12)
self.arrow.draw(at:CGPoint(0,0))
// ... and so on
```

It may not be evident from Figure 2-21, but we are adding a shadow each time we draw. This means the arrows are able to cast shadows on one another. Suppose, instead, that we want all the arrows to cast a single shadow collectively. The way to achieve this is with a *transparency layer*; this is basically a subcontext that accumulates all drawing and then adds the shadow. Our code for drawing the shadowed arrows now looks like this:

```
let con = UIGraphicsGetCurrentContext()!
con.setShadow(offset: CGSize(7, 7), blur: 12)
con.beginTransparencyLayer(auxiliaryInfo: nil)
self.arrow.draw(at:CGPoint(0,0))
for _ in 0..<3 {
    con.translateBy(x: 20, y: 100)
    con.rotate(by: 30 * .pi/180.0)
    con.translateBy(x: -20, y: -100)
    self.arrow.draw(at:CGPoint(0,0))
}
con.endTransparencyLayer()
```

Erasing

The CGContext clear(_:) function erases all existing drawing in a CGRect; combined with clipping, it can erase an area of any shape. The result can "punch a hole" through all existing drawing.

The behavior of clear(_:) depends on whether the context is transparent or opaque. This is particularly obvious and intuitive when drawing into an image context. If the image context is transparent, clear(_:) erases to transparent; otherwise it erases to black.

When drawing directly into a view, if the view's background color is nil or a color with even a tiny bit of transparency, the result of clear(_:) will appear to be transparent, punching a hole right through the view including its background color; if the background color is completely opaque, the result of clear(_:) will be black. This is because the view's background color determines whether the view's graphics context is transparent or opaque, so this is essentially the same behavior that I described in the preceding paragraph.

Figure 2-22 illustrates; the blue square on the left has been partly cut away to black, while the blue square on the right has been partly cut away to transparency. Yet these are instances of the same UIView subclass, drawn with exactly the same code! The UIView subclass's draw(_:) looks like this:

```
let con = UIGraphicsGetCurrentContext()!
con.setFillColor(UIColor.blue.cgColor)
con.fill(rect)
con.clear(CGRect(0,0,30,30))
```

The difference between the views in Figure 2-22 is that the backgroundColor of the first view is solid red with an alpha of 1, while the backgroundColor of the second view is solid red with an alpha of 0.99. This difference is imperceptible to the eye — not to mention that the red color never appears, as it is covered with a blue fill! Nevertheless, it completely changes the effect of clear(_:).

Figure 2-22. The very strange behavior of the clear function

If you find this as confusing as I do, the simplest solution may be to drop down to the level of the view's `layer` and set its `isOpaque` property after setting the view's background color:

```
self.backgroundColor = .red
self.layer.isOpaque = false
```

That gives you a final and dependable say on the behavior of `clear(_:)`. If `layer.isOpaque` is `false`, `clear(_:)` erases to transparency; if it is `true`, it erases to black.

Points and Pixels

A point is a dimensionless location described by an x-coordinate and a y-coordinate. When you draw in a graphics context, you specify the points at which to draw, and this works regardless of the device's resolution, because Core Graphics maps your drawing nicely onto the physical output using the base CTM and anti-aliasing. Therefore, throughout this chapter I've concerned myself with graphics context points, disregarding their relationship to screen pixels.

Nonetheless, pixels do exist. A pixel is a physical, integral, dimensioned unit of display in the real world. Whole-numbered points effectively lie between pixels, and this can matter if you're fussy, especially on a single-resolution device. If a vertical path with whole-number coordinates is stroked with a line width of 1, half the line falls on each side of the path, and the drawn line on the screen of a single-resolution device will seem to be 2 pixels wide (because the device can't illuminate half a pixel).

You may sometimes encounter the suggestion that if this effect is objectionable, you should try shifting the line's position by `0.5`, to center it in its pixels. This advice may appear to work, but it makes some simpleminded assumptions. A more sophisticated approach is to obtain the UIView's `contentScaleFactor` property. You can divide by this value to convert from pixels to points. Consider also that the most accurate way to draw a vertical or horizontal line is not to stroke a path but to fill a rectangle. This UIView subclass code will draw a perfect 1-pixel-wide vertical line on any device (con is the current graphics context):

```
con.fill(CGRect(100,0,1.0/self.contentScaleFactor,100))
```

Figure 2-23. Automatic stretching of content

Content Mode

A view that draws something within itself, as opposed to merely having a background color and subviews (as in the previous chapter), has *content*. This means that its contentMode property becomes important whenever the view is resized. As I mentioned earlier, the drawing system will avoid asking a view to redraw itself from scratch if possible; instead, it will use the cached result of the previous drawing operation (the bitmap backing store). If the view is resized, the system may simply stretch or shrink or reposition the cached drawing, if your contentMode setting instructs it to do so.

It's a little tricky to illustrate this point when the view's content is coming from draw(_:), because I have to arrange for the view to obtain its content from draw(_:) and then cause it to be resized without draw(_:) being called *again*. As the app starts up, I'll create an instance of a UIView subclass, MyView, that knows how to draw our arrow; then I'll use delayed performance to resize the instance after the window has shown and the interface has been initially displayed (for my delay function, see Appendix B):

```
delay(0.1) {
    mv.bounds.size.height *= 2 // mv is the MyView instance
}
```

We double the height of the view without causing draw(_:) to be called. The result is that the view's drawing appears at double its correct height. If our view's draw(_:) code is the same as the code that generated Figure 2-18, we get Figure 2-23.

Sooner or later, however, draw(_:) will be called, and the drawing will be refreshed in accordance with our code. Our code doesn't say to draw the arrow at a height that is relative to the height of the view's bounds; it draws the arrow at a fixed height. Therefore, the arrow will snap back to its original size.

A view's contentMode property should therefore usually be in agreement with how the view draws itself. Our draw(_:) code dictates the size and position of the arrow relative to the view's bounds origin, its top left; so we could set its contentMode to .topLeft. Alternatively, we could set it to .redraw; this will cause automatic scaling of the cached content to be turned off — instead, when the view is resized, its setNeedsDisplay method will be called, ultimately triggering draw(_:) to redraw the content.

Layers

The tale told in Chapters 1 and 2 of how a UIView draws itself is only half the story. A UIView has a partner called its *layer*, a CALayer. A UIView does not actually draw itself onto the screen; it draws itself into its layer, and it is the layer that is portrayed on the screen. As I've already mentioned, a view is not redrawn frequently; instead, its drawing is cached, and the cached version of the drawing (the bitmap backing store) is used where possible. The cached version is, in fact, the layer. What I spoke of in Chapter 2 as the view's graphics context is actually the layer's graphics context.

This might seem to be a mere implementation detail, but layers are important and interesting in their own right. To understand layers is to understand views more deeply; layers extend the power of views:

Layers have properties that affect drawing
> Layers have drawing-related properties beyond those of a UIView. Because a layer is the recipient and presenter of a view's drawing, you can modify how a view is drawn on the screen by accessing the layer's properties. By reaching down to the level of its layer, you can make a view do things you can't do through UIView methods alone.

Layers can be combined within a single view
> A UIView's partner layer can contain additional layers. Since the purpose of layers is to draw, portraying visible material on the screen, this allows a UIView's drawing to be composited of multiple distinct pieces. This can make drawing easier, with the constituents of a drawing being treated as objects.

Layers are the basis of animation
> Animation allows you to add clarity, emphasis, and just plain coolness to your interface. Layers are made to be animated; the "CA" in "CALayer" stands for "Core Animation." Animation is the subject of Chapter 4.

Figure 3-1. A compass, composed of layers

Suppose we want to add a compass indicator to our app's interface. Figure 3-1 portrays a simple version of such a compass. It takes advantage of the arrow that we drew in Chapter 2; the arrow is drawn into a layer of its own. The other parts of the compass are layers too: the circle is a layer, and each of the cardinal point letters is a layer. The drawing is easy to assemble in code (and later in this chapter, that's exactly what we'll do); even more intriguing, the pieces can be repositioned and animated separately, so it's easy to rotate the arrow without moving the circle (and in Chapter 4, that's exactly what we'll do).

View and Layer

A UIView instance has an accompanying CALayer instance, accessible as the view's `layer` property. This layer has a special status: it is partnered with this view to embody all of the view's drawing. The layer has no corresponding `view` property, but the view is the layer's `delegate` (adopting CALayerDelegate). The documentation sometimes speaks of this layer as the view's *underlying layer*.

Because every view has an underlying layer, there is a tight integration between the two. The layer portrays all the view's drawing; if the view draws, it does so by contributing to the layer's drawing. The view is the layer's delegate. And the view's properties are often merely a convenience for accessing the layer's properties. When you set the view's `backgroundColor`, you are really setting the layer's `backgroundColor`, and if you set the layer's `backgroundColor` directly, the view's `backgroundColor` is set to match. Similarly, the view's `frame` is really the layer's `frame` and *vice versa*.

The view draws into its layer, and the layer caches that drawing; the layer can then be manipulated, changing the view's appearance, without necessarily asking the view to redraw itself. This is a source of great efficiency in the drawing system. It also explains such phenomena as the content stretching that we encountered in the last section of Chapter 2: when the view's bounds size changes, the drawing system, by default, simply stretches or repositions the cached layer image, until such time as the view is told to draw freshly, replacing the layer's content.

By default, when a UIView is instantiated, its layer is a plain vanilla CALayer. But that might not be what you want. Suppose you have declared a UIView subclass, and you want your subclass's underlying layer to be an instance of a CALayer subclass (built-in or your own). Then override your UIView subclass's layerClass class property to return that CALayer subclass.

That is how the compass in Figure 3-1 is created. We have a UIView subclass, CompassView, and a CALayer subclass, CompassLayer. Here is CompassView's implementation:

```
class CompassView : UIView {
    override class var layerClass : AnyClass {
        return CompassLayer.self
    }
}
```

When CompassView is instantiated, its underlying layer is a CompassLayer. In this example, there is no drawing in CompassView; its job — in this case, its *only* job — is to give CompassLayer a place in the visible interface, because a layer cannot appear without a view.

Layers and Sublayers

A layer can have sublayers, and a layer has at most one superlayer. We may say there is a *tree* of layers. This is similar and parallel to the tree of views (Chapter 1). In fact, so tight is the integration between a view and its underlying layer that these hierarchies are effectively the *same* hierarchy. Given a view and its underlying layer, that layer's superlayer is the view's superview's underlying layer, and that layer has as sublayers all the underlying layers of all the view's subviews. Indeed, because the layers are how the views actually get drawn, one might say that the view hierarchy really *is* a layer hierarchy (Figure 3-2).

At the same time, the layer hierarchy can go *beyond* the view hierarchy. A view has exactly one underlying layer, but a layer can have sublayers that are *not the underlying layers of any view*. So the hierarchy of layers that underlie views exactly matches the hierarchy of views, but the total layer tree may be a superset of that hierarchy. In Figure 3-3, we see the same view-and-layer hierarchy as in Figure 3-2, but two of the layers have additional sublayers that are theirs alone (that is, sublayers that are not any view's underlying layers).

From a visual standpoint, there may be nothing to distinguish a hierarchy of views from a hierarchy of layers. In Chapter 1 we drew three overlapping rectangles using

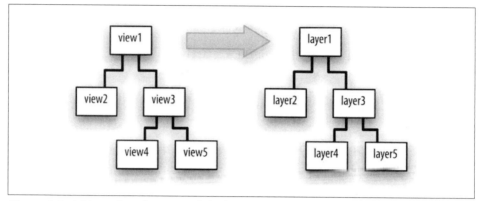

Figure 3-2. A hierarchy of views and the hierarchy of layers underlying it

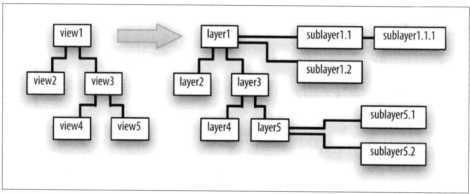

Figure 3-3. Layers that have sublayers of their own

a hierarchy of views (Figure 1-1). This code gives exactly the same visible display by manipulating layers (Figure 3-4):

```
let lay1 = CALayer()
lay1.backgroundColor = UIColor(red: 1, green: 0.4, blue: 1, alpha: 1).cgColor
lay1.frame = CGRect(113, 111, 132, 194)
self.view.layer.addSublayer(lay1)
let lay2 = CALayer()
lay2.backgroundColor = UIColor(red: 0.5, green: 1, blue: 0, alpha: 1).cgColor
lay2.frame = CGRect(41, 56, 132, 194)
lay1.addSublayer(lay2)
let lay3 = CALayer()
lay3.backgroundColor = UIColor(red: 1, green: 0, blue: 0, alpha: 1).cgColor
lay3.frame = CGRect(43, 197, 160, 230)
self.view.layer.addSublayer(lay3)
```

In Figure 3-4, Layer 1 and Layer 2 are siblings — they are sublayers of the main view's underlying layer — while Layer 3 is a sublayer of Layer 2. That's exactly parallel to the situation in Figure 1-1.

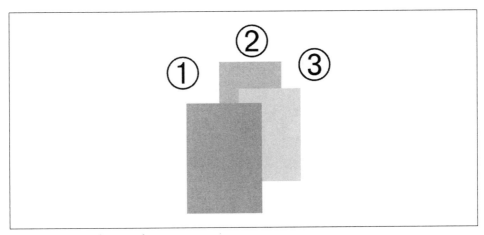

Figure 3-4. Overlapping layers

A view's subview's underlying layer is a sublayer of the view's underlying layer. Therefore, it can be positioned anywhere in the drawing order among any *other* sublayers the view may have. In other words: a view can be interspersed among layers! To illustrate, let's construct Figure 3-4 again, but between adding lay2 and lay3 to the interface, we'll add a subview:

```
// ...
lay1.addSublayer(lay2) // Layer 3
let iv = UIImageView(image:UIImage(named:"smiley"))
self.view.addSubview(iv) // Smiley view
iv.frame.origin = CGPoint(180,180)
let lay3 = CALayer() // Layer 1
// ...
```

The result is Figure 3-5. The smiley face (iv) was added to the interface before Layer 1 (lay3), so it appears behind it. The smiley face is a *view*, whereas Layer 1 is just a *layer*; so they are not siblings as views, since Layer 1 is not a view. But the smiley face is both a view and a layer; as layers, the smiley face and Layer 1 *are* siblings, since they have the same superlayer, namely the main view's layer. As siblings, either one can be made to appear in front of the other.

Whether a layer displays regions of its sublayers that lie outside that layer's own bounds depends upon the value of its masksToBounds property. This is parallel to a view's clipsToBounds property, and indeed, for a layer that is a view's underlying layer, they are the same thing. In Figures 3-4 and 3-5, the layers all have clipsToBounds set to false (the default); that's why Layer 3 is visible beyond the bounds of Layer 2, which is its superlayer.

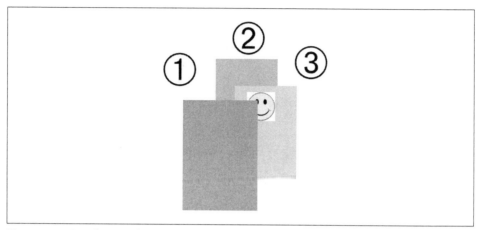

Figure 3-5. Overlapping layers and a view

Manipulating the Layer Hierarchy

Layers come with a full set of methods for reading and manipulating the layer hierarchy, parallel to the methods for reading and manipulating the view hierarchy. A layer has a superlayer property and a sublayers property, along with these methods:

- addSublayer(_:)
- insertSublayer(_:at:)
- insertSublayer(_:below:), insertSublayer(_:above:)
- replaceSublayer(_:with:)
- removeFromSuperlayer

Unlike a view's subviews property, a layer's sublayers property is writable. You can give a layer multiple sublayers in a single move, by assigning to its sublayers property. To remove all of a layer's sublayers, set its sublayers property to nil.

Although a layer's sublayers have an order, reflected in the sublayers order and regulated with the methods I've just mentioned, this is not necessarily the same as their back-to-front drawing order. By default, it is, but a layer also has a zPosition property, a CGFloat, and this also determines drawing order. The rule is that all sublayers with the same zPosition are drawn in the order they are listed among their sublayers siblings, but lower zPosition siblings are drawn before higher zPosition siblings. (The default zPosition is 0.0.)

Sometimes, the zPosition property is a more convenient way of dictating drawing order than sibling order is. If layers represent playing cards laid out in a solitaire game, it will likely be a lot easier and more flexible to determine how the cards overlap by setting their zPosition than by rearranging their sibling order.

Moreover, a subview's layer is itself just a layer, so you can rearrange the drawing order of subviews by setting the zPosition of their underlying layers! In our code constructing Figure 3-5, if we assign the image view's underlying layer a zPosition of 1, it is drawn in front of Layer 1:

```
self.view.addSubview(iv)
iv.layer.zPosition = 1
```

Like a UIView, a CALayer also has an isHidden property that can be set to take it and its sublayers out of the visible interface without actually removing it from the layer hierarchy.

Positioning a Sublayer

Layer coordinate systems and positioning are similar to those of views. A layer's own internal coordinate system is expressed by its bounds, just like a view; its size is its bounds size, and its bounds origin is the internal coordinate at its top left.

A sublayer's position within its superlayer is not described by its center, like a view; a layer does not have a center. Instead, a sublayer's position within its superlayer is defined by a combination of *two* properties:

position
> A point expressed in the superlayer's coordinate system.

anchorPoint
> Where the position point is located, with respect to the layer's own bounds. It is a CGPoint describing a fraction (or multiple) of the layer's own bounds width and bounds height. (0.0,0.0) is the top left of the layer's bounds, and (1.0,1.0) is the bottom right of the layer's bounds.

Here's an analogy; I didn't make it up, but it's pretty apt. Think of the sublayer as pinned to its superlayer; then you have to say both where the pin passes through the sublayer (the anchorPoint) and where it passes through the superlayer (the position).

If the anchorPoint is (0.5,0.5) (the default), the position property works like a view's center property. A view's center is actually a special case of a layer's position. This is quite typical of the relationship between view properties and layer properties; the view properties are often a simpler — but less powerful — version of the layer properties.

A layer's position and anchorPoint are orthogonal (independent); changing one does not change the other. Therefore, changing either of them without changing the other changes where the layer is drawn within its superlayer.

In Figure 3-1, the most important point in the circle is its center; all the other objects need to be positioned with respect to it. Therefore, they all have the same position: the center of the circle. But they differ in their anchorPoint. The arrow's anchor-Point is (0.5,0.8), the middle of the shaft, near the tail. But the anchorPoint of a cardinal point letter is (0.5,3.0), well outside the letter's bounds, so as to place the letter near the edge of the circle.

A layer's frame is a purely derived property. When you get the frame, it is calculated from the bounds size along with the position and anchorPoint. When you set the frame, you set the bounds size and position. In general, you should regard the frame as a convenient façade and no more. Nevertheless, it is convenient! To position a sub-layer so that it exactly overlaps its superlayer, you can just set the sublayer's frame to the superlayer's bounds.

 A layer created in code (as opposed to a view's underlying layer) has a frame and bounds of CGRect.zero and will not be visible on the screen even when you add it to a superlayer that is on the screen. Be sure to give your layer a nonzero width and height if you want to be able to see it! Creating a layer and adding it to a superlayer and then wondering why it isn't appearing in the interface is a common beginner error.

CALayer instance methods are provided for converting between the coordinate systems of layers within the same layer hierarchy; the first parameter can be a CGPoint or a CGRect, and the second parameter is another CALayer:

- convert(_:from:)
- convert(_:to:)

CAScrollLayer

If you're going to be moving a layer's bounds origin as a way of repositioning its sub-layers *en masse*, you might like to make the layer a CAScrollLayer, a CALayer sub-class that provides convenience methods for this sort of thing. (Despite the name, a CAScrollLayer provides no scrolling interface; the user can't scroll it by dragging.) By default, a CAScrollLayer's masksToBounds property is true, so that the CAScrollLayer acts like a window through which you see only what is within its bounds. (You can set its masksToBounds to false, but this would be an odd thing to do, as it somewhat defeats the purpose.)

To move the CAScrollLayer's bounds, you can talk either to it or to a sublayer (at any depth):

Talking to the CAScrollLayer
    Call this CAScrollLayer method:

`scroll(to:)`

> If the parameter is a CGPoint, changes the CAScrollLayer's bounds origin to that point. If the parameter is a CGRect, changes the CAScrollLayer's bounds origin minimally so that the given portion of the bounds rect is visible.

Talking to a sublayer

> Call these CALayer methods on sublayers of the CAScrollLayer:

`scroll(_:)`

> Changes the CAScrollLayer's bounds origin so that the given point *of the sublayer* is at the top left of the CAScrollLayer.

`scrollRectToVisible(_:)`

> Changes the CAScrollLayer's bounds origin so that the given rect *of the sublayer's bounds* is within the CAScrollLayer's bounds area. You can also ask the sublayer for its `visibleRect`, the part of this sublayer now within the CAScrollLayer's bounds.

Layer and Delegate

A CALayer's `delegate` property is settable (to an instance of any class adopting CALayerDelegate). If a layer is *not* the underlying layer of a view, it can be useful to give it a delegate; you might do this in order to give another object a hand in the layer's layout or its drawing, both of which I'll discuss later. A layer's delegate can also participate in certain aspects of animation, as I'll explain in Chapter 4.

But be careful! Do *not*, under any circumstances, set the `delegate` of a layer that *is* the underlying layer of a UIView; and do *not* make a UIView the `delegate` of any layer other than its underlying layer. A UIView *must* be the delegate of its underlying layer; moreover, it must *not* be the delegate of any *other* layer. *Don't do anything to mess this up.* If you do, extremely bad things will happen; for instance, drawing will stop working correctly.

Layout of Layers

The view hierarchy is actually a layer hierarchy (Figure 3-2). The positioning of a view within its superview is actually the positioning of its layer within its superlayer (the superview's layer). A view can be repositioned and resized automatically in accordance with its `autoresizingMask` or through autolayout based on its constraints. So there is automatic layout of layers *if they are the underlying layers of views.* Otherwise, there is *no* automatic layout of layers in iOS; the only option for layout of layers that are not the underlying layers of views is manual layout that you perform in code.

When a layer needs layout, either because its bounds have changed or because you called `setNeedsLayout`, you can respond in either of two ways:

- The layer's `layoutSublayers` method is called; to respond, override `layoutSublayers` in your CALayer subclass.

- Alternatively, implement `layoutSublayers(of:)` in the layer's delegate. (Remember, if the layer is a view's underlying layer, the view is its delegate.)

For your layer to do effective manual layout of its sublayers, you'll probably need a way to identify or refer to the sublayers. There is no layer equivalent of `viewWith-Tag(_:)`, so such identification and reference is entirely up to you. A CALayer does have a `name` property that you might misuse for your own purposes. Key–value coding can also be helpful here; layers implement key–value coding in a special way, discussed at the end of this chapter.

For a view's underlying layer, `layoutSublayers` or `layoutSublayers(of:)` is called after the view's `layoutSubviews`. Under autolayout, you must call `super` or else autolayout will break. Moreover, these methods may be called more than once during the course of autolayout; if you're looking for an automatically generated signal that it's time to do manual layout of sublayers, a view layout event might be a better choice (see "Layout Events" on page 79).

Drawing in a Layer

The simplest way to make something appear in a layer is through its `contents` property. This is parallel to the `image` in a UIImageView (Chapter 2). It is expected to be a CGImage (or `nil`, signifying no image). Here's how we might modify the code that generated Figure 3-5 in such a way as to generate the smiley face as a layer rather than a view:

```
let lay4 = CALayer()
let im = UIImage(named:"smiley")!
lay4.frame = CGRect(origin:CGPoint(180,180), size:im.size)
lay4.contents = im.cgImage
self.view.layer.addSublayer(lay4)
```

 Unfortunately, the CALayer `contents` property is typed as Any (wrapped in an Optional). That means you can assign *anything* to it. Setting a layer's `contents` to a UIImage, rather than a CGImage, will *fail silently* — the image doesn't appear, but there is no error either. This is absolutely maddening, and I wish I had a nickel for every time I've done it and then wasted hours figuring out why my layer isn't appearing.

There are also four methods that can be implemented to provide or draw a layer's content on demand, similar to a UIView's `draw(_:)`. A layer is very conservative about calling these methods (and you must not call any of them directly). When a layer *does* call these methods, I will say that the layer *redisplays itself.* Here is how a layer can be caused to redisplay itself:

- If the layer's needsDisplayOnBoundsChange property is false (the default), then the only way to cause the layer to redisplay itself is by calling setNeedsDisplay (or setNeedsDisplay(_:), specifying a CGRect). Even this might not cause the layer to redisplay itself right away; if that's crucial, then you will also call display-IfNeeded.

- If the layer's needsDisplayOnBoundsChange property is true, then the layer will also redisplay itself when the layer's bounds change (rather like a view's .redraw content mode).

Here are the four methods that can be called when a layer redisplays itself; pick one to implement (don't try to combine them, you'll just confuse things):

display *in a subclass*
: Your CALayer subclass can override display. There's no graphics context at this point, so display is pretty much limited to setting the contents image.

display(_:) *in the delegate*
: You can set the CALayer's delegate property and implement display(_:) in the delegate. As with CALayer's display, there's no graphics context, so you'll just be setting the contents image.

draw(in:) *in a subclass*
: Your CALayer subclass can override draw(in:). The parameter is a graphics context into which you can draw directly; it is *not* automatically made the current context.

draw(_:in:) *in the delegate*
: You can set the CALayer's delegate property and implement draw(_:in:) in the delegate. The second parameter is a graphics context into which you can draw directly; it is *not* automatically made the current context.

Assigning a layer a contents image and drawing directly into the layer are, in effect, mutually exclusive:

- If a layer's contents is assigned an image, this image is shown immediately and replaces whatever drawing may have been displayed in the layer.

- If a layer redisplays itself and draw(in:) or draw(_:in:) draws into the layer, the drawing replaces whatever image may have been displayed in the layer.

- If a layer redisplays itself and none of the four methods provides any content, the layer will be empty.

If a layer is a view's underlying layer, you usually won't use any of the four methods to draw into the layer: you'll use the view's draw(_:). But you *can* use these methods if you really want to. In that case, you will probably want to implement draw(_:) anyway, leaving that implementation empty. The reason is that this causes the layer to redisplay itself at appropriate moments.

Here's why. When a view is sent setNeedsDisplay — including when the view first appears — the view's underlying layer is also sent setNeedsDisplay, *unless the view has no draw(_:) implementation* (because in that case, it is assumed that the view never needs redrawing). So if you're drawing a view entirely by drawing to its underlying layer directly, and if you want the underlying layer to be redisplayed automatically when the view is told to redraw itself, you should implement draw(_:) to do nothing. (This technique has no effect on sublayers of the underlying layer.)

These are legitimate (but unusual) techniques for drawing into a view:

- The view subclass implements an empty draw(_:), along with either display-Layer: or draw(_:in:).

- The view subclass implements an empty draw(_:) plus layerClass, to give the view a custom layer subclass — and the custom layer subclass implements either display or draw(in:).

Drawing-Related Layer Properties

Here are some layer properties that affect what the layer displays:

contentsScale
> Maps point distances in the layer's graphics context to pixel distances on the device. A layer that's managed by Cocoa, if it has contents, will adjust its contentsScale automatically as needed; if a view implements draw(_:), then on a device with a double-resolution screen its underlying layer is assigned a contentsScale of 2.
>
> But a layer that you are creating and managing yourself has no such automatic behavior; it's up to you, if you plan to draw into the layer, to set its contents-Scale appropriately. Content drawn into a layer with a contentsScale of 1 may appear pixelated or fuzzy on a high-resolution screen. And when you're starting with a UIImage and assigning its CGImage as a layer's contents, if there's a mismatch between the UIImage's scale and the layer's contentsScale, then the image may be displayed at the wrong size.

backgroundColor
> Equivalent to a view's backgroundColor (and if this layer is a view's underlying layer, it *is* the view's backgroundColor). Changing the backgroundColor takes

effect immediately. Think of the `backgroundColor` as separate from the layer's own drawing, and as painted *behind* the layer's own drawing.

`opacity`

Affects the overall apparent transparency of the layer. It is equivalent to a view's `alpha` (and if this layer is a view's underlying layer, it *is* the view's `alpha`). It affects the apparent transparency of the layer's sublayers as well. It affects the apparent transparency of the background color and the apparent transparency of the layer's content separately (just as with a view's `alpha`). Changing the `opacity` property takes effect immediately.

`isOpaque`

Determines whether the layer's graphics context is opaque. An opaque graphics context is black; you can draw on top of that blackness, but the blackness is still there. A nonopaque graphics context is clear; where no drawing is, it is completely transparent.

Changing the `isOpaque` property has no effect until the layer redisplays itself. A view's underlying layer's `isOpaque` property is independent of the view's `isOpaque` property; they are unrelated and do entirely different things. But if the view implements `draw(_:)`, then setting the view's `backgroundColor` changes the layer's `isOpaque`! The latter becomes `true` if the new background color is opaque (alpha component of 1), and `false` otherwise. That's the reason behind the strange behavior of CGContext's `clear(_:)` method, described in Chapter 2.

 When drawing directly into a *layer*, the behavior of `clear(_:)` differs from what was described in Chapter 2 for drawing into a *view*: instead of punching a hole through the background color, it effectively paints with the layer's background color. This can have curious side effects, and I regard it as deeply weird.

Content Resizing and Positioning

A layer's content is stored (cached) as a bitmap which is then treated like an image:

- If the content came from setting the layer's `contents` property to an image, the cached content is that image; its size is the point size of the CGImage we started with.
- If the content came from drawing directly into the layer's graphics context, the cached content is the layer's entire graphics context; its size is the point size of the layer itself at the time the drawing was performed.

The layer's content is drawn in relation to the layer's bounds in accordance with various layer properties, which cause the cached content to be resized, repositioned, cropped, and so on, as it is displayed. The properties are:

contentsGravity

This property (CALayerContentsGravity) is parallel to a UIView's contentMode property, and describes how the content should be positioned or stretched in relation to the bounds. .center means the content is centered in the bounds without resizing; .resize (the default) means the content is sized to fit the bounds, even if this means distorting its aspect; and so forth.

 For historical reasons, the terms bottom and top in the names of the contents-Gravity settings have the opposite of their expected meanings. Reverse them in your mind: when you mean the top, say .bottom; when you mean the top left, say .bottomLeft; and so on.

contentsRect

A CGRect expressing the proportion of the content that is to be displayed. The default is (0.0,0.0,1.0,1.0), meaning the entire content is displayed. The specified part of the content is sized and positioned in relation to the bounds in accordance with the contentsGravity. By setting the contentsRect, you can scale up part of the content to fill the bounds, or slide part of a larger image into view without redrawing or changing the contents image.

You can also use the contentsRect to scale down the content, by specifying a larger contentsRect such as (-0.5,-0.5,1.5,1.5); but any content pixels that touch the edge of the contentsRect will then be extended outward to the edge of the layer (to prevent this, make sure that the outermost pixels of the content are all empty).

contentsCenter

A CGRect, structured like the contentsRect, expressing the central region of nine rectangular regions of the contentsRect that are variously allowed to stretch if the contentsGravity calls for stretching. The central region (the actual value of the contentsCenter) stretches in both directions. Of the other eight regions (inferred from the value you provide), the four corner regions don't stretch, and the four side regions stretch in one direction. (This should remind you of how a resizable image stretches; see Chapter 2.)

If a layer's content comes from drawing directly into its graphics context, then the layer's contentsGravity, of itself, has no effect, because the size of the graphics context, by definition, fits the size of the layer exactly; there is nothing to stretch or reposition. But the contentsGravity *will* have an effect on such a layer if its contentsRect is not (0.0,0.0,1.0,1.0), because now we're specifying a rectangle of some *other* size; the contentsGravity describes how to fit that rectangle into the layer.

Figure 3-6. One way of resizing the compass arrow

Again, if a layer's content comes from drawing directly into its graphics context, then when the layer is resized, if the layer is asked to display itself again, the drawing is performed again, and once more the layer's content fits the size of the layer exactly. But if the layer's bounds are resized when `needsDisplayOnBoundsChange` is `false`, then the layer does *not* redisplay itself, so its cached content no longer fits the layer, and the `contentsGravity` matters.

By a judicious combination of settings, you can get the layer to perform some clever drawing for you that might be difficult to perform directly. Figure 3-6 shows the result of the following settings:

```
arrow.needsDisplayOnBoundsChange = false
arrow.contentsCenter = CGRect(0.0, 0.4, 1.0, 0.6)
arrow.contentsGravity = .resizeAspect
arrow.bounds = arrow.bounds.insetBy(dx: -20, dy: -20)
```

Because `needsDisplayOnBoundsChange` is `false`, the content is not redisplayed when the arrow's bounds are increased; instead, the cached content is used. The `contents-Gravity` setting tells us to resize proportionally; therefore, the arrow is both longer and wider than in Figure 3-1, but not in such a way as to distort its proportions. Notice that although the triangular arrowhead is wider, it is not longer; the increase in length is due entirely to the stretching of the arrow's shaft. That's because the `contentsCenter` region is within the shaft.

A layer's `masksToBounds` property has the same effect on its content that it has on its sublayers. If it is `false`, the whole content is displayed, even if that content (after taking account of the `contentsGravity` and `contentsRect`) is larger then the layer. If it is `true`, only the part of the content within the layer's bounds will be displayed.

> The value of a layer's bounds origin does not affect where its content is drawn. It affects only where its sublayers are drawn.

Layers that Draw Themselves

A few built-in CALayer subclasses provide some basic but helpful self-drawing ability:

CATextLayer

A CATextLayer has a `string` property, which can be an NSString or NSAttributedString (Chapter 11), along with other text formatting properties, somewhat like a simplified UILabel; it draws its `string`. The default text color, the `foregroundColor` property, is white, which is unlikely to be what you want. The text is different from the `contents` and is mutually exclusive with it: either the contents image or the text will be drawn, but not both, so in general you should not give a CATextLayer any contents image. In Figures 3-1 and 3-6, the cardinal point letters are CATextLayer instances.

CAShapeLayer

A CAShapeLayer has a `path` property, which is a CGPath. It fills or strokes this path, or both, depending on its `fillColor` and `strokeColor` values, and displays the result; the default is a `fillColor` of black and no `strokeColor`. It has properties for line thickness, dash style, end-cap style, and join style, similar to a graphics context; it also has the remarkable ability to draw only part of its path (`strokeStart` and `strokeEnd`), making it very easy to draw things like an arc of an ellipse. A CAShapeLayer may also have `contents`; the shape is displayed on top of the contents image, but there is no property permitting you to specify a compositing mode. In Figures 3-1 and 3-6, the background circle is a CAShapeLayer instance, stroked with gray and filled with a lighter, slightly transparent gray.

CAGradientLayer

A CAGradientLayer covers its background with a gradient, whose type (CAGradientLayerType) can be `.axial` (linear), `.radial`, or `.conic` (starting in iOS 12). It's an easy way to draw a gradient in your interface. The gradient is defined much as in the Core Graphics gradient example in Chapter 2, an array of locations and an array of corresponding colors, along with a start and end point. To clip the gradient's shape, you can add a mask to the CAGradientLayer (masks are discussed later in this chapter). A CAGradientLayer's `contents` are not displayed. Figure 3-7 shows our compass drawn with a linear CAGradientLayer behind it.

Transforms

The way a layer is drawn on the screen can be modified though a transform. This is not surprising, because a view can have a transform (see Chapter 1), and a view is

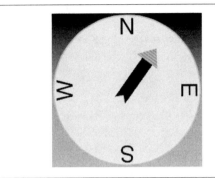

Figure 3-7. A gradient drawn behind the compass

drawn on the screen by its layer. You can treat a layer's transform as two-dimensional or as three-dimensional; with some additional preparation, you can even make a three-dimensional transform *look* three-dimensional (in a cartoony way).

Affine Transforms

In the simplest case, when a transform is two-dimensional, you can access a layer's transform through the `affineTransform` method (and the corresponding setter, `setAffineTransform(_:)`). The value is a CGAffineTransform, familiar from Chapters 1 and 2.

A layer's `affineTransform` is analogous to a view's `transform`. For details, see "Transform" on page 21. The chief difference is that a view's `transform` is applied around its `center`, whereas a layer's transform is applied around the `anchorPoint`, which might not be at its center. (So the `anchorPoint` has a second purpose that I didn't tell you about when discussing it earlier.)

You now know everything needed to understand the code that generated Figure 3-7. In this code, `self` is the CompassLayer; it does no drawing of its own, but merely assembles and configures its sublayers. The four cardinal point letters are each drawn by a CATextLayer; they are drawn at the same coordinates, but they have different rotation transforms, and are anchored so that their rotation is centered at the center of the circle. For the arrow, CompassLayer adopts CALayerDelegate, makes itself the arrow layer's delegate, and calls `setNeedsDisplay` on the arrow layer; this causes `draw(_:in:)` to be called in CompassLayer (that code is just the same code we developed for drawing the arrow in Chapter 2, and is not repeated here). The arrow layer is positioned by an `anchorPoint` pinning its tail to the center of the circle, and rotated around that pin by a transform:

```
// the gradient
let g = CAGradientLayer()
g.contentsScale = UIScreen.main.scale
g.frame = self.bounds
g.colors = [
    UIColor.black.cgColor,
    UIColor.red.cgColor
]
g.locations = [0.0,1.0]
self.addSublayer(g)
// the circle
let circle = CAShapeLayer()
circle.contentsScale = UIScreen.main.scale
circle.lineWidth = 2.0
circle.fillColor = UIColor(red:0.9, green:0.95, blue:0.93, alpha:0.9).cgColor
circle.strokeColor = UIColor.gray.cgColor
let p = CGMutablePath()
p.addEllipse(in: self.bounds.insetBy(dx: 3, dy: 3))
circle.path = p
self.addSublayer(circle)
circle.bounds = self.bounds
circle.position = self.bounds.center
// the four cardinal points
let pts = "NESW"
for (ix,c) in pts.enumerated() {
    let t = CATextLayer()
    t.contentsScale = UIScreen.main.scale
    t.string = String(c)
    t.bounds = CGRect(0,0,40,40)
    t.position = circle.bounds.center
    let vert = circle.bounds.midY / t.bounds.height
    t.anchorPoint = CGPoint(0.5, vert)
    t.alignmentMode = .center
    t.foregroundColor = UIColor.black.cgColor
    t.setAffineTransform(
        CGAffineTransform(rotationAngle:CGFloat(ix) * .pi/2.0))
    circle.addSublayer(t)
}
// the arrow
let arrow = CALayer()
arrow.contentsScale = UIScreen.main.scale
arrow.bounds = CGRect(0, 0, 40, 100)
arrow.position = self.bounds.center
arrow.anchorPoint = CGPoint(0.5, 0.8)
arrow.delegate = self // we will draw the arrow in the delegate method
arrow.setAffineTransform(CGAffineTransform(rotationAngle:.pi/5.0))
self.addSublayer(arrow)
arrow.setNeedsDisplay() // draw, please
```

3D Transforms

A layer's affineTransform is merely a façade for accessing its transform. A layer's transform is a three-dimensional transform, a CATransform3D; when the layer is a view's underlying layer, this property is exposed at the level of the view through the view's transform3D. For details, see "Transform3D" on page 25. The chief difference is that a view's transform3D takes place around the view's center, whereas a layer's three-dimensional transform takes place around a three-dimensional extension of the anchorPoint, whose z-component is supplied by the anchorPointZ property. Most of the time, you'll probably leave the anchorPointZ at its default of 0.0.

The following rotation flips a layer around its y-axis:

```
someLayer.transform = CATransform3DMakeRotation(.pi, 0, 1, 0)
```

What will we see after we do that? By default, the layer is considered double-sided, so when it is flipped to show its "back," what's drawn is an appropriately reversed version of the content of the layer — along with its sublayers, which by default are still drawn in front of the layer, but reversed and positioned in accordance with the layer's transformed coordinate system. (For a simple example, see xref: FIGbackwardsLabel[].) But if the layer's isDoubleSided property is false, then when it is flipped to show its "back," the layer disappears (along with its sublayers); its "back" is transparent and empty.

Depth

Layers do not magically give you realistic three-dimensional rendering — for that you would use Metal, which is beyond the scope of this discussion. Layers are two-dimensional objects, and they are designed for speed and simplicity. But read on, because I'm about to talk about adding an illusion of depth.

There are two ways to place layers at different nominal depths with respect to their siblings:

- Through the z-component of their position, which is the zPosition property. (So the zPosition has a second purpose that I didn't tell you about earlier.)
- By applying a transform that translates the layer's position in the z-direction.

These two values, the z-component of a layer's position and the z-component of its translation transform, are related; in some sense, the zPosition is a shorthand for a translation transform in the z-direction. (If you provide both a zPosition and a z-direction translation, you can rapidly confuse yourself.)

In the real world, changing an object's zPosition would make it appear larger or smaller, as it is positioned closer or further away; but this, by default, is not the case in the world of layer drawing. There is no attempt to portray perspective; the layer

Figure 3-8. A disappointing page-turn rotation

planes are drawn at their actual size and flattened onto one another, with no illusion of distance. (This is called *orthographic projection*, and is the way blueprints are often drawn to display an object from one side.) If we want to portray a visual sense of depth using layers, we're going to need some additional techniques, as I shall now explain.

Sublayer transform

Here's a widely used trick for adding a sense of perspective to the way layers are drawn: make them sublayers of a layer whose `sublayerTransform` property maps all points onto a "distant" plane. (This is probably just about the only thing the `sublayerTransform` property is ever used for.) Combined with orthographic projection, the effect is to apply one-point perspective to the drawing, so that things get perceptibly smaller in the negative z-direction.

Let's try applying a sort of "page-turn" rotation to our compass: we'll anchor it at its right side and then rotate it around the y-axis. Here, the sublayer we're rotating (accessed through a property, `rotationLayer`) is the gradient layer, and the circle and arrow are its sublayers so that they rotate with it:

```
self.rotationLayer.anchorPoint = CGPoint(1,0.5)
self.rotationLayer.position = CGPoint(self.bounds.maxX, self.bounds.midY)
self.rotationLayer.transform = CATransform3DMakeRotation(.pi/4.0, 0, 1, 0)
```

The results are disappointing (Figure 3-8); the compass looks more squashed than rotated. But now we'll also apply the distance-mapping transform. The superlayer here is `self`:

```
var transform = CATransform3DIdentity
transform.m34 = -1.0/1000.0
self.sublayerTransform = transform
```

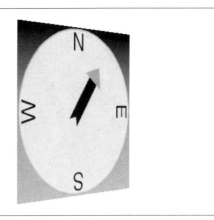

Figure 3-9. A dramatic page-turn rotation

The results (shown in Figure 3-9) are better, and you can experiment with values to replace 1000.0; for an even more exaggerated effect, try 500.0. Also, the zPosition of the rotationLayer will now affect how large it is.

Transform layers

Another way to draw layers with depth is to use CATransformLayer. This CALayer subclass doesn't do any drawing of its own; it is intended solely as a host for other layers. It has the remarkable feature that you can apply a transform to it and it will maintain the depth relationships among its own sublayers. In this example, how things look depends on whether or not lay1 is a CATransformLayer:

```
let lay2 = CALayer()
lay2.frame = f // some CGRect
lay2.backgroundColor = UIColor.blue.cgColor
lay1.addSublayer(lay2)
let lay3 = CALayer()
lay3.frame = f.offsetBy(dx: 20, dy: 30)
lay3.backgroundColor = UIColor.green.cgColor
lay3.zPosition = 10
lay1.addSublayer(lay3)
lay1.transform = CATransform3DMakeRotation(.pi, 0, 1, 0)
```

In that code, the superlayer lay1 has two sublayers, lay2 and lay3. The sublayers are added in that order, so lay3 is drawn in front of lay2. Then lay1 is flipped like a page being turned by setting its transform:

- If lay1 is a normal CALayer, the sublayer drawing order doesn't change; lay3 is *still* drawn in front of lay2, even after the transform is applied.

- If lay1 is a CATransformLayer, lay3 is drawn *behind* lay2 after the transform; they are both sublayers of lay1, so their depth relationship is maintained.

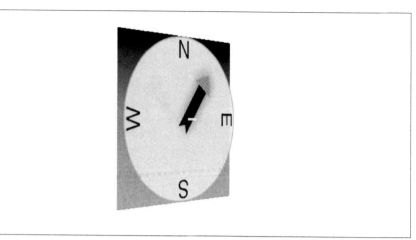

Figure 3-10. Page-turn rotation applied to a CATransformLayer

Figure 3-10 shows our page-turn rotation yet again, still with the sublayerTransform applied to self, but this time the only sublayer of self is a CATransformLayer:

```
var transform = CATransform3DIdentity
transform.m34 = -1.0/1000.0
self.sublayerTransform = transform
let master = CATransformLayer()
master.frame = self.bounds
self.addSublayer(master)
self.rotationLayer = master
```

The CATransformLayer, to which the page-turn transform is applied, holds the gradient layer, the circle layer, and the arrow layer. Those three layers are at different depths (using different zPosition settings), and I've tried to emphasize the arrow's separation from the circle by adding a shadow (discussed in the next section):

```
circle.zPosition = 10
arrow.shadowOpacity = 1.0
arrow.shadowRadius = 10
arrow.zPosition = 20
```

You can see from its apparent offset that the circle layer floats in front of the gradient layer, but I wish you could see this page-turn as an animation, which makes the circle jump right out from the gradient as the rotation proceeds.

Even more remarkable, I've added a little white peg sticking through the arrow and running into the circle! It is a CAShapeLayer, rotated to be perpendicular to the CATransformLayer (I'll explain the rotation code later in this chapter):

```
let peg = CAShapeLayer()
peg.contentsScale = UIScreen.main.scale
peg.bounds = CGRect(0,0,3.5,50)
let p2 = CGMutablePath()
```

```
p2.addRect(peg.bounds)
peg.path = p2
peg.fillColor = UIColor(red:1.0, green:0.95, blue:1.0, alpha:0.95).cgColor
peg.anchorPoint = CGPoint(0.5,0.5)
peg.position = master.bounds.center
master.addSublayer(peg)
peg.setValue(Float.pi/2, forKeyPath:"transform.rotation.x")
peg.setValue(Float.pi/2, forKeyPath:"transform.rotation.z")
peg.zPosition = 15
```

In that code, the peg runs straight out of the circle toward the viewer, so it is initially seen end-on, and because a layer has no thickness, it is invisible. But as the CATransformLayer pivots in our page-turn rotation, the peg maintains its orientation relative to the circle, and comes into view. In effect, the drawing portrays a 3D model constructed entirely out of layers!

There is, I think, a slight additional gain in realism if the same sublayerTransform is applied also to the CATransformLayer, but I have not done so here.

Further Layer Features

A CALayer has many additional properties that affect details of how it is drawn. Since these drawing details can be applied to a UIView's underlying layer, they are effectively view features as well.

Shadows

A CALayer can have a shadow, defined by its shadowColor, shadowOpacity, shadow-Radius, and shadowOffset properties. To make the layer draw a shadow, set the shadowOpacity to a nonzero value. The shadow is normally based on the shape of the layer's nontransparent region, but deriving this shape can be calculation-intensive (so much so that in early versions of iOS, layer shadows weren't implemented). You can vastly improve performance by defining the shape yourself as a CGPath and assigning it to the layer's shadowPath property.

If a layer's masksToBounds is true, no part of its shadow lying outside its bounds is drawn. (This includes the underlying layer of a view whose clipsToBounds is true.) Wondering why the shadow isn't appearing for a layer that masks to its bounds is a common beginner mistake.

This in turn poses a puzzle. Suppose we have a view for which clipsToBounds *must* be true, but we want that view to cast a shadow anyway. How can we do that? Figure 3-11 shows an example. The kitten image is shown in an image view whose contentMode is .scaleAspectFill. The original kitten image is rectangular, not square; the scaled image is therefore *larger* than the image view. But we don't want

Figure 3-11. A clipping view with a shadow?

the excess part of the image to be visible, so the image view's clipsToBounds is true. Yet we also want the image view to cast a shadow. How can that be done?

It *can't* be done. Figure 3-11 may *look* like that's what it's doing, but it isn't. It's a trick. There's another view that you don't see. It has the same frame as the image view, its background color is black, and it's behind the image view. Its clipsToBounds is false, and its layer has a shadow.

Borders and Rounded Corners

A CALayer can have a border (borderWidth, borderColor); the borderWidth is drawn inward from the bounds, potentially covering some of the content unless you compensate.

A CALayer's corners can be rounded, effectively bounding the layer with a rounded rectangle, by giving it a cornerRadius greater than zero. If the layer has a border, the border has rounded corners too. If the layer has a backgroundColor, that background is clipped to the shape of the rounded rectangle. If the layer's masksToBounds is true, the layer's content and its sublayers are clipped by the rounded corners (and then if you also want a shadow, you'll have to use the trick I described in the previous section).

Starting in iOS 11, you can round individual corners of a CALayer rather than having to round all four corners at once. To do so, set the layer's maskedCorners property to a CACornerMask, a bitmask whose values have these dreadful names:

- layerMinXMinYCorner
- layerMaxXMinYCorner

Figure 3-12. A layer with a mask

- `layerMinXMaxYCorner`
- `layerMaxXMaxYCorner`

Even if you set the `maskedCorners`, you won't see any corner rounding unless you also set the `cornerRadius` to a nonzero number.

Masks

A CALayer can have a `mask`. This is itself a layer, whose content must be provided somehow. The transparency of the mask's content in a particular spot becomes (all other things being equal) the transparency of the layer at that spot. The mask's colors (hues) are irrelevant; only transparency matters. To position the mask, pretend it's a sublayer.

Figure 3-12 shows our arrow layer, with the gray circle layer behind it, and a mask applied to the arrow layer. The mask is silly, but it illustrates very well how masks work: it's an ellipse, with an opaque fill and a thick, semitransparent stroke. Here's the code that generates and applies the mask:

```
let mask = CAShapeLayer()
mask.frame = arrow.bounds
let path = CGMutablePath()
path.addEllipse(in: mask.bounds.insetBy(dx: 10, dy: 10))
mask.strokeColor = UIColor(white:0.0, alpha:0.5).cgColor
mask.lineWidth = 20
mask.path = path
arrow.mask = mask
```

Using a mask, we can do more generally what the `cornerRadius` and `masksToBounds` properties do. Here's a utility method that generates a CALayer suitable for use as a rounded rectangle mask:

```
func mask(size sz:CGSize, roundingCorners rad:CGFloat) -> CALayer {
    let rect = CGRect(origin:.zero, size:sz)
    let r = UIGraphicsImageRenderer(bounds:rect)
    let im = r.image { ctx in
        let con = ctx.cgContext
        con.setFillColor(UIColor(white:0, alpha:0).cgColor)
        con.fill(rect)
        con.setFillColor(UIColor(white:0, alpha:1).cgColor)
        let p = UIBezierPath(roundedRect:rect, cornerRadius:rad)
```

```
            p.fill()
    }
    let mask = CALayer()
    mask.frame = rect
    mask.contents = im.cgImage
    return mask
}
```

The CALayer returned from that method can be placed as a mask anywhere in a layer by adjusting its frame origin and assigning it as the layer's mask. The result is that all of that layer's content drawing and its sublayers (including, if this layer is a view's underlying layer, the view's subviews) are clipped to the rounded rectangle shape; everything outside that shape is not drawn.

A mask drawing can have values between opaque and transparent, and can mask to any shape. The transparent region doesn't have to be on the outside of the mask; you can use a mask that's opaque on the outside and transparent on the inside to "punch a hole" in a layer (or a view).

A mask is like a sublayer, in that there is no built-in mechanism for automatically resizing the mask as the layer is resized. If *you* don't resize the mask when the layer is resized, the mask *won't* be resized. A common beginner mistake is to apply a mask to a view's underlying layer before the view has been fully laid out; when the view *is* laid out, its size changes, but the mask's size doesn't, and now the mask doesn't "fit."

Alternatively, you can apply a mask as a view directly to another view through the *view's* mask property, rather than having to drop down to the level of layers. This is not functionally distinct from applying the mask view's layer to the view's layer — under the hood, in fact, it *is* applying the mask view's layer to the view's layer. Using a mask view does nothing directly to help with the problem of resizing the mask when the view's size changes; a mask view isn't a subview, so it is not subject to autoresizing or autolayout. On the other hand, if you resize a mask view manually, you can do so using view properties; that's very convenient if you're already resizing the view itself manually (such as when using view property animation, as discussed in the next chapter).

Layer Efficiency

By now, you're probably envisioning all sorts of compositing fun, with layers masking sublayers and laid semitransparently over other layers. There's nothing wrong with that, but when an iOS device is asked to shift its drawing from place to place, the movement may stutter because the device lacks the necessary computing power to composite repeatedly and rapidly. This sort of issue is likely to emerge particularly when your code performs an animation (Chapter 4) or when the user is able to animate drawing through touch, as when scrolling a table view (Chapter 8).

You may be able to detect these problems by eye, and you can quantify them on a device by using the Core Animation template in Instruments, which shows the frame rate achieved during animation. New in Xcode 12, animation "hitches" (as Apple now calls them) can be measured with XCTMetrics during performance testing. Also, the Simulator's Debug menu lets you summon colored overlays that provide clues as to possible sources of inefficient drawing that can lead to such problems; when running on a device, similar overlays are available by choosing from the hierarchical menu under Debug → View Debugging → Rendering. New in Xcode 12, the view debugger ("View Debugger" on page 75) can display layers — choose Editor → Show Layers — and can offer suggestions for improving layer rendering efficiency.

Tricks like shadows and rounded corners and masks may be easy and fun, but in general, opaque drawing is most efficient. (Nonopaque drawing is what the Simulator marks when you check Debug → Color Blended Layers.) You may think that for some particular use case you *have* to do nonopaque drawing, but think again, because you might be wrong about that. If a layer will always be shown over a background consisting of a single color, you can give the layer its own background of that same color; when additional layer content is supplied, the visual effect will be the same as if that additional layer content were composited over a transparent background.

Another way to gain some efficiency is by "freezing" the entirety of the layer's drawing as a bitmap. In effect, you're drawing everything in the layer to a secondary cache and using the cache to draw to the screen. Copying from a cache is less efficient than drawing directly to the screen, but this inefficiency may be compensated for, if there's a deep or complex layer tree, by not having to composite that tree every time we render. To do this, set the layer's `shouldRasterize` to `true` and its `rasterizationScale` to some sensible value (probably `UIScreen.main.scale`). You can always turn rasterization off again by setting `shouldRasterize` to `false`, so it's easy to rasterize just before some massive or sluggish rearrangement of the screen and then unrasterize afterward.

In addition, there's a layer property `drawsAsynchronously`. The default is `false`. If set to `true`, the layer's graphics context accumulates drawing commands and obeys them later on a background thread; the drawing commands themselves run very quickly, because they are not being obeyed at the time you issue them. I haven't had occasion to use this, but presumably there could be situations where it keeps your app responsive when drawing would otherwise be time-consuming.

Layers and Key–Value Coding

All of a layer's properties are accessible through Cocoa key–value coding by way of keys with the same name as the property. These are two ways of doing the same thing:

```
layer.mask = mask
// or:
layer.setValue(mask, forKey: "mask")
```

In addition, CATransform3D and CGAffineTransform values can be expressed through key–value coding and key paths. Again, these are equivalent:

```
self.rotationLayer.transform = CATransform3DMakeRotation(.pi/4.0, 0, 1, 0)
// or:
self.rotationLayer.setValue(.pi/4.0, forKeyPath:"transform.rotation.y")
```

That notation is possible because CATransform3D is key–value coding compliant for a repertoire of keys and key paths. These are not properties; a CATransform3D doesn't have a `rotation` property. It doesn't have *any* properties, because it isn't even an object. You cannot say:

```
self.rotationLayer.transform.rotation.y = //... no, sorry
```

The transform key paths you'll use most often are:

- `"rotation.x"`, `"rotation.y"`, `"rotation.z"`
- `"rotation"` (same as `"rotation.z"`)
- `"scale.x"`, `"scale.y"`, `"scale.z"`
- `"translation.x"`, `"translation.y"`, `"translation.z"`
- `"translation"` (two-dimensional, a CGSize)

The Quartz Core framework also injects key–value coding compliance into CGPoint, CGSize, and CGRect, allowing you to use keys and key paths matching their struct component names. For a complete list of KVC compliant classes related to CALayer, along with the keys and key paths they implement, see "Core Animation Extensions to Key-Value Coding" in Apple's *Core Animation Programming Guide* in the documentation archive.

Moreover, you can treat a CALayer as a kind of dictionary, and get and set the value for *any* key. This means you can attach arbitrary information to an individual layer instance and retrieve it later. Earlier I mentioned that to apply manual layout to a layer's sublayers, you will need a way of identifying those sublayers. This feature could provide a way of doing that:

```
myLayer1.setValue("manny", forKey:"pepboy")
myLayer2.setValue("moe", forKey:"pepboy")
```

A layer doesn't have a `pepboy` property; the `"pepboy"` key is something I'm attaching to these layers arbitrarily. Now I can identify them later by getting the value of their respective `"pepboy"` keys.

Also, CALayer has a `defaultValue(forKey:)` class method; to implement it, you'll need to subclass and override. In the case of keys whose value you want to provide a default for, return that value; otherwise, return the value that comes from calling `super`. In this way, a key can have a non-`nil` value even if no value has ever been explicitly provided for that key.

The truth is that this feature, though delightful (and I often wish that all classes behaved like this), is not put there solely for your convenience and enjoyment. It's there to serve as the basis for animation, which is the subject of the next chapter.

Animation

Animation is an attribute changing over time. This will typically be a visible attribute of something in the interface. The changing attribute might be positional: something moves or changes size, not jumping abruptly, but sliding smoothly. Other kinds of attribute can animate as well. A view's background color might change from red to green, not switching colors abruptly, but blending from one to the other. A view might change from opaque to transparent, not vanishing abruptly, but fading away.

Without help, most of us would find animation beyond our reach. There are just too many complications — complications of calculation, of timing, of screen refresh, of threading, and many more. Fortunately, help is provided. You don't perform an animation yourself; you describe it, you order it, and it is performed for you. You get *animation on demand.*

Asking for an animation can be as simple as setting a property value; under some circumstances, a single line of code will result in animation:

```
myLayer.backgroundColor = UIColor.red.cgColor // animate to red
```

Animation is easy because Apple wants to facilitate your use of it. Animation isn't just cool and fun; it clarifies that something is changing or responding. It is crucial to the character of the iOS interface.

One of my first iOS apps was based on a macOS game in which the user clicks cards to select them. In the macOS version, a card was highlighted to show it was selected, and the computer would beep to indicate a click on an ineligible card. On iOS, these indications were insufficient: the highlighting felt weak, and you can't use a sound warning in an environment where the user might have the volume turned off or be listening to music. So in the iOS version, animation is the indicator for card selection (a selected card waggles eagerly) and for tapping on an ineligible card (the whole interface shudders, as if to shrug off the tap).

The purpose of this chapter is to explain the basics of animation itself; how you use it is another matter. Using animation effectively, especially in relation to touch (the subject of the next chapter), is a deep and complex subject involving psychology, biology, and other fields outside mere programming. Apple's own use of animation is deep and pervasive. It is used to make the interface feel live, fluid, responsive, intuitive, and natural. It helps to provide the user with a sense of what the user can do and is doing, of where the user is, of how things on the screen are related. Many WWDC videos go into depth about what Apple achieves with animation, and these can assist you in your own design.

Drawing, Animation, and Threading

Here's an interesting fact about how iOS draws to the screen: drawing doesn't actually take place at the time you give your drawing commands (Chapter 2). When you give a command that requires a view to be redrawn, the system remembers your command and marks the view as needing to be redrawn. Later, when all your code has run to completion and the system has, as it were, a free moment, then it redraws all views that need redrawing. Let's call this the *redraw moment*. (I'll explain what the redraw moment really is later in this chapter.)

Animation works the same way, and is part of the same process. When you ask for an animation to be performed, the animation doesn't start happening on the screen until the next redraw moment. (You can force an animation to start immediately, but this is unusual.)

Like a movie (especially an old-fashioned animated cartoon), an animation has "frames." An animated value does not change smoothly and continuously; it changes in small, individual increments that give the *illusion* of smooth, continuous change. This illusion works because the device itself undergoes periodic, rapid, more or less regular screen refreshes — a perpetual succession of redraw moments — and the incremental changes are made to fall between these refreshes. Apple calls the system component responsible for this the *animation server*.

Think of the "animation movie" as being interposed between the user and the "real" screen. While the animation lasts, this movie is superimposed onto the screen. When the animation is finished, the movie is removed, revealing the state of the "real" screen behind it. The user is unaware of all this, because (if you've done things correctly) at the time that it starts, the movie's first frame looks just like the state of the "real" screen at that moment, and at the time that it ends, the movie's last frame looks just like the state of the "real" screen at *that* moment.

When you animate a view's movement from position 1 to position 2, you can envision a typical sequence of events like this:

1. You reposition the view. The view is now set to position 2, but there has been no redraw moment, so it is still portrayed at position 1.

2. You order an animation of the view from position 1 to position 2.

3. The rest of your code runs to completion.

4. The redraw moment arrives. If there were no animation, the view would now suddenly be portrayed at position 2. But there *is* an animation, and so the "animation movie" appears. It starts with the view portrayed at position 1, so that is still what the user sees.

5. The animation proceeds, each "frame" portraying the view at intermediate positions between position 1 and position 2. (The documentation describes the animation as *in-flight*.)

6. The animation ends, portraying the view ending up at position 2.

7. The "animation movie" is removed, revealing the view indeed at position 2 — where you put it in the first step.

Realizing that the "animation movie" is different from what happens to the *real* view is key to configuring an animation correctly. A frequent complaint of beginners is that a position animation is performed as expected, but then, at the end, the view "jumps" to some other position. This happens because you set up the animation but failed to move the view to match its final position in the "animation movie"; when the "movie" is whipped away at the end of the animation, the real situation that's revealed doesn't match the last frame of the "movie," so the view appears to jump.

There isn't really an "animation movie" in front of the screen — but it's a good analogy, and the effect is much the same. To explain what's actually happening, I have to reveal something about layers that I omitted from Chapter 3. It is not a layer itself that is portrayed on the screen; it's a derived layer called the *presentation layer*. When you animate the change of a view's position or a layer's position from position 1 to position 2, its nominal position changes immediately; meanwhile, the presentation layer's position remains unchanged until the redraw moment, and then changes over time, and because that's what's actually drawn on the screen, that's what the user sees.

(A layer's presentation layer can be accessed through its `presentation` method — and the layer itself may be accessed through the presentation layer's `model` method. I'll give examples, in this chapter and the next, of situations where accessing the presentation layer is a useful thing to do.)

The animation server operates on an independent thread. You don't have to worry about that fact (thank heavens, because multithreading is generally rather tricky and complicated), but you can't ignore it either. Your code runs independently of and possibly simultaneously with the animation — that's what multithreading means — so communication between the animation and your code can require some planning.

Arranging for your code to be notified when an animation ends is a common need. Most of the animation APIs provide a way to set up such a notification. One use of an "animation ended" notification might be to chain animations together: one animation ends and then another begins, in sequence. Another use is to perform some sort of cleanup. A very frequent kind of cleanup has to do with handling of touches: what a touch means while an animation is in-flight might be quite different from what a touch means when no animation is taking place.

Since your code can run even after you've set up an animation, or might start running while an animation is in-flight, you need to be careful about setting up conflicting animations. Multiple animations can be set up (and performed) simultaneously, but an attempt to animate or change a property that's already in the middle of being animated may be incoherent. You'll want to take care not to let your animations step on each other's feet accidentally.

Outside forces can interrupt your animations. The user might send your app to the background, or an incoming phone call might arrive while an animation is in-flight. The system deals neatly with this situation by simply cancelling all in-flight animations when an app is backgrounded; you've already arranged *before* the animation for your views to assume the final states they will have *after* the animation, so no harm is done — when your app resumes, everything is in the final state that you arranged beforehand. But if you wanted your app to resume an animation where it left off when it was interrupted, that would require some canny coding on your part.

Image View and Image Animation

UIImageView (Chapter 2) provides a form of animation so simple as to be scarcely deserving of the name; still, sometimes it might be all you need. You supply a UIImageView with an array of UIImages, as the value of its `animationImages` or `highlightedAnimationImages` property. This array represents the "frames" of a simple cartoon; when you send the `startAnimating` message, the images are displayed in turn, at a frame rate determined by the `animationDuration` property, repeating as many times as specified by the `animationRepeatCount` property (the default is 0, meaning to repeat forever), or until the `stopAnimating` message is received. Before and after the animation, the image view continues displaying its `image` (or `highlightedImage`).

Suppose we want an image of Mars to appear out of nowhere and flash three times on the screen. This might seem to require some sort of Timer-based solution, but it's far simpler to use an animating UIImageView:

```
let mars = UIImage(named: "Mars")!
let empty = UIGraphicsImageRenderer(size:mars.size).image { _ in }
let arr = [mars, empty, mars, empty, mars]
let iv = UIImageView(image:empty)
```

```
iv.frame.origin = CGPoint(100,100)
self.view.addSubview(iv)
iv.animationImages = arr
iv.animationDuration = 2
iv.animationRepeatCount = 1
iv.startAnimating()
```

You can combine UIImageView animation with other kinds of animation. You could flash the image of Mars while at the same time sliding the UIImageView rightward, using view animation as described in the next section.

UIImage provides a form of animation parallel to that of UIImageView: an image can itself be an *animated image*. Just as with UIImageView, this means that you've prepared multiple images that form a sequence serving as the "frames" of a simple cartoon. You can create an animated image with one of these UIImage class methods:

animatedImage(with:duration:)

> As with UIImageView's animationImages, you supply an array of UIImages. You also supply the duration for the whole animation.

animatedImageNamed(_:duration:)

> You supply the name of a single image file, as with init(named:), with no file extension. The runtime appends "0" (or, if that fails, "1") to the name you supply and makes *that* image file the first image in the animation sequence. Then it increments the appended number, gathering images and adding them to the sequence (until there are no more, or we reach "1024").

animatedResizableImageNamed(_:capInsets:resizingMode:duration:)

> Combines an animated image with a resizable image (Chapter 2).

You do not tell an animated image to start animating, nor are you able to tell it how long you want the animation to repeat. Rather, an animated image is *always* animating, repeating its sequence once every duration seconds, so long as it appears in your interface; to control the animation, add the image to your interface or remove it from the interface, possibly exchanging it for a similar image that isn't animated.

An animated image can appear in the interface anywhere a UIImage can appear as a property of some interface object. In this example, I construct a sequence of red circles of different sizes, in code, and build an animated image which I then display in a UIButton:

```
var arr = [UIImage]()
let w : CGFloat = 18
for i in 0 ..< 6 {
    let r = UIGraphicsImageRenderer(size:CGSize(w,w))
    arr += [r.image { ctx in
        let con = ctx.cgContext
        con.setFillColor(UIColor.red.cgColor)
        let ii = CGFloat(i)
```

```
        con.addEllipse(in:CGRect(0+ii,0+ii,w-ii*2,w-ii*2))
        con.fillPath()
    }]
}
let im = UIImage.animatedImage(with:arr, duration:0.5)
b.setImage(im, for:.normal) // b is a button in the interface
```

 Images are memory hogs, and an array of images can cause your app to run completely out of memory. Confine your use of image view and image animation to a *few small images.*

View Animation

All animation is ultimately layer animation, which I'll discuss later in this chapter. However, for a limited range of properties, you can animate a UIView directly: these are its alpha, bounds, center, frame, transform, transform3D, and, if the view doesn't implement draw(_:), its backgroundColor (Chapter 1). You can also animate a UIView's change of contents. In addition, the UIVisualEffectView effect property is animatable between nil and a UIBlurEffect (Chapter 2); and, starting in iOS 11, a view's underlying layer's cornerRadius (Chapter 3) is animatable under view animation as well. This list of animatable features, despite its brevity, will often prove quite sufficient.

A Brief History of View Animation

The view animation API has evolved historically by way of three distinct major stages:

Begin and commit
    Way back at the dawn of iOS time, a view animation was constructed imperatively using a sequence of UIView class methods. To use this API, you call begin-Animations, configure the animation, set an animatable property, and *commit* the animation by calling commitAnimations:

```
    UIView.beginAnimations(nil, context: nil)
    UIView.setAnimationDuration(1)
    self.v.backgroundColor = .red
    UIView.commitAnimations()
```

Block-based animation
    When Objective-C blocks were introduced in iOS 4, the entire operation of configuring a view animation was reduced to a single UIView class method, to which you pass a block in which you set an animatable property. In Swift, an Objective-C block is a function — usually an anonymous function. We can call this the *animations function:*

```
UIView.animate(withDuration: 1) {
    self.v.backgroundColor = .red
}
```

Property animator

iOS 10 introduced a new object — a property animator (UIViewPropertyAnimator). It, too, receives an animations function in which you set an animatable property:

```
let anim = UIViewPropertyAnimator(duration: 1, curve: .linear) {
    self.v.backgroundColor = .red
}
anim.startAnimation()
```

Although begin-and-commit animation still exists, it is deprecated and you're unlikely to use it; block-based animation completely supersedes it. The property animator does *not* supersede block-based animation; rather, it supplements and expands it. There are certain kinds of animation (repeating animation, autoreversing animation, transition animation) where a property animator can't help you, and you'll go on using block-based animation. For the bulk of basic view animations, however, the property animator brings some valuable advantages — a full range of timing curves, multiple completion functions, and the ability to pause, resume, and reverse the animation, and to interact by touch with the animated view.

Property Animator Basics

The UIViewPropertyAnimator class adopts the UIViewImplicitlyAnimating protocol, which itself adopts the UIViewAnimating protocol:

UIViewAnimating protocol

A UIViewAnimating adopter can have its animation started, paused, and stopped:

- `startAnimation`

- `pauseAnimation`

- `stopAnimation(_:)`

- `finishAnimation(at:)`

Its `state` property reflects its current animation state (UIViewAnimatingState):

- `.inactive`

- `.active` (and if its `isRunning` property is `false`, the animation is paused, as I'll explain later)

- `.stopped`

UIViewAnimating also provides two settable properties:

`fractionComplete`
> Essentially, the current "frame" of the animation.

`isReversed`
> Determines whether the animation is running forward or backward.

UIViewImplicitlyAnimating protocol
> A UIViewImplicitlyAnimating adopter can be given animations functions:
>
> - `addAnimations(_:)`
> - `addAnimations(_:delayFactor:)`
>
> It can be given completion functions:
>
> - `addCompletion(_:)`
>
> UIViewImplicitlyAnimating also provides a `continueAnimation(withTiming-Parameters:durationFactor:)` method that allows a paused animation to be resumed with altered timing and duration; the `durationFactor` is the desired fraction of the animation's original duration, or zero to mean whatever remains of the original duration.

UIViewPropertyAnimator
> UIViewPropertyAnimator's own methods consist solely of initializers; I'll discuss those later, when I talk about timing curves. It has some read-only properties describing how it was configured and started (such as its animation's `duration`), along with five settable properties:

`isInterruptible`
> If `true` (the default), the animator can be paused or stopped.

`isUserInteractionEnabled`
> If `true` (the default), animated views can be tapped midflight.

`scrubsLinearly`
> If `true` (the default), then when the animator is paused, the animator's animation curve is temporarily replaced with a linear curve.

`isManualHitTestingEnabled`
> If `true`, hit-testing is up to you; the default is `false`, meaning that the animator performs hit-testing on your behalf, which is usually what you want. (See Chapter 5 for more about hit-testing animated views.)

`pausesOnCompletion`
> If `true`, then when the animation finishes, it does not revert to `.inactive`; the default is `false`.

As you can see, a property animator comes packed with power for controlling the animation after it starts. You can pause the animation in midflight, allow the user to manipulate the animation gesturally, resume the animation, reverse the animation, and much more. I'll illustrate those features in this and subsequent chapters.

In the simplest case, you'll just launch the animation and stand back, as I demonstrated earlier:

```
let anim = UIViewPropertyAnimator(duration: 1, curve: .linear) {
    self.v.backgroundColor = .red
}
anim.startAnimation()
```

In that code, the UIViewPropertyAnimator object anim is instantiated as a local variable, and we are not retaining it in a persistent property; yet the animation works because the animation server retains it. We *can* keep a persistent reference to the property animator if we're going to need it elsewhere, and I'll give examples later showing how that can be a useful thing to do.

When a property animator's animation is started, it transitions through state changes:

1. The animator starts life in the .inactive state with isRunning set to false.

2. When startAnimation is called, the animator enters the .active state with isRunning *still* set to false (paused).

3. The animator then immediately transitions to the .active state with isRunning set to true.

The "animation movie" starts running at the next redraw moment. Once the animation is set in motion, it continues to its finish and then passes through those same states in reverse:

1. The running animator was in the .active state with isRunning set to true.

2. When the animation finishes, the animator switches to .active with isRunning set to false (paused).

3. The animator then immediately transitions back to the .inactive state with isRunning set to false.

If you have set the animator's pausesOnCompletion to true, the final step is omitted; the animation pauses, *without* transitioning back to the .inactive state. Ultimately returning the animator to .inactive is then left up to you. To do that, you first send the animator the stopAnimation(_:) message, causing the animator to enter the special .stopped state. What happens next depends on the parameter you passed to stopAnimation(_:); it's a Bool:

stopAnimation(_:) *parameter is* `false`

You will ultimately call `finishAnimation(at:)`, after which the animator returns to `.inactive`.

stopAnimation(_:) *parameter is* `true`

You want to dispense with `finishAnimation(at:)` and let the runtime clean up for you. The runtime will bring the animator back to `.inactive` immediately, without running any completion handlers.

It is a runtime error to let an animator go out of existence while paused (`.active` but `isRunning` is `false`) or stopped (`.stopped`). Your app will crash unceremoniously if you allow that to happen. If you pause an animator, you *must* eventually bring it back to the `.inactive` state in good order before the animator goes out of existence.

When the animator finishes and reverts to the `.inactive` state, it jettisons its animations. This means that the animator, if you've retained it, is reusable after finishing only if you supply new animations.

View Animation Basics

The most important elements of view animation are the animations function and the completion function:

Animations function

Any change to an animatable view property made within an animations function will be animated.

Completion function

The completion function lets us specify what should happen after the animation ends.

More than one animatable view property can be animated at the same time. Here, we animate simultaneous changes both in a view's color and in its position:

```
let anim = UIViewPropertyAnimator(duration: 1, curve: .linear) {
    self.v.backgroundColor = .red
    self.v.center.y += 100
}
anim.startAnimation()
```

More than one view can be animated at the same time. Suppose we want to replace a view in the view hierarchy with another view, not suddenly, but making the first view dissolve into the second. We start by placing the second view into the view hierarchy, with the same frame as the first view, but with an `alpha` of 0, so that it is invisible. Then we animate the change of the first view's `alpha` to 0 and the second view's `alpha` to 1. Finally, in the completion function, we remove the first view after the animation ends (invisibly, because its `alpha` ends at 0):

```
let v2 = UIView()
v2.backgroundColor = .black
v2.alpha = 0
v2.frame = self.v.frame
self.v.superview!.addSubview(v2)
let anim = UIViewPropertyAnimator(duration: 1, curve: .linear) {
    self.v.alpha = 0
    v2.alpha = 1
}
anim.addCompletion { _ in
    self.v.removeFromSuperview()
}
anim.startAnimation()
```

 Another way to remove a view from the view hierarchy with animation is to call the UIView class method `perform(_:on:options:animations:completion:)` with .delete as its first argument (this is, in fact, the only possible first argument). This causes the view to blur, shrink, and fade, and sends it removeFrom-Superview() afterward.

Preventing animation

Code that isn't about animatable view properties can appear in an animations function with no problem. But we must be careful to keep any changes to animatable properties that we do *not* want animated out of the animations function. In the preceding example, in setting v2.alpha to 0, I just want to set it right now, instantly; I don't want that change to be animated. So I've put that line *outside* the animations function (and in particular, *before* it).

Sometimes, though, that's not so easy; perhaps, within the animations function, we must call a method that might perform unwanted animatable changes. The UIView class method performWithoutAnimation(_:) solves the problem; it goes inside an animations function, but whatever happens in *its* function is *not* animated. In this rather artificial example, the view jumps to its new position and then slowly turns red:

```
let anim = UIViewPropertyAnimator(duration: 1, curve: .linear) {
    self.v.backgroundColor = .red
    UIView.performWithoutAnimation {
        self.v.center.y += 100
    }
}
anim.startAnimation()
```

Conflicts and additive animations

The material inside an animations function (but not inside a performWithout-Animation function) *orders* the animation — that is, it gives instructions for what the animation will be when the redraw moment comes. If you change an animatable view property as part of the animation, you should *not* change that property again afterward; the results can be confusing, because there's a conflict with the animation you've already ordered. This code is essentially incoherent:

```
let anim = UIViewPropertyAnimator(duration: 2, curve: .linear) {
    self.v.center.y += 100
}
self.v.center.y += 300 // bad idea
anim.startAnimation()
```

What actually happens is that the view *jumps* 300 points down and then *animates* 100 points further down. That's probably not what you intended. After you've ordered an animatable view property to be animated inside an animations function, *don't change that view property's value again* until after the animation is over.

On the other hand, this code, while somewhat odd, nevertheless does a smooth single animation to a position 400 points further down:

```
let anim = UIViewPropertyAnimator(duration: 2, curve: .linear) {
    self.v.center.y += 100
    self.v.center.y += 300
}
anim.startAnimation()
```

That's because basic positional view animations are *additive* by default. This means that the second animation is run simultaneously with the first, and is blended with it.

To illustrate what it means for animations to be additive, let's take advantage of the fact that a property animator allows us to add a second animation that doesn't take effect until some amount of the first animation has elapsed:

```
let anim = UIViewPropertyAnimator(duration: 2, curve: .easeInOut) {
    self.v.center.y += 100
}
anim.addAnimations({
    self.v.center.x += 100
}, delayFactor: 0.5)
anim.startAnimation()
```

The delayFactor: of 0.5 means that the second animation will start halfway through the duration, which is 2 seconds. So the animated view heads straight downward for 1 second and then smoothly swoops off to the right while continuing down for another second, ending up 100 points down and 100 points to the right of where it started. The two animations might appear to conflict — they are both changing the center of our view, and they have different durations and therefore different speeds — but instead they blend together seamlessly.

An even stronger example is what happens when the two animations directly oppose one another:

```
let yorig = self.v.center.y
let anim = UIViewPropertyAnimator(duration: 2, curve: .easeInOut) {
    self.v.center.y += 100
}
anim.addAnimations({
    self.v.center.y = yorig
}, delayFactor: 0.5)
anim.startAnimation()
```

Amazingly, there's no conflict; instead, we get a smooth autoreversing animation. The animated view starts marching toward a point 100 points down from its original position, but at about the halfway point it smoothly — not abruptly or sharply — slows and reverses itself and returns to its original position.

View Animation Configuration

The details of how you configure a view animation differ depending on whether you're using a property animator or calling one of the UIView class methods. With a property animator, you configure the animator before telling it to start animating. With a UIView class method, on the other hand, everything has to be supplied in a single command, which both configures and orders the animation. The full form of the chief UIView class method is:

- `animate(withDuration:delay:options:animations:completion:)`

There are shortened versions of the same command; you can omit the `delay:` and `options:` parameters, and even the `completion:` parameter. But it's still the same command, and the configuration of the animation is effectively complete at this point.

Animations function

The animations function contains the commands that set animatable view properties:

- With a block-based UIView class method, you supply the animations function as the `animations:` parameter.

- With a property animator, the animations function is usually provided as the `animations:` argument when the property animator is instantiated. But you can add an animations function to a property animator after instantiating it; indeed, the `init(duration:timingParameters:)` initializer requires that you do this, as it lacks an `animations:` parameter. Multiple animations functions will be executed *simultaneously*:

```
let anim = UIViewPropertyAnimator(duration: 1,
    timingParameters: UICubicTimingParameters(animationCurve:.linear))
anim.addAnimations {
    self.v.backgroundColor = .red
}
```

```
anim.addAnimations {
    self.v.center.y += 100
}
anim.startAnimation() // view moves and turns red simultaneously
```

Completion function

A completion function contains commands that are to be executed when the animation finishes:

- With a UIView class method, you supply the completion function as the `completion:` parameter. It takes one parameter, a Bool reporting whether the animation finished.

- A property animator can have multiple completion functions, provided by calling `addCompletion(_:)`. As with the animations functions, a property animator can be assigned more than one completion function; but multiple completion functions will be executed *sequentially*, in the order in which they were added:

```
var anim = UIViewPropertyAnimator(duration: 1, curve: .linear) {
    self.v.backgroundColor = .red
    self.v.center.y += 100
}
anim.addCompletion { _ in
    print("hey")
}
anim.addCompletion { _ in
    print("ho")
}
anim.startAnimation() // animates, finishes, prints "hey" and "ho"
```

A property animator's completion function takes one parameter, a UIViewAnimatingPosition reporting where the animation ended up: `.end`, `.start`, or `.current`. (I'll talk later about what those values mean.)

A property animator that is told to stop its animation with `stopAnimation(_:)` does *not* execute its completion functions at that time:

- If you called `stopAnimation(false)`, the animator's completion functions are executed when you call `finishAnimation(at:)`.

- If you called `stopAnimation(true)`, the animator's completion functions are not executed at all.

Animation duration

The duration of an animation represents how long it takes (in seconds) to run from start to finish:

- With a block-based UIView class method, the animation duration is the `duration:` parameter.

- With a property animator, the animation duration is the `duration:` parameter when the property animator is initialized.

You can also think of the duration as the animation's speed. Obviously, if two views are told to move different distances in the same time, the one that must move further must move faster.

A duration of `0` doesn't really mean `0`. It means "use the default duration." This fact will be of interest later when we talk about nesting animations. Outside of a nested animation, the default is two-tenths of a second.

Animation delay

It is permitted to order the animation along with a delay before the animation goes into action. The default is no delay. A delay is *not* the same as applying the animation using delayed performance; the animation is applied immediately, but when it starts running it spins its wheels, with no visible change, until the delay time has elapsed:

- With a block-based UIView class method, the delay is the `delay:` parameter.

- To apply a delay to an animation with a property animator, call `start-Animation(afterDelay:)` instead of `startAnimation`.

Animation timing

Specifying a change in a value and a time over which it should be changed is insufficient to describe what should happen. Should we change at a constant rate the whole time? Should we change slowly at first and more quickly later? Questions like these are answered by *timing curves*. An animation's timing curve maps interpolated values to time:

- With a UIView class method, you get a choice of just four timing curves (supplied as part of the `options:` argument, as I'll explain in a moment).

- A property animator gives you very broad powers to configure the timing curve the way you want. This is such an important topic that I'll deal with it in a separate section later.

Animation options

In a UIView class method, the `options:` argument is a bitmask combining additional options. Here are some of the chief `options:` values (UIView.AnimationOptions) that you might wish to use:

Timing curve

When supplied in this way, only four built-in timing curves are available. The term "ease" means that there is a gradual acceleration or deceleration between the animation's central speed and the zero speed at its start or end. Specify one at most:

- `.curveEaseInOut` (the default)
- `.curveEaseIn`
- `.curveEaseOut`
- `.curveLinear` (constant speed throughout)

`.repeat`

If included, the animation will repeat indefinitely.

`.autoreverse`

If included, the animation will run from start to finish (in the given duration time), and will then run from finish to start (also in the given duration time). The documentation's claim that you can autoreverse only if you also repeat is incorrect; you can use either or both (or neither).

When using `.autoreverse`, you will want to clean up at the end so that the view is back in its original position when the animation is over. To see what I mean, consider this code:

```
let opts : UIView.AnimationOptions = .autoreverse
let xorig = self.v.center.x
UIView.animate(withDuration: 1, delay: 0, options: opts) {
    self.v.center.x += 100
}
```

The view animates 100 points to the right and then animates 100 points back to its original position — and then *jumps* 100 points *back to the right*. The reason is that the last actual value we assigned to the view's center x is 100 points to the right, so when the animation is over and the "animation movie" is whipped away, the view is revealed still sitting 100 points to the right. The solution is to move the view back to its original position in the completion function:

```
let opts : UIView.AnimationOptions = .autoreverse
let xorig = self.v.center.x
UIView.animate(withDuration: 1, delay: 0, options: opts) {
    self.v.center.x += 100
} completion: { _ in
    self.v.center.x = xorig // *
}
```

There seems to be a major hole in the design of the block-based animation API; if you say `.repeat`, you must repeat indefinitely. What if your goal is to repeat a finite number of times? In the past, the solution was to resort to a command from the earliest generation of animation methods:

```
let opts : UIView.AnimationOptions = .autoreverse
let xorig = self.v.center.x
UIView.animate(withDuration: 1, delay: 0, options: opts) {
    UIView.setAnimationRepeatCount(3) // *
    self.v.center.x += 100
} completion: { _ in
    self.v.center.x = xorig
}
```

Starting in iOS 13, the solution is to omit .autoreverse and .repeat from the animation options, and instead call another UIView class method, modify-Animations(withRepeatCount:autoreverses:), inside the animations function, containing the actual animations:

```
let xorig = self.v.center.x
UIView.animate(withDuration: 1) {
    UIView.modifyAnimations(withRepeatCount: 3, autoreverses: true) {
        self.v.center.x += 100
    }
} completion: { _ in
    self.v.center.x = xorig
}
```

There are also some options saying what should happen if we order an animation when another animation is already ordered or in-flight (so that we are effectively *nesting* animations):

.overrideInheritedDuration
: Prevents inheriting the duration from a surrounding or in-flight animation (the default is to inherit it).

.overrideInheritedCurve
: Prevents inheriting the timing curve from a surrounding or in-flight animation (the default is to inherit it).

.beginFromCurrentState
: Suppose this animation animates a property already being animated by an animation that is previously ordered or in-flight. Starting this animation might cancel the previous animation, completing the requested change instantly. But with .beginFromCurrentState, this animation will use the presentation layer to decide where to start, and, if possible, will "blend" its animation with the previous animation. There is usually little need for .beginFromCurrentState, because simple view animations are additive by default; however, I'll demonstrate one possible use later in this chapter.

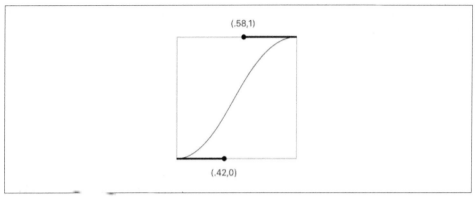

Figure 4-1. An ease-in-out Bézier curve

Timing Curves

A timing curve describes how an animation's speed should vary during the course of the animation. It does this by mapping the fraction of the animation's time that has elapsed (the x-axis) against the fraction of the animation's change that has occurred (the y-axis); its endpoints are therefore at `(0.0,0.0)` and `(1.0,1.0)`, because at the beginning of the animation there has been no elapsed time and no change, and at the end of the animation all the time has elapsed and all the change has occurred. There are two kinds of timing curve: cubic Bézier curves and springing curves.

Cubic timing curves

A cubic Bézier curve is defined by its endpoints, where each endpoint needs only one Bézier control point to define the tangent to the curve. Because the curve's endpoints are known, defining the two control points is sufficient to describe the entire curve. That is, in fact, how a cubic timing curve is expressed.

The built-in ease-in-out timing function is defined by the two control points `(0.42,0.0)` and `(0.58,1.0)` — that is, it's a Bézier curve with one endpoint at `(0.0,0.0)`, whose control point is `(0.42,0.0)`, and the other endpoint at `(1.0,1.0)`, whose control point is `(0.58,1.0)` (Figure 4-1).

With a UIView class method, you have a choice of four built-in timing curves; you specify one of them through the `options:` argument, as I've already explained.

With a property animator, you specify a timing curve as part of initialization. That's why I postponed telling you how to initialize a property animator until now. Here are three property animator initializers and how the timing curve is expressed:

`init(duration:curve:animations:)`
> The `curve:` is a built-in timing curve, specified as a UIView.AnimationCurve enum. These are the same built-in timing curves as for a UIView class method:

- `.easeInOut`
- `.easeIn`
- `.easeOut`
- `.linear`

`init(duration:controlPoint1:controlPoint2:animations:)`
> The timing curve is supplied as the two control points that define it.

`init(duration:timingParameters:)`
> This is most general form of initializer; the other two are convenience initializers that call it. There's no `animations:` parameter, so you'll have to call `add-Animations` later to supply the animations function. The `timingParameters:` is an object adopting the UITimingCurveProvider protocol, which can be a UICubicTimingParameters instance or a UISpringTimingParameters instance (I'll talk about springing timing curves in a moment). The UICubicTimingPara-meters initializers are:

`init(animationCurve:)`
> The value is one of the four built-in timing curves that I already mentioned, specified as a UIView.AnimationCurve enum.

`init()`
> Provides a fifth built-in timing curve, used as the default for many built-in behaviors.

`init(controlPoint1:controlPoint2:)`
> Defines the timing curve by its control points.

Defining a custom cubic timing curve is not difficult. Here's a cubic timing curve that eases in very slowly and finishes up all in a rush, whipping quickly into place after about two-thirds of the time has elapsed. I call this the "clunk" timing function:

```
anim = UIViewPropertyAnimator(
    duration: 1, timingParameters:
        UICubicTimingParameters(
            controlPoint1:CGPoint(0.9,0.1),
            controlPoint2:CGPoint(0.7,0.9)))
```

Springing timing curves

A springing timing curve is the solution to a physics problem whose initial conditions describe a mass attached to a stretched spring. The animation mimics releasing the spring and letting it rush toward and settle down at the destination value.

Springing timing curves are much more useful and widespread than you might suppose. A springing animation doesn't have to animate a view from place to place, and doesn't have to look particularly springy to be effective. A small initial spring velocity and a high damping gives a normal animation that wouldn't particularly remind anyone of a spring, but that does have a pleasingly rapid beginning and slow ending; many of Apple's own system animations are actually spring animations of that type (consider the way folders open in the home screen).

To use a springing timing curve with UIView block-based animation, you call a different class method:

- `animate(withDuration:delay:usingSpringWithDamping:initialSpring-Velocity:options:animations:completion:)`

You're supplying two parameters that vary the nature of the initial conditions, and hence the behavior of the animation over time.

Damping ratio
> The `damping:` parameter is a number between `0.0` and `1.0` that describes the amount of final oscillation. A value of `1.0` is *critically damped* and settles directly into place; lower values are *underdamped*. A value of `0.8` just barely overshoots and snaps back to the final value. A value of `0.1` waggles around the final value for a while before settling down.

Initial velocity
> The default is zero, and you'll usually leave it there. A nonzero initial velocity is useful particularly when converting from a gesture to an animation — that is, where the user is moving a view and releases it, and you want a springing animation to take over from there, starting out at the same velocity that the user was applying at the moment of release. Higher values cause greater overshoot, depending on the damping ratio. With a damping ratio of `0.3`, an initial velocity value of `1` overshoots a little and bounces about twice before settling into place, a value of `10` overshoots a bit further, and a value of `100` overshoots by more than twice the distance.

With a property animator, once again, you'll supply the timing curve as part of initialization:

`init(duration:dampingRatio:animations:)`
> The `dampingRatio:` argument is the same as the `damping:` in the UIView class method I just described. The initial velocity is zero.

`init(duration:timingParameters:)`
> This is the same initializer I discussed in connection with cubic timing curves. Recall that the `timingParameters:` is a UITimingCurveProvider; this can be a UISpringTimingParameters object, whose initializers are:

`init(dampingRatio:)`

You supply a damping ratio, and the initial velocity is zero.

`init(dampingRatio:initialVelocity:)`

The `initialVelocity:` is similar to the `initialSpringVelocity:` in the UIView class method I described a moment ago, except that it is a CGVector. Normally, only the x-component matters, in which case they are effectively the same thing; the y-component is considered only if what's being animated follows a two-dimensional path, as when you're changing both components of a view's `center`.

`init(mass:stiffness:damping:initialVelocity:)`

A slightly different way of looking at the initial conditions. The overall `duration:` value is ignored; the actual duration will be calculated from the other parameters (and this calculated duration can be discovered by reading the resulting property animator's `duration`). The first three parameters are in proportion to one another. A high `mass:` can cause a vast overshoot. A low `stiffness:` or a low `damping:` can result in a long settle-down time. The mass is usually quite small, while the stiffness and damping are usually quite large.

`init()`

The default spring animation; it is quite heavily damped, and settles into place in about half a second. The overall `duration:` value is ignored. In terms of the previous initializer, the `mass:` is 3, the `stiffness:` is 1000, the `damping:` is 500, and the `initialVelocity:` is (0,0).

Cancelling a View Animation

Once a view animation is in-flight, how can you cancel it? And what should "cancel" mean in the first place? This is one of the key areas where a property animator shows off its special powers. To illustrate why, I'll start by showing what you have to do to cancel a block-based animation.

Cancelling a block-based animation

Imagine a simple unidirectional positional animation, with a long duration so that we can interrupt it in midflight. To facilitate the explanation, I'll conserve both the view's original position and its final position in properties:

```
self.pOrig = self.v.center
self.pFinal = self.v.center
self.pFinal.x += 100
UIView.animate(withDuration: 4) {
    self.v.center = self.pFinal
}
```

We have a button that we can tap during that animation, and this button is supposed to cancel the animation. How can we do that?

One possibility is to reach down to the CALayer level and call `removeAllAnimations`:

```
self.v.layer.removeAllAnimations()
```

That has the advantage of simplicity, but the effect is jarring: the "animation movie" is whipped away instantly, "jumping" the view to its final position, effectively doing what the system does automatically when the app goes into the background.

So let's try to devise a more subtle form of cancellation: the view should *hurry* to its final position. This is a case where the additive nature of animations actually gets in our way. We cannot merely impose another animation that moves the view to its final position with a short duration, because this doesn't cancel the existing animation. Therefore, we must remove the first animation manually. We already know how to do that: call `removeAllAnimations`. But we also know that if we do that, the view will jump to its final position; we want it to remain, for the moment, at its current position — meaning *the animation's* current position. But where on earth is that?

To find out, we have to ask the view's *presentation layer* where it currently is. We reposition the view at the location of its presentation layer, and *then* remove the animation, and *then* perform the final "hurry home" animation:

```
self.v.layer.position = self.v.layer.presentation()!.position
self.v.layer.removeAllAnimations()
UIView.animate(withDuration: 0.1) {
    self.v.center = self.pFinal
}
```

Another alternative is that cancellation means hurrying the view back to its *original* position. In that case, animate the view's `center` to its original position instead of its destination position:

```
self.v.layer.position = self.v.layer.presentation()!.position
self.v.layer.removeAllAnimations()
UIView.animate(withDuration: 0.1) {
    self.v.center = self.pOrig
}
```

Yet another possibility is that cancellation means just *stopping* wherever we happen to be. In that case, omit the final animation:

```
self.v.layer.position = self.v.layer.presentation()!.position
self.v.layer.removeAllAnimations()
```

Cancelling a property animator's animation

Now I'll show how do those things with a property animator. We don't have to reach down to the level of the layer. We don't call `removeAllAnimations`. We don't query the presentation layer. We don't have to memorize the start position or the end position. The property animator does all of that for us!

For the sake of ease and generality, let's hold the animator in an instance property where all of our code can see it. Here's how it is configured:

```
self.anim = UIViewPropertyAnimator(
    duration: 4, timingParameters: UICubicTimingParameters())
self.anim.addAnimations {
    self.v.center.x += 100
}
self.anim.startAnimation()
```

Here's how to cancel the animation by hurrying home to its end:

```
self.anim.pauseAnimation()
self.anim.continueAnimation(withTimingParameters: nil, durationFactor: 0.1)
```

We first *pause* the animation, because otherwise we can't make changes to it. But the animation does not visibly pause, because we resume at once with a modification of the original animation, which is smoothly blended into the existing animation. The short durationFactor: is the "hurry" part; we want a much shorter duration than our animation's original duration. We don't have to tell the animator where to animate to; in the absence of any other commands, it animates to its original destination. The nil value for the timingParameters: tells the animation to use the existing timing curve.

What about cancelling the animation by hurrying home to its beginning? It's exactly the same, except that we reverse the animation:

```
self.anim.pauseAnimation()
self.anim.isReversed = true
self.anim.continueAnimation(withTimingParameters: nil, durationFactor: 0.1)
```

Again, we don't have to tell the animator where to animate to; it knows where we started, and reversing means to go there.

Using the same technique, we could interrupt the animation and hurry to anywhere we like — by adding another animations function before continuing. Here, cancellation causes us to rush right off the screen:

```
self.anim.pauseAnimation()
self.anim.addAnimations {
    self.v.center = CGPoint(-200,-200)
}
self.anim.continueAnimation(withTimingParameters: nil, durationFactor: 0.1)
```

What about cancelling the animation by stopping wherever we are? Just stop the animation:

```
self.anim.stopAnimation(false)
self.anim.finishAnimation(at: .current)
```

Recall that the `false` argument means: "Please allow me to call `finish-Animation(at:)`." We want to call `finishAnimation(at:)` in order to specify where the view should end up when the "animation movie" is removed. By passing in `.current`, we state that we want the animated view to end up right where it is now. If we were to pass in `.start` or `.end`, the view would *jump* to that position (if it weren't there already).

We can now understand the incoming parameter in the completion function! It is the position where we ended up:

- If the animation finished by proceeding to its end, the completion function parameter is `.end`.

- If we reversed the animation and it finished by proceeding back to its start, as in our second cancellation example, the parameter is `.start`.

- If we called `finishAnimation(at:)`, the parameter is the `at:` argument we specified in the call.

Cancelling a repeating animation

Suppose that the animation we want to cancel is an infinitely repeating autoreversing animation. It will presumably be created with the UIView class method:

```
self.pOrig = self.v.center
let opts : UIView.AnimationOptions = [.autoreverse, .repeat]
UIView.animate(withDuration: 1, delay: 0, options: opts) {
    self.v.center.x += 100
}
```

Let's say our idea of cancellation is to have the animated view hurry back to its original position; that is why we have saved the original position as an instance property. This is a situation where the `.beginFromCurrentState` option is useful! That's because a repeating animation is *not* additive with a further animation. It is therefore sufficient simply to impose the "hurry" animation on top of the existing repeating animation, because it contradicts the repeating animation and therefore also cancels it. The `.beginFromCurrentState` option prevents the view from jumping momentarily to the "final" position, 100 points to the right, to which we set it when we initiated the repeating animation:

```
let opts : UIView.AnimationOptions = .beginFromCurrentState
UIView.animate(withDuration: 0.1, delay: 0, options: opts) {
    self.v.center = self.pOrig
}
```

Frozen View Animation

Another important feature of a property animator is that its animation can be *frozen*. We already know that the animation can be paused — or never even started. A frozen animation is simply left in this state. It can be started or resumed at any time subsequently; or we can keep the animation frozen, but move it to a different "frame" of the animation by setting its `fractionComplete`, controlling the frozen animation manually.

In this simple example, we have in the interface a slider (a UISlider) and a small red square view. As the user slides the slider from left to right, the red view follows along — and gradually turns green, depending how far the user slides the slider. If the user slides the slider all the way to the right, the view is at the right and is fully green. If the user slides the slider all the way back to the left, the view is at the left and is fully red. To the user, this doesn't look like it involves any animation; it looks like the view just obeys the slider. But in fact a frozen animation is the way accomplish it.

The property animator is configured with an animation moving the view all the way to right and turning it all the way green. But the animation is never started:

```
self.anim = UIViewPropertyAnimator(duration: 1, curve: .easeInOut) {
    self.v.center.x = self.rightmostPoint.x
    self.v.backgroundColor = .green()
}
```

The slider, whenever the user moves it, simply changes the animator's `fraction-Complete` to match its own percentage:

```
self.anim.fractionComplete = CGFloat(slider.value)
```

Apple refers to this technique of manually moving a frozen animation back and forth from frame to frame as *scrubbing*. A common use case is that the user will touch and move the animated view itself. This will come in handy in connection with interactive view controller transitions in Chapter 6.

In that example, I deliberately set the timing curve to `.easeInOut` in order to illustrate the real purpose of the `scrubsLinearly` property. You would think that a nonlinear timing curve would affect the relationship between the position of the slider and the position of the view: with an `.easeInOut` timing curve, the view would arrive at the far right before the slider does. But that doesn't happen, because a nonrunning animation switches its timing curve to `.linear` *automatically* for as long as it is nonrunning. The purpose of the `scrubsLinearly` property, whose default property is `true`, is to allow you to turn *off* that behavior by setting it to `false` on the rare occasions when this might be desirable.

Custom Animatable View Properties

By default, as I explained earlier, only a few basic view properties are animatable through view animation. Changing some other view property in an animations function won't animate anything. But you can define a custom view property that *can* be animated in an animations function, provided the custom view property itself changes an animatable view property.

Imagine a UIView subclass, MyView, which has a Bool swing property. All this does is reposition the view: when swing is set to true, the view's center x-coordinate is increased by 100; when swing is set to false, it is decreased by 100. A view's center is animatable, so the swing property *itself* can be animatable.

The trick (suggested by an Apple WWDC 2014 video) is to implement MyView's swing setter with a zero-duration animation:

```
class MyView : UIView {
    var swing : Bool = false {
        didSet {
            var p = self.center
            p.x = self.swing ? p.x + 100 : p.x - 100
            UIView.animate(withDuration: 0) {
                self.center = p
            }
        }
    }
}
```

If we now change a MyView's swing directly, the view jumps to its new position; there is no animation. But if an animations function changes the swing property, the swing setter's animation inherits the duration of the surrounding animations function — because such inheritance is, as I mentioned earlier, the default. So the change in position is animated, with the specified duration:

```
let anim = UIViewPropertyAnimator(duration: 1, curve: .easeInOut) {
    self.v.swing.toggle()
}
anim.startAnimation()
```

Keyframe View Animation

A view animation can be described as a set of keyframes. This means that, instead of a simple beginning and end point, you specify multiple *stages* in the animation and those stages are joined together for you. This can be useful as a way of chaining animations together, or as a way of defining a complex animation that can't be described as a single change of value.

To create a keyframe animation, you call this UIView class method:

- animateKeyframes(withDuration:delay:options:animations:completion:)

It takes an animations function, and inside that function you call this UIView class method multiple times to specify each stage:

- addKeyframe(withRelativeStartTime:relativeDuration:animations:)

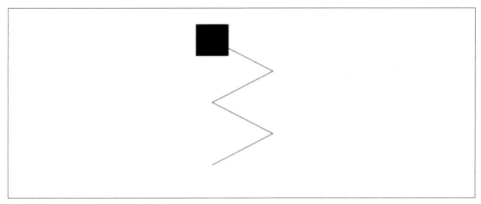

Figure 4-2. A zig-zag animation

Each keyframe's start time and duration is between 0 and 1, *relative to the animation as a whole*. (Giving a keyframe's start time and duration in seconds is a common beginner mistake.)

To illustrate, I'll oscillate a view back and forth horizontally while moving it down the screen vertically, forming a zig-zag (Figure 4-2):

```
var p = self.v.center
let dur = 0.25
var start = 0.0
let dx : CGFloat = 100
let dy : CGFloat = 50
var dir : CGFloat = 1
UIView.animateKeyframes(withDuration: 4, delay: 0) {
    UIView.addKeyframe(withRelativeStartTime:start,
        relativeDuration: dur) {
            p.x += dx*dir; p.y += dy
            self.v.center = p
    }
    start += dur; dir *= -1
    UIView.addKeyframe(withRelativeStartTime:start,
        relativeDuration: dur) {
            p.x += dx*dir; p.y += dy
            self.v.center = p
    }
    start += dur; dir *= -1
    UIView.addKeyframe(withRelativeStartTime:start,
        relativeDuration: dur) {
            p.x += dx*dir; p.y += dy
            self.v.center = p
    }
    start += dur; dir *= -1
    UIView.addKeyframe(withRelativeStartTime:start,
        relativeDuration: dur) {
```

```
                p.x += dx*dir; p.y += dy
                self.v.center = p
            }
        }
    }
```

In that code, there are four keyframes, evenly spaced: each is 0.25 in duration (one-fourth of the whole animation) and each starts 0.25 later than the previous one (as soon as the previous one ends). In each keyframe, the view's center x-coordinate increases or decreases by 100, alternately, while its center y-coordinate keeps increasing by 50.

The keyframe values are points in space and time; the actual animation interpolates between them. How this interpolation is done depends upon the options: parameter (omitted in the preceding code). Several UIView.KeyframeAnimationOptions values have names that start with calculationMode; pick one. The default is .calculation-ModeLinear. In our example, this means that the path followed by the view is a sharp zig-zag; the view seems to bounce off invisible walls at the right and left. But if our choice is .calculationModeCubic, our view describes a smooth S-curve, starting at the view's initial position and ending at the last keyframe point, and passing through the three other keyframe points like the maxima and minima of a sine wave.

Because my keyframes are perfectly even, I could achieve the same effects by using .calculationModePaced or .calculationModeCubicPaced, respectively. The paced options ignore the relative start time and relative duration values of the key-frames; you might as well pass 0 for all of them. Instead, they divide up the times and durations evenly, exactly as my code has done.

Finally, .calculationModeDiscrete means that the changed animatable properties don't animate: the animation jumps to each keyframe.

The outer animations function can contain other changes to animatable view proper-ties, as long as they don't conflict with the addKeyframe animations; these are animated over the total duration:

```
UIView.animateKeyframes(withDuration: 4, delay: 0) {
    self.v.alpha = 0
    // ...
```

The result is that as the view zigzags back and forth down the screen, it also gradually fades away.

It is legal and meaningful, although the documentation fails to make this clear, to supply a timing curve as part of the options: argument. If you don't do that, the default is .curveEaseInOut, which may not be what you want. Unfortunately Swift's obsessive-compulsive attitude toward data types resists folding a UIView.Animation-Options timing curve directly into a value that is typed as a UIView.Keyframe-

AnimationOptions; so you have to trick the compiler into letting you do it. Here's how to combine .calculationModeLinear with .curveLinear:

```
var opts : UIView.KeyframeAnimationOptions = .calculationModeLinear
let opt2 : UIView.AnimationOptions = .curveLinear
opts.insert(UIView.KeyframeAnimationOptions(rawValue:opt2.rawValue))
```

That's two different senses of linear! The first means that the path described by the moving view is a sequence of straight lines. The second means that the moving view's speed along that path is steady.

You might want to pause or reverse a keyframe view animation by way of a property animator. To do so, nest your call to UIView.animateKeyframes... inside the property animator's animations function. The property animator's duration and timing curve are then inherited, so this is another way to dictate the keyframe animation's timing:

```
let anim = UIViewPropertyAnimator(
    duration: 4, timingParameters: UICubicTimingParameters())
anim.addAnimations {
    UIView.animateKeyframes(withDuration: 0, delay: 0) {
        UIView.addKeyframe(withRelativeStartTime: 0,
            relativeDuration: 1) {
                self.v.center.x += 100
        }
        UIView.addKeyframe(withRelativeStartTime: 0.5,
            relativeDuration: 0.25) {
                self.v.backgroundColor = .red
        }
    }
}
anim.startAnimation()
```

In that example, our view animates slowly to the right, and changes color suddenly in the middle of its movement. As the example demonstrates, keyframes do not have to be sequential, nor do they all have to involve the same property. They can be used to coordinate different animations; they are a good way to overlap animations, as well as to chain animations. These aspects of the power and utility of keyframe animations often go unappreciated by beginners. There are other ways to arrange the same outward effect, but this way, the entire animation is placed under the control of a single property animator, and is easy to pause, scrub, reverse, and so on.

Transitions

A *transition* is an animation that emphasizes a view's change of content. Transitions are ordered using one of two UIView class methods:

- transition(with:duration:options:animations:completion:)
- transition(from:to:duration:options:completion:)

The transition animation types are expressed as part of the `options:` bitmask:

- `.transitionFlipFromLeft, .transitionFlipFromRight`
- `.transitionCurlUp, .transitionCurlDown`
- `.transitionFlipFromBottom, .transitionFlipFromTop`
- `.transitionCrossDissolve`

Transitioning one view

`transition(with:...)` takes one UIView parameter, and performs the transition animation on that view. In this example, a UIImageView containing an image of Mars flips over as its image changes to a smiley face; it looks as if the image view were two-sided, with Mars on one side and the smiley face on the other:

```
let opts : UIView.AnimationOptions = .transitionFlipFromLeft
UIView.transition(with: self.iv, duration: 0.8, options: opts) {
    self.iv.image = UIImage(named:"Smiley")
}
```

In that example, I've put the content change inside the animations function. That's conventional but misleading; the truth is that if all that's changing is the content, *nothing* needs to go into the animations function. The change of content can be anywhere, before or even after this entire line of code. It's the flip that's being animated. You might use the animations function here to order additional animations, such as a change in a view's center.

You can do the same sort of thing with a custom view that does its own drawing. Let's say that I have a UIView subclass, MyView, that draws either a rectangle or an ellipse depending on the value of its Bool `reverse` property:

```
class MyView : UIView {
    var reverse = false
    override func draw(_ rect: CGRect) {
        let f = self.bounds.insetBy(dx: 10, dy: 10)
        let con = UIGraphicsGetCurrentContext()!
        if self.reverse {
            con.strokeEllipse(in:f)
        }
        else {
            con.stroke(f)
        }
    }
}
```

This code flips a MyView instance while changing its drawing from a rectangle to an ellipse or *vice versa*:

```
let opts : UIView.AnimationOptions = .transitionFlipFromLeft
self.v.reverse.toggle()
UIView.transition(with: self.v, duration: 1, options: opts) {
    self.v.setNeedsDisplay()
}
```

By default, if a view has subviews whose layout changes as part of a transition animation, that change in layout is *not* animated: the layout changes directly to its final
appearance when the transition ends. If you want to display a subview of the transitioning view being animated as it assumes its final state, include .allowAnimated-
Content in the options: bitmask.

Transitioning two views and their superview

transition(from:to:...) takes two UIView parameters; the first view is *replaced* by
the second, while *their superview* undergoes the transition animation. There are two
possible configurations, depending on the options: you provide:

Remove one subview, add the other

If .showHideTransitionViews is *not* one of the options:, then the second subview is not in the view hierarchy when we start; the transition removes the first
subview from its superview and adds the second subview to that same superview.

Hide one subview, show the other

If .showHideTransitionViews *is* one of the options:, then both subviews are in
the view hierarchy when we start; the isHidden of the first is false, the isHidden
of the second is true, and the transition reverses those values.

In this example, a label self.lab is already in the interface. The animation causes the
superview of self.lab to flip over, while at the same time a different label, lab2, is
substituted for the existing label:

```
let lab2 = UILabel(frame:self.lab.frame)
lab2.text = self.lab.text == "Hello" ? "Howdy" : "Hello"
lab2.sizeToFit()
let opts : UIView.AnimationOptions = .transitionFlipFromLeft
UIView.transition(from: self.lab, to: lab2, duration: 0.8, options: opts) {
    _ in self.lab = lab2
}
```

It's up to you to make sure beforehand that the second view has the desired position,
so that it will appear in the right place in its superview.

Transitions are another handy but probably underutilized iOS animation feature.
Earlier, I demonstrated how to replace one view with another by adding the second
view, animating the alpha values of both views, and removing the first view in the
completion function. That's a common technique for implementing a dissolve, but

calling `transition(from:to:...)` with a `.transitionCrossDissolve` animation is simpler and does the same thing.

Implicit Layer Animation

All animation is ultimately layer animation. Up to now, we've been talking about view animation, which uses layer animation under the hood. Now we're going to talk about how to animate a layer directly.

Amazingly, animating a layer can be as simple as setting a layer property. A change in what the documentation calls an *animatable property* of a CALayer is *automatically* interpreted as a request to animate that change. In other words, animation of layer property changes is the default! Multiple property changes are considered part of the same animation. This mechanism is called *implicit animation.*

In Chapter 3 we constructed a compass out of layers. Suppose we have created that interface, and that we have a reference to the arrow layer (`arrow`). If we rotate the arrow layer by changing its `transform` property, *the arrow rotation is animated:*

```
arrow.transform = CATransform3DRotate(arrow.transform, .pi/4.0, 0, 0, 1)
```

You may be wondering: if implicit animation is the default, why didn't we notice it happening in any of the layer examples in Chapter 3? It's because there are two common situations where implicit layer animation *doesn't* happen:

View's underlying layer
Implicit layer animation doesn't operate on a UIView's underlying layer. You *can* animate a UIView's underlying layer directly, but you must use explicit layer animation (discussed later in this chapter).

During layer tree preparation
Implicit layer animation doesn't affect a layer as it is being created, configured, and added to the interface. Implicit animation comes into play when you change an animatable property of a layer that is *already* present in the interface.

Animatable Layer Properties

CALayer properties listed in the documentation as animatable are `anchorPoint` and `anchorPointZ`, `backgroundColor`, `borderColor`, `borderWidth`, `bounds`, `contents`, `contentsCenter`, `contentsRect`, `cornerRadius`, `isDoubleSided`, `isHidden`, `masksTo-Bounds`, `opacity`, `position` and `zPosition`, `rasterizationScale` and `should-Rasterize`, `shadowColor`, `shadowOffset`, `shadowOpacity`, `shadowRadius`, and `sublayerTransform` and `transform`.

In addition, a CAShapeLayer's `path`, `strokeStart`, `strokeEnd`, `fillColor`, `stroke-Color`, `lineWidth`, `lineDashPhase`, and `miterLimit` are animatable; so are a

CATextLayer's `fontSize` and `foregroundColor`, and a CAGradientLayer's `colors`, `locations`, and `endPoint`.

Basically, a property is animatable because there's some sensible way to interpolate the intermediate values between one value and another. The nature of the animation attached to each property is therefore generally just what you would intuitively expect. When you change a layer's `isHidden` property, it fades out of view (or into view). When you change a layer's `contents`, the old contents are dissolved into the new contents. And so forth.

 A layer's `cornerRadius` is animatable by explicit layer animation, or by view animation, but not by implicit layer animation.

Animating a Custom Layer Subclass

Suppose you create a custom CALayer subclass that has custom properties and a custom initializer. Then if you animate any property of that layer, it is possible that you'll crash with this message in the Xcode console: "Fatal error: Use of unimplemented initializer `init(layer:)`."

The reasons for this crash have to do with how layer animation works behind the scenes. The runtime has to create a *presentation layer* that will portray the animation of your custom layer on the screen. And in order to do that, the runtime will call this layer's `init(layer:)`. So you have to implement `init(layer:)`, to help the runtime create the presentation layer.

The parameter to `init(layer:)` is the existing instance of your layer subclass, typed as Any. Your implementation should set all custom properties of the new instance, based on their values in the old instance. Typically what you'll do is cast the parameter to your layer subclass and copy the old values directly into the new instance:

```
class MyLayer: CALayer {
    var prop: Int
    override init() {
        self.prop = 0
        super.init()
    }
    required init?(coder: NSCoder) {
        fatalError("init(coder:) has not been implemented")
    }
    override init(layer: Any) {
        guard let oldLayer = layer as? MyLayer else {
            fatalError("init(layer:) called with wrong layer type")
        }
```

```
        self.prop = oldLayer.prop
        super.init(layer: layer)
    }
}
```

That's a minimal, almost trivial implementation of init(layer:) — but without it, animating any property of a MyLayer instance will crash.

Animation Transactions

Animation operates with respect to a *transaction* (a CATransaction), which collects all animation requests and hands them over to the animation server in a single batch. Every animation request takes place in the context of some transaction. You can make this explicit by wrapping your animation requests in calls to the CATransaction class methods begin and commit; the result is a *transaction block*. Additionally, there is always an *implicit transaction* surrounding your code, and you can operate on this implicit transaction without any begin and commit.

To modify the characteristics of an implicit animation, you modify the transaction that surrounds it. Typically, you'll use these CATransaction class methods:

setAnimationDuration(_:)
>   The duration of the animation.

setAnimationTimingFunction(_:)
>   A CAMediaTimingFunction; layer timing functions are discussed in the next section.

setDisableActions(_:)
>   Toggles implicit animations for this transaction.

setCompletionBlock(_:)
>   A function (taking no parameters) to be called when the animation ends; it is called even if no animation is triggered during this transaction.

flush()
>   Pauses subsequent code until the current transaction has finished.

CATransaction also implements key–value coding to allow you to set and retrieve a value for an arbitrary key, similar to CALayer.

By nesting transaction blocks, you can apply different animation characteristics to different elements of an animation. You can also use transaction commands outside of any transaction block to modify the implicit transaction. In our previous example, we could slow down the animation of the arrow like this:

```
CATransaction.setAnimationDuration(0.8)
arrow.transform = CATransform3DRotate(arrow.transform, .pi/4.0, 0, 0, 1)
```

An important use of transactions is to turn implicit animation *off.* This is valuable because implicit animation is the default, and can be unwanted (and a performance drag). To turn off implicit animation, call `setDisableActions(true)`. There are other ways to turn off implicit animation (discussed later in this chapter), but this is the simplest.

`setCompletionBlock(_:)` establishes a completion function that signals the end, not only of the implicit layer property animations you yourself have ordered as part of this transaction, but of *all* animations ordered during this transaction, including Cocoa's own animations. It's a way to be notified when any and all animations come to an end.

The `flush` method can solve the problem of implicit animation not working during preparation of the layer tree. This attempt to add a layer and make it appear by growing from a point doesn't animate:

```
// ... create and configure lay ...
lay.bounds.size = .zero
self.view.layer.addSublayer(lay)
CATransaction.setAnimationDuration(2)
lay.bounds.size = CGSize(100,100) // no animation
```

But this does animate:

```
// ... create and configure lay ...
lay.bounds.size = .zero
self.view.layer.addSublayer(lay)
CATransaction.flush() // *
CATransaction.setAnimationDuration(2)
lay.bounds.size = CGSize(100,100) // animation
```

A better alternative, perhaps, would be to use explicit layer animation (discussed in the next section) rather than implicit layer animation.

And now for a revelation. The "redraw moment" that I've spoken of earlier is actually the end of the current transaction:

- You set a view's background color; the displayed color of the background is changed when the transaction ends.
- You call `setNeedsDisplay`; `draw(_:)` is called when the transaction ends.
- You call `setNeedsLayout`; layout happens when the transaction ends.
- You order an animation; the animation starts when the transaction ends.

What's really happening is this. Your code runs within an implicit transaction. Your code comes to an end, and the transaction commits itself. It is then, as part of the transaction commit procedure, that the screen is updated: first layout, then drawing, then obedience to layer property changes, then the start of any animations. The animation server then continues operating on a background thread; it has kept a reference to the transaction, and calls its completion function, if any, when the animations are over.

 An explicit transaction block that orders an animation to a layer, if the block is *not preceded by any other changes to the layer,* can cause animation to begin immediately when the CATransaction class method commit is called, without waiting for the redraw moment, while your code continues running. In my experience, this can cause trouble (animation delegate messages cannot arrive, and the presentation layer can't be queried properly) and should be avoided.

Media Timing Functions

The CATransaction class method setAnimationTimingFunction(_:) takes as its parameter a media timing function (CAMediaTimingFunction). This is the Core Animation way of describing the same cubic Bézier timing curves I discussed earlier.

To specify a built-in timing curve, call the CAMediaTimingFunction initializer init(name:) with one of these parameters (CAMediaTimingFunctionName):

- .linear
- .easeIn
- .easeOut
- .easeInEaseOut
- .default

To define your own timing curve, supply the coordinates of the two Bézier control points by calling init(controlPoints:). Here we define the "clunk" timing curve and apply it to the rotation of the compass arrow:

```
let clunk = CAMediaTimingFunction(controlPoints: 0.9, 0.1, 0.7, 0.9)
CATransaction.setAnimationTimingFunction(clunk)
arrow.transform = CATransform3DRotate(arrow.transform, .pi/4.0, 0, 0, 1)
```

Core Animation

Core Animation is the fundamental underlying iOS animation technology. View animation and implicit layer animation are both merely convenient façades for Core Animation. Core Animation is *explicit layer animation.*

Core Animation is vastly more powerful than simple implicit layer animation. Also, it works on a view's underlying layer, so it's the only way to apply full-on layer property animation to a view, letting you transcend the limited repertoire of animatable view properties. On the other hand, animating a view's underlying layer with Core Animation is layer animation, not view animation, so you don't get any automatic layout of that view's subviews; that can be a reason for preferring view animation.

CABasicAnimation and Its Inheritance

The simplest way to animate a property with Core Animation is with a CABasic-Animation object. CABasicAnimation derives much of its power through its inheritance, so I'll describe that inheritance along with CABasicAnimation itself. You will readily see that all the property animation features we have met already are embodied in a CABasicAnimation instance:

CAAnimation

CAAnimation is an abstract class, meaning that you'll only ever use a subclass of it. Some of CAAnimation's powers come from its implementation of the CAMediaTiming protocol.

delegate

An adopter of the CAAnimationDelegate protocol. The delegate messages are:

- animationDidStart(_:)

- animationDidStop(_:finished:)

A CAAnimation instance *retains its delegate*; this is very unusual behavior and can cause trouble if you're not conscious of it (as I know all too well from experience). Alternatively, don't set a delegate; to make your code run after the animation ends, call the CATransaction class method set-CompletionBlock(_:) before configuring the animation.

duration, timingFunction

The length of the animation, and its timing function (a CAMediaTiming-Function). A duration of 0 (the default) means 0.25 seconds unless overridden by the transaction.

autoreverses, repeatCount, repeatDuration

For an infinite repeatCount, use Float.greatestFiniteMagnitude. The repeatDuration property is a different way to govern repetition, specifying how long the repetition should continue rather than how many repetitions should occur; don't specify both a repeatCount and a repeatDuration.

beginTime

The delay before the animation starts. To delay an animation with respect to now, call CACurrentMediaTime and add the desired delay in seconds. The delay does not eat into the animation's duration.

timeOffset

A shift in the animation's overall timing; looked at another way, specifies the starting frame of the "animation movie," which is treated as a loop. An animation with a duration of 8 and a time offset of 4 plays its second half followed by its first half.

CAAnimation, along with all its subclasses, implements key–value coding to allow you to set and retrieve a value for an arbitrary key, similar to CALayer (Chapter 3) and CATransaction.

CAPropertyAnimation

CAPropertyAnimation is a subclass of CAAnimation. It too is abstract, and adds the following:

isAdditive

If true, the values supplied by the animation are added to the current presentation layer value.

isCumulative

If true, a repeating animation starts each repetition where the previous repetition ended rather than jumping back to the start value.

valueFunction

Converts a simple scalar value that you supply into a transform.

keyPath

The all-important string specifying the CALayer key that is to be animated. Recall from Chapter 3 that CALayer properties are accessible through KVC keys; now we are using those keys! The convenience initializer init(key-Path:) creates the instance and assigns it a keyPath.

 There is no animatable keyPath called "frame". To animate a layer's frame using explicit layer animation, if both its position and bounds are to change, you must animate both. Similarly, you cannot use explicit layer animation to animate a layer's affineTransform property, because affineTransform is not a property (it's a pair of convenience methods); you must animate its transform instead. Attempting to form a property animation with a keyPath value of "frame" or "affineTransform" is a common beginner error.

CABasicAnimation

CABasicAnimation is a subclass (not abstract!) of CAPropertyAnimation. It adds the following:

fromValue, toValue

The starting and ending values for the animation. These values must be Objective-C objects, so numbers and structs will have to be wrapped accordingly, using NSNumber and NSValue; fortunately, Swift will automatically take care of this for you. If neither fromValue nor toValue is provided, the former and current values of the property are used. If just one of them is provided, the other uses the current value of the property.

byValue

Expresses one of the endpoint values as a *difference* from the other rather than in absolute terms. So you would supply a byValue instead of a from-Value or instead of a toValue, and the actual fromValue or toValue would be calculated for you by subtraction or addition with respect to the other value. If you supply *only* a byValue, the fromValue is the property's current value.

Using a CABasicAnimation

Having constructed and configured a CABasicAnimation, the way you order it to be performed is to *add it to a layer*. This is done with the CALayer instance method add(_:forKey:). (I'll discuss the purpose of the forKey: parameter later; it's fine to ignore it and use nil, as I do in the examples that follow.)

But there's a slight twist. A CAAnimation is merely an animation; all it does is describe the hoops that the presentation layer is to jump through, the "animation movie" that is to be presented. It has no effect on the layer itself. If you naïvely create a CABasicAnimation and add it to a layer with add(_:forKey:), the animation happens and then the "animation movie" is whipped away to reveal the layer sitting there in exactly the same state as before. It is up to *you* to change the layer to match what the animation *will* ultimately portray. The converse, of course, is that you *don't* have to change the layer if it *doesn't* change as a result of the animation.

To ensure good results, start by taking a plodding, formulaic approach to the use of CABasicAnimation, like this:

1. Capture the start and end values for the layer property you're going to change, because you're likely to need these values in what follows.

2. Change the layer property to its end value, first calling setDisable-Actions(true) if necessary to prevent implicit animation.

3. Construct the explicit animation, using the start and end values you captured earlier, and with its keyPath corresponding to the layer property you just changed.

4. Add the explicit animation to the layer. An explicit animation is *copied* when it is added to a layer, and the copy added to the layer is immutable, so the animation must be configured beforehand.

Here's how you'd use this approach to animate our compass arrow rotation:

```
// capture the start and end values
let startValue = arrow.transform
let endValue = CATransform3DRotate(startValue, .pi/4.0, 0, 0, 1)
// change the layer, without implicit animation
CATransaction.setDisableActions(true)
arrow.transform = endValue
// construct the explicit animation
let anim = CABasicAnimation(keyPath:#keyPath(CALayer.transform))
anim.duration = 0.8
let clunk = CAMediaTimingFunction(controlPoints:0.9, 0.1, 0.7, 0.9)
anim.timingFunction = clunk
anim.fromValue = startValue
anim.toValue = endValue
// ask for the explicit animation
arrow.add(anim, forKey:nil)
```

Once you're comfortable with the full form, you will find that in many cases it can be condensed. When the fromValue and toValue are not set, the former and current values of the property are used automatically. (This magic is possible because, at the time the CABasicAnimation is added to the layer, the presentation layer still has the former value of the property, while the layer itself has the new value — and so the CABasicAnimation is able to retrieve them.) In our example, therefore, there is no need to set the fromValue and toValue, and no need to capture the start and end values beforehand. We can also omit disabling implicit animations, perhaps because the explicit animation of the transform cancels the implicit animation for us. Here's the condensed version:

```
arrow.transform = CATransform3DRotate(arrow.transform, .pi/4.0, 0, 0, 1)
let anim = CABasicAnimation(keyPath:#keyPath(CALayer.transform))
anim.duration = 0.8
let clunk = CAMediaTimingFunction(controlPoints:0.9, 0.1, 0.7, 0.9)
anim.timingFunction = clunk
arrow.add(anim, forKey:nil)
```

There's no need to change the layer if it doesn't change as a result of the animation. Let's make the compass arrow appear to vibrate rapidly, without ultimately changing its current orientation. To do this, we'll waggle it back and forth, using a repeated animation, between slightly clockwise from its current position and slightly counterclockwise from its current position. The "animation movie" neither starts nor stops at the current position of the arrow, but for this animation it doesn't matter, because it all happens so quickly as to appear natural:

```
// capture the start and end values
let nowValue = arrow.transform
let startValue = CATransform3DRotate(nowValue, .pi/40.0, 0, 0, 1)
let endValue = CATransform3DRotate(nowValue, -.pi/40.0, 0, 0, 1)
// construct the explicit animation
let anim = CABasicAnimation(keyPath:#keyPath(CALayer.transform))
anim.duration = 0.05
anim.timingFunction = CAMediaTimingFunction(name:.linear)
```

```
anim.repeatCount = 3
anim.autoreverses = true
anim.fromValue = startValue
anim.toValue = endValue
// ask for the explicit animation
arrow.add(anim, forKey:nil)
```

That code, too, can be shortened considerably from its full form. We can avoid calculating the new rotation values based on the arrow's current transform by setting our
animation's isAdditive property to true; the animation's property values are then
added to the existing property value for us (they are relative, not absolute). For a
transform, "added" means "matrix-multiplied," so we can describe the waggle
without any reference to the arrow's current rotation. Moreover, because our rotation
is so simple (around a cardinal axis), we can take advantage of CAProperty-
Animation's valueFunction; the animation's property values can then be simple
scalars (in this case, angles), because the valueFunction tells the animation to interpret them as rotations around the z-axis:

```
let anim = CABasicAnimation(keyPath:#keyPath(CALayer.transform))
anim.duration = 0.05
anim.timingFunction = CAMediaTimingFunction(name:.linear)
anim.repeatCount = 3
anim.autoreverses = true
anim.isAdditive = true
anim.valueFunction = CAValueFunction(name:.rotateZ)
anim.fromValue = Float.pi/40
anim.toValue = -Float.pi/40
arrow.add(anim, forKey:nil)
```

 Instead of using a valueFunction, we could have set the animation's key path to
"transform.rotation.z" to achieve the same effect. Apple advises against this,
though, as it can result in mathematical trouble when there is more than one
rotation.

Let's return once more to our arrow "clunk" rotation for another implementation,
this time using the isAdditive and valueFunction properties. We set the arrow
layer to its final transform at the outset, so when the time comes to configure the
animation, its toValue, in isAdditive terms, will be 0; the fromValue will be its current value expressed *negatively*, like this:

```
let rot = CGFloat.pi/4.0
CATransaction.setDisableActions(true)
arrow.transform = CATransform3DRotate(arrow.transform, rot, 0, 0, 1)
// construct animation additively
let anim = CABasicAnimation(keyPath:#keyPath(CALayer.transform))
anim.duration = 0.8
let clunk = CAMediaTimingFunction(controlPoints:0.9, 0.1, 0.7, 0.9)
anim.timingFunction = clunk
anim.fromValue = -rot
```

```
anim.toValue = 0
anim.isAdditive = true
anim.valueFunction = CAValueFunction(name:.rotateZ)
arrow.add(anim, forKey:nil)
```

That is an interesting way of describing the animation; in effect, it expresses the animation in reverse, regarding the final position as correct and the current position as an aberration to be corrected. It also happens to be how additive view animations are rewritten behind the scenes, and explains their behavior.

Springing Animation

Springing animation is exposed at the Core Animation level through the CASpring-Animation class (a CABasicAnimation subclass). Its properties are the same as the parameters of the fullest form of the UISpringTimingParameters initializer, except that its initialVelocity is a CGFloat, not a CGVector. The duration is ignored, but don't omit it. The actual duration calculated from your specifications can be extracted as the settlingDuration property:

```
CATransaction.setDisableActions(true)
self.v.layer.position.y += 100
let anim = CASpringAnimation(keyPath: #keyPath(CALayer.position))
anim.damping = 0.7
anim.initialVelocity = 20
anim.mass = 0.04
anim.stiffness = 4
anim.duration = 1 // ignored, but you need to supply something
self.v.layer.add(anim, forKey: nil)
```

Keyframe Animation

Keyframe animation (CAKeyframeAnimation) is an alternative to basic animation (CABasicAnimation); they are both subclasses of CAPropertyAnimation, and they are used in similar ways. The difference is that you need to tell the keyframe animation what the keyframes are. In the simplest case, you can just set its values array. This tells the animation its starting value, its ending value, and some specific values through which it should pass on the way between them.

Here's a new version of our animation for waggling the compass arrow, expressing it as a keyframe animation. The stages include the start and end states along with eight alternating waggles in between, with the degree of waggle becoming progressively smaller:

```
var values = [0.0]
let directions = sequence(first:1) {$0 * -1}
let bases = stride(from: 20, to: 60, by: 5)
for (base, dir) in zip(bases, directions) {
    values.append(Double(dir) * .pi / Double(base))
}
```

```
values.append(0.0)
let anim = CAKeyframeAnimation(keyPath:#keyPath(CALayer.transform))
anim.values = values
anim.isAdditive = true
anim.valueFunction = CAValueFunction(name: .rotateZ)
arrow.add(anim, forKey:nil)
```

Here are some CAKeyframeAnimation properties:

`values`
> The array of values that the animation is to adopt, including the starting and ending value.

`timingFunctions`
> An array of timing functions, one for each stage of the animation (this array will be one element shorter than the `values` array).

`keyTimes`
> An array of times to accompany the array of values, defining when each value should be reached. The times start at 0 and are expressed as increasing fractions of 1, ending at 1.

`calculationMode`
> Describes how the `values` are treated to create *all* the values through which the animation must pass (CAAnimationCalculationMode):

> `.linear`
> > The default. A simple straight-line interpolation from value to value.

> `.cubic`
> > Constructs a single smooth curve passing through all the values (and additional advanced properties, `tensionValues`, `continuityValues`, and `biasValues`, allow you to refine the curve).

> `.paced, .cubicPaced`
> > The timing functions and key times are ignored, and the velocity is made constant through the whole animation.

> `.discrete`
> > No interpolation: we jump directly to each value at the corresponding key time.

`path`
> When you're animating a property whose values are pairs of floats (CGPoints), this is an alternative way of describing the values; instead of a `values` array, which must be interpolated to arrive at the intermediate values along the way, you supply the entire interpolation as a single CGPath. The points used to define

the path are the keyframe values, so you can still apply timing functions and key times. If you're animating a position, the rotationMode property lets you ask the animated object to rotate so as to remain perpendicular to the path.

In this example, the values array is a sequence of five images (self.images) to be presented successively and repeatedly in a layer's contents, like the frames in a movie; the effect is similar to image animation, discussed earlier in this chapter:

```
let anim = CAKeyframeAnimation(keyPath:#keyPath(CALayer.contents))
anim.values = self.images.map {$0.cgImage!}
anim.keyTimes = [0.0, 0.25, 0.5, 0.75, 1.0]
anim.calculationMode = .discrete
anim.duration = 1.5
anim.repeatCount = .greatestFiniteMagnitude
self.sprite.add(anim, forKey:nil) // sprite is a CALayer
```

Making a Property Animatable

So far, we've been animating built-in animatable properties. If you define your own property on a CALayer subclass, you can easily make that property animatable through a CAPropertyAnimation. Here we animate the increase or decrease in a CALayer subclass property called thickness, using essentially the pattern for explicit animation that we've already developed:

```
let lay = self.v.layer as! MyLayer
let cur = lay.thickness
let val : CGFloat = cur == 10 ? 0 : 10
lay.thickness = val
let ba = CABasicAnimation(keyPath:#keyPath(MyLayer.thickness))
ba.fromValue = cur
lay.add(ba, forKey:nil)
```

To make our layer responsive to such a command, it needs a thickness property (obviously), and it must return true from the class method needsDisplay(forKey:) for this property:

```
class MyLayer : CALayer {
    @objc var thickness : CGFloat = 0
    override class func needsDisplay(forKey key: String) -> Bool {
        if key == #keyPath(thickness) {
            return true
        }
        return super.needsDisplay(forKey:key)
    }
}
```

Returning true from needsDisplay(forKey:) causes this layer to be redisplayed repeatedly as the thickness property changes. So if we want to *see* the animation, this layer also needs to draw itself in some way that depends on the thickness

property. Here, I'll implement the layer's draw(in:) to make thickness the thickness
of the black border around a red rectangle:

```
override func draw(in con: CGContext) {
    let r = self.bounds.insetBy(dx:20, dy:20)
    con.setFillColor(UIColor.red.cgColor)
    con.fill(r)
    con.setLineWidth(self.thickness)
    con.stroke(r)
}
```

At every frame of the animation, draw(in:) is called, and because the thickness
value differs at each step, the rectangle's border appears animated.

We have made MyLayer's thickness property animatable when using explicit layer
animation, but it would be even cooler to make it animatable when using implicit
layer animation (that is, when setting lay.thickness directly). Later in this chapter,
I'll show how to do that.

A custom animatable CALayer property is a solution to a much more general problem. Consider layer animation abstractly as a way of getting the runtime to calculate
and send us a series of *timed interpolated values*. Those values arrive through the runtime repeatedly calling our draw(in:) implementation, but no law says that we have
to *draw* in that implementation: we are free to use those values in some other way. In
fact, we don't even have to use the values! We can implement draw(in:) purely as a
way to get an event on every frame of an animation, responding to that event however we like.

Grouped Animations

An animation group (CAAnimationGroup) combines multiple animations — its
animations, an array of animations — into a single animation. By delaying and timing the various component animations, complex effects can be achieved.

A CAAnimationGroup is a CAAnimation subclass, so it has a duration and other
animation features. Think of the CAAnimationGroup as the parent, and its
animations as its children. The children *inherit* default property values from their
parent. If you don't set a child's duration explicitly, for instance, it will inherit the
parent's duration.

Let's use an animation group to construct a sequence where the compass arrow
rotates and then waggles. This requires very little modification of code we've already
written. We express the first animation in its full form, with explicit fromValue and
toValue. We postpone the second animation using its beginTime property; notice
that we express this in relative terms, as a number of seconds into the parent's
duration, not with respect to CACurrentMediaTime. Finally, we set the overall parent
duration to the sum of the child durations, so that it can embrace both of them

(failing to do this, and then wondering why some child animations never occur, is a common beginner error):

```
// capture current value, set final value
let rot = .pi/4.0
CATransaction.setDisableActions(true)
let current = arrow.value(forKeyPath:"transform.rotation.z") as! Double
arrow.setValue(current + rot, forKeyPath:"transform.rotation.z")
// first animation (rotate and clunk)
let anim1 = CABasicAnimation(keyPath:#keyPath(CALayer.transform))
anim1.duration = 0.8
let clunk = CAMediaTimingFunction(controlPoints:0.9, 0.1, 0.7, 0.9)
anim1.timingFunction = clunk
anim1.fromValue = current
anim1.toValue = current + rot
anim1.valueFunction = CAValueFunction(name:.rotateZ)
// second animation (waggle)
var values = [0.0]
let directions = sequence(first:1) {$0 * -1}
let bases = stride(from: 20, to: 60, by: 5)
for (base, dir) in zip(bases, directions) {
    values.append(Double(dir) * .pi / Double(base))
}
values.append(0.0)
let anim2 = CAKeyframeAnimation(keyPath:#keyPath(CALayer.transform))
anim2.values = values
anim2.duration = 0.25
anim2.isAdditive = true
anim2.beginTime = anim1.duration - 0.1
anim2.valueFunction = CAValueFunction(name: .rotateZ)
// group
let group = CAAnimationGroup()
group.animations = [anim1, anim2]
group.duration = anim1.duration + anim2.duration
arrow.add(group, forKey:nil)
```

In that example, I grouped two animations that animated the *same* property *sequentially*. Now let's do the opposite: we'll group some animations that animate *different* properties *simultaneously*.

I have a small view (self.v), located near the top-right corner of the screen, whose layer contents are a picture of a sailboat facing to the left. I'll "sail" the boat in a curving path, both down the screen and left and right across the screen, like an extended letter "S" (Figure 4-3). Each time the boat comes to a vertex of the curve, changing direction across the screen, I'll flip the boat so that it faces the way it's about to move. At the same time, I'll constantly rock the boat, so that it always appears to be pitching a little on the waves.

Here's the first animation, the movement of the boat (its position) along its curving path. It illustrates the use of a CAKeyframeAnimation with a CGPath; once we've

Figure 4-3. A boat and the course she'll sail

calculated the path, we know the final position of the boat, and we set it so the boat won't jump back to the start afterward. The `calculationMode` of `.paced` ensures an even speed over the whole path. We don't set an explicit duration because we want to adopt the duration of the group:

```
let h : CGFloat = 200
let v : CGFloat = 75
let path = CGMutablePath()
var leftright : CGFloat = 1
var next : CGPoint = self.v.layer.position
var pos : CGPoint
path.move(to:CGPoint(next.x, next.y))
for _ in 0 ..< 4 {
    pos = next
    leftright *= -1
    next = CGPoint(pos.x+h*leftright, pos.y+v)
    path.addCurve(to:CGPoint(next.x, next.y),
        control1: CGPoint(pos.x, pos.y+30),
        control2: CGPoint(next.x, next.y-30))
}
CATransaction.setDisableActions(true)
self.v.layer.position = next
let anim1 = CAKeyframeAnimation(keyPath:#keyPath(CALayer.position))
anim1.path = path
anim1.calculationMode = .paced
```

Here's the second animation, the reversal of the direction the boat is facing. This is simply a rotation around the y-axis. It's another CAKeyframeAnimation, but we make no attempt at visually animating this reversal: the `calculationMode` is `.discrete`, so that the boat image reversal is a sudden change, as in our earlier "sprite" example. There is one less value than the number of points in our first animation's path, and the first animation has an even speed, so the reversals take place at each curve apex with no further effort on our part. (If the pacing were more complicated, we could give both the first and the second animation identical key-Times arrays, to coordinate them.) Once again, we don't set an explicit duration:

```
let revs = [0.0, .pi, 0.0, .pi]
let anim2 = CAKeyframeAnimation(keyPath:#keyPath(CALayer.transform))
anim2.values = revs
anim2.valueFunction = CAValueFunction(name:.rotateY)
anim2.calculationMode = .discrete
```

Here's the third animation, the rocking of the boat. It has a short duration, and repeats indefinitely:

```
let pitches = [0.0, .pi/60.0, 0.0, -.pi/60.0, 0.0]
let anim3 = CAKeyframeAnimation(keyPath:#keyPath(CALayer.transform))
anim3.values = pitches
anim3.repeatCount = .greatestFiniteMagnitude
anim3.duration = 0.5
anim3.isAdditive = true
anim3.valueFunction = CAValueFunction(name:.rotateZ)
```

Finally, we combine the three animations, assigning the group an explicit duration that will be adopted by the first two animations:

```
let group = CAAnimationGroup()
group.animations = [anim1, anim2, anim3]
group.duration = 8
self.v.layer.add(group, forKey:nil)
```

Here are some further CAAnimation properties (from the CAMediaTiming protocol) that come into play especially when animations are grouped:

speed
> The ratio between a child's timescale and the parent's timescale. If a parent and child have the same duration, but the child's speed is 1.5, the child's animation runs one-and-a-half times as fast as the parent.

fillMode
> Suppose the child animation begins after the parent animation, or ends before the parent animation, or both. What should happen to the appearance of the property being animated, outside the child animation's boundaries? The answer depends on the child's fillMode (CAMediaTimingFillMode):

.removed
> The child animation is removed, revealing the layer property at its actual current value whenever the child is not running.

.forwards
> The final presentation layer value of the child animation remains afterward.

`.backwards`

    The initial presentation layer value of the child animation appears right from the start.

`.both`

    Combines the previous two.

Animating Multiple Layers

Beginners are often excited, when they discover grouped animations, at the prospect of a single complex animation that coordinates animations of multiple different layers. But is that possible? An animation must be added to a single layer, and a property animation's keyPath must refer to a property of just that *one* layer — right?

Actually, a keyPath is a key *path*. That means that it can represent a chain of properties. And a layer's sublayers are such a property, represented by the keyPath value "sublayers". Continuing the chain from there, we can refer to a particular sublayer by the value of its name property — and from there we can refer to a property of that sublayer. In this way, we can add a single animation to a superlayer and animate properties of *different* sublayers.

In this example, I have a superlayer with two sublayers. They portray a left footprint and a right footprint, and I assign values to their name properties so I can refer to them later:

```
self.leftfoot.name = "left"
self.leftfoot.contents = UIImage(named:"leftfoot")!.cgImage
self.rightfoot.name = "right"
self.rightfoot.contents = UIImage(named:"rightfoot")!.cgImage
```

Now I'll construct an animation group that makes each footprint step forward in turn:

```
func rightStepAfter(_ t: Double) -> CABasicAnimation {
    let rightStep = CABasicAnimation(keyPath: "sublayers.right.position.y")
    rightStep.byValue = -160
    rightStep.beginTime = t
    rightStep.duration = 2
    rightStep.fillMode = .forwards
    return rightStep
}
func leftStepAfter(_ t: Double) -> CABasicAnimation {
    let leftStep = CABasicAnimation(keyPath: "sublayers.left.position.y")
    leftStep.byValue = -160
    leftStep.beginTime = t
    leftStep.duration = 2
    leftStep.fillMode = .forwards
    return leftStep
}
```

```
let group = CAAnimationGroup()
group.duration = 11
group.animations = []
for i in stride(from: 0, through: 8, by: 4) {
    group.animations?.append(rightStepAfter(Double(i)))
    group.animations?.append(leftStepAfter(Double(i+2)))
}
```

The keyPath value "sublayers.right.position.y" means that the animation changes the y value of the position of the sublayer named "right", and the keyPath value "sublayers.left.position.y" means that the animation changes the y value of the position of the sublayer named "left". So if I now add the group animation to the superlayer of the two footprint layers, the footprints "walk" up the screen alternately; one animation group is animating two layers individually.

Freezing an Animation

An animation can be frozen using Core Animation at the level of the animation or of the layer, with an effect similar to what we did with a property animator earlier.

This feature depends upon the fact that the CAMediaTiming protocol is adopted by CALayer. CAMediaTiming properties of a layer affect the behavior of any animation attached to that layer. The speed property effectively changes the animation's duration: a speed of 2 means that a 10-second animation plays in 5 seconds, and a speed of 0 means the animation is frozen. When the animation is frozen, the timeOffset property dictates what frame of the animation is displayed.

To illustrate, let's explore the animatable path property of a CAShapeLayer. Consider a layer that can display a rectangle or an ellipse *or any of the intermediate shapes between them*. I can't imagine what the notion of an intermediate shape between a rectangle or an ellipse may mean, let alone how to draw such an intermediate shape; but thanks to frozen animations, I don't have to. Here, I'll construct the CAShapeLayer, add it to the interface, give it an animation from a rectangle to an ellipse, and keep a reference to it as a property:

```
let shape = CAShapeLayer()
shape.frame = v.bounds
v.layer.addSublayer(shape)
shape.fillColor = UIColor.clear.cgColor
shape.strokeColor = UIColor.red.cgColor
let path = CGPath(rect:shape.bounds, transform:nil)
shape.path = path
let path2 = CGPath(ellipseIn:shape.bounds, transform:nil)
let ba = CABasicAnimation(keyPath:#keyPath(CAShapeLayer.path))
ba.duration = 1
ba.fromValue = path
ba.toValue = path2
```

```
shape.speed = 0
shape.timeOffset = 0
shape.add(ba, forKey: nil)
self.shape = shape
```

I've added the animation to the layer, but I've also set the layer's speed to 0, so no animation takes place; the rectangle is displayed and that's all. As in my earlier example, there's a UISlider in the interface. I'll respond to the user changing the value of the slider by setting the frame of the animation:

```
self.shape.timeOffset = Double(slider.value)
```

Transitions

A layer transition is an animation involving two "copies" of a single layer, in which the second "copy" appears to replace the first. It is described by an instance of CATransition (a CAAnimation subclass), which has these chief properties specifying the animation:

type
> Your choices are (CATransitionType):
>
> - .fade
> - .moveIn
> - .push
> - .reveal

subtype
> If the type is not .fade, your choices are (CATransitionSubtype):
>
> - .fromRight
> - .fromLeft
> - .fromTop
> - .fromBottom

 For historical reasons, the terms bottom and top in the names of the subtype settings have the opposite of their expected meanings. Reverse them in your mind: when you mean the top, say .fromBottom.

Consider first what happens when we perform a layer transition without changing anything else about the layer:

Figure 4-4. A push transition

```
let t = CATransition()
t.type = .push
t.subtype = .fromBottom
t.duration = 2
lay.add(t, forKey: nil)
```

The entire layer exits moving down from its original place while fading away, and another copy of the very same layer enters moving down from above while fading in. If, at the same time, we change something about the layer's contents, then the old contents will appear to exit downward while the new contents appear to enter from above:

```
// ... configure the transition as before ...
CATransaction.setDisableActions(true)
lay.contents = UIImage(named: "Smiley")!.cgImage
lay.add(t, forKey: nil)
```

Typically, the layer that is to be transitioned will be inside a superlayer that has the same size and whose masksToBounds is true. This confines the visible transition to the bounds of the layer itself. In Figure 4-4, which shows a smiley face pushing an image of Mars out of the layer, I've emphasized this arrangement by giving the super-layer a border as well.

A transition on a superlayer can happen simultaneously with animation of a sublayer. The animation will be seen to occur on the second "copy" of the layer as it moves into position. This is analogous to the .allowAnimatedContent option for a view animation.

Animations List

To understand how CALayer's add(_:forKey:) actually works (and what the "key" is), you need to know about a layer's *animations list*.

An animation is an object (a CAAnimation) that modifies how a layer is drawn. It does this merely by being attached to the layer; the layer's drawing mechanism does the rest. A layer maintains a list of animations that are currently in force. To add an animation to this list, you call add(_:forKey:). When the time comes to draw itself, the layer looks through its animations list and draws itself in accordance with whatever animations it finds there. (The list of things the layer must do in order to draw itself is sometimes referred to by the documentation as the *render tree*.) The order in which animations were added to the list is the order in which they are applied.

The animations list behaves somewhat like a dictionary. An animation has a key — the forKey: parameter in add(_:forKey:). If an animation with a certain key is added to the list when an animation with that key is already in the list, the one that is already in the list is removed. So *only one animation with a given key* can be in the list at a time; I call this the *exclusivity rule*.

The exclusivity rule explains why ordering an animation can sometimes cancel an animation already ordered or in-flight: the two animations had the same key, so the first one was removed. (Additive view animations affecting the same property work around this limitation by giving the additional animations a *different key name* — for example, "position" and "position-2".)

Unlike a dictionary, the animations list will also accept an animation with *no key* — the key is nil. Animations with a nil key are *not* subject to the exclusivity rule; there can be more than one animation in the list with no key.

The forKey: parameter in add(_:forKey:) is *not a property name*. It *could* be a property name, but it can be any arbitrary value. Its purpose is to enforce the exclusivity rule. It does *not* have any meaning with regard to what property a CAProperty-Animation animates; that is the job of the animation's keyPath. Apple's use of the term "key" in add(_:forKey:) is somewhat confusing in this regard; I wish they had named this method something like add(_:identifier:).

Nevertheless, a relationship between the "key" in add(_:forKey:) and the keyPath of a CAPropertyAnimation does exist: if a CAPropertyAnimation's keyPath is nil at the time that it is added to a layer with add(_:forKey:), that keyPath is set to the value of the forKey: parameter! Therefore you can *misuse* the forKey: parameter in add(_:forKey:) as a way of specifying what keyPath an animation animates — and implicit layer animation crucially depends on this fact.

 Many Core Animation examples *do* misuse forKey: in just that way, supplying nil as the animation's keyPath and specifying the property to be animated as the "key" in add(_:forKey:). This is *wrong!* Set the animation's keyPath explicitly.

You can use the exclusivity rule to your own advantage, to keep your code from stepping on its own feet. Some code of yours might add an animation to the list using a certain key; then later, some other code might come along and correct this, removing that animation and replacing it with another. By using the same key, the second code is easily able to override the first: "You may have been given some other animation with this key, but throw it away; play this one instead."

In some cases, the key you supply is ignored and a different key is substituted. In particular, the key with which a CATransition is added to the list is always `"transition"` — and so there can be only one transition animation in the list.

You can think of an animation in a layer's animations list as being the "animation movie" I spoke of at the start of this chapter. As long as an animation is in the list, the movie is present, either waiting to be played or actually playing. An animation that has finished playing is, in general, pointless; the animation should now be removed from the list, as its presence serves no purpose and it imposes an extra burden on the render tree. Therefore, an animation has an `isRemovedOnCompletion` property, which defaults to `true`: when the "movie" is over, the animation removes itself from the list.

 Many Core Animation examples set `isRemovedOnCompletion` to `false` and set the animation's `fillMode` to `.forwards` or `.both` as a lazy way of preventing a property from jumping back to its initial value when the animation ends. This is *wrong!* An animation needs to be removed when it is completed; the `fillMode` is intended for use with a child animation within an animation group. To prevent jumping at the end of the animation, set the animated property value to match the final frame of the animation.

You can't access the entire animations list directly. You can access the key names of the animations in the list, with `animationKeys`; and you can obtain or remove an animation with a certain key, with `animation(forKey:)` and `removeAnimation(forKey:)`; but animations with a `nil` key are inaccessible. You can remove all animations, including animations with a `nil` key, using `removeAllAnimations`. When your app is suspended, `removeAllAnimations` is called on all layers for you; that is why it is possible to suspend an app coherently in the middle of an animation.

If an animation is in-flight when you remove it from the animations list, it will stop; but that doesn't happen until the next redraw moment. If you need an animation to be removed immediately, you might be able to make that happen by wrapping the `remove` call in an explicit transaction block.

Actions

For the sake of completeness, I will explain how implicit animation really works — that is, how implicit animation is turned into explicit animation behind the scenes. The basis of implicit animation is the *action mechanism*. Your code can hook into the action mechanism to *change* the behavior of implicit animation in interesting ways. Feel free to skip this section if you don't want to get into the under-the-hood nitty-gritty of implicit animation.

What an Action Is

An *action* is an object that adopts the CAAction protocol. This means simply that it implements `run(forKey:object:arguments:)`. The action object could do *anything* in response to this message. The notion of an action is completely general. The only built-in class that adopts the CAAction protocol happens to be CAAnimation, but in fact the action object doesn't have to be an animation — it doesn't even have to perform an animation.

You would never send `run(forKey:object:arguments:)` to an object directly. Rather, this message is sent to an action object for you, as the basis of implicit animation. The `key` is the property that was set, and the `object` is the layer whose property was set.

What an animation does when it receives `run(forKey:object:arguments:)` is to assume that the `object:` is a layer, and to add itself to that layer's animations list. For an animation, receiving the `run(forKey:object:arguments:)` message is like being told: "Play yourself!"

Recall that if an animation's `keyPath` is `nil`, the key by which the animation is assigned to a layer's animations list is used as the `keyPath`. When an animation is sent `run(forKey:object:arguments:)`, it calls `add(_:forKey:)` to add itself to the layer's animation's list, *using the name of the property as the key*. The animation's `key-Path` for an implicit layer animation is usually `nil`, so the animation's `keyPath` winds up being set to the same key! That is how the property that you set ends up being the property that is animated.

Action Search

Now we know what a CAAction is. But what's the connection between a CALayer and a CAAction? It all starts with the CALayer instance method `action(forKey:)`. The following events cause a layer's `action(forKey:)` method to be called:

- A CALayer property is set, directly or using `setValue(_:forKey:)`. For most built-in properties, the layer's response is to call `action(forKey:)`, passing along the name of the property as the key. Certain properties get special treatment:

  - Setting a layer's `frame` property sets its `position` and `bounds` and calls `action(forKey:)` for the `"position"` and `"bounds"` keys.

  - Calling a layer's `setAffineTransform(_:)` method sets its `transform` and calls `action(forKey:)` for the `"transform"` key.

  - You can configure a custom property to call `action(forKey:)` by designating it as `@NSManaged`, as I'll demonstrate later in this chapter.

- The layer is sent setValue(_:forKey:) with a key that is *not* a property; by default, CALayer's setValue(_:forUndefinedKey:) calls action(forKey:).

- Various other miscellaneous types of event take place, such as the layer being added to the interface. I'll give some examples later.

All of that presupposes that CATransaction.disableActions() is false. If CATransaction.setDisableActions(true) has been called, it *prevents* the action(forKey:) message from being sent, and that's the end of the story: there can be no implicit animation in this transaction.

Very well, but let's say that a layer's action(forKey:) *is* called. The layer now embarks upon an elaborate search for an action object (a CAAction) to which it can send the run(forKey:object:arguments:) message. This is the *action search.*

At each stage of the action search, the following rules are obeyed regarding what is returned from that stage of the search:

An action object
> If an action object is produced, that is the end of the search. The action mechanism sends that action object the run(forKey:object:arguments:) message; if this an animation, the animation responds by adding itself to the layer's animations list.

NSNull()
> If NSNull() is produced, that is the end of the search. There will be no implicit animation; NSNull() means, "Do nothing and stop searching."

nil
> If nil is produced, the search continues to the next stage.

The action search proceeds by stages:

1. The layer's action(forKey:) might terminate the search before it even starts. The layer will do this if it is the underlying layer of a view, or if the layer is not part of a window's layer hierarchy; there should be no implicit animation, so the whole mechanism is nipped in the bud. (This stage is special in that a returned value of nil ends the search and no animation takes place.)

2. If the layer has a delegate that implements action(for:forKey:), that message is sent to the delegate, with this layer as the first parameter and the property name as the key. If an action object or NSNull() is returned, the search ends.

3. The layer has a property called actions, which is a dictionary. If there is an entry in this dictionary with the given key, that value is used, and the search ends.

4. The layer has a property called style, which is a dictionary. If there is an entry in this dictionary with the key actions, it is assumed to be a dictionary; if this

`actions` dictionary has an entry with the given key, that value is used, and the search ends. Otherwise, if there is an entry in the `style` dictionary called `style`, the same search is performed within it, and so on recursively until either an `actions` entry with the given key is found (the search ends) or there are no more `style` entries (the search continues).

(If the `style` dictionary sounds profoundly weird, that's because it is profoundly weird. It is actually a special case of a larger, separate mechanism, which is also profoundly weird, having to do not with actions, but with a CALayer's implementation of KVC. When you call `value(forKey:)` on a layer, if the key is undefined by the layer itself, the `style` dictionary is consulted. I have never written or seen code that uses this mechanism for anything.)

5. The layer's class is sent `defaultAction(forKey:)`, with the property name as the key. If an action object or `NSNull()` is returned, the search ends.

6. If the search reaches this last stage, a default animation is supplied, as appropriate. For a property animation, this is a plain vanilla CABasicAnimation.

Hooking Into the Action Search

You can affect the action search at any of its various stages to modify what happens when the search is triggered. This is where the fun begins!

You can turn off implicit animation just for a particular property. One way would be to return `nil` from `action(forKey:)` itself, in a CALayer subclass. Here's the code for a CALayer subclass that doesn't have implicit animation for its `position` property:

```
override func action(forKey key: String) -> CAAction? {
    if key == #keyPath(position) {
        return nil
    }
    return super.action(forKey:key)
}
```

For more precise control, we can take advantage of the fact that a CALayer acts like a dictionary, allowing us to set an arbitrary key's value. We'll embed a switch in our CALayer subclass that we can use to turn implicit `position` animation on and off:

```
override func action(forKey key: String) -> CAAction? {
    if key == #keyPath(position) {
        if self.value(forKey:"suppressPositionAnimation") != nil {
            return nil
        }
    }
    return super.action(forKey:key)
}
```

To turn off implicit `position` animation for an instance of this layer, we set its "suppressPositionAnimation" key to a non-nil value:

```
layer.setValue(true, forKey:"suppressPositionAnimation")
```

Another possibility is to intervene at some stage of the search to produce an action object of your own. You would then be affecting how implicit animation behaves. Let's say we want a certain layer's duration for an implicit `position` animation to be 5 seconds. We can achieve this with a minimally configured animation, like this:

```
let ba = CABasicAnimation()
ba.duration = 5
```

The idea now is to situate this animation where it will be produced by the action search for the "position" key. We could, for instance, put it into the layer's `actions` dictionary:

```
layer.actions = ["position": ba]
```

The only property of this animation that we have set is its duration; that setting, however, is final. Although animation properties that you don't set can be set through CATransaction, in the usual manner for implicit property animation, animation properties that you *do* set *can't* be overridden through CATransaction. When we set this layer's `position`, if an implicit animation results, its duration is 5 seconds, even if we try to change it through CATransaction:

```
CATransaction.setAnimationDuration(1.5) // won't work
layer.position = CGPoint(100,100) // animated, takes 5 seconds
```

Storing an animation in the `actions` dictionary is a somewhat inflexible way to hook into the action search. If we have to write our animation beforehand, we know nothing about the layer's starting and ending values for the changed property. A much more powerful approach is to make our action object a custom CAAction object — because in that case, it will be sent `run(forKey:...)`, and we can construct and run an animation *now*, when we are in direct contact with the layer to be animated. Here's a barebones version of such an object:

```
class MyAction : NSObject, CAAction {
    func run(forKey event: String, object anObject: Any,
        arguments dict: [AnyHashable : Any]?) {
            let anim = CABasicAnimation(keyPath: event)
            anim.duration = 5
            let lay = anObject as! CALayer
            let newP = lay.value(forKey:event)
            let oldP = lay.presentation()!.value(forKey:event)
            lay.add(anim, forKey:nil)
    }
}
```

A MyAction instance might then be the action object that we store in the `actions` dictionary:

```
layer.actions = ["position": MyAction()]
```

Our custom CAAction object, MyAction, doesn't do anything very interesting — but it could. That's the point. As the code demonstrates, we have access to the name of the animated property (event), the old value of that property (from the layer's presentation layer), and the new value of that property (from the layer itself). That's enough information to build a complete animation from the ground up and add it to the layer.

Here's a modification of our MyAction object that creates and runs a keyframe animation that "waggles" as it goes from the start value to the end value:

```
class MyWagglePositionAction : NSObject, CAAction {
    func run(forKey event: String, object anObject: Any,
        arguments dict: [AnyHashable : Any]?) {
            let lay = anObject as! CALayer
            let newP = lay.value(forKey:event) as! CGPoint
            let oldP = lay.presentation()!.value(forKey:event) as! CGPoint
            let d = sqrt(pow(oldP.x - newP.x, 2) + pow(oldP.y - newP.y, 2))
            let r = Double(d/3.0)
            let theta = Double(atan2(newP.y - oldP.y, newP.x - oldP.x))
            let wag = 10 * .pi/180.0
            let p1 = CGPoint(
                oldP.x + CGFloat(r*cos(theta+wag)),
                oldP.y + CGFloat(r*sin(theta+wag)))
            let p2 = CGPoint(
                oldP.x + CGFloat(r*2*cos(theta-wag)),
                oldP.y + CGFloat(r*2*sin(theta-wag)))
            let anim = CAKeyframeAnimation(keyPath: event)
            anim.values = [oldP,p1,p2,newP]
            anim.calculationMode = .cubic
            lay.add(anim, forKey:nil)
    }
}
```

By adding this CAAction object to a layer's `actions` dictionary under the `"position"` key, we have created a CALayer that waggles when its `position` property is set. Our CAAction doesn't set the animation's `duration`, so our own call to CATransaction's `setAnimationDuration(_:)` works. The power of this mechanism is simply staggering. We can modify *any* layer in this way — even one that doesn't belong to us. (And we don't actually have to add an animation to the layer; we are free to interpret the setting of this property however we like!)

Instead of modifying a layer's `actions` dictionary, we could hook into the action search by setting the layer's delegate to an instance that responds to `action(for:for-Key:)`. The delegate can behave differently depending on what key this is (and even what *layer* this is). Here's an implementation that does exactly what the `actions` dictionary did — it returns an instance of our custom CAAction object, so that setting the layer's position waggles it into place:

```
func action(for layer: CALayer, forKey key: String) -> CAAction? {
    if key == #keyPath(CALayer.position) {
        return MyWagglePositionAction()
    }
}
```

Finally, I'll demonstrate overriding `defaultAction(forKey:)`. This code would go into a CALayer subclass; setting this layer's `contents` will automatically trigger a push transition from the left:

```
override class func defaultAction(forKey key: String) -> CAAction? {
    if key == #keyPath(contents) {
        let tr = CATransition()
        tr.type = .push
        tr.subtype = .fromLeft
        return tr
    }
    return super.defaultAction(forKey:key)
}
```

 Both the delegate's `action(for:forKey:)` and the subclass's `defaultAction(for-Key:)` are declared as returning a `CAAction`. Therefore, to return `NSNull()` from your implementation of one of these methods, you'll need to cast it to `CAAction` to quiet the compiler; you're lying (NSNull does not adopt CAAction), but it doesn't matter.

Making a Custom Property Implicitly Animatable

Earlier in this chapter, we made a custom layer's `thickness` property animatable through explicit layer animation. Now that we know how implicit layer animation works, we can make our layer's `thickness` property animatable through implicit animation as well. We will then be able to animate our layer's thickness with code like this:

```
let lay = self.v.layer as! MyLayer
let cur = lay.thickness
let val : CGFloat = cur == 10 ? 0 : 10
lay.thickness = val // implicit animation
```

We have already implemented `needsDisplay(forKey:)` to return `true` for the `"thickness"` key, and we have provided an appropriate `draw(in:)` implementation. Now we'll add two further pieces of the puzzle. As we now know, to make our MyLayer class respond to direct setting of a property, we need to hook into the action search and return a CAAction. The obvious place to do this is in the layer itself, at the very start of the action search, in an `action(forKey:)` implementation:

```
    override func action(forKey key: String) -> CAAction? {
        if key == #keyPath(thickness) {
            let ba = CABasicAnimation(keyPath: key)
            ba.fromValue = self.presentation()!.value(forKey:key)
            return ba
        }
        return super.action(forKey:key)
    }
}
```

Finally, we must declare MyLayer's `thickness` property `@NSManaged`. Otherwise, `action(forKey:)` won't be called in the first place and the action search will never happen:

```
class MyLayer : CALayer {
    @NSManaged var thickness : CGFloat
    // ...
}
```

(The `@NSManaged` declaration invites Cocoa to generate and dynamically inject getter and setter accessors into our layer class; it is the equivalent of Objective-C's `@dynamic` — and is completely different from Swift's `dynamic`.)

Nonproperty Actions

An action search is triggered when a layer is added to a superlayer (key `"onOrderIn"`) and when a layer's sublayers are changed by adding or removing a sublayer (key `"sublayers"`).

In this example, we use our layer's delegate so that when our layer is added to a superlayer, it will "pop" into view:

```
let layer = CALayer()
// ... configure layer here ...
layer.delegate = self
self.view.layer.addSublayer(layer)
```

In the layer's delegate (`self`), we implement the actual animation as an animation group, fading the layer quickly in from an opacity of 0 and at the same time scaling its transform to make it momentarily appear a little larger:

```
func action(for layer: CALayer, forKey key: String) -> CAAction? {
    if key == "onOrderIn" {
        let anim1 = CABasicAnimation(keyPath:#keyPath(CALayer.opacity))
        anim1.fromValue = 0.0
        anim1.toValue = layer.opacity
        let anim2 = CABasicAnimation(keyPath:#keyPath(CALayer.transform))
        anim2.toValue = CATransform3DScale(layer.transform, 1.2, 1.2, 1.0)
        anim2.autoreverses = true
        anim2.duration = 0.1
        let group = CAAnimationGroup()
        group.animations = [anim1, anim2]
```

```
        group.duration = 0.2
        return group
    }
}
```

The documentation says that when a layer is removed from a superlayer, an action is sought under the key "onOrderOut". This is true but useless, because by the time the action is sought, the layer has already been removed from the superlayer, so returning an animation has no visible effect. A possible workaround is to trigger the animation in some other way (and remove the layer afterward, if desired). To illustrate, let's implement an arbitrary key "farewell" so that it shrinks and fades the layer and then removes it from its superlayer:

```
layer.delegate = self
layer.setValue("", forKey:"farewell")
```

The supplier of the action object — in this case, the layer's delegate — returns the shrink-and-fade animation; it also sets itself as that animation's delegate, and removes the layer when the animation ends:

```
func action(for layer: CALayer, forKey key: String) -> CAAction? {
    if key == "farewell" {
        let anim1 = CABasicAnimation(keyPath:#keyPath(CALayer.opacity))
        anim1.fromValue = layer.opacity
        anim1.toValue = 0.0
        let anim2 = CABasicAnimation(keyPath:#keyPath(CALayer.transform))
        anim2.toValue = CATransform3DScale(layer.transform, 0.1, 0.1, 1.0)
        let group = CAAnimationGroup()
        group.animations = [anim1, anim2]
        group.duration = 0.2
        group.delegate = self
        group.setValue(layer, forKey:"remove")
        layer.opacity = 0
        return group
    }
}
func animationDidStop(_ anim: CAAnimation, finished flag: Bool) {
    if let layer = anim.value(forKey:"remove") as? CALayer {
        layer.removeFromSuperlayer()
    }
}
```

Emitter Layers

Emitter layers (CAEmitterLayer) are, to some extent, on a par with animated images: once you've set up an emitter layer, it just sits there animating all by itself. The nature of this animation is rather narrow: an emitter layer emits particles, which are CAEmitterCell instances. But by clever setting of the properties of an emitter layer and its emitter cells, you can achieve some astonishing effects. Moreover, the animation is itself animatable using Core Animation.

Here are some basic properties of a CAEmitterCell:

contents, contentsRect
> These are modeled after the eponymous CALayer properties, although CAEmitterCell is not a CALayer subclass; so, respectively, an image (a CGImage) and a CGRect specifying a region of that image. They define the image that a cell will portray.

birthrate, lifetime
> How many cells per second should be emitted, and how many seconds each cell should live before vanishing, respectively.

velocity
> The speed at which a cell moves. The unit of measurement is not documented; perhaps it's points per second.

emissionLatitude, emissionLongitude
> The angle at which the cell is emitted from the emitter, as a variation from the perpendicular. Longitude is an angle within the plane; latitude is an angle out of the plane.

Here's some code to create a very elementary emitter cell:

```
// make a gray circle image
let r = UIGraphicsImageRenderer(size:CGSize(10,10))
let im = r.image {
    ctx in let con = ctx.cgContext
    con.addEllipse(in:CGRect(0,0,10,10))
    con.setFillColor(UIColor.gray.cgColor)
    con.fillPath()
}
// make a cell with that image
let cell = CAEmitterCell()
cell.contentsScale = UIScreen.main.scale
cell.birthRate = 5
cell.lifetime = 1
cell.velocity = 100
cell.contents = im.cgImage
```

The result is that little gray circles should be emitted slowly and steadily, five per second, each one vanishing in one second. Now we need an emitter layer from which these circles are to be emitted. Here are some basic CAEmitterLayer properties (beyond those it inherits from CALayer); these define an imaginary object, an emitter, that will be producing the emitter cells:

emitterPosition
> The point at which the emitter should be located, in superlayer coordinates. You can optionally add a third dimension to this point, emitterZPosition.

emitterSize
> The size of the emitter.

emitterShape
> The shape of the emitter. The dimensions of the shape depend on the emitter's size; the cuboid shape depends also on a third size dimension, emitterDepth. Your choices are (CAEmitterLayerEmitterShape):
>
> - .point
> - .line
> - .rectangle
> - .cuboid
> - .circle
> - .sphere

emitterMode
> The region of the shape from which cells should be emitted. Your choices are (CAEmitterLayerEmitterMode):
>
> - .points
> - .outline
> - .surface
> - .volume

Let's start with the simplest possible case, a single point emitter:

```
let emit = CAEmitterLayer()
emit.emitterPosition = CGPoint(30,100)
emit.emitterShape = .point
emit.emitterMode = .points
```

We tell the emitter what types of cell to emit by assigning those cells to its emitter-Cells property (an array of CAEmitterCell). We then add the emitter to our interface, and presto, it starts emitting:

```
emit.emitterCells = [cell]
self.view.layer.addSublayer(emit)
```

The result is a constant stream of gray circles emitted from the point (30.0,100.0), each circle marching steadily to the right and vanishing after one second (Figure 4-5).

Figure 4-5. A really boring emitter layer

Now that we've succeeded in creating a boring emitter layer, we can start to vary some parameters. The `emissionRange` defines a cone in which cells will be emitted; if we increase the `birthRate` and widen the `emissionRange`, we get something that looks like a stream shooting from a water hose:

```
cell.birthRate = 100
cell.lifetime = 1.5
cell.velocity = 100
cell.emissionRange = .pi/5.0
```

In addition, as the cell moves, it can be made to accelerate (or decelerate) in each dimension, using its `xAcceleration`, `yAcceleration`, and `zAcceleration` properties. Here, we turn the stream into a falling cascade, like a waterfall coming from the left:

```
cell.xAcceleration = -40
cell.yAcceleration = 200
```

All aspects of cell behavior can be made to vary randomly, using the following CAEmitterCell properties:

`lifetimeRange, velocityRange`
> How much the lifetime and velocity values are allowed to vary randomly for different cells.

`scale`
`scaleRange, scaleSpeed`
> The scale alters the size of the cell; the range and speed determine how far and how rapidly this size alteration is allowed to change over the lifetime of each cell.

`spin`
`spinRange`
> The spin is a rotational speed (in radians per second); its range determines how far this speed is allowed to change over the lifetime of each cell.

`color`
`redRange, greenRange, blueRange, alphaRange`
`redSpeed, greenSpeed, blueSpeed, alphaSpeed`
> The color is painted in accordance with the opacity of the cell's contents image; it combines with the image's color, so if we want the color stated here to appear in full purity, our contents image should use only white. The range and speed determine how far and how rapidly each color component is to change.

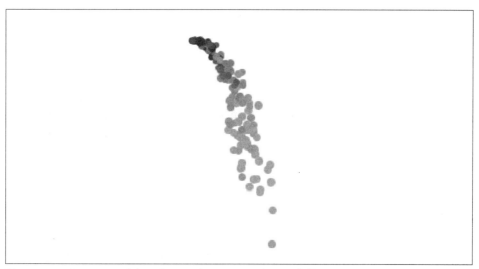

Figure 4-6. An emitter layer that makes a sort of waterfall

Here we add some variation so that the circles behave a little more independently of one another. Some live longer than others, some come out of the emitter faster than others. And they all start out a shade of blue, but change to a shade of green about halfway through the stream (Figure 4-6):

```
cell.lifetimeRange = 0.4
cell.velocityRange = 20
cell.scaleRange = 0.2
cell.scaleSpeed = 0.2
cell.color = UIColor.blue.cgColor
cell.greenRange = 0.5
cell.greenSpeed = 0.75
```

Once the emitter layer is in place and animating, you can change its parameters and the parameters of its emitter cells through key–value coding on the emitter layer. You can access the emitter cells through the emitter layer's "emitterCells" key path; to specify a cell type, use its name property as the next piece of the key path. Suppose we've set cell.name to "circle"; now we'll change the cell's greenSpeed so that each cell changes from blue to green much earlier in its lifetime:

```
emit.setValue(3.0, forKeyPath:"emitterCells.circle.greenSpeed")
```

The significance of this is that such changes can themselves be animated! Here, we'll attach to the emitter layer a repeating animation that causes our cell's greenSpeed to move slowly back and forth between two values. The result is that the stream varies, over time, between being mostly blue and mostly green:

```
let key = "emitterCells.circle.greenSpeed"
let ba = CABasicAnimation(keyPath:key)
ba.fromValue = -1.0
ba.toValue = 3.0
ba.duration = 4
ba.autoreverses = true
ba.repeatCount = .greatestFiniteMagnitude
emit.add(ba, forKey:nil)
```

A CAEmitterCell can itself function as an emitter — that is, it can have cells of its own. Both CAEmitterLayer and CAEmitterCell conform to the CAMediaTiming protocol, and their beginTime and duration properties can be used to govern their times of operation, much as in an animation group. This code causes our existing waterfall to spray tiny droplets in the region of the "nozzle" (the emitter):

```
let cell2 = CAEmitterCell()
cell.emitterCells = [cell2]
cell2.contents = im.cgImage
cell2.emissionRange = .pi
cell2.birthRate = 200
cell2.lifetime = 0.4
cell2.velocity = 200
cell2.scale = 0.2
cell2.beginTime = 0.04
cell2.duration = 0.2
```

But if we change the beginTime to be larger (hence later), the tiny droplets happen near the bottom of the cascade. We must also increase the duration, or stop setting it altogether, since if the duration is less than the beginTime, no emission takes place at all (Figure 4-7):

```
cell2.beginTime = 1.4
cell2.duration = 0.4
```

We can also alter the picture by changing the behavior of the emitter itself. This change turns the emitter into a line, so that our cascade becomes broader (more like Niagara Falls):

```
emit.emitterPosition = CGPoint(100,25)
emit.emitterSize = CGSize(100,100)
emit.emitterShape = .line
emit.emitterMode = .outline
cell.emissionLongitude = 3 * .pi/4
```

There's more to know about emitter layers and emitter cells, but at this point you know enough to understand Apple's sample code simulating such things as fire and smoke and pyrotechnics, and you can explore further on your own.

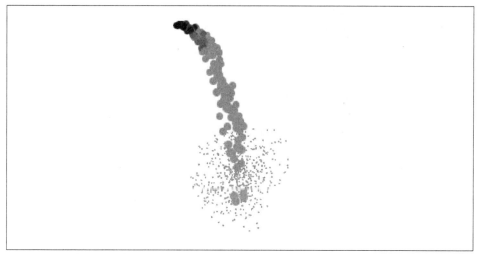

Figure 4-7. The waterfall makes a kind of splash

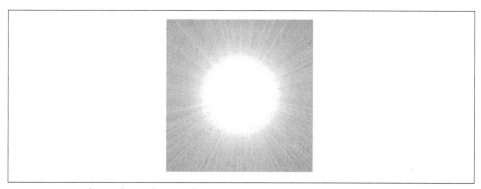

Figure 4-8. Midway through a starburst transition

CIFilter Transitions

Core Image filters (Chapter 2) include transitions. You supply two images and a frame time between 0 and 1; the filter supplies the corresponding frame of a one-second animation transitioning from the first image to the second. Figure 4-8 shows the frame at frame time 0.75 for a starburst transition from a solid red image to a photo of me. (You don't see the photo of me, because this transition, by default, "explodes" the first image to white first, and then quickly fades to the second image.)

Animating a Core Image transition filter is up to us. We need a way of rapidly calling the same method repeatedly; in that method, we'll request and draw each frame of the transition. This could be a job for a Timer, but a better way is to use a *display link* (CADisplayLink), a form of timer that's linked directly to the refreshing of the display (hence the name). The display refresh rate is hardware-dependent, but is typically every sixtieth of a second or faster; `UIScreen.maximumFramesPerSecond` will tell you the nominal value, and the nominal time between refreshes is the display link's `duration`.

 For the smoothest display of a Core Image transition filter animation with the least strain on the device's CPU, you would use Metal. But that's outside the scope of this book.

Like a timer, the display link calls a designated method of ours every time it fires. We can slow the rate of calls by setting the display link's `preferredFramesPerSecond`. We can learn the exact time when the display link last fired by querying its `timestamp`, and that's the best way to decide what frame needs displaying now.

In this example, I'll display the animation in a view's layer. We initialize ahead of time, in properties, everything we'll need later to obtain an output image for a given frame of the transition — the CIFilter, the image's `extent`, and the CIContext. We also have a `timestamp` property, which we initialize as well:

```
let moi = CIImage(image:UIImage(named:"moi")!)!
self.moiextent = moi.extent
let tran = CIFilter.flashTransition()
tran.inputImage = CIImage(color: CIColor(color:.red))
tran.targetImage = moi
tran.center = self.moiextent.center
self.tran = tran
self.timestamp = 0.0 // signal that we are starting
self.context = CIContext()
```

We create the display link, setting it to call into our `nextFrame` method, and start it going by adding it to the main run loop, which retains it:

```
let link = CADisplayLink(target:self, selector:#selector(self.nextFrame))
link.add(to:.main, forMode:.default)
```

Our `nextFrame(_:)` method is called with the display link as parameter (`sender`). We store the initial `timestamp` in our property, and use the difference between that and each successive `timestamp` value to calculate our desired frame. We ask the filter for the corresponding image and display it. When the frame value exceeds 1, the animation is over and we invalidate the display link (just like a repeating timer), which releases it from the run loop:

```
let scale = 1.0
@objc func nextFrame(_ sender:CADisplayLink) {
    if self.timestamp < 0.01 { // pick up and store first timestamp
        self.timestamp = sender.timestamp
        self.frame = 0.0
    } else { // calculate frame
        self.frame = (sender.timestamp - self.timestamp) * scale
    }
    sender.isPaused = true // defend against frame loss
```

```
    self.tran.setValue(self.frame, forKey:"inputTime")
    let moi = self.context.createCGImage(
        tran.outputImage!, from:self.moiextent)
    CATransaction.setDisableActions(true)
    self.v.layer.contents = moi
    if self.frame > 1.0 {
        sender.invalidate()
    }
    sender.isPaused = false
}
```

I have surrounded the time-consuming calculation and drawing of the image with calls to the display link's `isPaused` property, in case the calculation time exceeds the time between screen refreshes; perhaps this isn't necessary, but it can't hurt. Our animation occupies one second; changing that value is merely a matter of multiplying by a different `scale` value when we set our `frame` property.

UIKit Dynamics

UIKit dynamics comprises a suite of classes supplying a convenient API for animating views in a manner reminiscent of real-world physical behavior. Views can be subjected to gravity, collisions, bouncing, and transient forces, with effects that would otherwise be difficult to achieve.

UIKit dynamics should not be treated as a game engine. It is deliberately quite cartoony and simple, animating only the position (`center`) and rotation transform of views within a flat two-dimensional space. UIKit dynamics relies on CADisplayLink, and the calculation of each frame takes place on the main thread (not on the animation server's background thread). There's no "animation movie" and no distinct presentation layer; the views really are being repositioned in real time. UIKit Dynamics is not intended for extended use; it is a way of momentarily emphasizing or clarifying functional transformations of your interface.

The Dynamics Stack

Implementing UIKit dynamics involves configuring a "stack" of three things:

A dynamic animator
> A dynamic animator, a UIDynamicAnimator instance, is the ruler of the physics world you are creating. It has a reference view, whose bounds define the coordinate system of the animator's world. A view to be animated must be a subview of the reference view (though it does not have to be within the reference view's bounds). Retaining the animator is up to you, typically with an instance property. It's fine for an animator to sit empty until you need it; an animator whose world is empty (or at rest) is not running, and occupies no processor time.

A behavior

A UIDynamicBehavior is a rule describing how a view should behave. You'll typically use a built-in subclass, such as UIGravityBehavior or UICollisionBehavior. You configure the behavior and add it to the animator; an animator has methods and properties for managing its behaviors, such as addBehavior(_:), behaviors, removeBehavior(_:), and removeAllBehaviors. Even if an animation is already in progress, a behavior's configuration can be changed and behaviors can be added to and removed from the animator.

An item

An item is any object that implements the UIDynamicItem protocol. A UIView is such an object! You add a UIView (one that's a subview of your animator's reference view) to a behavior (one that belongs to that animator) — and at that moment, the view comes under the influence of that behavior. If this behavior is one that causes motion, and if no other behaviors prevent, the view will now move (the animator is running).

Some behaviors can accept multiple items, and have methods and properties such as addItem(_:), items, and removeItem(_:). Others can have just one or two items and must be initialized with these from the outset.

A UIDynamicItemGroup is a way of combining multiple items to form a single item. Its only property is its items. You apply behaviors to the resulting grouped item, not to the subitems that it comprises. Those subitems maintain their physical relationship to one another. For purposes of collisions, the boundaries of the individual subitems are respected.

That's sufficient to get started, so let's try it! First I'll create my animator and store it in a property:

```
self.anim = UIDynamicAnimator(referenceView: self.view)
```

Now I'll cause an existing subview of self.view (a UIImageView, self.iv, displaying the planet Mars) to drop off the screen, under the influence of gravity. I create a UIGravityBehavior, add it to the animator, and add self.iv to it:

```
let grav = UIGravityBehavior()
self.anim.addBehavior(grav)
grav.addItem(self.iv)
```

As a result, self.iv comes under the influence of gravity and is now animated downward off the screen. (A UIGravityBehavior object has properties configuring the strength and direction of gravity, but I've left them here at their defaults.)

An immediate concern is that our view falls forever. This is a serious waste of memory and processing power. If we no longer need the view after it has left the screen, we should take it out of the influence of UIKit dynamics by removing it from any behaviors to which it belongs (and we can also remove it from its superview). One way to do this is by removing from the animator any behaviors that are no longer needed. In our simple example, where the animator's entire world contains just this one item, it will be sufficient to call `removeAllBehaviors`.

But how will we know when the view is off the screen? A UIDynamicBehavior can be assigned an `action` function, which is called repeatedly as the animator drives the animation. I'll configure our gravity behavior's `action` function to check whether `self.iv` is still within the bounds of the reference view, by calling the animator's `items(in:)` method. Actually, `items(in:)` returns an array of UIDynamicItem, but I want an array of UIView, so I have a UIDynamicAnimator extension that will cast down safely:

```
extension UIDynamicAnimator {
    func views(in rect: CGRect) -> [UIView] {
        let nsitems = self.items(in: rect) as NSArray
        return nsitems.compactMap {$0 as? UIView}
    }
}
```

Here's my first attempt:

```
grav.action = {
    let items = self.anim.views(in:self.view.bounds)
    let ix = items.firstIndex(of:self.iv)
    if ix == nil {
        self.anim.removeAllBehaviors()
        self.iv.removeFromSuperview()
    }
}
```

This works in the sense that, after the image view leaves the screen, the image view is removed from the window and the animation stops. Unfortunately, there is also a memory leak: neither the image view nor the gravity behavior has been released. One solution is, in `grav.action`, to set `self.anim` (the animator property) to `nil`, breaking the retain cycle. This is a perfectly appropriate solution if, as here, we no longer need the animator for anything; a UIDynamicAnimator is a lightweight object and can very reasonably come into existence only for as long as we need to run an animation. Another possibility is to use delayed performance; even a delay of 0 solves the problem, presumably because the behavior's `action` function is no longer running at the time we remove the behavior:

```
grav.action = {
    let items = self.anim.views(in:self.view.bounds)
    let ix = items.firstIndex(of:self.iv)
    if ix == nil {
        delay(0) {
            self.anim.removeAllBehaviors()
```

```
                    self.iv.removeFromSuperview()
            }
        }
    }
```

Now let's add some further behaviors. If falling straight down is too boring, we can add a UIPushBehavior to apply a slight rightward impulse to the view as it begins to fall:

```
let push = UIPushBehavior(items:[self.iv], mode:.instantaneous)
push.pushDirection = CGVector(1,0)
self.anim.addBehavior(push)
```

The view now falls in a parabola to the right. Next, let's add a UICollisionBehavior to make our view strike the "floor" of the screen:

```
let coll = UICollisionBehavior()
coll.collisionMode = .boundaries
coll.collisionDelegate = self
let b = self.view.bounds
coll.addBoundary(withIdentifier:"floor" as NSString,
    from:CGPoint(b.minX, b.maxY), to:CGPoint(b.maxX, b.maxY))
self.anim.addBehavior(coll)
coll.addItem(self.iv)
```

The view now falls in a parabola onto the floor of the screen, bounces a tiny bit, and comes to rest. It would be nice if the view bounced a bit more. Characteristics internal to a dynamic item's physics, such as bounciness (`elasticity`), are configured by assigning it to a UIDynamicItemBehavior:

```
let bounce = UIDynamicItemBehavior()
bounce.elasticity = 0.8
self.anim.addBehavior(bounce)
bounce.addItem(self.iv)
```

Our view now bounces higher; nevertheless, when it hits the floor, it stops moving to the right, so it just bounces repeatedly, less and less, and ends up at rest on the floor. I'd prefer that, after it bounces, it should roll to the right, so that it eventually leaves the screen. Part of the problem here is that, in the mind of the physics engine, our view, even though it displays a round image, is itself *not* round. We can change that. We'll have to subclass our view class (UIImageView) and make sure our view is an instance of this subclass:

```
class MyImageView : UIImageView {
    override var collisionBoundsType: UIDynamicItemCollisionBoundsType {
        return .ellipse
    }
}
```

Our image view now has the ability to roll. The effect is quite realistic: the image itself appears to roll to the right after it bounces. But it isn't rolling very fast (because we didn't initially push it very hard). To remedy that, I'll add some rotational velocity as part of the first bounce. A UICollisionBehavior has a delegate to which it sends messages when a collision occurs. I'll make `self` the collision behavior's delegate, and when the delegate message arrives, I'll add rotational velocity to the existing dynamic item bounce behavior, so that our view starts spinning clockwise:

```
func collisionBehavior(_ behavior: UICollisionBehavior,
    beganContactFor item: UIDynamicItem,
    withBoundaryIdentifier identifier: NSCopying?,
    at p: CGPoint) {
        // look for the dynamic item behavior
        let b = self.anim.behaviors
        if let bounce = (b.compactMap {$0 as? UIDynamicItemBehavior}).first {
            let v = bounce.angularVelocity(for:item)
            if v <= 6 {
                bounce.addAngularVelocity(6, for:item)
            }
        }
    }
```

The view now falls in a parabola to the right, strikes the floor, spins clockwise, and bounces off the floor and continues bouncing its way off the right side of the screen.

Custom Behaviors

You will commonly find yourself composing a complex behavior out of a combination of several built-in UIDynamicBehavior subclass instances. It might make sense to express that combination as a single custom UIDynamicBehavior subclass.

To illustrate, I'll turn the behavior from the previous section into a custom subclass of UIDynamicBehavior. Let's call it MyDropBounceAndRollBehavior. Now we can apply this behavior to our view, `self.iv`, very simply:

```
self.anim.addBehavior(MyDropBounceAndRollBehavior(view:self.iv))
```

All the work is now done by the MyDropBounceAndRollBehavior instance. I've designed it to affect just one view, so its initializer looks like this:

```
let v : UIView
init(view v:UIView) {
    self.v = v
    super.init()
}
```

A UIDynamicBehavior can receive a reference to its dynamic animator just before being added to it, by implementing `willMove(to:)`, and can refer to it subsequently as `self.dynamicAnimator`. To incorporate actual behaviors into itself, our custom UIDynamicBehavior subclass creates and configures each behavior and calls `addChildBehavior(_:)`; it can refer to the array of its child behaviors as `self.childBehaviors`. When our custom behavior is added to or removed from the dynamic animator, the effect is the same as if its child behaviors themselves were added or removed.

Here is the rest of MyDropBounceAndRollBehavior. Our precautions in the gravity behavior's action function so as not to cause a retain cycle are simpler than before; it suffices to designate `self` as an unowned reference and remove `self` from the animator explicitly:

```
override func willMove(to anim: UIDynamicAnimator?) {
    guard let anim = anim else { return }
    let sup = self.v.superview!
    let b = sup.bounds
    let grav = UIGravityBehavior()
    grav.action = { [unowned self] in
        let items = anim.views(in: b)
        if items.firstIndex(of:self.v) == nil {
            anim.removeBehavior(self)
            self.v.removeFromSuperview()
        }
    }
    self.addChildBehavior(grav)
    grav.addItem(self.v)
    let push = UIPushBehavior(items:[self.v], mode:.instantaneous)
    push.pushDirection = CGVector(1,0)
    self.addChildBehavior(push)
    let coll = UICollisionBehavior()
    coll.collisionMode = .boundaries
    coll.collisionDelegate = self
    coll.addBoundary(withIdentifier:"floor" as NSString,
        from: CGPoint(b.minX, b.maxY), to:CGPoint(b.maxX, b.maxY))
    self.addChildBehavior(coll)
    coll.addItem(self.v)
    let bounce = UIDynamicItemBehavior()
    bounce.elasticity = 0.8
    self.addChildBehavior(bounce)
    bounce.addItem(self.v)
}
func collisionBehavior(_ behavior: UICollisionBehavior,
    beganContactFor item: UIDynamicItem,
    withBoundaryIdentifier identifier: NSCopying?,
    at p: CGPoint) {
        // look for the dynamic item behavior
        let b = self.childBehaviors
        if let bounce = (b.compactMap {$0 as? UIDynamicItemBehavior}).first {
            let v = bounce.angularVelocity(for:item)
            if v <= 6 {
                bounce.addAngularVelocity(6, for:item)
            }
        }
    }
}
```

Animator and Behaviors

Here are some further UIDynamicAnimator methods and properties:

delegate
> The delegate (UIDynamicAnimatorDelegate) is sent messages dynamicAnimator-DidPause(_:) and dynamicAnimatorWillResume(_:). The animator is paused when it has nothing to do: it has no dynamic items, or all its dynamic items are at rest.

isRunning
> If true, the animator is not paused; some dynamic item is being animated.

elapsedTime
> The total time during which this animator has been running since it first started running. The elapsedTime does not increase while the animator is paused, nor is it reset. You might use this in a delegate method or action method to decide that the animation is over.

updateItem(usingCurrentState:)
> Once a dynamic item has come under the influence of the animator, the animator is responsible for positioning that dynamic item. If your code manually changes the dynamic item's position or other relevant attributes, call this method so that the animator can take account of those changes.

 You can turn on a display that reveals visually what the animator is doing, showing its attachment lines and so forth; assuming that self.anim refers to the dynamic animator, you would say:

```
self.anim.perform(Selector(("setDebugEnabled:")), with:true)
```

UIDynamicItemBehavior

A UIDynamicItemBehavior doesn't apply any force or velocity; it is a way of endowing items with internal physical characteristics that will affect how they respond to other dynamic behaviors. Here are some of them:

density
> Changes the impulse-resisting mass in relation to size. When we speak of an item's mass, we mean a combination of its size and its density.

elasticity
> The item's tendency to bounce on collision.

friction
> The item's tendency to be slowed by sliding past another item.

`isAnchored`

An anchored item is not affected by forces that would make an item move; it remains stationary. This can give you something with friction and elasticity off of which you can bounce and slide other items.

`resistance, angularResistance, allowsRotation`

The item's tendency to come to rest unless forces are actively applied. `allows-Rotation` can prevent the item from acquiring any angular velocity at all.

`charge`

Meaningful only with respect to magnetic and electric fields, which I'll get to in a moment.

`addLinearVelocity(_:for:), linearVelocity(for:)`
`addAngularVelocity(_:for:), angularVelocity(for:)`

Methods for tweaking linear and angular velocity.

UIGravityBehavior

UIGravityBehavior imposes an acceleration on its dynamic items. By default, this acceleration is downward with a magnitude of 1 (arbitrarily defined as 1000 points per second per second). You can customize gravity by changing its `gravity-Direction` (a CGVector) or its `angle` and `magnitude`.

UIFieldBehavior

UIFieldBehavior is a generalization of UIGravityBehavior. A field affects any of its items for as long as they are within its area of influence, as described by these properties:

`position`

The center of the field's effective area of influence, in reference view coordinates. The default `position` is `CGPoint.zero`, the reference view's top left corner.

`region`

The shape of the field's effective area of influence; a UIRegion. The default is that the region is infinite, but you can limit it to a circle by its radius or to a rectangle by its size. More complex region shapes can be achieved by taking the union, intersection, or difference of two regions, or the inverse of a region.

`strength`

The magnitude of the field. It can be negative to reverse the directionality of the field's forces.

`falloff`

Defines a change in strength proportional to the distance from the center.

minimumRadius
Specifies a central circle within which there is no field effect.

direction, smoothness, animationSpeed
Applicable only to those built-in field types that define them.

The built-in field types are obtained by calling a class factory method:

linearGravityField(direction:)
Like UIGravityBehavior. Accelerates the item in the direction of a vector that you supply, proportionally to its mass, the length of the vector, and the strength of the field. The vector is the field's direction, and can be changed

velocityField(direction:)
Like UIGravityBehavior, but it doesn't apply an acceleration (a force) — instead, it applies a constant velocity.

radialGravityField(position:)
Like a point-oriented version of UIGravityBehavior. Accelerates the item toward, or pushes it away from, the field's designated central point (its position).

springField
Behaves as if there were a spring stretching from the item to the center, so that the item oscillates back and forth across the center until it settles there.

electricField
Behaves like an electric field emanating from the center. The default strength and falloff are both 1. If you set the falloff to 0, then a negatively charged item, all other things being equal, will oscillate endlessly across the center.

magneticField
Behaves like a magnetic field emanating from the center. A moving charged item's path is bent away from the center.

vortexField
Accelerates the item sideways with respect to the center.

dragField
Reduces the item's speed.

noiseField(smoothness:animationSpeed:)
Adds random disturbance to the position of the item. The smoothness is between 0 (noisy) and 1 (smooth). The animationSpeed is how many times per second the field should change randomly. Both can be changed in real time.

turbulenceField(smoothness:animationSpeed:)
Like a noise field, but takes the item's velocity into account.

Think of a field as an infinite grid of CGVectors, with the potential to affect the speed and direction (that is, the velocity) of an item within its borders; at every instant of time the vector applicable to a particular item can be recalculated. You can write a custom field by calling the UIFieldBehavior class method `field(evaluationBlock:)` with a function that takes the item's position, velocity, mass, and charge, along with the animator's elapsed time, and returns a CGVector.

In this (silly) example, we create a delayed drag field: for the first quarter second it does nothing, but then it suddenly switches on and applies the brakes to its items, bringing them to a standstill if they don't already have enough velocity to escape the region's boundaries:

```
let b = UIFieldBehavior.field { beh, pt, v, m, c, t in
    if t > 0.25 {
        return CGVector(-v.dx, -v.dy)
    }
    return CGVector(0,0)
}
```

The evaluation function receives the behavior itself as a parameter, so it can consult the behavior's properties in real time. You can define your own properties by sub-classing UIFieldBehavior. If you're going to do that, you might as well also define your own class factory method to configure and return the custom field. To illustrate, I'll turn the hard-coded `0.25` delay from the previous example into an instance property:

```
class MyDelayedFieldBehavior : UIFieldBehavior {
    var delay = 0.0
    class func dragField(delay del:Double) -> Self {
        let f = self.field { beh, pt, v, m, c, t in
            if t > (beh as! MyDelayedFieldBehavior).delay {
                return CGVector(-v.dx, -v.dy)
            }
            return CGVector(0,0)
        }
        f.delay = del
        return f
    }
}
```

Here's an example of creating and configuring our delayed drag field:

```
let b = MyDelayedFieldBehavior.dragField(delay:0.95)
b.region = UIRegion(size: self.view.bounds.size)
b.position = self.view.bounds.center
b.addItem(v)
self.anim.addBehavior(b)
```

UIPushBehavior

UIPushBehavior applies a force either instantaneously or continuously (mode), the latter constituting an acceleration. How this force affects an object depends in part upon the object's mass. The effect of a push behavior can be toggled with the `active` property; an instantaneous push is repeated each time the `active` property is set to `true`.

To configure a push behavior, set its `pushDirection` or its `angle` and `magnitude`. In addition, a push may be applied at an offset from the center of an item. This will apply an additional angular acceleration. In my earlier example, I could have started the view spinning clockwise by means of its initial push, like this:

```
push.setTargetOffsetFromCenter(
    UIOffset(horizontal:0, vertical:-200), for: self.iv)
```

UICollisionBehavior

UICollisionBehavior watches for collisions either between items belonging to this same behavior or between an item and a boundary (mode). One collision behavior can have multiple items and multiple boundaries. A boundary may be described as a line between two points or as a UIBezierPath, or you can turn the reference view's bounds into boundaries (`setTranslatesReferenceBoundsIntoBoundary(with:)`). Boundaries that you create can have an identifier. The `collisionDelegate` (UICollision-BehaviorDelegate) is called when a collision begins and again when it ends.

How a given collision affects the item(s) involved depends on the physical characteristics of the item(s), which may be configured through a UIDynamicItemBehavior.

A dynamic item, such as a UIView, can have a customized collision boundary, rather than its collision boundary being merely the edges of its frame. You can have a rectangle dictated by the frame, an ellipse dictated by the frame, or a custom shape — a convex counterclockwise simple closed UIBezierPath. The relevant properties, `collisionBoundsType` and (for a custom shape) `collisionBoundingPath`, are read-only, so you will have to subclass, as I did in my earlier example.

UISnapBehavior

UISnapBehavior causes one item to snap to one point as if pulled by a spring. Its `damping` describes how much the item should oscillate as its settles into that point. This is a very simple behavior: the snap occurs immediately when the behavior is added to the animator, and there's no notification when it's over.

The snap behavior's `snapPoint` is a settable property. Having performed a snap, you can subsequently change the `snapPoint` and cause another snap to take place.

UIAttachmentBehavior

UIAttachmentBehavior attaches an item to another item or to a point in the reference view, depending on how you initialize it:

- `init(item:attachedTo:)`
- `init(item:attachedToAnchor:)`

The attachment point is, by default, the item's center; to change that, there's a different pair of initializers:

- `init(item:offsetFromCenter:attachedTo:offsetFromCenter:)`
- `init(item:offsetFromCenter:attachedToAnchor:)`

The attaching medium's physics are governed by the behavior's `length`, `frequency`, and `damping`. If the `frequency` is `0` (the default), the attachment is like a bar; otherwise, and especially if the `damping` is very small, it is like a spring.

If the attachment is to another item, that item might move. If the attachment is to an anchor, you can move the `anchorPoint`. When that happens, this item moves too, in accordance with the physics of the attaching medium. An `anchorPoint` is particularly useful for implementing a draggable view within an animator world, as I'll demonstrate in the next chapter.

There are several more varieties of attachment:

Limit attachment
A limit attachment is created with this class method:

- `limitAttachment(with:offsetFromCenter:attachedTo:offsetFrom-Center:)`

It's like a rope running between two items. Each item can move freely and independently until the `length` is reached, at which point the moving item drags the other item along.

Fixed attachment
A fixed attachment is created with this class method:

- `fixedAttachment(with:attachedTo:attachmentAnchor:)`

It's as if there are two rods; each rod has an item at one end, with the other ends of the rods being welded together at the anchor point. If one item moves, it must remain at a fixed distance from the anchor, and will tend to rotate around it while pulling it along, at the same time making the other item rotate around the anchor.

Pin attachment

A pin attachment is created with this class method:

- `pinAttachment(with:attachedTo:attachmentAnchor:)`

A pin attachment is like a fixed attachment, but instead of the rods being welded together, they are hinged together. Each item is free to rotate around the anchor point, at a fixed distance from it, *independently*, subject to the pin attachment's `frictionTorque` which injects resistance into the hinge.

Sliding attachment

A sliding attachment can involve one or two items, and is created with one of these class methods:

- `slidingAttachment(with:attachmentAnchor:axisOfTranslation:)`
- `slidingAttachment(with:attachedTo:attachmentAnchor:axisOf-Translation:)`

Imagine a channel running through the anchor point, its direction defined by the axis of translation (a CGVector). Then an item is attached to a rod whose other end slots into that channel and is free to slide up and down it, but whose angle relative to the channel is fixed by its initial definition (given the item's position, the anchor's position, and the channel axis) and cannot change.

The channel is infinite by default, but you can add end caps that define the limits of sliding. To do so, you specify the attachment's `attachmentRange`; this is a UIFloatRange, which has a `minimum` and a `maximum`. The anchor point is 0, and you are defining the `minimum` and `maximum` with respect to that; a float range (`-100.0,100.0`) provides freedom of movement up to 100 points away from the initial anchor point. It may take some experimentation to discover whether the end cap along a given direction of the channel is the `minimum` or the `maximum`.

If there is one item, the anchor is fixed. If there are two items, they can slide independently, and the anchor is free to follow along if one of the items pulls it.

Here's an example of a sliding attachment. We start with a black square and a red square, sitting on the same horizontal, and attached to an anchor midway between them:

```
// first view
let v = UIView(frame:CGRect(0,0,50,50))
v.backgroundColor = .black
self.view.addSubview(v)
// second view
let v2 = UIView(frame:CGRect(200,0,50,50))
v2.backgroundColor = .red
self.view.addSubview(v2)
// sliding attachment
```

```
let a = UIAttachmentBehavior.slidingAttachment(with:v,
    attachedTo: v2, attachmentAnchor: CGPoint(125,25),
    axisOfTranslation: CGVector(0,1))
a.attachmentRange = UIFloatRange(minimum: -200, maximum: 200)
self.anim.addBehavior(a)
```

The axis through the anchor point is vertical, and we have permitted a maximum of 200. We now apply a slight vertical downward push to the black square:

```
let p = UIPushBehavior(items: [v], mode: .continuous)
p.pushDirection = CGVector(0,0.05)
self.anim.addBehavior(p)
```

The black square moves slowly vertically downward, with its rod sliding down the channel, until its rod hits the maximum end cap at 200. At that point, the anchor breaks free and begins to move, dragging the red square with it, the two of them continuing downward and slowly rotating round their connection of two rods and the channel.

Motion Effects

A view can respond in real time to the way the user tilts the device. Typically, the view's response will be to shift its position slightly. This is used in various parts of the interface, to give a sense of the interface's being layered (parallax). When an alert is present, if the user tilts the device, the alert shifts its position; the effect is a subtle suggestion that the alert is floating slightly in front of everything else on the screen.

Your own views can behave in the same way. A view will respond to shifts in the position of the device if it has one or more motion effects (UIMotionEffect), provided the user has not turned off motion effects in the device's Accessibility settings. A view's motion effects are managed with methods addMotionEffect(_:) and remove-MotionEffect(_:), and the motionEffects property.

The UIMotionEffect class is abstract. The chief subclass provided is UIInterpolating-MotionEffect. Every UIInterpolatingMotionEffect has a single key path, which uses key–value coding to specify the property of its view that it affects. It also has a type, specifying which axis of the device's tilting (horizontal tilt or vertical tilt) is to affect this property. Finally, it has a maximum and minimum relative value, the furthest distance that the affected property of the view is to be permitted to wander from its actual value as the user tilts the device.

Related motion effects should be combined into a UIMotionEffectGroup (a UIMotionEffect subclass), and the group added to the view:

```
let m1 = UIInterpolatingMotionEffect(
    keyPath:"center.x", type:.tiltAlongHorizontalAxis)
m1.maximumRelativeValue = 10.0
m1.minimumRelativeValue = -10.0
```

```
let m2 = UIInterpolatingMotionEffect(
    keyPath:"center.y", type:.tiltAlongVerticalAxis)
m2.maximumRelativeValue = 10.0
m2.minimumRelativeValue = -10.0
let g = UIMotionEffectGroup()
g.motionEffects = [m1,m2]
v.addMotionEffect(g)
```

You can write your own UIMotionEffect subclass by implementing a single method, keyPathsAndRelativeValues(forViewerOffset:), but this will rarely be necessary.

Animation and Layout

As I've already explained, layout ultimately takes place at the end of a CATransaction, when layoutSubviews is sent down the view hierarchy and autolayout constraints are obeyed. It turns out that the layout performed at this moment can be animated! To make that happen, order an animation of layoutIfNeeded:

```
UIView.animate(withDuration: 0.5) {
    self.layoutIfNeeded()
}
```

That code means: when layout takes place at the end of this transaction, all changes in the size or position of views should be performed, not instantly, but over a period of half a second.

Animating layout can be useful when you're trying to mediate between animation and autolayout. You may not have thought of those two things as needing mediation, but they do: they are, in fact, diametrically opposed to one another. As part of an animation, you may be changing a view's frame (or bounds, or center). You're really not supposed to do that when you're using autolayout. If you do, an animation may not work correctly — or it may appear to work at first, before any layout has happened, but then there can be undesirable side effects when layout *does* happen.

The reason, as I explained in Chapter 1, is that when layout takes place under autolayout, what matters are a view's constraints. If the constraints affecting a view don't resolve to the size and position that the view has at the moment of layout, the view will jump as the constraints are obeyed. That is almost certainly not what you want.

To persuade yourself that this can be a problem, just animate a view's position and then ask for immediate layout, like this:

```
UIView.animate(withDuration: 1) {
    self.v.center.x += 100
} completion: { _ in
    self.v.superview!.setNeedsLayout()
    self.v.superview!.layoutIfNeeded()
}
```

If we're using autolayout, the view slides to the right and then jumps back to the left. This is bad. It's up to us to keep the constraints synchronized with the reality, so that when layout comes along in the natural course of things, our views don't jump into undesirable states.

One option is to revise the violated constraints to match the new reality. If we've planned far ahead, we may have armed ourselves in advance with a reference to those constraints; in that case, our code can now remove and replace them — or, if the only thing that needs changing is the constant value of a constraint, we can change that value in place. Otherwise, discovering what constraints are now violated, and getting a reference to them, is not at all easy.

But there's a better way. Instead of performing the animation first and then revising the constraints, we can change the constraints first and then animate layout. (Again, this assumes that we have a reference to the constraints in question.) If we are animating a view (self.v) 100 points rightward, and if we have a reference (con) to the constraint whose constant positions that view horizontally, we would say:

```
con.constant += 100
UIView.animate(withDuration: 1) {
    self.v.superview!.layoutIfNeeded()
}
```

This technique is not limited to a simple change of constant. You can overhaul the constraints quite dramatically and still animate the resulting change of layout. In this example, I animate a view (self.v) from one side of its superview (self.view) to the other by removing its leading constraint and replacing it with a trailing constraint:

```
let c = self.oldConstraint.constant
NSLayoutConstraint.deactivate([self.oldConstraint])
let newConstraint = v.trailingAnchor.constraint(
    equalTo:self.view.layoutMarginsGuide.trailingAnchor, constant:-c)
NSLayoutConstraint.activate([newConstraint])
UIView.animate(withDuration: 0.4) {
    self.v.superview!.layoutIfNeeded()
}
```

Another possibility is to use a snapshot of the original view (Chapter 1). Add the snapshot temporarily to the interface — without using autolayout, and perhaps hiding the original view — and animate the snapshot:

```
let snap = self.v.snapshotView(afterScreenUpdates:false)!
snap.frame = self.v.frame
self.v.superview!.addSubview(snap)
self.v.isHidden = true
UIView.animate(withDuration: 1) {
    snap.center.x += 100
}
```

That works because the snapshot view is not under the influence of autolayout, so it stays where we put it even if layout takes place. But if we need to remove the snapshot view and reveal the real view, then the real view's constraints will probably still have to be revised.

Yet another approach is to animate the view's transform instead of the view itself:

```
UIView.animate(withDuration: 1) {
    self.v.transform = CGAffineTransform(translationX: 100, y: 0)
}
```

That's extremely robust, but of course it works only if the animation *can* be expressed as a transform, and it leaves open the question of how long we want a transformed view to remain lying around in our interface.

Touches

[Winifred the Woebegone illustrates hit-testing:] Hey nonny nonny, is it you? — Hey nonny nonny nonny no! — Hey nonny nonny, is it you? — Hey nonny nonny nonny no!

—Marshall Barer,
Once Upon a Mattress

A *touch* is an instance of the user putting a finger on the screen. The system and the hardware, working together, know *when* a finger contacts the screen and *where* it is. A finger is fat, but its location is cleverly reduced to a single point.

A UIResponder is a potential recipient of touches. A UIView is a UIResponder and is the *visible* recipient of touches. There are other UIResponder subclasses, but none of them is visible on the screen. The user *sees* a view by virtue of its underlying layer; the user *touches* a view by virtue of the fact that it is a UIResponder.

A touch is represented as an object (a UITouch instance) that is bundled up in an envelope (a UIEvent) that the system delivers to your app. It is then up to your app to deliver the envelope to the appropriate UIView. In the vast majority of cases, this will happen automatically the way you expect, and you will respond to a touch by way of the view in which the touch occurred.

Most built-in interface views deal with these low-level UITouch deliveries for you. They analyze and reduce the touches, and then notify your code at a higher level — you hear about functionality and intention rather than raw touches:

- A UIButton reports that it was tapped.
- A UITextField reports that its text changed.
- A UITableView reports that the user selected a cell.
- A UIScrollView, when dragged, reports that it scrolled; when pinched outward, it reports that it zoomed.

Nevertheless, it is useful to know how to respond to touches yourself, so that you can implement your own touchable views, and so that you understand what Cocoa's built-in views are actually doing.

In this chapter, I'll start by discussing touch detection and response by views (and other UIResponders) at their lowest level. Then I'll proceed to describe the higher-level, more practical mechanism that you'll use most of the time — gesture recognizers, which categorize touches into gesture types for you. Finally, I'll deconstruct the touch-delivery architecture whereby touches are reported to your views in the first place.

Touches nowadays are not the only means by which the user can communicate a gesture to your app. On an iPad, the user might wield an Apple Pencil, or attach a pointing device, such as a trackpad or mouse. This might not call for any special adaptation on your part; I was astounded the first time I hooked up a Bluetooth trackpad to my iPad and discovered that my own apps behaved perfectly.

Still, you might want to take advantage of the special things that a pointing device can do that a finger can't. With a pointing device, the cursor (which Apple calls the *pointer*) can be detected without a click — it can *hover* over a view, purely by virtue of its position on the screen. The user can make a scroll gesture, using a mouse scroll wheel or a two-finger swipe on a trackpad. A mouse can have multiple buttons; on a trackpad, the user can perform a two-finger pinch or rotation gesture. I'll make passing reference to these facilities in this chapter, and I'll say more in Chapter 10.

Touch Events and Views

Imagine a screen that the user is not touching at all: the screen is "finger-free." Now the user touches the screen with one or more fingers. From that moment until the time the screen is once again finger-free, all touches and finger movements together constitute what Apple calls a single *multitouch sequence*.

The system reports to your app, during a given multitouch sequence, every change in finger configuration, so that your app can figure out what the user is doing. Every such report is a UIEvent. In fact, every report having to do with the same multitouch sequence is *the same UIEvent instance*, arriving repeatedly, each time there's a change in finger configuration.

Every UIEvent reporting a change in the user's finger configuration contains one or more UITouch objects. Each UITouch object corresponds to a single finger; conversely, every finger touching the screen is represented in the UIEvent by a UITouch object. Once a UITouch instance has been created to represent a finger that has touched the screen, *the same UITouch instance* is used to represent that finger throughout this multitouch sequence until the finger leaves the screen.

Now, it might sound as if the system, during a multitouch sequence, constantly has to bombard the app with huge numbers of reports. But that's not really true. The system needs to report only *changes* in the finger configuration. For a given UITouch object (representing, remember, a specific finger), only four things can happen. These are called *touch phases*, and are described by a UITouch instance's phase property (UITouch.Phase):

.began
> The finger touched the screen for the first time; this UITouch instance has just been created. This is always the first phase, and arrives only once.

.moved
> The finger moved upon the screen.

.stationary
> The finger remained on the screen without moving. Why is it necessary to report this? Well, remember, once a UITouch instance has been created, it must be present every time the UIEvent for this multitouch sequence arrives. So if the UIEvent arrives because something *else* happened (e.g., a new finger touched the screen), the UIEvent must report what *this* finger has been doing, even if it has been doing nothing.

.ended
> The finger left the screen. Like .began, this phase arrives only once. The UITouch instance will now be destroyed and will no longer appear in UIEvents for this multitouch sequence.

Those four phases are sufficient to describe everything that a finger can do. Actually, there is one more possible phase:

.cancelled
> The system has aborted this multitouch sequence because something interrupted it. What might interrupt a multitouch sequence? There are many possibilities. Perhaps the user clicked the Home button or the screen lock button in the middle of the sequence. A local notification alert may have appeared (Chapter 14); on an iPhone, a call may have come in. And as we shall see, a gesture recognizer recognizing its gesture may also trigger touch cancellation. If you're dealing with touches yourself, you cannot afford to ignore touch cancellations; they are your opportunity to get things into a coherent state when the sequence is interrupted.

When a UITouch first appears (.began), your app works out which UIView it is associated with. (I'll give full details, later in this chapter, as to how it does that.) This view is then set as the touch's view property, and *remains* so; from then on, this UITouch is *always* associated with this view (until that finger leaves the screen).

The UITouches that constitute a UIEvent might be associated with different views. Accordingly, one and the same UIEvent is distributed to *all the views of all the UITouches it contains*. Conversely, if a view is sent a UIEvent, it's because that UIEvent contains at least one UITouch whose `view` is this view.

If every UITouch in a UIEvent associated with a certain UIView has the phase `.stationary`, that UIEvent is *not* sent to that UIView. There's no point, because as far as that view is concerned, nothing happened.

 Do not retain a reference to a UITouch or UIEvent object over time; it is mutable and doesn't belong to you. If you want to save touch information, extract and save the information, not the touch itself.

Receiving Touches

A UIResponder, and therefore a UIView, has four *touch methods* corresponding to the four UITouch phases that require UIEvent delivery. A UIEvent is delivered to a view by calling one of these methods:

`touchesBegan(_:with:)`
> A finger touched the screen, creating a UITouch.

`touchesMoved(_:with:)`
> A finger previously reported to this view with `touchesBegan(_:with:)` has moved. (On a device with 3D touch, "moved" might mean a change of pressure rather than location.)

`touchesEnded(_:with:)`
> A finger previously reported to this view with `touchesBegan(_:with:)` has left the screen.

`touchesCancelled(_:with:)`
> We are bailing out on a finger previously reported to this view with `touchesBegan(_:with:)`.

The parameters of the touch methods are:

The relevant touches
> These are the event's touches whose phase corresponds to the name of the method and (normally) whose `view` is this view. They arrive as a Set. If there is only one touch in the set, or if any touch in the set will do, you can retrieve it with `first` (a set is unordered, so *which* element is `first` is arbitrary).

The event
> This is the UIEvent instance. It contains its touches as a Set, which you can retrieve with the `allTouches` message. This means *all* the event's touches,

including but not necessarily limited to those in the first parameter; there might be touches in a different phase or intended for some other view. You can call touches(for:) to ask for the set of touches associated with a particular view or window.

When we say that a certain view *is receiving a touch*, that is a shorthand expression meaning that it is being sent a UIEvent containing this UITouch, over and over, by calling one of its touch methods, corresponding to the phase this touch is in, from the time the touch is created until the time it is destroyed.

A UITouch has some useful methods and properties:

location(in:), previousLocation(in:)
: The current and previous location of this touch with respect to the coordinate system of a given view. The view you'll be interested in will often be self or self.superview; supply nil to get the location with respect to the window. The previous location will be of interest only if the phase is .moved.

timestamp
: When the touch last changed. A touch is timestamped when it is created (.began) and each time it moves (.moved). There can be a delay between the occurrence of a physical touch and the delivery of the corresponding UITouch; to learn about the timing of touches, consult the timestamp, not the clock.

tapCount
: If two touches are in roughly the same place in quick succession, and the first one is brief, the second one may be characterized as a repeat of the first. They are different touch objects, but the second will be assigned a tapCount one larger than the previous one. The default is 1, so if a touch's tapCount is 3, then this is the third tap in quick succession in roughly the same spot.

view
: The view with which this touch is associated.

majorRadius, majorRadiusTolerance
: Respectively, the radius of the touch (approximately half its size) and the uncertainty of that measurement, in points.

A UITouch carries some additional information that may be useful if the touch arrived through an Apple Pencil rather than a finger, such as how the pencil is oriented.

Here are some additional UIEvent properties:

type

> For touches with a finger or clicks with a pointing device, this will be UIEvent.EventType.touches. A pointing device might alternatively generate a .hover event, a .scroll event, or a .transform event (signifying a rotation), possibly with no associated touches.

timestamp

> When the event occurred.

You can reduce the latency between the user's touches and your app's rendering to the screen. On certain devices, the touch detection rate is doubled or even quadrupled, and you can ask for the extra touches. On all devices, a few future touches may be predicted, and you can ask for these. Such features would be useful particularly in a drawing app.

Restricting Touches

A number of UIView properties restrict the delivery of touches to particular views:

isUserInteractionEnabled

> If set to false, this view (along with its subviews) is excluded from receiving touches. Touches on this view or one of its subviews fall through to a view behind it.

alpha

> If set to 0.0 (or extremely close to it), this view (along with its subviews) is excluded from receiving touches. Touches on this view or one of its subviews fall through to a view behind it.

isHidden

> If set to true, this view (along with its subviews) is excluded from receiving touches. This makes sense, since from the user's standpoint, the view and its subviews are not even present.

isMultipleTouchEnabled

> If set to false, this view never receives more than one touch simultaneously; once it receives a touch, it doesn't receive any other touches until the first touch has ended.

isExclusiveTouch

> A view whose isExclusiveTouch is true receives a touch only if no other views in the same window have touches associated with them; conversely, once a view whose isExclusiveTouch is true has received a touch, then while that touch exists, no other view in the same window receives any touches. (This is the only one of these properties that can't be set in the nib editor.)

A view can receive touches and yet be completely invisible because its background color is `.clear`. So this is an *invisible touchable view*. You can configure an invisible touchable view so that touches on this view do *not* fall through to the views behind it; that can be a useful trick. Later I'll give an example of an invisible touchable view that lets some touches fall through but not others.

If a superview's `clipsToBounds` is `false`, then a subview that is outside the bounds of the superview is *visible*. But any part of a subview that is outside the bounds of its superview *cannot be touched*. So you can end up unintentionally with a view that is visible but partially or totally untouchable. That's very confusing to your users, and might be confusing to you! Getting yourself into this situation, and then wondering why your view isn't responding normally to touches, is a common beginner mistake. This behavior has to do with how hit-testing works; later in this chapter, I'll explain that, along with a way of changing it.

Interpreting Touches

Once you receive calls in your touch methods, what do those touches *mean?* Sometimes they don't mean anything special; the raw touches are all you need. In a drawing program, you might want to know quite literally what the user's finger is doing and no more, and the touch methods will tell you. Most of the time, however, the user's touches *do* have meaning, and you will want to *interpret* those touches. What is the user doing? What are the user's intentions?

Thanks to gesture recognizers (discussed later in this chapter), in most cases you won't have to interpret touches at all; you'll let a gesture recognizer do most of that work. Even so, it is beneficial to be conversant with the nature of touch interpretation; this will help you use, subclass, and create gesture recognizers. Furthermore, not every touch sequence can be codified through a gesture recognizer; sometimes, directly interpreting touches is the best approach.

To figure out what's going on as touches are received by a view, your code must essentially function as a kind of state machine. You'll receive various touch method calls, and your response will depend in part upon what happened previously, so you'll have to record somehow, probably in instance properties, whatever information you'll need subsequently in order to decide what to do when the *next* touch method is called. Such an architecture can make writing and maintaining touch-analysis code quite tricky.

To illustrate the business of interpreting touches, we'll start with a view that can be dragged with the user's finger. For simplicity, I'll assume that this view receives only a single touch at a time. (This assumption is easy to enforce by setting the view's `isMultipleTouchEnabled` to `false`, which is the default.)

The trick to making a view follow the user's finger is to realize that a view is positioned by its center, which is in superview coordinates, but the user's finger might not be at the center of the view. So at every stage of the drag we must change the view's center by the change in the user's finger position in superview coordinates:

```
override func touchesMoved(_ touches: Set<UITouch>, with e: UIEvent?) {
    let t = touches.first!
    let loc = t.location(in:self.superview)
    let oldP = t.previousLocation(in:self.superview)
    let deltaX = loc.x - oldP.x
    let deltaY = loc.y - oldP.y
    var c = self.center
    c.x += deltaX
    c.y += deltaY
    self.center = c
}
```

Next, let's add a restriction that the view can be dragged only vertically or horizontally. All we have to do is hold one coordinate steady; but which coordinate? Everything seems to depend on what the user does initially. So we'll do a one-time test the first time we receive touchesMoved(_:with:). Now we're maintaining two Bool state properties, self.decided and self.horiz:

```
override func touchesBegan(_ touches: Set<UITouch>, with e: UIEvent?) {
    self.decided = false
}
override func touchesMoved(_ touches: Set<UITouch>, with e: UIEvent?) {
    let t = touches.first!
    if !self.decided {
        self.decided = true
        let then = t.previousLocation(in:self)
        let now = t.location(in:self)
        let deltaX = abs(then.x - now.x)
        let deltaY = abs(then.y - now.y)
        self.horiz = deltaX >= deltaY
    }
    let loc = t.location(in:self.superview)
    let oldP = t.previousLocation(in:self.superview)
    let deltaX = loc.x - oldP.x
    let deltaY = loc.y - oldP.y
    var c = self.center
    if self.horiz {
        c.x += deltaX
    } else {
        c.y += deltaY
    }
    self.center = c
}
```

Look at how things are trending. We are maintaining multiple state properties, which we are managing across multiple methods, and our touch method implementation is divided into branches that depend on the state of our state machine. Our state machine is very simple, but already our code is becoming difficult to read and to maintain — and things will only become more messy as we try to make our view's behavior more sophisticated.

Another area in which manual touch handling can rapidly prove overwhelming is when it comes to distinguishing between different gestures that the user might perform on a view. Imagine a view that distinguishes between a finger tapping briefly and a finger remaining down for a longer time. We can't know how long a tap is until it's over, so we must wait until then before deciding; once again, this requires maintaining state in a property (self.time):

```
override func touchesBegan(_ touches: Set<UITouch>, with e: UIEvent?) {
    self.time = touches.first!.timestamp
}
override func touchesEnded(_ touches: Set<UITouch>, with e: UIEvent?) {
    let diff = e!.timestamp - self.time
    if (diff < 0.4) {
        print("short")
    } else {
        print("long")
    }
}
```

A similar challenge is distinguishing between a single tap and a double tap. The UITouch tapCount property already makes this distinction, but that, by itself, is not enough to help us react differently to the two. Having received a tap whose tapCount is 1, we must wait long enough (using delayed performance) to give a second tap a chance to arrive. This is unfortunate, because it means that if the user intends a single tap, some time will elapse before anything happens in response to it. But there's nothing we can readily do about that.

Distributing our various tasks correctly is tricky. We *know* when we have a double tap as early as touchesBegan(_:with:), but we *respond* to the double tap in touches-Ended(_:with:). Therefore, we use a property (self.single) to communicate between the two. We don't start our delayed response to a single tap until touches-Ended(_:with:), because what matters is the time between the taps as a whole, not between the starts of the taps:

```
override func touchesBegan(_ touches: Set<UITouch>, with e: UIEvent?) {
    let ct = touches.first!.tapCount
    switch ct {
    case 2:
        self.single = false
    default: break
    }
}
override func touchesEnded(_ touches: Set<UITouch>, with e: UIEvent?) {
    let ct = touches.first!.tapCount
```

```
        switch ct {
        case 1:
            self.single = true
            delay(0.3) {
                if self.single { // no second tap intervened
                    print("single tap")
                }
            }
        case 2:
            print("double tap")
        default: break
        }
    }
```

As if that code weren't confusing enough, let's now consider combining our detection for a single or double tap with our earlier code for dragging a view horizontally or vertically. This is to be a view that can detect four kinds of gesture: a single tap, a double tap, a horizontal drag, and a vertical drag. We must include the code for all possibilities and make sure they don't interfere with each other. The result is horrifying — a forced join between two already complicated sets of code, along with an additional pair of state properties (self.drag, self.decidedTapOrDrag) to track the decision between the tap gestures on the one hand and the drag gestures on the other:

```
override func touchesBegan(_ touches: Set<UITouch>, with e: UIEvent?) {
    // be undecided
    self.decidedTapOrDrag = false
    // prepare for a tap
    let ct = touches.first!.tapCount
    switch ct {
    case 2:
        self.single = false
        self.decidedTapOrDrag = true
        self.drag = false
        return
    default: break
    }
    // prepare for a drag
    self.decidedDirection = false
}
override func touchesMoved(_ touches: Set<UITouch>, with e: UIEvent?) {
    if self.decidedTapOrDrag && !self.drag {return}
    self.superview!.bringSubviewToFront(self)
    let t = touches.first!
    self.decidedTapOrDrag = true
    self.drag = true
    if !self.decidedDirection {
        self.decidedDirection = true
        let then = t.previousLocation(in:self)
        let now = t.location(in:self)
        let deltaX = abs(then.x - now.x)
        let deltaY = abs(then.y - now.y)
```

```
            self.horiz = deltaX >= deltaY
        }
        let loc = t.location(in:self.superview)
        let oldP = t.previousLocation(in:self.superview)
        let deltaX = loc.x - oldP.x
        let deltaY = loc.y - oldP.y
        var c = self.center
        if self.horiz {
            c.x += deltaX
        } else {
            c.y += deltaY
        }
        self.center = c
    }
    override func touchesEnded(_ touches: Set<UITouch>, with e: UIEvent?) {
        if !self.decidedTapOrDrag || !self.drag {
            // end for a tap
            let ct = touches.first!.tapCount
            switch ct {
            case 1:
                self.single = true
                delay(0.3) {
                    if self.single {
                        print("single tap")
                    }
                }
            case 2:
                print("double tap")
            default: break
            }
        }
    }
}
```

That code seems to work, but it's hard to say whether it covers all possibilities coherently; it's barely legible and the logic borders on the mysterious. This is the kind of situation for which gesture recognizers were devised.

Gesture Recognizers

Writing and maintaining a state machine that interprets touches across a combination of three or four touch methods is hard enough when a view confines itself to expecting only one kind of gesture, such as dragging. It becomes even more involved when a view wants to accept and respond differently to different kinds of gesture. Furthermore, many types of gesture are conventional and standard; it seems insane to require every developer, independently, to devise a way of responding to what is, in effect, a universal vocabulary.

The solution is gesture recognizers, which standardize common gestures and allow the code for different gestures to be separated and encapsulated into different objects.

And thanks to gesture recognizers, it is unnecessary to subclass UIView merely in order to implement touch interpretation.

Gesture Recognizer Classes

A *gesture recognizer* (a subclass of UIGestureRecognizer) is an object whose job is to detect that a multitouch sequence equates to one particular type of gesture. It is attached to a UIView. The gesture recognizers attached to a view are its `gesture-Recognizers`; this property is settable (and might be `nil`). You can also manage gesture recognizers individually with these methods:

- `addGestureRecognizer(_:)`
- `removeGestureRecognizer(_:)`

A UIGestureRecognizer implements the four touch methods, but it is not a responder (a UIResponder), so it does not participate in the responder chain. If, however, a new touch is going to be delivered to a view, it is also associated with and delivered to that view's gesture recognizers if it has any, *and* to that view's *superview's* gesture recognizers if *it* has any, and so on up the view hierarchy. So the place of a gesture recognizer in the view hierarchy matters, even though it isn't part of the responder chain.

UITouch and UIEvent provide complementary ways of learning how touches and gesture recognizers are associated:

- UITouch's `gestureRecognizers` lists the gesture recognizers that are currently handling this touch.
- UIEvent's `touches(for:)` can take a gesture recognizer parameter; it then lists the touches that are currently being handled by that gesture recognizer.

Each gesture recognizer maintains its own state as touch events arrive, building up evidence as to what kind of gesture this is. When one of them decides that it has recognized its own particular type of gesture, it emits either a single message (a finger has tapped) or a series of messages (a finger is moving); the distinction here is between a *discrete* and a *continuous* gesture.

What message a gesture recognizer emits, and what object it sends that message to, is configured through a target–action dispatch table attached to the gesture recognizer. A gesture recognizer is rather like a UIControl in this regard; indeed, one might say that a gesture recognizer simplifies the touch handling of *any* view to be like that of a control. The difference is that one control may report several different control events, whereas each gesture recognizer reports only one gesture type, with different gestures being reported by different gesture recognizers.

UIGestureRecognizer itself is abstract, providing methods and properties to its subclasses. Among these are:

`init(target:action:)`

The designated initializer. The gesture recognizer will signal that something has happened by sending the action message to the target. Further target–action pairs may be added with `addTarget(_:action:)` and removed with `removeTarget(_:action:)`.

Two forms of `action:` selector are possible: either there is no parameter, or there is a single parameter which will be the gesture recognizer. Most commonly, you'll use the second form, so that the target can identify, query, and communicate with the gesture recognizer.

`numberOfTouches`

How many touches the gesture recognizer is tracking. In general, this is the number of fingers the user must employ to make the gesture that this gesture recognizer is interested in. The touches themselves are inaccessible by way of the gesture recognizer.

`location(ofTouch:in:)`

The first parameter is an index number (smaller than `numberOfTouches`) identifying the touch. The second parameter is the view whose coordinate system you want to use.

`isEnabled`

A convenient way to turn a gesture recognizer off without having to remove it from its view.

`state, view`

I'll discuss state later on. The `view` is the view to which this gesture recognizer is attached; it is an Optional.

`allowedTouchTypes`

An array of NSNumbers representing raw values of the UITouch.TouchType enum, designating the types of input device you're willing to handle:

- `.direct`: A finger.
- `.pencil`: An Apple pencil.
- `.indirectPointer`: A pointing device, such as a mouse or trackpad.
- `.indirect`: Not a finger, but not a mouse or trackpad pointer either; for instance, a scroll wheel.

The default is `[0,1,2,3]` — that is, all of them.

Built-in UIGestureRecognizer subclasses are provided for six common gesture types: tap, pinch (inward or outward), pan (drag), swipe, rotate, and long press. Each embodies properties and methods likely to be needed for each type of gesture, either in order to *configure* the gesture recognizer beforehand or in order to query it as to the *status* of an ongoing gesture:

UITapGestureRecognizer (discrete)
> Configuration: `numberOfTapsRequired`, `numberOfTouchesRequired` ("touches" means simultaneous fingers).

UIPinchGestureRecognizer (continuous)
> Two fingers moving toward or away from each other. Status: `scale`, `velocity`.

UIRotationGestureRecognizer (continuous)
> Two fingers moving round a common center. Status: `rotation`, `velocity`.

UISwipeGestureRecognizer (discrete)
> A straight-line movement in one of the four cardinal directions. Configuration: `direction` (meaning permitted directions, a bitmask), `numberOfTouches-Required`.

UIPanGestureRecognizer (continuous)
> Dragging. Configuration: `minimumNumberOfTouches`, `maximumNumberOfTouches`. Status: `translation(in:)`, `setTranslation(_:in:)`, `velocity(in:)`; the coordinate system of the specified view is used.
>
> On an iPad, UIPanGestureRecognizer is also the locus of mouse and trackpad scroll gesture detection; to receive scroll gestures, set the `allowedScrollTypes-Mask` to `.all`.

UIScreenEdgePanGestureRecognizer
> A UIPanGestureRecognizer subclass. It recognizes a pan gesture that starts at an edge of the screen. It adds a configuration property, `edges`, a UIRectEdge; despite the name (and the documentation), this must be set to a single edge.

UILongPressGestureRecognizer (continuous)
> Configuration: `numberOfTapsRequired`, `numberOfTouchesRequired`, `minimum-PressDuration`, `allowableMovement`. The `numberOfTapsRequired` is the count of taps *before* the tap that stays down, so it can be 0 (the default). The `allowable-Movement` setting lets you compensate for the fact that the user's finger is unlikely to remain steady during an extended press: we need to provide some limit before deciding that this gesture is, say, a drag, and not a long press after all. On the other hand, once the long press is recognized, the finger is permitted to drag as part of the long press gesture.

On an iPad, an additional gesture recognizer subclass, UIHoverGestureRecognizer, can detect a mouse or trackpad cursor entering and leaving a view.

UIGestureRecognizer also provides a location(in:) method. This is a single point, even if there are multiple touches. The subclasses implement this variously. Typically, the location is where the touch is if there's a single touch, but it's a sort of midpoint ("centroid") if there are multiple touches.

For a continuous gesture like dragging, we need to know both when the gesture is in progress and when the gesture ends. This brings us to the subject of a gesture recognizer's state.

Gesture Recognizer States

A gesture recognizer implements a notion of *states* (the state property, UIGesture-Recognizer.State); it passes through these states in a definite progression. The gesture recognizer remains in the .possible state until it can make a decision one way or the other as to whether this is in fact the correct gesture. The documentation neatly lays out the possible progressions:

Wrong gesture
.possible → .failed. No action message is sent.

Discrete gesture (like a tap), recognized
.possible → .ended. One action message is sent, when the state changes to .ended.

Continuous gesture (like a drag), recognized
.possible → .began → .changed (repeatedly) → .ended. Action messages are sent once for .began, as many times as necessary for .changed, and once for .ended.

Continuous gesture, recognized but later cancelled
.possible → .began → .changed (repeatedly) → .cancelled. Action messages are sent once for .began, as many times as necessary for .changed, and once for .cancelled.

The same action message arrives at the same target every time, so the action method must differentiate by asking about the gesture recognizer's state. The usual implementation involves a switch statement.

Gesture Recognizer Examples

The simplest use of a gesture recognizer is to implement a view that responds to a single tap, or a view that responds to a double tap. Here's code (probably from our view controller's viewDidLoad) that implements a view (self.v) that responds to a single tap by calling our singleTap method:

```
let t = UITapGestureRecognizer(target:self, action:#selector(singleTap))
self.v.addGestureRecognizer(t)
```

And here's code that implements a view (self.v2) that responds to a double tap by calling our doubleTap method:

```
let t = UITapGestureRecognizer(target:self, action:#selector(doubleTap))
t.numberOfTapsRequired = 2
self.v2.addGestureRecognizer(t)
```

Next, let's use a UIPanGestureRecognizer for one of its most common purposes — a view that lets itself be dragged around in any direction by a single finger. Our maintenance of state is greatly simplified, because a UIPanGestureRecognizer maintains a delta (translation) for us. This delta, available using translation(in:), is reckoned from the touch's initial position. We don't even need to record the view's original center, because we can call setTranslation(_:in:) to reset the UIPanGesture-Recognizer's delta every time:

```
func viewDidLoad {
    super.viewDidLoad()
    let p = UIPanGestureRecognizer(target:self, action:#selector(dragging))
    self.v.addGestureRecognizer(p)
}
@objc func dragging(_ p : UIPanGestureRecognizer) {
    let v = p.view!
    switch p.state {
    case .began, .changed:
        let delta = p.translation(in:v.superview)
        var c = v.center
        c.x += delta.x; c.y += delta.y
        v.center = c
        p.setTranslation(.zero, in: v.superview)
    default: break
    }
}
```

To illustrate the use of a UIPanGestureRecognizer's velocity(in:), let's imagine a view that the user can drag, but which then springs back to where it was. We can express "springs back" with a spring animation (Chapter 4). We'll just add an .ended case to our dragging(_:) method (dest is the original center of our view v):

```
case .ended, .cancelled:
    let anim = UIViewPropertyAnimator(
        duration: 0.4,
        timingParameters: UISpringTimingParameters(
            dampingRatio: 0.6,
            initialVelocity: .zero))
    anim.addAnimations {
        v.center = dest
    }
    anim.startAnimation()
```

That's good, but it would be more realistic if the view had some momentum at the moment the user lets go of it. If the user drags the view quickly away from its home and releases it, the view should keep moving a little in the same direction before springing back into place. That's what the spring animation's `initialVelocity:` parameter is for! We can easily find out what the view's velocity is, at the moment the user releases it, by asking the gesture recognizer:

```
let vel = p.velocity(in: v.superview!)
```

Unfortunately, we cannot use this value directly as the spring animation's `initial-Velocity`; there's a type impedance mismatch. The view's velocity is expressed as a CGPoint measured in points per second; but the spring's `initialVelocity` is expressed as a CGVector measured as a proportion of the distance to be traveled over the course of the animation. Fortunately, the conversion is easy:

```
case .ended, .cancelled:
    let vel = p.velocity(in: v.superview!)
    let c = v.center
    let distx = abs(c.x - dest.x)
    let disty = abs(c.y - dest.y)
    let anim = UIViewPropertyAnimator(
        duration: 0.4,
        timingParameters: UISpringTimingParameters(
            dampingRatio: 0.6,
            initialVelocity: CGVector(vel.x/distx, vel.y/disty)))
    anim.addAnimations {
        v.center = dest
    }
    anim.startAnimation()
```

A pan gesture recognizer can be used also to make a view draggable under the influence of a UIDynamicAnimator (Chapter 4). The strategy here is that the view is attached to one or more anchor points through a UIAttachmentBehavior; as the user drags, we move the anchor point(s), and the view follows. In this example, I set up the whole UIKit dynamics "stack" of objects as the gesture begins, anchoring the view at the point where the touch is; then I move the anchor point to stay with the touch. Instance properties `self.anim` and `self.att` store the UIDynamicAnimator and the UIAttachmentBehavior, respectively; `self.view` is our view's superview, and is the animator's reference view:

```
@objc func dragging(_ p: UIPanGestureRecognizer) {
    switch p.state {
    case .began:
        self.anim = UIDynamicAnimator(referenceView:self.view)
        let loc = p.location(ofTouch:0, in:p.view)
        let cen = p.view!.bounds.center
        let off = UIOffset(horizontal: loc.x-cen.x, vertical: loc.y-cen.y)
        let anchor = p.location(ofTouch:0, in:self.view)
        let att = UIAttachmentBehavior(item:p.view!,
```

```
                offsetFromCenter:off, attachedToAnchor:anchor)
        self.anim.addBehavior(att)
        self.att = att
    case .changed:
        self.att.anchorPoint = p.location(ofTouch:0, in: self.view)
    default:
        self.anim = nil
    }
}
```

The outcome is that the view both moves and rotates in response to dragging, like a plate being pulled about on a table by a single finger.

By adding behaviors to the dynamic animator, we can limit further what the view is permitted to do as it is being dragged by its anchor. Imagine a view that can be lifted vertically and dropped, but cannot be moved horizontally. As I demonstrated earlier, you can prevent horizontal dragging through the implementation of your response to touch events (and later in this chapter, I'll show how to do this by subclassing UIPan-GestureRecognizer). But the same sort of limitation can be imposed by way of the underlying physics of the world in which the view exists, perhaps with a sliding attachment.

Gesture Recognizer Conflicts

A view can have more than one gesture recognizer associated with it. This isn't a matter merely of multiple recognizers attached to a single view; as I have said, if a view is touched, not only its own gesture recognizers but also any gesture recognizers attached to views further up the view hierarchy are in play simultaneously. I like to think of a view as surrounded by a *swarm* of gesture recognizers — its own, and those of its superview, and so on. (In reality, it is a *touch* that has a swarm of gesture recognizers; that's why a UITouch has a `gestureRecognizers` property, in the plural.)

The superview gesture recognizer swarm comes as a surprise to beginners, but it makes sense, because without it, certain gestures would be impossible. Imagine a pair of views, each of which the user can tap individually, but which the user can also touch simultaneously (one finger on each view) to rotate them together around their mutual centroid. Neither view can detect the rotation *qua* rotation, because neither view receives both touches; only the superview can detect it, so the fact that the views themselves respond to touches must not prevent the superview's gesture recognizer from operating.

The question naturally arises, then, of what happens when multiple gesture recognizers are in play. There is a conflict between these gesture recognizers, each trying to recognize the current multitouch sequence as its own appropriate gesture. How will it be resolved?

The rule is simple. In general, by default, once a gesture recognizer succeeds in recognizing its gesture, any *other* gesture recognizers associated with its touches are *forced into the* .failed *state*, and whatever touches were associated with those gesture recognizers are no longer sent to them; in effect, the first gesture recognizer in a swarm that recognizes its gesture owns the gesture (and its touches) from then on.

In many cases, this "first past the post" behavior, on its own, will yield exactly the desired behavior. We can add both our single tap UITapGestureRecognizer and our UIPanGestureRecognizer to a view and everything will just work; dragging works, and single tap works:

```
let t = UITapGestureRecognizer(target:self, action:#selector(singleTap))
self.v.addGestureRecognizer(t)
let p = UIPanGestureRecognizer(target: self, action: #selector(dragging))
self.v.addGestureRecognizer(p)
```

You can take a hand in how conflicts are resolved, and sometimes you will need to do so. What happens if we add a double tap gesture recognizer and a single tap gesture recognizer to the same view? Double tap works, but without preventing the single tap from working: on a double tap, *both* the single tap action method *and* the double tap action method are called.

If that isn't what we want, we don't have to use delayed performance, as we did earlier. Instead, we can create a *dependency* between one gesture recognizer and another. One way to do that is with the UIGestureRecognizer require(toFail:) method. This method is rather badly named; it doesn't mean "force this other recognizer to fail," but rather, "you can't succeed unless this other recognizer has failed." It tells its recipient to suspend judgment about whether this is its gesture until some *other* gesture recognizer (the parameter) has had a chance to decide whether this is *its* gesture. In the case of the single tap gesture recognizer and the double tap gesture recognizer, we want the single tap gesture to suspend judgment until the double tap gesture recognizer can decide whether this is a double tap:

```
let t2 = UITapGestureRecognizer(target:self, action:#selector(doubleTap))
t2.numberOfTapsRequired = 2
self.v.addGestureRecognizer(t2)
let t1 = UITapGestureRecognizer(target:self, action:#selector(singleTap))
t1.require(toFail:t2) // *
self.v.addGestureRecognizer(t1)
```

Another conflict that can arise is between a gesture recognizer and a view that already knows how to respond to the same gesture, such as a UIControl. This problem pops up particularly when the gesture recognizer belongs to the UIControl's superview. The UIControl's mere presence does not "block" the superview's gesture recognizer from recognizing a gesture on the UIControl, even if it is a UIControl that responds autonomously to touches. Your window's root view might have a UITapGesture-Recognizer attached to it (perhaps because you want to be able to recognize taps on the background); if there is also a UIButton within that view, how is the tap gesture recognizer to ignore a tap on the button?

The UIView instance method `gestureRecognizerShouldBegin(_:)` solves the problem. It is called automatically; to modify its behavior, use a custom UIView subclass and override it. Its parameter is a gesture recognizer belonging to this view or to a view further up the view hierarchy. That gesture recognizer has recognized its gesture as taking place in this view; but by returning `false`, the view can tell the gesture recognizer to bow out and do nothing, not sending any action messages, and permitting this view to respond to the touch as if the gesture recognizer weren't there.

For example, a UIButton could return `false` for a single tap UITapGesture-Recognizer; a single tap on the button would then trigger the button's action message and not the gesture recognizer's action message. And in fact a UIButton, by default, *does* return `false` for a single tap UITapGestureRecognizer whose view is not the UIButton itself.

Other built-in controls may also implement `gestureRecognizerShouldBegin(_:)` in such a way as to prevent accidental interaction with a gesture recognizer; the documentation says that a UISlider implements it in such a way that a UISwipeGesture-Recognizer won't prevent the user from sliding the "thumb," and there may be other cases that aren't documented explicitly. Naturally, you can take advantage of this feature in your own UIView subclasses as well.

There are additional ways of resolving possible gesture recognizer conflicts through a gesture recognizer's delegate or with a gesture recognizer subclass.

Gesture Recognizer Delegate

A gesture recognizer can have a delegate (UIGestureRecognizerDelegate), which can perform two types of task: blocking operation and mediating conflict.

These delegate methods can *block a gesture recognizer's operation*:

`gestureRecognizer(_:shouldReceive:)`
    The second parameter can be a UITouch or a UIEvent:

    Second parameter is a UITouch
        Sent to the delegate before a touch is sent to the gesture recognizer's `touches-Began(_:with:)` method; return `false` to prevent that touch from ever being sent to the gesture recognizer.

    Second parameter is a UIEvent
        Sent to the delegate before any other message arrives at the gesture recognizer; return `false` to block that event or any of its touches from being considered. This is a generalized version of the preceding delegate method, new

in iOS 13.4, and is probably to be preferred. You can distinguish the event's type (`.touches`, `.hover`, `.scroll`, or `.transform`); you can determine whether there are any touches (`event.allTouches?.count ?? 0`); and if there are touches, you can examine them.

`gestureRecognizerShouldBegin(_:)`

Sent to the delegate before the gesture recognizer passes out of the `.possible` state; return `false` to force the gesture recognizer to proceed to the `.failed` state. This happens *after* `gestureRecognizerShouldBegin(_:)` has been sent to the view in which the touch took place; that view must not have returned `false`, or we wouldn't have reached this stage.

These delegate methods can *mediate gesture recognition conflict*:

`gestureRecognizer(_:shouldRecognizeSimultaneouslyWith:)`

Sent when a gesture recognizer, having recognized its gesture, is about to force another gesture recognizer to fail, to the delegates of *both* gesture recognizers. Return `true` to prevent that failure, allowing both gesture recognizers to operate simultaneously.

`gestureRecognizer(_:shouldRequireFailureOf:)`
`gestureRecognizer(_:shouldBeRequiredToFailBy:)`

Sent very early in the life of a gesture, when all gesture recognizers in a view's swarm are still in the `.possible` state, to the delegates of *all* of them, pairing the gesture recognizer whose delegate this is with each of the other gesture recognizers in the swarm. Return `true` to prioritize between this pair of gesture recognizers, saying that one cannot succeed until the other has first failed. In essence, these delegate methods turn the decision made once and permanently in `require(toFail:)` into a live decision that can be made freshly every time a gesture occurs.

As an example, we will use delegate messages to combine a UILongPressGesture-Recognizer and a UIPanGestureRecognizer. The user must perform a tap-and-a-half (tap, then tap and hold) to "get the view's attention," which we will indicate by a pulsing animation on the view; then and only then, the user can drag the view.

The UIPanGestureRecognizer's action method will take care of the drag, using the code shown earlier in this chapter. The UILongPressGestureRecognizer's action method will take care of starting and stopping the animation:

```
@objc func longPress(_ lp:UILongPressGestureRecognizer) {
    switch lp.state {
    case .began:
        let anim = CABasicAnimation(keyPath: #keyPath(CALayer.transform))
        anim.toValue = CATransform3DMakeScale(1.1, 1.1, 1)
        anim.fromValue = CATransform3DIdentity
```

```
        anim.repeatCount = .greatestFiniteMagnitude
        anim.autoreverses = true
        lp.view!.layer.add(anim, forKey:nil)
    case .ended, .cancelled:
        lp.view!.layer.removeAllAnimations()
    default: break
    }
}
```

As we created our gesture recognizers, we kept a reference to the UILongPress-
GestureRecognizer (`self.longPresser`). We also made ourself the UIPanGesture-
Recognizer's delegate, so we will receive delegate messages. If the
UIPanGestureRecognizer tries to declare success while the UILongPressGesture-
Recognizer's state is `.failed` or still at `.possible`, we prevent it. If the UILongPress-
GestureRecognizer succeeds, we permit the UIPanGestureRecognizer to operate as
well:

```
func gestureRecognizerShouldBegin(_ g: UIGestureRecognizer) -> Bool {
    switch self.longPresser.state {
    case .possible, .failed:
        return false
    default:
        return true
    }
}
func gestureRecognizer(_ g: UIGestureRecognizer,
    shouldRecognizeSimultaneouslyWith g2: UIGestureRecognizer) -> Bool {
        return true
}
```

The result is that the view can be dragged only while it is pulsing; in effect, what
we've done is to compensate, using delegate methods, for the fact that UIGesture-
Recognizer has no `require(toSucceed:)` method.

Subclassing Gesture Recognizers

To subclass UIGestureRecognizer or a built-in gesture recognizer subclass:

- You'll need to `import UIKit.UIGestureRecognizerSubclass`. This allows you to
  set a gesture recognizer's `state` property (which is otherwise read-only), and
  exposes declarations for the methods you may need to override.

- Override any relevant touch methods (as if the gesture recognizer were a UIResponder); if you're subclassing a built-in gesture recognizer subclass, you will
  almost certainly call `super` so as to take advantage of the built-in behavior. In
  overriding touch methods, try to think like a gesture recognizer: as these methods are called, the gesture recognizer is setting its state, and you must participate
  coherently in that process.

To illustrate, we will subclass UIPanGestureRecognizer so as to implement a view that can be moved only horizontally or vertically. Our strategy will be to make *two* UIPanGestureRecognizer subclasses — one that allows only horizontal movement, and another that allows only vertical movement. They will make their recognition decisions in a mutually exclusive manner, so we can attach an instance of each to the same view. This encapsulates the decision-making logic in a gorgeously object-oriented way — a far cry from the spaghetti code we wrote earlier to do this same task.

I will show only the code for the horizontal drag gesture recognizer, because the vertical recognizer is symmetrically identical. We maintain just one property, self.origLoc, which we will use once to determine whether the user's initial movement is horizontal. We override touchesBegan(_:with:) to set our property with the first touch's location:

```
override func touchesBegan(_ touches: Set<UITouch>, with e: UIEvent) {
    self.origLoc = touches.first!.location(in:self.view!.superview)
    super.touchesBegan(touches, with:e)
}
```

We then override touchesMoved(_:with:); all the recognition logic is here. This method will be called for the first time with the state still at .possible. At that moment, we look to see if the user's movement is more horizontal than vertical. If it isn't, we set the state to .failed. But if it is, we just step back and let the superclass do its thing:

```
override func touchesMoved(_ touches: Set<UITouch>, with e: UIEvent) {
    if self.state == .possible {
        let loc = touches.first!.location(in:self.view!.superview)
        let deltaX = abs(loc.x - self.origLoc.x)
        let deltaY = abs(loc.y - self.origLoc.y)
        if deltaY >= deltaX {
            self.state = .failed
        }
    }
    super.touchesMoved(touches, with:e)
}
```

If this gesture recognizer is attached to a view, we now have a view that moves only if the user's initial gesture is horizontal. But that isn't the entirety of what we want; we want a view that moves only horizontally. To implement that, we'll override translation(in:) so that our gesture recognizer lies to its client about where the user's finger is:

```
override func translation(in view: UIView?) -> CGPoint {
    var proposedTranslation = super.translation(in:view)
    proposedTranslation.y = 0
    return proposedTranslation
}
```

That example was simple, because we subclassed a fully functional built-in UIGestureRecognizer subclass. If you were to write your own UIGestureRecognizer subclass entirely from scratch, there would be more work to do:

Touch methods

You should definitely implement all four touch methods. Their job, at a minimum, is to advance the gesture recognizer through the canonical progression of its states. When the first touch arrives at a gesture recognizer, its state will be .possible; you never explicitly set the recognizer's state to .possible yourself. As soon as you know this can't be our gesture, you set the state to .failed. (Apple says that a gesture recognizer should "fail early, fail often.") If the gesture gets past all the failure tests, you set the state instead either to .ended (for a discrete gesture) or to .began (for a continuous gesture); if .began, then you might set it to .changed, and ultimately you must set it to .ended. Don't concern yourself with the sending of action messages; they will be sent automatically at the appropriate moments.

reset *method*

You should also probably implement reset. This is called after you reach the end of the progression of states to notify you that the gesture recognizer's state is about to be set back to .possible; it is your chance to return your state machine to its starting configuration. This is important because your gesture recognizer might stop receiving touches without notice. Just because it gets a touches-Began(_:with:) call for a particular touch doesn't mean it will ever get touches-Ended(_:with:) for that touch. If your gesture recognizer fails to recognize its gesture, either because it declares failure or because it is still in the .possible state when another gesture recognizer recognizes, it won't get any more touch method calls for any of the touches that were being sent to it. reset is the one reliable signal that it's time to clean up and get ready to receive the beginning of another possible gesture.

You can incorporate delegate-like behavior into a gesture recognizer subclass, by overriding the following methods:

- canPrevent(_:)
- canBePrevented(by:)
- shouldRequireFailure(of:)
- shouldBeRequiredToFail(by:)
- shouldReceive(_:) (introduced in iOS 13.4)

The prevent methods are similar to the delegate shouldBegin method, and the fail methods are similar to the delegate fail methods. By implementing them, you can mediate gesture recognizer conflict at the class level. The built-in gesture recognizer subclasses already do this; that is why a single tap UITapGestureRecognizer does not, by recognizing its gesture, cause the failure of a double tap UITapGestureRecognizer.

The `shouldReceive(_:)` method is similar to the delegate `gestureRecognizer(_:shouldReceive:)` method for an event. It hands you a UIEvent parameter, giving you the opportunity to turn that event away at the door before the event or any touches associated with it can affect the gesture recognizer.

You can also, in a gesture recognizer subclass, send `ignore(_:for:)` directly to a gesture recognizer (typically to `self`) to ignore a specific touch of a specific event. This has the same effect as returning `false` from the delegate `gestureRecognizer(_:shouldReceive:)` method for a touch, blocking all future delivery of that touch to the gesture recognizer. You might use this to ignore a new touch that arrives when you're in the middle of an already recognized gesture.

Gesture Recognizers in the Nib

Instead of instantiating a gesture recognizer in code, you can create and configure it in a *.xib* or *.storyboard* file. In the nib editor, drag a gesture recognizer from the Library onto a view; the gesture recognizer becomes a top-level nib object, and the view's `gestureRecognizers` outlet is connected to the gesture recognizer. (You can add more than one gesture recognizer to a view in the nib: the view's `gestureRecognizers` property is an array, and its `gestureRecognizers` outlet is an outlet collection.) The gesture recognizer is a full-fledged nib object, so you can make an outlet to it. A view retains its gesture recognizers, so there will usually be no need for additional memory management on a gesture recognizer instantiated from a nib.

The gesture recognizer's properties are configurable in the Attributes inspector, and the gesture recognizer has a `delegate` outlet. To configure a gesture recognizer's target–action pair in the nib editor, treat it like a UIControl's control event. The action method's signature should be marked `@IBAction`, and it should take a single parameter, which will be a reference to the gesture recognizer. You can form the action in any of the same ways as for a control action. A gesture recognizer can have multiple target–action pairs, but only one target–action pair can be configured for a gesture recognizer using the nib editor.

Touch Delivery

Here's the full standard procedure by which a touch is delivered to views and gesture recognizers:

- When a new touch appears, the application performs hit-testing to determine the view that was touched. This view will be permanently associated with this touch, and is called, appropriately, the *hit-test view*. The logic of ignoring a view in response to its `isUserInteractionEnabled`, `isHidden`, and `alpha` properties is implemented by denying this view the ability to become the hit-test view.

- When the touch situation changes, the application calls its own `sendEvent(_:)`, which in turn calls the window's `sendEvent(_:)`. The window delivers each of an event's touches by calling the appropriate touch method(s):

  - As a touch first appears, the logic of obedience to `isMultipleTouchEnabled` and `isExclusiveTouch` is considered. If permitted by that logic:

    - The touch is delivered to the hit-test view's swarm of gesture recognizers.

    - The touch is delivered to the hit-test view itself.

  - If a gesture is recognized by a gesture recognizer, then for any touch associated with this gesture recognizer:

    - `touchesCancelled(_:for:)` is sent to the touch's view, and the touch is no longer delivered to its view.

    - If the touch was associated with any other gesture recognizer, that gesture recognizer is forced to fail.

  - If a gesture recognizer fails, either because it declares failure or because it is forced to fail, its touches are no longer delivered to it, but (except as already specified) they continue to be delivered to their view.

The rest of this chapter discusses the details of touch delivery. As you'll see, nearly every bit of the standard procedure can be customized to some extent.

Hit-Testing

Hit-testing is the determination of what view the user touched. View hit-testing uses the UIView instance method `hitTest(_:with:)`, whose first parameter is the CGPoint of interest. It returns either a view (the hit-test view) or `nil`. The idea is to find the frontmost view containing the touch point.

The first thing a view's `hitTest(_:with:)` does is to implement the logic of touch restrictions exclusive to a view. If the view's `isUserInteractionEnabled` is `false`, or its `isHidden` is `true`, or its `alpha` is close to `0.0`, it immediately returns `nil`, meaning that neither it nor any of its subviews can be the hit-test view. Observe that these restrictions do not, of themselves, exclude a view from being hit-tested; on the contrary, they operate precisely by affecting a view's hit-test result.

(Hit-testing knows nothing about `isMultipleTouchEnabled`, which involves multiple touches, or `isExclusiveTouch`, which involves multiple views. The logic of obedience to these properties is implemented at a later stage of the story.)

If the view has not returned `nil` for any of those reasons, the `hitTest(_:with:)` method proceeds by an elegant recursive algorithm:

1. A view's `hitTest(_:with:)` first calls the same method on its own subviews, if it has any, because a subview is considered to be in front of its superview. The subviews are queried in front-to-back order (Chapter 1), so if two sibling views overlap, the one in front reports the hit first.

2. If, as a view hit-tests its subviews, any of those subviews responds by returning a view, it stops querying its subviews and immediately returns the view that was returned to it. In this way, the very first view to declare itself the hit-test view percolates all the way to the top of the call chain and *is* the hit-test view.

3. If, on the other hand, a view has no subviews, or if all of its subviews return `nil` (indicating that neither they nor their subviews was hit), then the view calls `point(inside:with:)` on itself:

   - If this call reveals that the touch was inside this view, the view returns itself, and so this view *is* the hit-test view, as I just explained.

   - Otherwise this view returns `nil` and the search continues.

No problem arises if a view being hit-tested has a transform, because `point(inside:with:)` takes the transform into account. That's why a rotated button continues to work correctly.

Performing Hit-Testing

You can perform hit-testing yourself at any moment where it might prove useful. In calling `hitTest(_:with:)`, supply a point *in the coordinates of the view to which the message is sent*. The second parameter is supposed to be a UIEvent, but it can be `nil` if you have no event.

Suppose we have a superview with two UIImageView subviews. We want to detect a tap in either UIImageView, but we want to handle this *at the level of the superview*. We can attach a UITapGestureRecognizer to the superview, but then the gesture recognizer's `view` is the superview, so how will we know which subview, if any, the tap was in?

First, ensure that `isUserInteractionEnabled` is `true` for both UIImageViews. UIImageView is one of the few built-in view classes where this property is `false` by default, and a view whose `isUserInteractionEnabled` is `false` won't normally be the result of a call to `hitTest(_:with:)`. Then, when our gesture recognizer's action method is called, we can perform hit-testing to determine where the tap was:

```
// g is the gesture recognizer
let p = g.location(ofTouch:0, in: g.view)
let v = g.view?.hitTest(p, with: nil)
if let v = v as? UIImageView { // ...
```

Hit-Test Munging

You can override hitTest(_:with:) in a UIView subclass, to alter its results during touch delivery, customizing the touch delivery mechanism. I call this *hit-test munging*. Hit-test munging can be used selectively as a way of turning user interaction on or off in an area of the interface. In this way, some unusual effects can be achieved. I'll give a couple of examples and leave the other possibilities to your imagination.

Suppose we want to permit the touching of subviews outside the bounds of their superview. As I mentioned earlier, if a view's clipsToBounds is false, a paradox arises: the user can *see* the regions of its subviews that are outside its bounds, but can't *touch* them. This behavior can be changed by a view that overrides hit-Test(_:with:):

```
override func hitTest(_ point: CGPoint, with e: UIEvent?) -> UIView? {
    if let result = super.hitTest(point, with:e) {
        return result
    }
    for sub in self.subviews.reversed() {
        let pt = self.convert(point, to:sub)
        if let result = sub.hitTest(pt, with:e) {
            return result
        }
    }
    return nil
}
```

In this next example, we implement a pass-through view. The idea is that only one object in our interface should be touchable; everything else should behave as if isUserInteractionEnabled were false. In a complex interface, actually cycling through all our subviews and toggling isUserInteractionEnabled might be too much trouble. As a shortcut, we place an invisible view in front of the entire interface and use hit-test munging so that only one view behind it (self.passthruView) is touchable. In effect, this is a view that is (selectively) touchable even though the user can't see it:

```
class MyView: UIView {
    weak var passthruView : UIView?
    override func hitTest(_ point: CGPoint, with e: UIEvent?) -> UIView? {
        if let pv = self.passthruView {
            let pt = pv.convert(point, from: self)
            if pv.point(inside: pt, with: e) {
                return nil
            }
        }
```

```
        }
        return super.hitTest(point, with: e)
    }
}
```

Hit-Testing for Layers

Layers do *not* receive touches. A touch is reported to a view, not a layer. A layer, except insofar as it is a view's underlying layer and gets touch reporting because of its view, is completely untouchable; from the point of view of touches and touch reporting, it's as if the layer weren't on the screen at all. No matter where a layer may appear to be, a touch falls through the layer to whatever view is behind it.

In the case of a layer that is a view's underlying layer, you don't need layer hit-testing, because you've got view hit-testing. The layer is the view's drawing; where it appears is where the view is. So a touch in that layer is equivalent to a touch in its view. Indeed, one might say (and it is often said) that this is what views are actually for: to provide layers with touchability.

Nevertheless, hit-testing for layers is possible. It doesn't happen automatically, as part of sendEvent(_:) or anything else; it's up to you. It's just a convenient way of finding out which layer *would* receive a touch at a point, if layers *did* receive touches. To hit-test layers, call hitTest(_:) on a layer, with a point *in superlayer coordinates*. Layer hit-testing knows nothing of the restrictions on touch delivery; it just reports on every sublayer, even one whose view has isUserInteractionEnabled set to false.

The only layers on which you'd need special hit-testing would presumably be layers that are not themselves any view's underlying layer. Still, all layers are part of the layer hierarchy and can participate in layer hit-testing. So the most comprehensive way to hit-test layers is to start with the topmost layer, the window's layer. In this example, we subclass UIWindow and override its hitTest(_:with:) so as to get layer hit-testing every time there is view hit-testing:

```
override func hitTest(_ point: CGPoint, with e: UIEvent?) -> UIView? {
    let lay = self.layer.hitTest(point)
    // ... possibly do something with that information
    return super.hitTest(point, with:e)
}
```

In that code, self is the window, which is a special case. In general, you'll have to convert to superlayer coordinates. I'll demonstrate in the next example.

Let's return to the CompassView developed in Chapter 3, in which all the parts of the compass are layers; we want to know whether the user tapped on the arrow layer, and if so, we'll rotate the arrow. For simplicity, we've given the CompassView a UITap-GestureRecognizer, and this is its action method, in the CompassView itself. We convert to our superview's coordinates, because these are also our layer's superlayer coordinates:

```
@objc func tapped(_ t:UITapGestureRecognizer) {
    let p = t.location(ofTouch:0, in: self.superview)
    let hitLayer = self.layer.hitTest(p)
    if let arrow = (self.layer as? CompassLayer)?.arrow {
        if hitLayer == arrow { // respond to touch
            arrow.transform = CATransform3DRotate(
                arrow.transform, .pi/4.0, 0, 0, 1)
        }
    }
}
```

Hit-Testing for Drawings

The preceding example (letting the user tap on the compass arrow) does work, but we might complain that it is reporting a hit on the arrow layer even if the hit misses the *drawing* of the arrow. That's true for view hit-testing as well. A hit is reported if we are within the view or layer as a whole; hit-testing knows nothing of drawing, transparent areas, and so forth.

If you know how the region is drawn and can reproduce the edge of that drawing as a CGPath, you can call contains(_:using:transform:) to test whether a point is inside it. So, in our compass layer, we could override hitTest(_:) along these lines:

```
override func hitTest(_ p: CGPoint) -> CALayer? {
    var lay = super.hitTest(p)
    if lay == self.arrow {
        let pt = self.arrow.convert(p, from:self.superlayer)
        let path = CGMutablePath()
        path.addRect(CGRect(10,20,20,80))
        path.move(to:CGPoint(0, 25))
        path.addLine(to:CGPoint(20, 0))
        path.addLine(to:CGPoint(40, 25))
        path.closeSubpath()
        if !path.contains(pt, using: .winding) {
            lay = nil
        }
    }
    return lay
}
```

Alternatively, it might be the case that if a pixel of the drawing is transparent, it's outside the drawn region, so that it suffices to detect whether the tapped pixel is transparent. Unfortunately, there's no built-in way to ask a drawing (or a view, or a layer) for the color of a pixel. Instead, you have to make a *bitmap graphics context* and copy the drawing into it, and then ask the bitmap for the color of a pixel. If you can reproduce the content as an image, and all you care about is transparency, you can make a one-pixel alpha-only bitmap, draw the image in such a way that the pixel you want to test is the pixel drawn into the bitmap, and examine the transparency of the resulting pixel. In this example, `im` is our UIImage and `point` is the coordinates of the pixel we want to test:

```
let info = CGImageAlphaInfo.alphaOnly.rawValue
let pixel = UnsafeMutablePointer<UInt8>.allocate(capacity:1)
pixel.initialize(to: 0)
defer {
    pixel.deinitialize(count: 1)
    pixel.deallocate()
}
let sp = CGColorSpaceCreateDeviceGray()
let context = CGContext(data: pixel,
    width: 1, height: 1, bitsPerComponent: 8, bytesPerRow: 1,
    space: sp, bitmapInfo: info)!
UIGraphicsPushContext(context)
im.draw(at:CGPoint(-point.x, -point.y))
UIGraphicsPopContext()
let p = pixel[0]
let alpha = Double(p)/255.0
let transparent = alpha < 0.01
```

There may not be a one-to-one relationship between the pixels of the underlying drawing and the points of the drawing as portrayed on the screen. (Perhaps the drawing is stretched.) In many cases, the CALayer method `render(in:)` can be helpful here. This method allows you to copy a layer's actual drawing into a graphics context of your choice. If that context is an image context (Chapter 2), you can use the resulting image as `im` in the preceding code.

Hit-Testing During Animation

Making a view touchable by the user while it is being animated is a tricky business, because the view may not be located where the user sees it. Recall (from Chapter 4) that the animation is just an "animation movie" — what the user sees is the *presentation layer*. The view itself, which the user is trying to touch, is at the location of the *model layer*. If user interaction is allowed during an animation that moves a view from one place to another, and if the user taps where the animated view appears to be, the tap might mysteriously fail because the actual view is elsewhere; conversely, the user might accidentally tap where the view actually is, and the tap will hit the animated view even though it appears to be elsewhere.

For this reason, view animation ordered through a UIView class method, by default, turns off touchability of a view while it is being animated — though you can override that with `.allowUserInteraction` in the `options:` argument.

If you're not using a property animator, you can make an animated view touchable if you really want to, but it takes some work: you have to *hit-test the presentation layer*. In this simple example, we implement hit-test munging in the view being animated:

```
override func hitTest(_ point: CGPoint, with e: UIEvent?) -> UIView? {
    let pres = self.layer.presentation()!
    let suppt = self.convert(point, to: self.superview!)
    let prespt = self.superview!.layer.convert(suppt, to: pres)
    return super.hitTest(prespt, with: e)
}
```

That works, but the animated view, as Apple puts it in the WWDC 2011 videos, "swallows the touch." Suppose the view in motion is a button. Although our hit-test munging makes it possible for the user to tap the button as it is being animated, and although the user sees the button highlight in response, the button's action message is not sent in response to this highlighting if the animation is in-flight when the tap takes place. This behavior seems unfortunate, though it's generally possible to work around it (perhaps with a gesture recognizer).

A property animator makes things far simpler. By default, a property animator's isUserInteractionEnabled is true. That means the animated view *is* touchable. As long as you don't also set the property animator's isManualHitTestingEnabled to true, the property animator will hit-test the animated view's presentation layer for you. (If you *do* set isManualHitTestingEnabled to true, the job of hit-testing is turned back over to you; you might want to do this in complicated situations where the property animator's hit-test munging isn't sufficient.) Moreover, the animated view *doesn't* "swallow the touch."

So, to animate a button that remains tappable while the animation is in-flight, just animate the button:

```
let goal : CGPoint = // whatever
let anim = UIViewPropertyAnimator(duration: 10, curve: .linear) {
    self.button.center = goal // button can be tapped while moving
}
anim.startAnimation()
```

By combining the power of a property animator to make its animated view touchable with its power to make its animation interruptible, we can make a view alternate between being animated and being manipulated by the user. To illustrate, I'll extend the preceding example. The view is slowly animating its way toward the goal position. But at any time, the user can grab it and drag it around, during which time the animation is interrupted. As soon as the user releases the view, the animation resumes: the view continues on its way toward the goal position.

In order to be draggable, the view has a UIPanGestureRecognizer. The property animator is now retained in an instance property (self.anim) so that the gesture recognizer's action method can access it; we have a method that creates the property animator (you'll see in a moment what the factor: parameter is for):

```
func configAnimator(factor:Double = 1) {
    self.anim = UIViewPropertyAnimator(
        duration: 10 * factor, curve: .linear) {
            self.button.center = self.goal
    }
}
```

All the work takes place in the gesture recognizer's action method; as usual, we have a switch statement that tests the gesture recognizer's state. In the .began case, we interrupt the animation so that dragging can happen:

```
case .began:
    if self.anim.state == .active {
        self.anim.stopAnimation(true)
    }
    fallthrough
```

The .changed case is our usual code for making a view draggable:

```
case .changed:
    let delta = p.translation(in:v.superview)
    var c = v.center
    c.x += delta.x; c.y += delta.y
    v.center = c
    p.setTranslation(.zero, in: v.superview)
```

The .ended case is the really interesting part. Our aim is to resume animating the view from wherever it is now toward the goal. In my opinion, this feels most natural if the *speed* at which the view moves remains the same. The ratio between durations is the ratio between the distance of the view's *original* position from the goal and its *current* distance from the goal:

```
case .ended:
    // how far are we from the goal relative to original distance?
    func pyth(_ pt1:CGPoint, _ pt2:CGPoint) -> CGFloat {
        return hypot(pt1.x - pt2.x, pt1.y - pt2.y)
    }
    let origd = pyth(self.oldButtonCenter, self.goal)
    let curd = pyth(v.center, self.goal)
    let factor = curd/origd
    self.configAnimator(factor:Double(factor))
    self.anim.startAnimation()
```

Initial Touch Event Delivery

Whenever the multitouch situation changes, an event containing all touches is handed to the UIApplication instance by calling its sendEvent(_:), and the UIApplication in turn hands it to the UIWindow by calling *its* sendEvent(_:). The UIWindow then performs the complicated logic of examining, for every touch, the hit-test view and its superviews and their gesture recognizers, and deciding which of them should be sent a touch method call.

You can override sendEvent(_:) in a subclass of UIWindow or UIApplication. These are delicate and crucial maneuvers, however, and you wouldn't want to lame your application by interfering with them. Moreover, it is unlikely, nowadays, that you would need to resort to such measures. A typical use case before the advent of gesture recognizers was that you needed to detect touches directed to an object of some built-in interface class that you couldn't subclass; but gesture recognizers exist now, and solve the problem nicely.

Gesture Recognizer and View

When a touch first appears and is delivered to a gesture recognizer, it is *also* delivered to its hit-test view, the same touch method being called on both.

This is the most reasonable approach, as it means that touch interpretation by a view isn't jettisoned just because gesture recognizers are in the picture. Later on in the multitouch sequence, if all the gesture recognizers in a view's swarm declare failure to recognize their gesture, that view's internal touch interpretation continues as if gesture recognizers had never been invented. Moreover, touches and gestures are two different things; sometimes you want to respond to both. In one of my apps, where the user can tap cards, each card has a single tap gesture recognizer and a double tap gesture recognizer, but it also responds directly to touchesBegan(_:with:) by reducing its own opacity, and to touchesEnded(_:with:) and touches-Cancelled(_:with:) by restoring its opacity. The result is that the user always sees *some* feedback when touching a card, *instantly*, regardless of what the gesture turns out to be.

Later, if a gesture recognizer in a view's swarm recognizes its gesture, that view is sent touchesCancelled(_:with:) for any touches that went to that gesture recognizer and were hit-tested to that view, and subsequently the view *no longer receives those touches*. This behavior can be changed by setting a gesture recognizer's cancels-TouchesInView property to false; if you were to do that for every gesture recognizer in a view's swarm, the view would receive touch events more or less as if no gesture recognizers were in the picture.

If a gesture recognizer happens to be ignoring a touch — perhaps it was told to do so with ignore(_:for:) — then touchesCancelled(_:with:) *won't* be sent to the view for that touch when that gesture recognizer recognizes its gesture. A touch ignored by a gesture recognizer effectively falls through to the view, as if the gesture recognizer didn't exist.

Gesture recognizers can also *delay* the delivery of some touch methods to a view, by means of these properties:

`delaysTouchesEnded`

> If `true` (the default), then when a touch reaches `.ended` and the gesture recognizer's `touchesEnded(_:with:)` is called, if the gesture recognizer is still allowing touches to be delivered to the view because its state is still `.possible`, it doesn't deliver this touch until it has resolved the gesture. When it does, either it will recognize the gesture, in which case the view will have `touchesCancelled(_:with:)` called instead (as already explained), or it will declare failure and *now* the view will have `touchesEnded(_:with:)` called.
>
> The reason for this behavior is most obvious with a gesture where multiple taps are required. Consider a double tap gesture recognizer. The first tap ends, but this is insufficient for the gesture recognizer to declare success or failure, so it withholds that `touchesEnded(_:with:)` from the view. If there is a second tap, the gesture recognizer will succeed and send `touchesCancelled(_:with:)` to the view — but it can't do that if the view has already been sent `touches-Ended(_:with:)`! So it was right to withhold `touchesEnded(_:with:)` in the first place.

`delaysTouchesBegan`

> If `true`, we delay the *entire* suite of touch methods from being called on a view. Again, this delay would be until the gesture recognizer can resolve the gesture: either it will recognize it, in which case the view will have `touches-Cancelled(_:with:)` called, or it will declare failure, in which case the view will receive `touchesBegan(_:with:)` plus any further touch method calls that were withheld — except that it will receive *at most* one `touchesMoved(_:with:)` call, the last one, because if a lot of these were withheld, to queue them all up and send them all at once now would be insane.

When touches are delayed and then delivered, what's delivered is the original touch with the original event, which still have their original timestamps. Because of the delay, these timestamps may differ significantly from now. As I've already said, analysis that is concerned with timing of touches should consult the timestamp, not the clock.

Touch Exclusion Logic

It is up to the UIWindow's `sendEvent(_:)` to implement the logic of `isMultipleTouchEnabled` and `isExclusiveTouch`:

`isMultipleTouchEnabled`

> If a new touch is hit-tested to a view whose `isMultipleTouchEnabled` is `false` and that already has an existing touch hit-tested to it, then `sendEvent(_:)` never delivers the new touch to that view. But that touch *is* delivered to the view's

swarm of gesture recognizers; in other words, gesture recognizers are *not* affected by the existence of the `isMultipleTouchEnabled` property.

`isExclusiveTouch`

If there's an `isExclusiveTouch` view in the window, then `sendEvent(_:)` must decide whether a particular touch should be delivered, in accordance with the meaning of `isExclusiveTouch`, which I described earlier. If a touch is not delivered to a view because of `isExclusiveTouch` restrictions, it is *not* delivered to its swarm of gesture recognizers either; in other words, gesture recognizers *are* affected by the existence of the `isExclusiveTouch` property.

To illustrate, suppose you have two views with touch handling, and their common superview has a pinch gesture recognizer. Normally, if you touch both views simultaneously and pinch, the pinch gesture recognizer recognizes. But if both views are marked `isExclusiveTouch`, the pinch gesture recognizer does *not* recognize.

Gesture Recognition Logic

When a gesture recognizer recognizes its gesture, everything changes. As we've already seen, the touches for this gesture recognizer are sent to their hit-test views as a `touchesCancelled(_:with:)` message, and then no longer arrive at those views (unless the gesture recognizer's `cancelsTouchesInView` is `false`). Moreover, all other gesture recognizers pending with regard to these touches are made to fail, and then are no longer sent the touches they were receiving either.

If the very same event might cause more than one gesture recognizer to recognize, there's an algorithm for picking the one that will succeed and make the others fail: a gesture recognizer lower down the view hierarchy (closer to the hit-test view) prevails over one higher up the hierarchy, and a gesture recognizer more recently added to its view prevails over one less recently added.

There are various ways to modify this "first past the post" behavior:

Dependency order
Certain methods institute a dependency order, causing a gesture recognizer to be put on hold when it tries to transition from the `.possible` state to the `.began` (continuous) or `.ended` (discrete) state; only if a certain other gesture recognizer fails is this one permitted to perform that transition:

- `require(toFail:)`
  sent to a gesture recognizer
- `shouldRequireFailure(of:)`
  in a subclass

- `shouldBeRequiredToFail(by:)`
  in a subclass

- `gestureRecognizer(_:shouldRequireFailureOf:)`
  in the delegate

- `gestureRecognizer(_:shouldBeRequiredToFailBy:)`
  in the delegate

The first of those methods sets up a permanent relationship between two gesture recognizers, and cannot be undone; but the others are sent every time a gesture starts in a view whose swarm includes both gesture recognizers, and the result is applied only on this occasion.

The delegate methods work together as follows. For each pair of gesture recognizers in the hit-test view's swarm, the members of that pair are arranged in a fixed order (as I've already described). The first of the pair is sent `shouldRequire` and then `shouldBeRequired`, and then the second of the pair is sent `should-Require` and then `shouldBeRequired`. But if any of those four methods returns `true`, the relationship between that pair is settled and we proceed immediately to the next pair.

(Apple says that in a dependency like this, the gesture recognizer that fails first is not sent `reset`, and won't receive any touches, until the second finishes its state sequence and is sent `reset`, so that they resume recognizing together.)

Success into failure

Certain methods, by returning `false`, turn success into failure; at the moment when a gesture recognizer is about to declare that it recognizes its gesture, transitioning from the `.possible` state to the `.began` (continuous) or `.ended` (discrete) state, it is forced to fail instead:

- `gestureRecognizerShouldBegin(_:)`
  in a view

- `gestureRecognizerShouldBegin(_:)`
  in the delegate

Simultaneous recognition

Certain methods ensure that when a gesture recognizer succeeds, some other gesture recognizer is *not* forced to fail:

- `gestureRecognizer(_:shouldRecognizeSimultaneouslyWith:)`
  in the delegate

- `canPrevent(_:)`
  in a subclass

- `canBePrevented(by:)`
  in a subclass

In the subclass methods, `prevent` means "by succeeding, you force failure upon this other," and `bePrevented` means "by succeeding, this other forces failure on you." They work together as follows. `canPrevent` is called first; if it returns `false`, that's the end of the story for that gesture recognizer, and `canPrevent` is called on the other gesture recognizer. But if `canPrevent` returns `true` when it is first called, the other gesture recognizer is sent `canBePrevented`. If it returns `true`, that's the end of the story; if it returns `false`, the process starts over the other way round, sending `canPrevent` to the second gesture recognizer, and so forth. In this way, conflicting answers are resolved without the device exploding: prevention is regarded as exceptional (even though it is in fact the norm) and will happen only if it is acquiesced to by everyone involved.

Interface

This part of the book describes view controllers, the major building blocks of an app's interface and functionality, along with the views provided by the UIKit framework:

- Chapter 6 is about view controllers, the basis of a Cocoa app's architecture. View controllers manage interface and respond to user actions.
- Chapter 7 is about scroll views, which let the user slide and zoom the interface.
- Chapter 8 explains table views, which are scroll views for navigating through data.
- Chapter 9 discusses collection views, which generalize table views, providing more flexible layout.
- Chapter 10 is about popovers, split views, iPad multitasking, drag and drop, external hardware input, and multiple windows on iPad.
- Chapter 11 describes how text is presented in a Cocoa app's interface.
- Chapter 12 explains how to put a web browser inside your app.
- Chapter 13 describes all the remaining built-in UIKit interface objects.
- Chapter 14 is about various forms of modal dialog that can appear in front of an app's interface.

.

View Controllers

An iOS app's interface is dynamic, and with good reason. The entire interface has to fit into a single display consisting of a single window, which in the case of the iPhone can be forbiddingly tiny. The solution is to change the interface. In response to some event — typically a user action — a new view, possibly with an elaborate hierarchy of subviews, replaces or covers the previous interface.

For this to work, regions of interface material — often the entire contents of the screen — must come and go in an agile fashion that is understandable to the user. There will typically be a logical, structural, and functional relationship between the view that was showing and the view that replaces or covers it. This relationship will need to be maintained behind the scenes, in your code.

The relationship between views also needs to be indicated to the user. Multiple views may be pure alternatives or siblings of one another, or one view may be a temporary replacement for another, or views may be like successive pages of a book. Animation is often used to emphasize and clarify these relationships as one view is superseded by another. Navigational interface and a vivid, suggestive gestural vocabulary give the user an ability to control what's seen and an understanding of the possible options: a tab bar whose buttons summon alternate views, a back button or a swipe gesture for returning to a previously visited view, a tap on an interface element to dive deeper into a conceptual world, a Done or Cancel button to escape from a settings screen, and so forth.

In Cocoa apps, the management of this dynamic interface is performed through view controllers. A *view controller* is an instance of UIViewController. Actually, it will be an instance of a UIViewController *subclass*; UIViewController is designed to be subclassed. You might write your own UIViewController subclass; you might use a built-in subclass such as UINavigationController or UITabBarController; or you might subclass a built-in subclass such as UITableViewController (Chapter 8).

A view controller manages a view together with that view's subviews, their subviews, and so on. The single superview at the top of that hierarchy is the view controller's *main view*, or simply its *view*; the view controller's `view` property points to it. A view controller's main view has no explicit pointer to the view controller that manages it, but a view controller is a UIResponder and is in the responder chain just above its view, so it is its view's `next` responder.

View Controller Responsibilities

For a view controller to be useful, its view must somehow *get into the visible interface*; a view controller is usually responsible for that, but typically *not* the view controller whose view this is — rather, this will be some view controller whose view is *already* in the interface. In many cases, that will happen automatically (I'll talk more about that in the next section), but you can participate in the process, and for some view controllers you may have to do the work yourself. A view that comes may also eventually go, and the view controller responsible for putting a view into the interface will usually be responsible also for removing it.

A view controller will typically provide *animation* of the interface as a view comes or goes. Built-in view controller subclasses, and built-in ways of summoning or removing a view controller and its view, come with built-in animations. We are all familiar with tapping something to make new interface slide in from the side of the screen, and then later tapping a back button to make that interface slide back out again. Whoever is responsible for getting a view controller's view into the interface is also responsible for providing the animation.

The most powerful view controller is the *top-level view controller*. This might be a fullscreen presented view controller, as I'll explain later in this chapter; but most of the time it will be your app's *root view controller*. This is the view controller managing the *root view*, the view that sits at the top of the entire view hierarchy, as the one and only direct subview of the window, acting as the superview for the rest of the app's interface (Chapter 1). The root view controller attains this lofty position because `UIApplicationMain`, or your code, puts it there, instantiating it and assigning it to the window's `rootViewController` property. The window responds by taking the view controller's main view, giving it the correct frame (resizing it if necessary), and making it its own subview ("How an App Launches" on page 6).

The top-level view controller bears ultimate responsibility for some important decisions about the behavior of your app:

Manipulation of the status bar
> The status bar is actually a secondary window belonging to the runtime. The runtime consults the top-level view controller as to whether the status bar should be present and, if so, whether its text should be light or dark.

Rotation of the interface

    The user can rotate the device, and you might like the interface to rotate in response, to compensate. The runtime consults the top-level view controller about whether to permit such rotation.

Above and beyond all this, view controllers are important because they manage views! Views display information for the user to see. The task of determining, at any given moment, what views are shown and what they display, typically belongs to the view controller that manages them. Views give the user something to interact with. When the user performs an interactive action such as tapping a view, that action will typically be reported to the view controller that manages that view. View controllers are the key mediators between what the user sees and does, on the one hand, and what the app does, on the other.

View Controller Hierarchy

There is always one root view controller, along with its view, the root view. There may also be other view controllers, each of which has its own main view. Those other view controllers are *subordinate* to the root view controller. There are two subordination relationships between view controllers:

Parentage (containment)

    A view controller can *contain* another view controller. The containing view controller is the *parent* of the contained view controller; the contained view controller is a *child* of the containing view controller. A containment relationship between two view controllers is reflected in their views: the child view controller's view, if it is in the interface at all, is a *subview* (at some depth) of the parent view controller's view.

    The parent view controller is responsible for getting a child view controller's view into the interface, by making it a subview of its own view, and (if necessary) for removing it later. Introduction of a view, removal of a view, and replacement of one view with another often involve a parent view controller managing its children and their views.

Presentation (modal)

    A view controller can *present* another view controller. The first view controller is the *presenting* view controller of the second; the second view controller is the *presented* view controller of the first. The second view controller's view replaces or covers, completely or partially, the first view controller's view.

    The name of this mechanism, and of the relationship between the view controllers, has evolved over time. In iOS 4 and before, the presented view controller was called a *modal view controller*, and its view was a *modal view*; there is an analogy here to the desktop, where a window is modal if it sits in front of, and

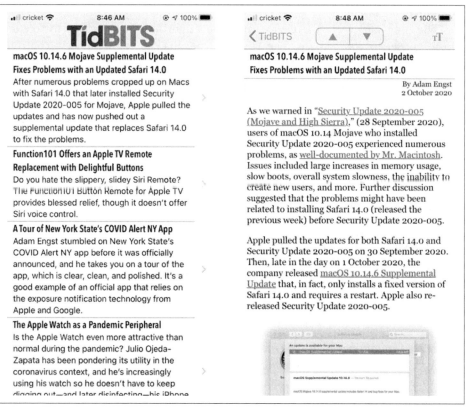

Figure 6-1. The TidBITS News app

denies the user access to, the rest of the interface until it is explicitly dismissed. The terms *presented view controller* and *presented view* are more recent and more general, but the historical term "modal" still appears in the documentation and in the API.

Here's an example of a parent view controller and a child view controller — the familiar navigation interface, where the user taps something and new interface slides in from the side, replacing the current interface. Figure 6-1 shows the TidBITS News app displaying a list of story headlines and summaries (on the left). The user taps an entry in the list, and the whole list slides away to one side, and the text of that story slides in from the other side (on the right).

The list and the story are both child view controllers. The parent view controller is a UINavigationController, which manipulates the views of its children to bring about this animated change of the interface. The parent view controller (the navigation controller) stays put, and so does its own view, which functions as a fixed superview within which all this view-swapping takes place.

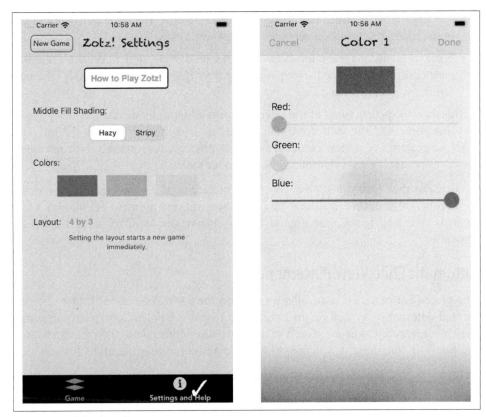

Figure 6-2. The Zotz! app

Here's an example of a presenting view controller and a presented view controller. Figure 6-2 shows the Zotz! app's settings screen (on the left). The user can edit a color by tapping a color swatch; a new screen then slides up from the bottom, offering three color sliders (on the right). The color editing interface is modal; it is being presented from the settings screen. The color editing interface has a Cancel button and a Done button, clearly implying that this is a place where the user must make a decision and can do nothing else until the decision is made. (But as I'll explain later, that isn't the only use of a presented view controller.)

There is a *hierarchy of view controllers*. It starts with the root view controller, which is the *only* nonsubordinate view controller. Every other view controller, if its view is to appear in the interface, *must* be a subordinate view controller. It can be a *child* view controller of some parent view controller; or it can be a *presented* view controller of some presenting view controller. And those are the only possibilities!

There is also a *hierarchy of views*. And there is a well-defined relationship between the view controller hierarchy and the view hierarchy:

- For a parent view controller and child view controller, the child's view, if present in the interface, must be a *subview* of the parent's view.

- For a presenting view controller and presented view controller, the presented view controller's view either *replaces* or *covers* (partially or completely) the presenting view controller's view.

In this way, the actual views of the interface form a hierarchy dictated by *and parallel to* some portion of the view controller hierarchy: *every* view visible in the interface owes its presence to a view controller's view, either because it *is* a view controller's view, or because it's a *subview* of a view controller's view.

It is *crucial* that your app's view controller hierarchy and view hierarchy be structured coherently, in the way I have just described, at every moment of your app's lifetime. If your app behaves as a good Cocoa citizen, they will be — as I will now illustrate.

Automatic Child View Placement

The placement of a view controller's view into the view hierarchy will often be performed automatically. You might never need to put a UIViewController's view into the view hierarchy yourself. You'll manipulate view controllers; their hierarchy and their built-in functionality will construct and manage the view hierarchy for you.

In Figure 6-1, on the left, we see two interface elements:

- The navigation bar, containing the TidBITS logo.
- The list of stories, which is actually a UITableView.

I will describe how all of this comes to appear on the screen through the view controller hierarchy and the view hierarchy. The relationship between view controllers and views is diagrammed in Figure 6-3. In the diagram, notice the word "automatic" in the two large right-pointing arrows associating a view controller with its view; this tells you how the view controller's view became part of the view hierarchy:

Root view controller
  The window's root view controller is a UINavigationController:

  - The UINavigationController's view is the window's sole immediate subview (the root view). That happened *automatically*, by virtue of the UINavigation-Controller being the window's `rootViewController`.
  - The navigation bar is a subview of that view.

Child view controller
  The UINavigationController has a child UIViewController (a parent–child relationship). The child is a custom UIViewController subclass, which I've called MasterViewController:

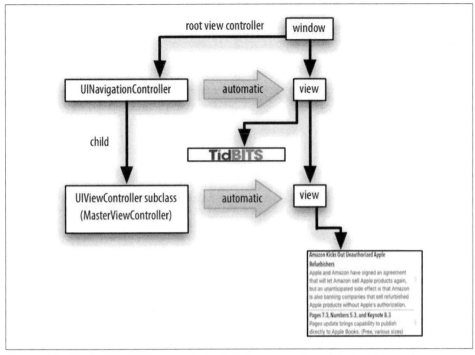

Figure 6-3. The TidBITS News app's initial view controller and view hierarchy

- MasterViewController's view is the UITableView, and it is *another* subview of the UINavigationController's view. That happened *automatically*, by virtue of the MasterViewController being the UINavigationController's child.

Manual Child View Placement

Sometimes, you'll write your own parent view controller class. In that case, *you* will be doing the kind of work that the UINavigationController was doing in that example, so you will need to put a child view controller's view into the interface *manually*, as a subview (at some depth) of the parent view controller's view.

I'll illustrate with another app of mine (Figure 6-4). The interface displays a flashcard containing information about a Latin word, along with a toolbar (the dark area at the bottom) where the user can tap an icon to choose additional functionality.

The app actually contains over a thousand of these Latin words, and I want the user to be able to navigate between flashcards to see the next or previous word; there is an excellent built-in UIViewController subclass for this purpose, the UIPageView-Controller. But the toolbar at the bottom stays put, so the toolbar can't be inside the UIPageViewController's view. How is this going to work?

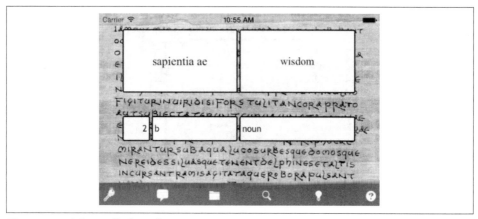

Figure 6-4. A Latin flashcard app

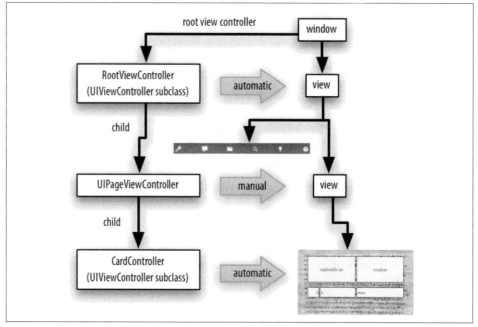

Figure 6-5. The Latin flashcard app's initial view controller and view hierarchy

Again, I will describe how the interface comes to appear on the screen through the view controller hierarchy and the view hierarchy. The relationships are diagrammed in Figure 6-5:

Root view controller

The window's root view controller is my own UIViewController subclass, called RootViewController:

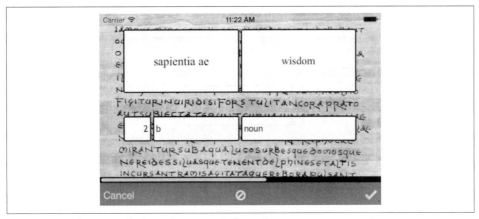

Figure 6-6. The Latin flashcard app, in drill mode

- RootViewController's view becomes the window's subview (the root view) *automatically*, by virtue of the RootViewController being the window's `root-ViewController`.

- The toolbar is a subview of RootViewController's view.

Child view controller
In order for the UIPageViewController's view to appear in the interface, since it is not the root view controller, it *must* be some view controller's child. My RootViewController is the only possible parent, so it must function as a custom parent view controller, with the UIPageViewController as its child. So I have made that happen, and therefore:

- I myself have had to put the UIPageViewController's view *manually* as a subview into my RootViewController's view.

Child view controller
I hand the UIPageViewController, as its child, an instance of another custom UIViewController subclass, called CardController (representing a flashcard):

- The UIPageViewController displays the CardController's view as a subview of its own view *automatically*.

Presented View Placement

My Latin flashcard app has a second mode, where the user is drilled on a subset of the cards in random order; the interface looks very much like the first mode's interface (Figure 6-6), but it behaves completely differently.

In reality, this is a presented view controller. The relationship between view controllers and views is diagrammed in Figure 6-7:

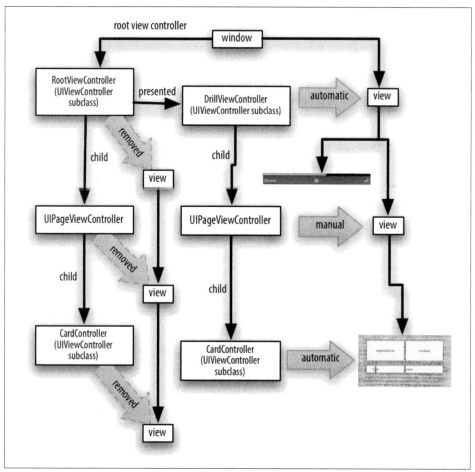

Figure 6-7. The Latin flashcard app's drill mode view controller and view hierarchy

Presented view controller

I have a UIViewController subclass called DrillViewController; it is structured very much like RootViewController. When the user is in drill mode, a DrillView-Controller is *presented* by the RootViewController. This means that the Drill-ViewController's interface takes over the screen *automatically*:

- The DrillViewController's view, with its whole subview hierarchy, including the views of the DrillViewController's children in the view controller hierarchy, *replaces* the RootViewController's view and *its* whole subview hierarchy.

Presenting view controller

The RootViewController is still the window's `rootViewController`, and its hierarchy of child view controllers remains in place while the DrillViewController is being presented. But:

- The RootViewController's view and its subviews are not in the interface.

- They will be returned to the interface automatically when we leave drill mode (because the presented DrillViewController is dismissed), and the situation will look like Figure 6-5 once again.

Ensuring a Coherent Hierarchy

For any app that you write, for every moment in the lifetime of that app, you should be able to construct a diagram showing the hierarchy of view controllers and charting how each view controller's view fits into the view hierarchy. The diagram should be similar to mine! The view hierarchy should run in neat parallel with the view controller hierarchy; there should be no crossed wires or orphan views. Every view controller's view should be placed *automatically* into the view hierarchy, *except* in the following two situations:

- You have created a custom parent view controller, and this view controller is its child ("Container View Controllers" on page 379).

- You're doing a custom transition animation ("Custom Transition" on page 354).

You can *see* the view controller hierarchy in schematic form by pausing in the debugger and giving this incantation:

```
(lldb) e -l objc -O -- [UIViewController _printHierarchy]
```

If I give that command when my Latin flashcard app is in the state shown in Figure 6-4, the output looks like this (omitting some of the information):

```
<JS_Latin_Vocab_iPhone_3.RootViewController ... >
   | <UIPageViewController ... >
   |   | <JS_Latin_Vocab_iPhone_3.CardController ... >
```

The analysis accords with mine: The window's root view controller is my RootViewController, which has a child UIPageViewController, which has a child CardController.

Another way to inspect the view controller hierarchy is the view debugger (Figure 6-8). This provides even more information. The view controller hierarchy is displayed with circular icons; interleaved with those, the corresponding view hierarchy is displayed with square icons.

Together, the view controller hierarchy and the view hierarchy constitute the bulk of the *responder chain*. What you're really doing by following the rules is ensuring a coherent responder chain.

Figure 6-8. The view debugger displays the view controller hierarchy

View Controller Creation

A view controller is an instance like any other, and it is created like any other instance — by instantiating its class. You might perform this instantiation in code; in that case, you'll also initialize and configure the instance as needed. Here's an example from one of my own apps:

```
let llc = LessonListController(terms: self.terms)
let nav = UINavigationController(rootViewController: llc)
```

In that example:

- LessonListController is my own UIViewController subclass, so I have called its designated initializer, which I myself have defined.
- UINavigationController is a built-in UIViewController subclass, and I have called one of its convenience initializers.

Once a view controller comes into existence, it must be retained so that it will persist. That will happen automatically when the view controller is assigned a place in the view controller hierarchy:

- A view controller assigned as a window's rootViewController is retained by the *window*.
- A view controller assigned as another view controller's child is retained by the *parent* view controller.
- A presented view controller is retained by the *presenting* view controller.

The retaining view controller then takes ownership, and will release the other view controller in good order if and when it is no longer needed.

Here's an example, from one of my apps, of view controllers being instantiated and then retained through their insertion into the view controller hierarchy:

```
let llc = LessonListController(terms: self.terms) ❶❷
let nav = UINavigationController(rootViewController: llc) ❸
self.present(nav, animated: true) ❹
```

That's the same code I showed a moment ago, extended by one line. It comes from a view controller class called RootViewController. Here's how view controller creation and memory management works in those three lines:

❶ The current view controller, `self`, is a RootViewController instance. It is already the window's `rootViewController`, and is retained by the window.

❷ I instantiate LessonListController.

❸ I instantiate UINavigationController, and I assign the LessonListController instance to the UINavigationController instance as its child; the navigation controller retains the LessonListController instance and takes ownership of it.

❹ I present the UINavigationController instance on `self`, the RootViewController instance; the RootViewController instance is the presenting view controller, and it retains and takes ownership of the UINavigationController instance as its presented view controller.

Whenever you instantiate a view controller, you should ask yourself who will be retaining it. Everything works fine if you do things correctly, but it is possible to do things incorrectly. If you're not careful, you might put a view controller's view into the interface while permitting the view controller itself to go out of existence. If that happens, the view will mysteriously fail to perform its intended functionality, because that functionality is embodied in the view controller, which no longer exists. (Yes, I've made this mistake.)

How a View Controller Obtains Its View

When it first comes into existence, a view controller *has no view*. A view is a relatively heavyweight object, involving interface elements that can entail a significant amount of memory. Therefore, a view controller postpones obtaining its view until it is first asked for the value of its `view` property. At that moment, if its `view` property is `nil`, the view controller sets about obtaining its view. (We say that a view controller loads its view *lazily*.) Typically, this happens because the time has come to put the view controller's view into the interface.

In working with a newly instantiated view controller, be careful not to refer to its `view` property if you don't need to, as that can cause the view controller to obtain its view prematurely. (As usual, I speak from experience.) To learn whether a view controller *has* a view without causing it to *load* its view, consult its `isViewLoaded` property. You can also refer to a view controller's view safely, without loading it, as its `viewIfLoaded` (an Optional).

As soon as a view controller has its view, its `viewDidLoad` method is called. If this view controller is an instance of your own UIViewController subclass, `viewDidLoad` is your opportunity to modify the contents of this view — to populate it with subviews, to tweak the subviews it already has, and so forth — as well as to perform other initializations of the view controller and its properties. `viewDidLoad` is generally regarded as a valuable place to put initialization code, because it is one of the *earliest* events in the life of the view controller instance, and it is called only *once* in the instance's lifetime.

When `viewDidLoad` is called, the view controller's `view` property is pointing to the view, so it is safe to refer to `self.view`. Bear in mind that the view may not yet be part of the interface! In fact, it almost certainly is not. (To confirm this, check whether `self.view.window` is `nil`.) And you cannot necessarily rely on the *dimensions* of the view at this point to be the dimensions that the view will assume when it becomes visible in the interface. Performing dimension-dependent customizations prematurely in `viewDidLoad` is a common beginner mistake, and I'll talk about that in detail later in this chapter.

Before `viewDidLoad` is called, the view controller must *obtain* its view. The question of where and how the view controller will get its view is often crucial. In some cases, to be sure, you won't care about this. In particular, when a view controller is an instance of a built-in UIViewController subclass such as UINavigationController or UITabBarController, its view is out of your hands; you might never have cause to refer to this view over the entire course of your app's lifetime, and you simply trust that the view controller will generate its view somehow. But when the view controller is an instance of your own subclass of UIViewController, and when you yourself will design or modify its view, it becomes essential to understand the process whereby a view controller gets its view.

This process is not difficult to understand. It is rather elaborate, because there are multiple possibilities, but it is *not magic*. Nevertheless it probably causes beginners more confusion than any other aspect of Cocoa programming. The main alternatives are:

- The view may be instantiated in the view controller's own code, manually.
- The view may be created as an empty generic UIView, automatically.
- The view may be loaded from a nib file.

To demonstrate, we'll need a view controller that we instantiate manually. For the sake of simplicity, I'll use the window's `rootViewController`.

To follow along hands-on, start with a clean project created from the basic App template. The template includes a storyboard and a UIViewController subclass called ViewController, but we're going to ignore both of those, behaving as if the storyboard didn't exist. Instead, we'll have a class called RootViewController; in code, at launch, we'll instantiate it and make that instance the window's root view controller (see "App Without a Storyboard" on page 7). When you launch the project, you'll know that the root view controller has obtained its view, because you'll *see* it.

Manual View

To supply a UIViewController's view manually, in code, override its `loadView` method. Your job here is to obtain an instance of UIView (or a subclass of UIView) — typically by instantiating it directly — and *assign it to `self.view`*. You must *not* call `super` (for reasons that I'll make clear later on).

Let's try it:

1. We need a UIViewController subclass, so choose File → New → File; specify iOS → Source → Cocoa Touch Class. Click Next.

2. Name the class RootViewController, and specify that it is to be a UIView-Controller subclass. Uncheck "Also create XIB file" (if it happens to be checked). Click Next.

3. Confirm that we're saving into the appropriate folder and group, and that these files will be part of the app target. Click Create.

We now have a RootViewController class, and we proceed to edit its code. In *Root-ViewController.swift*, we'll implement `loadView`. To convince ourselves that the example is working correctly, we'll give the view that we create manually an identifiable color, and we'll put some interface inside it, namely a "Hello, world" label:

```swift
override func loadView() {
    let v = UIView()
    v.backgroundColor = .green
    self.view = v // *
    let label = UILabel()
    v.addSubview(label)
    label.text = "Hello, world"
    label.autoresizingMask = [
        .flexibleTopMargin,
        .flexibleLeftMargin,
        .flexibleBottomMargin,
        .flexibleRightMargin
    ]
    label.sizeToFit()
    label.center = v.bounds.center
    label.frame = label.frame.integral
}
```

The starred line is the key: we made a view and we assigned it to `self.view`. To see that that code works, we need to instantiate RootViewController and place that instance into our view controller hierarchy. Edit *SceneDelegate.swift* to look like this:

```
import UIKit
class SceneDelegate: UIResponder, UIWindowSceneDelegate {
    var window: UIWindow?
    func scene(_ scene: UIScene,
            willConnectTo session: UISceneSession,
            options connectionOptions: UIScene.ConnectionOptions) {
        if let windowScene = scene as? UIWindowScene {
            self.window = UIWindow(windowScene: windowScene)
            let rvc = RootViewController() // *
            self.window!.rootViewController = rvc // *
            self.window!.backgroundColor = .white
            self.window!.makeKeyAndVisible()
        }
    }
}
```

Again, the starred lines are the key: we instantiate RootViewController and make that instance the window's root view controller. Build and run the app. Sure enough, there's our green background and our "Hello, world" label!

When we created our view controller's view (`self.view`), we never gave it a reasonable frame. This is because we are relying on someone else to frame the view appropriately. In this case, the "someone else" is the window. When the window's `rootViewController` property is set to a view controller, it responds by giving the view controller's view a frame and putting it into the window as a subview, making it the root view.

In general, it is the responsibility of whoever puts a view controller's view into the interface to give the view the correct frame — and this will never be the view controller itself (although under some circumstances the view controller can express a preference in this regard). Indeed, the size of a view controller's view may be changed as it is placed into the interface, and you must keep that possibility in mind as you design your view controller's view and its subviews. (That's why, in the preceding code, I used autoresizing to keep the label centered in the view, no matter how the view may be resized.)

Generic Automatic View

We should distinguish between *creating* a view and *populating* it. The preceding example fails to draw this distinction. The lines that create our RootViewController's view are merely these:

```
let v = UIView()
self.view = v
```

Everything else configures and populates the view, turning it green and putting a label into it. A more appropriate place to populate a view controller's view is its `view-DidLoad` implementation, which, as I've already mentioned, is called after the view exists and can be referred to as `self.view`. We could therefore rewrite the preceding example like this (just for fun, I'll use autolayout this time):

```
override func loadView() {
    let v = UIView()
    self.view = v
}
override func viewDidLoad() {
    super.viewDidLoad()
    let v = self.view!
    v.backgroundColor = .green
    let label = UILabel()
    v.addSubview(label)
    label.text = "Hello, world"
    label.translatesAutoresizingMaskIntoConstraints = false
    NSLayoutConstraint.activate([
        label.centerXAnchor.constraint(equalTo:v.centerXAnchor),
        label.centerYAnchor.constraint(equalTo:v.centerYAnchor)
    ])
}
```

But if we're going to do that, we can go even further and remove our implementation of `loadView` entirely! It turns out that if you *don't* implement `loadView`, and if no view is supplied in any other way, then UIViewController's default implementation of `loadView` will do *exactly* what we are doing: it creates a generic UIView object and assigns it to `self.view`. If we needed our view controller's view to be a particular UIView subclass, that wouldn't be acceptable; but in this case, our view controller's view *is* a generic UIView object, so it *is* acceptable.

Comment out or delete the entire `loadView` implementation from the preceding code, and build and run the app; our example still works!

View in a Separate Nib

In the preceding examples, we supplied and designed our view controller's view in code. That works, but of course we're missing out on the convenience of configuring and populating the view by designing it graphically in Xcode's nib editor. So now let's see how a view controller can obtain its view, ready-made, from a nib file.

To make this work, the nib file must be properly configured in accordance with the demands of the nib-loading mechanism. The view controller instance will already have been created. It will load the nib, *setting itself as the nib's owner*. The nib must be prepared for this situation:

- The owner object must have the same class as the view controller. This will also cause the owner object to have a `view` outlet.
- The owner object's `view` outlet must point to the view object in the nib.

The consequence is that when the view controller loads the nib, the view instantiated from the nib is assigned to the view controller's `view` property automatically.

Let's try it with a *.xib* file. In a *.xib* file, the owner object is the File's Owner proxy object. We can use the example we've already developed, with our RootViewController class. Delete the implementation of `loadView` (if you haven't already) and `viewDidLoad` from *RootViewController.swift*, because we want the view to come from a nib and we're going to populate it in the nib. Then:

1. Choose File → New → File and specify iOS → User Interface → View. This will be a *.xib* file containing a UIView object. Click Next.

2. Name the file *MyNib* (meaning *MyNib.xib*). Confirm the appropriate folder and group, and make sure that the file will be part of the app target. Click Create.

3. Edit *MyNib.xib*. Prepare it in the way I described a moment ago:

   a. Select the File's Owner object; in the Identity inspector, set its class to RootViewController. As a result, the File's Owner now has a `view` outlet.

   b. Connect the File's Owner `view` outlet to the View object.

4. Design the view. To make it clear that this is not the same view we were creating previously, perhaps you should give the view a red background color (in the Attributes inspector). Drag a UILabel into the middle of the view and give it some text, such as "Hello, world."

When our RootViewController instance wants its view, we want it to load the *MyNib* nib. To make it do that, we must associate this nib with our RootViewController instance. Recall these two lines in *SceneDelegate.swift*:

```
let rvc = RootViewController()
self.window!.rootViewController = rvc
```

We're going to change the first of those two lines. A UIViewController has a `nibName` property that tells it what nib, if any, it should load to obtain its view. But we are not allowed to set the `nibName` property of rvc; it is read-only, meaning that only RootViewController can set its own `nibName`. Instead, as we instantiate the view controller, we use the designated initializer, `init(nibName:bundle:)`, like this:

```
let rvc = RootViewController(nibName:"MyNib", bundle:nil)
self.window!.rootViewController = rvc
```

(The `nil` argument to the `bundle:` parameter specifies the main bundle, which is almost always what you want.) The result is that RootViewController *does* set its own `nibName` to `"MyNib"`, and obtains its view by locating that nib file and loading it.

To prove that this works, build and run. The red background appears! Our view controller's view is being obtained by loading it from the nib.

The eponymous nib

Now I'm going to describe a shortcut, based on the *name* of the nib. It turns out that if the nib name passed to `init(nibName:bundle:)` is nil, a nib will be sought automatically *with the same name as the view controller's class.* Moreover, UIView-Controller's `init()` turns out to be a convenience initializer: it actually calls `init(nibName:bundle:)`, passing `nil` for both arguments.

This means that we can return to using `init()` to initialize the view controller, provided that the nib file's name *matches the name* of the view controller class. Let's try it:

1. Rename *MyNib.xib* to *RootViewController.xib*.

2. Change the code that instantiates and initializes our RootViewController back to what it was before:

```
let rvc = RootViewController()
self.window!.rootViewController = rvc
```

Build and run. It works!

There's an additional aspect to that shortcut. It seems ridiculous that we should end up with a nib that has "Controller" in its name merely because our view controller, as is so often the case, has "Controller" in *its* name. A nib, after all, is not a controller. It turns out that the runtime, in looking for a view controller's corresponding nib, will in fact try stripping "Controller" off the end of the view controller class's name. We can name our nib file *RootView.xib* instead of *RootViewController.xib*, and it will *still* be properly associated with our RootViewController instance.

Automatic XIB file creation

When we created our UIViewController subclass, RootViewController, we saw in the Xcode dialog a checkbox offering to create an eponymous *.xib* file at the same time: "Also create XIB file." We deliberately unchecked it. We are now in a position to understand what happens if we check that checkbox:

- Xcode creates *RootViewController.swift* and *RootViewController.xib*.

- Xcode configures *RootViewController.xib*:

  - The File's Owner's class is set to the view controller's class, RootView-Controller.

  - The File's Owner's `view` outlet is hooked up to the view.

The view controller and *.xib* file are ready for use together: you instantiate the view controller with a `nil` nib name, and it gets its view from the eponymous nib.

(The *.xib* file created by Xcode in response to checking "Also create XIB file" does *not* have "Controller" stripped off the end of its name; you can rename it manually later if the default name bothers you.)

Summary

We can now summarize the sequence whereby a view controller's view is obtained. It turns out that the entire process is driven by loadView:

1. When the view controller first decides that it needs its view, loadView is *always* called:
    *   If we override loadView, we supply and set the view in code, and we do *not* call super. Therefore, the process of seeking a view comes to an end.
    *   If we *don't* override loadView, UIViewController's built-in default implementation of loadView takes over, and performs the rest of the process.

2. UIViewController's default implementation of loadView looks for a nib:
    *   If the view controller's nibName property is not nil, a nib with that name is sought, and the process comes to an end.
    *   If the view controller's nibName property *is* nil, then:
        1. An eponymous nib is sought. If it is found, it is loaded and the process comes to an end.
        2. If the view controller's name ends in "Controller," an eponymous nib without the "Controller" is sought. If it is found, it is loaded and the process comes to an end.

3. If we reach this point, UIViewController's default implementation of loadView creates a generic UIView.

If things go wrong during that process, at best the wrong view might appear; at worst the app might crash. Typically a crash happens because the view controller tries to obtain its view by loading a nib, but it fails, because:

*   A nibName is specified but there is no such nib.
*   A nib is found but the nib itself is not correctly configured: the file's owner is not of the right class, or its view outlet is not set.

How Storyboards Work

Up to this point, in explaining where a view controller comes from and how it gets its view, I've been ignoring the existence of storyboards. That's not because storyboards work differently from what I've been describing; it's because storyboards work *the same way* as what I've been describing!

First of all, what *is* a storyboard? It's actually a collection of nib files, along with some ancillary information about them (stored in an *Info.plist* file). And what's a nib file? It's just a set of instructions for creating and configuring instances. When a nib is loaded during the running of the app, those instructions are obeyed and the instances are created and configured. The instances in question will mostly be UIView instances; the advantage of a nib as a way of making view instances is that you get to design those views graphically, as in a drawing program, instead of having to describe them in code. But it is also legal for a nib object to be a view controller. So it is possible to store the instructions for creating and configuring a view controller in a nib file, and to obtain the actual view controller instance at runtime by loading the nib.

Storyboards contain *scenes*. Each scene consists of a view controller. Each view controller goes into a nib file. When the app runs, if an instance of that view controller is needed, that nib is loaded — and so that view controller's class is instantiated and the instance is configured. That answers the question about where the view controller comes from.

And how does this view controller get its view? Well, it *can* get its view in any of the ways I've just finished describing, but usually it will use the third way: it will get its view from a nib. By default, a storyboard scene contains *two* things: a view controller *and its main view*. The view controller goes into a nib file, and its main view goes into *another* nib file. This second nib file configures the view, its subviews, and any other top-level objects such as gesture recognizers. The view nib has a special name, such as *01J-lp-oVM-view-Ze5-6b-2t3.nib*, so that the view controller can find it later. And the view nib is correctly configured: its File's Owner class is the view controller's class, with its view outlet hooked to the view. When the view controller has been instantiated and needs its view, it loads the corresponding view nib.

As a result of this architecture, a storyboard has all the memory management advantages of nib files: none of these nib files are loaded until the instances that they contain are needed, and they can be loaded multiple times to give additional instances of the same nib objects. At the same time, you get the convenience of being able, through the nib editor, to see and edit a lot of your app's interface simultaneously in one place.

How a Storyboard View Controller Nib is Loaded

A storyboard is first and foremost a source of view controller instances. In fact, you can set up your app in such a way that a storyboard is the source of *every* view controller that your app will ever instantiate; what's more, you can usually configure the storyboard in such a way that every view controller your app will ever need will be instantiated *automatically* at exactly the moment it is needed.

To instantiate a view controller from a storyboard, we must load a view controller nib from that storyboard. The process therefore starts with a reference to the storyboard. You can get a reference to a storyboard chiefly in one of two ways:

- Through the storyboard's name, by calling the UIStoryboard initializer `init(name:bundle:)`.

- Through the `storyboard` property of a view controller that has already been instantiated from that storyboard.

When a view controller needs to be instantiated from a storyboard, its nib can be loaded in one of four main ways:

Initial view controller

> One view controller in the storyboard may be designated the storyboard's *initial view controller* (also called its *entry point*). To instantiate that view controller, call this UIStoryboard instance method:
>
> - `instantiateInitialViewController`
>
> The view controller instance is returned, or `nil` if the storyboard has no initial view controller.

By identifier

> A view controller in a storyboard may be assigned an arbitrary string identifier; this is its Storyboard ID in the Identity inspector. To instantiate that view controller, call this UIStoryboard instance method:
>
> - `instantiateViewController(withIdentifier:)`
>
> The view controller instance is returned, or you'll crash if the storyboard has no such view controller.

By relationship

> A parent view controller in a storyboard may have immediate children, such as a UINavigationController and its initial child view controller. The nib editor will show a *relationship* connection between them. When the parent is instantiated (the source of the relationship), the initial children (the destination of the relationship) are *automatically* instantiated at the same time.

By a triggered segue

> A view controller in a storyboard may be the source of a *segue* whose destination is a child or presented view controller. When the segue is triggered and performed, it *automatically* instantiates the destination view controller.

How a Storyboard View Nib is Loaded

When a view controller is instantiated from its storyboard nib, it has no view, because (as we know) view controller views are loaded lazily. Sooner or later, the view controller will probably want its view (typically because it is time to put that view into the interface). How will it get it?

The view nib, as I already mentioned, has been assigned a special name, such as *01J-lp-oVM-view-Ze5-6b-2t3.nib*. It turns out that the view controller, in *its* nib, was handed that same special name: its `nibName` property was set to the name of the view nib. So when the view controller wants its view, it loads it in the normal way! Its `nibName` is not `nil`, so it looks for a nib by that name — and finds it. The nib is loaded and the view becomes the view controller's `view`.

Alternatively, it is possible (though not common), in the nib editor, to select the view inside a view controller in a storyboard and *delete* it. That view controller then will *not* have a corresponding view nib in the storyboard, and will have to obtain its view in some *other* way:

- Through an implementation of `loadView` in the corresponding class's code.
- By loading an eponymous nib that you supply as a *.xib* file.
- As a generic UIView created automatically.

View Resizing

It's important to be prepared for the possibility that your view controller's main view will be resized. This might happen because:

- The view is put into the interface.
- The app rotates.
- The surrounding interface changes; for example, a navigation bar gets taller or shorter, appears or disappears.
- The window itself is resized in the iPad multitasking interface.

You'll want to use layout to help your app cope with all this resizing. Autolayout is likely to be your most important ally (Chapter 1). If your code also needs to take a hand in responding to a change in the view controller's view size, that code will probably go into the view controller itself. A view controller has properties and receives events connected to the resizing of its view, so it can respond when resizing takes place, and can even help dictate the arrangement of the interface if needed.

View Size in the Nib Editor

Of the various ways in which a view controller's view may be resized, the one that surprises beginners most is when they design a view controller's main view in the storyboard, and then it looks all wrong when they run the app — because the view is resized when it is put into the interface.

When you design your interface in the nib editor, there are various settings for specifying the size of a view controller's main view:

The View As button at the lower left of the canvas
> You can specify that you want all view controller main views displayed at the size of a particular device, along with an orientation.

The Simulated Metrics pop-up menus in the Attributes inspector
> You can adjust for the presence or absence of interface elements that can affect layout (status bar, top bar, bottom bar).

The Simulated Size pop-up menu in the Size inspector
> By choosing Freeform, you can display a view controller's view at *any* size.

But here's the problem: all of that is just a way of *displaying* the view. It tells you *nothing* about the size that the view will be *when the app runs!* There's a wide range of possible sizes that the view may assume when the app runs on different devices, in different orientations, and with different surroundings. No single device size, orientation, or metrics can reflect all of these.

If you design the interface only for the size you see in the nib editor, you can get a rude surprise when you actually run the app and the view appears at some *other* size! Failing to take account of this possibility is a common beginner mistake. Be sure to design your app's interface to be coherent at *any* size it may actually assume. Use every tool at your disposal, including building and running on every simulator, to ensure this.

Bars and Underlapping

A view controller's view will often have to adapt to the presence of bars at the top and bottom of the screen:

The status bar
> The status bar is transparent, so that the region of a view behind it is visible through it. The root view, and any other fullscreen view, must occupy the *entire window*, including the status bar area. The top of the view will be behind the status bar, underlapping it and visible through it; a view behind the status bar can't be touched. You'll want to design your view so that interface objects that the user needs to see or touch are not covered by the status bar.

Top and bottom bars

Top and bottom bars may be displayed by a navigation controller (navigation bar, toolbar) or tab bar controller (tab bar). Your view controller's view may extend *behind* a bar, underlapping it. You'll want to design your view so that top and bottom bars don't conceal any of your view's important interface.

Safe area

The status bar may be present or absent. Top and bottom bars may be present or absent, and, if present, their height can change. How will your interface cope with such changes? The primary coping mechanism is the view controller's *safe area* (see "Safe area" on page 48). The top and bottom of the safe area move automatically at runtime to reflect the view's environment.

Here's how the safe area top is determined:

- If there is a status bar and no top bar, the safe area top is at the bottom of the status bar.
- If there is a top bar, the safe area top is at the bottom of the top bar.
- If there is no top bar and no status bar, the safe area top is at the top of the view.

Here's how the safe area bottom is determined:

- If there is a bottom bar, the safe area bottom is at the top of the bottom bar.
- If there is no bottom bar, the safe area bottom is at the bottom of the view.

(On a device without a bezel, the safe area top and bottom will take account of the "notch" and home indicator, so they might not be at the top and bottom of the view.)

The easiest way to involve the safe area in your view layout is through autolayout and constraints. A view vends the safe area as its `safeAreaLayoutGuide`. Typically, the view whose `safeAreaLayoutGuide` you'll be interested in is the view controller's main view. By constraining a subview to the `topAnchor` or `bottomAnchor` of the `safeArea-LayoutGuide`, you guarantee that the subview will move when the top or bottom of the safe area changes. Such constraints are easy to form in the nib editor — they are the default when you form a constraint from a subview to the main view.

Status bar

The status bar can be present or absent. The default behavior is that it is present, except in landscape orientation on an iPhone, where it is absent. If the status bar is present, its background is transparent and it contains text; that text can be light or dark, so as to show up against whatever is behind the status bar. The default behavior (starting in iOS 13) is that the text color responds so as to contrast with the user interface style (light mode or dark mode).

The top-level view controller — which is usually the root view controller — gets a say in this behavior. Your UIViewController subclass, if an instance of it is the top-level view controller, can exercise this power by overriding these properties:

preferredStatusBarStyle

Your choices (UIStatusBarStyle) are:

.default

In iOS 13 and later, this means automatic in response to the user interface style. If the interface is in dark mode, the text will be light; if the interface is in light mode, the text will be dark.

.lightContent

The text will be light.

.darkContent

The text will be dark.

prefersStatusBarHidden

A value of true makes the status bar invisible; a value of false makes the status bar visible, even in landscape orientation on an iPhone.

Your override will be a computed variable with a getter function; your getter can return the result of a call to super to get the default behavior.

Even if your view controller is *not* the top-level view controller, those properties might *still* be consulted and obeyed, because your view controller might be the child of a parent that *is* the top-level view controller but *delegates* the decision-making power to one of its children, through an override of these properties:

childForStatusBarStyle
childForStatusBarHidden

Used to delegate the decision on the status bar style or visibility to a child view controller's preferredStatusBarStyle or prefersStatusBarHidden.

A tab bar controller is a case in point. It implements those properties to allow its selected child (the child view controller whose view is currently being displayed) to decide the status bar style and visibility.

You are not in charge of when status bar–related properties are consulted, but you can provide a nudge: if the situation has changed and one of those properties would now give a different answer, call setNeedsStatusBarAppearanceUpdate on your view controller.

If you call setNeedsStatusBarAppearanceUpdate and the status bar style or visibility changes, the change will be sudden. If you prefer to animate the change over time, call setNeedsStatusBarAppearanceUpdate inside an animations function. If the visibility changes, the nature of the animation is set by your view controller's override of `preferredStatusBarUpdateAnimation`; the value you return (UIStatusBar-Animation) can be `.fade`, `.slide`, or `.none`.

When you change the visibility of the status bar, the top of the safe area may move up or down. If your main view has subviews with constraints to the safe area's top anchor, those subviews will move. By default, the user will see this movement as a jump. If you prefer that the movement of the subviews should be animated, animate the change in layout by calling `layoutIfNeeded` on your view ("Animation and Layout" on page 246). If you are also animating the change in the status bar's visibility, you'll do that in the same animations function in which you call `setNeedsStatusBar-AppearanceUpdate`. In this example, a button's action method toggles the visibility of the status bar with smooth animation:

```
var hide = false
override var prefersStatusBarHidden : Bool {
    return self.hide
}
@IBAction func doButton(_ sender: Any) {
    self.hide.toggle()
    UIView.animate(withDuration: 0.4) {
        self.setNeedsStatusBarAppearanceUpdate()
        self.view.layoutIfNeeded()
    }
}
```

If you want to know the current state of the status bar, you should ask the window scene's status bar manager (UIStatusBarManager). It has properties `statusBarFrame`, `isStatusBarHidden`, and `statusBarStyle` (always reported as `.darkContent` or `.lightContent`). This works even if your app doesn't explicitly support window scenes, because there is always an implicit window scene:

```
if let sbman = self.view.window?.windowScene?.statusBarManager {
    let isHidden = sbman.isStatusBarHidden
    // ...
}
```

Extended layout

If a view controller is the child of a navigation controller or tab bar controller, you can govern whether its view underlaps a top bar (navigation bar) or bottom bar (toolbar, tab bar) with these UIViewController properties:

`edgesForExtendedLayout`
    A UIRectEdge governing what bars this view controller's view is permitted to underlap:

.all
> A top bar or a bottom bar. The default.

.top
> Top bars only.

.bottom
> Bottom bars only.

.none
> This view controller's view won't underlap top and bottom bars.

extendedLayoutIncludesOpaqueBars
> Top and bottom bars can be translucent or not, according to the value of their isTranslucent property. If a view controller's extendedLayoutIncludesOpaque-Bars property is true, then if its edgesForExtendedLayout permits underlapping of bars, those bars will be underlapped even if their isTranslucent is false. The default is false, meaning that *only* translucent bars are underlapped.

Resizing and Layout Events

A view controller receives *resizing events* that notify it of changes related to the main view being resized:

willTransition(to:with:) *(UIContentContainer protocol)*
> Sent when the view controller's *trait collection* is about to change. This can happen for many reasons, but one possibility is a size change that causes the size classes to change, such as the app rotating 90 degrees on an iPhone. The first parameter is the *new* trait collection (a UITraitCollection). The old trait collection is still available as self.traitCollection. If you override this method, call super.

viewWillTransition(to:with:) *(UIContentContainer protocol)*
> Sent when the main view's *size* is about to change. The app might be about to undergo rotation, or the user might be widening or narrowing the window under iPad multitasking (see Chapter 10). The first parameter is the *new* size (a CGSize). The old size is still available as self.view.bounds.size. If you override this method, call super.

traitCollectionDidChange(_:) *(UITraitEnvironment protocol)*
> Sent after the trait collection changes. The parameter is the *old* trait collection; the new trait collection is available as self.traitCollection. If you override this method, call super *first* before doing anything else.

Do not do anything time-consuming or irrelevant in the resizing events! These events can arrive multiple times in quick succession when the app (or scene) goes into the background, so that the runtime can obtain screenshots in both orientations and in both user interface styles (light and dark mode).

The `with:` parameter in the first two methods is a *transition coordinator* (UIViewControllerTransitionCoordinator). If we're getting these events because rotation is about to take place, we can hook into the rotation animation by calling this method of the coordinator:

`animate(alongsideTransition:completion:)`
> The first parameter is an animations function; animations we supply here will be performed in coordination with the rotation animation. The second parameter is an optional completion function to be executed when the rotation animation is over.

If you need to know what the rotation is, look at the coordinator's `targetTransform`, a CGAffineTransform. Here's a useful trick in case you need to keep a view (`self.v`) oriented the same way with respect to the *device* regardless of how the interface rotates:

```
self.v.transform =
    coordinator.targetTransform.inverted().concatenating(self.v.transform)
```

In addition, a UIViewController receives *layout events* related to the layout of its view (and compare "Layout Events" on page 79 for the corresponding UIView events):

`updateViewConstraints`
> The view is about to be told to update its constraints (`updateConstraints`), including at application launch. If you override this method, call `super`.

`viewWillLayoutSubviews`
`viewDidLayoutSubviews`
> These events surround the moment when the view is sent `layoutSubviews`, including at application launch. They are important and useful events, but they can arrive more often than you might expect, so don't do any work that you don't have to.

Layout events can be a more reliable way to detect a size change than the resizing events. There are many circumstances, such as the showing and hiding of a navigation bar that isn't underlapped, under which your view can be resized *without* a size change being reported; and you don't necessarily get any resizing event when your view is added to the interface, or at launch, even though it probably is resized at that moment. (I regard this as a flaw in the view controller event architecture.) But under those same circumstances you'll always get layout events.

Rotation

Your app can rotate, moving its top to correspond to a different edge of the device's screen. Your view controller will be intimately concerned with rotation of the app.

 A Simulator window can automatically rotate if the orientation of the app changes. Choose Device → Rotate Device Automatically to toggle this setting. Oddly, your choice applies to *all* Simulator windows.

Uses of Rotation

There are two complementary uses of rotation:

Compensatory rotation
> The app rotates to compensate for the orientation of the device, so that the interface appears right way up with respect to how the user is holding the device.

Forced rotation
> The app rotates when a particular view appears in the interface, or when the app launches, to indicate that the user needs to reorient the device in order to view the interface the right way up. This is typically because the interface has been specifically designed, in view of the fact that the screen is not square, to appear in just one orientation (portrait or landscape).

In the case of the iPhone, no law says that your app has to perform compensatory rotation. Most of my iPhone apps do not do so. My view controller views often look best in just one orientation (either just portrait or just landscape), and they stubbornly stay there regardless of how the user holds the device.

Some of those same apps may have some view controller views that look best in portrait and others that look best in landscape. In that case, I have no compunction about forcing the user to rotate the device differently depending on what view is being displayed. This is reasonable, because the iPhone has a natural right way up, and because it is small and easily reoriented 90 degrees with a twist of the user's wrist.

On the other hand, Apple thinks of an iPad as having no natural top, and would prefer iPad apps to rotate to at least two opposed orientations (such as both landscape orientations), and preferably to all four possible orientations, so that the user isn't restricted as to how the device is held.

Allowing a single interface to rotate between two orientations that are 90 degrees apart is tricky, because its dimensions must change — roughly speaking, its height and width are transposed — and this may require a change of layout, perhaps with quite substantial alterations, such as removal or addition of part of the interface. A good example is the behavior of Apple's Files app on the iPad, which displays the

Files list (showing locations and tags) as a sidebar in landscape but an overlay in portrait.

Permitting Compensatory Rotation

By default, when you create an Xcode project, the app will perform compensatory rotation in response to the user's rotation of the device. For an iPhone app, this means that the app can appear with its top at the top or either side of the device. For an iPad app, it means that the app can assume any of the four orientations.

If the default behavior isn't what you want, it is up to you to change it. There are three levels at which you can make changes:

The app's Info.plist
> The app itself, in its *Info.plist*, declares once and for all every orientation the interface will ever be permitted to assume. It does this under the "Supported interface orientations" key, `UISupportedInterfaceOrientations`. For a universal app, this is supplemented by "Supported interface orientations (iPad)," `UISupportedInterfaceOrientations~ipad`. These keys can be set through checkboxes when you edit the app target, in the General tab (under Deployment Info, Device Orientation).

The app delegate's `application(_:supportedInterfaceOrientationsFor:)`
> This method, if implemented, returns a bitmask listing every orientation the interface is permitted to assume at that moment. This list *overrides* the *Info.plist* settings. In this way, the app delegate can do dynamically what the *Info.plist* can do only statically. This method is called at least once every time the device rotates.

The top-level view controller's `supportedInterfaceOrientations`
> The top-level view controller — that is, the root view controller, or a view controller presented fullscreen — may override the `supportedInterfaceOrientations` property, returning a bitmask listing every orientation that the interface is permitted to assume at that moment. Starting in iOS 13, if both the app delegate and the view controller participate in this decision, the view controller wins outright. (In iOS 12 and before, their contributions must intersect or the app will crash.)
>
> The top-level view controller can also override `shouldAutorotate`. This is a Bool, and the default is `true`. It is consulted at least once every time the device rotates; if it returns `false`, that's the end of the matter — `supportedInterfaceOrientations` is not consulted and the interface does not perform compensatory rotation.

Built-in parent view controllers, when they are the top-level view controller, do *not* automatically consult their children about rotation. If your view controller is a child view controller of a UITabBarController or a UINavigationController, it has no direct say in how the app rotates. Those parent view controllers, however, do consult their *delegates* about rotation, as I'll explain later.

You can call the UIViewController class method `attemptRotationToDevice-Orientation` to prompt the runtime to do immediately what it would do if the user were to rotate the device, namely to walk the three levels I've just described and, if the results permit rotation of the interface to match the current device orientation, to rotate the interface at that moment. This would be useful if, say, your view controller had previously returned false from `shouldAutorotate`, but is now for some reason prepared to return true and wants to be asked again, immediately.

The bitmask you return from `application(_:supportedInterfaceOrientations-For:)` or `supportedInterfaceOrientations` is a UIInterfaceOrientationMask. It may be one of these values, or multiple values combined:

- `.portrait`
- `.landscapeLeft`
- `.landscapeRight`
- `.portraitUpsideDown`
- `.landscape` (a combination of `.left` and `.right`)
- `.all` (a combination of `.portrait`, `.upsideDown`, `.left`, and `.right`)
- `.allButUpsideDown` (a combination of `.portrait`, `.left`, and `.right`)

For example:

```
override var supportedInterfaceOrientations : UIInterfaceOrientationMask {
    return .portrait
}
```

If your code needs to know the current physical orientation of the *device* (as opposed to the current orientation of the interface), it is `UIDevice.current.orientation`. Possible values (UIDeviceOrientation) are `.unknown`, `.portrait`, and so on. The `orientation` also has two convenience properties, `isPortrait` and `isLandscape`, that return a Bool.

 On iPad, if your app permits all four orientations, and if it doesn't opt out of iPad multitasking, then `supportedInterfaceOrientations` and `should-Autorotate` are *never* consulted, because the answer is known in advance: compensatory rotation is always performed.

Initial Orientation

I've talked about how to determine what orientations your app can support in the course of its lifetime; but what about its *initial* orientation, the very first orientation your app will assume when it launches? In general, an app will launch directly into whatever permitted orientation is closest to the device's current orientation at launch time; this makes sense and is generally what you expect.

There can be a complication when the orientation in which the device is held would have been legal, but the initial root view controller rules it out. Suppose the device is held in portrait, and the *Info.plist* permits all orientations, but the root view controller's `supportedInterfaceOrientations` is set to return `.landscape`. Then the app starts to launch into portrait, realizes its mistake, and finishes launching in landscape. On the iPhone, this entails a kind of semirotation: `willTransition(to:with:)` is sent to report a trait collection change, but oddly there is *no size change*.

To work around that problem, here's a trick that I use. Let's say that my app needs *eventually* to be able to rotate to portrait, so I need to permit all orientations, but its *initial* root view controller must appear only in landscape. In my *Info.plist*, I permit *only* landscape; that way, my app launches directly into landscape, no matter how the device is oriented. But in my app delegate's `application(_:supportedInterface-OrientationsFor:)`, I return `.all`; that way, my app can rotate *subsequently* to portrait if it needs to.

Detecting Rotation

On the whole, you are unlikely to want to detect rotation *per se*. You are more likely to want to respond to a change of size classes, or a change of layout; you'll use a trait collection event or a layout event. If you really do need to detect that rotation is taking place, even on an iPad, the best way is through the size change event `willTransition(to:with:)`. Size changes can happen for other reasons, so to determine that this really was a rotation, compare the orientation of the interface before and after the transition. You can find out the interface orientation by asking the window scene:

```
override func viewWillTransition(to size: CGSize,
    with coordinator: UIViewControllerTransitionCoordinator) {
        super.viewWillTransition(to:size, with: coordinator)
        let before = self.view.window?.windowScene?.interfaceOrientation
        coordinator.animate(alongsideTransition: nil) { _ in
            let after = self.view.window?.windowScene?.interfaceOrientation
            if before != after {
                // we rotated
            }
        }
}
```

The `interfaceOrientation` is a UIInterfaceOrientation; possible values are .`portrait` and so on. Two convenient `interfaceOrientation` properties, `isLandscape` and `isPortrait`, return a Bool.

View Controller Manual Layout

What if a view controller wants to participate directly, in code, in the layout of its main view's subviews? A view controller's view can be resized, both as the view is first put into the interface and later as the app runs and is rotated. Where should your view controller's layout code be placed in order to behave coherently in the face of these potential size changes?

Initial Manual Layout

There is a natural temptation to perform initial layout-related tasks in `viewDidLoad`. This method is extraordinarily convenient. It is guaranteed to be called exactly once very early in the life of the view controller; the view controller has its view, and if it got that view from a nib, properties connected to outlets from that nib have been set. This seems like the perfect place for initializations. But initialization and layout are not the same thing.

At the time `viewDidLoad` is called, the view controller's view has been loaded, but it has *not* yet been inserted into the interface, the view has *not* been fully resized for the first time, and initial layout has *not* yet taken place. You cannot do anything here that depends upon knowing the dimensions of the view controller's view or any other nib-loaded view — for the simple reason that you do *not* know them. Performing layout-related tasks in `viewDidLoad` and then wondering why things are sized or positioned incorrectly is a common beginner mistake.

Imagine that our view controller is the child of a navigation controller, and that our view controller does *not* underlap top and bottom bars. And suppose we wish, in code, before our view controller's view appears, to create a label and place it in the lower left corner of our main view. This code looks as if it should do that:

```
override func viewDidLoad() {
    super.viewDidLoad()
    let lab = UILabel()
    lab.text = "Hello"
    lab.sizeToFit()
    lab.frame.origin.y = self.view.bounds.height - lab.frame.height // *
    self.view.addSubview(lab)
}
```

The app launches, our main view appears — and there's no label. Where did it go? The view debugger reveals the answer: it's below the bottom of the screen. `viewDidLoad` runs *before* the main view is resized. The starred line calculates the label's `frame.origin.y` based on our main view's `bounds.height`, and *then* the main view's `bounds.height` changes, so the calculation is wrong. `viewDidLoad` is *too soon*.

The natural place to put that sort of code is an event related to resizing and layout of the main view — such as `viewWillLayoutSubviews`. But we need to be careful, because `viewWillLayoutSubviews` may be called many times over the life of our view controller. We can *position* our label in `viewWillLayoutSubviews` each time it is called, and indeed that's probably a good thing to do, because it takes care of repositioning the label when the main view's size changes on rotation; but we don't want to *create* our label more than once. A neat solution is to create the view (once) in `view-DidLoad` and position it (whenever layout is needed) in `viewWillLayoutSubviews`:

```
var lab : UILabel!
override func viewDidLoad() {
    super.viewDidLoad()
    self.lab = UILabel()
    self.lab.text = "Hello"
    self.lab.sizeToFit()
    self.view.addSubview(lab)
}
override func viewWillLayoutSubviews() {
    self.lab.frame.origin.y = self.view.bounds.height - self.lab.frame.height
}
```

If possible, you shouldn't do manual layout in the first place. You can create and insert this label in `viewDidLoad` and configure it for future layout by giving it autolayout constraints:

```
override func viewDidLoad() {
    let lab = UILabel()
    lab.text = "Hello"
    self.view.addSubview(lab)
    lab.translatesAutoresizingMaskIntoConstraints = false
    NSLayoutConstraint.activate([
        lab.leadingAnchor.constraint(equalTo: self.view.leadingAnchor),
        lab.bottomAnchor.constraint(equalTo: self.view.bottomAnchor)
    ])
}
```

That is *not* a case of doing manual layout in `viewDidLoad`. The constraints are not layout; they are instructions as to how this view should be sized and positioned by the runtime when layout does happen. (Autoresizing would work fine here too.)

Manual Layout During Rotation

The same principles apply to manual layout later in the life of the app. Let's say that rotation is taking place, and we want to respond by changing the layout in some way. Again, `viewWillLayoutSubviews` is an excellent place to do that:

Order of events

By the time layout occurs, all the *other* initial conditions are already in place. If the trait collection needed to change, it *has* changed. If our main view needed to be resized, it *has* been resized.

Animation

Rotation of the interface is animated. If the layout is changing in response to rotation, we want the change to be animated in coordination with the rotation animation. If we perform our changes in a layoutSubviews event, it *will* be animated during rotation!

Let's say I have a large green rectangle that should occupy the left one-third of the interface, but only when we are in landscape orientation (the main view's width is larger than its height) and only when we are in a .regular horizontal size class. This rectangle should come and go in a smooth animated fashion; let's decide to have it appear from, or vanish off to, the left of the interface.

I can manage all of that entirely by means of manual layout. As in the previous example, I'll distribute responsibilities between viewDidLoad (creating the view) and view-WillLayoutSubviews (positioning the view):

```
var greenView : UIView!
override func viewDidLoad() {
    super.viewDidLoad()
    self.greenView = UIView()
    self.greenView.backgroundColor = .green
    self.view.addSubview(self.greenView)
}
override func viewWillLayoutSubviews() {
    func greenViewShouldAppear() -> Bool {
        let tc = self.traitCollection
        let sz = self.view.bounds.size
        if tc.horizontalSizeClass == .regular {
            if sz.width > sz.height {
                return true
            }
        }
        return false
    }
    if greenViewShouldAppear() {
        self.greenView.frame = CGRect(0, 0,
            self.view.bounds.width/3.0, self.view.bounds.height
        )
    } else {
        self.greenView.frame = CGRect(
            -self.view.bounds.width/3.0, 0,
            self.view.bounds.width/3.0, self.view.bounds.height
        )
    }
}
```

This is a very handy technique. The change of a subview's frame in `viewWillLayout-Subviews` is animated, automatically, in coordination with a rotation animation. Moreover, if a view is under the influence of autolayout and we change its constraints instead of its frame in `viewWillLayoutSubviews`, the change in layout is *still* animated in coordination with a rotation animation!

Presented View Controller

Back when the only iOS device was an iPhone, a presented view controller was called a *modal* view controller. Under that original architecture, when a view controller is *presented*, the root view controller remains in place, but the root view controller's view is taken out of the interface and the modal view controller's view is used instead (Figure 6-7). There is usually a general sense that this replacement is temporary; eventually, the presented view controller will be *dismissed*. The presented interface will then be removed and the original interface will be restored.

Presented view controllers have evolved since the early days, particularly with regard to how their views relate to the existing interface. Instead of replacing the entire interface, a presented view controller's view can:

- Replace a *subview* within the existing interface.
- Cover the existing interface completely or partially, *without* removing any existing interface.

For the most part, the "modal" characterization still applies. A presented view controller's view generally blocks access to the "real" view, and the user must work there until it is removed and the "real" view is visible again.

The color picker view in my Zotz! app (Figure 6-2) is modal in that sense. It is an interface that says, "You are now configuring a color, and that's all you can do; change the color or cancel, or you'll be stuck here forever." The user can't get out of this view without tapping Cancel or Done, and the view that the user was previously using is visible as a blur behind this view, waiting for the user to return to it.

Presentation and Dismissal

The key methods for presenting and dismissing a view controller are:

`present(_:animated:completion:)`
> To make a view controller present another view controller, you send the first view controller this message, handing it the second view controller, which you will probably instantiate for this purpose. The first view controller will typically be `self`.

We now have two view controllers that stand in the relationship of being one another's `presentingViewController` and `presentedViewController` respectively. The presented view controller is retained, and its view replaces or covers the presenting view controller's view in the interface.

`dismiss(animated:completion:)`
The "presented" state of affairs persists until the presenting view controller is sent this message. The presented view controller's view is then removed from the interface, the original interface is restored, and the presented view controller is released; it will thereupon typically go out of existence.

As the view of the presented view controller appears, and again when it is dismissed, there's an option for animation to be performed as the transition takes place (the `animated:` argument, a Bool). The `completion:` parameter, which can be `nil`, lets you supply a function to be run after the transition (including the animation) has finished.

View controller relationships during presentation

The presenting view controller (the presented view controller's `presentingView-Controller`) is not necessarily the same view controller to which you sent `present(_:animated:completion:)`. It will help if we distinguish *three* roles that view controllers can play in presenting a view controller:

Presented view controller
The first argument to `present(_:animated:completion:)`.

Original presenter
The view controller to which `present(_:animated:completion:)` was sent. Apple sometimes refers to this view controller as the *source*; "original presenter" is my own term.

The presented view controller is set as the original presenter's `presentedView-Controller`.

Presenting view controller
The view controller whose view is replaced or covered by the presented view controller's view. By default, it is the view controller that was the top-level view controller prior to the presentation. It might not be the same as the original presenter.

This view controller is set as the presented view controller's `presentingView-Controller`. The presented view controller is set as the presenting view controller's `presentedViewController`. (This means that the presented view controller might be the `presentedViewController` of two different view controllers.)

When you want to dismiss a presented view controller, you can send `dismiss(animated:completion:)` to *any* of those three objects; the runtime will use the linkages between them to transmit the necessary messages up the chain on your behalf to the `presentingViewController`.

You can test whether a view controller's `presentedViewController` or `presentingViewController` is `nil` to learn whether presentation is occurring. A view controller whose `presentingViewController` is `nil` is not a presented view controller at this moment.

A view controller can present only one view controller at a time. If you send `present(_:animated:completion:)` to a view controller whose `presentedViewController` isn't `nil`, nothing will happen and the completion function is not called (and you'll get a warning from the runtime). A presented view controller can itself present a view controller, though, so there can be a chain of presented view controllers.

If you send `dismiss(animated:completion:)` to a view controller in the middle of a presentation chain — a view controller that has both a `presentingViewController` and a `presentedViewController` — then its `presentedViewController` is dismissed.

If you send `dismiss(animated:completion:)` to a view controller whose `presentedViewController` is `nil` and that has no `presentingViewController`, nothing will happen (not even a warning in the console), and the completion function is not called.

Manual view controller presentation

To illustrate, let's make one view controller present another, by calling `present(_:animated:completion:)`. (I'll talk later about how to arrange things in a storyboard with a modal segue so that `present(_:animated:completion:)` is called for you.)

Start with an iPhone project made from the basic App template. It contains one view controller class, called ViewController. We'll need a second view controller class:

1. Choose File → New → File and specify iOS → Source → Cocoa Touch Class. Click Next.
2. Name the class SecondViewController, make it a subclass of UIViewController, and check the XIB checkbox so that we can design this view controller's view in the nib editor. Click Next.
3. Confirm the folder, group, and app target membership, and click Create.

4. Edit *SecondViewController.xib*, and do something there to make the view distinctive, so that you'll recognize it when it appears; you might give it a red background color.

5. In *ViewController.swift*, give ViewController an action method that instantiates SecondViewController and presents it:

```
@IBAction func doPresent(_ sender: Any) {
    let svc = SecondViewController()
    svc.modalPresentationStyle = .fullScreen
    self.present(svc, animated:true)
}
```

6. Edit *Main.storyboard* and add a button to the ViewController's main view. Make an action connecting that button's Touch Up Inside control event to ViewController's doPresent.

Run the project. In ViewController's view, tap the button. SecondViewController's view slides into place over ViewController's view. We've presented a view controller!

In our lust for instant gratification, we have neglected to provide a way to dismiss the presented view controller. If you'd like to do that:

1. In *SecondViewController.swift*, give SecondViewController an action method that dismisses SecondViewController:

```
@IBAction func doDismiss(_ sender: Any) {
    self.presentingViewController?.dismiss(animated:true)
}
```

2. Edit *SecondViewController.xib* and add a button to SecondViewController's view. Connect that button to SecondViewController's doDismiss.

Run the project. You can now alternate between ViewController's view and SecondViewController's view, presenting and dismissing in turn. Go ahead and play for a while with your exciting new app; I'll wait.

Configuring a Presentation

This section describes some configurable aspects of how a view controller's view behaves as the view controller is presented.

Transition style

When a view controller is presented and later when it is dismissed, a simple animation of its view can be performed, according to whether the animated: parameter of the corresponding method is true. The animation type is the presented view controller's *modal transition style*. To choose an animation type, set the presented view controller's `modalTransitionStyle` property prior to the presentation. This value can be set in code or in the nib editor. Your choices (UIModalTransitionStyle) are:

`.coverVertical` *(the default)*
> The view slides up from the bottom on presentation and down on dismissal. The definition of "bottom" depends on the orientation of the device and the orientations the view controllers support.

`.flipHorizontal`
> The view flips on the vertical axis. If this is a `.fullScreen` or `.currentContext` presentation (as I'll describe in the next section), the presenting and presented views behave like the front and back of a piece of paper. The "vertical axis" is the device's long axis, regardless of the app's orientation.

`.crossDissolve`
> The views effectively remain stationary, and one fades into the other.

 A fourth option, `.partialCurl`, is completely unusable and should be avoided.

Alternatively, instead of a built-in modal transition style, you can substitute your own custom transition animation, as I'll explain later in this chapter.

Presentation style

When a view controller is presented, its view appears. Where that view is placed is determined by the presented view controller's *modal presentation style*. To choose a presentation style, set the presented view controller's `modalPresentationStyle` property prior to the presentation. This value can be set in code or in the nib editor. Your choices (UIModalPresentationStyle) are:

`.fullScreen`
> The presented view controller covers the entire screen. The presenting view controller is the top-level view controller, and its view — meaning the entire interface — is replaced. This was the default before iOS 13.

`.overFullScreen`
> Similar to `.fullScreen`, but the presenting view controller's view is *not* replaced; instead, it stays where it is, possibly being visible during the transition, and remaining visible behind the presented view controller's view if the latter has some transparency.

`.pageSheet`
> Starting in iOS 13, this is the default and its appearance is different from earlier systems. On the iPad it is smaller than the screen. On the iPhone in portrait

(`.compact` horizontal size class), it covers the screen but leaves a gap at the top, while the existing interface shrinks a little behind it. (It can look like that on the iPad too if the dynamic text size is very large.) On the iPhone in landscape (`.compact` vertical size class), visually indistinguishable from `.overFullScreen`.

`.formSheet`

On the iPad, similar to `.pageSheet` but smaller (and it has a `.compact` horizontal size class). As the name implies, this is intended to allow the user to fill out a form (Apple describes this as "gathering structured information from the user"). On the iPhone, visually indistinguishable from `.pageSheet`.

`.currentContext`

The presenting view controller can be *any* view controller, such as a child view controller. The presented view controller's view replaces the presenting view controller's view, which may have been occupying only a portion of the screen. I'll explain later how to specify the presenting view controller.

`.overCurrentContext`

Like `.currentContext`, but the presented view controller's view covers the presenting view controller's view rather than replacing it. This will often be a better choice than `.currentContext`, because some subviews don't behave well when automatically removed from their superview and restored later.

`.automatic`

Okay, I lied when I said that `.pageSheet` is the default starting in iOS 13. *This* is the default! You'll rarely need to set it explicitly. In general it resolves to `.pageSheet`, but it also allows certain built-in view controllers to choose their own presentation style. In the storyboard, the Automatic presentation style is backward compatible, resolving to `.fullScreen` on iOS 12 and before.

Alternatively, instead of a built-in modal presentation style, you can create your own custom transition that places the presented view controller's view anywhere you like, as I'll explain later in this chapter.

User dismissal of a sheet

By default, a sheet (page sheet or form sheet) in iOS 13 and later can be dismissed by the user dragging down (except on an iPhone in landscape where it is treated as if it were `.fullScreen`).

That might not be what you want. To prevent it, set the presented view controller's `isModalInPresentation` to `true`; the user will still be able to drag the sheet down, but it will snap back into place instead of being dismissed. To detect this gesture, use the *presentation controller delegate*. (I'll talk later about what the presentation controller is.) Set the presented view controller's `presentationController?.delegate` to an object adopting the UIAdaptivePresentationControllerDelegate protocol and implement this delegate method:

presentationControllerDidAttemptToDismiss(_:)
> Called when the user attempts to dismiss a sheet by dragging down but is prevented from doing so. The idea is that you might put up some interface explaining *why* the user can't dismiss the sheet this way.

Instead of setting isModalInPresentation permanently, you can make the same decision in real time in a different presentation controller delegate method:

presentationControllerShouldDismiss(_:)
> If you return false, it is as if you had momentarily set isModalInPresentation to true: the user is attempting to drag down and failing to dismiss, so presentationControllerDidAttemptToDismiss(_:) is called immediately.

If isModalInPresentation is not true and presentationControllerShould-Dismiss(_:) does not return false, the user's drag can succeed in dismissing the presented view controller. To let you detect what's happening, there are two more presentation controller delegate methods:

presentationControllerWillDismiss(_:)
> The user is starting to drag down. This does *not* necessarily mean that the user will complete the drag gesture; the user might release the sheet, in which case it will pop back into place and won't be dismissed. The idea is that you might want to coordinate some change of interface with the dismissal gesture (by means of the presented view controller's transitionCoordinator, as I'll explain later).

presentationControllerDidDismiss(_:)
> The user has completed the drag gesture and the sheet has been dismissed.

You don't get any delegate event when you dismiss the sheet in code with dismiss(animated:completion:), because you already know that the sheet is being dismissed.

 The drag gesture is implemented by a UIPanGestureRecognizer further up the view hierarchy. If you need to immobilize the presented view so that it doesn't move in response to the user's gesture, implement gestureRecognizerShould-Begin (in a view subclass or a gesture recognizer delegate) to return false.

Current context presentation

When the presented view controller's modalPresentationStyle is .currentContext or .overCurrentContext, a decision has to be made by the runtime as to what view controller should be the presenting view controller. This will determine what view will be replaced or covered by the presented view controller's view. The decision involves another UIViewController property, `definesPresentationContext` (a Bool), and possibly still *another* UIViewController property, `providesPresentation-ContextTransitionStyle`:

1. Starting with the original presenter — that is, the view controller to which `present(_:animated:completion:)` was sent — we (the runtime) walk up the chain of parent view controllers, looking for one whose `definesPresentation-Context` property is `true`.

   - If we *don't* find one, the search has failed. Things work as if the presented view controller's `modalPresentationStyle` were `.automatic`, and we don't proceed to the next step.

   - If we *do* find one, that's the one — it will be the `presentingView-Controller`, and its view will be replaced or covered by the presented view controller's view — and we do proceed to the next step.

2. If we get here, we have found a `presentingViewController` whose `defines-PresentationContext` property is `true`. We now look to see if its `provides-PresentationContextTransitionStyle` property is *also* `true`. If so, *that* view controller's `modalTransitionStyle` is used for this transition animation, rather than the presented view controller's `modalTransitionStyle`.

To illustrate, I need a parent–child view controller arrangement to work with. This chapter hasn't yet discussed any parent view controllers in detail, but the simplest is UITabBarController, which I discuss in the next section, and it's easy to create a working app with a UITabBarController-based interface, so that's the example I'll use:

1. Make a new project with the basic App template. Edit *Main.storyboard*. Select the existing view controller and choose Editor → Embed In → Tab Bar Controller.

2. As in the previous example, I want us to create and present the presented view controller manually, rather than letting the storyboard do it automatically; so make another view controller class, with an accompanying *.xib* file, to use as a presented view controller — call it ExtraViewController.

3. In *ExtraViewController.xib*, give the view a distinctive background color, so you'll recognize it when it appears.

4. In the storyboard, put a button in the View Controller view (Item Scene), and connect it to an action method in *ViewController.swift* that summons the new view controller as a presented view controller:

```
@IBAction func doPresent(_ sender: Any) {
    let vc = ExtraViewController()
    self.present(vc, animated: true)
}
```

Run the project and tap the button. In iOS 13 and later, we get the default `.page-Sheet` presentation style. The presenting view controller is the root view controller, which is the UITabBarController. The entire interface, *including the tab bar*, is covered by the presented view controller's view.

Now change the `doPresent` code in *ViewController.swift* to look like this:

```
@IBAction func doPresent(_ sender: Any) {
    let vc = ExtraViewController()
    self.definesPresentationContext = true // *
    vc.modalPresentationStyle = .currentContext // *
    self.present(vc, animated: true)
}
```

Run the project and tap the button. This time, the presented view controller's view replaces the first view controller's view, while *the tab bar remains visible.* That's because the presented view controller's `modalPresentationStyle` is `.currentContext`, and `definesPresentationContext` is `true` in ViewController. The search for a context stops in ViewController, which becomes the presenting view controller — meaning that the presented view replaces ViewController's view instead of the root view.

We can also override the presented view controller's transition animation through the `modalTransitionStyle` property of the presenting view controller:

```
@IBAction func doPresent(_ sender: Any) {
    let vc = ExtraViewController()
    self.definesPresentationContext = true
    self.providesPresentationContextTransitionStyle = true // *
    self.modalTransitionStyle = .flipHorizontal // *
    vc.modalPresentationStyle = .currentContext
    self.present(vc, animated: true)
}
```

Because the presenting view controller's `providesPresentationContextTransitionStyle` is `true`, the transition now uses the `.flipHorizontal` animation belonging to the presenting view controller, rather than the default `.coverVertical` animation of the presented view controller.

Configuration in the nib editor

Most of what I've described so far can be configured in a *.storyboard* or *.xib* file. A view controller's Attributes inspector lets you set its transition style and presentation style, as well as `definesPresentationContext` and `providesPresentationContextTransitionStyle`.

If you're using a storyboard, you can configure one view controller to present another view controller by connecting them with a Present Modally segue; to do the presentation, you trigger the segue (or give the user a way to trigger it) instead of calling `present(_:animated:completion:)`. The segue's Attributes inspector lets you set the presentation style and transition style (and whether there is to be animation). Dismissal is a little more involved; either you must dismiss the presented view controller in code, by calling `dismiss(animated:completion:)`, or you must use an unwind segue. I'll discuss triggered segues and unwind segues in detail later in this chapter.

Communication with a Presented View Controller

In real life, when you present a view controller, the original presenter will probably have information to impart to the presented view controller as the latter is created and presented, and the presented view controller will probably want to pass information back to the original presenter as it is dismissed. Knowing how to arrange this exchange of information can be very important.

Passing information from the original presenter to the presented view controller is usually easy, because the original presenter typically has a reference to the presented view controller before the latter's view appears in the interface. Suppose the presented view controller has a public `data` property. Then the original presenter can easily set this property as it instantiates the presented view controller:

```
@IBAction func doPresent(_ sender: Any) {
    let svc = SecondViewController()
    svc.data = "This is very important data!" // *
    self.present(svc, animated:true)
}
```

You might even give the presented view controller a designated initializer that accepts — and requires — the data that it needs to do its job, so that whoever creates it *must* pass it that data.

(If you're using a storyboard and a Present Modally segue, things are a bit different. In the original presenter, you typically implement `prepare(for:sender:)` as a moment when the original presenter and the presented view controller will meet, and the former can hand across any needed data. Alternatively, you can have the segue call an `@IBSegueAction` method in the original presenter, to accomplish the same thing a bit more cleanly. I'll give more details later in this chapter.)

Passing information back from the presented view controller to the original presenter is a more interesting problem. The presented view controller will need to know who the original presenter is, but it doesn't automatically have a reference to it (the original presenter, remember, is not necessarily the same as the `presentingViewController`). Moreover, the presented view controller will need to know the signature of some method, implemented by the original presenter, that it can call in order to hand over the information — and this needs to work regardless of the original presenter's class.

The standard solution is to use *delegation*:

1. The presented view controller defines a *protocol* declaring a method that it wants to call before it is dismissed.

2. The presented view controller provides a means whereby it can be handed a reference to an object conforming to this protocol. Think of that reference as the presented view controller's *delegate*. Very often, this will be a property — perhaps called `delegate` — typed *as the protocol*. Such a property should probably be weak, since an object usually has no business retaining its delegate.

3. The original presenter *conforms* to this protocol: it declares adoption of the protocol, and it implements the required method.

4. As the original presenter creates and configures the presented view controller, it hands the presented view controller a reference to itself, in its role as adopter of the protocol, by *assigning itself as the delegate* of the presented view controller.

5. As the presented view controller is dismissed, it looks to see if it has a delegate. If so, it calls the required method on that delegate, passing it the associated information.

This sounds elaborate, but with practice you'll find yourself able to implement it very quickly. To illustrate, suppose that (as in our earlier example) the root view controller, ViewController, presents SecondViewController. Then our code in *SecondViewController.swift* would look like this:

```
protocol SecondViewControllerDelegate : class {
    func accept(data:Any)
}
class SecondViewController : UIViewController {
    var data : Any?
    weak var delegate : SecondViewControllerDelegate?
    @IBAction func doDismiss(_ sender: Any) {
        self.delegate?.accept(data:"Even more important data!")
        self.presentingViewController?.dismiss(animated:true)
    }
}
```

It is now ViewController's job to adopt the SecondViewControllerDelegate protocol, and to set itself as the SecondViewController's delegate. If it does so, then when the delegate method is called, ViewController will be handed the data:

```
class ViewController : UIViewController, SecondViewControllerDelegate {
    @IBAction func doPresent(_ sender: Any) {
        let svc = SecondViewController()
        svc.data = "This is very important data!"
        svc.delegate = self // *
        self.present(svc, animated:true)
    }
}
```

```
        func accept(data:Any) {
            // do something with data here
        }
    }
```

But the presented view controller can also be dismissed by the user dragging down the view. That *won't* cause doDismiss to be called, and SecondViewController won't call the delegate method. We need a way for the presented view controller to hear about its own dismissal *no matter how* that dismissal is triggered.

A good solution is to override the UIViewController method viewDidDisappear (discussed later in this chapter). There is more than one reason why viewWill-Disappear might be called; we can ensure that this really is the moment of our own dismissal by consulting isBeingDismissed. Here's how SecondViewController would look now:

```
    protocol SecondViewControllerDelegate : class {
        func accept(data:Any)
    }
    class SecondViewController : UIViewController {
        var data : Any?
        weak var delegate : SecondViewControllerDelegate?
        @IBAction func doDismiss(_ sender: Any) {
            self.presentingViewController?.dismiss(animated:true)
        }
        override func viewDidDisappear(_ animated: Bool) {
            super.viewDidDisappear(animated)
            if self.isBeingDismissed {
                self.delegate?.accept(data:"Even more important data!")
            }
        }
    }
```

Adaptive Presentation

When a view controller is about to appear with a modalPresentationStyle of .page-Sheet or .formSheet, you get a second opportunity to change its effective modal-PresentationStyle, and even to substitute a different view controller, based on the current trait collection environment. This is called *adaptive presentation*. The idea is that your presented view controller might appear one way for certain trait collections and another way for others — on an iPad as opposed to an iPhone, for instance.

The adaptations you can perform are:

- You can adapt .pageSheet or .formSheet to .fullScreen or .overFullScreen.

- You can adapt .pageSheet to .formSheet; this will make a visible difference only on an iPad.

(It isn't illegal to try to perform another adaptation, but it isn't going to work either.)

To implement adaptive presentation, use the presentation controller delegate: set the presented view controller's `presentationController?.delegate` to an object adopting the UIAdaptivePresentationControllerDelegate protocol, *before* presenting the view controller. When you *do* present the view controller, but before its view actually appears, the delegate is sent these messages:

`adaptivePresentationStyle(for:traitCollection:)`
> The first parameter is the presentation controller, and its `presentationStyle` is the `modalPresentationStyle` it proposes to use. Return a different modal presentation style to use instead (or `.none` if you don't want to change the presentation style).

`presentationController(_:willPresentWithAdaptiveStyle:transition-Coordinator:)`
> Called just before the presentation takes place. If the `adaptiveStyle:` is `.none`, adaptive presentation is *not* going to take place.

`presentationController(_:viewControllerForAdaptivePresentationStyle:)`
> Called only if adaptive presentation *is* going to take place. The first parameter is the presentation controller, and its `presentedViewController` is the view controller it proposes to present. Return a different view controller to present instead (or `nil` to keep the current presented view controller).

Here's how to present a view controller as a `.pageSheet` on iPad but as `.overFull-Screen` on iPhone:

```
extension ViewController : UIAdaptivePresentationControllerDelegate {
    @IBAction func doPresent(_ sender: Any) {
        let svc = SecondViewController()
        svc.modalPresentationStyle = .pageSheet
        svc.presentationController!.delegate = self // *
        self.present(svc, animated:true)
    }
    func adaptivePresentationStyle(for controller: UIPresentationController,
        traitCollection: UITraitCollection) -> UIModalPresentationStyle {
            if traitCollection.horizontalSizeClass == .compact ||
                traitCollection.verticalSizeClass == .compact {
                    return .overFullScreen
            }
            return .none // don't adapt
    }
}
```

Now let's extend that example by presenting one view controller on iPad but a different view controller on iPhone; this method won't be called when `adaptive-PresentationStyle` returns `.none`, so it affects iPhone only:

```
extension ViewController : UIAdaptivePresentationControllerDelegate {
    func presentationController(_ controller: UIPresentationController,
        viewControllerForAdaptivePresentationStyle: UIModalPresentationStyle)
        -> UIViewController? {
            let newvc = ThirdViewController()
            return newvc
    }
}
```

In real life, of course, when substituting a different view controller, you might need to configure it before returning it, doing things like giving it data or setting its delegate. A common scenario is to return the *same* view controller wrapped in a navigation controller; I'll illustrate in Chapter 10.

Presentation, Rotation, and the Status Bar

A .fullScreen presented view controller, even though it is not the root view controller, is the *top-level view controller*, and acquires some of the same mighty powers as if it *were* the root view controller:

- Its supportedInterfaceOrientations and shouldAutorotate are honored; this view controller gets to limit your app's legal orientations.

- Its prefersStatusBarHidden and preferredStatusBarStyle are honored; this view controller gets to dictate the appearance of the status bar.

When you present a view controller whose modalPresentationStyle is .fullScreen, if its supportedInterfaceOrientations do not include the app's current orientation, the app's orientation *will rotate*, as the presented view appears, to an orientation that the presented view controller supports — and the same thing will be true in reverse when the presented view controller is dismissed. This is the *only* officially sanctioned way to perform *forced rotation* (as I called it earlier in this chapter).

 On an iPad, if your app permits all four orientations and does not opt out of iPad multitasking, its view controllers' supportedInterfaceOrientations are not even consulted, so forced rotation doesn't work.

The presented view controller's supportedInterfaceOrientations bitmask might permit multiple possible orientations. The view controller may then also wish to specify which of those multiple orientations it should have *initially* when it is presented. To do so, override preferredInterfaceOrientationForPresentation; this property is consulted before supportedInterfaceOrientations, and its value is a single UIInterfaceOrientation (*not* a bitmask).

When a view controller is presented, if its presentation style is *not* .fullScreen, a question arises of whether its status bar properties (prefersStatusBarHidden and preferredStatusBarStyle) should be consulted. By default, the answer is no, because this view controller is not the top-level view controller. To make the answer be yes, set this view controller's `modalPresentationCapturesStatusBarAppearance` to `true`.

Tab Bar Controller

A *tab bar* (UITabBar, see also Chapter 13) is a horizontal bar containing tab bar items. A tab bar item (UITabBarItem) displays, by default, an image and a title. The title usually appears *beside* the image; on an iPhone in portrait orientation, the title appears *below* the image. At all times, exactly one of a tab bar's items is selected (highlighted); when the user taps an item, it becomes the selected item.

If there are too many items to fit on a tab bar, the excess items are subsumed into a final More item. When the user taps the More item, a list of the excess items appears, and the user can select one; the user can also be permitted to edit the tab bar, determining which items appear in the tab bar itself and which ones spill over into the More list.

A tab bar is an independent interface object, but it is nearly always used in conjunction with a *tab bar controller* (UITabBarController, a subclass of UIViewController) to form a *tab bar interface*. The tab bar controller displays the tab bar at the bottom of its own view. From the user's standpoint, the tab bar items correspond to views; when the user selects a tab bar item, the corresponding view appears, filling the remainder of the space. The user is employing the tab bar to choose an entire area of your app's functionality.

In reality, the UITabBarController is a parent view controller; you give it child view controllers, which the tab bar controller then contains. Tapping a tab bar item changes which child view controller is currently selected, and the view that appears in response is that child view controller's view.

Familiar examples of a tab bar interface on the iPhone are Apple's Clock app and Music app.

You can get a reference to the tab bar controller's tab bar through its `tabBar` property. In general, you won't need this. When using a UITabBarController, you do not interact (as a programmer) with the tab bar itself; you don't create it or set its items. You provide the UITabBarController with children, and it does the rest; when the UITabBarController's view is displayed, there's the tab bar along with the view of the selected item. You can, however, customize the *look* of the tab bar (see Chapter 13 for details).

Tab Bar Items

For each view controller you assign as a tab bar controller's child, you'll need to create and configure the tab bar item that will appear as its representative in the tab bar.

This tab bar item will be your child view controller's `tabBarItem`, a UITabBarItem; this is a subclass of UIBarItem, an abstract class that provides some of its most important properties, such as `title`, `image`, and `isEnabled`.

There are two ways to make a tab bar item:

By borrowing it from the system
> Instantiate UITabBarItem using `init(tabBarSystemItem:tag:)`, and assign the instance to your child view controller's `tabBarItem`. Consult the documentation for the list of available system items. You can't customize a system tab bar item's title; you must accept the title the system hands you.

By making your own
> Instantiate UITabBarItem using `init(title:image:tag:)` and assign the instance to your child view controller's `tabBarItem`. Alternatively, use the view controller's existing `tabBarItem` and set its `image` and `title`. Instead of setting the `title` of the `tabBarItem`, you can set the `title` property of the view controller itself; doing this automatically sets the `title` of its current `tabBarItem` (unless the tab bar item is a system tab bar item), though the converse is not true.

> You can also add a separate `selectedImage` later, or by initializing with `init(title:image:selectedImage:)`. The `selectedImage` will be displayed in place of the normal `image` when this tab bar item is selected in the tab bar.

The `image` (and `selectedImage`) for a tab bar item should be a 30×30 PNG, or a vector image (see Chapter 2). Apple prefers you to use a vector image; the vast repertoire of standard symbol images is available. By default, the image will be treated as a transparency mask (a template). You can instead display the image as is, and not as a transparency mask, by deriving an image whose rendering mode is `.always-Original`.

A tab bar controller automatically reduces the height of its tab bar when the vertical size class is `.compact` (an iPhone in landscape orientation, except for a big iPhone). If the image is not a vector image, you will have to cope with the possibility that the tab bar item will be displayed at reduced size when the tab bar's height is reduced. The solution is to set the tab bar item's `landscapeImagePhone` to a 20×20 PNG; it will be used when the vertical size class is `.compact`.

 A tab bar item's `selectedImage` is not used in a `.compact` vertical size class environment if it also has a separate `landscapeImagePhone`. I regard this as a bug.

Other ways in which you can customize the look of a tab bar item are discussed in Chapter 13.

Configuring a Tab Bar Controller

Basic configuration of a tab bar controller is simple: just hand it the view controllers that will be its children. To do so, collect those view controllers into an array and set the UITabBarController's `viewControllers` property to that array. The view controllers in the array are now the tab bar controller's child view controllers; the tab bar controller is the `parent` of the view controllers in the array. The tab bar controller is also the `tabBarController` of the view controllers in the array and of all their children; a child view controller at any depth can learn that it is contained by a tab bar controller and can get a reference to that tab bar controller. The tab bar controller retains the array, and the array retains the child view controllers.

Here's a simple example from one of my apps, in which I construct a tab bar interface in code; the tab bar controller later becomes the window's root view controller:

```
let vc1 = GameBoardController()
let sc = SettingsController()
let vc2 = UINavigationController(rootViewController:sc)
let tabBarController = UITabBarController()
tabBarController.viewControllers = [vc1, vc2]
tabBarController.selectedIndex = 0
tabBarController.delegate = self
```

A tab bar controller's tab bar displays the `tabBarItem` of each child view controller. The order of the tab bar items is the order of the view controllers in the tab bar controller's `viewControllers` array. A child view controller will probably want to configure its `tabBarItem` property early in its lifetime, so that the `tabBarItem` is ready by the time the view controller is handed as a child to the tab bar controller. `viewDidLoad` is *not* early enough! That's because the view controllers (other than the initially selected view controller) have no view when the tab bar controller initially appears. It is common to implement an initializer for this purpose.

Here's an example from the same app as the previous code (in the GameBoardController class):

```
init() {
    super.init(nibName:nil, bundle:nil)
    // tab bar configuration
    self.tabBarItem.image = UIImage(named: "game")
    self.title = "Game"
}
```

If you change the tab bar controller's view controllers array later in its lifetime and you want the corresponding change in the tab bar's display of its items to be animated, call `setViewControllers(_:animated:)`.

To ask the tab bar controller which tab bar item the user has selected, you can couch your query in terms of the child view controller (`selectedViewController`) or by index number in the array (selectedIndex). You can also *set* those properties to switch between displayed child view controllers programmatically. If you don't do that before the tab bar controller appears, then initially the first tab bar item will be selected by default.

 You can supply a view animation when a tab bar controller's selected tab item changes and one child view controller's view is replaced by another, as I'll explain later in this chapter.

You can also set the UITabBarController's delegate (adopting UITabBarController-Delegate). The delegate gets messages allowing it to prevent a given tab bar item from being selected, and notifying it when a tab bar item is selected and when the user is customizing the tab bar from the More item

If a tab bar controller is the top-level view controller, it determines your app's compensatory rotation behavior. To take a hand in that determination without having to subclass UITabBarController, make one of your objects the tab bar controller's delegate and implement these methods, as needed:

- `tabBarControllerSupportedInterfaceOrientations(_:)`
- `tabBarControllerPreferredInterfaceOrientationForPresentation(_:)`

A top-level tab bar controller also determines your app's status bar appearance. However, a tab bar controller implements `childForStatusBarStyle` and `childForStatusBarHidden` so that the actual decision is relegated to the child view controller whose view is currently being displayed: the child's `preferredStatusBarStyle` and `prefersStatusBarHidden` are consulted and obeyed.

If the tab bar contains few enough items that it doesn't need a More item, there won't be one, and the tab bar won't be user-customizable. If there *is* a More item, you can exclude some tab bar items from being customizable by setting the `customizableViewControllers` property to an array that lacks them; setting this property to `nil` means that the user can see the More list but can't rearrange the items. Setting the `viewControllers` property sets the `customizableViewControllers` property to the same value, so if you're going to set the `customizableViewControllers` property, do it *after* setting the `viewControllers` property. The `moreNavigationController` property can be compared with the `selectedViewController` property to learn whether the user is currently viewing the More list.

You can configure a UITabBarController in a storyboard. The UITabBarController's contained view controllers can be set directly — there will be a "view controllers" relationship between the tab bar controller and each of its children — and the contained view controllers will be instantiated together with the tab bar controller. When you drag a tab bar controller from the Library into the canvas in the nib editor, you get the tab bar controller and two child view controllers automatically.

In the nib editor, each contained view controller has a Tab Bar Item; you can select this and set many aspects of the `tabBarItem`, such as its system item or its title, image, selected image, and tag, directly in the nib editor. (If a view controller in a nib doesn't have a Tab Bar Item and you want to configure this view controller for use in a tab bar interface, drag a Tab Bar Item from the Library onto the view controller.)

 You will rarely if ever have a need to subclass UITabBar. If you do, and if you want to use an instance of your subclass as a tab bar controller's tab bar, you'll have to create the tab bar controller in a storyboard. A tab bar controller configured in a storyboard can easily have a custom tab bar subclass, but it's much harder to do that with a tab bar controller created in code.

Navigation Controller

A *navigation bar* (UINavigationBar, see also Chapter 13) is a horizontal bar displaying, in its simplest form, a center title and a right button. When the user taps the right button, the navigation bar animates, sliding its interface out to the left and replacing it with a new interface that enters from the right. The new interface displays a back button at the left side, and a new center title — and possibly a new right button. The user can tap the back button to go back to the first interface, which slides in from the left; or, if there's a right button in the second interface, the user can tap it to go further forward to a third interface, which slides in from the right.

The successive interfaces of a navigation bar behave like a stack. In fact, a navigation bar does represent an actual stack — an internal stack of *navigation items* (UINavigationItem). It starts out with one navigation item: the *root item* or *bottom item* of the stack. Since there is initially just one navigation item, it is also initially the *top item* of the stack (the navigation bar's `topItem`). The navigation bar's interface is always representing whatever its top item is at that moment. When the user taps a right button, a new navigation item is *pushed* onto the stack; it becomes the top item, and its interface is seen. When the user taps a back button, the top item is *popped* off the stack, and the navigation item that was previously beneath it in the stack — the *back item* (the navigation bar's `backItem`) — becomes the top item, and its interface is seen.

A navigation bar is an independent interface object, but it is most commonly used in conjunction with a *navigation controller* (UINavigationController, a subclass of UIViewController) to form a *navigation interface*. Just as there is a stack of navigation items in the navigation bar, there is a stack of view controllers in the navigation controller. These view controllers are the navigation controller's children, and each navigation item belongs to a view controller — it is a view controller's `navigationItem`.

The navigation controller performs automatic coordination of the navigation bar and the overall interface. Whenever a view controller comes to the top of the navigation controller's stack, its view is displayed in the interface; at the same time, its navigationItem is pushed onto the top of the navigation bar's stack, and is displayed in the navigation bar as its top item. Moreover, the animation in the navigation bar is reinforced by animation of the interface as a whole: by default, a view controller's view slides into the main interface from the side just as its navigation item slides into the navigation bar from the same side.

 You can substitute a different view animation when a view controller is pushed onto or popped off a navigation controller's stack, as I'll explain later in this chapter.

With a navigation controller, your code can control the overall navigation. So you can let the user navigate in any way that suits the interface. There is only one back item, and the back button in the navigation bar is a standard convention telling the user what it is and providing a way to navigate to it by tapping, so you'll usually display the back button. But for letting the user push a new view controller, instead of a right button in the navigation bar, there might be something the user taps inside the main interface, such as a listing in a table view. (Figure 6-1 is a navigation interface that works this way.) Your app can decide in real time, in response to the user's tap, what the next view controller should be; typically, you won't even create the next view controller until the user asks to navigate to it. The navigation interface becomes a *master–detail interface*.

You can get a reference to the navigation controller's navigation bar through its navigationBar property. In general, you won't need this. When using a UINavigationController, you do not interact (as a programmer) with the navigation bar itself; you don't create it or manipulate its navigation items. You provide the UINavigationController with children, and it does the rest, handing each child view controller's navigationItem to the navigation bar for display and showing the child view controller's view each time navigation occurs. You can, however, customize the *look* of the navigation bar (see Chapter 13 for details).

A navigation interface may optionally display a *toolbar* at the bottom. A toolbar (UIToolbar) is a horizontal view displaying a row of toolbar items. A toolbar item may provide information, or it may be something the user can tap. A tapped item is not selected, as in a tab bar; rather, it represents the initiation of an action, like a button. You can get a reference to a UINavigationController's toolbar through its toolbar property. The look of the toolbar can be customized (Chapter 13). In a navigation interface, the contents of the toolbar are determined automatically by the view controller that is currently the top item in the stack: they are its toolbarItems.

A familiar example of a navigation interface is Apple's Settings app on the iPhone. The Mail app on the iPhone is a navigation interface that includes a toolbar.

A toolbar can be used independently, and often is. An independent toolbar, not in a navigation interface, may appear at the top on an iPad, where it plays something of the role that the menu bar plays on the desktop; but it typically appears at the bottom on an iPhone (Figure 6-4 has a toolbar at the bottom). If you need a top bar on the iPhone, you might put a view controller inside a navigation controller even if no actual navigation is going to take place, just for the convenience of the navigation bar with its title and buttons at the top of the screen.

Bar Button Items

The items in a UIToolbar or a UINavigationBar are *bar button items* — UIBar-ButtonItem, a subclass of UIBarItem. A bar button item comes in one of two broadly different flavors:

Basic bar button item
> The bar button item behaves like a simple button.

Custom view
> The bar button item has no inherent behavior, but has (and displays) a custom-View.

UIBarItem is not a UIView subclass. A basic bar button item is button-like, but it has no frame, no UIView touch handling, and so forth. But a UIBarButtonItem's custom-View, if it has one, *is* a UIView, so you can display any sort of view in a toolbar or navigation bar, and that view can have subviews, touch handling, and so on.

Let's start with the basic bar button item (no custom view). A bar button item, like a tab bar item, inherits from UIBarItem the title, image, and isEnabled properties. The title text color, by default, comes from the bar button item's tintColor, which may be inherited from the bar itself or from higher up the view hierarchy. *Assigning an image removes the title;* you can't display both. The image should usually be quite small; Apple recommends 22×22. By default, it will be treated as a transparency mask (a template): the hue of its pixels will be ignored, and the transparency of its pixels will be combined with the bar button item's tint color. You can instead display an image as is, and not as a transparency mask, by deriving an image whose rendering mode is .alwaysOriginal (see Chapter 2).

A basic bar button item has a style property (UIBarButtonItem.Style); this will usually be .plain. The alternative, .done, causes the title to be bold. You can further refine the title font and style. In addition, a bar button item can have a background image; this will typically be a small resizable image, and can be used to provide a border. Full details appear in Chapter 13.

A bar button item also has target and action properties. These facilitate its button-like behavior: tapping a bar button item calls the action method on the target, so you can handle the tap in some object that makes sense for your architecture, such as the view controller.

New in iOS 14, instead of the target–action mechanism, you can attach a `primary-Action`, a UIAction object with a `handler:` action function, directly to the bar button item. (In that case, the `target` and `action` are ignored.) Also new in iOS 14, you can give a bar button item a `menu`. The menu items will appear when the user long presses the bar button item if the bar button item has a `target` and `action` or a `primary-Action`; otherwise, they will appear when the user simply taps the bar button item. I'll give details in Chapter 13.

There are three ways to make a bar button item:

By borrowing it from the system
> Make a UIBarButtonItem with `init(barButtonSystemItem:target:action:)` — or, new in iOS 14, with `init(systemItem:primaryAction:menu:)`. Consult the documentation for the list of available system items; they are not the same as for a tab bar item. You can't assign a title or change the image. (But you can change the tint color or assign a background image.)

By making your own basic bar button item
> Make a UIBarButtonItem with `init(title:style:target:action:)` or with `init(image:style:target:action:)` — or, new in iOS 14, you can call `init(title:image:primaryAction:menu:)`. The repertoire of standard symbol images is available to use here.
>
> Also, `init(image:landscapeImagePhone:style:target:action:)` lets you specify a second image for use when the vertical size class is `.compact`, because the bar's height might be smaller in this situation.

By making a custom view bar button item
> Make a UIBarButtonItem with `init(customView:)`, supplying a UIView that the bar button item is to display. The bar button item has no action and target; the UIView itself must somehow implement button behavior if that's what you want. For instance, the `customView` might be a UISegmentedControl, but then it is the UISegmentedControl's target and action that give it button behavior.
>
> Your custom view can and should use autolayout internally. Provide sufficient constraints to size the view from the inside out; otherwise, it may have no size (and might be invisible).

Bar button items in a toolbar are horizontally positioned automatically by the system. You can't control their position precisely, but you can provide hints. You can give a bar button item an absolute `width`, and you can incorporate spacers into the toolbar. Spacers are bar button items that have no visible appearance, and cannot be tapped.

You can make one using a UIBarButtonItem class method. Use `flexibleSpace()` bar button items between the visible items to distribute the visible items equally across the width of the toolbar. Use a `fixedSpace(width:)` bar button item to insert a space of defined size. (These class methods are new in iOS 14, superseding the old `.flexibleSpace` and `.fixedSpace` system bar button items; the latter are not yet deprecated.)

Navigation Items and Toolbar Items

What appears in a navigation bar (UINavigationBar) depends upon the navigation items (UINavigationItem) in its stack. In a navigation interface, the navigation controller will manage the navigation bar's stack for you; your job is to configure the `navigationItem` of each child view controller. The UINavigationItem properties are (see also Chapter 13):

`title`
`titleView`

> The `title` is a string. Setting a view controller's `title` property sets the `title` of its `navigationItem` automatically, and is usually the best approach. The `titleView` can be any kind of UIView, and can implement further UIView functionality such as touchability.
>
> In iOS 10 and before, the `title` and the `titleView` are displayed in the same spot — the center of the navigation bar. So there can be only one: if there is a `titleView`, it is shown instead of the `title`. Starting in iOS 11, the `title` may be shown at the *bottom* of the navigation bar, in which case both the `title` and the `titleView` can appear; I'll explain more about that in a moment.
>
> As with a custom view, the `titleView` should use autolayout internally, with sufficient constraints to size the view from the inside out.

`prompt`

> An optional string to appear centered above everything else in the navigation bar. The navigation bar's height will be increased to accommodate it.

`rightBarButtonItem` *or* `rightBarButtonItems`

> A bar button item or, respectively, an array of bar button items to appear at the right side of the navigation bar; the first item in the array will be rightmost.

`backBarButtonItem`, `backButtonTitle`

> When a view controller is pushed on top of this view controller, the navigation bar will display at its left a button pointing to the left, whose title is *this* view controller's `title`. That button is *this* view controller's navigation item's `backBarButtonItem`. In other words, the back button displayed in the navigation bar belongs, not to the top item (the `navigationItem` of the current view controller),

but to the back item (the `navigationItem` of the view controller that is one level down in the stack).

If you wish, you can customize the back button. If you just want to change its title to be different from the view controller's `title`, set the navigation item's `backButtonTitle`. To go further, perhaps to give the back button an image, set the navigation item's `backBarButtonItem` to a bar button item whose target and action are `nil`; the runtime will add a correct target and action, so as to create a working back button:

```
let b = UIBarButtonItem(image: UIImage(named: "files.png"))
self.navigationItem.backBarButtonItem = b
```

A Bool property, `hidesBackButton`, allows the top navigation item to suppress display of the back button. If you set this to `true`, you'll probably want to provide some other means of letting the user navigate back.

The visible indication that the back button *is* a back button is a chevron (the *back indicator*) that's separate from the button itself. This chevron can also be customized, but it's a feature of the navigation bar, not the bar button item. (I'll give an example in Chapter 13.)

`leftBarButtonItem` *or* `leftBarButtonItems`
A bar button item or, respectively, an array of bar button items to appear at the left side of the navigation bar; the first item in the array will be leftmost. The `leftItemsSupplementBackButton` property, if set to `true`, allows both the back button and one or more left bar button items to appear.

Starting in iOS 11, a navigation bar can adopt an increased height in order to display the top item's `title` in a large font *below* the bar button items. This is a navigation bar feature, its `prefersLargeTitles` property. In order to accommodate the possibility that different view controllers will have different preferences in this regard, a navigation item has a `largeTitleDisplayMode`, which may be one of the following:

`.always`
The navigation item's `title` is displayed large if the navigation bar's `prefersLargeTitles` is `true`.

`.never`
The navigation item's `title` is *not* displayed large.

`.automatic`
The navigation item's `title` display is the same as the `title` display of the back item — that is, of the navigation item preceding this one in the navigation bar's stack. This is the default. The idea is that all navigation items pushed onto a

navigation bar will display their titles in the same way, until a pushed navigation item declares .always or .never.

The navigation controller may grow or shrink its navigation bar to display or hide the large title as the contents of its view are scrolled — yet another reason why a nimble interface based on autolayout and the safe area is crucial.

 Starting in iOS 13, a navigation bar with a large title is transparent by default. I'll talk in Chapter 13 about how to change that.

A view controller's navigationItem is not just something to be prepared before that view controller is pushed onto a navigation controller's stack; it is *live*. You can change its properties while its interface is being displayed in the navigation bar. In one of my apps, we play music from the user's library using interface in the navigation bar. The titleView is a progress view (UIProgressView, Chapter 13) that needs updating every second to reflect the playback position in the current song, and the right bar button should be either the system Play button or the system Pause button, depending on whether we are paused or playing. So I have a timer that periodically checks the state of the music player (self.mp); we access the progress view and the right bar button by way of self.navigationItem:

```
// change the progress view
let prog = self.navigationItem.titleView!.subviews[0] as! UIProgressView
if let item = self.nowPlayingItem {
    let current = self.mp.currentPlaybackTime
    let total = item.playbackDuration
    prog.progress = Float(current / total)
} else {
    prog.progress = 0
}
// change the bar button
let whichButton : UIBarButtonItem.SystemItem? = {
    switch self.mp.currentPlaybackRate {
    case 0..<0.1:
        return .play
    case 0.1...1.0:
        return .pause
    default:
        return nil
    }
}()
if let which = whichButton {
    let bb = UIBarButtonItem(barButtonSystemItem: which,
        target: self, action: #selector(doPlayPause))
    self.navigationItem.rightBarButtonItem = bb
}
```

Each view controller to be pushed onto the navigation controller's stack is responsible also for supplying the items to appear in the navigation interface's toolbar, if there is one: set the view controller's `toolbarItems` property to an array of UIBarButton-Item instances. You can change the toolbar items even while the view controller's view and current `toolbarItems` are showing, optionally with animation, by sending `setToolbarItems(_:animated:)` to the view controller.

Configuring a Navigation Controller

You configure a navigation controller by manipulating its stack of view controllers. This stack is the navigation controller's `viewControllers` array property, though you will rarely need to manipulate that property directly.

The view controllers in a navigation controller's `viewControllers` array are the navigation controller's child view controllers; the navigation controller is the `parent` of the view controllers in the array. The navigation controller is also the `navigation-Controller` of the view controllers in the array and of all their children; a child view controller at any depth can learn that it is contained by a navigation controller and can get a reference to that navigation controller. The navigation controller retains the array, and the array retains the child view controllers.

The normal way to manipulate a navigation controller's stack is by pushing or popping one view controller at a time. When the navigation controller is instantiated, it is usually initialized with `init(rootViewController:)`; this is a convenience method that assigns the navigation controller a single initial child view controller, the root view controller that goes at the bottom of the stack:

```
let fvc = FirstViewController()
let nav = UINavigationController(rootViewController:fvc)
```

Instead of `init(rootViewController:)`, you might choose to create the navigation controller with `init(navigationBarClass:toolbarClass:)` in order to set a custom subclass of UINavigationBar or UIToolbar. If you do that, you'll have to set the navigation controller's root view controller separately.

You can also set the UINavigationController's delegate (adopting UINavigation-ControllerDelegate). The delegate receives messages before and after a child view controller's view is shown.

If a navigation controller is the top-level view controller, it determines your app's compensatory rotation behavior. To take a hand in that determination without having to subclass UINavigationController, make one of your objects the navigation controller's delegate and implement these methods, as needed:

- `navigationControllerSupportedInterfaceOrientations(_:)`
- `navigationControllerPreferredInterfaceOrientationForPresentation(_:)`

But don't try to use those methods to implement forced rotation between one view controller and the next as it is pushed onto the stack. That isn't going to work. The way to implement forced rotation is to use a fullscreen presented view controller, as I explained earlier.

A top-level navigation controller also determines your app's status bar visibility. However, a navigation controller implements childForStatusBarHidden so that the actual decision is relegated to the child view controller whose view is currently being displayed: the child's prefersStatusBarHidden is consulted and obeyed. But on a device without a bezel, such as the iPhone X, if the navigation bar is present, the status bar cannot be hidden and the child's prefersStatusBarHidden is not called.

Determining the status bar *style* (light or dark content) is more complicated:

The navigation bar is hidden
> If the navigation bar is hidden but the status bar is showing, then your view controller's preferredStatusBarStyle override gets to determine the status bar style. That's because the navigation controller's childForStatusBarStyle points to the child view controller whose view is currently being displayed.

The navigation bar is showing
> If the navigation bar is showing, the navigation controller does not relegate the decision to its child view controller. Before iOS 13, the status bar content color depends on the navigation bar's barStyle — the status bar content is dark if the navigation bar style is .default, and light if the navigation bar style is .black. But in iOS 13 and later, where the user interface style (light or dark mode) can change, you should leave the navigation bar style at .default and give the navigation bar a sensible dynamic color; the status bar content will change automatically between dark and light to contrast with the user interface style, as I've already described.

A navigation controller will typically appear on the screen initially containing just its root view controller and displaying its root view controller's view, with no back button (because there is nowhere to go back to). Subsequently, when the user asks to navigate to a new view, you create the next view controller and push it onto the stack by calling pushViewController(_:animated:) on the navigation controller. The navigation controller performs the animation, and displays the new view controller's view:

```
let svc = SecondViewController()
self.navigationController!.pushViewController(svc, animated: true)
```

(There's a second way to push a view controller onto the navigation controller's stack, without referring to the navigation controller: show(_:sender:). This method *pushes* the view controller if we are in a navigation interface, but otherwise *presents* it as a presented view controller. I'll talk more about that in Chapter 10.)

The command for going back is popViewController(animated:), but you might never need to call it yourself, as the runtime will call it for you when the user taps the back button. When a view controller is popped from the stack, the viewControllers array removes and releases the view controller, which is usually permitted to go out of existence at that point.

Instead of tapping the back button, the user can go back by dragging a pushed view controller's view from the left edge of the screen. This is actually a way of calling popViewController(animated:), with the difference that the animation is interactive. The UINavigationController uses a UIScreenEdgePanGestureRecognizer to detect and track the user's gesture. You can obtain a reference to this gesture recognizer as the navigation controller's interactivePopGestureRecognizer; you can disable the gesture recognizer to prevent this way of going back, or you can mediate between your own gesture recognizers and this one (see Chapter 5).

You can manipulate the stack more directly if you wish. You can call popViewController(animated:) explicitly; to pop multiple items so as to leave a particular view controller at the top of the stack, call popToViewController(_:animated:), or to pop all the items down to the root view controller, call popToRootViewController(animated:). All of these methods return the popped view controller (or view controllers, as an array) in case you want to do something with them. To set the entire stack at once, call setViewControllers(_:animated:). You can access the stack through the viewControllers property. Manipulating the stack directly is the only way, for instance, to remove or insert a view controller in the middle of the stack.

 If a view controller needs a signal that it is being popped, override viewWillDisappear and see if self.isMovingFromParent is true.

The view controller at the top of the stack is the topViewController; the view controller whose view is displayed is the visibleViewController. Those will normally be the same, but they needn't be, as the topViewController might present a view controller, in which case the presented view controller will be the visibleViewController. Other view controllers can be accessed through the viewControllers array by index number. The root view controller is at index 0; if the array's count is c, the back view controller (the one whose navigationItem.backBarButtonItem is currently displayed in the navigation bar) is at index c-2.

The topViewController may need to communicate with the next view controller as the latter is pushed onto the stack, or with the back view controller as it itself is popped off the stack. The problem is parallel to that of communication between an original presenter and a presented view controller, which I discussed earlier in this chapter ("Communication with a Presented View Controller" on page 334), so I won't say more about it here.

A child view controller will probably want to configure its navigationItem early in its lifetime, so as to be ready for display in the navigation bar by the time the view controller is handed as a child to the navigation controller. Apple warns (in the UIViewController class reference, under navigationItem) that loadView and view-DidLoad are not appropriate places to do this, because the circumstances under which the view is needed are not related to the circumstances under which the navigation item is needed. Apple's own code examples routinely violate this warning, but it is probably best to override a view controller initializer for this purpose.

A navigation controller's navigation bar is accessible as its navigationBar, and can be hidden and shown with setNavigationBarHidden(_:animated:). (It is possible, though not common, to maintain and manipulate a navigation stack through a navigation controller whose navigation bar never appears.) Its toolbar is accessible as its toolbar, and can be hidden and shown with setToolbarHidden(_:animated:). Do *not* reach into the navigation controller's interface and set a bar's isHidden property directly!

A view controller also has the power to specify that its ancestor's bottom bar (a navigation controller's toolbar, or a tab bar controller's tab bar) should be hidden as this view controller is pushed onto a navigation controller's stack. To do so, set the view controller's hidesBottomBarWhenPushed property to true. The trick is that you must do this very early, before the view loads; the view controller's initializer is a good place. The bottom bar remains hidden from the time this view controller is pushed to the time it is popped, even if other view controllers are pushed and popped on top of it in the meantime.

A navigation controller can perform automatic hiding and showing of its navigation bar (and, if normally shown, its toolbar) in response to various situations, as configured by properties:

When tapped

If the navigation controller's hidesBarsOnTap is true, a tap that falls through the top view controller's view is taken as a signal to toggle bar visibility. The relevant gesture recognizer is the navigation controller's barHideOnTapGesture-Recognizer.

When swiped

If the navigation controller's hidesBarsOnSwipe is true, an upward or downward swipe respectively hides or shows the bars. The relevant gesture recognizer is the navigation controller's barHideOnSwipeGestureRecognizer.

In landscape

> If the navigation controller's `hidesBarsWhenVerticallyCompact` is `true`, bars are automatically hidden when the app rotates to landscape on the iPhone (and `hidesBarsOnTap` is treated as `true`, so the bars can be shown again by tapping).

When the user is typing

> If the navigation controller's `hidesBarsWhenKeyboardAppears` is `true`, bars are automatically hidden when the virtual keyboard appears (see Chapter 11).

In the nib editor, you can configure a UINavigationController and any view controller that is to serve in a navigation interface. In the Attributes inspector, use a navigation controller's Bar Visibility and Hide Bars checkboxes to determine the presence of the navigation bar and toolbar. The navigation bar and toolbar are themselves subviews of the navigation controller, and you can configure them with the Attributes inspector as well. A navigation bar has a Prefers Large Titles checkbox. A navigation controller's root view controller can be specified; in a storyboard, there will be a "root view controller" relationship between the navigation controller and its root view controller. The root view controller is automatically instantiated together with the navigation controller.

A view controller in the nib editor has a Navigation Item where you can specify its title, its prompt, and the title of its back button. A navigation item has a Large Title pop-up menu, where you can set its `largeTitleDisplayMode`. You can drag Bar Button Items into a view controller's navigation bar in the canvas to set the left buttons and right buttons of its `navigationItem`. Moreover, the Navigation Item has outlets, one of which permits you to set its `titleView`. Similarly, you can give a view controller Bar Button Items that will appear in the toolbar. (If a view controller in a nib doesn't have a Navigation Item and you want to configure this view controller for use in a navigation interface, drag a Navigation Item from the Library onto the view controller.)

To create an iPhone project with a main storyboard that has a UINavigationController as its initial view controller, start with the basic App template, select the existing view controller, and choose Editor → Embed In → Navigation Controller (or choose Navigation Controller from the Embed button at the lower right of the canvas). A view controller to be subsequently pushed onto the navigation stack can be configured in the storyboard as the destination of a push segue; I'll talk more about that later in this chapter.

Custom Transition

You can customize the transitions when certain built-in view controllers change views:

Tab bar controller

When a tab bar controller changes which of its child view controllers is selected, by default there is no view animation; you can add a custom animation.

Navigation controller

When a navigation controller pushes or pops a child view controller, by default there is a sideways sliding view animation; you can replace this with a custom animation.

Presented view controller

When a view controller is presented or dismissed, there is a limited set of built-in view animations (`modalTransitionStyle`); you can substitute a custom animation. Moreover, you can customize the ultimate size and position of the presented view, and how the presenting view is seen behind it; you can also provide ancillary views that remain during the presentation.

Given the extensive animation resources of iOS (see Chapter 4), this is an excellent chance for you to provide your app with variety, distinction, and clarity. The view of a child view controller pushed onto a navigation controller's stack needn't arrive sliding from the side; it can expand by zooming from the middle of the screen, drop from above and fall into place with a bounce, snap into place like a spring, or whatever else you can dream up. A familiar example is Apple's Calendar app, which transitions from a year to a month, in a navigation controller, by zooming in.

A custom transition animation can optionally have some extra capabilities:

It can be interactive

Instead of tapping and causing an animation to take place, the user performs an extended gesture and gradually summons the new view to supersede the old one. A familiar example is the Photos app, which lets the user pinch a photo, in a navigation controller, to pop to the album containing it.

It can be interruptible

You can provide a way for the user to pause the animation, possibly interact with the animated view by means of a gesture, and then resume (or cancel) the animation.

Noninteractive Custom Transition Animation

In the base case, you provide a custom animation that is *not* interactive. Configuring your custom animation requires three steps:

1. Before the transition begins, you give the view controller in charge of the transition a delegate.

2. As the transition begins, the delegate will be asked for an *animation controller*. You will return a reference to some object adopting the UIViewController-

AnimatedTransitioning protocol (or `nil` to specify that the default animation, if any, should be used).

The delegate and the animation controller are often the same object, and in my examples they will be; but they don't have to be. The animation controller can be any object, possibly a dedicated lightweight object instantiated just to govern this transition. The animation controller needn't even be the same object every time; depending on the circumstances, we could readily return a different animation controller, or `nil` to specify the default transition.

3. The animation controller will be sent these messages:

`transitionDuration(using:)`
The animation controller must return the duration of the custom animation.

`animateTransition(using:)`
The animation controller should perform the animation.

`interruptibleAnimator(using:)`
Optional; if implemented, the animation controller should return an object adopting the UIViewImplicitlyAnimating protocol, which may be a property animator.

`animationEnded(_:)`
Optional; if implemented, the animation controller may perform cleanup following the animation.

I like to use a property animator to govern the animation; it will need to be accessible from multiple methods, so it must live in an instance property. I like to type this instance property as `UIViewImplicitlyAnimating?`; that way, I can use `nil` to indicate that the property animator doesn't exist. Here's what the four animation controller methods will need to do:

`transitionDuration(using:)`
We'll return the property animator's animation duration.

`animateTransition(using:)`
We'll call `interruptibleAnimator(using:)` to obtain the property animator, and we'll tell the property animator to start animating.

`interruptibleAnimator(using:)`
This is where all the real work happens. We're being asked for the property animator. There is a danger that we will be called multiple times during the animation, so if the property animator already exists in our instance property, we simply return it; if it doesn't exist, we create and configure it and assign it to our instance property, and *then* return it.

`animationEnded(_:)`

> We'll clean up any instance properties; at a minimum, we'll set our property animator instance property to `nil`.

The heart of the matter is what `interruptibleAnimator(using:)` does to configure the property animator and its animation. In general, a custom transition animation works like this:

1. The `using:` parameter is the *transition context* (adopting the UIViewControllerContextTransitioning protocol). By querying the transition context, you can obtain:

   - The *container view*, an already existing view within which all the action is to take place.

   - The outgoing and incoming view controllers.

   - The outgoing and incoming views. These are probably the main views of the outgoing and incoming view controllers, but you should obtain the views directly from the transition context, just in case they aren't. The outgoing view is already inside the container view.

   - The initial `frame` of the outgoing view, and the ultimate `frame` where the incoming view must end up.

2. Having gathered this information, your mission is:

   a. Put the incoming view into the container view.

   b. Animate the incoming view so as to end up at its correct ultimate `frame`. (You may also animate the outgoing view if you wish.)

3. When the animation ends, your completion function *must* call the transition context's `completeTransition` to tell it that the animation is over. In response, the outgoing view is removed automatically, and the animation comes to an end (and our `animationEnded` will be called).

I'll illustrate with the transition between two child view controllers of a tab bar controller, when the user taps a different tab bar item. By default, this transition isn't animated; one view just replaces the other. A possible custom animation is that the new view controller's view should slide in from one side while the old view controller's view should slide out the other side. The direction of the slide should depend on whether the index of the new view controller is greater or less than that of the old view controller. Let's implement that.

For simplicity, I'll do all the work in a single custom class called Animator:

```
class Animator : NSObject {
    var anim : UIViewImplicitlyAnimating?
    unowned var tbc : UITabBarController
    init(tabBarController tbc: UITabBarController) {
        self.tbc = tbc
    }
}
```

I'll keep an Animator instance as a property of some stable object, such as the app delegate. The tab bar controller is in charge of the transition, so the first step is to make the Animator its delegate:

```
if let tbc = self.window?.rootViewController as? UITabBarController {
    self.animator = Animator(tabBarController: tbc)
    tbc.delegate = self.animator
}
```

As the UITabBarControllerDelegate, the Animator will be sent a message whenever the tab bar controller is about to change view controllers. That message is:

- `tabBarController(_:animationControllerForTransitionFrom:to:)`

The second step is to implement that method. We must return an animation controller, namely, some object implementing UIViewControllerAnimatedTransitioning. I'll return self:

```
extension Animator : UITabBarControllerDelegate {
    func tabBarController(_ tabBarController: UITabBarController,
        animationControllerForTransitionFrom fromVC: UIViewController,
        to toVC: UIViewController) -> UIViewControllerAnimatedTransitioning? {
            return self
    }
}
```

The third step is to implement the animation controller (UIViewControllerAnimated-Transitioning). I'll start with stubs for the four methods we're going to write:

```
extension Animator : UIViewControllerAnimatedTransitioning {
    func transitionDuration(using ctx: UIViewControllerContextTransitioning?)
        -> TimeInterval {
            // ...
    }
    func animateTransition(using ctx: UIViewControllerContextTransitioning) {
        // ...
    }
    func interruptibleAnimator(using ctx: UIViewControllerContextTransitioning)
        -> UIViewImplicitlyAnimating {
            // ...
    }
    func animationEnded(_ transitionCompleted: Bool) {
        // ...
    }
}
```

Our `transitionDuration` must reveal in advance the duration of our animation:

```
func transitionDuration(using ctx: UIViewControllerContextTransitioning?)
    -> TimeInterval {
        return 0.4
}
```

Our `animateTransition` simply calls `interruptibleAnimator` to obtain the property animator, and tells it to animate:

```
func animateTransition(using ctx: UIViewControllerContextTransitioning) {
    let anim = self.interruptibleAnimator(using: ctx)
    anim.startAnimation()
}
```

The workhorse is `interruptibleAnimator`. If the property animator already exists, we unwrap it and return it, and that's all:

```
func interruptibleAnimator(using ctx: UIViewControllerContextTransitioning)
    -> UIViewImplicitlyAnimating {
        if self.anim != nil {
            return self.anim!
        }
        // ...
}
```

If we haven't returned, we need to construct the property animator. First, we thoroughly query the transition context `ctx` about the parameters of this animation:

```
let vc1 = ctx.viewController(forKey:.from)!
let vc2 = ctx.viewController(forKey:.to)!
let con = ctx.containerView
let r1start = ctx.initialFrame(for:vc1)
let r2end = ctx.finalFrame(for:vc2)
let v1 = ctx.view(forKey:.from)!
let v2 = ctx.view(forKey:.to)!
```

Now we can prepare for our intended animation. In this case, we are sliding the views, so we need to decide the final frame of the outgoing view and the initial frame of the incoming view. We are sliding the views sideways, so those frames should be positioned sideways from the initial frame of the outgoing view and the final frame of the incoming view, which the transition context has just given us. *Which* side they go on depends upon the relative place of these view controllers among the children of the tab bar controller:

```
let ix1 = self.tbc.viewControllers!.firstIndex(of:vc1)!
let ix2 = self.tbc.viewControllers!.firstIndex(of:vc2)!
let dir : CGFloat = ix1 < ix2 ? 1 : -1
var r1end = r1start
r1end.origin.x -= r1end.size.width * dir
var r2start = r2end
r2start.origin.x += r2start.size.width * dir
```

Now we're ready for the animations function. We put the second view controller's view into the container view at its initial frame, and animate our views:

```
v2.frame = r2start
con.addSubview(v2)
let anim = UIViewPropertyAnimator(duration: 0.4, curve: .linear) {
    v1.frame = r1end
    v2.frame = r2end
}
```

We must not neglect to supply the completion function that calls `complete-Transition`:

```
anim.addCompletion { _ in
    ctx.completeTransition(true)
}
```

Our property animator is ready! We retain it in our `self.anim` property, and we also return it:

```
self.anim = anim
return anim
```

That completes `interruptibleAnimator`. Finally, our `animationEnded` cleans up by destroying the property animator:

```
func animationEnded(_ transitionCompleted: Bool) {
    self.anim = nil
}
```

That's all there is to it. Our example animation wasn't very complex, but an animation needn't be complex to be interesting, significant, and helpful to the user; I use this animation in my own apps, and I think it enlivens and clarifies the transition.

One possibility that I didn't illustrate in my example is that you are free to introduce additional views temporarily into the container view during the course of the animation; you'll probably want to remove them in the completion function. You might use this to make some interface object appear to migrate from one view controller's view into the other (in reality you'd probably use a snapshot view; see Chapter 1).

Interactive Custom Transition Animation

With an interactive custom transition animation, the idea is that we track something the user is doing, typically by means of a gesture recognizer (see Chapter 5), and perform the "frames" of the transition in response.

To make a custom transition animation interactive, you supply, in addition to the animation controller, an *interaction controller*. This is an object adopting the UIViewControllerInteractiveTransitioning protocol. Again, this object needn't be the same as the animation controller, but it often is, and in my examples it will be. The runtime calls the interaction controller's `startInteractiveTransition(_:)` *instead* of the animation controller's `animateTransition(using:)`.

Configuring your custom animation requires the following steps:

1. Before the transition begins, you give the view controller in charge of the transition a delegate.

2. You'll need a gesture recognizer that tracks the interactive gesture. When the gesture recognizer recognizes, make it trigger the transition to the new view controller.

3. As the transition begins, the delegate will be asked for an animation controller. You will return a UIViewControllerAnimatedTransitioning object.

4. The delegate will also be asked for an interaction controller. You will return a UIViewControllerInteractiveTransitioning object (or nil to prevent the transition from being interactive). This object implements `startInteractive-Transition(_:)`.

5. The gesture recognizer continues by repeatedly calling `updateInteractive-Transition(_:)` on the transition context, as well as managing the frames of the animation.

6. Sooner or later the gesture will end. At this point, decide whether to declare the transition completed or cancelled. A typical approach is to say that if the user performed more than half the full gesture, that constitutes completion; otherwise, it constitutes cancellation. Finish the animation accordingly.

7. The animation is now completed, and its completion function is called. You *must* call the transition context's `finishInteractiveTransition` or `cancel-InteractiveTransition`, and then call its `completeTransition(_:)` with an argument stating whether the transition was finished or cancelled.

8. Finally, `animationEnded` is called, and you can clean up.

(You may be asking: why is it necessary to keep talking to the transition context throughout the process? The reason is that the animation might have a component separate from what you're doing, such as the change in the appearance of the navigation bar during a navigation controller push or pop transition. The transition context, in order to coordinate that animation with the interactive gesture and with your animation, needs to be kept abreast of where things are throughout the course of the interaction.)

I'll describe how to make an interactive version of the tab bar controller transition animation that we developed in the previous section. The user will be able to drag from the edge of the screen to bring the tab bar controller's adjacent view controller in from the right or from the left.

In the previous section, I cleverly planned ahead for this section. Almost all the code from the previous section can be left as is! I'll build on that code, in such a way that the same custom transition animation can be *either* noninteractive (the user taps a tab bar item) *or* interactive (the user drags from one edge).

In my Animator object, I'm going to need two more instance properties, in addition to self.anim and self.tbc:

```
var anim : UIViewImplicitlyAnimating?
unowned var tbc : UITabBarController
weak var context : UIViewControllerContextTransitioning?
var interacting = false
```

The interacting property will be used as a signal that our transition is to be interactive. The context property is needed because the gesture recognizer's action method is going to need access to the transition context.

To track the user's gesture, I'll put a pair of UIScreenEdgePanGestureRecognizers into the interface. The gesture recognizers are attached to the tab bar controller's view (tbc.view), as this will remain constant while the views of its view controllers are sliding across the screen. In the Animator's initializer, I create the gesture recognizers and make the Animator their delegate, so I can dictate which of them is applicable to the current situation:

```
init(tabBarController tbc: UITabBarController) {
    self.tbc = tbc
    super.init()
    let sep = UIScreenEdgePanGestureRecognizer(
        target:self, action:#selector(pan))
    sep.edges = UIRectEdge.right
    tbc.view.addGestureRecognizer(sep)
    sep.delegate = self
    let sep2 = UIScreenEdgePanGestureRecognizer(
        target:self, action:#selector(pan))
    sep2.edges = UIRectEdge.left
    tbc.view.addGestureRecognizer(sep2)
    sep2.delegate = self
}
```

Acting as the delegate of the two gesture recognizers, we prevent either pan gesture recognizer from operating unless there is another child of the tab bar controller available on that side of the current child:

```
extension Animator : UIGestureRecognizerDelegate {
    func gestureRecognizerShouldBegin(_ g: UIGestureRecognizer) -> Bool {
        let ix = self.tbc.selectedIndex
        return
            (g as! UIScreenEdgePanGestureRecognizer).edges == .right ?
                ix < self.tbc.viewControllers!.count - 1 : ix > 0
    }
}
```

If the gesture recognizer action method `pan` is called, our interactive transition animation is to take place. I'll break down the discussion according to the gesture recognizer's states. In `.began`, I raise the `self.interacting` flag and trigger the transition by setting the tab bar controller's `selectedIndex`:

```
@objc func pan(_ g:UIScreenEdgePanGestureRecognizer) {
    switch g.state {
    case .began:
        self.interacting = true
        if g.edges == .right {
            self.tbc.selectedIndex = self.tbc.selectedIndex + 1
        } else {
            self.tbc.selectedIndex = self.tbc.selectedIndex - 1
        }
    // ...
    }
}
```

The transition begins. We are asked for our animation controller and our transition controller. We will supply a transition controller only if the `self.interacting` flag was raised; if the `self.interacting` flag is *not* raised, the user tapped a tab bar item and we are back in the preceding example:

```
extension AppDelegate: UITabBarControllerDelegate {
    func tabBarController(_ tabBarController: UITabBarController,
        animationControllerForTransitionFrom fromVC: UIViewController,
        to toVC: UIViewController) -> UIViewControllerAnimatedTransitioning? {
            return self
    }
    func tabBarController(_ tabBarController: UITabBarController,
        interactionControllerFor ac: UIViewControllerAnimatedTransitioning)
        -> UIViewControllerInteractiveTransitioning? {
            return self.interacting ? self : nil
    }
}
```

As a UIViewControllerInteractiveTransitioning adopter, our `startInteractive-Transition(_:)` is called instead of `animateTransition(using:)`. Our `animate-Transition(using:)` is still in place, and still does the same job it did in the previous section. So we call it to obtain the property animator, and set the property animator instance property. But we do *not* tell the property animator to animate! We are interactive; we intend to manage the "frames" of the animation ourselves (see "Frozen View Animation" on page 186). We also set the UIViewControllerContextTransitioning property, so that the gesture recognizer's action method can access it:

```
extension AppDelegate : UIViewControllerInteractiveTransitioning {
    func startInteractiveTransition(_ c:UIViewControllerContextTransitioning) {
        self.anim = self.interruptibleAnimator(using: c)
        self.context = c
    }
}
```

The user's gesture proceeds, and we are now back in the gesture recognizer's action method, in the `.changed` state. We calculate the completed percentage of the gesture, and update both the property animator's "frame" and the transition context:

```
case .changed:
    let v = g.view!
    let delta = g.translation(in:v)
    let percent = abs(delta.x/v.bounds.size.width)
    self.anim?.fractionComplete = percent
    self.context?.updateInteractiveTransition(percent)
```

Ultimately, the user's gesture ends, and we must finish the animation. Our goal is to "hurry" to the start of the animation or the end of the animation, depending on how far the user got through the gesture. With a property animator, that's really easy (see "Cancelling a View Animation" on page 183):

```
case .ended:
    let anim = self.anim as! UIViewPropertyAnimator
    anim.pauseAnimation()
    if anim.fractionComplete < 0.5 {
        anim.isReversed = true
    }
    anim.continueAnimation(
        withTimingParameters:
        UICubicTimingParameters(animationCurve:.linear),
        durationFactor: 0.2)
```

The animation comes to an end, and the completion function that we gave our property animator in `interruptibleAnimator` is called. Unlike the preceding example, we must send *different* messages to the transition context depending on whether we finished at the end or reversed to the start:

```
anim.addCompletion { finish in
    if finish == .end {
        ctx.finishInteractiveTransition()
        ctx.completeTransition(true)
    } else {
        ctx.cancelInteractiveTransition()
        ctx.completeTransition(false)
    }
}
```

Finally, our `animationEnded` is called, and we clean up our instance properties:

```
func animationEnded(_ transitionCompleted: Bool) {
    self.interacting = false
    self.anim = nil
}
```

Another variation would be to make the custom transition animation interruptible. Again, this is straightforward thanks to the existence of property animators. While a view is in the middle of being animated, the property animator implements touchability of the animated view, and allows you to pause the animation. The user can be permitted to do such things as grab the animated view in the middle of the animation and move it around with the animation paused, and the animation can then resume when the user lets go of the view (as I demonstrated in "Hit-Testing During Animation" on page 279). You could equally incorporate these features into a custom transition animation.

Custom Presented View Controller Transition

With a presented view controller transition, you can customize not only the *animation* but also the final *position* of the presented view. Moreover, you can introduce ancillary views which *remain in the scene* while the presented view is presented, and are not removed until after dismissal is complete; for instance, if the presented view is smaller than the presenting view and covers it only partially, you might add a dimming view between them, to darken the presenting view (just as a .formSheet presentation does).

There is no existing view to serve as the container view; therefore, when the presentation starts, the runtime constructs the container view and inserts it into the interface, leaving it there while the view remains presented. In the case of a .fullScreen presentation, the runtime also rips the presenting view out of the interface and inserts it into the container view, in case you want to animate it as well. For other styles of presentation, the container view is in front of the presenting view.

The work of customizing a presentation is distributed between *two* objects:

The animation controller
> The animation controller should be responsible for only the animation, the movement of the presented view into its final position.

The custom presentation controller
> The determination of the presented view's final position is the job of the presentation controller. The presentation controller is also responsible for inserting any extra views, such as a dimming view, into the container view; Apple says that the animation controller animates the content, while the presentation controller animates the "chrome."

This distribution of responsibilities may sound rather elaborate, but in fact the opposite is true: it greatly simplifies things, because if you don't need one kind of customization you can omit it:

Animation controller only
> If you supply an animation controller and no custom presentation controller, you dictate the animation, but the presented view will end up wherever the modal presentation style puts it.

Presentation controller only
> If you supply a custom presentation controller and no animation controller, a default modal transition style animation will be performed, but the presented view will end up at the position your custom presentation controller dictates.

Customizing the animation

I'll start with a situation where we don't use the presentation controller: all we want to do is customize the animation part of a built-in presentation style. The steps are almost completely parallel to how we customized a tab bar controller animation:

1. Give the presented view controller a delegate. This means that you set the presented view controller's `transitioningDelegate` property to an object adopting the UIViewControllerTransitioningDelegate protocol.

2. The delegate will be asked for an animation controller, and will return an object adopting the UIViewControllerAnimatedTransitioning protocol. Unlike a tab bar controller or navigation controller, a presented view controller's view undergoes *two* animations — the presentation and the dismissal — and therefore the delegate is asked *separately* for controllers:

   - `animationController(forPresented:presenting:source:)`
   - `interactionControllerForPresentation(using:)`
   - `animationController(forDismissed:)`
   - `interactionControllerForDismissal(using:)`

   You are free to customize just one animation, leaving the other at the default by not providing a controller for it.

3. The animation controller will implement its four methods as usual — `transitionDuration`, `animateTransition`, `interruptibleAnimator`, and `animationEnded`.

To illustrate, let's say we're running on an iPad, and we want to present a view using the `.formSheet` presentation style. But instead of using any of the built-in animation types (transition styles), we'll have the presented view appear to grow from the middle of the screen.

The only mildly tricky step is the first one. The `transitioningDelegate` must be set very early in the presented view controller's life — before the presentation begins. But the presented view controller doesn't exist before the presentation begins. The most reliable solution is for the presented view controller to assign its own delegate in its own initializer:

```
required init?(coder: NSCoder) {
    super.init(coder:coder)
    self.transitioningDelegate = self
}
```

The presentation begins, and we're on to the second step. The transitioning delegate (UIViewControllerTransitioningDelegate) is asked for an animation controller; here, I'll have it supply `self` once again, and I'll do this only for the presentation, leaving the dismissal to use the default animation (and I'm not making this example interactive, so I don't implement the `interactionController` methods):

```
func animationController(forPresented presented: UIViewController,
    presenting: UIViewController, source: UIViewController)
    -> UIViewControllerAnimatedTransitioning? {
        return self
}
```

The third step is that the animation controller (UIViewControllerAnimatedTransitioning) is called upon to implement the animation. Our implementations of `transitionDuration`, `animateTransition`, and `animationEnded` are the usual boilerplate, so I'll show only `interruptibleAnimator`, which configures the property animator; observe that we don't care about the `.from` view controller (its view isn't even in the container view):

```
func interruptibleAnimator(using ctx: UIViewControllerContextTransitioning)
    -> UIViewImplicitlyAnimating {
        if self.anim != nil {
            return self.anim!
        }
        let vc2 = ctx.viewController(forKey:.to)
        let con = ctx.containerView
        let r2end = ctx.finalFrame(for:vc2!)
        let v2 = ctx.view(forKey:.to)!
        v2.frame = r2end
        v2.transform = CGAffineTransform(scaleX: 0.1, y: 0.1)
        v2.alpha = 0
        con.addSubview(v2)
        let anim = UIViewPropertyAnimator(duration: 0.4, curve: .linear) {
            v2.alpha = 1
            v2.transform = .identity
        }
        anim.addCompletion { _ in
            ctx.completeTransition(true)
```

```
        }
        self.anim = anim
        return anim
    }
```

If we wish to customize both animation and dismissal using the same animation controller, there is a complication: the roles of the view controllers are reversed in the mind of the transition context. On presentation, the presented view controller is the .to view controller, but on dismissal, it is the .from view controller. For a presentation that isn't .fullScreen, the unused view is nil, so you can distinguish the cases by structuring your code like this:

```
let v1 = ctx.view(forKey:.from)
let v2 = ctx.view(forKey:.to)
if let v2 = v2 { // presenting
    // ...
} else if let v1 = v1 { // dismissing
    // ...
}
```

Customizing the presentation

Now let's involve the presentation controller: we will customize the final frame of the presented view controller's view, and we'll even add some "chrome" to the presentation. This will require some additional steps:

1. In addition to setting the presented view controller's transitioningDelegate, you set its modalPresentationStyle to .custom.

2. The result of the preceding step is that the delegate (the adopter of UIViewControllerTransitioningDelegate) is sent an additional message:

   • presentationController(forPresented:presenting:source:)

   Your mission is to return an instance of a *custom UIPresentationController subclass*. This will then be the presented view controller's presentation controller from the time presentation begins to the time dismissal ends. You create this instance by calling (directly or indirectly) the designated initializer:

   • init(presentedViewController:presenting:)

3. By means of appropriate overrides in the UIPresentationController subclass, you participate in the presentation, dictating the presented view's final position (frameOfPresentedViewInContainerView) and adding "chrome" to the presentation as desired.

The UIPresentationController has properties pointing to the presentingViewController as well the presentedViewController and the presentedView, plus the presentationStyle set by the presented view controller. It also obtains the containerView, which it subsequently communicates to the animation controller's

---

transition context. It has some methods and properties that can be overridden in the subclass; you only need to override the ones that require customization for your particular implementation:

`frameOfPresentedViewInContainerView`
> The final position of the presented view. The animation controller, if there is one, will receive this from the transition context's `finalFrame(for:)` method.

`presentationTransitionWillBegin`
`presentationTransitionDidEnd`
`dismissalTransitionWillBegin`
`dismissalTransitionDidEnd`
> Use these events as signals to add or remove "chrome" (extra views) to the container view.

`containerViewWillLayoutSubviews`
`containerViewDidLayoutSubviews`
> Use these layout events as signals to update the "chrome" views if needed.

A presentation controller is not a view controller, but UIPresentationController adopts some protocols that UIViewController adopts, and gets the same resizing-related messages that a UIViewController gets, as I described earlier in this chapter. It adopts UITraitEnvironment, meaning that it has a `traitCollection` and participates in the trait collection inheritance hierarchy, and receives the `traitCollectionDidChange(_:)` message. It also adopts UIContentContainer, meaning that it receives `willTransition(to:with:)` and `viewWillTransition(to:with:)`.

I'll expand the preceding example to implement a custom presentation style that looks like a `.formSheet` *even on an iPhone*. The first step is to set the presentation style to `.custom` when we set the transitioning delegate:

```
required init?(coder: NSCoder) {
    super.init(coder:coder)
    self.transitioningDelegate = self
    self.modalPresentationStyle = .custom // *
}
```

The result (step two) is that this extra UIViewControllerTransitioningDelegate method is called so that we can provide a custom presentation controller:

```
func presentationController(forPresented presented: UIViewController,
    presenting: UIViewController?, source: UIViewController)
    -> UIPresentationController? {
        let pc = MyPresentationController(
            presentedViewController: presented, presenting: presenting)
        return pc
}
```

Everything else happens in the implementation of our UIPresentationController subclass (named MyPresentationController). To make the presentation look like an iPad .formSheet, we inset the presented view's frame:

```
override var frameOfPresentedViewInContainerView : CGRect {
    return super.frameOfPresentedViewInContainerView.insetBy(dx:40, dy:40)
}
```

We could actually stop at this point! The presented view now appears in the correct position. Unfortunately, the presenting view is appearing undimmed behind it. Let's add dimming, by inserting a translucent dimming view into the container view, being careful to deal with the possibility of subsequent rotation:

```
override func presentationTransitionWillBegin() {
    let con = self.containerView!
    let shadow = UIView(frame:con.bounds)
    shadow.backgroundColor = UIColor(white:0, alpha:0.4)
    con.insertSubview(shadow, at: 0)
    shadow.autoresizingMask = [.flexibleWidth, .flexibleHeight]
}
```

Again, this works perfectly, but now I don't like what happens when the presented view is dismissed: the dimming view vanishes suddenly at the end of the dismissal. I'd rather have the dimming view fade out, and I'd like it to fade out *in coordination with the dismissal animation.* The way to arrange that is through the object vended by the presented view controller's transitionCoordinator property (a UIViewController-TransitionCoordinator); in particular, we can call its animate(alongside-Transition:completion:) method to add our own animation:

```
override func dismissalTransitionWillBegin() {
    let con = self.containerView!
    let shadow = con.subviews[0]
    if let tc = self.presentedViewController.transitionCoordinator {
        tc.animate { _ in
            shadow.alpha = 0
        }
    }
}
```

Once again, we could stop at this point. But I'd like to add a further refinement. A .formSheet view has rounded corners. I'd like to make our presented view look the same way:

```
override var presentedView : UIView? {
    let v = super.presentedView!
    v.layer.cornerRadius = 6
    v.layer.masksToBounds = true
    return v
}
```

Finally, for completeness, it would be nice, during presentation, to dim the appearance of any button titles and other tinted interface elements visible through the dimming view, to emphasize that they are disabled:

```
override func presentationTransitionDidEnd(_ completed: Bool) {
    let vc = self.presentingViewController
    let v = vc.view
    v?.tintAdjustmentMode = .dimmed
}
override func dismissalTransitionDidEnd(_ completed: Bool) {
    let vc = self.presentingViewController
    let v = vc.view
    v?.tintAdjustmentMode = .automatic
}
```

Transition Coordinator

In the previous section, I mentioned that a view controller has a transition-Coordinator, which is typed as a UIViewControllerTransitionCoordinator. A view controller's transitionCoordinator exists only during a transition between view controllers, such as presentation or pushing. Its actual class is of no importance; UIViewControllerTransitionCoordinator is a protocol. This protocol, in turn, conforms to the UIViewControllerTransitionCoordinatorContext protocol, just like a transition context; indeed, it is a kind of wrapper around the transition context.

A view controller can use its transitionCoordinator to find out about the transition it is currently involved in. Moreover, as I've already said, it can take advantage of animate(alongsideTransition:completion:) to add animation of its view's internal interface as part of a transition animation. This works equally for a custom animation or a built-in animation; in fact, the point is that the view controller can behave agnostically with regard to how its own view is being animated.

In this example, a presented view controller animates part of its interface into place as the transition animation proceeds (whatever that animation may be):

```
override func viewWillAppear(_ animated: Bool) {
    super.viewWillAppear(animated)
    if let tc = self.transitionCoordinator {
        tc.animate { _ in
            self.buttonTopConstraint.constant += 200
            self.view.layoutIfNeeded()
        }
    }
}
```

The same technique works equally well if the transition animation is interactive. Here, a .pageSheet presented view controller fades out its subviews as the user drags down the view to dismiss it:

```
func presentationControllerWillDismiss(_ pc: UIPresentationController) {
    if let tc = pc.presentedViewController.transitionCoordinator {
        tc.animate { _ in
            for v in pc.presentedViewController.view.subviews {
                v.alpha = 0
            }
        }
    }
}
```

The transition coordinator implements an additional method that might be of occasional interest:

notifyWhenInteractionChanges(:)
    The argument you pass is a function to be called; the transition context is the function's parameter. Your function is called whenever the transition changes between being interactive and being noninteractive; this might be because the interactive transition was cancelled.

In this example, a navigation controller has pushed a view controller, and now the user is popping it interactively (using the default drag-from-the-left-edge gesture). If the user cancels, the back view controller can hear about it, like this:

```
override func viewWillAppear(_ animated: Bool) {
    super.viewWillAppear(animated)
    let tc = self.transitionCoordinator
    tc?.notifyWhenInteractionChanges { ctx in
        if ctx.isCancelled {
            // ...
        }
    }
}
```

 I have not found any occasion when the child of a tab bar controller has a non-nil transition coordinator — even though you may have given the tab bar controller's transition a custom animation. I regard this as a bug.

Page View Controller

A page view controller (UIPageViewController) is like a book that can be viewed one page at a time. The user, by a gesture, can navigate in one direction or the other to see the next or the previous page, successively — like turning the pages of a book.

A page view controller only *seems* to have multiple pages. In reality, it has only the one page that the user is looking at. That page is the view of its one child view controller. The page view controller navigates to another page essentially by releasing its existing child view controller and replacing it with another. This is a very efficient architecture: it makes no difference whether the page view controller lets the user page through three pages or ten thousand pages, because each page is created in real time, on demand, and exists only as long as the user is looking at it.

The page view controller's children are its `viewControllers`. In general, there will be at most one of them (though there is a rarely used configuration in which a page view controller can have two pages at a time, as I'll explain in a moment). The page view controller is its current child's `parent`.

Preparing a Page View Controller

To create a UIPageViewController in code, use its designated initializer:

- `init(transitionStyle:navigationOrientation:options:)`

Here's what the parameters mean:

`transitionStyle:`
:   The animation type during navigation (UIPageViewController.TransitionStyle). Your choices are:

    - `.pageCurl`
    - `.scroll` (sliding)

`navigationOrientation:`
:   The direction of navigation (UIPageViewController.NavigationOrientation). Your choices are:

    - `.horizontal`
    - `.vertical`

`options:`
:   A dictionary. Possible keys are (UIPageViewController.OptionsKey):

    `.spineLocation`
    :   If you're using the `.pageCurl` transition style, this is the position of the pivot line around which those page curl transitions rotate. The value (UIPageView-Controller.SpineLocation) is one of the following:

        - `.min` (left or top)
        - `.mid` (middle; in this configuration there are *two* children, and *two* pages are shown at once)
        - `.max` (right or bottom)

    `.interPageSpacing`
    :   If you're using the `.scroll` transition style, this is the spacing between successive pages, visible as a gap during the transition (the default is 0).

You configure the page view controller's initial content by handing it its initial child view controller(s). You do that by calling this method:

- setViewControllers(_:direction:animated:completion:)

Here's what the parameters mean:

viewControllers:
> An array of one view controller — unless you're using the .pageCurl transition style and the .mid spine location, in which case it's an array of two view controllers.

direction:
> The animation direction (UIPageViewController.NavigationDirection). This probably won't matter when you're assigning the page view controller its initial content, as you are not likely to want any animation. Possible values are:
>
> - .forward
> - .backward

animated:, completion:
> A Bool and a completion function.

To allow the user to page through the page view controller, you assign the page view controller a dataSource, which should conform to the UIPageViewControllerData-Source protocol. The dataSource is told whenever the user starts to change pages, and should respond by immediately providing another view controller whose view will constitute the new page. Typically, the data source will create this view controller on the spot.

Here's a minimal example. Each page in the page view controller is to portray an image of a named Pep Boy. The first question is where the pages will come from. My data model consists of an array (self.pep) of the string names of the three Pep Boys:

```
let pep : [String] = ["Manny", "Moe", "Jack"]
```

To match these, I have three eponymous image files (manny, moe, and jack), portraying each Pep Boy. I've also got a UIViewController subclass called Pep, capable of displaying a Pep Boy's image in an image view. I initialize a Pep object with its designated initializer init(pepBoy:), supplying the name of a Pep Boy from the array; the Pep object sets its own boy property:

```
let boy : String
init(pepBoy boy:String) {
    self.boy = boy
    super.init(nibName: nil, bundle: nil)
}
```

Pep's `viewDidLoad` fetches the corresponding image and assigns it as the image of a UIImageView (`self.pic`) within its own view:

```
override func viewDidLoad() {
    super.viewDidLoad()
    self.pic.image = UIImage(named:self.boy.lowercased())
}
```

At any given moment, our page view controller is to have one Pep instance as its child; its current page will portray a Pep Boy. Here's how I create the page view controller itself (in my scene delegate):

```
// make a page view controller
let pvc = UIPageViewController(
    transitionStyle: .scroll, navigationOrientation: .horizontal)
// give it an initial page
let page = Pep(pepBoy: self.pep[0])
pvc.setViewControllers([page], direction: .forward, animated: false)
// give it a data source
pvc.dataSource = self
// put its view into the interface
self.window!.rootViewController = pvc
```

That's sufficient to show the first page, but I haven't yet explained how to allow the user to navigate to a new page! That's the job of the data source, as I'll describe in the next section.

The page view controller is a UIViewController, and its view must get into the interface by standard means. You can make the page view controller the window's `rootViewController`, as I do here; you can make it a presented view controller; you can make it a child view controller of a tab bar controller or a navigation controller. If you want the page view controller's view to be a subview of a custom view controller's view, the custom view controller must be configured as a container view controller, as I'll describe later in this chapter.

Page View Controller Navigation

We now have a page view controller's view in our interface, itself containing and displaying the view of the one Pep view controller that is its child. In theory, we have *three* pages, because we have three Pep Boys and their images — but the page view controller knows about only one of them.

You don't supply (or even create) another page until the page view controller asks for it by calling one of these data source methods:

- `pageViewController(_:viewControllerAfter:)`

- `pageViewController(_:viewControllerBefore:)`

The job of those methods is to return the requested successive view controller — or nil, to signify that there is no further page in this direction. Your strategy for doing that will depend on how your model maintains the data. My data, as you'll recall, is an array of unique strings:

```
let pep : [String] = ["Manny", "Moe", "Jack"]
```

And a Pep view controller has one of those strings as its boy property. So all I have to do is start with the current Pep view controller's boy and find the previous name or the next name in the array:

```
func pageViewController(_ pvc: UIPageViewController,
    viewControllerAfter vc: UIViewController) -> UIViewController? {
        let boy = (vc as! Pep).boy
        let ix = self.pep.firstIndex(of:boy)! + 1
        if ix >= self.pep.count {
            return nil
        }
        return Pep(pepBoy: self.pep[ix])
}
func pageViewController(_ pvc: UIPageViewController,
    viewControllerBefore vc: UIViewController) -> UIViewController? {
        let boy = (vc as! Pep).boy
        let ix = self.pep.firstIndex(of:boy)! - 1
        if ix < 0 {
            return nil
        }
        return Pep(pepBoy: self.pep[ix])
}
```

We now have a working page view controller! The user, with a sliding gesture, can page through it, one page at a time. When the user reaches the first page or the last page, it is impossible to go further in that direction.

 A .scroll style page view controller may cache some of its view controllers in advance. Therefore you should make no assumptions about *when* these data source methods will be called. If you need to be notified when the user is actually turning the page, use the delegate (which I'll describe later), not the data source.

You can also, at any time, call setViewControllers to change programmatically what page is being displayed, possibly with animation. In this way, you can "jump" to a page other than a successive page (something that the user cannot do with a gesture).

Page indicator

If you're using the .scroll transition style, the page view controller can optionally display a page indicator (a UIPageControl, see Chapter 13). The user can look at this to get a sense of what page we're on, and can tap or drag on it to navigate.

To get the page indicator, you must implement two more data source methods; they are consulted in response to setViewControllers. We called that method initially to configure the page view controller; if we never call it again (because the user simply keeps navigating to the next or previous page), these data source methods won't be called again either, because they don't need to be: the page view controller will keep track of the current index on its own:

```
func presentationCount(for pvc: UIPageViewController) -> Int {
    return self.pep.count
}
func presentationIndex(for pvc: UIPageViewController) -> Int {
    let page = pvc.viewControllers![0] as! Pep
    let boy = page.boy
    return self.pep.firstIndex(of:boy)!
}
```

Unfortunately, the page view controller's page indicator by default has white dots and a clear background, so it is invisible in front of a white background. You'll want to customize it to change that. There is no direct access to it, so it's simplest to use the appearance proxy (Chapter 13):

```
let proxy = UIPageControl.appearance()
proxy.pageIndicatorTintColor = UIColor.red.withAlphaComponent(0.6)
proxy.currentPageIndicatorTintColor = .red
proxy.backgroundColor = .yellow
```

Navigation gestures

If you've assigned the page view controller the .pageCurl transition style, the user can navigate by tapping at either edge of the view or by dragging across the view. These gestures are detected through two gesture recognizers, which you can access through the page view controller's gestureRecognizers property. The documentation suggests that you might change where the user can tap or drag, by attaching those gesture recognizers to a different view, and other customizations are possible as well. In this code, I change the behavior of a .pageCurl page view controller (pvc) so that the user must double tap to request navigation:

```
for g in pvc.gestureRecognizers {
    if let g = g as? UITapGestureRecognizer {
        g.numberOfTapsRequired = 2
    }
}
```

Of course you are also free to add to the user's stock of gestures for requesting navigation. You can supply any controls or gesture recognizers that make sense for your app. Suppose you're using the .scroll transition style; by default, there's no tap gesture recognizer, so the user can't tap to request navigation (unless there's also a page control). Let's change that. I've added invisible views at either edge of my Pep view controller's view, with tap gesture recognizers attached. When the user taps, the tap gesture recognizer fires, and the action method posts a notification whose `object` is the tap gesture recognizer:

```
@IBAction func tap (_ sender: UIGestureRecognizer?) {
    NotificationCenter.default.post(name:Pep.tap, object: sender)
}
```

Elsewhere, I have registered to receive this notification. When it arrives, I use the tap gesture recognizer's view's `tag` to learn which view was tapped; I then navigate accordingly by calling `setViewControllers` (pvc is the page view controller):

```
NotificationCenter.default.addObserver(
    forName:Pep.tap, object: nil, queue: .main) { n in
        let g = n.object as! UIGestureRecognizer
        let which = g.view!.tag
        let vc0 = pvc.viewControllers![0]
        guard let vc = (which == 0 ?
            self.pageViewController(pvc, viewControllerBefore: vc0) :
            self.pageViewController(pvc, viewControllerAfter: vc0))
            else {return}
        let dir : UIPageViewController.NavigationDirection =
            which == 0 ? .reverse : .forward
        pvc.view.isUserInteractionEnabled = false
        pvc.setViewControllers([vc], direction: dir, animated: true) { _ in
            pvc.view.isUserInteractionEnabled = true
        }
    }
```

In that code, I turn off user interaction when the page animation starts and turn it back on when the animation ends. Otherwise we can crash (or get into an incoherent state) if the user taps during the animation.

Other Page View Controller Configurations

It is possible to assign a page view controller a delegate (UIPageViewController-Delegate), which gets an event when the user starts turning the page and when the user finishes turning the page, and can change the spine location dynamically in response to a change in device orientation. As with a tab bar controller's delegate or a navigation controller's delegate, a page view controller's delegate also gets messages allowing it to specify the page view controller's app rotation policy, so there's no need to subclass UIPageViewController solely for that purpose.

One further bit of configuration applicable to a `.pageCurl` page view controller is the `isDoubleSided` property. If it is `true`, the next page occupies the back of the previous page. The default is `false`, unless the spine is in the middle, in which case it's `true` and can't be changed. Your only option here, therefore, is to set it to `true` when the spine isn't in the middle, and in that case the back of each page would be a sort of throwaway page, glimpsed by the user during the page curl animation.

A page view controller in a storyboard lets you configure its transition style, navigation orientation, page spacing, spine location, and `isDoubleSided` property. (It also has delegate and data source outlets, but you're not allowed to connect them to other view controllers, because you can't draw an outlet from one scene to another in a storyboard.) It has no child view controller relationship, so you can't set the page view controller's initial child view controller in the storyboard; you'll have to complete the page view controller's initial configuration in code.

Container View Controllers

UITabBarController, UINavigationController, and UIPageViewController are all built-in *parent view controllers*: you hand them a child view controller and they do all the work, retaining that child view controller and putting its view into the interface inside their own view. What if you wanted your own view controller to do the same sort of thing?

Your UIViewController subclass can act as a *custom* parent view controller, managing child view controllers and putting their views into the interface. Your view controller becomes a *container view controller*. It does what the built-in parent view controllers do, except that *you* get to specify the details — what it means for a view controller to be a child of this kind of parent view controller, how many children it has, which of its children's views appear in the interface and where they appear, and so on. A container view controller can also participate actively in the business of trait collection inheritance and view resizing.

An example appears in Figure 6-4 — and the construction of that interface is charted in Figure 6-5. We have a page view controller, but it is not the root view controller, and its view does not occupy the entire interface. How is that achieved? It is *not* achieved by simply grabbing the page view controller's view and plopping it into the interface. You must *never* do that.

To put a view controller's view into the interface manually, you *must* have a container view controller, and it must *follow certain rules*. The container view controller must act as a well-behaved parent view controller. If another view controller is formally made its child, then the parent is permitted — as long it follows the rules — to put that child view controller's view into the interface as a subview of its own view.

 Custom parent view controllers are an important and probably underutilized Cocoa feature. They allow you to compose view controllers, manually assembling them into a hierarchy similar (and parallel) to views. Using child view controllers, you can partition a single screen among multiple view controllers, each responsible for a confined region of the interface. Indeed, a splendid lecture by Dave DeLong (available on YouTube) cogently argues that in fact, thanks to this feature, view controllers effectively *are* views.

Adding and Removing Children

A view controller has a `children` array; that's what gives it the power to be a parent. But you must not directly manipulate this array. A child view controller needs to receive certain definite events at particular moments:

- As it becomes a child view controller
- As its view is added to and removed from the interface
- As it ceases to be a child view controller

Therefore, to act as a parent view controller, your UIViewController subclass must fulfill certain responsibilities:

Adding a child

When a view controller is to *become your view controller's child*, your view controller must do these things, in this order:

1. Send `addChild(_:)` to itself, with the child as argument. The child is automatically added to your `children` array and is retained.

2. Get the child view controller's view into the interface (as a subview of your view controller's view), if that's what adding a child view controller means.

3. Send `didMove(toParent:)` to the child view controller, with your view controller as argument.

Removing a child

When a view controller is to *cease being your view controller's child*, your view controller must do these things, in this order:

1. Send `willMove(toParent:)` to the child, with a `nil` argument.

2. Remove the child view controller's view from the interface.

3. Send `removeFromParent` to the child. The child is automatically removed from your `children` array and is released.

That little dance ensures that a child view controller will always receive `willMove(toParent:)` followed by `didMove(toParent:)`. But you don't actually send both those messages explicitly:

- `addChild(_:)` sends `willMove(toParent:)` for you *automatically*.
- `removeFromParent` sends `didMove(toParent:)` for you *automatically*.

In each case, therefore, you *do* send explicitly the *other* message, the one that adding or removing a child view controller *doesn't* send for you — and of course you must send it so that everything happens in the correct order.

When you do this dance correctly, the proper parent–child relationship results: the container view controller can refer to its children as its `children`, and any child has a reference to the parent as its `parent`. If you don't do it correctly, all sorts of bad things can happen; in a worst-case scenario, the child view controller won't even survive, and its view won't work correctly, because the view controller was never properly retained as part of the view controller hierarchy (see "View Controller Hierarchy" on page 291). So do the dance correctly!

The initial child view controller

Example 6-1 provides a schematic approach for how to obtain an initial child view controller and put its view into the interface. (Alternatively, a storyboard can do this work for you, with no code, as I'll explain later in this chapter.)

Example 6-1. Adding an initial child view controller

```
let vc = // whatever; this is the initial child view controller
self.addChild(vc) // "will" called for us
// insert view into interface between "will" and "did"
self.view.addSubview(vc.view)
vc.view.frame = // whatever, or use constraints
// when we call add, we must call "did" afterward
vc.didMove(toParent: self)
```

In many cases, that's all you'll need. You have a parent view controller and a child view controller, and they are paired *permanently*, for the lifetime of the parent. That's how Figure 6-4 behaves: RootViewController has the UIPageViewController as its child, and the page view controller's view as its own view's subview, for the entire lifetime of the app.

To illustrate, I'll use the same page view controller that I used in my earlier examples, the one that displays Pep Boys; but this time, its view won't occupy the entire interface. My window's root view controller, in its `viewDidLoad`, will create and configure the page view controller as its child. Note how I perform the dance:

```
let pep : [String] = ["Manny", "Moe", "Jack"]
override func viewDidLoad() {
    super.viewDidLoad()
    let pvc = UIPageViewController(
        transitionStyle: .scroll, navigationOrientation: .horizontal)
    pvc.dataSource = self
    self.addChild(pvc) // dance, step 1
    self.view.addSubview(pvc.view) // dance, step 2
    // ... configure frame or constraints here ...
    pvc.didMove(toParent: self) // dance, step 3
    let page = Pep(pepBoy: self.pep[0])
    pvc.setViewControllers([page], direction: .forward, animated: false)
}
```

Replacing a child view controller

It is also possible to *replace* one child view controller's view in the interface with another (comparable to how UITabBarController behaves when a different tab bar item is selected). The simplest way is with this parent view controller instance method:

- `transition(from:to:duration:options:animations:completion:)`

That method manages the stages in good order, adding the view of one child view controller (`to:`) to the interface before the transition and removing the view of the other child view controller (`from:`) from the interface after the transition, and seeing to it that the child view controllers receive lifetime events (such as `viewWill-Appear(_:)`) at the right moment. Here's what the last three arguments are for:

`options:`
> A bitmask (UIView.AnimationOptions) comprising the same possible options that apply to any view transition (see "Transitions" on page 191).

`animations:`
> An animations function. This may be used for animating views other than the two views being managed by the transition animation specified in the `options:` argument; alternatively, if none of the built-in transition animations is suitable, you can animate the transitioning views yourself here (they are both in the interface when the animations function is called).

`completion:`
> A completion function. This will be important if the transition involves the removal or addition of a child view controller. At the time when you call `transition`, both view controllers must be children of the parent view controller; so if you're going to remove one of the view controllers as a child, you'll do it in the completion function. Similarly, if you owe a new child view controller a `did-Move(toParent:)` call, you'll use the completion function to fulfill that debt.

Here's an example. To keep things simple, suppose that our view controller has just one child view controller at a time, and displays the view of that child view controller within its own view. When our view controller is handed a new child view controller, it substitutes that new child view controller for the old child view controller, and replaces the old child view controller's view with the new child view controller's view in the interface. Here's code that does that correctly; the view controllers are `fromvc` and `tovc`:

```
// we have already been handed the new view controller
// set up the new view controller's view's frame
tovc.view.frame = // ... whatever
// must have both as children before we can transition between them
self.addChild(tovc) // "will" called for us
```

```
// when we call remove, we must call "will" (with nil) beforehand
fromvc.willMove(toParent: nil)
// then perform the transition
let opts = UIView.AnimationOptions.transitionFlipFromLeft
self.transition(from: fromvc, to: tovc, duration: 0.4, options: opts) {
} completion: { _ in
    // when we call add, we must call "did" afterward
    tovc.didMove(toParent: self)
    fromvc.removeFromParent() // "did" called for us
}
```

If we're using constraints to position the new child view controller's view, where will we set up those constraints? Before you call `transition...` is too soon, as the new child view controller's view is not yet in the interface. The completion function is too late: if the view is added with no constraints, it will have no initial size or position, so the animation will be performed and then the view will suddenly seem to pop into existence as we provide its constraints. The animations function turns out to be a very good place:

```
// must have both as children before we can transition between them
self.addChild(tovc) // "will" called for us
// when we call remove, we must call "will" (with nil) beforehand
fromvc.willMove(toParent: nil)
// then perform the transition
let opts = UIView.AnimationOptions.transitionFlipFromLeft
self.transition(from: fromvc, to: tovc, duration: 0.4, options: opts) {
    tovc.view.translatesAutoresizingMaskIntoConstraints = false
    // ... configure tovc.view constraints here ...
} completion: { _ in
    // when we call add, we must call "did" afterward
    tovc.didMove(toParent: self)
    fromvc.removeFromParent() // "did" called for us
}
```

If the built-in transition animations are unsuitable, you can omit the `options:` argument and provide your own animation in the animations function, at which time both views are in the interface. In this example, I animate a substitute view (an image view showing a snapshot of `tovc.view`) to grow from the top left corner; then I configure the real view's constraints and remove the substitute:

```
// tovc.view.frame is already set
let r = UIGraphicsImageRenderer(size:tovc.view.bounds.size)
let im = r.image { ctx in
    tovc.view.layer.render(in:ctx.cgContext)
}
let iv = UIImageView(image:im)
iv.frame = .zero
self.view.addSubview(iv)
tovc.view.alpha = 0 // hide the real view
// must have both as children before we can transition between them
self.addChild(tovc) // "will" called for us
```

```
// when we call remove, we must call "will" (with nil) beforehand
fromvc.willMove(toParent: nil)
// then perform the transition
self.transition(from:fromvc, to:tovc, duration:0.4) { // no options
    iv.frame = tovc.view.frame // animate bounds change
    // ... configure tovc.view constraints here ...
} completion: { _ in
    tovc.view.alpha = 1
    iv.removeFromSuperview()
    // when we call add, we must call "did" afterward
    tovc.didMove(toParent: self)
    fromvc.removeFromParent() // "did" called for us
}
```

Status Bar, Traits, and Resizing

A parent view controller, instead of dictating the status bar appearance through its own implementation of `preferredStatusBarStyle` or `prefersStatusBarHidden`, can defer the responsibility to one of its children, by overriding these properties:

- `childForStatusBarStyle`

- `childForStatusBarHidden`

That's what a UITabBarController does (as I've already mentioned). Your custom parent view controller can do the same thing.

A container view controller also participates in trait collection inheritance. In fact, you might insert a container view controller into your view controller hierarchy just to take advantage of this feature. A parent view controller has the amazing ability to lie to a child view controller about the environment, thanks to this method:

- `setOverrideTraitCollection(_:forChild:)`

The first parameter is a UITraitCollection that will be combined with the inherited trait collection and communicated to the specified child.

Why would you want to lie to a child view controller about its environment? Well, imagine that we're writing an iPad app, and we have a view controller whose view can appear either fullscreen or as a small subview of a parent view controller's main view. The view's interface might need to be different when it appears in the smaller size. You could configure that difference using size classes (conditional constraints) in the nib editor, with one interface for a `.regular` horizontal size class (iPad) and another interface for a `.compact` horizontal size class (iPhone). Then, when the view is to appear in its smaller size, we lie to its view controller and tell it that the horizontal size class *is* `.compact`:

```
let vc = // the view controller we're going to use as a child
self.addChild(vc) // "will" called for us
let tc = UITraitCollection(horizontalSizeClass: .compact)
self.setOverrideTraitCollection(tc, forChild: vc) // heh heh
vc.view.frame = // whatever
self.view.addSubview(vc.view)
vc.didMove(toParent: self)
```

UIPresentationController has a similar power, through its overrideTrait-
Collection property, allowing it to lie to its presented view controller about the
inherited trait collection. That is how a .formSheet presented view controller comes
to have a .compact horizontal size class even on an iPad.

 If your only reason for overriding the trait collection is to affect the user interface
style (light or dark), you can set the .overrideUserInterfaceStyle of a view
controller or view instead.

A parent view controller sets the size of a child view controller's view. A child view
controller, however, can express a preference as to what size it would like its view to
be, by setting its own preferredContentSize property. The chief purpose of this
property is to be consulted by a parent view controller when this view controller is its
child. It is a preference and no more; no law says that the parent must consult the
child, or that the parent must obey the child's preference.

If a view controller's preferredContentSize is set while it is already a child view
controller, the runtime automatically communicates this fact to the parent view controller by calling this UIContentContainer method:

- preferredContentSizeDidChange(forChildContentContainer:)

The parent view controller may implement this method to consult the child's
preferredContentSize, and may change the child's view's size in response if it so
chooses.

A parent view controller, as an adopter of the UIContentContainer protocol, is also
responsible for communicating to its children that their sizes are changing and what
their new sizes will be. It is the parent view controller's duty to implement this
method:

size(forChildContentContainer:withParentContainerSize:)
　　Should be implemented to return each child view controller's correct size at any
　　moment.

　　Failure to implement this method will cause the child view controller to be
　　handed the wrong size in its viewWillTransition(to:with:) — it will be given
　　the *parent's* new size rather than its own new size!

If your parent view controller implements `viewWillTransition(to:with:)`, it should call `super` so that `viewWillTransition(to:with:)` will be passed down to its children. This works even if your implementation is explicitly changing the size of a child view controller, provided you have implemented `size(forChildContent-Container:withParentContainerSize:)` to return the new size.

Previews and Context Menus

You can permit the user to summon a preview by long pressing on a view. The preview is a view controller's view. The runtime can create a view controller to show a view as a preview, but the real power of this feature lies in the fact that *you* can create the view controller.

Moreover, you can respond to the user tapping the preview; one possible response is to transition to a *real* view controller. That's why the preview is a preview: you're letting the user look at a view controller's view *without* actually transitioning to it, but then the user can *perform* the transition by tapping the preview.

The preview can be accompanied by a menu of tappable menu items. For that reason, this entire mechanism is referred to as a *context menu.*

(The overall context menu mechanism, introduced in iOS 13, is similar to the sequence of actions known in iOS 12 and before as *peek and pop.* But peek and pop was available only on devices with 3D touch, whereas this sort of preview is available on any device.)

To illustrate, imagine that we have a superview containing three image views, each portraying one of the three Pep Boys. Let's allow the user to long press on a Pep Boy image in order to summon a preview of that Pep Boy. At first, to keep things simple, I'll have this preview be the default view controller image generated by the runtime. But then I'll change the example to supply a custom view controller — and then I'll allow the user to tap the preview to transition to that view controller. Finally, to complete the example, I'll add menu items (Figure 6-9).

Context Menu Interaction and Configuration

Everything starts with a UIContextMenuInteraction and its delegate (UIContext-MenuInteractionDelegate). You add the interaction to a view, and a special long press gesture recognizer is installed for you. In our `viewDidLoad`, I'll add the interaction to the superview of the three image views:

Figure 6-9. A context menu and preview

```
@IBOutlet weak var imageBackground: UIView!
override func viewDidLoad() {
    super.viewDidLoad()
    let interaction = UIContextMenuInteraction(delegate: self)
    self.imageBackground.addInteraction(interaction)
}
```

That compiles just so long as `self` does in fact conform to UIContextMenuInteractionDelegate. To make it do that, we need an implementation of this delegate method:

- `contextMenuInteraction(_:configurationForMenuAtLocation:)`

The job here is to create a UIContextMenuConfiguration, configure it, and return it. The initializer is:

- `init(identifier:previewProvider:actionProvider:)`

Here's what the parameters mean:

`indentifier`
:   An arbitrary string. I'll demonstrate its use later on.

`previewProvider`
:   The preview provider is a function that returns a view controller whose view will be displayed as the preview.

`actionProvider`
:   The action provider is a function that returns a UIMenu whose items will be displayed below the preview.

Both the preview and the menu are optional; you can return `nil` from either function:

- If you supply a menu but a `nil` preview, the runtime creates a view controller whose view is a snapshot of the pressed view.

- If you supply a preview but a `nil` menu, just the preview is displayed.

- If you return `nil` for both the preview and the menu, the long pressed view waggles but nothing else happens.

- If you return `nil` as the UIContextMenuConfiguration, nothing happens at all.

Configuring the Preview

Let's start with minimal code just to make something happen when the user long presses on an image of a Pep Boy:

```
func contextMenuInteraction(_ inter: UIContextMenuInteraction,
    configurationForMenuAtLocation loc: CGPoint)
    -> UIContextMenuConfiguration? {
        let config = UIContextMenuConfiguration(
            identifier: nil, previewProvider: nil) { _ in
                let simpleAction = UIAction(title: "Testing") { _ in }
                return UIMenu(title: "", children: [simpleAction])
        }
        return config
}
```

We've provided a menu with a single menu item, and no preview view controller. So what appears when the user long presses on a Pep Boy image is the runtime-supplied preview along with a single Testing menu item. There's no other code, so when the user taps on the preview or the menu item, the whole thing just goes away.

I've deliberately built some wrong behavior into that setup. Because we attached the UIContextMenuInteraction to the background superview of the three image views, the default preview displays that superview; no matter which image view the user long pressed, all three image views appear as the preview. To fix that, there's another delegate method that lets you designate a view to be wrapped up as the preview. To prepare for this, I've given each Pep Boy image view a different `tag`; the `tag` values are 1, 2, and 3 respectively. The `tag` value will let me find the image view the user long pressed:

```
func contextMenuInteraction(_ interaction: UIContextMenuInteraction,
    previewForHighlightingMenuWithConfiguration
    config: UIContextMenuConfiguration)
    -> UITargetedPreview? {
        if let tag = config.identifier as? Int {
            if let imageView = self.imageBackground.viewWithTag(tag) {
                return UITargetedPreview(view: imageView)
            }
        }
        return nil
}
```

Our job here is to return a UITargetedPreview, which is basically a snapshot of a view along with a location where it should appear. This can be a view already in the interface, in which case the location is already known.

That example still isn't working yet, because it assumes that the UIContextMenu-Configuration has an `identifier` that comes from the `tag` of the image view that the user is long pressing. We need to set that `identifier` when we initialize the UICon-textMenuConfiguration. Currently, we are passing `nil` as the `identifier:` argument. We'll revise that, as follows:

```
guard let imageView =
    inter.view?.hitTest(loc, with: nil) as? UIImageView else {
        return nil
    }
let tag = imageView.tag as NSNumber
let config = UIContextMenuConfiguration(
    identifier: tag, previewProvider: nil) { _ in
```

The example now works! The user long presses a Pep Boy image, and that image is displayed as the preview.

But that *still* isn't what we really want to do. Recall that our goal is to supply our own view controller as the preview. I have a Pep view controller whose initializer takes the name of a Pep Boy, and whose view displays the name and image of that Pep Boy. So let's return an instance of that view controller, and no menu:

```
let boys = ["manny", "moe", "jack"]
func contextMenuInteraction(_ inter: UIContextMenuInteraction,
    configurationForMenuAtLocation loc: CGPoint)
    -> UIContextMenuConfiguration? {
        guard let imageView =
            inter.view?.hitTest(loc, with: nil) as? UIImageView else {
                return nil
            }
        let boy = boys[imageView.tag - 1]
        let tag = imageView.tag as NSNumber
        let config = UIContextMenuConfiguration(identifier: tag) {
            let pep = Pep(pepBoy: boy)
            pep.preferredContentSize = CGSize(width: 240, height: 300)
            return pep
        }
        return config
    }
```

Now the user long presses a Pep Boy image, and that Pep Boy's name and image appear as the preview. We don't really have to supply a `preferredContentSize` for the view controller, but the preview may be too large otherwise.

And now for the icing on the cake. Currently, when the user taps the preview, it just goes away. Let's change that so that tapping the preview actually navigates to that view controller. To do that, we implement yet another delegate method:

```
func contextMenuInteraction(_ interaction: UIContextMenuInteraction,
    willPerformPreviewActionForMenuWith
    configuration: UIContextMenuConfiguration,
    animator: UIContextMenuInteractionCommitAnimating) {
        if let vc = animator.previewViewController as? Pep {
            animator.preferredCommitStyle = .pop
            animator.addCompletion {
                vc.modalTransitionStyle = .crossDissolve
                self.present(vc, animated: true)
            }
        }
}
```

The object that arrives as the `animator:` parameter accepts an animation function and a completion function, and hands us the preview's view controller if there is one. I've performed the full transition to that view controller in the completion function.

Configuring the Menu

If we want to display a menu, we must return a UIMenu from the `actionProvider` function of the UIContextMenuConfiguration. This will be the *main* UIMenu, which typically will have no title and will itself act as a wrapper for its menu *elements*. Menu elements are effectively menu items; they are visible and tappable, and can have a title and an image. They are of two types:

UIAction
> A UIAction has a `handler:` function. When the user taps it, the entire menu interface (including the preview) is dismissed and the `handler:` function runs.

UIMenu
> A UIMenu (other than the main menu) looks like a UIAction, but it also has menu elements of its own, which the user does not see at first. When the user taps the UIMenu, the entire menu vanishes and is replaced by the elements of this UIMenu. In this way, you can create a menu with hierarchical levels.

As an example of a simple UIAction, I'll create a Favorites menu item. The user can tap this to make the currently previewed Pep Boy the favorite. The user's current favorite is stored in the user defaults. If this Pep Boy is already the user's favorite, the menu item has a filled star; otherwise it has an empty star.

I'll also create a hierarchical UIMenu. Here, I'll pretend that the user can colorize the current Pep Boy in a choice of red, green, or blue; I have no actual colorization functionality, so I'll just print to the console for purposes of the example.

I'll rewrite the `actionProvider` function of our UIContextMenuConfiguration initializer to incorporate those menu elements:

```
// Favorite menu item
let favKey = "favoritePepBoy"
let fav = UserDefaults.standard.string(forKey:favKey)
let star = boy == fav ? "star.fill" : "star"
let im = UIImage(systemName: star)
let favorite = UIAction(title: "Favorite", image: im) { _ in
    UserDefaults.standard.set(boy, forKey:favKey)
}
// Colorize menu item
let red = UIAction(title: "Red") {action in
    print ("coloring", boy, action.title.lowercased())
}
let green = UIAction(title: "Green") {action in
    print ("coloring", boy, action.title.lowercased())
}
let blue = UIAction(title: "Blue") {action in
    print ("coloring", boy, action.title.lowercased())
}
let color = UIMenu(title: "Colorize", children: [red,green,blue])
// Actual menu
return UIMenu(title: "", children: [favorite, color])
```

The result is that our menu is displayed along with the preview image (Figure 6-9).

New in iOS 14, a menu item can be a UIDeferredMenuElement. This permits a placeholder menu item to be presented to the user until your time-consuming code is ready with the actual UIAction elements to go in its place. This toy example is just to demonstrate the syntax:

```
let def = UIDeferredMenuElement { f in
    delay(2) {
        let action = UIAction(title: "Yoho") { action in
            // do nothing
        }
        f([action])
    }
}
```

If `def` is included as one of the `children` of our main UIMenu, it appears as a menu item with the title Loading and a spinner for two seconds, and is then replaced by a menu item with the title Yoho. Include more UIActions in the array to replace the Loading menu with multiple menu items.

Storyboards

A storyboard is a way of *automatically* creating view controllers and performing the kind of coherent view controller management and transitions that I've described throughout this chapter. A storyboard doesn't necessarily reduce the amount of code you'll have to write, but it does clarify the relationships between your view controllers over the course of your app's lifetime. Instead of having to hunt around in your code to see which class creates which view controller and when, you can view and manage the chain of view controller creation graphically in the nib editor.

A storyboard is a collection of view controller nibs, which are displayed as its scenes. Each view controller is instantiated from its own nib, as needed, and will then obtain its view, as needed — typically from a view nib that you've configured in the same scene by editing the view controller's view. I described this in "How Storyboards Work" on page 308. As I explained there, a view controller may be instantiated from a storyboard *automatically* in various ways:

Initial view controller

If your app (or window scene) has a main storyboard, as specified in the *Info.plist*, that storyboard's initial view controller will be instantiated and assigned as the window's `rootViewController` *automatically* as the app launches. To specify that a view controller is a storyboard's initial view controller, check the "Is Initial View Controller" checkbox in its Attributes inspector. This will cause any existing initial view controller to lose its initial view controller status. The initial view controller is distinguished graphically in the canvas by an arrow pointing to it from the left, and in the document outline by the presence of the Storyboard Entry Point.

Relationship

Two built-in parent view controllers can specify their children directly in the storyboard, setting their `viewControllers` array:

- UITabBarController can specify multiple children (its "view controllers").
- UINavigationController can specify its single initial child (its "root view controller").

To add a view controller as a child to one of those parent view controller types, Control-drag from the parent view controller to the child view controller; in the little HUD that appears, choose the appropriate listing under Relationship Segue. The result is a *relationship* whose source is the parent and whose destination is the child. The destination view controller will be instantiated *automatically* when the source view controller is instantiated, and will be assigned into its `view-Controllers` array, making it a child and retaining it.

Triggered segue

A triggered segue configures a *future* situation, when, while the app is running, the segue will somehow be *triggered*. At that time, one view controller that already exists (the source) will cause the instantiation of another view controller (the destination), bringing the latter into existence *automatically*. Two types of triggered segue are particularly common (their names in the nib editor depend on whether the "Use Trait Variations" checkbox is checked in the File inspector):

Show (formerly Push)
> The future view controller will be *pushed* onto the stack of the navigation controller of which the existing view controller is already a child.
>
> The name Show comes from the show(_:sender:) method, which pushes a view controller onto the parent navigation controller if there is one, but behaves adaptively if there is not (I'll talk more about that in Chapter 10). A Show segue from a view controller that is *not* a navigation controller's child will *present* the future view controller rather than pushing it, as there is no navigation stack to push onto. Setting up a Show segue without a navigation controller and then wondering why there is no push is a common beginner mistake.

Present Modally (formerly Modal)
> The future view controller will be a *presented* view controller (and the existing view controller will be its original presenter).

A triggered segue may emanate from the source view controller itself, and is then a *manual* segue; it must be triggered in code, using the segue's identifier. Alternatively, it can emanate from something in the source view controller's view that the user can interact with — a gesture recognizer, or a tappable view such as a button or a table view cell — and is then an *action* segue, meaning that the segue will be triggered *automatically*, bringing the destination view controller into existence and displaying its view, when a tap or other gesture occurs.

To create a triggered segue, Control-drag from the tappable object in the first view controller, or from the first view controller itself, to the second view controller. In the little HUD that appears, choose the type of segue you want. If you dragged from the view controller, this will be a manual segue; if you dragged from a tappable object, it will be an action segue.

Figure 6-10 shows the storyboard of a small test app. The initial view controller (at the left) is a tab bar controller. It will be instantiated automatically when the app launches. Through two "view controllers" relationships, it has two children, which will both be instantiated automatically together with the tab bar controller:

- The tab bar controller's first child (upper row) is a navigation controller, which itself, through a "root view controller" relationship, has one child, which will also be instantiated automatically and will be placed at the bottom of the navigation controller's stack when the navigation controller is instantiated.

Figure 6-10. The storyboard of an app

- That child has a triggered Show segue to *another* view controller, giving it the ability in the future to create that view controller and *push* it onto the navigation controller's stack.

- The tab bar controller's second child (lower row) has a triggered Present Modally segue to another view controller, giving it the ability in the future to create that view controller and *present* it.

It is also possible to instantiate a view controller from a storyboard *manually*, in code. That way, you are still creating the view controller instance on demand, but you also get the convenience of designing its view in the nib editor, and the instance comes with the segues that emanate from it in the storyboard.

Your code can instantiate a view controller manually from a storyboard by calling one of these methods:

- `instantiateInitialViewController`

- `instantiateViewController(withIdentifier:)`

The `identifier:` in the second method is a string that must match the Storyboard ID in the Identity inspector of some view controller in the storyboard (or you'll crash).

Starting in iOS 13, each of those methods has a variant that takes a function:

- `instantiateInitialViewController(creator:)`

- `instantiateViewController(identifier:creator:)`

The `creator:` is a function whose parameter is an NSCoder and that returns a view controller. Your function must call `init(coder:)`, using that same NSCoder as the argument. You might prefer these variants, for two reasons:

- Your function can call a custom initializer that does other things besides calling `init(coder:)`, and it can perform additional configurations on the view controller that's being instantiated.

- These methods are generics, so the return type is your view controller's type, rather than a plain UIViewController that you then have to cast down.

To illustrate, here's a rewrite of an earlier example ("App Without a Storyboard" on page 7) where we used a condition in our `scene(_:willConnectTo:options:)` implementation in order to decide at launch time what the window's root view controller should be. In the case where the user has not yet logged in, where we currently call `instantiateViewController(identifier:)`, we'll call `instantiateViewController(identifier:creator:)` instead.

To prepare, I've given my LoginViewController a custom initializer, `init(coder:message:)`, like this:

```
class LoginViewController: UIViewController {
    var message : String = ""
    convenience init(coder:NSCoder, message:String) {
        self.init(coder:coder)!
        self.message = message
    }
    // ...
}
```

When the time comes to instantiate the LoginViewController from the storyboard, I call `instantiateViewController(identifier:creator:)`; in my `creator:` function, I call `init(coder:message:)` — which I am allowed to do, because this initializer obeys the rule that we must call `init(coder:)` as part of initialization:

```
self.window = UIWindow(windowScene: windowScene)
let userHasLoggedIn : Bool = // ...
let sb = UIStoryboard(name: "Main", bundle: nil)
if userHasLoggedIn {
    let vc = sb.instantiateViewController(identifier: "UserHasLoggedIn")
    self.window!.rootViewController = vc
} else {
    let lvc = sb.instantiateViewController(identifier: "LoginScreen") { // *
        LoginViewController(coder:$0, message:"You need to log in first.")
    }
```

```
    // could perform further initializations here
    self.window!.rootViewController = lvc
}
self.window!.makeKeyAndVisible()
```

Moreover, we could now perform further configuration of the view controller without casting it down; lvc is already typed, not as a vanilla UIViewController, but as a LoginViewController. None of that was possible before iOS 13.

Triggered Segues

A triggered segue is a true segue (as opposed to a relationship, which isn't). The most common types are Show (Push) and Present Modally (Modal). A segue is a full-fledged object, an instance of UIStoryboardSegue, and it can be configured in the nib editor through its Attributes inspector. However, it is not instantiated by the loading of a nib, and it cannot be pointed to by an outlet. Rather, it will be instantiated *when the segue is triggered*, at which time its designated initializer will be called, namely init(identifier:source:destination:).

A segue's source and destination are the two view controllers between which it runs. The segue is directional, so the source and destination are clearly distinguished. The source view controller is the one that will exist already, before the segue is triggered; the destination view controller will be instantiated when the segue is triggered, along with the segue itself.

A segue's identifier is a string. You can set this string for a segue in a storyboard in the Attributes inspector; that's useful when you want to trigger the segue manually in code (you'll specify it by means of its identifier), or when you have code that can receive a segue as parameter and you need to distinguish which segue this is.

Triggered segue behavior

The default behavior of a segue when it is triggered is exactly the behavior of the corresponding manual transition described earlier in this chapter:

Show (Push)
> The segue is going to call pushViewController(_:animated:) (if we are in a navigation interface). To set animated: to false, uncheck the Animates checkbox in the Attributes inspector.

Present Modally (Modal)
> The segue is going to call present(_:animated:completion:). To set animated: to false, uncheck the Animates checkbox in the Attributes inspector. Other presentation options, such as the modal presentation style and the modal transition style, can be set in Attributes inspector either for the destination view controller or for the segue; the segue settings take precedence.

You can further customize a triggered segue's behavior by providing your own UIStoryboardSegue subclass. The key thing is that you must implement your custom segue's perform method, which will be called after the segue is triggered and instantiated, to do the actual transition from one view controller to another.

If this is a push segue or a modal segue, it already knows how to do the transition; therefore, in the Attributes inspector for the segue, you specify your UIStoryboardSegue subclass, and in that subclass, you call super in your perform implementation.

Let's say that you want to add a custom transition animation to a modal segue. You can do this by writing a segue class that makes itself the destination view controller's transitioning delegate in its perform implementation before calling super:

```
class MyCoolSegue: UIStoryboardSegue {
    override func perform() {
        let dest = self.destination
        dest.modalPresentationStyle = .custom
        dest.transitioningDelegate = self
        super.perform()
    }
}
extension MyCoolSegue: UIViewControllerTransitioningDelegate {
    func animationController(forPresented presented: UIViewController,
        presenting: UIViewController,
        source: UIViewController) -> UIViewControllerAnimatedTransitioning? {
            return self
    }
    // ...
}
extension MyCoolSegue: UIViewControllerAnimatedTransitioning {
    func transitionDuration(using ctx: UIViewControllerContextTransitioning?)
        -> TimeInterval {
            return 0.8
    }
    // ...
}
```

The rest is then exactly as in "Custom Presented View Controller Transition" on page 365. MyCoolSegue is the UIViewControllerTransitioningDelegate, so its animation-Controller(forPresented:...) will be called. MyCoolSegue is also the UIViewControllerAnimatedTransitioning object, so its transitionDuration and so forth will be called. In short, we are now off to the races with a custom presented view controller transition, with all the code living inside MyCoolSegue — a pleasant encapsulation of functionality.

You can also create a *completely* custom segue. To do so, in the HUD when you Control-drag to create the segue, ask for a Custom segue, and then, in the Attributes inspector, specify your UIStoryboardSegue subclass. Again, you must override perform, but now you *don't* call super — the *whole transition* is up to you! Your perform implementation can access the segue's `identifier`, `source`, and `destination` properties. The `destination` view controller has already been instantiated, but that's all; it is entirely up to your code to make this view controller either a child view controller or a presented view controller, and to cause its view to appear in the interface.

How a segue is triggered

A triggered segue will be triggered in one of two ways:

Through a user gesture

If a segue emanates from a gesture recognizer or from a tappable view, it is an *action segue*, meaning that it will be triggered automatically when the tap or other gesture occurs.

Your source view controller class can prevent an action segue from being triggered. To do so, override this method:

`shouldPerformSegue(withIdentifier:sender:)`

Sent when an action segue is about to be triggered. Returns a Bool (and the default is `true`), so if you don't want this segue triggered on this occasion, return `false`.

In code

If a segue emanates from a view controller as a whole, it is a *manual segue*, and triggering it is up to your code. Send this message to the source view controller:

`performSegue(withIdentifier:sender:)`

Triggers a segue whose source is this view controller. The segue will need an identifier in the storyboard so that you can specify it here! `shouldPerform-Segue(withIdentifier:sender:)` will *not* be called, because if you didn't want the segue triggered, you wouldn't have called `performSegue` in the first place.

An action segue with an identifier can be treated as a manual segue: that is, you can trigger it by calling `performSegue`, doing in code what the user could have done by tapping.

View controller communication

When a segue is triggered, the destination view controller is instantiated automatically; your code does not instantiate it. This raises a crucial question: how are you going to communicate between the source view controller and the destination view controller? This, you'll remember, was the subject of an earlier section of this chapter ("Communication with a Presented View Controller" on page 334), where I used this code as an example:

```
let svc = SecondViewController()
svc.data = "This is very important data!"
svc.delegate = self
self.present(svc, animated:true)
```

In that code, the first view controller creates the second view controller, and therefore has a reference to it at that moment — so it has an opportunity to communicate with it, passing along some data to it, and setting itself as its delegate, before presenting it. With a modal segue, however, the second view controller is instantiated for you, and the segue itself is going to call present(_:animated:completion:). So when and how will the first view controller be able to set svc.data and set itself as svc's delegate?

One solution is for the source view controller to override prepare(for:sender:). After a segue has instantiated the destination view controller but before the segue is actually performed, the source view controller's prepare(for:sender:) is called. The first parameter is the segue, and the segue has a reference to the destination view controller — so this is the moment when the source view controller and the destination view controller meet! The source view controller can now perform configurations on the destination view controller, hand it data, and so forth. The source view controller can work out which segue is being triggered by examining the segue's identifier and destination properties, and the sender is the interface object that was tapped to trigger the segue (or, if performSegue(withIdentifier:sender:) was called in code, whatever object was supplied as the sender: argument):

```
override func prepare(for segue: UIStoryboardSegue, sender: Any?) {
    if segue.identifier == "second" {
        let svc = segue.destination as! SecondViewController
        svc.data = "This is very important data!"
        svc.delegate = self
    }
}
```

That solves the communication problem, but in a clumsy way. The fact is that prepare(for:sender:) is a blunt instrument:

- The destination arrives typed as a plain UIViewController, and it is up to your code to know its actual type and cast it down before configuring it.

- The destination view controller is instantiated for you, by calling init(coder:). That means you can't call a custom initializer; in prepare(for:sender:), you can only set properties after initialization is over.

- If more than one segue emanates from a view controller, they are all bottlenecked through the same prepare(for:sender:) implementation, which devolves into an ugly series of conditions to distinguish them.

Starting in iOS 13, there's an elegant alternative architecture. In the source view controller, you implement a method marked @IBSegueAction, with this signature:

```
@IBSegueAction
func f(coder:NSCoder, sender:Any?, ident:String?) -> UIViewController? {
```

The method name is up to you; so are the external parameter names. The third parameter, or the second and third parameters, may be omitted. The second parameter is just like the sender: in prepare(for:sender:). The third parameter is the segue's identifier. The result type can be a specific UIViewController subclass. It doesn't have to be an Optional; if it is, and if you return nil, everything proceeds as if this IBSegueAction method didn't exist.

To arrange for an IBSegueAction method to be called, you create an action connection in the storyboard *from the segue* to the view controller and hook it to this method. (Technically, this is an *instantiation action*.) When the IBSegueAction method is called, the segue has been triggered. You must now instantiate the correct class of view controller by directly or indirectly calling init(coder:) with the coder that was passed to you, and *return* that view controller instance (or nil if the return type is an Optional).

To illustrate, I'll rewrite the preceding code. Let's give SecondViewController an initializer that accepts the data it needs to do its work:

```
init(coder:NSCoder, data:Any) {
    self.data = data
    super.init(coder:coder)!
}
```

And here's an IBSegueAction method that calls that initializer:

```
@IBSegueAction func config(coder:NSCoder) -> SecondViewController { ❶
    let svc = SecondViewController( ❷
        coder:coder, data:"This is very important data!") { ❸
    svc.delegate = self ❹
    return svc
}
```

❶ We can give our IBSegueAction method any name we like. We can give the parameters any external names we like. We can omit the second and third parameters. We can specify a particular view controller class as the return type, and it doesn't have to be an Optional.

❷ We have to know the class of the segue's destination view controller, so that we can instantiate it. If we instantiate a view controller that is not of the right class, we'll crash at runtime. But we can configure the storyboard so that only one segue ever calls this IBSegueAction method, and so we can be confident about its destination without checking its identifier.

❸ We are able to call a custom initializer, something that a segue on its own could not have done. Our custom initializer *must* call `init(coder:)` with the same coder we received as our first parameter; otherwise, we'll crash at runtime.

❹ We are able to perform additional customizations, just as we would have done in `prepare(for:sender:)`. But there is no need to cast down first!

Even if you use the IBSegueAction mechanism, `prepare(for:sender:)` will still be called afterward if you've implemented it. Nevertheless, you might end up never implementing `prepare(for:sender:)` at all! Instead, you might rely entirely on the IBSegueAction mechanism.

Container Views and Embed Segues

The only parent view controllers for which you can create relationship segues specifying their children in a storyboard are the built-in UITabBarController and UINavigationController. That's because the nib editor understands how they work. If you write your own custom container view controller ("Container View Controllers" on page 379), the nib editor doesn't even know that your view controller *is* a container view controller, so it can't be the source of a relationship segue.

Nevertheless, you can perform some initial parent–child configuration of your custom container view controller in a storyboard, if you want your parent view controller to have one or more child view controllers whose views are to be placed somewhere in the parent view controller's view.

To give your view controller a child view controller in a storyboard, drag a Container View object from the Library into the parent view controller's view in the canvas. This gives you three things:

- A container view. This is a generic UIView that is now a subview in your view controller's view.

- An additional view controller. This is the view controller that will become your view controller's child.

- An *embed segue* leading from the container view to the child view controller.

You can then specify the child view controller's correct class in its Identity inspector. Alternatively, delete the child view controller, Control-drag from the container view to some *other* view controller that already exists in the storyboard, and specify an Embed segue in the HUD.

The container view is not only a way of generating the embed segue, but also a way of specifying where you want the child view controller's view to go. When an embed segue is triggered, the destination view controller is instantiated and made the source view controller's child, and its view becomes the container view's subview, with its frame matching the container view's bounds. The entire child-addition dance is performed correctly and automatically for you: addChild(_:) is called, the child's view is put into the interface, and didMove(toParent:) is called.

If the frame of the container view is going to change during the lifetime of the app, you're probably going to want the frame of the embedded child view controller's view to change with it. In the child view controller scene, use its view's Size inspector to set the Layout pop-up menu to Translates Mask Into Constraints, and give the view autoresizing struts externally on all four sides. (This may have been done for you by default when you created the container view.)

An embed segue is a triggered segue. It can have an identifier, and the standard messages are sent to the source view controller when the segue is triggered. At the same time, it has this similarity to a relationship: when the source (parent) view controller is instantiated, the runtime wants to trigger the segue automatically, instantiating the child view controller and embedding its view in the container view *now*. If that isn't what you want, override shouldPerformSegue(withIdentifier:sender:) in the parent view controller to return false for this segue, and call performSegue(withIdentifier:sender:) later when you *do* want the child view controller instantiated.

The parent view controller is sent prepare(for:sender:) before the child's view loads. At this time, the child has not been added to the parent's children array. If you allow the segue to be triggered when the parent view controller is instantiated, then by the time the parent's viewDidLoad is called, the child's viewDidLoad has already been called, the child has already been added to the parent's children, and the child's view is already inside the parent's view.

If, as the app runs, you subsequently want to replace the child view controller's view with another child view controller's view in the interface, you can call transition(from:to:duration:options:animations:completion:) as I described earlier in this chapter; sizing the new view and configuring it so that it is pinned to the container view will be up to you. (If you really want to, you can arrange that in the storyboard by means of a custom segue.)

Storyboard References

A storyboard reference is a *placeholder* for a specific view controller. Instead of a large and complicated network of segues running all over your storyboard, possibly crisscrossing in confusing ways, you can effectively *jump* through the storyboard reference to the actual destination view controller. You add a storyboard reference to the canvas of the storyboard, and then, when you create a segue, you can Control-drag to the storyboard reference.

To specify what view controller a storyboard reference stands for, you need to perform two steps:

1. Select the view controller and, in the Identity inspector, give it a Storyboard ID.

2. Select the storyboard reference and, in the Attributes inspector, enter that same Storyboard ID as its Referenced ID.

But wait — there's more! The referenced view controller doesn't even have to be in the same storyboard as the storyboard reference. You can use a storyboard reference to jump to a view controller in *a different storyboard*. This allows you to organize your app's interface into multiple storyboards.

To configure a storyboard reference to refer to a view controller in a different storyboard, use the Storyboard pop-up menu in its Attributes inspector. The rule is that if you specify the Storyboard but not the Referenced ID, the storyboard reference stands for the target storyboard's initial view controller. But it is better to specify *both* the Storyboard *and* the Referenced ID.

Unwind Segues

Here's an interesting puzzle: Storyboards and segues would appear to be useful only half the time, because segues are asymmetrical. There is a push segue but no pop segue. There is a present modally segue but no dismiss segue.

The reason, in a nutshell, is that a triggered segue cannot "go back." A triggered segue *instantiates* the destination view controller; it creates a new view controller instance. But when dismissing a presented view controller or popping a pushed view controller, we don't need any *new* view controller instances. We want to return, somehow, to an *existing* instance of a view controller.

Beginners sometimes make a triggered segue from view controller A to view controller B, and then try to express the notion "go back" by making *another* triggered segue from view controller B to view controller A. The result is a vicious cycle of segues, with presentation piled on presentation, or push piled on push, one view controller instantiated on top of another on top of another. *Don't do that.* (Unfortunately, the nib editor doesn't alert you to this mistake.)

The correct storyboard solution is an *unwind segue*. An unwind segue *does* let you express the notion "go back" in a storyboard. Basically, it lets you jump to any view controller that is already instantiated further up your view controller hierarchy, destroying the source view controller and any intervening view controllers in good order.

Creating an unwind segue

Before you can create an unwind segue, you must implement an *unwind method* in the class of some view controller represented in the storyboard. This should be a method marked @IBAction as a hint to the storyboard editor, and taking a single

Figure 6-11. Creating an unwind segue

parameter, a UIStoryboardSegue. You can name it unwind if you like, but the name doesn't really matter:

```
@IBAction func unwind(_ seg: UIStoryboardSegue) {
    // ...
}
```

Think of this method as a marker, specifying that the view controller in which it appears can be the destination for an unwind segue. It is, in fact, a little more than a marker: it will also be called when the segue is triggered. But its marker functionality is much more important — so much so that, in many cases, you won't give this method any code at all. Its *presence* is what matters.

Now you can create an unwind segue. Doing so involves the use of the Exit proxy object that appears in every scene of a storyboard. This is what the Exit proxy is for! Control-drag from the view controller you want to go back *from* (for a manual segue), or from something like a button in that view controller's view (for an action segue), connecting it to the Exit proxy object *in the same scene* (Figure 6-11). A little HUD appears, listing all the known unwind methods (similar to how action methods are listed in the HUD when you connect a button to its target). Click the name of the unwind method you want. You have now made an unwind segue, bound to that unwind method.

How an unwind segue works

An unwind segue works in an ingenious and rather elaborate way. It has to, because (as I've just shown) it can't possibly work like a normal segue! So how *does* it work?

When an unwind segue is *triggered*:

1. If this is an action segue, the source view controller's shouldPerformSegue(with-Identifier:sender:) is called — just as for a normal segue. This is your chance to forestall the whole process by returning false.

2. The name of the unwind method to which the unwind segue is bound is *only* a name. The unwind segue's actual destination view controller is unknown! Therefore, the runtime now starts walking up the view controller hierarchy looking for

a destination view controller. The first view controller it finds that *implements* the unwind method will, by default, be the destination view controller.

Assume now that the destination view controller has been found. Then the runtime proceeds to *perform* the segue:

1. The source view controller's `prepare(for:sender:)` is called with the segue as the first parameter — just as for a normal segue. The two view controllers are now in contact (because the other view controller is the segue's `destination`). This is an opportunity for the source view controller to hand information to the destination view controller before being destroyed! An unwind segue is an alternative to delegation in this regard.

2. The destination view controller's unwind method is called. Its parameter is the segue. The two view controllers are now in contact *again* (because the other view controller is the segue's `source`). It is perfectly reasonable for the unwind method body to be empty; its real purpose is to mark this view controller as the destination view controller.

3. The source view controller is *destroyed* along with any intervening view controllers up to (but not including) the destination view controller, in good order. We have "gone back" to the destination view controller.

In general, that's all you need to know about unwind segues.

Now I'll go back and explain in detail *how* the destination view controller is found, and *how* the segue is actually performed. This is partly out of sheer interest — they are both devilishly clever — and partly in case you need to customize the process. You can skip the discussion if the technical details aren't of interest.

How the destination view controller is found

The process of locating the destination view controller starts by walking *up* the view controller hierarchy. Every view controller has either a `parent` or a `presentingViewController`, so the next view controller up the hierarchy is that view controller — though it might also be necessary to walk back *down* the hierarchy, to a child (at some depth) of one of the parents we encounter:

1. At each step up the view controller hierarchy, the runtime sends this view controller the following event:

   • `allowedChildrenForUnwinding(from:)`

   This view controller's job is to supply an *array of its own direct children*. The array can be empty, but it must be an array. To help form this array, the view controller calls this method:

   • `childContaining(_:)`

This tells the view controller which of its own children is, or is the ultimate parent of, the source view controller. We don't want to go down *that* branch of the view hierarchy; that's the branch we just came *up*. So this view controller *subtracts* that view controller from the array of its own child view controllers, and returns the resulting array.

2. There are two possible kinds of result from the previous step (the value returned from `allowedChildren...`):

There are children

> If the previous step yielded an array with one or more child view controllers in it, the runtime performs step 1 on all of them (stopping if it finds the destination), going *down* the view hierarchy

There are no children

> If, on the other hand, the previous step yielded an *empty* array, the runtime asks *this same* view controller the following question:
>
> • `canPerformUnwindSegueAction(_:from:sender:)`

The default implementation of this method is simply to call `responds(to:)` on `self`, asking whether this view controller contains an implementation of the unwind method we're looking for. The result is a Bool. If it is `true`, we *stop. This is the destination view controller.* If it is `false`, we continue with the search *up* the view controller hierarchy, finding the next view controller and performing step 1 again.

The recursive application of this algorithm will eventually arrive at an existing view controller instance with an implementation of the unwind method if there is one.

How an unwind segue is performed

The way an unwind segue is performed is just as ingenious as how the destination is found. During the walk in search of the destination view controller, the runtime *remembers* the walk. There's a *path* of view controllers between the source and the destination, and the runtime walks that path:

• If it encounters a *presented* view controller on the path, the runtime calls `dismiss(animated:completion:)` on the presenting view controller.

• If it encounters a *parent* view controller on the path, the runtime tells it to `unwind(for:towards:)`.

The second parameter of `unwind(for:towards:)` is the *direct child* of this parent view controller leading down the branch where the destination lives. This child might or might not *be* the destination, but that's no concern of this parent view controller. Its job is merely to *get us onto that branch*, whatever that may mean for this kind of parent view controller.

If this procedure (called *incremental unwind*) is followed correctly, we will in fact end up at the destination, releasing in good order all intervening view controllers that need to be released.

Unwind segue customization

Knowing how an unwind segue works, you can see how to intervene in and customize the process:

- In a custom view controller that contains an implementation of the unwind method, you might implement canPerformUnwindSegueAction(_:from:withSender:) to return false instead of true so that it doesn't become the destination on this occasion.

- In a custom parent view controller, you might implement allowedChildrenForUnwinding(from:). In all probability, your implementation will consist simply of listing your children, calling childContaining(_:) to find out which of your children is or contains the source, subtracting that child from the array, and returning the array — just as the built-in parent view controllers do.

- In a custom container view controller, you might implement unwind(for:towards:). The second parameter is one of your current children; you will do whatever it means for this parent view controller to make this the currently displayed child.

In allowedChildrenForUnwinding(from:) and childContaining(_:), the parameter is not a UIStoryboardSegue. It's an instance of a special value class called UIStoryboardUnwindSegueSource, which has no other job than to communicate, in these two methods, the essential information about the unwind segue needed to make a decision. It has a source, a sender, and an unwindAction (the Selector specified when forming the unwind segue).

 Do *not* override childContaining(_:). It knows more than you do; you wouldn't want to interfere with its operation.

View Controller Lifetime Events

As views come and go, driven by view controllers and the actions of the user, events arrive that give your view controller the opportunity to respond to the various stages of its own existence and the management of its view. By overriding these methods, your UIViewController subclass can perform appropriate tasks at appropriate moments:

`viewDidLoad`

> The view controller has obtained its view (as explained earlier in this chapter); `self.view` exists, and if obtaining the view involved loading a nib, outlets have been hooked up. This does *not* mean that the view is in the interface or that it has been given its correct size. You should call `super` in your implementation, just in case a superclass has work to do in *its* implementation.

`willTransition(to:with:)`
`viewWillTransition(to:with:)`
`traitCollectionDidChange(_:)`

> The view controller's view is being resized or the trait environment is changing, or both (as explained earlier in this chapter). Your implementation of these methods should call `super`.

`updateViewConstraints`
`viewWillLayoutSubviews`
`viewDidLayoutSubviews`

> The view is receiving `updateConstraints` and `layoutSubviews` events (as explained earlier in this chapter). Your implementation of `updateView-Constraints` should call `super`.

`willMove(toParent:)`
`didMove(toParent:)`

> The view controller is being added or removed as a child of another view controller (as explained earlier in this chapter). Your implementation of these methods should call `super`.

`viewWillAppear(_:)`
`viewDidAppear(_:)`
`viewWillDisappear(_:)`
`viewDidDisappear(_:)`

> The view is being added to or removed from the interface. This includes being supplanted by another view controller's view or being restored through the removal of another view controller's view. A view that has appeared is in the window; it is part of your app's active view hierarchy. A view that has disappeared is not in the window; its `window` is `nil`. Your implementation of these methods should call `super`.

> To distinguish more precisely *why* your view is appearing or disappearing, consult any of these properties of the view controller:

> - `isBeingPresented`
> - `isBeingDismissed`

- isMovingtoParent

- isMovingFromParent

Order of Events

To get a sense for when view controller lifetime events arrive, it helps to examine some specific scenarios in which they normally occur. Consider a UIViewController being pushed onto the stack of a navigation controller. It receives, in this order, the following messages:

1. `willMove(toParent:)`

2. `viewWillAppear(_:)`

3. `viewWillLayoutSubviews`

4. `viewDidLayoutSubviews`

5. `viewDidAppear(_:)`

6. `didMove(toParent:)`

When this same UIViewController is popped off the stack of the navigation controller, it receives, in this order, the following messages:

1. `willMove(toParent:)` (with parameter `nil`)

2. `viewWillDisappear(_:)`

3. `viewDidDisappear(_:)`

4. `didMove(toParent:)` (with parameter `nil`)

Disappearance, as I mentioned a moment ago, can happen because another view controller's view supplants this view controller's view. Consider a UIViewController functioning as the top (and visible) view controller of a navigation controller. When another view controller is pushed on top of it, the first view controller gets these messages:

1. `viewWillDisappear(_:)`

2. `viewDidDisappear(_:)`

The converse is also true. When a view controller is popped from a navigation controller, the view controller that was below it in the stack (the back view controller) receives these messages:

1. `viewWillAppear(_:)`

2. `viewDidAppear(_:)`

Appear and Disappear Events

The appear and disappear events are particularly appropriate for making sure that a view controller's view reflects your app's underlying data each time it appears. These methods are useful also when something must be true exactly so long as a view is in the interface. A repeating Timer that must be running while a view is present might be started in the view controller's viewDidAppear(_:) and stopped in its viewWill-Disappear(_:). (This architecture also allows you to avoid the retain cycle that could result if you waited to invalidate the timer in a deinit that might otherwise never arrive.)

Changes to the interface performed in viewDidAppear(_:) or viewWill-Disappear(_:) may be visible to the user as they occur. If that's not what you want, use the other member of the pair, viewWillAppear(_:) or viewDidDisappear(_:). In a certain view containing a long scrollable text, I want the scroll position to be the same when the user returns to this view as it was when the user left it, so I save the scroll position in viewWillDisappear(_:) and restore it in viewWillAppear(_:) — not viewDidAppear(_:), where the user might see the scroll position jump.

The appear events are not layout events. Don't make any assumptions about whether your views have achieved their correct size just because the view is appearing — even if those assumptions seem to be correct. To respond when layout is taking place, implement layout events.

A view does not disappear if a presented view controller's view merely covers it rather than supplanting it. A view controller that presents another view controller as a sheet (.pageSheet or .formSheet) gets no lifetime events during presentation and dismissal.

A view does not disappear merely because the app is backgrounded and suspended. That fact sometimes surprises beginners, and has important implications for how you save data in case the app is terminated in the background. You cannot rely solely on a disappear event for saving data that the app will need the next time it launches; if you are to cover every case, you may need to ensure that your data-saving code also runs in response to a lifetime event sent to your app delegate or scene delegate (see Appendix A).

 Sometimes a will event arrives without the corresponding did event. A case in point is when an interactive transition animation begins and is cancelled. I regard this as a bug.

Event Forwarding to a Child View Controller

A custom container view controller must effectively send willMove(toParent:) and didMove(toParent:) to its children manually, and it will do so if you perform the dance correctly when your view controller acquires or loses a child view controller (see "Container View Controllers" on page 379).

A custom container view controller must forward resizing events to its children. This will happen automatically if you call super in your implementation of the will-Transition methods.

The appear and disappear events are normally passed along automatically. However, you can take charge by overriding this property:

shouldAutomaticallyForwardAppearanceMethods
> If you override this property to return false, you are responsible for seeing that the four appear and disappear methods are called on your view controller's children. You do *not* do this by calling these methods directly. The reason is that you have no access to the correct moment for sending them. Instead, you call these two methods on your child view controller:

beginAppearanceTransition(_:animated:)
endAppearanceTransition
> The first parameter of the first method is a Bool saying whether this view controller's view is about to appear (true) or disappear (false).

Here's an example of the kind of thing you'll have to do in the appear methods if your shouldAutomaticallyForwardAppearanceMethods is false:

```
override func viewWillAppear(_ animated: Bool) {
    super.viewWillAppear(animated)
    let child = // whatever
    if child.isViewLoaded && child.view.superview != nil {
        child.beginAppearanceTransition(true, animated: true)
    }
}
override func viewDidAppear(_ animated: Bool) {
    super.viewDidAppear(animated)
    let child = // whatever
    if child.isViewLoaded && child.view.superview != nil {
        child.endAppearanceTransition()
    }
}
```

The disappear methods will be similar, except that the first argument for begin-AppearanceTransition is false.

When your custom container view controller swaps one child for another in the interface, you should *not* call the UIViewController transition... method if your shouldAutomaticallyForwardAppearanceMethods is false. Instead, you perform the transition animation directly, calling beginAppearanceTransition(_:animated:) and endAppearanceTransition yourself. A minimal correct implementation might involve a UIView transition... animation class method ("Transitions" on page 191). Here's an example; I've put asterisks to call attention to the additional method calls that forward the appear and disappear events to the children (fromvc and tovc):

```
self.addChild(tovc) // "will" called for us
fromvc.willMove(toParent: nil)
fromvc.beginAppearanceTransition(false, animated:true) // *
tovc.beginAppearanceTransition(true, animated:true) // *
UIView.transition(
    from:fromvc.view, to:tovc.view,
    duration:0.4, options:.transitionFlipFromLeft) { _ in
        tovc.endAppearanceTransition() // *
        fromvc.endAppearanceTransition() // *
        tovc.didMove(toParent: self)
        fromvc.removeFromParent()
}
```

View Controller Memory Management

Memory is at a premium on a mobile device, so you want to minimize your app's use of memory. Your motivations are partly altruistic and partly selfish. While your app is running, other apps are suspended in the background; you want to keep your memory usage as low as possible so that those other apps have room to remain suspended and the user can readily switch to them from your app. You also want to prevent your own app from being terminated! If your app is backgrounded and suspended while using a lot of memory, it may be terminated in the background when memory runs short. If your app uses an inordinate amount of memory while in the foreground, it may be summarily killed before the user's very eyes.

One strategy for avoiding using too much memory is to release any memory-hogging objects you're retaining if they are not needed at this moment. Because a view controller is the basis of so much of your application's architecture, it is likely to be a place where you'll concern yourself with releasing unneeded memory.

One of your view controller's most memory-intensive objects is its view. Fortunately, the iOS runtime manages a view controller's view's memory for you. If a view controller's view is not in the interface, it can be temporarily dispensed with. In such a situation, if memory is getting tight, then even though the view controller itself persists, and even though it retains its actual view, the runtime may release the view's backing store (the cached bitmap representing the view's drawn contents). The view will then be redrawn when and if it is to be shown again later.

Your view controller should override this method so that it can receive an event when memory runs low:

`didReceiveMemoryWarning`

> Sent to a view controller to advise it of a low-memory situation. It is preceded by a call to the app delegate's `applicationDidReceiveMemoryWarning`, together with a `UIApplication.didReceiveMemoryWarningNotification` posted to any registered objects. You are invited to respond by releasing any data that you can do without. Do not release data that you can't readily and quickly recreate! The documentation advises that you should call `super`.

To test the behavior of your app under low-memory circumstances, run your app in the Simulator and choose Debug → Simulate Memory Warning. I don't believe this has any actual effect on memory, but a memory warning of sufficient severity is sent to your app, so you can see the results of triggering your low-memory response code.

Another approach, which works also on a device, is to call an undocumented method. First, define a dummy protocol to make the selector legal:

```
@objc protocol Dummy {
    func _performMemoryWarning()
}
```

Now you can send that selector to the shared application:

```
UIApplication.shared.perform(#selector(Dummy._performMemoryWarning))
```

(Be sure to remove that code when it is no longer needed for testing, as the App Store won't accept it.)

There are no hard and fast rules about what might be occupying your app's memory unnecessarily. Use the Allocations template in Instruments to find out! When multiple view controllers exist simultaneously, interface objects and data in a view controller whose view is not currently visible are obvious candidates for purging when memory is tight. You might also discover that you are retaining large objects that you don't really need. It will come as no surprise that the most common source of accidental memory bloat is images; a retained array of images, or an image that is much larger than the size at which it needs to be displayed in the interface, can waste a lot of memory and should always be avoided.

Lazy Loading

If you're going to release data in `didReceiveMemoryWarning`, you must concern yourself with how you're going to get it back. A simple and reliable mechanism is *lazy loading* — a getter that reconstructs or fetches the data if it is `nil`.

Suppose we have a property `myBigData` which might be a big piece of data. We make this a computed property, storing the real data in a private property (I'll call it `_myBigData`). Our computed property's setter simply writes through to the private property. In `didReceiveMemoryWarning`, we write `myBigData` out as a file (Chapter 23) and set myBigData to nil, which sets _myBigData to nil as well, releasing the big data from memory. The getter for myBigData implements lazy loading: if we try to get myBig-Data when _myBigData is nil, we attempt to fetch the data from the file — and if we succeed, we delete the file (to prevent stale data):

```
private let fnam = "myBigData"
private var _myBigData : Data!
var myBigData : Data! {
    set (newdata) { self._myBigData = newdata }
    get {
        if _myBigData == nil {
            let fm = FileManager.default
            let f = fm.temporaryDirectory.appendingPathComponent(self.fnam)
            if let d = try? Data(contentsOf:f) {
                self._myBigData = d
                do {
                    try fm.removeItem(at:f)
                } catch {
                    print("Couldn't remove temp file")
                }
            }
        }
        return self._myBigData
    }
}
func saveAndReleaseMyBigData() {
    if let myBigData = self.myBigData {
        let fm = FileManager.default
        let f = fm.temporaryDirectory.appendingPathComponent(self.fnam)
        if let _ = try? myBigData.write(to:f) {
            self.myBigData = nil
        }
    }
}
override func didReceiveMemoryWarning() {
    super.didReceiveMemoryWarning()
    self.saveAndReleaseMyBigData()
}
```

NSCache, NSPurgeableData, and Memory-Mapping

When your big data can be reconstructed from scratch on demand, you can take advantage of the built-in NSCache class, which is like a dictionary with the ability to clear out its own entries automatically under memory pressure. As in the previous example, a computed property can be used as a façade:

```
private let _cache = NSCache<NSString, NSData>()
var cachedData : Data {
    let key = "somekey" as NSString
    if let olddata = self._cache.object(forKey:key) {
        return olddata as Data
```

```
    }
    let newdata = // ... recreate data ...
    self._cache.setObject(newdata as NSData, forKey: key)
    return newdata
}
```

Another built-in class that knows how to clear itself out is NSPurgeableData. It is a subclass of NSMutableData. To signal that the data should be discarded, send your object `discardContentIfPossible`. Wrap any access to data in calls to `beginContentAccess` and `endContentAccess`; the former returns a Bool to indicate whether the data was accessible. The tricky part is getting those access calls right; when you create an NSPurgeableData, you must send it an unbalanced `endContentAccess` to make its content discardable:

```
private var _purgeable = NSPurgeableData()
var purgeabledata : Data {
    if self._purgeable.beginContentAccess() && self._purgeable.length > 0 {
        let result = self._purgeable.copy() as! Data
        self._purgeable.endContentAccess()
        return result
    } else {
        let data = // ... recreate data ...
        self._purgeable = NSPurgeableData(data:data)
        self._purgeable.endContentAccess()
        return data
    }
}
```

(For more about NSCache and NSPurgeableData, see the "Caching and Purgeable Memory" chapter of Apple's *Memory Usage Performance Guidelines* in the documentation archive.)

At an even lower level, you can store your data as a file (in some reasonable location such the Caches directory) and read it using the Data initializer `init(contentsOfURL:options:)` with an `options:` argument `.alwaysMapped`. This creates a memory-mapped data object, which has the remarkable feature that it isn't considered to belong to your memory at all; the system has no hesitation in clearing it from RAM, because it is backed through the virtual memory system by the file, and will be read back into memory automatically when you next access it. This is suitable only for large immutable data, because small data might fragment a virtual memory page.

Background Memory Usage

You will also wish to concern yourself with releasing memory when your app is about to be suspended. If your app has been backgrounded and suspended and the system later discovers it is running short of memory, it will go hunting through the suspended apps, looking for memory hogs that it can kill in order to free up that memory. If the system decides that your suspended app is a memory hog, it isn't politely going to wake your app and send it a memory warning; it's just going to terminate your app in its sleep (see Appendix A).

There is nothing you can really do to guarantee that your app won't be terminated while suspended in the background. Apple advises that reducing your memory usage to less than 200MB before going into the background is a good idea, and less than 50MB is even better. All the same, being terminated while suspended is not, of itself, a bug. It's a normal part of how multitasking works on iOS. All you can do is release as much memory as you can, *before* the app is suspended, and hope for the best.

To help with that, you'll probably want your view controller to be registered to receive a notification from the application or scene that we are about to go into the background. The arrival of this notification is an opportunity to release any easily restored memory-hogging objects, such as `myBigData` in the previous example:

```
var didAppearInitially = false
override func viewDidAppear(_ animated: Bool) {
    super.viewDidAppear(animated)
    if !didAppearInitially {
        didAppearInitially = true
        NotificationCenter.default.addObserver(self,
            selector: #selector(backgrounding),
            name: UIScene.didEnterBackgroundNotification,
            object: self.view.window?.windowScene)
    }
}
@objc func backgrounding(_ n:Notification) {
    self.saveAndReleaseMyBigData()
}
```

In real life, we should be returning from our `backgrounding` method as quickly as possible; the way to do that is to get onto a background thread and call `begin-BackgroundTask` (see Chapter 25).

 A nice feature of NSCache is that it evicts its objects automatically when your app goes into the background.

Scroll Views

A scroll view (UIScrollView) is a view whose content is larger than its bounds. To reveal a desired area, the user can scroll the content by dragging, or you can reposition the content in code. The scroll view functions as a limited window on a larger world of content.

A scroll view isn't magic; it takes advantage of ordinary UIView features (Chapter 1). The content is simply the scroll view's subviews. When the scroll view scrolls, what's really changing is the scroll view's own bounds origin; the subviews are positioned with respect to the bounds origin, so they move with it. The scroll view's clipsTo-Bounds is true, so any content positioned within the scroll view is visible and any content positioned outside it is not.

A scroll view has the following specialized abilities:

- It knows how to shift its bounds origin in response to the user's gestures.
- It provides scroll indicators whose size and position give the user a clue as to the content's size and position.
- It can enforce paging, whereby the user can scroll only by a fixed amount.
- It supports zooming, so that the user can resize the content with a pinch gesture.
- It provides delegate methods so that your code knows how the user is scrolling and zooming.

Content Size

How *far* should a scroll view scroll? Clearly, that depends on how much *content* it has. The scroll view already knows how far it should be allowed to slide its subviews downward and rightward: the limit is reached when the scroll view's bounds origin is

CGPoint.zero. What the scroll view *needs* to know is how far it should be allowed to slide its subviews upward and leftward. That is the scroll view's *content size* — its contentSize property.

The scroll view uses its contentSize, in combination with its own bounds size, to set the limits on how large its bounds origin can become. It may be helpful to think of the scroll view's scrollable content as the rectangle defined by CGRect(origin:.zero, size:contentSize); this is the rectangle that the user can inspect by scrolling. If a dimension of the contentSize isn't larger than the same dimension of the scroll view's own bounds, the content won't be scrollable in that dimension: there is nothing to scroll, as the entire scrollable content is already showing.

The default is that the contentSize is .zero — meaning that the scroll view *isn't scrollable*. To get a working scroll view, therefore, it will be crucial to set its content-Size correctly. You can do this directly, in code; or, if you're using autolayout, the contentSize can be calculated for you based on the autolayout constraints of the scroll view's subviews (as I'll demonstrate in a moment).

How big should a scroll view's content size be? Clearly that depends on the size of its subviews. Typically, you'll want the content size to be just large enough to embrace all the subviews: they, after all, are the content the user needs to be able to see. You'll likely want to set the content size correctly at the outset. You can subsequently alter a scroll view's content (subviews) or contentSize, or both, dynamically as the app runs; in and of themselves, they are independent. You can change the contentSize at any time; it does not change by itself just because, for instance, the scroll view's bounds size changes due to rotation of the app.

Creating a Scroll View in Code

Let's start by creating a scroll view, providing it with subviews, and making those subviews viewable by scrolling, entirely in code. There are two ways to set the contentSize, so I'll demonstrate each of them in turn.

Manual Content Size

In the first instance, let's not use autolayout at all. Our project is based on the basic App template, with a single view controller class, ViewController. In View-Controller's viewDidLoad, I'll create the scroll view to fill the main view, and populate it with a vertical column of 30 UILabels whose text contains a sequential number so that we can see where we are when we scroll:

```
let sv = UIScrollView(frame: self.view.bounds)
sv.autoresizingMask = [.flexibleWidth, .flexibleHeight]
self.view.addSubview(sv)
sv.backgroundColor = .white
```

```
var y : CGFloat = 10
for i in 0 ..< 30 {
    let lab = UILabel()
    lab.text = "This is label \(i+1)"
    lab.sizeToFit()
    lab.frame.origin = CGPoint(10,y)
    sv.addSubview(lab)
    y += lab.bounds.size.height + 10
}
var sz = sv.bounds.size
sz.height = y
sv.contentSize = sz // *
```

The crucial move is the last line, where we tell the scroll view how large its content-Size is to be. Our sz.height accommodates all the labels, but sz.width matches the scroll view's width; the scroll view will be scrollable vertically but not horizontally (a common scenario).

There is no rule about the order in which you perform the two operations of setting the contentSize and populating the scroll view with subviews. In that example, we set the contentSize afterward because it is more convenient to track the heights of the subviews as we add them than to calculate their total height in advance.

Automatic Content Size with Autolayout

With autolayout, things are different. Under autolayout, a scroll view interprets the constraints of its immediate subviews in a special way. Constraints between a scroll view and its direct subviews are *not* a way of positioning the subviews relative to the scroll view (as they would be if the superview were an ordinary UIView). Rather, they are a way of describing the scroll view's contentSize *from the inside out*.

To see this, let's rewrite the preceding example to use autolayout. The scroll view and its subviews have their translatesAutoresizingMaskIntoConstraints set to false, and we're giving them explicit constraints:

```
let sv = UIScrollView()
sv.backgroundColor = .white
sv.translatesAutoresizingMaskIntoConstraints = false
self.view.addSubview(sv)
NSLayoutConstraint.activate([
    sv.topAnchor.constraint(equalTo:self.view.topAnchor),
    sv.bottomAnchor.constraint(equalTo:self.view.bottomAnchor),
    sv.leadingAnchor.constraint(equalTo:self.view.leadingAnchor),
    sv.trailingAnchor.constraint(equalTo:self.view.trailingAnchor),
])
var previousLab : UILabel? = nil
for i in 0 ..< 30 {
    let lab = UILabel()
    // lab.backgroundColor = .red
    lab.translatesAutoresizingMaskIntoConstraints = false
```

```
lab.text = "This is label \(i+1)"
sv.addSubview(lab)
lab.leadingAnchor.constraint(
    equalTo: sv.leadingAnchor, constant: 10).isActive = true
lab.topAnchor.constraint(
    // first one, pin to top; all others, pin to previous
    equalTo: previousLab?.bottomAnchor ?? sv.topAnchor,
    constant: 10).isActive = true
previousLab = lab
}
```

The labels are correctly positioned relative to one another, but the scroll view isn't scrollable. Moreover, setting the `contentSize` manually doesn't help; it has no effect!

Why is that? It's because we're using autolayout, so we must generate the `content-Size` by means of constraints between the scroll view and its immediate subviews. We've almost done that, but not quite. We are *missing a constraint.* We have to add one more constraint, showing the scroll view what the height of its `contentSize` should be:

```
sv.bottomAnchor.constraint(
    equalTo: previousLab!.bottomAnchor, constant: 10).isActive = true
```

The constraints of the scroll view's subviews now describe the `contentSize` height: the top label is pinned to the top of the scroll view, the next one is pinned to the one above it, and so on — *and the bottom one is pinned to the bottom of the scroll view.* Consequently, the runtime calculates the `contentSize` height from the inside out as the sum of all the vertical constraints (including the intrinsic heights of the labels), and the scroll view is vertically scrollable to show all the labels.

We should also provide a `contentSize` width; here, I'll add a trailing constraint from the bottom label, which will be narrower than the scroll view, so we won't actually scroll horizontally:

```
previousLab!.trailingAnchor.constraint(
    equalTo:sv.trailingAnchor).isActive = true
```

Scroll View Layout Guides

Starting in iOS 11, there's another way to determine a scroll view's content size. A UIScrollView has a `contentLayoutGuide`. There are two ways to use it:

Direct dimension constraints
    If we give the content layout guide a width constraint or a height constraint, we can determine the `contentSize` directly.

Self-sizing based on subviews

If we pin the scroll view's subviews to the content layout guide, we can determine the contentSize from the inside out; this is like pinning the subviews to the scroll view itself, but it's preferable, because it's clearer what we're doing.

I'll rewrite the preceding example to use the contentLayoutGuide:

```
let sv = UIScrollView()
sv.backgroundColor = .white
sv.translatesAutoresizingMaskIntoConstraints = false
self.view.addSubview(sv)
NSLayoutConstraint.activate([
    sv.topAnchor.constraint(equalTo:self.view.topAnchor),
    sv.bottomAnchor.constraint(equalTo:self.view.bottomAnchor),
    sv.leadingAnchor.constraint(equalTo:self.view.leadingAnchor),
    sv.trailingAnchor.constraint(equalTo:self.view.trailingAnchor),
])
let svclg = sv.contentLayoutGuide // *
var previousLab : UILabel? = nil
for i in 0 ..< 30 {
    let lab = UILabel()
    // lab.backgroundColor = .red
    lab.translatesAutoresizingMaskIntoConstraints = false
    lab.text = "This is label \(i+1)"
    sv.addSubview(lab)
    lab.leadingAnchor.constraint(
        equalTo: svclg.leadingAnchor,
        constant: 10).isActive = true
    lab.topAnchor.constraint(
        // first one, pin to top; all others, pin to previous
        equalTo: previousLab?.bottomAnchor ?? svclg.topAnchor,
        constant: 10).isActive = true
    previousLab = lab
}
svclg.bottomAnchor.constraint(
    equalTo: previousLab!.bottomAnchor, constant: 10).isActive = true
svclg.widthAnchor.constraint(equalToConstant:0).isActive = true // *
```

The last line demonstrates that we can set the content layout guide's height or width constraint *directly* to determine that dimension of the content size. Thanks to the content layout guide, I'm able to set the content size width directly to zero, which states precisely what I mean: don't scroll horizontally.

Also starting in iOS 11, there's a second UIScrollView property, its frameLayoutGuide, which is pinned to the scroll view's frame. This gives us an even better way to state that the scroll view should not scroll horizontally, by making the content layout guide width the same as the frame layout guide width:

```
let svflg = sv.frameLayoutGuide
svclg.widthAnchor.constraint(equalTo:svflg.widthAnchor).isActive = true
```

Using a Content View

A commonly used arrangement is to give a scroll view just *one* immediate subview; all other views inside the scroll view are subviews of this single immediate subview of the scroll view, which is often called the *content view*. The content view is usually a generic UIView; the user won't even know it's there. It has no purpose other than to contain the other subviews — and to help determine the scroll view's content size. The usual idea is that the scroll view's `contentSize` should exactly match the dimensions of the content view. There are two ways to achieve that, depending on whether we want to set the content size manually or using autolayout:

- Set the content view's `translatesAutoresizingMaskIntoConstraints` to `true`, and set the scroll view's `contentSize` manually to the size of the content view.

- Set the content view's `translatesAutoresizingMaskIntoConstraints` to `false`, set its size with constraints, and pin its edges with constraints to the scroll view's content layout guide. If all four of those edge constraints have a `constant` of `0`, the scroll view's `contentSize` will be the same as the size of the content view.

This arrangement works independently of whether the content view's own subviews are positioned explicitly by their frames or using constraints, so there are four possible combinations:

No constraints
  The content view is sized by its frame, its contents are positioned by their frames, and the scroll view's `contentSize` is set explicitly.

Content view constraints
  The content view is sized by its own height and width constraints, and its edges are pinned to the content layout guide to set the scroll view's content size.

Content view and content constraints
  The content view is sized from the inside out by the constraints of its subviews, and its edges are pinned to the content layout guide to set the scroll view's content size.

Content constraints only
  The content view is sized by its frame, and the scroll view's `contentSize` is set explicitly; but the content view's subviews are positioned using constraints. (This option is rather far-fetched, but I list it for the sake of completeness.)

I'll illustrate by rewriting the previous example to use a content view (v) in each of those ways. All four possible combinations start the same way:

```
let sv = UIScrollView()
sv.backgroundColor = .white
sv.translatesAutoresizingMaskIntoConstraints = false
self.view.addSubview(sv)
NSLayoutConstraint.activate([
    sv.topAnchor.constraint(equalTo:self.view.topAnchor),
    sv.bottomAnchor.constraint(equalTo:self.view.bottomAnchor),
    sv.leadingAnchor.constraint(equalTo:self.view.leadingAnchor),
    sv.trailingAnchor.constraint(equalTo:self.view.trailingAnchor),
])
let v = UIView() // content view!
sv.addSubview(v)
```

The differences lie in what happens next. The first combination is that no constraints
are used, and the scroll view's content size is set explicitly. It's very like the first
example in this chapter, except that the labels are added to the content view, not to
the scroll view. The content view's height is a little taller than the bottom of the lowest label, and its width is a little wider than the widest label, so it neatly contains all
the labels:

```
var y : CGFloat = 10
var maxw : CGFloat = 0
for i in 0 ..< 30 {
    let lab = UILabel()
    lab.text = "This is label \(i+1)"
    lab.sizeToFit()
    lab.frame.origin = CGPoint(10,y)
    v.addSubview(lab)
    y += lab.bounds.size.height + 10
    maxw = max(maxw, lab.frame.maxX + 10)
}
// set content view frame and content size explicitly
v.frame = CGRect(0,0,maxw,y)
sv.contentSize = v.frame.size
```

The second combination is that the content view is sized by explicit width and height
constraints, and its edges are pinned by constraints to the scroll view's content layout
guide to give the scroll view a content size:

```
var y : CGFloat = 10
var maxw : CGFloat = 0
for i in 0 ..< 30 {
    let lab = UILabel()
    lab.text = "This is label \(i+1)"
    lab.sizeToFit()
    lab.frame.origin = CGPoint(10,y)
    v.addSubview(lab)
    y += lab.bounds.size.height + 10
    maxw = max(maxw, lab.frame.maxX + 10)
}
// set content view width, height, and edge constraints
// content size is calculated for us
```

```
v.translatesAutoresizingMaskIntoConstraints = false
let svclg = sv.contentLayoutGuide
NSLayoutConstraint.activate([
    v.widthAnchor.constraint(equalToConstant:maxw),
    v.heightAnchor.constraint(equalToConstant:y),
    svclg.topAnchor.constraint(equalTo:v.topAnchor),
    svclg.bottomAnchor.constraint(equalTo:v.bottomAnchor),
    svclg.leadingAnchor.constraint(equalTo:v.leadingAnchor),
    svclg.trailingAnchor.constraint(equalTo:v.trailingAnchor),
])
```

The third combination is that the content view is self-sizing based on constraints from its subviews ("Self-Sizing Views" on page 56), and the content view's edges are pinned by constraints to the scroll view's content layout guide. In a very real sense, the scroll view gets its content size *from the labels*. This is similar to the second example in this chapter, except that the labels are added to the content view:

```
var previousLab : UILabel? = nil
for i in 0 ..< 30 {
    let lab = UILabel()
    // lab.backgroundColor = .red
    lab.translatesAutoresizingMaskIntoConstraints = false
    lab.text = "This is label \(i+1)"
    v.addSubview(lab)
    lab.leadingAnchor.constraint(
        equalTo: v.leadingAnchor,
        constant: 10).isActive = true
    lab.topAnchor.constraint(
        // first one, pin to top; all others, pin to previous
        equalTo: previousLab?.bottomAnchor ?? v.topAnchor,
        constant: 10).isActive = true
    previousLab = lab
}
// last one, pin to bottom, this dictates content size height
v.bottomAnchor.constraint(
    equalTo: previousLab!.bottomAnchor, constant: 10).isActive = true
// need to do something about width
v.trailingAnchor.constraint(
    equalTo: previousLab!.trailingAnchor, constant: 10).isActive = true
// pin content view to scroll view, sized by its subview constraints
// content size is calculated for us
v.translatesAutoresizingMaskIntoConstraints = false
let svclg = sv.contentLayoutGuide
NSLayoutConstraint.activate([
    svclg.topAnchor.constraint(equalTo:v.topAnchor),
    svclg.bottomAnchor.constraint(equalTo:v.bottomAnchor),
    svclg.leadingAnchor.constraint(equalTo:v.leadingAnchor),
    svclg.trailingAnchor.constraint(equalTo:v.trailingAnchor),
])
```

The fourth (and somewhat improbable) combination is that the content view's subviews are positioned using constraints, but we set the content view's frame and the scroll view's content size explicitly. How can we derive the content view size from the constraints of its subviews? By calling `systemLayoutSizeFitting(_:)` to perform layout for us:

```
var previousLab : UILabel? = nil
for i in 0 ..< 30 {
    let lab = UILabel()
    // lab.backgroundColor = .red
    lab.translatesAutoresizingMaskIntoConstraints = false
    lab.text = "This is label \(i+1)"
    v.addSubview(lab)
    lab.leadingAnchor.constraint(
        equalTo: v.leadingAnchor,
        constant: 10).isActive = true
    lab.topAnchor.constraint(
        // first one, pin to top; all others, pin to previous
        equalTo: previousLab?.bottomAnchor ?? v.topAnchor,
        constant: 10).isActive = true
    previousLab = lab
}
// last one, pin to bottom, this dictates content size height!
v.bottomAnchor.constraint(
    equalTo: previousLab!.bottomAnchor, constant: 10).isActive = true
// need to do something about width
v.trailingAnchor.constraint(
    equalTo: previousLab!.trailingAnchor, constant: 10).isActive = true
// autolayout helps us learn the consequences of those constraints
let minsz = v.systemLayoutSizeFitting(UIView.layoutFittingCompressedSize)
// set content view frame and content size explicitly
v.frame = CGRect(origin:.zero, size:minsz)
sv.contentSize = minsz
```

Scroll View in a Nib

A UIScrollView object is available in the nib editor's Library, so you can drag it into a view in the canvas and give it subviews. Alternatively, you can wrap existing views in the canvas in a UIScrollView: to do so, select the views and choose Editor → Embed In → Scroll View (or choose Scroll View from the Embed button at the lower right of the canvas).

There is no provision for entering a scroll view's `contentSize` numerically in the nib editor, so you'll have to use autolayout. Starting in Xcode 11, a scroll view's content layout guide and frame layout guide are present in the nib editor (if you don't see them, check Content Layout Guides in the scroll view's Size inspector). Unfortunately, you can't configure the content layout guide's width or height constraints directly (I regard that as a bug). But you can constrain subviews of the scroll view in terms of the layout guides, and so you can use autolayout to configure a scroll view in the nib editor much as you'd configure it in code. The nib editor understands how

Figure 7-1. Designing a scroll view's contents

scroll view configuration works, and will alert you with a warning (about the "scrollable content size") until you've provided enough constraints to determine unambiguously the scroll view's `contentSize`.

While designing the scroll view's subviews initially, you might need to make the view controller's main view large enough to accommodate them. One solution is to set the view controller's Simulated Size pop-up menu in its Size inspector to Freeform; now you can change the main view's size. But you might not need to do that, because once you've provided sufficient constraint information, the scroll view is scrollable *directly in the nib editor.*

To illustrate, consider a scroll view whose content size is configured in the nib editor using a content view. The content view is the scroll view's subview; it has explicit width and height constraints and is pinned with zero-constant constraints to the scroll view's content layout guide.

We can now proceed to populate the content view with subviews. Purely for demonstration purposes, I'll use four plain vanilla UIViews, and I won't use autolayout. I can design the first three views directly, because they fit within the main view

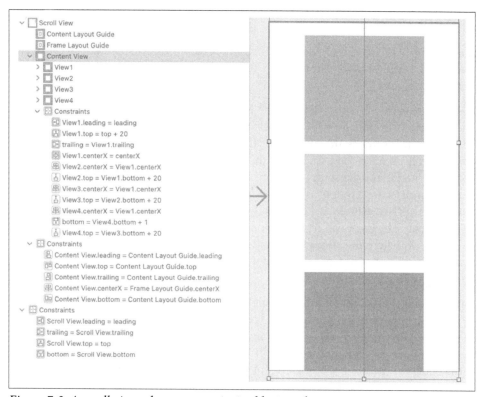

Figure 7-2. A scroll view whose content is sized by its subviews

(Figure 7-1, left). But what about the last view? The scroll view's content size is determined, so I can scroll the scroll view directly in the nib editor; once the bottom of the content view is within the main view, I can add the fourth view (Figure 7-1, right).

Instead of dictating the scroll view's content size numerically with explicit width and height constraints on the content view, you can apply constraints to the content view from its subviews and let those subviews size the content view from the inside out, setting the scroll view's `contentSize` as a result. In Figure 7-2, the subviews have explicit height and width constraints and are pinned to one another and to the top and bottom of the content view, and the content view is pinned to the scroll view's content layout guide, so the scroll view is scrollable to view all of the subviews. Moreover, I've given the subviews zero-constant leading and trailing constraints to the content view, and I've centered the content view horizontally within the scroll view's frame layout guide; the result is that the subviews are centered horizontally on any screen size.

(Strictly speaking, I suppose the content view in that example is unnecessary; we could pin the scroll view's subviews directly to its content layout guide.)

Content Inset

The content inset of a scroll view is a margin space around its content. In effect, it changes where the content stops when the scroll view is scrolled all the way to its extreme limit.

The main reason why this is important is that a scroll view will typically underlap other interface. In the app with 30 labels that we created at the start of this chapter, the scroll view occupies the entirety of the view controller's main view — and the view controller's main view underlaps the status bar. That means that the top of the scroll view underlaps the status bar. And *that* means that at launch time, and whenever the scroll view's content is scrolled all the way down, there's a danger that the first label, which is now as far down as it can go, will be partly hidden by the text of the status bar. The issue will be even more acute on a device without a bezel, such as the iPhone X, where the status bar is taller to accommodate the "notch" containing the front camera; the "notch" will prevent the user from *ever* being able to see the top center of the scroll view's content.

You might say: Well, don't do that! Don't let the scroll view underlap the status bar in the first place; pin the top of the scroll view to the bottom of the status bar. But that isn't necessarily what we want; and in any case, the problem is not where the top of the scroll view is, but where the top of its *content* is considered to be. When the content is being scrolled *upward*, it's fine for that content to pass behind the status bar! The problem is what happens when the content is moved *downward* as far as it can go. Its content top shouldn't stop at the top of the scroll view; the stopping point should be further down, at the *bottom* of the status bar.

That's the problem that the scroll view's content inset solves. It positions the top of the scroll view's content lower than the top of the scroll view, by the amount that the scroll view underlaps the status bar.

But there's more. The content inset can't be a simple static value; it needs to be *live*. The status bar can come and go. The top of the scroll view's content should be further down than the top of the scroll view itself when the iPhone is in portrait orientation and the status bar is present; but when the iPhone is in landscape orientation and the status bar vanishes, the content inset needs to be adjusted so that the top of the content will be identical to the top of the scroll view.

And the status bar isn't the only kind of top bar; there's also the navigation bar, which can come and go as well, and can change its height. Plus there are bottom bars, which can *also* come and go, and can change *their* heights. The runtime would like your view to underlap those bars. With a scroll view, this looks cool, because the scroll view's contents are visible in a blurry way through the translucent bar; but clearly the top and bottom values of the scroll view's content inset need to be adjusted so that the scrolling limits stay between the top bar and the bottom bar, even as these bars can come and go and change their heights.

The boundaries I'm describing here, as has no doubt already occurred to you, are the boundaries of the safe area ("Safe area" on page 48). If a scroll view would simply adjust its content inset automatically to correspond to the safe area, its content would scroll in exactly the right way so as to be visible regardless of how any bars are underlapped.

That, by default, is in fact exactly what *does* happen! A scroll view knows where the top and bottom bars are because the safe area is propagated down the view hierarchy, and it knows how to adjust its content inset to correspond to the safe area. It will do that in accordance with its `contentInsetAdjustmentBehavior` property (UIScroll-View.ContentInsetAdjustmentBehavior):

`.always`
> The content is inset to match the safe area.

`.never`
> The content is not inset to match the safe area.

`.scrollableAxes`
> The content is inset to match the safe area only for a dimension in which the scroll view is scrollable.

`.automatic`
> Similar to `scrollableAxes`, but is also backward compatible. In iOS 10 and before, a view controller had an `automaticallyAdjustsScrollViewInsets` property (now deprecated); `.automatic` means that the scroll view can respond to that as well.

The default `contentInsetAdjustmentBehavior` is `.automatic` — which means that your scroll view will probably adjust its content inset appropriately with no work on your part! (To see what *would* have happened without adjustment of the content inset, set the scroll view's `contentInsetAdjustmentBehavior` to `.never`.)

To learn numerically how the scroll view has set its content inset, consult its `adjustedContentInset` property. Suppose we're in a navigation interface, where the scroll view coincides with the view controller's main view and underlaps the top bars. Suppose further that the navigation bar doesn't have a large title. Then in portrait orientation on an iPhone, the status bar and the navigation bar together add 64 points of height to the top of the safe area. So if the scroll view's content inset adjustment behavior isn't `.never`, its `adjustedContentInset` is (64.0,0.0,0.0,0.0).

A scroll view also has a separate `contentInset` property; unlike the `adjustedContent-Inset`, it is settable. It will usually be `.zero`; if you set it to some other value, that value is applied *additively* to the `adjustedContentInset`. In the navigation interface scenario from the preceding paragraph, if we also set the scroll view's `contentInset` to a UIEdgeInsets whose `top:` is 30, then the `adjustedContentInset` will have a `top` value of 94, and there will be an additional 30-point gap between the top of the content and the bottom of the navigation bar when the content is scrolled all the way down.

The scroll view's delegate (discussed later in this chapter) receives `scrollViewDidChangeAdjustedContentInset(_:)` whenever the adjusted content inset changes. This is matched by a method `adjustedContentInsetDidChange` that can be overridden in a UIScrollView subclass.

 Starting in iOS 13, if a navigation bar has a large title, then as the scroll view's content is scrolled downward and the large title appears, the navigation bar becomes transparent by default, revealing the scroll view behind it. This shouldn't make any appreciable difference, because *ex hypothesi* the entire content of the scroll view is already scrolled down past the bottom of the navigation bar, so the navigation bar won't overlap that content.

Scrolling

For the most part, the purpose of a scroll view will be to let the user scroll. Here are some scroll view properties that affect the user experience with regard to scrolling:

`isScrollEnabled`

If `false`, the user can't scroll, but you can still scroll in code (as explained later in this section). You could put a UIScrollView to various creative purposes other than letting the user scroll; scrolling in code to a different region of the content might be a way of replacing one piece of interface by another, possibly with animation.

`scrollsToTop`

If `true` (the default), and assuming scrolling is enabled, the user can tap on the status bar as a way of making the scroll view scroll its content to the top (that is, the content moves all the way down). You can override this setting dynamically through the scroll view's delegate, discussed later in this chapter.

`bounces`

If `true` (the default), then when the user scrolls to a limit of the content, it is possible to scroll somewhat further (possibly revealing the scroll view's `backgroundColor` behind the content, if a subview was covering it); the content then snaps back into place when the user releases it. Otherwise, the user experiences the limit as a sudden inability to scroll further in that direction.

`alwaysBounceVertical`
`alwaysBounceHorizontal`

   If `true`, and assuming that `bounces` is `true`, then even if the `contentSize` in the given dimension isn't larger than the scroll view (so that no scrolling is actually possible in that dimension), the user can scroll somewhat and the content then snaps back into place when the user releases it. Otherwise, the user experiences a simple inability to scroll in this dimension.

`isDirectionalLockEnabled`

   If `true`, and if scrolling is possible in both dimensions (even if only because `alwaysBounce` is `true`), then the user, having begun to scroll in one dimension, can't scroll in the other dimension without ending the gesture and starting over. In other words, the user is constrained to scroll vertically or horizontally but not both at once.

`decelerationRate`

   The rate at which scrolling is damped out, and the content comes to a stop, after the user's gesture ends. As convenient examples, standard constants are provided (UIScrollView.DecelerationRate):

   - `.normal` (0.998)
   - `.fast` (0.99)

   Lower values mean faster damping; experimentation suggests that values lower than 0.5 are viable but barely distinguishable from one another. You can effectively override this value dynamically through the scroll view's delegate, discussed later in this chapter.

`showsHorizontalScrollIndicator`
`showsVerticalScrollIndicator`

   The scroll indicators are bars that appear only while the user is scrolling in a scrollable dimension (where the content is larger than the scroll view); they indicate both the size of the content in that dimension and the user's position within it. The default is `true` for both.

   Because the user cannot see the scroll indicators except when actively scrolling, there is normally no indication that the view is scrollable. I regard this as somewhat unfortunate, because it makes the possibility of scrolling less discoverable; I'd prefer an option to make the scroll indicators constantly visible. Apple suggests that you call `flashScrollIndicators` when the scroll view appears, to make the scroll indicators visible momentarily.

`indicatorStyle`

The way the scroll indicators are drawn. Your choices (UIScrollView.Indicator-Style) are `.black`, `.white`, and `.default`; like the status bar style, `.default` responds to the user interface style (light or dark mode), contrasting with a system background color.

 The scroll indicators are subviews of the scroll view (they are actually UIImage-Views). Do not assume that the subviews you add to a UIScrollView are its only subviews!

Scrolling in Code

You can scroll in code, and you can do so even if the user can't scroll. The content moves to the position you specify, with no bouncing and no exposure of the scroll indicators. You can specify the new position in two ways:

`scrollRectToVisible(_:animated:)`

Adjusts the content so that the specified CGRect of the content is within the scroll view's bounds. This is imprecise, because you're not saying exactly what the resulting scroll position will be, but sometimes guaranteeing the visibility of a certain portion of the content is exactly what you're after.

`contentOffset`

A property signifying the point (CGPoint) of the content that is located at the scroll view's top left (effectively the same thing as the scroll view's bounds origin). Setting it changes the current scroll position, or call `setContent-Offset(_:animated:)` to set the `contentOffset` with animation. The values normally go up from (`0.0,0.0`) until the limit dictated by the `contentSize` and the scroll view's own bounds size is reached.

The `adjustedContentInset` (discussed in the previous section) can affect the meaning of the `contentOffset`. Recall the scenario where the scroll view underlaps the status bar and a navigation bar and acquires an `adjustedContentInset` with a top of 64. Then when the scroll view's content is scrolled all the way down, the `contentOffset` is not (`0.0,0.0`) but (`0.0,-64.0`). The (`0.0,0.0`) point is the top of the content rect, which is located at the bottom of the navigation bar; the point at the top left of the scroll view itself is 64 points above that.

That fact manifests itself particularly when *you* want to scroll, in code. If you scroll by setting the `contentOffset`, you need to subtract the corresponding `adjustedContent-Inset` value. Staying with our scroll view that underlaps a navigation bar, if your goal is to scroll the scroll view so that the top of its content is visible, you do *not* say this (the scroll view is `self.sv`):

```
self.sv.contentOffset.y = 0
```

Instead, you say this:

```
self.sv.contentOffset.y = -self.sv.adjustedContentInset.top
```

Paging

If its `isPagingEnabled` property is `true`, the scroll view doesn't let the user scroll freely; instead, the content is considered to consist of equal-sized sections. The user can scroll only in such a way as to move to a different section. The size of a section is set automatically to the size of the scroll view's bounds. The sections are the scroll view's *pages*. This is a *paging* scroll view.

When the user stops dragging, a paging scroll view gently snaps automatically to the nearest whole page. Let's say that a paging scroll view scrolls only horizontally, and that its subviews are image views showing photos, sized to match the scroll view's bounds:

- If the user drags horizontally to the left to a point where *less* than half of the next photo to the right is visible, and raises the dragging finger, the paging scroll view snaps its content back to the right until the entire first photo is visible again.

- If the user drags horizontally to the left to a point where *more* than half of the next photo to the right is visible, and raises the dragging finger, the paging scroll view snaps its content further to the left until the entire second photo is visible.

The usual arrangement is that a paging scroll view is as large, or nearly as large, in its scrollable dimension, as the window. Under this arrangement, it is impossible for the user to move the content more than a single page in any direction with a single gesture; the size of the page is the size of the scroll view's bounds, so the user will run out of surface area to drag on before being able to move the content the distance of a page and a half, which is what would be needed to make the scroll view skip a page.

Another possibility is for the paging scroll view to be slightly *larger* than the window in its scrollable dimension. This allows each page's content to fill the scroll view while also providing gaps between the pages, visible when the user starts to scroll. The user is still able to move from page to page, because it is still possible to drag more than half a new page into view.

When the user raises the dragging finger, the scroll view's action in adjusting its content is considered to be *decelerating*, and the scroll view's delegate (discussed in more detail later in this chapter) will receive `scrollViewWillBeginDecelerating(_:)`, followed by `scrollViewDidEndDecelerating(_:)` when the scroll view's content has stopped moving and a full page is showing. These messages can be used to detect efficiently that the page may have changed.

Using the delegate methods, a paging scroll view can be coordinated with a UIPage-Control (Chapter 13). In this example, a page control (`self.pager`) is updated whenever the user causes a horizontally scrollable scroll view (`self.sv`) to display a different page:

```
func scrollViewDidEndDecelerating(_ scrollView: UIScrollView) {
    let x = self.sv.contentOffset.x
    let w = self.sv.bounds.size.width
    self.pager.currentPage = Int(x/w)
}
```

Conversely, we can scroll the scroll view to a new page manually when the user taps the page control:

```
@IBAction func userDidPage(_ sender: Any) {
    let p = self.pager.currentPage
    let w = self.sv.bounds.size.width
    self.sv.setContentOffset(CGPoint(CGFloat(p)*w,0), animated:true)
}
```

A useful interface is a paging scroll view where you supply pages dynamically as the user scrolls. In this way, you can display a huge number of pages without having to put them all into the scroll view at once. In fact, a scrolling UIPageViewController (Chapter 6) implements exactly that interface! Its `.interPageSpacing` options key even provides the gap between pages that I mentioned earlier.

A compromise between a UIPageViewController and a completely preconfigured paging scroll view is a scroll view whose `contentSize` can accommodate all pages, but whose actual page content is supplied lazily. The only pages that have to be present at all times are the page visible to the user and the two pages adjacent to it on either side, so that there is no delay in displaying a new page's content when the user starts to scroll. (This approach is exemplified by Apple's PageControl sample code.)

Tiling

Suppose we have some finite but really big content that we want to display in a scroll view, such as a very large image that the user can inspect piecemeal by scrolling. To hold the entire image in memory may be onerous or impossible. One solution to this kind of problem is *tiling*.

The idea behind tiling is that there's no need to hold the entire image in memory; all we need at any given moment is the part of the image visible to the user right now. Mentally, divide the content rectangle into a matrix of rectangles; these rectangles are the tiles. In reality, divide the huge image into corresponding rectangles. Then whenever the user scrolls, we look to see whether part of any empty tile has become visible, and if so, we supply its content. At the same time, we can release the content of all tiles that are completely offscreen. At any given moment, only the tiles that are showing have content. There is some latency associated with this approach (the user scrolls, then any newly visible empty tiles are filled in), but we will have to live with that.

There is actually a built-in CALayer subclass for helping us implement tiling — CATiledLayer. Its `tileSize` property sets the dimensions of a tile. The usual approach to using CATiledLayer is to implement `draw(_:)` in a UIView whose underlying layer is the CATiledLayer; under that arrangement, the host view's `draw(_:)` is called every time a new tile is needed, and its parameter is the rect of the tile we are to draw.

The `tileSize` may need to be adjusted for the screen resolution. On a double-resolution device, the CATiledLayer's `contentsScale` will be doubled, and the tiles will be half the size that we ask for. If that isn't acceptable, we can double the `tileSize` dimensions.

To illustrate, I'll use as my tiles a few of the "CuriousFrog" images already created for us as part of Apple's own PhotoScroller sample code. The images have names of the form *CuriousFrog_500_x_y.png*, where *x* and *y* are integers corresponding to the picture's position within the matrix. The images are 256×256 pixels; for this example, I've selected a 3×3 matrix of images.

We will give our scroll view (`self.sv`) one subview, a UIView subclass (called Tiled-View) that exists purely to give our CATiledLayer a place to live. TILESIZE is defined as 256, to match the image dimensions:

```
override func viewDidLoad() {
    let f = CGRect(0,0,3*TILESIZE,3*TILESIZE)
    let content = TiledView(frame:f)
    let tsz = TILESIZE * content.layer.contentsScale
    (content.layer as! CATiledLayer).tileSize = CGSize(tsz, tsz)
    self.sv.addSubview(content)
    self.sv.contentSize = f.size
    self.content = content
}
```

Here's the code for TiledView. As Apple's sample code points out, we must fetch images with `init(contentsOfFile:)` in order to avoid the automatic caching behavior of `init(named:)` — after all, we're going to all this trouble exactly to avoid using more memory than we have to:

```
override class var layerClass : AnyClass {
    return CATiledLayer.self
}
override func draw(_ r: CGRect) {
    let tile = r
    let x = Int(tile.origin.x/TILESIZE)
    let y = Int(tile.origin.y/TILESIZE)
    let tileName = String(format:"CuriousFrog_500_\(x+3)_\(y)")
    let path = Bundle.main.path(forResource: tileName, ofType:"png")!
    let image = UIImage(contentsOfFile:path)!
    image.draw(at:CGPoint(CGFloat(x)*TILESIZE,CGFloat(y)*TILESIZE))
}
```

Figure 7-3. A tiled frog

In this configuration, our TiledView's `drawRect` is called *on a background thread.* This is unusual, but it shouldn't cause any trouble as long as you confine yourself to standard thread-safe activities. Fortunately, fetching the tile image and drawing it *are* thread-safe.

In Figure 7-3, I've modified that code to add borders around the tiles, so that you can see how the image is constructed. Parts of just six tiles are visible, so the remaining tile images have not been loaded at all; they will be loaded only if we scroll to view them.

There is no special call for invalidating an offscreen tile. You're just supposed to trust that the CATiledLayer will eventually clear offscreen tiles if needed in order to conserve memory.

CATiledLayer has a class method `fadeDuration` that dictates the duration of the animation that fades a new tile into view. You can create a CATiledLayer subclass and override this method to return a value different from the default (`0.25`), but this is probably not worth doing, as the default value is a good one. Returning a smaller value won't make tiles appear faster; it just replaces the nice fade-in with an annoying flash.

Zooming

To implement zooming of a scroll view's content, you set the scroll view's `minimum-ZoomScale` and `maximumZoomScale` so that at least one of them isn't 1 (the default). You also implement `viewForZooming(in:)` in the scroll view's delegate to tell the scroll view which of its subviews is to be the scalable view. The scroll view then zooms by applying a scale transform to this subview. The amount of that transform is the scroll view's `zoomScale` property.

Typically, you'll want the scroll view's entire content to be scalable, so you'll have one direct subview of the scroll view that acts as the scalable view, and anything else inside the scroll view will be a subview of the scalable view, so as to be scaled together with it. This is another reason for arranging your scroll view's subviews inside a single content view, as I suggested earlier.

To illustrate, we can start with any of the four content view–based versions of our scroll view containing 30 labels from earlier in this chapter ("Using a Content View" on page 422). I called the content view v. Now we add these lines:

```
v.tag = 999
sv.minimumZoomScale = 1.0
sv.maximumZoomScale = 2.0
sv.delegate = self
```

We have assigned a tag to the view that is to be scaled, so that we can refer to it later. We have set the scale limits for the scroll view. And we have made ourselves the scroll view's delegate. Now all we have to do is implement `viewForZooming(in:)` to return the scalable view:

```
func viewForZooming(in scrollView: UIScrollView) -> UIView? {
    return scrollView.viewWithTag(999)
}
```

This works: the scroll view now responds to pinch gestures by scaling! Recall that in our 30 labels example, the scroll view is not scrollable horizontally. Nevertheless, in this scenario, the width of the content view matters, because when it is scaled up, including during the act of zooming, the user will be able to scroll to see any part of it. So a good policy would be for the content view to embrace its content quite tightly.

The user can actually scale considerably beyond the limits we set in both directions; in that case, when the gesture ends, the scale snaps back to the limit value. If we wish to confine scaling strictly to our defined limits, we can set the scroll view's `bounces-Zoom` to `false`; when the user reaches a limit, scaling will simply stop.

If the `minimumZoomScale` is less than 1, then when the scalable view becomes smaller than the scroll view, it is pinned to the scroll view's top left. If you don't like this, you can change it by subclassing UIScrollView and overriding `layoutSubviews`, or by implementing the scroll view delegate method `scrollViewDidZoom(_:)`. Here's a simple example (drawn from a WWDC 2010 video) demonstrating an override of `layoutSubviews` that keeps the scalable view centered in either dimension whenever it is smaller than the scroll view in that dimension:

```
override func layoutSubviews() {
    super.layoutSubviews()
    if let v = self.delegate?.viewForZooming?(in:self) {
        let svw = self.bounds.width
        let svh = self.bounds.height
        let vw = v.frame.width
        let vh = v.frame.height
        var f = v.frame
        if vw < svw {
            f.origin.x = (svw - vw) / 2.0
        } else {
            f.origin.x = 0
        }
        if vh < svh {
            f.origin.y = (svh - vh) / 2.0
        } else {
            f.origin.y = 0
        }
        v.frame = f
    }
}
```

Zooming is, in reality, the application of a scale transform to the scalable view. This has two important consequences that can surprise you if you're unprepared:

The `frame` *of the scalable view*
> The frame of the scalable view is scaled to match the current `zoomScale`. This follows as a natural consequence of applying a scale transform to the scalable view.

The `contentSize` *of the scroll view*
> The scroll view is concerned to make scrolling continue to work correctly: the limits as the user scrolls should continue to match the limits of the content, and commands like `scrollRectToVisible(_:animated:)` should continue to work the same way for the same values. Therefore, the scroll view automatically scales its own `contentSize` to match the current `zoomScale`.

Zooming Programmatically

To zoom programmatically, you have two choices:

`zoomTo(_:animated:)`
> Zooms so that the given rectangle of the content occupies as much as possible of the scroll view's bounds. The `contentOffset` is automatically adjusted to keep the content occupying the entire scroll view.

```
setZoomScale(_:animated:)
```
Zooms in terms of scale value. The `contentOffset` is automatically adjusted to keep the current center centered, with the content occupying the entire scroll view.

In this example, I implement double tapping as a zoom gesture. In my action method for the double tap UITapGestureRecognizer attached to the scalable view, a double tap means to zoom to maximum scale, minimum scale, or actual size, depending on the current scale value:

```
@IBAction func tapped(_ tap : UIGestureRecognizer) {
    let v = tap.view!
    let sv = v.superview as! UIScrollView
    if sv.zoomScale < 1 {
        sv.setZoomScale(1, animated:true)
        let pt = CGPoint((v.bounds.width - sv.bounds.width)/2.0,0)
        sv.setContentOffset(pt, animated:false)
    }
    else if sv.zoomScale < sv.maximumZoomScale {
        sv.setZoomScale(sv.maximumZoomScale, animated:true)
    }
    else {
        sv.setZoomScale(sv.minimumZoomScale, animated:true)
    }
}
```

Zooming with Detail

Sometimes, you may want more from zooming than the mere application of a scale transform to the scaled view. The scaled view's drawing is cached beforehand into its layer, so when we zoom in, the bits of the resulting bitmap are drawn larger. This means that a zoomed-in scroll view's content may be fuzzy (pixelated). You might prefer the content to be redrawn more sharply at its new size.

(On a high-resolution device, this might not be an issue. If the user is allowed to zoom only up to double scale, you can draw at double scale right from the start; the results will look good at single scale, because the screen has high resolution, as well as at double scale, because that's the scale you drew at.)

One solution is to take advantage of a CATiledLayer feature that I didn't mention earlier. It turns out that CATiledLayer is aware not only of scrolling but also of scaling: you can configure it to ask for tiles to be redrawn when the layer is scaled to a new order of magnitude. When your drawing routine is called, the graphics context itself has already been scaled by a transform.

In the case of an image into which the user is to be permitted to zoom deeply, you might be forearmed with multiple tile sets constituting the image, each set having double the tile size of the previous set (as in Apple's PhotoScroller example). In other cases, you may not need tiles at all; you'll just draw again, at the new resolution.

Besides its `tileSize`, you'll need to set two additional CATiledLayer properties:

`levelsOfDetail`
> The number of different resolutions at which you want to redraw, where each level has twice the resolution of the previous level.

`levelsOfDetailBias`
> The number of levels of detail that are *larger* than single size (1x).

Those two properties work together. To illustrate, suppose we specify two levels of detail. Then we can ask to redraw when zooming to double size (2x) and when zooming back to single size (1x). But that isn't the *only* thing two levels of detail might mean; to complete the meaning, we need to set the `levelsOfDetailBias`. If `levelsOfDetail` is 2, then if we want to redraw when zooming to 2x and when zooming back to 1x, the `levelsOfDetailBias` needs to be 1, because one of those levels is larger than 1x. If we were to leave `levelsOfDetailBias` at 0, the default, we would be saying we want to redraw when zooming to 0.5x and back to 1x — we have two levels of detail but neither is larger than 1x, so one must be smaller than 1x.

The CATiledLayer will ask for a redraw at a higher resolution as soon as the view's size becomes larger than the previous resolution. In other words, if there are two levels of detail with a bias of 1, the layer will be redrawn at 2x as soon as it is zoomed even a little bit larger than 1x. This is an excellent approach, because although a level of detail would look blurry if scaled up, it looks pretty good scaled down.

Let's say I have a TiledView that hosts a CATiledLayer, in which I intend to draw an image. I haven't broken the image into tiles, because the maximum size at which the user can view it isn't prohibitively large; the original image happens to be 838×958, and can be held in memory easily. Rather, I'm using a CATiledLayer in order to take advantage of its ability to change resolutions automatically. The image will be drawn initially at less than quarter-size (namely 208×238), and we will permit the user to zoom in to the full size of the image. If the user never zooms in to view the image larger than the initial display, we will be saving a considerable amount of memory; if the user does zoom in, that will cost us more memory, but we have determined that this won't be prohibitive.

The CATiledLayer is configured like this:

```
let scale = lay.contentsScale
lay.tileSize = CGSize(208*scale,238*scale)
lay.levelsOfDetail = 3
lay.levelsOfDetailBias = 2
```

The `tileSize` has been adjusted for screen resolution, so the result is:

- As originally displayed at 208×238, there is one tile and we can draw our image at quarter size.

- If the user zooms in, to show the image larger than its originally displayed size, there will be 4 tiles and we can draw our image at half size.

- If the user zooms in still further, to show the image larger than double its originally displayed size (416×476), there will be 16 tiles and we can draw our image at full size, which will continue to look good as the user zooms all the way in to the full size of the original image.

We don't need to draw each tile individually. Each time we're called upon to draw a tile, we'll draw the entire image into the TiledView's bounds; whatever falls outside the requested tile will be clipped out and won't be drawn.

Here's my TiledView's draw(_:) implementation. I have an Optional UIImage property currentImage, initialized to nil, and a CGSize property currentSize initialized to .zero. Each time draw(_:) is called, I compare the tile size (the incoming rect parameter's size) to currentSize. If it's different, I know that we've changed by one level of detail and we need a new version of currentImage, so I create the new version of currentImage at a scale appropriate to this level of detail. Finally, I draw current-Image into the TiledView's bounds:

```
override func drawRect(rect: CGRect) {
    let (lay, bounds) = DispatchQueue.main.sync {
        return (self.layer as! CATiledLayer, self.bounds)
    }
    let oldSize = self.currentSize
    if !oldSize.equalTo(rect.size) {
        // make a new size
        self.currentSize = rect.size
        // make a new image
        let tr = UIGraphicsGetCurrentContext()!.ctm
        let sc = tr.a/lay.contentsScale
        let scale = sc/4.0
        let path = Bundle.main.path(
            forResource: "earthFromSaturn", ofType:"png")!
        let im = UIImage(contentsOfFile:path)!
        let sz = CGSize(im.size.width * scale, im.size.height * scale)
        let f = UIGraphicsImageRendererFormat.default()
        f.opaque = true; f.scale = 1 // *
        let r = UIGraphicsImageRenderer(size: sz, format: f)
        self.currentImage = r.image { _ in
            im.draw(in:CGRect(origin:.zero, size:sz))
        }
    }
    self.currentImage?.draw(in:bounds)
}
```

(The `DispatchQueue.main.sync` call at the start initializes my local variables `lay` and `bounds` on the main thread, even though `drawRect` is called on a background thread; see Chapter 25.)

An alternative approach (from a WWDC 2011 video) is to make yourself the scroll view's delegate so that you get an event when the zoom ends, and then change the scalable view's `contentScaleFactor` to match the current zoom scale, compensating for the high-resolution screen at the same time:

```
func scrollViewDidEndZooming(_ scrollView: UIScrollView,
    with view: UIView?, atScale scale: CGFloat) {
        if let view = view {
            scrollView.bounces = self.oldBounces
            view.contentScaleFactor = scale * UIScreen.main.scale // *
        }
}
```

In response, the scalable view's `draw(_:)` will be called, and its `rect` parameter will be the CGRect to draw into. The view may appear fuzzy for a while as the user zooms in, but when the user stops zooming, the view is redrawn sharply. That approach comes with a caveat: you mustn't overdo it. If the zoom scale, screen resolution, and scalable view size are high, you will be asking for a very large graphics context, which could cause your app to use too much memory.

For more about displaying a large image in a zoomable scroll view, see Apple's Large Image Downsizing example.

Scroll View Delegate

The scroll view's delegate (adopting the UIScrollViewDelegate protocol) receives messages that let you track in great detail what the scroll view is up to:

scrollViewDidScroll(_:)
> If you scroll in code without animation, you will receive this message *once* afterward. If the user scrolls, either by dragging or with the scroll-to-top feature, or if you scroll in code with animation, you will receive this message *repeatedly* throughout the scroll, including during the time the scroll view is decelerating after the user's finger has lifted; there are other delegate messages that tell you, in those cases, when the scroll has finally ended.

scrollViewDidEndScrollingAnimation(_:)
> If you scroll in code with animation, you will receive this message afterward, when the animation ends.

```
scrollViewWillBeginDragging(_:)
scrollViewWillEndDragging(_:withVelocity:targetContentOffset:)
scrollViewDidEndDragging(_:willDecelerate:)
```
If the user scrolls by dragging, you will receive these messages at the start and end of the user's finger movement. If the user brings the scroll view to a stop before lifting the finger, `willDecelerate` is `false` and the scroll is over. If the user lets go of the scroll view while the finger is moving, or when paging is turned on, `willDecelerate` is `true` and we proceed to the delegate messages reporting deceleration.

The purpose of `scrollViewWillEndDragging` is to let you customize the outcome of the content's deceleration. The third argument is a pointer to a CGPoint; you can use it to set a different CGPoint, specifying the `contentOffset` value the scroll view should have when the deceleration is over. By taking the `velocity:` into account, you can allow the user to "fling" the scroll view with momentum before it comes to a halt.

```
scrollViewWillBeginDecelerating(_:)
scrollViewDidEndDecelerating(_:)
```
Sent once each after `scrollViewDidEndDragging(_:willDecelerate:)` arrives with a value of `true`. When `scrollViewDidEndDecelerating(_:)` arrives, the scroll is over.

```
scrollViewShouldScrollToTop(_:)
scrollViewDidScrollToTop(_:)
```
These have to do with the feature where the user can tap the status bar to scroll the scroll view's content to its top. You won't get either of them if `scrollsToTop` is `false`, because the scroll-to-top feature is turned off. The first lets you prevent the user from scrolling to the top on this occasion even if `scrollsToTop` is `true`. The second tells you that the user has employed this feature and the scroll is over.

If you wanted to do something after a scroll ends completely regardless of how the scroll was performed, you'd need to implement multiple delegate methods:

- `scrollViewDidEndDragging(_:willDecelerate:)` in case the user drags and stops (`willDecelerate` is `false`).
- `scrollViewDidEndDecelerating(_:)` in case the user drags and the scroll continues afterward.
- `scrollViewDidScrollToTop(_:)` in case the user uses the scroll-to-top feature.
- `scrollViewDidEndScrollingAnimation(_:)` in case you scroll with animation.

In addition, the scroll view has read-only properties reporting its state:

isTracking
: The user has touched the scroll view, but the scroll view hasn't decided whether this is a scroll or some kind of tap.

isDragging
: The user is dragging to scroll.

isDecelerating
: The user has scrolled and has lifted the finger, and the scroll is continuing.

There are also three delegate messages that report zooming:

scrollViewWillBeginZooming(_:with:)
: If the user zooms or you zoom in code, you will receive this message as the zoom begins.

scrollViewDidZoom(_:)
: If you zoom in code, even with animation, you will receive this message *once*. If the user zooms, you will receive this message *repeatedly* as the zoom proceeds. (You will probably also receive scrollViewDidScroll(_:), possibly many times, as the zoom proceeds.)

scrollViewDidEndZooming(_:with:atScale:)
: If the user zooms or you zoom in code, you will receive this message after the last scrollViewDidZoom(_:).

In addition, the scroll view has read-only properties reporting its state during a zoom:

isZooming
: The scroll view is zooming. It is possible for isDragging to be true at the same time.

isZoomBouncing
: The scroll view's bouncesZoom is true, and now it *is* bouncing: it was zoomed beyond its minimum or maximum limit, and now it is returning automatically to that limit. As far as I can tell, you'll get only one scrollViewDidZoom(_:) while the scroll view is in this state.

Scroll View Touches

Since the early days of iOS, improvements in UIScrollView's internal implementation have eliminated most of the worry once associated with touches inside a scroll view. A scroll view will interpret a drag or a pinch as a command to scroll or zoom, and any other gesture will fall through to the subviews; buttons and similar interface objects inside a scroll view work just fine.

You can even put a scroll view inside a scroll view, and this can be a useful thing to do, in contexts where you might not think of it at first. Apple's PhotoScroller example, based on principles discussed in a delightful WWDC 2010 video, is an app where a single photo fills the screen: you can page-scroll from one photo to the next, and you can zoom into the current photo with a pinch gesture. This is implemented as a scroll view inside a scroll view: the outer scroll view is for paging between images, and the inner scroll view contains the current image and is for zooming (and for scrolling to different parts of the zoomed-in image). Similarly, a WWDC 2013 video deconstructs the iOS 7 lock screen in terms of scroll views embedded in scroll views.

Gesture recognizers (Chapter 5) have also greatly simplified the task of adding custom gestures to a scroll view. For instance, some older code in Apple's documentation, showing how to implement a double tap to zoom in and a two-finger tap to zoom out, used old-fashioned touch handling; but this is no longer necessary. Simply attach to your scroll view's scalable subview any gesture recognizers for these sorts of gesture, and they will mediate automatically among the possibilities.

In the past, making something inside a scroll view draggable required setting the scroll view's canCancelContentTouches property to false. (The reason for the name is that the scroll view, when it realizes that a gesture is a drag or pinch gesture, normally sends touchesCancelled(_:with:) to a subview tracking touches, so that the scroll view and not the subview will be affected.) But unless you're implementing old-fashioned direct touch handling, you probably won't have to concern yourself with this.

Some draggable controls might benefit from setting the scroll view's delaysContent-Touches to false; for instance, a UISwitch or a UISlider in a horizontally scrollable scroll view might be more responsive to a sliding gesture. Nevertheless, the user *can* slide the control even if delaysContentTouches is true; it's just that the user might need to hold down on the control a bit longer first, to get the scroll view's gesture recognizer to bow out.

(You can set both delaysContentTouches and canCancelContentTouches in the nib editor.)

Here's an example of a draggable object inside a scroll view implemented through a gesture recognizer. Suppose we have an image of a map, larger than the screen, and we want the user to be able to scroll it in the normal way to see any part of the map, but we also want the user to be able to drag a flag into a new location on the map. We'll put the map image in an image view and wrap the image view in a scroll view, with the scroll view's contentSize the same as the map image view's size. The flag is a small image view; it's another subview of the scroll view, and it has a UIPan-GestureRecognizer. The pan gesture recognizer's action method allows the flag to be dragged, exactly as described in Chapter 5:

Figure 7-4. A scrollable map with a draggable flag

```
@IBAction func dragging (_ p: UIPanGestureRecognizer) {
    let v = p.view!
    switch p.state {
    case .began, .changed:
        let delta = p.translation(in:v.superview!)
        v.center.x += delta.x
        v.center.y += delta.y
        p.setTranslation(.zero, in: v.superview)
    default: break
    }
}
```

The user can now drag the map or the flag (Figure 7-4). Dragging the map brings the flag along with it, but dragging the flag doesn't move the map.

An interesting addition to that example would be to implement *autoscrolling*, meaning that the scroll view scrolls itself when the user drags the flag close to its edge. This, too, is greatly simplified by gesture recognizers; in fact, we can add autoscrolling code directly to the dragging(_:) action method:

```
@IBAction func dragging (_ p: UIPanGestureRecognizer) {
    let v = p.view!
    switch p.state {
    case .began, .changed:
        let delta = p.translation(in:v.superview!)
        v.center.x += delta.x
        v.center.y += delta.y
```

```
                    p.setTranslation(.zero, in: v.superview)
                    // autoscroll
                    let sv = self.sv!
                    let loc = p.location(in:sv)
                    let f = sv.bounds
                    var off = sv.contentOffset
                    let sz = sv.contentSize
                    var c = v.center
                    // to the right
                    if loc.x > f.maxX - 30 {
                        let margin = sz.width - sv.bounds.maxX
                        if margin > 6 {
                            off.x += 5
                            sv.contentOffset = off
                            c.x += 5
                            v.center = c
                            self.keepDragging(p)
                        }
                    }
                    // to the left
                    if loc.x < f.origin.x + 30 {
                        let margin = off.x
                        if margin > 6 {
                            // ...
                        }
                    }
                    // to the bottom
                    if loc.y > f.maxY - 30 {
                        let margin = sz.height - sv.bounds.maxY
                        if margin > 6 {
                            // ...
                        }
                    }
                    // to the top
                    if loc.y < f.origin.y + 30 {
                        let margin = off.y
                        if margin > 6 {
                            // ...
                        }
                    }
                default: break
                }
            }
            func keepDragging (_ p: UIPanGestureRecognizer) {
                let del = 0.1
                delay(del) {
                    self.dragging(p)
                }
            }
        }
```

The delay in keepDragging (see Appendix B), combined with the change in offset,
determines the speed of autoscrolling. The material omitted in the second, third, and

fourth cases is obviously parallel to the first case, and is left as an exercise for the reader.

A scroll view's touch handling is itself based on gesture recognizers attached to the scroll view, and these are available to your code through the scroll view's panGesture-Recognizer and pinchGestureRecognizer properties. This means that if you want to customize a scroll view's touch handling, it's easy to add more gesture recognizers and mediate between them and the gesture recognizers already attached to the scroll view.

To illustrate, I'll build on the previous example. Suppose we want the flag to start out offscreen, and we'd like the user to be able to summon it with a rightward swipe. We can attach a UISwipeGestureRecognizer to our scroll view, but it will never recognize its gesture because the scroll view's own pan gesture recognizer will recognize first. But we have access to the scroll view's pan gesture recognizer, so we can compel it to yield to our swipe gesture recognizer by sending it require(toFail:):

```
self.sv.panGestureRecognizer.require(toFail:self.swipe)
```

The UISwipeGestureRecognizer can now recognize a rightward swipe. The flag has been waiting invisibly offscreen; in the gesture recognizer's action method, we position the flag just off to the top left of the scroll view's visible content and animate it onto the screen. We then disable the swipe gesture recognizer; its work is done:

```
@IBAction func swiped (_ g: UISwipeGestureRecognizer) {
    let sv = self.sv!
    let p = sv.contentOffset
    self.flag.frame.origin = p
    self.flag.frame.origin.x -= self.flag.bounds.width
    self.flag.isHidden = false
    UIView.animate(withDuration: 0.25) {
        self.flag.frame.origin.x = p.x
        // thanks for the flag, now stop operating altogether
        g.isEnabled = false
    }
}
```

Floating Scroll View Subviews

A scroll view's subview will appear to "float" over the scroll view if it remains stationary while the rest of the scroll view's content is being scrolled.

Before autolayout, that sort of thing was rather tricky to arrange; you had to use a delegate event to respond to every change in the scroll view's bounds origin by shifting the "floating" view's position to compensate, so as to appear to remain fixed. With autolayout, an easy solution is to set up constraints pinning the subview to something *outside* the scroll view. Even better, the scroll view itself provides a `frameLayoutGuide`; pin a subview to that, to make the subview stand still while the scroll view scrolls.

In this example, the image view is a subview of the scroll view that doesn't move during scrolling:

```
let iv = UIImageView(image:UIImage(named:"smiley"))
iv.translatesAutoresizingMaskIntoConstraints = false
self.sv.addSubview(iv)
let svflg = self.sv.frameLayoutGuide
NSLayoutConstraint.activate([
    iv.rightAnchor.constraint(equalTo:svflg.rightAnchor, constant: -5),
    iv.topAnchor.constraint(equalTo:svflg.topAnchor, constant: 25)
])
```

Scroll View Performance

Several times in earlier chapters I've mentioned performance problems and ways to increase drawing efficiency. The likeliest place to encounter such issues is in connection with a scroll view. As a scroll view scrolls, views must be drawn very rapidly as they appear on the screen. If the drawing system can't keep up with the speed of the scroll, the scrolling will visibly stutter.

Performance testing and optimization is a big subject, so I can't tell you exactly what to do if you encounter stuttering while scrolling. But certain general suggestions, mostly extracted from a really great WWDC 2010 video, should come in handy (and see also "Layer Efficiency" on page 158, some of which I'm repeating here):

- Everything that can be opaque should be opaque: don't force the drawing system to composite transparency, and remember to tell it that an opaque view or layer *is* opaque by setting its isOpaque property to true. If you really must composite transparency, keep the size of the nonopaque regions to a minimum.

- If you're drawing shadows, don't make the drawing system calculate the shadow shape for a layer: supply a shadowPath, or use Core Graphics to create the shadow with a drawing. Similarly, avoid making the drawing system composite the shadow as a transparency against another layer; if the background layer is white, your opaque drawing can itself include a shadow already drawn on a white background.

- Don't make the drawing system scale images for you; supply the images at the target size for the correct resolution.

- Coalesce layers (including views). The fewer layers constitute the render tree, the less work the drawing system has to do in order to render them.

- In a pinch, you can just eliminate massive swatches of the rendering operation by setting a layer's `shouldRasterize` to `true`. You could do this when scrolling starts and then set it back to `false` when scrolling ends.

Apple's documentation also says that setting a view's `clearsContextBeforeDrawing` to `false` may make a difference. I can't confirm or deny this; it may be true, but I haven't encountered a case that positively proves it.

Xcode provides tools that will help you detect inefficiencies in the drawing system. In the Simulator, the Debug menu lets you display blended layers (where transparency is being composited) and images that are being copied, misaligned, or rendered off-screen; the Xcode Debug → View Debugging → Rendering hierarchical menu provides even more options. On a device, the Core Animation template of Instruments tracks the frame rate for you, allowing you to measure performance objectively while scrolling. New in Xcode 12, in a UI test, XCTOSSignpostMetric lets you track the efficiency of scroll dragging and deceleration by measuring the ratio of animation "hitches," as well as frame rate, between `os_signpost` calls; create the starting signpost with the OSSignpostAnimationBegin case `.animationBegin`, as explained in the WWDC 2020 video on this topic.

Table Views

I'm gonna ask you the three big questions. — Go ahead. — Who made you? — You did. —
Who owns the biggest piece of you? — You do. — What would happen if I dropped you? —
I'd go right down the drain.
—Dialogue by Garson Kanin
and Ruth Gordon,
Pat and Mike

A table view (UITableView) is a vertically scrolling UIScrollView (Chapter 7) containing a single column of rectangular cells. Each cell is a UITableViewCell, a UIView subclass. A table view has three main purposes:

Information
> The cells constitute a list, which will often be text. The cells are usually quite small, in order to maximize the quantity appearing on the screen at once, so the information may be condensed, truncated, or summarized.

Choice
> The cells may represent choices. The user chooses by tapping a cell, which selects the cell; the app responds appropriately to that choice.

Navigation
> The response to the user's choosing a cell might be navigation to another interface.

An extremely common configuration is a *master–detail interface*, a navigation interface where the master view is a table view (Chapter 6): the user taps a table view cell to navigate to the details about that cell. This is one reason why the information in a table view cell can be a summary: to see the full information, the user can ask for the detail view. Figure 6-1 is an example.

In addition to its column of cells, a table view can have a number of other features:

- A table can include a header view at the top and a footer view at the bottom.

- The cells can be clumped into sections. Each section can have a header and a footer, which may explain the section and tell the user where we are within the table.

- If the table has sections, a section index can be provided as an overlay column of abbreviated section titles, which the user can tap or drag to jump to the start of a section; this makes a long table tractable.

- Tables can be editable: the user can be permitted to insert, delete, and reorder cells, and to edit information within a cell.

- Cells can have actions: the user can swipe a cell sideways to reveal buttons that act in relation to that cell.

- Cells can have menus: the user can long press a cell to pop up a menu with tappable menu items.

- A table can have a grouped format, where the cells are embedded into a common background that includes the section header and footer information. This format is often used for clumping small numbers of related cells, with explanations provided by the headers and footers.

Table view cells themselves can be extremely flexible. Some basic cell formats are provided, such as a text label along with a small image view, but you are free to design your own cell as you would any other view. There are also some standard interface items that are commonly used in a cell, such as a checkmark to indicate selection, or a right-pointing chevron to indicate that tapping the cell navigates to a detail view.

Figure 8-1 shows a familiar table view: Apple's Music app. Each table cell displays a song's name and artist, in truncated form; the user can tap to play the song. The table can be navigated using the section index at the right.

Figure 8-2 shows a familiar grouped table: Apple's Settings app. It's a master–detail interface. The master view has sections, but they aren't labeled with headers: they merely clump related topics. The detail view sometimes has just a single cell per section, using section headers and footers to explain what that cell does.

It would be difficult to overstate the importance of table views. An iOS app without a table view somewhere in its interface would be a rare thing, especially on the small iPhone screen. Indeed, table views are key to the small screen's viability. I've written apps consisting entirely of table views.

It is not uncommon to use a table view even in situations that have nothing particularly table-like about them, simply because it is so convenient. In one of my apps I want the user to be able to choose between three levels of difficulty and two sets of images. In a desktop application I'd probably use radio buttons; but there are no radio buttons among the standard iOS interface objects. Instead, I use a grouped

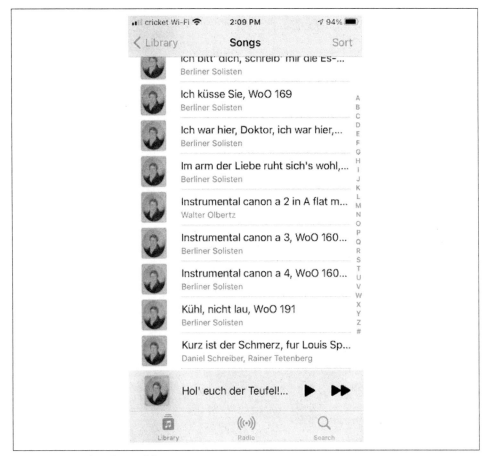

Figure 8-1. A familiar table view

table view so small that it doesn't even scroll. This gives me section headers, tappable cells, and a checkmark indicating the current choice (Figure 8-3).

Table View Controller

In the examples throughout this chapter, I'll use a table view controller in conjunction with a table view. This is a built-in view controller subclass, UITableViewController, whose main view is a table view. You're not obliged to use a UITableViewController with every table view — it doesn't do anything that you couldn't do yourself by other means — but it is certainly convenient. Here are some features of a table view controller:

- UITableViewController's `init(style:)` initializer creates the table view with a plain or grouped format.

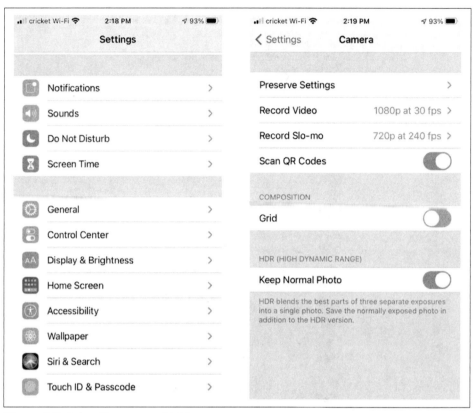

Figure 8-2. A familiar grouped table

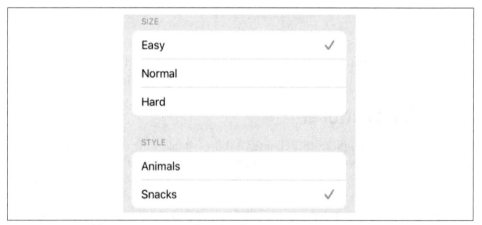

Figure 8-3. A table view as an interface for choosing options

- Every table view needs a data source and a delegate (as I'll explain later); a table view controller is its table view's data source and delegate by default.

- The table view is the table view controller's `tableView`. It is also the table view controller's `view`, but the `tableView` property is typed as a UITableView, so you can send table view messages to it without casting down.

- A table view controller lets you configure the layout and content of an entire table in a storyboard (a static table).

- A table view controller provides interface for automatic toggling of its table view's edit mode.

A table view controller is so convenient, in fact, that it might make sense to use one with *every* table view. Suppose a table view is to be a subview of some view controller's main view. That could be a "loose" table view. But it might be better to make the view controller a custom container view controller with a table view controller as its child ("Container View Controllers" on page 379).

Table View Cells

A table view's structure and contents are generally not configured in advance. Rather, you supply the table view with a data source and a delegate (which will often be the same object), and the table view turns to these in real time, as the app runs, whenever it needs a piece of information about its own structure and contents.

This architecture (which might surprise beginners) is part of a brilliant strategy to conserve resources. Imagine a long table consisting of thousands of rows. It must appear to consist of thousands of cells as the user scrolls. But a cell is a UIView; to maintain thousands of cells internally would put a terrible strain on memory. Therefore, the table typically maintains only as many cells as are showing simultaneously at any one moment. As the user scrolls to reveal new cells, those cells are created on the spot; meanwhile, the cells that have been scrolled out of view are permitted to die.

That's ingenious, but wouldn't it be even cleverer if, instead of letting a cell die as it scrolls *out* of view, we whisked it around to the other end and reused it as one of the cells being scrolled *into* view? Yes, and in fact that's exactly what you're supposed to do. You do it by assigning each cell a *reuse identifier*.

As cells with a given reuse identifier are scrolled out of view, the table view maintains a bunch of them in a pile. As a cell is about to be scrolled into view, you ask the table view for a cell from that pile, specifying the pile by means of the reuse identifier. The table view hands an old used cell back to you, and now you can configure it as the cell that is about to be scrolled into view. Cells are *reused* to minimize not only the number of actual cells in existence at any one moment but the number of actual cells *ever created*. A table of 1000 rows might very well never need to create more than about a dozen cells *over the entire lifetime of the app!*

To facilitate this architecture, your code must be prepared, on demand, to supply the table with pieces of requested data. Of these, the most important is the cell to be slotted into a given position. A position in the table is specified by means of an index path (IndexPath), used here to combine a section number with a row number; it is often referred to as a *row* of the table. Your data source object may at any moment be sent the message tableView(_:cellForRowAt:), and you must respond by returning the UITableViewCell to be displayed at that row of the table. And you must return it *fast*: the user is scrolling *now*, so the table needs that cell *now*.

Built-In Cell Styles

A simple way to obtain a table view cell is to start with one of the four built-in table view cell styles. A cell using a built-in style is created by calling init(style:reuse-Identifier:). The reuseIdentifier: is what allows cells previously assigned to rows that are no longer showing to be reused for cells that are; it will usually be the same for all cells in a table. Your choices of cell style (UITableViewCell.CellStyle) are:

.default
> The cell has a UILabel (its textLabel), with an optional UIImageView (its image-View) at the left. If there is no image, the label occupies the width of the cell.

.value1
> The cell has two UILabels (its textLabel and its detailTextLabel) side by side, with an optional UIImageView (its imageView) at the left. The first label is left-aligned; the second label is right-aligned. If the first label's text is too long, the second label won't appear.

.value2
> The cell has two UILabels (its textLabel and its detailTextLabel) side by side. No UIImageView will appear. The first label is right-aligned; the second label is left-aligned. The label sizes are fixed, and the text of either will be truncated if it's too long.

.subtitle
> The cell has two UILabels (its textLabel and its detailTextLabel), one above the other, with an optional UIImageView (its imageView) at the left.

 New in iOS 14, Apple appears to be on the point of deprecating the textLabel, detailTextLabel, and imageView properties; I'll explain later in this chapter what's intended to replace them ("Apple's Cell Configuration Architecture" on page 478). Nevertheless, these properties do still work, and they are an excellent way to start experimenting with table view cells, so I'll continue using them in my examples.

To experiment with the built-in cell styles, do this:

1. Start with the basic App template.

2. We're going to ignore the storyboard ("App Without a Storyboard" on page 7). So we need a class to serve as our root view controller. Choose File → New → File and specify iOS → Source → Cocoa Touch Class. Click Next.

3. Make this class a UITableViewController subclass called RootViewController. The XIB checkbox should be *checked*; Xcode will create an eponymous *.xib* file containing a table view, correctly configured with its File's Owner as our Root-ViewController class. Click Next.

4. Make sure you're saving into the correct folder and group, and that the app target is checked. Click Create.

5. Rewrite SceneDelegate's scene(_:willConnectTo:options:) to make our Root-ViewController the window's rootViewController:

   ```
   if let windowScene = scene as? UIWindowScene {
       self.window = UIWindow(windowScene: windowScene)
       self.window!.rootViewController = RootViewController()
       self.window!.backgroundColor = .white
       self.window!.makeKeyAndVisible()
   }
   ```

6. Now modify the RootViewController class (which comes with a lot of templated code), as in Example 8-1.

Example 8-1. Basic table data source schema

```
let cellID = "Cell"
override func numberOfSections(in tableView: UITableView) -> Int {
    return 1 ❶
}
override func tableView(_ tableView: UITableView,
    numberOfRowsInSection section: Int) -> Int {
        return 20 ❷
}
override func tableView(_ tableView: UITableView,
    cellForRowAt indexPath: IndexPath) -> UITableViewCell {
        var cell : UITableViewCell! = tableView.dequeueReusableCell(
            withIdentifier: self.cellID) ❸
        if cell == nil {
            cell = UITableViewCell(style:.default,
                reuseIdentifier: self.cellID) ❹
            cell.textLabel!.textColor = .red ❺
        }
        cell.textLabel!.text = "Hello there! \(indexPath.row)" ❻
        return cell
}
```

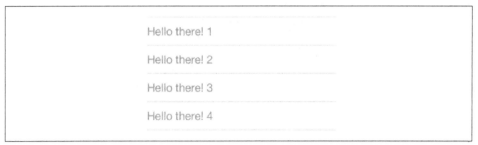

Figure 8-4. The world's simplest table

The key parts of the code are:

❶ Our table will have one section.

❷ Our table will consist of 20 rows. Having multiple rows will give us a sense of how our cell looks when placed among other cells.

❸ In `tableView(_:cellForRowAt:)`, you should *always* start by asking the table view for a reusable cell. Here, we will receive either an already existing reused cell or `nil`.

❹ If we received `nil`, we create the cell from scratch, ourselves. This is where you specify the built-in table view cell style you want to experiment with.

❺ At this point in the code you can modify characteristics of the cell (`cell`) that are to be the same for *every* cell of the table. For the moment, I've symbolized this by assuming that every cell's text is to be the same color.

❻ We now have the cell to be used for *this* row of the table, so at this point in the code you can modify features of the cell (`cell`) that are unique to this row. I've symbolized this by appending the row number to the text of each row.

Run the app to see the world's simplest table (Figure 8-4).

Now you can experiment with your cell's appearance by tweaking the code and running the app. Feel free to try different built-in cell styles in the place where we are now specifying `.default`.

Label features

Our built-in cell style's `textLabel` is a UILabel, so further flexibility within each built-in style comes from the flexibility of a label. Not everything can be customized, because after you return the cell some further configuration takes place, which may override your settings; for instance, the size and position of the cell's subviews are not up to you. (I'll explain, a little later, how to get around that.) But you get a remarkable degree of freedom. Here are a few basic UILabel properties for you to play with now, and I'll talk much more about UILabels in Chapter 11:

text
> The string shown in the label.

textColor, highlightedTextColor
> The color of the text. The highlightedTextColor applies when the cell is highlighted or selected (tap on a cell to select it).

textAlignment
> How the text is aligned; some possible choices (NSTextAlignment) are .left, .center, and .right.

numberOfLines
> The maximum number of lines of text to appear in the label. Text that is long but permitted to wrap, or that contains explicit linefeed characters, can appear completely in the label if the label is tall enough and the number of permitted lines is sufficient. 0 means there's no maximum; the default is 1.

font
> The label's font. You could reduce the font size as a way of fitting more text into the label. A font name includes its style:
>
> ```
> cell.textLabel!.font = UIFont(name:"Helvetica-Bold", size:12.0)
> ```

shadowColor, shadowOffset
> The text shadow. Adding a little shadow can increase clarity and emphasis for large text.

Image view features

You can also assign the image view (cell.imageView) an image. The frame of the image view can't be changed, but you can inset its apparent size by supplying a smaller image and setting the image view's contentMode to .center. It's a good idea in any case, for performance reasons, to supply images at their drawn size and resolution rather than making image views scale them down for you (see "UIImage Drawing" on page 100).

Cell features

The cell itself also has some properties you can play with:

accessoryType
> A built-in type (UITableViewCell.AccessoryType) of accessory view, which appears at the cell's right end:

```
cell.accessoryType = .disclosureIndicator
```

`accessoryView`

Your own UIView, which appears at the cell's right end (overriding the `accessoryType`):

```
let b = UIButton(type:.system)
b.setTitle("Tap Me", for:.normal)
b.sizeToFit()
// ... add action and target here ...
cell.accessoryView = b
```

`indentationLevel`, `indentationWidth`

These properties give the cell a left margin, useful for suggesting a hierarchy among cells. You can also set a cell's indentation level in real time, with respect to the table row into which it is slotted, by implementing the delegate's `tableView(_:indentationLevelForRowAt:)` method.

`separatorInset`

This property affects both the drawing of the separator between cells and the indentation of content of the built-in cell styles. A UIEdgeInsets; only the left and right insets matter. The default is a left inset of 15, but the built-in table view cell styles may shift it to match the left layout margin of the root view (16 or 20).

`selectionStyle`

How the background looks when the cell is selected (UITableViewCell.Selection-Style). The default is solid gray (`.default`), or you can choose `.none`. Solid colors of cell subviews can obscure the default gray.

`backgroundColor`
`backgroundView`
`selectedBackgroundView`

What's behind everything else drawn in the cell. Solid colors of cell subviews can obscure any of these. The `selectedBackgroundView` is drawn in front of the `backgroundView` (if any) when the cell is selected, and will appear instead of whatever the `selectionStyle` dictates. The `backgroundColor` is behind the `backgroundView`. There is no need to set the frame of the `backgroundView` and `selectedBackgroundView`; they will be resized automatically to fit the cell.

`multipleSelectionBackgroundView`

If the table's `allowsMultipleSelection` or `allowsMultipleSelectionDuring-Editing` is true, used instead of the `selectedBackgroundView` when the cell is selected.

In this example, we set the cell's `backgroundView` to display an image with some transparency at the outside edges, so that the `backgroundColor` shows behind it, and

Figure 8-5. A cell with an image background

we set the `selectedBackgroundView` to an almost transparent blue rectangle, to darken that image when the cell is selected (Figure 8-5):

```
cell.textLabel!.textColor = .white
let v = UIImageView(image: UIImage(named:"linen")) // no need to set frame
v.contentMode = .scaleToFill
cell.backgroundView = v
let v2 = UIView() // no need to set frame
v2.backgroundColor = UIColor.blue.withAlphaComponent(0.2)
cell.selectedBackgroundView = v2
cell.backgroundColor = .red
```

If those features are to be true of every cell ever displayed in the table, then that code should go in the spot numbered 5 in Example 8-1; it would be wasteful to do the same thing all over again when an existing cell is reused.

Table view features

Finally, here are a few properties of the table view itself worth playing with:

`rowHeight`
> The height of every cell. Taller cells may accommodate more information. You can also change this value in the nib editor; the table view's row height appears in the Size inspector. With a built-in cell style, the cell's subviews have their autoresizing set so as to compensate correctly. You can also set a cell's height in real time by implementing the delegate's `tableView(_:heightForRowAt:)` method, so that a table's cells may differ from one another in height (more about that later in this chapter).

`separatorStyle`, `separatorColor`
> These can also be set in the nib. Separator styles (UITableViewCell.Separator-Style) are `.none` and `.singleLine`.

`separatorInset`, `separatorInsetReference`
> These can also be set in the nib. The table view's `separatorInset` is adopted by individual cells that don't have their own explicit `separatorInset`; to put it another way, the table view's `separatorInset` is the default, but a cell can override it.

The `separatorInsetReference` (introduced in iOS 11) determines how the separator inset is understood, either `.fromCellEdges` or `.fromAutomaticReference` (meaning from the margins). The default is `.fromCellEdges`.

`backgroundColor, backgroundView`
What's behind all the cells of the table; this may be seen if the cells have transparency, or if the user scrolls the cells beyond their limit. The `backgroundView` is drawn on top of the `backgroundColor`.

`tableHeaderView, tableFooterView`
Views to be shown before the first row and after the last row, respectively, as part of the table's scrolling content. You must dictate their heights explicitly, by setting their frame or bounds height; their widths will be dynamically resized to fit the table. You can allow the user to interact with these views (and their subviews); for example, a view can be (or can contain) a UIButton.

You can alter a table header or footer view dynamically during the lifetime of the app; if you change its height, you must set the corresponding table view property afresh to notify the table view of what has happened.

`insetsContentViewsToSafeArea`
The cell's contents, such as its `textLabel`, are inside an unseen view called the `contentView`; those contents are positioned with respect to the content view's bounds. If this property is `true` (the default), the safe area insets will inset the frame of the content view; that's significant in landscape on an iPhone without a bezel, such as the iPhone X. (The `backgroundColor` and `backgroundView` are *not* inset by the safe area insets.)

`cellLayoutMarginsFollowReadableWidth`
If this property is `true`, the content view margins will be inset on a wide screen (such as an iPad in landscape) to prevent text content from becoming overly wide. Starting in iOS 12, the default is `false`.

Registering a Cell Class

In Example 8-1, I used this method to obtain the reusable cell:

- `dequeueReusableCell(withIdentifier:)`

But there's a better way:

- `dequeueReusableCell(withIdentifier:for:)`

The *outward* difference is that the second method has a second parameter — an IndexPath. But that's mere boilerplate; you received an index path as the last parameter of `tableView(_:cellForRowAt:)`, and you'll just pass it along as the second parameter here. The *functional* difference is very dramatic:

The result is never nil

Unlike `dequeueReusableCell(withIdentifier:)`, the value returned by `dequeueReusableCell(withIdentifier:for:)` is never `nil` (in Swift, it isn't an Optional). If there is a free reusable cell with the given identifier, it is returned. If there isn't, a new one is created for you, automatically. Step 4 of Example 8-1 can be eliminated!

The cell size is known earlier

Unlike `dequeueReusableCell(withIdentifier:)`, the cell returned by `dequeueReusableCell(withIdentifier:for:)` has its final bounds. That's possible because you've passed the index path as an argument, so the runtime knows this cell's ultimate destination within the table, and has already consulted the table's `rowHeight` or the delegate's `tableView(_:heightForRowAt:)`. This can make laying out the cell's contents much easier.

The identifier is consistent

A danger with `dequeueReusableCell(withIdentifier:)` is that you may accidentally pass an incorrect reuse identifier and end up not reusing cells. With `dequeueReusableCell(withIdentifier:for:)`, that can't happen.

Those are powerful advantages, and for that reason I suggest always using `dequeueReusableCell(withIdentifier:for:)`. This will mean that Example 8-1 is wrong and will have to be modified; in a moment, that's just what I'll do. But first we need to talk about some more implications of using `dequeueReusableCell(withIdentifier:for:)`.

Let's go back to the first advantage of `dequeueReusableCell(withIdentifier:for:)` — if there isn't a reusable cell with the given identifier, *the table view will create the cell;* you never instantiate the cell yourself. But how does the table view know how to do that? You have to tell it in advance, associating the reuse identifier with the correct means of instantiation. There are three possibilities:

Provide a class

You *register* a class with the table view, associating that class with the reuse identifier. The table view will instantiate that class.

Provide a nib

You *register* a .*xib* file with the table view, associating that nib with the reuse identifier. The table view will load the nib to instantiate the cell.

Provide a storyboard

If you're getting the cell from a storyboard, you *don't* register anything with the table view! Instead, you associate the cell in the storyboard with the reuse identifier by entering that reuse identifier in the Identifier field of the cell's Attributes inspector. The table view will instantiate the cell from the storyboard.

In my examples so far, we're not using a storyboard (I'll discuss that approach later). So let's use the first approach: we'll *register a class* with the table view. To do so, before we call dequeueReusableCell(withIdentifier:for:) for the first time, we call register(_:forCellReuseIdentifier:), where the first parameter is the UITableViewCell class or a subclass thereof. That will associate this class with our reuse identifier. It will also add a measure of safety, because henceforth if we pass a bad identifier into dequeueReusableCell(withIdentifier:for:), the app will crash (with a helpful log message); we are forcing ourselves to reuse cells properly.

This is a very elegant mechanism. It also raises some new questions:

When should I register with the table view?

Do it early, before the table view starts generating cells; viewDidLoad is a good place:

```
let cellID = "Cell"
override func viewDidLoad() {
    super.viewDidLoad()
    self.tableView.register(
        UITableViewCell.self, forCellReuseIdentifier: self.cellID)
}
```

How do I specify a built-in table view cell style?

We are no longer calling init(style:reuseIdentifier:), so where do we make our choice of built-in cell style? The default cell style is .default, so if that's what you wanted, the problem is solved. Otherwise, subclass UITableViewCell and register the subclass; in the subclass, override init(style:reuseIdentifier:) to substitute the cell style you're after (passing along the reuse identifier you were handed).

Suppose we want the .subtitle style. Let's call our UITableViewCell subclass MyCell. So we now specify MyCell.self in our call to register(_:forCell-ReuseIdentifier:). MyCell's initializer looks like this:

```
override init(style: UITableViewCell.CellStyle,
    reuseIdentifier: String?) {
        super.init(style:.subtitle, reuseIdentifier: reuseIdentifier)
}
```

How do I know whether the returned cell is new or reused?

Good question! dequeueReusableCell(withIdentifier:for:) never returns nil, so we need some *other* way to distinguish between configurations that are to apply once and for all to a *new cell* (step 5 of Example 8-1) and configurations that differ for *each row* (step 6). It's up to you, when performing one-time configuration on a cell, to give that cell some distinguishing mark that you can look for later to determine whether a cell requires one-time configuration.

Suppose every cell is to have a two-line text label. Then there is no point configuring the text label of *every* cell returned by dequeueReusableCell(withIdentifier:for:) to have two lines; the reused cells have already been configured. But how will we know which cells need their text label to be configured? It's easy: they are the ones whose text label *hasn't* been configured:

```
override func tableView(_ tableView: UITableView,
    cellForRowAt indexPath: IndexPath) -> UITableViewCell {
        let cell = tableView.dequeueReusableCell(
            withIdentifier: self.cellID, for: indexPath) as! MyCell
        if cell.textLabel!.numberOfLines != 2 { // not configured!
            cell.textLabel!.numberOfLines = 2
            // other one-time configurations here ...
        }
        cell.textLabel!.text = // ...
        // other individual configurations here ...
        return cell
}
```

We are now ready to rewrite Example 8-1 to use dequeueReusableCell(withIdentifier:for:). The result is Example 8-2.

Example 8-2. Basic table data source schema, revised

```
let cellID = "Cell"
override func viewDidLoad() {
    super.viewDidLoad()
    self.tableView.register(
        UITableViewCell.self, forCellReuseIdentifier: self.cellID) ❶
}
override func numberOfSections(in tableView: UITableView) -> Int {
    return 1 ❷
}
override func tableView(_ tableView: UITableView,
    numberOfRowsInSection section: Int) -> Int {
        return 20 ❸
}
override func tableView(_ tableView: UITableView,
    cellForRowAt indexPath: IndexPath) -> UITableViewCell {
        let cell = tableView.dequeueReusableCell(
            withIdentifier: self.cellID, for: indexPath) ❹
        if cell.textLabel!.numberOfLines != 2 { ❺
            cell.textLabel!.numberOfLines = 2
            // ... other universal configurations here ...
        }
        cell.textLabel!.text = "Hello there! \(indexPath.row)" ❻
        // ... other individual configurations here ...
        return cell
}
```

❶ Register the cell identifier with the table view. No law requires that this be done in `viewDidLoad`, but it's a good place because it's called once, early. (This step *must be omitted* if the cell is to come from a storyboard, as I'll explain later.)

❷ Give the number of sections our table is to have.

❸ Give the number of rows each section is to have.

❹ Call `dequeueReusableCell(withIdentifier:for:)` to obtain a cell for this reuse identifier, passing along the incoming index path. If the registered cell class is a UITableViewCell subclass, you'll probably need to cast down here; this is a situation where a forced downcast is justified, because if the cast fails something is very wrong and we can't proceed.

❺ If there are configurations to be performed that are the same for *every* cell, look to see whether *this* cell has already been configured. If not, configure it.

❻ Modify features of the cell that are *unique to this row*, and return the cell.

Custom Cells

In real life it is unusual to rest content with the built-in cell styles. They give the beginner a leg up in getting started with table views, but there is nothing sacred about them, and soon you'll surely want to transcend them, putting yourself in charge of how a table's cells look and what subviews they contain. You want a *custom cell.*

Keep in mind, as you design your custom cell, that the cell has a `contentView` property, which is one of its subviews; things like the `accessoryView` are outside the `contentView`, but all *your* custom subviews must be subviews of the `contentView`. This allows the cell to continue working correctly.

 New in iOS 14, you are penalized if you mistakenly add a subview directly to a cell: the `contentView` covers the subview and prevents the user from interacting with it.

I'll illustrate four possible approaches to customizing the contents of a cell:

- Start with a built-in cell style, but supply a UITableViewCell subclass and override `layoutSubviews` to alter the frames of the built-in subviews.
- In `tableView(_:cellForRowAt:)`, add subviews to each cell's `contentView` as the cell is created.
- Design the cell in a nib, and load that nib in `tableView(_:cellForRowAt:)` each time a cell needs to be created.
- Design the cell in a storyboard.

The author of this book, who would rather be out dirt biking	

Figure 8-6. A cell with its label and image view swapped

Overriding a cell's subview layout

You can't directly change the frame of a built-in cell style subview in `table-View(_:cellForRowAt:)`, because the cell's `layoutSubviews` comes along later and overrides your changes. The workaround is to override the cell's `layoutSubviews`! This is a straightforward solution if your main objection to a built-in style is the frame of an existing subview.

To illustrate, let's modify a `.default` cell so that the image is at the right end instead of the left end (Figure 8-6). We'll make a UITableViewCell subclass called MyCell; here is MyCell's `layoutSubviews`:

```
override func layoutSubviews() {
    super.layoutSubviews()
    let cvb = self.contentView.bounds
    let imf = self.imageView!.frame
    self.imageView!.frame.origin.x = cvb.size.width - imf.size.width - 15
    self.textLabel!.frame.origin.x = 15
}
```

We must also make sure to *use* our subclass as the cell type:

```
self.tableView.register(MyCell.self, forCellReuseIdentifier: self.cellID)
```

Adding subviews in code

Instead of modifying the existing default subviews, you can add completely new views to each UITableViewCell's content view. The best place to do this in code is `tableView(_:cellForRowAt:)`. Here are some things to keep in mind:

- The new views must be added when we configure a brand new cell — but not when we reuse a cell, because a reused cell already has them. (Adding multiple copies of the same subview repeatedly, as the cell is reused, is a common beginner mistake.)

- We must never send `addSubview(_:)` to the cell itself — only to its `contentView` (or some subview thereof).

- We should assign the new views an appropriate `autoresizingMask` or constraints, because the cell's content view might be resized.

- Each new view needs a way to be identified and referred to elsewhere. A `tag` is a simple solution.

I'll rewrite the previous example to use this technique. We don't need a UITable-ViewCell subclass; the registered cell class can be UITableViewCell itself. If this is a new cell, we add the subviews, position them, and assign them tags. If this is a reused cell, we *don't* add the subviews — the cell already has them! Either way, we then use the tags to refer to the subviews:

```
override func tableView(_ tableView: UITableView,
    cellForRowAt indexPath: IndexPath) -> UITableViewCell {
        let cell = tableView.dequeueReusableCell(
            withIdentifier: self.cellID, for: indexPath)
        if cell.viewWithTag(1) == nil { // no subviews! add them
            let iv = UIImageView(); iv.tag = 1
            cell.contentView.addSubview(iv)
            let lab = UILabel(); lab.tag = 2
            cell.contentView.addSubview(lab)
            // ... position the subviews ...
        }
        // can refer to subviews by their tags
        let lab = cell.viewWithTag(2) as! UILabel
        let iv = cell.viewWithTag(1) as! UIImageView
        // ...
        return cell
}
```

Designing a cell in a nib

We can avoid the verbosity of the previous code by designing the cell in a nib. We start by creating a *.xib* file that will consist, in effect, solely of this one cell; then we design the cell:

1. In Xcode, create the *.xib* file by specifying iOS → User Interface → View. Let's call it *MyCell.xib*.

2. Edit *MyCell.xib*. In the nib editor, delete the existing View and replace it with a Table View Cell from the Library.

   The cell's design window shows a standard-sized cell; you can resize it as desired, but the actual size of the cell in the interface will be dictated by the table view's width and its rowHeight (or the delegate's response to tableView(_:heightFor-RowAt:)). The cell already has a contentView, and any subviews you add will be inside that; do not subvert that arrangement.

3. You can choose a built-in table view cell style in the Style pop-up menu of the cell's Attributes inspector, which gives you the default subviews, locked in their standard positions. But if you set the Style pop-up menu to Custom, you start with a blank slate; let's do that.

4. Design the cell! Let's implement, from scratch, the same subviews we've already implemented in the preceding two examples: a UILabel on the left side of the cell, and a UIImageView on the right side. Just as when adding subviews in code, we

should set each subview's autoresizing behavior or constraints, and *give each sub-view a tag*, so that later, in `tableView(_:cellForRowAt:)`, we'll be able to refer to the label and the image view using `viewWithTag(_:)`, exactly as in the previous example.

The only remaining question is how to load the cell from the nib. It's simple. When we register with the table view, which we're currently doing in `viewDidLoad`, in our call to `register(_:forCellReuseIdentifier:)`, we supply a nib instead of a class. To specify the nib, call UINib's initializer `init(nibName:bundle:)`, like this:

```
self.tableView.register(
    UINib(nibName:"MyCell", bundle:nil), forCellReuseIdentifier:self.cellID)
```

That's all there is to it. In `tableView(_:cellForRowAt:)`, when we call `dequeue-ReusableCell(withIdentifier:for:)`, if the table has no free reusable cell already in existence, the nib will automatically be loaded and the cell will be instantiated from it and returned to us.

You may wonder how that's possible, when we haven't specified a File's Owner class or added an outlet from the File's Owner to the cell in the nib. The answer is that the nib conforms to a specific format. The UINib instance method `instantiate(with-Owner:options:)` can load a nib with a `nil` owner, and it returns an array of the nib's instantiated top-level objects. A nib registered with the table view is expected to have exactly one top-level object, and that top-level object is expected to be a UITable-ViewCell; the cell can easily be extracted from the resulting array, as it is the array's only element. Our nib meets those expectations!

 The nib *must* conform to that format: it must have *exactly* one top-level object, a UITableViewCell. Unfortunately, this means that some configurations are diffi-cult or impossible in the nib. A cell's `backgroundView` cannot be configured in the nib, because this would require the presence of a second top-level nib object. The simplest workaround is to add the `backgroundView` in code.

The advantages of this approach should be immediately obvious. The subviews can now be designed in the nib editor, and code that was creating and configuring each subview can be deleted. All code that sizes and positions our subviews can be removed; we can specify the constraints in the nib editor. If we were configuring the label — assigning it a font, a line break mode, a `numberOfLines` — all of that code can be removed; we can specify those things in the nib editor.

But we can go further. In `tableView(_:cellForRowAt:)`, we are still referring to the cell's subviews by way of `viewWithTag(_:)`. There's nothing wrong with that, but it would be nice to use names instead. Now that we're designing the cell in a nib, that's easy. Provide a UITableViewCell subclass with outlet properties, and configure the nib file accordingly:

1. Create a UITableViewCell subclass — let's call it MyCell — and declare two outlet properties:

```
class MyCell : UITableViewCell {
    @IBOutlet var theLabel : UILabel!
    @IBOutlet var theImageView : UIImageView!
}
```

That is the *entirety* of MyCell's code; it exists solely so that we can create these outlets.

2. Edit the table view cell nib *MyCell.xib*. Change the class of the cell (in the Identity inspector) to MyCell, and connect the outlets from the cell to the respective subviews.

The result is that in our implementation of `tableView(_:cellForRowAt:)`, once we've typed the cell as a MyCell, the compiler will let us use the property names to access the subviews:

```
let cell = tableView.dequeueReusableCell(
    withIdentifier: self.cellID, for: indexPath) as! MyCell // *
let lab = cell.theLabel // *
let iv = cell.theImageView // *
// ... configure lab and iv ...
```

Designing a cell in a storyboard

If your table view is instantiated from a storyboard, then along with all the ways of obtaining and designing its cells that I've already described, there is an additional option. You can have the table view obtain its cells *from the storyboard itself*. This means you can also *design* the cell in the storyboard.

Let's experiment with this way of obtaining and designing a cell:

1. Start with a project based on the basic App template.

2. In the project, create a file for a UITableViewController subclass called RootViewController, *without* a corresponding *.xib* file.

3. In the storyboard, delete the View Controller scene. Drag a Table View Controller into the empty canvas, and set its class to RootViewController. Make sure to designate it as the initial view controller.

4. The table view controller in the storyboard comes with a table view. In the storyboard, select that table view and, in the Attributes inspector, set the Content popup menu to Dynamic Prototypes, and set the number of Prototype Cells to 1 (those are the defaults).

The table view in the storyboard now contains a single table view cell with a content view. You can do in this cell exactly what we were doing before when designing a table view cell in a *.xib* file! I like being able to refer to my custom cell subviews with property names, so we'll use a table view cell subclass with outlets. Our procedure is just like what we did in the previous example:

1. In code, declare a UITableViewCell subclass — let's call it MyCell — with two outlet properties:

```
class MyCell : UITableViewCell {
    @IBOutlet var theLabel : UILabel!
    @IBOutlet var theImageView : UIImageView!
}
```

2. In the storyboard, select the table view's prototype cell and change its class in the Identity inspector to MyCell.

3. Drag a label and an image view into the prototype cell, position and configure them as desired, and connect the outlets from the cell to the respective subviews.

So far, so good; but there is one crucial question I have not yet answered: how will you tell the table view to get its cells from the storyboard? The answer is: by *not* calling register(_:forCellReuseIdentifier:)! Instead, when you call dequeue-ReusableCell(withIdentifier:for:), you supply an identifier that matches the *prototype cell's identifier* in the storyboard:

1. If you are calling register(_:forCellReuseIdentifier:) in RootView-Controller's code, *delete that line.*

2. In the storyboard, select the prototype cell. In the Attributes inspector, enter Cell (or whatever the string value of self.cellID is) in the Identifier field.

Now RootViewController's tableView(_:cellForRowAt:) works exactly as it did in the previous example:

```
let cell = tableView.dequeueReusableCell(
    withIdentifier: self.cellID, for: indexPath) as! MyCell
let lab = cell.theLabel
let iv = cell.theImageView
```

When your UITableViewController is to get its cells from the UITableView-Controller scene in the storyboard, there are several ways to go wrong. These are all common beginner mistakes:

Wrong view controller class

In the storyboard, make sure that your UITableViewController's class, in the Identity inspector, matches the class of your UITableViewController subclass in code. If you get this wrong, none of your table view controller code will run.

Wrong cell identifier

In the storyboard, make sure that the prototype cell identifier matches the reuse identifier in your code's dequeueReusableCell(withIdentifier:for:) call. If you get this wrong, your app will crash (with a helpful message in the console).

Wrong cell class

In the storyboard, make sure that your prototype cell's class, in the Identity inspector, is the class you expect to receive from dequeueReusableCell(with-Identifier:for:). If you get this wrong, your app will crash when the cell can't be cast down.

Wrong registration

In your table view controller code, make sure you do *not* call register(_:for-CellReuseIdentifier:). If you do call it, you will be telling the runtime *not* to get the cell from the storyboard. If you get this wrong by registering a nib, then (if you're lucky) your app will crash (with a helpful message in the console). If you get it wrong by registering a class, your cells might be mysteriously empty and your app might even crash when you access outlets that have never been connected.

Table View Data

As the preceding examples have shown, the structure and content of the actual data portrayed in a table view comes from the *data source*, an object pointed to by the table view's dataSource property and adopting the UITableViewDataSource protocol. The data source is the heart and soul of the table. What surprises beginners is that the data source operates not by *setting* the table view's structure and content, but by *responding on demand*. The data source, *qua* data source, consists of a set of methods that the table view will call whenever it needs information; in effect, the table view will ask your data source some questions. This architecture has important consequences for how you write your code, which can be summarized by these simple guidelines:

Be ready

Your data source cannot know *when* or *how often* any of these methods will be called, so it must be prepared to answer *any question at any time*.

Be fast

The table view is asking for data in real time; the user is probably scrolling through the table *right now*. So you mustn't gum up the works; you must be ready to supply responses as fast as possible.

Be consistent

There are multiple data source methods, and you cannot know *which* one will be called at a given moment. So you must make sure your responses are mutually consistent at *any* moment. A common beginner error is forgetting to take into account, in your data source methods, the possibility that the data might not yet be ready.

Another source of confusion for beginners is that methods are rather oddly distributed between the data source and the *delegate*, an object pointed to by the table view's delegate property and adopting the UITableViewDelegate protocol; in some cases, one may seem to be doing the job of the other. This is not usually a cause of any real difficulty, because the object serving as data source might also be the object serving as delegate. Nevertheless, it is rather inconvenient when you're consulting the documentation; you'll probably want to keep the data source and delegate documentation pages open simultaneously as you work.

 When you're using a table view controller with a corresponding table view in the storyboard (or in a *.xib* file created at the same time), the table view controller comes to you already configured as both the table view's data source and the table view's delegate. Creating a table view in some other way, and then forgetting to set its dataSource and delegate, is a common beginner mistake.

The Three Big Questions

Pretend now that you are the data source. Like Katherine Hepburn in *Pat and Mike*, the basis of your success is your ability, at any time, to answer the Three Big Questions; you must know the answers and be able to recite them at any moment:

How many sections does this table have?
> The table will call numberOfSections(in:); respond with an integer. In theory you can sometimes omit this method, as the default response is 1, which is often correct. However, I never omit it; for one thing, returning 0 is a good way to say that you've no data yet, and will prevent the table view from asking any other questions.

How many rows does this section have?
> The table will call tableView(_:numberOfRowsInSection:). The table supplies a section number — the first section is numbered 0 — and you respond with an integer. In a table with only one section there is probably no need to examine the incoming section number.

What cell goes in this row of this section?
> The table will call tableView(_:cellForRowAt:). The index path is expressed as an IndexPath; UITableView extends IndexPath to add two read-only properties — section and row. Using these, you extract the requested section number and row number, and return a fully configured UITableViewCell, ready for display in the table view. The first row of a section is numbered 0. I have already explained how to obtain the cell in the first place, by calling dequeueReusableCell(withIdentifier:for:) (see Example 8-2).

How you're going to fulfill these obligations depends on your data model and what your table is trying to portray. You can acquire and store and arrange your data whenever and however you like. The important thing is that you're going to be receiving an IndexPath specifying a section and a row, and you need to be able to lay your hands on the data corresponding to that slot *now* and configure the cell *now*. So construct your model, and your algorithm for consulting it in the Three Big Questions, in such a way that the data source can access any requested piece of data instantly.

Suppose our table is to list the names of the Pep Boys. Our table has only one section, so our data model can be very simple — an array of string names (`self.pep`). We're using a UITableViewController, and it is the table view's data source. So our code might look like this:

```
let pep = ["Manny", "Moe", "Jack"]
override func numberOfSections(in tableView: UITableView) -> Int {
    return 1
}
override func tableView(_ tableView: UITableView,
    numberOfRowsInSection section: Int) -> Int {
        return self.pep.count
}
override func tableView(_ tableView: UITableView,
    cellForRowAt indexPath: IndexPath) -> UITableViewCell {
        let cell = tableView.dequeueReusableCell(
            withIdentifier: self.cellID, for: indexPath)
        cell.textLabel!.text = pep[indexPath.row]
        return cell
}
```

At this point you may be feeling some exasperation. You want to object: "But that's trivial!" Exactly so! Your access to the data model *should* be trivial. That's the sign of a data model that's well designed for access by your table view's data source. There might be some interesting work to do in order to configure the *form* of the cell, but accessing the actual *data* should be simple and boring.

Above all, your data source methods must be *fast*. In particular, when `table-View(_:cellForRowAt:)` is called, the user is probably scrolling; you have only a few milliseconds to supply a cell, or else that scrolling will stutter. And the runtime itself is competing with you for those milliseconds, because even after you provide the cell, the runtime must perform layout and drawing on it, which are relatively expensive operations. You may be able to speed up layout and drawing by paying attention to the suggestions in the last section of Chapter 7. You may be able to obtain the data in advance of `tableView(_:cellForRowAt:)` by implementing *prefetching* in your data source. If that's not sufficient, you may have to skip portraying this data in the table, supply a placeholder, and insert the data into the table later. I'll give an example in Chapter 24.

There are two other ways to supply a table view with data; I'll discuss them later in this chapter:

- If the table view's entire structure and contents are known beforehand and won't change, you can design it in a storyboard as a *static* table and omit the Three Big Questions. See "Cell Choice and Static Tables" on page 505.
- Starting in iOS 13, you can use a *diffable data source* to hold the data and answer the Three Big Questions for you. This is useful especially when the table view's structure and contents can change before the user's eyes. See "Table View Diffable Data Source" on page 516.

Reusing Cells

An important goal of tableView(_:cellForRowAt:) is to conserve resources by reusing cells. As I've already explained, once a cell's row is no longer visible on the screen, that cell can be slotted into a row that *is* visible — with its portrayed data appropriately modified, of course! — so that only a few more than the number of simultaneously visible cells will ever need to be instantiated.

A table view is ready to implement this strategy for you; all you have to do is call dequeueReusableCell(withIdentifier:for:). For any given identifier, you'll be handed either a newly minted cell or a reused cell that previously appeared in the table view but is now no longer needed because it has scrolled out of view.

To prove to yourself the efficiency of the cell-caching architecture, do something to differentiate newly instantiated cells from reused cells, and keep track of the newly instantiated cells, like this:

```
override func numberOfSections(in tableView: UITableView) -> Int {
    return 1
}
override func tableView(_ tableView: UITableView,
    numberOfRowsInSection section: Int) -> Int {
        return 1000 // make a lot of rows this time!
}
var cells = 0
override func tableView(_ tableView: UITableView,
    cellForRowAt indexPath: IndexPath) -> UITableViewCell {
    let cell = tableView.dequeueReusableCell(
        withIdentifier: self.cellID, for: indexPath) as! MyCell
    let lab = cell.theLabel!
    lab.text = "Row \(indexPath.row) of section \(indexPath.section)"
    if lab.tag != 999 {
        lab.tag = 999
        self.cells += 1; print("New cell \(self.cells)")
    }
    return cell
}
```

When we run this code and scroll through the table, every cell is numbered correctly, so there appear to be 1000 cells. But the console messages show that only about a dozen distinct cells are ever actually created.

Be certain that *your* table view code passes that test, and that you are truly reusing cells! Fortunately, one of the benefits of calling dequeueReusableCell(with-Identifier:for:) is that it forces you to supply a valid reuse identifier. But it is still possible to subvert the architecture of cell reuse.

(For instance, you might obtain a cell in some improper way, such as instantiating it directly every time tableView(_:cellForRowAt:) is called; I have even seen beginners call dequeueReusableCell(withIdentifier:for:), only to throw away that cell and instantiate a fresh cell manually in the next line. Don't do that!)

Forgetting that cells are reused is the *single most common beginner mistake* associated with table views. Typically, everything in the table may look fine at first, but then when the table view is scrolled, incorrect values or incorrect interface will appear in some of the cells. The reason is that the cell you are configuring for a particular row in tableView(_:cellForRowAt:) (step 6 in Example 8-2) may already have been configured for some other row. Therefore you must configure *everything* about the cell that might need configuring, with your logic covering *every* possible case, making *no assumptions* about the prior state of the cell. Otherwise, the cell may retain unwanted state from its previous use in a different row.

As usual, I learned that lesson the hard way. (I was a beginner once!) In the TidBITS News app, there was a little loudspeaker icon that should appear in a given cell in the master view's table view only if a recording was associated with this article. So I initially wrote this code:

```
if item.enclosures != nil && item.enclosures.count > 0 {
    cell.speaker.isHidden = false
}
```

At first, everything seemed to be fine; but after scrolling the table view up and down a few times, I ended up with a loudspeaker icon in just about every cell! Do you see why? Once you start scrolling, your cells are likely to be reused. Based on my code, a reused cell will *always* have a visible loudspeaker icon if, in a previous usage, that cell has *ever* had a visible loudspeaker icon!

The solution was to rewrite the logic to *cover all possibilities completely*, like this:

```
cell.speaker.isHidden =
    !(item.enclosures != nil && item.enclosures.count > 0)
```

You do get a sort of second bite of the cherry: there's a delegate method, table-View(_:willDisplay:forRowAt:), that is called for every cell just before it appears in the table. This is absolutely the last minute to configure a cell. But don't misuse this method. You're functioning as the delegate here, not the data source; you may set the final details of the cell's appearance, but you shouldn't be consulting the data model at this point. It is of great importance that you not do anything even slightly time-consuming in `tableView(_:willDisplay:forRowAt:)`; the cell is literally just milliseconds away from appearing in the interface.

An additional delegate method is `tableView(_:didEndDisplaying:forRowAt:)`. This tells you that the cell no longer appears in the interface and has become free for reuse. You could take advantage of this to tear down any resource-heavy customization of the cell or simply to prepare it somehow for subsequent future reuse.

The table view can maintain more than one cache of reusable cells; this could be useful if your table view contains more than one type of cell (where the meaning of "type of cell" is pretty much up to you). This is why you must *name* each cache by attaching a reuse identifier string to each cell. All the examples in this chapter use just one cache and just one identifier, but there can be more than one. If you're using a storyboard as a source of cells, there would then need to be more than one prototype cell.

Self-Configuring Cells

There is a school of thought according to which our implementation of the data source method `tableView(_:cellForRowAt:)` is doing too much work. In particular, it knows too much:

```
let cell = tableView.dequeueReusableCell(
    withIdentifier: self.cellID, for: indexPath) as! MyCell
let lab = cell.theLabel
let iv = cell.theImageView
// ... configure lab and iv here ...
```

Arguably, it should be none of the data source's business to know about the subviews of the cell. The only thing that should matter to the data source is the *data* — the information to be displayed in the cell. How the cell displays that data should be the *cell's* business.

When we're using a custom UITableViewCell subclass, it's easy to conform to that philosophy. Our cell subclass needs two things:

A configuration type
> The cell subclass declares a value type (a collection of properties) sufficient for transporting all the relevant data from the data source to the cell.

A configuration method
> The cell subclass declares a method that accepts an instance of the configuration type. When this method is called, the cell applies the data to its own interface. In this way, the cell configures itself.

Let's modify the custom cell subclass MyCell to embody this approach. The data consists of the text and the image, so that's what the cell's configuration type asks for:

```
struct Configuration {
    let text: String
    let image: UIImage
}
```

The cell subclass also needs a configuration method. This method does exactly what tableView(_:cellForRowAt:) was doing previously; the only difference is that the data comes from the Configuration object that's passed in to the method call:

```
func configure(_ configuration: Configuration) {
    let lab = self.theLabel!
    lab.text = configuration.text
    let iv = self.theImageView!
    let im = configuration.image
    let r = UIGraphicsImageRenderer(
        size:CGSize(36,36), format:im.imageRendererFormat)
    let im2 = r.image { _ in
        im.draw(in:CGRect(0,0,36,36))
    }
    iv.image = im2
    iv.contentMode = .center
}
```

The work of the data source's tableView(_:cellForRowAt:) is now greatly reduced; it passes the data across to the cell and returns the cell:

```
override func tableView(_ tableView: UITableView,
    cellForRowAt indexPath: IndexPath) -> UITableViewCell {
        let cell = tableView.dequeueReusableCell(
            withIdentifier: self.cellID, for: indexPath) as! MyCell
        let s = "The author of this book, who would rather be out dirt biking"
        let im = UIImage(named:"moi.png")!
        let config = MyCell.Configuration(text: s, image: im)
        cell.configure(config)
        return cell
}
```

That's a toy example, but it has broad implications. This approach might seem to be more work at the outset, but it makes for a clean, small data source, and it scales up brilliantly; there might be lots of data to be displayed in a cell, and there might be more than one type of cell displaying different kinds of data, but the data source doesn't become significantly bigger. There are programmers who use that sort of architecture for every table view.

Apple's Cell Configuration Architecture

New in iOS 14, Apple has adopted the sort of philosophy I described in the preceding section. UITableViewCell itself now has a contentConfiguration property and a backgroundConfiguration property, and you can set these to configure the cell.

What you set them to are a UIContentConfiguration and a UIBackgroundConfiguration, respectively.

Content configuration

For the cell's content, you will typically ask the cell for its `defaultContent-Configuration()`; the cell hands you a UIListContentConfiguration object (conforming to UIContentConfiguration). You assign values to the desired properties of the configuration object, and assign it to the cell's `contentConfiguration`. The runtime uses the content configuration to form a new content view for the cell, literally replacing the cell's content view with this one.

This approach is useful particularly if your cell is one of the built-in cell styles. UIListContentConfiguration has data properties `text`, `secondaryText`, and `image`, along with properties for dictating how that data should be displayed: `textProperties`, `secondaryTextProperties`, and `imageProperties`. Text properties are somewhat like label properties; you can dictate font, color, number of lines, alignment, and so forth. Image properties include symbol configuration, tint color, corner radius, and maximum size. In addition, you get a little flexibility in the layout; UIListContentConfiguration properties let you specify the margins and the padding between the subviews.

To illustrate, here's what you'd say to get Figure 8-4 using a cell's built-in UIListContentConfiguration:

```
override func tableView(_ tableView: UITableView,
    cellForRowAt indexPath: IndexPath) -> UITableViewCell {
        let cell = tableView.dequeueReusableCell(
            withIdentifier: self.cellID, for: indexPath)
        var config = cell.defaultContentConfiguration()
        config.textProperties.color = .red
        config.text = "Hello there! \(indexPath.row)"
        cell.contentConfiguration = config
        return cell
}
```

Under this architecture, your code no longer speaks of the cell's subviews. You don't refer to the cell's `textLabel`, its `detailTextLabel`, or its `imageView`. You just provide textual and image data, along with some formatting instructions, and let the configuration worry about how to display the data.

Another benefit is that you no longer have to worry about what features of the cell have already been configured due to cell reuse. You simply describe the cell and let the runtime concern itself with display. Apple assures us that the configuration is applied in an efficient manner.

Apple apparently feels so strongly about the superiority of this approach that the textLabel, detailTextLabel, and imageView cell properties are slated for eventual deprecation.

You are free to insert your own cell subviews together with those created by the UIListContentConfiguration. For example, in tableView(_:cellForRowAt:), as soon as you have set the cell's contentConfiguration property, you can fetch the cell's contentView, which is now a UIListContentView, and add subviews to it, just as we were doing earlier. You can't access the views added by the configuration — there is no textLabel, for example — but you can find out where they are, for purposes of autolayout, by accessing the content view's textLayoutGuide, secondaryTextLayout-Guide, and imageLayoutGuide. Here, picking up from the previous example, I'll add an image to the right of the label inserted by the configuration's text property:

```
// ... as before ...
cell.contentConfiguration = config
if let cv = cell.contentView as? UIListContentView,
    cv.viewWithTag(1) == nil {
        let guide = cv.textLayoutGuide!
        let iv = UIImageView(image: UIImage(systemName: "hand.point.left"))
        iv.tag = 1
        iv.tintColor = .black
        iv.translatesAutoresizingMaskIntoConstraints = false
        cv.addSubview(iv)
        iv.leadingAnchor.constraint(
            equalToSystemSpacingAfter: guide.trailingAnchor,
            multiplier: 1).isActive = true
        iv.centerYAnchor.constraint(
            equalTo: guide.centerYAnchor).isActive = true
}
return cell
```

Custom content configuration

The preceding examples assume that we are starting with one of the built-in cell styles. But what if the cell subviews are completely custom? Can you still take advantage of Apple's configuration architecture?

You can, but to do so, you would need to supply your own configuration type that adopts UIContentConfiguration, so that you can define your own properties. This means that your configuration type must implement makeContentView() and updated(for:).

To illustrate, pretend that we have four pieces of text to display in the cell. Presumably these pieces of text would appear as UILabels, but the point of a configuration is that that's a display implementation detail, irrelevant to the configuration's own public interface. Here's how we might define a custom configuration type that adopts UIContentConfiguration:

```
struct Configuration : UIContentConfiguration {
    let text1: String
    let text2: String
    let text3: String
    let text4: String
    func makeContentView() -> UIView & UIContentView {
        let c = MyContentView(configuration: self) // *
        return c
    }
    func updated(for state: UIConfigurationState) -> Self {
        return self
    }
}
```

(The state in updated(for:) refers primarily to whether the cell is selected. I'll talk about cell selection later in this chapter. In real life, our updated(for:) implementation might respond to a change in state by returning a version of this configuration with some property changed; but in this case there is nothing to do, so we just return self.)

In that code, we have posited the existence of MyContentView, a UIView subclass that adopts UIContentView, meaning that it has a configuration property. Now we need to declare that class! This is where we'll give the view its subviews and apply the configuration; in this case, applying the configuration means simply setting the text of the four labels. I'll separate those two tasks. Our initializer adds the subviews; a private configure method gives them their content:

```
class MyContentView: UIView, UIContentView {
    var configuration: UIContentConfiguration {
        didSet {
            self.configure()
        }
    }
    // the subviews
    private let lab1 = UILabel()
    private let lab2 = UILabel()
    private let lab3 = UILabel()
    private let lab4 = UILabel()
    init(configuration: UIContentConfiguration) {
        self.configuration = configuration
        super.init(frame: .zero)
        // ... set up the labels ...
        // add them as subviews to self
        self.addSubview(lab1)
        self.addSubview(lab2)
        self.addSubview(lab3)
        self.addSubview(lab4)
        // ... set up autolayout constraints ...
        self.configure()
    }
    required init?(coder: NSCoder) {
```

```
        fatalError("init(coder:) has not been implemented")
    }
    private func configure() {
        guard let config = self.configuration as? Configuration else {
            return
        }
        self.lab1.text = config.text1
        self.lab2.text = config.text2
        self.lab3.text = config.text3
        self.lab4.text = config.text4
    }
}
```

Note the implementation of the `configuration` setter observer. If at some point in the future we are assigned a new `configuration` because of a state change, the setter observer simply calls `self.configure()` to set the texts of the labels again, with no need to reconstruct the subviews themselves. In real life, we could gain some further efficiency by examining the incoming configuration; if it is identical to the current configuration, there's no need to call `self.configure()`.

The upshot is that we can now talk like this in our `tableView(_:cellForRowAt:)` implementation:

```
override func tableView(_ tableView: UITableView,
    cellForRowAt indexPath: IndexPath) -> UITableViewCell {
        let cell = tableView.dequeueReusableCell(
            withIdentifier: self.cellID, for: indexPath) as! MyCell
        let config = MyCell.Configuration(
            text1: "Harpo",
            text2: "Groucho",
            text3: "Chico",
            text4: "Zeppo"
        )
        cell.contentConfiguration = config
        return cell
}
```

Unfortunately, it seems that the content view interface *must* be created in code. We can't load the cell ready-made from a nib, because the content view of the cell loaded from the nib, along with all its subviews, will be *replaced* by the content view returned from our `makeContentView` implementation! So Apple's configuration architecture can't be used with a cell that you've designed in the storyboard or a *.xib* file.

Background configuration

Adapting your code to use the UIBackgroundConfiguration object is slightly different. You start by calling a UIBackgroundConfiguration static method to create the background configuration. The configuration object has properties like `customView` and `backgroundColor`, and you set them to configure the background.

To illustrate, here's how to use a UIBackgroundConfiguration to get the cell background shown in Figure 8-5:

```
override func tableView(_ tableView: UITableView,
    cellForRowAt indexPath: IndexPath) -> UITableViewCell {
        let cell = tableView.dequeueReusableCell(
            withIdentifier: self.cellID, for: indexPath)
        var config = cell.defaultContentConfiguration()
        config.textProperties.color = .red
        config.text = "Hello there! \(indexPath.row)"
        cell.contentConfiguration = config
        var back = UIBackgroundConfiguration.listPlainCell()
        back.backgroundColor = .red
        let v = UIImageView(image: UIImage(named:"linen.png"))
        v.contentMode = .scaleToFill
        back.customView = v
        cell.backgroundConfiguration = back
        return cell
}
```

So far, so good. Recall, however, that Figure 8-5 was generated by setting the cell's selectedBackgroundView, putting a transparent blue cast over the background when the cell is selected. Unfortunately, a UIBackgroundConfiguration has no such property; there is nothing about our back object that responds to the cell being selected.

To work around that, we have to remove our background configuration code from tableView(_:cellForRowAt:) and instead override the cell's update-Configuration(using:) method. This method, new in iOS 14, is called whenever the background is needed, including when the cell's state changes. The state parameter tells us whether the cell is selected, so we can respond differently if so. There is *still* no selectedBackgroundView, so we have to modify the customView directly with the blue transparent cast:

```
override func updateConfiguration(using state: UICellConfigurationState) {
    var back = UIBackgroundConfiguration.listPlainCell().updated(for: state)
    let v = UIImageView(image: UIImage(named:"linen.png"))
    v.contentMode = .scaleToFill
    if state.isSelected || state.isHighlighted {
        let v2 = UIView()
        v2.backgroundColor = UIColor.blue.withAlphaComponent(0.2)
        v.addSubview(v2)
        v2.frame = v.bounds
        v2.autoresizingMask = [.flexibleWidth, .flexibleHeight]
    }
    back.customView = v
    back.backgroundColor = .red
    self.backgroundConfiguration = back
}
```

Table View Sections

Your table data may be grouped into multiple sections. Here are some reasons why you might do that:

- You want to clump the table cells into groups in the table view.
- You want to display section headers (or footers, or both) in the table view.
- You want to make navigation of the table view easier through an index.
- You want to facilitate rearranging entire portions of the table view contents.

A table that is to have sections may require some planning in the construction and architecture of its data model. In order to answer the Three Big Questions, you need to know immediately how many sections your data has and how many rows a given section has; then, given a section number and a row number, you need to be able to fetch the data for that row. Clearly a simple array of individual row data, like the array of strings listing the names of the Pep Boys in our earlier example, is not going to be sufficient.

A section-based data structure typically needs two levels. A standard minimal approach is an array of sections, each section containing an array of row data, as shown in Example 8-3.

Example 8-3. Section-based data

```
struct Row {
    // properties pertaining to each row
}
struct Section {
    // properties pertaining to each section
    var rowData : [Row]
}
var sections = [Section]() // data model
```

Now the Three Big Questions are easy to answer:

- The number of sections is `self.sections.count`.
- The number of rows in the section numbered `section` is `self.sections[section].rowData.count`.
- Your implementation of `tableView(_:cellForRowAt:)` can index into the section with `indexPath.section`, and from there into the row data with `indexPath.row`:

  ```
  let data = self.sections[indexPath.section].rowData[indexPath.row]
  ```

The details will depend on the exact nature of your data and what you want to portray in your table. You will very likely want a section-based table view to have section headers, so I'll talk about that before giving an example.

Section Headers and Footers

A section header or footer appears between the cells, before the first row of a section or after the last row of a section, respectively. In a nongrouped table, a section header or footer detaches itself while the user scrolls the table, pinning itself to the top or bottom of the table view and floating over the scrolled rows, giving the user a clue, at every moment, as to where we are within the table. Also, a section header or footer can contain custom views, so it's a place where you might put additional information, or even functional interface, such as a button the user can tap.

 Don't confuse the section headers and footers with the header and footer of the table as a whole. The latter are properties of the table view itself, its `tableHeaderView` and `tableFooterView`, discussed earlier in this chapter. The table header view appears only when the table is scrolled all the way down; the table footer view appears only when the table is scrolled all the way up.

The number of sections is determined by your reply to the first Big Question, `numberOfSections(in:)`. For each section, the table view will consult your data source and delegate to learn whether this section has a header or a footer, or both, or neither (the default).

A section header or footer in the table view will usually be a UITableViewHeaderFooterView. This is a UIView subclass intended specifically for this purpose; much like a table view cell, it is reusable. It has the following properties:

`textLabel`
A label (UILabel) for displaying the text of the header or footer.

`detailTextLabel`
This label, if you set its text, appears only in a grouped style table.

`contentView`
A subview of the header or footer, to which you can add custom subviews.

`backgroundView`
Any view you want to assign. The `contentView` is in front of the `backgroundView`. The `contentView` has a clear background by default, so the `backgroundView` shows through.

If the `backgroundView` is `nil` (the default), the header or footer view will supply its own background view whose `backgroundColor` is derived (in some unspecified way) from the table's `backgroundColor`. You shouldn't set a UITableView-

HeaderFooterView's `backgroundColor`; instead, give it a `backgroundView` and set that view's `backgroundColor`.

New in iOS 14, just as I described for cells in the previous section, Apple wants to deprecate `textLabel` and `detailTextLabel` and replace them with the new configuration-based architecture. A UITableViewHeaderFooterView has `content-Configuration` and `backgroundConfiguration` properties, and if your needs are simple, you can easily populate the view by passing data to them. You can set the `text`, `secondaryText` (even in a nongrouped table), and `image` properties of the content configuration just as you would in a cell; so in that respect this approach gives you more built-in views to play with.

There are two ways in which you can supply a header or footer. You can use both, but it will be less confusing if you pick just one:

Header or footer title string

You implement one or both of these data source methods:

- `tableView(_:titleForHeaderInSection:)`
- `tableView(_:titleForFooterInSection:)`

Return `nil` to indicate that the given section has no header (or footer). The header or footer view itself is a UITableViewHeaderFooterView, and is reused automatically. The string you supply becomes the view's `textLabel.text`.

(In a grouped style table, the string's capitalization may be changed. To avoid that, use the second way of supplying the header or footer.)

Header or footer view

You implement one or both of these delegate methods:

- `tableView(_:viewForHeaderInSection:)`
- `tableView(_:viewForFooterInSection:)`

The view you supply is used as the entire header or footer and is automatically resized to the table's width and the section header or footer height. (I'll discuss in a moment how the height is determined.)

When you implement `viewFor...`, you are not required to return a UITableView-HeaderFooterView, but you should do so. The procedure is much like making a cell reusable:

1. You register beforehand with the table view by calling `register(_:forHeader-FooterViewReuseIdentifier:)` with the UITableViewHeaderFooterView class or a subclass.

Designing a Section Header View in the Nib Editor

It would be great to be able to design a table view section header (or footer) view in the nib editor — but you can't. That's because of a massive shortcoming in Xcode: The nib editor's Library doesn't include a UITableViewHeaderFooterView!

The irony is that there's a UITableView method that *would* allow you to do this *if* the Library included a UITableViewHeaderFooterView. In theory, you can call `register(_:forHeaderFooterViewReuseIdentifier:)` to register a nib instead of a class, just as with a UITableViewCell. But without a UITableViewHeaderFooterView in the nib, you can never call that method; it is useless.

Some popular "solutions" attempt to circumvent this shortcoming by misusing a UITableViewCell prototype as a header, or by putting a UIView in a nib and setting its class in the Identity inspector to be UITableViewHeaderFooterView. Those don't work; don't try them. Unless Apple fixes this bug, you *can't* design a header or footer view in a nib and that's that. A viable workaround is: Design an ordinary UIView in a nib. Implement the `viewFor` delegate method to load that nib, obtain the view, and insert it inside a UITableViewHeaderFooterView's `contentView`.

2. To obtain the reusable view, call `dequeueReusableHeaderFooterView(with-Identifier:)` on the table view; the result will be either a newly instantiated view or a reused view.

3. You can then configure this view as desired. You can set its `textLabel.text`; you can give its `contentView` custom subviews. In the latter case, use autoresizing or constraints to ensure that the subviews will be positioned and sized appropriately when the view itself is resized. Alternatively, new in iOS 14, use the `content-Configuration` and `backgroundConfiguration` properties.

In addition, these delegate methods permit you to perform final configurations on your header or footer views:

`tableView(_:willDisplayHeaderView:forSection:)`
`tableView(_:willDisplayFooterView:forSection:)`

You can perform further configurations here, if desired. If you generated the default UITableViewHeaderFooterView by implementing `titleFor...`, you can tweak it here. These delegate methods are matched by `didEndDisplaying` methods.

The runtime resizes your header or footer before displaying it. Its width will be the table view's width; its height will be the table view's `sectionHeaderHeight` or `sectionFooterHeight` unless you implement one of these delegate methods to say otherwise:

```
tableView(_:heightForHeaderInSection:)
tableView(_:heightForFooterInSection:)
```
Returning 0 (or failing to dictate the height at all) hides the header or footer.

Returning UITableView.automaticDimension means 0 if titleFor... returns nil or the empty string (or isn't implemented); otherwise, it means the table view's sectionHeaderHeight or sectionFooterHeight.

 Starting in iOS 11, you can size a section header or footer from the inside out, using autolayout constraints. I'll talk about that later in this chapter.

A header or footer view in a nongrouped table is in front of the table's cells. Moreover, when a header or footer view is not pinned to the top or bottom of the table view, there is a transparent gap behind it. You'll want to take that into account when designing your header or footer view.

Table View Section Example

Here's a simple example to illustrate a table view with sections. Suppose we intend to display the names of all 50 U.S. states in alphabetical order as the rows of a table view, and that we wish to divide the table into sections according to the first letter of each state's name. We'll have section headers, each consisting of a single letter of the alphabet; the cells of each section will list the names of the states that start with that letter.

Let's adapt the sectioned data scheme from Example 8-3 to our use case. The only section-related property we need, besides the rowData, is the name of the section; the only thing we intend to display in our table view cells is the name of the state, so the row data for each cell can be a String:

```
struct Section {
    var sectionName : String
    var rowData : [String]
}
var sections : [Section]() // data model
```

Let's say I have the alphabetized list of state names as a text file, which starts like this:

```
Alabama
Alaska
Arizona
Arkansas
California
Colorado
Connecticut
Delaware
...
```

I'll prepare the data model by loading the text file and parsing it into a Section array:

```
override func viewDidLoad() {
    super.viewDidLoad()
    let s = try! String(
        contentsOfFile: Bundle.main.path(
            forResource: "states", ofType: "txt")!)
    let states = s.components(separatedBy:"\n")
    let d = Dictionary(grouping: states) {String($0.prefix(1))}
    self.sections = Array(d).sorted {$0.key < $1.key}.map {
        Section(sectionName: $0.key, rowData: $0.value)
    }
    // ...
}
```

The value of this preparatory dance is evident when we are bombarded with questions from the table view about cells and headers; supplying the answers is trivial, just as it should be:

```
override func numberOfSections(in tableView: UITableView) -> Int {
    return self.sections.count
}
override func tableView(_ tableView: UITableView,
    numberOfRowsInSection section: Int) -> Int {
        return self.sections[section].rowData.count
}
override func tableView(_ tableView: UITableView,
    cellForRowAt indexPath: IndexPath) -> UITableViewCell {
        let cell = tableView.dequeueReusableCell(
            withIdentifier: self.cellID, for: indexPath)
        let s = self.sections[indexPath.section].rowData[indexPath.row]
        cell.textLabel!.text = s
        return cell
}
override func tableView(_ tableView: UITableView,
    titleForHeaderInSection section: Int) -> String? {
        return self.sections[section].sectionName
}
```

Let's modify that example to illustrate creation of a custom section header view with tableView(_:viewForHeaderInSection:). I register my header identifier in viewDid-Load:

```
let headerID = "Header"
override func viewDidLoad() {
    super.viewDidLoad()
    // ...
    self.tableView.register(UITableViewHeaderFooterView.self,
        forHeaderFooterViewReuseIdentifier: self.headerID)
}
```

We delete `tableView(_:titleForHeaderInSection:)` and implement `table-View(_:viewForHeaderInSection:)` instead. For completely new views, I'll place my own label inside the `contentView` and give it some basic configuration; then I'll perform individual configuration on all views, new or reused:

```
override func tableView(_ tableView: UITableView,
    viewForHeaderInSection section: Int) -> UIView? {
        let h = tableView.dequeueReusableHeaderFooterView(
            withIdentifier: self.headerID)!
        if h.viewWithTag(1) == nil {
            h.backgroundView = UIView()
            h.backgroundView?.backgroundColor = .black
            let lab = UILabel()
            lab.tag = 1
            lab.font = UIFont(name:"Georgia-Bold", size:22)
            lab.textColor = .green
            lab.backgroundColor = .clear
            h.contentView.addSubview(lab)
            // ... add constraints ...
        }
        let lab = h.contentView.viewWithTag(1) as! UILabel
        lab.text = self.sections[section].sectionName
        return h
}
```

Just as I suggested earlier that one might move the physical configuration of a cell off into a cell subclass, so here we can neaten things up considerably by subclassing UITableViewHeaderFooterView and moving most of that code into the subclass. I'll call the subclass MyHeader, and I'll remember to register it, instead of UITableViewHeaderFooterView, as the class of the header. I'll give it a Configuration struct with a `sectionName` property, and a `configure(_:)` method that does almost everything from my `tableView(_:viewForHeaderInSection:)` implementation, which becomes much simpler:

```
override func tableView(_ tableView: UITableView,
    viewForHeaderInSection section: Int) -> UIView? {
        let h = tableView.dequeueReusableHeaderFooterView(
            withIdentifier: self.headerID) as! MyHeader
        let config = MyHeader.Configuration(
            sectionName: self.sections[section].sectionName)
        h.configure(config)
        return h
}
```

Alternatively, new in iOS 14, we can use Apple's configuration architecture:

```
override func tableView(_ tableView: UITableView,
    viewForHeaderInSection section: Int) -> UIView? {
        let h = tableView.dequeueReusableHeaderFooterView(
            withIdentifier: self.headerID)!
        var config = h.defaultContentConfiguration()
```

```
        config.text = self.sections[section].sectionName
        config.textProperties.color = .green
        config.textProperties.font = UIFont(name:"Georgia-Bold", size:22)!
        var back = UIBackgroundConfiguration.listPlainHeaderFooter()
        back.backgroundColor = .black
        h.contentConfiguration = config
        h.backgroundConfiguration = back
        return h
    }
```

Section Index

If your table view has the plain style, you can add an index down the side of the table, where the user can tap or drag to jump to the start of a section — helpful for navigating long tables. To generate the index, implement the data source method `section-IndexTitles(for:)`, returning an array of string titles to appear as entries in the index.

For our list of state names, that's trivial, just as it should be:

```
override func sectionIndexTitles(for tv: UITableView) -> [String]? {
    return self.sections.map {$0.sectionName}
}
```

The index can appear even if there are no section headers. It will appear only if the number of rows exceeds the table view's `sectionIndexMinimumDisplayRowCount` property value; the default is 0, so the index is always displayed by default. You will want the index entries to be short — preferably just one character — because each cell's content view will shrink to compensate, so you're sacrificing some cell real estate.

You can modify three table view properties that affect the index's appearance:

`sectionIndexColor`
> The index text color.

`sectionIndexBackgroundColor`
> The index background color. I advise giving the index some background color, because otherwise the index distorts the colors of what's behind it in a distracting way.

`sectionIndexTrackingBackgroundColor`
> The index background color while the user's finger is sliding over it. By default, it's the same as the `sectionIndexBackgroundColor`.

Normally, there will be a one-to-one correspondence between the index entries and the sections; when the user taps an index entry, the table jumps to the start of the corresponding section. But under certain circumstances you may want to customize this correspondence. Suppose there are 100 sections, but there isn't room to display

100 index entries comfortably on the iPhone. The index will automatically curtail itself, omitting some index entries and inserting bullets to suggest the omission, but you might prefer to take charge of the situation.

To do so, supply a shorter index, and implement the data source method `table-View(_:sectionForSectionIndexTitle:at:)`, returning the number of the section to jump to. You are told both the title and the index number of the section index listing that the user chose, so you can use whichever is convenient.

 If the table view has a section index, its scroll indicators will never appear.

Variable Row Heights

Most tables have rows that are all the same height, as set by the table view's `row-Height`. It is possible, though, for different rows to have different heights. You can see an example in the TidBITS News app (Figure 6-1).

Back when I first wrote my TidBITS News and Albumen apps for iOS 4, variable row heights were possible but virtually unheard-of; I knew of no other app that was using them, and Apple provided no guidance, so I had to invent my own technique by trial and error. There were three main challenges:

Measurement
    What should the height of a given row be?

Timing
    When should the determination of each row's height be made?

Layout
    How should the *subviews* of each cell be configured for its individual height?

Over the years since then, implementing variable row heights has become considerably easier:

- In iOS 6, with the advent of autolayout, both measurement and layout became much simpler.

- In iOS 7, new table view properties made it possible to improve the timing.

- iOS 8 permitted variable row heights to be implemented *automatically* using autolayout, without your having to worry about any of these problems.

- Starting in iOS 11, section header and footer heights can be implemented automatically as well.

I will briefly describe, in historical order, four different techniques that I have used over the years in my own apps.

Manual Row Height Measurement

In its earliest incarnation, my variable row heights technique depends on the delegate's `tableView(_:heightForRowAt:)`. Whatever height I return for a given row, that's the height that the cell at that row will be given.

The timing is interesting. Before our `tableView(_:cellForRowAt:)` is called for even *one* row, we are sent `tableView(_:heightForRowAt:)` for *every* row. In preparation for this situation, I start with an array of Optional CGFloats stored in a property, `self.rowHeights`. (Assume, for simplicity, that the table has just one section, so that the row number can serve directly as an index into the array.) Initially, all the values in the array are `nil`. Once the real values have been filled in, the array can be used to supply a requested height instantly.

To calculate the cell heights, I have a utility method, `setUpCell(_:for:)`. It takes a cell and an index path, lays out the cell using the actual data for that row, and returns (as a CGFloat) the height required for the cell to accommodate that layout.

(Before the days of autolayout, doing the actual work of measurement in `setUpCell(_:for:)` was laborious; I had to lay out the cell manually, assigning a frame to each subview, one by one. The main challenge was dealing with labels whose text, and therefore height, could vary from row to row. I'll spare you the gory details!)

When the delegate's `tableView(_:heightForRowAt:)` is called, either this is the very first time it has been called or it isn't. So either we've already constructed `self.rowHeights` or we haven't. If we haven't, we construct it now, by immediately calling the `setUpCell(_:for:)` utility method for *every row* and storing each resulting height in `self.rowHeights`. The cell that I'm passing to `setUpCell(_:for:)` isn't going into the table; it's just a dummy copy of the cell, to give me something to configure and work out the resulting cell height. From now on, I'm ready to answer `tableView(_:heightForRowAt:)` for *any* row, *immediately* — all I have to do is return the appropriate value from the `self.rowHeights` array:

```
override func tableView(_ tableView: UITableView,
    heightForRowAt indexPath: IndexPath) -> CGFloat {
        let ix = indexPath.row
        if self.rowHeights[ix] == nil {
            let objects = UINib(nibName: "MyCell", bundle: nil)
                .instantiate(withOwner: nil)
            let cell = objects.first as! UITableViewCell
            for ix in 0..<self.rowHeights.count {
                let indexPath = IndexPath(row: ix, section: 0)
                let h = self.setUpCell(cell, for: indexPath)
                self.rowHeights[ix] = h
```

```
        }
    }
    return self.rowHeights[ix]!
}
```

My `setUpCell(_:for:)` utility is also called by `tableView(_:cellForRowAt:)`, but now I'm laying out the *real* cell (and ignoring the returned height value):

```
override func tableView(_ tableView: UITableView,
    cellForRowAt indexPath: IndexPath) -> UITableViewCell {
        let cell = tableView.dequeueReusableCell(
            withIdentifier: self.cellID, for: indexPath)
        self.setUpCell(cell, for:indexPath)
        return cell
}
```

Measurement and Layout with Constraints

With autolayout in the picture, constraints are of great assistance. They obviously perform layout of each cell for us, because that's what constraints do. But they can also perform measurement of the height of each cell. If constraints ultimately pin every subview to the `contentView` in such a way as to size the `contentView` height unambiguously *from the inside out*, then we can simply call `systemLayoutSize-Fitting(_:)` on the `contentView` to learn the resulting height of the cell.

My `setUpCell(_:for:)` no longer needs to perform any layout, calculate any heights, or return a value; I hand it a reference to a cell, it puts the data into the cell, and now I can do whatever I like with that cell. If this is the model cell being used for measurement in `tableView(_:heightForRowAt:)`, I call `systemLayoutSizeFitting(_:)` to get the height:

```
override func tableView(_ tableView: UITableView,
    heightForRowAt indexPath: IndexPath) -> CGFloat {
        let ix = indexPath.row
        if self.rowHeights[ix] == nil {
            let objects = UINib(nibName: "MyCell", bundle: nil)
                .instantiate(withOwner: nil)
            let cell = objects.first as! UITableViewCell
            for ix in 0..<self.rowHeights.count {
                let indexPath = IndexPath(row: ix, section: 0)
                self.setUpCell(cell, for: indexPath)
                let v = cell.contentView                  // *
                let sz = v.systemLayoutSizeFitting(
                    UIView.layoutFittingCompressedSize)   // *
                self.rowHeights[ix] = sz.height
            }
        }
        return self.rowHeights[ix]!
}
```

If this is the real cell generated by dequeuing in `tableView(_:cellForRowAt:)`, I simply set up the cell and return it, as before.

Estimated Height

In iOS 7, three new table view properties were introduced:

- `estimatedRowHeight`
- `estimatedSectionHeaderHeight`
- `estimatedSectionFooterHeight`

To accompany those, there are also three table view delegate methods:

- `tableView(_:estimatedHeightForRowAt:)`
- `tableView(_:estimatedHeightForHeaderInSection:)`
- `tableView(_:estimatedHeightForFooterInSection:)`

The idea here is to reduce the amount of time spent calculating row heights at the outset. If you supply an estimated row height, then when `tableView(_:heightForRowAt:)` is called initially, before the table is displayed, it is called *only for the visible cells* of the table; for the remaining cells, the *estimated* height is used. In this way, the runtime obtains enough information to lay out the entire table very quickly: the only real heights you have to provide up front are those of the initially visible rows. The downside is that this layout is only an approximation, and will have to be corrected later. As new rows are scrolled into view, `tableView(_:heightForRowAt:)` will be called for those new rows, and the layout of the whole table will be revised accordingly.

In my implementation, the estimated height is set in `viewDidLoad` (it can alternatively be set in the nib editor):

```
self.tableView.estimatedRowHeight = 75
```

Now in my `tableView(_:heightForRowAt:)` implementation, when I find that a requested height value in `self.rowHeights` is nil, I don't fill in *all* the values of `self.rowHeights` — I fill in *just that one height*. It's simply a matter of removing the for loop:

```
override func tableView(_ tableView: UITableView,
    heightForRowAt indexPath: IndexPath) -> CGFloat {
        let ix = indexPath.row
        if self.rowHeights[ix] == nil {
            let objects = UINib(nibName: "MyCell", bundle: nil)
                .instantiate(withOwner: nil)
            let cell = objects.first as! UITableViewCell
            let indexPath = IndexPath(row: ix, section: 0)
            self.setUpCell(cell, for: indexPath)
```

```
            let v = cell.contentView
            let sz = v.systemLayoutSizeFitting(
                UIView.layoutFittingCompressedSize)
            self.rowHeights[ix] = sz.height
        }
        return self.rowHeights[ix]!
    }
```

Automatic Row Height

Starting in iOS 8, a completely automatic calculation of variable row heights was introduced. This, in effect, does behind the scenes what I'm doing in `table-View(_:heightForRowAt:)` in the preceding code: it relies upon autolayout to calculate a cell's height from the inside out based on the constraints of its subviews, and it performs that calculation and caches a row's height the first time it is needed, before it appears on the screen.

To use the automatic row height mechanism, all you have to do is to set the table view's `estimatedRowHeight` — and *don't* implement `tableView(_:heightForRow-At:)`. In some cases, it may be necessary to set the table view's row height to `UITable-View.automaticDimension` as well (again, this can be configured in the nib editor):

```
self.tableView.rowHeight = UITableView.automaticDimension
self.tableView.estimatedRowHeight = 75
```

Once I've done that, I can adopt this approach in my app just by deleting my `table-View(_:heightForRowAt:)` implementation entirely!

Starting in iOS 11, you don't even have to supply an `estimatedRowHeight`; it can be `UITableView.automaticDimension` as well. Basically, the rule is that if the `rowHeight` is `UITableView.automaticDimension`, then as long as the `estimatedRowHeight` isn't 0, you'll get automatic row heights:

```
self.tableView.rowHeight = UITableView.automaticDimension
self.tableView.estimatedRowHeight = UITableView.automaticDimension
```

Also starting in iOS 11, section headers and footers participate in the same variable height mechanism. If the table view's `sectionHeaderHeight` and `estimatedSection-HeaderHeight` are both `UITableView.automaticDimension`, the headers will have their heights determined by autolayout from the inside out.

I have said that adopting automatic row heights allows you to delete your implementation of the `height` delegate method, such as `tableView(_:heightForRowAt:)`. But you don't *have* to delete it, and you don't have to adopt automatic height calculation for *every* row. Whatever your table view's `height` settings may be, you can still override them for *individual* rows, so long as the `estimatedRowHeight` isn't 0:

- If `tableView(_:heightForRowAt:)` returns `UITableView.automaticDimension`, you'll get automatic determination of this row's height, even if the table view's `rowHeight` is absolute.

- If `tableView(_:heightForRowAt:)` returns an absolute height, that height will be used for this row, even if the table view's `rowHeight` is `UITableView.automatic-Dimension`.

The same technique works for individual section headers and footers. But it *doesn't* work for the *table view's* header and footer, the `tableHeaderView` and `tableFooter-View`; their heights are not determined for you by means of internal constraints. (I regard this as a bug.)

The automatic row height mechanism is particularly well suited to cells containing UILabels whose height will depend upon their text contents, because the label provides that height in its `intrinsicContentSize`. If you want to use the automatic row height mechanism in conjunction with a *custom* UIView subclass whose height can vary, you should make your view behave like a label! Don't set your view's height constraint directly; instead, have your UIView subclass override `intrinsicContent-Size`, and set some property on which that override depends:

```
class MyView : UIView {
    var internalHeight : CGFloat = 200 {
        didSet {
            self.invalidateIntrinsicContentSize()
        }
    }
    override var intrinsicContentSize: CGSize {
        return CGSize(width:300, height:self.internalHeight)
    }
}
```

Obviously, taking advantage of the automatic row height mechanism is very easy: but easy does not necessarily mean best. There is also a question of performance. The four techniques I've outlined here run not only from oldest to newest but also from fastest to slowest. Manual layout is faster than calling `systemLayoutSize-Fitting(_:)`, and calculating the heights of all rows up front, though it may cause a longer pause initially, makes scrolling faster for the user because no row heights have to be calculated while scrolling. You will have to measure and decide which approach is most suitable.

Also, I said earlier that the cell returned to you from `dequeueReusableCell(with-Identifier:for:)` in your implementation of `tableView(_:cellForRowAt:)` already has its final size. But if you use automatic row heights, that's not true, because automatic calculation of a cell's height can't take place until after the cell exists! Any code that relies on the cell having its final size in `tableView(_:cellForRowAt:)` will break when you switch to automatic row heights. You can probably work around this by moving that code to `tableView(_:willDisplay:forRowAt:)`, where the final cell size has definitely been achieved.

 If you implement `tableView(_:heightForRowAt:)`, don't make any assumptions about how many times or how often it will be called. It can be called multiple times in succession for the same row. Your implementation needs to be as fast and efficient as possible; if it involves work, cache the results so as not to waste time doing the same work twice.

Table View Selection

One of the chief purposes of your table view is likely to be to let the user *select* a cell by tapping it. Selection of a cell involves a change of *state*. A table view cell has a normal state, a highlighted state (according to its `isHighlighted` property), and a selected state (according to its `isSelected` property). You can change these states directly, optionally with animation, by calling `setHighlighted(_:animated:)` or `setSelected(_:animated:)` on the cell; but you don't want to act behind the table's back, so you are more likely to manage selection through the table view, letting the table view manage and track the state of its cells.

Although selection and highlighting are different states, selection implies highlighting. When a cell is selected, it propagates the highlighted state down through its subviews by setting each subview's `isHighlighted` property if it has one. That is why a UILabel's `highlightedTextColor` applies when the cell is selected. Similarly, a UIImageView (such as the cell's `imageView`) can have a `highlightedImage` that is shown when the cell is selected. The cell's background can also change in response to selection, as I've already explained.

The user can tap a cell to select it if you have not set the table view's `allowsSelection` property to `false`. You can also permit the user to select multiple cells; to do so, set the table view's `allowsMultipleSelection` property to `true`. If the user taps an already selected cell, by default it stays selected if the table doesn't allow multiple selection, but it is deselected if the table does allow multiple selection.

Managing Cell Selection

Your code can learn and manage the selection through these UITableView properties and instance methods:

`indexPathForSelectedRow`
`indexPathsForSelectedRows`
> These read-only properties report the currently selected row(s), or `nil` if there is no selection.

Don't accidentally examine the wrong property! Asking for `indexPathFor-SelectedRow` when the table view allows multiple selection gives a result that will have you scratching your head in confusion. (As usual, I speak from experience.)

`selectRow(at:animated:scrollPosition:)`

The animation involves fading in the selection, but the user may not see this unless the selected row is already visible.

The last parameter dictates whether and how the table view should scroll to reveal the newly selected row; your choices (UITableView.ScrollPosition) are `.top`, `.middle`, `.bottom`, and `.none`. For the first three options, the table view scrolls (with animation, if the second parameter is `true`) so that the selected row is at the specified position among the visible cells. For `.none`, the table view does not scroll; if the selected row is not already visible, it does not become visible.

`deselectRow(at:animated:)`

Deselects the given row (if it is selected); the optional animation involves fading out the selection. No automatic scrolling takes place.

To deselect *all* currently selected rows, call `selectRow(at:...)` with a `nil` index path.

Selection is preserved when a selected cell is scrolled off the screen; the row is still reported as selected, and the cell will still appear selected when it is scrolled back on screen.

Responding to Cell Selection

Response to user selection is through these table view delegate methods:

- `tableView(_:shouldHighlightRowAt:)`
- `tableView(_:didHighlightRowAt:)`
- `tableView(_:didUnhighlightRowAt:)`
- `tableView(_:willSelectRowAt:)`
- `tableView(_:didSelectRowAt:)`
- `tableView(_:willDeselectRowAt:)`
- `tableView(_:didDeselectRowAt:)`

The delegate method you'll be most interested in with regard to selection is `tableView(_:didSelectRowAt:)`. This is your signal that the user has selected a cell! Your response will depend upon the purpose of this table view and what selection is supposed to mean.

Despite their names, the two `will` methods are actually `should` methods and expect a return value:

- Return `nil` to prevent the selection (or deselection) from taking place.

- Return the same index path to permit the selection (or deselection), or a different index path to cause a different cell to be selected (or deselected).

The `highlight` methods arrive first, so you can return `false` from `table-View(_:shouldHighlightRowAt:)` to prevent a cell from being selected. When the user taps a cell and `willSelect` is called, then if this table view permits only single cell selection, `willDeselect` will be called subsequently for any previously selected cells.

Here's an example of implementing `tableView(_:willSelectRowAt:)`. When `allowsSelection` is `true` and `allowsMultipleSelection` is `false`, the default behavior is that if the user taps an already selected row, the selection does not change. We can alter this so that tapping a selected row deselects it:

```
override func tableView(_ tableView: UITableView,
    willSelectRowAt indexPath: IndexPath) -> IndexPath? {
        if tableView.indexPathForSelectedRow == indexPath {
            tableView.deselectRow(at:indexPath, animated:false)
            return nil
        }
        return indexPath
}
```

A cell's highlighted state and its selected state are, in fact, two different states, even though the user doesn't know the difference between them: whether the cell is highlighted or selected, the cell's subviews are highlighted and the `selectedBackground-View` appears. There are two different states because the user might touch a cell in two different ways:

The user touches and scrolls
The cell is *highlighted, then unhighlighted*; the user sees the flash of the cell's selected appearance, until the table begins to scroll and the cell returns to normal.

The user touches and lifts the finger
The cell is *highlighted, then selected*; the cell takes on its selected appearance and keeps it. There is actually a moment in the sequence where the cell has been highlighted and then unhighlighted and not yet selected, but the user doesn't see any momentary unhighlighting of the cell, because no redraw moment occurs (see Chapter 4).

Navigation from a Table View

A common response to user selection is navigation. A master–detail architecture is typical: the table view lists things the user can see in more detail, and a tap displays the detailed view of the tapped thing. On the iPhone, very often the table view will be in a navigation interface, and you will respond to user selection by creating the detail view and pushing it onto the navigation controller's stack.

Here's the code from my Albumen app that navigates from the list of albums to the list of songs in the album that the user has tapped:

```
override func tableView(_ tableView: UITableView,
    didSelectRowAt indexPath: IndexPath) {
        let t = TracksViewController(
            mediaItemCollection: self.albums[indexPath.row])
        self.navigationController!.pushViewController(t, animated: true)
}
```

In a storyboard, when you draw a segue from a UITableViewCell, you are given a choice of two segue triggers: Selection Segue and Accessory Action. If you create a selection segue, the segue will be triggered *automatically* when the user selects a cell; in this way, you can arrange to push or present another view controller in response to cell selection without implementing `tableView(_:didSelectRowAt:)`.

 Do not create a selection segue and *also* implement `tableView(_:didSelectRow-At:)` so as to perform a transition (such as calling `performSegue` or `pushView-Controller`). This is a common beginner mistake, and can have confusing consequences because you're trying to perform two transitions simultaneously when the user taps a cell.

If you're using a UITableViewController, then by default, whenever the table view appears, the selection is cleared automatically in `viewWillAppear(_:)`, and the scroll indicators are flashed in `viewDidAppear(_:)`. You can prevent the automatic clearing of the selection by setting the table view controller's `clearsSelectionOnViewWill-Appear` to `false`. You can get a nice effect by implementing deselection in `viewDid-Appear(_:)` instead: when the user returns to the table, the row remains momentarily selected before it deselects itself.

By convention, if selecting a table view cell causes navigation, the cell should be given an `accessoryType` (UITableViewCell.AccessoryType) of `.disclosureIndicator`. This is a plain gray right-pointing chevron at the right end of the cell. The chevron itself doesn't respond to user interaction; it is not a button, but rather a visual cue that the user can tap the cell to learn more.

Two additional `accessoryType` settings *are* buttons:

`.detailButton`
> Drawn as a letter "i" in a circle.

`.detailDisclosureButton`
> Drawn like `.detailButton`, along with a disclosure indicator chevron to its right.

To respond to the tapping of a detail button, implement the table view delegate's `tableView(_:accessoryButtonTappedForRowWith:)`. Alternatively, in a storyboard, you can Control-drag a connection from a cell and choose an Accessory Action segue. A common convention is that selecting the cell as a whole does one thing and tapping the detail button does something else. In Apple's Phone app, tapping a contact's listing in the Recents table places a call to that contact — has anyone *not* made that mistake? — but tapping the detail button navigates to that contact's detail view.

Table View Scrolling and Layout

A UITableView is a UIScrollView, so everything you already know about scroll views is applicable (Chapter 7). In addition, a table view supplies two convenience methods for scrolling in code:

- `scrollToRow(at:at:animated:)`
- `scrollToNearestSelectedRow(at:animated:)`

One of the parameters is a scroll position, like the `scrollPosition` parameter for `selectRow`, discussed earlier in this chapter.

The following UITableView methods mediate between the table's bounds coordinates on the one hand and table structure on the other:

- `indexPathForRow(at:)`
- `indexPathsForRows(in:)`
- `rect(forSection:)`
- `rectForRow(at:)`
- `rectForFooter(inSection:)`
- `rectForHeader(inSection:)`

The table view's own table header view and table footer view are its direct subviews, so their positions within the table's bounds are given by their frames.

If you want to receive UIScrollView delegate messages from the table view, implement them in the table view's delegate. The table view's delegate *is* its scroll view delegate; there is no need to set a scroll view delegate explicitly or adopt UIScrollViewDelegate formally, because UITableViewDelegate conforms to UIScrollViewDelegate.

Refreshing a Table View

If you want a table view's contents to change, you first change the underlying data and then inform the table view that the data have changed. This causes the table view to refresh itself; basically, you're requesting that the Three Big Questions be asked all over again. At first blush, this seems inefficient; but it isn't. Remember, in a table that caches reusable cells, there are no cells of interest other than those actually showing in the table at this moment. Having worked out the layout of the table through the section header and footer heights and row heights, the table has to regenerate only those cells that are actually visible.

You can cause the table data to be refreshed using any of several methods:

reloadData
> The table view will ask the Three Big Questions all over again, including heights of rows and section headers and footers, and the index, much as when the table view first appears.

reloadRows(at:with:)
> The first parameter is an array of index paths. The table view will ask the Three Big Questions all over again, including heights, but not index entries. Cells are requested only for visible cells among those you specify.

reloadSections(_:with:)
> The first parameter is an IndexSet. The table view will ask the Three Big Questions all over again, including heights of rows and section headers and footers, and the index. Cells, headers, and footers are requested only for visible elements of the sections you specify.

The latter two methods can perform animations that cue the user as to what's changing. For the with: argument, you'll specify what animation you want by passing one of the following (UITableView.RowAnimation):

.fade
> The old fades into the new.

.right, .left, .top, .bottom
> The old slides out in the stated direction, and is replaced from the opposite direction.

.middle
> Hard to describe; it's a sort of venetian blind effect on each cell individually.

`.automatic`

The table view just "does the right thing." This is especially useful for grouped style tables, because if you pick the wrong animation, the display can look very funny as it proceeds.

`.none`

No animation.

If all you need is to refresh the index, call `reloadSectionIndexTitles`; this calls the data source's `sectionIndexTitles(for:)`.

 Calling a `reload` method deselects any affected cells; calling `reloadData` deselects *all* selected cells. Calling `reloadData`, and then calling `indexPathFor-SelectedRow` and wondering what happened to the selection, is a common beginner mistake.

Call `reloadData` whenever the model data has changed and you want to alert the table view to that fact. The usual scenario in my own apps is that the data may take time to assemble or prepare.

My Albumen app consists of a table view controller whose table view lists the albums in the user's music library. Gathering that data takes time. Therefore I must instantiate the table view controller *first* and gather the data *later*, because if we pause to gather the data *before* instantiating the table view controller, the app will take too long to launch — the delay will be perceptible, and we might even crash (because iOS forbids long launch times). Therefore the data properties that will be used to populate the table view are all Optionals; they are set to `nil` until the data are gathered, at which time they are assigned their "real" values:

```
class RootViewController : UITableViewController {
    var albums : [MPMediaItemCollection]?
    override func tableView(_ tableView: UITableView,
        numberOfRowsInSection section: Int) -> Int {
            return self.albums?.count ?? 0
    }
    // ...
}
```

When the app launches and the table view appears, the table view turns to the table view controller and asks the Three Big Questions. My implementation of `tableView(_:numberOfRowsInSection:)` sees that `albums` is `nil` and returns 0 — and so the table is initially empty. Meanwhile, the data are being gathered. After gathering the data, I call `reloadData` to tell my table view to ask the Three Big Questions *again*. This time, `albums` is *not* `nil`, but rather consists of actual data — and so now `tableView(_:numberOfRowsInSection:)` returns the `count` of the `albums` array, and `tableView(_:cellForRowAt:)` is called to populate the table.

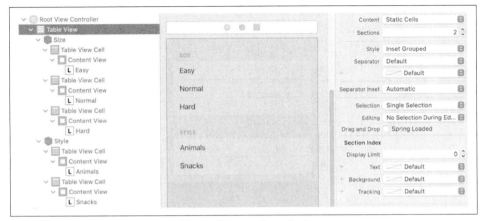

Figure 8-7. Designing a static table in the storyboard editor

Cell Choice and Static Tables

As a further example of using `reloadData`, I'll implement the interface shown in Figure 8-3. The idea here is to give the user a choice among cells, where a section of a table effectively functions as an iOS equivalent of macOS radio buttons, with an `accessoryType` of `.checkmark` to indicate the current choice. My table view has a grouped style (it looks particularly nice with the `.insetGrouped` style, which was introduced in iOS 13), and consists of two sections. The first section, with a "Size" header, has three mutually exclusive choices: "Easy," "Normal," or "Hard." The second section, with a "Style" header, has two choices: "Animals" or "Snacks."

This table's entire contents, except for the checkmark, are known beforehand and won't change. It is, in effect, a *static* table. If we're using a UITableViewController subclass instantiated from a storyboard, the nib editor lets us design a static table, including the headers and the cells *and their content*, directly in the storyboard. Select the table and set its Content pop-up menu in the Attributes inspector to Static Cells to make the table editable in this way (Figure 8-7).

When you're using a static table, you are still free to implement table view data source and delegate methods, provided you cooperate with what the static table is already doing for you. This is useful when you'll have relevant information at run-time that you don't have while designing the storyboard. You can implement `table-View(_:cellForRowAt:)`, but your implementation must not dequeue a cell explicitly; instead, obtain the cell by calling `super`. Now you can add runtime modifications to the cell.

I'll add the checkmarks to our static table by implementing `tableView(_:cellForRow-At:)` to set the cell's `accessoryType`. Note the call to `super`, as well as the call to `tableView(_:titleForHeaderInSection:)` to learn the title of the current section.

The user defaults will store the current choice in each of the two categories; in both cases, the key is the section title and the value is the label text of the chosen cell:

```
override func tableView(_ tv: UITableView,
    cellForRowAt ix: IndexPath) -> UITableViewCell {
        let cell = super.tableView(tv, cellForRowAt:ix)
        let ud = UserDefaults.standard
        cell.accessoryType = .none
        if let title = self.tableView(
            tv, titleForHeaderInSection:ix.section) {
                if let label = ud.object(forKey:title) as? String {
                    if label == cell.textLabel!.text {
                        cell.accessoryType = .checkmark
                    }
                }
        }
        return cell
}
```

The position of the checkmark needs to change in response to the user tapping a cell. When the user taps a cell, the cell is selected. I want the user to see that selection momentarily, as feedback, but then I want to deselect, adjusting the checkmarks so that that cell is the only one checked in its section. In `tableView(_:didSelectRow-At:)`, I set the user defaults, and then I reload the table view's data. This removes the selection and causes `tableView(_:cellForRowAt:)` to be called to adjust the checkmarks:

```
override func tableView(_ tv: UITableView, didSelectRowAt ix: IndexPath) {
    let ud = UserDefaults.standard
    let setting = tv.cellForRow(at:ix)!.textLabel!.text
    let header = self.tableView(tv, titleForHeaderInSection:ix.section)!
    ud.setValue(setting, forKey:header)
    tv.reloadData()
}
```

Direct Access to Cells

It is possible to access and alter a table's individual cells directly. This can be a lightweight approach to refreshing the table, plus you can supply your own animation within the cell as it alters its appearance. But don't forget that the cells are not the data! If you change the content of a cell manually, make sure that you have *also* changed the model corresponding to it, so that the row will appear correctly if its data is reloaded later. Do *not* change the display of a table cell directly *without* also changing the underlying data! The "source of truth" for a table view is the data, not the transient appearance of the cells. Be sure to design your data model and your implementation of `tableView(_:cellForRowAt:)` to accommodate any real-time changes you'll need to make.

When accessing a cell directly, you'll probably want to check first that the cell is visible within the table view's bounds; nonvisible cells don't really exist (except as potential cells waiting in the reuse cache), and there's no point changing them manually, as they'll be configured in accordance with the data model when they are scrolled into view, through the usual call to `tableView(_:cellForRowAt:)`.

Here are some UITableView properties and methods that mediate between cells, rows, and visibility:

`visibleCells`
: An array of the cells actually showing within the table's bounds.

`indexPathsForVisibleRows`
: An array of the rows actually showing within the table's bounds.

`cellForRow(at:)`
: Returns a UITableViewCell if the table is maintaining a cell for the given row (typically because this is a visible row); otherwise, returns `nil`.

`indexPath(for:)`
: Given a cell obtained from the table view, returns the row into which it is slotted.

By the same token, you can get access to the views constituting headers and footers, by calling `headerView(forSection:)` or `footerView(forSection:)`. You should assume that if a section is returned by `indexPathsForVisibleRows`, its header or footer might be visible.

Refresh Control

If you want to grant the user some interface for requesting that a table view be refreshed, you might like to use a UIRefreshControl. You aren't required to use this; it's just Apple's attempt to provide a standard interface.

To give a table view a refresh control, assign a UIRefreshControl to the table view's `refreshControl` property; this property is actually inherited from UIScrollView. You can also configure this in the nib editor through a table view controller's Refreshing pop-up menu in the Attributes inspector.

To request a refresh, the user scrolls the table view downward to display the refresh control and holds long enough to indicate that this scrolling is deliberate. The refresh control then acknowledges visually that it is refreshing, and remains visible until refreshing is complete.

The refresh control is normally displayed at the top of the scrolling part of the table view. Starting in iOS 11, if we're in a navigation interface (UINavigationController) with a navigation bar that displays large titles, the refresh control appears in the navigation bar, which stretches to accommodate it when visible; for this to work properly, it is *crucial* that the table view should underlap the navigation bar.

A refresh control is a control (UIControl, Chapter 13), and you will want to hook its Value Changed event to an action method; you can do that in the nib editor by making an action connection, or you can do it in code:

```
self.tableView.refreshControl = UIRefreshControl()
self.tableView.refreshControl!.addTarget(
    self, action: #selector(doRefresh), for: .valueChanged)
```

Once a refresh control's action message has fired, the control remains visible and indicates by animation (similar to an activity indicator) that it is refreshing, until you send it the endRefreshing message.

```
@IBAction func doRefresh(_ sender: Any) {
    // ...
    (sender as! UIRefreshControl).endRefreshing()
}
```

You can initiate a refresh animation in code with beginRefreshing, but this does not fire the action message. It also doesn't display the refresh control; to display it, scroll the table view:

```
self.refreshControl!.sizeToFit()
let top = self.tableView.adjustedContentInset.top
let y = self.refreshControl!.frame.maxY + top
self.tableView.setContentOffset(CGPoint(0, -y), animated:true)
self.refreshControl!.beginRefreshing()
self.doRefresh(self.refreshControl!)
```

(The sizeToFit call works around a bug where the refresh control may otherwise report its own frame height as less than 1 point.)

A refresh control also has these properties:

isRefreshing *(read-only)*
  Whether the refresh control is refreshing.

tintColor
  The refresh control's color. It is *not* inherited from the view hierarchy (I regard this as a bug).

attributedTitle
  Styled text displayed below the refresh control's activity indicator. On attributed strings, see Chapter 11.

`backgroundColor` *(inherited from UIView)*

> If you give a table view controller's `refreshControl` a background color, that color completely covers the table view's own background when the refresh control is revealed.

The `attributedTitle` sometimes fails to appear unless the refresh control has a background color (I regard this as a bug); on the other hand, a refresh control background color that's different from the table view's own background can ruin the entire look of the refresh control. A good compromise is to give the table view and the refresh control the same background color.

Editing a Table View

A table view cell has a normal state and an editing state, according to its `isEditing` property. The editing state (or *edit mode*) is typically indicated visually by one or more of the following:

Editing controls
> At least one editing control will usually appear, such as a Minus button (for deletion) at the left side.

Shrinkage
> The content of the cell will usually shrink to allow room for an editing control. If there is no editing control, you can prevent a cell shifting its left end rightward in edit mode with the delegate's `tableView(_:shouldIndentWhileEditingRowAt:)`.

Changing accessory view
> The cell's accessory view will change automatically in accordance with its `editingAccessoryType` or `editingAccessoryView`. If you assign neither, so that they are `nil`, the cell's existing accessory view will vanish when in edit mode.

You could set a cell's `isEditing` property directly, but you don't want to act behind the table's back, so you are more likely to let the table view manage editability. Table view editability is controlled through the table view's `isEditing` property, usually by sending the table the `setEditing(_:animated:)` message. The table responds by changing the edit mode of its cells.

Toggling a Table View's Edit Mode

Putting the table into edit mode is usually left up to the user. A typical interface would be an Edit button that the user can tap. In a navigation interface, we might have our view controller supply the button as a bar button item in the navigation bar:

```
let b = UIBarButtonItem(barButtonSystemItem: .edit,
    target: self, action: #selector(doEdit))
self.navigationItem.rightBarButtonItem = b
```

Our action method will be responsible for putting the table into edit mode, so in its simplest form it might look like this:

```
@objc func doEdit(_ sender: Any) {
    self.tableView.setEditing(true, animated:true)
}
```

But now we face the problem of getting *out* of edit mode. The standard interface is that the Edit button replaces itself with a Done button; the same button, either Edit or Done, now switches the table view into or out of edit mode:

```
@objc func doEdit(_ sender: Any) {
    var which : UIBarButtonItem.SystemItem
    if !self.tableView.isEditing {
        self.tableView.setEditing(true, animated:true)
        which = .done
    } else {
        self.tableView.setEditing(false, animated:true)
        which = .edit
    }
    let b = UIBarButtonItem(barButtonSystemItem: which,
        target: self, action: #selector(doEdit))
    self.navigationItem.rightBarButtonItem = b
}
```

But it turns out that all of that is completely unnecessary; if we want standard behavior, it's already implemented for us! A UIViewController has an `editButtonItem` property, which vends a bar button item that does precisely what we need:

- It calls the UIViewController's `setEditing(_:animated:)` when tapped.
- It tracks the UIViewController's `isEditing` property, and changes its own title accordingly (Edit or Done).

Moreover, UITableViewController's implementation of `setEditing(_:animated:)` is to call `setEditing(_:animated:)` on its table view. So if we're using a UITable-ViewController, we get all of the desired behavior for free, just by retrieving the `edit-ButtonItem` and inserting the resulting button into our interface:

```
self.navigationItem.rightBarButtonItem = self.editButtonItem
```

When the table view enters edit mode, it consults its data source and delegate about the editability of individual rows:

`tableView(_:canEditRowAt:)` *to the data source*
> The default is `true`. The data source can return `false` to prevent the given row from entering edit mode.

`tableView(_:editingStyleForRowAt:)` *to the delegate*
> Each standard editing style corresponds to a control that will appear in the cell. The choices (UITableViewCell.EditingStyle) are:

`.delete`

> The cell shows a Minus button at its left end. The user can tap this to summon a Delete button, which the user can then tap to confirm the deletion. This is the default.

`.insert`

> The cell shows a Plus button at its left end; this is usually taken to be an insert button.

`.none`

> No editing control appears.

If the user taps an insert button (the Plus button) or a delete button (the Delete button that appears after the user taps the Minus button), the data source is sent the `tableView(_:commit:forRowAt:)` message. That's where the actual insertion or deletion needs to happen. I'll talk more about that in a moment.

Edit Mode and Selection

When a table view is in edit mode, a cell can be selected by the user if the table view's `allowsSelectionDuringEditing` is `true`. (The default is `false`.)

If both `allowsSelectionDuringEditing` and `allowsMultipleSelectionDuring-Editing` are `true`, the user can select multiple cells when the table view is in edit mode. In that case, `tableView(_:editingStyleForRowAt:)` is ignored; neither a Minus button nor a Plus button will appear at the left end of any cell. Instead, a cell shows an empty circle at its left end, which will be filled with a checkmark if the cell is selected.

The empty circle and checkmark can be suppressed for an individual cell if `tableView(_:canEditRowAt:)` for that cell returns `false`. The user can still select a cell for which the empty circle is suppressed, unless selection for that cell is *also* suppressed by `tableView(_:willSelectRowAt:)`.

Starting in iOS 13, if multiple selection during editing is enabled, the user can select multiple cells with a gesture, panning across cells with two fingers, when the table view is in edit mode. Moreover, a delegate method lets the user perform multiple selection with this panning gesture even if the table view is *not* in edit mode:

`tableView(_:shouldBeginMultipleSelectionInteractionAt:)`

> Consulted only if both `allowsSelectionDuringEditing` and `allowsMultiple-SelectionDuringEditing` are `true`, and when the table view is not in edit mode. Return `true` to permit multiple selection with the panning gesture. The default is `false`. If `true`, then as the gesture begins, the table enters edit mode and the circles appear.

(If the table view controller's editButtonItem is displayed, it does *not* change modes automatically at that moment; I regard that as a bug. You can work around it by calling self.setEditing(true, animated: true) before returning true.)

Two more delegate methods report that the user is changing a multiple selection:

tableView(_:didBeginMultipleSelectionInteractionAt:)
tableViewDidEndMultipleSelectionInteraction(_:)

> Sent at the beginning and end, respectively, of a change in a multiple selection. This might be due to a multiple selection gesture or to tapping rows individually.

Changing a Table View's Structure

When you want to alter the structure of the table before the user's eyes, you can call one or more of the following UITableView methods:

- insertRows(at:with:)
- deleteRows(at:with:)
- insertSections(_:with:)
- deleteSections(_:with:)
- moveSection(_:toSection:)
- moveRow(at:to:)

The with: parameters are row animations that are effectively the same ones discussed earlier in connection with refreshing table data. For an insertion, .left means to slide in from the left, and for a deletion it means to slide out to the left. The two move methods provide animation with no provision for customizing it.

Before you change the table with these commands, you *must* first change the data model, so that when the changes are over, the table view can coherently refresh itself. Before you delete a row, you must first remove from the model the datum that it represents — and so on, for any structural change. Coordinating between the state of the data model and the state of the table view can be tricky. The runtime will alert you with error messages if you do it incorrectly.

A further difficulty arises when multiple changes are to be made in a single move. If you were to delete row 1 of a certain section and then row 2 of the same section, you might reasonably worry that the notion "row 2" would have changed its meaning after row 1 is removed, so that you might need to delete row 1 twice, or change the order of your deletions.

To help with this problem, there's a UITableView instance method, performBatch-Updates(_:completion:). When you issue *any* commands that alter a table view's structure, you should do so inside a call to that method! It takes two functions, similar to an animation: the first function contains the commands and their animations, and the second function is a completion function that will be called after the animations have finished.

Combining multiple commands into a single batch update ensures that those commands are coherent. When there are multiple commands, the batch reorders them for you and interprets them correctly:

- If you perform insertions and deletions, the deletions are performed first.
- If you perform multiple deletions, they are performed in reverse index order, and the indexes refer to the state of the table *before* the deletions.
- If you perform insertions, they are performed in ascending index order, and the indexes refer to the state of the table *after* the deletions.
- If you perform moves, they are decomposed into deletions and insertions; the source index refers to the state of the table *before* the deletions, while the destination index refers to the state of the table *after* the deletions.

(A batch update can also include `reloadRows` and `reloadSections` commands — but not `reloadData`.)

But the help that `performBatchUpdates` gives you does *not* apply to the commands with which you alter your data model. When you alter the data model, *you* need to behave like the batch update engine! Otherwise you can crash, or wind up with your data model in an incoherent state.

Deleting a Cell

The simplest case of editing a table view's structure is deletion of a single cell. In effect, deletion of cells is the default, because:

- If you don't implement `tableView(_:canEditRowAt:)`, the default for all rows is that they are editable.
- If you don't implement `tableView(_:editingStyleForRowAt:)`, the default editing style for all rows is `.delete`.

What you *do* need to implement is `tableView(_:commit:forRowAt:)`. You then get two features automatically:

Minus button and Delete button
    If the table view is in edit mode, all editable cells get a Minus button at the left end, and if the user taps it, the cell displays a Delete button at the right end. If the user taps the Delete button, `tableView(_:commit:forRowAt:)` is called with the `.delete` action.

Swipe-to-delete

All editable cells permit swipe-to-delete when the table view is *not* in edit mode. The user can swipe left on a cell and the Delete button appears; if the user taps the Delete button, or if the user keeps swiping left, `tableView(_:commit:forRow-At:)` is called with the `.delete` action.

You can customize the Delete button's title with the table view delegate method `tableView(_:titleForDeleteConfirmationButtonForRowAt:)`.

Let's modify our table of state names so that the user can delete any cell. All we have to do is implement `tableView(_:commit:forRowAt:)` to get swipe-to-delete. In that implementation, we proceed in two stages. First, we remove the deleted row — from the data and then from the table. Second, if the deletion of that row emptied a section, we remove the deleted section — from the data and then from the table:

```
override func tableView(_ tableView: UITableView,
    commit editingStyle: UITableViewCell.EditingStyle,
    forRowAt ip: IndexPath) {
    switch editingStyle {
    case .delete:
        tableView.performBatchUpdates {
            self.sections[ip.section].rowData.remove(at:ip.row)
            tableView.deleteRows(at:[ip], with: .automatic)
            if self.sections[ip.section].rowData.count == 0 {
                self.sections.remove(at:ip.section)
                tableView.deleteSections(
                    IndexSet(integer: ip.section), with:.fade)
            }
        }
    default: break
    }
}
```

We can also allow the user to delete a row when the table view is in edit mode. All we have to do is provide the user with a way to get the table view *into* edit mode! If the table view is managed by a table view controller in a navigation interface, we can simply supply the built-in Edit button:

```
self.navigationItem.rightBarButtonItem = self.editButtonItem
```

The user can now tap the Edit button to put the table view into edit mode, tap a row's Minus button to reveal the Delete button, and tap the Delete button to delete the row.

An interesting question is how to turn swipe-to-delete *off* while still allowing the user to delete rows when the table view is in edit mode. We get swipe-to-delete "for free" by virtue of our having supplied an implementation of `tableView(_:commit:forRow-At:)`, and we cannot remove that implementation — we need it so that when the user taps the Minus button and the Delete button in edit mode, deletion actually occurs.

One solution is to make all rows noneditable unless the table view is already in edit mode:

```
override func tableView(_ tableView: UITableView,
    editingStyleForRowAt indexPath: IndexPath)
    -> UITableViewCell.EditingStyle {
        return tableView.isEditing ? .delete : .none
}
```

Deleting Multiple Cells

Now let's talk about deletion of multiple cells. A reasonable interface would be to allow the user to perform multiple selection and then delete the selected cells. If we allow multiple selection in edit mode, or if we permit two-finger panning to perform multiple selection, we get the circles that are filled with checkmarks as the user selects cells — but we don't get any Minus editing controls, so there will have to be a Delete button elsewhere to act upon the current selection.

What should that button do? We can easily learn the index paths of the selected rows. Using those index paths, we'll delete the corresponding rows — from the data and then from the table. Now we'll look to see if any sections in the data model are empty. If they are, we'll delete those sections — from the data and then from the table.

If we do all that in a `performBatchUpdates` call, we don't have to worry about the order in which we delete rows and sections from the table view. But we *do* have to worry about the order in which we delete items from our data model!

Suppose a section's `rowData` has four elements and the selected rows include that section's row 0 and row 3. If we delete element 0 and then element 3, we'll crash — because after deleting element 0, there is no longer an element 3. Similarly, if we want to delete sections 1 and 2, and we start by deleting `self.sections[1]`, the section we were calling 2 has become the new `self.sections[1]`; if we now delete `self.sections[2]`, either we'll crash or we'll delete the wrong section.

The solution is to ensure that deletions are performed in reverse index order:

```
guard let sel = self.tableView.indexPathsForSelectedRows else {return}
self.tableView.performBatchUpdates {
    for ip in sel.sorted().reversed() { // *
        self.sections[ip.section].rowData.remove(at:ip.row)
    }
    self.tableView.deleteRows(at:sel, with: .automatic)
    let secs = self.sections.indices.filter {
        self.sections[$0].rowData.count == 0
    }
    for sec in secs.reversed() { // *
```

```
        self.sections.remove(at:sec)
    }
    self.tableView.deleteSections(IndexSet(secs), with: .fade)
}
```

Table View Diffable Data Source

Even a fairly simple structural rearrangement of a table view, such as deleting multiple rows, is beset with pitfalls, as the preceding example demonstrates. We have to call performBatchUpdates; we have to delete from the data model before deleting physical rows or sections from the table view; and we have to be careful about the order of operations when changing the data model. If the desired rearrangement is more elaborate, involving both deletions and insertions or moving rows from place to place, the complexity increases. The procedures are delicate and tedious; the code is difficult to write and difficult to read.

That's the motivation behind an alternative data source architecture that was introduced in iOS 13 — the *diffable data source.*

In this architecture, the data source is a special class of object that maintains a special relationship with the table view. You don't have to answer the Three Big Questions; you don't have to query your data. Instead, you supply the data, and the data source automatically feeds it to the table view for you. And when you *change* the data in your data source, the data source knows the difference between the new data and the old data — hence the term *diffable* — and *automatically* performs the corresponding changes in the table view, with appropriate animations!

For this to work, the data — both section data and row data — must be Hashable. This allows the data to be queried efficiently. And that means that each piece of section data and each piece of row data must be *unique.* Hashable implies Equatable; two pieces of data that are equal to one another will be seen as the same piece of data, and cannot go into two different rows or two different sections. For this reason, the diffable data source is considered to contain, not actual data, but *identifiers,* called the *section identifiers* and the *item identifiers.* (Both a table view and a collection view can have a diffable data source; so a diffable data source uses the term *item* rather than *row,* because that's the term a collection view uses.)

In practice, the Hashable requirement should not prove troublesome. Making your section data and row data types Hashable will probably be easy. If your data type is a struct, most likely either it is Hashable already or you can make it Hashable just by declaring conformance to Hashable.

The only difficulty arises if there is a danger of duplication. Suppose your row data is just a name, which is a String. And suppose the strings for two different rows might be the same. Then a mere String cannot be your row data type, because values for different rows need to be unique. Instead, turn your data into a struct that associates the string with a unique identifier, and base your conformance to Equatable and Hashable on that identifier:

```
struct RowData : Hashable {
    let name : String
    let uid = UUID()
    static func ==(lhs:RowData, rhs:RowData) -> Bool {
        return lhs.uid == rhs.uid
    }
    func hash(into hasher: inout Hasher) {
        hasher.combine(uid)
    }
}
```

The diffable data source architecture revolves around two objects: a *data source* (a UITableViewDiffableDataSource) and a *snapshot* (an NSDiffableDataSourceSnapshot). These are generic types, parameterized on the section identifier type and the item identifier type. The data source has a reference to the table view, and it keeps the table view updated with its data. But its data is immutable; you cannot directly set it or change it. Instead, when you want to alter the data source's data, either to populate it initially or to change it, you create a snapshot and *apply* the snapshot to the data source (and you then let the snapshot go out of existence). The data source can calculate the difference between its existing data and the snapshot's data, and can make the table view animate that change.

A question that arises when you use a diffable data source is where the "real" data will live:

Separately
> You maintain the data separately (probably in an instance property). You structure the data in any way that's convenient and appropriate. Each time you want to change what the table view displays, you construct a snapshot based on the data and apply it to the data source.

In the data source itself
> There is no data instance property other than the data source itself. To change the table's data, you obtain a snapshot from the data source, change it, and apply it to the data source.

I prefer the second approach wherever possible; after all, the data source is going to store internally whatever data we hand it, so why bother storing another version of the same data elsewhere? Nevertheless, sometimes the first approach will be better — as when the data might at any time be updated automatically through some independent or asynchronous mechanism.

Populating a Diffable Data Source

To populate a table view with a diffable data source requires two steps:

1. Initialize a UITableViewDiffableDataSource instance with your table view; in response, the table view's `dataSource` is set automatically to this instance. Retain the instance, typically as an instance property.

2. Create an NSDiffableDataSourceSnapshot and feed it your section and row data (the section identifiers and item identifiers). Apply the snapshot to the data source. You can now release the snapshot; it has done its work.

Let's rewrite our table of state names to use a diffable data source. Keep in mind that there are no longer any Three Big Questions! We may have a UITableViewController, but it is not the table view's data source and it does not implement any data source methods. The diffable data source is going to be the table view's data source.

We have, as you remember, an alphabetized list of state names as a text file. Previously, we prepared the data model in `viewDidLoad` by parsing that text file into an instance property called `self.sections`, which is an array of Section structs. Now we don't need `self.sections`, and we don't need any Section struct! Instead, we have an instance property that I'll call `self.datasource`, which is a UITableViewDiffableDataSource.

I'm going to describe the two steps in reverse order. So pretend for now that `self.datasource` has already been declared and initialized; I'll return to that in a moment.

Our section data is a letter of the alphabet, and our row data consists of just the name of a state. Both the letters and the state names are unique, and they are Strings, a Hashable type. So the data source's parameterized types can be simply `<String, String>`.

Here's how we previously parsed the text file into an array of Section objects:

```
let s = try! String(
    contentsOfFile: Bundle.main.path(
        forResource: "states", ofType: "txt")!)
let states = s.components(separatedBy:"\n")
let d = Dictionary(grouping: states) {String($0.prefix(1))}
self.sections = Array(d).sorted {$0.key < $1.key}.map { // *
    Section(sectionName: $0.key, rowData: $0.value)
}
```

We now remove the last statement, where we assign into `self.sections`. Instead, we create an NSDiffableDataSourceSnapshot and parse the text file into that. We then apply the snapshot to `self.datasource`:

```
let sections = Array(d).sorted {$0.key < $1.key} // *
var snap = NSDiffableDataSourceSnapshot<String,String>()
for section in sections {
    snap.appendSections([section.0])
    snap.appendItems(section.1)
}
self.datasource.apply(snap, animatingDifferences: false)
```

The structure of that code is typical. We are giving the data source its initial data, so we start with an empty snapshot. We then append a section and its items, then another section and its items, and so on. There is a method `appendItems(_:to-Section:)`, but we don't have to use it here, because there's a convenient shortcut: when we call `appendItems`, those items are appended to the most recently appended section.

Finally, we apply the snapshot to the data source. The `apply` method takes three parameters, two of which can be omitted:

• `apply(_:animatingDifferences:completion:)`

If we don't set `animatingDifferences:` to `false`, we'll get animation. But we don't want any animation here, as the table view is about to appear for the first time and we want it simply to appear populated.

Now I'll go back and write the declaration for `self.datasource`. The initializer for UITableViewDiffableDataSource takes two parameters: the table view, and a function. I'll start by writing the declaration without the function body. I'll make `datasource` a `lazy` instance property so that its initializer can legally refer to the table view, which is also an instance property:

```
lazy var datasource =
    UITableViewDiffableDataSource(tableView:self.tableView) {
        // ...
    }
```

What goes into the anonymous function body? Basically, the function must do what `tableView(_:cellForRowAt:)` would do: it must dequeue, populate, and return a cell. The function receives the same two parameters as `tableView(_:cellForRowAt:)` — the table view and an index path. But it also receives a third parameter — the data for this row! There is no need to use the index path to look up the cell data in an array; the index path is needed only to dequeue the cell:

```
lazy var datasource =
    UITableViewDiffableDataSource(tableView:self.tableView) { tv, ip, s in
        let cell =
            tv.dequeueReusableCell(withIdentifier: self.cellID, for: ip)
        cell.textLabel!.text = s
        return cell
    }
```

That is sufficient to make our table view display a list of state names! But the list is not visibly divided into sections; it has no section headers. How we generate section headers depends on whether we want to call `tableView(_:titleForHeaderIn-Section:)` or `tableView(_:viewForHeaderInSection:)`.

Previously, we were using `tableView(_:viewForHeaderInSection:)`; let's go on using it. It's a delegate method. Our table view's data source has changed, but its delegate has not. If the UITableViewController was the table view's delegate, it can *still* be the table view's delegate. And the code remains almost exactly the same as before. Here's how it looked previously:

```
override func tableView(_ tableView: UITableView,
    viewForHeaderInSection section: Int) -> UIView? {
        let h = tableView.dequeueReusableHeaderFooterView(
            withIdentifier: self.headerID)!
        // ...
        let lab = h.contentView.viewWithTag(1) as! UILabel
        lab.text = self.sections[section].sectionName // *
        return h
}
```

Only the starred line needs to change. It refers to `self.sections`, the Section array. There is no longer any `self.sections`! The data lives inside `self.datasource`. To access it, we ask `self.datasource` for a snapshot; now we can interrogate the data:

```
lab.text = self.datasource.snapshot().sectionIdentifiers[section]
```

In that line, we're working around an impedance mismatch. The diffable data source and the snapshot can access identifiers in terms of the identifier itself — that's why identifiers are unique and Hashable. But `tableView(_:viewForHeaderInSection:)` knows nothing of that; it provides us with a section *number*. So we end up indexing into the section identifier array, much as we would have done before diffable data sources existed.

Subclassing a Diffable Data Source

When you're using a diffable data source, the table view's `dataSource` is now a UITableViewDiffableDataSource. This means that any UITableViewDataSource functionality not implemented automatically by the UITableViewDiffableDataSource must be implemented explicitly by subclassing. Our `self.datasource` instance property must now be an instance of the subclass, which I'll call MyDataSource.

If we want a section index down the side of our table view, we need to override the relevant data source methods in the subclass:

```
class MyDataSource : UITableViewDiffableDataSource<String,String> {
    override func sectionIndexTitles(for tv: UITableView) -> [String]? {
        let snap = self.snapshot()
        return snap.sectionIdentifiers
```

```
    }
    override func tableView(_ tableView: UITableView,
        sectionForSectionIndexTitle title: String, at index: Int) -> Int {
            let snap = self.snapshot()
            return snap.indexOfSection(title) ?? 0
    }
}
```

Similarly, if we want the table cells to be editable when the table view enters edit mode, we must explicitly enable editability in our subclass:

```
override func tableView(_ tableView: UITableView,
    canEditRowAt indexPath: IndexPath) -> Bool {
        return true
}
```

And if we wanted to supply header titles rather than header views, `table-View(_:titleForHeaderInSection:)` is a data source method, not a delegate method, and we'd need to implement it in the subclass.

Changing a Diffable Data Source

The real power of diffable data sources emerges when we alter the data source and the corresponding changes in the table view are performed and animated for us. To illustrate, let's implement deletion of multiple rows of the table view. We do *not* call `performBatchUpdates`! We do *not* call `deleteRows(at:with:)` or `delete-Sections(_:with:)`! We just change the snapshot and apply it, and both the data and the table view are updated for us — with animation of the table view changes.

(The magic ability of the diffable data source to deduce how a new snapshot differs from the old one, and to express that through animated changes in the table view, comes from the CollectionDifference struct and the `difference(from:)` and `applying` Array instance methods.)

To illustrate, let's say we have permitted the user to select multiple rows while the table view is in edit mode, and we have supplied a Delete button that the user can tap to delete the selected rows. Now we are going to implement the Delete button's action method.

If the user deletes all the rows of a section, we also want to delete that section. All the work takes place in the snapshot, so it will be useful to extend NSDiffableDataSource-Snapshot to enforce that rule:

```
extension NSDiffableDataSourceSnapshot {
    mutating func deleteWithSections(_ items : [ItemIdentifierType]) {
        self.deleteItems(items)
        let empties = self.sectionIdentifiers.filter {
            self.numberOfItems(inSection: $0) == 0
```

```
        }
        self.deleteSections(empties)
    }
}
```

Our Delete button obtains a snapshot from the data source, gathers the item identifiers for the selected rows, calls that method, and applies the snapshot:

```
guard let sel = self.tableView.indexPathsForSelectedRows else {return}
let rowids = sel.map {
    self.datasource.itemIdentifier(for: $0)
}.compactMap {$0}
var snap = self.datasource.snapshot()
snap.deleteWithSections(rowids)
self.datasource.apply(snap)
```

That's all there is to it! Once again, we're working around an impedance mismatch: the table view describes the selected rows in terms of their index paths, but the snapshot wants lists of item identifiers and section identifiers. Luckily, the data source provides methods such as `itemIdentifier(for:)` to convert between index paths and identifiers. And the resulting code is far simpler and more robust than what we were previously doing in `performBatchUpdates`. We just change the data and the table view changes to match, automatically, with animation. The animation looks particularly nice, I think, if we set the data source's default animation beforehand:

```
self.datasource.defaultRowAnimation = .left
```

Pros and Cons of the Diffable Data Source

Should you adopt a diffable data source for your table view? Or should you stick with the old-style Three Big Questions data source? Here are some arguments in favor of the diffable data source:

Less code
> The Three Big Questions are eliminated. You still have to write code equivalent to the third Big Question, but it is nicely encapsulated in the function you supply to the data source initializer, and the actual data for each row arrives directly into the function as a parameter.

No custom data model storage
> There may be no need to devise a structure for your data model and store it in an instance property, because the diffable data source stores the data for you.

Easy data modification
> It's easy to insert, delete, or move data items or sections directly in a snapshot and keep those changes synchronized with the table view by applying the snapshot to the data source.

In other respects, a diffable data source may feel like a step backward:

Impedance mismatch

The table view thinks in terms of cells and index paths, and the UITableView-DataSource and UITableViewDelegate methods are couched in those terms. But the diffable data source thinks in terms of unique identifiers, so you may end up converting back and forth. Conversion isn't difficult, but it can feel inelegant.

No `performBatchUpdates`

With a diffable data source, calling `performBatchUpdates` is illegal. But certain techniques involving animated layout (described later in this chapter) depend upon calling `performBatchUpdates`.

One of the nicest aspects of a diffable data source is that it makes the table view data source an independent object. That's probably a good architecture in any case, but the diffable data source enforces it. By subclassing UITableViewDiffableDataSource and overriding data source methods there, and by also making the diffable data source the table view's delegate, you can move the functionality associated with populating and configuring the table view out of the view controller entirely.

Let's take our table of U.S. states as an example. We have a UITableViewDiffableData-Source subclass, MyDataSource, living in its own file, *MyDataSource.swift*. We provide an initializer where all the table view configuration takes place, including cell registration and the initial population of the data source; all the data source and delegate methods are here as well:

```
class MyDataSource: UITableViewDiffableDataSource<String, String> {
    let cellID = "Cell"
    let headerID = "Header"
    init(tableView: UITableView) {
        tableView.register(UITableViewCell.self,
            forCellReuseIdentifier: self.cellID)
        // ... other table view configurations ...
        let cellID = self.cellID
        super.init(tableView: tableView) { tv, ip, s in
            let cell = tv.dequeueReusableCell(withIdentifier:cellID, for:ip)
            // ... configure cell, Third Big Question ...
            return cell
        }
        self.populate()
    }
    private func populate() {
        let s = try! String(
            contentsOfFile: Bundle.main.path(
                forResource: "states", ofType: "txt")!)
        // ... parse text file, create initial snapshot ...
        self.apply(snap, animatingDifferences: false)
    }
    override func sectionIndexTitles(for tableView: UITableView)
        -> [String]? {
            return self.snapshot().sectionIdentifiers
```

```
        }
        override func tableView(_ tableView: UITableView,
            sectionForSectionIndexTitle title: String, at index: Int) -> Int {
                return self.snapshot().sectionIdentifiers
                    .firstIndex(of: title) ?? 0
        }
    }
    extension MyDataSource : UITableViewDelegate {
        func tableView(_ tableView: UITableView,
            viewForHeaderInSection section: Int) -> UIView? {
                // ... as before ...
                let lab = h.contentView.viewWithTag(1) as! UILabel
                lab.text = self.snapshot().sectionIdentifiers[section]
                return h
        }
    }
```

The result is that the view controller has very little to say about the table view:

```
lazy var datasource = MyDataSource(tableView: self.tableView)
override func viewDidLoad() {
    super.viewDidLoad()
    self.tableView.delegate = self.datasource
}
```

More Table View Editing

This section describes some further types of change you can permit the user to perform in a table view.

Rearranging Cells

When a table view is in edit mode, it can display a reordering control at the right end of each cell. The user can drag this to rearrange the cells:

- To make the reordering control appear, the data source must implement table-View(_:moveRowAt:to:). That method will be called when the user does rearrange cells, and you should respond by rearranging the data model to match.

- To suppress the reordering control for an individual row, implement the data source method tableView(_:canMoveRowAt:).

- To limit where a particular row can be moved to, implement the delegate method tableView(_:targetIndexPathForMoveFromRowAt:toProposedIndexPath:).

To illustrate, let's permit the user to rearrange cells within the table of U.S. states. Let's decide that rows can be rearranged only within their section; the user can reverse the order of Kansas and Kentucky, but can't drag either Kansas or Kentucky outside of the K section. Since a one-row section can't be rearranged, we'll suppress the reordering control when a cell is the only one in its section.

For simplicity, I'll assume the data model is our old-fashioned `self.sections` instance property, an array of Section where each Section has a `rowData` property that's an array of state names. To make the reordering controls spring to life when the table view is in edit mode, we have to implement `tableView(_:moveRowAt:to:)`. We're going to guarantee that a row can't move out of its section, so all we have to do is rearrange the `rowData` within the section to match what the user did:

```
override func tableView(_ tableView: UITableView,
    moveRowAt srcip: IndexPath, to destip: IndexPath) {
        let sec = srcip.section
        let srcrow = srcip.row
        let destrow = destip.row
        self.sections[sec].rowData.swapAt(srcrow, destrow)
}
```

We prevent the reordering control from appearing if the section has only one row:

```
override func tableView(_ tableView: UITableView,
    canMoveRowAt ip: IndexPath) -> Bool {
        return self.sections[ip.section].rowData.count > 1
}
```

We prevent the user from dragging a row out of its section, by substituting the source index path for the destination index path unless they are in the same section; if the user drops the cell in a different section, it snaps back into its original place:

```
override func tableView(_ tableView: UITableView,
    targetIndexPathForMoveFromRowAt srcip: IndexPath,
    toProposedIndexPath destip: IndexPath) -> IndexPath {
        if destip.section != srcip.section {
            return srcip
        }
        return destip
}
```

Editable Content in Cells

A cell might have content that the user can edit directly, such as a UISwitch that the user can switch on or off (Chapter 13), or a UITextField where the user can change the text (Chapter 11). In this situation, you must reflect the user's changes back into the data model. But there's no built-in data source method to tell us what's happening. *You* need to arrange to hear that the user has made a change in a row of the table view, and you need a way to find out *which* row the user changed.

To illustrate, imagine an app that maintains a list of names and phone numbers. The data are displayed as a grouped style table, and they become editable when the user taps the Edit button (Figure 8-8).

The table displays just one name but can display multiple phone numbers, so my data model looks like this:

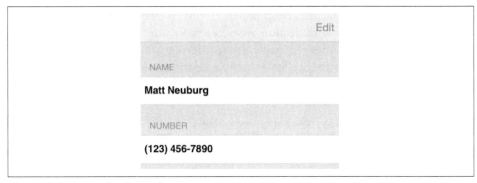

Figure 8-8. A simple phone directory app

```
var name = ""
var numbers = [String]()
```

We don't need an editing control at the left end of a cell when it's being edited:

```
override func tableView(_ tableView: UITableView,
    editingStyleForRowAt indexPath: IndexPath)
    -> UITableViewCell.EditingStyle {
        return .none
}
```

A UITextField is editable if its `isEnabled` is `true`. To tie this to the cell's `isEditing` state, I'll use a custom UITableViewCell class called MyCell with a single UITextField connected to an outlet property called `textField`:

```
class MyCell : UITableViewCell {
    @IBOutlet weak var textField : UITextField!
    override func didTransition(to state: UITableViewCell.StateMask) {
        self.textField.isEnabled = state.contains(.showingEditControl)
        super.didTransition(to:state)
    }
}
```

How will we hear that the user is editing a text field? One obvious way is to be the text field's delegate (adopting the UITextFieldDelegate protocol; I'll talk more about that in Chapter 11). We can conveniently set that up when we configure the cell:

```
override func tableView(_ tableView: UITableView,
    cellForRowAt indexPath: IndexPath) -> UITableViewCell {
        let cell = tableView.dequeueReusableCell(
            withIdentifier: self.cellID, for: indexPath) as! MyCell
        switch indexPath.section {
        case 0:
            cell.textField.text = self.name
        case 1:
            cell.textField.text = self.numbers[indexPath.row]
            cell.textField.keyboardType = .numbersAndPunctuation
        default: break
```

```
        }
        cell.textField.delegate = self // *
        return cell
    }
```

Acting as the text field's delegate, we are responsible for implementing the Return button in the keyboard to dismiss the keyboard; we can do so by implementing `text-FieldShouldReturn(_:)`:

```
func textFieldShouldReturn(_ textField: UITextField) -> Bool {
    textField.endEditing(true)
    return false
}
```

Still acting as the text field's delegate, we can hear that the user has changed the text field's text, by implementing `textFieldDidEndEditing(_:)`:

```
func textFieldDidEndEditing(_ textField: UITextField) {
    // ???
}
```

Now we face a fundamental challenge. We know which text field this is, because it arrives as the parameter to the delegate method. But we don't know the index path of the cell containing this text field! And we need to know that in order to update the data model correctly.

There are various solutions to this problem, usually involving the text field's `tag` or some custom property. But the approach I favor is this: The table view knows what index path corresponds to this cell, and the cell is a superview of the text field, so I just walk up the responder chain from the text field to the cell (for the `next(ofType:)` method, see Appendix B). It is then trivial to update the model:

```
func textFieldDidEndEditing(_ textField: UITextField) {
    if let cell = textField.next(ofType: MyCell.self) {
        // update data model to match
        if let ip = self.tableView.indexPath(for:cell) {
            let s = cell.textField.text ?? ""
            switch ip.section {
            case 0: self.name = s
            case 1: self.numbers[ip.row] = s
            default: break
            }
        }
    }
}
```

Expandable Cell

A useful trick is to animate a change in the height of one or more cells by performing an empty batch operation:

```
self.tableView.performBatchUpdates(nil)
```

This causes the section and row *structure* of the table to be asked for, along with calculation of all heights, but no *views* are requested; the table view is laid out freshly without reloading any cells. And if any heights have changed since the last time the table view was laid out, the change in height is animated!

Apple's Calendar app is an example. When you're editing an event and you tap on the Starts or Ends date, a space opens up just below that row of the table, revealing a date picker. When you tap the date again, the space closes again.

How might we implement that? Presume that the date picker is in its own table view cell. It is there all along, but you can't normally see it because the cell has zero height and its clipsToBounds is true. When you tap on the date, performBatchUpdates is called. This causes tableView(_:heightForRowAt:) to be called, and a different answer is given for the height of this cell. The cell expands to reveal the date picker:

```
var showDatePicker = false
let expandedHeight: CGFloat = 200
func toggleDatePickerCell() {
    self.showDatePicker.toggle()
    self.tableView.performBatchUpdates(nil)
}
func tableView(_ tableView: UITableView,
    heightForRowAt indexPath: IndexPath) -> CGFloat {
        if indexPath == datePickerPath {
            return self.showDatePicker ? self.expandedHeight : 0
        }
        return tableView.rowHeight
}
```

(A cell that behaves this way is sometimes called an *accordion* cell.)

Table View Swipe Action Buttons

We've already seen that you can swipe a cell sideways to reveal a Delete button. You can customize that interface, introducing additional buttons that the user can reveal by swiping a cell sideways. That's how Apple's Mail app works: the user can swipe a message listing left to reveal three buttons, or swipe right to reveal one button, and can tap a button to perform an action on that message.

Starting in iOS 11, Apple provides an API that allows your app to have the same kind of interface as the Mail app. For each row of the table view, you specify *swipe actions;* these are buttons that can appear at the right or left (leading or trailing) end of the cell when the user swipes sideways. There are two delegate methods that you can implement:

- tableView(_:leadingSwipeActionsConfigurationForRowAt:)

- tableView(_:trailingSwipeActionsConfigurationForRowAt:)

Your job here is to return a UISwipeActionsConfiguration object (or nil), which wraps an array of UIContextualAction objects; a UIContextualAction is a button, initialized with a style (.normal or .destructive), a title, and an action function that will be called when the action is to be executed. The title can be nil, because you might set the UIContextualAction's image instead. Here's a simple example, where we implement a Delete button with a trash-can icon, along with a blue Mark button; the user can swipe left to see them:

```
override func tableView(_ tableView: UITableView,
    trailingSwipeActionsConfigurationForRowAt ip: IndexPath)
    -> UISwipeActionsConfiguration? {
        let d = UIContextualAction(style: .destructive, title: nil) {
            action, view, completion in
            tableView.performBatchUpdates {
                self.sections[ip.section].rowData.remove(at:ip.row)
                tableView.deleteRows(at:[ip], with: .automatic)
                if self.sections[ip.section].rowData.count == 0 {
                    self.sections.remove(at:ip.section)
                    tableView.deleteSections(
                        IndexSet(integer: ip.section), with:.fade)
                }
            }
            completion(true)
        }
        d.image = UIGraphicsImageRenderer(size:CGSize(30,30)).image { _ in
            UIImage(named:"trash")?.draw(in: CGRect(0,0,30,30))
        }
        let m = UIContextualAction(style: .normal, title: "Mark") {
            action, view, completion in
            print("Mark") // in real life, do something here
            completion(true)
        }
        m.backgroundColor = .blue
        let config = UISwipeActionsConfiguration(actions: [d,m])
        return config
}
```

The code for the first button (d) comes directly from the .delete case of the table-View(_:commit:forRowAt:) implementation we developed earlier. In fact, if the table view is in edit mode with a Minus button and the user taps the Minus button, the custom contextual actions are revealed; they have replaced the default Delete button! So if you use a trailing swipe action, you probably won't need to implement table-View(_:commit:forRowAt:) at all.

The action function receives as its parameters the UIContextualAction itself, the view (which you probably won't need), and a completion function. You *must* call this completion function, with a Bool argument, to signal that the action is over and the swiped cell should slide back into place.

The `actions` for the UISwipeActionsConfiguration object are supplied in order, starting at the far end of the cell. A UISwipeActionsConfiguration object has one additional property, a Bool called `performsFirstActionWithFullSwipe`. If this is `true`, the user can keep swiping to perform the first action; if `false`, the user must swipe to reveal the button and then tap the button. The default is `true` for trailing actions, `false` for leading actions.

Table View Menus

You can permit the user to summon a menu by long pressing on a table view cell. In iOS 12 and before, this menu was managed through the UIMenuController class, and the menu was similar to what appears above a text field when you double tap or long press within the text (saying Copy, Paste, Select, and so forth). In iOS 13 and later, it's the same UIContextMenuConfiguration architecture that I discussed in Chapter 6 ("Previews and Context Menus" on page 386). With a table view, you don't need to add a UIContextMenuInteraction or declare a delegate; instead, the table view is ready for the user to long press on a cell, and the delegate is the table view's delegate. The key method is:

- `tableView(_:contextMenuConfigurationForRowAt:point:)`

You return a UIContextMenuConfiguration instance (or `nil` to opt out on this occasion). The second parameter is the index path for the cell the user is pressing.

Here's a minimal example where we allow the user to summon a Copy context menu item by long pressing a cell. Presume this is our table view listing U.S. states, and we want the user to be able to copy the name of a state:

```
override func tableView(_ tableView: UITableView,
    contextMenuConfigurationForRowAt ip: IndexPath, point: CGPoint)
    -> UIContextMenuConfiguration? {
        let config = UIContextMenuConfiguration(
            identifier:nil, previewProvider: nil) { _ in
                let action = UIAction(title: "Copy") { _ in
                    let state = self.sections[ip.section].rowData[ip.row]
                    UIPasteboard.general.string = state
                }
                let menu = UIMenu(title: "", children: [action])
                return menu
            }
        return config
}
```

The user can now long press a cell to summon a menu consisting of single menu item labeled "Copy." If the user taps that item, the name of the corresponding state is copied onto the pasteboard.

There are three additional delegate methods, similar to the UIContextMenuInteractionDelegate methods I discussed earlier:

- `tableView(_:previewForHighlightingContextMenuWithConfiguration:)`
- `tableView(_:previewForDismissingContextMenuWithConfiguration:)`
- `tableView(_:willPerformPreviewActionForMenuWith:)`

If you don't supply a preview, the entire cell is used as a preview. If you return a subview of the cell as the UITargetedPreview in `previewForHighlighting`, it looks best if you return the same subview in `previewForDismissing`.

For all three of these delegate methods, you'll likely want to know what cell the user is pressing. But no incoming parameter tells you that; all you get is the UIContextMenuConfiguration. One solution is to use the index path (or, if you're using a diffable data source, a unique item identifier) as the `identifier:` when you initialize the configuration; then, in these delegate methods, you can ask the configuration for its `identifier`. Another possibility might be to subclass UIContextMenuConfiguration and give the subclass properties that carry any needed data into the delegate methods.

Table View Searching

A common need is to make a table view searchable, typically through a search field (a UISearchBar; see Chapter 13). A standard interface for listing the results of such a search is itself a table view. The interface should respond to what the user types in the search field by changing what appears in the list of results. To help you, there's a UIViewController subclass, UISearchController.

UISearchController has nothing to do, *per se*, with table views! It's completely agnostic about what is being searched and about the form in which the results are presented. Still, using a table view to present the results of searching a table view is a common interface, so this is a good place to introduce UISearchController.

Basic Configuration of a Search Controller

A UISearchController is a view controller; it provides an interface containing a search bar and the results of the search. The search controller vends its search bar, and you'll put that search bar into your initial interface. When the user taps in the search bar to begin searching, the search controller will take over the screen. And that's basically *all* the search controller does. It knows nothing about doing any actual searching or about showing the user the results of the search. All of that is up to you. You provide two things:

Search results controller

> The search results controller is your view controller that shows the user the results of the search. The UISearchController will display the search results controller's view, but what happens in that view is up to you.

Search results updater

> The search results updater is the search controller's conduit to you; basically, it's a kind of delegate. The search results controller will be repeatedly informing you that the user has edited the text in the search field; in response, you'll perform the actual search and update the results.

Here's what's going to happen:

- When the time comes to display search results (because the user has tapped inside the search bar in your initial interface), the search controller will present itself as a presented view controller, displaying the same search bar, with the search results controller's view embedded inside its own view.

- When the user edits in the search bar, the search controller will notify the search results updater.

- When the user taps the search bar's Cancel button, the search controller will dismiss itself.

The minimalistic nature of the search controller's behavior is exactly the source of its power and flexibility, because it leaves you free to manage the details of what searching means and what displaying search results means.

Here are the general steps for configuring a UISearchController (and I'll talk about exceptions in subsequent sections):

1. Instantiate a view controller whose job will be to display the results of the search. This is the search results controller. (In this discussion, the search results controller will be a UITableViewController, but no law requires this.)

2. Instantiate UISearchController, calling the designated initializer, `init(search-ResultsController:)`, with the search results controller as argument.

3. *Retain the search controller.* The search controller, in turn, will retain the search results controller as a child view controller.

4. Assign to the search controller's `searchResultsUpdater` an object to be notified when the search results change. This is the search results updater. It must adopt the UISearchResultsUpdating protocol, which means that it implements one method: `updateSearchResults(for:)`. Often, the search results updater will be the search results controller, but no law requires this.

5. Acquire the search controller's `searchBar` and put it into the interface.

Nowhere in that description did I mention table views. As I've said, a search controller has nothing to do, in and of itself, with table views. To see that this is so, we can experiment with a minimal search controller that doesn't cause any information to be displayed:

```
class ViewController: UIViewController {
    var sc : UISearchController?
    override var prefersStatusBarHidden: Bool { true }
    override func viewDidLoad() {
        super.viewDidLoad()
        let vc2 = ViewController2()                             // step 1
        let sc = UISearchController(searchResultsController: vc2) // step 2
        self.sc = sc                                            // step 3
        sc.searchResultsUpdater = vc2                           // step 4
        let sb = sc.searchBar                                   // step 5
        self.view.addSubview(sb)
    }
}
class ViewController2: UIViewController, UISearchResultsUpdating {
    override func viewDidLoad() {
        super.viewDidLoad()
        self.view.backgroundColor = .green
    }
    func updateSearchResults(for searchController: UISearchController) {
        guard searchController.isActive else {return}
        if let t = searchController.searchBar.text, !t.isEmpty {
            print("You are searching for", t)
        }
    }
}
```

That is actually a working UISearchController! As you can see, I perform all five steps. I perform them in a very simple-minded way; I don't worry about *where* the search controller's search bar is displayed (it just appears at the top of the first view controller's view), and I don't attempt to display any search results either (the second view controller is just a big green background). Nevertheless, we are in fact responding to the user typing in the search field — by printing to the console. In real life, the second view controller will have an interface, such as a table view, and we will respond to the user typing by modifying that interface.

More Search Controller Configuration

A UISearchController has just a few other properties you might want to configure:

obscuresBackgroundDuringPresentation

Whether a "dimming view" should appear behind the search controller's own view. Defaults to true, but there are situations where it needs to be set to false (as I'll demonstrate later).

`hidesNavigationBarDuringPresentation`
> Whether a navigation bar, if present, should be hidden. Defaults to `true`, but there are situations where it needs to be set to `false` (as I'll demonstrate later).

A UISearchController has its own ideas about when it wants to show the search bar's scope bar if it has one, the search bar's Cancel button, and the search results controller's view. Starting in iOS 13, that automatic behavior is governed by three properties:

- `automaticallyShowsCancelButton`
- `automaticallyShowsScopeBar`
- `automaticallyShowsSearchResultsController`

If you set any of the corresponding properties — the search bar's `showsCancel-Button`, the search bar's `showsScopeBar`, or the search controller's `showsSearch-ResultsController` — that `automaticallyShows` property is set to `false` and control of that property is turned over to you.

A UISearchController can also be assigned a real delegate (UISearchController-Delegate), which is notified before and after presentation and dismissal. The delegate works in one of two ways:

`presentSearchController(_:)`
> If you implement this method, then you are expected to present the search controller yourself, by calling `present(_:animated:completion:)`. In that case, the other delegate methods are *not* called.

`willPresentSearchController(_:)`
`didPresentSearchController(_:)`
`willDismissSearchController(_:)`
`didDismissSearchController(_:)`
> Called only if you didn't implement `presentSearchController(_:)`.

Using a Search Controller

I'll demonstrate several variations on the theme of using a search controller to make a table view searchable. In these examples, the searchable table view will be (you guessed it) the list of U.S. states, with sections and an index, developed earlier in this chapter. Searching will mean finding the search text within the text displayed in the single label in each of the table view's cells — that is, we will search the state names.

Minimal search results table

Let's start with the simplest possible case. We will have two table view controllers — one managing the original table view, the other managing the search results table view. I propose to make the search results table view as minimal as possible, a

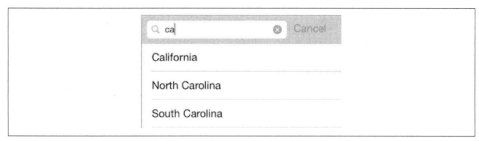

Figure 8-9. Searching a table

rock-bottom table view with `.default` style cells, where each search result will be the text of a cell's `textLabel` (Figure 8-9).

In the original table's UITableViewController, I configure the UISearchController, in accordance with the steps that I described earlier. I have a property, `self.searcher`, waiting to retain the search controller. I also have a second UITableViewController subclass, boringly named SearchResultsController, whose job will be to obtain and present the search results. In `viewDidLoad`, I instantiate SearchResultsController, create and configure the UISearchController, and put the search controller's search bar into the interface as the table view's header view (and scroll to hide that search bar initially, a common convention):

```
let src = SearchResultsController(data: self.sections)
let searcher = UISearchController(searchResultsController: src)
self.searcher = searcher
searcher.searchResultsUpdater = src
let b = searcher.searchBar
b.autocapitalizationType = .none
self.tableView.tableHeaderView = b
self.tableView.reloadData()
self.tableView.scrollToRow(
    at:IndexPath(row: 0, section: 0), at:.top, animated:false)
```

 Adding the search bar as the table view's header view has an odd side effect: it causes the table view's background color to be covered by an ugly gray color, visible above the search bar when the user scrolls down. The official workaround is to assign the table view a `backgroundView` with the desired color.

Now we turn to SearchResultsController. It's a table view controller. I'm not using sections in the SearchResultsController's table, so as I receive the searchable data, I flatten it to a simple array:

```
var originalData : [String]
var filteredData = [String]()
init(data:[RootViewController.Section]) {
    self.originalData = data.map {$0.rowData}.flatMap {$0}
    super.init(nibName: nil, bundle: nil)
}
```

What I display in the table view is not `self.originalData` but a *different* array, `self.filteredData`. This is initially empty, because there are no search results until the user starts typing in the search field. So how does our search results table go from being empty to displaying any search results? SearchResultsController is also the `searchResultsUpdater` of our UISearchController. It adopts the UISearchResultsUpdating protocol, so it implements `updateSearchResults(for:)`, which will be called each time the user changes the text of the search bar. This method simply uses the current text of the search controller's `searchBar` to filter `self.originalData` into `self.filteredData`, and reloads the table view:

```
func updateSearchResults(for searchController: UISearchController) {
    let sb = searchController.searchBar
    let target = sb.text!
    self.filteredData = self.originalData.filter { s in
        let found = s.range(of:target, options: .caseInsensitive)
        return (found != nil)
    }
    self.tableView.reloadData()
}
```

That's all! Of course, it's an artificially simple example; in real life you would presumably want to allow the user to *do* something with the search results, perhaps by tapping on a cell in the search results table.

Using a diffable data source instead of a Three Big Questions data source is a nice way to animate the results table as the user types in the search bar. Now there's no need for a `filteredData` instance property; we simply filter the original data into a snapshot and apply it:

```
func updateSearchResults(for searchController: UISearchController) {
    let sb = searchController.searchBar
    let target = sb.text!
    var snap = NSDiffableDataSourceSnapshot<Int,String>()
    snap.appendSections([0])
    snap.appendItems(self.originalData.filter { s in
        let found = s.range(of:target, options: .caseInsensitive)
        return (found != nil)
    })
    self.datasource.apply(snap)
}
```

Search bar in navigation bar

In a navigation interface, you can put the UISearchController's search bar into the navigation bar. Starting in iOS 11, Apple seems to prefer that interface over putting it into the table view's header view, and facilitates it through a UINavigationItem property: instead of finding a place for the search bar in the navigation bar yourself — as its `titleView`, for instance — you set the `searchController` of your view controller's `navigationItem` directly to your UISearchController instance. When you do that, you don't need to retain the search controller; the navigation item will retain it for you:

```
let src = SearchResultsController(data: self.sections)
let searcher = UISearchController(searchResultsController: src)
searcher.searchResultsUpdater = src
self.navigationItem.searchController = searcher // *
```

Nothing else needs to change; our search results controller just keeps right on working.

The consequences of this arrangement are:

- The navigation bar stretches to accommodate the search bar, which appears *below* everything else in the navigation bar; the search bar makes no inroads on the space used by the title and the bar button items.

- If the navigation bar's `prefersLargeTitles` is `true`, the interface still works just fine, with the search bar displayed below the large title if there is one.

- If the navigation item's `hidesSearchBarWhenScrolling` property is `true`, the navigation bar expands and contracts to reveal or hide the search bar as the user scrolls.

- You can decide whether the overall navigation bar should remain present when the search controller's view is being presented, by setting the search controller's `hidesNavigationBarDuringPresentation`. The default is `true`, which means that the navigation bar shrinks to show just the search bar at the top during the search.

- The search bar can have scope buttons! Set the search bar's `scopeButtonTitles` as desired. By default, the scope buttons will appear when the search controller presents its view.

I'll demonstrate the use of scope buttons. Let's say we've configured this search bar with two scope buttons:

```
let b = searcher.searchBar
b.scopeButtonTitles = ["Contains", "Starts With"]
```

We must take account of the currently selected scope button whenever we set `self.filteredData`. Starting in iOS 13, `updateSearchResults` is called when the user changes the selected scope button, so its implementation is simple:

```
func updateSearchResults(for sc: UISearchController) {
    if let target = sc.searchBar.text {
        let selectedIndex = sc.searchBar.selectedScopeButtonIndex
        self.filteredData = self.originalData.filter { s in
            var options = String.CompareOptions.caseInsensitive
            if selectedIndex == 1 { // 1 means "starts with"
                options.insert(.anchored)
```

```
            }
            let found = s.range(of:target, options: options)
            return (found != nil)
        }
        self.tableView.reloadData()
    }
}
```

No search results controller

You can also use a search controller *without* a search results controller. Instead, you can present the search results *in the original table view.*

To configure our search controller, we pass nil as its searchResultsController and set the original table view controller as the searchResultsUpdater. We must also set the search controller's obscuresBackgroundDuringPresentation to false; this allows the original table view to remain *visible and touchable* behind the search controller's view:

```
let searcher = UISearchController(searchResultsController:nil) // *
self.searcher = searcher
searcher.obscuresBackgroundDuringPresentation = false // *
searcher.searchResultsUpdater = self
searcher.delegate = self
```

We have also made ourselves the search controller's delegate, because we might need to distinguish whether we're in the middle of a search or not. We have a Bool property, self.searching, that acts as a flag; we raise and lower the flag when searching begins and ends. We also create a copy of our data model whenever we're about to start searching; the reason for that will be clear in a moment:

```
func willPresentSearchController(_ searchController: UISearchController) {
    self.originalSections = self.sections // keep copy of original data
    self.searching = true
}
func willDismissSearchController(_ searchController: UISearchController) {
    self.searching = false
}
```

Our table view data source and delegate methods don't need to change unless there's a difference in the interface depending on whether or not we're searching. Let's say we want to remove the index while searching is in progress:

```
override func sectionIndexTitlesForTableView(tableView: UITableView)
    -> [String]? {
        return self.searching ? nil : self.sections.map {$0.sectionName}
}
```

All that remains is to implement updateSearchResults(for:). Similar to our search results controller, whenever we're doing a search we're going to filter self.original-Sections into self.sections based on the search bar text:

```
func updateSearchResults(for searchController: UISearchController) {
    let sb = searchController.searchBar
    let target = sb.text!
    if target == "" {
        self.sections = self.originalSections
    } else {
        self.sections = self.originalSections.reduce(into:[Section]()) {
            acc, sec in
            let rowData = sec.rowData.filter {
                $0.range(of:target, options: .caseInsensitive) != nil
            }
            if rowData.count > 0 {
                acc.append(Section(
                    sectionName: sec.sectionName, rowData: rowData))
            }
        }
    }
    self.tableView.reloadData()
}
```

Collection Views

A collection view (UICollectionView) is a UIScrollView that generalizes the notion of a table view (Chapter 8). Where a table view has *rows*, a collection view has *items*. (UICollectionView extends IndexPath so that you can refer to its `item` property instead of its `row` property, though in fact they are interchangeable.)

If you mentally substitute for items for rows, you'll find that, knowing about table views, you know a great deal about collection views already:

- The items are portrayed by reusable cells. These are UICollectionViewCell instances. If the collection view is instantiated from a storyboard, you can get reusable cells from the storyboard; otherwise, you'll register a class or nib with the collection view.

- A collection view can clump its items into sections.

- A collection view has a data source (UICollectionViewDataSource) and a delegate (UICollectionViewDelegate), and it's going to ask the data source Three Big Questions:

  - `numberOfSections(in:)`

  - `collectionView(_:numberOfItemsInSection:)`

  - `collectionView(_:cellForItemAt:)`

  Alternatively, starting in iOS 13, you can use a UICollectionViewDiffableData-Source.

- To answer the third Big Question, your data source will obtain a reusable cell by dequeuing it from the collection view:

  - `dequeueReusableCell(withReuseIdentifier:for:)`

- A collection view allows the user to select a cell, or multiple cells. The delegate is notified of highlighting and selection.

- Your code can rearrange the cells, inserting, moving, and deleting cells or entire sections, with animation.

- If the delegate permits, the user can long press a cell to produce a menu, or to rearrange the cells by dragging.

- You can scroll your collection view in code by calling `scrollToItem(at:at:animated:)`. The collection view's delegate is its scroll view delegate (and UICollectionViewDelegate conforms to UIScrollViewDelegate).

- A collection view can have a refresh control.

- You can manage your UICollectionView through a UICollectionViewController.

A collection view section can have a header and footer, but the collection view itself does not call them that; instead, it generalizes its subview types into cells, on the one hand, and *supplementary views*, on the other. A supplementary view is just a UICollectionReusableView, which is UICollectionViewCell's superclass. A supplementary view is associated with a *kind*, an arbitrary string that categorizes it however you like; you can have a header as one kind, a footer as another kind, and anything else you can imagine. Supplementary views behave quite similarly to section header or footer views in a table view:

- Supplementary views are reusable.

- You are asked for a supplementary view in a data source method (*not* a delegate method):

  - `collectionView(_:viewForSupplementaryElementOfKind:at:)`

- In that method, your data source will obtain a reusable supplementary view by dequeuing it from the collection view:

  - `dequeueReusableSupplementaryView(ofKind:withReuseIdentifier:for:)`

The big difference between a table view and a collection view is how the collection view lays out its elements (cells and supplementary views). A table view lays out its cells in just one way: a vertically scrolling column, where the cell widths are the width of the table view, their heights are dictated by the table view or the delegate, and the cells are touching one another. A collection view has no such rules. In fact, a collection view doesn't lay out its elements at all! That job is left to another object — a *collection view layout*.

A collection view layout is an instance of a UICollectionViewLayout subclass. It is responsible for the overall layout of the collection view that owns it. It does this by answering some Big Questions of its own, posed by the collection view; the most important are these:

`collectionViewContentSize`

> How big is the entire content? The collection view needs to know this, because it is a scroll view (Chapter 7), and this will be the content size of the scrollable material that it will display.

`layoutAttributesForElements(in:)`

> Where are the elements to be positioned within the content rectangle? The layout attributes, as I'll explain in more detail in a moment, are bundles of positional information.

To answer these questions, the collection view layout needs to ask the collection view some questions as well. It will want to know the collection view's bounds; also, it will probably call such methods as `numberOfSections` and `numberOfItems(inSection:)`, and the collection view, in turn, will get the answers to those questions from its data source.

The collection view layout can assign the elements any positions it likes, and the collection view will faithfully draw them in those positions within its content rectangle. That seems very open-ended, and indeed it is. To get you started, there are two built-in UICollectionViewLayout subclasses:

- UICollectionViewFlowLayout
- UICollectionViewCompositionalLayout (introduced in iOS 13)

UICollectionViewFlowLayout arranges its cells in something like a grid. The grid can be scrolled either horizontally or vertically, but not both, so it's a series of rows or columns. Through properties and a delegate protocol of its own (UICollectionView-DelegateFlowLayout), the UICollectionViewFlowLayout instance lets you provide instructions about how big the cells are and how they should be spaced. It defines two supplementary view kinds to let you give each section a header and a footer.

Figure 9-1 shows a collection view, laid out with a flow layout, from my Latin flash-card app. This interface lists the chapters and lessons into which the flashcards are divided, and allows the user to jump to a desired lesson by tapping it. Originally, I was using a table view to present this list; when collection views were introduced (in iOS 6), I adopted one for this interface, and you can see why. Instead of a lesson item like "1a" occupying an entire row that stretches the whole width of a table, it's just a little rectangle; in landscape orientation, the flow layout fits about half a dozen of these rectangles into a line for me. So a collection view is a much more compact and appropriate way to present this interface than a table view.

If UICollectionViewFlowLayout doesn't quite meet your needs, you can subclass it. Alternatively, you can subclass UICollectionViewLayout itself to create a layout from scratch. Starting in iOS 13, there's a third possibility: you can use a UICollectionView-CompositionalLayout. This is a powerful and flexible layout that does all the heavy lifting for you; it can do everything a flow layout can do, and much more.

Figure 9-1. A collection view in my Latin flashcard app

Collection View Classes

Here's a conceptual overview of the main classes associated with UICollectionView; I don't recite all the properties and methods of each class, because you can gather them from the documentation:

UICollectionViewController
> A UIViewController subclass. Like a table view controller, UICollectionView-Controller is convenient if a UICollectionView is to be a view controller's view, but using it is not required. It is the delegate and data source of its collection-View by default. The designated initializer requires you to supply a collection view layout instance, which will be assigned to the collection view as its layout. In the nib editor, there is a Collection View Controller nib object, which comes with a collection view.

UICollectionView
> A UIScrollView subclass. Its capabilities are parallel to those of a UITableView, as I outlined in the preceding section. It has a backgroundColor (because it's a view) and optionally a backgroundView in front of that. Its designated initializer requires you to supply a collection view layout instance, which will be its collectionViewLayout. In the nib editor, there is a Collection View nib object, which comes with a Collection View Flow Layout by default; you can change the collection view layout class with the Layout pop-up menu in the Attributes inspector.

UICollectionViewLayoutAttributes
> A value class (a bunch of properties) tying together an element's indexPath with the specifications for how and where it should be drawn. These specifications are

reminiscent of view or layer properties, with names like `frame`, `center`, `size`, `transform`, and so forth. Instances of this class function as the mediators between the collection view layout and the collection view; they are what the collection view layout passes to the collection view to tell it where all the elements of the view should go.

UICollectionViewCell

An extremely minimal view class. It has an `isHighlighted` property and an `isSelected` property. It has a `contentView`, a `selectedBackgroundView`, a `backgroundView`, and of course (since it's a view) a `backgroundColor`, layered in that order, just like a table view cell; everything else is up to you. However, new in iOS 14, a UICollectionViewCell has `contentConfiguration` and `background-Configuration` properties ("Apple's Cell Configuration Architecture" on page 478); it does not vend a default content configuration, but you are free to apply a UIListContentConfiguration, which lets you set the `text` and so on.

If you start with a collection view in a storyboard, you get prototype cells, which you obtain by dequeuing. Otherwise, you obtain cells through registration and dequeuing.

UICollectionReusableView

The superclass of UICollectionViewCell — so it is even more minimal! This is the class of supplementary views such as headers and footers. (You can use UICollectionViewCell as the supplementary view class if you like.) If you're using a flow layout in a storyboard, you are given header and footer prototype views, which you obtain by dequeuing; otherwise, you obtain reusable views through registration and dequeuing.

UICollectionViewLayout

The layout workhorse class for a collection view. A collection view cannot exist without a collection view layout instance! As I've already said, the collection view layout knows how much room all the subviews occupy, and supplies the `collectionViewContentSize` that sets the `contentSize` of the collection view, *qua* scroll view. In addition, the collection view layout must answer questions from the collection view, by supplying a UICollectionViewLayoutAttributes object, or an array of such objects, saying where and how elements should be drawn. These questions come in two categories:

Static attributes

The collection view wants to know the layout attributes of an element (an item or supplementary view), specified by the element's index path, or of all elements within a given rect.

Dynamic attributes

The collection view is inserting or removing elements. It asks for the layout attributes that an element, specified by index path, should have as insertion begins or removal ends. The collection view can animate between the element's static attributes and these dynamic attributes. If an element's dynamic layout attributes `alpha` is 0 as removal ends, the element will appear to fade away as it is removed.

The collection view also notifies the collection view layout of pending changes through some methods whose names start with `prepare` and `finalize`. This is another way for the collection view layout to participate in animations, or to perform other kinds of preparation and cleanup.

UICollectionViewLayout is an abstract class; to use it, you must subclass it, or start with a built-in subclass, either UICollectionViewFlowLayout or UICollectionViewCompositionalLayout.

 When you choose File → New → File to create a new UICollectionViewController subclass, the template code's implementation of `viewDidLoad` calls `register(_:forCellWithReuseIdentifier:)` to register the UICollectionViewCell class. As a result, if you design a prototype cell in the storyboard, it will not be loaded; you'll get empty cells instead. The solution is to delete that line of code; I regard its presence as a bug in the template.

Flow Layout

UICollectionViewFlowLayout is a concrete subclass of UICollectionViewLayout. It lays out items in a grid that can be scrolled either horizontally or vertically, and it defines two supplementary element types to serve as the header and footer of a section. A collection view in the nib editor has a Layout pop-up menu that lets you choose a Flow layout, and you can configure the flow layout in the Size inspector; in a storyboard, you can even add and design a header and a footer.

A flow layout has the following configurable properties:

- `scrollDirection`, either `.vertical` or `.horizontal`
- `sectionInset` (the margins for a section); starting in iOS 11, the `sectionInset-Reference` property lets you specify where the inset is measured from (`.from-ContentInset`, `.fromLayoutMargins`, or `.fromSafeArea`)
- `itemSize`, along with `minimumLineSpacing` (spacing in the scroll direction) and `minimumInteritemSpacing` (spacing in the other direction)
- `headerReferenceSize`, `footerReferenceSize`

- `sectionHeadersPinToVisibleBounds`, `sectionFootersPinToVisibleBounds`; if `true`, they cause the headers and footers to behave like table view section headers and footers when the user scrolls

At a minimum, if you want to see any section headers, you must assign the flow layout a `headerReferenceSize`, because the default is `.zero`. Apart from that, you get initial defaults that will at least allow you to see something immediately, such as an `itemSize` of (50.0,50.0) along with reasonable default spacing between items and rows (or columns).

UICollectionViewFlowLayout also defines a delegate protocol of its own, UICollectionViewDelegateFlowLayout. The flow layout automatically treats the collection view's delegate as its own delegate. However, you must explicitly declare that the collection view's delegate adopts the UICollectionViewDelegateFlowLayout protocol; otherwise, your flow layout delegate methods won't be called. The section margins, item size, item spacing, line spacing, and header and footer size can be set for individual sections, cells, and supplementary views through this delegate.

To illustrate, here's how the view shown in Figure 9-1 is created. I have a UICollectionViewController subclass, LessonListController. Every collection view must have a collection view layout, so LessonListController's designated initializer initializes itself with a UICollectionViewFlowLayout:

```
init(terms data:[Term]) {
    // ... other self-initializations here ...
    let layout = UICollectionViewFlowLayout()
    super.init(collectionViewLayout:layout)
}
```

In `viewDidLoad`, we give the flow layout hints about the sizes of the margins, cells, and headers, as well as registering for cell and header reusability:

```
let headerID = "LessonHeader"
let cellID = "LessonCell"
override func viewDidLoad() {
    super.viewDidLoad()
    let layout = self.collectionView.collectionViewLayout
        as! UICollectionViewFlowLayout
    layout.sectionInset = UIEdgeInsets(top:10, left:20, bottom:10, right:20)
    layout.headerReferenceSize = CGSize(0,40)
    layout.itemSize = CGSize(70,45)
    self.collectionView.register(
        UINib(nibName: self.cellID, bundle: nil),
        forCellWithReuseIdentifier: self.cellID)
    self.collectionView.register(
        UICollectionReusableView.self,
        forSupplementaryViewOfKind: UICollectionView.elementKindSectionHeader,
```

```
        withReuseIdentifier: self.headerID)
    self.collectionView.backgroundColor = .myGolden
    self.collectionView.contentInsetAdjustmentBehavior = .always
}
```

My data model is just like the model for the table of U.S. states I've been using throughout this chapter. (What are the chances of *that?*) The difference is that my rowData, instead of being an array of Strings, is an array of Terms. (Term is basically a custom value class.) The first two of the Three Big Questions are extremely familiar:

```
override func numberOfSections(
    in collectionView: UICollectionView) -> Int {
        return self.sections.count
}
override func collectionView(_ collectionView: UICollectionView,
    numberOfItemsInSection section: Int) -> Int {
        return self.sections[section].rowData.count
}
```

The third of the Three Big Questions creates and configures the cells. In a *.xib* file, I've designed the cell with a single subview, a UILabel with tag 1; if the text of that label is still "Label", the cell has come freshly minted from the nib and needs further initial configuration. Among other things, I assign each new cell a selected-BackgroundView and give the label a highlightedTextColor, to get an automatic indication of selection:

```
override func collectionView(_ collectionView: UICollectionView,
    cellForItemAt indexPath: IndexPath) -> UICollectionViewCell {
        let cell = collectionView.dequeueReusableCell(
            withReuseIdentifier: self.cellID, for: indexPath)
        let lab = cell.viewWithTag(1) as! UILabel
        if lab.text == "Label" {
            lab.highlightedTextColor = .white
            cell.backgroundColor = .myPaler
            cell.layer.borderColor = UIColor.brown.cgColor
            cell.layer.borderWidth = 5
            cell.layer.cornerRadius = 5
            let v = UIView()
            v.backgroundColor = UIColor.blue.withAlphaComponent(0.8)
            cell.selectedBackgroundView = v
        }
        let term = self.sections[indexPath.section].rowData[indexPath.item]
        lab.text = term.lesson + term.sectionFirstWord
        return cell
}
```

The data source is also asked for the supplementary element views; in my case, these are the section headers. I configure the header entirely in code. Again I distinguish between newly minted views and reused views; the latter will already have a single subview, a UILabel:

```
override func collectionView(_ collectionView: UICollectionView,
    viewForSupplementaryElementOfKind kind: String,
    at indexPath: IndexPath) -> UICollectionReusableView {
        let v = collectionView.dequeueReusableSupplementaryView(
            ofKind: kind,
            withReuseIdentifier: self.headerID, for: indexPath)
        if v.subviews.count == 0 {
            let lab = UILabel(frame:CGRect(10,0,100,40))
            lab.font = UIFont(name:"GillSans-Bold", size:20)
            lab.backgroundColor = .clear
            v.addSubview(lab)
            v.backgroundColor = .black
            lab.textColor = .myPaler
        }
        let lab = v.subviews[0] as! UILabel
        lab.text = self.sections[indexPath.section].sectionName
        return v
}
```

As you can see from Figure 9-1, the first section is treated specially — it has no header, and its cell is wider. I take care of that with two UICollectionViewDelegateFlowLayout methods:

```
func collectionView(_ collectionView: UICollectionView,
    layout lay: UICollectionViewLayout,
    sizeForItemAt indexPath: IndexPath) -> CGSize {
        var sz = (lay as! UICollectionViewFlowLayout).itemSize
        if indexPath.section == 0 {
            sz.width = 150
        }
        return sz
}
func collectionView(_ collectionView: UICollectionView,
    layout lay: UICollectionViewLayout,
    referenceSizeForHeaderInSection section: Int) -> CGSize {
        var sz = (lay as! UICollectionViewFlowLayout).headerReferenceSize
        if section == 0 {
            sz.height = 0
        }
        return sz
}
```

When the user taps a cell, I hear about it through the delegate method collectionView(_:didSelectItemAt:) and respond accordingly. And that's the entire code for managing this collection view!

When you create a new collection view (or collection view controller) with a flow layout in the nib editor, its Estimate Size pop-up menu in the Size inspector is set to Automatic, and the prototype cell's Size pop-up menu is set to Automatic as well. This means that cells are *self-sizing by default*; they expect to be sized from the inside out by their contents, using autolayout. If that's not what you're expecting, your cells may appear at the wrong size, and implementing the flow layout delegate method collectionView(_:layout:sizeForItemAt:) might not help. Try changing one or both of those pop-up menus to fix it.

Compositional Layout

In iOS 13, a new concrete UICollectionViewLayout subclass was introduced — UICollectionViewCompositionalLayout. It can do everything UICollectionView-FlowLayout can do; even more important, it can achieve layouts that previously required you to write a custom UICollectionViewLayout subclass from scratch.

In general, you construct a compositional layout by building up a description from the smallest element to the largest (hence the term *compositional*). The elements are:

item (NSCollectionLayoutItem)
    In effect, a cell.

group (NSCollectionLayoutGroup)
    A single unidimensional set of items, either horizontal or vertical. Think of it as a single row or column. In most layouts, a group will run along the other axis from the layout's scrolling direction. If a layout scrolls vertically, a group will typically be horizontal and will represent one row of cells.

section (NSCollectionLayoutSection)
    A section repeats a group. If a group is a row, a section may contain many rows. Your data may have one or more sections. Sections can be laid out differently from one another.

layout (UICollectionViewCompositionalLayout)
    The object that will actually be handed to the collection view as its layout.

Size, Count, Spacing, and Insets

As you construct a compositional layout, you must specify the *size* of a section's group, the *size* of an item in the group, and the *count* of items per group. These are the most important determinants of how the cells will be laid out in the section; further refinements are provided through various spacing and inset properties.

A size is an NSCollectionLayoutSize. Its initializer is init(widthDimension:height-Dimension:). A dimension is an NSCollectionLayoutDimension, which has four class methods:

absolute
> A definite number of points.

fractionalWidth
fractionalHeight
> A proportion, between 0 and 1, of the container. For an item, the container is the group. For a group, the container is the collection view bounds. These are just numbers, so it is legal for the heightDimension: to be a fractionalWidth and *vice versa.*

estimated
> A number of points, but you are inviting the layout engine to measure cells using internal autolayout constraints to determine the actual value. A common situation is that one dimension of a size is fixed while the other is estimated.

A group (NSCollectionLayoutGroup) is instantiated using a horizontal or vertical class method. You supply parameters in two different ways:

horizontal(layoutSize:subitems:)
vertical(layoutSize:subitems:)
> The group repeats one or more item types, as many per group as will fit. Suppose the subitems: consists of two item types, one wide and one narrow; then the layout will alternate wide item with narrow item, filling a group before going on to the next group.

horizontal(layoutSize:subitem:count:)
vertical(layoutSize:subitem:count:)
> The group repeats a single item type, a fixed number of times per group. The items will be equally sized, possibly overriding the item's own size in that dimension. For instance, you can specify that there should be exactly three equally sized items per group.

Apple's own examples illustrate some basic combinations of item size, group size, and item count; these are all vertically scrolling collection views, so a group is a row:

- The item has width dimension fractional width 1 and height dimension fractional height 1. The group has width dimension fractional width 1 and height dimension absolute 44, and the subitems: initializer is used.

  So each row is as wide as the collection view and 44 points tall, with one item per row, filling the row. It looks rather like a table view.

- Like the previous layout, but the group's subitem:count: initializer is used with a count: of 2.

  So there are exactly two cells per row and they have equal widths; the item's layoutSize: width dimension is effectively ignored.

- The item has width dimension fractional width `0.2` and height dimension fractional height `1`. The group has width dimension `1` and height dimension fractional *width* `0.2`, and the `subitems:` initializer is used.

  So an item's width is one-fifth the width of the collection view, and a row's height is that same value — and an item's height fills it, resulting in a grid of square cells, five per row.

Further size refinements are applied through spacing and insets properties of the item, group, and section:

Item `edgeSpacing`
> An NSLayoutEdgeSpacing object with `leading:`, `top:`, `trailing:`, and `bottom:` parameters. A parameter is either `nil` or an NSCollectionLayoutSpacing object, instantiated through a class method, either `flexible` or `fixed`. For instance, in a vertically scrolling layout whose group uses the `subitems:` initializer, if there is room for only one cell per group, then a `leading:` and `trailing:` spacing of `.flexible(0)` will center the cell horizontally.

Group `interItemSpacing`
> The distance between items within the group. This is also an NSCollection-LayoutSpacing, so it can be `flexible`, causing the items to be spaced out equally and justified at both extremes.

Section `interGroupSpacing`
> A CGFloat determining absolutely the distance between rows (or columns) in the section.

Layout `interSectionSpacing`
> A CGFloat. A property, not of the layout itself, but of its `configuration`, a UICollectionViewCompositionalLayoutConfiguration (a value class). The configuration is also how you specify the layout's `scrollDirection`; the default is `.vertical`, so if that's what you want, and if you don't need to set the section spacing, you might not need a layout configuration.

Item, group, or section `contentInsets`
> An NSDirectionalEdgeInsets (Chapter 1). Content insets are applied *after* the sizing and layout have been worked out. In Apple's example of a grid with 5 square cells per row, if a positive `contentInsets` is applied to the item, there are *still* five cells per row, each in a square area, but a cell itself is inset within that square area. (Any `contentInsets` along an `estimated` dimension are ignored.)

You now know almost enough to achieve the layout shown in Figure 9-1 as a compositional layout! I haven't talked yet about section headers, and the first section's single item needs to be wider than all other items; but if we concentrate on just the items of the remaining sections, we can construct the layout like this:

```
private static func prepareLayout() -> UICollectionViewLayout {
    let itemSize = NSCollectionLayoutSize(
        widthDimension: .absolute(70),
        heightDimension: .fractionalHeight(1))
    let item = NSCollectionLayoutItem(layoutSize: itemSize)
    let groupSize = NSCollectionLayoutSize(
        widthDimension: .fractionalWidth(1),
        heightDimension: .absolute(45))
    let group = NSCollectionLayoutGroup.horizontal(
        layoutSize: groupSize, subitems: [item])
    group.interItemSpacing = .flexible(10)
    group.contentInsets = NSDirectionalEdgeInsets(
        top: 0, leading: 20, bottom: 0, trailing: 20)
    let section = NSCollectionLayoutSection(group: group)
    let vSpace = CGFloat(10)
    section.contentInsets = NSDirectionalEdgeInsets(
        top: vSpace, leading: 0, bottom: vSpace, trailing: 0)
    section.interGroupSpacing = vSpace
    let layout = UICollectionViewCompositionalLayout(section: section)
    return layout
}
```

Here's how that compositional layout mimics the flow layout shown in Figure 9-1:

Flow behavior

The compositional layout lays out its rows like a flow layout, because:

- The group uses the `subitems:` initializer, meaning that a row consists of as many cells as will fit.

- The group uses `flexible` interitem spacing, which causes the cells to be justified at the leading and trailing edges with equal spacing between them.

Cell size

In the flow layout, we set an `itemSize` of `CGSize(70,45)`. In the compositional layout, the same effect is achieved like this:

- An item has width dimension absolute `70` and height dimension fractional height `1`.

- The group has width dimension fractional width `1` and height dimension absolute `45`.

Margins

The flow layout has a `sectionInset` with a UIEdgeInsets value of (`10.0,20.0,10.0,20.0`). In the compositional layout:

- Horizontally, each group has leading and trailing margins.
- Vertically, each section has top and bottom margins along with spacing between the rows.

Supplementary Items

In a compositional layout, supplementary items come in two main categories:

NSCollectionLayoutSupplementaryItem
> An item or group's `supplementaryItems`. An item's supplementary items must be declared in the item initializer; a group has a settable `supplementaryItems` property.
>
> The initializer is `init(layoutSize:elementKind:containerAnchor:item-Anchor:)`:
>
> - The `elementKind:` is an arbitrary string.
> - The anchors are NSCollectionLayoutAnchor objects; the item anchor is optional. An anchor has `edges` (an NSDirectionalRectEdge) along with an optional `absoluteOffset` or `fractionalOffset`, which is a CGPoint.
>
>   An NSDirectionalRectEdge is an option set consisting of static properties `.top`, `.trailing`, `.leading`, and `.bottom`.
>
> A supplementary item also has a `zIndex` for front-to-back layering.
>
> Apple's example of an item's supplementary item has edges [`.top`, `.trailing`] and a `fractionalOffset` of `CGPoint(x:0.5,y:-0.5)`; that's a badge centered at the upper right corner.

NSCollectionLayoutBoundarySupplementaryItem
> An NSCollectionLayoutSupplementaryItem subclass. Can be applied to a section or a layout:
>
> - A section has a settable `boundarySupplementaryItems` property.
> - A layout's `configuration` has a `boundarySupplementaryItems` property.
>
> A boundary supplementary item has an `alignment` which is an NSRectAlignment, along with a possible `absoluteOffset`. The NSRectAlignment is an enum specifying a single edge or corner: `.top`, `.topLeading`, `.leading`, and so on; a header in a vertically scrolling layout would be attached to the section's `.top`. If the supplementary item's `extendsBoundary` is true (the default), it lies *outside* what would otherwise be the layout size of its container. There is also a `pinToVisibleBounds` property so that a section header or footer can behave like a table header or footer.

We are now ready to add section headers to the Latin LessonListController example! As we construct the section, we insert these lines:

```
let headerSize = NSCollectionLayoutSize(
    widthDimension: .fractionalWidth(1),
    heightDimension: .absolute(40))
let headerKind = UICollectionView.elementKindSectionHeader
let header = NSCollectionLayoutBoundarySupplementaryItem(
    layoutSize: headerSize, elementKind: headerKind, alignment: .top)
section.boundarySupplementaryItems = [header]
```

Our implementation of `collectionView(_:viewForSupplementaryElementOf-Kind:at:)` is called, and section headers now appear in the layout! Our compositional layout now looks almost identical to the original flow layout in Figure 9-1. Only the first section is wrong; I'll deal with that now.

Multiple Section Layouts

In the layout shown in Figure 9-1, the first section needs to be special. It should have no section header, and its single cell needs to be wider than the subsequent cells. With a flow layout, we took care of these differences with two UICollectionView-DelegateFlowLayout methods. With a compositional layout, we handle section differences by changing the layout initialization slightly. Currently, we have this:

```
let itemSize = NSCollectionLayoutSize( // ...
// ...
let section = NSCollectionLayoutSection(group: group)
// ...
let layout = UICollectionViewCompositionalLayout(section: section)
return layout
```

We change it to this:

```
let layout = UICollectionViewCompositionalLayout { index, env in
    let itemSize = NSCollectionLayoutSize( // ...
    // ...
    let section = NSCollectionLayoutSection(group: group)
    // ...
    return section
}
return layout
```

Instead of the UICollectionViewCompositionalLayout initializer `init(section:)`, we are now using `init(sectionProvider:)`. The parameter is a *section provider* function that is called for each section. Each time, it is fed the index number of that section, and returns the section.

The idea is that the section we construct can differ depending on the index number. In our section provider function, the first section is a special case:

```
let layout = UICollectionViewCompositionalLayout { index, env in
    let itemSize = NSCollectionLayoutSize(
        widthDimension: .absolute(index == 0 ? 150 : 70), // *
        heightDimension: .fractionalHeight(1))
    // ...
    let section = NSCollectionLayoutSection(group: group)
    // ...
    let header = NSCollectionLayoutBoundarySupplementaryItem(
        layoutSize: headerSize, elementKind: headerKind, alignment: .top)
    if index != 0 { // *
        section.boundarySupplementaryItems = [header]
    }
    return section
}
return layout
```

In that code, the starred comments mark the lines where we behave differently; if this is the first section, an item is 150 points wide instead of 70 points wide, and we don't attach the header.

The second parameter in the section provider function (env) is an NSCollection-LayoutEnvironment object, a value class consisting of two properties:

container
> An NSCollectionLayoutContainer telling us the contentSize and content-Insets of the overall layout.

traitCollection
> The current UITraitCollection for this view.

The section provider function is also called whenever the layout environment changes. Using the environment object, you can make your layout differ depending on the size or orientation of the view. Apple's example is a grid of cells that has five cells per row, unless the view is wider than a certain amount — in which case it has ten cells per row.

Other Compositional Layout Features

This section describes some further compositional layout features.

Manual cell layout

So far, we've been sizing our cells (items) by initializing a group with the horizontal or vertical class methods and giving an item a layoutSize. But there's another way. You initialize the group with the custom class method. You supply an *item provider* function: it receives an NSCollectionLayoutEnvironment (whose container reports the content size and content insets of this group), and returns an array of NSCollec-tionLayoutGroupCustomItem objects. This is a value class consisting of a frame and

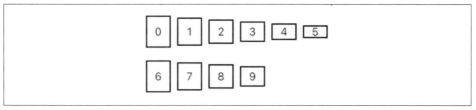

Figure 9-2. Manual cell layout

an optional zIndex. You are now in complete charge of how many cells this group contains and what their frames should be.

In this example, the height of each cell in the row is a little smaller than that of the preceding cell; we return the items, ending the row and causing a new row to start, when otherwise there would be too many cells to fit into the collection view's width, or the cell height would become vanishingly small (Figure 9-2):

```
let sz = NSCollectionLayoutSize(
    widthDimension: .fractionalWidth(1), heightDimension: .absolute(50))
let group = NSCollectionLayoutGroup.custom(layoutSize: sz) { env in
    var items = [NSCollectionLayoutGroupCustomItem]()
    let w = CGFloat(40)
    var frame = CGRect(0, 0, w, env.container.contentSize.height)
    while true {
        items.append(NSCollectionLayoutGroupCustomItem(frame: frame))
        frame.origin.x += w + 10
        frame.size.height -= 6; frame.origin.y += 3
        if frame.size.height < 20 {
            return items
        }
        if frame.maxX > env.container.contentSize.width {
            return items
        }
    }
}
```

Nested groups

A group is an item (NSCollectionLayoutGroup is a subclass of NSCollectionLayout-Item). This means that a group can contain a group. A nested group can have a different orientation (horizontal or vertical) from its container group.

In this example, the section's group is a horizontal group composed of two vertical groups of two items. The result is that items are clumped into blocks of four, in the order upper left, lower left, upper right, lower right (Figure 9-3):

```
let itemSize = NSCollectionLayoutSize(
    widthDimension: .fractionalWidth(1),
    heightDimension: .fractionalHeight(0.5))
let item = NSCollectionLayoutItem(layoutSize: itemSize)
```

Figure 9-3. Nested groups

```
let vgroupSize = NSCollectionLayoutSize(
    widthDimension: .fractionalWidth(0.48),
    heightDimension: .absolute(60))
let vgroup = NSCollectionLayoutGroup.vertical(
    layoutSize: vgroupSize, subitems: [item])
let hgroupSize = NSCollectionLayoutSize(
    widthDimension: .fractionalWidth(1),
    heightDimension: .absolute(60))
let hgroup = NSCollectionLayoutGroup.horizontal(
    layoutSize: hgroupSize, subitems: [vgroup])
hgroup.interItemSpacing = .flexible(1)
let section = NSCollectionLayoutSection(group: hgroup)
```

Orthogonal scrolling

A section has an `orthogonalScrollingBehavior` property, a UICollectionLayout-SectionOrthogonalScrollingBehavior enum. By default, this is `.none`. If you change it to anything else, the section's groups are arranged in a *single* row (or column) along the other axis from the layout's scrolling direction, and the section is *scrollable* so that the user can view all the items. For instance, if the layout scrolls vertically, a scrolling section lines up all its groups in a single horizontal row, which scrolls horizontally. It's like having a collection view inside a collection view, scrolling at right angles to it.

The scrolling behavior values are:

`continuous`
    Normal unrestricted scrolling.

`continuousGroupLeadingBoundary`
    Normal unrestricted scrolling, but comes to rest with the leading edge of a group at the leading edge of the collection view.

`paging`
    The user can scroll only one collection view width at a time.

```
groupPaging
```
The user can scroll only one group at a time.

```
groupPagingCentered
```
The user can scroll only one group at a time, and a group comes to rest centered in the collection view.

Collection View Diffable Data Source

A collection view's data source can be a diffable data source (UICollectionViewDiffableDataSource). It works similarly to a table view's diffable data source ("Table View Diffable Data Source" on page 516), but there are some extra requirements (and failure to fulfill them will result in a crash at runtime):

- Any calls to the collection view's `register(_:forCellWithReuseIdentifier:)` or `register(_:forSupplementaryViewOfKind:)` must take place *before* an initial snapshot is applied to the data source.

- If any supplementary views are to be displayed, the diffable data source's `supplementaryViewProvider` property must be set *before* an initial snapshot of data is applied to the data source. Basically, this function replaces the data source method `collectionView(_:viewForSupplementaryElementOfKind:at:)`, and must do the same work that that method would have done. Its parameters are the collection view, the supplementary view kind (a string), and the index path, and it returns a UICollectionReusableView that has been dequeued from the collection view.

Diffable Data Source Construction

To illustrate, I'll create a simple collection view (with a flow layout) based on the Three Big Questions; then I'll convert it to use a diffable data source. This will be a collection view version of the table view displaying the names of the U.S. states in sections, and the conversion will be exactly parallel to what I did in "Populating a Diffable Data Source" on page 518.

First I'll construct the Three Big Questions version of my collection view. The data model initially will be our familiar array of Section objects:

```
struct Section {
    var sectionName : String
    var itemData : [String]
}
var sections : [Section]()
```

I'll also declare instance property constants for our registration identifiers, as usual:

```
let cellID = "Cell"
let headerID = "Header"
```

When the view loads (viewDidLoad), we parse the text file of state names into the self.sections array as usual:

```
let s = try! String(
    contentsOfFile: Bundle.main.path(
        forResource: "states", ofType: "txt")!)
let states = s.components(separatedBy:"\n")
let d = Dictionary(grouping: states) {String($0.prefix(1))}
self.sections = Array(d).sorted {$0.key < $1.key}.map {
    Section(sectionName: $0.key, itemData: $0.value)
}
```

We register our cell and header types; our cell is a UICollectionViewCell subclass called Cell, designed in a nib called *Cell.xib*, with a lab outlet to a UILabel:

```
self.collectionView.register(UINib(nibName:"Cell", bundle:nil),
    forCellWithReuseIdentifier: self.cellID)
self.collectionView.register(UICollectionReusableView.self,
    forSupplementaryViewOfKind: UICollectionView.elementKindSectionHeader,
    withReuseIdentifier: self.headerID)
```

We also configure the flow layout (I won't bother showing that code). Now for the data source methods. Here are the Three Big Questions:

```
override func numberOfSections(
    in collectionView: UICollectionView) -> Int {
        return self.sections.count
}
override func collectionView(_ collectionView: UICollectionView,
    numberOfItemsInSection section: Int) -> Int {
        return self.sections[section].itemData.count
}
override func collectionView(_ collectionView: UICollectionView,
    cellForItemAt indexPath: IndexPath) -> UICollectionViewCell {
        let cell = collectionView.dequeueReusableCell(
            withReuseIdentifier: self.cellID, for: indexPath) as! Cell
        // ...
        cell.lab.text =
            self.sections[indexPath.section].itemData[indexPath.row]
        return cell
}
```

And here's how we provide the header views:

```
override func collectionView(_ collectionView: UICollectionView,
    viewForSupplementaryElementOfKind kind: String,
    at indexPath: IndexPath) -> UICollectionReusableView {
        let v = collectionView.dequeueReusableSupplementaryView(
            ofKind: kind, withReuseIdentifier: self.headerID, for: indexPath)
        if v.subviews.count == 0 {
            let lab = UILabel()
```

```
            v.addSubview(lab)
            // ...
        }
        let lab = v.subviews[0] as! UILabel
        lab.text = self.sections[indexPath.section].sectionName
        return v
    }
```

That's a working collection view! Now I'll convert it to use a diffable data source.

We start by deleting the Section struct and the `sections` instance property:

```
// this is gone!
// struct Section {
//      var sectionName : String
//      var itemData : [String]
// }
// var sections : [Section]()
```

Instead, we now have a diffable data source instance property. I'll make this an implicitly unwrapped Optional, automatically initialized to `nil`:

```
var datasource : UICollectionViewDiffableDataSource<String,String>!
```

In `viewDidLoad`, we do things in a definite order — registration, instantiation, and population:

```
// registration ❶
self.collectionView.register(UINib(nibName:"Cell", bundle:nil),
    forCellWithReuseIdentifier: self.cellID)
self.collectionView.register(UICollectionReusableView.self,
    forSupplementaryViewOfKind: UICollectionView.elementKindSectionHeader,
    withReuseIdentifier: self.headerID)
// instantiation ❷
self.datasource = UICollectionViewDiffableDataSource<String,String>(
    collectionView:self.collectionView) { [weak self] cv,ip,s in
        return self?.makeCell(cv,ip,s) // *
}
self.datasource.supplementaryViewProvider = { [weak self] cv,kind,ip in
    return self?.makeSupplementaryView(cv,kind,ip) // *
}
// population ❸
// ... parse the data into `sections` ...
var snap = NSDiffableDataSourceSnapshot<String,String>()
for section in sections {
    snap.appendSections([section.0])
    snap.appendItems(section.1)
}
self.datasource.apply(snap, animatingDifferences: false)
```

❶ We *register* our cell and supplementary view.

❷ We *instantiate* the diffable data source and configure it with two functions, one for producing cells, and one for producing supplementary views. I've coded speculatively, postponing the actual code of those functions by moving them into instance methods.

❸ We *populate* the diffable data source with data. This part is identical to how we populated the table view diffable data source with the same data.

Now I'll write the two functions from step 2, which I called makeCell and make-SupplementaryView. These are effectively the same as what we were already doing in our data source methods!

makeCell replaces collectionView(_:cellForItemAt:), and does the same thing, except that we receive the actual data from the diffable data source:

```
func makeCell(_ collectionView:UICollectionView,
    _ indexPath:IndexPath, _ s:String) -> UICollectionViewCell {
    let cell = collectionView.dequeueReusableCell(
        withReuseIdentifier: self.cellID, for: indexPath) as! Cell
    // ...
    cell.lab.text = s // *
    return cell
}
```

makeSupplementaryView replaces collectionView(_:viewForSupplementary-ElementOfKind:at:), and does the same thing, except that we look up the data in the diffable data source:

```
func makeSupplementaryView(_ collectionView:UICollectionView,
    _ kind:String, _ indexPath:IndexPath) -> UICollectionReusableView {
    let v = collectionView.dequeueReusableSupplementaryView(
        ofKind: kind, withReuseIdentifier: self.headerID, for: indexPath)
    if v.subviews.count == 0 {
        let lab = UILabel()
        v.addSubview(lab)
        // ...
    }
    let lab = v.subviews[0] as! UILabel
    let snap = self.datasource.snapshot() // *
    lab.text = snap.sectionIdentifiers[indexPath.section] // *
    return v
}
```

Registration Objects

In the preceding section, the first step was to register the cell and the supplementary view. New in iOS 14, we can effectively skip that step. Actually, we don't so much skip it as combine it with the data source's cell provider and supplementary view provider functions.

To demonstrate, I'll rewrite the preceding example a bit more. We start by deleting the reuse identifiers:

```
// this is gone!
// let cellID = "Cell"
// let headerID = "Header"
```

Instead of calling `self.collectionView.register`, we create two *registration objects*. These are generic types with rather long names, so to save space later I'll declare a couple of type aliases:

```
typealias CellReg = UICollectionView.CellRegistration
typealias SuppReg = UICollectionView.SupplementaryRegistration
```

The cell registration type is generic over the view type and the data source's item type; the supplementary view registration type is generic over the view type. The supplementary view registration initializer takes an `elementKind:` string. The registration initializer takes a nib, if we are registering a nib.

The registration initializer also takes a function; this is where we configure the view! The view is passed to us by reference as a parameter, so we do not need to return it:

```
let cellReg = CellReg<Cell, String>(
    cellNib: UINib(nibName:"Cell", bundle:nil)) { [weak self]
        cell, ip, s in self?.configureCell(cell, ip, s) // *
}
let headReg = SuppReg<UICollectionReusableView> (
    elementKind: UICollectionView.elementKindSectionHeader) { [weak self]
        v, kind, ip in self?.configureHeader(v, kind, ip) // *
}
```

As usual, I've coded speculatively; I'll write `configureCell` and `configureHeader` later.

In the data source's cell provider and supplementary view provider functions, when we dequeue, we call a method, new in iOS 14, that has `Configured` in its name, and that takes a registration object as its first parameter — and we immediately *return the result*:

```
self.datasource = UICollectionViewDiffableDataSource<String,String>(
    collectionView:self.collectionView) { cv,ip,s in
        cv.dequeueConfiguredReusableCell(using: cellReg, for: ip, item: s)
}
self.datasource.supplementaryViewProvider = { cv,kind,ip in
    cv.dequeueConfiguredReusableSupplementary(using: headReg, for: ip)
}
```

Let's pause for a moment to appreciate what's just happened. Consider the cell provider function. We call `dequeueConfiguredReusableCell`, supplying as the first parameter the cell registration object `cellReg` that we declared a moment before. The runtime looks at the cell registration object and *dequeues the cell* for us. In this case, it discovers that the cell is to come from a nib; so if there is no existing cell among the pile of reusable cells, it loads the nib to instantiate the cell. It then passes the cell down into the body of the function we supplied to the cell registration initializer, and all we have to do is configure it.

How do we do that? The same way as before! Our `configureCell` and `configure-Header` methods are just like the `makeCell` and `makeSupplementaryView` methods from the previous section. The difference is that they don't need to dequeue anything or return anything; they receive the view as a parameter, and they configure it:

```
func configureCell(_ cell:Cell,
    _ indexPath:IndexPath, _ s:String) {
        // ...
        cell.lab.text = s
}
func configureHeader(_ v:UICollectionReusableView,
    _ kind:String, _ indexPath:IndexPath) {
        // ...
        lab.text = snap.sectionIdentifiers[indexPath.section]
}
```

Section Snapshots

New in iOS 14, a UICollectionView's diffable data source's snapshot can refer to a *single section* of the diffable data source. Instead of (or alongside) NSDiffableData-SourceSnapshot, you can use NSDiffableDataSourceSectionSnapshot:

Obtaining a section snapshot
> To obtain a section snapshot from the diffable data source, call `snapshot(for:)`; the parameter is the section identifier.

Applying a section snapshot
> To apply a section snapshot to the diffable data source, call `apply(_:to:animatingDifferences:completion:)` The second parameter is the section identifier; if the section doesn't exist, it is created.

Section snapshots allow you to construct a multisection diffable data source in a somewhat cleaner way. That's useful especially when the model data itself comes from different sources for different sections, but we can illustrate well enough just by using our U.S. states data source once again. Previously, we were saying this:

```
var snap = NSDiffableDataSourceSnapshot<String,String>()
for section in sections {
    snap.appendSections([section.0])
    snap.appendItems(section.1)
}
self.datasource.apply(snap, animatingDifferences: false)
```

Now we can rewrite it like this:

```
    for section in sections {
        var snap = NSDiffableDataSourceSectionSnapshot<String>()
        snap.append(section.1)
        datasource.apply(snap, to: section.0, animatingDifferences: false)
    }
```

Also, unlike normal data source snapshots, a section snapshot permits its items to be arranged *hierarchically,* so that you can implement an outline interface. I'll demonstrate that in a moment.

Collection View Lists

New in iOS 14, a collection view can imitate most features of a table view. Its cells can look like table view cells, including accessory views, swipe actions, and more. A collection view that behaves this way is called a *list.* This is a compositional layout feature. Either the entire layout or a section of it can be a list:

Entire collection view
> To ask for a list layout for the entire collection view, create a UICollectionLayoutListConfiguration and pass it into the UICollectionViewCompositionalLayout list(using:) static method. Now use the result as your collection view's layout.

Compositional layout section
> To ask for a list layout for a section of a compositional list, create the layout with a section provider function, and call the NSCollectionLayoutSection static method list(using:layoutEnvironment:) to create the section.

The UICollectionLayoutListConfiguration initializer takes an appearance: value that corresponds to the style of a table view: .plain, .grouped, and so on. You can also use the configuration to determine the overall background color and the visibility of separators.

 In a list, self-sizing of a cell's height using autolayout internally is the default. If that's not what you want, you have to use a cell subclass and override preferredLayoutAttributesFitting(_:).

To demonstrate, I'll make a small table-like collection view showing the names of the three Pep Boys. I'm using a UICollectionViewController. I'll configure the layout in viewDidLoad:

```
    private let cellId = "Cell"
    override func viewDidLoad() {
        super.viewDidLoad()
        let config = UICollectionLayoutListConfiguration(appearance: .plain)
        let layout = UICollectionViewCompositionalLayout.list(using: config)
        self.collectionView.collectionViewLayout = layout
```

```
    self.collectionView.register(
        UICollectionViewListCell.self,
        forCellWithReuseIdentifier: self.cellId)
}
```

I have registered the UICollectionViewListCell class for our collection view cells. Just like a table view cell, it offers a defaultContentConfiguration that we can use to set up our contentConfiguration ("Apple's Cell Configuration Architecture" on page 478). Here are the data source methods for our simple list:

```
let data = ["Manny", "Moe", "Jack"]
override func numberOfSections(
    in collectionView: UICollectionView) -> Int {
        return 1
}
override func collectionView(
    _ collectionView: UICollectionView,
    numberOfItemsInSection section: Int) -> Int {
        return data.count
}
override func collectionView(
    _ collectionView: UICollectionView,
    cellForItemAt indexPath: IndexPath) -> UICollectionViewCell {
        let cell = collectionView.dequeueReusableCell(
            withReuseIdentifier: self.cellId, for: indexPath)
            as! UICollectionViewListCell
        var contentConfig = cell.defaultContentConfiguration()
        contentConfig.text = data[indexPath.item]
        cell.contentConfiguration = contentConfig
        return cell
}
```

That's all: we've made a simple list!

To make things more interesting, let's say I want the user to be able to select a cell to make that Pep Boy the favorite. I'll signify that with a checkmark accessory. A collection view list cell has an accessories property that lets us specify accessory views. I'll keep track of who the favorite is with an instance property:

```
var favorite: Int?
```

In collectionView(_:cellForItemAt:), I'll insert a line to determine the presence of the checkmark:

```
cell.accessories = self.favorite == indexPath.item ? [.checkmark()] : []
```

Finally, I'll implement a delegate method to respond to selection by changing the favorite:

```
override func collectionView(_ collectionView: UICollectionView,
    didSelectItemAt indexPath: IndexPath) {
        self.favorite = indexPath.item
        delay(0.2) {
            collectionView.reloadData()
        }
}
```

To get something that looks like a table view section header or footer, we need to set the headerMode or footerMode of our UICollectionLayoutListConfiguration. We can set it to .supplementary if we want to supply a supplementary view. But for headers only, there's a more lightweight approach; we can set the header mode to .firstItem-InSection, in which case the first item in the section is treated as a header:

```
var config = UICollectionLayoutListConfiguration(appearance: .plain)
config.headerMode = .firstItemInSection
let layout = UICollectionViewCompositionalLayout.list(using: config)
```

I'll change my data model to start with the header text:

```
let data = ["Pep", "Manny", "Moe", "Jack"]
```

And I'll add a delegate method to prevent the "header" from being selectable:

```
override func collectionView(_ collectionView: UICollectionView,
    shouldSelectItemAt indexPath: IndexPath) -> Bool {
        return indexPath.item != 0
}
```

The list now works just as before, with the addition of the Pep header, which has a default gray background. It isn't a real header, though; it's a cell, so it acts like a cell, scrolling with the other cells rather than staying pinned to the top of the view like a table view section header.

If you want a header that acts like a real header, use a supplementary view instead. As we're not using a diffable data source, I can simply set a headerId constant instance property and register it with the collection view to get a reusable view. Apple suggests that we use UICollectionViewListCell as the class for the header view; when we do, we still get the default gray background, and we can use the built-in configuration architecture:

```
var config = UICollectionLayoutListConfiguration(appearance: .plain)
config.headerMode = .supplementary
let layout = UICollectionViewCompositionalLayout.list(using: config)
// ...
self.collectionView.register(UICollectionViewListCell.self,
    forSupplementaryViewOfKind: UICollectionView.elementKindSectionHeader,
    withReuseIdentifier: self.headerId)
```

Now I implement the data source method to configure the supplementary view:

```
override func collectionView(_ collectionView: UICollectionView,
    viewForSupplementaryElementOfKind kind: String,
    at indexPath: IndexPath) -> UICollectionReusableView {
        let v = collectionView.dequeueReusableSupplementaryView(
            ofKind: kind,
            withReuseIdentifier: self.headerId,
            for: indexPath) as! UICollectionViewListCell
        var contentConfig = v.defaultContentConfiguration()
        contentConfig.text = "Pep"
        v.contentConfiguration = contentConfig
        return v
}
```

What about swipe actions? The UICollectionLayoutListConfiguration has leading-
SwipeActionsConfigurationProvider and trailingSwipeActionsConfiguration-
Provider properties that are functions taking an index path. Your function can
return different swipe actions, or nil, for different rows of the list (see "Table View
Swipe Action Buttons" on page 528).

To illustrate, let's give each Pep Boy a Delete button as its trailing action. Go back
once again to the point where we created our layout list configuration:

```
var config = UICollectionLayoutListConfiguration(appearance: .plain)
config.trailingSwipeActionsConfigurationProvider = { indexPath in
    let del = UIContextualAction(style: .destructive, title: "Delete") {
        [weak self] action, view, completion in
        self?.delete(at: indexPath) // *
        completion(true)
    }
    return UISwipeActionsConfiguration(actions: [del])
}
```

I'm coding speculatively here; we haven't written any method delete(at:) for
actually deleting a cell. I'll talk later about how to do that.

As my examples have already shown, a UICollectionViewListCell has an
accessories property, which is an array of UICellAccessory instances. These are
powerful little objects, not only decorating the cell but in some cases acting as key to
the user's ancillary interaction with the cell. For example, if there's a reorder accessory, the user can reorder the cells.

You create an accessory using a UICellAccessory static method:

- disclosureIndicator(displayed:options:)

- checkmark(displayed:options:)

- delete(displayed:options:actionHandler:) (leading Minus button)

- insert(displayed:options:actionHandler:) (leading Plus button)

- reorder(displayed:options:)

- `multiselect(displayed:options:)` (leading circle with checkmark)
- `outlineDisclosure(displayed:options:actionHandler:)`
- `label(text:displayed:options:)` (brief text)
- `customView(configuration:)` (any UIView)

Here's what the parameters mean:

`displayed:`

Lets you specify the cell states in which the accessory should be visible: `.always`, `.when-Editing`, and `.whenNotEditing`. The default, if you omit this parameter, will be the value appropriate to the particular accessory; a checkmark's default is `.always`, but a delete button's default is `.whenEditing`.

`options:`

The `options:` depend on the particular accessory and have mostly to do with color and layout.

`actionHandler:`

Some interactive accessories let you intervene with a custom response when the user taps the accessory. For the most part, you won't need to do so; for example, a delete accessory, by default, when the user taps it, reveals the trailing swipe actions, which is usually what you want.

`text:`

The text for the label accessory.

`configuration:`

This is how you set up a custom view accessory. It's a UICellAccessory.Custom-ViewConfiguration, which is a value type (a bunch of properties). The most important property is the `customView`! You can also configure the view's size, position, and tint color.

Most parameters are optional; recall that earlier I made a checkmark by saying `checkmark()`, with no parameters.

Hierarchical Items

New in iOS 14, a collection view section can be hierarchical. This, as I mentioned earlier, is actually a feature of the diffable data source, and in particular of the section snapshot. You can make any sort of collection view section behave hierarchically, but a demonstration is especially easy with a section that's a list, because everything is configured for you automatically.

To illustrate, I'll use the little list of Pep Boys from the previous section and make it hierarchical. The plan is to lay out the list elements like this:

```
Pep
    Manny
    Moe
    Jack
```

Pep will be a parent in our outline; Manny, Moe, and Jack will be Pep's children. The user will be able to expand and collapse Pep to show and hide Manny, Moe, and Jack.

To get started, I have to replace my string array data model with a diffable data source:

```
var datasource: UICollectionViewDiffableDataSource<String, String>!
```

In viewDidLoad, when I create the data source, I'll take advantage of the new cell registration object that I described earlier. I need to give my parent cell an outline disclosure accessory, so that the user has a way to expand and collapse it:

```
typealias CellReg = UICollectionView.CellRegistration
let reg = CellReg<UICollectionViewListCell, String> { cell, ip, s in
    var contentConfig = cell.defaultContentConfiguration()
    contentConfig.text = s
    if ip.item == 0 {
        cell.accessories = [.outlineDisclosure()]
    } else {
        cell.accessories = []
    }
    cell.contentConfiguration = contentConfig
}
let ds = UICollectionViewDiffableDataSource<String, String>(
    collectionView:self.collectionView) { cv, ip, s in
        cv.dequeueConfiguredReusableCell(using: reg, for: ip, item: s)
}
self.datasource = ds
```

Now we'll populate the data source. We must use a section snapshot, because that's where the ability to specify the hierarchy is implemented:

```
var snap = NSDiffableDataSourceSectionSnapshot<String>()
snap.append(["Pep"]) // to:nil
snap.append(["Manny", "Moe", "Jack"], to: "Pep")
self.datasource.apply(snap, to: "Dummy", animatingDifferences: false)
```

We append Pep as a root-level item by not appending it to anything. (Optionally, we could say to:nil to make that explicit.) But we append Manny, Moe, and Jack to Pep as their parent. The result is that the user initially sees *just Pep* — with a disclosure icon. The user taps Pep, and the disclosure icon swivels to point down, and Manny, Moe, and Jack are revealed — with their text indented (Figure 9-4).

A section snapshot has numerous properties reflecting the possibility that the items might be hierarchical:

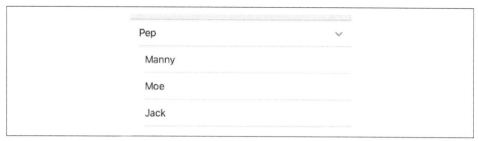

Figure 9-4. A hierarchical list

- It has a `rootItems` property; a root item is an item whose parent is `nil` (it is at the top level of the outline).

- It has a `visibleItems` property; a visible item is either a root item or a child of an expanded item.

- You can ask for an item's parent.

- You can ask for an item's level; a root item's level is `0`.

- You can ask whether an item is expanded; an item with no children is considered collapsed.

- You can replace an item's children.

You can also obtain an item's children, but the procedure is a little tricky. You call `snapshot(of:includingParent:)` on an existing snapshot; the first parameter is the item. This gives you, in effect, a *partial* snapshot. The default is not to include the parent, and in that case the root items of the result are the children:

```
let snap = self.datasource.snapshot(for: "Dummy")
let snap2 = snap.snapshot(of: "Pep")
let children = snap2.rootItems // Manny, Moe, Jack
```

That technique gives us a way to ask whether an item *is* a parent. Using it, we can improve our earlier code. Here, I hard-coded a knowledge that item `0` of my data is a parent:

```
if ip.item == 0 {
    cell.accessories = [.outlineDisclosure()]
} else {
    cell.accessories = []
}
```

A better way would be to give a cell an outline disclosure accessory just in case it is a parent:

```
let snap = self.datasource.snapshot(for: "Dummy")
let snap2 = snap.snapshot(of: s)
if snap2.items.count > 0 { // it's a parent
    cell.accessories = [.outlineDisclosure()]
} else {
    cell.accessories = [.delete()]
}
```

You can expand or collapse a parent item in code; indeed, when the user taps to expand or collapse a parent item, by default the runtime takes a snapshot, expands or collapses that item, and applies the resulting snapshot. To illustrate, I'll make an improvement to our interface. At the moment, the parent cell, Pep, is selectable by the user, and the user must tap directly on the outline disclosure accessory to expand it. Let's fix both of those things, so that a parent cell is *not* selectable, and the user can tap *anywhere* in a parent cell to toggle its expansion (Apple's own outlines generally work this way):

```
override func collectionView(_ collectionView: UICollectionView,
    shouldSelectItemAt indexPath: IndexPath) -> Bool {
        var snap = self.datasource.snapshot(for: "Dummy")
        let s = self.datasource.itemIdentifier(for: indexPath)!
        let snap2 = snap.snapshot(of: s)
        let hasChildren = snap2.items.count > 0
        if hasChildren {
            if snap.isExpanded(s) {
                snap.collapse([s])
            } else {
                snap.expand([s])
            }
            self.datasource.apply(snap, to: "Dummy")
        }
        return !hasChildren
}
```

To be notified when the user expands or collapses an item, use the diffable data source's sectionSnapshotHandlers property; this is a SectionSnapshotHandlers instance, a struct consisting entirely of properties whose values are functions:

- shouldExpandItem

- shouldCollapseItem

- willExpandItem

- willCollapseItem

- snapshotForExpandingParent

The last one lets you determine in real time what the user should see when expanding this item. That's valuable in case actually obtaining the data in question is expensive; instead of obtaining the data and storing it in the diffable data source up front, you obtain it only if the user happens to expand the parent.

Another way to interfere when the user taps a parent item to toggle expansion is to give the outline disclosure accessory an action handler function. You do that when you initialize the accessory:

```
let f : () -> () = { /* ... */ }
cell.accessories = [.outlineDisclosure(options: opts, actionHandler: f)]
```

In that case, you've replaced all automatic behavior; collapsing or expanding the item is now completely up to you.

Basic Cell Manipulation

This section describes some basic manipulations you can perform on collection view cells.

Selecting Cells

A collection view has a notion of cell selection, similar to a table view ("Table View Selection" on page 498):

- A collection view has `allowsSelection` and `allowsMultipleSelection` properties; if these are not `false`, the user can tap a cell to select it.

- A collection view has an `indexPathsForSelectedItems` property, along with methods for selecting and deselecting an item. (Unlike a table view, there is no singular `indexPathForSelectedItem` to add confusion.)

- A cell has an `isSelected` property and a `selectedBackgroundView` property.

- The delegate has a full complement of `should` and `did` methods for highlighting and unhighlighting, selecting and deselecting. When the user taps to select a cell, the cell highlights, unhighlights, and selects.

- Starting in iOS 13, the delegate has three `multipleSelectionInteraction` methods for when the user pans with two fingers to perform multiple selection; unlike a table view, a collection view has no notion of edit mode to complicate matters. You can permit multiple selection by gesture even if the collection view's `allowsMultipleSelection` is `false`.

As with a table view, you can indicate selection visually with subviews that respond to highlighting and with the `selectedBackgroundView` property. Earlier in this chapter, I configured a cell containing a label like this:

```
lab.highlightedTextColor = .white
cell.backgroundColor = .myPaler
let v = UIView()
v.backgroundColor = UIColor.blue.withAlphaComponent(0.8)
cell.selectedBackgroundView = v
```

Deleting Cells

In general, collection views don't provide any standard interface for allowing the user to delete cells. You are free to display a UICollectionViewController's `editButton-Item`, and when the user taps it, the collection view controller's `set-Editing(_:animated:)` is called. But the interface does not automatically change in response, and neither a collection view nor a collection view cell has an `isEditing` property. Providing interface that lets the user express a desire to delete a cell is left completely up to you. For instance, you might have a Delete button that appears in every cell when the view controller's `isEditing` is `true`, parallel to the Minus editing control of a table view cell.

A collection view list, on the other hand, behaves like a table view: its cells have state, and it *does* respond automatically when the collection view controller's `set-Editing(_:animated:)` is called. If you give a list cell a delete accessory (a Minus button), then by default that accessory will appear automatically when the cell is in editing mode — and when the user taps it, the trailing swipe actions will appear. Provide a delete accessory plus a Delete trailing swipe action, and you have the standard interface for letting the user ask to delete a cell.

How should you respond to the user asking to delete a cell? With a Three Big Questions data source, you have to alter the data, being careful about the order of operations, and then call `performBatchUpdates` to remove items and sections from the collection view with `deleteItems(at:)` and `deleteSections(_:)`.

Deleting cells is a lot simpler if you're using a diffable data source: you just manipulate a snapshot and apply it. Earlier in this chapter, I made a collection view list where the cells have a Delete trailing swipe action; the user taps Delete, and we respond by calling our own `delete(at:)` method. Now let's write that method:

```
func delete(at ip: IndexPath) {
    var snap = self.datasource.snapshot()
    if let ident = self.datasource.itemIdentifier(for: ip) {
        snap.deleteItems([ident])
    }
    self.datasource.apply(snap)
}
```

Here's another example. Imagine a collection view where the user has selected multiple cells and has tapped a Delete button; I want to respond by deleting the selected cells, along with any sections that are now empty. Unsurprisingly, the code for doing that is almost exactly the same as what we developed earlier for doing this in a table view ("Changing a Diffable Data Source" on page 521):

```
    guard let sel = self.collectionView.indexPathsForSelectedItems,
        sel.count > 0 else {return}
    let rowids = sel.map {
        self.datasource.itemIdentifier(for: $0)
    }.compactMap {$0}
    var snap = self.datasource.snapshot()
    snap.deleteWithSections(rowids) // implemented in an extension
    self.datasource.apply(snap)
```

Menu Handling

Menu handling is completely parallel to a table view, using the context menu interface based on UIMenu and UIAction. Here's some code that lets the user long press a
cell to produce a Copy menu item; as usual, I have a collection view displaying U.S.
state names, and the name of the long pressed cell's state is copied to the clipboard if
the user taps Copy:

```
override func collectionView(_ collectionView: UICollectionView,
    contextMenuConfigurationForItemAt indexPath: IndexPath,
    point: CGPoint) -> UIContextMenuConfiguration? {
        let config = UIContextMenuConfiguration(
            identifier:nil, previewProvider: nil) { _ in
                let action = UIAction(title: "Copy") { _ in
                    let d = self.datasource
                    if let state = d.itemIdentifier(for: indexPath) {
                        UIPasteboard.general.string = state
                    }
                }
                let menu = UIMenu(title: "", children: [action])
                return menu
            }
        return config
}
```

 Menus don't play very well with selection, because the long pressed cell visibly
highlights first, after which the long press gesture recognizer recognizes, unhighlights the cell, and produces the menu.

Rearranging Cells

You can permit the user to rearrange cells by dragging them. If you're using a collection view controller, it supplies a gesture recognizer ready to respond to the user's
long press gesture followed by a drag. (This is incompatible with a menu, because the
menu long press gesture recognizer recognizes first.)

To permit the drag to proceed, you implement two data source methods:

collectionView(_:canMoveItemAt:)
    Return true to allow this item to be moved.

`collectionView(_:moveItemAt:to:)`
>The item has been moved to a new index path. Update the data model, and reload cells as needed.

You can also limit where the user can drag with this delegate method:

`collectionView(_:targetIndexPathForMoveFromItemAt:toProposedIndexPath:)`
>Return either the proposed index path or some other index path. To prevent the drag entirely, return the original index path (the second parameter).

If you're using a diffable data source, dealing with user rearrangement of cells was extremely tricky in iOS 13. You had to implement the data source methods, and the implementation was difficult to get right. New in iOS 14, it's trivial: do nothing! Do *not* implement the data source methods. The data source responds automatically; the user rearranges cells, and the data source is rearranged to match.

New in iOS 14, if you need an event related to the user rearranging cells, use the data source's `reorderingHandlers` property; this is a ReorderingHandlers struct consisting of properties that are functions you can set:

- `canReorderItem`
- `willReorder`
- `didReorder`

You *must* supply a `canReorderItem` function, even if it always just returns `true`; otherwise, user reordering of cells will not be possible.

By the time you receive `didReorder`, the data inside the diffable data source has *already* been reordered. The purpose of this method is just in case you are also storing your model data somewhere else and you need to update it. The parameter is an NSDiffableDataSourceTransaction (new in iOS 14) that you can use to work out what happened.

Even if you're using a diffable data source, you can still use the delegate method. In this example, the delegate method prevents the move if the drag crosses a section boundary:

```
override func collectionView(_ collectionView: UICollectionView,
    targetIndexPathForMoveFromItemAt orig: IndexPath,
    toProposedIndexPath prop: IndexPath) -> IndexPath {
        if orig.section != prop.section {
            return orig
        }
        return prop
}
```

If you prefer to provide your own gesture recognizer, then if you're using a collection view controller, set its `installsStandardGestureForInteractiveMovement` to `false`.

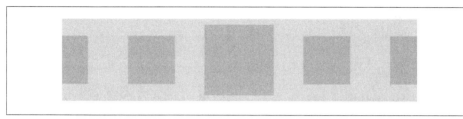

Figure 9-5. A carousel layout

Your gesture recognizer action method will need to call these collection view methods to keep the collection view apprised of what's happening (and the data source and delegate methods will then be called appropriately):

- `beginInteractiveMovementForItem(at:)`
- `updateInteractiveMovementTargetPosition(_:)`
- `endInteractiveMovement`
- `cancelInteractiveMovement`

Custom Collection View Layouts

It is possible that neither a flow layout nor a compositional layout does quite what you want, and that you'll want to tweak its behavior or even write your own UICollectionViewLayout subclass. The topic is a very large one, but getting started is not difficult; this section explores the basics.

Tweaking a Layout

Both UICollectionViewFlowLayout and UICollectionViewCompositionalLayout constitute powerful starting points, so it may be that all you need is to tweak what they already do. To illustrate, I'll use an example from a WWDC 2012 video.

Suppose we have a horizontally scrolling collection view as wide as the screen and 128 points tall. Centered vertically in this collection view is a horizontal series of single square cells 75 points on a side, spaced fairly well apart. About three cells fit completely on the screen; the user can scroll horizontally to see more cells.

Our goal is to modify the behavior of the collection view such that as the user scrolls horizontally, the currently central cell is emphasized. As a cell approaches the horizontal center of the screen, it grows, and as it moves away from the horizontal center, it returns to its normal size. This sort of interface is commonly referred to as a *carousel* (Figure 9-5).

I'll describe how to make a carousel layout, first using a flow layout, then using a compositional layout.

Flow layout subclass

We can easily configure our collection view with a flow layout:

```
lay.itemSize = CGSize(width: 75, height: 75)
lay.minimumLineSpacing = 65
```

To achieve our "carousel" tweak, we subclass UICollectionViewFlowLayout and set our collection view's `collectionViewLayout` to an instance of the subclass. In the subclass, we override the method that describes how each cell should be laid out, namely `layoutAttributesForElements(in:)`.

The parameter of the `layoutAttributesForElements(in:)` method is a CGRect, and the method returns an array of UICollectionViewLayoutAttributes objects describing all the subviews of the collection view within that CGRect. The properties of each attributes object are the `indexPath` identifying the view, along with the `frame`, `center`, `size`, `transform`, `transform3D`, and `zIndex` that it should have. All of these properties are basically correct already in the default implementation, so we can call `super` and make modifications as necessary. All we have to do is to change the `transform3D` when this cell is near the center of the screen.

A layout has a `collectionView` property, which we can use to work out the collection view's visible bounds and the horizontal center of those bounds. Having called `super`, we have the array of attributes objects that the method would return. We copy the attribute objects (that's crucial) and examine the `frame` and `center` of each one in turn. If it isn't within the visible bounds, or if it isn't a cell, or if it isn't sufficiently close to the horizontal center of the screen, there's nothing more to do. Otherwise, we change the `transform3D` in proportion to the distance of the `center` from the collection view's horizontal center, and substitute the copy for the original. Finally, we return the whole array of copies:

```
override func layoutAttributesForElements(in rect: CGRect)
    -> [UICollectionViewLayoutAttributes]? {
        guard let cv = self.collectionView else { return nil }
        let r = CGRect(origin:cv.contentOffset, size:cv.bounds.size)
        let arr = super.layoutAttributesForElements(in: rect)!
        return arr.map { atts in
            let atts = atts.copy() as! UICollectionViewLayoutAttributes
            if atts.representedElementCategory == .cell {
                if atts.frame.intersects(r) {
                    let d = abs(r.midX - atts.center.x)
                    let act = CGFloat(70)
                    let nd = d/act
                    if d < act {
                        let scale = 1 + 0.5*(1-(abs(nd)))
                        let t = CATransform3DMakeScale(scale,scale,1)
                        atts.transform3D = t
                    }
                }
            }
```

```
        }
            return atts
        }
    }
```

We also override another method:

```
override func shouldInvalidateLayout(
    forBoundsChange newBounds: CGRect) -> Bool {
        return true
}
```

This override ensures that the collection view will ask for layout repeatedly as the user scrolls. Our flow layout subclass is complete!

Compositional layout invalidation handler

Exactly the same overrides work if we are using a compositional layout instead of a flow layout, and we could do the same thing by subclassing UICollectionViewCompositionalLayout. But there's no need for that! It turns out that a compositional layout provides a hook method that lets us modify the attributes of visible items directly.

To do so, we set the section's visibleItemsInvalidationHandler to a function that takes three parameters:

- An array of NSCollectionLayoutVisibleItems. These are just like UICollectionViewLayoutAttributes objects, except that you can set their properties directly. Moreover, the array contains only objects representing those collection view subviews that are actually visible at the moment.

- A CGPoint representing the collection view's current scrolling offset.

- The NSCollectionLayoutEnvironment.

Here's a compositional layout that looks and behaves like our tweaked flow layout:

```
let itemSize = NSCollectionLayoutSize(
    widthDimension: .fractionalWidth(1),
    heightDimension: .absolute(75))
let item = NSCollectionLayoutItem(layoutSize: itemSize)
item.edgeSpacing = NSCollectionLayoutEdgeSpacing(
    leading: nil, top: .flexible(0),
    trailing: nil, bottom: .flexible(0))
let groupSize = NSCollectionLayoutSize(
    widthDimension: .absolute(75),
    heightDimension: .fractionalHeight(1))
let group = NSCollectionLayoutGroup.vertical(
    layoutSize: groupSize, subitems: [item])
let section = NSCollectionLayoutSection(group: group)
section.interGroupSpacing = 65
section.contentInsets = NSDirectionalEdgeInsets(
    top: 0, leading: 75, bottom: 0, trailing: 75)
section.visibleItemsInvalidationHandler = { items, offset, env in
```

```
    let r = CGRect(origin:offset, size:env.container.contentSize)
    let cells = items.filter {$0.representedElementCategory == .cell}
    for item in cells {
        let d = abs(r.midX - item.center.x)
        let act = CGFloat(70)
        let nd = d/act
        if d < act {
            let scale = 1 + 0.5*(1-(abs(nd)))
            let t = CATransform3DMakeScale(scale,scale,1)
            item.transform3D = t
        }
    }
}
let config = UICollectionViewCompositionalLayoutConfiguration()
config.scrollDirection = .horizontal
let layout = UICollectionViewCompositionalLayout(
    section: section, configuration:config)
```

Collection View Layout Subclass

For total freedom, you can subclass UICollectionViewLayout itself. The WWDC
2012 videos demonstrate a UICollectionViewLayout subclass that arranges its cells in
a circle; the WWDC 2013 videos demonstrate a UICollectionViewLayout subclass
that piles its cells into a single stack in the center of the collection view, like a deck of
cards seen from above. For my example, I'll write a simple collection view layout that
ignores sections and presents all cells as a plain grid of squares. This is unnecessary
now that compositional layouts exist, but it demonstrates nicely the basics of writing
a layout from scratch.

In my UICollectionViewLayout subclass, called MyLayout, the big questions I will
need to answer are collectionViewContentSize and layoutAttributesFor-
Elements(in:). To answer them, I'll calculate the entire layout of my grid beforehand. The prepare method is the perfect place to do this; it is called every time
something about the collection view or its data changes. I'll calculate the grid of cells
and express their positions as an array of UICollectionViewLayoutAttributes objects;
I'll store that information in a property self.atts, which is a dictionary keyed by
index path so that I can retrieve a given layout attributes object by its index path
quickly. I'll also store the size of the grid in a property self.sz:

```
override func prepare() {
    let sections = self.collectionView.numberOfSections
    // work out cell size based on bounds size
    let sz = self.collectionView!.bounds.size
    let width = sz.width
    let shortside = (width/100).rounded(.down)
    let side = width/shortside
    // generate attributes for all cells
    var (x,y) = (0,0)
    var atts = [UICollectionViewLayoutAttributes]()
```

```
        for i in 0 ..< sections {
            let jj = self.collectionView!.numberOfItems(inSection:i)
            for j in 0 ..< jj {
                let att = UICollectionViewLayoutAttributes(
                    forCellWith: IndexPath(item:j, section:i))
                att.frame = CGRect(CGFloat(x)*side,CGFloat(y)*side,side,side)
                atts += [att]
                x += 1
                if CGFloat(x) >= shortside {
                    x = 0; y += 1
                }
            }
        }
        for att in atts {
            self.atts[att.indexPath] = att
        }
        let fluff = (x == 0) ? 0 : 1
        self.sz = CGSize(width, CGFloat(y+fluff) * side)
    }
```

It is now trivial to implement collectionViewContentSize, layoutAttributesFor-
Elements(in:), and layoutAttributesForItem(at:). I'll just fetch the requested
information from the sz or atts property:

```
override var collectionViewContentSize : CGSize {
    return self.sz
}
override func layoutAttributesForElements(in rect: CGRect)
    -> [UICollectionViewLayoutAttributes]? {
        return Array(self.atts.values)
}
override func layoutAttributesForItem(at indexPath: IndexPath)
    -> UICollectionViewLayoutAttributes? {
        return self.atts[indexPath]
}
```

Finally, I want to implement shouldInvalidateLayout(forBoundsChange:) to
return true, so that if the interface is rotated, my prepare method will be called again
to recalculate the grid. There's a potential source of inefficiency here, though: the
user scrolling the collection view counts as a bounds change as well. Therefore, I
return false unless the bounds size has changed:

```
var oldBoundsSize = CGSize.zero
override func shouldInvalidateLayout(forBoundsChange newBounds: CGRect)
    -> Bool {
        let ok = newBounds.size != self.oldBoundsSize
        if ok {
            self.oldBoundsSize = newBounds.size
        }
        return ok
}
```

Decoration Views

A *decoration view* is a third type of collection view subview, on a par with cells and supplementary views. The difference is that it is implemented entirely by the collection view layout. You register a decoration view class (or nib) with the layout — not with the collection view. A collection view will faithfully draw a decoration view imposed by the collection view layout, but none of the methods and properties of a collection view, its data source, or its delegate involve decoration views. There is no support for letting the user select a decoration view or reposition a decoration view. There aren't even any collection view methods for finding out what decoration views exist or where they are located.

A flow layout comes with no built-in support for adding a decoration view, but a compositional layout does. It is of class NSCollectionLayoutDecorationItem (an NSCollectionLayoutItem subclass), and represents just one kind of decoration, a background behind a section. So there's a single class method, background, which takes an elementKind, and you set the section's decorationItems. There must be a corresponding UICollectionReusableView (or a nib containing such a view) registered with the layout.

As a simple example, I'll put a pale blue background behind each section of a compositional layout. Here's my view class:

```
class Deco : UICollectionReusableView {
    override init(frame: CGRect) {
        super.init(frame: frame)
        self.backgroundColor = UIColor.blue.withAlphaComponent(0.1)
    }
    required init?(coder: NSCoder) {
        fatalError("init(coder:) has not been implemented")
    }
}
```

Here's how I register that class with the layout when I configure the collection view:

```
let layout = self.createLayout()
layout.register(Deco.self, forDecorationViewOfKind: "background")
self.collectionView.collectionViewLayout = layout
```

And here's how the decoration view is added to the section (in createLayout):

```
let deco = NSCollectionLayoutDecorationItem.background(
    elementKind: "background")
deco.contentInsets = NSDirectionalEdgeInsets(
    top: 5, leading: 5, bottom: 5, trailing: 5)
section.decorationItems = [deco]
```

You can also implement a decoration view in a layout subclass that you write, and you are free to define any desired mechanism for allowing a user of this collection view layout to customize your decoration views. You implement layoutAttributes-

ForDecorationView(ofKind:at:) to return a UICollectionViewLayoutAttributes object that positions the UICollectionReusableView. To construct this object, you call init(forDecorationViewOfKind:with:) and configure its properties. Finally, you implement layoutAttributesForElements(in:) such that the result of layout-AttributesForDecorationView(ofKind:at:) is included in the returned array.

Switching Layouts

An astonishing feature of a collection view is that its collection view layout object can be swapped out on the fly. You can substitute one collection view layout for another, by calling setCollectionViewLayout(_:animated:completion:). The data hasn't changed, and the collection view can identify each element uniquely and persistently, so it responds by moving every element from its position according to the old layout to its position according to the new layout — and, if the animated: argument is true, it does this *with animation!* The elements are seen to rearrange themselves, as if by magic.

This animated change of layout can even be driven interactively in response to a user gesture. You call startInteractiveTransition(to:completion:) on the collection view, and a special layout object is returned — a UICollectionViewTransitionLayout instance (or a subclass thereof; to make it a subclass, you need to have implemented collectionView(_:transitionLayoutForOldLayout:newLayout:) in your collection view delegate). This transition layout is temporarily made the collection view's layout, and your job is then to keep it apprised of the transition's progress (through its transitionProgress property) and ultimately to call finishInteractive-Transition or cancelInteractiveTransition on the collection view.

Furthermore, when one collection view controller is pushed on top of another in a navigation interface, the runtime will do exactly the same thing for you, as a custom view controller transition. To arrange this, the first collection view controller's use-LayoutToLayoutNavigationTransitions property must be false and the second collection view controller's useLayoutToLayoutNavigationTransitions property must be true. The result is that when the second collection view controller is pushed onto the navigation controller, *the collection view remains in place*, and the collection view layout specified by the second collection view controller is substituted for the collection view's existing collection view layout, with animation of the elements as they adopt their new positions.

During the transition, as the second collection view controller is pushed onto the navigation stack, the two collection view controllers share the same collection view, and the collection view's data source and delegate remain the first view controller. After the transition is complete, however, the collection view's delegate becomes the *second* view controller, even though its data source is still the *first* view controller. I find this profoundly weird; why does the runtime change who the delegate is, and why would I want the delegate to be different from the data source? I solve the problem by resetting the delegate in the second view controller, like this:

```
override func viewDidAppear(_ animated: Bool) {
    super.viewDidAppear(animated)
    let oldDelegate = self.collectionView.delegate
    DispatchQueue.main.async {
        self.collectionView.delegate = oldDelegate
    }
}
```

Collection Views and UIKit Dynamics

The UICollectionViewLayoutAttributes class adopts the UIDynamicItem protocol (see Chapter 4). This means that collection view elements can be animated under UIKit dynamics. The world of the animator here is not a superview but the collection view layout itself:

- Instead of `init(referenceView:)`, you'll create the UIDynamicAnimator by calling `init(collectionViewLayout:)`.
- When adding an item to a UIDynamicBehavior, instead of being a UIView, the item is a UICollectionViewLayoutAttributes object.

But there's a tricky bit. On every frame of its animation, the UIDynamicAnimator is going to change the layout attributes of some items — but the collection view knows nothing of that! It still wants to draw those items in accordance with the collection view layout's `layoutAttributesForElements(in:)`. We need to make the collection view modify its `layoutAttributesForElements(in:)` so as to obtain those layout attributes from the UIDynamicAnimator. There are some helpful UIDynamicAnimator convenience methods:

`layoutAttributesForCell(at:)`
`layoutAttributesForSupplementaryView(ofKind:at:)`

> The layout attributes for the requested item, in accordance with where the animator wants to put them — or `nil` if the specified item is not being animated.

How will we hook into the layout's `layoutAttributesForElements(in:)`? One possibility is to create a custom subclass of UICollectionViewLayout so that you can override `layoutAttributesForElements(in:)` directly. If you're using a compositional layout, however, you can use the section's `visibleItemsInvalidationHandler` instead.

In this example, I'm using a compositional layout to arrange the collection view's cells in a grid. I'll animate the visible cells to fall off the screen with random rates and random rotation. As usual, I have an Optional UIDynamicAnimator instance property called self.anim:

```
let layout = cv.collectionViewLayout
let anim = UIDynamicAnimator(collectionViewLayout: layout)
var atts = [UICollectionViewLayoutAttributes]()
for ip in cv.indexPathsForVisibleItems {
    if let att = cv.layoutAttributesForItem(at: ip) {
        let beh = UIDynamicItemBehavior(items:[att])
        beh.resistance = CGFloat.random(in: 0.2...6)
        beh.addAngularVelocity(CGFloat.random(in: -2...2), for: att)
        anim.addBehavior(beh)
        atts.append(att)
    }
}
let grav = UIGravityBehavior(items: atts)
grav.action = { [unowned self] in
    let items = anim.items(in: self.collectionView.bounds)
    if items.count == 0 {
        anim.removeAllBehaviors()
        self.anim = nil
    }
}
anim.addBehavior(grav)
self.anim = anim
```

We run that code, and nothing appears to happen. In reality, the animator runs, and it stops as expected when all the cells are off the screen. But the cells drawn by the collection view are not moving! This is where the visibleItemsInvalidationHandler comes in, when we construct our compositional layout:

```
let section = NSCollectionLayoutSection(group: group)
section.visibleItemsInvalidationHandler = { [unowned self] items, _, _ in
    if let anim = self.anim {
        for item in items {
            if let atts = anim.layoutAttributesForCell(at:item.indexPath) {
                item.center = atts.center
                item.transform3D = atts.transform3D
            }
        }
    }
}
```

While the animator is running, the invalidation handler is called on every frame. We cycle through the NSCollectionLayoutVisibleItem objects (items), replacing their center and transform3D values with those provided by the animator. The cells now visibly fall off the screen when the animator runs.

iPad Interface

This chapter discusses some iOS interface features that differ between the iPad and the iPhone:

Popovers and split views
> Popovers and split views were exclusive to the iPad when they were introduced in iOS 3.2. Starting in iOS 8, they became available also on the iPhone, where they typically adapt, appearing in an altered form more appropriate to the smaller screen. New in iOS 14, split views have been completely overhauled.

iPad multitasking
> iPad multitasking, introduced in iOS 9, is an interface confined to the iPad, where two apps can occupy the screen simultaneously.

Drag and drop
> Drag and drop was introduced in iOS 11 primarily to allow the user to drag from one app to another in an iPad multitasking interface. It can also be used within a single app, even on the iPhone.

Pointer and keyboard handling
> New in iOS 14, an iPad user can attach a pointing device, such as a mouse or trackpad; your app can respond to and manipulate the onscreen cursor. If an external keyboard is attached, your app can also detect keyboard shortcuts.

Multiple windows
> Starting in iOS 13, an app can display multiple windows on the iPad.

Popovers

A *popover* is a temporary view layered in front of the main interface. It is usually associated, through a sort of arrow, with a view in the main interface; typically, this

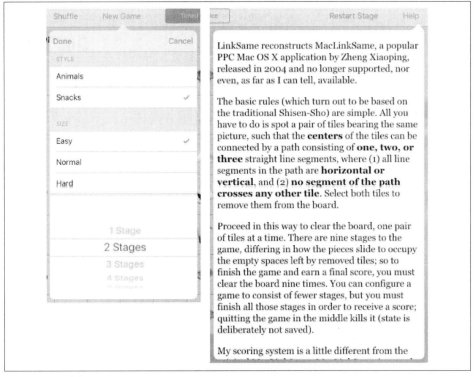

LinkSame reconstructs MacLinkSame, a popular PPC Mac OS X application by Zheng Xiaoping, released in 2004 and no longer supported, nor even, as far as I can tell, available.

The basic rules (which turn out to be based on the traditional Shisen-Sho) are simple. All you have to do is spot a pair of tiles bearing the same picture, such that the **centers** of the tiles can be connected by a path consisting of **one, two, or three** straight line segments, where (1) all line segments in the path are **horizontal or vertical**, and (2) **no segment of the path crosses any other tile**. Select both tiles to remove them from the board.

Proceed in this way to clear the board, one pair of tiles at a time. There are nine stages to the game, differing in how the pieces slide to occupy the empty spaces left by removed tiles; so to finish the game and earn a final score, you must clear the board nine times. You can configure a game to consist of fewer stages, but you must finish all those stages in order to receive a score; quitting the game in the middle kills it (state is deliberately not saved).

My scoring system is a little different from the

Figure 10-1. Two popovers

will be the button that the user tapped to summon the popover. The popover might be effectively modal, preventing the user from working in the rest of the interface; alternatively, it might vanish if the user taps outside it.

Popovers bring to the larger iPad the smaller, more lightweight flavor of the iPhone. In my LinkSame app, both the settings view (where the user configures the game) and the help view (which describes how to play the game) are popovers (Figure 10-1). On the iPhone, these views occupy the entire screen; the user navigates to one of them and later has to navigate back to the main game interface. But on the larger iPad screen, neither view is large enough, or important enough, to occupy the entire screen exclusively. A popover is the perfect solution. A popover view is small and secondary, and the user summons it temporarily, works with it, and then dismisses it, while the main interface continues to occupy the rest of the screen.

A popover is actually a form of presented view controller — a presented view controller with a `modalPresentationStyle` of `.popover` (which I didn't tell you about in Chapter 6). There's a guideline that a maximum of one popover at a time should be shown; a view controller can't have more than one presented view controller at a time, so the guideline is enforced automatically.

Like a sheet presented view controller, a popover can adapt, depending on the size class environment. The default adaptation of a popover on the iPhone depends on what system we're running on:

iOS 12 and before
The default adaptation on the iPhone is `.fullScreen`.

iOS 13 and later
The default adaptation on the iPhone is `.formSheet`. This is indistinguishable from `.pageSheet`, meaning that it leaves a gap at the top in portrait, but behaves like `.overFullScreen` in landscape.

You don't have to accept the default; you can customize how the popover adapts. It can appear on the iPhone as `.fullScreen` even in portrait; it can even appear *as a popover!* I'll explain later how to make it do that.

 A popover presented view controller that appears as a popover has a `.compact` horizontal size class, even on an iPad.

To display a popover, you're going to present a view controller. Before that presentation takes place, you'll turn this into a popover presentation by setting the view controller's `modalPresentationStyle` to `.popover`:

```
let vc = MyViewController()
vc.modalPresentationStyle = .popover
self.present(vc, animated: true)
```

But that code is insufficient. In fact, it will crash at runtime when the popover is presented! The reason is that some further configuration of the popover is required before it appears. To configure a popover, you'll talk to its *presentation controller.* Setting the view controller's `modalPresentationStyle` to `.popover`, as in the preceding code, causes its `presentationController` to become a UIPopoverPresentation-Controller (a UIPresentationController subclass). The popover view controller's `popoverPresentationController` property points to the presentation controller as a popover presentation controller (or to `nil`). That's the object you need to talk to.

In general, it is permissible to perform your configurations just *after* telling your view controller to present the popover, because even though you have ordered the presentation, it hasn't actually started yet. This is a common pattern:

```
let vc = MyViewController()
vc.modalPresentationStyle = .popover
self.present(vc, animated: true)
if let pop = vc.popoverPresentationController {
    // ... configure pop here ...
}
```

Arrow Source and Direction

At a minimum, the popover presentation controller needs to know where its arrow should point. You'll specify this by setting one of the following:

`barButtonItem`
> A bar button item in the interface, with which the popover should be associated. The popover's arrow will point to this bar button item. Typically, this will be the bar button item that was tapped in order to summon the popover (as in Figure 10-1).

`sourceView, sourceRect`
> A UIView in the interface, along with a CGRect *in that view's coordinate system*, with which the popover should be associated. The popover's arrow will point to this rect. Typically, the `sourceView` will be the view that was tapped in order to summon the popover, and the `sourceRect` will be that view's bounds.

Here's a minimal popover presentation that works without crashing; the popover is summoned by tapping a UIButton in the interface, and this is that button's action method:

```
@IBAction func doButton(_ sender: Any) {
    let vc = MyViewController()
    vc.modalPresentationStyle = .popover
    self.present(vc, animated: true)
    if let pop = vc.popoverPresentationController {
        let v = sender as! UIView
        pop.sourceView = v
        pop.sourceRect = v.bounds
    }
}
```

In addition to the arrow source, you can set the desired arrow direction, as the popover presentation controller's `permittedArrowDirections`. This is a bitmask with possible values `.up`, `.down`, `.left`, and `.right`. The default is `.any`, comprising all four bitmask values; that will usually be what you want.

Popover Size

You can specify the desired size of the popover view. This information is provided through the presented view controller's `preferredContentSize`. Recall (from Chapter 6) that a view controller can use its `preferredContentSize` to communicate to its container view controller, *qua* UIContentContainer, the size that it would like to be. The popover presentation controller is a presentation controller (UIPresentationController), which is also a UIContentContainer; it will consult the presented view controller's `preferredContentSize` and will try, within limits, to respect it. The presentation of the popover won't fail if you don't supply a size for the popover, but you probably will want to supply one, as the default is unlikely to be desirable.

Who will set the presented view controller's `preferredContentSize`, and when? It's up to you. The presented view controller might set its own `preferredContentSize`; its `viewDidLoad` is a reasonable place, or, if the view controller is instantiated from a nib, the nib editor provides Content Size fields in the Attributes inspector. Alternatively, you can set the presented view controller's `preferredContentSize` when you configure the popover presentation controller:

```
if let pop = vc.popoverPresentationController {
    let v = sender as! UIView
    pop.sourceView = v
    pop.sourceRect = v.bounds
    vc.preferredContentSize = CGSize(200,500) // *
}
```

It is possible to change the presented view controller's `preferredContentSize` while the popover is showing. The popover presentation controller will hear about this (through the `preferredContentSizeDidChange` mechanism discussed in Chapter 6), and may respond by changing the popover's size, with animation.

The popover presentation controller's `canOverlapSourceViewRect` can be set to `true` to permit the popover to cover the source view if space becomes tight while attempting to comply with the `preferredContentSize`. The default is `false`.

You can also set the popover presentation controller's `popoverLayoutMargins` as a way of encouraging the popover to maintain some distance from the edges of the presenting view controller's view. (This property was broken starting about iOS 8, but works correctly again starting in iOS 13.)

Popover Appearance

By default, a popover presentation controller bases the arrow color on the color of the presented view controller's view. Alternatively, you can set the popover presentation controller's `backgroundColor`; this sets the arrow color as well. But the presented view controller's own view color will override this, unless it is `.clear` or `nil`.

For full control, you can customize the entire outside of the popover — that is, the "frame" surrounding the content, *including* the arrow. To do so, you set the UIPopoverPresentationController's `popoverBackgroundViewClass` to your own subclass of UIPopoverBackgroundView (a UIView subclass). You then implement the UIPopoverBackgroundView's `draw(_:)` method to draw the arrow and the frame. The size of the arrow is dictated by your implementation of the `arrowHeight` property. The thickness of the frame is dictated by your implementation of the `contentViewInsets` property.

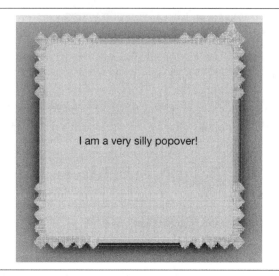

Figure 10-2. A very silly popover

A very silly example is shown in Figure 10-2. Here's how that result was achieved. I start by implementing five inherited members that we are required to override, along with our initializer:

```
class MyPopoverBackgroundView : UIPopoverBackgroundView {
    override class func arrowBase() -> CGFloat { return 20 }
    override class func arrowHeight() -> CGFloat { return 20 }
    override class func contentViewInsets() -> UIEdgeInsets {
        return UIEdgeInsets(top: 20, left: 20, bottom: 20, right: 20)
    }
    // we are required to implement these, even trivially
    var arrOff : CGFloat
    var arrDir : UIPopoverArrowDirection
    override var arrowDirection : UIPopoverArrowDirection {
        get { return self.arrDir }
        set { self.arrDir = newValue }
    }
    override var arrowOffset : CGFloat {
        get { return self.arrOff }
        set { self.arrOff = newValue }
    }
    override init(frame:CGRect) {
        self.arrOff = 0
        self.arrDir = .any
        super.init(frame:frame)
        self.isOpaque = false
    }
    // ...
}
```

Now I'll implement draw(_:). Its job is to draw the frame and the arrow. This can be a bit tricky, because we need to draw differently depending on the arrow direction (which we can learn from the UIPopoverBackgroundView's arrowDirection property). I'll simplify by assuming that the arrow direction will always be .up.

I'll start with the frame. I divide the view's overall rect into two areas, the arrow area on top and the frame area on the bottom, and I draw the frame into the bottom area as a resizable image (Chapter 2):

```
override func draw(_ rect: CGRect) {
    let linOrig = UIImage(named: "linen.png")!
    let capw = linOrig.size.width / 2.0 - 1
    let caph = linOrig.size.height / 2.0 - 1
    let lin = linOrig.resizableImage(
        withCapInsets:
            UIEdgeInsets(top: caph, left: capw, bottom: caph, right: capw),
        resizingMode:.tile)
    let arrowHeight = Self.arrowHeight()
    let arrowBase = Self.arrowBase()
    // ... draw arrow here ...
    let (_,body) = rect.divided(atDistance: arrowHeight, from: .minYEdge)
    lin.draw(in:body)
}
```

Our next task is to fill in the blank left by the "draw arrow here" comment in the preceding code. We don't actually have to do that; we could quite legally stop at this point. Our popover would then have no arrow, but that's no disaster; many developers dislike the arrow and seek a way to remove it, and this constitutes a legal way. But let's continue by drawing the arrow.

My arrow will consist simply of a texture-filled isosceles triangle, with an excess base rectangle joining it to the frame. The runtime has set the arrowOffset property to tell us where to draw the arrow: this offset measures the positive distance between the center of the view's edge and the center of the arrow. However, the runtime will have no hesitation in setting the arrowOffset all the way at the edge of the view, or even beyond its bounds (in which case it won't be drawn); to prevent this, I impose a maximum offset limit:

```
let con = UIGraphicsGetCurrentContext()!
con.saveGState()
// clamp offset
var propX = self.arrowOffset
let limit : CGFloat = 22.0
let maxX = rect.size.width/2.0 - limit
propX = min(max(propX, limit), maxX)
// draw!
con.translateBy(x: rect.size.width/2.0 + propX - arrowBase/2.0, y: 0)
con.move(to:CGPoint(0, arrowHeight))
con.addLine(to:CGPoint(arrowBase / 2.0, 0))
con.addLine(to:CGPoint(arrowBase, arrowHeight))
```

```
con.closePath()
con.addRect(CGRect(0,arrowHeight,arrowBase,15))
con.clip()
lin.draw(at:CGPoint(-40,-40))
con.restoreGState()
```

Passthrough Views

When you're configuring your popover, you'll want to plan ahead for how the popover is to be dismissed. The default behavior is that the user can tap anywhere *outside* the popover to dismiss it, but it can be modified through two properties:

UIPopoverPresentationController's passthroughViews *property*
   An array of views in the interface behind the popover; the user can interact normally with these views while the popover is showing, and the popover will *not* be dismissed.

UIViewController's isModalInPresentation *property*
   If this is true for the presented view controller (or for its current child view controller, as in a tab bar interface or navigation interface), then if the user taps outside the popover, the popover is *not* dismissed. The default is false. The user can still interact with any of the passthroughViews, even if isModalInPresentation is true.

If you've set the presented view controller's isModalInPresentation to true, you've removed the user's ability to dismiss the popover by tapping outside it. You would then presumably provide some *other* way of letting the user dismiss the popover — typically, a button *inside* the popover which the user can tap in order to call dismiss(animated:completion:).

Surprisingly, if a popover is summoned by the user tapping a UIBarButton item in a toolbar, other UIBarButtonItems in that toolbar are automatically turned into passthrough views! This means that, while the popover is showing, the user can tap any other button in the toolbar. I regard this as a bug; working around it is remarkably difficult. If you set the popover presentation controller's passthroughViews too soon, your setting is overridden by the runtime. The best place is the presentation's completion function:

```
self.present(vc, animated: true) {
    vc.popoverPresentationController?.passthroughViews = nil
}
```

Popover Presentation, Dismissal, and Delegate

A popover is a form of presented view controller. To show a popover, you'll call present(_:animated:completion:). If you want to dismiss a popover in code, you'll call dismiss(animated:completion:).

Messages to the popover presentation controller's delegate (UIPopoverPresentation-ControllerDelegate) provide further information and control. Typically, you'll set the delegate in the same place you're performing the other configurations:

```
if let pop = vc.popoverPresentationController {
    // ... other configurations go here ...
    pop.delegate = self
}
```

The most commonly used delegate methods are:

prepareForPopoverPresentation(_:)
> The popover is being presented. This is another opportunity to perform initial configurations, such as what interface object the arrow points to. (But this method is still called too early for you to work around the passthroughViews issue I discussed a moment ago.)

presentationControllerShouldDismiss(_:)
> The user is dismissing the popover by tapping outside it. Return false to prevent dismissal. *Not* called when you dismiss the popover in code.

presentationControllerWillDismiss(_:)
> The user has dismissed the popover by tapping outside it. The popover is still on the screen. *Not* called when you dismiss the popover in code.

presentationControllerDidDismiss(_:)
> The user has dismissed the popover by tapping outside it. The popover is gone from the screen and dismissal is complete, even though the popover presentation controller still exists. *Not* called when you dismiss the popover in code.

popoverPresentationController(_:willRepositionPopoverTo:in:)
> The popover's sourceView is involved in new layout activity. This might be because the interface is rotating. The to: and in: parameters are mutable pointers to the popover's sourceRect and sourceView respectively, so you can change the attachment of the arrow through their pointee properties.

The delegate methods provide the popover presentation controller as parameter, and if necessary you can use it to identify the popover more precisely; the view controller being presented is the popover presentation controller's presentedViewController. The delegate dismiss methods make up for the fact that, when the user dismisses the popover, you don't have the sort of direct information and control that you would get if *you* had dismissed the popover by calling dismiss(animated:completion:) with a completion function.

If a popover can be dismissed *both* by tapping outside the popover *and* by tapping an interface item that calls dismiss(animated:completion:), you may have to duplicate some code in order to cover all cases. Consider the first popover shown in

Figure 10-1. It has a Done button and a Cancel button; the idea here is that the user sets up a desired game configuration and then, while dismissing the popover, either saves it (Done) or doesn't (Cancel). But what if the user taps outside the popover? I interpret that as cancellation. If the Cancel button's action function does any work besides dismissing the popover, my `presentationControllerDidDismiss(_:)` implementation will have to do the same thing.

Adaptive Popovers

A popover is a presented view controller, so it's *adaptive* (see "Adaptive Presentation" on page 336). By default, on an iPhone, the `.popover` modal presentation style will adapt as `.formSheet`, which is identical in appearance to `.pageSheet`, the default for a presented view controller on an iPhone; and so with no extra code you'll get something eminently sensible on both types of device.

But sometimes the default is not quite what you want. A case in point appears in Figure 10-1. The popover on the right, containing our help info, has no internal button for dismissal. It doesn't need one on the iPad, because the user can dismiss the popover by tapping outside it. But this is a universal app. On the iPhone, the popover will adapt to `.formSheet`. In landscape on the iPhone, a `.formSheet` presentation appears as fullscreen — and the user will have *no way to dismiss* this view controller! Clearly, we need a Done button that appears inside the presented view controller's view — but only on the iPhone.

To achieve this, we can take advantage of UIPresentationController delegate methods. The popover presentation controller *is* a UIPresentationController, and its delegate (UIPopoverPresentationControllerDelegate) *is* a UIPresentationController delegate (UIAdaptivePresentationControllerDelegate). Set the presentation controller's delegate *before* calling `present(_:animated:completion:)`; otherwise, the adaptive presentation delegate methods won't be called:

```
let vc = MyViewController()
vc.modalPresentationStyle = .popover
if let pop = vc.popoverPresentationController {
    pop.delegate = self // *
}
self.present(vc, animated: true)
```

We'll implement the delegate method `presentationController(_:viewController-ForAdaptivePresentationStyle:)` to substitute a different view controller. The substitute view controller can be the original view controller wrapped in a UINavigationController; if we also give our original view controller a `navigation-Item` with a working Done button, the problem is solved:

```
func presentationController(_ controller: UIPresentationController,
    viewControllerForAdaptivePresentationStyle
    style: UIModalPresentationStyle) -> UIViewController? {
        let vc = controller.presentedViewController
        let nav = UINavigationController(rootViewController: vc)
        let b = UIBarButtonItem(barButtonSystemItem: .done,
            target: self, action: #selector(dismissHelp))
        vc.navigationItem.rightBarButtonItem = b
        return nav
}
@objc func dismissHelp(_ sender: Any) {
    self.dismiss(animated:true)
}
```

The outcome is that in a situation where we don't adapt (such as an iPad) we get an ordinary popover; otherwise, we get a presented view controller that can be dismissed with a Done button in a navigation bar.

You can also implement the delegate method adaptivePresentation-Style(for:traitCollection:). You might use this to return something other than a sheet in a .compact size class environment. One possibility is to return .none, in which case the presented view controller will be a popover *even on iPhone*:

```
func adaptivePresentationStyle(for controller: UIPresentationController,
    traitCollection: UITraitCollection) -> UIModalPresentationStyle {
        return .none
}
```

Popover Segues

If you're using a storyboard (with Use Trait Variations checked), you can configure a popover presentation with little or no code. Draw (Control-drag) a segue from a button or view controller that is to *summon* the popover to a view controller that is to *be* the popover, and specify Present As Popover as the segue type. The result is a *popover segue*.

The segue, as it is triggered, configures the presentation just as you would configure it in code. It instantiates and initializes the presented view controller, sets its modal presentation style to .popover, and presents it. The sourceView, barButtonItem, and permittedArrowDirections can be set in the segue's Attributes inspector. You can also set the passthrough views in the nib editor — but not in such a way as to override the unwanted bar button item behavior I discussed earlier.

To perform additional configurations in code, implement prepare(for:sender:). At the time prepare(for:sender:) is called, the popoverPresentationController of the segue's destination view controller exists, but the presentation has not yet begun, so you can successfully set the popover presentation controller's delegate here if desired:

```
override func prepare(for segue: UIStoryboardSegue, sender: Any?) {
    if segue.identifier == "MyPopover" {
        let dest = segue.destination
        if let pop = dest.popoverPresentationController {
            pop.delegate = self
        }
    }
}
```

The popover version of an unwind segue is dismissal of the popover, and so both presentation and dismissal can be managed through the storyboard. A further possibility is to specify a custom segue class (as I explained in Chapter 6).

Popover Presenting a View Controller

A popover can present a view controller internally; you'll specify a `modalPresentationStyle` of `.currentContext` or `.overCurrentContext`, because otherwise the presented view will appear over the entire screen (see Chapter 6).

What happens when the user taps outside a popover that is currently presenting a view controller's view internally? Unfortunately, different systems behave differently. Here's a sample:

iOS 7 and before
> Nothing happens.

iOS 8.1
> The entire popover, including the internal presented view controller, is dismissed.

iOS 8.3
> The internal presented view controller is dismissed, while the popover remains.

iOS 9 and later
> Like iOS 8.1.

In my opinion, the iOS 7 behavior was correct. Presented view controllers are supposed to be modal. They don't spontaneously dismiss themselves because the user taps elsewhere; there has to be some internal interface, such as a Done button or a Cancel button, that the user must tap in order to dismiss the view controller and proceed. You can restore the iOS 7 behavior by implementing the delegate method `presentationControllerShouldDismiss(_:)` to prevent dismissal if the popover is itself presenting a view controller:

```
func presentationControllerShouldDismiss(
    _ pc: UIPresentationController) -> Bool {
        return pc.presentedViewController.presentedViewController == nil
}
```

Figure 10-3. A familiar split view controller interface

Split Views

A *split view* is a way of displaying the views of multiple view controllers simultaneously on an iPad. The interface is managed by a *split view controller* (UISplitView-Controller). The split view controller acts as a parent view controller, maintaining and managing the other view controllers as its children. A UIViewController that is a child, at any depth, of a UISplitViewController has a reference to the UISplitView-Controller through its `splitViewController` property.

New in iOS 14, UISplitViewController has been completely overhauled, giving it an improved architecture. I will discuss the new architecture; the old architecture is documented in earlier editions of this book. If you were using split view controllers in the past, prepare to forget just about everything you knew about them!

In iOS 14, a split view controller can have two or even three children whose views can appear simultaneously. (Apple's Mail and Contacts apps are examples where a split view controller has three child views.) There are various ways of displaying the children's views, as I'll describe later, but the most characteristic is on an iPad in landscape orientation, where by default the child views appear side by side (Figure 10-3).

The typical purpose of a split view controller is to implement a *master-detail architecture*. The first view is the master view, and is usually a list. It generally occupies a third of the screen or less. The majority of the screen displays the second view, which is the detail view. The user taps an item of the list in the master view to determine what should appear in the the detail view. We may speak of the two children of the split view controller as the *master* view controller and the *detail* view controller. Officially, they are the *primary* and *secondary* view controllers; in iOS 14, they are said to occupy the primary and secondary *columns* of the split view controller. If a third view controller's view is displayed as well, it is the *supplementary* view controller, and its view appears to the right of the primary view.

The split view controller's display is *adaptive*, meaning that, by default, it differs depending on the environment. I'll describe a split view controller with a primary and a secondary view controller:

iPad in landscape
> The primary and secondary views appear *side by side*; by default, there is a way for the user to dismiss and summon the primary view, so another possibility is that the secondary view occupies the entire screen.

iPad in portrait
> By default, the secondary view occupies the entire screen; the user can summon the primary view as an *overlay* and can then dismiss it again. The overlay, when present, is modal; it covers part of the secondary view, which is dimmed.

Big iPhone in landscape
> Like the iPad in portrait.

iPhone in general
> A completely different interface is substituted. In addition to the primary, secondary, and (optional) supplementary child view controllers, the split view controller has a *compact* child view controller. This is the view controller whose view appears in a horizontally `.compact` size class situation — an iPhone in portrait, a normal iPhone in landscape, or an iPad involved in multitasking (as I'll describe later in this chapter). Typically it will be a navigation controller, implementing the master–detail interface familiar from Chapter 6.

 The introduction of the separate compact child view controller is the most significant innovation in the iOS 14 overhaul of the split view controller architecture.

Those are the defaults, but there are many other possible variations. In the Settings app, for example, on an iPad, the master and detail views appear side by side even in portrait, and there is no option to dismiss the master view. I'll talk later about those sorts of customizations.

To get started with split view controllers, there's no better approach than to construct one. I'll proceed in three stages. First, I'll make a basic split view controller on an iPad. Second, I'll add more code so that the same split view controller works on an iPhone as well. Finally, I'll talk about the tricky case where the same split view controller toggles between iPad and iPhone configurations.

Expanded Split View Controller

For reasons that will be clear later, a split view controller on the iPad is called an *expanded* split view controller; its isCollapsed property is false. For our example, I'll create a split view controller with a master (primary) child view controller and a detail (secondary) child view controller:

Master view
> The master view will be a collection view list displaying the names of the three Pep Boys. Its name is PepListViewController.

Detail view
> The detail view will contain a label and an image view, displaying the name and face of the Pep Boy selected in the master view. Its name is Pep.

The app's root view controller is called ViewController. It creates the split view controller, puts it into the interface as a standard child view controller, and populates it with a PepListViewController and a Pep view controller:

```
// create the split view and put it in the interface
let split = UISplitViewController(style: .doubleColumn) ❶
self.addChild(split)
self.view.addSubview(split.view)
split.view.frame = self.view.bounds
split.view.autoresizingMask = [.flexibleHeight, .flexibleWidth]
split.didMove(toParent: self)
// populate the split view
let pepList = PepListViewController()
let pep = Pep()
let pepNav = UINavigationController(rootViewController: pep)
split.setViewController(pepList, for: .primary) ❷
split.setViewController(pepNav, for: .secondary)
```

❶ The UISplitViewController is initialized with a style: parameter. It is this move that alerts the runtime to the fact that this is going to be a new-style iOS 14 split view controller. Our choices are .doubleColumn and .tripleColumn; a third option, .unspecified, would throw us back to the UISplitViewController from iOS 13 and earlier.

❷ Having asked for two columns, we must also populate those columns by providing the child view controllers. We do that by calling setView-Controller(_:for:). The second parameter is an enum that specifies the column — here, either .primary or .secondary.

I'll tackle the master and detail view controllers in reverse order. First, the detail view controller, Pep:

```
class Pep: UIViewController {
    let boy : String
    @IBOutlet var name : UILabel!
    @IBOutlet var pic : UIImageView!
    override var nibName: String? { "Pep" }
    init(pepBoy boy:String = "Manny") {
        self.boy = boy
        super.init(nibName: nil, bundle: nil)
    }
    required init(coder: NSCoder) {
        fatalError("NSCoding not supported")
    }
    override func viewDidLoad() {
        super.viewDidLoad()
        self.name.text = self.boy
        self.pic.image = UIImage(named:self.boy.lowercased())
    }
}
```

The master detail view controller, PepListViewController, in its viewDidLoad, constructs the collection view list, just as in Chapter 9:

```
class PepListViewController: UICollectionViewController {
    var datasource: UICollectionViewDiffableDataSource<String, String>!
    convenience init() {
        self.init(collectionViewLayout: UICollectionViewLayout())
    }
    override func viewDidLoad() {
        super.viewDidLoad()
        self.title = "Pep"
        self.navigationController?.navigationBar.prefersLargeTitles = true
        let config = UICollectionLayoutListConfiguration(
            appearance: .sidebarPlain) ❶
        let layout = UICollectionViewCompositionalLayout.list(using: config)
        self.collectionView.collectionViewLayout = layout
        typealias CellReg = UICollectionView.CellRegistration
        let reg = CellReg<UICollectionViewListCell, String> { cell, ip, s in
            var contentConfig = cell.defaultContentConfiguration()
            contentConfig.text = s
            cell.contentConfiguration = contentConfig
        }
        let ds = UICollectionViewDiffableDataSource<String, String>(
            collectionView:self.collectionView) { cv, ip, s in
                cv.dequeueConfiguredReusableCell(using: reg, for: ip, item: s)
        }
        self.datasource = ds
        var snap = NSDiffableDataSourceSectionSnapshot<String>()
        snap.append(["Manny", "Moe", "Jack"])
        self.datasource.apply(snap, to: "Dummy", animatingDifferences: false)
    }
    fileprivate func respondToSelection(_ indexPath: IndexPath) {
        ❷
    }
}
```

```
        override func collectionView(_ collectionView: UICollectionView,
            didSelectItemAt indexPath: IndexPath) {
                self.respondToSelection(indexPath)
        }
    }
```

All of that is standard boilerplate code for making a collection view list. There are just two things to notice:

❶ When we create our list configuration, we use the `.sidebarPlain` appearance. That's what this sort of primary view in a split view controller is — it's a sidebar. Apple wants us to use `.sidebar` or `.sidebarPlain` here, and I think `.sidebar-Plain` is more appropriate for this list.

❷ What should happen when the user taps a Pep Boy's name? We need to supply that code.

The idea of selection in the master view controller is that we should make the detail view controller change to match the tapped item. The way to do that, it turns out, is to call `showDetailViewController` on the master controller. Here's the missing content of our `respondToSelection` method:

```
    fileprivate func respondToSelection(_ indexPath: IndexPath) {
        let snap = self.datasource.snapshot()
        let boy = snap.itemIdentifiers[indexPath.row]
        let pep = Pep(pepBoy: boy)
        let nav = UINavigationController(rootViewController: pep)
        self.showDetailViewController(nav, sender: self) // *
    }
```

The starred line is the key to the entire implementation of the master–detail architecture. Despite being sent to `self`, the call to `showDetailViewController(_:sender:)` actually walks up the view controller hierarchy until it arrives at the split view controller. (The mechanism of this walk is quite interesting of itself; I'll discuss it later.) The split view controller responds by making the nav view controller its `.secondary` child, replacing the existing detail view and causing the selected Pep Boy's name and face to appear in the interface.

In that code, I've created a Pep view controller corresponding to the selected name; but before handing it over to the split view controller as the detail view controller, I've wrapped it in a navigation controller. That's deliberate; I did the same thing in the root view controller when I initially populated the `.secondary` column. Why?

It turns out that if we *don't* wrap a child view controller in a navigation controller, the runtime will do it for us; and I have relied on that behavior in populating the `.primary` column. But when the runtime creates this navigation controller, it adds some default behavior. For the secondary view controller, that behavior is to *push* each new view controller onto the existing navigation controller's stack every time `showDetailViewController(_:sender:)` is called. If we permit that, then when the user taps Manny and then Moe, the detail view displaying Moe will have a Back button which, when tapped, leads back to Manny. That isn't what I want; I want the detail view to be just one Pep Boy, not a navigation stack of Pep Boys. So I supply my own navigation controller, to prevent the default behavior; I *replace* the existing navigation controller rather than *pushing* onto it.

We now have a complete working split view controller on iPad! Moreover, we get a lot of elaborate and powerful functionality "for free":

In landscape
> The master and detail views appear side by side. The runtime has supplied a button (as the master view navigation bar's left bar button item) that the user can tap to dismiss the master view, and when it has been dismissed, the same button (as the detail view navigation bar's left bar button item) summons the master view. Alternatively, the user can swipe from the left edge to summon the master view interactively as an overlay; the overlay is dismissed whenever the user chooses a Pep Boy or taps outside the overlay.

In portrait
> The detail view always occupies the whole screen. The master view, if it appears, is an overlay; the overlay is dismissed when the user chooses a Pep Boy or taps outside the overlay. To summon the overlay, there's a chevron button (like a back button) at the left of the detail view's navigation bar, or the user can swipe from the left edge.

Collapsed Split View Controller

A split view controller on a normal iPhone is a *collapsed* split view controller; its `isCollapsed` property is `true`. Now, we can in fact launch the app we've already created on an iPhone — and, incredibly, it works almost perfectly. However, what we're seeing is merely the automatic adaptive behavior left over from iOS 13 and before. In iOS 14, there's a different mechanism entirely, and we should use it.

In addition to the primary and secondary child view controllers, we will give the split view controller *another* child view controller — the `.compact` view controller. This is the view controller that provides the split view controller's single visible child view in a compact environment. The idea is that there are *two separate view controller hierarchies* — one for a compact environment (when the split view controller is collapsed), and one for a regular environment (when the split view controller is expanded).

In our app, what should the compact view controller be? Our case is pretty simple and clear-cut: it should be a navigation controller whose root view controller is similar to the PepListViewController — except that it should use the `.plain` appearance and the cells should have disclosure indicators. And when the user taps a row of the list, we should create something similar to a Pep view controller and just *push* it onto the navigation controller.

So now we're going to create two new view controllers, remarkably similar to the existing view controllers. I'll call them PepListCompactViewController and PepCompact. Here's the compact master view controller PepListCompactViewController; there are just three differences from PepListViewController, which I've marked with comments:

```swift
class PepListCompactViewController: UICollectionViewController {
    var datasource: UICollectionViewDiffableDataSource<String, String>!
    convenience init() {
        self.init(collectionViewLayout: UICollectionViewLayout())
    }
    override func viewDidLoad() {
        super.viewDidLoad()
        self.title = "Pep"
        self.navigationController?.navigationBar.prefersLargeTitles = true
        // ** plain appearance! **
        let config = UICollectionLayoutListConfiguration(appearance: .plain)
        let layout = UICollectionViewCompositionalLayout.list(using: config)
        self.collectionView.collectionViewLayout = layout
        typealias CellReg = UICollectionView.CellRegistration
        let reg = CellReg<UICollectionViewListCell, String> { cell, ip, s in
            var contentConfig = cell.defaultContentConfiguration()
            contentConfig.text = s
            cell.contentConfiguration = contentConfig
            // ** disclosure indicators! **
            cell.accessories = [.disclosureIndicator()]
        }
        let ds = UICollectionViewDiffableDataSource<String, String>(
            collectionView:self.collectionView) { cv, ip, s in
            cv.dequeueConfiguredReusableCell(using: reg, for: ip, item: s)
        }
        self.datasource = ds
        var snap = NSDiffableDataSourceSectionSnapshot<String>()
        snap.append(["Manny", "Moe", "Jack"])
        self.datasource.apply(snap, to: "Dummy", animatingDifferences: false)
    }
    fileprivate func respondToSelection(_ indexPath: IndexPath) {
        let snap = self.datasource.snapshot()
        let boy = snap.itemIdentifiers[indexPath.row]
        let pep = PepCompact(pepBoy: boy)
        // ** just push! **
        self.navigationController?.pushViewController(pep, animated: true)
    }
    override func collectionView(_ collectionView: UICollectionView,
        didSelectItemAt indexPath: IndexPath) {
            self.respondToSelection(indexPath)
    }
}
```

The compact detail view controller, PepCompact, is identical to Pep in this example, so I won't show it. (Nevertheless, for clarity, I'm treating them as different view controllers.)

To make our app work in a compact environment, we now go back to the View-Controller class, where we configure the split view controller, and give the split view controller a `.compact` view controller:

```
let pepListCompact = PepListCompactViewController()
let nav = UINavigationController(rootViewController: pepListCompact)
split.setViewController(nav, for: .compact)
```

Our interface now works perfectly on an iPhone as well as on an iPad.

Collapsing and Expanding Split View Controller

If life consisted entirely of just fullscreen iPad apps, on the one hand, and normal iPhones, on the other, we would be finished now. The fact is, however, that there are hybrid situations in which your app can sometimes think it is effectively running on an iPad and sometimes think it is effectively running on an iPhone:

"Big" iPhones
> A "big" iPhone is a hybrid device: its horizontal size class is `.regular` in landscape orientation but `.compact` in portrait orientation.

iPad multitasking
> An iPad app can participate in iPad multitasking: it might appear in slideover mode, occupying only part of the screen, or it might be made to share the screen horizontally with another app in splitscreen mode. The horizontal size class is `.regular` when the app is fullscreen but might be `.compact` during iPad multitasking.

Our split view controller can thus *alternate* between being collapsed and being expanded on a single device, in real time. This is not as daunting a prospect as you might suppose. In fact, our app does work in these hybrid situations. The only problem is that, as things stand, when the user causes this alternation to happen, the app *loses the user's place.*

Let's take the "big" iPhone as an example. The user launches the app in portrait orientation, sees the list of Pep Boys, and taps Jack. Now the user is looking at Jack's face in the detail view. The user now rotates the device to landscape — and sees Manny's face! This is bad.

Why is this happening? The split view controller can be displaying either of two completely separate view controller hierarchies, depending on whether it is expanded or collapsed. The expanded view controllers are expressed through its `.primary` and `.secondary` columns; the collapsed view controllers are expressed through its `.compact` column. In rotating the device, we have switched from a hierarchy with PepListCompactViewController and PepCompact, on the one hand, to a hierarchy with PepListViewController and Pep, on the other — and the two hierarchies know nothing about one another's states. We need to fix that. When the split view controller collapses or expands, the view controller hierarchy that the user *now* sees needs to be in the same "place" — expressing the same state, or data — as the view controller hierarchy that the user was seeing a moment ago.

But how? Unfortunately, Apple is rather coy on this topic; but I believe that what we're intended to do is as follows. Back in ViewController, where we configure the split view controller, we append to our existing code this single line:

```
split.delegate = self
```

The result is that we can now adopt the UISplitViewControllerDelegate protocol and receive callbacks through delegate methods as the user expands and collapses the interface:

```
extension ViewController : UISplitViewControllerDelegate {
    func splitViewController(_ svc: UISplitViewController,
        topColumnForCollapsingToProposedTopColumn
        proposedTopColumn: UISplitViewController.Column)
        -> UISplitViewController.Column {
            // ...
            return proposedTopColumn
    }
    func splitViewController(_ svc: UISplitViewController,
        displayModeForExpandingToProposedDisplayMode
        proposedDisplayMode: UISplitViewController.DisplayMode)
        -> UISplitViewController.DisplayMode {
            // ...
            return proposedDisplayMode
    }
}
```

I'm going to implement those delegate methods — but not because I intend to change the `proposedTopColumn` or the `proposedDisplayMode`. I'm going to use them as hooks to make adjustments in the split view controller itself as it collapses or expands.

My approach is crude but effective. First, I'll give ViewController a state variable to track what Pep Boy the user is looking at:

```
var chosenBoy : String?
```

In PepListViewController and PepListCompactViewController, when the user chooses a Pep Boy's name, we also set the state variable:

```
(self.splitViewController?.parent as? ViewController)?.chosenBoy = boy
```

In the delegate methods, I call a utility method that will be responsible for adjusting the split view controller. I use delayed performance so as not to be changing the split view controller during the delegate method:

```
func splitViewController(_ svc: UISplitViewController,
    topColumnForCollapsingToProposedTopColumn
    proposedTopColumn: UISplitViewController.Column)
    -> UISplitViewController.Column {
        delay(0.1) {
            self.swap(svc, collapsing: true) // *
        }
    return proposedTopColumn
}
func splitViewController(_ svc: UISplitViewController,
    displayModeForExpandingToProposedDisplayMode
    proposedDisplayMode: UISplitViewController.DisplayMode)
    -> UISplitViewController.DisplayMode {
        delay(0.1) {
            self.swap(svc, collapsing: false) // *
        }
    return proposedDisplayMode
}
```

My utility method, swap(_:collapsing:), does all the work. When the split view controller is collapsing, whatever Pep Boy the user has chosen for display from the .primary column in its expanded state, that same Pep Boy needs to be displayed in the PepCompact view controller pushed onto the navigation controller in the .compact column in its collapsed state. When the split view controller is expanding, whatever Pep Boy the user has chosen for display in the .compact column in its collapsed state, that same Pep Boy needs to be displayed in the .secondary column in its expanded state:

```
if collapsing {
    if let boy = self.chosenBoy,
    let nav = svc.viewController(for: .compact) as? UINavigationController {
        let newPep = PepCompact(pepBoy: boy)
        nav.popToRootViewController(animated: false)
        nav.pushViewController(newPep, animated: false)
    }
} else {
    if let boy = self.chosenBoy,
    let list = svc.viewController(for: .primary) as? PepListViewController {
        let newPep = Pep(pepBoy: boy)
        let nav = UINavigationController(rootViewController: newPep)
        list.showDetailViewController(nav, sender: self)
    }
}
```

The example is simple, but it illustrates the underlying principle neatly. The split view controller expresses to the user some state or data, and it must continue to express that same state or data even when we switch between view controller hierarchies. Depending on the nature of your data and how the split view controller expresses it, you'll devise a way to *transfer* that state from one view controller hierarchy to the other at the moment the user collapses or expands the split view controller.

Customizing a Split View Controller

The most important determinant of an expanded split view controller's interface appearance is its *display mode,* describing what columns are visible and how the .secondary column relates to the others. To learn the actual display mode being used, ask for the current displayMode. To alter the display mode, set the preferred-DisplayMode property; use .automatic to allow the display mode to adopt its default value. Possible values are (UISplitViewController.DisplayMode):

.secondaryOnly
> Just the .secondary column is visible, occupying the entire interface.

.oneBesideSecondary
.oneOverSecondary
> There are two columns, either side by side or with the .secondary column full-screen and overlaid by the one. The name is coy about *which* column is the one, because this will be different depending on whether there are two columns or three columns:

> *Two-column layout*
> > The one is the .primary column.

> *Three-column layout*
> > The one is the .supplementary column.

> The rule for a three-column layout is that the .supplementary column can appear without the .primary column — but the .primary column cannot appear without the .supplementary column.

.twoBesideSecondary
.twoOverSecondary
.twoDisplaceSecondary
> Applicable *only* in a three-column layout. two means both the .primary and .supplementary columns appear; the difference is in how the .secondary column appears:

> beside
> > All three columns are side by side.

over

> The `.primary` and `.supplementary` columns constitute an overlay.

displace

> The `.secondary` column is beside the other two, but *without* being reduced in width — instead, it is darkened, as in an overlay mode, and pushed partially offscreen. This is the default in a three-column layout in landscape on an iPad when both the `.primary` and `.supplementary` columns are visible.

Your preferred display mode is only a preference; the runtime remembers and applies it as appropriate in terms of the interface's orientation and the user's actions. If the goal is to change the display mode on just one occasion, you might be better off calling `show(_:)` or `hide(_:)`, which take a column.

For instance, I happen to think that the default policy of hiding the `.primary` column in portrait on an iPad is wrong if we *launch* into portrait; I'd rather have the user see the `.primary` column on that one occasion:

```
var initial = true
override func viewDidLayoutSubviews() {
    super.viewDidLayoutSubviews()
    if self.initial {
        if self.traitCollection.userInterfaceIdiom == .pad {
            if self.view.bounds.width < self.view.bounds.height {
                let svc = self.children[0] as! UISplitViewController
                svc.show(.primary)
            }
        }
    }
    self.initial = false
}
```

The split view controller's response to your `preferredDisplayMode` setting is mediated also by its *split behavior*. To learn the actual split behavior in effect, ask for the current `splitBehavior`. To alter the split behavior, set the `preferredSplitBehavior` property; use `.automatic` to allow the split behavior to adopt its default value. Possible values are (UISplitViewController.SplitBehavior):

tile

> No over or displace display mode is allowed.

overlay

> No beside or displace display mode is allowed.

displace

> No over display mode is allowed; `.twoBesideSecondary` is not allowed, but `.one-BesideSecondary` *is* allowed, as otherwise we'd never see the `.primary` column in a double-column layout.

If you ask for a display mode that isn't permitted by the split behavior, you'll get a different display mode. For instance, if you ask for `.oneBesideSecondary` when the split behavior is `.overlay`, you'll get `.oneOverSecondary`.

The user's ability to switch between display modes using buttons and gestures is affected by two properties:

`presentsWithGesture`

> The default is `true`. Despite the name, it actually affects *two* things: the enablement of the swipe gesture, and the presence of the toggle button. If this property is `false`, the user cannot hide the `.primary` column if it is showing in a `beside` display mode, and cannot summon the `.primary` column if it is not showing; giving the user a way to do those things, if desired, would then be up to you.

`showsSecondaryOnlyButton`

> The default is `false`. If `true`, then in a three-column layout, a button is present that allows the user to dismiss all columns except the `.secondary` column, or to summon the `.supplementary` column if it is not showing.

Here are some further properties of a UISplitViewController that allow it to be customized:

`primaryEdge`

> Which side the `.primary` column (and `.supplementary` column) appears on. Your choices are `.leading` and `.trailing`. A `.trailing` split view controller is a rarity, but clearly it isn't illegal.

`preferredPrimaryColumnWidth`, `preferredPrimaryColumnWidthFraction`
`minimumPrimaryColumnWidth`, `maximumPrimaryColumnWidth`
`preferredSupplementaryColumnWidth`
`preferredSupplementaryColumnWidthFraction`
`minimumSupplementaryColumnWidth`, `maximumSupplementaryColumnWidth`

> Sets the widths that the `.primary` and `.supplementary` columns will have when showing:
>
> - To specify the default width, use `UISplitViewController.automaticDimension`.
> - To let the `.supplementary` column fill the remainder of the screen, use `UISplitViewController.automaticSupplementaryFillDimension`.
> - To learn the actual width being used, ask for the current `primaryColumnWidth` and `supplementaryColumnWidth`.

If you set both a fractional and an absolute width, the absolute width takes precedence. You must set the preferred *maximum* width before any other width setting will take effect!

Split View Controller Delegate Methods

These are the split view controller delegate methods (UISplitViewController-Delegate) that you're most likely to use in iOS 14:

`splitViewController(_:willShow:)`
`splitViewController(_:willHide:)`
> The split view controller is about to show or hide a column.

`splitViewController(_:topColumnForCollapsingToProposedTopColumn:)`
`splitViewController(_:displayModeForExpandingToProposedDisplayMode:)`
> The split view controller is collapsing or expanding, respectively. You can change the column that will be used in the collapsed state or the initial display mode in the expanded state; but, as I've already shown, these methods are more important as being the moment when you can transfer data state information between the two view controller hierarchies.

`splitViewControllerDidCollapse(_:)`
`splitViewControllerDidExpand(_:)`
> The split view controller has switched between the collapsed and expanded state.

`splitViewController(_:willChangeTo:)`
> The split view controller is about to change its display mode.

`splitViewControllerInteractivePresentationGestureWillBegin(_:)`
`splitViewControllerInteractivePresentationGestureDidEnd(_:)`
> The user is employing the edge swipe gesture. Confusingly, the gesture may end without completing (because it was cancelled instead).

If a split view controller is the top-level view controller, it determines your app's compensatory rotation behavior. To take a hand in that determination without having to subclass UISplitViewController, make one of your objects the split view controller's delegate and implement these methods, as needed:

- `splitViewControllerSupportedInterfaceOrientations(_:)`

- `splitViewControllerPreferredInterfaceOrientationForPresentation(_:)`

A split view controller does not relegate decisions about the status bar appearance to its children. To hide the status bar when a split view controller is the root view controller, you might have to subclass UISplitViewController.

Expanding a Split View Controller

Suppose you want a split view controller to behave like a split view controller, showing its `.primary` and `.secondary` columns, *on an iPhone*. The problem here is that we need to control the value of the split view controller's `isCollapsed` property — but we can't just set it directly, because this property is read-only.

The split view controller decides its own expanded or collapsed state depending on the environment — in particular, on whether the current trait collection's horizontal size class is `.compact`. We need, therefore, to *lie to the split view controller* about its trait collection environment, effectively making it believe that it's on an iPad even though it's really on an iPhone.

We can do that through a custom container view controller that sits above the split view controller in the view controller hierarchy. By sending this container view controller the `setOverrideTraitCollection(_:forChild:)` message, we cause it to pass a trait collection of our choosing down the view controller hierarchy to the split view controller.

In this example, suppose our app runs on an iPhone only. Nevertheless, it has a side-by-side split view controller interface:

```
var didInitialSetup = false
override func viewWillLayoutSubviews() {
    if !self.didInitialSetup {
        self.didInitialSetup = true
        let svc = self.children[0] as! UISplitViewController
        svc.preferredSplitBehavior = .tile
        svc.preferredDisplayMode = .oneBesideSecondary
        svc.maximumPrimaryColumnWidth = 200
        svc.preferredPrimaryColumnWidthFraction = 0.5
        let reg = UITraitCollection(horizontalSizeClass: .regular)
        let traits = UITraitCollection(traitsFrom: [reg])
        self.setOverrideTraitCollection(traits, forChild: svc)
    }
}
```

View Controller Message Percolation

As I mentioned earlier, my code sends `showDetailViewController(_:sender:)` to `self` (the `.primary` view controller), but it is actually the split view controller that responds. How is that possible? The answer is that this message *percolates up* the view controller hierarchy to the split view controller.

Only two built-in UIViewController methods are implemented to behave in this way: `show(_:sender:)` and `showDetailViewController(_:sender:)`. Underlying this behavior is a *general* architecture for percolating a message up the view controller hierarchy, which I will now describe.

The heart of the message-percolation architecture is the method `targetView-Controller(forAction:sender:)`, where the `action:` parameter is the selector for the method we're inquiring about. This method, using some deep introspective voodoo, looks to see whether the view controller to which the message was sent *overrides the UIViewController implementation* of the method in question. If so, it returns `self`; if not, it effectively recurses *up* the view controller hierarchy by returning the result of calling `targetViewController(forAction:sender:)` with the same parameters on its own parent view controller or presenting view controller — or `nil` if no view controller is ultimately returned to it.

(A view controller subclass that *does* override the method in question but does *not* want to be the target view controller can implement the UIResponder method `canPerformAction(_:withSender:)` to return `false`.)

So `show(_:sender:)` and `showDetailViewController(_:sender:)` are implemented to call `targetViewController(forAction:sender:)`. If this call returns a target, they send themselves to that target. If it *doesn't* return a target, they call `present(_:animated:completion:)` as a kind of fallback.

The reason for the percolation architecture is that it allows `show(_:sender:)` and `showDetailViewController(_:sender:)` to work *differently* depending on how the view controller to which they are originally sent is situated in the view controller hierarchy. There are two built-in UIViewController subclasses, UINavigationController and UISplitViewController, whose overrides of these methods matter; if they are *further up the view controller hierarchy* than the view controller on which these methods are called, they will take charge of what happens:

UINavigationController `show(_:sender:)`
UINavigationController implements `show(_:sender:)` to call `pushViewController(_:animated:)`. That explains the dual behavior of `show(_:sender:)` — everything depends on whether or not we're in a navigation interface:

In a navigation interface
If you send `show(_:sender:)` to a view controller whose parent is a UINavigationController, it is the navigation controller's implementation that will be called, meaning that the parameter view controller is *pushed* onto the stack.

Not in a navigation interface
If you send `show(_:sender:)` to a view controller *without* a parent that overrides this method, it can't find a target, so it executes its fallback, meaning that the parameter view controller is *presented*.

UISplitViewController showDetailViewController(_:sender:)

UISplitViewController implements showDetailViewController(_:sender:) as follows:

If the split view controller is expanded

The split view controller replaces its .secondary child view controller with the parameter view controller.

If the split view controller is collapsed

If the split view controller's .compact child view controller is a UINavigationController, it sends show(_:sender:) to it — and the navigation controller responds by pushing the parameter view controller onto its own stack.

If not, the split view controller calls present(_:animated:completion:).

Now that you understand the percolation mechanism, perhaps you'd like to know whether your own custom methods can participate in it. They can! Extend UIView-Controller to implement your method such that it calls targetViewController(for-Action:sender:) on self and sends the action method to the target if there is one:

```
extension UIViewController {
    @objc func showHide(_ sender: Any) {
        if let target = self.targetViewController(
            forAction:#selector(showHide), sender: sender) {
                target.showHide(self)
        }
    }
}
```

In that example, I don't know what any particular UIViewController subclass's override of showHide(_:) may do, and I don't care! What matters is that if showHide(_:) is sent to a view controller that *doesn't* override it, it will percolate up the view controller hierarchy until we find a view controller that *does* override it, and it is *that override* that will be called.

iPad Multitasking

Current iPad models can perform a kind of multitasking where the windows of two different apps can appear simultaneously. There are two multitasking modes (Figure 10-4):

Slideover

One app appears in a narrow format in front of the other, occupying roughly one-third of the screen's width. The rear app continues to occupy the full width of the screen. On newer iPad models, the rear app remains active and the user can interact with either app.

Figure 10-4. Slideover (left) and splitscreen (right) multitasking modes

Splitscreen

The two apps appear side by side and are both active simultaneously; the user can interact with either app. One of the two apps can occupy roughly one-third of the screen's width; in landscape orientation, the apps can also divide the screen's width equally.

Your iPad or universal app, by default, will participate in iPad multitasking if your *Info.plist* permits all four orientations. If you would like to opt out of participation in iPad multitasking, set the *Info.plist* key `UIRequiresFullScreen` to `YES`; you can do that conveniently while editing the app target by checking Requires Full Screen in the General tab. But Apple warns that this option is slated to be removed; multitasking will become a requirement.

If your app participates in iPad multitasking, its size can change from occupying the device's entire screen to a narrower size. This, in turn, may be accompanied by a change in the trait collection to a `.compact` horizontal size class. So your app can be toggled between a `.compact` horizontal size class and a `.regular` horizontal size class, and it must be prepared to cope with that change.

When your app changes size because of multitasking, your view controller will receive events to signal what's happening (see "Resizing and Layout Events" on page 316); the application or scene (or both) may be *inactive* at the time these events arrive:

- Your view controller will receive `viewWillTransition(to:with:)` to report the *size* change.

- If the size change also involves a transition from one horizontal size class to another, then your view controller will also receive `willTransition(to:with:)` and `traitCollectionDidChange(_:)` to report the *trait collection* change.

The good news is that, if your app is a universal app, it is probably prepared *already* to respond coherently to these events, and might well be able to participate in iPad multitasking with no significant change. Your code should already be thinking in terms of size classes, not device type. A view controller on an iPad can have a `.compact` horizontal size class quite apart from iPad multitasking (it might be a popover or form sheet presented view controller), so your code is already prepared for that possibility.

View controllers that respond to a size class change will do so in real time:

- If a view controller is a presented view controller, then if the size transition involves a trait collection transition, the view controller will adapt, there and then. An iPad popover will transform into a sheet before the user's eyes as the app transitions from a .regular horizontal size class to .compact (and you can take a hand in how the presented view controller adapts by functioning as the presentation controller's delegate).

- In a split view controller interface, the split view controller will collapse and expand before the user's eyes as the app transitions from a .regular horizontal size class to .compact and back again. This is no different from the ability of a split view controller to collapse and expand when a big iPhone is rotated, and essentially the same precautions will take care of it satisfactorily.

Here are some of the likely challenges you'll face in adapting your app to cope with iPad multitasking:

Size ratio

The variety of *absolute* sizes that your app's interface might assume under iPad multitasking is unlikely to raise any new concerns. If this is a universal app, then you are *already* taking care of a wide range of possible sizes through size classes and autolayout, and you probably won't have to do anything new to cover these new sizes. But there's a large possible range of *ratios* between the longer and shorter dimensions of your window's size. On a large iPad Pro, the window can go from a roughly square height-to-width ratio all the way up to a very tall and narrow height-to-width ratio. Designing an interface that looks decent and can be operated correctly under such widely variable size ratios can be tricky.

Window bounds and screen bounds

Under iPad multitasking, you can't assume that window bounds are screen bounds (see "Window Coordinates and Screen Coordinates" on page 27). What actually changes when your app is resized is the size of its *window*. Under iPad multitasking, your app's window bounds can be different from screen bounds. Moreover, if your app appears on the right, its window origin is shifted to the right; this changes the relationship between a view's position in window coordinates and its position in screen coordinates. You probably weren't using screen coordinates for anything anyway, but if you were, your code will need to change.

Resource sharing

An important implication of iPad multitasking is that your app may effectively be frontmost *at the same time* as some other app. This means that the other app can be using both the processor (especially the main thread) and memory at a time when your app is not suspended. For this to work, all apps participating in iPad multitasking need to be on good behavior, adhering to best practices with regard to threading (see Chapter 25) and memory usage (see "View Controller Memory Management" on page 412).

Drag and Drop

Drag and drop, introduced in iOS 11, allows the user to drag something from one app into another; it can also be used within a single app. What the user appears to drag is a view, but what is actually communicated to the target app is data. Drag and drop is effectively a visual form of copy and paste — with this important difference·

Copy and paste uses a clipboard
Typically, copy and paste starts by copying the actual data to be communicated onto a clipboard. The data sits in the clipboard, ready to paste anywhere. The data in the clipboard can be pasted multiple times in multiple places.

Drag and drop uses a promise
With drag and drop between apps, no actual data is carried around during the drag. The data might be large; it might take time to acquire. What's carried is effectively a promise to supply a certain type of data on request; that promise isn't fulfilled until the drop takes place. Only the drop target can receive the data.

Drag and Drop Architecture

From an app's point of view, drag and drop operates at the level of individual views. The user performs a set sequence of actions:

1. The user long presses on a view; if this is a view from which dragging is possible (a *drag source*), a visible avatar — a *preview* — appears under the user's finger.
2. The user may then start dragging the preview.
3. The user drags the preview over some other view, possibly in a different app; if this is a view on which dropping is possible (a *drop destination*), the preview is badged to indicate this.
4. If the user releases the preview over a drop destination, the preview disappears, and the actual data is communicated from the source to the destination. (If the user releases the preview when it is *not* badged, the drag and drop is cancelled and no data is communicated.)

To prepare for drag and drop, therefore, your app will need either a drag source view or a drop destination view (or both):

Configuring a drag source view

To configure a view so that dragging from it is possible, you create a UIDrag-Interaction object and attach it to that view. You don't subclass UIDragInteraction; rather, you give it a *delegate* (adopting the UIDragInteractionDelegate protocol). From your app's standpoint, it is this delegate that does all the work if the user actually tries to perform a drag from the source view.

Configuring a drop destination view

To configure a view so that dropping onto it is possible, you create a UIDrop-Interaction object and attach it to that view. You don't subclass UIDropInteraction; rather, you give it a *delegate* (adopting the UIDropInteractionDelegate protocol). From your app's standpoint, it is this delegate that does all the work if the user actually tries to drop onto the destination view.

Drag and drop needs to operate between apps and outside of any app; it is a system-level technology. Between the start of the drag and the ultimate drop, the user, moving the preview, is interacting with the runtime — not the source app or the destination app. The preview being dragged doesn't belong to either app. In a sense, while dragging, the user isn't "in" any app at all; by the same token, while dragging, the user is not prevented from interacting with your app.

The runtime sends messages to the drag interaction delegate or the drop interaction delegate, as appropriate, at the start and end of the drag and drop. In those messages, the runtime presents two different faces:

- To the drag interaction delegate, it presents a UIDragSession object (a UIDragDropSession subclass).
- To the drop interaction delegate, it presents a UIDropSession object (another UIDragDropSession subclass).

More than one piece of data can be supplied through a single drag and drop session. The data itself is accessed through a nest of envelopes. Here's how the session is initially configured by the drag interaction delegate:

1. At the heart of each envelope is a single NSItemProvider representing a single piece of data.
2. Each item provider is wrapped in a UIDragItem.
3. The drag items are attached to the drag session.

At the other end of the process, the drop interaction delegate reverses the procedure:

1. The drop session contains drag items.
2. Each drag item contains a single NSItemProvider.
3. Each item provider is the conduit for fetching the corresponding piece of data.

Basic Drag and Drop

You now know enough for an example! I'll talk through a basic drag and drop operation. In my example, the source view will be a simple color swatch; it vends a color. The destination view will receive that color as the session's data. The source view and the destination view could be in two different apps, but the architecture is completely general, so they could be in the same app — it makes no difference.

The drag source view

The drag source view (which I'm calling `dragView`) can be configured like this:

```
@IBOutlet weak var dragView: UIView!
override func viewDidLoad() {
    super.viewDidLoad()
    let dragger = UIDragInteraction(delegate: self)
    self.dragView.addInteraction(dragger)
}
```

The user long presses on the source view, and the UIDragInteraction detects this. (If you think this makes a UIDragInteraction rather like a gesture recognizer, you're exactly right; in fact, adding a drag interaction to a view installs *four* gesture recognizers on that view.) The drag interaction turns to its delegate (UIDragInteractionDelegate) to find out what to do. A UIDragInteractionDelegate has just one required method, and this is it:

```
func dragInteraction(_ interaction: UIDragInteraction,
    itemsForBeginning session: UIDragSession) -> [UIDragItem] {
        let ip = NSItemProvider(object:UIColor.red)
        let di = UIDragItem(itemProvider: ip)
        return [di]
}
```

The drag delegate's `dragInteraction(_:itemsForBeginning:)` must return an array of drag items. If the array is empty, that's the end of the story; there will be no drag. In our case, we want to permit the drag. Our data is very simple, so we just package it up inside an item provider, pop the item provider into a drag item, and return an array consisting of that drag item.

The user now sees the preview and can drag it. The source effectively retires from the story. So much for the source view!

You may be wondering: where did the preview come from? We didn't supply a custom preview, so the system takes a snapshot of the drag source view, enlarges it slightly, makes it somewhat transparent, and uses that as the draggable preview. For our color swatch example, that might be perfectly acceptable.

The drop destination view

The drop destination view (which I'm calling `dropView`) can be configured in a manner remarkably similar to how we configured the source view:

```
@IBOutlet weak var dropView: UIView!
override func viewDidLoad() {
    super.viewDidLoad()
    let dropper = UIDropInteraction(delegate: self)
    self.dropView.addInteraction(dropper)
}
```

A drop interaction delegate has no required methods, but nothing is going to happen unless we implement this method:

```
func dropInteraction(_ interaction: UIDropInteraction,
    sessionDidUpdate session: UIDropSession) -> UIDropProposal {
        return UIDropProposal(operation: .copy)
}
```

In `dropInteraction(_:sessionDidUpdate:)`, our job is to return a UIDropProposal. This will be initialized with a UIDropOperation that will usually be `.cancel` or `.copy`. If it's `.cancel`, the user won't see any feedback while dragging over this view, and if the user drops onto this view, nothing will happen (the entire operation will be cancelled). If it's `.copy`, the preview is badged with a Plus sign while the user is dragging over this view, and if the user drops onto this view, we can be notified of this and can proceed to ask for the data.

In our implementation of `dropInteraction(_:sessionDidUpdate:)`, we have expressed a willingness to accept a drop regardless of what sort of data is associated with this session. Let's refine that. If what we accept is a color, we should base our response on whether any of the session's item providers promise us color data. We can query the item providers individually, or we can ask the session itself:

```
func dropInteraction(_ interaction: UIDropInteraction,
    sessionDidUpdate session: UIDropSession) -> UIDropProposal {
        let op : UIDropOperation =
            session.canLoadObjects(ofClass: UIColor.self) ? .copy : .cancel
        return UIDropProposal(operation:op)
}
```

Finally, let's say the drop actually occurs on the destination view. The drop interaction delegate's opportunity to obtain the data is its implementation of `dropInteraction(_:performDrop:)`. In this method, there are two ways to ask for the data. The simple way is to ask the session itself:

```
func dropInteraction(_ interaction: UIDropInteraction,
    performDrop session: UIDropSession) {
        session.loadObjects(ofClass: UIColor.self) { colors in
            if let color = colors[0] as? UIColor {
```

```
                    // do something with color here
                }
            }
        }
    }
```

The more elaborate way is to get a reference to an item provider and ask the item
provider to load the data:

```
    func dropInteraction(_ interaction: UIDropInteraction,
        performDrop session: UIDropSession) {
            for item in session.items {
                let ip = item.itemProvider
                ip.loadObject(ofClass: UIColor.self) { (color, error) in
                    if let color = color as? UIColor {
                        // do something with color here
                    }
                }
            }
    }
```

There's an important difference between those two approaches:

loadObjects(ofClass:)
> When calling the session's loadObjects(ofClass:), the completion function is
> called on the *main* thread.

loadObject(ofClass:)
> When calling an item provider's loadObject(ofClass:), the completion func-
> tion is called on a *background* thread.

If you use the second way and you intend to update or otherwise communicate with
the interface, you'll need to step out to the main thread (see Chapter 25); I'll show an
example later in this chapter.

Item Providers

It's no coincidence that my color swatch example in the preceding section uses a
UIColor as the data passed through the drag and drop session. UIColor implements
two key protocols, NSItemProviderWriting and NSItemProviderReading. That's why
my code was able to make two important method calls:

The drag source and init(object:)
> At the drag source end of things, I was able to construct my item provider by
> calling NSItemProvider's initializer init(object:). That's because UIColor
> adopts the NSItemProviderWriting protocol; the parameter of init(object:)
> must be an instance of an NSItemProviderWriting adopter.

The drop destination and `loadObject(ofClass:)`

At the drop destination end of things, I was able to get the data from my item provider by calling `loadObject(ofClass:)`. That's because UIColor adopts the NSItemProviderReading protocol; the parameter of `loadObject(ofClass:)` must be an NSItemProviderReading adopter.

Other common classes that adopt these protocols include NSString, UIImage, NSURL, MKMapItem, and CNContact. But what if your data's class isn't one of those? Then adopt those protocols in *your* class!

To illustrate, I'll create a Person class and then configure it so that Person data can be passed through drag and drop. Here's the basic Person class:

```
final class Person : NSObject, Codable {
    let firstName: String
    let lastName: String
    init(firstName:String, lastName:String) {
        self.firstName = firstName
        self.lastName = lastName
        super.init()
    }
    override var description : String {
        return self.firstName + " " + self.lastName
    }
    enum MyError : Error { case oops }
    static let personUTI = "neuburg.matt.person"
}
```

It turns out that the only kind of data that can actually pass through a drag and drop session is a Data object. Therefore, I'm going to need a way to serialize a Person as Data to pass it from the source to the destination. That's why my Person class adopts the Codable protocol, which makes serialization trivial (Chapter 23). I also supply a simple Error type, to use as a signal if things go wrong. Finally, there is no standard UTI (universal type identifier) for my Person type, so I've made one up.

NSItemProviderWriting

Now I'll make it possible to call NSItemProvider's `init(object:)` when the `object:` is a Person. To do so, I adopt NSItemProviderWriting, which has two required members:

```
extension Person : NSItemProviderWriting {
    static var writableTypeIdentifiersForItemProvider = [personUTI] ❶
    func loadData(withTypeIdentifier typeid: String,
        forItemProviderCompletionHandler
        ch: @escaping (Data?, Error?) -> Void) -> Progress? { ❷
            switch typeid {
            case Self.personUTI:
                do {
                    ch(try PropertyListEncoder().encode(self), nil)
```

```
        } catch {
            ch(nil, error)
        }
    default: ch(nil, MyError.oops)
    }
    return nil
    }
}
```

❶ The `writableTypeIdentifiersForItemProvider` property lists type identifiers for the various representations in which we are willing to supply our data. At the moment, I'm willing to supply a Person only as a Person.

❷ `loadData(withTypeIdentifier:forItemProviderCompletionHandler:)` will be called when a drop destination asks for our data. The drop has occurred, and our Person object, originally passed into NSItemProvider's `init(object:)`, is going to package itself up as a Data object. That's easy, because Person is Codable. There are no existing conventions for the format in which a Person is coded as Data, so I use a property list. Whatever happens, I make sure to *call the completion function* — either I pass in a Data object as the first parameter, or I pass in an Error object as the second parameter. That's crucial!

Our data doesn't take any time to generate, so I'm returning `nil` from the `loadData` method. If our data were time-consuming to supply, we might wish to return a Progress object with the fetching of our data tied to the updating of that object. I'll talk more about the purpose of the Progress object later.

NSItemProviderReading

Next I'll make it possible to call NSItemProvider's `loadObject(ofClass:)` when the `class:` is `Person.self`. To do so, I adopt NSItemProviderReading, which has two required members:

```
extension Person : NSItemProviderReading {
    static var readableTypeIdentifiersForItemProvider = [personUTI]  ❶
    static func object(withItemProviderData data: Data,
        typeIdentifier typeid: String) throws -> Self {  ❷
            switch typeid {
            case personUTI:
                do {
                    let p = try PropertyListDecoder().decode(self, from: data)
                    return p
                } catch {
                    throw error
                }
            default: throw MyError.oops
            }
    }
}
```

Everything I'm doing to implement NSItemProviderReading complements what I did to implement NSItemProviderWriting:

❶ The `readableTypeIdentifiersForItemProvider` property lists type identifiers for any representations that we know how to transform into a Person. At the moment, we do this only for an actual Person.

❷ When `object(withItemProviderData:typeIdentifier:)` is called with the Person type identifier, this means that a Person object is arriving at the destination, packaged up as a Data object. Our job is to extract it and return it. Well, we know how it has been encoded; it's a property list! So we decode it and return it. If anything goes wrong, we throw an error instead.

The upshot is that drag and drop of a Person object now works perfectly within our app, if we drop on a view whose UIDropInteractionDelegate expects a Person object.

Vending additional representations

What if we want a Person to be draggable from our app to some other app? It's unlikely that another app will know about our Person class. Or what if we want a Person to be draggable within our app to a view that expects some other kind of data?

So far, our `writableTypeIdentifiersForItemProvider` property declares just one UTI, signifying that we dispense a Person object. But we can add other UTIs, signifying that we provide alternate representations of a Person. Let's decide to vend a Person as text:

```
static var writableTypeIdentifiersForItemProvider =
    [personUTI, UTType.plainText.identifier]
```

(The UTType struct is new in iOS 14, replacing the CFString constants starting with kUTType. To use it, you might have to `import UniformTypeIdentifiers`.)

Now we need to supplement our implementation of `loadData(withTypeIdentifier:forItemProviderCompletionHandler:)` to take account of the possibility that we may be called by someone who is expecting a String instead of a Person. What string shall we provide? How about a string rendering of the Person's name? It happens that our `description` property is ready and willing to provide that. And there's a simple standard way to wrap a UTF-8 string as Data: just call `data(using: .utf8)`. So all we have to do is add this case to our switch statement:

```
case UTType.plainText.identifier:
    ch(self.description.data(using: .utf8)!, nil)
```

The result is that if a Person is dragged and dropped onto a view that expects a string to be dropped on it, the Person's name is provided as the data. A UITextField is such a view; if a Person is dragged and dropped onto a text field, the Person's name is inserted into the text field!

Receiving additional representations

We can also extend our implementation of the NSItemProviderReading protocol in a similar way. Here, our app contains a view that expects a Person to be dropped onto it, and we want it to have the ability to accept data of some other kind. Suppose the user drags a String and drops it onto our view. A String is not a Person, but perhaps this String is in fact a person's name. We could make a Person from that String.

To make that possible, we add a UTI to our readableTypeIdentifiersForItemProvider property, signifying that we can derive a Person from text:

```
static var readableTypeIdentifiersForItemProvider =
    [personUTI, UTType.plainText.identifier]
```

To go with that, we add a case to the switch statement in our `object(withItemProviderData:typeIdentifier:)` implementation. We pull the String out of the Data object, parse it in a crude way into a first and last name, and create a Person object:

```
case UTType.plainText.identifier:
    if let s = String(data: data, encoding: .utf8) {
        let arr = s.split(separator:" ")
        let first = arr.dropLast().joined(separator: " ")
        let last = arr.last ?? ""
        return self.init(firstName: first, lastName: String(last))
    }
    throw MyError.oops
```

The result is that if the string `"Matt Neuburg"` is dragged onto a view that expects a Person object, the drop is accepted, because our Person type has signified that it knows how to turn a string into a Person, and the result of the drop is a Person with first name "Matt" and last name "Neuburg".

Slow Data Delivery

Pretend that you are the drop interaction delegate, and you are now asking for the data in your implementation of `dropInteraction(_:performDrop:)`. Whether you call the session's `loadObjects(ofClass:)` or an item provider's `loadObject(ofClass:)`, your completion function is called *asynchronously* when the data arrives. This could take some considerable time, depending on the circumstances. (See Appendix C for more about what "asynchronous" means.)

Therefore, by default, if things take too long, the runtime puts up a dialog tracking the overall progress of data delivery and allowing the user to cancel it. If you like, you can replace the runtime's dialog with your own progress interface. (If you intend to do that, set the drop session's `progressIndicatorStyle` to `.none`, to suppress the default dialog — and make sure that your interface gives the user a way to cancel.)

You can stay informed about the supplying of the data through a Progress object (Chapter 13). A Progress object has `fractionCompleted` and `isFinished` properties that you can track through key–value observing in order to update your interface; you can also cancel the loading process by telling the Progress object to `cancel`. There are two ways to get such an object:

- The session vends an overall Progress object as its `progress` property.
- An individual item provider's `loadObject` method can return a Progress object tracking the delivery of its own data.

Even if you rely on the runtime's default progress dialog, there can be a disconcerting effect of blankness when all the apparent action comes to an end without any data to display. You can discover this situation by implementing your drop interaction delegate's `dropInteraction(_:concludeDrop:)` method. When that method is called, all visible activity in the interface has stopped. If you discover here that the drop session's `progress.isFinished` is `false`, then depending on the nature of your interface, you might need to provide some sort of temporary view, to show the user that something has happened, until the actual data arrives.

Additional Delegate Methods

Additional UIDragInteractionDelegate and UIDropInteractionDelegate methods allow the delegate to dress up the drag or drop process in more detail:

Drag interaction delegate
> Drag interaction delegate methods let the delegate supply drag items, provide a preview, restrict the type of drag permitted, animate along with the start of the drag, and hear about each stage of the entire session.

Drop interaction delegate
> Drop interaction delegate methods let the delegate signify willingness to accept the drop, track the user's finger dragging over the view, and, when an actual drop takes place, provide a preview, perform an animation, and request the associated data.

Here are some examples; for full details, consult the documentation.

Custom drag preview

The drag interaction delegate can supply a preview to replace the snapshot of its view. Let's modify our earlier color swatch example to illustrate. Our color swatch is red; it will create a label containing the word "RED" and provide that as the preview.

The trick is that we have to say where this label should initially appear. To do that, we create a UIDragPreviewTarget, which specifies a container view in the interface to which our preview will be added as a subview, along with a center for the preview in that view's coordinate system. This view will be removed from the container when the user either fails to initiate the drag or does in fact start dragging; in the latter case, it will be replaced by a snapshot. Then we combine our preview with that target as a UITargetedDragPreview. In this case, we want the center of the label under the user's finger; we can find out from the session where the user's finger is:

```
func dragInteraction(_ interaction: UIDragInteraction,
    previewForLifting item: UIDragItem, session: UIDragSession)
    -> UITargetedDragPreview? {
        let lab = UILabel()
        lab.text = "RED"
        lab.textAlignment = .center
        lab.textColor = .red
        lab.layer.borderWidth = 1
        lab.layer.cornerRadius = 10
        lab.sizeToFit()
        lab.frame = lab.frame.insetBy(dx: -10, dy: -10)
        let v = interaction.view!
        let ptrLoc = session.location(in: v)
        let targ = UIDragPreviewTarget(container: v, center: ptrLoc)
        let params = UIDragPreviewParameters()
        params.backgroundColor = .white
        return UITargetedDragPreview(view: lab,
            parameters: params, target: targ)
}
```

In addition to a view and a target, a UITargetedDragPreview is initialized with a UIDragPreviewParameters object. In the preceding code, I used the UIDragPreview-Parameters object to make the preview's background white, just to give it a role in the example. Another useful possibility is to set the UIDragPreviewParameters visible-Path property, supplying a clipping path, in case you want the preview to be a snapshot of a certain subregion of the source view.

The drag interaction delegate can also *change* the preview in the course of the drag. To do so, it will set the drag item's previewProvider to a function returning a UIDragPreview (which has no target, because it has no relationship to the app's interface). If the drag interaction delegate does this in, say, drag-Interaction(_:itemsForBeginning:), the previewProvider function won't be called until the drag begins, so the user will see the lifting preview first, and will see the previewProvider preview after the drag starts. Another strategy is to implement dragInteraction(_:sessionDidMove:) and set the previewProvider there; the preview will change at that moment. But dragInteraction(_:sessionDidMove:) is called repeatedly, so be careful not to set the same drag item's previewProvider to the same function over and over.

In addition, the drag interaction delegate can set a cancel preview, with drag-Interaction(_:previewForCancelling:withDefault:). This is used if the user begins to drag the preview but then releases it while not over a drop destination. A nice effect is to keep the existing drag preview (accessible through the third parameter) but retarget it to say where it should fall to as it vanishes; and in fact UITargeted-DragPreview has a retargetedPreview(with:) method for this very purpose. Furthermore, the UIDragPreviewTarget initializer lets you supply a transform: parameter that will be applied over the course of the animation as the preview falls.

The drop interaction delegate, too, can provide a preview to replace the dragged preview when the drop animation occurs; it works just like the cancel preview.

Additional animation

The drag interaction delegate can make the source view perform some sort of animation along with the runtime's initial animated display of the preview. In this example, I'll fade the color swatch slightly:

```
func dragInteraction(_ interaction: UIDragInteraction,
    willAnimateLiftWith anim: UIDragAnimating, session: UIDragSession) {
        if let v = interaction.view {
            anim.addAnimations {
                v.alpha = 0.5
            }
        }
}
```

I could have supplied a completion function by calling addCompletion, but I didn't, so the color swatch stays faded throughout the drag. Clearly, I don't want it to stay faded forever; when the drag ends, I'll be called back again, and I'll restore the swatch's alpha then:

```
func dragInteraction(_ interaction: UIDragInteraction,
    session: UIDragSession, willEndWith operation: UIDropOperation) {
        if let v = interaction.view {
            UIView.animate(withDuration: 0.3) {
                v.alpha = 1
            }
        }
}
```

 The animations you pass with addAnimations are applied *before* the runtime takes its snapshot to form the default preview. Therefore, the results of those animations appear *in* the default preview. To avoid that, supply your own preview.

The drop interaction delegate receives a corresponding message, dropInteraction(_:item:willAnimateDropWith:). By retargeting the drop preview and performing its own animations alongside the drop, the drop interaction delegate can create some vivid effects.

Flocking

If a source view's drag interaction delegate implements `dragInteraction(_:items-ForAddingTo:withTouchAt:)`, and if that implementation returns a nonempty array of drag items, then the user can tap on this source view *while already dragging a preview*, as a way of adding *more* drag items to the existing session. Apple refers to this as *flocking*.

If you permit flocking, be careful of unintended consequences. If the user can tap a source view to get flocking *once* during a drag, the user can tap the *same* source view to get flocking *again* during that drag. This will result in the session effectively carrying multiple copies of the same data, which is probably not what you want. You can solve this problem by examining the session's current drag items to make sure you're not adding another drag item whose item provider refers to the same data.

Table Views and Collection Views

Table views and collection views get a special implementation of drag and drop, focusing on their cells. There is no need to supply a UIDragInteraction or UIDrop-Interaction; instead, simply give the table view or collection view an appropriate delegate:

UITableView
> The delegate properties are:
>
> - `dragDelegate` (UITableViewDragDelegate)
> - `dropDelegate` (UITableViewDropDelegate)

UICollectionView
> The delegate properties are:
>
> - `dragDelegate` (UICollectionViewDragDelegate)
> - `dropDelegate` (UICollectionViewDropDelegate)

The methods of these delegates are generally analogous to, but simpler than, those of UIDragInteractionDelegate and UIDropInteractionDelegate. I'll discuss some table view drag and drop delegate methods; collection views work very similarly.

Table view dragging

To illustrate dragging, let's return to the table of U.S. states developed in Chapter 8, and make it possible to drag a cell and drop it on a view that expects text. Our text will be, appropriately enough, the name of the state. The implementation is trivial. First, in some early event such as `viewDidLoad`, we give our table view a drag delegate:

```
self.tableView.dragDelegate = self
```

Then, acting as drag delegate, we implement the only required method, table-View(_:itemsForBeginning:at:). There's nothing new or surprising about our implementation:

```
func tableView(_ tableView: UITableView,
    itemsForBeginning session: UIDragSession,
    at indexPath: IndexPath) -> [UIDragItem] {
        let s = self.sections[indexPath.section].rowData[indexPath.row]
        let ip = NSItemProvider(object:s as NSString)
        let di = UIDragItem(itemProvider: ip)
        return [di]
}
```

That's all we have to do! It is now possible to long press on a cell to get a drag preview snapshotting the cell, and that preview can be dropped on any drop target that expects text.

Table view dropping

Now let's do the converse: we'll make it possible to drop on a table. Imagine that I have a table of person names, whose underlying model is an array containing a single Section whose rowData is an array of Person. I want the user to be able to drop a Person onto the table view; in response, I'll insert that person into the data, and I'll insert a cell representing that person into the table. We give our table view a drop delegate:

```
self.tableView.dropDelegate = self
```

Acting as the drop delegate, I implement two delegate methods. First, I implement tableView(_:dropSessionDidUpdate:withDestinationIndexPath:) to determine, as the user's finger passes over the table view, whether the drop should be possible. The destination index path might be nil, indicating that the user's finger is not over a row of the table. Also, the dragged data might not be something that can generate a Person. In either case, I return the .cancel operation. Otherwise, I return the .copy operation to badge the dragged preview and permit the drop:

```
func tableView(_ tableView: UITableView,
    dropSessionDidUpdate session: UIDropSession,
    withDestinationIndexPath ip: IndexPath?) -> UITableViewDropProposal {
        if ip == nil {
            return UITableViewDropProposal(operation: .cancel)
        }
        if !session.canLoadObjects(ofClass: Person.self) {
            return UITableViewDropProposal(operation: .cancel)
        }
        return UITableViewDropProposal(operation: .copy,
            intent: .insertAtDestinationIndexPath)
}
```

In the UITableViewDropProposal initializer, the `intent:` argument (UITableViewDropProposal.Intent) tells the table view how to animate as the user's finger hovers over it:

`.insertAtDestinationIndexPath`
For when the drop would insert rows; the table view opens a gap between rows under the user's finger.

`.insertIntoDestinationIndexPath`
For when the drop would not insert rows; the row under the user's finger highlights, suggesting that the dropped material will be incorporated into that row in some way.

`.automatic`
A combination of the previous two, depending on precisely where the user's finger is.

`.unspecified`
The table doesn't respond while the user's finger is over it.

Next, I implement the required `tableView(_:performDropWith:)` method. The drop is now happening; we need to retrieve the incoming data and update the table. The second parameter is a UITableViewDropCoordinator; everything we need to know about what's happening, such as the index path and the session, is available through the coordinator:

```
func tableView(_ tableView: UITableView,
    performDropWith coord: UITableViewDropCoordinator) {
        if let ip = coord.destinationIndexPath {
            coord.session.loadObjects(ofClass: Person.self) { persons in
                for person in (persons as! [Person]).reversed() {
                    tableView.performBatchUpdates {
                        self.sections[ip.section].rowData.insert(
                            person, at: ip.row)
                        tableView.insertRows(at: [ip], with: .none)
                    }
                }
            }
        }
}
```

Time-consuming table view drop data delivery

The preceding example works, but we are not updating the table until the data arrives. We are skirting the issue of what will happen if the data takes time to arrive. The drop happens, and we should insert a row *right now* — that is, *before* asking for the data. But at that moment, we obviously don't yet have the data! So either we must freeze the interface while we wait for the data to arrive, which sounds like very bad interface, or we must update the table with data that we don't yet have, which sounds like a metaphysical impossibility.

The solution is to use a *placeholder cell* for each new row while we wait for its data. The technique is best understood through an example. I'll use the item provider to fetch the data this time:

```
func tableView(_ tableView: UITableView,
    performDropWith coord: UITableViewDropCoordinator) {
        guard let ip = coord.destinationIndexPath else {return}
        for item in coord.items {
            let item = item.dragItem
            guard item.itemProvider.canLoadObject(ofClass: Person.self)
                else {continue}
            let ph = UITableViewDropPlaceholder( ❶
                insertionIndexPath: ip,
                reuseIdentifier: self.cellID,
                rowHeight: self.tableView.rowHeight)
            ph.cellUpdateHandler = { cell in ❷
                cell.textLabel?.text = ""
            }
            let con = coord.drop(item, to: ph) ❸
            item.itemProvider.loadObject(ofClass: Person.self) { p, e in ❹
                DispatchQueue.main.async { ❺
                    guard let p = p as? Person else { ❻
                        con.deletePlaceholder(); return
                    }
                    con.commitInsertion { ip in ❼
                        tableView.performBatchUpdates {
                            self.sections[ip.section].rowData.insert(
                                p, at: ip.row)
                        }
                    }
                }
            }
        }
    }
}
```

For each drag item capable of providing a Person object, this is what we do:

❶ We make a UITableViewDropPlaceholder, supplying our cell's `reuseIdentifier` so that the table view can dequeue a cell for us to use as a placeholder cell.

❷ We set the placeholder's `cellUpdateHandler` to a function that will be called to configure the placeholder cell. In my simple table, we're using a basic default cell with a `textLabel` that normally displays the full name of a Person; for the placeholder cell, the `textLabel` should be blank.

❸ We call the coordinator's `drop(_:to:)` with the placeholder, to perform the drop animation and create the placeholder cell; a context object (UITableViewDropPlaceholderContext) is returned. The placeholder cell is now visible in the table. The important thing is that the table view knows that this is not a real cell! For purposes of all data source and delegate methods, it will behave as if the cell didn't exist. In particular, it won't call `tableView(_:cellForRowAt:)` for this cell; the cell is static and is already completely configured by the `cellUpdateHandler` function we supplied earlier.

❹ Now, at long last, we call `loadObject(ofClass:)` to ask for the actual data!

❺ Eventually, we are called with the data on a background thread. We step out to the main thread, because we're about to talk to the interface.

❻ If we didn't get the expected data, the placeholder cell is no longer needed, and we remove it by calling the context object's `deletePlaceholder`.

❼ If we reach this point, we've got data! We call the context object's `commit-Insertion(dataSourceUpdates:)` with a function that updates *the model only*. As a result, `tableView(_:cellForRowAt:)` is called to supply the real cell, which quietly replaces the placeholder cell in good order.

While your table view contains placeholders, the table view's `hasUncommitted-Updates` is `true`. Use that property as a flag to prevent your other code from calling `reloadData` on the table view, which would cause the placeholders to be lost and the entire table view update process to get out of whack.

Table view drop animations

In step 3 of the preceding example, we gave the UITableViewDropCoordinator a drop animation command to create the placeholder cell. This command must be given outside of the `loadObject` completion function, because the drop is about to happen *now*, so the animation must replace the default drop animation *now*, not at some asynchronous future time. The drop coordinator obeys four drop animation commands:

`drop(_:to:)`
  The second parameter is a UITableViewDropPlaceholder.

`drop(_:intoRowAt:rect:)`
  Animates the drop preview into the cell at the specified row, to the frame specified in that cell's bounds coordinates.

`drop(_:to:)`

Animates the drop preview *anywhere*. The second parameter is a UIDragPreview-Target combining a container and a center in the container's bounds coordinates.

`drop(_:toRowAt:)`

Snapshots the cell at the given row, replaces the drop preview with that snapshot, and animates the snapshot to fit the cell. This is useful under a very limited set of circumstances:

- You want to give the impression that the drop *replaces* the contents of a cell.

- The drag and drop must be *local* (see later in this chapter), so that the model can be updated with the new data and the row can be reloaded *before* the snapshot is taken.

Spring Loading

Spring loading is an effect similar to what happens on an iOS device's home screen when the user goes into "jiggly mode" and then drags an app's icon over a folder: the folder highlights, then flashes several times, then opens. In this way, the user can open the folder as part of the drag, and can then continue the drag, dropping the icon inside the opened folder.

You can use spring loading in an analogous way. Suppose there's a button in your interface that the user can tap to transition to a presented view controller. You can make that button be spring loaded, so that the user, in the middle of a drag, can hover over that button to make it perform that transition — and can then drop on something inside the newly presented view.

To make a button be spring loaded, set its `isSpringLoaded` property to `true`, and call its `addInteraction(_:)` method with a UISpringLoadedInteraction object. That object's initializer takes a function to be performed when the spring loaded interaction actually fires; the button's normal control event action function, which fires in response to the button being tapped, does *not* fire as a result of spring loading, though of course you can make the spring loaded interaction function fire it:

```
self.button.isSpringLoaded = true
self.button.addInteraction(UISpringLoadedInteraction { int, con in
    let vc = // some view controller
    // ... other preparations ...
    self.present(vc, animated: true)
})
```

In the spring loaded interaction function, the second parameter (con in the preceding code) is a UISpringLoadedInteractionContext object providing information about the interaction. It reports the location of the drag, and it has a `state` describing how the view is currently responding. The first parameter (int) is the UISpringLoaded-Interaction itself.

A fuller form of initializer lets you give the UISpringLoadedInteraction object two further properties:

An interaction behavior
> A UISpringLoadedInteractionBehavior, to which you can attach two functions — one to be called when the interaction wants permission to proceed, the other to be called when the interaction has finished.

An interaction effect
> A UISpringLoadedInteractionEffect, to which you can attach a function to be called every time the interaction's state changes.

Spring loading is available for buttons and button-like interface objects such as bar button items and tab bar items, as well as for UIAlertController (Chapter 14), where the spring loading is applied to the alert's buttons. It is also supported by table views and collection views, where it applies to the cells; if turned on, it can be turned off for individual cells by delegate methods:

- `tableView(_:shouldSpringLoadRowAt:with:)`
- `collectionView(_:shouldSpringLoadItemAt:with:)`

iPhone and Local Drag and Drop

By default, a UIDragInteraction comes into existence with its `isEnabled` property set to `false` on an iPhone. To bring dragging to life on an iPhone, set that property to `true`. Similarly, table views and collection views have a `dragInteractionEnabled` property that you'll need to set explicitly to `true` on an iPhone if you want dragging to work.

There's no iPad multitasking interface on the iPhone, so the only drag and drop your app will be capable of will be *local* drag and drop, within the app itself.

On an iPad, local drag and drop is always *possible*, of course, but you can also *restrict* a drag originating in your app to remain local to the app by implementing the drag interaction delegate method `dragInteraction(_:sessionIsRestrictedToDragging-Application:)` to return `true`. That situation can subsequently be detected by reading the session's `isRestrictedToDraggingApplication` property.

A drag that is dropped within the same app can provide the drop destination with more information, and more directly, than the same drag can provide to another app. We no longer have to pipe the data asynchronously through the session by means of a Data object; instead (or in addition), we can use these properties:

UIDragItem `localObject`

> The drag item can carry actual data with it, or a reference to an object that can provide the data, in its `localObject` property, and the drop interaction delegate can read this value directly, in real time, on the main thread — but only in the same app. If you try to read the `localObject` in an app different from the one where the drag originated, it will be `nil`.

UIDragSession `localContext`

> The drag session can maintain state, in its `localContext` property, and the drop interaction delegate can read this value directly, in real time, on the main thread, by way of the drop session's `localDragSession` — but only in the same app. If you try to read the `localDragSession` in an app different from the one where the drag originated, it will be `nil`.

Table and collection view `sourceIndexPath`

> If drag and drop takes place within a table view or collection view, the UITable-ViewDropItem or UICollectionViewDropItem has a `sourceIndexPath` revealing where the drag started. If you try to read the `sourceIndexPath` in an app different from the one where the drag originated, it will be `nil`.

Pointer and Keyboard

Apple is gradually reducing the distinctions between mobile and desktop devices, and this can affect the way the user interacts with your app. An iPad can be connected to a trackpad (or mouse) and a keyboard. iPad apps can be ported to Mac using Mac Catalyst, and future Macs will run mobile apps natively; again, a Mac will have a trackpad (or mouse) and a keyboard. This means that your app can find itself in a world where literal touch — a finger on a screen — is not the only form of user input.

Don't panic! Your app will probably behave just fine in such environments right off the bat. Many built-in UIView subclasses already respond coherently to this situation. UIBarButtonItem and UISegmentedControl animate as the pointer passes within them. Scroll views respond to a scroll wheel. In a table view for which `allows-MultipleSelectionDuringEditing` is `true`, the user can Shift-click to select a range of rows. And so on.

Still, it may be that your app can benefit from customizations that enhance the user experience when hardware input is present. The full details are beyond the scope of this book, but in this section I'll suggest some of the areas you might want to consider.

I already mentioned in Chapter 5 that, new in iOS 14, gesture recognizers and events can take hardware input into account:

- UIHoverGestureRecognizer has `.began`, `.changed`, and `.ended` states that report when the pointer passes into, through, and out of a view.

- A UITouch has a `type`, distinguishing between physical touches and hardware input, and UIGestureRecognizer's `allowedTouchTypes` lets you filter out touches of a particular type.

- UIGestureRecognizer's `modifierFlags` let you distinguish what modifier keys the user is holding down during a gesture.

- A tap gesture recognizer's `buttonMaskRequired` property lets you specify which mouse button must be used.

- A pan gesture recognizer can respond to a scroll wheel or trackpad scroll gesture, and has an `allowedScrollTypesMask`.

- Pinch and rotate gesture recognizers can receive transform events from a trackpad.

You can also govern the behavior of the pointer itself (the "cursor") as it passes within a view. The idea is that the view should respond to suggest what the user can do; often, you'll just be making the view tell the user, "Click me!" The key class here is UIPointerStyle, which is initialized with two parameters:

`effect:`
A UIPointerEffect. Your choices are:

`.hover`
The pointer passes in front of the view, which is optionally scaled up slightly, tinted, and given a shadow. The default is scaling and tinting but no shadow.

`.lift`
The pointer disappears behind the view, which is scaled up slightly and given a shadow and a parallax effect.

`.highlight`
Similar to `lift`, but the pointer, behind the view, adopts the shape of the view, and there's no shadow.

All three pointer effects are initialized with a UITargetedPreview, which is the superclass of UITargetedDragPreview, discussed in the preceding section. This is how the runtime knows what view to snapshot and portray while the pointer is within a view; typically, the targeted view will *be* that view.

`shape:`
A UIPointerShape. The pointer has some default shapes, such as a small circle for most views, and a vertical beam for text. You can change the shape, specifying a horizontal or vertical beam, a rounded rect, or an arbitrary UIBezierPath. In

specifying a path, you'll probably want the origin to have a negative offset so as to keep the path centered around the center of the pointer.

To give a view a pointer style, create a UIPointerInteraction, specifying a delegate, and attach it to the view with addInteraction(_:). Now, acting as the delegate (UIPointerInteractionDelegate), implement pointerInteraction(_:styleFor:). In your implementation, construct and return a UIPointerStyle as desired. Here's a minimal example:

```
func pointerInteraction(_ interaction: UIPointerInteraction,
    styleFor region: UIPointerRegion) -> UIPointerStyle? {
        let view = interaction.view
        let target = UITargetedPreview(view: view!)
        return UIPointerStyle(effect: UIPointerEffect.lift(target))
}
```

The result is that the view to which this pointer interaction is attached does a lift effect animation as the pointer passes across it.

You can get some powerful additional mileage out of a pointer interaction by implementing the delegate method pointerInteraction(_:regionFor:defaultRegion:). This lets you subdivide your view into regions that can respond separately to the pointer; these will typically be areas of drawing, or subviews. In this example, my view contains three image views that I want to respond individually to the pointer; I've given them tags to distinguish them (and I've set their isUserInteraction-Enabled to true):

```
func pointerInteraction(_ inter: UIPointerInteraction,
    regionFor request: UIPointerRegionRequest,
    defaultRegion: UIPointerRegion) -> UIPointerRegion? {
        let loc = request.location
        if let iv = inter.view!.hitTest(loc, with: nil) as? UIImageView {
            let rect = inter.view!.convert(iv.bounds, from: iv)
            let region = UIPointerRegion(rect: rect, identifier: iv.tag)
            return region
        }
        return nil
}
```

Back in pointerInteraction(_:styleFor:), I use the region identifier to find the image view the pointer is passing over, so I can use it as the targeted preview:

```
func pointerInteraction(_ interaction: UIPointerInteraction,
    styleFor region: UIPointerRegion) -> UIPointerStyle? {
        if let tag = region.identifier as? Int {
            if let view = interaction.view?.viewWithTag(tag) {
                let target = UITargetedPreview(view: view)
                return UIPointerStyle(effect: UIPointerEffect.hover(target))
```

```
            }
        }
        return nil
    }
```

A UIButton works differently. It has a `pointerStyleProvider` property that you can set to a function. This function receives the button, a pointer effect, and a pointer shape; your job is to return a pointer style, and you can use the incoming effect or shape to initialize it if you have no changes to make. In this example, I enlarge the shape of the preview area, calling attention more strongly to the button:

```
self.button.pointerStyleProvider = { button, effect, shape in
    let params = UIPreviewParameters()
    params.shadowPath = UIBezierPath(
        rect: button.bounds.insetBy(dx: -24, dy: -24))
    let effect = UIPointerEffect.lift(
        UITargetedPreview(view: button, parameters: params))
    return UIPointerStyle(effect: effect, shape: shape)
}
```

Another nice touch is to permit the user with an external keyboard to press a keyboard shortcut as a way of taking action. If you have a commonly used button, for instance, you might have a keyboard shortcut that effectively "presses" that button, triggering the same functionality.

Response to the keyboard requires that your view controller be the first responder (I'll have a lot more to say about that in the next chapter). You'll override `canBecome-FirstResponder` to return `true`. You can then install UIKeyCommand objects on your view controller with `addKeyCommand(_:)`. In this example, I'll make it possible for the user to type Shift-Command-T as way of triggering some test functionality; `self` is the view controller:

```
self.becomeFirstResponder()
let command = UIKeyCommand(
    title: "Test", action: #selector(doTest),
    input: "t", modifierFlags: [.command, .shift])
self.addKeyCommand(command)
```

It isn't strictly necessary to give the command a title, but if you do, it shows up in the list of shortcuts that the user can see by holding down the Command key.

Multiple Windows

Starting in iOS 13, your app running on an iPad with iPad multitasking can have more than one window. Once there are two windows on a single app, the user can arrange them with multitasking so as to see two things at once. Apple's own apps illustrate this: using multiple windows, you can see simultaneously two contacts in the Contacts app, two maps in the Maps app, two tabs in Safari, and so on. Sometimes you can also drag something from one window to another.

There are various ways to make a new window in an app that supports this feature. The user can long press on an app's icon, choose Show All Windows (to enter what Apple calls App Exposé), and tap the Plus button, or drag the app's icon from the Dock onto its own window. Some apps also provide an internal means of generating a new window, such as tapping a button, or dragging something to the side of the screen. In Apple's Maps app, a marked location can be dragged to the side of the screen to become a new window.

Your app might wish to participate in this architecture if the user might benefit from it. To opt in, in the "Application Scene Manifest" entry in your *Info.plist*, switch "Enable Multiple Windows" to YES.

The Window Architecture

Here are the classes and objects involved in the window architecture:

Scene
> The app's *scenes* are instances of UIWindowScene, a UIScene subclass. Each scene can be in the foreground or in the background, activated or deactivated.

Window
> Each UIWindowScene owns a *window*. Actually, a window scene can have multiple windows (its `windows`), but only one of these is what you would think of as *your* app's window, holding your view controllers and your app's interface. The window is created with a `windowScene` and maintains a reference to it.

Session
> Every scene has associated with it one *session*. This is a UISceneSession. The scene and the session have pointers to one another. The reason for this pairing is that a session can persist even if its scene has been *disconnected* in the background to save memory. The snapshots in the app switcher interface belong to scene sessions; there may or may not be a connected scene associated with a snapshot.

Delegate
> Your live link to a scene is the scene's *delegate*, a UIResponder adopting the UIWindowSceneDelegate protocol. In the app templates, this is an instance of the SceneDelegate class. It gets events when the scene is connected to or disconnected from its session, and when its activation or foreground state changes. In the app templates, the scene delegate also has a `window` property that retains the window.

You're going to want to know how to get references to the pieces of that architecture. Here are some common approaches:

From the scene delegate
> All the scene delegate events come with a reference to the scene.

From the application
> The shared application has references to all sessions as its `openSessions`, and to all scenes that are connected to sessions as its `connectedScenes`, and to all windows as its `windows`, so you can get a needed reference from the top down.

From a view controller
> A view controller has no direct reference to any part of the architecture. But it has a `view`, which (if it is in the interface) has a `window`, which has a `windowScene`, which has a `session`, so you can assemble a reference from the bottom up.

Scene Creation

At launch time and whenever a new window is created, the runtime creates these objects in this order:

1. The scene session
2. The scene configuration
3. The window scene
4. The scene delegate
5. The window

The *scene configuration* is a value class (UISceneConfiguration) containing instructions for instantiating the window scene and the scene delegate. It is the object described in the *Info.plist* by the "Scene Configuration" entry in the "Application Scene Manifest." This is an array of "Application Session Role" entries, each of which is a dictionary uniting a "Configuration Name" and a "Delegate Class Name" (the name of the class that is to be instantiated as the scene delegate), along with an optional "Storyboard Name." (You can also include the "Class Name" if you want the scene's class to be a custom subclass of UIWindowScene; but this is unlikely.)

Early in the window creation process, the runtime may turn to your app delegate and call `application(_:configurationForConnecting:options:)` if it exists. This is your chance to construct or modify the scene configuration *in code*. Here's an implementation that does the same thing that the default *Info.plist* "Scene Configuration" entry does; in fact, if you have this implementation, you can delete the "Scene Configuration" entry from the *Info.plist* altogether:

```
func application(_ application: UIApplication,
    configurationForConnecting connectingSceneSession: UISceneSession,
    options: UIScene.ConnectionOptions) -> UISceneConfiguration {
        let config = UISceneConfiguration(
            name: "Default Configuration", sessionRole: .windowApplication)
        config.delegateClass = SceneDelegate.self
        config.storyboard = UIStoryboard(name: "Main", bundle: nil)
        return config
}
```

What might be the purpose of having more than one scene configuration? Well, if you have several window types and your implementation of the SceneDelegate class threatens to become overly complex, you might use a different scene configuration to specify a different scene delegate class for each window type. To know whether you need to do that on any particular call to your `application(_:configurationFor-Connecting:options:)` implementation, you'd look at the incoming `options`. It's a value class that tells you why this window is being created. I'll talk more about that later.

When a window closes, its scene session can persist, identified by its `persistent-Identifier`, in order to be reused when the window is created again. This persistence is the basis of scene saving and restoration, which operates even between runs of your app. When a window is created with a scene session that has survived from earlier, you *won't* get a call to `application(_:configurationForConnecting:options:)` — even if the app is launching from scratch — because the configuration for this scene session is already known.

The next important event your code receives during the window creation process is the scene delegate's `scene(_:willConnectTo:options:)`. At this point, if this scene uses a storyboard, the window has already been created and assigned to the scene delegate's `window` property, and it has a `rootViewController` instantiated from the storyboard's initial view controller — and if you do nothing, the window will be made visible for you. But if the scene doesn't use a storyboard, or if you want to substitute a different window class or a different root view controller, this is your chance to do so (see "App Without a Storyboard" on page 7).

Window Creation and Closing

If the user asks directly within your app to create a new window — by tapping a New Window button in your interface, for instance — you can call this UIApplication method to create the window:

- `requestSceneSessionActivation(_:userActivity:options:errorHandler:)`

If the first parameter (the session) is `nil`, a new window is created.

The most important parameter is the `userActivity`. This is an NSUserActivity object that will arrive into the `options` parameter of `application(_:configurationFor-Connecting:options:)` and `scene(_:willConnectTo:options:)`, in that parameter's `userActivities` property. Your code will examine this to learn what sort of window this is to be, in order to configure things appropriately. So the NSUserActivity object is a kind of message to yourself. By setting its `activityType` and its `userInfo` (a dictionary), you can encode the needed information into that message.

Suppose my app's root view controller allows the user to display any of the three Pep Boys, and has a button the user can tap to open a new window for editing the current Pep Boy (whatever "editing" may mean for this app). Clearly the NSUserActivity object needs to say which Pep Boy is current. Let's say that this information is stored in an instance property, `self.pepName`. Here's a possible implementation:

```
let opts = UIScene.ActivationRequestOptions()
opts.requestingScene = self.view.window?.windowScene
let act = NSUserActivity(activityType:
    PepEditorViewController.newEditorActivityType)
let key = PepEditorViewController.whichPepBoyWeAreEditing
act.userInfo = [key: self.pepName]
UIApplication.shared.requestSceneSessionActivation(
    nil, userActivity: act, options: opts, errorHandler: nil)
```

So now there are two reasons why a new window might be created in my app, and my `scene(_:willConnectTo:options:)` needs to behave differently depending on why *this* window is being created. On the one hand, we might be launching, or the user may have requested a new window from the App Exposé interface; in that case, I should just allow my window to be populated with the normal root view controller. On the other hand, the user may have tapped the button asking to edit the current Pep Boy; in that case, I should instantiate the editing view controller, populate it with the information about what Pep Boy to display, and set it as the window's root view controller.

And how will I distinguish those two cases? By looking for the NSUserActivity that I provided in my call to `requestSceneSessionActivation`:

```
var pepName = ""
let key = PepEditorViewController.whichPepBoyWeAreEditing
let type = PepEditorViewController.newEditorActivityType
if let act = connectionOptions.userActivities.first(where: {
    $0.activityType == type
}) {
    if let pep = act.userInfo?[key] as? String {
        pepName = pep
    }
}
if !pepName.isEmpty {
    let s = scene.session.configuration.storyboard!
    let pepEditor = s.instantiateViewController(identifier: "pepEditor")
```

```
        as! PepEditorViewController
    pepEditor.pepName = pepName
    self.window?.rootViewController = pepEditor
}
// ... and otherwise, do nothing ...
```

Subsequently, PepEditorViewController's `viewDidLoad` comes along and configures the actual interface based on which Pep Boy it finds in its `pepName` property.

Closing a window is even simpler. You call this UIApplication method:

- `requestSceneSessionDestruction(_:options:errorHandler:)`

The `options` should specify the animation as the window vanishes. Your choices are (UIWindowScene.DismissalAnimation):

- `.standard`
- `.commit` (the user was asked whether to save something, and said yes)
- `.decline` (the user was asked whether to save something, and said no)

Here's an example of a Close Window button implementation:

```
guard let session = self.view.window?.windowScene?.session else {return}
let opts = UIWindowSceneDestructionRequestOptions()
opts.windowDismissalAnimation = .standard
UIApplication.shared.requestSceneSessionDestruction(
    session, options: opts, errorHandler: nil)
```

State Saving and Restoration

While a window session persists, its scene might be disconnected and destroyed in the background. When the user taps that window session's snapshot in the app switcher, a new window will be created, and you'll need to recreate the entire view controller hierarchy and state to populate it.

For this purpose, a session maintains a `stateRestorationActivity` property, which is an NSUserActivity. You are supposed to use this for state saving and restoration:

State saving
    When the scene is backgrounded, the scene delegate is asked what the value of the `stateRestorationActivity` property should be. Your job is to supply an NSUserActivity populated with all the information needed later to restore state for this scene's window.

State restoration
    When the same session recreates its window and your scene delegate's `scene(_:willConnectTo:options:)` is called, the session gives back this NSUser-Activity in its `stateRestorationActivity` property. (This works even if the app

was completely terminated in the background.) Your job is to extract the NSUserActivity and recreate the window's contents.

An NSUserActivity works in a special way with a UIResponder. A UIResponder has a `userActivity` property. When a UIResponder's `userActivity` actually holds an NSUserActivity, that NSUserActivity is "saved" automatically as needed by the runtime, by calling the responder's implementation of `updateUserActivityState(_:)`, which can write into the NSUserActivity's `userInfo`. If multiple responders share the same NSUserActivity instance, they *all* get an opportunity to write into the same NSUserActivity's `userInfo`. The state-saving mechanism takes advantage of this architecture:

- A UIScene, by virtue of being a UIResponder, has a `userActivity` property, which can hold an NSUserActivity and cause it to persist for the lifetime of the scene.

- From time to time, and especially when the scene goes into the background, the scene delegate method `stateRestorationActivity(for:)` is called. It should simply return the scene's `userActivity`.

- When `stateRestorationActivity(for:)` returns an NSUserActivity, all responders that are holding that NSUserActivity in their `userActivity` property are automatically sent an `updateUserActivityState(_:)` event with that NSUserActivity as the parameter, and can contribute to its `userInfo`.

- The session will then keep that NSUserActivity as its expression of saved state, and will supply it in its `stateRestorationActivity` property at restoration time.

An implementation might look like this. The scene delegate either creates the scene's `userActivity` or passes the received restoration activity into it, and returns that as its own user activity:

```
func scene(_ scene: UIScene, willConnectTo session: UISceneSession,
    options connectionOptions: UIScene.ConnectionOptions) {
        guard let scene = scene as? UIWindowScene else { return }
        scene.userActivity =
            session.stateRestorationActivity ??
            NSUserActivity(activityType: "com.neuburg.mw.restoration")
}
func stateRestorationActivity(for scene: UIScene) -> NSUserActivity? {
    return scene.userActivity
}
```

Every view controller should use its own `viewDidAppear(_:)` to share that user activity object. That way, its own `updateUserActivityState(_:)` will be called automatically when we go into the background, and it has a chance to contribute to the global pool of the `userInfo`:

```
    override func viewDidAppear(_ animated: Bool) {
        super.viewDidAppear(animated)
        self.userActivity = self.view.window?.windowScene?.userActivity
    }
    // called automatically at saving time
    override func updateUserActivityState(_ activity: NSUserActivity) {
        super.updateUserActivityState(activity)
        // gather info into `info`
        activity.addUserInfoEntries(from: info)
    }
```

If every view controller does that, then every view controller that is alive at the time we go into background gets a chance to contribute to the user info of the shared user activity object, and so every view controller's state can be saved. Later, if the window needs to be recreated, that same user activity object will return as the session's `state-RestorationActivity`; the scene delegate can extract its `userInfo` and use it as a guide to restoration of the interface.

Further Multiple Window Considerations

Adopting multiple windows is not trivial. Here are some further considerations to be aware of (and there are many other details you'll want to look into on your own).

Drag and drop

Drag and drop works just as described earlier in this chapter, except for one thing: what if you want the user to be able to drag something to the edge of the screen in order to create a new window? In that case, call `registerObject(_:visibility:)` on the UIDragItem's NSItemProvider, with the first parameter being (you guess it) an NSUserActivity. This NSUserActivity's `activityType` must be listed in your *Info.plist* under the NSUserActivityTypes key; that allows the drag to pass out of your app into the system and back into your app as a call to create a new window. In the call to your scene delegate's `scene(_:willConnectTo:options:)`, the same NSUserActivity will arrive in the `userActivities` of the `options` parameter, and you can detect this and configure the new window, just as I described earlier.

Data sharing

The relationship between your data and your interface becomes more complicated when there are multiple windows, because more than one window might hold an instance of the very same view controller. No individual view controller instance can be used as the "source of truth" for the app's data. Instead, the data will need to be stored in some persistent central location. When the user (or some other outside force) makes a change in the data, you'll need to send that information up to the persistent central data model, and the central data model will then send that information back down (probably by means of a notification or a similar publish-and-subscribe mechanism) to all instances of that view controller, each of which will update its view's interface accordingly.

The session has a userInfo object of its own. You can use this for any purpose you like, including storing data to be preserved in case the window is opened later. It can also be used as a global repository of data among view controllers within this window, as an alternative to the app's user defaults.

If a scene is in the foreground when its interface is updated, the interface will change before the user's eyes. If the scene is in the background, the user can't see it, but you *still* might want to change the interface so that the app switcher snapshot is updated. To do so, call the UIApplication method requestSceneSessionRefresh(;).

Memory management

When a scene is about to be disconnected from its session, and the window and scene delegate are about to be released, the scene delegate is sent sceneDidDisconnect(_:). If there is data to be preserved, this is a key moment to preserve it. If the scene was maintaining any scratch files or other independently persistent objects, this is a key moment to delete them.

A scene session has a persistentIdentifier, a unique string that persists for the lifetime of the session, even if the app is terminated and relaunched, even across restarts of the device. This can help you associate saved data with the session to which it belongs.

Text

Drawing text into your app's interface is one of the most complex and powerful things that iOS does for you. But iOS also shields you from much of that complexity; all you need is some text to draw, and possibly an interface object to draw it for you.

Text to appear in your app's interface will be an NSString (bridged from Swift String) or an NSAttributedString. NSAttributedString adds text styling to an NSString, including runs of different character styles, along with paragraph-level features such as alignment, line spacing, and margins.

To make your NSString or NSAttributedString appear in the interface, you can hand it to an interface object that knows how to draw it, or you can draw it into a graphics context yourself:

Text-drawing interface objects
> Interface objects that know how to draw an NSString or NSAttributedString are:

> *UILabel*
>> Displays text, possibly consisting of multiple lines; neither scrollable nor editable.

> *UITextField*
>> Displays a single line of editable text.

> *UITextView*
>> Displays multiline text; can be scrollable and editable.

Self-drawing text
> Both NSString and NSAttributedString have methods for drawing themselves into any graphics context.

Deep under the hood, all text drawing is performed through a low-level technology with a C API called Core Text. At a higher level, iOS provides Text Kit, a middle-level technology lying on top of Core Text. UITextView is largely just a lightweight wrapper around Text Kit, and Text Kit can also draw directly into a graphics context. By working with Text Kit, you can readily do all sorts of useful text-drawing tricks without having to sweat your way through Core Text.

(Another way of drawing text is to use a web view, a scrollable view displaying rendered HTML. A web view can also display various additional document types, such as PDF, RTF, and *.doc*. Web views draw their text using a somewhat different technology, and are discussed in Chapter 12. For display of PDFs, see also the discussion of PDF Kit in Chapter 23.)

Fonts and Font Descriptors

There are two ways of specifying a font: as a UIFont suitable for use with strings, attributed strings, and UIKit interface objects; or as a CTFont suitable for Core Text. You're unlikely to use CTFont; I'll focus exclusively on UIFont.

To describe a UIFont in terms of its features, and to perform transformations between fonts, you use UIFontDescriptor; you can convert both ways between UIFont and UIFontDescriptor. The Core Text analog is CTFontDescriptor, which is toll-free bridged to UIFontDescriptor so that you can cast between them (and this bridging can be used to convert between UIFont and CTFont).

Fonts

A font (UIFont) is a simple object. You specify a font by its name and size by calling the UIFont initializer `init(name:size:)`, and you can transform a font to the same font in a different size by calling the `withSize(_:)` instance method. UIFont also provides some properties for learning a font's various metrics, such as its `lineHeight` and `capHeight`.

To ask for a font by name, you have to *know* the font's name. Every font variant (bold, italic, and so on) counts as a different font, and font variants are clumped into families. UIFont has class methods that tell you the names of the families and the names of the fonts within them. To learn, in the console, the name of every built-in font, you would say:

```
UIFont.familyNames.forEach {
    UIFont.fontNames(forFamilyName:$0).forEach {print($0)}}
```

When calling `init(name:size:)`, you can specify a font by its family name or by its font name (technically, its PostScript name). For example, `"Avenir"` is a family name; the plain font within that family is `"Avenir-Book"`. Either of those is legal as the `name:` argument. The initializer is failable, so you'll know if you've specified the font incorrectly — you'll get `nil`.

System font

The system font, used by default for things like UILabel text and UIButton titles, can be obtained by calling the UIFont class method `systemFont(ofSize:weight:)`. A UIFont class property such as `buttonFontSize` will give you the standard size. Possible weights, in order from lightest to heaviest, are (UIFont.Weight):

- `.ultraLight`
- `.thin`
- `.light`
- `.regular`
- `.medium`
- `.semibold`
- `.bold`
- `.heavy`
- `.black`

Starting in iOS 9, the system font (which was formerly Helvetica) is San Francisco, and comes in all of those weights, except at sizes smaller than 20 points, where the extreme ultralight, thin, and black are missing. A variant of the system font whose digits are monospaced can be obtained by calling `monospacedDigitSystemFont(ofSize:weight:)`. I'll talk later about how to obtain additional variants.

Dynamic type

If you have text for the user to read or edit — in a UILabel, a UITextField, or a UITextView (all discussed later in this chapter) — you are encouraged to take advantage of *dynamic type*. If a font is linked to dynamic type, then:

Text size is up to the user
    The user specifies a size preference using a slider in the Settings app. Additional larger sizes may be enabled under Accessibility. Possible sizes (UIContentSize-Category) are:

- `.unspecified`
- `.extraSmall`
- `.small`
- `.medium`

- `.large`
- `.extraLarge`
- `.extraExtraLarge`
- `.extraExtraExtraLarge`
- `.accessibilityMedium`
- `.accessibilityLarge`
- `.accessibilityExtraLarge`
- `.accessibilityExtraExtraLarge`
- `.accessibilityExtraExtraExtraLarge`

You specify a role

You specify a dynamic type font in terms of the *role* it is to play in your layout. The size and weight are determined for you by the system, based on the user's text size preference. Possible roles that you can specify (UIFont.TextStyle) are:

- `.largeTitle`
- `.title1`
- `.title2`
- `.title3`
- `.headline`
- `.subheadline`
- `.body`
- `.callout`
- `.footnote`
- `.caption1`
- `.caption2`

You'll probably want to experiment with specifying various roles for your individual pieces of text, to see which looks appropriate in context. (In Figure 6-1, the headlines are `.subheadline` and the blurbs are `.caption1`.)

When dynamic type was first introduced, in iOS 7, it wasn't actually dynamic. The user could change the preferred text size, but responding to that change, by refreshing the fonts of your interface objects, was left up to you. But starting in iOS 10, you can set the `adjustsFontForContentSizeCategory` property of your UILabel, UIText-Field, or UITextView to `true` (in code or in the nib editor); if this interface object uses dynamic type, it will then respond *automatically* if the user changes the text size preference in the Settings app.

One way to make your text use dynamic type is to specify a dynamic type font supplied by the system. To do that in the nib editor, summon the font popover and, in the Font pop-up menu, choose one of the Text Style menu items. To do the same thing in code, call the UIFont class method `preferredFont(forTextStyle:)`:

```
self.label.font = UIFont.preferredFont(forTextStyle: .headline)
self.label.adjustsFontForContentSizeCategory = true
```

The font, in that case, is effectively the system font in another guise. But you might prefer to use some other font. Starting in iOS 11, there's an easy way to do that:

1. Instantiate a UIFontMetrics object by calling `init(forTextStyle:)`, or use the `default` class property, which corresponds to the `.body` text style).

2. Call `scaledFont(for:)` with your base font.

To illustrate, I'll convert an existing label (`self.label2`) to respond to the user's dynamic text size preference, even though its font is *not* the system font:

```
if let f = self.label2.font {
    let f2 = UIFontMetrics(forTextStyle: .caption1).scaledFont(for: f)
    self.label2.font = f2
    self.label2.adjustsFontForContentSizeCategory = true
}
```

Adoption of dynamic type means that your interface must now respond to the possibility that text will grow and shrink, with interface objects changing size in response. Obviously, autolayout can be a big help here (Chapter 1). A standard vertical spacing constraint between labels, from the upper label's last baseline to the lower label's first baseline, will respond to dynamic text size preference changes. You can configure this in the nib editor, or in code by calling `constraint(equalToSystemSpacing-Below:multiplier:)`. If the distance you want is not identically the standard system spacing, set the constraint's `multiplier`.

Sometimes, more radical adjustments of the overall layout may be needed, especially when we get into the five very large `.accessibility` text sizes. You'll have to respond to text size changes in code in order to make those adjustments. To do so, implement `traitCollectionDidChange(_:)`. The text size preference is reported through the trait collection's `preferredContentSizeCategory`. UIContentSizeCategory overloads the comparison operators so that you can determine easily whether one size is larger than another; also, the `isAccessibilityCategory` property tells you whether this size is one of the `.accessibility` text sizes. To help you scale actual numeric values, the UIFontMetrics instance method `scaledValue(for:)` adjusts a CGFloat with respect to the user's current text size preferences.

A wild and crazy label

A wild and crazy label

Figure 11-1. A dynamic text label with a symbol image

To test your app's response to changes in the user's dynamic text size preference, click the Environment Overrides button in the project window's debug bar to summon a popover where you can use the Text switch and slider.

Symbol Images and Text

The built-in symbol images (Chapter 2) are intended for use in conjunction with text. That is why a symbol configuration (UIImage.SymbolConfiguration) is constructed in terms of text features such as font, weight, and point size. If you derive the symbol configuration from the characteristics of the text with which it is to be associated, it will harmonize with that text.

Symbol configurations also work with dynamic text. Set up the symbol configuration in terms of a dynamic text style, and the symbol image will respond automatically when the user changes the text size preference in the Settings app, changing its own size just like text.

A symbol image configuration also has a scale: `.default`, `.small`, `.medium`, or `.large`. This is so that the image size can be adjusted relative to any associated text without breaking the harmonization between them.

A typical arrangement is that the symbol image is in a UIImageView while the text is in a label. If you have configured them so that their their size and weight harmonize, they will also align correctly with one another if they are aligned by their vertical centers. (If you have a multiline label and you prefer that the image should be aligned with the first line of the label, align them by their first baselines instead.)

Figure 11-1 demonstrates how an image view and label can resize themselves together in response to a change in the user's text size preference. The label's font is the `.headline` text style. The image view displays a symbol image, and its symbol configuration has the `.headline` text style with a `.large` scale for emphasis. The label and image view are aligned by their vertical centers. Thanks to autolayout, the image view changes size in response to the image's size while the label maintains a fixed horizontal spacing from it. No code was involved in preparing this example! Everything was configured in the nib editor.

A *wild* and crazy label

Figure 11-2. A dynamic type font with an italic variant

Font Descriptors

A font descriptor (UIFontDescriptor, toll-free bridged to Core Text's CTFont-Descriptor) describes a font in terms of its features. You can then use those features to convert between font descriptors, and ultimately to derive a new font. Given a font descriptor `desc`, you can ask for a corresponding italic font descriptor like this:

```
let desc2 = desc.withSymbolicTraits(.traitItalic)
```

If `desc` was originally a descriptor for Avenir-Book 15, `desc2` is now a descriptor for Avenir-BookOblique 15. However, it is not the *font* Avenir-BookOblique 15; a font descriptor is not a font. The question is how to get from a font to a corresponding font descriptor, and *vice versa*:

To convert from a font to a font descriptor
Ask for the font's `fontDescriptor` property. Alternatively, you can obtain a font descriptor directly just as you would obtain a font, by calling its initializer `init(name:size:)` or its class method `preferredFontDescriptor(withText-Style:)`.

To convert from a font descriptor to a font
Call the UIFont initializer `init(descriptor:size:)`, typically supplying a size of `0` to signify that the size should not change. This can be slow, because the entire font collection must be searched, so don't do it in speed-sensitive situations.

This will be a common pattern in your code, as you convert from font to font descriptor to perform some transformation, and then back to font:

```
let f = UIFont(name: "Avenir", size: 15)!
let desc = f.fontDescriptor
let desc2 = desc.withSymbolicTraits(.traitItalic)
let f2 = UIFont(descriptor: desc2!, size: 0) // Avenir-BookOblique 15
```

The same technique is useful for obtaining styled variants of the dynamic type fonts. Here I prepare to form an NSAttributedString whose font is mostly UIFont.Text-Style.body, but with one italicized word (Figure 11-2):

```
let body = UIFontDescriptor.preferredFontDescriptor(withTextStyle:.body)
let emphasis = body.withSymbolicTraits(.traitItalic)!
let fbody = UIFont(descriptor: body, size: 0)
let femphasis = UIFont(descriptor: emphasis, size: 0)
```

> A *wild* and crazy label

Figure 11-3. A dynamic type font with a serif design

Starting in iOS 13, using the same technique, you can obtain alternative variants of the system font. These are referred to as system *designs;* they are actually distinct fonts. The designs are (UIFontDescriptor.SystemDesign):

- .default
- .rounded
- .monospaced
- .serif

To access a system design font, start with a dynamic type font descriptor and call withDesign(_:). To illustrate, I'll modify the previous code; now my fonts have a serif, because they come from the .serif system design (Figure 11-3):

```
var body = UIFontDescriptor.preferredFontDescriptor(withTextStyle:.body)
if let desc = body.withDesign(.serif) { // *
    body = desc
}
let emphasis = body.withSymbolicTraits(.traitItalic)!
let fbody = UIFont(descriptor: body, size: 0)
let femphasis = UIFont(descriptor: emphasis, size: 0)
```

 In iOS 14, as of this writing, system font variants based on a dynamic font (like fbody and femphasis in the preceding code) are not themselves dynamic. I regard that as a bug.

Exploring font features

You can explore a font's features by way of a UIFontDescriptor. Some features are available directly as properties, such as postscriptName and symbolicTraits. The symbolicTraits is expressed as a bitmask:

```
let f = UIFont(name: "GillSans-BoldItalic", size: 20)!
let d = f.fontDescriptor
let traits = d.symbolicTraits
let isItalic = traits.contains(.traitItalic) // true
let isBold = traits.contains(.traitBold) // true
```

For other types of information, call object(forKey:), where the key: will be a UIFontDescriptor.AttributeName:

```
let f = UIFont(name: "GillSans-BoldItalic", size: 20)!
let d = f.fontDescriptor
let vis = d.object(forKey:.visibleName)!
// Gill Sans Bold Italic
```

THIS IS VERY IMPORTANT!

Figure 11-4. A small caps font variant

Accessing typographical variants

Another use of font descriptors is to access typographical variants of a font. To do so, you construct a dictionary whose keys (UIFontDescriptor.FeatureKey) specify two pieces of information: the feature type (`.featureIdentifier`) and the feature selector (`.typeIdentifer`). To illustrate, I'll obtain a variant of the Didot font that draws its minuscules as small caps (Figure 11-4):

```
let desc = UIFontDescriptor(name:"Didot", size:18)
let d = [
    UIFontDescriptor.FeatureKey.featureIdentifier: kLowerCaseType,
    UIFontDescriptor.FeatureKey.typeIdentifier: kLowerCaseSmallCapsSelector
]
let desc2 = desc.addingAttributes([.featureSettings:[d]])
let f = UIFont(descriptor: desc2, size: 0)
```

(Typographical identifier constants such as `kLowerCaseSmallCapsSelector` come from the Core Text header *SFNTLayoutTypes.h*.)

The system (and dynamic type) font can also portray small caps; in fact, it can do this in two different ways: in addition to `kLowerCaseType` and `kLowerCaseSmallCaps-Selector`, where lowercase characters are shown as small caps, it implements `kUpper-CaseType` and `kUpperCaseSmallCapsSelector`, where uppercase characters are shown as small caps.

Another system (and dynamic type) font feature is an alternate set of glyph forms designed for legibility, with a type of `kStylisticAlternativesType`. If the selector is `kStylisticAltOneOnSelector`, the 6 and 9 glyphs have straight tails. If the selector is `kStylisticAltSixOnSelector`, certain letters also have special distinguishing shapes, such as the lowercase "l" (ell) which has a curved bottom, to distinguish it from capital "I" which has a top and bottom bar.

How are you supposed to discover what typographical variants a particular font supports? In code, you have to drop down to the level of Core Text:

```
let desc = UIFontDescriptor(name: "Didot", size: 20) as CTFontDescriptor
let f = CTFontCreateWithFontDescriptor(desc,0,nil)
let arr = CTFontCopyFeatures(f)
```

The resulting array of dictionaries includes entries [`CTFeatureTypeIdentifier:37`], which is `kLowerCaseType`, and [`CTFeatureSelectorIdentifier:1`], which is `kLower-CaseSmallCapsSelector`.

A more practical (and fun) approach to exploring a font's typographical variants is to obtain a copy of the font on the desktop, install it, launch TextEdit, choose Format → Font → Show Fonts, select the font, and open the Typography panel, exposing the font's various features. Now you can experiment on selected text.

Choosing a Font

Starting in iOS 13, there's a standard interface for letting the user pick a font. This is the UIFontPickerViewController. To use it, create a configuration (UIFontPicker-ViewController.Configuration) and set its properties as desired, and initialize the picker with the configuration. Then assign the picker a delegate and present the picker as a presented view controller.

Configuration properties are:

displayUsingSystemFont
> The default is false, meaning that each font name is shown in that font. If true, all font names are shown in a system font.

includeFaces
> The default is false, meaning that only font families are listed. If true, a listed font family comprising multiple fonts can reveal the names of those fonts, and the user can choose a specific font.

filteredTraits
> Symbolic traits to which the listed fonts should be limited. This is a bitmask, so you can combine multiple font family classes and features. Only fonts matching one or more of those traits will be listed.

filteredLanguagesPredicate
> A language predicate formed with the class method filterPredicate(for-FilteredLanguages:). Only fonts appropriate to that language will be listed.

The delegate (UIFontPickerViewControllerDelegate) can implement two methods:

fontPickerViewControllerDidCancel(_:)
> Called when the user cancels using the Cancel button (but not when the user manually swipes the presented view down to dismiss it).

fontPickerViewControllerDidPickFont(_:)
> The user has tapped on a font listing and the picker has been dismissed. You should ask the picker for its selectedFontDescriptor. This might be the descriptor for a font family or (if the configuration's includeFaces is true) for a font name.

	Application requires iPhone envi... ⌄	Boolean	YES
⊿ SourceCodePro-Regular.ttf	⌄ Fonts provided by application ⌄	Array	(1 item)
🗎 Info.plist	Item 0	String	SourceCodePro-Regular.ttf
> 🗁 Products	Launch screen interface file bas... ⌄	String	LaunchScreen
	Main storyboard file base name ⌄	String	Main
	> Required device capabilities ⌄	Array	(1 item)
	> Supported interface orientations ⌄	Array	(3 items)

Figure 11-5. Embedding a font in an app bundle

Adding Fonts

You are not limited to the fonts that are built in by default as part of the system. There are ways to obtain additional fonts.

Fonts in the app bundle

A font included at the top level of your app bundle will be loaded at launch time and available to your app if your *Info.plist* lists it under the "Fonts provided by application" key (UIAppFonts).

Figure 11-5 shows a font included in the app bundle, along with the *Info.plist* entry that lists it. Observe that what you're listing here is the name of the font *file*.

Downloadable Apple fonts

All macOS fonts are available for download from Apple's servers; you can obtain and start using one while your app is running.

To download a font in real time, you'll have to specify the font as a font descriptor and drop down to the level of Core Text (import CoreText) to call CTFont-DescriptorMatchFontDescriptorsWithProgressHandler. It takes a function which is called repeatedly at every stage of the download process; it will be called on a background thread, so if you want to use the downloaded font immediately in the interface, you must step out to the main thread (see Chapter 25).

I'll attempt to use Nanum Brush Script as my UILabel's font; if it isn't installed, I'll attempt to download it and *then* use it as my UILabel's font. I've inserted a lot of unnecessary logging to mark the stages of the download process:

```
let name = "NanumBrush"
let size : CGFloat = 24
let f : UIFont! = UIFont(name:name, size:size)
if f != nil {
    self.lab.font = f
    print("already installed")
    return
}
print("attempting to download font")
let desc = UIFontDescriptor(name:name, size:size)
```

```
CTFontDescriptorMatchFontDescriptorsWithProgressHandler(
    [desc] as CFArray, nil) { state, prog in
        switch state {
        case .didBegin:
            NSLog("%@", "matching did begin")
        case .willBeginDownloading:
            NSLog("%@", "downloading will begin")
        case .downloading:
            let d = prog as NSDictionary
            let key = kCTFontDescriptorMatchingPercentage
            let cur = d[key]
            if let cur = cur as? NSNumber {
                NSLog("progress: %@%%", cur)
            }
        case .didFinishDownloading:
            NSLog("%@", "downloading did finish")
        case .didFailWithError:
            NSLog("%@", "downloading failed")
        case .didFinish:
            NSLog("%@", "matching did finish")
            DispatchQueue.main.async {
                let f : UIFont! = UIFont(name:name, size:size)
                if f != nil {
                    NSLog("%@", "got the font!")
                    self.lab.font = f
                }
            }
        default:break
        }
        return true
}
```

Installed fonts

The preceding ways of adding fonts make those fonts available within your app but
nowhere else. Starting in iOS 13, apps can install fonts to be made available system-
wide. Apple calls an app that does this a *font provider* app, and it calls fonts provided
in this way *installed* fonts (as opposed to the built-in fonts that come with the system). A font provider app can include its fonts at the top level of the app bundle or in
the asset catalog as on-demand resources ("On-Demand Resources" on page 1128).

To act as a font provider requires a special entitlement; in the Signing & Capabilities
tab of the target editor, choose the Fonts capability and check "Install Fonts." The
fonts must be approved by Apple during the app review process. The user has the
final say, so an attempt to install a font will cause the system to put up a dialog asking
for the user's approval, and fonts installed by a font provider app can be deleted in
the Settings app (under General → Fonts); if the user deletes a font provider app, all
the fonts it provides are deleted as well.

Just as installing a font system-wide is a special privilege, so is using a font installed in this way. An app that wants access to fonts installed by a font provider app requires the same entitlement as a font provider, except that you check "Use Installed Fonts." An app that uses installed fonts needs to be aware that the user can install or remove fonts at any time; a notification lets you know when the list has changed.

Installing fonts and using installed fonts in code involves talking to Core Text (import CoreText) using a C API. As a simple demonstration, I'll use the app from the start of this section, where I included the SourceCodePro font in my app bundle. I'll act as a font provider and attempt to install that font for use system-wide:

```
if let url = Bundle.main.url(
    forResource: "SourceCodePro-Regular", withExtension: "ttf") {
        let urls = [url] as CFArray
        CTFontManagerRegisterFontURLs(urls, .persistent, true) { errs, ok in
            // ... user is asked for permission to install ...
            return true
        }
}
```

To act as a user of that font, I can also use a C API; if I know the descriptor of the font I want to use, I can call CTFontManagerRequestFonts. Moreover, because my app has the "Use Installed Fonts" entitlement, UIFontPickerViewController will include installed fonts in its list, and if the user picks one, that font will be available to my app immediately without any further action on my part.

For more information, look at the *CTFontManager.h* header (and Apple has a WWDC 2019 video on this topic).

Attributed Strings

Styled text, possibly consisting of multiple style runs with different font, size, color, and other text features in different parts of the text, is expressed as an *attributed string* (NSAttributedString and its mutable subclass, NSMutableAttributedString). An NSAttributedString consists of an NSString (its string) plus the attributes, applied in ranges.

The way the ranges are applied when configuring an attributed string is not quite the same as what the resulting style runs will be. Suppose the string "one red word" is to be blue, except for the word "red," which is to be red. We can apply the attributes in two steps, first making the whole string blue, and then making the word "red" red. If these are the only changes over the course of the string, then the result is that are three distinct style runs — everything before the word "red," the word "red" itself, and everything after the word "red."

Attributed String Attributes

The attributes applied to a range of an attributed string are described in dictionaries. Each possible attribute has a predefined name, used as a key in these dictionaries; here are some of the most important attributes (NSAttributedString.Key):

`.font`
> A UIFont. The default is Helvetica 12 (*not* San Francisco, the system font).

`.foregroundColor`
> The text color, a UIColor.

`.backgroundColor`
> The color *behind* the text, a UIColor. You could use this to highlight a word.

`.ligature`
> An NSNumber wrapping 0 or 1, expressing whether or not you want ligatures used. Some fonts, such as Didot, have ligatures that are on by default.

`.kern`
> An NSNumber wrapping the floating-point amount by which the built-in kerning between letter pairs is to be adjusted. A negative value brings a glyph closer to the following glyph; a positive value adds space between them.

`.tracking`
> An NSNumber wrapping the floating-point amount by which the overall tracking — the ratio of spacing to size — is to be adjusted. A negative value brings glyphs closer together; a positive value adds space between them. (New in iOS 14, though it has been available in Core Text since iOS 10.)

`.strikethroughStyle`
`.underlineStyle`
> An NSNumber wrapping one of these values (NSUnderlineStyle, an option set) describing the line weight:
>
> - `.none`
> - `.single`
> - `.double`
> - `.thick`
>
> In addition, you may specify a line pattern; the line pattern settings have names that start with `pattern`, such as `.patternDot`, `.patternDash`, and so on. Also, you may specify `.byWord`; if you do not, then if the underline or strikethrough range spans multiple words, the whitespace between the words will be underlined or struck through.

`.strikethroughColor`
`.underlineColor`
   A UIColor. If not defined, the foreground color is used.

`.strokeWidth`
   An NSNumber wrapping a Float. The stroke width is peculiarly coded. If it's positive, then the text glyphs are stroked but not filled, giving an outline effect, and the foreground color is used unless a separate stroke color is defined. If it's negative, then its absolute value is the width of the stroke, and the glyphs are both filled (with the foreground color) and stroked (with the stroke color).

`.strokeColor`
   The stroke color, a UIColor.

`.shadow`
   An NSShadow object. An NSShadow is just a value class, combining a `shadow-Offset`, `shadowColor`, and `shadowBlurRadius`.

`.textEffect`
   An NSAttributedString.TextEffectStyle. The only text effect style you can specify is `.letterpressStyle`.

`.attachment`
   An NSTextAttachment object. A text attachment is basically an inline image. I'll discuss text attachments later on.

`.link`
   A URL. This may give the style range a default appearance, such as color and underlining, but you can override this by adding attributes to the same style range. In a noneditable, selectable UITextView, the link is tappable to go to the URL (as I'll explain later in this chapter).

`.baselineOffset`
`.obliqueness`
`.expansion`
   An NSNumber wrapping a Float.

`.paragraphStyle`
   An NSParagraphStyle object. This is basically just a value class, assembling text features that apply properly to paragraphs as a whole, not merely to characters. Here are its most important properties:

   • `alignment` (NSTextAlignment)

      ▪ `.left`

      ▪ `.center`

- .right
- .justified
- .natural (left-aligned or right-aligned depending on the localization; a right-to-left language will be right-aligned)

- lineBreakMode (NSLineBreakMode)
  - .byWordWrapping
  - .byCharWrapping
  - .byClipping
  - .byTruncatingHead
  - .byTruncatingTail
  - .byTruncatingMiddle

- firstLineHeadIndent, headIndent (left margin), tailIndent (right margin)
- lineHeightMultiple, maximumLineHeight, minimumLineHeight
- lineSpacing
- paragraphSpacing, paragraphSpacingBefore
- hyphenationFactor (0 or 1)
- defaultTabInterval, tabStops (the tab stops are an array of NSTextTab objects; I'll give an example in a moment)
- allowsDefaultTighteningForTruncation (if true, permits some negative tracking to be applied automatically to a truncating paragraph if this would prevent truncation)

To construct an NSAttributedString, you can call init(string:attributes:) if the entire string has the same attributes; otherwise, you'll use its mutable subclass NSMutableAttributedString, which lets you set attributes over a range.

To construct an NSParagraphStyle, you'll use its mutable subclass NSMutable-ParagraphStyle. You should apply a paragraph style to the *first character* of a paragraph; that dictates how the whole paragraph is rendered. (Applying a paragraph style to a character other than the first character of a paragraph can cause the paragraph style to be ignored.)

Both NSAttributedString and NSParagraphStyle come with default values for all attributes, so you only have to set the attributes you care about. However, Apple says that explicitly supplying a font, foreground color, and paragraph style makes attributed strings more efficient.

Figure 11-6. An attributed string

Making an Attributed String

We now know enough for an example! I'll draw my attributed strings in a disabled (noninteractive) UITextView; its background is white, but its superview's background is gray, so you can see the text view's bounds relative to the text. (Ignore the text's vertical positioning, which is configured independently as a feature of the text view itself.)

First, two words of my attributed string are made extra-bold by stroking in a different color. I start by dictating the entire string and the overall style of the text; then I apply the special style to the two stroked words (Figure 11-6):

```
let s1 = """
    The Gettysburg Address, as delivered on a certain occasion \
    (namely Thursday, November 19, 1863) by A. Lincoln
    """
let content = NSMutableAttributedString(string:s1, attributes:[
    .font: UIFont(name:"Arial-BoldMT", size:15)!,
    .foregroundColor: UIColor(red:0.251, green:0.000, blue:0.502, alpha:1)
])
let r = (content.string as NSString).range(of:"Gettysburg Address")
content.addAttributes([
    .strokeColor: UIColor.red,
    .strokeWidth: -2.0
], range: r)
self.tv.attributedText = content
```

Carrying on from the previous code, I'll also make the whole paragraph centered and indented from the edges of the text view. To do so, I create a paragraph style and apply it to the first character. Note how the margins are dictated: the tailIndent is negative, to bring the right margin leftward, and the firstLineHeadIndent must be set separately, as the headIndent does not automatically apply to the first line (Figure 11-7):

```
let para = NSMutableParagraphStyle()
para.headIndent = 10
para.firstLineHeadIndent = 10
para.tailIndent = -10
```

Figure 11-7. An attributed string with a paragraph style

Figure 11-8. An attributed string with an expanded first character

```
para.lineBreakMode = .byWordWrapping
para.alignment = .center
para.paragraphSpacing = 15
content.addAttribute(
    .paragraphStyle,
    value:para, range:NSMakeRange(0,1))
self.tv.attributedText = content
```

Next, I'll enlarge the first character of a paragraph. I assign the first character a larger font size, I expand its width slightly, and I reduce its kerning (Figure 11-8):

```
let s2 = """
    Fourscore and seven years ago, our fathers brought forth \
    upon this continent a new nation, conceived in liberty and \
    dedicated to the proposition that all men are created equal.
    """
content2 = NSMutableAttributedString(string:s2, attributes: [
    .font: UIFont(name:"HoeflerText-Black", size:16)!
])
content2.addAttributes([
    .font: UIFont(name:"HoeflerText-Black", size:24)!,
    .expansion: 0.3,
    .kern: -4
], range:NSMakeRange(0,1))
self.tv.attributedText = content2
```

Figure 11-9. An attributed string with justification and autohyphenation

Carrying on from the previous code, I'll once again construct a paragraph style and add it to the first character. My paragraph style illustrates full justification and automatic hyphenation (Figure 11-9):

```
content2.addAttribute(.paragraphStyle,
    value:lend { (para:NSMutableParagraphStyle) in
        para.headIndent = 10
        para.firstLineHeadIndent = 10
        para.tailIndent = -10
        para.lineBreakMode = .byWordWrapping
        para.alignment = .justified
        para.lineHeightMultiple = 1.2
        para.hyphenationFactor = 1.0
    }, range:NSMakeRange(0,1))
self.tv.attributedText = content2
```

When working temporarily with a value class such as NSMutableParagraphStyle, it feels clunky to be forced to instantiate the class and configure the instance before using it for the one and only time. So I've written a little Swift generic function, lend (see Appendix B), that lets me do all that in an anonymous function at the point where the value class is actually used.

Now we come to the Really Amazing Part. I can make a *single* attributed string consisting of *both* paragraphs, and a single text view can portray it (Figure 11-10):

```
let end = content.length
content.replaceCharacters(in:NSMakeRange(end, 0), with:"\n")
content.append(content2)
self.tv.attributedText = content
```

Tab stops

A tab stop is an NSTextTab, a value class whose initializer lets you set its location (points from the left edge) and alignment.

The initializer also lets you include an options: dictionary whose key (NSText-Tab.OptionKey) is .columnTerminators, as a way of setting the tab stop's column terminator characters. A common use is to create a decimal tab stop, for aligning

**The Gettysburg Address, as
delivered on a certain occasion
(namely Thursday, November 19,
1863) by A. Lincoln**

Fourscore and seven years ago,
our fathers brought forth upon
this continent a new nation,
conceived in liberty and dedicated to the proposition that all
men are created equal.

Figure 11-10. A single attributed string comprising differently styled paragraphs

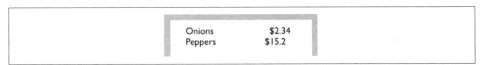

| Onions | $2.34 |
| Peppers | $15.2 |

Figure 11-11. Tab stops in an attributed string

currency values at their decimal point. You can obtain a value appropriate to a given locale by calling NSTextTab's class method `columnTerminators(for:)`.

Here's a demonstration (Figure 11-11); I have deliberately omitted the last digit from the second currency value, to prove that the tab stop really is aligning the numbers at their decimal points:

```
let s = "Onions\t$2.34\nPeppers\t$15.2\n"
let mas = NSMutableAttributedString(string:s, attributes:[
    .font:UIFont(name:"GillSans", size:15)!,
    .paragraphStyle:lend { (p:NSMutableParagraphStyle) in
        let terms = NSTextTab.columnTerminators(for:Locale.current)
        let tab = NSTextTab(textAlignment:.right, location:170,
            options:[.columnTerminators:terms])
        p.tabStops = [tab]
        p.firstLineHeadIndent = 20
    }
])
self.tv.attributedText = mas
```

The `tabStops` array can also be modified by calling `addTabStop(_:)` or `removeTab-Stop(_:)` on the paragraph style. Note that a paragraph style comes with some default tab stops.

Text attachments

A text attachment is basically an inline image. To make one, you need an instance of NSTextAttachment initialized with image data; the easiest way is to start with a

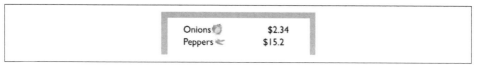

Figure 11-12. Text attachments in an attributed string

UIImage and assign it directly to the NSTextAttachment's image property. You must also give the NSTextAttachment a nonzero bounds; the image will be scaled to the size of the bounds you provide, and a .zero origin places the image on the text baseline.

A text attachment is attached to an NSAttributedString using the .attachment key; the text attachment itself is the value. The range to which this attribute is applied must consist of a special nonprinting character whose UTF-16 codepoint is NSText-Attachment.character (0xFFFC). The simplest way to arrange that is to call the NSAttributedString initializer init(attachment:); you hand it an attachment, and it hands you an attributed string consisting of the NSTextAttachment character with its .attachment attribute set to that text attachment. You can then insert this attributed string into your own attributed string at the point where you want the image to appear.

To illustrate, I'll add an image of onions and an image of peppers just after the words "Onions" and "Peppers" in the attributed string (mas) that I created in the previous example (Figure 11-12):

```
let onions = // ... get image ...
let peppers = // ... get image ...
let onionatt = NSTextAttachment()
onionatt.image = onions
onionatt.bounds = CGRect(0,-5,onions.size.width,onions.size.height)
let onionattchar = NSAttributedString(attachment:onionatt)
let pepperatt = NSTextAttachment()
pepperatt.image = peppers
pepperatt.bounds = CGRect(0,-1,peppers.size.width,peppers.size.height)
let pepperattchar = NSAttributedString(attachment:pepperatt)
let r = (mas.string as NSString).range(of:"Onions")
mas.insert(onionattchar, at:(r.location + r.length))
let r2 = (mas.string as NSString).range(of:"Peppers")
mas.insert(pepperattchar, at:(r2.location + r2.length))
self.tv.attributedText = mas
```

You might want to use a built-in symbol image as a text attachment. To do so, do *not* create the NSTextAttachment object and then assign the symbol to its image property; instead, use the initializer init(image:). This causes the symbol image's configuration, including its point size and baseline offset, to be set automatically to harmonize with the surrounding text. If you want the symbol image to pick up its tint color from the foreground color of the surrounding text, specify an `.alwaysOriginal` rendering mode:

```
let checkim = UIImage(systemName:"checkmark.circle")!
    .withRenderingMode(.alwaysOriginal)
let check = NSTextAttachment(image:checkim) // *
let checkchar = NSAttributedString(attachment:check)
let index = // ...
mas.insert(checkchar, at:index)
```

Other ways to create an attributed string

In the nib editor, the Attributes inspector for an interface object with an attributed string property, such as a UILabel or UITextView, provides an ingenious interface for letting you construct the attributed string; it's not perfect, though, and isn't suitable for lengthy or complex text.

It is also possible to import an attributed string from text in some other standard format, such as HTML or RTF. (There are also corresponding export methods.) To import, get the target text into a Data object and call `init(data:options:document-Attributes:)`; alternatively, start with a file and call `init(url:options:document-Attributes:)`. The `options:` allow you to specify the source text's format. Here we read an RTF file from the app bundle as an attributed string and show it in a text view (`self.tv`):

```
let url = Bundle.main.url(forResource: "test", withExtension: "rtf")!
let opts : [NSAttributedString.DocumentReadingOptionKey : Any] =
    [.documentType : NSAttributedString.DocumentType.rtf]
let s = try! NSAttributedString(
    url: url, options: opts, documentAttributes: nil)
self.tv.attributedText = s
```

Modifying and Querying an Attributed String

We can coherently modify just the character content of a mutable attributed string by calling `replaceCharacters(in:with:)`, which takes an NSRange and a substitute string. This method can do two different kinds of thing, depending whether the range has zero length:

Replacement
> If the range has *nonzero* length, we're *replacing* characters. The replacement characters all take on the attributes of the *first replaced* character.

Insertion
> If the range has *zero* length, we're *inserting* characters. The inserted characters all take on the attributes of the character *preceding* the insertion — except that, if we insert at the *start*, there is no preceding character, so the inserted characters take on the attributes of the character *following* the insertion.

You can query an attributed string about the attributes applied to a single character, asking either about all attributes at once with `attributes(at:effectiveRange:)`, or about a particular attribute by name with `attribute(_:at:effectiveRange:)`. The `effectiveRange:` argument is a pointer to an NSRange variable, which will be set by indirection to the range over which the same attribute value, or set of attribute values, applies.

In this example, we ask about the last character of our `content` attributed string:

```
var range : NSRange = NSMakeRange(0,0)
let d = content.attributes(at:content.length-1, effectiveRange:&range)
```

After that, `range` is `{111,175}`, and `d` is:

```
[__C.NSAttributedStringKey(_rawValue: NSFont):
    <UICTFont: 0x7ff533904ae0>
        font-family: "HoeflerText-Black";
        font-weight: bold;
        font-style: normal;
        font-size: 16.00pt]
```

So now we know that the last character's `.font` attribute is Hoefler Text 16, and that that attribute is applied over a stretch of 175 characters starting at character 111.

Because style runs are something of an artifice, the `effectiveRange` might not be what you would think of as the *entire* style run. The methods with `longestEffective-Range:` parameters work out the entire style run range for you; but this comes at the cost of some efficiency, and in practice you typically won't need this information anyway, because you're cycling through ranges — so that speed, even at the cost of *more* iterations, matters more than getting the longest effective range on *every* iteration.

In this example, I start with the `content` attributed string and change all the size 15 material to Arial Bold 20. I don't care whether I'm handed longest effective ranges (and my code explicitly says so); I just want to cycle efficiently:

```
content.enumerateAttribute(.font,
    in:NSMakeRange(0,content.length),
    options:.longestEffectiveRangeNotRequired) { value, range, stop in
        let font = value as! UIFont
        if font.pointSize == 15 {
            content.addAttribute(.font,
                value:UIFont(name: "Arial-BoldMT", size:20)!,
                range:range)
        }
    }
```

Custom Attributes

You are permitted to apply your own custom attributes to a stretch of text in an attributed string. Your attributes won't directly affect how the string is drawn, because the text engine doesn't know what to make of them; but it doesn't object to them either. In this way, you can mark a stretch of text invisibly for your own future use.

In this example, I have a UILabel whose text includes a date. Every so often, I want to replace the date by the current date. The problem is that when the moment comes to replace the date, I don't know where it is: I know neither its length nor the length of the text that precedes it. The solution is to use an attributed string where the date part is marked with a custom attribute.

My custom attribute is defined by extending NSAttributedString.Key:

```
extension NSAttributedString.Key {
    static let date = NSAttributedString.Key("date")
}
```

I've applied this attribute to the date part of my label's attributed text, with an arbitrary value of 1. Now I can readily find the date again later, because the text engine will tell me where it is:

```
let mas = NSMutableAttributedString(
    attributedString: self.lab.attributedText!)
mas.enumerateAttribute(.date, in:NSMakeRange(0, mas.length)) { val, r, stop in
    if val as? Int == 1 {
        mas.replaceCharacters(in: r, with: Date().description)
        stop.pointee = true
    }
}
self.lab.attributedText = mas
```

Drawing and Measuring an Attributed String

You can draw an attributed string yourself, rather than having a built-in interface object do it for you; and sometimes this will prove to be the most reliable approach. An NSString can be drawn into a rect with draw(in:withAttributes:) and related methods; an NSAttributedString can be drawn with draw(at:), draw(in:), and draw(with:options:context:).

Here, I draw an attributed string (content) into an image graphics context and extract the image, which might then be displayed by an image view:

```
let rect = CGRect(0,0,280,250)
let r = UIGraphicsImageRenderer(size:rect.size)
let im = r.image { ctx in
    UIColor.white.setFill()
    ctx.cgContext.fill(rect)
    content.draw(in:rect)
}
```

Similarly, you can draw an attributed string directly in a UIView's `draw(_:)` override. Imagine that we have a UIView subclass called StringDrawer that has an `attributedText` property; the idea is that we just assign an attributed string to that property and the StringDrawer redraws itself:

```
self.drawer.attributedText = content
```

And here's StringDrawer:

```
class StringDrawer : UIView {
    @NSCopying var attributedText : NSAttributedString! {
        didSet {
            self.setNeedsDisplay()
        }
    }
    override func draw(_ rect: CGRect) {
        let r = rect.offsetBy(dx: 0, dy: 2)
        let opts : NSStringDrawingOptions = .usesLineFragmentOrigin
        self.attributedText.draw(with:r, options: opts, context: context)
    }
}
```

The `.usesLineFragmentOrigin` option is crucial here. Without it, the string is drawn with its *baseline* at the rect origin (so that it appears *above* that rect), and it doesn't wrap. The rule is that `.usesLineFragmentOrigin` is the implicit default for simple `draw(in:)`, but for `draw(with:options:context:)` you must specify it explicitly.

NSAttributedString also provides methods to *measure* an attributed string, such as `boundingRect(with:options:context:)`. As before, the `.usesLineFragmentOrigin` option is crucial; without it, the measured text doesn't wrap and the returned height will be very small. The documentation warns that the returned height can be fractional and that you should round up to an integer if the height of a view is going to depend on this result.

The `context:` parameter of methods such as `draw(with:options:context:)` lets you supply an instance of NSStringDrawingContext, a simple value class whose `totalBounds` property tells you where you just drew.

 The documentation lists additional features of NSStringDrawingContext, such as its `minimumScaleFactor`; but these appear to be nonfunctional.

Labels

A label (UILabel) is a simple built-in interface object for displaying text. I listed some of its chief properties in Chapter 8 ("Built-In Cell Styles" on page 456).

If you're displaying a plain NSString in a label, by way of the label's text property, then you are likely also to set the label's font, textColor, and textAlignment properties, and possibly its shadowColor and shadowOffset properties. The label's text can have an alternate highlightedTextColor, to be used when its isHighlighted property is true, as when the label is in a selected cell of a table view.

On the other hand, if you're using an NSAttributedString, then you'll set just the label's attributedText property and let the attributes dictate things like color, alignment, and shadow. In general, if your intention is to display text in a single font, size, color, and alignment, you probably won't bother with attributedText; but if you *do* set the attributedText, you should make it your *only* way of dictating text style features. Those other UILabel properties do mostly work when you have set the attributedText, but they're going to change the attributes of your *entire* attributed string, with results that you might not intend. Setting the text of a UILabel that has attributedText will effectively override the attributes.

 The highlightedTextColor property affects the attributedText only if the latter is the same color as the textColor.

Number of Lines

A UILabel's numberOfLines property is extremely important. Together with the label's line breaking behavior and resizing behavior, it determines how much of the text will appear. The default is 1 — a single line — which can come as a surprise. To make a label display more than one line of text, you must explicitly set its numberOfLines to a value greater than 1, or to 0 to indicate that there is to be no maximum.

Line break characters in a label's text are honored. In a single-line label, you won't see whatever follows the first line break character.

Wrapping and Truncation

UILabel line breaking (wrapping) and truncation behavior, which applies to both single-line and multiline labels, is determined by the lineBreakMode (of the label or the attributed string). The options (NSLineBreakMode) are those that I listed earlier in discussing NSParagraphStyle, but their *behavior* within a label needs to be described:

.byClipping
    Lines break at word-end, but the *last* line can continue past its boundary, even if this leaves a character showing only partially.

`.byWordWrapping`

> Lines break at word-end, but if this is a single-line label, indistinguishable from `.byClipping`.

`.byCharWrapping`

> Lines break in midword in order to maximize the number of characters in each line.

`.byTruncatingHead`
`.byTruncatingMiddle`
`.byTruncatingTail`

> Lines break at word-end; if the text is too long for the label, then the *last* line displays an ellipsis at the start, middle, or end of the line respectively, and text is omitted at the point of the ellipsis.

> The `allowsDefaultTighteningForTruncation` property, if `true`, permits some negative tracking to be applied automatically to a `truncating` label if this would prevent truncation.

A UILabel's line break behavior is *not* the same as what happens when an NSAttributedString draws itself into a graphics context:

- The default line break mode for an NSAttributedString's NSParagraphStyle is `.byWordWrapping`, but the default line break mode for a new label is `.byTruncatingTail`.

- An NSAttributedString whose NSParagraphStyle's `lineBreakMode` doesn't have `wrapping` in its name *doesn't wrap* when it draws itself (it consists of a single line), but a multiline UILabel *always* wraps, regardless of its line break mode.

Fitting Label to Text

If a label is too small for its text, the entire text won't show. If a label is too big for its text, the text is vertically centered in the label, with space above and below. Either of those might be undesirable; you might prefer the label to *fit* its text.

If you're not using autolayout, in most simple cases `sizeToFit` will do the right thing; I believe that behind the scenes it is calling `boundingRect(with:options:context:)`.

If you're using autolayout, a label will correctly configure its own `intrinsicContentSize` automatically, based on its contents — and therefore, all other things being equal, the label will size itself to fit its contents *with no code at all!* Every time you reconfigure the label in a way that affects its contents (setting its text, changing its font, setting its attributed text, and so forth), the label *automatically* invalidates and recalculates its intrinsic content size and resizes itself to fit. There are two general cases to consider:

Short single-line label

You might give the label no width or height constraints; you'll constrain its position, but you'll let the label's `intrinsicContentSize` provide both the label's width and its height.

Multiline label

Most likely, you'll want to dictate the label's width, while letting the label's height change automatically to accommodate its contents. There are two ways to do this:

Set the label's internal width constraint

This is appropriate particularly when the label's width is to remain fixed ever after.

Set the label's `preferredMaxLayoutWidth`

This property is a hint to help the label's calculation of its `intrinsicContentSize`. It is the width at which the label, as its contents increase, will stop growing horizontally to accommodate those contents, and start growing vertically instead.

Consider a label whose top, left, and right edges are pinned to its superview, while its height is free to change based on its `intrinsicContentSize`. Presume also that the superview's width can change, possibly due to rotation, changing the width of the label. Then the label's height will always perfectly fit its contents, provided that, after every width change, the label's `preferredMaxLayoutWidth` is adjusted *to match its current width*.

How can we make that happen? It's easy. It turns out that if we simply set the label's `preferredMaxLayoutWidth` to 0, that will be taken as a signal that the label should change its `preferredMaxLayoutWidth` to match its width *automatically* whenever its width changes. Moreover, that happens to be the default `preferredMaxLayoutWidth` value! (In the nib editor, at the top of a label's Size inspector, when the Explicit checkbox is unchecked and the Desired Width field says "Automatic," that means the label's `preferredMaxLayoutWidth` is 0; again, this is the default.) So a label in this configuration will *always* fit its contents, with no effort on your part.

Instead of letting a label grow, you can permit its text font size to shrink if this would allow more of the text to fit. How the text is repositioned when the font size shrinks is determined by the label's `baselineAdjustment` property. For this feature to operate, *all* of the following conditions must be met:

- The label's `adjustsFontSizeToFitWidth` property must be `true`.
- The label's `minimumScaleFactor` must be less than `1.0`.
- The label's size must be limited.

- *Either* this must be a single-line label (numberOfLines is 1) *or* the line break mode (of the label or the attributed string) must *not* have wrapping in its name.

Customized Label Drawing

Methods that you can override in a subclass to modify a label's drawing are drawText(in:) and textRect(forBounds:limitedToNumberOfLines:). This is the code for a UILabel subclass that outlines the label with a black rectangle and puts a five-point inset around the label's contents:

```
class BoundedLabel: UILabel {
    override func awakeFromNib() {
        super.awakeFromNib()
        self.layer.borderWidth = 2.0
        self.layer.cornerRadius = 3.0
    }
    override func drawText(in rect: CGRect) {
        super.drawText(in: rect.insetBy(dx: 5, dy: 5).integral)
    }
}
```

 A CATextLayer (Chapter 3) is like a lightweight, layer-level version of a UILabel. If the width of the layer is insufficient to display the entire string, we can get truncation behavior with the truncationMode property. If the isWrapped property is set to true, the string will wrap. We can also set the alignment with the alignmentMode property. And its string property can be an attributed string.

Text Fields

A text field (UITextField) is for brief user text entry. It portrays just a single line of text; any line break characters in its text are treated as spaces. It has many of the same properties as a label. You can provide it with a plain NSString, setting its text, font, textColor, and textAlignment, or provide it with an attributed string, setting its attributedText. You can learn (and set) a text field's overall text attributes as an attributes dictionary through its defaultTextAttributes property.

UITextField adopts the UITextInput protocol, which itself adopts the UIKeyInput protocol. These protocols endow a text field with methods for such things as obtaining the text field's current selection and inserting text at the current selection. I'll give examples later in this section.

Under autolayout, a text field's intrinsicContentSize will attempt to set its width to fit its contents; if its width is fixed, you can set its adjustsFontSizeToFitWidth and minimumFontSize properties to allow the text size to shrink somewhat.

Text that is too long for the text field is displayed with an ellipsis at the end. To change the position of the ellipsis, assign the text field an attributed string with different truncation behavior, such as `.byTruncatingHead`. When long text is being edited, the ellipsis is removed and the text shifts to show the insertion point.

Regardless of whether you originally supplied a plain string or an attributed string, if the text field's `allowsEditingTextAttributes` property is `true`, the user, when editing in the text field, can summon a menu toggling the selected text's bold, italics, or underline features.

A text field has a `placeholder` property, which is the text that appears faded within the text field when it has no text (its `text` or `attributedText` has been set to `nil`, or the user has removed all the text); the idea is that you can use this to suggest to the user what the text field is for. It has a styled text alternative, `attributedPlaceholder`.

If a text field's `clearsOnBeginEditing` property is `true`, it automatically deletes its existing text (and displays the placeholder) when editing begins within it. If a text field's `clearsOnInsertion` property is `true`, then when editing begins within it, the text remains, but is invisibly selected, and will be replaced by the user's typing.

A text field's border drawing is determined by its `borderStyle` property. Your options (UITextField.BorderStyle) are:

`.none`
> No border.

`.line`
> A plain black rectangle.

`.bezel`
> A gray rectangle, where the top and left sides have a very slight, thin shadow.

`.roundedRect`
> A larger rectangle with slightly rounded corners and a flat, faded gray color.

If the `borderStyle` is not `.roundedRect`, you can supply a background image (`background`). In iOS 13 and before, the background image is drawn on top of the border; new in iOS 14, the border is removed. You can use the background image to draw your own border if you wish. The image is automatically resized, and you will probably want to supply a resizable image. A second image, `disabledBackground`, can be displayed when the text field's `isEnabled` property, inherited from UIControl, is `false`. The user can't interact with a disabled text field, but without a `disabledBackground` image, the user may lack a sufficient visual clue to this fact. You can't set the `disabledBackground` unless you have also set the `background`.

A text field may contain one or two ancillary overlay views, its leftView and right-View, and possibly a Clear button (a gray circle with a white X). The automatic visibility of each of these is determined by the leftViewMode, rightViewMode, and clearButtonMode, respectively. The view mode values (UITextField.ViewMode) are:

.never
> The view never appears.

.whileEditing
> A Clear button appears if there is text in the field and the user is editing. A left or right view appears if the user is editing, even if there is no text in the field.

.unlessEditing
> A Clear button appears if there is text in the field and the user is not editing. A left or right view appears if the user is not editing, or if the user is editing but there is no text in the field.

.always
> A Clear button appears if there is text in the field. A left or right view always appears.

Depending on what sort of view you use, your leftView and rightView may have to be sized manually (possibly using internal constraints) so as not to overwhelm the text view contents. If a right view and a Clear button appear at the same time, the right view may cover the Clear button unless you reposition it.

The positions and sizes of *any* of the components of the text field can be set in relation to the text field's bounds by overriding the appropriate method in a subclass:

- clearButtonRect(forBounds:)
- leftViewRect(forBounds:)
- rightViewRect(forBounds:)
- borderRect(forBounds:)
- textRect(forBounds:)
- placeholderRect(forBounds:)
- editingRect(forBounds:)

You should make no assumptions about when or how frequently these methods will be called; the same method might be called several times in quick succession.

 These methods should all be called with a parameter that is the bounds of the text field, but some are sometimes called with a 100×100 bounds. This feels like a bug.

You can also override in a subclass the methods `drawText(in:)` and `draw-Placeholder(in:)`. You should either draw the specified text or call `super` to draw it; if you do neither, the text won't appear. Both these methods are called with a parameter whose size is the dimensions of the text field's text area, but whose origin is `.zero`. In effect what you've got is a graphics context for just the text area; any drawing you do outside the given rectangle will be clipped.

Summoning and Dismissing the Keyboard

The presence or absence of the virtual keyboard is intimately tied to a text field's editing state. They both have to do with the text field's status as the *first responder*:

- When a text field is first responder, it is being edited and the keyboard is present.
- When a text field is no longer first responder, it is no longer being edited, and if no other text field (or text view) becomes first responder, the keyboard is not present. The keyboard is not dismissed if one text field takes over first responder status from another.

When the user taps in a text field, by default that text field *is* first responder, and so the virtual keyboard appears automatically if it was not already present.

You can also control the presence or absence of the keyboard in code, together with a text field's editing state, by way of the text field's first responder status:

Becoming first responder
> To make the insertion point appear within a text field and to cause the keyboard to appear, you send `becomeFirstResponder` to that text field.

Resigning first responder
> To make a text field stop being edited and to cause the keyboard to disappear, you send `resignFirstResponder` to that text field. (Actually, `resignFirstResponder` returns a Bool, because a responder might return `false` to indicate that for some reason it refuses to obey this command.)
>
> Alternatively, call the UIView `endEditing(_:)` method on the first responder *or any superview* (including the window) to ask or compel the first responder to resign first responder status.

The `endEditing(_:)` method is useful particularly because there may be times when you want to dismiss the keyboard without knowing who the first responder is. You can't send `resignFirstResponder` if you don't know who to send it to. And, amazingly, there is no simple way to learn what view is first responder!

In a view presented in the `.formSheet` modal presentation style on the iPad (Chapter 6), the keyboard, by default, does *not* disappear when a text field resigns first responder status. This is presumably because a form sheet is intended primarily for text input, so the keyboard is felt as accompanying the form as a whole, not individual text fields. Optionally, you can prevent this exceptional behavior: in your UIViewController subclass, override `disables-AutomaticKeyboardDismissal` to return `false`.

Once the user has tapped in a text field and the keyboard has automatically appeared, how is the user supposed to get rid of it? On the iPad, the keyboard may contain a button that dismisses the keyboard. Otherwise, this is an oddly tricky issue. You would think that the Return key in the keyboard would dismiss the keyboard, since you can't enter a Return character in a text field; but, of itself, it doesn't.

One solution is to be the text field's delegate and to implement a text field delegate method, `textFieldShouldReturn(_:)`. When the user taps the Return key in the keyboard, we hear about it through this method, and we receive a reference to the text field; we can respond by telling the text field to resign its first responder status, which dismisses the keyboard:

```
func textFieldShouldReturn(_ tf: UITextField) -> Bool {
    tf.resignFirstResponder()
    return false
}
```

Certain virtual keyboards, however, lack a Return key. In that case, you'll need some other way to allow the user to dismiss the keyboard, such as a button elsewhere in the interface. If there's a scroll view in the interface, you can set its `keyboardDismissMode` to provide a way of letting the user dismiss the keyboard. The options (UIScroll-View.KeyboardDismissMode) are:

`.none`
: The default; if the keyboard doesn't contain a button that lets the user dismiss it, we must use code to dismiss it.

`.interactive`
: The user can dismiss the keyboard by dragging it down.

`.onDrag`
: The keyboard dismisses itself if the user scrolls the scroll view.

A scroll view with a `keyboardDismissMode` that isn't `.none` also calls `resignFirst-Responder` on the text field when it dismisses the keyboard.

Keyboard Covers Text Field

The keyboard, having appeared from offscreen, occupies on the iPhone a position "docked" at the bottom of the screen. This may cover the text field in which the user wants to type, even if it is first responder.

This is not likely to be a major issue on the iPad, because the user has ways of moving the keyboard. Starting in iOS 13, the user has a choice of three ways to unmoor the text field from its "docked" position at the bottom of the screen on the iPad:

Undock
> The keyboard moves up slightly while continuing to occupy the full width of the screen; the user can drag it up and down.

Split
> The keyboard becomes smaller and splits into two separate parts pinned to opposite edges of the screen; the user can drag them up and down together.

Floating
> The keyboard becomes even smaller and looks like an iPhone keyboard, less than half the width of the screen; the user can drag it anywhere.

So on the iPad your interface probably won't need to compensate for the keyboard, because the user can move the keyboard instead.

On the iPhone, however, you'll typically want to reveal the text field so as to ensure that it is not covered by the keyboard. To help with this, you can register for keyboard-related notifications:

- `UIResponder.keyboardWillShowNotification`
- `UIResponder.keyboardDidShowNotification`
- `UIResponder.keyboardWillHideNotification`
- `UIResponder.keyboardDidHideNotification`

Those notifications all have to do with the docked position of the keyboard. On the iPhone, keyboard docking and keyboard visibility are equivalent: the keyboard is visible if and only if it is docked.

Two additional notifications are sent *both* when the keyboard enters and leaves the screen *and* (on the iPad) when the user drags it, splits or unsplits it, and docks or undocks it:

- `UIResponder.keyboardWillChangeFrameNotification`
- `UIResponder.keyboardDidChangeFrameNotification`

(On the iPad, where the user can undock the keyboard, the keyboard is said to show if it is being docked, whether that's because it is appearing from offscreen or because the user is docking it, and it is said to hide if it is being undocked, whether that's because it is moving offscreen or because the user is undocking it. If the keyboard is already undocked and the user moves it around the screen, or if the keyboard appears into or disappears from an undocked configuration, you get *only* changeFrame notifications.)

The most important situations to respond to on the iPhone are those corresponding to the willShow and willHide notifications, when the keyboard is attaining or leaving its docked position at the bottom of the screen. You might think that it would also be necessary to handle the changeFrame notification, in case the keyboard changes its height — as when the user switches from the text keyboard to the emoji keyboard. But the willShow notification is sent in that situation too.

Each notification's userInfo dictionary contains information describing what the keyboard will do or has done, under these keys:

- UIResponder.keyboardFrameBeginUserInfoKey
- UIResponder.keyboardFrameEndUserInfoKey
- UIResponder.keyboardAnimationDurationUserInfoKey
- UIResponder.keyboardAnimationCurveUserInfoKey

When you receive a willShow notification, you can look at the user info's UIResponder.keyboardFrameEndUserInfoKey to learn what position the keyboard is moving to. It is an NSValue wrapping a CGRect *in screen coordinates*. By converting the coordinate system as appropriate, you can compare the keyboard's new frame with the frame of your interface items. If the keyboard's new frame intersects a text field's frame (in the same coordinates), the keyboard is going to cover that text field. You're going to want to take evasive maneuvers.

A natural-looking approach is to slide the entire interface upward as the keyboard appears, just enough to expose the text field being edited above the top of the keyboard. The simplest way to do that is for the entire interface to be inside a scroll view — which is, after all, a view that knows how to slide its contents. This scroll view need not be ordinarily scrollable by the user; in fact, the user may be completely unaware of its existence. But *after* the keyboard appears, the scroll view *should* be scrollable by the user, so that the user can inspect the entire interface at will, even while the keyboard is covering part of it. We can ensure that by adjusting the scroll view's content-Inset.

This behavior is in fact implemented automatically by a UITableViewController. When a text field inside a table cell is first responder, the table view controller adjusts the bottom of the table view's adjustedContentInset to compensate for the keyboard. The result is that the entire table view content is available within the space between the top of the table view and the top of the keyboard.

Moreover, a scroll view has two additional bits of built-in behavior that will help us:

- It scrolls automatically to reveal the first responder. This will make it easy for us to expose the text field being edited.
- It has, as I already mentioned, a keyboardDismissMode, which can give us an additional way to allow the user to dismiss the keyboard.

Let's imitate UITableViewController's behavior with a scroll view containing text fields. In particular, our interface consists of a scroll view containing a content view; the content view contains several text fields.

In viewDidLoad, we register for keyboard notifications:

```
NotificationCenter.default.addObserver(self,
    selector: #selector(keyboardShow),
    name: UIResponder.keyboardWillShowNotification, object: nil)
NotificationCenter.default.addObserver(self,
    selector: #selector(keyboardHide),
    name: UIResponder.keyboardWillHideNotification, object: nil)
```

We are the delegate of the text fields, so that we can hear about it when the user taps the Return key in the keyboard. We use that as a signal to dismiss the keyboard, as I suggested earlier:

```
func textFieldShouldReturn(_ tf: UITextField) -> Bool {
    tf.resignFirstResponder()
    return false
}
```

It will help to have on hand a utility function that works out the geometry based on the notification's userInfo dictionary and the bounds of the view we're concerned with (which will be the scroll view). If the keyboard wasn't within the view's bounds and now it will be, it is entering; if it was within the view's bounds and now it won't be, it is exiting. We return that information, along with the keyboard's frame in the view's bounds coordinates:

```
enum KeyboardState {
    case unknown
    case entering
    case exiting
}
func keyboardState(for d:[AnyHashable:Any], in v:UIView?)
    -> (KeyboardState, CGRect?) {
        var rold = d[UIResponder.keyboardFrameBeginUserInfoKey] as! CGRect
        var rnew = d[UIResponder.keyboardFrameEndUserInfoKey] as! CGRect
        var ks : KeyboardState = .unknown
        var newRect : CGRect? = nil
        if let v = v {
            let co = UIScreen.main.coordinateSpace
            rold = co.convert(rold, to:v)
            rnew = co.convert(rnew, to:v)
```

```
            newRect = rnew
            if !rold.intersects(v.bounds) && rnew.intersects(v.bounds) {
                ks = .entering
            }
            if rold.intersects(v.bounds) && !rnew.intersects(v.bounds) {
                ks = .exiting
            }
        }
        return (ks, newRect)
    }
```

We maintain some state variables:

```
var oldContentInset = UIEdgeInsets.zero
var oldIndicatorInset = UIEdgeInsets.zero
var oldOffset = CGPoint.zero
var prevr = CGRect.zero
```

Here's what we do when we get a willShow notification (self.sv is the scroll view):

```
@objc func keyboardShow(_ n:Notification) {
    let d = n.userInfo!
    let (state, rnew) = keyboardState(for:d, in:self.sv)
    if state == .entering { ❶
        self.oldContentInset = self.sv.contentInset
        self.oldIndicatorInset = self.sv.verticalScrollIndicatorInsets
        self.oldOffset = self.sv.contentOffset
    }
    if let rnew = rnew, rnew != self.prevr { ❷
        self.prevr = rnew
        let h = rnew.intersection(self.sv.bounds).height + 6 ❸
        self.sv.contentInset.bottom = h
        self.sv.verticalScrollIndicatorInsets.bottom = h
    }
}
```

❶ We check whether the keyboard is about to enter the bounds of our scroll view; if so, we store the scroll view's current content offset, content inset, and scroll indicator insets.

❷ We deal with the fact that we might get extra willShow notifications, as when the user taps in a different text field. If the keyboard rect hasn't actually changed since the previous willShow notification, there's no point doing anything; that is what my state variable self.prevr is for.

❸ If the keyboard rect *has* changed, we alter the scroll view's insets to match the virtual keyboard (plus a little extra space), allowing the scroll view itself to scroll the first responder into view if needed.

When the keyboard hides, we reverse the process, restoring the saved values:

```
@objc func keyboardHide(_ n:Notification) {
    let d = n.userInfo!
    let (state, _) = keyboardState(for:d, in:self.sv)
    if state == .exiting {
        self.sv.contentOffset = self.oldOffset
        self.sv.verticalScrollIndicatorInsets = self.oldIndicatorInset
        self.sv.contentInset = self.oldContentInset
        self.prevr = .zero
    }
}
```

Behind the scenes, we are inside an animations function at the time that our notifications arrive. This means that our changes to the scroll view are nicely animated in coordination with the keyboard appearing and disappearing.

Under iPad multitasking (Chapter 10), your app can receive keyboard show and hide notifications if *another* app summons or dismisses the keyboard. This makes sense because the keyboard is, after all, covering your app. You can distinguish whether your app was responsible for summoning the keyboard by examining the show notification userInfo dictionary's UIResponder.keyboardIsLocalUserInfoKey; but in general you probably won't have to, provided you handle keyboard notifications coherently in the first place.

Text Field Delegate and Control Event Messages

As editing begins and proceeds in a text field, various messages are sent to the text field's delegate, adopting the UITextFieldDelegate protocol. Some of these messages are also available as notifications. Using them, you can customize the text field's behavior during editing:

textFieldShouldBeginEditing(_:)
> Return false to prevent the text field from becoming first responder.

textFieldDidBeginEditing(_:)
UITextField.textDidBeginEditingNotification
> The text field has become first responder.

textFieldShouldClear(_:)
> Return false to prevent the operation of the Clear button or of automatic clearing on entry (clearsOnBeginEditing). This event is *not* sent when the text is cleared because clearsOnInsertion is true, presumably because the user is not clearing the text but rather changing it.

textFieldShouldReturn(_:)
> The user has tapped the Return button in the keyboard. We have already seen that this can be used as a signal to dismiss the keyboard.

`textFieldDidChangeSelection(_:)`

The text field selection has changed. This happens any time the position of the insertion point or the selection changes for any reason, so this delegate message reports almost any editing action. Merely typing a character changes the selection, because the insertion point position is now greater by one character.

`textField(_:shouldChangeCharactersIn:replacementString:)`
`UITextField.textDidChangeNotification`

The notification is a signal that the user *has* edited the text, but the delegate method is your chance to *interfere* with the user's editing *before* it takes effect. You can return `false` to prevent the proposed change; if you're going to do that, you can replace the user's edit with your own, by changing the text field's text directly (there is no circularity, as this delegate method is not called when you do that). You are *not* notified when the user changes text styling through the Bold, Italics, or Underline menu items.

`textFieldShouldEndEditing(_:)`

Return `false` to prevent the text field from resigning first responder (even if you just sent `resignFirstResponder` to it). You might do this because the text is invalid or unacceptable in some way. The user will not know why the text field is refusing to end editing, so the usual thing is to put up an alert (Chapter 14) explaining the problem.

`textFieldDidEndEditing(_:)`
`UITextField.textDidEndEditingNotification`

The text field has resigned first responder. See "Editable Content in Cells" on page 525 for an example of using the delegate method to fetch the text field's current text and store it in the model.

The `shouldChangeCharactersIn` delegate method is of particular interest, because it's your chance to filter what the user can enter into the text field. In this example, the user can enter only lowercase characters (the `insertText` method comes from the UIKeyInput protocol, which UITextField adopts):

```
func textField(_ textField: UITextField,
    shouldChangeCharactersIn range: NSRange,
    replacementString string: String) -> Bool {
        if string.isEmpty { // backspace
            return true
        }
        let lc = string.lowercased()
        textField.insertText(lc)
        return false
}
```

As the example shows, you can distinguish whether the user is typing or pasting, on the one hand, or backspacing or cutting, on the other; in the latter case, the replacement string will be empty.

In this example, we want to limit (to a maximum of 10) the number of characters the user can enter:

```
func textField(_ textField: UITextField,
    shouldChangeCharactersIn range: NSRange,
    replacementString string: String) -> Bool {
        if string.isEmpty { // backspace
            return true
        }
        let text = textField.text ?? ""
        guard let rangeSwift = Range(range, in: text) else { return true }
        let stringToReplace = text[rangeSwift]
        let result = text.replacingCharacters(in: rangeSwift, with: string)
        return result.count <= 10
}
```

A text field is also a control (UIControl; see Chapter 13). That means you can attach a target–action pair to any of the events that it reports in order to receive a message when that event occurs. Of the various control event messages emitted by a text field, the two most useful (in my experience) are:

Editing Changed (`.editingChanged`*)*

Sent after the user performs any editing. If your goal is to respond to changes, rather than to forestall them, this is a better way than the delegate method `text-Field(_:shouldChangeCharactersIn:replacementString:)`, because it arrives at the right moment, namely *after* the change has occurred, and because it can detect attributes changes, which the delegate method can't do.

Did End on Exit (`.editingDidEndOnExit`*)*

Sent when the user taps the Return button in the text field's keyboard. Surprisingly, if this control event is configured to trigger an action message, the keyboard is dismissed *automatically* — even if the action method does nothing. In fact, the action method doesn't even have to exist! The action can be `nil`-targeted. There is no penalty for implementing a `nil`-targeted action that walks up the responder chain without finding a method that handles it.

In this example, I use the Did End on Exit control event to create a UITextField subclass that *automatically dismisses itself* when the user taps Return:

```
@objc protocol Dummy {
    func dummy(_ sender: Any)
}
class MyTextField: UITextField {
    required init?(coder: NSCoder) {
        super.init(coder:coder)
```

```
        self.addTarget(nil,
            action:#selector(Dummy.dummy), for:.editingDidEndOnExit)
    }
}
```

You can configure the same thing in the nib editor. Edit the First Responder proxy object in the Attributes inspector, adding a new First Responder Action; call it dummy:. Now hook the Did End on Exit event of the text field to the dummy: action of the First Responder proxy object.

Text Field Menu

When the user double taps or long presses in a text field, a menu appears. It contains menu items such as Select, Select All, Paste, Copy, Cut, and Replace; which menu items appear depends on the circumstances. Many of the selectors for these standard menu items are listed in the UIResponderStandardEditActions protocol. Commonly used standard actions are:

- cut(_:)
- copy(_:)
- select(_:)
- selectAll(_:)
- paste(_:)
- delete(_:)
- toggleBoldface(_:)
- toggleItalics(_:)
- toggleUnderline(_:)

Some other menu items are known only through their Objective-C selectors:

- _promptForReplace:
- _define:
- _showTextStyleOptions:

The menu can be customized; this involves setting the shared UIMenuController object's menuItems property to an array of UIMenuItem instances representing the menu items that may appear in addition to those that the system puts there.

Actions for menu items are nil-targeted, so they percolate up the responder chain. You can implement a menu item's action anywhere up the responder chain; if you do this for a standard menu item at a point in the responder chain before the system receives it, you can interfere with and customize what it does. You govern the

presence or absence of a menu item by implementing the UIResponder method can-
PerformAction(_:withSender:) in the responder chain.

To illustrate, we'll devise a text field whose menu includes our own menu item,
Expand. I'm imagining a text field where the user can select a U.S. state's two-letter
abbreviation (such as "CA") and can then summon the menu and tap Expand to
replace it with the state's full name (such as "California"). I'll implement this in a
UITextField subclass called MyTextField, in order to guarantee that the Expand
menu item will be available when an instance of this subclass is first responder, but at
no other time.

At some moment before the user taps in an instance of MyTextField (such as our
view controller's viewDidLoad), we modify the global menu:

```
let mi = UIMenuItem(title:"Expand", action:#selector(MyTextField.expand))
let mc = UIMenuController.shared
mc.menuItems = [mi]
```

The text field subclass has a property, self.list, which has been set to a dictionary
whose keys are state name abbreviations and whose values are the corresponding
state names. A utility function looks up an abbreviation in the dictionary:

```
func state(for abbrev:String) -> String? {
    return self.list[abbrev.uppercased()]
}
```

We implement canPerformAction(_:withSender:) to govern the contents of the
menu. Let's presume that we want our Expand menu item to be present only if the
selection consists of a two-letter state abbreviation. UITextField conforms to the
UITextInput protocol, which lets us learn the selected text:

```
override func canPerformAction(_ action: Selector,
    withSender sender: Any?) -> Bool {
        if action == #selector(expand) {
            if let r = self.selectedTextRange, let s = self.text(in:r) {
                return (s.count == 2 && self.state(for:s) != nil)
            }
        }
        return super.canPerformAction(action, withSender:sender)
}
```

When the user chooses the Expand menu item, the expand message is sent up the responder chain. We catch it in our UITextField subclass and obey it by replacing the
selected text with the corresponding state name:

```
@objc func expand(_ sender: Any) {
    if let r = self.selectedTextRange, let s = self.text(in:r) {
        if let ss = self.state(for:s) {
            self.replace(r, withText:ss)
        }
    }
}
```

We can also implement the selector for, and modify the behavior of, any of the standard menu items. Here, I'll implement `copy(_:)` and modify its behavior. First we call `super` to get standard copying behavior; then we modify what's now on the pasteboard:

```
override func copy(_ sender: Any?) {
    super.copy(sender)
    let pb = UIPasteboard.general
    if let s = pb.string {
        let ss = // ... alter s here ...
        pb.string = ss
    }
}
```

Drag and Drop

A text field implements drag and drop (Chapter 10) by way of the UITextDraggable and UITextDroppable protocols. By default, a text field's text is draggable, but you can set the `isEnabled` property of its `textDragInteraction` to change that. If a text field's text is draggable, then by default its dragged text can be dropped within the same text field.

To customize a text field's drag and drop behavior, provide a `textDragDelegate` (UITextDragDelegate) or `textDropDelegate` (UITextDropDelegate) and implement any of their various methods. You can change the drag preview, change the drag items, and so forth. To turn a text field's droppability on or off depending on some condition, give it a `textDropDelegate` and implement `textDroppableView(_:proposalForDrop:)` to return an appropriate UITextDropProposal.

Keyboard and Input Configuration

There are various ways to configure the virtual keyboard that appears when a text field becomes first responder. This configuration is performed through properties, not of the keyboard, but of the text field.

Text input traits

A UITextField adopts the UITextInputTraits protocol. This protocol's properties customize physical features and behaviors of the keyboard, as well as the text field's response to input (and these properties can also be set in the nib editor):

- Set the `keyboardType` to choose one of many alternate built-in keyboard layouts. For instance, set it to `.numberPad` to make the virtual keyboard for this text field consist of digits.

  Setting the keyboard type does *not* dictate what characters the user can enter into this text field. On an iPhone, even with a `.numberPad` keyboard type, the user can paste letters or type them with an external keyboard; on an iPad, the user can switch the `.numberPad` keyboard to show letters. To limit what characters can be entered into a text field, use the `textField(_:shouldChangeCharacters-In:replacementString:)` delegate method that I described earlier.

- Set the `returnKeyType` to determine the text of the Return key (if the keyboard is of a type that has one).

- Give the keyboard a dark or light shade (`keyboardAppearance`).

- Turn off autocapitalization or autocorrection (`autocapitalizationType`, `autocorrectionType`).

- Use or don't use smart quotes, smart dashes, and smart spaces during insertion and deletion (`smartQuotesType`, `smartDashesType`, `smartInsertDeleteType`).

- Make the Return key disable itself if the text field has no content (`enablesReturn-KeyAutomatically`).

- Make the text field a password field (`secureTextEntry`).

- Set the `textContentType` to assist the system in making semantically appropriate spelling and autofill suggestions.

Accessory view

You can attach an accessory view to the top of the keyboard by setting the text field's `inputAccessoryView`. For instance, an accessory view containing a button can serve as a way to let the user dismiss keyboards whose type has no Return key, such as `.numberPad`, `.phonePad`, and `.decimalPad`.

Figure 11-13 shows a `.phonePad` keyboard. It has no Return key, so we've added a Done button in its accessory view. The accessory view itself is designed in a view *.xib* file. We (the view controller) are the text field's delegate; when the text field becomes first responder, we configure the keyboard:

```
func textFieldDidBeginEditing(_ tf: UITextField) {
    self.currentField = tf // keep track of first responder
    let arr =
        UINib(nibName:"AccessoryView", bundle:nil).instantiate(withOwner:nil)
    let accessoryView = arr[0] as! UIView
    let b = accessoryView.subviews[0] as! UIButton
    b.addTarget(self, action:#selector(doNextButton), for:.touchUpInside)
    let b2 = accessoryView.subviews[1] as! UIButton
```

Figure 11-13. A phonePad keyboard with an accessory view

```
    b2.addTarget(self, action:#selector(doDone), for:.touchUpInside)
    tf.inputAccessoryView = accessoryView
    tf.keyboardAppearance = .dark
    tf.keyboardType = .phonePad
}
```

When the Done button is tapped, we dismiss the keyboard:

```
@objc func doDone(_ sender: Any) {
    self.currentField = nil
    self.view.endEditing(false)
}
```

The Next button lets the user navigate to the next text field. I have an array property (`self.textFields`) populated with references to all the text fields in the interface. My `textFieldDidBeginEditing` implementation stores a reference to the current text field in a property (`self.currentField`), because in order to determine the *next* text field, I need to know which one is *this* text field:

```
@objc func doNextButton(_ sender: Any) {
    var ix = self.textFields.firstIndex(of:self.currentField)!
    ix = (ix + 1) % self.textFields.count
    let v = self.textFields[ix]
    v.becomeFirstResponder()
}
```

Input view

Going even further, you can replace the system keyboard entirely with a view of your own creation. This is done by setting the text field's `inputView`. For best results, the custom view should be a UIInputView, and ideally it should be the `inputView` (and `view`) of a UIInputViewController. The input view controller needs to be retained, but not as a child view controller in the view controller hierarchy; the keyboard is not one of your app's views, but is layered by the system in front of your app. The input view's contents might imitate a standard system keyboard, or may consist of any interface you like.

An input view controller, used in this way, is also the key to supplying *other* apps with a keyboard. See the "Custom Keyboard" chapter of Apple's *App Extension Programming Guide* in the documentation archive.

To illustrate, I'll implement a standard beginner example: I'll replace a text field's keyboard with a UIPickerView. Here's the input view controller, MyPickerVC. Its viewDidLoad puts the UIPickerView into the inputView and positions it with auto-layout constraints:

```
class MyPickerVC : UIInputViewController {
    override func viewDidLoad() {
        let iv = self.inputView!
        iv.translatesAutoresizingMaskIntoConstraints = false
        let p = UIPickerView()
        p.delegate = self
        p.dataSource = self
        iv.addSubview(p)
        p.translatesAutoresizingMaskIntoConstraints = false
        NSLayoutConstraint.activate([
            p.topAnchor.constraint(equalTo: iv.topAnchor),
            p.bottomAnchor.constraint(equalTo: iv.bottomAnchor),
            p.leadingAnchor.constraint(equalTo: iv.leadingAnchor),
            p.trailingAnchor.constraint(equalTo: iv.trailingAnchor),
        ])
    }
}
extension MyPickerVC : UIPickerViewDelegate, UIPickerViewDataSource {
    // ...
}
```

The text field itself is configured in our main view controller:

```
class ViewController: UIViewController {
    @IBOutlet weak var tf: UITextField!
    let pvc = MyPickerVC()
    override func viewDidLoad() {
        super.viewDidLoad()
        self.tf.inputView = self.pvc.inputView
    }
}
```

It is also possible to use an input view controller to manage a text field's input-AccessoryView. To do that, you set the text field's inputAccessoryViewController instead of its inputAccessoryView. To do *that*, you have to subclass UITextField to give it a writable inputAccessoryViewController (because this property, as inherited from UIResponder, is read-only):

```
class MyTextField : UITextField {
    var _iavc : UIInputViewController?
    override var inputAccessoryViewController: UIInputViewController? {
        get {
            return self._iavc
```

```
        }
        set {
            self._iavc = newValue
        }
    }
}
```

Let's use that feature to give the user a way to dismiss the "keyboard" consisting entirely of a UIPickerView. We'll attach a Done button as the text field's accessory input view and manage it with another input view controller, MyDoneButtonVC. I'll configure the button much as I configured the picker view, by putting it into the input view controller's inputView:

```
class MyDoneButtonVC : UIInputViewController {
    weak var delegate : UIViewController?
    override func viewDidLoad() {
        let iv = self.inputView!
        iv.translatesAutoresizingMaskIntoConstraints = false
        iv.allowsSelfSizing = true // crucial
        let b = UIButton(type: .system)
        b.tintColor = .black
        b.setTitle("Done", for: .normal)
        b.sizeToFit()
        b.addTarget(self, action: #selector(doDone), for: .touchUpInside)
        b.backgroundColor = UIColor.lightGray
        iv.addSubview(b)
        b.translatesAutoresizingMaskIntoConstraints = false
        NSLayoutConstraint.activate([
            b.topAnchor.constraint(equalTo: iv.topAnchor),
            b.bottomAnchor.constraint(equalTo: iv.bottomAnchor),
            b.leadingAnchor.constraint(equalTo: iv.leadingAnchor),
            b.trailingAnchor.constraint(equalTo: iv.trailingAnchor),
        ])
    }
    @objc func doDone() {
        if let del = self.delegate {
            (del as AnyObject).doDone?()
        }
    }
}
```

Now our main view controller configures the text field like this:

```
class ViewController: UIViewController {
    @IBOutlet weak var tf: UITextField!
    let pvc = MyPickerVC()
    let mdbvc = MyDoneButtonVC()
    override func viewDidLoad() {
        super.viewDidLoad()
        self.tf.inputView = self.pvc.inputView
```

```
        (self.tf as! MyTextField).inputAccessoryViewController = self.mdbvc
        self.mdbvc.delegate = self
    }
}
```

When the Done button is tapped, MyDoneButtonVC's doDone method is called. It, in turn, calls the doDone method of its delegate, if there is one. Its delegate is our original ViewController, which can implement doDone to set the text of the text field and dismiss the keyboard.

An important advantage of using an input view controller is that it is a view controller. Despite not being part of the app's view controller hierarchy, it is sent standard view controller messages such as viewDidLayoutSubviews and traitCollectionDid-Change, allowing you to respond coherently to rotation and other changes.

Input view without a text field

With only a slight modification, you can use the techniques described in the preceding section to present a custom input view to the user *without* the user editing any text field. Suppose we have a label in our interface; we can allow the user to tap a button to summon our custom input view and use that input to change the text of the label. (See Figure 11-14; as usual, my example revolves around letting the user specify one of the Pep Boys.)

The trick here is that the relevant UITextField properties and methods are all inherited from UIResponder — and a UIViewController is a UIResponder. All we have to do is override our view controller's canBecomeFirstResponder to return true, and then call its becomeFirstResponder — just like a text field. If the view controller has overridden inputView, our custom input view will appear as the virtual keyboard. If the view controller has overridden inputAccessoryView or inputAccessoryView-Controller, the accessory view will be attached to that keyboard.

Here's an implementation of that scenario. Normally, our view controller's can-BecomeFirstResponder returns false, so that the input view won't appear. But when the user taps the button in our interface, we switch to returning true and call become-FirstResponder. Presto, the input view appears along with the accessory view, because we've also overridden inputView and inputAccessoryViewController. When the user taps the Done button in the accessory view, we update the label and dismiss the keyboard:

```
class ViewController: UIViewController {
    @IBOutlet weak var lab: UILabel!
    let pvc = MyPickerVC()
    let mdbvc = MyDoneButtonVC()
    override func viewDidLoad() {
        super.viewDidLoad()
        self.mdbvc.delegate = self // for dismissal
```

Figure 11-14. Editing a label with a custom input view

```
    }
    var showKeyboard = false
    override var canBecomeFirstResponder: Bool {
        return showKeyboard
    }
    override var inputView: UIView? {
        return self.pvc.inputView
    }
    override var inputAccessoryViewController: UIInputViewController? {
        return self.mdbvc
    }
    @IBAction func doPickBoy(_ sender: Any) { // button in the interface
        self.showKeyboard = true
        self.becomeFirstResponder()
    }
    @objc func doDone() { // user tapped Done button in accessory view
        self.lab.text = pvc.currentPep // update label
        self.resignFirstResponder() // dismiss keyboard
        self.showKeyboard = false
    }
}
```

Shortcuts bar

On the iPad, the shortcuts bar appears along with spelling suggestions at the top of the keyboard. You can customize it by adding bar button items.

The shortcuts bar is the text field's inputAssistantItem (inherited from UIResponder), and it has leadingBarButtonGroups and trailingBarButtonGroups. A button group is a UIBarButtonItemGroup, an array of UIBarButtonItems along with an optional representativeItem to be shown if there isn't room for the whole array; if the representative item has no target–action pair, tapping it will summon a popover containing the actual group.

In this example, we add a Camera bar button item to the right (trailing) side of the shortcuts bar for our text field (`self.tf`):

```
let bbi = UIBarButtonItem(
    barButtonSystemItem: .camera, target: self, action: #selector(doCamera))
let group = UIBarButtonItemGroup(
    barButtonItems: [bbi], representativeItem: nil)
let shortcuts = self.tf.inputAssistantItem
shortcuts.trailingBarButtonGroups.append(group)
```

Keyboard language

Suppose your app performs a Russian dictionary lookup. It would be nice to be able to force the keyboard to appear as Russian in conjunction with your text field. But you can't. You can't access the Russian keyboard unless the user has explicitly enabled it; and even if the user *has* explicitly enabled it, your text field can only express a preference as to the language in which the keyboard initially appears. To do so, override your view controller's `textInputMode` property along these lines:

```
override var textInputMode: UITextInputMode? {
    for tim in UITextInputMode.activeInputModes {
        if tim.primaryLanguage == "ru-RU" {
            return tim
        }
    }
    return super.textInputMode
}
```

Another keyboard language–related property is `textInputContextIdentifier`. You can use this to ensure that the runtime remembers the language to which the keyboard was set the last time each text field was edited. To do so, override `textInput-ContextIdentifier` in your view controller as a computed variable whose getter fetches the value of a stored variable, and set that stored variable to some appropriate unique value whenever the editing context changes, whatever that may mean for your app.

Text Views

A text view (UITextView) is a scroll view subclass (UIScrollView); it is *not* a control. It displays multiline text, possibly scrollable, possibly editable. Many of its properties are similar to those of a text field:

- A text view has `text`, `font`, `textColor`, and `textAlignment` properties.

- A text view has `attributedText`, `allowsEditingTextAttributes`, and `typing-Attributes` properties, as well as `clearsOnInsertion`.

- An editable text view governs its keyboard just as a text field does: when it is first responder, it is being edited and shows the keyboard, and it adopts the UIText-Input protocol and has `inputView` and `inputAccessoryView` properties.
- A text view's menu works the same way as a text field's.
- A text view implements drag and drop similarly to a text field.

A text view can be editable or not, according to its `isEditable` property. You can do things with a noneditable text view that you can't do otherwise, as I'll explain later. A text field can be selectable without being editable, if its `isEditable` property is `false` but its `isSelectable` property is `true`; in that case, the user can select text and copy it.

A text view is a scroll view, so everything you know about scroll views applies (see Chapter 7). It can be scrollable (by the user) or not. Its `contentSize` is maintained for you automatically as the text changes, so as to contain the text exactly; if the text view is scrollable, the user can see any of its text. The text view's delegate (UITextView-Delegate) is its scroll view delegate (UIScrollViewDelegate). A text view has a `scroll-RangeToVisible(_:)` method so that you can scroll in terms of a range of its text.

A text view provides information about, and control of, its selection: it has a `selectedRange` property which you can get and set.

A text view's delegate messages (UITextViewDelegate) and notifications are similar to those of a text field. The following delegate methods and notifications should have a familiar ring:

- `textViewShouldBeginEditing(_:)`
- `textViewDidBeginEditing(_:)`
  `UITextView.textDidBeginEditingNotification`
- `textViewShouldEndEditing(_:)`
- `textViewDidEndEditing(_:)`
  `UITextView.textDidEndEditingNotification`
- `textView(_:shouldChangeTextIn:replacementText:)`
- `textViewDidChange(_:)`
  `UITextView.textDidChangeNotification`

Links, Text Attachments, and Data

A link is a stretch of attributed text to which the `.link` attribute has been applied. The default appearance of links in a text view is determined by the text view's `link-TextAttributes`. By default, this is a bluish color with no underline, but you can change it. Alternatively, you can apply any desired attributes to the individual links in the text view's `attributedText`; in that case, set the text view's `linkTextAttributes` to an empty dictionary to prevent it from overriding the individual link attributes.

The user can tap on a link, or on a text attachment, if the text view is selectable but not editable. The text view's delegate can then decide how to respond to the tap:

`textView(_:shouldInteractWith:in:interaction:)`
> The third parameter is a range. The last parameter tells you what the user is doing (UITextItemInteraction):
>
> - `.invokeDefaultAction` means tap.
> - `.presentActions` means long press.
> - `.preview` means 3D touch, but in iOS 13 and later it won't occur.

That delegate method comes in two forms:

The second parameter is a URL
> The user is interacting with a link. The default return value, if you don't implement the delegate method, is `true`.

The second parameter is an NSTextAttachment
> The user is interacting with an inline image. The default return value, if you don't implement the delegate method, is `false`.

If you implement this delegate method and return `true`, you get a default response. By returning `false`, you can prevent interaction; but you can also substitute your own response, effectively treating the link or image as a button.

Default responses when the second parameter is a URL are:

`.invokeDefaultAction`
> The URL is opened in Safari.

`.presentActions`
> A UIMenu is presented, previewing the URL, with menu items Open Link, Add to Reading List, Copy Link, and Share. The user can tap the preview to open the URL in Safari.

Default responses when the second parameter is a text attachment are:

`.invokeDefaultAction`
> Nothing happens.

`.presentActions`
> A UIMenu is presented, previewing the image, with menu items Copy Image and Save to Camera Roll. Tapping the preview dismisses the menu.

A text view also has a dataDetectorTypes property; if the text view is selectable but not editable, this allows text of these types, specified as a UIDataDetectorTypes bit-mask (and presumably located using NSDataDetector), to be treated as tappable links.

textView(_:shouldInteractWith:in:interaction:) will catch these taps as well; the second parameter will be a URL, but it won't necessarily be much use to you. You can distinguish a phone number through the URL's scheme (it will be "tel"), and the rest of the URL is the phone number; but other types will be more or less opaque (the scheme is "x-apple-data-detectors"). More important, you have the range, so you can obtain the tapped text. You can return true for the default response, or return false and substitute your own response. Some common UIDataDetectorTypes are:

.phoneNumber
>   Default responses are:
>
>   .invokeDefaultAction
>   >   An alert is presented, with an option to call the number.
>
>   .presentActions
>   >   A UIMenu presented, with menu items Call, FaceTime Audio, FaceTime, Send Message, Add to Contacts, and Copy.

.address
>   Default responses are:
>
>   .invokeDefaultAction
>   >   The address is looked up in the Maps app.
>
>   .presentActions
>   >   A UIMenu is presented, with menu items Get Directions, Open in Maps, Add to Contacts, and Copy Address, and a preview displaying a map showing the address if possible.

.calendarEvent
>   Default responses are:
>
>   .invokeDefaultAction
>   >   An action sheet is presented, with menu items Create Event, Create Reminder, Show in Calendar, and Copy Event.
>
>   .presentActions
>   >   A UIMenu is presented, with the same menu items as the default action, along with a preview showing the relevant time in the user's Calendar.

(There are three more data detector types: .shipmentTrackingNumber, .flightNumber, and .lookupSuggestion.)

Self-Sizing Text View

On some occasions, you may want a *self-sizing* text view — that is, a text view that adjusts its height automatically to embrace the amount of text it contains.

The simplest approach, under autolayout, is to prevent the text view from scrolling by setting its isScrollEnabled to false. The text view now has an *intrinsic content size* — and will behave just like a label ("Fitting Label to Text" on page 675). Pin the top and sides of the text view, and the bottom will shift automatically to accommodate the content as the user types. In effect, you've made a cross between a label and a text field: like a label, there are multiple lines and the height adjusts to fit the text; but like a text field, the user can edit the text.

To put a limit on how tall a self-sizing text view can grow, keep track of the height of its contentSize (perhaps in viewDidLayoutSubviews) and, if it gets too big, set the text view's isScrollEnabled to true and constrain its height.

Text View and Keyboard

The fact that a text view is a scroll view comes in handy when the keyboard partially covers a text view. The text view usually dominates the screen, and you can respond to the keyboard partially covering it by adjusting the text view's contentInset and scrollIndicatorInsets, exactly as we did earlier in this chapter with a scroll view containing a text field ("Keyboard Covers Text Field" on page 682). There is no need to worry about the text view's contentOffset; the text view will scroll as needed to reveal the insertion point as the keyboard shows, and will scroll itself correctly as the keyboard hides.

How is the keyboard to be dismissed? The Return key is meaningful for character entry, so you won't want to use it to dismiss the keyboard. On the iPad, there is usually a separate button in the keyboard that dismisses the keyboard, solving the problem; on the iPhone there might be no such button.

On the iPhone, the interface might consist of a text view and the keyboard, which is *always* showing. Instead of dismissing the keyboard, the user dismisses the entire interface. In Apple's Mail app on the iPhone, when the user is composing a message, the keyboard is present; if the user taps Cancel or Send, the mail composition interface is dismissed and so is the keyboard.

Alternatively, you can provide interface for dismissing the keyboard explicitly. In Apple's Notes app, when a note is being edited, the keyboard is present and a Done button appears; the user taps the Done button to dismiss the keyboard. If there's no good place to put a Done button in the interface, you could attach an accessory view to the keyboard itself, as I did in an earlier example.

Also, being a scroll view, a text view has a `keyboardDismissMode`. By setting this to `.interactive` or `.onDrag`, you can permit the user to hide the keyboard by scrolling or dragging. Apple does that in both the Mail app and the Notes app.

Text Kit

Text Kit comes originally from macOS, where you may already be more familiar with it than you realize. Much of the text-editing "magic" of Xcode itself is due to Text Kit; and the TextEdit app is just a thin wrapper around Text Kit. Text Kit comprises a small group of classes that are responsible for drawing text; simply put, they turn an NSAttributedString into graphics. You can take advantage of Text Kit to modify text drawing in ways that were once possible only by dipping down to the low-level C-based world of Core Text.

Text Kit has three chief classes: NSTextStorage, NSLayoutManager, and NSTextContainer. Instances of these three classes join to form a "stack" of objects that allow Text Kit to operate. In the minimal and most common case, a text storage has a layout manager, and a layout manager has a text container, forming the "stack."

Here's what the three chief Text Kit classes do:

NSTextStorage
> A subclass of NSMutableAttributedString. It is, or holds, the underlying text. It has one or more layout managers, and notifies them when the text changes.
>
> By subclassing and delegation (NSTextStorageDelegate), a text storage's behavior can be modified so that it applies attributes in a custom fashion.

NSLayoutManager
> This is the master text drawing class. It has one or more text containers, and is owned by a text storage. It draws the text storage's text into the boundaries defined by the text container(s).
>
> A layout manager can have a delegate (NSLayoutManagerDelegate), and can be subclassed. This, as you may well imagine, is a powerful and sophisticated class.

NSTextContainer
> Owned by a layout manager; helps that layout manager by defining the region in which the text is to be laid out. It does this in three primary ways:

> *Size*
>> The text container's top left is the origin for the text layout coordinate system, and the text will be laid out within the text container's rectangle.

Exclusion paths
> The `exclusionPaths` property consists of UIBezierPath objects within which no text is to be drawn.

Subclassing
> By subclassing, you can place each chunk of text drawing anywhere at all (except inside an exclusion path).

Text View and Text Kit

A UITextView provides direct access to the underlying Text Kit engine. It has the following Text Kit–related properties:

`textContainer`
> The text view's text container (an NSTextContainer instance). UITextView's designated initializer is `init(frame:textContainer:)`; the `textContainer:` can be `nil` to get a default text container, or you can supply your own custom text container.

`textContainerInset`
> The margins of the text container, designating the area within the `contentSize` rectangle in which the text as a whole is drawn. Changing this value changes the margins immediately, causing the text to be freshly laid out. The default is a top and bottom of 8.

`layoutManager`
> The text view's layout manager (an NSLayoutManager instance).

`textStorage`
> The text view's text storage (an NSTextStorage instance).

When you initialize a text view with a custom text container, you hand it the entire "stack" of Text Kit instances, the stack is retained, and the text view is operative. The simplest case might look like this:

```
let r = // ... frame for the new text view
let lm = NSLayoutManager()
let ts = NSTextStorage()
ts.addLayoutManager(lm)
let tc = NSTextContainer(size:CGSize(r.width, .greatestFiniteMagnitude))
lm.addTextContainer(tc)
let tv = UITextView(frame:r, textContainer:tc)
```

Text Container

An NSTextContainer has a `size`, within which the text will be drawn.

In a text view, by default, the text container's width is the width of the text view, while its height is effectively infinite, allowing the drawing of the text to grow vertically but not horizontally beyond the bounds of the text view, and making it possible to scroll the text vertically.

NSTextContainer also has `heightTracksTextView` and `widthTracksTextView` properties, causing the text container to be resized to match changes in the size of the text view — if the text view is resized because of interface rotation, for instance. By default, as you might expect, `widthTracksTextView` is `true`, while `heightTracksText-View` is `false`: the text fills the width of the text view, and is laid out freshly if the text view's width changes, but its height remains effectively infinite. The text view itself configures its own `contentSize` so that the user can scroll just to the bottom of the existing text.

When you change a text view's `textContainerInset`, it modifies its text container's size as necessary. In the default configuration, this means that it modifies the text container's width; the top and bottom insets are implemented through the text container's position within the content rect. Within the text container, additional side margins are imposed by the text container's `lineFragmentPadding`; the default is 5, but you can change it.

If the text view's `isScrollEnabled` is `false`, then by default its text container's `heightTracksTextView` and `widthTracksTextView` are both `true`, and the text container size is adjusted so that the text fills the text view. In that case, you can also set the text container's `lineBreakMode`. This works like the line break mode of a UILabel: for instance, if the line break mode is `.byTruncatingTail`, then the last line has an ellipsis at the end (if the text is too long for the text view). You can also set the text container's `maximumNumberOfLines`, which is like a UILabel's `numberOfLines`. In effect, you've turned the text view into a label!

But a nonscrolling text view isn't *just* a label, because you've got access to the Text Kit stack that backs it. For example, you can apply exclusion paths to the text container. Figure 11-15 shows a case in point. The text wraps in longer and longer lines, and then in shorter and shorter lines, because there's an exclusion path on the right side of the text container that's a rectangle with a large V-shaped indentation.

In Figure 11-15, the text view (`self.tv`) is initially configured in the view controller's `viewDidLoad`:

Figure 11-15. A text view with an exclusion path

```
self.tv.attributedText = // ...
self.tv.textContainerInset =
    UIEdgeInsets(top: 20, left: 20, bottom: 20, right: 0)
self.tv.isScrollEnabled = false
```

The exclusion path is then drawn and applied in `viewDidLayoutSubviews`:

```
override func viewDidLayoutSubviews() {
    let sz = self.tv.textContainer.size
    let p = UIBezierPath()
    p.move(to: CGPoint(sz.width/4.0,0))
    p.addLine(to: CGPoint(sz.width,0))
    p.addLine(to: CGPoint(sz.width,sz.height))
    p.addLine(to: CGPoint(sz.width/4.0,sz.height))
    p.addLine(to: CGPoint(sz.width,sz.height/2.0))
    p.close()
    self.tv.textContainer.exclusionPaths = [p]
}
```

You can also subclass NSTextContainer to modify the rectangle in which the layout manager wants to position a piece of text. (Each piece of text is actually a line fragment; I'll explain in the next section what a line fragment is.) In Figure 11-16, the text is inside a circle.

The text displayed in the text view is an attributed string (NSAttributedString), and I have given its paragraph style a `lineBreakMode` of `.byCharWrapping`, to bring the right edge of each line as close as possible to the circular shape. I have constructed the text view's Text Kit stack by hand, to include an instance of my NSTextContainer subclass:

Figure 11-16. A text view with a subclassed text container

```
let r = self.tv.frame
let lm = NSLayoutManager()
let ts = NSTextStorage()
ts.addLayoutManager(lm)
let tc = MyTextContainer(size:CGSize(r.width, r.height))
lm.addTextContainer(tc)
let tv = UITextView(frame:r, textContainer:tc)
```

Here's my NSTextContainer subclass; it overrides just one property and one method, to dictate the rect of each line fragment:

```
class MyTextContainer : NSTextContainer {
    override var isSimpleRectangularTextContainer : Bool { return false }
    override func lineFragmentRect(forProposedRect proposedRect: CGRect,
        at characterIndex: Int,
        writingDirection baseWritingDirection: NSWritingDirection,
        remaining remainingRect: UnsafeMutablePointer<CGRect>?) -> CGRect {
            var result = super.lineFragmentRect(
                forProposedRect:proposedRect, at:characterIndex,
                writingDirection:baseWritingDirection,
                remaining:remainingRect)
            let r = self.size.height / 2.0
            // convert initial y so that circle is centered at origin
            let y = r - result.origin.y
            let theta = asin(y/r)
            let x = r * cos(theta)
            // convert resulting x from circle centered at origin
            let offset = self.size.width / 2.0 - r
            result.origin.x = r-x+offset
            result.size.width = 2*x
            return result
    }
}
```

| Twas brillig, and the slithy toves did gyre and gimble in the wabe; all mimsy were the borogoves, and the mome raths outgrabe. Beware the Jabberwock, my son! The jaws that bite, the claws that catch! Beware the Jubjub bird, and shun the frumious | Bandersnatch! He took his vorpal sword in hand: long time the manxome foe he sought — so rested he by the Tumtum tree, and stood awhile in thought. And as in uffish thought he stood, the Jabberwock, with eyes of flame, came whif- |

Figure 11-17. A layout manager with two text containers

Alternative Text Kit Stack Architectures

The default Text Kit stack consists of one text storage, which has one layout manager, which has one text container. But a text storage can have multiple layout managers, and a layout manager can have multiple text containers. What's that all about?

Multiple text containers

If one layout manager has multiple text containers, the overflow from each text container is drawn in the next one. In Figure 11-17, there are two text views; the text has filled the first text view, and has then continued by flowing into and filling the second text view. As far as I can tell, the text views can't be made editable in this configuration; but clearly this is a way to achieve a multicolumn or multipage layout, or you could use text views of different sizes for a magazine-style layout.

It is possible to achieve that arrangement by disconnecting the layout managers of existing text views from their text containers and rebuilding the stack from below. In this example, though, I'll build the entire stack by hand:

```
let r = // frame
let r2 = // frame
let mas = // content
let ts1 = NSTextStorage(attributedString:mas)
let lm1 = NSLayoutManager()
ts1.addLayoutManager(lm1)
let tc1 = NSTextContainer(size:r.size)
lm1.addTextContainer(tc1)
let tv = UITextView(frame:r, textContainer:tc1)
let tc2 = NSTextContainer(size:r2.size)
lm1.addTextContainer(tc2)
let tv2 = UITextView(frame:r2, textContainer:tc2)
```

Figure 11-18. A text storage with two layout managers

Multiple layout managers

If one text storage has multiple layout managers, then each layout manager is laying out the same text. In Figure 11-18, there are two text views displaying the same text. The remarkable thing is that if you edit one text view, the other changes to match. (That's how Xcode lets you edit the same code file in different windows, tabs, or panes.)

Again, this arrangement is probably best achieved by building the entire text stack by hand:

```
let r = // frame
let r2 = // frame
let mas = // content
let ts1 = NSTextStorage(attributedString:mas)
let lm1 = NSLayoutManager()
ts1.addLayoutManager(lm1)
let lm2 = NSLayoutManager()
ts1.addLayoutManager(lm2)
let tc1 = NSTextContainer(size:r.size)
let tc2 = NSTextContainer(size:r2.size)
lm1.addTextContainer(tc1)
lm2.addTextContainer(tc2)
let tv = UITextView(frame:r, textContainer:tc1)
let tv2 = UITextView(frame:r2, textContainer:tc2)
```

Layout Manager

The first thing to know about a layout manager is the geometry in which it thinks. To envision a layout manager's geometrical world, think in terms of glyphs and line fragments:

Glyph

The drawn analog of a character. The correspondence is not one-to-one; multiple glyphs can correspond to one character, and multiple characters can correspond to one glyph. The layout manager's job is to translate the characters into glyphs, get those glyphs from a font, and draw them.

Line fragment

A rectangle in which glyphs are drawn, one after another. (The reason it's a line *fragment*, and not simply a line, is that a line might be interrupted by the text container's exclusion paths.)

A glyph has a location in terms of the line fragment into which it is drawn. A line fragment's coordinates are in terms of the text container. The layout manager can convert between these coordinate systems, and between text and glyphs:

- Given a range of text in the text storage, the layout manager knows where the corresponding glyphs are drawn in the text container.

- Conversely, given a location in the text container, the layout manager knows what glyph is drawn there and what range of text in the text storage that glyph represents.

What's missing from that geometry is what, if anything, the text container corresponds to in the real world. A text container is not, itself, a real rectangle in the real world; it's just a class that tells the layout manager a size to draw into. Making that rectangle meaningful for drawing purposes is up to some *other* class outside the Text Kit stack.

A UITextView is a case in point. It has a text container, which it shares with a layout manager. The text view knows how its own content is scrolled and how the rectangle represented by its text container is inset within that scrolling content. The layout manager doesn't know anything about that; it sees the text container as a purely theoretical rectangular boundary. Only when the layout manager actually draws does it make contact with the real world of some graphics context — and it must be told, on those occasions, how the text container's rectangle is offset within that graphics context.

Layout geometry of a text view

As an example, consider a text view scrolled so as to place some word at the top left of its visible bounds. I'll use the layout manager to learn what word it is.

I can ask the layout manager what character or glyph corresponds to a certain point in the text container, but what point should I ask about? Translating from the real world to text container coordinates is up to me; I must take into account both the scroll position of the text view's content and the inset of the text container within that content:

```
let off = self.tv.contentOffset
let top = self.tv.textContainerInset.top
let left = self.tv.textContainerInset.left
var tctopleft = CGPoint(off.x - left, off.y - top)
```

Now I'm speaking in text container coordinates, which are layout manager coordinates. One possibility is then to ask directly for the index (in the text storage's string) of the corresponding character:

```
let ixx = self.tv.layoutManager.characterIndex(for:tctopleft,
    in:self.tv.textContainer,
    fractionOfDistanceBetweenInsertionPoints:nil)
```

That, however, does not give quite the results one might intuitively expect. If *any* of a word is poking down from above into the visible area of the text view, that is the word whose first character is returned. I think we intuitively expect, if a word isn't fully visible, that the answer should be the word that starts the *next* line, which *is* fully visible. So I'll modify that code in a simpleminded way. I'll obtain the index of the *glyph* at my initial point; from this, I can derive the rect of the line fragment containing it. If that line fragment is not at least three-quarters visible, I'll add one line fragment height to the starting point and derive the glyph index again. Then I'll convert the glyph index to a character range:

```
var ix = self.tv.layoutManager.glyphIndex(for:tctopleft,
    in:self.tv.textContainer, fractionOfDistanceThroughGlyph:nil)
let frag = self.tv.layoutManager.lineFragmentRect(
    forGlyphAt:ix, effectiveRange:nil)
if tctopleft.y > frag.origin.y + 0.5*frag.size.height {
    tctopleft.y += frag.size.height
    ix = self.tv.layoutManager.glyphIndex(for:tctopleft,
        in:self.tv.textContainer, fractionOfDistanceThroughGlyph:nil)
}
let charRange = self.tv.layoutManager.characterRange(
    forGlyphRange: NSMakeRange(ix,0), actualGlyphRange:nil)
```

Finally, I'll use NLTokenizer (`import NaturalLanguage`) to get the range of the entire word to which this character belongs:

```
let tokenizer = NLTokenizer(unit: .word)
tokenizer.setLanguage(.english)
let text = self.tv.text!
tokenizer.string = text
let range = NSMakeRange(charRange.location, 100)
let words = tokenizer.tokens(for: Range(range, in:text)!)
if let word = words.first {
    print(text[word])
}
```

Clearly, the same sort of technique could be used to formulate a custom response to a tap — answering the question, "What word did the user just tap on?"

Layout manager drawing

By subclassing NSLayoutManager (and by implementing its delegate), many power-ful effects can be achieved. To illustrate, I'll carry on from the preceding code by drawing a rectangular outline around the word we just located. To make this possi-ble, I have an NSLayoutManager subclass, MyLayoutManager, an instance of which is built into the Text Kit stack for this text view. MyLayoutManager has a public NSRange property, wordRange. Having worked out what word I want to outline, I set the layout manager's wordRange and invalidate its drawing of that word, to force a redraw:

```
let range = NSRange(word, in:text)
let lm = self.tv.layoutManager as! MyLayoutManager
lm.wordRange = range
lm.invalidateDisplay(forCharacterRange:range)
```

In MyLayoutManager, I've overridden the method that draws the background behind glyphs, drawBackground(forGlyphRange:at:). At the moment this method is called, there is already a graphics context, so all we have to do is draw.

First, I call super. Then, if the range of glyphs to be drawn includes the glyphs for the range of characters in self.wordRange, I ask for the rect of the bounding box of those glyphs, and stroke it to form the rectangle. As I mentioned earlier, the bounding box is in text container coordinates, but now we're drawing in the real world, so I have to compensate by offsetting the drawn rectangle by the same amount that the text con-tainer is supposed to be offset in the real world; fortunately, the text view tells us (through the origin: parameter) what that offset is:

```
override func drawBackground(forGlyphRange glyphsToShow: NSRange,
    at origin: CGPoint) {
        super.drawBackground(forGlyphRange:glyphsToShow, at:origin)
        if self.wordRange.length == 0 {
            return
        }
        var range = self.glyphRange(forCharacterRange:self.wordRange,
            actualCharacterRange:nil)
        range = NSIntersectionRange(glyphsToShow, range)
        if range.length == 0 {
            return
        }
        if let tc = self.textContainer(forGlyphAt:range.location,
            effectiveRange:nil, withoutAdditionalLayout:true) {
                var r = self.boundingRect(forGlyphRange:range, in:tc)
                r.origin.x += origin.x
                r.origin.y += origin.y
                let c = UIGraphicsGetCurrentContext()!
                c.saveGState()
                c.setStrokeColor(UIColor.black.cgColor)
                c.setLineWidth(1.0)
```

```
            c.stroke(r)
            c.restoreGState()
        }
    }
```

Text Kit Without a Text View

UITextView is the only built-in iOS class that has a Text Kit stack to which you are given programmatic access. But that doesn't mean it's the only place where you can draw with Text Kit! You can draw with Text Kit *anywhere you can draw* — that is, in any graphics context (Chapter 2). When you do so, you should always call two NSLayoutManager methods, `drawBackground(forGlyphRange:at:)` (the method I overrode in the previous example) and `drawGlyphs(forGlyphRange:at:)`, in that order. The `at:` argument is the point where you consider the text container's origin to be within the current graphics context.

To illustrate, I'll change the implementation of the StringDrawer class that I described earlier in this chapter. Previously, StringDrawer's `draw(_:)` implementation told the attributed string (`self.attributedText`) to draw itself:

```
override func draw(_ rect: CGRect) {
    let r = rect.offsetBy(dx: 0, dy: 2)
    let opts : NSStringDrawingOptions = .usesLineFragmentOrigin
    self.attributedText.draw(with:r, options: opts, context: context)
}
```

Instead, I'll construct the Text Kit stack and tell its layout manager to draw the text:

```
override func draw(_ rect: CGRect) {
    let lm = NSLayoutManager()
    let ts = NSTextStorage(attributedString:self.attributedText)
    ts.addLayoutManager(lm)
    let tc = NSTextContainer(size:rect.size)
    lm.addTextContainer(tc)
    tc.lineFragmentPadding = 0
    let r = lm.glyphRange(for:tc)
    lm.drawBackground(forGlyphRange:r, at:CGPoint(0,2))
    lm.drawGlyphs(forGlyphRange: r, at:CGPoint(0,2))
}
```

Building the entire Text Kit stack by hand may seem like overkill for that simple example, but imagine what *else* I could do now that I have access to the entire Text Kit stack! I can use properties, subclassing, delegation, and alternative stack architectures to achieve customizations and effects that, before Text Kit was migrated to iOS, were difficult or impossible to achieve without dipping down to the level of Core Text.

The two-column display of U.S. state names on the iPad shown in Figure 11-19 was a Core Text example in early editions of this book, requiring 50 or 60 lines of elaborate

ALABAMA	MONTANA
ALASKA	NEBRASKA
ARIZONA	NEVADA
ARKANSAS	NEW HAMPSHIRE
CALIFORNIA	NEW JERSEY
COLORADO	NEW MEXICO
CONNECTICUT	NEW YORK
DELAWARE	NORTH CAROLINA
FLORIDA	NORTH DAKOTA
GEORGIA	OHIO
HAWAII	OKLAHOMA
IDAHO	OREGON
ILLINOIS	PENNSYLVANIA
INDIANA	RHODE ISLAND
IOWA	SOUTH CAROLINA
KANSAS	SOUTH DAKOTA
KENTUCKY	TENNESSEE
LOUISIANA	TEXAS
MAINE	UTAH
MARYLAND	VERMONT
MASSACHUSETTS	VIRGINIA
MICHIGAN	WASHINGTON
MINNESOTA	WEST VIRGINIA
MISSISSIPPI	WISCONSIN
MISSOURI	WYOMING

Figure 11-19. Two-column text in small caps

ARIZONA
ARKANSAS
CALIFORNIA
COLORADO
CONNECTICUT

Figure 11-20. The user has tapped on California

C code, complicated by the necessity of flipping the context to prevent the text from being drawn upside-down. Nowadays, it can be achieved easily through Text Kit — effectively just by reusing code from earlier examples in this chapter.

We can also make the display of state names interactive, with the name of the tapped state briefly outlined with a rectangle (Figure 11-20). When I implemented this using Core Text in early editions of the book, it was insanely difficult, not least because we had to keep track of all the line fragment rectangles ourselves. But it's easy with Text Kit, because the layout manager knows all the answers.

We have a UIView subclass, StyledText. In its `layoutSubviews`, it creates the Text Kit stack — a layout manager with two text containers, to achieve the two-column layout — and stores the whole stack, along with the rects at which the two text containers are to be drawn, in properties:

```
override func layoutSubviews() {
    super.layoutSubviews()
    var r1 = self.bounds
    r1.origin.y += 2 // a little top space
    r1.size.width /= 2.0 // column 1
    var r2 = r1
    r2.origin.x += r2.size.width // column 2
    let lm = MyLayoutManager()
    let ts = NSTextStorage(attributedString:self.text)
    ts.addLayoutManager(lm)
    let tc = NSTextContainer(size:r1.size)
    lm.addTextContainer(tc)
    let tc2 = NSTextContainer(size:r2.size)
    lm.addTextContainer(tc2)
    self.lm = lm; self.ts = ts; self.tc = tc; self.tc2 = tc2
    self.r1 = r1; self.r2 = r2
}
```

Our `draw(_:)` is just like the previous example, except that we have two text containers to draw:

```
override func draw(_ rect: CGRect) {
    let range1 = self.lm.glyphRange(for:self.tc)
    self.lm.drawBackground(forGlyphRange:range1, at: self.r1.origin)
    self.lm.drawGlyphs(forGlyphRange:range1, at: self.r1.origin)
    let range2 = self.lm.glyphRange(for:self.tc2)
    self.lm.drawBackground(forGlyphRange:range2, at: self.r2.origin)
    self.lm.drawGlyphs(forGlyphRange:range2, at: self.r2.origin)
}
```

So much for drawing the text! We now have Figure 11-19.

On to Figure 11-20. When the user taps on our view, a tap gesture recognizer's action method is called. We are using the same layout manager subclass developed in the preceding section of this chapter: it draws a rectangle around the glyphs corresponding to the characters of its `wordRange` property. All we have to do in order to make the flashing rectangle around the tapped word is work out what that range is, set our layout manager's `wordRange` property and redraw ourselves, and then (after a short delay) set the `wordRange` property back to a zero range and redraw ourselves again to remove the rectangle.

We start by working out which column the user tapped in; this tells us which text container it is, and what the tapped point is in text container coordinates (g is the tap gesture recognizer):

```
    var p = g.location(in:self)
    var tc = self.tc!
    if !self.r1.contains(p) {
        tc = self.tc2!
        p.x -= self.r1.size.width
    }
```

Now we can ask the layout manager what glyph the user tapped on, and hence the whole range of glyphs within the line fragment the user tapped in. If the user tapped to the left of the first glyph or to the right of the last glyph, no word was tapped:

```
    var f : CGFloat = 0
    let ix =
        self.lm.glyphIndex(for:p, in:tc, fractionOfDistanceThroughGlyph:&f)
    var glyphRange : NSRange = NSMakeRange(0,0)
    self.lm.lineFragmentRect(forGlyphAt:ix, effectiveRange:&glyphRange)
    if ix == glyphRange.location && f == 0.0 {
        return
    }
    if ix == glyphRange.location + glyphRange.length - 1 && f == 1.0 {
        return
    }
```

If the last glyph of the line fragment is a whitespace glyph, we don't want to include it in our rectangle, so we subtract it from the end of our range. Then we're ready to convert to a character range, and we can learn the name of the tapped state:

```
    func lastCharIsControl () -> Bool {
        let lastCharRange = glyphRange.location + glyphRange.length - 1
        let property = self.lm.propertyForGlyph(at:lastCharRange)
        return property.contains(.controlCharacter)
    }
    while lastCharIsControl() {
        glyphRange.length -= 1
    }
    let characterRange =
        self.lm.characterRange(forGlyphRange:glyphRange, actualGlyphRange:nil)
    let s = self.text.string
    if let r = Range(characterRange, in:s) {
        let stateName = s[r]
        print("you tapped \(stateName)")
    }
```

Finally, we flash the rectangle around the state name by setting and resetting the word-Range property of the subclassed layout manager:

```
    let lm = self.lm as! MyLayoutManager
    lm.wordRange = characterRange
    self.setNeedsDisplay()
    delay(0.3) {
        lm.wordRange = NSMakeRange(0, 0)
        self.setNeedsDisplay()
    }
```

Web Views

A web view is a web browser, which is a powerful thing: it knows how to fetch resources through the internet, and it can render HTML and CSS, and can respond to JavaScript. It is a network communication device, as well as an interactive layout, animation, and media display engine.

In a web view, links and other ancillary resources work automatically. If your web view's HTML refers to an image, the web view will fetch it and display it. If the user taps on a link, the web view will fetch that content and display it; if the link is to some sort of media (a sound or video file), the web view will allow the user to play it.

A web view can also display some other types of content commonly encountered as internet resources. It can display PDF files, as well as documents in such formats as *.rtf*, Microsoft Word (*.doc* and *.docx*), and Pages. (A Pages file that is actually a bundle must be compressed to form a single *.pages.zip* resource.)

 A web view should also be able to display *.rtfd* files, but this feature is not working properly; Apple suggests that you convert to an attributed string as I described in Chapter 11 (specifying a document type of NSRTFDTextDocument-Type), or use a QLPreviewController (Chapter 23).

The loading and rendering of a web view's content takes time, and may involve networking. Your app's interface, however, is not blocked or frozen while the content is loading. On the contrary, your interface remains accessible and operative. The web view, in fetching and rendering a web page and its linked components, is doing something quite complex, involving both threading and network interaction — I'll have a lot more to say about this in Chapters 24 and 25 — but it shields you from this complexity, and it operates in the background, off the main thread. Your own interaction with the web view stays on the main thread and is straightforward. You ask the web view to load some content; then you sit back and let it worry about the details.

iOS 9 introduced App Transport Security. Your app, by default, cannot load external URLs that are not secure (`https:`). You can turn off this restriction completely or in part in your *Info.plist*. See Chapter 24 for details.

WKWebView

WKWebView is part of the WebKit framework (`import WebKit`). The designated initializer is `init(frame:configuration:)`. The second parameter, `configuration:`, is a WKWebViewConfiguration. You can create a configuration beforehand:

```
let config = WKWebViewConfiguration()
// ... configure config here ...
let wv = WKWebView(frame: rect, configuration:config)
```

Alternatively, you can modify the web view's configuration later, through its `configuration` property. Either way, you'll probably want to perform configurations before the web view has a chance to load any content, because some settings will affect *how* it loads or renders that content. Here are some of the more important WKWebViewConfiguration properties:

suppressesIncrementalRendering
> If `true`, the web view's visible content doesn't change until all linked renderable resources (such as images) have finished loading. The default is `false`.

allowsInlineMediaPlayback
> If `true`, linked media are played inside the web page. The default is `false` (the fullscreen player is used).

mediaTypesRequiringUserActionForPlayback
> Types of media that *won't* start playing automatically, without a user gesture. A bitmask (WKAudiovisualMediaTypes) with possible values `.audio`, `.video`, and `.all`.

allowsPictureInPictureMediaPlayback
> See Chapter 16 for a discussion of picture-in-picture playback.

dataDetectorTypes
> Types of content that may be transformed automatically into tappable links. Similar to a text view's data detectors (Chapter 11).

websiteDataStore
> A WKWebsiteDataStore. By supplying a data store, you get control over stored resources. Its `httpCookieStore` is a WKHTTPCookieStore where you can examine, add, and remove cookies.

`preferences`

A WKPreferences object. This is a value class embodying these properties:

- `minimumFontSize`
- `javaScriptCanOpenWindowsAutomatically`
- `isFraudulentWebsiteWarningEnabled`

(New in iOS 14, the `javaScriptEnabled` property is deprecated; JavaScript enablement is now moved to the WKWebpagePreferences class, as I'll explain later.)

`userContentController`

A WKUserContentController object. This is how you can inject JavaScript into a web page and communicate between your code and the web page's content. I'll give an example later. Also, you can give the `userContentController` a rule list (WKContentRuleList) that filters the web view's content.

`limitsNavigationsToAppBoundDomains`

New in iOS 14. If `true`, the user will be unable to navigate to any domains other than those listed in your *Info.plist* under the key `WKAppBoundDomains`, whose value is an array of strings. The default is `false`.

 The *Info.plist* `WKAppBoundDomains` value has another purpose: the listed domains are the only ones for which JavaScript injection, custom style sheets, cookie manipulation, and message handlers are enabled. Disabling those features effectively wards off malicious user tracking; an empty array disables them for *all* domains.

A WKWebView is not a scroll view, but it *has* a scroll view (`scrollView`). You can use this to scroll the web view's content programmatically and to respond as the scroll view's delegate when the user scrolls, plus you can get references to the scroll view's gesture recognizers and add gesture recognizers of your own.

You can take a snapshot of a web view's content by calling `take-Snapshot(with:completionHandler:)`. The snapshot image is passed into the completion function as a UIImage. New in iOS 14, you can snapshot the content as a PDF with `createPDF(configuration:completionHandler:)`, and you can export the content as a web archive with `createWebArchiveData(completionHandler:)`.

In the nib editor, the Objects library contains a WKWebView object, referred to as a WebKit View, that you can drag into your interface as you design it; you might need to link to the WebKit framework manually (in the app target's Link Binary With Libraries build phase) to prevent the app from crashing as the nib loads. Many WKWebViewConfiguration and WKPreferences properties can be configured in the nib editor as well.

Web View Content

You can supply a web view with content using one of four methods, depending on the content's type:

A URLRequest

Form a URLRequest from a URL and call load(_:). The URLRequest initializer is init(url:cachePolicy:timeoutInterval:), but the second and third parameters are optional and will often be omitted. Additional URLRequest configuration includes such properties as allowsExpensiveNetworkAccess (see Chapter 24):

```
let url = URL(string: "https://www.apple.com")!
let req = URLRequest(url: url)
// could set req.allowsExpensiveNetworkAccess here
self.wv.load(req)
```

A local file

Obtain a local file URL and call loadFileURL(_:allowingReadAccessTo:). The second parameter effectively sandboxes the web view into a single file or directory. In this example from one of my apps, the HTML file *zotzhelp.html* refers to images in the same directory as itself:

```
let url = Bundle.main.url(
    forResource: "zotzhelp", withExtension: "html")!
view.loadFileURL(url, allowingReadAccessTo: url)
```

An HTML string

Prepare a string consisting of valid HTML, and call loadHTMLString(_:baseURL:). The baseURL: specifies how partial URLs in your HTML are to be resolved (as when the HTML refers to resources in your app bundle). Starting with an HTML string is useful particularly when you want to construct your HTML programmatically or make changes to it before handing it to the web view. In this example from the TidBITS News app, my HTML consists of two strings: a wrapper with the usual <html> tags, and the body content derived from an RSS feed. I assemble them and hand the resulting string to my web view for display:

```
let templatepath = Bundle.main.path(
    forResource: "htmlTemplate", ofType:"txt")!
let base = URL(fileURLWithPath:templatepath)
var s = try! String(contentsOfFile:templatepath)
let ss = // actual body content for this page
s = s.replacingOccurrences(of:"<content>", with:ss)
self.wv.loadHTMLString(s, baseURL:base)
```

A Data object

Call `load(_:MIMEType:characterEncodingName:baseURL:)`. This is useful particularly when the content has itself arrived from the network, as the parameters correspond to the properties of a URLResponse. This example will be more meaningful to you after you've read Chapter 24:

```
let sess = URLSession.shared
let url = // whatever
let task = sess.dataTask(with: url) { data, response, err in
    if let response = response,
        let mime = response.mimeType,
        let enc = response.textEncodingName,
        let data = data {
            self.wv.load(data, mimeType: mime,
                characterEncodingName: enc, baseURL: url)
    }
}
```

All four methods return a WKNavigation object; I've ignored it in my examples. If you like, you can capture it to identify an individual page-loading operation, as I'll explain later.

Tracking Changes in a Web View

A WKWebView has properties that can be tracked with key–value observing, such as:

- `isLoading`
- `estimatedProgress`
- `url`
- `title`

You can observe these properties to be notified as a web page loads or changes.

To illustrate, I'll give the user feedback while a page is loading by displaying an activity indicator (Chapter 13). I'll start by putting the activity indicator in the center of my web view and keeping a reference to it:

```
let act = UIActivityIndicatorView(style:.large)
act.backgroundColor = UIColor(white:0.1, alpha:0.5)
act.color = .white
self.wv.addSubview(act)
act.translatesAutoresizingMaskIntoConstraints = false
NSLayoutConstraint.activate([
    act.centerXAnchor.constraint(equalTo:wv.centerXAnchor),
    act.centerYAnchor.constraint(equalTo:wv.centerYAnchor)
])
self.activity = act
```

Now I observe the web view's isLoading property (self.obs is a Set instance property). When the web view starts loading or stops loading, I'm notified, so I can show or hide the activity view:

```
let ob = self.wv.observe(\.isLoading, options:.new) {[unowned self] wv, ch in
    if let val = ch.newValue {
        if val {
            self.activity.startAnimating()
        } else {
            self.activity.stopAnimating()
        }
    }
}
self.obs.insert(ob)
```

Web View Navigation

A WKWebView maintains a back and forward list of the URLs to which the user has navigated. The list is its backForwardList, a WKBackForwardList, which is a collection of read-only properties (and one method):

- currentItem
- backItem
- forwardItem
- item(at:)

Each item in the list is a WKBackForwardItem, a simple value class basically consisting of a url and a title.

A WKWebView responds to goBack, goForward and go(to:), so you can tell it in code to navigate the list. Its properties canGoBack and canGoForward are key–value observable; typically you would use that fact to enable or disable a Back and Forward button in your interface in response to the list changing.

A WKWebView also has a settable property, allowsBackForwardNavigation-Gestures. The default is false; if true, the user can swipe sideways to go back and forward in the list. This property can also be set in the nib editor.

To prevent or reroute navigation that the user tries to perform by tapping links, set yourself as the WKWebView's navigationDelegate (WKNavigationDelegate) and implement webView(_:decidePolicyFor:preferences:decisionHandler:). The for: parameter is a WKNavigationAction that you can examine to help make your decision. Among other things, its request property is the URLRequest we are proposing to perform — look at its url to see where we are proposing to go — along with a navigationType, which will be one of the following (WKNavigationType):

- `.linkActivated`
- `.backForward`
- `.reload`
- `.formSubmitted`
- `.formResubmitted`
- `.other`

You are also handed a `decisionHandler` function which you *must* call with a WKNavigationActionPolicy argument — either `.cancel` or `.allow`. You must also pass a WKWebpagePreferences object in your call to this function; I'll talk in a moment about what it's for, but in general you can just pass the `preferences` object that arrived as a parameter.

In this example, I permit navigation in the most general case — otherwise nothing would ever appear in my web view! — but if the user taps a link, I forbid it and load that URL in Mobile Safari instead:

```
func webView(_ webView: WKWebView,
    decidePolicyFor navigationAction: WKNavigationAction,
    preferences: WKWebpagePreferences, decisionHandler:
    @escaping (WKNavigationActionPolicy, WKWebpagePreferences) -> Void) {
        if navigationAction.navigationType == .linkActivated {
            if let url = navigationAction.request.url {
                UIApplication.shared.open(url)
                decisionHandler(.cancel, preferences) // *
                return
            }
        }
        decisionHandler(.allow, preferences)
}
```

Starting in iOS 13, a web view has a *content mode* (WKWebpagePreferences.Content-Mode), determining how the web view represents itself as a browser to the server:

`.desktop`
> The default on an iPad when the web view is fullscreen. Websites will appear in their desktop version.

`.mobile`
> The default on an iPhone, or on the iPad when the web view is not fullscreen (perhaps it's in a popover, or we're doing iPad multitasking). Websites will appear in their mobile version.

To access desktop mode in a WKWebView, you'll need to set the configuration's `applicationNameForUserAgent` property to a desktop browser's user agent string, such as `"Version/14.0 Safari/605.1.15"`. You can set this in the nib editor.

To change the content mode for a particular web page during navigation, use your implementation of `webView(_:decidePolicyFor:preferences:decisionHandler:)`. The third parameter, `preferences`, is a WKWebpagePreferences object, a simple value class. Set its `preferredContentMode` to `.desktop` or `.mobile`, and pass the revised object into the `decisionHandler` call as the second argument.

New in iOS 14, another use of the `preferences` object is to enable or disable Java-Script; set its `allowsContentJavaScript` as desired. This toggles JavaScript on a per-page basis. It applies, as the name suggests, to JavaScript that comes from the loaded content; JavaScript that you inject into the page from your code, as I'll describe in the next section, is effective even if this property is `false`.

Several other WKNavigationDelegate methods can notify you as a page loads (or fails to load). Under normal circumstances, you'll receive them in this order:

- `webView(_:didStartProvisionalNavigation:)`
- `webView(_:didCommit:)`
- `webView(_:didFinish:)`

Those delegate methods, and all navigation commands, including the four ways of loading your web view with initial content, supply a WKNavigation object. You can use this in an equality comparison to determine whether the navigations referred to in different methods are the same navigation (roughly speaking, the same page-loading operation). This object also has an `effectiveContentMode` property that tells you the current content mode (`.desktop` or `.mobile`).

Communicating with a Web Page

Your code can pass JavaScript messages into and out of a WKWebView's web page, allowing you to change the page's contents or respond to changes within it, even while it is being displayed.

Communicating into a web page

To send a message into an already loaded WKWebView web page, call `evaluateJava-Script(_:in:in:completionHandler:)`. This method is new in iOS 14, superseding `evaluateJavaScript(_:completionHandler:)`. With the new method, you can specify the WKFrameInfo context in which your JavaScript should run, as well as a WKContentWorld, which will usually be `.defaultClient`; this keeps your JavaScript and the content's JavaScript from impinging on one another, whether accidentally or maliciously.

In this example, the user is able to decrease the size of the text in the web page. We have prepared some JavaScript that generates a `<style>` element containing CSS that sets the `font-size` for the page's `<body>` in accordance with a property, `self.fontsize`:

```
var fontsize = 18
var cssrule : String {
    return """
    var s = document.createElement('style');
    s.textContent = 'body { font-size: \(self.fontsize)px; }';
    document.documentElement.appendChild(s);
    """
}
```

When the user taps a button, we decrement `self.fontsize`, construct that Java-Script, and send it to the web page:

```
func doDecreaseSize (_ sender: Any) {
    self.fontsize -= 1
    if self.fontsize < 10 {
        self.fontsize = 20
    }
    let s = self.cssrule
    self.wv.evaluateJavaScript(s, in: nil, in: .defaultClient)
}
```

But there's something rather inelegant about that. Our `cssrule` getter is performing string interpolation in order to assemble the JavaScript. That's ugly, and it would be a lot uglier if there were additional interpolations. New in iOS 14, there's an elegant solution. Instead of `evaluateJavaScript(_:in:in:completionHandler:)`, you can call `callAsyncJavaScript(_:arguments:in:in:completionHandler:)`. This lets you pass an `arguments:` dictionary of substitutions to be performed for you.

To demonstrate, I'll construct our JavaScript a different way:

```
var cssrule2 : String {
    return """
    var s = document.createElement('style');
    s.textContent = `body { font-size: ${thefontsize}px; }`;
    document.documentElement.appendChild(s);
    """
}
```

That JavaScript uses JavaScript string interpolation (a template literal). There's no variable called `thefontsize`; that's what we have to supply as an argument:

```
self.wv.callAsyncJavaScript(self.cssrule2,
    arguments: ["thefontsize": self.fontsize],
    in: nil, in: .defaultClient)
```

Finally, we have not done anything about setting the web page's *initial* `font-size`. Let's fix that.

A WKWebView allows us to inject JavaScript into the web page *at the time it is loaded*. To do so, we use the userContentController of the WKWebView's configuration. We create a WKUserScript, specifying the JavaScript it contains, along with an injectionTime which can be either before (.documentStart) or after (.documentEnd) a page's content has loaded. In this case, we want it to be before; otherwise, the user will see the font size change suddenly:

```
let script = WKUserScript(source: self.cssrule,
    injectionTime: .atDocumentStart, forMainFrameOnly: true,
    in: .defaultClient)
let config = self.wv.configuration
config.userContentController.addUserScript(script)
```

(It's a pity that we can't supply substitution arguments in that call.)

Communicating out of a web page

To communicate out of a web page, you need first to install a message handler to receive the communication. Again, this involves the userContentController. You call add(_:contentWorld:name:). Again, this method is new in iOS 14, replacing add(_:name:) so that you can specify a content world for the JavaScript to run in. The first argument is an object that must implement the WKScriptMessageHandler protocol, so that its userContentController(_:didReceive:) method can be called later:

```
let config = self.wv.configuration
config.userContentController.add(self,
    contentWorld: .defaultClient, name: "playbutton")
```

We have just installed a playbutton message handler. This means that the DOM for our web page now contains an element, among its window.webkit.messageHandlers, called playbutton. A message handler sends its message when it receives a post-Message() function call. The WKScriptMessageHandler (self in this example) will get a call to its userContentController(_:didReceive:) method if JavaScript inside the web page sends postMessage() to the window.webkit.message-Handlers.playbutton object.

To make that actually happen, I've put an <img> tag into my web page's HTML, defining an image that will act as a tappable button:

```
<img src="listen.png"
  onclick="window.webkit.messageHandlers.playbutton.postMessage('play')">
```

When the user taps that image, the message is posted, and so my code runs and I can respond:

```
func userContentController(_ userContentController: WKUserContentController,
    didReceive message: WKScriptMessage) {
        if message.name == "playbutton" {
            if let body = message.body as? String {
                if body == "play" {
                    // ... do stuff here ...
                }
            }
        }
}
```

There's just one little problem: that code causes a retain cycle! The reason is that a WKUserContentController leaks, and it retains the WKScriptMessageHandler, which in this case is `self` — and so `self` will never be deallocated. But `self` is the view controller, so that's very bad. My solution is to create an intermediate trampoline object that can be harmlessly retained, and that has a weak reference to `self`:

```
class MyMessageHandler : NSObject, WKScriptMessageHandler {
    weak var delegate : WKScriptMessageHandler?
    init(delegate:WKScriptMessageHandler) {
        self.delegate = delegate
        super.init()
    }
    func userContentController(_ ucc: WKUserContentController,
        didReceive message: WKScriptMessage) {
            self.delegate?.userContentController(ucc, didReceive: message)
    }
}
```

Now when I add myself as a script message handler, I do it by way of the trampoline object:

```
let config = self.wv.configuration
let handler = MyMessageHandler(delegate:self)
config.userContentController.add(handler, name: "playbutton")
```

Now that I've broken the retain cycle, my own `deinit` is called, and I can release the offending objects:

```
deinit {
    let ucc = self.wv.configuration.userContentController
    ucc.removeAllUserScripts()
    ucc.removeScriptMessageHandler(forName:"playbutton")
}
```

New in iOS 14, if you need to receive a message from the web page and reply to it, you can. Instead of calling add(_:contentWorld:name:), you call addScriptMessage-Handler(_:contentWorld:name:). Instead of conforming to WKScriptMessageHandler, the first parameter conforms to WKScriptMessageHandlerWithReply, meaning that it implements userContentController(_:didReceive:replyHandler:). The JavaScript sends a Promise, so your reply can be asynchronous.

JavaScript alerts

If a web page tries to put up a JavaScript alert, nothing will happen in your app unless you assign the WKWebView a `uiDelegate`, an object adopting the WKUIDelegate protocol, and implement these methods:

`webView(_:runJavaScriptAlertPanelWithMessage:initiatedByFrame:completion-Handler:)`

Called by JavaScript `alert`.

`webView(_:runJavaScriptConfirmPanelWithMessage:initiatedByFrame:completionHandler:)`

Called by JavaScript `confirm`.

`webView(_:runJavaScriptTextInputPanelWithPrompt:defaultText:initiatedByFrame:completionHandler:)`

Called by JavaScript `prompt`.

Your implementation should put up an appropriate alert (UIAlertController, see Chapter 14) and call the completion function when it is dismissed. Here's a minimal implementation for the `alert` method:

```
func webView(_ webView: WKWebView,
    runJavaScriptAlertPanelWithMessage message: String,
    initiatedByFrame frame: WKFrameInfo,
    completionHandler: @escaping () -> Void) {
        let host = frame.request.url?.host
        let alert = UIAlertController(title: host, message: message,
            preferredStyle: .alert)
        alert.addAction(UIAlertAction(title: "OK", style: .default) { _ in
            completionHandler()
        })
        self.present(alert, animated:true)
}
```

Similarly, if a web page's JavaScript calls `window.open`, implement this method:

- `webView(_:createWebViewWith:for:windowFeatures:)`

Your implementation can return `nil`, or else create a new WKWebView, get it into the interface, and return it.

Custom Schemes

Starting in iOS 11, you can feed data into a web page by implementing a custom URL scheme. When the web page asks for the data by way of the scheme, the WKWebView turns to your code to supply the data.

Let's say I have an MP3 file called `"theme"` in my app's asset catalog, and I want the user to be able to play it through an `<audio>` tag in my web page. I've invented a custom scheme that signals to my app that we want this audio data, and my web page's <source> tag asks for its data using that scheme:

```
weak var wv: WKWebView!
let sch = "neuburg-custom-scheme-demo-audio" // custom scheme
override func viewDidLoad() {
    super.viewDidLoad()
    let config = WKWebViewConfiguration()
    // ... configure the web view ...
    let r = // ... CGRect for web view frame ...
    let wv = WKWebView(frame: r, configuration: config)
    self.view.addSubview(wv)
    self.wv = wv
    let s = """
    <!DOCTYPE html><html><head>
    <meta name="viewport" content="initial-scale=1.0, user-scalable=no" />
    </head><body>
    <p>Here you go:</p>
    <audio controls>
    <source src="\(sch)://theme" />
    </audio>
    </body></html>
    """
    self.wv.loadHTMLString(s, baseURL: nil)
}
```

Now let's fill in the missing code, where we configure the web view to accept sch as a custom scheme:

```
let sh = SchemeHandler()
sh.sch = self.sch
config.setURLSchemeHandler(sh, forURLScheme: self.sch)
```

The call to setURLSchemeHandler requires that we provide an object that adopts the WKURLSchemeHandler protocol. That object cannot be self, or we'll get ourselves into a retain cycle (similar to the problem we had with WKScriptMessageHandler earlier); so I'm configuring and passing a custom SchemeHandler helper object instead.

The WKURLSchemeHandler protocol methods are where the action is. When the web page wants data with our custom scheme, it calls our SchemeHandler's webView(_:start:) method. The second parameter is a WKURLSchemeTask that operates as our gateway back to the web view. Its request property contains the URLRequest from the web page. We must call the WKURLSchemeTask's methods, first supplying a URLResponse, then handing it the data, then telling it that we've finished:

```
class SchemeHandler : NSObject, WKURLSchemeHandler {
    var sch : String?
    func webView(_ webView: WKWebView, start task: WKURLSchemeTask) {
        if let url = task.request.url,
```

```
                    let sch = self.sch,
                    url.scheme == sch,
                    let host = url.host,
                    let theme = NSDataAsset(name:host) {
                        let data = theme.data
                        let resp = URLResponse(url: url, mimeType: "audio/mpeg",
                            expectedContentLength: data.count,
                            textEncodingName: nil)
                        task.didReceive(resp)
                        task.didReceive(data)
                        task.didFinish()
                } else {
                    task.didFailWithError(NSError(domain: "oops", code: 0))
                }
            }
            func webView(_ webView: WKWebView, stop task: WKURLSchemeTask) {
                print("stop")
            }
        }
```

The outcome is that the audio controls appear in our web page, and when the user
taps the Play button, what plays is the MP3 file from the app's asset catalog.

 This feature works only if we create the web view ourselves, in code, using the
init(frame:configuration:) initializer, with the WKWebViewConfiguration
object prepared beforehand. So we can't use a custom scheme with a web view
instantiated from a nib. I regard this limitation as a bug.

Web View Previews and Context Menus

As I described earlier ("Previews and Context Menus" on page 386), 3D touch peek
and pop was superseded in iOS 13 by the use of a long press to summon a preview
with a context menu. If a WKWebView's allowsLinkPreview property is true, the
user can long press on a link to summon a preview of the linked page, along with
default menu items Open Link, Add to Reading List, Copy Link, Share, and Hide
Link Previews. (This property can be set in the nib editor.)

The default response to the user tapping on the preview is to open the link in Safari.
This mechanism does *not* pass through your navigation delegate's implementation of
webView(_:decidePolicyFor:preferences:decisionHandler:). Instead, if you
wish to customize your app's response to the user previewing links, you can implement methods in your uiDelegate (WKUIDelegate) that are parallel to the
UIContextMenuInteractionDelegate methods:

webView(_:contextMenuConfigurationForElement:completionHandler:)
    The element: is a WKContextMenuElementInfo, which is merely a value class
    carrying a single property, the linkURL for the link that the user is pressing on.
    Your job is to call the completionHandler with one of these as argument:

- A fully configured UIContextMenuConfiguration. If you supply an action provider function, the incoming parameter is an array of the default UIActions, so you can keep any or all of those as menu items if you want to.

- nil to permit the default behavior.

- An empty UIContextMenuConfiguration (no preview provider, no action provider) to prevent anything from happening.

webView(_:contextMenuWillPresentForElement:)
The context menu is about to appear.

webView(_:contextMenuForElement:willCommitWithAnimator:)
The user has tapped the preview. You might add a completion handler to the animator to perform a view controller transition.

webView(_:contextMenuDidEndForElement:)
The preview and menu have been dismissed, no matter how.

Safari View Controller

A Safari view controller (SFSafariViewController, import SafariServices) embeds the Mobile Safari interface in a separate process inside your app. It provides the user with a browser interface familiar from Mobile Safari itself. In a toolbar, which can be shown or hidden by scrolling, there are Back and Forward buttons, a Share button including standard Safari features such as Add Bookmark and Add to Reading List, and a Safari button that lets the user load the same page in the real Safari app. In a navigation bar, which can be shrunk or grown by scrolling, are a read-only URL field, a Text button where the user can change the text size, enter Reader view, and configure site settings, plus a Refresh button, along with a Done button. The user has access to autofill and to Safari cookies with no intervention by your app.

The idea, according to Apple, is that when you want to present internal HTML content, such as an HTML string, you'll use a WKWebView, but when you really want to allow the user to access the web, you'll use a Safari view controller. In this way, you are saved from the trouble of trying to build a full-fledged web browser yourself.

To use a Safari view controller, create the SFSafariViewController, initialize it with a URL, and present it:

```
let svc = SFSafariViewController(url: url)
self.present(svc, animated: true)
```

In this example, we interfere (as a WKWebView's navigationDelegate) with the user tapping on a link in our web view, so that the linked page is displayed in an SFSafariViewController within our app:

```
func webView(_ webView: WKWebView,
    decidePolicyFor navigationAction: WKNavigationAction,
    preferences: WKWebpagePreferences, decisionHandler:
    @escaping (WKNavigationActionPolicy, WKWebpagePreferences) -> Void) {
        if navigationAction.navigationType == .linkActivated {
            if let url = navigationAction.request.url {
                let svc = SFSafariViewController(url: url)
                self.present(svc, animated: true)
                decisionHandler(.cancel, preferences)
                return
            }
        }
        decisionHandler(.allow, preferences)
}
```

When the user taps the Done button in the navigation bar, the Safari view controller is dismissed. You can change the title of the Done button; to do so, set the Safari view controller's dismissButtonStyle to .done, .close, or .cancel.

You can set the color of the Safari view controller's navigation bar (preferredBar-TintColor) and bar button items (preferredControlTintColor). This allows the look of the view to harmonize with the rest of your app.

You can configure a Safari view controller by creating an SFSafariView-Controller.Configuration object and passing it to the Safari view controller through its initializer init(url:configuration:). Using the configuration object, you can prevent the Safari view controller's top and bottom bars from collapsing when the user scrolls; to do so, set its barCollapsingEnabled property to false.

You can make yourself the Safari view controller's delegate (SFSafariViewController-Delegate) and implement any of these methods:

safariViewController(_:didCompleteInitialLoad:)
safariViewControllerDidFinish(_:)
> Called on presentation and dismissal of the Safari view controller, respectively.

func safariViewController(_:initialLoadDidRedirectTo:)
> Reports that the Safari view controller's initial web page differs from the URL you originally provided, because redirection occurred.

safariViewController(_:activityItemsFor:title:)
> Allows you to supply your own Share button items; I'll explain what activity items are in Chapter 14.

safariViewController(_:excludedActivityTypesFor:title:)
> In a sense, the converse of the preceding: allows you to eliminate unwanted activity types from the Share button.

`safariViewControllerWillOpenInBrowser(_:)`
> (New in iOS 14.) The user has tapped the button that reopens the current page in Mobile Safari.

Developing Web View Content

Before designing the HTML to be displayed in a web view, you might want to read up on the brand of HTML native to the mobile WebKit rendering engine. There are certain limitations; mobile WebKit doesn't use plug-ins such as Flash, and it imposes limits on the size of resources (such as images) that it can display. On the plus side, WebKit is in the vanguard of the march toward HTML5 and CSS3, and has many special capabilities suited for display on a mobile device. For documentation and other resources, see Apple's Safari Dev Center (*https://developer.apple.com/safari*).

A good place to start is the *Safari Web Content Guide* (in the documentation archive). It contains links to other relevant documentation, such as the *Safari CSS Visual Effects Guide*, which describes some things you can do with WebKit's implementation of CSS3 (like animations), and the *Safari HTML5 Audio and Video Guide*, which describes WebKit's audio and video player support.

If nothing else, you'll want to be aware of one important aspect of web page content — the *viewport*. This is typically set through a `<meta>` tag in the `<head>` area:

```
<meta name="viewport" content="initial-scale=1.0, user-scalable=no">
```

Without that line, or something similar, a web page may be laid out incorrectly when it is rendered: your content may appear tiny (because it is being rendered as if the screen were large), or it may be too wide for the view, forcing the user to scroll horizontally to read it. The viewport's `user-scalable` attribute can be treated as `yes` by setting the WKWebViewConfiguration's `ignoresViewportScaleLimits` to `true`.

Another important section of the *Safari Web Content Guide* describes how you can use a `media` attribute in the `<link>` tag that loads your CSS to load different CSS depending on what kind of device your app is running on (also known as a *responsive* web page); you might have one CSS file that lays out your web view's content on an iPhone, and another that lays it out on an iPad. New in iOS 14, the WKWebView `mediaType` property lets you set the string that will be matched by the CSS `@media` rule; in addition to the built-in `screen` and `print` types, you can supply your own type using this property.

Another new iOS 14 WKWebView property related to CSS is `pageZoom`; this is equivalent to the CSS `zoom` property, but it applies to all page content and is injected before the page even starts to load.

Inspecting, debugging, and experimenting with web view content is greatly eased by the Web Inspector, built into Safari on the desktop. It can see a web view in your app running on a device or the Simulator, and lets you analyze every aspect of how it works. You can hover the mouse over a web page element in the Web Inspector to highlight the rendering of that element in the running app. Moreover, the Web Inspector lets you change your web view's content in real time, with many helpful features such as CSS autocompletion.

JavaScript and the document object model (*DOM*) are also extremely powerful. Event listeners allow JavaScript code to respond directly to touch and gesture events, so that the user can interact with elements of a web page much as if they were iOS-native touchable views; it can also take advantage of Core Location and Core Motion facilities to respond to where the user is on earth and how the device is positioned (see Chapter 22). Additional helpful documentation includes Apple's *WebKit DOM Programming Topics* and the WebKit JS framework reference page.

Controls and Other Views

This chapter discusses all UIView subclasses provided by UIKit that haven't been discussed already. It's remarkable how few of them there are; UIKit exhibits a notable economy of means in this regard.

Additional UIView subclasses, as well as UIViewController subclasses that create interface, are provided by other frameworks. There will be examples in Part III.

UIActivityIndicatorView

An activity indicator (UIActivityIndicatorView) appears as the spokes of a small wheel. You set the spokes spinning with `startAnimating`, giving the user a sense that some time-consuming process is taking place. You stop the spinning with `stopAnimating`. If the activity indicator's `hidesWhenStopped` is `true` (the default), it is visible only while spinning.

An activity indicator comes in a `style`; if it is created in code, you'll set its style with `init(style:)`. Your choices (UIActivityIndicatorView.Style) are:

- `.large`
- `.medium`

An activity indicator has a standard size, which depends on its style. Changing its size in code changes the size of the view, but not the size of the spokes. For bigger spokes, you can resort to a scale transform.

You can assign an activity indicator a `color`; this overrides the default gray color of the spokes. An activity indicator is a UIView, so you can also set its `backgroundColor`; a nice effect is to give an activity indicator a contrasting background color and to round its corners by way of the view's layer.

Figure 13-1. A large activity indicator

Here's some code from a UITableViewCell subclass in one of my apps. In this app, it takes some time, after the user taps a cell to select it, for me to construct the next view and navigate to it; to cover the delay, I show a spinning activity indicator in the center of the cell while it's selected (Figure 13-1):

```
override func setSelected(_ selected: Bool, animated: Bool) {
    if selected {
        let v = UIActivityIndicatorView(style:.large)
        v.color = .yellow
        v.backgroundColor = UIColor(white:0.2, alpha:0.6)
        v.layer.cornerRadius = 10
        v.frame = v.frame.insetBy(dx: -10, dy: -10)
        v.center = self.contentView.convert(self.bounds.center, from: self)
        v.tag = 1001
        self.contentView.addSubview(v)
        v.startAnimating()
    } else {
        self.viewWithTag(1001)?.removeFromSuperview()
    }
    super.setSelected(selected, animated: animated)
}
```

If activity involves the network, you might want to set the UIApplication's isNetwork-ActivityIndicatorVisible to true. This displays a small spinning activity indicator in the status bar. The indicator is not reflecting actual network activity; if it's visible, it's spinning. Be sure to set it back to false when the activity is over.

An activity indicator is simple and standard, but you can't change the way it's drawn. One obvious alternative would be a UIImageView with an animated image, as described in Chapter 4. Another solution is a CAReplicatorLayer, a layer that makes multiple copies of its sublayer; by animating the sublayer, you animate the copies. This is a very common approach. Here's an example:

```
let lay = CAReplicatorLayer()
lay.frame = CGRect(0,0,100,20)
let bar = CALayer()
bar.frame = CGRect(0,0,10,20)
bar.backgroundColor = UIColor.red.cgColor
lay.addSublayer(bar)
lay.instanceCount = 5
lay.instanceTransform = CATransform3DMakeTranslation(20, 0, 0)
let anim = CABasicAnimation(keyPath: #keyPath(CALayer.opacity))
anim.fromValue = 1.0
anim.toValue = 0.2
```

Figure 13-2. A custom activity indicator

```
anim.duration = 1
anim.repeatCount = .greatestFiniteMagnitude
bar.add(anim, forKey: nil)
lay.instanceDelay = anim.duration / Double(lay.instanceCount)
self.view.layer.addSublayer(lay)
// ... give the replicator layer a position ...
```

Our single red vertical bar (bar) is replicated to make five red vertical bars. We repeatedly fade the bar from opaque to transparent, but because we've set the replicator layer's instanceDelay, the replicated bars fade in sequence, so that the darkest bar appears to be marching repeatedly to the right (Figure 13-2).

UIProgressView

A progress view (UIProgressView) is a "thermometer" graphically displaying a percentage. This may be a static percentage, or it might represent a time-consuming process whose percentage of completion is known (if the percentage of completion is unknown, you're more likely to use an activity indicator). In one of my apps, I use a progress view to show how many cards are left in the deck; in another of my apps, I use a progress view to show the current position within the song being played by the built-in music player.

A progress view comes in a style, its progressViewStyle; if the progress view is created in code, you'll set its style with init(progressViewStyle:). Your choices (UIProgressView.Style) are:

- .default (the ends are drawn slightly rounded)
- .bar (thinner; the ends are squared off)

A .bar progress view is intended for use in a UIBarButtonItem, as the title view of a navigation item, and so on. Both styles draw the thermometer quite thin — just 4 points and 2.5 points, respectively. Figure 13-3 shows a .default progress view. Changing a progress view's frame height directly has no visible effect on how the thermometer is drawn. Under autolayout, to make a thicker thermometer, supply a height constraint with a larger value, overriding the intrinsic content height. Alternatively, subclass UIProgressView and override sizeThatFits(_:).

The fullness of the thermometer is the progress view's progress property. This is a value between 0 and 1, inclusive; you'll usually do some elementary arithmetic to

Figure 13-3. A progress view

Figure 13-4. A thicker progress view using a custom progress image

convert from the value you're reflecting to a value within that range. It is also a Float; in Swift, you may have to coerce explicitly. A change in progress value can be animated by calling setProgress(_:animated:). This progress view reflects the number of cards remaining in a deck of 52 cards:

```
let r = self.deck.cards.count
self.prog.setProgress(Float(r)/52, animated: true)
```

The default color of the filled portion of a progress view is the tintColor (which may be inherited from higher up the view hierarchy). The default color for the unfilled portion is gray for a .default progress view and transparent for a .bar progress view. You can customize the colors; set the progress view's progressTintColor and trackTintColor, respectively. This can also be done in the nib editor.

Alternatively, you can customize the image used to draw the filled portion of the progress view (its progressImage), along with the image used to draw the unfilled portion (its trackImage). This can also be done in the nib editor. Each image must be stretched to the length of the filled or unfilled area, so you'll want to use a resizable image. Be sure to give the progress view sufficient height, as I explained earlier, to accommodate your images. Here's a simple example from one of my apps (Figure 13-4):

```
let r = UIGraphicsImageRenderer(size:CGSize(10,10))
var trackim : UIImage?
let im = r.image { ctx in
    let con = ctx.cgContext
    // track
    con.setFillColor(UIColor.black.cgColor)
    con.fill(CGRect(0,0,10,10))
    trackim = ctx.currentImage
    // progress
    con.setFillColor(UIColor.yellow.cgColor)
    con.fillEllipse(in: CGRect(2,2,6,6))
}
self.prog.trackImage = trackim?.resizableImage(
    withCapInsets:UIEdgeInsets(top: 4, left: 4, bottom: 4, right: 4),
```

Figure 13-5. A circular custom progress view

```
    resizingMode:.stretch)
self.prog.progressImage = im.resizableImage(
    withCapInsets:UIEdgeInsets(top: 4, left: 4, bottom: 4, right: 4),
    resizingMode:.stretch)
```

Progress View Alternatives

For maximum flexibility, you can design your own UIView subclass that behaves like a thermometer. It doesn't have to *look* like a thermometer! A common interface (as in Apple's App Store app during a download) is to draw the arc of a circle. This effect is easily achieved by setting the strokeEnd of a CAShapeLayer with a circular path. Here's a UIButton subclass that implements it (Figure 13-5):

```
class MyCircularProgressButton : UIButton {
    var progress : Float = 0 {
        didSet {
            self.shapelayer?.strokeEnd = CGFloat(self.progress)
        }
    }
    private weak var shapelayer : CAShapeLayer?
    override func layoutSubviews() {
        super.layoutSubviews()
        guard self.shapelayer == nil else {return}
        let layer = CAShapeLayer()
        layer.frame = self.bounds
        layer.lineWidth = 3
        layer.lineCap = .round
        layer.fillColor = nil
        layer.strokeColor = UIColor.red.cgColor
        let b = UIBezierPath(ovalIn: self.bounds.insetBy(dx: 3, dy: 3))
        layer.path = b.cgPath
        layer.strokeStart = 0
        layer.strokeEnd = 0
        layer.setAffineTransform(CGAffineTransform(rotationAngle: -.pi/2.0))
        self.layer.addSublayer(layer)
        self.shapelayer = layer
    }
}
```

The Progress Class

A progress view has an observedProgress property that you can set to a Progress object. Progress is a Foundation class that abstracts the notion of task progress: it has a `totalUnitCount` property and a `completedUnitCount` property, and their ratio generates its `fractionCompleted`, which is read-only and observable with KVO.

If you assign a Progress object to a progress view's `observedProgress` property and configure and update it, the progress view will *automatically* use the changes in the Progress object's `fractionCompleted` to update its own `progress`. That's useful because you might already have a time-consuming process that maintains and vends its own Progress object. (For a case in point, see "Slow Data Delivery" on page 626.)

How should your progress view's `observedProgress` be related to the Progress object vended by the time-consuming process? There are two possibilities:

- In simple cases, you might assign the process's Progress object *directly* to your progress view's `observedProgress`.

- Alternatively, you can configure your progress view's `observedProgress` as the *parent* of the process's Progress object.

When Progress objects stand in a parent–child relationship, the progress of an operation reported to the child automatically forms an appropriate fraction of the progress reported by the parent; this allows a single Progress object, acting as the ultimate parent, to conglomerate the progress of several individual operations. There are two ways to put two Progress objects into a parent–child relationship:

Explicit parent
> Call the parent's `addChild(_:withPendingUnitCount:)` method. Alternatively, create the child by initializing it with reference to the parent, by calling `init(totalUnitCount:parent:pendingUnitCount:)`.

Implicit parent
> This approach uses the notion of the *current* Progress object. The rule is that while a Progress object is current, any new Progress objects will become its child automatically. The whole procedure comes down to doing things in the right order:
>
> 1. Tell the prospective parent Progress object to `becomeCurrent(withPending-UnitCount:)`.
>
> 2. Create the child Progress object without an explicit parent, by calling `init(totalUnitCount:)`. As if by magic, it becomes the other Progress object's child (because the other Progress object is current).
>
> 3. Tell the parent to `resignCurrent`. This balances the earlier `become-Current(withPendingUnitCount:)` and completes the configuration.

UIPickerView

A picker view (UIPickerView) displays selectable choices using a rotating drum metaphor. Its default height is adaptive — 162 in an environment with a `.compact` vertical size class (an iPhone in landscape orientation) and 216 otherwise — but you are free to set its height to something else. Its width is generally up to you.

Each drum, or column, is called a *component*. Your code configures the UIPickerView's content through its data source (UIPickerViewDataSource) and delegate (UIPickerViewDelegate), which are usually the same object. Your data source and delegate must answer some Big Questions similar to those posed by a UITableView (Chapter 8):

`numberOfComponents(in:)`
> How many components (drums) does this picker view have?

`pickerView(_:numberOfRowsInComponent:)`
> How many rows does this component have? The first component is numbered 0.

`pickerView(_:titleForRow:forComponent:)`
`pickerView(_:attributedTitleForRow:forComponent:)`
`pickerView(_:viewForRow:forComponent:reusing:)`
> What should this row of this component display? The first row is numbered 0. You can supply a simple string, an attributed string (Chapter 11), or an entire view such as a UILabel; but you should supply every row of every component the same way.

 In `pickerView(_:viewForRow:forComponent:reusing:)`, the `reusing:` parameter, if not `nil`, is supposed to be a view that you supplied for a row now no longer visible, giving you a chance to reuse it, much as cells are reused in a table view. In actual fact, the `reusing:` parameter is *always* `nil`. Views don't leak — they go out of existence in good order when they are no longer visible — but they aren't reused. I regard this as a bug.

Here's the code for a UIPickerView (Figure 13-6) that displays the names of the 50 U.S. states, stored in an array (`self.states`). We implement `pickerView(_:viewForRow:forComponent:reusing:)` just because it's the most interesting case; as our views, we supply UILabel instances. The `view` parameter is always `nil`, so we ignore it and make a new UILabel every time we're called. The state names appear centered because the labels are centered within the picker view:

```
func numberOfComponents(in pickerView: UIPickerView) -> Int {
    return 1
}
func pickerView(_ pickerView: UIPickerView,
    numberOfRowsInComponent component: Int) -> Int {
```

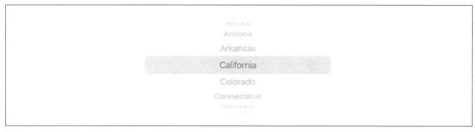

Figure 13-6. A picker view

```
        return self.states.count
    }
    func pickerView(_ pickerView: UIPickerView,
        viewForRow row: Int,
        forComponent component: Int,
        reusing view: UIView?) -> UIView {
            let lab = UILabel()
            lab.text = self.states[row]
            lab.backgroundColor = .clear
            lab.sizeToFit()
            return lab
    }
```

The delegate may further configure the UIPickerView's physical appearance by means of these methods:

- `pickerView(_:rowHeightForComponent:)`

- `pickerView(_:widthForComponent:)`

The delegate may implement `pickerView(_:didSelectRow:inComponent:)`, so as to be notified each time the user spins a drum to a new position. You can also query the picker view directly by sending it `selectedRow(inComponent:)`.

You can set the value to which any drum is turned by calling `selectRow(_:in-Component:animated:)`. Other handy picker view methods allow you to request that the data be reloaded, and there are properties and methods to query the picker view's structure:

- `reloadComponent(_:)`

- `reloadAllComponents`

- `numberOfComponents`

- `numberOfRows(inComponent:)`

- `view(forRow:forComponent:)`

By implementing `pickerView(_:didSelectRow:inComponent:)` and calling `reload-Component(_:)`, you can make a picker view where the values displayed by one drum depend dynamically on what is selected in another. One can imagine extending our U.S. states example to include a second drum listing major cities in each state; when the user switches to a different state in the first drum, a different set of major cities appears in the second drum.

UIColorPickerViewController

New in iOS 14, a color picker interface is provided as a view controller. To use it, create a UIColorPickerViewController, give it a delegate, set its `supportsAlpha` if desired (the default is `true`, meaning that the user can choose a nonopaque color), and present the view controller. Before presenting the picker, you can set its `title` to replace the prompt that appears at the top. You can also set the `selectedColor` to dictate what color should be selected initially; the default is black.

Acting as the delegate (UIColorPickerViewControllerDelegate), implement these methods:

`colorPickerViewControllerDidSelectColor(_:)`
> The user has selected a color. In your implementation, fetch the color picker's `selectedColor`.

`colorPickerViewControllerDidFinish(_:)`
> The user has dismissed the picker, using the X button. If the user dismisses the picker by dragging it down, this method won't be called.

The user can keep selecting colors while the picker is displayed, and can dismiss the picker either with the X button or by dragging. There's no Cancel button, so let's presume dragging to dismiss signifies cancellation. Then we can store the user's selection in an instance property, using it only if the picker is dismissed with the X button:

```
var chosenColor: UIColor?
@IBAction func doButton(_ sender: Any) {
    let cp = UIColorPickerViewController()
    cp.delegate = self
    self.present(cp, animated: true)
    self.chosenColor = nil
}
func colorPickerViewControllerDidSelectColor(
    _ viewController: UIColorPickerViewController) {
        self.chosenColor = viewController.selectedColor
}
func colorPickerViewControllerDidFinish(
    _ viewController: UIColorPickerViewController) {
        if let color = self.chosenColor {
            // use color here
        }
}
```

Figure 13-7. A search bar with a search results button

UISearchBar

A search bar (UISearchBar) is essentially a wrapper for a text field; it has a text field as one of its subviews. It is displayed by default as a rounded rectangle containing a magnifying glass icon, where the user can enter text (Figure 13-7). It does not, of itself, do any searching or display the results of a search; a common interface involves displaying the results of a search in a table view, and the UISearchController class makes this easy to do (see Chapter 8).

A search bar's current text is its `text` property. It can have a `placeholder`, which appears when there is no text. A `prompt` can be displayed above the search bar to explain its purpose. Delegate methods (UISearchBarDelegate) notify you of editing events; for their use, compare the text field and text view delegate methods discussed in Chapter 11:

- `searchBarShouldBeginEditing(_:)`
- `searchBarTextDidBeginEditing(_:)`
- `searchBar(_:textDidChange:)`
- `searchBar(_:shouldChangeTextIn:replacementText:)`
- `searchBarShouldEndEditing(_:)`
- `searchBarTextDidEndEditing(_:)`

A search bar has a `barStyle` (UIBarStyle):

- `.default`, a white background and a light gray search field
- `.black`, a black background and a black search field (with white text)

In addition, there's a `searchBarStyle` property (UISearchBar.Style):

- `.default`, as already described
- `.prominent`, identical to `.default`
- `.minimal`, transparent background without a border

Alternatively, you can set a search bar's `barTintColor` to change its background color; if the bar style is `.black`, the `barTintColor` will also tint the search field itself. The `tintColor` property, whose value may be inherited from higher up the view hierarchy, governs the color of search bar components such as the Cancel button title and the flashing insertion cursor.

A search bar can also have a custom backgroundImage; this will be treated as a resizable image. The backgroundImage overrides all other ways of determining the background, and the search bar's backgroundColor, if any, appears behind it — though under some circumstances, if the search bar's isTranslucent is false, the barTintColor may appear behind it instead.

The search field area where the user enters text can be offset with respect to its background, using the searchFieldBackgroundPositionAdjustment property; you might do this if you have enlarged the search bar's height and want to reposition the search field within that height. The text can be offset within the search field with the searchTextPositionAdjustment property.

You can also replace the image of the search field itself; this is the image that is normally a rounded rectangle. To do so, call setSearchFieldBackgroundImage(_:for:). The second parameter is a UIControl.State; the possible states are .normal and .disabled. But a search bar has no disabled state; the state here refers to the search field, which is a text field and *can* be disabled. Before iOS 13, there was no official access to this text field; you had to cycle through the search bar's subviews recursively to find it (for subviews(ofType:), see Appendix B):

```
if let tf = self.sb.subviews(ofType: UITextField.self).first {
    tf.isEnabled = false
}
```

Starting in iOS 13, the search field is directly exposed through the search bar's searchTextField property:

```
self.sb.searchTextField.isEnabled = false
```

The search field image will be drawn vertically centered in front of the background and behind the contents of the search field (such as the text); its width will be adjusted for you, but it is up to you choose an appropriate height, and to ensure an appropriate background color so that the user can read the text.

A search bar displays an internal cancel button automatically (normally an X in a circle) if there is text in the search field. Internally, at its right end, a search bar may display a search results button (showsSearchResultsButton), which may be selected or not (isSearchResultsButtonSelected), or a bookmark button (showsBookmarkButton); if you ask to display both, you'll get the search results button. These buttons vanish if text is entered in the search bar so that the cancel button can be displayed. There is also an option to display a Cancel button externally (showsCancelButton, or call setShowsCancelButton(_:animated:)). The internal cancel button works automatically to remove whatever text is in the field; the other buttons do nothing, but delegate methods notify you when they are tapped:

- searchBarResultsListButtonClicked(_:)
- searchBarBookmarkButtonClicked(_:)
- searchBarCancelButtonClicked(_:)

You can customize the images used for the search icon (a magnifying glass, by default) and any of the internal right icons (the internal cancel button, the search results button, and the bookmark button) with setImage(_:for:state:); about 20×20 seems to be a good size. The icon in question (the for: parameter) is specified using one of these values (UISearchBar.Icon):

- .search
- .clear (the internal cancel button)
- .bookmark
- .resultsList

The documentation says that the possible state: values are .normal and .disabled, but this is wrong; the choices are .normal and .highlighted. The highlighted image appears while the user taps on the icon (except for the search icon, which isn't a button). If you don't supply a normal image, the default image is used; if you supply a normal image but no highlighted image, the normal image is used for both. Setting isSearchResultsButtonSelected to true reverses the search results button's behavior: it displays the highlighted image, but when the user taps it, it displays the normal image. To change an icon's location, call setPositionAdjustment(_:for:).

It may appear that there is no way to customize the external Cancel button, but in fact, although you've no official direct access to it through the search bar, you can customize it using the UIBarButtonItem appearance proxy, as discussed later in this chapter.

A search bar may also display scope buttons. These are intended to let the user alter the meaning of the search; precisely how you use them is up to you. To make the scope buttons appear, use the showsScopeBar property. The actual button titles are the scopeButtonTitles property; the currently selected scope button is the selectedScopeButtonIndex property. The delegate is notified when the user taps a different scope button:

- searchBar(_:selectedScopeButtonIndexDidChange:)

The overall look of the scope bar can be heavily customized, using these properties and methods:

scopeBarBackgroundImage
    The scope bar background. It will be stretched or tiled as needed.

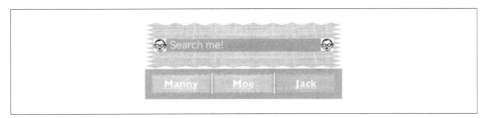

Figure 13-8. A horrible search bar

`setScopeBarButtonBackgroundImage(_:for:)`
Sets the background of the smaller area constituting the actual buttons; the states (the `for:` parameter) are `.normal` and `.selected`. You should supply a resizable image; if you don't, the image will be made resizable for you, but you might not like the way the runtime decides what region of the image will be stretched behind each button.

`setScopeBarButtonDividerImage(_:forLeftSegmentState:rightSegmentState:)`
The dividers between the buttons are normally vertical lines, but you can customize them with this method. A full complement of dividers consists of three images, one when the buttons on both sides of the divider are normal (unselected) and one each when a button on one side or the other is selected; if you supply an image for just one state combination, it is used for the other two state combinations. The height of the divider image is adjusted for you, but the width is not; you'll normally use an image just a few pixels wide.

`setScopeBarButtonTitleTextAttributes(_:for:)`
The text attributes of the titles of the scope buttons. The attributes are specified like the attributes dictionary of an NSAttributedString (Chapter 11).

By combining the various customization possibilities, a completely unrecognizable search bar of inconceivable ugliness can easily be achieved (Figure 13-8). Let's be careful out there.

The problem of allowing the keyboard to appear without covering the search bar is exactly as for a text field (Chapter 11). Text input properties of the search bar configure its keyboard and typing behavior like a text field as well. When the user taps the Search key in the keyboard, the delegate is notified, and it is then up to you to dismiss the keyboard (`resignFirstResponder`) and perform the search:

- `searchBarSearchButtonClicked(_:)`

Starting in iOS 13, a search bar's text field (UISearchTextField) lets you display *search tokens* (UISearchToken). A search token is initialized with text (and possibly an image) and is displayed as a rounded-rectangle cartouche; you should also set its `representedObject` so you know what the search token signifies. The user can select and delete an entire token, unless you set the field's `allowsDeletingTokens` to `false`.

Each search token is a single-length "character," and any search tokens in the search field must precede any actual text; if you try to put a search token anywhere else, you'll crash. The field's `textualRange` tells you what part of the field consists of real text.

A search bar can be embedded in a toolbar or navigation bar as a bar button item's custom view, or in a navigation bar as a `titleView`. A common configuration is a UISearchController's search bar in a navigation bar; see the discussion of the UINavigationItem `searchController` property in Chapter 8. Alternatively, a UISearchBar can *itself* function as a top bar, without being inside any other bar. In that case, you'll want the search bar's height to be extended automatically under the status bar; I'll explain later in this chapter how to arrange that.

UIControl

UIControl is a subclass of UIView whose chief purpose is to be the superclass of several further built-in classes (controls) and to endow them with common behavior.

A text field (UITextField) is a control; see Chapter 11. A refresh control (UIRefreshControl) is a control; see Chapter 8. The remaining controls are covered in this section, and then I'll give a simple example of writing your own custom control.

Control States

A control has `isEnabled`, `isSelected`, and `isHighlighted` properties; any of these can be `true` or `false` independently of the others. Together, they correspond to the control's `state`, a bitmask of three possible values (UIControl.State):

- `.highlighted` (`isHighlighted` is `true`)
- `.disabled` (`isEnabled` is `false`)
- `.selected` (`isSelected` is `true`)

A fourth state, `.normal`, corresponds to a zero `state` bitmask, meaning that `isEnabled` is `true` and that `isSelected` and `isHighlighted` are both `false`.

A control that is not enabled does not respond to user interaction. Whether the control also portrays itself differently, to cue the user to this fact, depends upon the control. A disabled UISwitch is faded, but a rounded rect text field, by default, gives the user no obvious cue that it is disabled. The visual nature of control selection and highlighting, too, depends on the control. Neither highlighting nor selection make any difference to the appearance of a UISwitch, but a highlighted UIButton usually looks quite different from a normal UIButton.

Control Events

The most important thing that controls have in common is that they automatically track and analyze touch events (Chapter 5) and report them to your code as significant *control events* by way of action messages. Each control implements some subset of the possible control events. The fundamental control events (UIControl.Event) are:

- `.touchDown`
- `.touchDownRepeat`
- `.touchDragInside`
- `.touchDragOutside`
- `.touchDragEnter`
- `.touchDragExit`
- `.touchUpInside`
- `.touchUpOutside`
- `.touchCancel`
- `.valueChanged`
- `.editingDidBegin`
- `.editingChanged`
- `.editingDidEnd`
- `.editingDidEndOnExit`

The control events also have informal names that are visible in the Connections inspector when you're editing a nib. I'll mostly use the informal names in the next couple of paragraphs.

Control events fall roughly into three groups:

- The user has touched the screen (Touch Down, Touch Drag Inside, Touch Up Inside, etc.).
- The user has edited text (Editing Did Begin, Editing Changed, etc.).
- The user has changed the control's value (Value Changed).

Apple's documentation is rather coy about which controls normally emit actions for which control events, so here's a list obtained through experimentation:

UIButton
    All Touch events

UIColorWell, UIDatePicker, UIRefreshControl, UISegmentedControl
   Value Changed

UIPageControl, UISlider, UISwitch, UIStepper
   All Touch events, Value Changed

UITextField
   All Touch events except the Up events, and all Editing events (see Chapter 11 for details)

UIControl (generic)
   All Touch events

There are also two specialized control events.

- `.primaryActionTriggered`
- `.menuActionTriggered` (new in iOS 14)

The `.primaryActionTriggered` event fires after a control's primary action event has fired. This is presumably to save you from having to remember what this control's primary control event is. The primary control event is Value Changed for all controls except for UIButton, where it is Touch Up Inside, and UITextField, where it is Did End On Exit.

I'll explain the `.menuActionTriggered` event a little later.

Control Actions

To hear about a control event occurring, there's an *action mechanism*. For each control event that you want to hear about, you attach to the control, in advance, an action — essentially, a function. The control maintains a dispatch table for each control event. The dispatch table permits multiple actions to be attached to the same control event (though that's not a common thing to do). Thenceforward, when that control event actually occurs, the control *calls* all the action functions for that event.

There are three ways to configure a control's dispatch table with an action.

Target-action pair

The oldest way to give a control an action, going right back to the beginnings of Cocoa itself, is through a target–action pair. The action here is a selector; the target is an object that will exist at the time the control event occurs. For this to work, the target object needs to be introspectable by Objective-C: it should be an NSObject subclass, it should implement the action method, and the action method should be marked `@objc` so that Objective-C can find and call it.

These methods and properties permit you to manipulate and query a control's action–target pairs:

- `addTarget(_:action:for:)`
- `removeTarget(_:action:for:)`
- `actions(forTarget:forControlEvent:)`
- `allTargets`
- `allControlEvents` (a bitmask of control events with at least one target–action pair attached)

An action method (the method that will be called on the target when the control event occurs) may adopt any of three signatures, whose parameters are:

- The control and the UIEvent
- The control only
- No parameters

The second signature is by far the most common. It's unlikely that you'd want to dispense altogether with the parameter telling you which control sent the control event. It's equally unlikely that you'd want to examine the original UIEvent that triggered this control event, since control events deliberately shield you from dealing with the nitty-gritty of touches. (I suppose you might, on rare occasions, have some reason to examine the UIEvent's `timestamp`.)

 The target–action messaging mechanism is actually more complex than I've just stated. The UIControl does not really send the action message directly; rather, it tells the shared application to send it. When a control wants to send an action message reporting a control event, it calls its own `sendAction(_:to:for:)` method. This in turn calls the shared application instance's `sendAction(_:to:from:for:)`, which actually sends the specified action message to the specified target. In theory, you could call or override either of these methods to customize this aspect of the message-sending architecture, but it is extremely unlikely that you would do so.

Nib editor

The second way to configure a control's dispatch table is in the nib editor. That's what an *action connection* is for. This is actually the target–action mechanism in another guise. An action connection is a effectively a graphical way of forming (and, at nib-loading time, running) the `addTarget(_:action:for:)` command. That's possible because an action connection in a nib specifies all the needed information:

- Its source is the control object.
- Its destination is the target.
- You tell the action connection, as you form it, what the control event should be (in the control) and what the action message should be (in the target).

UIActions

New in iOS 14, there's another way of expressing an action. Instead of specifying a target that implements the action as a method, you hand the action function directly to the control, which retains it. No explicit target is needed, because the function is now effectively inside the control itself.

This approach revolves around the UIAction class — the very same class that I described earlier in connection with UIMenu items ("Previews and Context Menus" on page 386). It wraps a function, supplied as the `handler:` parameter when the UIAction is initialized. In a UIMenu, the function is called when the menu item is tapped. In a control, the function is called when the control emits the control event. In general, the UIAction doesn't need a `title` or any property other than the `handler:` function, as it will never appear visibly as a menu item in the interface; it's just a wrapper for the function.

To attach a UIAction to an existing control, call the control's `addAction(_:for:)` method. In this example, I have a UIButton `button`, and I give it an action:

```
button.addAction(.init {action in
    print("Your \(type(of:action.sender!)) is calling you!")
}, for: .touchUpInside)
```

When the button is tapped, the console prints "Your UIButton is calling you!" As you can see, there is no explicit target, and there is no separate action method. The action is expressed by a function, which can be an anonymous function supplied inline. The function receives the UIAction as its parameter, and the UIAction has the `sender` as a property.

This notation is far more compact, legible, and maintainable than the Cocoa target–action notation. But I don't like the fact that `addAction(_:for:)` requires me to supply the UIAction as the first parameter; the anonymous function interrupts the flow of the method call. In fact, I don't like the fact that I have to form a UIAction in the first place; all that interests me is the `handler:` function, so why doesn't `addAction` just *take* that function?

Naturally, I've written an extension to fix that little problem (Appendix B); with it, I can add an action to a UIControl by calling `addAction(for:handler:)`, like this:

```
button.addAction(for: .touchUpInside) { action in
    print("This is so much nicer! Thanks", type(of:action.sender!))
}
```

If you are creating the control in code, there's an even more economical way; call the UIControl initializer `init(frame:primaryAction:)`. No control event is specified; you're associating the UIAction with the control's `.primaryActionTriggered` control event. That's almost certainly the control event you wanted, so that approach is likely to be extremely handy.

A UIAction attached to a control becomes part of the control's dispatch table for the control event you've specified, but it does *not* cause any target to be added to the control's list of targets as returned by `allTargets`, and a call to `actions(forTarget:for-ControlEvent:)` will not find the UIAction. Instead, there are additional methods for manipulating the list of UIActions attached to a control:

- `enumerateEventHandlers(_:)`
- `removeAction(_:for:)`
- `removeAction(identifiedBy:for:)`

The first of those methods, `enumerateEventHandlers(_:)`, is the key to introspecting the complete list of actions registered with the control's dispatch table. You supply a function that takes four parameters: an action, a target–action pair (expressed as a tuple), a control event, and a pointer to a Bool (so that you can stop the enumeration by setting its `pointee` to `true`). The function is called for each event handler in the dispatch table. The parameters reflect how the event handler was added:

As a UIAction

> If this event handler was added as a UIAction, the first parameter will be the UIAction and the second parameter will be nil.

As a target–action pair

> If this event handler was added as a target–action pair, the first parameter will be nil and the second parameter will be a tuple consisting of the target and the action selector.

The third parameter is the control event under which the action is registered. Here's a toy example for testing purposes:

```
button.enumerateEventHandlers { action, pair, event, stop in
    print("got an action for", event)
    if action != nil {
        print("This one is a UIAction")
    }
    if pair != nil {
        print("This one is a target-action and the target is", pair!.0)
    }
}
```

Running an action function manually

To make a control emit its action message(s) corresponding to a particular control event right now, in code, call its sendActions(for:) method (which is never called automatically by the runtime). This includes both any target–action pairs and any UIActions that have been attached to the control's dispatch table for the given control event.

Suppose you tell a UISwitch programmatically to change its setting from Off to On. This doesn't cause the switch to report a control event, as it would if the *user* had slid the switch from Off to On; if you wanted it to do so, you could use send-Actions(for:), like this:

```
self.sw.setOn(true, animated: true)
self.sw.sendActions(for:.valueChanged)
```

You might also use sendActions(for:) in a subclass to customize the circumstances under which a control reports control events. I'll give an example later in this chapter.

New in iOS 14, you can also make a control perform the handler for a UIAction that you supply at that moment, *without* attaching it to the dispatch table, by calling send-Action(_:). (But it's not clear to me what the purpose would be in doing that.)

Figure 13-9. A switch

Control Menus

New in iOS 14, a UIControl can have a menu, which will typically appear when the user long presses on the control. This is the same UIMenu mechanism that I discussed earlier ("Previews and Context Menus" on page 386): a UIContextMenuInteraction is attached to the control, and its delegate then supplies the menu.

In general, however, *you* won't attach the context menu interaction or act as its delegate. UIControl *itself* conforms to UIContextMenuInteractionDelegate and implements the delegate methods. A control that wants you to be able to attach a menu to it will give you a way to do that, and the control itself will then be responsible for the context menu interaction and its configuration. The main UIControl subclass that does that is UIButton, which has a menu property; I'll talk about that later. You could do something similar with your own UIControl subclass.

When a control is tappable, it may be that you want the tap, rather than a long press, to summon the menu. To accommodate that possibility, UIControl has a showsMenuAsPrimaryAction property; the default is false, but you can set it to true. The likely case in point, in real life, will be a UIButton once again.

Before the menu appears, the control emits a .menuActionTriggered control event. It is legal, at that moment, to construct the menu and assign it to the control, implementing a dynamic menu. I'll give an example later.

UISwitch

A switch (UISwitch, Figure 13-9) portrays a Bool value: it looks like a sliding switch, and its isOn property is either true or false. The user can slide or tap to toggle the switch's setting. When the user changes the switch's setting, the switch reports a Value Changed control event. To change the isOn property's value with accompanying animation, call setOn(_:animated:).

A switch has only one size; any attempt to set its size will be ignored. You can customize a switch's appearance by setting these properties:

onTintColor
    The color of the track when the switch is at the On setting.

thumbTintColor
    The color of the slidable button.

There is no offTintColor property. A switch's track when the switch is at the Off setting is a translucent gray, and its color can't be customized. I regard this as a bug. Merely changing the switch's backgroundColor is not a successful workaround, because the background color shows outside the switch's outline. A hacky workaround is to locate the switch's subview that draws its filled shape when the switch is off, and change *its* background color:

```
self.sw.subviews.first?.subviews.first?.backgroundColor = .green
```

UIColorWell

New in iOS 14, a color well (UIColorWell) displays itself by default as a color wheel; when tapped, it presents the UIColorPickerViewController (discussed earlier in this chapter). It has title, supportsAlpha, and selectedColor properties whose values are forwarded to the UIColorPickerViewController. When the user chooses a color, a Value Changed event is emitted, and the color well's display changes to a circular swatch of that color; you can respond by retrieving the selectedColor.

As of this writing, there is no color well in the storyboard editor's library, so you'll have to create the control in code:

```
let well = UIColorWell(frame: .zero)
well.addAction(UIAction { action in
    if let c = (action.sender as? UIColorWell)?.selectedColor {
        // use the color here
    }
}, for: .valueChanged)
well.title = "Pick a color:"
self.view.addSubview(well)
// position using autolayout, or set frame origin and call sizeToFit
```

Unfortunately, there is no way to learn when the view controller is dismissed or *how* it was dismissed (whether the user tapped the X button or cancelled by dragging down); so it might be better to use the color picker view controller directly.

UIStepper

A stepper (UIStepper, Figure 13-10) looks like two buttons side by side, one labeled (by default) with a minus sign, the other with a plus sign. The user can tap or hold a button, and can slide a finger from one button to the other as part of the same interaction with the stepper.

The stepper maintains a numeric value, which is its value; this is what the user is manipulating with the stepper's buttons, incrementing or decrementing it by 1. Each time the user increments or decrements the value, it changes by the stepper's stepValue. If the minimumValue or maximumValue is reached, the user can go no further in that direction, and to show this, the corresponding button is disabled — unless the

Figure 13-10. A stepper

stepper's `wraps` property is `true`, in which case the value goes beyond the maximum by starting again at the minimum, and *vice versa*.

As the user changes the stepper's `value`, a Value Changed control event is reported. Portraying the numeric value itself is up to you; you might use a label or (as here) a progress view:

```
@IBAction func doStep(_ sender: Any) {
    let step = sender as! UIStepper
    self.prog.setProgress(
        Float(step.value / (step.maximumValue - step.minimumValue)),
        animated:true)
}
```

If a stepper's `isContinuous` is `true` (the default), a long touch on one of the buttons will update the value repeatedly; the updates start slowly and get faster. If the stepper's `autorepeat` is `false`, the updated value is not reported as a Value Changed control event until the entire interaction with the stepper ends; the default is `true`.

A stepper has only one size, but most other aspects of the appearance of a stepper can be customized. The color of the outline and the button captions is the stepper's `tintColor`, which may be inherited from further up the view hierarchy. You can also dictate the images that constitute the stepper's structure with these methods:

- `setDecrementImage(_:for:)`
- `setIncrementImage(_:for:)`
- `setDividerImage(_:forLeftSegmentState:rightSegmentState:)`
- `setBackgroundImage(_:for:)`

The images work similarly to a search bar's scope bar (described earlier in this chapter). The background images should probably be resizable; they are stretched behind both buttons, half the image being seen as the background of each button. If the button is disabled (because we've reached the value's limit in that direction), it displays the `.disabled` background image; otherwise, it displays the `.normal` background image, except that it displays the `.highlighted` background image while the user is tapping it. You'll probably want to provide all three background images if you're going to provide any; the default is used if a state's background image is `nil`. You'll probably want to provide three divider images as well, to cover the three combinations of one or neither segment being highlighted. The increment and decrement

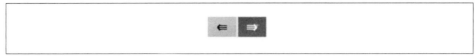

Figure 13-11. A customized stepper

images, replacing the default minus and plus signs, are composited on top of the background image; they are treated as template images, colored by the `tintColor`, unless you explicitly provide an `.alwaysOriginal` image. If you provide only a `.normal` image, it will be adjusted automatically for the other two states. Figure 13-11 shows a customized stepper.

UIPageControl

A page control (UIPageControl) is a row of dots; each dot is called a *page*, because it is intended to be used in conjunction with some other interface that portrays something analogous to pages, such as a UIScrollView with its `isPagingEnabled` set to `true`. Coordinating the page control with this other interface is usually up to you; see Chapter 7 for an example. A UIPageViewController in scroll style can optionally display a page control that's automatically coordinated with its content (Chapter 6).

The number of dots is the page control's `numberOfPages`. At all times, exactly one dot is selected; this is the page control's `currentPage`. To learn the minimum bounds size required to accommodate a given number of dots, call `size(forNumberOfPages:)`. New in iOS 14, the page control doesn't have to be wide enough to accommodate all the page dots at once; if there are too many dots for the space provided, the dots will scroll sideways automatically when the user selects the next-to-last dot currently displayed. If a page control's `hidesForSinglePage` is `true`, the page control becomes invisible when its `numberOfPages` changes to 1.

The dot colors differentiate the current page from the others; by default, the current page is portrayed as a solid dot, while the others are slightly transparent. You can customize a page control's `pageIndicatorTintColor` (the color of the dots in general) and `currentPageIndicatorTintColor` (the color of the current page's dot); you will almost certainly want to do this, as the default dot color is white, which under normal circumstances may be hard to see. It is possible to set a page control's `background-Color`; you might do this to show the user the tappable area, or to make the dots more clearly visible by contrast.

New in iOS 14, you can substitute a custom shape for the dots. Set the `preferred-IndicatorImage` property to set all the shapes; call `setIndicatorImage(_:forPage:)` to set one shape. The image is treated as a template image; setting the rendering mode to `.alwaysOriginal` has no effect. If the image is not a vector image (such as a symbol image), it is not resized automatically; on the contrary, the page control itself is sized up to embrace a large image.

Now let's talk about how the user interacts with the page control. One way is by tapping. This increments or decrements the current page. It doesn't matter what dot the user taps on, or even whether the user taps on a dot; all that matters is which side of the current dot the user taps on. In fact, you can make the page control wider than the dots to increase the target region on which the user can tap.

New in iOS 14, a page control permits another sort of user interaction — *continuous* interaction. A tapping interaction is a *discrete* interaction (during which the page control's `interactionState` is `.discrete`). But with continuous interaction, the user long presses on a dot, and can slide to another dot to change the page (and the page control's `interactionState` is `.continuous`). Continuous interaction is enabled by default, but you can turn it off by setting `allowsContinuousInteraction` to `false`.

The page control by default displays a cartouche around the dots during a continuous interaction; you can change that behavior by setting the page control's `background-Style`:

- `.automatic` (the default behavior)
- `.prominent` (the cartouche always appears)
- `.minimal` (the cartouche never appears)

When the cartouche is visible, the `pageIndicatorTintColor` is replaced by a default gray.

When the user changes what dot is currently selected, the page control reports a Value Changed control event.

UIDatePicker

A date picker (UIDatePicker) is a control that expresses the notion of a date and time, taking care of the calendrical and numerical complexities so that you don't have to. When the user changes its setting, the date picker reports a Value Changed control event.

New in iOS 14, the visible interface is completely overhauled. The old interface looks like a UIPickerView (discussed earlier in this chapter), but you might not get that interface unless you explicitly set your date picker's `preferredDatePickerStyle` to `.wheels`. To get the new interface, set the `preferredDatePickerStyle` to one of these:

`.inline`
    The full date picker interface is shown at all times.

`.compact`

    The date picker interface is just a line of text. When the user taps on it, it expands to reveal the full interface.

A UIDatePicker has one of four modes (`datePickerMode`) determining how it is drawn (UIDatePicker.Mode). The exact details depend upon the locale, meaning (by default) the user's region settings; I'll describe the United States appearance:

`.time`

    The date picker displays a time. The old `.wheels` style has an hour component and a minutes component. The new interface is a time label that you can tap to edit with the numeric keypad, along with an AM/PM segmented control.

`.date`

    The date picker displays a date. The old `.wheels` style has a month component, a day component, and a year component. The new style is a month calendar.

`.dateAndTime`

    The date picker displays a date and time. The old `.wheels` style has a component showing day of the week, month, and day, plus an hour component and a minutes component. The new style is a month calendar containing a time label and an AM/PM segmented control.

`.countDownTimer`

    The date picker displays a number of hours and minutes; for example, it has an hours component and a minutes component. The date picker style must *not* be `.compact` or `.inline` (if it is, the app will crash).

The interface may differ depending on the user's region. For instance, a U.S. time displays an hour numbered 1 through 12 plus minutes and AM or PM; but a British time displays an hour numbered 1 through 24 plus minutes, so there is no AM/PM component or segmented control. If the user changes the region format in the Settings app, the date picker's display will change immediately.

A date picker has `calendar` and `timeZone` properties, respectively a Calendar and a TimeZone; these are `nil` by default, meaning that the date picker responds to the user's system settings. You can also change these values manually; if you live in California and you set a date picker's `timeZone` to GMT, the displayed time is shifted forward by 8 hours, so that 11 AM is displayed as 7 PM (if it is winter).

For the old `.wheels` style, the minutes component defaults to showing every minute, but you can change this with the `minuteInterval` property. The maximum value is 30, in which case the minutes component values are 0 and 30. An attempt to set the `minuteInterval` to a value that doesn't divide evenly into 60 will be silently ignored.

The date represented by a date picker (unless its mode is .countDownTimer) is its date property, a Date. The default date is now, at the time the date picker is instantiated. For a .date date picker, the time by default is 12 AM (midnight), local time; for a .time date picker, the date by default is today. The internal value is reckoned in the local time zone, so it may be different from the displayed value, if you have changed the date picker's timeZone.

The maximum and minimum values enabled in the date picker are determined by its maximumDate and minimumDate properties. Values outside this range may appear, but they will be disabled and the user won't be able to choose one. There isn't really any practical limit on the range that a date picker can display, because the interface is dynamic. In this example, we set the initial minimum and maximum dates of a date picker (dp) to the beginning and end of 1954. We also set the actual date, so that the date picker will be set initially to a value within the minimum–maximum range:

```
dp.datePickerMode = .date
var dc = DateComponents(year:1954, month:1, day:1)
let c = Calendar(identifier:.gregorian)
let d1 = c.date(from: dc)!
dp.minimumDate = d1
dp.date = d1
dc.year = 1955
let d2 = c.date(from: dc)!
dp.maximumDate = d2
```

The value displayed in a .countDownTimer date picker is its countDownDuration; this is a TimeInterval, which is a Double representing a number of seconds, even though the minimum interval displayed is a minute. A .countDownTimer date picker does not actually do any counting down! You are expected to count down in some other way, and to use some other interface to display the countdown. The Timer tab of Apple's Clock app shows a typical interface; the user configures a picker view to set the countDownDuration initially, but once the counting starts, the picker view is hidden and a label displays the remaining time.

 Don't change the timeZone of a .countDownTimer date picker; if you do, the displayed value will be shifted, and you will confuse the heck out of yourself (and your users). Don't set the maximumDate and minimumDate properties values for a .countDownTimer date picker; if you do, you might cause a crash with an out-of-range exception. A nasty bug makes the Value Changed event from a .countDownTimer date picker unreliable (especially just after the app launches, and whenever the user has tried to set the timer to zero). The workaround is not to rely on the Value Changed event; you might provide a button in the interface that the user can tap to make your code read the date picker's countDownDuration.

UISlider

A slider (UISlider) is an expression of a continuously settable value (its value, a Float) between some minimum and maximum (its minimumValue and maximumValue; they are 0 and 1 by default). It is portrayed as an object, the *thumb*, positioned along a *track*. As the user changes the thumb's position, the slider reports a Value Changed control event; it may do this continuously as the user presses and drags the thumb (if the slider's isContinuous is true, the default) or only when the user releases the thumb (if isContinuous is false). While the user is pressing on the thumb, the slider is in the .highlighted state. To change a slider's value with animation of the thumb, call setValue(_:animated:); to set the speed of the animation, call that method in an animations function.

A commonly expressed desire is to modify a slider's behavior so that if the user taps on its track, the slider moves to the spot where the user tapped. Unfortunately, a slider does not, of itself, respond to taps on its track; no control event is reported. Still, with a gesture recognizer, most things are possible; here's the action method for a UITapGestureRecognizer attached to a UISlider:

```
@objc func tapped(_ g:UIGestureRecognizer) {
    let s = g.view as! UISlider
    if s.isHighlighted {
        return // tap on thumb, let slider deal with it
    }
    let pt = g.location(in:s)
    let track = s.trackRect(forBounds: s.bounds)
    if !track.insetBy(dx: 0, dy: -10).contains(pt) {
        return // not on track, forget it
    }
    let percentage = pt.x / s.bounds.size.width
    let delta = Float(percentage) * (s.maximumValue - s.minimumValue)
    let value = s.minimumValue + delta
    delay(0.1) {
        UIView.animate(withDuration: 0.15) {
            s.setValue(value, animated:true) // animate sliding the thumb
        }
    }
}
```

A slider's tintColor (which may be inherited from further up the view hierarchy) determines the color of the track to the left of the thumb. You can change the color of the two parts of the track with the minimumTrackTintColor and maximumTrackTint-Color properties. You can change the color of the thumb with the thumbTintColor property.

The images at the ends of the track are the slider's minimumValueImage and maximum-ValueImage, and they are nil by default. If you set them to actual images (which can also be done in the nib editor), the slider will attempt to position them within its own

Figure 13-12. Repositioning a slider's images and track

Figure 13-13. Replacing a slider's thumb

bounds, shrinking the drawing of the track to compensate. You can change that behavior by overriding these methods in a subclass:

- `minimumValueImageRect(forBounds:)`

- `maximumValueImageRect(forBounds:)`

- `trackRect(forBounds:)`

The bounds passed in are the slider's bounds. In this example (Figure 13-12), we expand the track width to the full width of the slider, and draw the images outside the slider's bounds. The images are still visible, because the slider does not clip its subviews to its bounds. In the figure, I've given the slider a background color so you can see how the track and images are related to its bounds:

```
override func maximumValueImageRect(forBounds bounds: CGRect) -> CGRect {
    return super.maximumValueImageRect(
        forBounds:bounds).offsetBy(dx: 31, dy: 0)
}
override func minimumValueImageRect(forBounds bounds: CGRect) -> CGRect {
    return super.minimumValueImageRect(
        forBounds: bounds).offsetBy(dx: -31, dy: 0)
}
override func trackRect(forBounds bounds: CGRect) -> CGRect {
    var result = super.trackRect(forBounds: bounds)
    result.origin.x = 0
    result.size.width = bounds.size.width
    return result
}
```

The thumb is also an image, and you set it with `setThumbImage(_:for:)`. There are two chiefly relevant states, `.normal` and `.highlighted`. If you supply images for both, the thumb will change automatically while the user is dragging it. By default, the image will be centered in the track at the point represented by the slider's current value; you can shift this position by overriding `thumbRect(forBounds:trackRect:value:)` in a subclass. In this example, the image is repositioned slightly upward (Figure 13-13):

Figure 13-14. Replacing a slider's track

```
override func thumbRect(forBounds bounds: CGRect,
    trackRect rect: CGRect, value: Float) -> CGRect {
        return super.thumbRect(forBounds: bounds,
            trackRect: rect, value: value).offsetBy(dx: 0, dy: -7)
}
```

Enlarging or offsetting a slider's thumb can mislead the user as to the area where it can be touched to drag it. The slider, not the thumb, is the touchable UIControl; only the part of the thumb that intersects the slider's bounds will be draggable. The user may try to drag the part of the thumb that is drawn outside the slider's bounds, and will fail (and be confused). One solution is to increase the slider's height; if you're using autolayout, you can add an explicit height constraint in the nib editor, or override `intrinsicContentSize` in code (Chapter 1). Another solution is to subclass and use hit-test munging (Chapter 5):

```
override func hitTest(_ point: CGPoint, with e: UIEvent?) -> UIView? {
    let tr = self.trackRect(forBounds: self.bounds)
    if tr.contains(point) { return self }
    let r = self.thumbRect(
        forBounds: self.bounds, trackRect: tr, value: self.value)
    if r.contains(point) { return self }
    return nil
}
```

The track is two images, one appearing to the left of the thumb, the other to its right. They are set with `setMinimumTrackImage(_:for:)` and `setMaximumTrack-Image(_:for:)`. If you supply images both for `.normal` state and for `.highlighted` state, the images will change while the user is dragging the thumb. The images should be resizable, because that's how the slider cleverly makes it look like the user is dragging the thumb along a single static track. In reality, there are two images; as the user drags the thumb, one image grows horizontally and the other shrinks horizontally. For the left track image, the right end will be hidden under the thumb; for the right track image, the left end will be hidden under the thumb. Figure 13-14 shows a track derived from a single 15×15 image of a circular object (a coin):

```
let coinEnd = UIImage(named:"coin")!.resizableImage(withCapInsets:
    UIEdgeInsets(top: 0, left: 7, bottom: 0, right: 7), resizingMode: .stretch)
self.setMinimumTrackImage(coinEnd, for:.normal)
self.setMaximumTrackImage(coinEnd, for:.normal)
```

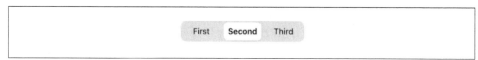

Figure 13-15. A segmented control

UISegmentedControl

A segmented control (UISegmentedControl, Figure 13-15) is a row of tappable seg-ments; a segment is rather like a button. The user taps a segment to select it, choosing among options. Starting in iOS 13, the selected segment is indicated by a rounded rectangle overlay. The behavior of this overlay depends on the segmented control's isMomentary property:

isMomentary *is* false
> The default. Tapping a segment causes the overlay to slide over to cover that seg-ment, where it remains.

isMomentary *is* true
> When a segment is tapped, the overlay appears momentarily and then vanishes, so that there is no visible indication that any segment is selected. Internally, the tapped segment remains the selected segment.

The selected segment can be set and retrieved with the selectedSegmentIndex prop-erty; when you set it in code, the selected segment remains visibly selected, even for an isMomentary segmented control. A selectedSegmentIndex value of UISegmented-Control.noSegment means no segment is selected. When the user taps a segment that isn't already visibly selected, the segmented control reports a Value Changed event.

A segment can be individually enabled or disabled with setEnabled(_:forSegment-At:), and its enabled state can be retrieved with isEnabledForSegment(at:). A disabled segment, by default, is drawn faded; the user can't tap it, but it can still be selected in code.

The background color of the selection overlay is dictated by the segmented control's selectedSegmentTintColor.

A segment has either a title or an image; when one is set, the other becomes nil. The methods for setting and fetching the title and image for existing segments are:

- setTitle(_:forSegmentAt:), titleForSegment(at:)
- setImage(_:forSegmentAt:), imageForSegment(at:)

An image is treated as a template image unless you explicitly provide an .always-Original image. A template image or a title gets its default color from the effective tint color. Starting in iOS 13, the effective tint color is *not* the segmented control's tintColor; the tintColor does nothing (I regard this as a bug). The default effective tint color is .label, and the way to change it is to set the segmented control's title text attributes to a different .foregroundColor, which then tints both titles and images:

```
self.seg.setTitleTextAttributes([
    .foregroundColor: UIColor.red
], for: .normal)
```

If you're creating the segmented control in code, you can configure the segments with init(items:), which takes an array, each item being either a string or an image:

```
let seg = UISegmentedControl(items: [
    UIImage(named:"one")!.withRenderingMode(.alwaysOriginal),
    "Two"
])
```

Methods for managing segments dynamically are:

- insertSegment(withTitle:at:animated:)
- insertSegment(with:at:animated:) (the first parameter is a UIImage)
- removeSegment(at:animated:)
- removeAllSegments

The number of segments can be retrieved with the read-only numberOfSegments property.

As I explained earlier, new in iOS 14, you can assign a UIAction to a control to supply the function to be triggered by a control event. A segmented control takes this idea even further: instead of assigning a single UIAction to the segmented control as a whole, you can assign UIActions to *individual segments*. That's a big improvement, because it means you don't have to examine the segmented control's selected-SegmentIndex to decide what to do.

Not only that, but a UIAction can contain title: and image: information, so this same mechanism becomes a way to configure the segments themselves! Whichever you supply, the title or the image, is displayed in the segment's interface. (If you supply both, the image wins.)

If you're creating the segmented control in code, you can use this initializer:

- init(frame:actions:)

In this example, a single call to the initializer creates the segments, sets the title and image for each one, and gives each segment its own action handler:

```
let im = UIImage(named:"one")!.withRenderingMode(.alwaysOriginal)
let action1 = UIAction(image: im) { action in
    print("segment zero selected")
}
let action2 = UIAction(title: "Two") { action in
    print("segment one selected")
}
let seg = UISegmentedControl(frame: .zero, actions:[action1, action2])
```

You can also insert a segment as a UIAction, set an existing segment's UIAction, and explore the relationship between segments and actions:

- `insertSegment(action:at:animated:)`

- `setAction(_:forSegmentAt:)`

- `segmentIndex(identifiedBy:)`

- `actionForSegment(at:)`

If the segmented control's `apportionsSegmentWidthsByContent` property is `false`, segment sizes will be made equal to one another; if it is `true`, each segment's width will be sized individually to fit its content. Alternatively, you can set a segment's width explicitly with `setWidth(_:forSegmentAt:)`; setting a segment's width to 0 means that this segment is to be sized automatically.

A segmented control has a standard height; if you're using autolayout, you can change the height through constraints or by overriding `intrinsicContentSize` — or by setting its background image, as I'll describe in a moment. A segmented control's height does *not* automatically increase to accommodate a segment image that's too tall; instead, the image's height is squashed to fit the segmented control's height.

To change the position of the content (title or image) within a segment, call `setContentOffset(_:forSegmentAt:)`.

Further methods for customizing a segmented control's appearance are parallel to those for setting the look of a stepper or the scope bar portion of a search bar:

- `setBackgroundImage(_:for:barMetrics:)`

- `setDividerImage(_:forLeftSegmentState:rightSegmentState:barMetrics:)`

- `setContentPositionAdjustment(_:forSegmentType:barMetrics:)`

I'll talk later about what the `barMetrics:` is ("Bar Metrics" on page 779); you'll usually pass `.default`. The `segmentType:` parameter is needed because, by default, the segments at the two extremes have rounded ends (and, if a segment is the lone segment, both its ends are rounded); the argument (UISegmentedControl.Segment) lets you distinguish among the possibilities:

Figure 13-16. A segmented control, customized

- `.any`
- `.left`
- `.center`
- `.right`
- `.alone`

As I mentioned a moment ago, setting a background image changes the segmented control's height. It also removes the selection overlay, leaving it up to you to indicate selection by supplying different background images for the `.normal` and `.selected` states (Figure 13-16):

```
let sz = CGSize(100,60)
let linen = UIImage(named:"linen")!
let im = UIGraphicsImageRenderer(size:sz).image { _ in
    linen.draw(in:CGRect(origin: .zero, size: sz))
    }.resizableImage(withCapInsets:
        UIEdgeInsets(top: 0,left: 10,bottom: 0,right: 10),
        resizingMode: .stretch)
self.seg.setBackgroundImage(im, for:.normal, barMetrics: .default)
let im2 = UIGraphicsImageRenderer(size:sz).image {ctx in
    let r = CGRect(origin: .zero, size: sz)
    ctx.cgContext.setFillColor(UIColor.blue.withAlphaComponent(0.1).cgColor)
    ctx.cgContext.fill(r)
    linen.draw(in: r, blendMode: .destinationAtop, alpha: 1)
    }.resizableImage(withCapInsets:
        UIEdgeInsets(top: 0,left: 10,bottom: 0,right: 10),
        resizingMode: .stretch)
self.seg.setBackgroundImage(im2, for:.selected, barMetrics: .default)
```

UIButton

A button (UIButton) is a fundamental tappable control, which may contain a title, an internal image (referred to simply as the button's "image"), and a background image:

Title

Along with the title, you can add a title color and a title shadow color — or you can supply an attributed title, dictating these features and more in a single value through an NSAttributedString (Chapter 11).

Image

The button can have both a title and an image, provided the image is small enough, in which case the image is shown to the left of the title by default; if the image is too large, the title won't appear.

Starting in iOS 13, a button can have a preferred symbol configuration, in case the internal image is a symbol image. This is similar to the UIImageView preferred symbol configuration: you apply it to the button and it is applied to the symbol image for you. If the button has both a symbol image and a title, and if the title font is not the default, matching the symbol configuration to the title is up to you.

Background image

The background image size will always match the button's bounds (technically, its `backgroundRect(forBounds:)`). Either it will resize the button to match its own size or it will stretch to match the button size. This is different from the behavior of the internal image, which might be sized down if the button is too small for it, but will never be sized up larger than its own actual size.

These features can vary depending on the button's current state, which may be either `.normal` or any combination of one or more of the other states — `.highlighted`, `.selected`, and `.disabled`. In this way, a state change, whether automatic (the button is highlighted while the user is tapping it) or programmatically imposed, can of itself alter a button's appearance. Therefore, you do not simply set them as properties; instead, you have to specify a corresponding state — or multiple states, using a bitmask:

- `setTitle(_:for:)`
- `setTitleColor(_:for:)`
- `setTitleShadowColor(_:for:)`
- `setAttributedTitle(_:for:)`
- `setImage(_:for:)`
- `setBackgroundImage(_:for:)`
- `setPreferredSymbolConfiguration(_:forImageIn:)`

Similarly, when getting these button features, you must either specify a single state you're interested in or ask about the feature as currently displayed:

- `title(for:)`, `currentTitle`
- `titleColor(for:)`, `currentTitleColor`
- `titleShadowColor(for:)`, `currentTitleShadowColor`
- `attributedTitle(for:)`, `currentAttributedTitle`

- `image(for:)`, `currentImage`

- `backgroundImage(for:)`, `currentBackgroundImage`

- `preferredSymbolConfigurationForImage(in:)`,
  `currentPreferredSymbolConfiguration`

When configuring these features with the `set` methods (or in the nib editor), if you don't specify a feature for a particular state, or if the button adopts more than one state at once, an internal heuristic is used to determine what to display. I can't describe all possible combinations, but here are some general observations:

- If you specify a feature for a particular state (highlighted, selected, or disabled), and the button is in *only* that state, that feature will be used.

- If you *don't* specify a feature for a particular state (highlighted, selected, or disabled), and the button is in *only* that state, the normal version of that feature will be used as fallback. (That's why many examples earlier in this book have assigned a title for `.normal` only; that's sufficient to give the button a title in every state.)

- Combinations of states often cause the button to fall back on the feature for normal state. If a button is both highlighted and selected, the button will display its normal title, even if it has a highlighted title, a selected title, or both.

Some of the `set` methods may be animated, and this can have unpleasant side effects. Preventing the animation can be tricky. A workaround that seems reliable is to ask for layout without animation, like this:

```
self.button.setAttributedTitle(t, for: .normal) // t is an attributed string
UIView.performWithoutAnimation {
    self.button.layoutIfNeeded()
}
```

A button has a type. You must initialize the button with its type; you can't change it later. The types (UIButton.ButtonType) are:

`.system`
> If you don't provide an attributed title with an explicit color, the title text appears in the button's `tintColor`, which may be inherited from further up the view hierarchy; when the button is tapped, the title text color momentarily changes to a color derived from what's behind it (which might be the button's `background-Color`). The image is treated as a template image, colored by the `tintColor`, unless you explicitly provide an `.alwaysOriginal` image; when the button is tapped, the image (even if it isn't a template image) is momentarily tinted to a color derived from what's behind it.

`.custom`
> There's no automatic coloring of the title or the image, and the image is a normal image by default. The title text color may be white by default! Creating a `.custom`

button and wondering why nothing appears, because the title is white on a white background, is a common beginner mistake.

.detailDisclosure, .infoLight, .infoDark, .contactAdd
System buttons whose image is set automatically to a standard image. The first three are an "i" in a circle, and are indistinguishable from one another. .contact-Add is a Plus in a circle.

.close
(Introduced in iOS 13.) A system button that has a dark gray "x" (the "xmark" symbol image) as its image and a light gray filled circle as its background image, both unaffected by the tint color. You probably should not add a title, as that would deform the filled circle.

There is no built-in button type with an outline (border), comparable to the Rounded Rect style of iOS 6 and before. You can provide an outline by some simple manipulation of the button's layer, or by constructing a background image (as in Figure 13-19).

If you're creating a button in code and you don't specify a type, you may get a .custom button by default. A common beginner mistake is to create a button with init(frame:) and then wonder why the button can't be seen; it's because this is a .custom button and the title is white. Even though init(frame:) is the designated initializer, it's better practice to call one of these methods (and supply the frame later):

init(type:)
A convenience initializer.

systemButton(with:target:action:)
A convenience class factory method. The first parameter is intended to be a symbol image. This is useful in the special case where you want a .system button consisting of a symbol image and nothing else.

init(type:primaryAction:)
New in iOS 14. The type: parameter is optional; if you omit it, it defaults to .system. The primaryAction: is a UIAction; in addition to setting the action function for when the button is tapped, the UIAction's title: is set as the button's title for the normal state, and its image: is set as the button's image for the normal state.

A UIButton has some properties determining how it draws its images in various states, which can save you the trouble of specifying different images for different states:

showsTouchWhenHighlighted

> If true, then the button projects a circular white glow when highlighted. If the button has an internal image, the glow is centered behind it. This feature is suitable particularly if the button image is small and circular. If the button has no internal image, the glow is centered at the button's center. The glow is drawn on top of the background image or color, if any.

adjustsImageWhenHighlighted

> In a .custom button, if this property is true (the default), then if there is no separate highlighted image (and if showsTouchWhenHighlighted is false), the normal image is darkened when the button is highlighted. This applies equally to the internal image and the background image. (A .system button is already tinting its highlighted image, so this property doesn't apply.)

adjustsImageWhenDisabled

> If true, then if there is no separate disabled image, the normal image is shaded when the button is disabled. This applies equally to the internal image and the background image. The default is true for a .custom button and false for a .system button.

A button has a natural size in relation to its contents. If you're using autolayout, the button can adopt that size automatically as its intrinsicContentSize, and you can modify the way it does this by overriding intrinsicContentSize in a subclass or by applying explicit constraints. If you're not using autolayout and you create a button in code, send it sizeToFit or give it an explicit size; otherwise, the button may have size .zero, making it invisible. Creating a zero-size button and then wondering why the button isn't visible in the interface is a common beginner mistake.

The title is displayed in a UILabel (Chapter 11), and the label features of the title can be accessed through the button's titleLabel. Beginners often wonder how to make a button's title consist of more than one line; the answer is obvious, once you remember that the title is displayed in a label: set the button's titleLabel.numberOfLines. In general, the label's properties may be set, provided they do not conflict with existing UIButton features. You can use the label to set the title's font and shadowOffset; but the title's text, color, and shadow color should be set using the appropriate button methods specifying a button state. If the title is given a shadow in this way, then the button's reversesTitleShadowWhenHighlighted property also applies: if true, the shadowOffset values are replaced with their additive inverses when the button is highlighted. But the modern way to do that sort of thing is through the button's attributed title.

The internal image is drawn by a UIImageView (Chapter 2), whose features can be accessed through the button's imageView. For instance, you can change the internal image view's alpha to make the image more transparent.

The internal position of the image and title as a whole are governed by the button's `contentVerticalAlignment` and `contentHorizontalAlignment` (actually, inherited from UIControl). You can also tweak the position of the image and title, together or separately, by setting the button's `contentEdgeInsets`, `titleEdgeInsets`, or `image-EdgeInsets`. Increasing an inset component increases that margin; a positive top component makes the distance between that object and the top of the button larger than normal (where "normal" is where the object would be according to the alignment settings). The `titleEdgeInsets` or `imageEdgeInsets` values are added to the overall `contentEdgeInsets` values. For instance, you could make the internal image appear to the right of the title by decreasing the left `titleEdgeInsets` and increasing the left `imageEdgeInsets`.

Four methods also let you customize a button's positioning of its elements by overriding them in a subclass:

- `titleRect(forContentRect:)`
- `imageRect(forContentRect:)`
- `contentRect(forBounds:)`
- `backgroundRect(forBounds:)`

Those methods are called whenever the button is redrawn, including every time it changes state. The content rect is the area in which the title and image are placed. By default, the content rect and the background rect are the same.

Here's an example of a customized button (Figure 13-17). In a UIButton subclass, we increase the button's `intrinsicContentSize` to give it larger margins around its content (for `withDelta`, see Appendix B), and we configure the background rect to shrink the button slightly when highlighted as a way of providing feedback when the user taps the button:

```
override var intrinsicContentSize : CGSize {
    return super.intrinsicContentSize.withDelta(dw:25, dh: 20)
}
override func backgroundRect(forBounds bounds: CGRect) -> CGRect {
    var result = super.backgroundRect(forBounds:bounds)
    if self.isHighlighted {
        result = result.insetBy(dx: 3, dy: 3)
    }
    return result
}
```

The button, which is a `.custom` button, is assigned an internal image and a background image from the same resizable image, along with attributed titles for the `.normal` and `.highlighted` states. The internal image glows when highlighted, thanks to `adjustsImageWhenHighlighted`.

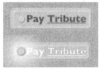

Figure 13-17. A customized button

New in iOS 14, a UIButton has a menu property. The goal here is to make it trivial to attach a UIMenu to a UIButton. Instead of working with a UIContextMenuInteraction and its delegate, you just set the menu to a UIMenu and walk away. That menu will appear when the user long presses on the button — or you can set the button's showsMenuAsPrimaryAction to true, in which case the menu will appear when the user taps the button.

Apple's expectation is that you'll be using button menus in a lot of places in your app, where previously you would have used a more elaborate interface. For example, in Chapter 8 I talked about letting the user make a choice between three options by means of a small table view. In iOS 14, I might use a button with a menu. In this example, I'll let the user pick a favorite Pep Boy. I'll store the name of the current favorite Pep Boy in an instance property (self.currentFavorite). I'll build my menu dynamically at the time the user taps the button, putting a checkmark next to whoever the favorite Pep Boy is now. When the user taps the name of a Pep Boy, I'll store the name as the current favorite, and I'll change the button title to reflect the current favorite:

```
b.menu = UIMenu()
b.addAction(for: .menuActionTriggered) { action in
    guard let b = action.sender as? UIButton else { return }
    func boyAction(for name: String) -> UIAction {
        let image : UIImage? =
            name == self.currentFavorite ?
            UIImage(systemName: "checkmark") :
            nil
        return UIAction(title: name, image: image) { [weak self] action in
            self?.currentFavorite = action.title
            b.setTitle("Favorite Pep Boy: \(name)", for: .normal)
            b.sizeToFit()
        }
    }
    b.menu = UIMenu(title: "", children: [
        boyAction(for: "Manny"),
        boyAction(for: "Moe"),
        boyAction(for: "Jack")
    ])
}
b.showsMenuAsPrimaryAction = true
```

Figure 13-18. A custom control

Custom Controls

If you create your own UIControl subclass, you automatically get the built-in Touch events; in addition, there are several methods that you can override in order to customize touch tracking, along with properties that tell you whether touch tracking is going on:

- `beginTracking(_:with:)`
- `continueTracking(_:with:)`
- `endTracking(_:with:)`
- `cancelTracking(with:)`
- `isTracking`
- `isTouchInside`

The main reason for using a custom UIControl subclass — rather than, say, a UIView subclass and gesture recognizers — would probably be to obtain the convenience of control events. Also, the touch-tracking methods, though not as high-level as gesture recognizers, are at least a level up from the UIResponder touch methods (Chapter 5): they track a single touch, and both `beginTracking` and `continueTracking` return a Bool, giving you a chance to stop tracking the current touch.

To illustrate, we'll build a simplified knob control (Figure 13-18). The control starts life at its minimum position, with an internal angle value of 0; it can be rotated clockwise with a single finger as far as its maximum position, with an internal angle value of 5 (radians). The words "Min" and "Max" appearing in the interface are actually labels; the control just draws the knob, and to rotate it we'll apply a rotation transform.

Our control is a UIControl subclass, MyKnob. It has a public CGFloat `angle` property, and there's a private CGFloat property `self.initialAngle` that we'll use internally during rotation. Because a UIControl is a UIView, it can draw itself, which it does with an image file included in our app bundle:

```
override func draw(_ rect: CGRect) {
    UIImage(named:"knob")!.draw(in: rect)
}
```

We'll need a utility function for transforming a touch's Cartesian coordinates into polar coordinates, giving us the angle to be applied as a rotation to the view:

```
func pToA (_ t:UITouch) -> CGFloat {
    let loc = t.location(in: self)
    let c = self.bounds.center
    return atan2(loc.y - c.y, loc.x - c.x)
}
```

Now we're ready to override the tracking methods. beginTracking simply notes down the angle of the initial touch location. continueTracking uses the difference between the current touch location's angle and the initial touch location's angle to apply a transform to the view, and updates the angle property. endTracking triggers the Value Changed control event. So our first draft looks like this:

```
override func beginTracking(_ t: UITouch, with _: UIEvent?) -> Bool {
    self.initialAngle = pToA(t)
    return true
}
override func continueTracking(_ t: UITouch, with _: UIEvent?) -> Bool {
    let ang = pToA(t) - self.initialAngle
    let absoluteAngle = self.angle + ang
    self.transform = self.transform.rotated(by: ang)
    self.angle = absoluteAngle
    return true
}
override func endTracking(_: UITouch?, with _: UIEvent?) {
    self.sendActions(for: .valueChanged)
}
```

That works: we can put a MyKnob into the interface and hook up its Value Changed control event (this can be done in the nib editor), and sure enough, when we run the app, we can rotate the knob and, when our finger lifts from the knob, the Value Changed action method is called.

However, our class needs modification. When the angle is set programmatically, we should respond by rotating the knob; at the same time, we need to clamp the incoming value to the allowable minimum or maximum:

```
var angle : CGFloat = 0 {
    didSet {
        self.angle = min(max(self.angle, 0), 5) // clamp
        self.transform = CGAffineTransform(rotationAngle: self.angle)
    }
}
```

Now we should revise continueTracking. We no longer need to perform the rotation, since setting the angle will do that for us. On the other hand, we do need to clamp the gesture when the minimum or maximum rotation is exceeded. My solution is simply to stop tracking; in that case, endTracking will never be called, so we also need to trigger the Value Changed control event. Also, it might be nice to give the programmer the option to have the Value Changed control event reported continuously as continueTracking is called repeatedly; so we'll add a public isContinuous Bool property and obey it:

```
override func continueTracking(_ t: UITouch, with _: UIEvent?) -> Bool {
    let ang = pToA(t) - self.initialAngle
    let absoluteAngle = self.angle + ang
    switch absoluteAngle {
    case -CGFloat.greatestFiniteMagnitude...0:
        self.angle = 0
        self.sendActions(for: .valueChanged)
        return false
    case 5...CGFloat.greatestFiniteMagnitude:
        self.angle = 5
        self.sendActions(for: .valueChanged)
        return false
    default:
        self.angle = absoluteAngle
        if self.isContinuous {
            self.sendActions(for: .valueChanged)
        }
        return true
    }
}
```

Bars

There are three bar types:

UINavigationBar

A navigation bar should appear only at the top of the screen. It is usually used in conjunction with a UINavigationController.

UIToolbar

A toolbar may appear at the bottom or at the top of the screen, though the bottom is more common. It is usually used in conjunction with a UINavigation-Controller, where it appears at the bottom.

UITabBar

A tab bar should appear only at the bottom of the screen. It is usually used in conjunction with a UITabBarController.

This section summarizes the three bar types and the items that populate them.

Bar Position

If a bar is to occupy the top of the screen, its apparent height should be increased to underlap the transparent status bar. This is taken care of for you in the case of a UINavigationBar owned by a UINavigationController; otherwise, it's up to you. The mechanism for doing that involves the notion of a *bar position*. The UIBarPositioning protocol is adopted by the bars that can go at the top of the screen, namely UINavigationBar and UIToolbar — along with UISearchBar, because it can be used independently as a top bar. This protocol defines one property, barPosition, whose possible values (UIBarPosition) are:

- .any
- .bottom
- .top
- .topAttached

But barPosition is read-only, so how are you supposed to set it? Use the bar's delegate! The delegate protocols UINavigationBarDelegate, UIToolbarDelegate, and UISearchBarDelegate all conform to UIBarPositioningDelegate, which defines one method, position(for:). This provides a way for a bar's delegate to dictate the bar's barPosition. In this example, we have a "loose" navigation bar that's not owned by a navigation controller:

```
class ViewController: UIViewController, UINavigationBarDelegate {
    @IBOutlet weak var navbar: UINavigationBar!
    override func viewDidLoad() {
        super.viewDidLoad()
        self.navbar.delegate = self
    }
    func position(for bar: UIBarPositioning) -> UIBarPosition {
        return .topAttached
    }
}
```

The bar's apparent height will be extended upward so as to underlap the status bar if the bar's delegate returns .topAttached from its implementation of position(for:). To get the final position right, the bar's top should also have a zero-constant constraint to the safe area layout guide's top.

Similarly, a toolbar or tab bar whose bottom has a zero-constant constraint to the safe area layout guide bottom will have its apparent height extended downward behind the home indicator on an iPhone without a bezel.

I say that a bar's *apparent* height is extended, because in fact its height remains untouched. It is *drawn* extended, and this drawing is visible because the bar's clipsToBounds is false. For this reason (and others), you should not set a bar's clipsToBounds to true.

Bar Metrics

Bars are almost always used in conjunction with standard parent view controllers, UINavigationController and UITabBarController. These parent view controllers will change the height of the bar in a .compact horizontal size class environment, depending on the vertical size class (reflecting the app's orientation), either .regular or .compact.

For this reason, some methods for setting features of a bar or a bar button item (or a view that might be used in a bar, such as a segmented control) take a *bar metrics* parameter — because you might want those features to vary depending on the automatic height applied to the bar. Possible bar metrics values are (UIBarMetrics):

- .default
- .compact
- .defaultPrompt
- .compactPrompt

The compact metrics apply in a .compact vertical size class environment. The prompt metrics apply to a bar whose height is extended downward to accommodate prompt text (and to a search bar whose scope buttons are showing). But in general you'll probably just supply .default; the feature you are configuring will then be set for *all* bar metrics that you don't specify separately.

Bar and Item Appearance

When you want to customize a bar, bar metrics alone are insufficient to distinguish amongst the possible bar configurations. For instance, a navigation controller's navigation bar can be extended downward in order to display a large title — and starting in iOS 13, it then takes on a special look (the bar becomes transparent). Similarly, a tab bar controller's tab bar on an iPhone in portrait orientation draws its tab bar items with the title under the image rather than beside it.

To handle this problem, a hierarchy of *appearances* was introduced in iOS 13:

- Each bar type has various appearance properties (UIBarAppearance); when you customize the bar, you do so by customizing a particular *bar appearance*.

- A bar appearance has various *bar item appearances*, so that you can dictate certain common features of bar button items belonging to that kind of bar.

- To complete the picture, each bar item appearance comes in different flavors corresponding to the bar item's *state*.

Here's a hierarchical outline of the various bar and bar item appearance properties:

UINavigationBar
> A navigation bar has three bar appearances with three item appearances:
>
> - `standardAppearance`, `compactAppearance`, `scrollEdgeAppearance`
>   (UINavigationBarAppearance, a UIBarAppearance subclass)
>   - `buttonAppearance`, `backButtonAppearance`, `doneButtonAppearance`
>   (UIBarButtonItemAppearance)
>   - `normal`, `disabled`, `highlighted`
>   (UIBarButtonItemStateAppearance)

UIToolbar
> A toolbar has two bar appearances with two item appearances:
>
> - `standardAppearance`, `compactAppearance`
>   (UIToolbarAppearance, a UIBarAppearance subclass)
>   - `buttonAppearance`, `doneButtonAppearance`
>   (UIBarButtonItemAppearance)
>   - `normal`, `disabled`, `highlighted`
>   (UIBarButtonItemStateAppearance)

UITabBar
> A tab bar has one bar appearance with three item appearances:
>
> - `standardAppearance`
>   (UITabBarAppearance, a UIBarAppearance subclass)
>   - `stackedLayoutAppearance`, `inlineLayoutAppearance`, `compactInline-LayoutAppearance`
>   (UITabBarItemAppearance)
>   - `normal`, `disabled`, `highlighted`
>   (UITabBarItemStateAppearance)

A bar's standard appearance always exists, but the others don't (they are Optionals and are `nil` by default). If a bar has no compact appearance, the standard appearance is used. You can create a bar appearance or item appearance and assign it to an appearance property; the state appearance properties are read-only, so you just set their properties as desired.

This architecture may seem elaborate, but in fact it makes customizing bars very straightforward. The actual properties of the various appearance objects are simple and direct, and your customization code is easy to read and understand, as subsequent examples will show.

Bar Background and Shadow

The default bar background, starting in iOS 13, is a *blur* of whatever is behind the bar, whitish in light mode and blackish in dark mode (`.systemChromeMaterial`) — except that a navigation bar, when extended to show the large title, is completely *transparent,* with no blur. To override those defaults, use these properties of the appropriate bar appearance (UIBarAppearance):

backgroundColor
   A UIColor that occupies the entire bar.

backgroundImage
backgroundImageContentMode
   A UIImage that appears in front of the background color, along with the content mode for drawing it. The default content mode is `.scaleToFill`, which is probably what you want. You can supply a resizable image if you like. If the image is a template image, its color is the bar's `tintColor` by default.

backgroundEffect
   A UIBlurEffect. If the background color is not opaque, and if the background image has some nonopaque pixels or does not completely fill the bar, content behind the bar will be visible; this property determines how that content will be blurred to get the standard translucent effect. The default is `.systemChrome-Material`, which is probably what you want. `nil` means no blur.

To illustrate, I'll configure a navigation bar to adopt three different colors depending on its configuration. By default, the `.compactAppearance` copies the `.standard-Appearance`, so I prevent that by setting it separately. The so-called `scrollEdge-Appearance` is used when the navigation bar is extended to show the large title; the explicit background color prevents the navigation bar from becoming transparent:

```
let bar = self.navigationController!.navigationBar
bar.prefersLargeTitles = true
let app = UINavigationBarAppearance()
app.backgroundColor = UIColor.red.withAlphaComponent(0.2)
bar.standardAppearance = app
app.backgroundColor = UIColor.blue.withAlphaComponent(0.2)
bar.compactAppearance = app
app.backgroundColor = UIColor.orange.withAlphaComponent(0.2)
bar.scrollEdgeAppearance = app
```

By default, a bar (except for the transparent large title navigation bar) casts a thin gray-tinted shadow upon whatever is behind it, at its bottom edge if it is a top bar, at its top edge if it is a bottom bar. To change the shadow, use these properties of the appropriate bar appearance:

shadowImage
> If nil, the default shadow is used. If you supply an image, it should probably be very small, just one or two pixels in height and one pixel in width; the image will be tiled to the width of the bar.

shadowColor
> If there is no shadow image, this color tints the default shadow. If there is an image and it is a template image, this color tints it. If there is an image and it is *not* a template image, the shadow color is ignored. If both the shadowImage and the shadowColor are nil, the bar will have no shadow.

As a shortcut, three convenience methods on UIBarAppearance are provided for setting a bar appearance's background properties:

configureWithDefaultBackground
> The background has the .systemChromeMaterial blur effect and the default shadow.

configureWithOpaqueBackground
> The background has the system background color and the default shadow.

configureWithTransparentBackground
> All properties are nil. There is no background color, no blur, and no shadow.

The old isTranslucent bar property is not needed in iOS 13 and later, and should probably be avoided. The default is true and you should leave it there. Setting it to false accomplishes nothing useful and can have unwanted side effects.

Bar Button Items

You don't add subviews to a bar. Instead, you populate the bar with *bar items*. For a navigation bar or toolbar, these will be bar button items (UIBarButtonItem, a subclass of UIBarItem). A bar button item is not a UIView, but you can still put an arbitrary view into a bar, because a bar button item can contain a custom view.

A bar button item may be instantiated with any of these methods:

- init(barButtonSystemItem:target:action:)
- init(systemItem:primaryAction:menu:)
- init(title:style:target:action:)
- init(image:style:target:action:)

Figure 13-19. A bar button item with a border

- init(title:image:primaryAction:menu:)
- init(image:landscapeImagePhone:style:target:action:)
- init(customView:)

The style: options (UIBarButtonItem.Style) are .plain and .done; the difference is that .done title text is bold. No bar button item style supplies an outline (border); the .bordered style is deprecated, and its appearance is identical to .plain. If you want an outline, you have to supply it yourself; for the left bar button item in the settings view of my Zotz! app (Figure 13-19), I use a custom view that's a UIButton with a background image.

The two initializers with primaryAction: and menu: parameters are new in iOS 14:

primaryAction:
    A UIAction. Its function will be called when the bar button item is tapped; if the bar button item also has a target: and action: selector, they will be ignored. Like a segmented control's segment, the UIAction's title: or image:, whichever you supply, becomes the bar button item's title or image. (If you supply both, the image wins.) If you supply neither, the bar button item will be invisible unless you set its title or image property later.

menu:
    A UIMenu. It will appear when the user taps or long presses the button. If the bar button item has either a target and action or a primaryAction, the action is called when the bar button item is tapped, so to summon the menu will require a long press. Otherwise, the menu appears on a tap.

A bar button item also has a primaryAction property and a menu property that you can set after initialization. You might need to do that for a bar button item with a custom view, for instance.

The image is not resized for you; roughly 24×24 is a reasonable size. If you provide both an image and a landscapeImagePhone, the latter is used when the bar is compact (on an iPhone in landscape orientation — hence the name). If the image is a symbol image, there is no need for a separate landscapeImagePhone, because the scale of the symbol image configuration is adjusted automatically. A bar button item's image is treated by default as a template image, unless you explicitly provide an .alwaysOriginal image.

A bar button item's tintColor property tints the title text or template image of the button; it is inherited from the tintColor of the bar, or you can override it for an individual bar button item.

A bar button item inherits from UIBarItem the ability to adjust the image position with imageInsets (and landscapeImagePhoneInsets), plus the isEnabled and tag properties.

You can set a bar button item's width property, but if the bar button item has a custom view, you can and should size the view from the inside out using autolayout constraints.

 Starting in iOS 13, a bar button item's background image is resized horizontally to fit the bar button item, *but not vertically* (unless this is a system button). This is a major change from iOS 12 and before, where the background image is resized in both dimensions; this change can break your existing interface, and I regard it as a bug.

You can give a bar button item a background image, and you can adjust the background image's position. In addition, you can apply text attributes to the bar button item's title, and you can adjust the title's position. Those settings can be performed either for *individual* bar button items or for a bar's bar button items *as a whole* (by way of the bar's appearance).

Individual bar button item settings

Here are the UIBarButtonItem methods for customizing the title and background image of an individual bar button item. Some of these methods take a parameter that's a UIControl.State (.normal, .highlighted, and so forth). Some of them take a UIBarMetrics parameter (.default, .compact, and so forth). Some take both. Confusingly, the for: parameter, if there is no separate barMetrics: parameter, is sometimes a UIControl.State and sometimes a UIBarMetrics (this is an unfortunate consequence of Swift 3 "renamification"). The backButton methods apply only if the bar button item is being used as a back button item in a navigation bar (as I'll describe in the next section):

Applying an attributes dictionary to a bar button item's title
- setTitleTextAttributes(_:for:)
- setTitlePositionAdjustment(_:for:)
- setBackButtonTitlePositionAdjustment(_:for:)

Giving a bar button item a background image
- setBackgroundImage(_:for:barMetrics:)
- setBackgroundImage(_:for:style:barMetrics:)

- setBackButtonBackgroundImage(_:for:barMetrics:)
- setBackgroundVerticalPositionAdjustment(_:for:)
- setBackButtonBackgroundVerticalPositionAdjustment(_:for:)

Appearance bar button item settings

The appearance properties (UIBarButtonItemStateAppearance) are:

- titleTextAttributes
- titlePositionAdjustment
- backgroundImage
- backgroundImagePositionAdjustment

They are useful particularly when you want to configure features of all (or most) of a bar's bar button items at once. You usually *do* want to do that, because uniformity is generally desirable; and if there's an exception, you can override the general appearance property settings with the individual setting methods.

Let's say I want every bar button item in my navigation bar to have a white background normally and a yellow background while the user is tapping it:

```
let bar = self.navigationController!.navigationBar
let r = UIGraphicsImageRenderer(size: CGSize(40,30))
let im = r.image { ctx in
    let con = ctx.cgContext
    con.setFillColor(UIColor.white.cgColor)
    ctx.fill(CGRect(0,0,40,30))
}
bar.standardAppearance.buttonAppearance.normal.backgroundImage = im
let im2 = r.image { ctx in
    let con = ctx.cgContext
    con.setFillColor(UIColor.yellow.cgColor)
    ctx.fill(CGRect(0,0,40,30))
}
bar.standardAppearance.buttonAppearance.highlighted.backgroundImage = im2
```

That code exemplifies how neatly we can express ourselves, thanks to the hierarchical organization of the appearance properties. If we want a different variant for a different bar configuration, we specify a different *bar* appearance; for example, if we want a smaller image height when the bar is compact, we set the bar's compactAppearance instead of its standardAppearance. If we want a different variant for a different type of bar button item, we specify a different *item* appearance; for example, if we don't want these settings to apply to the back button, we give the back button an empty (not nil!) image:

```
let none = UIImage()
bar.standardAppearance.backButtonAppearance.normal.backgroundImage = none
```

Navigation Bar

A navigation bar (UINavigationBar) is populated by navigation items (UINavigation-Item). The UINavigationBar maintains a stack; UINavigationItems are pushed onto and popped off of this stack. For a "loose" navigation bar, items are pushed and popped with pushItem(_:animated:) and popItemAnimated(_:), or you can call set-Items(_:animated:) to set all items on the stack at once. When a navigation bar is used as part of a navigation interface (UINavigationController, "Navigation Controller" on page 343), its items are set by each child view controller through its navigationItem property.

The UINavigationItem that is currently topmost in the stack (the UINavigationBar's topItem), in combination with the UINavigationItem just beneath it in the stack (the UINavigationBar's backItem), determines what appears in the navigation bar:

title, titleView
: The title (string) or titleView (UIView) of the topItem appears in the center of the navigation bar. You can and should size the titleView from the inside out using autolayout constraints.

largeTitleDisplayMode
: Whether the navigation bar's large title can be displayed; possible values are .always, .never, or .automatic (meaning inherited from further down the stack). The large title will not be displayed if this property is .never, or the navigation bar is compact, or the navigation bar's prefersLargeTitles is false. If the top view controller's main view is or contains a UIScrollView, the large title, if displayed, collapses as it is scrolled upward.

prompt
: The prompt (string) appears at the top of the navigation bar, whose height increases to accommodate it.

rightBarButtonItem, rightBarButtonItems
leftBarButtonItem, leftBarButtonItems
: The rightBarButtonItem and leftBarButtonItem appear at the right and left ends of the navigation bar. A UINavigationItem can have multiple right bar button items and multiple left bar button items; its rightBarButtonItems and left-BarButtonItems properties are arrays (of bar button items). The bar button items are displayed from the outside in: that is, the first item in the leftBar-ButtonItems is leftmost, while the first item in the rightBarButtonItems is rightmost. If there are multiple buttons on a side, the rightBarButtonItem is the first item of the rightBarButtonItems array, and the leftBarButtonItem is the first item of the leftBarButtonItems array.

Figure 13-20. A back button animating to the left

backBarButtonItem

The backBarButtonItem of the backItem appears at the left end of the navigation bar. It is automatically configured so that, when tapped, the topItem is popped off the stack. Even if the backItem has no backBarButtonItem, there is *still* a back button at the left end of the navigation bar, taking its title from the title of the backItem.

The back button can be suppressed, if:

- The topItem has its hidesBackButton set to true.

- The topItem has a leftBarButtonItem. But if the topItem has its leftItems-SupplementBackButton set to true, it can have both a leftBarButtonItem and a back button.

New in iOS 14, the back button also has a menu that appears when it is long pressed; it lists the titles from *all* the navigation items in the stack. This allows the user to pop back as far down the stack as desired in a single move. (I do not know how to suppress this menu.)

The indication that the back button *is* a back button is supplied by the navigation bar's backIndicatorImage, which by default is a left-pointing chevron appearing to the left of the back button. You can customize this image; the image that you supply is treated as a template image by default. You must also supply a backIndicator-TransitionMaskImage. The purpose of the mask image is to indicate the region where the back button should disappear as it slides out to the left when a new navigation item is pushed onto the stack. In Figure 13-20, the back button title, which is sliding out to the left, is visible to the right of the chevron but not to the left of the chevron; that's because on the left side of the chevron it is masked out.

We can and should perform this setting through a UINavigationBarAppearance property, by calling setBackIndicatorImage(_:transitionMaskImage:). In this example, I replace the chevron with a left-pointing triangle (a symbol image):

```
let sz = CGSize(20,20)
let arrow = UIImage(systemName:"arrowtriangle.left")!
let indic =
    UIGraphicsImageRenderer(size:sz).image { ctx in
        arrow.draw(in:CGRect(0,0,20,20)) // indicator is arrow
}
let indicmask =
    UIGraphicsImageRenderer(size:sz).image { ctx in
```

Figure 13-21. A toolbar

```
        ctx.fill(CGRect(0,0,20,20)) // mask is entire image
    }
bar.standardAppearance.setBackIndicatorImage(
    indic, transitionMaskImage: indicmask)
```

You can configure the attributes dictionary for the title by setting the navigation bar's `titleTextAttributes`, and you can shift the title's position through the title-PositionAdjustment. You can configure the large title's attributes dictionary by setting the navigation bar's `largeTitleTextAttributes`. Starting in iOS 13, these are all UINavigationBarAppearance properties. Here's how my Zotz! app configures the title shown in Figure 13-19:

```
bar.standardAppearance.titleTextAttributes = [
    .font: UIFont(name:"Chalkduster", size:20)!,
    .foregroundColor: UIColor.black
]
```

A view controller's `navigationItem`, like a UINavigationBar, has `standardAppearance`, `compactAppearance`, and `scrollEdgeAppearance` properties. Using these, different view controllers can configure the navigation bar differently, depending on which one is currently the navigation controller's `topViewController`.

Toolbar

A toolbar (UIToolbar, Figure 13-21) displays a row of UIBarButtonItems, which are its `items`. The items are displayed from left to right in the order in which they appear in the `items` array. For a "loose" toolbar, the items can be set with animation by calling `setItems(_:animated:)`. When a toolbar is used as part of a navigation interface (UINavigationController, "Navigation Controller" on page 343), its items are set by each child view controller through its `toolbarItems` property, and can be changed with animation by calling `setToolbarItems(_:animated:)`.

The items within the toolbar are positioned automatically; you can intervene in this positioning by using the bar button items generated by the UIBarButtonItem static methods `flexibleSpace()` and `fixedSpace(width:)`, along with the UIBarButtonItem `width` property.

To configure all of the toolbar's bar button items uniformly, use the `button-Appearance` (or `doneButtonAppearance`) of the toolbar's `standardAppearance` or `compactAppearance`.

Tab Bar

A tab bar (UITabBar) displays tab bar items (UITabBarItem), its items, each consist-ing of a title and an image. For a "loose" tab bar, to change the items with animation, call setItems(_:animated:). When a tab bar is owned by a UITabBarController ("Tab Bar Controller" on page 339), the tab bar items are the tabBarItem properties of the tab bar controller's children.

The tab bar maintains a current selection among its items, its selectedItem, which is a UITabBarItem, not an index number; you can set it in code, or the user can set it by tapping on a tab bar item. When the user changes the selection, tabBar(_:did-Select:) is sent to the delegate (UITabBarDelegate). With a UITabBarController, the tab bar controller is the delegate, and you'll use its selectedViewController or selectedIndex, along with its delegate (UITabBarControllerDelegate).

You get very little control over how the tab bar items are laid out, and even then only when the tab bar items are "stacked," meaning that the icon appears above the title (only on an iPhone in portrait orientation):

Item positioning
> This can be set through the tab bar's standardAppearance, using the UITabBar-Appearance stackedItemPositioning property. There are three possible values (UITabBar.ItemPositioning):

.centered
> The items are crowded together at the center.

.fill
> The items are spaced out evenly.

.automatic
> On the iPhone, the same as .fill. (On the iPad, the same as .centered; but tab bar items are never stacked on the iPad nowadays, so this appears to be a dead letter.)

Item spacing
> The standard appearance's stackedItemSpacing. The space between items, if the positioning is .centered. For the default space, specify 0.

Item width
> The standard appearance's stackedItemWidth. The width of the items, if the positioning is .centered. For the default width, specify 0.

Here's an example:

```
let tb = self.tabBarController!.tabBar
let tbapp = UITabBarAppearance()
tbapp.stackedItemPositioning = .centered
tbapp.stackedItemSpacing = 0
tbapp.stackedItemWidth = 35
tb.standardAppearance = tbapp
```

You can set an image to be drawn behind the selected tab bar item to indicate that it's selected; it is the tab bar's `selectionIndicatorImage`.

 The documentation claims that you can set the `selectionIndicatorImage`, along with the `selectionIndicatorTintColor`, through the tab bar's standard-Appearance; but in my tests these properties do nothing.

A UITabBarItem is created with one of these methods:

- `init(tabBarSystemItem:tag:)`
- `init(title:image:tag:)`
- `init(title:image:selectedImage:)`

UITabBarItem is a subclass of UIBarItem, so in addition to its `title` and `image` it inherits the ability to adjust the image position with `imageInsets`, plus the `isEnabled` and `tag` properties. The UITabBarItem itself adds the `selectedImage` property; this image replaces the `image` when this item is selected.

You can assign a tab bar item an alternate `landscapeImagePhone` (inherited from UIBarItem) to be used on the iPhone in landscape orientation. However, doing so disables the `selectedImage`; I regard that as a bug. The best workaround is to supply the `image` only, as a vector image or symbol image (Chapter 2).

A tab bar item's image is treated, by default, as a template image, tinted with the tab bar's `tintColor` when selected and with its `unselectedItemTintColor` otherwise. Starting in iOS 13, you can use the UITabBarItemStateAppearance `iconColor` property instead:

```
let app = UITabBarAppearance()
app.stackedLayoutAppearance.normal.iconColor = .red
app.stackedLayoutAppearance.selected.iconColor = .green
tb.standardAppearance = app
```

A tab bar item's title is also tinted when selected, by default, with the the tab bar's `tintColor`.

To configure fully the text features of a tab bar's items, set the `titleTextAttributes` of the appropriate UITabBarItemStateAppearance. In this example, I'm setting the font, and I'm making the text of the selected item red and the text of the unselected items green, on an iPhone in both orientations:

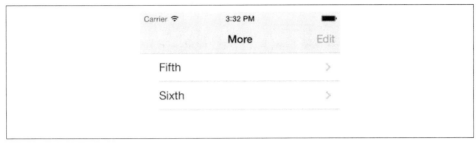

Figure 13-22. Automatically generated More list

```
let app = UITabBarAppearance()
app.stackedLayoutAppearance.normal.titleTextAttributes = [
    .font:UIFont(name:"Avenir-Heavy", size:14)!,
    .foregroundColor:UIColor.green
]
app.stackedLayoutAppearance.selected.titleTextAttributes = [
    .font:UIFont(name:"Avenir-Heavy", size:14)!,
    .foregroundColor:UIColor.red
]
app.compactInlineLayoutAppearance.normal.titleTextAttributes = [
    .font:UIFont(name:"Avenir-Heavy", size:14)!,
    .foregroundColor:UIColor.green
]
app.compactInlineLayoutAppearance.selected.titleTextAttributes = [
    .font:UIFont(name:"Avenir-Heavy", size:14)!,
    .foregroundColor:UIColor.red
]
self.tabBarController?.tabBar.standardAppearance = app
```

Starting in iOS 13, a tab bar item also has a `standardAppearance` property. Using this, different view controllers can configure the tab bar differently, depending on which one's tab bar item is currently selected.

The user can be permitted to alter the contents of the tab bar, setting its tab bar items from among a larger repertoire of tab bar items. When used in conjunction with a UITabBarController, the customization interface is provided automatically. If there are a lot of items, a More item is present as the last item in the tab bar; the user can tap this to access the remaining items through a table view. In this table view, the user can select any of the excess items to navigate to the corresponding view, or switch to the customization interface by tapping the Edit button. Figure 13-22 shows how a More list looks by default.

The way this works is that the automatically provided More item corresponds to a UINavigationController with a root view controller whose `view` is a UITableView. You have access to this navigation controller as the UITabBarController's `more-NavigationController`, and therefore you can customize its appearance to some extent.

Tint Color

Both UIView and UIBarButtonItem have a `tintColor` property. This property has a remarkable built-in feature: its value, if not set explicitly (or if set to nil), is inherited from its superview. (UIBarButtonItems don't have a superview, because they aren't views; but for purposes of this feature, pretend that they are views, and that the containing bar is their superview.)

The idea is to simplify the task of giving your app a consistent overall appearance. Many built-in interface objects use the `tintColor` for some aspect of their appearance, as I've already described. If a `.system` button's `tintColor` is red, either because you've set it directly or because it has inherited that color from higher up the view hierarchy, it will have red title text by default.

The inheritance architecture works exactly the way you would expect:

Superviews and subviews
> When you set the `tintColor` of a view, that value is inherited by all subviews of that view. The ultimate superview is the window; you can set the `tintColor` of your UIWindow instance, and its value will be inherited by *every* view that ever appears within it. At an even higher level, you can set the `tintColor` for the entire app; in the File inspector in the storyboard editor, set the Global Tint popup menu, or (new in Xcode 14) the AccentColor image set in the asset catalog.

Overriding
> The inherited `tintColor` can be overridden by setting a view's `tintColor` explicitly. You can set the `tintColor` of a view partway down the view hierarchy so that it and all its subviews have a different `tintColor` from the rest of the interface. In this way, you might subtly suggest that the user has entered a different world.

Propagation
> If you change the `tintColor` of a view, the change immediately propagates down the hierarchy of its subviews — except, of course, that a view whose `tintColor` has been explicitly set to a color of its own is unaffected, along with its subviews.

Whenever a view's `tintColor` changes, including when its `tintColor` is initially set at launch time, and including when *you* set it in code, this view and all its affected subviews are sent the `tintColorDidChange` message. A subview whose `tintColor` has been explicitly set to a color of its own is *not* sent the `tintColorDidChange` message merely because its superview's `tintColor` changes; that's because the subview's own `tintColor` *didn't* change.

When you ask a view for its `tintColor`, what you get is the `tintColor` of the view itself, if its own `tintColor` has been explicitly set to a color, or else the `tintColor` inherited from higher up the view hierarchy. In this way, you can always learn what the *effective* tint color of a view is.

A UIView also has a `tintAdjustmentMode`. Under certain circumstances, such as the summoning of an alert (Chapter 14) or a popover (Chapter 10), the system will set the `tintAdjustmentMode` of the view at the top of the view hierarchy to `.dimmed`. This causes the `tintColor` to change to a variety of gray. The idea is that the tinting of the background should become monochrome, emphasizing the primacy of the view that occupies the foreground (the alert or popover). See "Custom Presented View Controller Transition" on page 365 for an example of my own code making this change.

By default, a change in the `tintAdjustmentMode` propagates all the way down the view hierarchy, changing *all* `tintAdjustmentMode` values and *all* `tintColor` values — and sending *all* subviews the `tintColorDidChange` message. When the foreground view goes away, the system will set the topmost view's `tintAdjustmentMode` to `.normal`, and that change, too, will propagate down the hierarchy.

This propagation behavior is governed by the `tintAdjustmentMode` of the subviews. The default `tintAdjustmentMode` value is `.automatic`, meaning that you want this view's `tintAdjustmentMode` to adopt its superview's `tintAdjustmentMode` automatically. When you ask for a view's `tintAdjustmentMode`, what you get is just like what you get for `tintColor` — you're told the *effective* tint adjustment mode (`.normal` or `.dimmed`) inherited from up the view hierarchy.

If, on the other hand, you set a view's `tintAdjustmentMode` *explicitly* to `.normal` or `.dimmed`, this tells the system that you want to be left in charge of the `tintAdjustmentMode` for this part of the hierarchy, preventing automatic propagation. To turn automatic propagation back on, set the `tintAdjustmentMode` back to `.automatic`.

Appearance Proxy

When you want to customize the look of an interface object, instead of sending a message to the object itself, you can send that message to an *appearance proxy* for that object's class. The appearance proxy then passes that same message along to the actual *future* instances of that class. You'll usually configure your appearance proxies once very early in the lifetime of the app, and never again. The app delegate's `application(_:didFinishLaunchingWithOptions:)`, before the window has been displayed, is the obvious place to do this, because your code here runs before *any* instances of *any* interface objects are created, and affects *all* of them.

This architecture, like the `tintColor` that I discussed in the previous section, helps you give your app a consistent appearance with a minimum of code. Also, the appearance proxy sometimes allows customization of interface objects that you have no official way to refer to directly (such as a search bar's external Cancel button).

There are four class methods implemented by UIView and UIBarItem, through adoption of the UIAppearance protocol, for obtaining an appearance proxy:

`appearance`

> Returns a general appearance proxy for the receiver class. The method you call on the appearance proxy will be applied generally to future instances of this class.

`appearance(for:)`

> The parameter is a *trait collection*. The method you call on the appearance proxy will be applied to future instances of the receiver class when the environment matches the specified trait collection.

`appearance(whenContainedInInstancesOf:)`

> The argument is an *array of classes*, arranged in order of containment from inner to outer. The method you call on the appearance proxy will be applied only to instances of the receiver class that are actually contained in the way you describe. The notion of what "contained" means is deliberately left vague; basically, it works the way you intuitively expect it to work.

`appearance(for:whenContainedInInstancesOf:)`

> A combination of the preceding two.

When configuring appearance proxy objects, *specificity trumps generality*. You could call `appearance` to say what should happen for *most* instances of some class, and call the other methods to say what should happen instead for *certain* instances of that class. Similarly, longer `whenContainedInInstancesOf:` chains are more specific than shorter ones.

Here's some code from my Latin flashcard app (`myGolden` and `myPaler` are class properties defined by an extension on UIColor):

```
UIBarButtonItem.appearance().tintColor = .myGolden ❶
UIBarButtonItem.appearance(
    whenContainedInInstancesOf: [UIToolbar.self])
        .tintColor = .myPaler ❷
UIBarButtonItem.appearance(
    whenContainedInInstancesOf: [UIToolbar.self, DrillViewController.self])
        .tintColor = .myGolden ❸
```

That means:

❶ In general, bar button items should be tinted golden.

❷ But bar button items in a toolbar are an exception: they should be tinted paler.

❸ But bar button items in the toolbar in DrillViewController's view are an exception to the exception: they should be tinted golden.

Sometimes, in order to express sufficient specificity, I find myself defining subclasses for no other purpose than to refer to them when obtaining an appearance proxy. Here's some more code from my Latin flashcard app:

```
let app = UINavigationBarAppearance()
app.backgroundImage = marble
UINavigationBar.appearance().compactAppearance = app
let app2 = UINavigationBarAppearance()
app2.titleTextAttributes = [.foregroundColor: UIColor.white]
app2.backgroundColor = .black
BlackNavigationBar.appearance().compactAppearance = app2
```

In that code, BlackNavigationBar is a UINavigationBar subclass that does nothing whatever. Its sole purpose is to tag one navigation bar in my interface so that I can refer to it in that code! As a result, I'm able to say, in effect, "All navigation bars in this app should have `marble` as their background image, except for the one BlackNavigationBar."

(That code also demonstrates that the bar appearance properties, discussed earlier in this chapter, can themselves be applied to a class appearance proxy.)

The ultimate in specificity is to customize the look of an instance directly. If you set a bar button item's `tintColor`, then setting the tint color by way of a UIBarButtonItem appearance proxy will have no effect on that particular bar button item.

Not every message that can be sent to an instance of a class can be sent to that class's appearance proxy. Unfortunately, the compiler can't help you here; illegal code like this will compile, but will probably crash at runtime:

```
UIBarButtonItem.appearance().action = #selector(configureAppearance)
```

The problem is not that UIBarButtonItem has no `action` property; on the contrary, that code compiles because it *does* have an `action` property! But that property is not one that you can set by way of the appearance proxy, and the mistake isn't caught until that line executes and the runtime tries to configure an actual UIBarButtonItem.

When in doubt, look at the class documentation; there should be a section that lists the properties and methods applicable to the appearance proxy for this class. The UINavigationBar class documentation has a section called "Customizing the Bar Appearance," the UIBarButtonItem class documentation has a section called "Customizing Appearance," and so forth.

 To define your own appearance-compliant property, declare that property `@objc dynamic` in your UIView subclass.

Modal Dialogs

A modal dialog demands attention; while it is present, the user can do nothing other than work within it or dismiss it. This chapter discusses various forms of modal dialog:

- Within your app, you can show alerts and action sheets. An *alert* is basically a message, possibly with an opportunity for text entry, and some buttons. An *action sheet* is effectively a column of buttons.

- You can provide a sort of action sheet even when your app is not frontmost (or even running) by allowing the user to summon *quick actions* — also known as *shortcut items* — by long pressing on your app's icon.

- A *local notification* is an alert that the system presents on your app's behalf, even when your app isn't frontmost.

- An *activity view* is typically summoned by the user from a Share button. It displays possible courses of external and internal action (activities), such as handing off data to another app, or processing data within your app. Your app can also provide activities that *other* apps can display in *their* activity views, through an action extension or share extension.

Alerts and Action Sheets

Alerts and action sheets are both forms of presented view controller (Chapter 6). They are managed through the UIAlertController class, a UIViewController subclass. To show an alert or an action sheet is a three-step process:

1. Instantiate UIAlertController with `init(title:message:preferredStyle:)`. The `title:` and `message:` are large and small descriptive text to appear at the top

of the dialog. The `preferredStyle:` argument (UIAlertController.Style) will be either `.alert` or `.actionSheet`.

2. Configure the dialog by calling `addAction(_:)` on the UIAlertController as many times as needed. An action is a UIAlertAction, which basically means it's a button to appear in the dialog, along with a function to be executed when the button is tapped; to create one, call `init(title:style:handler:)`. Possible `style:` values are (UIAlertAction.Style):

   - `.default`
   - `.cancel`
   - `.destructive`

   An alert may also have text fields (I'll talk about that in a moment).

3. Call `present(_:animated:completion:)` to present the UIAlertController.

The dialog is automatically dismissed when the user taps any button.

Alerts

An alert (UIAlertController style `.alert`) pops up unexpectedly in the middle of the screen, with an elaborate animation, and may be thought of as an attention-getting interruption. It contains a title, a message, and some number of buttons, one of which may be the cancel button, meaning that it does nothing but dismiss the alert. In addition, an alert may contain one or two text fields.

Alerts are minimal, and intentionally so: they are meant for simple, quick interactions or display of information. Often there is only a cancel button, the primary purpose of the alert being to show the user the message ("You won the game!"); additional buttons can give the user a choice of how to proceed ("You won the game; would you like to play another?" "Cancel," "Play Another," "Replay").

Figure 14-1 shows a basic alert, illustrating the title, the message, and the three button styles: `.destructive`, `.default`, and `.cancel` respectively. Here's the code that generated it:

```
let alert = UIAlertController(title: "Not So Fast!",
    message: """
    Do you really want to do this \
    tremendously destructive thing?
    """,
    preferredStyle: .alert)
func handler(_ act:UIAlertAction) {
    print("User tapped \(act.title as Any)")
}
alert.addAction(UIAlertAction(title: "Cancel",
    style: .cancel, handler: handler))
alert.addAction(UIAlertAction(title: "Just Do It!",
```

Figure 14-1. An alert

```
        style: .destructive, handler: handler))
    alert.addAction(UIAlertAction(title: "Maybe",
        style: .default, handler: handler))
    self.present(alert, animated: true)
```

In Figure 14-1, the `.destructive` button appears first and the `.cancel` button appears last, without regard to the order in which they were added with `addAction`. The order in which the `.default` buttons were added, on the other hand, will be the order of the buttons themselves. If no `.cancel` button is added, the last `.default` button will be displayed as a `.cancel` button.

You can also designate an action as the alert's `preferredAction`. This appears to boldify the title of that button. Suppose I append this to the preceding code:

```
    alert.preferredAction = alert.actions[2]
```

The order of the `actions` array is the order in which we added actions, so the preferred action is now the Maybe button. The order isn't changed — the Maybe button still appears second — but the bold styling is removed from the Cancel button and placed on the Maybe button instead.

The dialog is dismissed automatically when the user taps a button. If you don't want to respond to the tap of a particular button, you can supply `nil` as the `handler:` argument (or omit it altogether), but the dialog will still be dismissed. In the preceding code, I've provided a minimal `handler:` function, just to show what one looks like. As the example demonstrates, the function receives the original UIAlertAction as a parameter, and can examine it as desired. The function can also access the alert controller itself, provided the alert controller is in scope at the point where the `handler:` function is defined (which will usually be the case). My example code assigns the same function to all three buttons, but more often you'll give each button its own individual `handler:` function, probably as an anonymous function using trailing closure syntax.

Text fields may be added to an alert. Because space is limited on the smaller iPhone screen, especially when the keyboard is present, an alert that is to contain a text field should probably be assigned at most two buttons, with short titles such as "OK" and "Cancel," and at most two text fields. To add a text field to an alert, call addText-Field(configurationHandler:). The configurationHandler: function is called *before* the alert appears; it will receive the text field as a parameter. Button handler: functions can access the text field through the alert's textFields property, which is an array.

In this example, the user is invited to enter a number in a text field. When the text field is added, its configurationHandler: function configures the keyboard. If the alert is dismissed with the OK button, the OK button's handler: function reads the text from the text field:

```
let alert = UIAlertController(title: "Enter a number:",
    message: nil, preferredStyle: .alert)
alert.addTextField { tf in
    tf.keyboardType = .numberPad
}
func handler(_ act:UIAlertAction) {
    let tf = alert.textFields![0]
    // ... can read tf.text here ...
}
alert.addAction(UIAlertAction(title: "Cancel", style: .cancel))
alert.addAction(UIAlertAction(title: "OK",
    style: .default, handler: handler))
self.present(alert, animated: true)
```

A puzzle arises as to how to prevent the user from dismissing the alert if the text fields are not acceptably filled in. The alert will be dismissed if the user taps a button, and no button handler: function can prevent this. The solution is to *disable* the relevant buttons until the text fields are satisfactory. A UIAlertAction has an isEnabled property for this very purpose. I'll modify the preceding example so that the OK button is disabled initially:

```
alert.addAction(UIAlertAction(title: "Cancel", style: .cancel))
alert.addAction(UIAlertAction(title: "OK",
    style: .default, handler: handler))
alert.actions[1].isEnabled = false
self.present(alert, animated: true)
```

But this raises a new puzzle: how will the OK button ever be enabled? The text field can have a delegate or a control event target–action pair (Chapter 11), and so we can hear about the user typing in it. I'll modify the example again so that I'm notified as the user edits the text field:

```
alert.addTextField { tf in
    tf.keyboardType = .numberPad
    tf.addTarget(self,
        action: #selector(self.textChanged), for: .editingChanged)
}
```

Our `textChanged` method will now be called when the user edits, but this raises a further puzzle: how will this method, which receives a reference to the text field, get a reference to the OK button in the alert in order to enable it? My approach is to walk my way up the responder chain from the text field to the alert controller (for the `next(ofType:)` method, see Appendix B). Here, I enable the OK button if and only if the text field contains some text:

```
@objc func textChanged(_ sender: Any) {
    let tf = sender as! UITextField
    let alert = tf.next(ofType: UIAlertController.self)
    alert?.actions[1].isEnabled = (tf.text != "")
}
```

But there is a hole in our implementation, because a user with a hardware keyboard can still enter nondigits and can still press Return to dismiss the alert even when the text field is empty. To prevent *that*, we also give the text field a delegate (in the `handler:` function for `alert.addTextField`) and implement the appropriate delegate methods:

```
func textField(_ textField: UITextField,
    shouldChangeCharactersIn range: NSRange,
    replacementString string: String) -> Bool {
        if string.isEmpty { return true }
        if Int(string) == nil { return false }
        return true
}
func textFieldShouldReturn(_ textField: UITextField) -> Bool {
    return textField.text != ""
}
```

Action Sheets

An action sheet (UIAlertController style `.actionSheet`) is similar to menu; it consists primarily of buttons. On the iPhone, it slides up from the bottom of the screen; on the iPad, it appears as a popover.

New in iOS 14, Apple expects your use of action sheets to be greatly reduced. The vast majority of the time, an action sheet appears in response to the user tapping a button or a bar button item — and in iOS 14, those have *real* menus! When your goal is to present courses of action between which the user is to choose, a menu effectively sprouts from the button the user tapped; the button *becomes* the choices. With an action sheet, especially on the iPhone, the user, having tapped a button, must look

Figure 14-2. An action sheet on the iPhone

elsewhere for the menu of options, down at the bottom of the screen; that creates more friction.

On the other hand, sometimes friction is exactly what you want; in those cases, an action sheet remains appropriate. An action sheet is the right way to give the user an opportunity for reflection before taking a possibly destructive action. In Apple's Photos app, asking to delete a photo brings up an action sheet whose buttons are Delete Photo and Cancel; in Apple's Calendar app, starting to create a new event and then cancelling brings up an action sheet whose buttons are Discard Changes and Keep Editing.

Perhaps the alert presented in Figure 14-1 would have been better as an action sheet. If we change the preferred style from .alert to .actionSheet, we get Figure 14-2.

On the iPad, an action sheet wants to be a popover. This means that a UIPopover-PresentationController will take charge of it. It is incumbent upon you to provide something for the popover's arrow to point to (as explained in Chapter 10) or you'll crash at runtime:

```
self.present(action, animated: true)
if let pop = action.popoverPresentationController {
    let v = sender as! UIView
    pop.sourceView = v
    pop.sourceRect = v.bounds
}
```

The cancel button for a popover action sheet on the iPad is suppressed, because the user can dismiss the popover by tapping outside it. On the iPhone, too, where the cancel button is displayed, the user can *still* dismiss the action sheet by tapping outside it. When the user does that, the cancel button's handler: function will be called, just as if the user had tapped the cancel button — even if the cancel button is not displayed.

Figure 14-3. A presented view behaving like an alert

Alert Alternatives

Alerts and action sheets are deliberately limited, inflexible, and inappropriate to any but the simplest cases. Their interface can contain title text, buttons, and (for an alert) one or two text fields, and that's all. What if you wanted more interface than that?

Some developers have hacked into their alerts or action sheets in an attempt to force them to be more customizable. *This is wrong*, and in any case there is no need for such extremes. These are just presented view controllers, and if you don't like what they contain, you can make your own presented view controller with its own customized view. If you also want that view to look and behave like an alert or an action sheet, then make it so!

As I have shown ("Custom Presented View Controller Transition" on page 365), it is easy to create a small presented view that looks and behaves quite like an alert or action sheet, floating in front of the main interface and darkening everything behind it — the difference being that this is an ordinary view controller's view, belonging entirely to you, so that you can populate it with any interface you like (Figure 14-3).

But a presented view controller doesn't have to look like an alert in order to have the same effect. A popover is virtually a secondary window, and can be truly modal; the popovers in Figure 10-1 are effectively modal dialogs. A presented view controller on an iPad can use the .formSheet presentation style, which is effectively a dialog window smaller than the screen. On the iPhone, *any* presented view is essentially a modal dialog, and can replace an alert or action sheet. In Apple's Mail app, when reading a mail message, the action button in iOS 12 and earlier summons an action sheet letting the user reply to the current message, forward it, or print it; starting in iOS 13, Apple wanted to add many more options, so that button now summons a custom presented view controller instead of an action sheet.

Quick Actions

Quick actions are essentially a column of buttons summoned when the user long presses on your app's icon. They should represent convenient ways of accessing functionality that the user could equally have performed from within your app.

Quick actions are of two kinds:

Static quick actions

Static quick actions are described in your app's *Info.plist*. The system can present them even if your app isn't running — indeed, even if your app has *never* run — because it can read your app's *Info.plist*.

Dynamic quick actions

Dynamic quick actions are configured in code. This means that they are not available until your app's code has actually run. Your code can alter and remove dynamic quick actions, but it cannot affect your app's static quick actions.

When the user taps a quick action, your app is brought to the front (launching it if necessary) and a delegate method is called. In iOS 12 and before, this was an app delegate method; now it's a scene delegate method. You'll be handed a UIApplicationShortcutItem describing the button the user tapped; now you can respond as appropriate.

A UIApplicationShortcutItem is just a value class, embodying five properties describing the button that will appear in the interface. Those five properties have analogs in the *Info.plist*, so that you can configure your static quick actions. The *Info.plist* UIApplicationShortcutItems entry is an array of dictionaries, one for each quick action, each containing the properties and values you wish to set.

The UIApplicationShortcutItem properties and corresponding *Info.plist* keys are:

type *property*
UIApplicationShortcutItemType *key*

An arbitrary string. You can use this string in your delegate method to distinguish which button was tapped. Required.

localizedTitle *property*
UIApplicationShortcutItemTitle *key*

The button title; a string. Required.

localizedSubtitle *property*
UIApplicationShortcutItemSubtitle *key*

The button subtitle; a string. Optional.

icon *property*
UIApplicationShortcutItemIconType *key*
UIApplicationShortcutItemIconFile *key*

An icon to appear in the button. Optional, but it's good to supply some icon, because if you don't, you'll get an ugly filled circle by default. When forming a UIApplicationShortcutItem in code, you'll supply a UIApplicationShortcutIcon object as its icon property. UIApplicationShortcutIcon has four initializers:

Figure 14-4. Quick actions

`init(type:)`
> A UIApplicationShortcutIcon.IconType. This is an enum of about 30 cases, each representing a built-in standard image, such as `.time` (a clock icon).

`init(templateImageName:)`
> Works like UIImage's `init(named:)`. The image will be treated as a template image. Apple says that the image should be 35×35, though a larger image will be scaled down appropriately.

`init(systemImageName:)`
> Works like UIImage's `init(systemName:)`. The image should be a symbol image.

`init(contact:)`
> A CNContact (see Chapter 19). The icon will be based on the contact's picture or initials.

In the *Info.plist*, you may use either the `IconType` key or the `IconFile` key. The value for the `IconType` key is the Objective-C name of a UIApplicationShortcut-Icon.IconType case, such as `UIApplicationShortcutIconTypeTime`. The value for the `IconFile` key is the name of an image file in your app, suitable for use with `UIImage(named:)`.

`userInfo` *property*
`UIApplicationShortcutItemUserInfo` *key*
> An optional dictionary of additional information, whose usage is completely up to you.

⌄ UIApplicationShortcutItems	⌃⌄	Array	(2 items)
⌄ Item 0		Dictionary	(5 items)
UIApplicationShortcutItemIconFile		String	cup
UIApplicationShortcutItemSubtitle		String	In 5 minutes...
UIApplicationShortcutItemTitle		String	Coffee Reminder
UIApplicationShortcutItemType		String	coffee.schedule
⌄ UIApplicationShortcutItemUserInfo		Dictionary	(1 item)
time		Number	5
⌄ Item 1		Dictionary	(5 items)
UIApplicationShortcutItemIconFile		String	cup
UIApplicationShortcutItemSubtitle		String	In 15 minutes...
UIApplicationShortcutItemTitle		String	Coffee Reminder
UIApplicationShortcutItemType		String	coffee.schedule
⌄ UIApplicationShortcutItemUserInfo		Dictionary	(1 item)
time		Number	15

Figure 14-5. Static quick actions in the Info.plist

To illustrate, imagine that our app's purpose is to remind the user periodically to go get a cup of coffee. Figure 14-4 shows a quick actions menu of three items generated when the user long presses our app's icon. The first two items are static items, generated by our settings in the *Info.plist*, which is shown in Figure 14-5.

The third quick action item in Figure 14-4 is a dynamic item. The idea is that our app lets the user set a time interval as a favorite default interval. We cannot know what this favorite interval will be until the app runs and the user sets it; that's why this item is dynamic. Here's the code that generates it; all we have to do is set our shared UIApplication object's shortcutItems property:

```
let subtitle = "In 1 hour..." // or whatever
let time = 60 // or whatever
let item = UIApplicationShortcutItem(type: "coffee.schedule",
    localizedTitle: "Coffee Reminder", localizedSubtitle: subtitle,
    icon: UIApplicationShortcutIcon(templateImageName: "cup"),
    userInfo: ["time":time as NSNumber])
UIApplication.shared.shortcutItems = [item]
```

Both in the *Info.plist* static quick actions and in this dynamic quick action, I've configured the userInfo so that when I receive this UIApplicationShortcutItem in my delegate method, I can look at the value of its "time" key to find out what time interval the user specified.

So now let's say the user taps one of the quick action buttons. Our delegate method is called! If our app is already running, this will be the scene delegate's window-Scene(_:performActionFor:completionHandler:) method. In our response, we are supposed to finish by calling the completionHandler, passing a Bool to indicate success or failure; but in fact I see no difference in behavior regardless of whether we pass true or false, or even if we omit to call the completionHandler entirely:

```
func windowScene(_ windowScene: UIWindowScene,
    performActionFor shortcutItem: UIApplicationShortcutItem,
    completionHandler: @escaping (Bool) -> Void) {
        if shortcutItem.type == "coffee.schedule" {
            if let d = shortcutItem.userInfo {
                if let time = d["time"] as? Int {
                    // ... do something with time ...
                    completionHandler(true)
                }
            }
        }
        completionHandler(false)
}
```

If our app is launched from scratch by the user tapping a quick action button, window-Scene(_:performActionFor:completionHandler:) is *not* called. Instead, we have to implement scene(_:willConnectTo:options:) and check whether the options: parameter's shortcutItem isn't nil:

```
func scene(_ scene: UIScene,
    willConnectTo session: UISceneSession,
    options connectionOptions: UIScene.ConnectionOptions) {
        if let shortcutItem = connectionOptions.shortcutItem {
            if shortcutItem.type == "coffee.schedule" {
                if let d = shortcutItem.userInfo {
                    if let time = d["time"] as? Int {
                        // ... do something with time ...
                    }
                }
            }
        }
}
```

If your app supports multiple windows on iPad, the runtime needs a way to know *which* window scene's delegate to call. To answer that question, use your UIScene's activationConditions: set it to a UISceneActivationConditions object whose can-ActivateForTargetContentIdentifierPredicate and prefersToActivateFor-TargetContentIdentifierPredicate properties specify appropriate predicates. The targetContentIdentifier in question is a property of UIApplicationShortcutItem; it's just a string, such as "myShortcutIdentifier". The predicate's self *is* the incoming targetContentIdentifier string, so the predicate will be something like this:

```
let pred = NSPredicate(format: "self == 'myShortcutIdentifier'")
```

 Apple has not explained how to specify a symbol image or a target content identifier for a static UIApplicationShortcutItem defined in the *Info.plist*.

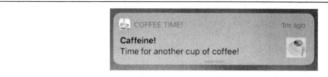

Figure 14-6. A local notification

Local Notifications

A local notification (Figure 14-6) is an alert to the user presented by the system — not by your app. You instruct the system as to when the notification should *fire*, and then you just stand back and let the system deal with it. At the time the system decides to present the alert, your app doesn't have to be frontmost; it doesn't even have to be running! The notification *can* appear when your app is frontmost, but even then it is the system that is presenting it on your behalf.

Notification alerts can appear in any of these venues:

- On the lock screen.
- In the notification center; this is the interface that appears when the user swipes down from the top screen edge.
- As a banner at the top of the screen.

A local notification, as it fires, can do other things:

- It can play a sound.
- It can cause a badge number to appear on, or to be removed from, your app's icon.

Taken together, those five possibilities constitute your app's *delivery options* for local notifications. The user, in the Settings app, can veto any of the delivery options for your app's local notifications, and can even turn off your app's local notifications entirely. The user can also do just the opposite, turning on delivery options that were previously turned off. A user who permits your notifications to appear as a banner also gets to choose between a *temporary* banner, which vanishes spontaneously after displaying itself briefly, and a *persistent* banner, which remains until the user dismisses it.

The user can also, upon receipt of a notification from your app, summon a Manage Notifications dialog, where a Deliver Quietly button limits your app's notifications to appear only in the notification center; there is also a Turn Off button that suppresses them entirely (Figure 14-7). Other user settings can affect notification delivery as well; for instance, the user turning on Do Not Disturb has the same effect as choosing Deliver Quietly.

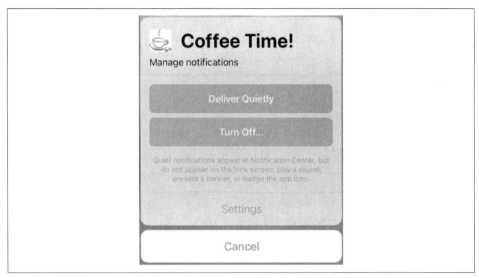

Figure 14-7. The user manages your app's notifications

The user can interact with local notification alerts in some rudimentary ways. At a minimum, a local notification alert can be tapped as a way for the user to summon your app, bringing it to the front if it is backgrounded, and launching it if it isn't running. This response to the notification is its *default action*. In the lock screen or notification center, the user can slide the notification to reveal standard buttons such as Clear (to close the alert), Manage (to bring up the dialog shown in Figure 14-7), and Open (to summon your app).

The user can also elect to *view* the notification. Depending on the circumstances, the user might slide the notification sideways to reveal the View button and tap it, or drag it downward, or long press it. This produces the notification's *secondary interface*, which you get to design.

You can add *custom actions*, in the form of buttons to appear in the secondary interface. A local notification can also carry an *attachment*, which may be an image, a sound file, or a video; in the secondary interface, if the attachment is an image, the image is displayed, and if the attachment is audio or video, interface is provided for playing it.

In Figure 14-6, the little image at the right of the alert is the thumbnail of an image attachment. In Figure 14-8, the user has summoned the alert's secondary interface, displaying the image as well as two custom action buttons.

But wait, there's more! You can modify the secondary interface still further by writing a *notification content extension*. This lets you design the interior of the secondary interface however you like. Figure 14-9 shows an example; I've replaced the default

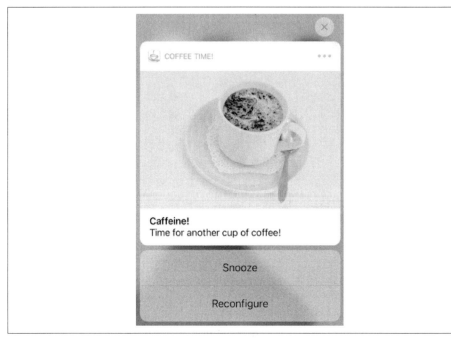

Figure 14-8. Local notification secondary interface

title and body with a caption in my own font, and I've shown the attachment image in a smaller size.

Use of a local notification involves several steps:

1. Your app must obtain *authorization* for notifications.

2. You might register a notification *category*.

3. Your app creates and *schedules* the local notification, handing it over to the system.

4. Your app is prepared to hear about the user *responding* to the notification after it fires.

I'll describe this sequence one step at a time; then I'll talk about writing a notification content extension.

You'll need to import the User Notifications framework (`import User-Notifications`). Most of your activity will ultimately involve the user notification center, a singleton UNUserNotificationCenter instance available by calling `UNUser-NotificationCenter.current()`.

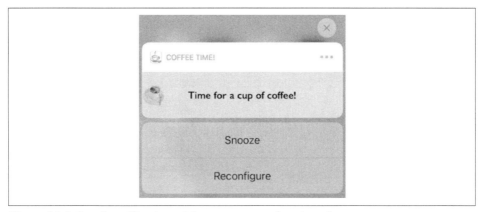

Figure 14-9. Local notification with custom secondary interface

Authorization for Local Notifications

You have a choice of two strategies for obtaining initial authorization for your app's notifications:

Full authorization

> Before trying to schedule any local notifications, you ask the system to present a one-time authorization alert on your behalf. The user must choose between granting and denying authorization to your app (Figure 14-10, on the left). An app that gains full authorization in this way is eligible initially for all delivery options.

Provisional authorization

> With *no* explicit user authorization, you can be *automatically* authorized for "quiet" delivery: your notifications can appear in the notification center *only*, with no sound and no icon badging. In the notification center, your notification is accompanied by options to keep or turn off your app's notifications (Figure 14-10, on the right). If the user ignores this choice, "quiet" delivery of your app's notifications will continue. If the user taps Keep, an action sheet lets the user grant your app full authorization. (This form of authorization was introduced in iOS 12.)

Which strategy should you choose? Full authorization, if you can obtain it, gives your notifications the widest range of possible venues immediately; but it can be hard to obtain. Who of us hasn't seen that alert (Figure 14-10, on the left) and wondered: "What's *that* all about?" If you're like me, you instinctively tap Don't Allow and move on. The idea of provisional authorization is that the user, having seen your notifications in the notification center, and having understood what they are for, might then grant full authorization. But no matter what sort of authorization you obtain, the

Figure 14-10. Two ways of requesting user authorization

user, at any time, can return to the Settings app and increase or decrease the powers of your local notifications.

Whichever strategy you decide on, your first step before scheduling any local notifications should be to find out whether we are already authorized. To do so, call the user notification center's `getNotificationSettings` method. It returns a UNNotificationSettings object asynchronously; examine the `authorizationStatus` property of that object. The possibilities are (UNAuthorizationStatus):

`.denied`
> The user has explicitly disallowed all notifications from your app. There may be no point scheduling any local notifications, as they will not fire unless the user's settings are changed. (You might put up an alert begging the user to switch to the Settings app and authorize your app's notifications.)

`.authorized`
`.provisional`
`.ephemeral`
> You have authorization! Your authorization is full, provisional, or ephemeral (new in iOS 14, applicable to app clips). Feel free to go ahead and schedule a local notification.

`.notDetermined`
> This is the really interesting case — the moment when you're going to try to get authorization! You should immediately send `requestAuthorization(options:)` to the user notification center. A Bool is returned asynchronously, telling you whether authorization was granted. The `options:` argument is a UNAuthorizationOptions object, an option set that can include any of the following:

`.badge`
`.sound`
`.alert`

> The maximum range of abilities you want your app to have. `.badge` means you might want your app's icon to be badged with a number when a notification fires. `.sound` means you might want a sound to play when a notification fires. `.alert` means you might want a notification alert to be presented when a notification fires. Be sure to include all choices that might be needed for any of your app's notifications, as you won't get another chance! For instance, if you don't include `.badge`, the switch that lets the user turn on badges for your app's notifications will never even appear in Settings.

`.provideAppNotificationSettings`

> I'll discuss this more in a moment.

`.provisional`

> You are opting for provisional authorization.

What happens as a result of your call to `requestAuthorization(options:)` when the authorization status is `.notDetermined` depends on whether your UNAuthorizationOptions does or doesn't include `.provisional`:

It doesn't include `.provisional`

> The authorization alert will appear (Figure 14-10, on the left), and the user must make a choice on the spot. The outcome of that choice is the Bool that is returned from the call to `requestAuthorization(options:)`.

It does include `.provisional`

> The authorization alert will *never* appear, and you will be granted provisional authorization immediately — the Bool will be `true`.

Both `getNotificationSettings` and `requestAuthorization(options:)` return their results *asynchronously* (see Appendix C) and possibly on a background thread (Chapter 25). This means that you cannot simply follow a call to `getNotificationSettings` with a call to `requestAuthorization(options:)`; if you do, `requestAuthorization(options:)` will run *before* `getNotificationSettings` has a chance to return its UNNotificationSettings object! Instead, you must *nest* the calls by means of their completion functions, like this:

```
let center = UNUserNotificationCenter.current()
center.getNotificationSettings { settings in
    switch settings.authorizationStatus {
    case .denied:
        break // or beg for authorization
    case .authorized, .provisional, .ephemeral:
        break // or schedule a notification
```

```
        case .notDetermined:
            center.requestAuthorization(options:[.alert, .sound]) { ok, err in
                if let err = err {
                    return // could do something with the error information
                }
                if ok {
                    // authorized; could schedule a notification
                }
            }
        }
    }
    @unknown default: fatalError()
}
```

The parameter that arrives in your `getNotificationSettings` completion function (`settings` in the preceding code) is a UNNotificationSettings object. This object describes your app's notification settings in the Settings app as they are configured at this moment. That information might be of interest at any time, especially because the user can change those settings. In addition to its `authorizationStatus`, a UNNotificationSettings object has the following properties:

soundSetting
badgeSetting
alertSetting
notificationCenterSetting
lockScreenSetting

How the user has configured the notification settings for your app:

- .enabled

- .disabled

- .notSupported

alertStyle

How the user has configured the alert style setting for your app:

- .banner

- .alert

- .none

showPreviewsSetting

How the user has configured previews for your app (I'll discuss the implications of this setting later:

- .always

- .whenAuthenticated

- .never

`providesAppNotificationSettings`

This depends on whether your app included `.provideAppNotification-Settings` when requesting authorization. I'll explain that later, when I talk about the user notification center delegate.

Notification Categories

A notification category is a somewhat nebulous entity, embracing a miscellany of possible settings to be associated with individual notifications. You register any desired categories with the user notification center; each category has an arbitrary string identifier. Later, when you create a notification, you associate it with a previously registered category by means of that string identifier.

Categories have grown over the years to embrace more and more settings, so a category (UNNotificationCategory) now has three initializers with increasingly more parameters. The fullest form is:

- `init(identifier:actions:intentIdentifiers:hiddenPreviewsBody-Placeholder:categorySummaryFormat:options:)`

The `identifier:` is how a subsequent notification will be matched to this category. I'll talk about the other parameters later (except for `intentIdentifiers:`; it has to do with SiriKit, which is not covered in this book).

To bring a category into force, you register it with the user notification center by calling `setNotificationCategories`. The parameter is an array of categories:

```
let cat1 = UNNotificationCategory(identifier: /* ... */)
let cat2 = UNNotificationCategory(identifier: /* ... */)
let cat3 = UNNotificationCategory(identifier: /* ... */)
let center = UNUserNotificationCenter.current()
center.setNotificationCategories([cat1, cat2, cat3])
```

There are no category management commands, in the sense of adding or removing individual categories. But the categories are maintained as a Set, so it does no harm to register the same identical category multiple times. Moreover, there is a command that allows you to *get* categories; you can retrieve the existing categories, add a category to the list, and set the categories again:

```
let center = UNUserNotificationCenter.current()
center.getNotificationCategories { cats in
    var cats = cats
    let newcat = UNNotificationCategory(identifier: /* ... */)
    cats.insert(newcat)
    center.setNotificationCategories(cats)
}
```

You might use a notification category for any of the following purposes:

- You want your notification's secondary interface to display custom actions.
- You want your app to be notified when the user dismisses your notification.
- You want to customize the text of your notification when the user has suppressed previews.
- You want to customize the text that summarizes your notifications when they are grouped.

I'll talk now about the first three of those uses, leaving grouped notifications for later.

Custom actions

Custom actions are basically buttons that appear in a notification's secondary interface (Figure 14-8). Before iOS 12, the only way to get these was through a notification category. In iOS 12 and later, you can create custom actions in a notification content extension, so you don't need to use a category for this unless your notification has no corresponding notification content extension.

A custom action is a UNNotificationAction, a value class whose initializer is:

- `init(identifier:title:options:)`

The `identifier:` is an arbitrary string; you might use it later to distinguish which button was tapped. The `title:` is the text to appear in the button. The `options:` are a UNNotificationActionOptions bitmask; here are the options and what they mean if you include them:

`.foreground`
> Tapping this button summons your app to the foreground. Otherwise, this button will call your app in the background; your app will be given just enough time to respond and will then be suspended.

`.destructive`
> This button will be marked in the interface as dangerous (by being displayed in red).

`.authenticationRequired`
> If this is not a `.foreground` button, then if the user's device requires authentication (such as a passcode) to go beyond the lock screen, tapping this button in the lock screen will also require authentication. The idea is to prevent performance of this action from the lock screen without the user explicitly unlocking it.

Alternatively, an action can be a text field where the user can type and then tap a button to send the text to your app. This is a UNTextInputNotificationAction, a UNNotificationAction subclass. Its initializer is:

- `init(identifier:title:options:textInputButtonTitle:textInput-`
  `Placeholder:)`

Having created your actions, initialize your UNNotificationCategory with the actions in an array as the `actions:` argument. I'll explain how your app responds to the tapping of a custom action button later, when I talk about the user notification center delegate (and custom content extensions).

Dismiss action

The user can dismiss your local notification (removing it from the notification center) without interacting with it in any other way that might cause your app to get an event — without tapping it to summon your app (the default action) and without tapping a custom action button. Normally, when that happens, your app will get no event at all, so you won't even know that the user has seen the notification.

However, you can change that. In the UNNotificationCategory initializer, the `options:` parameter is a UNNotificationCategoryOptions, an option set. Include `.customDismissAction` if you want your code to get an event under those circumstances. I'll explain how your app gets this event later, when I talk about the user notification center delegate.

 Unfortunately, there is no dismiss event when the user merely swipes up to remove a notification alert banner; perhaps this is because the notification is not truly dismissed (it might still be in the notification center).

Previews

Notifications can pop up unexpectedly, including on the lock screen. So the user might prefer, in the interests of privacy, to suppress the notification's text when the alert initially appears. The text would then be visible only in the notification's secondary interface. The text in a local notification alert when it initially appears is called the *preview* of the notification.

In the Settings app, the user has three choices about when previews should be permitted to appear: always, when the phone is unlocked (to prevent the previews on the lock screen only), and never.

By default, if previews are turned off, the title and subtitle of the notification are suppressed, and the body text is replaced by a placeholder — the word "Notification." Instead of "Notification," you can supply your own placeholder. In the UNNotificationCategory initializer, set the `hiddenPreviewsBodyPlaceholder:` argument to the desired placeholder.

If your notification's title and subtitle contain no sensitive information, you can cause them to appear even if previews are turned off. To do so, include the UNNotification-

CategoryOptions `.hiddenPreviewsShowTitle` and `.hiddenPreviewsShowSubtitle` in the `options:` argument when you initialize your UNNotificationCategory.

Scheduling a Local Notification

To schedule a notification, you create a UNNotificationRequest, by calling its designated initializer:

- `init(identifier:content:trigger:)`

You then tell the user notification center to `add(_:)` this notification to its internal list of scheduled notifications.

The `identifier:` is an arbitrary string. You might use this later on to distinguish which notification this is. And it lets you prevent clutter. If you schedule a notification when a previous notification with the same identifier is already scheduled, the previous notification is deleted; if a notification fires (is delivered) when a previous notification with the same identifier is already sitting in the notification center, the previous notification is deleted.

The `content:` is the heart and soul of this individual notification — what it is to display, what information it carries, and so forth. It is sometimes referred to as the *payload* of the notification. It is a UNNotificationContent object, but that class is immutable; in order to *form* the payload, you'll start by instantiating its mutable subclass, UNMutableNotificationContent. You will then assign values to as many of its properties as you like. Those properties are:

`title, subtitle, body`
> Text visible in the notification alert.

`attachments`
> UNNotificationAttachment objects. An attachment is created by calling its designated initializer:
>
> - `init(identifier:url:options:)`
>
> The `identifier:` is an arbitrary string. The `url:` is the attachment itself; it must be a file URL pointing to an image file, an audio file, or a video file on disk. The file must be fairly small, because the system, in order to present it on your behalf in the notification's interface after the notification fires some time in the future, is going to *copy* it off to a private secure area of its own.

`sound`
> A sound (UNNotificationSound) to be played when the notification fires. You can specify a sound file in your app bundle by name (UNNotificationSound-Name), or call `default` to specify the default sound:

```
content.sound =
    UNNotificationSound(named: UNNotificationSoundName("test.aif"))
```

badge

A number to appear on your app's icon after this notification fires. Specify 0 to remove an existing badge. (You can also set or remove your app's icon badge at any time by means of the shared application's `applicationIconBadgeNumber`.)

categoryIdentifier

The identifier string of a previously registered category. This is how your local notification will be associated with the settings you've applied to that category.

userInfo

An arbitrary dictionary, to carry extra information you'll retrieve later.

threadIdentifier

A string; notification alerts with the same thread identifier are grouped together physically in the lock screen and notification center. I'll talk more about that later.

launchImageName

Your app might be launched from scratch by the user tapping this notification's alert. Suppose that when this happens, you're going to configure your app so that it appears differently from how it normally launches. You might want the momentary launch screen, shown while your app starts up, to correspond to that different interface. This is how you specify the alternative launch image to be used in that situation.

The `trigger:` parameter tells the system how to know when it's time for this notification to fire. It will be expressed as a subclass of UNNotificationTrigger:

UNTimeIntervalNotificationTrigger

Fires starting a certain number of seconds from now, possibly repeating every time that number of seconds elapses. The initializer is:

- `init(timeInterval:repeats:)`

UNCalendarNotificationTrigger

Fires at a certain date-time, expressed using DateComponents, possibly repeating when the same DateComponents occurs again. For instance, if you use the Date-Components to express nine o'clock in the morning, without regard to date, then the trigger, if repeating, would be nine o'clock *every* morning. The initializer is:

- `init(dateMatching:repeats:)`

UNLocationNotificationTrigger
Fires when the user enters or leaves a certain geographical region. I'll discuss this further in Chapter 22.

As an example, here's the code that generated Figure 14-6:

```
let interval = // ... whatever ...
let trigger = UNTimeIntervalNotificationTrigger(
    timeInterval: interval, repeats: false)
let content = UNMutableNotificationContent()
content.title = "Caffeine!"
content.body = "Time for another cup of coffee!"
content.sound = UNNotificationSound.default
content.categoryIdentifier = self.categoryIdentifier
let url = Bundle.main.url(forResource: "cup", withExtension: "jpg")!
if let att = try? UNNotificationAttachment(
    identifier: "cup", url: url, options:nil) {
        content.attachments = [att]
}
let req = UNNotificationRequest(
    identifier: "coffeeNotification", content: content, trigger: trigger)
let center = UNUserNotificationCenter.current()
center.add(req)
```

Hearing About a Local Notification

In order to hear about your scheduled local notification after it fires, you need to configure some object to be the user notification center's `delegate`, adopting the UNUserNotificationCenterDelegate protocol. You'll want to do this very early in your app's lifetime, because you might need to be sent a delegate message immediately upon launching; `application(_:didFinishLaunchingWithOptions:)` is a good place. The user notification center delegate might be the app delegate itself, or it might be some helper object that the app delegate creates and retains:

```
func application(_ application: UIApplication,
    didFinishLaunchingWithOptions launchOptions:
    [UIApplication.LaunchOptionsKey : Any]?) -> Bool {
        let center = UNUserNotificationCenter.current()
        center.delegate = self // or whatever
        return true
}
```

The UNUserNotificationCenterDelegate protocol consists of three optional methods. All three of them provide you with a UNNotification object containing the fire `date` and your original `request` (UNNotificationRequest). You can identify the local notification, and you can extract information from it, such as an attachment or the `user-Info` dictionary. Here are the delegate methods:

`userNotificationCenter(_:willPresent:withCompletionHandler:)`

This method is called only if your app is frontmost when your local notification fires. By default, when that happens, the notification's entire user interface is suppressed: no sound is played, no banner appears, no notification is added to the notification center or the lock screen. This method lets *you* know that the notification fired, but the *user* has no way of knowing. The idea is that your app itself, as it is already frontmost, might inform the user of whatever the user needs to know.

However, you can opt to let the system do what it would have done if your app had *not* been frontmost. You are handed a completion function; your job is to call it with some combination of UNNotificationPresentationOptions values — .banner, .sound, and .badge — or else with an empty option set to get the default behavior. (The .banner option is new in iOS 14, replacing .alert, which is deprecated.) Here's an example where we tell the runtime to present the local notification alert within our app:

```
func userNotificationCenter(_ center: UNUserNotificationCenter,
    willPresent notification: UNNotification,
    withCompletionHandler completionHandler:
    @escaping (UNNotificationPresentationOptions) -> ()) {
        completionHandler([.sound, .banner])
}
```

`userNotificationCenter(_:didReceive:withCompletionHandler:)`

Called when the user interacts with your local notification alert. The second parameter is a UNNotificationResponse, consisting of two properties. One, the `notification`, is the UNNotification object. The other, the `actionIdentifier`, is a string telling you what the user did; there are three possibilities:

`UNNotificationDefaultActionIdentifier`

The user performed the default action, tapping the alert or the Open button to summon your app.

`UNNotificationDismissActionIdentifier`

The user dismissed the local notification alert. You won't hear about this (and this method won't be called) unless you specified the .customDismiss-Action option for this notification's category — and even then, as I mentioned earlier, the user merely swiping a banner up and off the screen does not count as dismissal in this sense.

A custom action identifier string

The user tapped a custom action button, and this is its `identifier`.

If the custom action was a text input action, then the UNNotificationResponse will be a subclass, UNTextInputNotificationResponse, which has an additional userText property. You'll cast down safely and retrieve the userText:

```
if let textresponse = response as? UNTextInputNotificationResponse {
    let text = textresponse.userText
    // ...
}
```

You are handed a completion function, which you *must* call when you're done. You must be quick, because it may be that you are being awakened momentarily in the background, and your code is running on the main thread. Here's an example where the user has tapped a custom action button; I use a background task (Chapter 25) and my delay utility (Appendix B) so as to return immediately before proceeding to obey the button:

```
func userNotificationCenter(_ center: UNUserNotificationCenter,
    didReceive response: UNNotificationResponse,
    withCompletionHandler completionHandler: @escaping () -> ()) {
        let id = response.actionIdentifier
        if id == "snooze" {
            var id = UIBackgroundTaskIdentifier.invalid
            id = UIApplication.shared.beginBackgroundTask {
                UIApplication.shared.endBackgroundTask(id)
            }
            delay(0.1) {
                self.createNotification()
                UIApplication.shared.endBackgroundTask(id)
            }
        }
        completionHandler()
}
```

If the user tapped on your notification alert (the default action), your app is activated and, if necessary, launched from scratch. If your app with window scene support is launched from scratch or if the notification is routed to a scene that was previously disconnected, your scene delegate's scene(_:willConnect-To:options:) is called with the notificationResponse in its options: parameter. As with a shortcut item, you can set your notification request content's targetContentIdentifier to specify which scene the notification should be routed to. In any case, userNotificationCenter(_:didReceive:with-CompletionHandler:) is still called.

userNotificationCenter(_:openSettingsFor:)
When you requested authorization, you may have included the .provideApp-NotificationSettings option. Doing so constitutes a promise that your app provides its own *internal interface* for letting the user manage notifications-

related settings. In response, the runtime provides on your behalf a special app notification settings button in appropriate places like the Settings app. The user has now tapped that button, and you should immediately display that interface.

How might you use this feature? Well, suppose your app has several clearly distinct categories of notification; you might want to allow the user to elect to turn notifications on or off for a particular category. Your app provides interface for letting the user do that, and the button in the Settings app provides a direct pathway to that interface. The idea is that permitting the user to perform fine-grained notification management will reduce clutter in the user's interface and might increase the chances that the user will allow your app to continue sending notifications.

Grouped Notifications

In iOS 12 and later, grouping of notifications by app is the default (though, as usual, the user can turn it off). So you do not need to set the `threadIdentifier` of a notification request's payload (UNMutableNotificationContent) merely in order to group your notifications in the lock screen and the notification center. Rather, the purpose of the `threadIdentifier` is so that, if you have multiple notification types, you can use different `threadIdentifier` values to subdivide your app's group into multiple groups.

Another way to tweak your grouped notifications is to change the summary text that labels each group. By default, some summary text such as "2 more notifications" is generated automatically to describe the group. It might be nice to customize it, depending on what sort of thing my notifications represent. For example, I might like to describe these notifications as "reminders." That's the purpose of the `category-SummaryFormat:` parameter of the UNNotificationCategory initializer.

The `categorySummaryFormat:` is a format string. At a minimum, it will contain a `"%u"` format specifier where the count is to go, such as `"%u more reminders"`.

When you create the payload for your notification, you can supply a `summary-Argument` string. By default, the summary text will then incorporate this as the sender or source of the notification; if the `summaryArgument` for three notifications is `"Matt"`, the summary text will say "2 more notifications from Matt." To customize that, my `categorySummaryFormat` string would need to contain a `"%@"` format specifier where the summary argument is to go, such as `"%u more reminders from %@"`.

(Rarely, an app might also include a `summaryArgumentCount` in the payload. This is to cover the special case where a single notification represents more than one of whatever is represented. In the summary text, the count will be sum of the `summary-ArgumentCount` values of the grouped notifications, rather than just the count of the grouped notifications.)

Managing Notifications

The user notification center is introspectable. It vends two lists of notifications: those that have been scheduled but have not yet fired, and those that have fired but have not yet been removed from the user's notification center:

Scheduled notifications

These are the methods for managing scheduled notifications:

- `getPendingNotificationRequests(completionHandler:)`
- `removePendingNotificationRequests(withIdentifiers:)`
- `removeAllPendingNotificationRequests`

You can examine the list of scheduled notifications, and you can remove a notification from the list to cancel it; that also means you can effectively reschedule a notification (by removing it, copying it with any desired alterations, and adding the resulting notification).

You can learn when each notification is scheduled to fire; if a notification has an interval trigger or a calendar trigger, you can ask for its `nextTriggerDate`.

 Unfortunately, the `nextTriggerDate` is useless for a time interval trigger notification request, because it adds the time interval to the *current* time rather than to the time at which the notification was scheduled. I regard this as a major bug.

Delivered notifications

These are the methods for managing delivered notifications:

- `getDeliveredNotifications(completionHandler:)`
- `removeDeliveredNotifications(withIdentifiers:)`
- `removeAllDeliveredNotifications`

By judicious removal of notifications from this list, you can keep the user's notification center trimmed. You might prefer that only your most recently delivered notification should appear in the notification center. You can even modify the text of a delivered notification, so that the notification will be up-to-date when the user gets around to dealing with it; to do so, you add a notification whose identifier is the same as that of an existing notification.

 Cancelling a repeating local notification is up to your code; if you don't provide a way of doing that, then if the user wants to prevent the notification from recurring, the only recourse may be to delete your app.

Notification Content Extensions

You can customize what appears in your notification's secondary interface. To do so, you write a *notification content extension*. This is a target, separate from your app target, because the system needs to access it outside your app, possibly when your app isn't even running.

To add a notification content extension to your app, create a new target and specify iOS → Application Extension → Notification Content Extension. The template gives you a good start on your extension. You have a storyboard with a single scene, and the code for a corresponding view controller. The code file imports both the User Notifications framework and the User Notifications UI framework, and the view controller adopts the UNNotificationContentExtension protocol.

The view controller code contains a stub implementation of the didReceive(_:) method, which is the only required method. The parameter is a UNNotification whose request is your original UNNotificationRequest; you can examine this and extract information from it as you configure your interface. The attachment URL is security scoped, so if you want to extract an attachment, you'll have to wrap your access in calls to these URL methods:

- startAccessingSecurityScopedResource
- stopAccessingSecurityScopedResource

The only other thing your view controller really needs to do is to set its own preferredContentSize to the desired dimensions of the custom interface. Alternatively, you can use autolayout to size the interface from the inside out.

To illustrate, here's how the custom interface in Figure 14-9 was attained. The interface consists of a label and an image view. The image view is to contain the image attachment from the local notification, so I extract the image from the attachment and set it as the image view's image. I find that the interface doesn't reliably appear unless we also call setNeedsLayout at the end:

```
override func viewDidLoad() {
    super.viewDidLoad()
    self.preferredContentSize = CGSize(320, 80)
}
func didReceive(_ notification: UNNotification) {
    let req = notification.request
    let content = req.content
    let atts = content.attachments
    if let att = atts.first, att.identifier == "cup" {
        if att.url.startAccessingSecurityScopedResource() {
            if let data = try? Data(contentsOf: att.url) {
                self.imageView.image = UIImage(data: data)
            }
            att.url.stopAccessingSecurityScopedResource()
```

∨ NSExtension	Dictionary ⟨⟩	(3 items)
∨ NSExtensionAttributes	Dictionary	(5 items)
UNNotificationExtensionCategory	String	coffee
UNNotificationExtensionDefaultContentHidden	Boolean	1
UNNotificationExtensionInitialContentSizeRatio	Number	0.25
UNNotificationExtensionOverridesDefaultTitle	Boolean	0

Figure 14-11. A content extension's Info.plist

```
        }
    }
    self.view.setNeedsLayout()
}
```

The template also includes an *Info.plist* for your extension. You will need to modify it by configuring these keys:

UNNotificationExtensionCategory
> A string corresponding to the `categoryIdentifier` of the local notification(s) to which this custom secondary interface is to be applied. This is how the runtime knows to associate this notification content extension with this notification! There does *not* have to be an actual category with this identifier.

UNNotificationExtensionInitialContentSizeRatio
> A number representing the width of your custom interface divided by its height. This doesn't have to be perfect — and indeed it probably can't be, since you don't know the actual width of the screen on which this interface will be displayed — but the idea is to give the system a rough idea of the size as it prepares to display the custom interface.

UNNotificationExtensionDefaultContentHidden
> Optional. A Boolean. Set to YES if you want to eliminate the default display of the local notification's title, subtitle, and body from the custom interface.

UNNotificationExtensionOverridesDefaultTitle
> Optional. A Boolean. Set to YES if you want to replace the default display of your app's name at the top of the interface (where it says "Coffee Time!" in Figure 14-9) with a title of your own choosing. To determine that title, set your view controller's `title` property in your `didReceive(_:)` implementation.

Figure 14-11 shows the relevant part of the *Info.plist* for my content extension.

Action button management

Your secondary interface may include custom action buttons. If the user taps one of these, your user notification center delegate's `userNotificationCenter(_:did-Receive:withCompletionHandler:)` is called, as I described earlier. However, your notification content extension view controller can intervene in this mechanism by implementing `didReceive(_:completionHandler:)`. This is different from `did-Receive(_:)`! The parameter is a UNNotificationResponse, not a UNNotification, and there's a second parameter, the completion function.

What you do in your implementation of `didReceive(_:completionHandler:)` is up to you. You might respond by changing the interface in some way. When you've finished doing whatever you came to do, the runtime needs to know how to proceed; you tell it by calling the completion function with one of these responses (UNNotificationContentExtensionResponseOption):

`.doNotDismiss`
> The local notification alert remains in place, still displaying the custom secondary interface.

`.dismiss`
> The alert is dismissed.

`.dismissAndForwardAction`
> The alert is dismissed and the action is passed along to your user notification center delegate's `userNotificationCenter(_:didReceive:withCompletion-Handler:)`.

Even if you tell the completion function to dismiss the alert, you can *still* modify the interface, delaying the call to the completion function so that the user has time to see the change.

Your notification content extension view controller can create and remove custom actions on the fly, in code. Your view controller inherits the UIViewController `extensionContext` property, which is an NSExtensionContext object. Its `notificationActions` property is an array of UNNotificationAction. A UNNotificationAction is an action button! This array therefore initially consists of whatever action buttons you configured in your category — and any changes you make to it will immediately be reflected in the action buttons the user sees.

This means you don't have to create your custom actions in your category configuration in the first place! Creating custom action buttons in your category configuration allows you to have custom buttons *without* a notification content extension; if you *do* have a notification content extension, you can create the custom actions in the view controller's `didReceive(_:completionHandler:)` instead.

Interface interaction

Prior to iOS 12, a custom secondary interface (the notification content extension view controller's main view) is *not interactive*. If the user taps it, nothing happens — except that the notification's default action is performed, which means that the notification is dismissed and your app is summoned. The exception is that the runtime can add a tappable play/pause button for you; this is useful if your custom interface contains video or audio material. Three UNNotificationContentExtension properties can be overridden to dictate that the play/pause button should appear and where it should go, and two methods can be implemented to hear when the user taps the play/pause button.

Starting in iOS 12, the view controller's main view *can* be interactive. This is an opt-in feature: under the `NSExtensionAttributes` in the *Info.plist*, add the `UNNotificationExtensionUserInteractionEnabled` Boolean key and set its value to `YES`. Now the entire mechanism for user interaction springs to life. For instance, your interface can contain a button; if you've configured its action in the storyboard to call a method in your view controller, the user can tap the button to call that method.

Making your content extension view interactive in this way means that the user can no longer tap in the view to trigger the notification's default action, dismissing the notification and summoning your app. Therefore, there is a way for your *code* to trigger the notification's default action: tell the extension context to `perform-NotificationDefaultAction`. In your app, the user notification center delegate's `userNotificationCenter(_:didReceive:withCompletionHandler:)` will be called with the `UNNotificationDefaultActionIdentifier`, as you would expect.

You can also dismiss the notification *without* summoning your app: tell the extension context to `dismissNotificationContentExtension`. In that case, `userNotification-Center(_:didReceive:withCompletionHandler:)` is *not* called, even if you have registered for the `.customDismissAction` (I regard that as a bug).

Activity Views

An activity view is the view belonging to a UIActivityViewController, typically appearing when the user taps a Share button. To display it, you start with one or more pieces of data, such as a string or an image, that you want the user to have the option of sharing or working with. The activity view, when it appears, will then contain a menu item or app icon for every activity (UIActivity) that can work with this type of data. The user may tap one of these to send the data to the activity, and is then perhaps shown additional interface belonging to the provider of the chosen activity.

Figure 14-12 shows an activity view from Mobile Safari. There's a row displaying the icons of some apps that provide applicable built-in system-wide activities; this is followed by menu items representing activities provided internally by Safari itself.

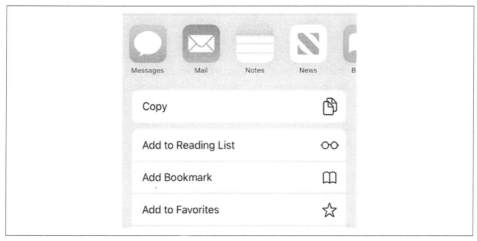

Figure 14-12. An activity view

When you present an activity view within your app, you can add menu items for activities provided internally by *your* app. Moreover, your app can provide system-wide activities that are available when *any* app presents an activity view; these come in two forms:

Share extensions
> A *share extension* is represented as an app icon in the upper row of an activity view. Share extensions are for apps that can accept information into themselves, either for storage, such as Notes and Reminders, or for sending out to a server, such as Twitter and Facebook.

Action extensions
> An *action extension* is represented among the menu items of an activity view. Action extensions offer to perform some kind of manipulation on the data provided by the host app.

I'll describe how to present an activity view and how to construct an activity that's internal to your app. Then I'll give an example of writing an action extension, and finally an example of writing a share extension.

Presenting an Activity View

You will typically want to present an activity view in response to the user tapping a Share button in your app. To do so:

1. Instantiate UIActivityViewController. The initializer you'll be calling is:

   - `init(activityItems:applicationActivities:)`

The `activityItems:` argument is an array of objects to be shared or operated on, such as string or image objects. Presumably these are objects associated somehow with the interface the user is looking at right now.

2. Set the activity view controller's `completionWithItemsHandler` property to a function that will be called when the user's interaction with the activity interface has finished.

3. Present the activity view controller, as a presented view controller; on the iPad, it will be a popover, so you'll also configure the popover presentation controller. The presented view will be dismissed automatically when the user cancels or chooses an activity.

Here's an example:

```
let url = Bundle.main.url(forResource:"sunglasses", withExtension:"png")!
let things : [Any] = ["This is a cool picture", url]
let avc = UIActivityViewController(
    activityItems:things, applicationActivities:nil)
avc.completionWithItemsHandler = { type, ok, items, err in
    // ...
}
self.present(avc, animated:true)
if let pop = avc.popoverPresentationController {
    let v = sender as! UIView
    pop.sourceView = v
    pop.sourceRect = v.bounds
}
```

The activity view is populated automatically with known system-wide activities that can handle any of the types of data you provided as the `activityItems:` argument. These activities represent UIActivity types (UIActivity.ActivityType):

- `.postToFacebook`
- `.postToTwitter`
- `.postToWeibo`
- `.message`
- `.mail`
- `.print`
- `.copyToPasteboard`
- `.assignToContact`
- `.saveToCameraRoll`
- `.addToReadingList`
- `.postToFlickr`

- `.postToVimeo`
- `.postToTencentWeibo`
- `.airDrop`
- `.openInIBooks`
- `.markupAsPDF`

Consult the UIActivity class documentation to learn what types of activity item each of these activities can handle. For instance, the `.mail` activity will accept a string, an image, or a file (such as an image file) designated by a URL; it will present a mail composition interface with the activity item(s) in the body.

Since the default is to include all the system-wide activities that can handle the provided data, if you *don't* want a certain system-wide activity included in the activity view, you must exclude it explicitly. You do this by setting the UIActivityView-Controller's `excludedActivityTypes` property to an array of activity type constants.

 Apps other than Messages, Mail, and Books have no corresponding UIActivity type, because they are implemented as share extensions; it is up to the *user* to include or exclude them.

In the UIActivityViewController initializer `init(activityItems:application-Activities:)`, if you would prefer that an element of the `activityItems:` array should be an object that will supply the data instead of the data itself, make it an object that adopts the UIActivityItemSource protocol. Typically, this object will be `self` (the view controller in charge of all this code). Here's a minimal, artificial example:

```
extension ViewController : UIActivityItemSource {
    func activityViewControllerPlaceholderItem(
        _ activityViewController: UIActivityViewController) -> Any {
            return ""
    }
    func activityViewController(
        _ activityViewController: UIActivityViewController,
        itemForActivityType activityType: UIActivity.ActivityType?) -> Any? {
            return "Coolness"
    }
}
```

The first method provides a placeholder that exemplifies the type of data that will be returned; the second method returns the actual data. The second method can return different data depending on the activity type that the user chose; in this way, you could provide one string to Notes and another string to Mail.

The UIActivitySource protocol also answers a commonly asked question about how to get the Mail activity to populate the mail composition form with a default subject:

```
extension ViewController : UIActivityItemSource {
    // ...
    func activityViewController(
        _ activityViewController: UIActivityViewController,
        subjectForActivityType activityType: UIActivity.ActivityType?)
        -> String {
            return "This is cool"
    }
}
```

If your `activityItems:` data is time-consuming to provide, substitute an instance of a UIActivityItemProvider subclass:

```
let avc = UIActivityViewController(
    activityItems:[MyProvider(placeholderItem: "")],
    applicationActivities:nil)
```

The `placeholderItem:` in the initializer signals the type of data that this UIActivity-ItemProvider object will actually provide. Your UIActivityItemProvider subclass should override the `item` property to return the actual object. This property will be consulted on a background thread, and UIActivityItemProvider is itself an Operation subclass (see Chapter 25).

Custom Activities

The purpose of the `applicationActivities:` parameter of `init(activityItems:applicationActivities:)` is for you to list any additional activities implemented internally by your own app. These will appear as menu items when your app presents an activity view. Each activity will be an instance of one of your own UIActivity subclasses.

To illustrate, I'll create a minimal (and nonsensical) activity called Be Cool that accepts string activity items. It is a UIActivity subclass called MyCoolActivity. So, to include Be Cool among the choices presented to the user by a UIActivityView-Controller, I'd say:

```
let things : [Any] = ["This is a cool picture", url]
let avc = UIActivityViewController(
    activityItems:things, applicationActivities:[MyCoolActivity()])
```

Now let's implement MyCoolActivity. It has an array property called `items`, for reasons that will be apparent in a moment. We need to arm ourselves with an image to represent this activity in the activity view; this will be treated as a template image and will be scaled down automatically. Here's the preparatory part of the implementation of MyCoolActivity:

```
var items : [Any]?
var image : UIImage
override init() {
    // ... construct self.image ...
```

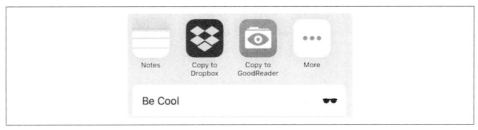

Figure 14-13. Our activity appears in our activity view

```
        super.init()
    }
    override class var activityCategory : UIActivity.ActivityCategory {
        return .action // the default
    }
    override var activityType : UIActivity.ActivityType {
        return UIActivity.ActivityType("com.neuburg.matt.coolActivity")
    }
    override var activityTitle : String? {
        return "Be Cool"
    }
    override var activityImage : UIImage? {
        return self.image
    }
    override func canPerform(withActivityItems activityItems: [Any]) -> Bool {
        for obj in activityItems {
            if obj is String {
                return true
            }
        }
        return false
    }
    override func prepare(withActivityItems activityItems: [Any]) {
        self.items = activityItems
    }
```

If we return `true` from `canPerform(withActivityItems:)`, then a menu item for this activity with title Be Cool and displaying our `activityImage` will appear in the activity view (Figure 14-13).

If the user taps our menu item, `prepare(withActivityItems:)` will be called. We retain the `activityItems` into our `items` property, because they won't be arriving again when we are actually told to perform the activity.

The next step is that we *are* told to perform the activity. To do so, we implement one of these:

`perform` *method*

We immediately perform the activity directly, using the activity items we've already retained. If the activity is time-consuming, it should be performed on a background thread (Chapter 25) so that we can return immediately; the activity view interface will be taken down and the user will be able to go on interacting with the app.

`activityViewController` *property*

We have further interface that we'd like to show the user as part of the activity, so we provide an instance of a UIViewController subclass. The activity view mechanism will present this view controller for us; it is not our job to present or dismiss it. (But we may subsequently present or dismiss dependent interface. If our view controller is a navigation controller with a custom root view controller, we might push another view controller onto its stack while the user is interacting with the activity.)

No matter which of those we implement, we *must* eventually call this activity instance's `activityDidFinish(_:)`. This is the signal to the activity view mechanism that the activity is over. If the activity view is still being presented, it will be taken down or not, depending on the argument we supply here, `true` or `false`; and the argument will be passed into the function we supplied earlier as the activity view controller's `completionWithItemsHandler`:

```
override func perform() {
    // ... do something with self.items here ...
    self.activityDidFinish(true)
}
```

If the UIActivity is providing a view controller as its `activityViewController`, it will want to hand that view controller a reference to `self` beforehand, so that the view controller can call the activity's `activityDidFinish(_:)` when the time comes. This reference will need to be weak; otherwise, a retain cycle ensues.

To illustrate, suppose our activity involves letting the user draw a mustache on a photo of someone. We need our own interface for that, so we return a view controller as the `activityViewController`. Our view controller will include some way of letting the user signal completion, such as a Cancel button and a Done button. When the user taps either of those, we'll do whatever else is necessary (such as saving the altered photo somewhere if the user tapped Done) and then call `activityDidFinish(_:)`. We could implement the `activityViewController` property like this:

```
override var activityViewController : UIViewController? {
    let mvc = MustacheViewController(activity: self, items: self.items!)
    return mvc
}
```

And then MustacheViewController would have code like this:

```
weak var activity : UIActivity?
var items: [Any]
init(activity:UIActivity, items:[Any]) {
    self.activity = activity
    self.items = items
    super.init(nibName: "MustacheViewController", bundle: nil)
}
// ... other stuff ...
@IBAction func doCancel(_ sender: Any) {
    self.activity?.activityDidFinish(false)
}
@IBAction func doDone(_ sender: Any) {
    self.activity?.activityDidFinish(true)
}
```

Our `activityViewController` is displayed as a presented view controller. Starting in iOS 13, this is a sheet that the user can dismiss by dragging down. If the user does that, the right thing happens automatically: `activityDidFinish` is called for us with an argument of `false`.

 The purpose of the SFSafariViewController delegate method `safariViewController(_:activityItemsFor:title:)` (Chapter 12) is now clear. This view controller's view appears inside your app, but it isn't your view controller, its Share button is not your button, and the activity view that it presents is not your activity view. Therefore, you need some other way to add custom UIActivity items to that activity view; to do so, implement this method.

Action Extensions

Your app's activity can appear among the menu items when some *other* app displays an activity view. To make that happen, you write an action extension. A single app can provide multiple action extensions.

To write an action extension, start with the appropriate target template, iOS → Application Extension → Action Extension. There are two kinds of action extension, with or without an interface; you'll make your choice in the second pane as you create the target.

In the *Info.plist*, in addition to setting the bundle name, which will appear below the activity's icon in the activity view, you'll need to specify what types of data this activity accepts as its operands. In the `NSExtensionActivationRule` dictionary, you'll provide one or more keys, such as:

- `NSExtensionActivationSupportsFileWithMaxCount`

- `NSExtensionActivationSupportsImageWithMaxCount`

- `NSExtensionActivationSupportsMovieWithMaxCount`

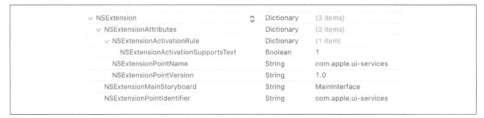

NSExtension	Dictionary	(3 items)
NSExtensionAttributes	Dictionary	(3 items)
NSExtensionActivationRule	Dictionary	(1 item)
NSExtensionActivationSupportsText	Boolean	1
NSExtensionPointName	String	com.apple.ui-services
NSExtensionPointVersion	String	1.0
NSExtensionMainStoryboard	String	MainInterface
NSExtensionPointIdentifier	String	com.apple.ui-services

Figure 14-14. An action extension Info.plist

- `NSExtensionActivationSupportsText`

- `NSExtensionActivationSupportsWebURLWithMaxCount`

For the full list, see the "Action Extension Keys" section of Apple's *Information Property List Key Reference*. It is also possible to declare in a more sophisticated way what types of data your activity accepts, by writing an NSPredicate string as the value of the `NSExtensionActivationRule` key. Figure 14-14 shows the relevant part of the *Info.plist* for an action extension that accepts one text object.

To supply the image that will appear in the menu item for your activity, add an asset catalog to the action extension target and create an iOS app icon in the asset catalog. The icon will be treated as a template image.

I'll describe how to implement an action extension with an interface. This, in effect, is your chance to inject an entire presented view controller into another app!

Our example extension accepts a string that might be the two-letter abbreviation of one of the U.S. states, and if it is, it provides the name of the state. The template provides a storyboard with one scene, along with the code for a corresponding UIView-Controller subclass called ActionViewController. I'll give the interface a Cancel button, a Done button (`self.doneButton`), and a label (`self.lab`). I'll also declare two Optional string properties to hold our data, `self.orig` (the incoming string) and `self.expansion` (the state name, if any). Finally, `self.list` will be a dictionary whose keys are state name abbreviations and whose values are the corresponding state names; that information comes from a text file in the action extension bundle:

```
let list : [String:String] = {
    let path = Bundle.main.url(forResource:"abbrevs", withExtension:"txt")!
    // ... load the text file as a string, parse into dictionary (result)
    return result
}()
```

I have a little utility method that looks up a string in that dictionary:

```
func state(for abbrev:String) -> String? {
    return self.list[abbrev]
}
```

Our view controller's `viewDidLoad` starts by preparing the interface:

```
override func viewDidLoad() {
    super.viewDidLoad()
    self.doneButton.isEnabled = false
    self.lab.text = "No expansion available."
    // ...
}
```

We turn next to the data from the host app, which is supposed to be a string that might be a state abbreviation. It arrives by way of the view controller `extension-Context` property, which is an NSExtensionContext (wrapped in an Optional). Think of this as a holding a nest of envelopes that we must examine and open:

- The NSExtensionContext's `inputItems` is an array of NSExtensionItem objects.

- An NSExtensionItem has an `attachments` array of NSItemProvider objects.

- An NSItemProvider vends items, each of which represents the data in a particular format. In particular:

  - We can *ask* whether an NSItemProvider has an item of a particular type, by calling `hasItemConformingToTypeIdentifier(_:)`.

  - We can *retrieve* the item of a particular type, by calling `loadItem(forType-Identifier:options:completionHandler:)`. The item may be vended lazily, and can take time to prepare and provide; so we proceed in the `completion-Handler:` function to receive the item and do something with it.

We are expecting only one item, so it will be provided by the first NSItemProvider inside the first NSExtensionItem. So my first move is to look inside that envelope and make sure it contains a string:

```
if self.extensionContext == nil {
    return
}
let items = self.extensionContext!.inputItems
let desiredType = UTType.plainText.identifier
guard let extensionItem = items[0] as? NSExtensionItem
    else {return}
guard let provider = extensionItem.attachments?.first
    else {return}
guard provider.hasItemConformingToTypeIdentifier(self.desiredType)
    else {return}
```

If we've gotten this far, there's a string in that envelope, and we're now ready to retrieve it and see if it is the abbreviation of a state. If it is, I'll enable the Done button and offer to place the abbreviation on the clipboard if the user taps that button:

```
provider.loadItem(forTypeIdentifier: desiredType) { item, err in
    DispatchQueue.main.async {
        if let orig = (item as? String)?.uppercased() {
            self.orig = orig
            if let exp = self.state(for:orig) {
```

```
            self.expansion = exp
            self.lab.text = """
                Can expand \(orig) to \(exp).
                Tap Done to place on clipboard.
                """
            self.doneButton.isEnabled = true
        }
      }
    }
  }
```

All that remains is to implement the action methods for the Cancel and Done buttons. They must both call this method of the extension context:

- `completeRequest(returningItems:completionHandler:)`

That call is the signal that our interface should be taken down. The only difference between the two buttons is that the Done button puts the expanded state name onto the clipboard:

```
@IBAction func cancel(_ sender: Any) {
    self.extensionContext?.completeRequest(returningItems: nil)
}
@IBAction func done(_ sender: Any) {
    UIPasteboard.general.string = self.expansion!
    self.extensionContext?.completeRequest(returningItems: nil)
}
```

Share Extensions

Your app can appear in the row of app icons when some *other* app displays an activity view. To make that happen, you write a share extension. A share extension is similar to an action extension, but instead of processing the data it receives, it is expected

Figure 14-15 A share extension

to deposit that data somehow, such as storing it or posting it to a server. Your app can provide at most one share extension.

The user, after tapping your app's icon in the activity view, is given an opportunity to interact further with the data before completing the share operation, possibly modifying it or cancelling altogether. To make this possible, the Share Extension template, when you create the target (iOS → Application Extension → Share Extension), will give you a storyboard and a view controller. This view controller can be one of two types:

An SLComposeServiceViewController
> The SLComposeServiceViewController provides a standard interface for displaying editable text in a UITextView along with a possible preview, plus user-configurable option buttons, along with a Cancel button and a Post button.

A plain view controller subclass
> If you opt for a plain view controller subclass, then designing its interface, including providing a way to dismiss it, will be up to you.

Whichever form of interface you elect to use, your way of dismissing it will be this familiar-looking incantation:

```
self.extensionContext?.completeRequest(returningItems:nil)
```

I'll describe the basics of working with an SLComposeServiceViewController, as it can be rather tricky. Its view contains a text view that is already populated with the text passed along from the host app when the view appears, so there's very little more for you to do; you can add a preview view and option buttons, and that's just about all. Figure 14-15 shows my share extension, summoned from within the Notes app; the text of the note has been copied automatically into the SLComposeServiceView-Controller's text view.

An option button displays a title string and a value string. When tapped, it will typically summon interface where the user can change the value string. My SLCompose-ServiceViewController implements an option button, visible in Figure 14-15. It's a Size button, whose value can be Large, Medium, or Small. (I have no idea what this choice is supposed to signify for my app; it's only an example!) I'll explain how I did that.

To create the configuration option, I override the SLComposeServiceViewController configurationItems method to return an array of one SLComposeSheetConfigurationItem. Its title and value are displayed in the button. Its tapHandler will be called when the button is tapped. Typically, you'll create a view controller and push it into the interface with pushConfigurationViewController:

```
weak var config : SLComposeSheetConfigurationItem?
var selectedText = "Large" {
    didSet {
        self.config?.value = self.selectedText
    }
}
override func configurationItems() -> [Any]! {
    let c = SLComposeSheetConfigurationItem()!
    c.title = "Size"
    c.value = self.selectedText
    c.tapHandler = { [unowned self] in
        let tvc = TableViewController(style: .grouped)
        tvc.selectedSize = self.selectedText
        tvc.delegate = self
        self.pushConfigurationViewController(tvc)
    }
    self.config = c
    return [c]
}
```

My TableViewController is a UITableViewController subclass. Its table view displays three rows whose cells are labeled Large, Medium, and Small, along with a checkmark (compare the table view described in "Cell Choice and Static Tables" on page 505). The tricky part is that I need a way to communicate with this table view controller: I need to tell it what the configuration item's value is now, and I need to hear from it what the user chooses in the table view. So I've given the table view controller a property (selectedSize) where I can deposit the configuration item's value, and I've declared a delegate protocol so that the table view controller can set the selected-Text of the SLComposeServiceViewController. This is the relevant portion of my TableViewController class:

```
protocol SizeDelegate : class {
    var selectedText : String {get set}
}
class TableViewController: UITableViewController {
    var selectedSize : String?
```

```
        weak var delegate : SizeDelegate?
        override func tableView(_ tableView: UITableView,
            didSelectRowAt indexPath: IndexPath) {
                let cell = tableView.cellForRow(at:indexPath)!
                let s = cell.textLabel!.text!
                self.selectedSize = s
                self.delegate?.selectedText = s
                tableView.reloadData()
        }
        // ...
    }
```

The navigation interface is provided for me, so I don't have to do anything about popping the table view controller: the user will do that by tapping the Back button after choosing a size. In my configurationItems implementation, I cleverly kept a reference to my configuration item as self.config. When the user chooses from the table view, its tableView(_:didSelectRowAt:) sets my selectedText, and my selectedText setter observer promptly changes the value of the configuration item to whatever the user chose.

The user, when finished interacting with the share extension interface, will tap one of the provided buttons, either Cancel or Post. The Cancel button is handled automatically: the interface is dismissed. The Post button is hooked automatically to my didSelectPost implementation, where I fetch the text from my own contentText property, do something with it, and dismiss the interface:

```
override func didSelectPost() {
    let s = self.contentText
    // ... do something with it ...
    self.extensionContext?.completeRequest(returningItems:nil)
}
```

If the material provided from the host app were more elaborate, I would pull it out of self.extensionContext in the same way as for an action extension. If there were networking to do at this point, I would initiate a background URLSession (as I'll explain in Chapter 24).

There is no official way, as far as I can tell, to change the title or appearance of the Cancel and Post buttons. Apps that show different buttons, such as Reminders and Notes, are either not using SLComposeServiceViewController or are using a technique available only to Apple. I was able to change my Post button to a Save button like this (though I've no idea if it's legal):

```
override func viewDidLayoutSubviews() {
    super.viewDidLayoutSubviews()
    self.navigationController?.navigationBar.topItem?
        .rightBarButtonItem?.title = "Save"
}
```

Some Frameworks

This part of the book gets you started on some of Cocoa's specialized frameworks:

- Chapter 15 talks about playing sound.
- Chapter 16 talks about playing video and introduces the powerful AV Foundation framework.
- Chapter 17 is about how to access the user's music library.
- Chapter 18 is about how to access the user's photo library, and discusses using the device's camera.
- Chapter 19 is about how to access the user's contacts.
- Chapter 20 is about how to access the user's calendars and reminders.
- Chapter 21 explains how to display and customize a map, how to show the user's current location, and how to convert between a location and an address.
- Chapter 22 is about the sensors that tell your app where the device is located and how it is oriented.

Audio

iOS provides various technologies that allow your app to produce, record, and process sound. The topic is a large one, so I'll concentrate on the basics. Suggestions for further exploration appear at the end of this chapter.

None of the classes discussed in this chapter provides any interface for allowing the user to stop and start playback of sound — also known as *transport* interface. If you want transport interface, here are some options:

- You can create your own interface.
- You can associate the built-in "remote control" buttons with your app, as I'll explain in this chapter.
- A web view (Chapter 12) supports the HTML5 <audio> tag; this can be a simple, lightweight way to play audio and to allow the user to control playback (including use of AirPlay).
- You could treat the sound as a movie and use the interface-providing classes that I'll discuss in Chapter 16; this can also be a good way to play a sound file located remotely over the internet.

System Sounds

The simplest form of sound is *system sound*, which is the iOS equivalent of the basic computer "beep." This is implemented through System Sound Services, part of the Audio Toolbox framework; you'll need to import AudioToolbox. The API for playing a system sound comes in two forms — the old form, and a new form that was introduced in iOS 9.

The old form involves calling one of two C functions, which behave very similarly to one another:

AudioServicesPlayAlertSound

On an iPhone, may also vibrate the device, depending on the user's settings.

AudioServicesPlaySystemSound

On an iPhone, there won't be an accompanying vibration, but you can elect to have this "sound" *be* a device vibration (by passing kSystemSoundID_Vibrate as the name of the "sound").

The sound file to be played needs to be an uncompressed AIFF or WAV file (or an Apple CAF file wrapping one of those). To hand the sound to these functions, you'll need a SystemSoundID, which you obtain by calling AudioServicesCreateSystem-SoundID with a URL that points to a sound file. In this example, the sound file is in our app bundle:

```
let sndurl = Bundle.main.url(forResource:"test", withExtension: "aif")!
var snd : SystemSoundID = 0
AudioServicesCreateSystemSoundID(sndurl as CFURL, &snd)
AudioServicesPlaySystemSound(snd)
```

That code works — we hear the sound — but there's a problem: we have failed to exercise proper memory management. We need to call AudioServicesDispose-SystemSoundID to release our SystemSoundID. But when shall we do this? Audio-ServicesPlaySystemSound executes *asynchronously*. So the solution can't be to call AudioServicesDisposeSystemSoundID in the next line, because this would release our sound just as it is about to start playing, resulting in silence:

```
let sndurl = Bundle.main.url(forResource:"test", withExtension: "aif")!
var snd : SystemSoundID = 0
AudioServicesCreateSystemSoundID(sndurl as CFURL, &snd)
AudioServicesPlaySystemSound(snd)
AudioServicesDisposeSystemSoundID(snd) // oops, no sound!
```

The correct approach is to implement a *sound completion function* to be called when the sound has finished playing. The sound completion function is specified by calling AudioServicesAddSystemSoundCompletion. It must be supplied as a C pointer-to-function, but Swift lets you pass a global or local Swift function (including an anonymous function) where a C pointer-to-function is expected. So our code now looks like this:

```
let sndurl = Bundle.main.url(forResource:"test", withExtension: "aif")!
var snd : SystemSoundID = 0
AudioServicesCreateSystemSoundID(sndurl as CFURL, &snd)
AudioServicesAddSystemSoundCompletion(snd, nil, nil, { snd, _ in
    AudioServicesRemoveSystemSoundCompletion(snd)
    AudioServicesDisposeSystemSoundID(snd)
}, nil)
AudioServicesPlaySystemSound(snd)
```

Note that when we are about to release the sound, we first release the sound completion function itself.

Now for the new form. The new calls take *two* parameters: a SystemSoundID and a completion function. The completion function takes no parameters; we can still refer to the SystemSoundID in order to dispose of its memory, because it is in scope. Here, we'll call `AudioServicesPlaySystemSoundWithCompletion` instead of `AudioServicesPlaySystemSound`; we no longer need to call `AudioServicesRemoveSystemSoundCompletion`, because we never called `AudioServicesAddSystemSoundCompletion`:

```
let sndurl = Bundle.main.url(forResource:"test", withExtension: "aif")!
var snd : SystemSoundID = 0
AudioServicesCreateSystemSoundID(sndurl as CFURL, &snd)
AudioServicesPlaySystemSoundWithCompletion(snd) {
    AudioServicesDisposeSystemSoundID(snd)
}
```

Audio Session

Audio on the device — *all* audio belonging to *all* apps and processes — is controlled and mediated by the *media services daemon*. This daemon must juggle many demands; your app is just one of many clamoring for its attention and cooperation. As a result, your app's audio can be affected and even overruled by other apps and external factors.

Your communication with the audio services daemon is conducted through an *audio session*, which is a singleton AVAudioSession instance created automatically as your app launches. This is part of the AV Foundation framework; you'll need to `import` AVFoundation. You'll refer to your app's AVAudioSession by way of the class method `sharedInstance`.

Category

Your app, if it is going to be producing sound, needs to specify a *policy* regarding that sound and tell the media services daemon about it. This policy will answer such questions as:

- Should your app's sound be stopped when the screen is locked?
- If other sound is being produced (as when the Music app is playing a song in the background), should your app stop that sound or be layered on top of it?

To declare your audio session's policy, you'll set its *category* (AVAudioSession.Category) by calling `setCategory(_:mode:options:)`. I'll explain later about the `mode:` and `options:`; the `options:` parameter may be omitted, and if you have no mode, you can use a mode of `.default`. Your app needn't set just one category for all time; different activities or stages in the lifetime of your app might require that the category should change.

The basic policies for audio playback are:

Ambient (`.ambient`*)*
Your app's audio plays even while another app is playing audio, and is stopped by the phone's Silent switch and screen locking.

Solo Ambient (`.soloAmbient`*, the default)*
Your app stops any audio being played by other apps, and is stopped by the phone's Silent switch and screen locking.

Playback (`.playback`*)*
Your app stops any audio being played by other apps, and is *not* stopped by the Silent switch. It is stopped by screen locking, unless it is also configured to play in the background (as explained later in this chapter).

Audio session category options (the `options:` parameter, AVAudioSession.Category-Options) allow you to modify the playback policies:

Mixable audio (`.mixWithOthers`*)*
You can override the Playback policy so as to allow other apps to continue playing audio. Your sound is then said to be *mixable*. Mixability can also affect you in the other direction: another app's mixable audio can continue to play even when your app's Playback policy is *not* mixable.

Mixable except for speech (`.interruptSpokenAudioAndMixWithOthers`*)*
Similar to `.mixWithOthers`, but although you are willing to mix with background music, you are electing to stop background speech. An app's audio is marked as speech by setting its audio session mode to `.spokenAudio`.

Ducking audio (`.duckOthers`*)*
You can override a policy that allows other audio to play, so as to *duck* (diminish the volume of) that other audio. Ducking is a form of mixing.

Activation and Deactivation

Your audio session policy is not in effect unless your audio session is also *active*. By default, it isn't. Asserting your audio session policy is done by a combination of configuring the audio session and activating the audio session. To activate your audio session, you call `setActive(true)`.

The question is *when* to call `setActive(true)`. This depends on whether you need your audio session to be active all the time or only when you are producing sound. In many cases, it will be best not to activate your audio session until just before you start to produce sound. But let's take a very simple case where our sounds are always occasional, intermittent, and nonessential. We want sound from other apps, such as the Music app, to be allowed to continue playing when the user launches or switches to our app. That's the Ambient policy. Our policy will never vary, and it doesn't stop other audio, so we might as well set our app's category and activate it at launch time:

```
func application(_ application: UIApplication,
    didFinishLaunchingWithOptions launchOptions:
    [UIApplication.LaunchOptionsKey : Any]?) -> Bool {
        let sess = AVAudioSession.sharedInstance()
        try? sess.setCategory(.ambient, mode:.default)
        try? sess.setActive(true)
        return true
}
```

It is also possible to call `setActive(false)`, deactivating your audio session. There are various reasons why you might deactivate (and perhaps reactivate) your audio session over the lifetime of your app.

One possible reason is that you want to *change* something about your audio session policy. Certain changes in your audio session category and options don't take effect unless you deactivate the existing policy and activate the new policy. Ducking is a good example; I'll demonstrate in the next section.

Another reason for deactivating your audio session is that you have stopped playing sound; you no longer need to hog the device's audio, and you want to yield to other apps that were stopped by your audio session policy, so that they can resume playing. You can even send a message to other apps as you do this, by supplying the `.notify-OthersOnDeactivation` option in a call to `setActive(_:options:)`, like this:

```
let sess = AVAudioSession.sharedInstance()
try? sess.setActive(false, options: .notifyOthersOnDeactivation)
```

 Apple suggests that you might want to register for `AVAudioSession.media-ServicesWereResetNotification`. If this notification arrives, the media services daemon was somehow hosed. In this situation, you should basically start from scratch, configuring your category and activating your audio session, as well as resetting and recreating any audio-related objects.

Ducking

As an example of deactivating and activating your audio session, I'll describe how to implement ducking.

Presume that we have configured and activated an Ambient category audio session, as described in the preceding sections. This category permits other audio to continue playing. Now let's say we do sometimes play a sound, but it's brief and doesn't require other sound to stop entirely — but we'd like other audio to be quieter momentarily while we're playing our sound. That's ducking!

Background sound is not ducked automatically just because we play a sound of our own. It is up to *us* to duck the background sound as we start to play our sound, and to stop ducking when our sound ends. We do this by changing our Ambient category to use or not to use the `.duckOthers` option. To make such a change, the most reliable approach is three steps:

1. Deactivate our audio session.
2. Reconfigure our audio session category with a changed set of options.
3. Activate our audio session

So, just before we play our sound, we duck any other sound by adding `.duckOthers` to the options on our Ambient category:

```
let sess = AVAudioSession.sharedInstance()
try? sess.setActive(false)
let opts = sess.categoryOptions.union(.duckOthers)
try? sess.setCategory(sess.category, mode: sess.mode, options: opts)
try? sess.setActive(true)
```

When our sound finishes playing, we unduck any other sound by removing `.duck-Others` from the options on our category:

```
let sess = AVAudioSession.sharedInstance()
try? sess.setActive(false)
let opts = sess.categoryOptions.subtracting(.duckOthers)
try? sess.setCategory(sess.category, mode: sess.mode, options:opts)
try? sess.setActive(true)
```

Interruptions

Management of your audio session is complicated by the fact that it can be *interrupted*. On an iPhone, a phone call can arrive or an alarm can go off. Or another app might assert its audio session over yours, possibly because your app went into the background and the other app came into the foreground. Under certain circumstances, merely going into the background will interrupt your audio session.

When your audio session is interrupted, *it is deactivated*. That means you need to know when the interruption ends, so that you can reactivate your audio session. In order to know that, you will need to register for the `AVAudioSession.interruptionNotification`. You should do this as early as possible, perhaps at launch time.

The `AVAudioSession.interruptionNotification` can arrive either because an interruption begins or because it ends. To learn whether the interruption began or ended, you'll examine the `AVAudioSessionInterruptionTypeKey` entry in the notification's userInfo dictionary; this will be a UInt encoding an AVAudioSession.Interruption-Type, either .began or .ended.

When an interruption to your audio session begins, your audio has already paused and your audio session has been deactivated. If your app contains interface for playing and pausing, you might change a Pause button to a Play button; but apart from this there's no particular work for you to do. When the interruption ends, on the other hand, activating your audio session and possibly resuming playback of your audio might be up to you:

```
NotificationCenter.default.addObserver(forName:
    AVAudioSession.interruptionNotification, object: nil, queue: nil) { n in
        let why = n.userInfo![AVAudioSessionInterruptionTypeKey] as! UInt
        let type = AVAudioSession.InterruptionType(rawValue: why)!
        switch type {
        case .began:
            // update interface if needed
        case .ended:
            try? AVAudioSession.sharedInstance().setActive(true)
            // update interface if needed
            // resume playback?
        @unknown default: fatalError()
        }
}
```

The notification telling you that the interruption is over can include a message from some other app that interrupted you and has now deactivated its audio session. The other app sends that message by deactivating its audio session along with the .notify-OthersOnDeactivation option, as I demonstrated earlier. You'll receive the message in the userInfo dictionary's AVAudioSessionInterruptionOptionKey entry; its value will be a UInt encoding an AVAudioSession.InterruptionOptions, which might be .shouldResume:

```
guard let opt = n.userInfo![AVAudioSessionInterruptionOptionKey] as? UInt
    else {return}
if AVAudioSession.InterruptionOptions(rawValue:opt).contains(.shouldResume) {
    // resume playback
}
```

Secondary Audio

Apple draws a fine-grained distinction between two types of audio, primary audio and secondary audio. Apple's example is a game app, where intermittent sound effects are the primary audio, while an ongoing underlying soundtrack is the secondary audio. The idea is that the user might be playing a song in the background (from the Music app, for instance), and that your app would therefore suppress its own secondary audio while continuing to produce its primary audio, allowing the user's chosen Music track to function as the soundtrack behind your game's sound effects.

At key moments, such as when your app is activated or when you're thinking of producing secondary audio, you should check your audio session's secondaryAudio-ShouldBeSilencedHint property. If it is true, don't play your secondary audio.

It is also possible, under certain circumstances, that the secondaryAudioShouldBe-SilencedHint will go from false to true while your app is frontmost. An example is when your app is frontmost with an .ambient audio session and the user brings up the control center and uses the Play button to resume the current Music app song. There may be no interruption of your audio session, because your app never went into the background — but the secondaryAudioShouldBeSilencedHint may now have become true.

To hear about this, register for AVAudioSession.silenceSecondaryAudioHint-Notification. To respond to this notification, examine the AVAudioSessionSilence-SecondaryAudioHintTypeKey entry in the notification's userInfo dictionary; this will be a UInt encoding an AVAudioSession.SilenceSecondaryAudioHintType, either .begin or .end:

```
NotificationCenter.default.addObserver(forName:
    AVAudioSession.silenceSecondaryAudioHintNotification,
    object: nil, queue: nil) { n in
        let why = n.userInfo![AVAudioSessionSilenceSecondaryAudioHintTypeKey]
            as! UInt
        let type = AVAudioSession.SilenceSecondaryAudioHintType(rawValue:why)!
        switch type {
        case .begin:
            // pause secondary audio
        case .end:
            // resume secondary audio
        @unknown default: fatalError()
        }
}
```

Routing Changes

Your audio is routed through a particular output (and input). External events, such as a phone call arriving, can cause a change in audio routing, and the user can also make changes in audio routing — for instance, by plugging headphones into the device, which causes sound to stop coming out of the speaker and to come out of the headphones instead. You can and should register for the AVAudioSession.route-ChangeNotification to hear about routing changes and respond to them.

The notification's userInfo dictionary is chock full of useful information about what just happened. Here's the console log of the dictionary that results when I detach headphones from the device:

```
AVAudioSessionRouteChangeReasonKey = 2;
AVAudioSessionRouteChangePreviousRouteKey =
    <AVAudioSessionRouteDescription: 0x174019ee0,
        inputs = (null);
        outputs = (
            <AVAudioSessionPortDescription: 0x174019f00,
                type = Headphones;
                name = Headphones;
                UID = Wired Headphones;
                selectedDataSource = (null)>
        )>;
```

Upon receipt of this notification, I can find out what the audio route is now, by calling AVAudioSession's currentRoute method; here's the result logged to the console:

```
<AVAudioSessionRouteDescription: 0x174019fc0,
    inputs = (null);
    outputs = (
        <AVAudioSessionPortDescription: 0x17401a000,
            type = Speaker;
            name = Speaker;
            UID = Speaker;
            selectedDataSource = (null)>
    )>
```

The classes mentioned here — AVAudioSessionRouteDescription and AVAudioSessionPortDescription — are value classes. The AVAudioSessionRouteChangeReasonKey refers to an AVAudioSessionRouteChangeReason; the value in this instance, 2, is .oldDeviceUnavailable — we stopped using the headphones and started using the speaker, because there are no headphones any longer.

A routing change may not of itself interrupt your sound, but Apple suggests that in this particular situation you should respond by stopping your audio deliberately, because otherwise sound may now suddenly be coming out of the speaker in a public place.

Audio Player

The easiest way to play sounds is to use an *audio player* (AVAudioPlayer). AVAudioPlayer is part of the AV Foundation framework; you'll need to import AVFoundation.

An audio player is initialized with its sound, using a local file URL or Data; optionally, the initializer can also state the expected sound file format. A wide range of sound types is acceptable, including MP3, AAC, and ALAC, as well as AIFF and WAV. Starting in iOS 11, FLAC is an acceptable format, as well as Opus (a lossy compression codec commonly used for streaming and VoIP). A single audio player can possess and play only one sound; but you can have multiple audio players, they can play separately or simultaneously, and you can synchronize them. You can set a sound's volume and stereo pan features, loop a sound, change the playing rate, and set playback to begin somewhere in the middle of a sound. You can even execute a fade in or fade out over time.

Having created and initialized an audio player, you must *retain it*, typically by assigning it to an instance property. Assigning an audio player to a *local* variable and telling it to play, and hearing nothing — because the player has gone out of existence immediately, before it even has a chance to start playing — is a common beginner mistake.

To play the sound, first make sure your audio session is configured correctly. Now tell the audio player to prepareToPlay, causing it to load buffers and initialize hardware; then tell it to play. The audio player's delegate (AVAudioPlayerDelegate) is notified when the sound has finished playing, through a call to audioPlayerDid-FinishPlaying(_:successfully:); do *not* repeatedly check the audio player's isPlaying property to learn its state.

The playAtTime(_:) method allows playing to be scheduled to start at a certain time. The time should be described in terms of the audio player's deviceCurrentTime property. Other useful methods include pause and stop; the chief difference between them is that pause doesn't release the buffers and hardware set up by prepareToPlay, but stop does, so you'd want to call prepareToPlay again before resuming play. Neither pause nor stop changes the playhead position, the point in the sound where playback will start if play is sent again; for that, use the currentTime property.

Devising a strategy for instantiating, retaining, and releasing your audio players is up to you. In one of my apps, I define a class called Player, which implements a play-File(atPath:) method expecting a string path to a sound file. This method creates a new AVAudioPlayer, stores it as a property, and tells it to play the sound file; it also sets itself as that audio player's delegate, and notifies its own delegate when the sound finishes playing (by way of a PlayerDelegate protocol that I define). In this way, by maintaining a single Player instance, I can play different sounds in succession:

```
protocol PlayerDelegate : class {
    func soundFinished(_ sender: Any)
}
class Player : NSObject, AVAudioPlayerDelegate {
    var player : AVAudioPlayer!
    weak var delegate : PlayerDelegate?
    func playFile(atPath path:String) {
        self.player?.delegate = nil
        self.player?.stop()
        let fileURL = URL(fileURLWithPath: path)
        guard let p = try? AVAudioPlayer(contentsOf:fileURL) else {return}
        self.player = p
        self.player.prepareToPlay()
        self.player.delegate = self
```

```
            self.player.play()
        }
        func audioPlayerDidFinishPlaying(_ player: AVAudioPlayer,
            successfully flag: Bool) {
                self.delegate?.soundFinished(self)
    }
```

Here are some useful AVAudioPlayer properties:

pan, volume
> Stereo positioning and loudness, respectively.

numberOfLoops
> How many times the sound should repeat after it finishes playing; 0 (the default) means it doesn't repeat. A negative value causes the sound to repeat indefinitely (until told to stop).

duration
> The length of the sound (read-only).

currentTime
> The playhead position within the sound. If the sound is paused or stopped, play will start at the currentTime. You can set this property in order to "seek" to a playback position within the sound.

enableRate, rate
> These properties allow the sound to be played at anywhere from half speed (0.5) to double speed (2.0). Set enableRate to true *before* calling prepareToPlay; you are then free to set the rate.

isMeteringEnabled
> If true (the default is false), you can call updateMeters followed by average-Power(forChannel:) or peakPower(forChannel:) periodically to track how loud the sound is. Presumably this would be so you could provide some sort of graphical representation of this value in your interface.

settings
> A read-only dictionary describing features of the sound, such as its bit rate (AVEncoderBitRateKey), its sample rate (AVSampleRateKey), and its data format (AVFormatIDKey). You can alternatively learn the sound's data format from the format property.

An audio player handles certain types of interruption seamlessly; in particular, if your sound was forced to stop playing when your app was moved to the background, then when your app comes to front, the audio player reactivates your audio session and resumes playing — and you won't get any interruption notifications. But resumption

Figure 15-1. The software remote controls in the control center

of play is not automatic for every kind of interruption, so you may still need to register for interruption notifications, as I described earlier.

Remote Control of Your Sound

Various sorts of signal constitute *remote control*. There is hardware remote control, such as the buttons on certain models of earbuds. There is also software remote control — the playback controls that you access through the control center (Figure 15-1) and the lock screen.

Your app can arrange to be targeted by *remote control events* reporting that the user has tapped a remote control, and can then respond to the remote play/pause button (probably by playing or pausing its sound). For this to work, your app's audio session category must be Solo Ambient or Playback, and your app must actually produce some sound; this causes your app's sound to become the device's *now playing* sound. The rule is that the running app that is capable of receiving remote control events and actually produced sound most recently is the target of remote control events. The Music app is the default remote control event target if no other app takes precedence by this rule.

To configure your app to receive remote control events, use the Media Player framework (`import MediaPlayer`). You talk to the *remote command center*, through the shared command center that you get from the MPRemoteCommandCenter `shared` class method, and configure its commands to send you messages, to which you then respond as appropriate. There are two ways to perform such configuration: you can give a command a target–action pair, or you can hand it a function directly.

Let's say that our app plays audio, and we want to respond to remote commands to pause or resume this audio. We will need to configure the play command and the pause command, because they are triggered by the software play/pause button, as well as the play/pause command, because it is triggered by an earbud button. I'll demonstrate the target–action style of configuration. This code could appear in our view controller's `viewDidLoad`:

```
let scc = MPRemoteCommandCenter.shared()
scc.playCommand.addTarget(self, action:#selector(doPlay))
scc.pauseCommand.addTarget(self, action:#selector(doPause))
scc.togglePlayPauseCommand.addTarget(self, action: #selector(doPlayPause))
```

Obviously, that code won't compile unless we also have doPlay, doPause, and doPlay-Pause methods. Each of these methods will be sent the appropriate remote command event (MPRemoteCommandEvent). Assuming that `self.player` is an AVAudio-Player, our implementations might look like this:

```
@objc func doPlayPause(_ event:MPRemoteCommandEvent)
    -> MPRemoteCommandHandlerStatus {
        let p = self.player
        if p.isPlaying { p.pause() } else { p.play() }
        return .success
}
@objc func doPlay(_ event:MPRemoteCommandEvent)
    -> MPRemoteCommandHandlerStatus {
        let p = self.player
        p.play()
        return .success
}
@objc func doPause(_ event:MPRemoteCommandEvent)
    -> MPRemoteCommandHandlerStatus {
        let p = self.player
        p.pause()
        return .success
}
```

This works! Once our app is playing a sound, that sound can be paused and resumed using the control center or an earbud switch. (It can also be paused and resumed using the lock screen, but only if our app is capable of playing sound in the background; I'll explain in the next section how to arrange that.)

However, we are not quite finished. Having registered a target with the remote command center, we must remember to unregister when that target is about to go out of existence; otherwise, there is a danger that the remote command center will attempt to send a remote command event to a nonexistent target, resulting in a crash. If we registered in our view controller's `viewDidLoad`, we can conveniently unregister in its `deinit`:

```
deinit {
    let scc = MPRemoteCommandCenter.shared()
    scc.togglePlayPauseCommand.removeTarget(self)
    scc.playCommand.removeTarget(self)
    scc.pauseCommand.removeTarget(self)
}
```

Having formed the connection between our app and the software remote control
interface, we can proceed to refine that interface. One refinement is to specify what
information is displayed about what's being played. For that, we use the MPNow-
PlayingInfoCenter. Call the class method default and set the resulting instance's now-
PlayingInfo property to a dictionary. The relevant keys are listed in the class
documentation; many of these are actually MPMediaItem properties, and will make
more sense after you've read Chapter 17. Here we make the command center show
the title and artist of the sound file our app is playing:

```
let mpic = MPNowPlayingInfoCenter.default()
mpic.nowPlayingInfo = [
    MPMediaItemPropertyArtist: "Matt Neuburg",
    MPMediaItemPropertyTitle: "About Tiagol",
]
```

To make the progress view appear in the software remote control interface, displaying our sound's duration and the current play position within it, we need to tell the
MPNowPlayingInfoCenter what that duration is. If we also tell it that we are actively
playing, it will automatically increment its display of the current play position as the
time goes by. So, when we start playing, we would say something like this:

```
let mpic = MPNowPlayingInfoCenter.default()
mpic.nowPlayingInfo = [
    MPMediaItemPropertyArtist: "Matt Neuburg",
    MPMediaItemPropertyTitle: "About Tiagol",
    MPMediaItemPropertyPlaybackDuration: self.player.duration,
    MPNowPlayingInfoPropertyElapsedPlaybackTime: 0,
    MPNowPlayingInfoPropertyPlaybackRate: 1
]
```

The MPNowPlayingInfoCenter is not actually watching our sound play; it just
blindly advances the current play position display. Therefore, if our sound pauses or
resumes, we need to keep the MPNowPlayingInfoCenter updated. When the sound
pauses, we need to tell it not only that we have paused, but also what the current play
position is; otherwise, it will assume that the play position is zero:

```
let p = self.player
let mpic = MPNowPlayingInfoCenter.default()
if var d = mpic.nowPlayingInfo {
    d[MPNowPlayingInfoPropertyPlaybackRate] = 0
    d[MPNowPlayingInfoPropertyElapsedPlaybackTime] = p.currentTime
    mpic.nowPlayingInfo = d
}
```

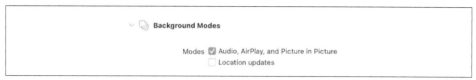

Figure 15-2. Using Capabilities to enable background audio

If we don't want the user to be able to slide the slider that would tell our app to change the current play position, we must use the MPRemoteCommandCenter to disable it:

```
let scc = MPRemoteCommandCenter.shared()
scc.changePlaybackPositionCommand.isEnabled = false
```

The MPRemoteCommandCenter offers many other commands you can configure. When you do so, the appropriate software remote control interface springs to life. For instance, if you assign a target–action pair to the likeCommand, a menu button appears in the control center; the user taps this button to see an action sheet that includes your like command button.

Playing Sound in the Background

When the user switches away from your app to another app, by default, your app is suspended and stops producing sound. But if the business of your app is to play sound, you might like your app to continue playing sound in the background. To play sound in the background, your app must do these things:

- In your *Info.plist*, you must include the "Required background modes" key (UIBackgroundModes) with an array value that includes "App plays audio or streams audio/video using AirPlay" (audio). The simplest way to arrange that is to add the Background Modes capability in the Signing & Capabilities tab of the target editor, and then check "Audio, AirPlay, and Picture in Picture" (Figure 15-2).
- Your audio session's policy must be active and must be Playback.

If those things are true, then the sound that your app is playing in the foreground will go right on playing when the user clicks the Home button and dismisses your app, or when the user switches to another app, or when the screen is locked. Your app is now running in the background for the purpose of playing sound.

Your app, playing in the background, may be interrupted by the foreground app's audio session policy. However, having registered for the AVAudio-Session.interruptionNotification, your app may receive this notification in the background, and, if the AVAudioSession.InterruptionType is .ended, may be able to resume playing — still in the background.

Remote control events continue to work when your app is in the background. In fact, even if your app was *not* actively playing at the time it was put into the background, it may nevertheless be the remote control target (because it *was* playing sound earlier, as explained in the preceding section). In that case, if the user causes a remote control event to be sent, your app, if suspended in the background, will be woken up (still in the background) in order to receive the remote control event, and can then begin playing sound. Your app may also be able to start playing in the background if it is mixable (.mixWithOthers, see earlier in this chapter), even if it was not playing previously.

While your app is playing sound in the background, there's an interesting byproduct: a Timer can fire. This is remarkable, because many other sorts of activity are forbidden when your app is running in the background. The timer must have been created and scheduled in the foreground, but after that, it will fire even while your app is in the background, unless your app is currently not playing any sound.

Another curious byproduct of your app playing sound in the background has to do with app delegate events (see Appendix A). Typically, your app delegate will probably never receive the applicationWillTerminate(_:) message, because by the time the app terminates, it will already have been suspended and incapable of receiving any events. However, an app that is playing sound in the background is obviously *not* suspended, even though it is in the background. If it is terminated while playing sound in the background, it *will* receive applicationWillTerminate(_:).

AVAudioRecorder

AVAudioRecorder is the simplest way to record sound through the device's microphone. To use it, your audio session category will need to be .record (or .playAnd-Record). You will also need the user's *permission* to use the microphone. You'll need to have a meaningful entry in your *Info.plist* under the "Privacy — Microphone Usage Description" key (NSMicrophoneUsageDescription) explaining to the user why you want to use the microphone. You don't have to request authorization explicitly; the system will put up an authorization request dialog on your behalf as soon as you try to use microphone. If you do want to request authorization explicitly, check your AVAudioSession's recordPermission to learn whether we have authorization, and call its requestRecordPermission, if it is .undetermined, to request authorization. A user who denies your app microphone authorization may grant it later in Settings. (See "Checking for Authorization" on page 899 for detailed discussion of user authorization requests.)

Here's a minimal example of recording through an AVAudioRecorder. The recorder is created with a file URL where the recording is to be saved, along with information about the format of the sound file to be created. It is then assigned to an instance property, just like an AVAudioPlayer, and is told to record:

```
var recorder : AVAudioRecorder?
let recurl : URL = {
    let temp = FileManager.default.temporaryDirectory
    return temp.appendingPathComponent("rec.m4a")
}()
func startRecording() {
    try? AVAudioSession.sharedInstance().setCategory(.record, mode:.default)
    try? AVAudioSession.sharedInstance().setActive(true)
    let format = AVAudioFormat(settings: [
        AVFormatIDKey : Int(kAudioFormatMPEG4AAC),
        AVSampleRateKey : 44100.0,
        AVEncoderBitRateKey : 192000,
        AVNumberOfChannelsKey : 2
    ])
    do {
        let rec = try AVAudioRecorder(url:self.recurl, format:format!)
        self.recorder = rec
        rec.record(forDuration: 10)
    } catch {
        print("oops")
    }
}
```

Our little sound recording app would presumably also have a way to tell the recorder to stop, but just in case, I've limited the recording time to ten seconds.

 When you're using the .playAndRecord audio session category, you can explicitly set the output and input sources with the AVAudioSession overrideOutput-AudioPort(_:) and setPreferredInput(_:) methods. New in iOS 14, some devices with four microphones can record in stereo.

AVAudioEngine

AVAudioEngine is modeled after a mixer board. You can construct and manipulate a graph of sound-producing objects in real time, varying their relative volumes and other attributes, mixing them down to a single sound. This is a deep topic; I'll provide an introductory overview.

The key classes are:

AVAudioEngine
> The overall engine object, representing the world in which everything else happens. You'll probably make and retain just one at a time; it is perfectly reasonable to replace your engine with a new one, as a way of starting over with a clean slate. Its chief jobs are:

- To connect and disconnect *nodes* (AVAudioNode), like configuring the patch cords on a mixer board. The engine itself has three built-in nodes — its inputNode, its mixerNode, and its outputNode — and you can add others.

- To start and stop the production of sound. The engine must be running if any sound is to be produced; on the other hand, configuration changes generally need to be made with the engine stopped.

AVAudioNode

An abstract class embracing the various types of object for producing, processing, mixing, and receiving sound. An audio node is useful only when it has been attached to the audio engine. An audio node has inputs and outputs, and the audio engine can connect the output of one node to the input of another. It is also possible to put a *tap* on a node, copying the node's sound data off into a buffer as it passes through the node; this might be for analysis, monitoring, or saving into a file.

Some AVAudioNode subclasses are:

AVAudioMixerNode

A node with an output volume; it mixes its inputs down to a single output. The AVAudioEngine's built-in mixerNode is an AVAudioMixerNode.

AVAudioIONode

A node that patches through to the system's (device's) own input (AVAudioInputNode) or output (AVAudioOutputNode). The AVAudioEngine's built-in inputNode and outputNode are AVAudioIONodes.

AVAudioPlayerNode

A node that produces sound, analogous to an AVAudioPlayer. It can play from a file or from a buffer.

AVAudioSourceNode
AVAudioSinkNode

Nodes that let you produce or process a buffer's contents directly.

AVAudioEnvironmentNode

Gives three-dimensional spatial control over sound sources (suitable for games). With it, a bunch of additional AVAudioNode properties spring to life.

AVAudioUnit

A node that processes its input with special effects before passing it to the output.

Built-in AVAudioUnit subclasses include:

AVAudioUnitTimePitch
> Independently changes the pitch and rate of the input.

AVAudioUnitVarispeed
> Changes the pitch and rate of the input together.

AVAudioUnitDelay
> Adds to the input a delayed version of itself.

AVAudioUnitDistortion
> Adds distortion to the input.

AVAudioUnitEQ
> Constructs an equalizer, for processing frequency bands separately.

AVAudioUnitReverb
> Adds a reverb effect to the input.

To give an idea of what working with AVAudioEngine looks like, I'll start by simply playing a file. Our AVAudioEngine has already been instantiated and assigned to an instance property, `self.engine`, so that it will persist for the duration of the exercise. We will need an AVAudioPlayerNode and an AVAudioFile. We attach the AVAudio-PlayerNode to the engine and patch it to the engine's built-in mixer node. (In this simple case, we could have patched the player node to the engine's output node; but the engine's mixer node is already patched to the output node, so it makes no difference.) We associate the file with the player node, supplying a completion function that stops the engine so as not to waste resources after the file finishes playing. Finally, we start the engine running and tell the player node to play:

```
let player = AVAudioPlayerNode()
let url = Bundle.main.url(forResource:"aboutTiagol", withExtension:"m4a")!
let f = try! AVAudioFile(forReading: url)
let mixer = self.engine.mainMixerNode
self.engine.attach(player)
self.engine.connect(player, to: mixer, format: f.processingFormat)
player.scheduleFile(f, at: nil) { [unowned self] in
    delay(0.1) {
        if self.engine.isRunning {
            self.engine.stop()
        }
    }
}
self.engine.prepare()
try! self.engine.start()
player.play()
```

(Instead of stopping the engine in our player node's completion function, we can configure the engine to stop automatically by setting its `isAutoShutdownEnabled` property to `true`.)

So far, we've done nothing that we couldn't have done with an AVAudioPlayer. But now let's start patching some more nodes into the graph. I'll play two sounds simultaneously, the first one directly from a file, the second one through a buffer — which will allow me to loop the second sound. I'll also pass the first sound through a time-pitch effect node and then through a reverb effect node. And I'll set the volumes and pan positions of the two sounds:

```
// first sound
let player = AVAudioPlayerNode()
let url = Bundle.main.url(forResource:"aboutTiagol", withExtension:"m4a")!
let f = try! AVAudioFile(forReading: url)
self.engine.attach(player)
// add some effect nodes to the chain
let effect = AVAudioUnitTimePitch()
effect.rate = 0.9
effect.pitch = -300
self.engine.attach(effect)
self.engine.connect(player, to: effect, format: f.processingFormat)
let effect2 = AVAudioUnitReverb()
effect2.loadFactoryPreset(.cathedral)
effect2.wetDryMix = 40
self.engine.attach(effect2)
self.engine.connect(effect, to: effect2, format: f.processingFormat)
// patch last node into engine mixer and start playing first sound
let mixer = self.engine.mainMixerNode
self.engine.connect(effect2, to: mixer, format: f.processingFormat)
player.scheduleFile(f, at: nil) {
    delay(0.1) {
        if self.engine.isRunning {
            self.engine.stop()
        }
    }
}
self.engine.prepare()
try! self.engine.start()
player.play()
// second sound; loop it
let url2 = Bundle.main.url(forResource:"Hooded", withExtension: "mp3")!
let f2 = try! AVAudioFile(forReading: url2)
let buffer = AVAudioPCMBuffer(
    pcmFormat: f2.processingFormat, frameCapacity: UInt32(f2.length))
try! f2.read(into:buffer!)
let player2 = AVAudioPlayerNode()
self.engine.attach(player2)
self.engine.connect(player2, to: mixer, format: f2.processingFormat)
player2.scheduleBuffer(buffer!, at: nil, options: .loops)
// mix down a little, start playing second sound
player.pan = -0.5
player2.volume = 0.5
player2.pan = 0.5
player2.play()
```

You can split a node's output between multiple nodes. Instead of calling connect(_:to:format:), you call connect(_:to:fromBus:format:), where the second argument is an array of AVAudioConnectionPoint objects, each of which is simply a node and a bus. In this example, I'll split my player's output three ways: I'll connect it simultaneously to a delay effect and a reverb effect, both of which are connected to the output mixer, and I'll connect the player itself directly to the output mixer as well:

```
let effect = AVAudioUnitDelay()
effect.delayTime = 0.4
effect.feedback = 0
self.engine.attach(effect)
let effect2 = AVAudioUnitReverb()
effect2.loadFactoryPreset(.cathedral)
effect2.wetDryMix = 40
self.engine.attach(effect2)
let mixer = self.engine.mainMixerNode
// patch player node to _both_ effect nodes _and_ the mixer
let cons = [
    AVAudioConnectionPoint(node: effect, bus: 0),
    AVAudioConnectionPoint(node: effect2, bus: 0),
    AVAudioConnectionPoint(node: mixer, bus: 1),
]
self.engine.connect(player, to: cons,
    fromBus: 0, format: f.processingFormat)
// patch both effect nodes into the mixer
self.engine.connect(effect, to: mixer, format: f.processingFormat)
self.engine.connect(effect2, to: mixer, format: f.processingFormat)
```

Finally, I'll demonstrate how to process sound into a file. When AVAudioEngine appeared in iOS 8, I was hoping that the processing might be done rapidly in the background, but that turned out to be impossible; you had to play the sound in real time, install a tap on a node to collect its sound into a buffer, and write the buffer into a file. Starting in iOS 11, rapid offline rendering through AVAudioEngine became possible.

To demonstrate, I'll pass a sound file through a reverb effect and save the output into a new file. Initial configuration is much as you would expect:

```
let url = Bundle.main.url(forResource:"Hooded", withExtension: "mp3")!
let f = try! AVAudioFile(forReading: url)
let player = AVAudioPlayerNode()
self.engine.attach(player)
// patch the player into the effect
let effect = AVAudioUnitReverb()
effect.loadFactoryPreset(.cathedral)
effect.wetDryMix = 40
```

```
self.engine.attach(effect)
self.engine.connect(player, to: effect, format: f.processingFormat)
let mixer = self.engine.mainMixerNode
self.engine.connect(effect, to: mixer, format: f.processingFormat)
```

We create an output file with an appropriate format:

```
let fm = FileManager.default
let doc = try! fm.url(for:.documentDirectory, in: .userDomainMask,
    appropriateFor: nil, create: true)
let outurl = doc.appendingPathComponent("myfile.aac", isDirectory:false)
let outfile = try! AVAudioFile(forWriting: outurl, settings: [
    AVFormatIDKey : kAudioFormatMPEG4AAC,
    AVNumberOfChannelsKey : 1,
    AVSampleRateKey : 22050,
])
```

Now comes the interesting part. Before we start playing through the audio engine, we configure it for offline rendering:

```
var done = false
player.scheduleFile(f, at: nil)
let sz : UInt32 = 4096
try! self.engine.enableManualRenderingMode(.offline,
    format: f.processingFormat, maximumFrameCount: sz)
self.engine.prepare()
try! self.engine.start()
player.play()
```

We have told the engine to start and the player to play, but nothing happens. That's because it's up to us to *pull* the sound data through the engine into a buffer one chunk at a time, and write the buffer into a file. I create the buffer, and then loop repeatedly until all the sound data has been read:

```
let outbuf = AVAudioPCMBuffer(
    pcmFormat: f.processingFormat, frameCapacity: sz)!
var rest : Int64 { return f.length - self.engine.manualRenderingSampleTime }
while rest > 0 {
    let ct = min(outbuf.frameCapacity, UInt32(rest))
    let stat = try! self.engine.renderOffline(ct, to: outbuf)
    if stat == .success {
        try! outfile.write(from: outbuf)
    }
}
```

The result is that the input file is processed very quickly into the output file. I have one quibble with the result: our reverb effect is not given a chance to fade away at the end of the output, because we stop writing to the output file as soon as the input file is exhausted. One solution might be to add a couple of seconds arbitrarily onto the size of rest; another might be to examine the contents of outbuf and keep looping after reading the input file until the amplitude of the sound data falls below some threshold.

MIDI Playback

Playing a MIDI file is as simple as playing an audio file. In this example, I'm already armed with a MIDI file, which provides the music, and a SoundFont file, which provides the instrument that will play it; `self.player` will be an AVMIDIPlayer:

```
let midurl = Bundle.main.url(forResource: "presto", withExtension: "mid")!
let sndurl = Bundle.main.url(forResource: "Piano", withExtension: "sf2")!
self.player = try! AVMIDIPlayer(contentsOf: midurl, soundBankURL: sndurl)
self.player.prepareToPlay()
self.player.play()
```

A MIDI player can also act as a source in an AVAudioEngine. In this case, you'll want an AVAudioUnitSampler as your starting AVAudioUnit. The MIDI file will be parsed by an AVAudioSequencer; this is not part of the audio engine node structure, but rather it *has* the audio engine as a property, so you'll need to retain it in a property (`self.seq` in this example):

```
let midurl = Bundle.main.url(forResource: "presto", withExtension: "mid")!
let sndurl = Bundle.main.url(forResource: "Piano", withExtension: "sf2")!
let unit = AVAudioUnitSampler()
self.engine.attach(unit)
let mixer = self.engine.outputNode
self.engine.connect(unit, to: mixer, format: mixer.outputFormat(forBus:0))
try! unit.loadInstrument(at:sndurl)
self.seq = AVAudioSequencer(audioEngine: self.engine)
try! self.seq.load(from:midurl)
self.engine.prepare()
try! engine.start()
try! self.seq.start()
```

That code is rather mysterious: where's the connection between the AVAudio-Sequencer and the AVAudioUnitSampler? The answer is that the sequencer just finds the first AVAudioUnitSampler in the audio engine graph and proceeds to drive it. If that isn't what you want, get the AVAudioSequencer's `tracks` property, which is an array of AVMusicTrack; now you can set each track's `destinationAudioUnit` explicitly.

Text to Speech

Text can be transformed into synthesized speech using the AVSpeechUtterance and AVSpeechSynthesizer classes. As with an AVAudioPlayer, you'll need to retain the AVSpeechSynthesizer (`self.talker` in my example); here, I also use the AVSpeech-SynthesisVoice class to make sure the device speaks the text in English, regardless of the user's language settings:

```
let utter = AVSpeechUtterance(string:"Polly, want a cracker?")
if let v = AVSpeechSynthesisVoice(language: "en-US") {
    utter.voice = v
    self.talker.delegate = self
    self.talker.speak(utter)
}
```

You can set the utterance's speech rate; the value ranges between 0 and 1, where 0.5 is normal. You can also set pitch (higher or lower voice) and volume (louder or softer). The delegate (AVSpeechSynthesizerDelegate) is told when the speech starts, when it comes to a new range of text (usually a word), and when it finishes.

To get the user's current language, call the AVSpeechSynthesisVoice class method currentLanguageCode. Instead of specifying a voice by language, you can use the system's identifier. To get a list of all voices, call the class method speechVoices.

If you don't specify a voice identifier, the user's preferred voice (set in the Accessibility settings, under Spoken Content) will be used — except that a fallback voice will be used instead of a Siri voice. For example, on my device, my spoken content voice is Siri Male, but the synthesizer falls back to Samantha. New in iOS 14, you can set the utterance's prefersAssistiveTechnologySettings property to true; in that case, user preferences for such things as speech rate will be honored.

If a word within your AVSpeechUtterance needs extra pronunciation guidance, you can write it out using the international phonetic alphabet (IPA):

1. Form an NSMutableAttributedString from your overall phrase.

2. Call addAttribute(_:value:range:):

   • The first parameter is NSAttributedString.Key(rawValue: AVSpeech-SynthesisIPANotationAttribute).

   • The second parameter is the IPA notation to be substituted at the range of that word.

3. Form the speech utterance from the attributed string with the initializer init(attributedString:).

Starting in iOS 13, you can set the speech synthesizer's usesApplicationAudio-Session property to false. When you do, the system manages your synthesized speech in its own audio session; it deals automatically with interruptions, and even ducks your app's other audio during speech.

Speech to Text

Your app can participate in the same speech recognition engine used by Siri and the virtual keyboard's Dictate button. In this way, you can transcribe speech to text. To do so, you'll use the Speech framework (import Speech).

Use of the speech recognition engine requires authorization from the user. You'll need to have a meaningful entry in your *Info.plist* under the "Privacy — Speech Recognition Usage Description" key (NSSpeechRecognitionUsageDescription) explaining to the user why you want to do speech recognition. In your code, check the value of SFSpeechRecognizer.authorizationStatus(). If it is .notDetermined, request authorization by calling SFSpeechRecognizer.requestAuthorization. The system will put up an alert requesting authorization from the user for your app to do speech recognition. A user who denies your app speech recognition authorization may grant it later in Settings.

Once you have authorization, the basic procedure is simple. You form a speech recognition request and hand it off to an SFSpeechRecognizer. Recognition can be performed in various languages, which are expressed as locales; to learn what these are, call the supportedLocales class method. The device's current locale is used by default, or you can specify a locale when you initialize the SFSpeechRecognizer.

There are two modes of speech recognition:

Over the air
> In this mode, recognition is performed by Apple's servers. This is a resource-heavy operation. It requires an internet connection, with the work being done by Apple's servers; such a connection can fail. Apple also warns that recognized snippets must be short, and that excessive use of the server may result in access being throttled.

On the device
> In this mode (introduced in iOS 13), recognition is performed on the device. This may be less accurate than over-the-air recognition, and only certain languages are recognized; but no internet connection is required, and there is no limit on the number and frequency of recognitions you can perform. To specify this mode, ask the SFSpeechRecognizer for its supportsOnDeviceRecognition and, if true, set the speech recognition request's requiresOnDeviceRecognition to true.

There are also two *kinds* of speech recognition: transcription of an existing file, and transcription of live speech. For transcription of a file, your speech recognition request will be an SFSpeechURLRecognitionRequest initialized with the file URL. In this example, I have a recording of myself saying "This is a test." I speak American English, so just to be on the safe side, I initialize my SFSpeechRecognizer with the "en-US" locale. Interestingly, none of the objects needs to be retained in an instance property:

```
let f = Bundle.main.url(forResource: "test", withExtension: "aif")!
let req = SFSpeechURLRecognitionRequest(url: f)
let loc = Locale(identifier: "en-US")
guard let rec = SFSpeechRecognizer(locale:loc)
```

```
        else {return} // no recognizer
    rec.recognitionTask(with: req) { result, err in
        if let result = result {
            let trans = result.bestTranscription
            let s = trans.formattedString
            print(s)
            if result.isFinal {
                print("finished!")
            }
        } else {
            print(err!)
        }
    }
}
```

In that code, we're calling recognitionTask(with:resultHandler:) with an anonymous function. The function is called several times, passing us an SFSpeechRecognitionResult containing possible transcriptions (an array of SFTranscription). We ignore these, asking instead for the bestTranscription and extracting its formattedString. We know when we've been called for the last time because the recognition result's isFinal is true. In real life, it might be sufficient to extract the transcription only on the final pass, but for the purposes of this demonstration, I've logged every call to the function; the resulting console log looks like this:

```
This
This is
This is
This is
This is a test
This is a test
finished!
```

For transcription of live speech, your app is going to be using the device's microphone, so you'll need microphone usage permission, as I described earlier in this chapter. Once you have authorization for both speech recognition and microphone usage, the procedure is almost exactly the same as before — except that the speech recognition request will be an SFSpeechAudioBufferRecognitionRequest, and we need a way to pass the microphone input to it. A buffer recognition request has an append method whose parameter is an AVAudioPCMBuffer. To obtain an AVAudioPCMBuffer, we can use AVAudioEngine and put a tap on a node. Here, that node will be the audio engine's inputNode, representing the device's microphone:

```
let engine = AVAudioEngine()
let req = SFSpeechAudioBufferRecognitionRequest()
func doLive() {
    let loc = Locale(identifier: "en-US")
    guard let rec = SFSpeechRecognizer(locale:loc)
        else {return} // no recognizer
    let input = self.engine.inputNode
    input.installTap(onBus: 0, bufferSize: 4096,
        format: input.outputFormat(forBus: 0)) { buffer, time in
```

```
                self.req.append(buffer)
        }
        self.engine.prepare()
        try! self.engine.start()
        // provide the user with "recording" feedback
        rec.recognitionTask(with: self.req) { result, err in
            // ... and the rest is as before ...
        }
    }
```

You must provide the user with a clear indication in the interface that the microphone is now live and the speech recognition engine is listening. You must also provide a way for the user to *stop* recognition, signaling that the speech is over (like the
Done button in the dictation interface). That's why our buffer recognition request is
an instance property (self.req); the buffer recognition request has an endAudio
instance method, which we need to able to call when the user taps our Done button. I
also stop the audio engine and remove the tap from its input node, so as to be ready if
the user wants to do more speech recognition later:

```
@IBAction func endLive(_ sender: Any) {
    self.engine.stop()
    self.engine.inputNode.removeTap(onBus: 0)
    self.req.endAudio()
    // take down "recording" feedback
}
```

Instead of calling recognitionTask(with:resultHandler:), you can call
recognitionTask(with:delegate:), providing an adopter of the SFSpeechRecogni-
tionTaskDelegate protocol. Here you can implement any of half a dozen optional
methods, called at various stages of the recognition process, to allow your response to
be more fine-grained. You can also assist the recognition request with hints, retrieve
confidence levels and alternatives from the segments of a transcription, and move the
task messages onto a background queue.

Further Topics in Sound

iOS is a powerful milieu for production and processing of sound; its sound-related
technologies are extensive. This is a big topic, and an entire book could be written
about it (in fact, such books do exist). I'll talk in Chapter 17 about accessing sound
files in the user's music library. Here are some further topics that there is no room to
discuss here (and see Apple's *Core Audio Overview* in the documentation archive):

Other audio session policies
    If your app accepts sound input or does audio processing, you'll want to look
    into audio session policies such as Record, Play and Record, and Audio Process-
    ing. In addition, if you're using Record or Play and Record, there are modes —

voice chat, video recording, and measurement (of the sound being input) — that optimize how sound is routed and how it is modified.

Audio queues

Audio queues — Audio Queue Services, part of the Audio Toolbox framework — implement sound playing and recording through a C API with more granularity than the Objective-C AVAudioPlayer and AVAudioRecorder (though it is still regarded as a high-level API), giving you access to the buffers used to move chunks of sound data between a storage format (a sound file) and sound hardware.

Extended Audio File Services

A C API for reading and writing sound files in chunks. It is useful in connection with technologies such as audio queues.

Audio Converter Services

Originally, a C API for converting sound files between formats. Starting in iOS 9, the AVAudioConverter class (along with AVAudioCompressedBuffer) gives this API an object-oriented structure.

Streaming audio

Audio streamed in real time over the network, such as an internet radio station, can be played with Audio File Stream Services, in connection with audio queues.

Audio units

Plug-ins that generate sound or modify sound as it passes through them. Starting in iOS 9, the API was migrated from C into Objective-C and given a modern object-oriented structure; audio units can vend interface (AUViewController); and an audio unit from one app can be hosted inside another (audio unit extensions).

Core MIDI

The CoreMIDI framework manages direct communication with MIDI devices.

Core Haptics

Introduced in iOS 13, the Core Haptics framework lets you construct precise vibration patterns to be played on certain iPhone models (iPhone 8 and higher); these are typically used to supplement and reinforce sounds.

Video

Video playback is performed using classes provided by the AV Foundation framework (import AVFoundation), such as AVPlayer. An AVPlayer is not a view; rather, an AVPlayer's content is made visible through a CALayer subclass, AVPlayerLayer, which can be added to your app's interface. An AV Foundation video playback interface can be wrapped in a simple view controller, AVPlayerViewController: you provide an AVPlayer, and the AVPlayerViewController *automatically* hosts an associated AVPlayerLayer in its own main view, providing standard playback transport controls so that the user can start and stop play, seek to a different frame, and so forth. AVPlayerViewController is provided by the AVKit framework; you'll need to import AVKit.

A simple interface for letting the user trim video (UIVideoEditorController) is also supplied. Sophisticated video editing can be performed in code through the AV Foundation framework.

If an AVPlayer produces sound, you may need to concern yourself with your application's audio session; see Chapter 15. You will almost certainly want the category to be .playback. AVPlayer deals gracefully with the app being sent into the background: it will pause when your app is backgrounded and resume when your app returns to the foreground.

A movie file can be in a standard movie format, such as *.mov* or *.mp4*, but it can also be a sound file. An AVPlayerViewController is an easy way to play a sound file, including a sound file obtained in real time over the internet, along with standard controls for pausing the sound and moving the playhead — unlike AVAudioPlayer, which, as I pointed out in Chapter 15, lacks a transport interface.

A web view (Chapter 12) supports the HTML5 `<video>` tag. This can be a simple lightweight way to present video and to allow the user to control playback. Both web view video and AVPlayer support AirPlay.

AVPlayerViewController

An AVPlayerViewController is a view controller whose view contains an AVPlayer-Layer and transport controls. It must be assigned a `player`, which is an AVPlayer. An AVPlayer can be initialized directly from the URL of the video it is to play, with `init(url:)`. You'll instantiate AVPlayerViewController, create and set its AVPlayer, and get the AVPlayerViewController into the view controller hierarchy. You can instantiate an AVPlayerViewController in code or from a storyboard; look for the AVKit Player View Controller object in the Library.

The simplest approach is to use an AVPlayerViewController as a presented view controller. In this example, I present a video from the app bundle:

```
let av = AVPlayerViewController()
let url = Bundle.main.url(forResource:"ElMirage", withExtension: "mp4")!
let player = AVPlayer(url: url)
av.player = player
self.present(av, animated: true)
```

The AVPlayerViewController is presented fullscreen. (This is a good example of the `.automatic` modal presentation style in action: normally, this would resolve to `.pageSheet`, but for an AVPlayerViewController it is `.fullScreen`.) It knows that it's being shown as a fullscreen presented view controller, so it provides fullscreen video controls, including a Done button which automatically dismisses the presented view controller. There is literally no further work for you to do.

Figure 16-1 shows a fullscreen presented AVPlayerViewController. Exactly what controls you'll see depends on the circumstances; in my case, at the top there's the Done button (which appears as an X), the zoom button, and a volume slider, and at the bottom are transport controls including the current playhead position slider, along with the AirPlay button. The user can hide or show the controls by tapping the video.

If the AVPlayer's file is in fact a sound file, the central region is blacked out, and the controls can't be hidden.

Instead of a presented AVPlayerViewController, you might push the AVPlayerViewController onto a navigation controller's stack. Again, the AVPlayerViewController behaves intelligently. The controls include a fullscreen button, which results in almost exactly the same interface shown in Figure 16-1. There is now no Done button, because the user can tap the back button when finished with this screen. Ensuring that the back button is visible is up to you! You might set the navigation

Figure 16-1. A presented AVPlayerViewController

controller's hidesBarsWhenVerticallyCompact to false and the AVPlayerViewController's edgesForExtendedLayout to [].

If you want the convenience and the control interface that come from using an
AVPlayerViewController, while displaying its view as a subview of your own view
controller's view, make your view controller a parent view controller with the
AVPlayerViewController as its child, adding the AVPlayerViewController's view in
good order (see "Container View Controllers" on page 379):

```
let url = Bundle.main.url(forResource:"ElMirage", withExtension:"mp4")!
let player = AVPlayer(url:url)
let av = AVPlayerViewController()
av.player = player
av.view.frame = CGRect(10,10,300,200)
self.addChild(av)
self.view.addSubview(av.view)
av.didMove(toParent:self)
```

Once again, the AVPlayerViewController behaves intelligently, reducing its controls
to a minimum to adapt to the reduced size of its view. On my device, at the given
view size, there is room for a fullscreen button, a volume button, a play button, the
playhead position slider, and the AirPlay button (Figure 16-2). From here, the user
can enter fullscreen mode, either by tapping the fullscreen button or by pinching outward on the video view, and now the full complement of controls is present (exactly
as in Figure 16-1).

Figure 16-2. An embedded AVPlayerViewController

Starting in iOS 13 (and backward compatible to iOS 12), the AVPlayerViewController's delegate (AVPlayerViewControllerDelegate) can be notified when the user enters and exits fullscreen mode. There are two relevant delegate methods:

- playerViewController(_:willBeginFullScreenPresentationWithAnimation-Coordinator:)

- playerViewController(_:willEndFullScreenPresentationWithAnimation-Coordinator:)

The user can start to enter fullscreen mode with an outward pinch without completing the gesture; to find out whether the user *really* entered fullscreen mode, check the transition coordinator to see whether the transition was cancelled:

```
func playerViewController(_ av: AVPlayerViewController,
    willBeginFullScreenPresentationWithAnimationCoordinator
    coordinator: UIViewControllerTransitionCoordinator) {
        coordinator.animate { con in
            // ...
        } completion: { con in
            if con.isCancelled {
                // ...
            } else {
                // really went fullscreen!
            }
        }
}
```

AVPlayerViewController Configuration

You configure an AVPlayerViewController through its properties:

player

The view controller's AVPlayer, whose AVPlayerLayer will be hosted in the view controller's view. You can set the player while the view is visible, to change what video it displays (though you are more likely to keep the player and tell *it* to change the video). It is legal to assign an AVQueuePlayer, an AVPlayer subclass; an AVQueuePlayer has multiple items, and the AVPlayerViewController will treat these as chapters of the video. An AVPlayerLooper object can be used in conjunction with an AVQueuePlayer to repeat play automatically. (I'll give an AVQueuePlayer example in Chapter 17, and an AVPlayerLooper example in Chapter 18.)

`showsPlaybackControls`

If `false`, the controls are hidden. This could be useful if you want to display a video for decorative purposes, or if you are substituting your own controls.

`contentOverlayView`

A UIView to which you are free to add subviews. These subviews will appear overlaid in front of the video but behind the playback controls. Starting in iOS 11, the content overlay is sized to fit its contents, or you can give it constraints to size it as you prefer.

`videoGravity`

How the video should be positioned within the view. Possible values are (AVLayerVideoGravity):

- `.resizeAspect` (the default)
- `.resizeAspectFill`
- `.resize` (fills the view, possibly distorting the video)

`videoBounds`
`isReadyForDisplay`

Read-only. The video position within the view, and the ability of the video to display its first frame and start playing, respectively. If the video is not ready for display, we probably don't yet know its bounds either. In any case, `isReadyFor-Display` will initially be `false` and the `videoBounds` will initially be reported as `.zero`. This is because, with video, things take time to prepare. I'll explain in detail later in this chapter.

`updatesNowPlayingInfoCenter`

If `true` (the default), the AVPlayerViewController keeps the MPNowPlaying-InfoCenter (Chapter 15) apprised of the movie's duration and current playhead position. If `false`, it doesn't do that, leaving your code in charge of managing the MPNowPlayingInfoCenter. Starting in iOS 13, you can leave this property at `true` and still govern what information appears in the remote control interface, by setting the player item's `externalMetadata`; here's an example (without further comment):

Figure 16-3. The picture-in-picture button appears

```
let metadata = AVMutableMetadataItem()
metadata.keySpace = .common
metadata.key = AVMetadataKey.commonKeyTitle as NSString
metadata.value = "El Mirage" as NSString
av.player?.currentItem?.externalMetadata = [metadata]
```

entersFullScreenWhenPlaybackBegins
exitsFullScreenWhenPlaybackEnds

> If true, a child AVPlayerViewController's view switches to and from fullscreen mode automatically when play begins and ends.

Everything else there is to know about an AVPlayerViewController comes from its player, an AVPlayer. I'll discuss AVPlayer in more detail in a moment.

Picture-in-Picture

A device capable of running iOS 14 supports picture-in-picture video playback. This means that the user can move your video into a small system window that floats in front of everything else on the screen. This floating window persists if your app is put into the background.

Your app will support picture-in-picture if it supports background audio, as I described in Chapter 15: you check the checkbox in the Signing & Capabilities tab of the target editor (Figure 15-2), and your audio session's policy must be active and must be Playback. If you want to do those things *without* your app being forced to support picture-in-picture, set the AVPlayerViewController's allowsPictureIn-PicturePlayback to false.

If picture-in-picture is supported, an extra button appears among the upper set of playback controls (Figure 16-3). When the user taps this button, the video is moved into the system window (and the AVPlayerViewController's view displays a place-holder). The user is now free to leave your app while continuing to see and hear the video. Moreover, if the video is being played fullscreen when the user leaves your app, the video is moved into the picture-in-picture system window *automatically* (unless the user turns this feature off in the Settings app).

The user can move the system window to any corner. Buttons in the system window, which can be shown or hidden by tapping, allow the user to play and pause the video or to dismiss the system window. There's also a button to dismiss the system window plus return to your app; if the user taps it while the video is playing, the video goes right on playing as it moves back into place within your app.

Various delegate methods keep you informed of when the user causes your app to enter and leave picture-in-picture mode; the most important are:

- `playerViewControllerDidStartPictureInPicture(_:)`

- `playerViewControllerDidStopPictureInPicture(_:)`

If your AVPlayerViewController is being presented fullscreen when the video is taken into picture-in-picture mode, then the presented view controller, by default, *is dismissed.* If the user tries to return to your app from the system picture-in-picture window, the video has no place to return to. To handle this situation, give the AVPlayerViewController a **delegate** (AVPlayerViewControllerDelegate) and deal with it in a delegate method. You have two choices; the outward difference between the two approaches lies in what happens if the user comes back to your app while picture-in-picture is still going on:

Don't dismiss the presented view controller
    Implement this method:

- `playerViewControllerShouldAutomaticallyDismissAtPictureInPicture-Start(_:)`

Return `false`. Now the presented view controller remains, and the video has a place in your app to which it can be restored. If the user returns to your app while picture-in-picture is still going on, the video's place in the app is black and empty, with a legend: "This video is playing picture in picture." The user can then animate the video back to its place.

Recreate the presented view controller
    Implement this method:

- `playerViewController(_:restoreUserInterfaceForPictureInPicture-StopWithCompletionHandler:)`

Do what the name tells you: restore the user interface! The first parameter is your original AVPlayerViewController; all you have to do is get it back into the view controller hierarchy. At the end of the process, *call the completion function:*

```
func playerViewController(_ pvc: AVPlayerViewController,
    restoreUserInterfaceForPictureInPictureStopWithCompletionHandler
    ch: @escaping (Bool) -> ()) {
        self.present(pvc, animated:true) {
            ch(true)
        }
}
```

If the user returns to your app while picture-in-picture is still going on, the presented AVPlayerViewController is gone, and if the user were to present it, you'd have *two* copies of the video, the one still playing picture-in-picture and the one now being presented. That's bad, so you need to prevent it from happening. In other words, while you are still in picture-in-picture mode, the second delegate method should be the *only* way that your app presents the AVPlayerViewController. Luckily, you know *when* you are in picture-in-picture mode, because the other delegate methods tell you.

 Once you've entered picture-in-picture mode, you are effectively a background app, and you should reduce resources and activity so that playing the video is *all* you're doing until picture-in-picture mode ends.

Introducing AV Foundation

The video display performed by AVPlayerViewController is supplied by classes from the AV Foundation framework. This is a big framework with a lot of classes, but there's a good reason for that: video has a lot of structure and can be manipulated in many ways, and AV Foundation very carefully and correctly draws all the distinctions needed for good object-oriented encapsulation. I'll just point out some of the principal classes, features, and techniques associated with video. Further AV Foundation examples will appear in Chapters 17 and 18.

Some AV Foundation Classes

The heart of AV Foundation video playback is AVPlayer. AVPlayer is not a UIView, but rather is the locus of video transport; the actual video, if shown, appears in an AVPlayerLayer associated with the AVPlayer. AVPlayerViewController provides a play button, but what if you wanted to start video playback in code? You'd talk to the AVPlayerViewController's `player` — an AVPlayer. You'd tell it to `play` or set its `rate` to 1.

An AVPlayer's video is its `currentItem`, an AVPlayerItem. In the examples earlier in this chapter we initialized an AVPlayer directly from a URL, with no reference to any AVPlayerItem; but that was just a shortcut. AVPlayer's *real* initializer is `init(playerItem:)`, which takes an AVPlayerItem; when we called `init(url:)`, the AVPlayerItem was created for us.

An AVPlayerItem, too, can be initialized from a URL with `init(url:)`, but again, this is just a shortcut. AVPlayerItem's *real* initializer is `init(asset:)`, which takes an AVAsset. An AVAsset is an actual video resource, and comes in one of two subclasses:

AVURLAsset

An asset specified through a URL.

AVComposition

An asset constructed by editing video in code. I'll give an example later in this chapter.

To configure an AVPlayer using the complete "stack" of objects that constitute it, you could say something like this:

```
let url = Bundle.main.url(forResource:"ElMirage", withExtension:"mp4")!
let asset = AVURLAsset(url:url)
let item = AVPlayerItem(asset:asset)
let player = AVPlayer(playerItem:item)
```

Once an AVPlayer exists and has an AVPlayerItem, that player item's tracks, as seen from the player's perspective, are AVPlayerItemTrack objects, which can be individually enabled or disabled. That's different from an AVAssetTrack, which is a fact about an AVAsset. This distinction is a good example of how AV Foundation encapsulates its objects correctly: an AVAssetTrack is a hard and fast reality, but an AVPlayerItemTrack lets a track be manipulated for purposes of playback on a particular occasion.

Things Take Time

Working with video is time-consuming. Just because you give an AVPlayer a command or set a property doesn't mean that it obeys immediately. All sorts of operations, from reading a video file and learning its metadata to transcoding and saving a video file, take a significant amount of time. The user interface must not freeze while a video task is in progress, so AV Foundation relies heavily on threading (Chapter 25). In this way, AV Foundation covers the complex and time-consuming nature of its operations; but your code must cooperate. You'll frequently use key-value observing and callbacks to run your code at the right moment.

Here's an example; it's slightly artificial, but it illustrates the principles and techniques you need to know about. There's an elementary interface flaw when we create an embedded AVPlayerViewController:

```
let url = Bundle.main.url(forResource:"ElMirage", withExtension:"mp4")!
let asset = AVURLAsset(url:url)
let item = AVPlayerItem(asset:asset)
let player = AVPlayer(playerItem:item)
let av = AVPlayerViewController()
av.view.frame = CGRect(10,10,300,200)
av.player = player
self.addChild(av)
self.view.addSubview(av.view)
av.didMove(toParent: self)
```

There are two issues here:

- The AVPlayerViewController's view is initially appearing empty in the interface, because the video is not yet ready for display. Then there's a *visible flash* when the video appears, because now it *is* ready for display.

- The proposed frame of the AVPlayerViewController's view doesn't fit the actual aspect ratio of the video, which results in the video being *letterboxed* within that frame (visible in Figure 16-2).

Fixing those issues requires us to grapple with the fact that it takes time to learn when the video is ready for display and what its aspect ratio is.

Key–value observing a property

To prevent the flash, we can start out with the AVPlayerViewController's view hidden, and not show it until `isReadyForDisplay` is `true`. But how will we know when that is? *Not* by repeatedly polling the `isReadyForDisplay` property! That sort of behavior is absolutely wrong. Rather, we should use KVO to register as an observer of this property. Sooner or later, `isReadyForDisplay` will become `true`, and we'll be notified. Now we can unregister from KVO and show the AVPlayerViewController's view:

```
av.view.isHidden = true
var ob : NSKeyValueObservation!
ob = av.observe(\.isReadyForDisplay, options: [.initial, .new]) { vc, ch in
    guard let ok = ch.newValue, ok else {return}
    self.obs.remove(ob)
    DispatchQueue.main.async {
        vc.view.isHidden = false
    }
}
self.obs.insert(ob) // obs is a Set<NSKeyValueObservation>
```

Note that, in that code, I make no assumptions about what thread KVO calls me back on: I intend to operate on the interface, so I step out to the main thread.

Asynchronous property loading

Next, let's talk about setting the AVPlayerViewController's `view.frame` in accordance with the video's aspect ratio. An AVAsset has `tracks` (AVAssetTrack); in particular, an AVAsset representing a video has a video track. A video track has a `naturalSize`, which will give me the aspect ratio I need. But we cannot access these properties immediately. For the sake of efficiency, these and many other AV Foundation object properties don't even *have* a value unless we specifically request that they be evaluated — and when we do, it takes time to fulfill our request.

AV Foundation objects that behave this way conform to the AVAsynchronousKey-ValueLoading protocol. You call `loadValuesAsynchronously(forKeys:completion-`

`Handler:)` ahead of time, for any properties you're going to be interested in. When your completion function is called, you check the status of a key and, if its status is `.loaded`, you are now free to access the property.

To obtain the video's aspect ratio, I'm going to need to do that twice — first for the AVAsset's `tracks` property, in order to get the video track, and then for the video track's `naturalSize` property, in order to get the aspect ratio. Let's go all the way back to the beginning. I'll start by creating the AVAsset *and then stop*, waiting to hear in the completion function that the AVAsset's `tracks` property is ready:

```
let url = Bundle.main.url(forResource:"ElMirage", withExtension:"mp4")!
let asset = AVURLAsset(url:url)
let track = #keyPath(AVURLAsset.tracks)
asset.loadValuesAsynchronously(forKeys:[track]) {
    let status = asset.statusOfValue(forKey:track, error: nil)
    if status == .loaded {
        DispatchQueue.main.async {
            self.getVideoTrack(asset)
        }
    }
}
```

When the `tracks` property is ready, my completion function is called, and I call my `getVideoTrack` method. Here, I obtain the video track *and then stop* once again, waiting to hear in the completion function that the video track's `naturalSize` property is ready:

```
func getVideoTrack(_ asset:AVAsset) {
    let visual = AVMediaCharacteristic.visual
    let vtrack = asset.tracks(withMediaCharacteristic: visual)[0]
    let size = #keyPath(AVAssetTrack.naturalSize)
    vtrack.loadValuesAsynchronously(forKeys: [size]) {
        let status = vtrack.statusOfValue(forKey: size, error: nil)
        if status == .loaded {
            DispatchQueue.main.async {
                self.getNaturalSize(vtrack, asset)
            }
        }
    }
}
```

When the video track's `naturalSize` property is ready, my completion function is called, and I call my `getNaturalSize` method. Here, at long last, I get the natural size and use it to finish constructing the AVPlayer and to set AVPlayerController's frame:

```
func getNaturalSize(_ vtrack:AVAssetTrack, _ asset:AVAsset) {
    let sz = vtrack.naturalSize
    let item = AVPlayerItem(asset:asset)
    let player = AVPlayer(playerItem:item)
    let av = AVPlayerViewController()
    av.view.frame = AVMakeRect(
```

```
            aspectRatio: sz, insideRect: CGRect(10,10,300,200))
        av.player = player
        // ... and the rest is as before ...
    }
```

AVPlayerItem provides another way of loading an asset's properties: initialize it with
`init(asset:automaticallyLoadedAssetKeys:)` and then observe its `status` using
KVO. When that `status` is `.readyToPlay`, you are guaranteed that the player item's
`asset` has attempted to load those keys, and you can query them just as you would in
`loadValuesAsynchronously`.

 Apple recommends that, as a matter of best practice, you should *always* use KVO
to observe the player item's status. The reason is that if that status changes
to `.failed`, you're going to want to know about it. Fetch the player item's `error`
property to find out more. For possible errors, consult the AVError
documentation. If the error is `.mediaServicesWereReset`, the media services
daemon is hosed (similar to `AVAudioSession.mediaServicesWereReset-`
`Notification` in Chapter 15), and you should recreate your AVFoundation
objects from scratch.

Remote assets

An AVURLAsset's URL doesn't have to be a local file URL; it can point to a resource
located across the internet. Now things *really* take time: the asset has to arrive by way
of the network, which may be slow, interrupted, or missing in action. There's a
buffer, and if it isn't sufficiently full of your AVAsset's data, playback will stutter
or stop.

Before iOS 10, you had to use your AVPlayer's AVPlayerItem as the locus of information about the arrival and playback of your AVAsset from across the network,
keeping track of properties such as `playbackLikelyToKeepUp` and the `accessLog`,
along with notifications such as `AVPlayerItemPlaybackStalled`, to keep abreast of
any issues, pausing and resuming to optimize the user experience.

Starting in iOS 10, Apple made this entire procedure much easier: just tell the
AVPlayer to play and stand back! Play won't start until the buffer has filled to the
point where the whole video can play without stalling, and if it *does* stall, it will
resume automatically. To learn what's happening, check the AVPlayer's `timeControl-`
`Status`; if it is `.waitingToPlayAtSpecifiedRate` and you want to know why, check
the AVPlayer's `reasonForWaitingToPlay`. To learn the actual current play rate, call
`CMTimebaseGetRate` with the AVPlayerItem's `timebase`.

Time Is Measured Oddly

Another peculiarity of AV Foundation is that time is measured in an unfamiliar way.
This is necessary because calculations using an ordinary built-in numeric class such

as CGFloat will always have slight rounding errors that quickly begin to matter when you're trying to specify a time within a large piece of media. Therefore, the Core Media framework provides the CMTime class, which under the hood is a pair of integers; they are called the value and the timescale, but they are simply the numerator and denominator of a rational number.

When you call the CMTime initializer init(value:timescale:) (equivalent to C CMTimeMake), that's what you're providing. The denominator represents the degree of granularity; a typical value is 600, sufficient to specify individual frames in common video formats.

In the convenience initializer init(seconds:preferredTimescale:) (equivalent to C CMTimeMakeWithSeconds), the two arguments are *not* the numerator and denominator; they are the time's equivalent in seconds and the denominator. For instance, CMTime(seconds:2.5, preferredTimescale:600) yields the CMTime (1500,600).

Constructing Media

AV Foundation allows you to construct your own media asset in code as an AVComposition, an AVAsset subclass, using *its* subclass, AVMutableComposition. An AVComposition is an AVAsset, so given an AVMutableComposition, we could make an AVPlayerItem from it (by calling init(asset:)) and hand it over to an AVPlayerViewController's player; we will be creating and displaying our own movie!

Cutting and pasting

In this example, I start with an AVAsset (asset1, a video file) and assemble its first 5 seconds of video and its last 5 seconds of video into an AVMutableComposition (comp):

```
let type = AVMediaType.video
let arr = asset1.tracks(withMediaType: type)
let track = arr.last!
let duration : CMTime = track.timeRange.duration
let comp = AVMutableComposition()
let comptrack = comp.addMutableTrack(withMediaType: type,
    preferredTrackID: Int32(kCMPersistentTrackID_Invalid))!
try! comptrack.insertTimeRange(CMTimeRange(
    start: CMTime(seconds:0, preferredTimescale:600),
    duration: CMTime(seconds:5, preferredTimescale:600)),
    of:track, at:CMTime(seconds:0, preferredTimescale:600))
try! comptrack.insertTimeRange(CMTimeRange(
    start: duration - CMTime(seconds:5, preferredTimescale:600),
    duration: CMTime(seconds:5, preferredTimescale:600)),
    of:track, at:CMTime(seconds:5, preferredTimescale:600))
```

This works perfectly. But we are not very good video editors, as we have forgotten the corresponding soundtrack from asset1. Let's go back and get it and add it to our AVMutableComposition (comp):

```
let type2 = AVMediaType.audio
let arr2 = asset1.tracks(withMediaType: type2)
let track2 = arr2.last!
let comptrack2 = comp.addMutableTrack(withMediaType: type2,
    preferredTrackID:Int32(kCMPersistentTrackID_Invalid))!
try! comptrack2.insertTimeRange(CMTimeRange(
    start: CMTime(seconds:0, preferredTimescale:600),
    duration: CMTime(seconds:5, preferredTimescale:600)),
    of:track2, at:CMTime(seconds:0, preferredTimescale:600))
try! comptrack2.insertTimeRange(CMTimeRange(
    start: duration - CMTime(seconds:5, preferredTimescale:600),
    duration: CMTime(seconds:5, preferredTimescale:600)),
    of:track2, at:CMTime(seconds:5, preferredTimescale:600))
```

To display our edited movie in an AVPlayerViewController, we would talk to its player, replacing its player item with a new player item made from our AVMutableComposition:

```
let item = AVPlayerItem(asset:comp)
let p = vc.player! // vc is an AVPlayerViewController
p.replaceCurrentItem(with: item)
```

Adding tracks

We can use the same technique to overlay *another* audio track from *another* asset; this might be, let's say, some additional narration taken from a sound file (comp is the AVMutableComposition from the previous example):

```
let type3 = AVMediaType.audio
let s = Bundle.main.url(forResource:"aboutTiagol", withExtension:"m4a")!
let asset2 = AVURLAsset(url:s)
let arr3 = asset2.tracks(withMediaType: type3)
let track3 = arr3.last!
let comptrack3 = comp.addMutableTrack(withMediaType: type3,
    preferredTrackID:Int32(kCMPersistentTrackID_Invalid))!
try! comptrack3.insertTimeRange(CMTimeRange(
    start: CMTime(seconds:0, preferredTimescale:600),
    duration: CMTime(seconds:10, preferredTimescale:600)),
    of:track3, at:CMTime(seconds:0, preferredTimescale:600))
```

Transitions

You can apply audio volume changes, and video opacity and transform changes, to the playback of individual tracks. I'll continue from the previous example, applying a fadeout to the second half of the narration track (comptrack3) by creating an AVAudioMix:

```
let params = AVMutableAudioMixInputParameters(track:comptrack3)
params.setVolume(1, at:CMTime(seconds:0, preferredTimescale:600))
params.setVolumeRamp(fromStartVolume: 1, toEndVolume:0,
    timeRange:CMTimeRange(
        start: CMTime(seconds:5, preferredTimescale:600),
        duration: CMTime(seconds:5, preferredTimescale:600)))
let mix = AVMutableAudioMix()
mix.inputParameters = [params]
```

The audio mix must be applied to a playback milieu, such as an AVPlayerItem. So when we make an AVPlayerItem out of our AVComposition, we can set its audioMix property to our AVAudioMix:

```
let item = AVPlayerItem(asset:comp)
item.audioMix = mix
```

Filters

You can add a CIFilter (Chapter 2) to be applied to your video. In this example, I'll apply a sepia filter to my entire edited video (comp from the previous examples):

```
let vidcomp = AVVideoComposition(asset: comp) { req in
    // req is an AVAsynchronousCIImageFilteringRequest
    let f = "CISepiaTone"
    let im = req.sourceImage.applyingFilter(
        f, parameters: ["inputIntensity":0.95])
    req.finish(with: im, context: nil)
}
```

Like an AVAudioMix, an AVVideoComposition must be applied to a playback milieu:

```
let item = AVPlayerItem(asset:comp)
item.videoComposition = vidcomp
```

You can also use an AVVideoComposition to dictate how video tracks are to be composited.

Synchronizing animation with video

AVSynchronizedLayer is a CALayer subclass that effectively crosses the bridge between video time (the CMTime within the progress of a movie) and Core Animation time (the time within the progress of an animation). This means that you can coordinate animation in your interface (Chapter 4) with the playback of a movie! You attach an animation to a layer in more or less the usual way, but the animation takes place in movie playback time: if the movie is stopped, the animation is stopped; if the movie is run at double rate, the animation runs at double rate; and the current "frame" of the animation always corresponds to the current frame of the video within its overall duration.

Figure 16-4. The black square's position is synchronized to the movie

The synchronization is performed with respect to an AVPlayer's AVPlayerItem. To demonstrate, I'll draw a long thin gray rectangle containing a little black square; the horizontal position of the black square within the gray rectangle will be synchronized to the movie playhead position:

```
let vc = self.children[0] as! AVPlayerViewController
let p = vc.player!
// create synch layer, put it in the interface
let item = p.currentItem!
let syncLayer = AVSynchronizedLayer(playerItem:item)
syncLayer.frame = CGRect(10,220,300,10)
syncLayer.backgroundColor = UIColor.lightGray.cgColor
self.view.layer.addSublayer(syncLayer)
// give synch layer a sublayer
let subLayer = CALayer()
subLayer.backgroundColor = UIColor.black.cgColor
subLayer.frame = CGRect(0,0,10,10)
syncLayer.addSublayer(subLayer)
// animate the sublayer
let anim = CABasicAnimation(keyPath:#keyPath(CALayer.position))
anim.fromValue = subLayer.position
anim.toValue = CGPoint(295,5)
anim.isRemovedOnCompletion = false
anim.beginTime = AVCoreAnimationBeginTimeAtZero // important trick
anim.duration = item.asset.duration.seconds
subLayer.add(anim, forKey:nil)
```

The result is shown in Figure 16-4. The long gray rectangle is the AVSynchronized-Layer, tied to our movie. The little black square inside it is its sublayer; when we animate the black square, that animation will be synchronized to the movie, changing its position from the left end of the gray rectangle to the right end, starting at the beginning of the movie and with the same duration as the movie. Although we attach this animation to the black square layer in the usual way, that animation is frozen: the black square *doesn't move* until we start the movie playing. Moreover, if we pause the movie, the black square stops. The black square is *automatically* representing the current play position within the movie. This may seem a silly example, but if you were to suppress the video controls it could prove downright useful.

Adding layers to video

Instead of adding a CALayer to the interface, you can *render* a CALayer into the video itself. In effect, you treat the video itself as a layer, combine it with other layers however you like, and then package everything into a new video.

Suppose, for instance, that we want to add a caption, title, or other text to our video. If the video itself is a layer, the text can obviously be a CATextLayer in front of it. I'll describe the procedure backward, starting with some boilerplate.

To render layers into a video, you have to *export* the video to a file on disk. That requires an AVExportSession. To demonstrate, I'll export comp, the AVMutable-Composition from the earlier examples, and load the exported video into our AVPlayerViewController:

```
let pre = AVAssetExportPresetHighestQuality
guard let exporter = AVAssetExportSession(asset:comp, presetName:pre) else {
    print("oops")
    return
}
// create a URL to export to
let fm = FileManager.default
var url = fm.temporaryDirectory
let uuid = UUID().uuidString
url.appendPathComponent(uuid + ".mov")
exporter.outputURL = url
exporter.outputFileType = AVFileType.mov
// warning: this can take a long time!
exporter.exportAsynchronously() {
    DispatchQueue.main.async {
        let item = AVPlayerItem(url: url)
        let p = vc.player! // vc is an AVPlayerViewController
        p.replaceCurrentItem(with:item)
    }
}
```

(In real life, you'd probably want to put up some kind of interface to cover the fact that exporting can take a significant amount of time.) The result of that code isn't very interesting, because we didn't make any *change* to our video. To make a change — in particular, to render the video as a layer along with other layers — we need to attach an AVVideoComposition to the exporter:

```
exporter.videoComposition = vidcomp
```

Very well, but what's vidcomp? I'll continue with some more boilerplate. First, we construct our layer architecture. At a minimum, you need two layers — a parent layer with the video layer as its sublayer:

```
let vidtrack = comp.tracks(withMediaType: .video)[0]
let sz = vidtrack.naturalSize
let parent = CALayer()
parent.frame = CGRect(origin: .zero, size: sz)
let child = CALayer()
child.frame = parent.bounds
parent.addSublayer(child)
```

Next, we package up that layer architecture into an *animation tool,* and attach it to an AVVideoComposition. There's a lot of boilerplate here, but if you don't perform this complete dance, you can crash at runtime or end up with a black video:

```
let tool = AVVideoCompositionCoreAnimationTool(
    postProcessingAsVideoLayer: child, in: parent)
let vidcomp = AVMutableVideoComposition()
vidcomp.animationTool = tool
vidcomp.renderSize = sz
vidcomp.frameDuration = CMTime(value: 1, timescale: 30)
let inst = AVMutableVideoCompositionInstruction()
let dur = comp.duration
inst.timeRange = CMTimeRange(start: .zero, duration: dur)
let layinst = AVMutableVideoCompositionLayerInstruction(assetTrack: vidtrack)
inst.layerInstructions = [layinst]
vidcomp.instructions = [inst]
```

If we now attach `vidcomp` to `exporter` as we export `comp`, we still end up with a video that looks like `comp` itself. But that's not bad; it's good! Our boilerplate is working, and now at long last we are ready to introduce more layers into the architecture. Let's go back and add our text layer:

```
let lay = CATextLayer()
lay.string = "This is cool!"
lay.alignmentMode = .center
lay.foregroundColor = UIColor.black.cgColor
lay.frame = child.bounds
child.addSublayer(lay)
// ... and the rest is as before ...
```

The exported version of `comp` now displays the words "This is cool!" superimposed in front of it.

We've accomplished our original goal, but let's go further. These are CALayers. That means we can animate them! To demonstrate, I'll cause our text to fade in slowly, starting one second after the start of the video. To do so, I simply add an opacity animation to the text layer (`lay`). As with a synchronized layer, it is crucial to coordinate our timing by starting at `AVCoreAnimationBeginTimeAtZero`:

```
let ba = CABasicAnimation(keyPath: #keyPath(CALayer.opacity))
ba.duration = 1
ba.fromValue = 0
ba.toValue = 1
ba.beginTime = AVCoreAnimationBeginTimeAtZero + 1 // crucial
ba.fillMode = .backwards
lay.add(ba, forKey: nil)
```

All of that is extremely cool, but keep in mind that exporting video can take quite a bit of time. You might want to give the user something to look at while waiting. An AVAssetExportSession has a `progress` property for this very purpose; it vends a Progress object (see "The Progress Class" on page 739).

AVPlayerLayer

An AVPlayer is not an interface object. The corresponding interface object — an AVPlayer made visible, as it were — is an AVPlayerLayer (a CALayer subclass). It has no controls for letting the user play and pause a movie and visualize its progress; it just shows the movie, acting as a bridge between the AV Foundation world of media and the CALayer world of things the user can see.

An AVPlayerViewController's view hosts an AVPlayerLayer for you automatically; otherwise you would not see any video in the AVPlayerViewController's view. But there may be situations where you find AVPlayerViewController too heavyweight, where you don't need the standard transport controls, where you don't want the video to be expandable or to have a fullscreen mode — you just want the simple direct power that can be obtained only by putting an AVPlayerLayer into the interface yourself.

Here, I'll display the same movie as before, but without an AVPlayerViewController:

```
let m = Bundle.main.url(forResource:"ElMirage", withExtension:"mp4")!
let asset = AVURLAsset(url:m)
let item = AVPlayerItem(asset:asset)
let p = AVPlayer(playerItem:item)
self.player = p // might need a reference later
let lay = AVPlayerLayer(player:p)
lay.frame = CGRect(10,10,300,200)
self.playerLayer = lay // might need a reference later
self.view.layer.addSublayer(lay)
```

As before, if we want to prevent a flash when the video becomes ready for display, we can postpone adding the AVPlayerLayer to our interface until its `isReadyForDisplay` property becomes `true` — which we can learn through KVO.

In a WWDC 2016 video, Apple suggests an interesting twist on the preceding code: create the AVPlayer *without* an AVPlayerItem, create the AVPlayerLayer, and *then* assign the AVPlayerItem to AVPlayer, like this:

```
let m = Bundle.main.url(forResource:"ElMirage", withExtension:"mp4")!
let asset = AVURLAsset(url:m)
let item = AVPlayerItem(asset:asset)
let p = AVPlayer() // *
self.player = p
let lay = AVPlayerLayer(player:p)
lay.frame = CGRect(10,10,300,200)
self.playerLayer = lay
p.replaceCurrentItem(with: item) // *
self.view.layer.addSublayer(lay)
```

Apparently, there is some increase in efficiency if you do things in that order. The reason, it turns out, is that when an AVPlayerItem is assigned to an AVPlayer that doesn't have an associated AVPlayerLayer, the AVPlayer assumes that only the audio track of the AVAsset is important — and then, when an AVPlayerLayer *is* assigned to it, the AVPlayer must scramble to pick up the video track as well.

The movie is now visible in the interface, but it isn't doing anything. We haven't told our AVPlayer to play, and there are no transport controls, so the user can't tell the video to play either. That's why I kept a reference to the AVPlayer in a property! We can start play either by calling play or by setting the AVPlayer's rate. Here, I imagine that we've provided a simple play/pause button that toggles the playing status of the movie by changing its rate:

```
@IBAction func doButton (_ sender: Any) {
    let rate = self.player.rate
    self.player.rate = rate < 0.01 ? 1 : 0
}
```

Without trying to replicate the full transport controls, we might also like to give the user a way to jump the playhead back to the start of the movie. The playhead position is a feature of an AVPlayerItem:

```
@IBAction func restart (_ sender: Any) {
    let item = self.player.currentItem!
    let time: CMTime = CMTime(seconds:0, preferredTimescale:600)
    item.seek(to:time, completionHandler:nil)
}
```

If we want our AVPlayerLayer to support picture-in-picture, then (in addition to making the app itself support picture-in-picture, as I've already described) we need to call upon AVKit to supply us with an AVPictureInPictureController. This is *not* a view controller; it merely endows our AVPlayerLayer with picture-in-picture behavior. You create the AVPictureInPictureController (checking first to see whether the environment supports picture-in-picture in the first place), initialize it with the AVPlayerLayer, *and retain it*:

```
if AVPictureInPictureController.isPictureInPictureSupported() {
    let pic = AVPictureInPictureController(playerLayer: self.playerLayer)
    self.pic = pic
}
```

There are no transport controls, so there is no picture-in-picture button. Supplying one is up to you. Don't show the button if picture-in-picture isn't supported! When the button is tapped, tell the AVPictureInPictureController to startPictureIn-Picture:

```
@IBAction func doPicInPic(_ sender: Any) {
    if self.pic.isPictureInPicturePossible {
        self.pic.startPictureInPicture()
    }
}
```

You might also want to set yourself as the AVPictureInPictureController's delegate (AVPictureInPictureControllerDelegate). As with the AVPlayerViewController delegate, you are informed of stages in the life of the picture-in-picture window so that you can adjust your interface accordingly. When the user taps the button that dismisses the system window and returns to your app, then if the AVPlayerLayer is still sitting in your interface, there may be no work to do. If you removed the AVPlayerLayer from your interface, and you now want to restore it, implement this delegate method:

- pictureInPictureController(_:restoreUserInterfaceForPictureInPicture-StopWithCompletionHandler:)

In your implementation, configure your interface so that the AVPlayerLayer is present. Make sure that the AVPlayerLayer that you now put into your interface is *the same one* that was removed earlier; in other words, your player layer must continue to be the same as the AVPictureInPictureController's playerLayer.

Further Exploration of AV Foundation

Here are some other things you can do with AV Foundation:

- Extract single images (sometimes referred to as *thumbnails* or *poster images*) from a movie (AVAssetImageGenerator). Displaying a poster image of a video's initial frame can help cover up for the delay before the video is ready to start playing.

- Export a movie in a different format (AVAssetExportSession), or read/write raw uncompressed data through a buffer to or from a track (AVAssetReader, AVAssetReaderOutput, AVAssetWriter, AVAssetWriterInput, and so on).

- Capture audio, video, and stills through the device's hardware (AVCapture-Session and so on). I'll say more about that in Chapter 18.

- Tap into video and audio being captured or played, including capturing video frames as still images (AVPlayerItemVideoOutput, AVCaptureVideoDataOutput, and so on; and see Apple's *Technical Q&A QA1702*).

The media capabilities of AV Foundation are nicely summarized in a classic WWDC video, *https://developer.apple.com/videos/play/wwdc2011/415*.

UIVideoEditorController

UIVideoEditorController is a view controller that presents an interface where the user can trim video. Its view and internal behavior are outside your control, and you're not supposed to subclass it. You are expected to treat the view controller as a presented view controller on the iPhone or as a popover on the iPad, and respond by way of its delegate.

 UIVideoEditorController is one of the creakiest pieces of interface in iOS. It dates back to iOS 3.1, and hasn't been revised since its inception — and it looks like it. It has *never* worked properly on the iPad, and still doesn't. I'm not going to dwell on its bugginess or we'd be here all day.

Before summoning a UIVideoEditorController, be sure to call its class method `canEditVideo(atPath:)`. (This call can take some noticeable time to return.) If it returns `false`, don't instantiate UIVideoEditorController to edit the given file. Not every video format is editable, and not every device supports video editing. You must also set the UIVideoEditorController instance's `delegate` and `videoPath` before presenting it; the delegate should adopt both UINavigationControllerDelegate and UIVideoEditorControllerDelegate. You must manually set the video editor controller's `modalPresentationStyle` to `.popover` on the iPad (a good instance of the creakiness I was just referring to):

```
let path = Bundle.main.path(forResource:"ElMirage", ofType: "mp4")!
let can = UIVideoEditorController.canEditVideo(atPath:path)
if !can {
    print("can't edit this video")
    return
}
let vc = UIVideoEditorController()
vc.delegate = self
vc.videoPath = path
if UIDevice.current.userInterfaceIdiom == .pad {
    vc.modalPresentationStyle = .popover
}
self.present(vc, animated: true)
if let pop = vc.popoverPresentationController {
    let v = sender as! UIView
```

```
    pop.sourceView = v
    pop.sourceRect = v.bounds
    pop.delegate = self
}
```

The view's interface (on the iPhone) contains Cancel and Save buttons, a trimming box displaying thumbnails from the movie, a play/pause button, and the movie itself. The user slides the ends of the trimming box to set the beginning and end of the saved movie. The Cancel and Save buttons do *not* dismiss the presented view; you must do that in your implementation of the delegate methods. There are three of them, and you should implement all three and dismiss the presented view in all of them:

- `videoEditorController(_:didSaveEditedVideoToPath:)`
- `videoEditorControllerDidCancel(_:)`
- `videoEditorController(_:didFailWithError:)`

Implementing the second two delegate methods is straightforward:

```
func videoEditorControllerDidCancel(_ editor: UIVideoEditorController) {
    self.dismiss(animated:true)
}
func videoEditorController(_ editor: UIVideoEditorController,
    didFailWithError error: Error) {
        self.dismiss(animated:true)
}
```

Saving the trimmed video is more involved. Like everything else about a movie, it takes time. When the user taps Save, there's a progress view while the video is trimmed and compressed. The trimmed video has *already* been saved to a file in your app's temporary directory by the time the delegate method `videoEditor-Controller(_:didSaveEditedVideoToPath:)` is called.

 `videoEditorController(_:didSaveEditedVideoToPath:)` is actually called *twice* in quick succession. That's more of its creaky bugginess.

Doing something useful with the saved file at this point is up to you; if you merely leave it in the temporary directory, you can't rely on it to persist. In this example, I copy the edited movie into the Camera Roll album of the user's photo library, by calling `UISaveVideoAtPathToSavedPhotosAlbum`. For this to work, our app's *Info.plist* must have a meaningful "Privacy — Photo Library Additions Usage Description" entry (`NSPhotoLibraryAddUsageDescription`) so that the runtime can ask for the user's permission on our behalf:

```
func videoEditorController(_ editor: UIVideoEditorController,
    didSaveEditedVideoToPath path: String) {
        self.dismiss(animated:true)
        if UIVideoAtPathIsCompatibleWithSavedPhotosAlbum(path) {
            UISaveVideoAtPathToSavedPhotosAlbum(path, self,
                #selector(savedVideo), nil)
        } else {
            // can't save to photo album, try something else
        }
}
```

The function reference `#selector(savedVideo)` in that code refers to a callback method that must take three parameters: a String (the path), an Optional wrapping an Error, and an UnsafeMutableRawPointer. It's important to check for errors, because things can still go wrong. In particular, the user could deny us access to the photo library (see Chapter 18 for more about that). If that's the case, we'll get an Error whose domain is `ALAssetsLibraryErrorDomain`:

```
@objc func savedVideo(at path: String,
    withError error: Error?,
    ci: UnsafeMutableRawPointer) {
        if let error = error {
            print("error: \(error)")
        }
}
```

Music Library

An iOS device can be used for the same purpose as the original iPod — to hold and play music, podcasts, and audiobooks. These items constitute the device's *music library*. iOS provides the programmer with various forms of access to the music library; you can:

- Explore the music library.
- Play an item from the music library.
- Control the Music app's music player.
- Present a standard interface where the user can select a music library item.

These features are all provided by the Media Player framework; you'll need to `import MediaPlayer`.

This chapter assumes that the user's music library consists of sound files that are actually present on the device. However, the user might be using the iCloud Music Library (iTunes Match) — and, starting in iOS 11, MusicKit allows your app to interface on the user's behalf with the cloud-based Apple Music service. That's beyond the scope of this book; see the *Apple Music API Reference* for information about it.

Music Library Authorization

Access to the music library requires authorization from the user. You'll need to include in your *Info.plist* a meaningful entry under the "Privacy — Media Library Usage Description" key (`NSAppleMusicUsageDescription`) justifying to the user your desire for access, to be displayed in the authorization alert that will be presented to the user on your behalf (Figure 17-1).

Figure 17-1. The system prompts for music library access

The system, by default, will automatically present the authorization alert the first time your app attempts to access the music library. But instead of letting that happen, you will probably want to take control by checking for authorization yourself and requesting it if necessary. To learn whether you already have authorization, call the MPMediaLibrary authorizationStatus class method. The result is an MPMedia-LibraryAuthorizationStatus:

.notDetermined

Authorization has never been requested. You should request authorization, causing the system's authorization alert to appear.

.authorized

You're already authorized. Go ahead and access the music library.

.denied

You have been refused authorization. If your app depends upon music library access, you might put up an alert begging for authorization. The alert can even take the user directly to the spot in the Settings app where the user can provide authorization:

```
let url = URL(string:UIApplication.openSettingsURLString)!
UIApplication.shared.open(url)
```

.restricted

You have been refused authorization and the user may not have the power to authorize you. There's no point harassing the user about this, so it is best to do nothing.

If the authorization status is .notDetermined and you want to request authorization, call the MPMediaLibrary class method requestAuthorization. This method executes asynchronously. To hear about the user's response to the alert, you pass a completion function as parameter; it will be called, possibly on a background thread, when the user dismisses the alert, with an MPMediaLibraryAuthorizationStatus parameter. If the status is now .authorized, you can go ahead and access the music

Taking the MPMediaLibrary as an example, let's construct a general strategy for performing an action if and only if we have or can obtain authorization. This is a little tricky, because we must proceed to our action by two different paths. If we are *already* authorized, we can take our action directly; but if we *request* authorization, the reply arrives asynchronously in the completion function (see Appendix C) and we take our action there. Since the same action appears in two places, we can encapsulate our strategy as a utility function that takes the action as a function parameter; it's an Optional in case we just want to request the authorization dialog and stop:

```
func checkForMusicLibraryAccess(andThen f:(()->())? = nil) {
    // check for authorization
    let status = MPMediaLibrary.authorizationStatus()
    switch status {
    case .authorized: f?() // already have it, proceed directly
    case .notDetermined:
        // request authorization
        MPMediaLibrary.requestAuthorization() { status in
            if status == .authorized {
                DispatchQueue.main.async {
                    f?() // got it, proceed asynchronously
                }
            }
        }
    case .restricted: break // do nothing
    case .denied: break // do nothing, or beg for authorization
    @unknown default: fatalError()
    }
}
```

To retest the system authorization request alert and other access-related behaviors, go to the Settings app and choose General → Reset → Reset Location & Privacy. For a simulator, the xcrun simctl command in the Terminal lets you reset permissions generally, or grant or deny them to your app.

library. (The sidebar "Checking for Authorization" encapsulates this entire procedure into a general utility function.)

Exploring the Music Library

Everything in the user's music library, as seen by your code, is an MPMediaEntity. This is an abstract class. It has two concrete subclasses:

MPMediaItem
    An MPMediaItem is a single item (a "song").

MPMediaCollection
>An MPMediaCollection is an ordered list of MPMediaItems, rather like an array; it has a count, and its items property *is* an array.

MPMediaEntity endows its subclasses with the ability to describe themselves through key–value pairs called *properties*. The property keys have names like MPMediaItem-PropertyTitle. To fetch a property's value, call value(forProperty:) with its key. You can fetch multiple properties with enumerateValues(forProperties:using:). As a convenience, MPMediaEntity and its subclasses also have instance properties whose names correspond to the property key names. With an MPMediaItem, for instance, you can say either myItem.value(forProperty:MPMediaItemProperty-Title) or myItem.title, and in most cases you will surely prefer the latter. But you'll still need the full property key name if you're going to form an MPMediaProperty-Predicate, as I'll demonstrate later.

An MPMediaItem has a type (mediaType, or MPMediaItemPropertyMediaType); it might be music, a podcast, or an audiobook. Different types of item have slightly different properties; these will be intuitively familiar from your use of iTunes or the Music app. A song (music) has a title, an album title, a track number, an artist, a composer, and so on; a podcast, in addition to its normal title, has a podcast title.

A playlist is an MPMediaPlaylist, a subclass of MPMediaCollection. Its properties include its name, along with its attributes (playlistAttributes), an option set that tells you (for instance) whether this is a "smart" playlist.

An item's artwork image is available through an instance of the MPMediaItem-Artwork class. From this, you are supposed to be able to get the image itself scaled to a specified size by calling image(at:). My experience is that in reality you'll receive an image of any old size the system cares to give you, so you may have to scale it further yourself (see "UIImage Drawing" on page 100).

Querying the Music Library

Obtaining actual information from the music library involves a *query*, an MPMedia-Query. Querying the music library can be time-consuming; it is perfectly reasonable to do this work on a background thread (see Chapter 25).

Forming a query

First, you *form* the query. There are three main ways to do this:

Without limits
>Create a simple MPMediaQuery by calling init (that is, MPMediaQuery()). The result is an unlimited query; it asks for everything in the music library.

With a convenience constructor

MPMediaQuery provides several class methods that form a query asking the music library for a limited subset of its contents — all of its songs, or all of its podcasts, and so on:

- songs
- podcasts
- audiobooks
- playlists
- albums
- artists
- composers
- genres
- compilations

With filter predicates

You can limit a query more precisely by attaching to it one or more MPMedia-PropertyPredicate instances. These predicates filter the music library according to criteria you specify; to be included in the result, a media item must successfully pass through all the filters (in other words, the predicates are combined using logical-and). A predicate is a simple comparison. It has three aspects:

A property

The key name of the property you want to compare against. Not every property can be used in a filter predicate; the documentation makes the distinction clear, and you can get additional help from an MPMediaEntity class method, canFilter(byProperty:).

A value

The value that the property must have in order to pass through the filter.

A comparison type (optional)

An MPMediaPredicateComparison. In order to pass through the filter, a media item's property value can either *match* the value you provide (the default, .equalTo) or *contain* the value you provide (.contains).

The two ways of forming a limited query are actually the same; a convenience constructor is just a quick way of obtaining a query already endowed with a filter predicate.

A query also *groups* its results, according to its groupingType (MPMediaGrouping). Your choices are:

- `.title`
- `.album`
- `.artist`
- `.albumArtist`
- `.composer`
- `.genre`
- `.playlist`
- `.podcastTitle`

The query convenience constructors all involve a `groupingType`. Indeed, the grouping is often the salient aspect of the query. An `albums` query, for instance, is merely a `songs` query grouped by album.

Performing a query

After you form the query, you *perform* the query. You do this by asking for the query's properties:

- You can ask for its `items`, an array of MPMediaItems, if you don't care about the groups returned from the query.
- Alternatively, you can ask for its `collections`, an array of MPMediaItemCollections each of which represents one group.

An MPMediaItemCollection has a `representativeItem` property that can come in handy when it is obtained from a grouped query. It gives you just one item from the collection, and the reason you need it is that properties of a group collection are often embodied in its items rather than in the collection itself. For example, an album has no title; rather, its items have album titles that are all the same. So to learn the title of an album, you ask for the album title of a representative item.

To illustrate, I'll discover the titles of all the albums:

```
let query = MPMediaQuery.albums() // form the query
guard let result = query.collections else {return} // perform the query
// prove we've performed the query, by logging the album titles
for album in result {
    print(album.representativeItem!.albumTitle!)
}
/*
Bach, CPE, Symphonies
Beethoven Canons
Beethoven Dances
Scarlatti Continuo
*/
```

Now let's make our query more elaborate; we'll get the titles of all the albums whose name contains "Beethoven." We simply add a filter predicate to the previous query:

```
let query = MPMediaQuery.albums()
let hasBeethoven = MPMediaPropertyPredicate(value:"Beethoven",
    forProperty:MPMediaItemPropertyAlbumTitle,
    comparisonType:.contains)
query.addFilterPredicate(hasBeethoven)
guard let result = query.collections else {return}
for album in result {
    print(album.representativeItem!.albumTitle!)
}
/*
Beethoven Canons
Beethoven Dances
*/
```

Similarly, we can get the titles of all the albums containing any songs whose name contains "Sonata." This is like the previous example, but here we are concerned with the song's own title rather than its album title:

```
let query = MPMediaQuery.albums()
let hasSonata = MPMediaPropertyPredicate(value:"Sonata",
    forProperty:MPMediaItemPropertyTitle,
    comparisonType:.contains)
query.addFilterPredicate(hasSonata)
guard let result = query.collections else {return}
for album in result {
    print(album.representativeItem!.albumTitle!)
}
/*
Scarlatti Continuo
*/
```

An album is a collection of songs (MPMediaItems). Let's modify the output from our previous query to print the titles of all the matching songs in the first album returned. We don't have to change our query, so I'll start at the point where we perform it; result is the array of collections returned from our query, so result[0] is an MPMediaItemCollection holding the filtered songs of one album:

```
// ... same as before ...
let album = result[0]
for song in album.items {
    print(song.title!)
}
/*
Sonata in E minor Kk 81 - I Grave
Sonata in E minor Kk 81 - II Allegro
Sonata in E minor Kk 81 - III Grave
Sonata in E minor Kk 81 - IV Allegro
... and so on ...
*/
```

Persistence and Change in the Music Library

One of the properties of an MPMediaEntity is its `persistentID`, which uniquely identifies it. All sorts of things have persistent IDs — entities in general, songs (media items), albums, artists, composers, and more. Two songs or two playlists can have the same title, but a persistent ID is unique. It is also persistent: using the persistent ID, you can retrieve again at a later time the same song or playlist you retrieved earlier, even across launches of your app.

While you are maintaining the results of a search, the contents of the music library may themselves change. For instance, the user might connect the device to a computer and add or delete music manually. This can put your results out of date. For this reason, the library's own modified date is available through the MPMediaLibrary class. Call the class method `default` to get the actual library instance; now you can ask for its `lastModifiedDate`.

You can also register to receive a notification, `.MPMediaLibraryDidChange`, when the music library is modified. This notification is not emitted unless you first call the MPMediaLibrary instance method `beginGeneratingLibraryChangeNotifications`; you should eventually balance this with a call to `endGeneratingLibraryChange-Notifications`.

Music Player

The music player (MPMusicPlayerController) is the Media Player framework class for playing an MPMediaItem. Actually the music player plays from a *queue* of items. This behavior is familiar from iTunes and the Music app: when you tap the first song of a playlist to start playing it, then when the end of that song is reached, we proceed by default to the next song in the playlist. That's because tapping the first song of a playlist causes the queue to be the totality of songs in the playlist. The music player behaves the same way: when it reaches the end of a song, it proceeds to the next song in its queue.

Your methods for controlling playback reflect the music player's queue-based orientation. In addition to the expected `play`, `pause`, and `stop` commands, there's a `skipTo-NextItem` and `skipToPreviousItem` command. Anyone who has ever used iTunes or the Music app (or, for that matter, an old-fashioned iPod) will have an intuitive grasp of this and everything else a music player does. You can even set a music player's `repeatMode` and `shuffleMode`.

The music player comes in two flavors, depending on which class property you use to get an instance:

`systemMusicPlayer`

The very same player used by the Music app. This might already be playing an item, or it might be paused with a current item, at any time while your app runs; you can learn or change what item this is. The system music player continues playing independently of the state of your app. It has a complete built-in user interface, namely the Music app itself, where the user can at any time alter what it is doing.

`applicationQueuePlayer`

A separate player, independent of the Music app; the song it is playing can be different from the Music app's current song. Nevertheless, this player isn't entirely inside your app. It has its own audio session. Telling it to play interrupts your app's audio session; if your app's capabilities include the Audio background mode (Chapter 15), then the player will keep playing when your app is backgrounded, even if your app's audio session category is not Playback.

Either version of the player will communicate automatically with the remote playback controls (Figure 15-1), allowing the user to control it by pausing, seeking, and skipping forward or backward in the queue.

Setting the Queue

To provide a music player with its queue, you call `setQueue(with:)`. The parameter can be:

A query

You hand the music player an MPMediaQuery. The query's `items` are the items of the queue.

A collection

You hand the music player an MPMediaItemCollection. This might be derived from a query you performed, but you can also assemble your own collection of MPMediaItems in any way you like, putting them into an array and calling MPMediaItemCollection's `init(items:)`.

A descriptor

You hand the music player an MPMusicPlayerQueueDescriptor. This class was introduced in iOS 10.1 to allow the queue to contain Apple Music songs. It is abstract; its concrete subclasses are:

- MPMusicPlayerMediaItemQueueDescriptor
- MPMusicPlayerPlayParametersQueueDescriptor
- MPMusicPlayerStoreQueueDescriptor

MPMusicPlayerMediaItemQueueDescriptor has two initializers, init(query:) and init(itemCollection:). You don't need this class merely to set a music player's queue, but you can use it if you like; it will come in handy particularly when you want to *modify* a music player's queue, as I'll explain a little later. (The other two descriptor classes have to do with Apple Music, which is outside the scope of this book.)

Here are some tips, based on my own experience, for configuring a music player with its queue and making it play:

- The player can behave in unexpected ways if you don't ask it to play immediately after setting the queue; apparently the queue does not actually take effect until you do that.

- Setting the queue seems to be most reliable if you command the player to stop beforehand.

- It may be useful to insert a brief delay between setting the queue and starting to play; otherwise, the player might silently fail to play, or you can even crash.

- The player behaves much better if you keep a persistent reference to it as an instance property.

In this example, we collect all songs actually present in the library that are shorter than 30 seconds, and set them playing in random order using the application queue player (self.player):

```
DispatchQueue.global(qos:.userInitiated).async {
    let query = MPMediaQuery.songs()
    let isPresent = MPMediaPropertyPredicate(value:false,
        forProperty:MPMediaItemPropertyIsCloudItem,
        comparisonType:.equalTo)
    query.addFilterPredicate(isPresent)
    guard let items = query.items else {return}
    let shorties = items.filter {
        let dur = $0.playbackDuration
        return dur < 30
    }
    guard shorties.count > 0 else { return }
    let queue = MPMediaItemCollection(items:shorties)
    DispatchQueue.main.async {
        if self.player.playbackState == .playing {
            self.player.stop()
        }
        self.player.shuffleMode = .songs
        self.player.setQueue(with:queue)
        delay(0.2) {
            self.player.play()
        }
    }
}
```

Modifying the Queue

You can modify a player's existing queue. There are two distinct approaches:

Play next and play later
> Call prepend(_:) or append(_:). Apple characterizes these as equivalent to Play Next and Play Later functionality; prepend(_:) inserts into the queue just after the currently playing item, while append(_:) inserts at the end of the queue. The parameter is an MPMusicPlayerQueueDescriptor.

Insert and remove
> This feature is available only for the application queue player:
>
> 1. Call perform(queueTransaction:completionHandler:). Be careful with this call; if calls overlap, you can crash ("Only one queue transaction may be performed at a time").
>
> 2. Inside the queueTransaction: function, the parameter is an MPMusicPlayerControllerMutableQueue. This is a mutable subclass of MPMusicPlayerControllerQueue; you can use its items property to examine the queue.
>
> 3. Call insert(_:after:) or remove(_:) on the mutable queue. The first parameter of insert(_:after:) is an MPMusicPlayerQueueDescriptor.
>
> 4. In the completionHandler: function, the first parameter is an MPMusicPlayerControllerQueue, so you can examine the effect of your insertion or removal on the queue. The second parameter tells you whether there was an error. You can have an empty completionHandler: function body, but you can't omit the function altogether.

Player State

You can ask a music player for its nowPlayingItem, and since this is an MPMediaItem, you can learn all about it through its properties. You can ask a music player which song within the queue is currently playing (indexOfNowPlayingItem). Unfortunately, you can't ask the system music player for its actual queue! You can obtain the application queue player's current queue by misusing perform(queueTransaction:completionHandler:).

A music player has a playbackState that you can query to learn what it's doing (whether it is playing, paused, stopped, or seeking). Do not use the music player's currentPlaybackRate to learn whether the player is playing; it is not as reliable as the playbackState.

The music player emits notifications informing you of various changes in its state:

- `.MPMusicPlayerControllerPlaybackStateDidChange`

- `.MPMusicPlayerControllerNowPlayingItemDidChange`

- `.MPMusicPlayerControllerVolumeDidChange`

- `.MPMusicPlayerControllerQueueDidChange`

You can arrange to receive notifications from either of the two music players. If you are receiving notifications from both, you can distinguish them by examining the Notification's `object` and comparing it to each player.

To illustrate, I'll extend the previous example to set the text of a UILabel in our interface (`self.label`) every time a different song starts playing. The player (`self.player`) is still the application queue player. Before we start the player playing, we insert these lines to generate the notifications:

```
NotificationCenter.default.addObserver(self,
    selector: #selector(self.changed),
    name: .MPMusicPlayerControllerNowPlayingItemDidChange,
    object: self.player)
```

And here's how we respond to those notifications:

```
@objc func changed(_ n:Notification) {
    self.label.text = ""
    let player = self.player
    guard let obj = n.object, obj as AnyObject === player else {return}
    guard let title = player.nowPlayingItem?.title else {return}
    let ix = player.indexOfNowPlayingItem
    guard ix != NSNotFound else {return}
    player.perform { _ in } completionHandler: { q,_ in
        self.label.text = "\(ix+1) of \(q.items.count): \(title)"
    }
}
```

There's no periodic notification as a song plays and the current playhead position advances. To get that information, you'll have to resort to polling. This is not objectionable as long as your polling interval is reasonably sparse; your display may occasionally fall a little behind reality, but that won't usually matter. To illustrate, let's add to our existing example a UIProgressView (`self.prog`) showing the current percentage of the current song being played by the music player. I'll use a Timer to poll the state of the player every second:

```
self.timer = Timer.scheduledTimer(timeInterval:1,
    target: self, selector: #selector(self.timerFired),
    userInfo: nil, repeats: true)
self.timer.tolerance = 0.1
```

When the timer fires, the progress view displays the state of the currently playing item:

```
@objc func timerFired(_: Any) {
    let player = self.player
    guard let item = player.nowPlayingItem,
        player.playbackState != .stopped else {
            self.prog.isHidden = true
            return
    }
    self.prog.isHidden = false
    let current = player.currentPlaybackTime
    let total = item.playbackDuration
    self.prog.progress = Float(current / total)
}
```

MPVolumeView

The Media Player framework offers a slider for letting the user set the system output volume, along with an AirPlay route button if appropriate; this is an MPVolume-View. It is customizable similarly to a UISlider (Chapter 13); you can set the images for the two halves of the track and the thumb for both the normal and the highlighted state (while the user is touching the thumb).

For further customization, you can subclass MPVolumeView and override volume-SliderRect(forBounds:). (An additional overridable method is documented, volumeThumbRect(forBounds:volumeSliderRect:value:), but in my testing it is never called; I regard this as a bug.)

Playing Songs with AV Foundation

MPMusicPlayerController is convenient and easy, but it's also restrictive. The music player doesn't really belong to you. It has a fixed set of music playing behaviors, similar to iTunes or the Music app. Its audio session isn't your audio session. It takes control of the remote command center. What if that isn't what you want? How else might you play an MPMediaItem?

An MPMediaItem representing a file in the user's music library has an assetURL property whose value is a file URL. Therefore, everything from Chapters 15 and 16 comes into play. Having obtained an MPMediaItem's asset URL, you can use that URL to initialize an AVAudioPlayer, an AVAsset, or an AVPlayer (which might be wrapped in an AVPlayerViewController).

In this example, I'll use an AVQueuePlayer (an AVPlayer subclass) to play a sequence of MPMediaItems, just as an MPMusicPlayerController does. The queue player is retained in an instance property, self.qp. We might be tempted to treat it as a playlist, handing it the entire array of songs to be played:

```
let arr = // array of MPMediaItem
let items = arr.map {
    let url = $0.assetURL!
    let asset = AVAsset(url:url)
    return AVPlayerItem(asset: asset)
}
self.qp = AVQueuePlayer(items:items)
self.qp.play()
```

Instead of adding a whole batch of AVPlayerItems to an AVQueuePlayer all at once, we should probably add just a few AVPlayerItems to start with, and then append each additional AVPlayerItem when an item finishes playing. So I'll start out by storing the array in a property (`self.items`) and I'll add just three AVPlayerItems to the queue player. Then I'll use key–value observing to watch for changes in the AVQueuePlayer's `currentItem`:

```
let arr = // array of MPMediaItem
self.items = arr.map {
    let url = $0.assetURL!
    let asset = AVAsset(url:url)
    return AVPlayerItem(asset: asset)
}
let seed = min(3,self.items.count)
self.qp = AVQueuePlayer(items:Array(self.items.prefix(upTo:seed)))
self.items = Array(self.items.suffix(from:seed))
// use .initial option so that we get an observation for the first item
let ob = qp.observe(\.currentItem, options: .initial) { _,_ in
    self.changed()
}
self.obs.insert(ob) // self.obs is a Set<NSKeyValueObservation>
self.qp.play()
```

In our `changed` method, we pull an AVPlayerItem off the front of our `items` array and add it to the end of the AVQueuePlayer's queue. The AVQueuePlayer itself deletes an item from the start of its queue after playing it, so in this way the queue never exceeds four items in length:

```
guard let item = self.qp.currentItem else {return}
guard self.items.count > 0 else {return}
let newItem = self.items.removeFirst()
self.qp.insert(newItem, after:nil) // means "at end"
```

Now let's go further. Since we're already being notified each time a new song starts playing, we can insert some code to update a label's text with the title of each successive song. This will demonstrate how to extract metadata from an AVAsset by way of an AVMetadataItem. Here, we fetch the `AVMetadata.commonKeyTitle` and get its `value` property:

```
var arr = item.asset.commonMetadata
arr = AVMetadataItem.metadataItems(from:arr,
    withKey:AVMetadataKey.commonKeyTitle,
    keySpace:.common)
let met = arr[0]
let value = #keyPath(AVMetadataItem.value)
met.loadValuesAsynchronously(forKeys:[value]) {
    if met.statusOfValue(forKey:value, error:nil) == .loaded {
        guard let title = met.value as? String else {return}
        DispatchQueue.main.async {
            self.label.text = "\(title)"
        }
    }
}
```

Going even further, we can also update a progress view to reflect the current item's current time and duration. Unlike an MPMusicPlayerController, we don't need to poll with a Timer; an AVPlayer can have a *time observer*. We need to retain the time observer in a property:

```
self.timeObserver = self.qp.addPeriodicTimeObserver(
    forInterval: CMTime(seconds:0.5, preferredTimescale:600),
    queue: nil) { [unowned self] t in
        self.timerFired(time:t)
}
```

To get our AVPlayerItems to load their `duration` property, we'll need to go back and modify the code we used to initialize them:

```
let url = $0.assetURL!
let asset = AVAsset(url:url)
return AVPlayerItem(asset: asset,
    automaticallyLoadedAssetKeys: [#keyPath(AVAsset.duration)])
```

Our time observer now causes our `timerFired` method to be called periodically, reporting the current time of the current player item; we obtain the current item's `duration` and update our progress view (`self.prog`):

```
func timerFired(time:CMTime) {
    if let item = self.qp.currentItem {
        let asset = item.asset
        let dur = #keyPath(AVAsset.duration)
        if asset.statusOfValue(forKey:dur, error: nil) == .loaded {
            let dur = asset.duration
            self.prog.setProgress(Float(time.seconds/dur.seconds),
                animated: false)
        }
    }
}
```

Media Picker

The media picker (MPMediaPickerController), supplied by the Media Player framework, is a view controller whose view is a self-contained navigation interface in which the user can select a media item from the music library, similar to the Music app. You are expected to treat the picker as a presented view controller. As with any access to the music library, the media picker requires user authorization ("Checking for Authorization" on page 899); if you don't have authorization, don't present the picker.

You can use the initializer, init(mediaTypes:), to limit the type of media items displayed. You can make a prompt appear at the top of the navigation bar (prompt). You can govern whether the user can choose multiple media items or just one, with the allowsPickingMultipleItems property. You can filter out items stored in the cloud, and items protected with DRM, by setting showsCloudItems and showsItemsWithProtectedAssets, respectively, to false.

 Starting in iOS 9, the mediaTypes: values .podcast and .audioBook don't work. I believe that this is because podcasts are considered to be the purview of the Podcasts app, and audiobooks are considered to be the purview of the Books app — not the Music app. You can see podcasts and audiobooks as MPMediaEntity objects in the user's music library, but *not* by way of an MPMediaPickerController.

While the media picker controller's view is showing, you learn what the user is doing through two delegate methods (MPMediaPickerControllerDelegate); the presented view controller is not automatically dismissed, so it is up to you dismiss it in these delegate methods:

- mediaPicker(_:didPickMediaItems:)
- mediaPickerDidCancel(_:)

The behavior of the delegate methods depends on the value of the controller's allowsPickingMultipleItems:

The controller's allowsPickingMultipleItems *is* false *(the default)*
There's a Cancel button. When the user taps a media item, your mediaPicker(_:didPickMediaItems:) is called, handing you an MPMediaItemCollection consisting of that item. When the user taps Cancel, your mediaPickerDidCancel(_:) is called.

The controller's `allowsPickingMultipleItems` *is* `true`

There's a Done button. Every time the user taps a media item, it is checked to indicate that it has been selected. When the user taps Done, your `media-Picker(_:didPickMediaItems:)` is called, handing you an MPMediaItem-Collection consisting of all items the user selected — unless the user selected no items, in which case your `mediaPickerDidCancel(_:)` is called.

In this example, we put up the media picker; we then play the user's chosen media item(s) with the application queue player. The example works equally well whether `allowsPickingMultipleItems` is `true` or `false`:

```
func presentPicker (_ sender: Any) {
    checkForMusicLibraryAccess {
        let picker = MPMediaPickerController(mediaTypes:.music)
        picker.delegate = self
        self.present(picker, animated: true)
    }
}
func mediaPicker(_ mediaPicker: MPMediaPickerController,
    didPickMediaItems mediaItemCollection: MPMediaItemCollection) {
        let player = MPMusicPlayerController.applicationQueuePlayer
        player.stop()
        player.setQueue(with:mediaItemCollection)
        delay(0.2) {
            player.play()
        }
        self.dismiss(animated:true)
}
func mediaPickerDidCancel(_ mediaPicker: MPMediaPickerController) {
    self.dismiss(animated:true)
}
```

On the iPad, the media picker can be presented as is, in which case it appears by default as a modal `.pageSheet`; but it also works reasonably well as a popover, especially if we increase its `preferredContentSize`. This code presents as fullscreen on an iPhone and as a popover on an iPad:

```
let picker = MPMediaPickerController(mediaTypes:.music)
picker.delegate = self
picker.modalPresentationStyle = .popover
picker.preferredContentSize = CGSize(500,600)
self.present(picker, animated: true)
if let pop = picker.popoverPresentationController {
    if let b = sender as? UIBarButtonItem {
        pop.barButtonItem = b
    }
}
```

Photo Library and Camera

The stored photos and videos accessed by the user through the Photos app constitute the device's photo library:

- The PHPickerViewController class (new in iOS 14) can give the user an interface for exploring the photo library and choosing a photo. You'll need to `import PhotosUI`.

- The Photos framework, also known as PhotoKit, lets you access the photo library and its contents programmatically — including the ability to modify a photo's image. You'll need to `import Photos`.

The user's device may include one or more cameras, and your app might want to let the user take (*capture*) a photo or video:

- The UIImagePickerController class can give the user an interface similar to the Camera app, letting the user capture photos and videos.

- At a deeper level, the AV Foundation framework (Chapter 16) provides direct control over the camera hardware. You'll need to `import AVFoundation`.

The two subjects are related, especially because having allowed the user to capture an image, you will typically store it in the photo library, just as the Camera app does. So this chapter treats them together.

Browsing the Photo Library

PHPickerViewController is a view controller providing an interface, similar to the Photos app, in which the user can choose an item from the photo library. (PHPickerViewController is new in iOS 14, superseding the use of UIImagePickerController for this purpose.) You are expected to treat the PHPickerViewController as a presented view controller.

PHPickerViewController Presentation

The first step in using PHPickerViewController is to create a *configuration,* an instance of PHPickerConfiguration. This is a struct, so in order to set any of its properties you'll need a `var` declaration. If you're going to want to access the user's selected items directly from the photo library yourself as a PHAsset (as I'll explain later in this chapter), you'll need to initialize the configuration with a reference to the photo library:

```
var config = PHPickerConfiguration(photoLibrary: PHPhotoLibrary.shared())
```

But in general you *won't* need to do that; my examples in this section don't. Just initialize the configuration using `init`:

```
var config = PHPickerConfiguration()
```

The configuration has just two settable properties:

`selectionLimit`
> How many items the user is permitted to select simultaneously. The default is 1. Specify a higher number to permit limited multiple selection, or 0 to mean unlimited multiple selection.

`filter`
> What types of item the user will see in the picker view. Your choices (PHPicker-Filter) are `.images`, `.videos`, and `.livePhotos` — or, to specify a combination of those, supply `.any` with an array of the permitted types. The default is no filter, meaning all three types will appear in the picker view.

 If your `filter` is just `.livePhotos`, the user sees only live photos; but if your filter includes `.images` and not `.livePhotos`, the user will see live photos anyway. I regard this as a bug.

Now create the picker, set its delegate, and present it:

```
var config = PHPickerConfiguration()
// ... set selectionLimit and filter as desired ...
let picker = PHPickerViewController(configuration: config)
picker.delegate = self
self.present(picker, animated: true)
```

PHPickerViewController Delegate

When the user has finished working with the PHPickerViewController, if the user actually selected one or more items and did not cancel, the delegate (PHPickerView-ControllerDelegate) will receive this message:

- `picker(_ :didFinishPicking:)`

You must respond by dismissing the picker, which arrives in the first parameter. The second parameter is an array of PHPickerResult objects, one for each item the user selected; use these to learn of and retrieve the actual chosen images, videos, and live photos.

A PHPickerResult has just two properties:

assetIdentifier
> A string suitable for obtaining from the photo library the PHAsset corresponding to the selected item. I'll talk later about the photo library and PHAssets. In general you won't need this, and it will be nil unless you initialized the PHPicker-Configuration with the photo library.

itemProvider
> An NSItemProvider. Use it to obtain the image, live photo, or video on demand.

NSItemProvider is the same class we talked about in connection with drag and drop in Chapter 10 and in connection with action extensions in Chapter 14. The idea behind the use of an NSItemProvider here is that no data has actually been handed to you; that's a good thing, because photos can be big, and videos can be *really* big. Instead, the item provider is your gateway to obtain the data if you want it.

To learn what sort of data the item provider can provide, corresponding to what sort of item the user chose, look at the item provider's registeredTypeIdentifiers, or just ask it whether it can provide data of the corresponding type:

```
// prov is the PHPickerResult's itemProvider
if prov.hasItemConformingToTypeIdentifier(UTType.movie.identifier) {
    // it's a video
} else if prov.canLoadObject(ofClass: PHLivePhoto.self) {
    // it's a live photo
} else if prov.canLoadObject(ofClass: UIImage.self) {
    // it's a photo
}
```

In that code, the order of the tests is deliberate. A live photo can be supplied in a simple UIImage representation, so if we test for images before live photos, we won't learn that the result is a live photo.

Dealing with PHPickerViewController Results

In the PHPickerViewController delegate, you don't have to extract the data for the user's chosen items immediately. A PHPickerResult is a tiny lightweight object, so there is no penalty if you store it for later retrieval of the data (except that in the meantime the user might alter the photo library in a way that puts the item provider out of date).

But let's assume that your goal *is* to extract the data immediately, and in particular that you want to display in your interface whatever the user chose. How would you do that?

The answer, obviously, depends on what sort of item this is. Suppose it's a UIImage. Then we just ask the item provider to obtain the image and hand it to us. We could then, for example, proceed to display it in a UIImageView:

```
prov.loadObject(ofClass: UIImage.self) { im, err in
    if let im = im as? UIImage {
        DispatchQueue.main.async {
            myImageView.image = im // or whatever
        }
    }
}
```

Observe that in that code I've stepped out to the main queue before doing anything to the interface (Chapter 25). That's crucial. `loadObject(ofClass:)` operates in the background, and calls its completion handler on a background thread; but we must talk to the interface on the main thread.

An interesting problem arises if you also want the metadata that accompanies the photo in the photo library. To get it, go back to the item provider and ask for the actual image data; then use the Image I/O framework to extract the metadata as a dictionary (`import ImageIO`, and see Chapter 23):

```
let im = UTType.image.identifier
prov.loadDataRepresentation(forTypeIdentifier: im) { data, err in
    if let data = data {
        let src = CGImageSourceCreateWithData(data as CFData, nil)!
        let d = CGImageSourceCopyPropertiesAtIndex(src,0,nil)
            as! [AnyHashable:Any]
        // ...
    }
}
```

The procedure for a live photo is exactly the same, except that if you want to display the live photo as a live photo, you need a PHLivePhoto:

```
prov.loadObject(ofClass: PHLivePhoto.self) { livePhoto, err in
    if let photo = livePhoto as? PHLivePhoto {
        DispatchQueue.main.async {
            // show the live photo
        }
    }
}
```

I'll talk about *how* to display a live photo as a live photo later in this chapter.

Finally, what about a video? This is the hard case. In the first place, there is no class that represents a video, so we can't call `loadObject(ofClass:)`. And even if we could, we wouldn't want to. The last thing we want on our hands is the entirety of a video's data held in memory! What we want is the URL of a file *on disk*. That way, we can hand the URL to an AVPlayer or whatever mechanism we intend to use to display the video, as I described in Chapter 16.

Fortunately, an NSItemProvider will happily write the data directly to disk for us as it retrieves it, handing us the URL; all we have to do is call `loadFile-Representation(forTypeIdentifier:)`, which takes a completion handler with a URL parameter. However, the file in question is a temporary file that will be erased as soon as the completion handler ends — and we are going to need to step out to the main thread in order to display the video in our interface, so the completion handler will end while we are doing that. One solution would be to copy the file immediately to something that won't be so temporary; but that would be time-consuming for a large video. A better approach is to step out to the main thread *synchronously;* that's a rare thing to do, but it does no harm here, and it preserves the file long enough for our interface to take charge of it (and see Chapter 25 for more on this topic):

```
let movie = UTType.movie.identifier
prov.loadFileRepresentation(forTypeIdentifier: movie) { url, err in
    if let url = url {
        DispatchQueue.main.sync {
            // ... give the url to an AVPlayer or whatever ...
        }
    }
}
```

Observe that the call to `loadFileRepresentation` returns a Progress object that we could use to supply some additional interface if saving the video to disk is likely to take a long time.

A curious twist is that the video might be a live photo to which the Loop or Bounce effect has been applied. Implementing the looping, in that case, is up to us. We can detect this situation by examining the types registered with the item provider; the type I'm specifying is private, but I don't know how else to learn that the video is supposed to loop:

```
let loopType = "com.apple.private.auto-loop-gif"
if prov.hasItemConformingToTypeIdentifier(loopType) { // it loops
```

The video can then be displayed from its URL using an AVPlayerLooper object (mentioned in Chapter 16). Start with an AVQueuePlayer rather than an AVPlayer, configure the AVPlayerLooper and retain it in an instance property, and use the AVQueuePlayer to show the video:

```
let av = AVPlayerViewController()
let player = AVQueuePlayer(url:url)
av.player = player
self.looper = AVPlayerLooper(
    player: player, templateItem: player.currentItem!)
// ... and so on ...
```

Photos Framework

The Photos framework (import Photos), also known as PhotoKit, does for the photo library roughly what the Media Player framework does for the music library (Chapter 17), letting your code explore the library's contents — and then some. You can manipulate albums, add photos, and even perform edits on the user's photos.

The photo library itself is represented by the PHPhotoLibrary class, and by its shared instance, which you can obtain through the shared method; you do not need to retain the shared photo library instance. Then there are the classes representing the kinds of things that inhabit the library (the *photo entities*):

PHAsset
> A single photo or video file.

PHCollection
> An abstract class representing collections of all kinds. Its concrete subclasses are:

> *PHAssetCollection*
>> A collection of photos. Albums and smart albums are PHAssetCollections.

> *PHCollectionList*
>> A collection of asset collections. A folder of albums, or a smart folder, is a collection list.

Finer typological distinctions are drawn, not through subclasses, but through a system of types and subtypes, which are properties:

- A PHAsset has mediaType and mediaSubtypes properties.
- A PHAssetCollection has assetCollectionType and assetCollectionSubtype properties.
- A PHCollectionList has collectionListType and collectionListSubtype properties.

So a PHAsset might have a type of .image and a subtype of .photoPanorama; a PHAssetCollection might have a type of .album and a subtype of .albumRegular; and so on. Smart albums on the user's device help draw further distinctions: a PHAssetCollection with a type of .smartAlbum and a subtype of .smartAlbumPanoramas contains all the user's panorama photos. A PHAsset's playbackStyle draws the distinction between a still image and an animated GIF, and between a video and a looped or bounced live photo.

The photo entity classes are actually all subclasses of PHObject, an abstract class that endows them with a localIdentifier property that functions as a persistent unique identifier. (For a PHAsset, this is the same identifier that a PHPickerResult supplies as its assetIdentifier string.)

Access to the photo library requires user authorization. You'll use the PHPhoto-Library class for this. New in iOS 14, there are two types of authorization you can talk about, distinguished by the PHAccessLevel enum:

.readWrite
> Full authorization for accessing the photo library. To obtain this type of authori-zation, you will need a key "Privacy — Photo Library Usage Description" (NSPhotoLibraryUsageDescription) in your *Info.plist,* whose value is some meaningful text that the system authorization request alert can use to explain why your app wants access.

.addOnly
> Authorization only to write new items into the photo library. To obtain this type of authorization, you will need a key "Privacy — Photo Library Additions Usage Description" (NSPhotoLibraryAddUsageDescription) in your *Info.plist,* whose value is some meaningful text that the system authorization request alert can use to explain why your app wants access. This type of authorization existed in ear-lier versions of iOS, but there was no way to ask for it explicitly or to learn whether it had been granted; you just had to attempt to write to the library and see what happened (I gave an example of doing that in Chapter 16).

The idea here is that .addOnly access might be easier to obtain than .readWrite access, so you'll ask for .readWrite access only if you really need it.

Nevertheless, the user might be hesitant to grant you .readWrite access even if you really *do* need it. Therefore, new in iOS 14, the user can specify a *lower level* of .read-Write access. When the dialog appears asking the user whether to grant access, one of the buttons says Select Photos. If the user taps it, an interface similar to the PHPick-erViewController appears, where the user can specify *which photos the app can access.* This is called *limited* access.

Corresponding to these options, in Settings, the possible privacy choices for your app are Add Photos Only, Selected Photos, All Photos, and None. (The effect of these set-tings is rather confusing, depending on the order in which the user taps the buttons; I'm not going to go into details, but in my view this is an inadequate user interface.) Selected Photos means limited access.

To learn what the current authorization status is, call the PHPhotoLibrary class method authorizationStatus(for:), where the parameter (new in iOS 14) is a PHAccessLevel. In addition to the usual .notDetermined, .restricted, .denied, and .authorized, there is another possibility (new in iOS 14): .limited.

If the status is .limited, you can go ahead and access the photo library, but be aware that some types of access won't succeed. You won't be able to get information about any assets except those to which the user has granted explicit access and those you add yourself. You won't be able to create albums, or access albums that the user has created. And you won't be able to access assets or albums that are shared into the cloud.

Moreover, if the status is .limited, the system may put up the Select Photos interface again from time to time to see whether the user wants to change what photos your app can access. You can prevent that from happening by adding to your *Info.plist* the key "Prevent limited photos access alert" (PHPhotoLibraryPreventAutomatic-LimitedAccessAlert). (This key does *not* prevent the user from specifying limited access in the initial authorization request alert or the Settings app.) In addition, *you* can put up the Select Photos interface, to ask the user to extend your access; call the PHPhotoLibrary instance method presentLimitedLibraryPicker(from:), where the parameter is your view controller.

A .limited status does not affect your ability to write into the library as a whole if you have .addOnly access. And the status in general does not affect your ability to use the PHPickerViewController! It is out of process and doesn't require access permission from the user.

To ask the system to put up the authorization request alert if the status is .notDetermined, you can call the PHPhotoLibrary class method requestAuthorization(for:handler:), where the first parameter (new in iOS 14) is a PHAccessLevel. The resulting status is reported to you asynchronously in the handler: function. See "Checking for Authorization" on page 899 for a discussion of authorization strategy.

In the rest of this chapter, for simplicity, I'll assume that we have full access to the photo library.

Querying the Photo Library

When you want to know what's in the photo library, start with the photo entity class that represents the type of entity you want to know about. It will supply class methods whose names begin with fetch; you'll pick the class method that expresses the kind of criteria you're starting with. So to fetch one or more PHAssets, you'll call a PHAsset fetch method; you can fetch by local identifier, by media type, or by containing asset collection. Similarly, to fetch one or more PHAssetCollections, you'll call a PHAssetCollection `fetch` method; you can fetch by identifier, by type and sub-type, or by whether they contain a given PHAsset.

In addition to the various `fetch` method parameters, you can supply a PHFetch-Options object letting you refine the results even further. You can set its `predicate` to limit your request results, and its `sortDescriptors` to determine the results order. Its `fetchLimit` can limit the number of results returned, and its `includeAssetSource-Types` can specify where the results should come from, such as eliminating cloud items.

What you get back from a `fetch` method query is not images or videos but *information*. A `fetch` method returns a list of PHObjects of the type to which you sent the `fetch` method originally; these *refer* to entities in the photo library, rather than handing you an entire file (which would be huge and might take considerable time). The list itself is expressed as a PHFetchResult, which behaves very like an array: you can ask for its `count`, obtain the object at a given index, look for an object within the collection, extract objects into an array, and enumerate the objects with an `enumerate` method.

 You cannot directly enumerate a PHFetchResult with `for...in` in Swift, even though you can do so in Objective-C. I regard this as a bug (caused by the fact that PHFetchResult is a generic).

Let's list all albums created by the user. An album is a PHAssetCollection, so the relevant class is PHAssetCollection:

```
let result = PHAssetCollection.fetchAssetCollections(
    with: .album, subtype: .albumRegular, options: nil)
let albums = result.objects(at: IndexSet(0..<result.count))
for album in albums {
    let count = album.estimatedAssetCount
    print("\(album.localizedTitle!):",
        "approximately \(count) photos")
}
```

In that code, we can learn how many assets are in each album only as its `estimated-AssetCount`. This is probably the right answer, but to obtain the real count, we'd have to dive one level deeper and fetch the album's actual assets. Let's do that: given an `album`, let's list its contents. An album's contents are its assets (photos and videos), so the relevant class is PHAsset:

```
let result = PHAsset.fetchAssets(in:album, options: nil)
let assets = result.objects(at: IndexSet(0..<result.count))
for asset in assets {
    print(asset.localIdentifier)
}
```

If the fetch method you need seems not to exist, don't forget about PHFetchOptions. There is no PHAsset fetch method for fetching from a certain collection all assets of a certain type; you cannot specify, for instance, that you want all photos (but no videos) from the user's Camera Roll. But you can perform such a fetch by setting the PHFetchOptions predicate property. To illustrate, I'll fetch ten ordinary photos (no videos, and no HDR photos) from the user's Recent smart album:

```
let recentAlbums = PHAssetCollection.fetchAssetCollections(
    with: .smartAlbum, subtype: .smartAlbumRecentlyAdded, options: nil)
guard let rec = recentAlbums.firstObject else {return}
let options = PHFetchOptions()
let pred = NSPredicate(
    format: "mediaType == %d && !((mediaSubtype & %d) == %d)",
    PHAssetMediaType.image.rawValue,
    PHAssetMediaSubtype.photoHDR.rawValue,
    PHAssetMediaSubtype.photoHDR.rawValue)
options.predicate = pred // photos only, please, no HDRs
options.fetchLimit = 10 // let's not take all day about it
let photos = PHAsset.fetchAssets(in:rec, options: options)
```

Modifying the Library

Structural modifications to the photo library are performed through a *change request class* corresponding to the class of photo entity we wish to modify. The name of the change request class is the name of a photo entity class followed by "ChangeRequest." For PHAsset, there's the PHAssetChangeRequest class — and so on.

To use a change request, you'll call a performChanges method on the shared photo library. Typically, that method will be performChanges(_:completionHandler:), which takes two functions. The first function, the *changes function*, is where you describe the changes you want performed; the second function, the *completion function*, is called back after the changes have been performed.

Each change request class comes with methods that ask for a change of some particular type. Here are some examples:

PHAssetChangeRequest

Class methods include deleteAssets(_:), creationRequestForAssetFromImage(atFileURL:), and so on.

If you're creating an asset and what you're starting with is raw data, call PHAssetCreationRequest.forAsset(). That gives you a PHAssetCreationRequest, a subclass of PHAssetChangeRequest that provides instance methods such as addResource(with:data:options:).

PHAssetCollectionChangeRequest

Class methods include `deleteAssetCollections(_:)` and `creationRequestFor-AssetCollection(withTitle:)`.

In addition, there are initializers like `init(for:)`, which takes an asset collection, along with instance methods `addAssets(_:)`, `removeAssets(_:)`, and so on.

A `creationRequest` class method also returns an instance of the change request class. You can throw this away if you don't need it for anything. Its purpose is to let you perform further changes as part of the same batch. For example, once you have a PHAssetChangeRequest instance, you can use its properties to initialize the asset's features, such as its creation date or its associated geographical location; those would be read-only if accessed through the PHAsset.

To illustrate, let's create an album called "Test Album." An album is a PHAsset-Collection, so we start with the PHAssetCollectionChangeRequest class and call its `creationRequestForAssetCollection(withTitle:)` class method in the `perform-Changes` function. This method returns a PHAssetCollectionChangeRequest instance, but we don't need that instance for anything, so we simply throw it away:

```
PHPhotoLibrary.shared().performChanges {
    let t = "TestAlbum"
    typealias Req = PHAssetCollectionChangeRequest
    Req.creationRequestForAssetCollection(withTitle:t)
}
```

(The class name PHAssetCollectionChangeRequest is very long, so I've shortened it with a type alias.)

It may appear, in that code, that we didn't actually *do* anything — we asked for a creation request, but we didn't tell it to do any creating. Nevertheless, that code is sufficient; generating the creation request for a new asset collection in the `perform-Changes` function constitutes an instruction to create an asset collection.

All the same, that code is rather silly. The album was created asynchronously, so to use it, we need a completion function (see Appendix C). Moreover, we're left with no reference to the album we created. For that, we need a PHObjectPlaceholder. This minimal PHObject subclass has just one property — `localIdentifier`, which it inherits from PHObject. That's sufficient to permit a reference to the created object to survive into the completion function, where we can do something useful with it, such as saving it off to an instance property:

```
var ph : PHObjectPlaceholder?
PHPhotoLibrary.shared().performChanges {
    let t = "TestAlbum"
    typealias Req = PHAssetCollectionChangeRequest
    let cr = Req.creationRequestForAssetCollection(withTitle:t)
    ph = cr.placeholderForCreatedAssetCollection
```

```
    } completionHandler: { ok, err in
        if ok, let ph = ph {
            self.newAlbumId = ph.localIdentifier
        }
    }
}
```

Now suppose we subsequently want to populate our newly created album. Let's say we want to make the first asset in the user's Recently Added smart album a member of our new album as well. No problem! First, we need a reference to the Recently Added album; then we need a reference to its first asset; and finally, we need a reference to our newly created album (whose identifier we've already captured as self.newAlbumId). Those are all basic fetch requests, which we can perform in succession, and we then use their results to form the change request:

```
// find Recently Added smart album
let result = PHAssetCollection.fetchAssetCollections(
    with: .smartAlbum, subtype: .smartAlbumRecentlyAdded, options: nil)
guard let rec = result.firstObject else { return }
// find its first asset
let result2 = PHAsset.fetchAssets(in:rec, options: nil)
guard let asset1 = result2.firstObject else { return }
// find our newly created album by its local id
let result3 = PHAssetCollection.fetchAssetCollections(
    withLocalIdentifiers: [self.newAlbumId], options: nil)
guard let alb2 = result3.firstObject else { return }
// ready to perform the change request
PHPhotoLibrary.shared().performChanges {
    typealias Req = PHAssetCollectionChangeRequest
    let cr = Req(for: alb2)
    cr?.addAssets([asset1] as NSArray)
}
```

A PHObjectPlaceholder has a further use. What if we created, say, an asset collection and wanted to add *it* to something (presumably to a PHCollectionList), all in one batch request? Requesting the creation of an asset collection gives us a PHAssetCollectionChangeRequest instance; you can't add *that* to a collection. And the requested PHAssetCollection itself hasn't been created yet! The solution is to obtain a PHObjectPlaceholder. Because it is a PHObject, it can be used as the argument of change request methods such as addChildCollections(_:).

Being Notified of Changes

When the library is modified, whether by your code or by some other means while your app is running, any information you've collected about the library — information which you may even be displaying in your interface at that very moment — may become out of date. To cope with this possibility, you should, perhaps very early in the life of your app, register a change observer (adopting the PHPhotoLibraryChangeObserver protocol) with the photo library:

```
PHPhotoLibrary.shared().register(self)
```

The outcome is that, whenever the library changes, the observer's `photoLibraryDid-Change(_:)` method is called, with a PHChange object encapsulating a description of the change. The observer can then probe the PHChange object by calling `change-Details(for:)`. The idea is that if you're hanging on to information in an instance property, you can use what the PHChange object tells you to modify that information (and possibly your interface). The parameter can be one of two types:

A PHObject

The parameter is a single PHAsset, PHAssetCollection, or PHCollectionList you're interested in. The result is a PHObjectChangeDetails object, with properties like `objectBeforeChanges`, `objectAfterChanges`, and `objectWasDeleted`.

A PHFetchResult

The result is a PHFetchResultChangeDetails object, with properties like `fetch-ResultBeforeChanges`, `fetchResultAfterChanges`, `removedObjects`, `inserted-Objects`, and so on.

Suppose my interface is displaying a list of album names, which I obtained originally through a PHAssetCollection fetch request. And suppose that, at the time that I performed the fetch request, I also retained as an instance property (`self.albums`) the PHFetchResult that it returned. Then if my `photoLibraryDidChange(_:)` method is called, I can update the fetch result and change my interface accordingly:

```
func photoLibraryDidChange(_ changeInfo: PHChange) {
    if self.albums !== nil {
        let details = changeInfo.changeDetails(for:self.albums)
        if details !== nil {
            self.albums = details!.fetchResultAfterChanges
            // ... and adjust interface if needed ...
        }
    }
}
```

New in iOS 14, `photoLibraryDidChange(_:)` is called when your app has `.limited` access and the user changes the set of photos to which your app has access in the Select Photos interface. The reason is that, as far as your app is concerned, it is as if the user had altered the contents of the photo library.

Fetching Images

Sooner or later, you'll probably want to go beyond information about the structure of the photo library and fetch an actual photo or video for display in your app. The process of obtaining an image can be time-consuming: not only may the image data be large, but also it may be stored in the cloud. Therefore you will typically supply a completion function that can be called back *asynchronously* with the data (see Appendix C).

To obtain an image, you'll need an *image manager*, which you'll get by calling the PHImageManager `default` class method. You then call a method whose name starts with `request`, supplying a completion function. For an image, you can ask for a UIImage or the original data; for a video, you can ask for an AVPlayerItem or an AVAsset configured for display of the video, or an AVAssetExportSession suitable for exporting the video to a new file (see Chapter 16). The result comes back to you as a parameter passed into your completion function.

Asking for a UIImage

If you're asking for a UIImage, information about the image may increase in accuracy and detail in the course of time — with the curious consequence that your completion function may be called multiple times. The idea is to give you *some* image to display as fast as possible, with better versions of the image arriving later. If you would rather receive just *one* version of the image, you can specify that through a PHImageRequestOptions object (as I'll explain in a moment).

The various `request` methods take parameters letting you refine the details of the data-retrieval process. When asking for a UIImage, you supply these parameters:

`targetSize:`
> The size of the desired image. It is a waste of memory to ask for an image larger than you need for actual display, and a larger image may take longer to supply (and a photo, remember, is a *very* large image). The image retrieval process performs the desired downsizing so that you don't have to. For the largest possible size, pass `PHImageManagerMaximumSize`.

`contentMode:`
> A PHImageContentMode, either `.aspectFit` or `.aspectFill`, with respect to your `targetSize`. With `.aspectFill`, the image retrieval process does any needed cropping so that you don't have to.

`options:`
> A PHImageRequestOptions object. This is a value class representing a grab-bag of additional tweaks, such as:
>
> `.version`
> > Do you want the original image (`.original`) or the edited image (`.current`)?

`.resizeMode`

Do you want the image sized exactly to your `targetSize` (`.exact`), or will you accept a larger version (`.fast`)?

`.normalizedCropRect`

Do you want custom cropping?

`.isNetworkAccessAllowed`, `.progressHandler`

Do you want the image fetched over the network if necessary, and if so, do you want to install a progress callback function?

`.deliveryMode`

Do you want one call to your completion function, or many (`.opportunistic`)? If one, do you want a degraded thumbnail which will arrive quickly (`.fastFormat`), or the best possible quality which may take some considerable time (`.highQualityFormat`)?

`.isSynchronous`

Do you want the image fetched synchronously? If you do, you will get only *one* call to your completion function — but then you *must* make your call *on a background thread*, and the image will arrive on that same background thread (see Chapter 25).

In this simple example, I have a view controller called DataViewController, good for displaying one photo in an image view (`self.iv`). It has a PHAsset property, `self.asset`, which is assumed to have been set when this view controller instance was created. In `viewDidLoad`, I call my `setUpInterface` utility method to populate the interface:

```
func setUpInterface() {
    guard let asset = self.asset else { return }
    let opts = PHImageRequestOptions()
    opts.resizeMode = .exact
    PHImageManager.default().requestImage(for: asset,
        targetSize: CGSize(300,300), contentMode: .aspectFit,
        options: opts) { im, info in
            if let im = im {
                self.iv.image = im
            }
    }
}
```

This may result in the image view's `image` being set multiple times, as the requested image is supplied repeatedly, with its quality improving each time; but there is nothing wrong with that. Using this technique with a UIPageViewController, you can easily write an app that allows the user to browse photos one at a time.

The second parameter in an image request's completion function is a dictionary whose elements may be useful in certain circumstances. Among the keys are:

PHImageResultRequestIDKey

Uniquely identifies a single image request for which this result function is being called multiple times. This value is also *returned* by the original request method call (I didn't bother to capture it in the previous example). You can also use this identifier to call cancelImageRequest(_:) if it turns out that you don't need this image after all.

PHImageCancelledKey

Reports that an attempt to cancel an image request with cancelImage-Request(_:) succeeded.

PHImageResultIsInCloudKey

Warns that the image is in the cloud and that your request must be resubmitted with the PHImageRequestOptions isNetworkAccessAllowed property set to true.

Cancelling and caching

If your interface is a table view or collection view, the asynchronous, time-consuming nature of image fetching is clearly significant. As the user scrolls, a cell comes into view and you request the corresponding image. But as the user keeps scrolling, that cell goes out of view, and now the requested image, if it hasn't arrived, is no longer needed, so you cancel the request. (I'll tackle the same sort of problem with regard to internet-based images in a table view in Chapter 24.)

There is also a PHImageManager subclass, PHCachingImageManager, that can help do the opposite: you can prefetch some images *before* the user scrolls to view them, improving response time. For an example that displays photos in a UICollection-View, look at Apple's PhotoBrowsing sample code (available from the "Browsing and Modifying Photo Albums" help document). It uses the PHImageManager class to fetch individual photos; but for the UICollectionViewCell thumbnails, it uses PHCachingImageManager.

Live photos, videos, and data

If a PHAsset represents a live photo, you can call the PHImageManager requestLive-Photo method, parallel to requestImage; what you get in the completion function is a PHLivePhoto. Here, I'll fetch a live photo (from a PHAsset called asset), and I'll display it in the interface; this illustrates the use of a PHLivePhotoView, which displays a live photo *as* a live photo:

```
let opts = PHLivePhotoRequestOptions()
opts.deliveryMode = .highQualityFormat
PHImageManager.default().requestLivePhoto(
    for: asset, targetSize: CGSize(300,300),
    contentMode: .aspectFit, options: opts) { photo, info in
        let v = PHLivePhotoView(frame: CGRect(20,20,300,300))
        v.contentMode = .scaleAspectFit
        v.livePhoto = photo
        self.view.addSubview(v)
}
```

Fetching a video resource is far simpler, and there's little to say about it. In this example, I fetch a reference to the first video in the user's photo library and display it in the interface (using an AVPlayerViewController); unlike an image, I am not guaranteed that the result will arrive on the main thread, so I must step out to the main thread before interacting with the app's user interface:

```
func fetchMovie() {
    let opts = PHFetchOptions()
    opts.fetchLimit = 1
    let result = PHAsset.fetchAssets(with: .video, options: opts)
    guard let asset = result.firstObject else {return}
    PHImageManager.default().requestPlayerItem(
        forVideo: asset, options: nil) { item, info in
            if let item = item {
                DispatchQueue.main.async {
                    self.display(item:item)
                }
            }
    }
}
func display(item:AVPlayerItem) {
    let player = AVPlayer(playerItem: item)
    let vc = AVPlayerViewController()
    vc.player = player
    vc.view.frame = self.v.bounds
    self.addChild(vc)
    self.v.addSubview(vc.view)
    vc.didMove(toParent: self)
}
```

You can also access an asset's various kinds of data directly through the PHAsset-ResourceManager class. The request method takes a PHAssetResource object based on a PHAsset or PHLivePhoto. You can retrieve an image's RAW and JPEG data separately. For a list of the data types we're talking about here, see the documentation on the PHAssetResourceType enum.

Editing Images

Astonishingly, PhotoKit allows you to *change* an image in the user's photo library. Why is this even legal? There are two reasons:

- The user will have to give permission every time your app proposes to modify a photo in the library, and will be shown the proposed modification beforehand.

- Changes to library photos are undoable, because the original image remains in the database along with the changed image that the user sees, and the user can revert to that original at any time.

How to change a photo image

To change a photo image is a three-step process:

1. You send a PHAsset this message:

    - `requestContentEditingInput(with:completionHandler:)`

   Your completion function is called, and is handed a PHContentEditingInput object. This object wraps some image data that you can display to the user (`displaySizeImage`), along with a pointer to the real image data as a file (`fullSizeImageURL`).

2. You create a PHContentEditingOutput object by calling its initializer:

    - `init(contentEditingInput:)`

   The argument is the PHContentEditingInput object. The PHContentEditing-Output object has a `renderedContentURL` property, representing a file URL. Your mission is to *write the edited photo image data to that URL*. What you'll typically do is:

    a. Fetch the image data from the PHContentEditingInput object's `fullSizeImageURL`.

    b. Process the image.

    c. Write the resulting image data to the PHContentEditingOutput object's `renderedContentURL`.

3. You notify the photo library that it should pick up the edited version of the photo. To do so, you call `performChanges(_:completionHandler:)` and, inside the changes function, create a PHAssetChangeRequest and set its `content-EditingOutput` property to the PHContentEditingOutput object. The user will now be shown the alert requesting permission to modify this photo; your completion function is then called, with a first parameter of `false` if the user refuses (or if anything else goes wrong).

Handling the adjustment data

So far, so good. However, if you do *only* what I have just described, your attempt to modify the photo will fail. The reason is that I have omitted something: before the third step, you *must* set the PHContentEditingOutput object's `adjustmentData` property to a newly instantiated PHAdjustmentData object. The initializer is:

- `init(formatIdentifier:formatVersion:data:)`

What goes into the initializer parameters is completely up to you, but the goal is to store with the photo a message to your future self in case you are called upon to edit the *same* photo again on some *later* occasion. In that message, you describe to yourself how you edited the photo on *this* occasion.

Your handling of the adjustment data works in three steps, interwoven with the three steps I already outlined. As you start to edit the photo, first you say whether you *can* read its existing PHAdjustmentData, and then you *do* read its existing PHAdjustmentData and use it as part of your editing; when you have finished editing the photo, you make a *new* PHAdjustmentData, ready for the *next* time you edit this same photo:

1. When you call `requestContentEditingInput`, the first argument (`with:`) should be a PHContentEditingInputRequestOptions object. You have created this object and set its `canHandleAdjustmentData` property to a function that takes a PHAdjustmentData and returns a Bool. This Bool will be based mostly on whether you recognize this photo's PHAdjustmentData as yours — typically because you recognize its `formatIdentifier`. That determines what image you'll get when you receive your PHContentEditingInput object:

   Your `canHandleAdjustmentData` *function returns* `false`
   The image you'll be editing is the edited image displayed in the Photos app.

   Your `canHandleAdjustmentData` *function returns* `true`
   The image you'll be editing is the *original* image, stripped of your edits. This is because, by returning `true`, you are asserting that you can reconstruct your edits based on what's in the PHAdjustmentData's `data`.

2. When your completion function is called and you receive your PHContent-EditingInput object, it has (you guessed it) an `adjustmentData` property, which is an Optional wrapping a PHAdjustmentData object. If this isn't `nil`, and if you edited this image previously, its `data` is the `data` you put in the last time you edited this image, and you are expected to extract it and use it to recreate the edited state of the image.

3. After editing the image, when you prepare the PHContentEditingOutput object, you give it a *new* PHAdjustmentData object whose `data` summarizes the *new*

edited state of the photo from your point of view — and so the whole cycle can start again if the same photo is to be edited again later.

Example: Before editing

An actual implementation is quite straightforward and almost pure boilerplate. The details will vary only in regard to the actual editing of the photo and the particular form of the data by which you'll summarize that editing — so, in constructing an example, I'll keep that part very simple. Recall my example of a custom "vignette" CIFilter called MyVignetteFilter ("CIFilter and CIImage" on page 106). I'll provide an interface whereby the user can apply that filter to a photo. My interface will include:

- A slider that allows the user to set the *degree* of vignetting that should be applied (MyVignetteFilter's `inputPercentage`).
- A button that lets the user remove *all* vignetting from the photo, even if that vignetting was applied in a previous editing session.

First, I'll plan the structure of the PHAdjustmentData:

`formatIdentifier`
> This can be any unique string; I'll use `"com.neuburg.matt.PhotoKit-Images.vignette"`, a constant that I'll store in a property (`self.myidentifier`).

`formatVersion`
> This is likewise arbitrary; I'll use `"1.0"`.

`data`
> This will express the only thing about my editing that is adjustable — the `input-Percentage`. The `data` will wrap an NSNumber which itself wraps a Double whose value is the `inputPercentage`.

As editing begins, I construct the PHContentEditingInputRequestOptions object that determines whether a photo's most recent editing belongs to me. Then, starting with the photo that is to be edited (a PHAsset), I ask for the PHContentEditingInput object:

```
let options = PHContentEditingInputRequestOptions()
options.canHandleAdjustmentData = { adjustmentData in
    return adjustmentData.formatIdentifier == self.myidentifier
}
var id : PHContentEditingInputRequestID = 0
id = self.asset.requestContentEditingInput(with: options) { input, info in
    // ...
}
```

In the completion function, I receive my PHContentEditingInput object as a parameter (`input`). I'm going to need this object later when editing ends, so I immediately store it in a property. I then unwrap its `adjustmentData`, extract the `data`, and construct the editing interface; in this case, that happens to be a presented view controller, but the details are irrelevant and are omitted here:

```
guard let input = input else {
    self.asset.cancelContentEditingInputRequest(id)
    return
}
self.input = input
let im = input.displaySizeImage! // show this to user during editing
if let adj = input.adjustmentData,
adj.formatIdentifier == self.myidentifier {
    if let vigNumber = try? NSKeyedUnarchiver.unarchivedObject(
        ofClass: NSNumber.self, from: adj.data),
    let vigAmount = vigNumber as? Double {
        // ... store vigAmount ...
    }
}
// ... present editing interface, passing it the vigAmount ...
```

The important thing about that code is how we deal with the `adjustmentData` and its `data`. The question is whether we *have* data, and whether we recognize this as *our* data from some previous edit on this image. This will affect how our editing interface needs to behave. There are two possibilities:

It's our data

> If we were able to extract a `vigAmount` from the `adjustmentData`, then the `displaySizeImage` is the original, unvignetted image. Therefore, our editing interface initially applies the `vigAmount` of vignetting to this image — *reconstructing* the vignetted state of the photo as shown in the Photos app, while allowing the user to *change* the amount of vignetting, or even to remove all vignetting entirely.

It's not our data

> On the other hand, if we *weren't* able to extract a `vigAmount` from the `adjustmentData`, then there is nothing to reconstruct; the `displaySizeImage` is the actual photo image from the Photos app, and our editing interface will apply vignetting to it directly.

Example: After editing

Let's skip ahead now to the point where the user's interaction with our editing interface comes to an end. If the user cancelled, that's all; the user doesn't want to modify the photo after all. Otherwise, the user either asked to apply a certain amount of vignetting (`vignette`) or asked to remove all vignetting; in the latter case, I use an arbitrary `vignette` value of -1 as a signal.

Up to now, our editing interface has been using the displaySizeImage to show the user a *preview* of what the edited photo would look like. Now the time has come to perform the vignetting that the user is asking us to perform — that is, we must apply this amount of vignetting to the *real* photo image, which has been sitting waiting for us all this time, untouched, at the PHContentEditingInput's fullSizeImageURL. This is a big image, which will take significant time to load, to alter, and to save (which is why we haven't been working with it in the editing interface).

So, depending on the value of vignette requested by the user, I either pass the input image from the fullSizeImageURL through my vignette filter or I don't:

```
let inurl = self.input.fullSizeImageURL!
let output = PHContentEditingOutput(contentEditingInput:self.input)
let outurl = output.renderedContentURL
var ci = CIImage(contentsOf: inurl, options: [.applyOrientationProperty:true])!
let space = ci.colorSpace!
if vignette >= 0.0 {
    let vig = MyVignetteFilter()
    vig.setValue(ci, forKey: "inputImage")
    vig.setValue(vignette, forKey: "inputPercentage")
    ci = vig.outputImage!
}
```

Don't forget about setting the PHContentEditingOutput's adjustmentData! My goal here is to send a message to myself, in case I am asked later to edit this same image again, stating what amount of vignetting is already applied to the image. That amount is represented by vignette — so that's the value I store in the adjustment-Data:

```
let data = try! NSKeyedArchiver.archivedData(
    withRootObject: vignette, requiringSecureCoding: true)
output.adjustmentData = PHAdjustmentData(
    formatIdentifier: self.myidentifier, formatVersion: "1.0", data: data)
```

Finally, I must write a JPEG to the PHContentEditingOutput's renderedContentURL:

```
try! CIContext().writeJPEGRepresentation(of:ci, to:outurl, colorSpace:space)
```

Some of that code is time-consuming, particularly where I read and write the data with these methods:

- CIImage init(contentsOf:options:)
- CIContext writeJPEGRepresentation(of:to:colorSpace:)

So in real life I call it on a background thread (Chapter 25), and I also show a UIActivityIndicatorView to let the user know that work is being done.

We conclude by telling the photo library to retrieve the edited image. This will cause the alert to appear, asking the user whether to allow us to modify this photo. If the user taps Modify, the modification is made, and if we are displaying the image, we should get onto the main thread and redisplay it:

```
PHPhotoLibrary.shared().performChanges {
    typealias Req = PHAssetChangeRequest
    let req = Req(for: self.asset)
    req.contentEditingOutput = output // triggers alert
} completionHandler: { ok, err in
    if ok {
        // if we are displaying the image, redisplay it on the main thread
    } else {
        // user refused to allow modification, do nothing
    }
}
```

You can also edit a live photo, using a PHLivePhotoEditingContext: you are handed each frame of the video as a CIImage, making it easy to apply a CIFilter. For a demonstration, see Apple's Photo Edit sample app (also known as Sample Photo Editing Extension).

Photo Editing Extension

A photo editing extension is photo-modifying code supplied by your app that is effectively injected into the Photos app. When the user edits a photo *from within the Photos app*, your extension appears as an option and can modify the photo being edited.

To make a photo editing extension, create a new target in your app, specifying iOS → Application Extension → Photo Editing Extension. The template supplies a storyboard containing one scene, along with the code file for a corresponding UIViewController subclass. This file imports not only the Photos framework but also the Photos UI framework, which supplies the PHContentEditingController protocol, to which the view controller conforms. This protocol specifies the methods through which the runtime will communicate with your extension's code.

A photo editing extension works almost exactly the same way as modifying photo library assets in general, as I described in the preceding section. The chief differences are:

- You don't put a Done or a Cancel button into your editing interface. The Photos app will wrap your editing interface in its own interface, providing those buttons when it presents your view.

- You must situate the pieces of your code so as to respond to the calls that will come through the PHContentEditingController methods.

The PHContentEditingController methods are:

`canHandle(_:)`

You will not be instantiating PHContentEditingInput; the runtime will do it for you. Therefore, instead of configuring a PHContentEditingInputRequestOptions object and setting its `canHandleAdjustmentData`, you implement this method; you'll receive the PHAdjustmentData and return a Bool.

`startContentEditing(with:placeholderImage:)`

The runtime has obtained the PHContentEditingInput object for you. Now it supplies that object to you, along with a very temporary initial version of the image to be displayed in your interface; you are expected to replace this with the PHContentEditingInput object's `displaySizeImage`. Just as in the previous section's code, you should retain the PHContentEditingInput object in a property, as you will need it again later.

`cancelContentEditing`

The user tapped Cancel. You may well have nothing to do here.

`finishContentEditing(completionHandler:)`

The user tapped Done. In your implementation, you get onto a background thread (the template configures this for you) and do *exactly* the same thing you would do if this were not a photo editing extension — get the PHContentEditing-Output object and set its `adjustmentData`; get the photo from the PHContent-EditingInput object's `fullSizeImageURL`, modify it, and save the modified image as a full-quality JPEG at the PHContentEditingOutput object's `renderedContent-URL`. When you're done, *don't* notify the PHPhotoLibrary; instead, call the `completionHandler` that arrived as a parameter, handing it the PHContent-EditingOutput object.

During the time-consuming part of this method, the Photos app puts up a UIActivityIndicatorView, just as I suggested you might want to do in your own app. When you call the `completionHandler`, there is no alert asking the user to confirm the modification of the photo; the user is already *in* the Photos app and has explicitly asked to edit the photo, so no confirmation is needed.

Using the Camera

Use of the camera requires user authorization. You'll use the AVCaptureDevice class for this (part of the AV Foundation framework; `import AVFoundation`). To learn what the current authorization status is, call the class method `authorization-Status(forMediaType:)`. To ask the system to put up the authorization request alert if the status is `.notDetermined`, call the class method `requestAccess(forMedia-Type:completionHandler:)`. The media type (AVMediaType) will be `.video`; this embraces capturing both still photos and movies. Your app's *Info.plist* must contain some meaningful text that the system authorization request alert can use to explain why your app wants camera use; the relevant key is "Privacy — Camera Usage Description" (NSCameraUsageDescription).

If your app will let the user capture movies (as opposed to still photos), you will also need to obtain permission from the user to access the microphone. The same methods apply, but with argument .audio. Your app's *Info.plist* must contain some explanatory text under the "Privacy — Microphone Usage Description" key (NSMicrophoneUsageDescription). See "Checking for Authorization" on page 899 for discussion of authorization strategy.

Having included the relevant *Info.plist* keys, it is quite reasonable *not* to ask explicitly for authorization, as the system will put up the appropriate authorization dialog on your behalf when the user attempts to capture a photo or a video. But you should still check the authorization status, because there is no point providing the user with any camera interface at all if you have already been denied authorization.

 Use of the camera is greatly curtailed, and is interruptible, under iPad multitasking. Watch WWDC 2015 video 211 for details.

Capture with UIImagePickerController

The simplest way to prompt the user to take a photo or video is with the UIImagePickerController class. It provides an interface that is effectively a limited subset of the Camera app. (In iOS 13 and before, UIImagePickerController was used also to let the user browse the photo library; now that iOS 14 provides the PHPickerViewController, the camera aspect of the UIImagePickerController will be the *only* aspect you'll use.)

Here's how to prepare:

1. Call the class method isSourceTypeAvailable(_:) with parameter .camera; if the result is false, the user's device has no camera or the camera is unavailable, so stop at this point.

2. Call the class method availableMediaTypes(for:.camera) to learn whether the user can take a still photo (UTType.image.identifier), a video (UTType.movie.identifier), or both.

3. Instantiate UIImagePickerController, set its source type to .camera, and set its mediaTypes in accordance with which types you just learned are available. If your setting is an array of both types, the user will see a Camera-like interface allowing a choice of either one.

4. Set a delegate, adopting UINavigationControllerDelegate and UIImagePickerControllerDelegate.

Now you can present the picker:

```
let src = UIImagePickerController.SourceType.camera
guard UIImagePickerController.isSourceTypeAvailable(src)
    else {return}
guard = UIImagePickerController.availableMediaTypes(for:src) != nil
    else {return}
let picker = UIImagePickerController()
picker.sourceType = src
picker.mediaTypes = arr
picker.delegate = self
self.present(picker, animated: true)
```

For video, you can also specify the videoQuality and videoMaximumDuration. More-over, these additional properties and class methods allow you to discover the camera capabilities:

isCameraDeviceAvailable:
> Checks to see whether the front or rear camera is available, using one of these values as argument (UIImagePickerController.CameraDevice):
>
> - .front
>
> - .rear

cameraDevice
> Lets you learn and set which camera is being used.

availableCaptureModes(for:)
> Checks whether the given camera can capture still photos, video, or both. You specify the front or rear camera; returns an array of integers. Possible modes are (UIImagePickerController.CameraCaptureMode):
>
> - .photo
>
> - .video

cameraCaptureMode
> Lets you learn and set the capture mode (still photo or video).

isFlashAvailable(for:)
> Checks whether flash is available.

cameraFlashMode
> Lets you learn and set the flash mode (or, for a movie, toggles the LED "torch"). Your choices are (UIImagePickerController.CameraFlashMode):
>
> - .off
>
> - .auto
>
> - .on

When the view controller's view appears, the user will see the interface for taking a picture, familiar from the Camera app, possibly including flash options, camera selection button, photo/video option (if your `mediaTypes` setting allows both), and Cancel and shutter buttons. If the user takes a picture, the presented view offers an opportunity to use the picture or to retake it. If you have set the picker's `allowsEditing` to `true`, the user will have an opportunity to crop a still photo.

In the delegate, implement these two methods:

`imagePickerControllerDidCancel(_:)`
> Dismiss the picker.

`imagePickerController(_:didFinishPickingMediaWithInfo:)`
> Obtain what the user captured and dismiss the picker. The `info:` is a dictionary whose keys are of type UIImagePickerController.InfoKey. You'll be interested in the following keys (any of which might be `nil`):
>
> `.mediaType`
> > A string, either `UTType.image.identifier` or `UTType.movie.identifier`, telling you whether the user captured a still photo or a video.
>
> `.originalImage`
> > A UIImage. If the user captured a still image, this is it. However, you should also check whether the `.editedImage` is not `nil`; if it is an actual UIImage, because you set `allowsEditing` to `true` and the user did in fact crop the image, you should use the `.editedImage` instead of the `.originalImage`.
>
> `.mediaMetadata`
> > An NSDictionary containing the metadata for a captured image.
>
> `.mediaURL`
> > If the user captured a video, the file URL where it has been saved.

The photo library was not involved in the process of media capture, so no user permission to access the photo library is needed. But if you *now* propose to save the media into the photo library, you *will* need permission. Suppose that the user takes a still image, and you now want to save it into the user's Camera Roll album. Creating the PHAsset is sufficient:

```
func imagePickerController(_ picker: UIImagePickerController,
    didFinishPickingMediaWithInfo
    info: [UIImagePickerController.InfoKey : Any]) {
        var image = info[.originalImage] as? UIImage
        if let edited = info[.editedImage] as? UIImage {
            image = edited
        }
        let metadata = info[.mediaMetadata] as? NSDictionary
```

```
        self.dismiss(animated:true) {
            let mediatype = info[.mediaType]
            guard let type = mediatype as? String else {return}
            switch type {
            case UTType.image.identifier:
                if image != nil {
                    checkForPhotoLibraryAccess {
                        let lib = PHPhotoLibrary.shared()
                        lib.performChanges {
                            typealias Req = PHAssetChangeRequest
                            Req.creationRequestForAsset(from: image!)
                        }
                    }
                }
            default:break
            }
        }
    }
```

In that code, the metadata associated with the photo is received (`metadata`), but
nothing is done with it, and it is not folded into the PHAsset created from the image
(`image`). To attach the metadata to the photo, use the Image I/O framework (`import
ImageIO`) to make a copy of the image data along with the metadata. Now you can use
a PHAssetCreationRequest to make the PHAsset from the data:

```
let jpeg = image!.jpegData(compressionQuality:1)
let src = CGImageSourceCreateWithData(jpeg as CFData, nil)!
let data = NSMutableData()
let uti = CGImageSourceGetType(src)!
let dest = CGImageDestinationCreateWithData(
    data as CFMutableData, uti, 1, nil)!
CGImageDestinationAddImageFromSource(dest, src, 0, metadata)
CGImageDestinationFinalize(dest)
let lib = PHPhotoLibrary.shared()
lib.performChanges {
    let req = PHAssetCreationRequest.forAsset()
    req.addResource(with: .photo, data: data as Data, options: nil)
}
```

You can customize the UIImagePickerController image capture interface. If you need
to do that, you should probably consider dispensing entirely with UIImagePicker-
Controller and instead designing your own image capture interface from scratch,
based around AV Foundation and AVCaptureSession, which I'll introduce in the
next section. Still, it may be that a modified UIImagePickerController is all you need.

In the image capture interface, you can hide the standard controls by setting `shows-
CameraControls` to `false`, replacing them with your own overlay view, which you
supply as the value of the `cameraOverlayView`. That removes the shutter button, so
you're probably going to want to provide some new means of allowing the user to
take a picture! You can do that through these methods:

- `takePicture`

- `startVideoCapture`

- `stopVideoCapture`

The UIImagePickerController is a UINavigationController, so if you need additional interface — possibly to let the user vet the captured picture before dismissing the picker — you can push it onto the navigation interface.

Capture with AV Foundation

Instead of using UIImagePickerController, you can control the camera directly using the AV Foundation framework (Chapter 16). You get no help with interface, but you get vastly more power than UIImagePickerController can give you. For stills, you can control focus and exposure directly and independently, and for video, you can determine the quality, size, and frame rate of the resulting movie.

To understand how AV Foundation classes are used for image capture, imagine how the Camera app works. When you are running the Camera app, you have, at all times, a "window on the world" — the screen is showing you what the camera sees. At some point, you might tap the button to take a still image or start taking a video; now what the camera sees goes into a file.

Think of all that as being controlled by an engine. This engine, the heart of all AV Foundation capture operations, is an AVCaptureSession object. It has inputs (such as a camera) and outputs (such as a file). It also has an associated layer in your interface. When you start the engine running, by calling `startRunning`, data flows from the input through the engine; that is how you get your "window on the world," displaying on the screen what the camera sees.

As a rock-bottom example, let's start by implementing just the "window on the world" part of the engine. Our AVCaptureSession is retained in an instance property (`self.sess`). We also need a special CALayer that will display what the camera is seeing — namely, an AVCaptureVideoPreviewLayer. This layer is not really an AVCaptureSession output; rather, the layer receives its imagery by association with the AVCaptureSession. Our capture session's input is the default camera. We have no intention, as yet, of capturing anything to a file, so no output is needed:

```
self.sess = AVCaptureSession()
guard let cam = AVCaptureDevice.default(for: .video),
    let input = try? AVCaptureDeviceInput(device:cam)
    else {return}
self.sess.addInput(input)
let lay = AVCaptureVideoPreviewLayer(session:self.sess)
lay.frame = // ... some reasonable frame ...
self.view.layer.addSublayer(lay)
self.sess.startRunning()
```

Presto! Our interface now displays a "window on the world," showing what the camera sees.

Suppose now that our intention is that, while the engine is running and the "window on the world" is showing, the user is to be allowed to tap a button that will capture a still photo. Now we *do* need an output for our AVCaptureSession. This will be an AVCapturePhotoOutput instance. We should also configure the session with a preset (AVCaptureSession.Preset) to match our intended use of it; in this case, the preset will be .photo.

So let's modify the preceding code to give the session an output and a preset. We can do this directly before we start the session running. We can also do it while the session is already running (and in general, if you want to reconfigure a running session, doing so while it is running is far more efficient than stopping the session and starting it again), but then we must wrap our configuration changes in begin-Configuration and commitConfiguration. We should also run this sort of code on a dedicated background dispatch queue (see Chapter 25), but I'm not bothering to show that here:

```
self.sess.beginConfiguration()
guard self.sess.canSetSessionPreset(self.sess.sessionPreset)
    else {return}
self.sess.sessionPreset = .photo
let output = AVCapturePhotoOutput()
guard self.sess.canAddOutput(output)
    else {return}
self.sess.addOutput(output)
self.sess.commitConfiguration()
```

The session is now running and is ready to capture a photo. The user taps the button that asks to capture a photo, and we respond by telling the session's photo output to capturePhoto(with:delegate:). To prepare for that, we're going to need a reference to that output, which we can obtain from the session. Also, the first parameter is an AVCapturePhotoSettings object, which we should create and configure beforehand. So we start out like this:

```
guard let output = self.sess.outputs[0] as? AVCapturePhotoOutput
    else {return}
let settings = AVCapturePhotoSettings()
```

What sort of configuration might our AVCapturePhotoSettings need? Well, if we intend to display the user's captured photo in our interface, we should request a preview image explicitly. It's a lot more efficient for AV Foundation to create an uncompressed preview image of the correct size than for us to try to display or downsize a huge photo image. Here's how we might ask for the preview image:

```
let pbpf = settings.availablePreviewPhotoPixelFormatTypes[0]
let len = // desired maximum dimension
settings.previewPhotoFormat = [
    kCVPixelBufferPixelFormatTypeKey as String : pbpf,
    kCVPixelBufferWidthKey as String : len,
    kCVPixelBufferHeightKey as String : len
]
```

Another good idea, when configuring the AVCapturePhotoSettings object, is to ask for a thumbnail image. This is different from the preview image: the preview image is for you to display in your interface, but the thumbnail image is stored with the photo and is suitable for rapid display by other applications. Here's how to request a thumbnail image at a standard size (160×120):

```
settings.embeddedThumbnailPhotoFormat = [
    AVVideoCodecKey : AVVideoCodecType.jpeg
]
```

Just to make things more interesting, I'll also specify explicitly that I want the camera to use automatic flash:

```
let supported = output.supportedFlashModes
if supported.contains(.auto) {
    settings.flashMode = .auto
}
```

When the AVCapturePhotoSettings object is fully configured, we're ready to call capturePhoto(with:delegate:) at last:

```
output.capturePhoto(with: settings, delegate: self)
```

In that code, I specified self as the delegate (an AVCapturePhotoCaptureDelegate adopter). Functioning as the delegate, we will now receive a sequence of events. The exact sequence depends on what sort of capture we're doing; in this case, it will be:

1. photoOutput(_:willBeginCaptureFor:)

2. photoOutput(_:willCapturePhotoFor:)

3. photoOutput(_:didCapturePhotoFor:)

4. photoOutput(_:didFinishProcessingPhoto:error:)

5. photoOutput(_:didFinishCaptureFor:)

The for: parameter throughout is an AVCaptureResolvedSettings object, embodying the settings actually used during the capture; for instance, we could use it to find out whether flash was actually used.

The delegate event of most interest to our example is the fourth one. This is where we receive the photo! It will arrive in the second parameter as an AVCapturePhoto object. This object contains a lot of information. It provides the resolved settings in its resolvedSettings property. Its previewPixelBuffer property contains the data for the preview image, if we requested one in our AVCapturePhotoSettings. We can extract the image data from the AVCapturePhoto by calling its fileData-Representation method.

In this example, we implement the fourth delegate method to store the preview image as a property, for subsequent display in our interface, and then save the actual image as a PHAsset in the user's photo library:

```
func photoOutput(_ output: AVCapturePhotoOutput,
    didFinishProcessingPhoto photo:
    AVCapturePhoto, error: Error?) {
        if let cgim =
            photo.previewCGImageRepresentation()?.takeUnretainedValue() {
                let orient = // work out desired UIImage.Orientation
                self.previewImage = UIImage(
                    cgImage: cgim, scale: 1, orientation: orient)
        }
        if let data = photo.fileDataRepresentation() {
            let lib = PHPhotoLibrary.shared()
            lib.performChanges {
                let req = PHAssetCreationRequest.forAsset()
                req.addResource(with: .photo, data: data, options: nil)
            }
        }
}
```

Image capture with AV Foundation is a huge subject, and our example of a simple photo capture has barely scratched the surface:

- AVCaptureVideoPreviewLayer provides methods for converting between layer coordinates and capture device coordinates; without such methods, this can be a very difficult problem to solve.

- You can scan bar codes, shoot video at 60 frames per second (on some devices), and more.

- You can turn on the LED "torch" by setting the back camera's torchMode to AVCaptureTorchModeOn, even if no AVCaptureSession is running.

- You get direct hardware-level control over the camera focus, manual exposure, and white balance.

- You can capture bracketed images; starting in iOS 10, you can capture live images on some devices, and you can capture RAW images on some devices; and since iOS 11 even more new features have been introduced, such as depth-based image capture and multicamera capture.

There are very good WWDC videos about all this, stretching back over the past several years, and the AVCam-iOS and AVCamManual sample code examples are absolutely superb, demonstrating how to deal with tricky issues such as orientation that would otherwise be very difficult to figure out.

Contacts

The user's contacts constitute a database. The user can interact with this database through the Contacts app. Your code can access the user's contacts database programmatically through the Contacts framework. You'll need to `import Contacts`. An interface similar to the Contacts app for letting the user interact with the contacts database from within your app is provided by the Contacts UI framework. You'll need to `import ContactsUI`.

Access to the contacts database requires user authorization. You'll use the CNContactStore class for this. To learn what the current authorization status is, call the class method `authorizationStatus(for:)` with a CNEntityType of `.contacts`. (This is a curious requirement, as `.contacts` is the *only* CNEntityType!) To ask the system to put up the authorization request alert if the status is `.notDetermined`, call the instance method `requestAccess(for:completionHandler:)`. The *Info.plist* must contain some meaningful text that the system authorization request alert can use to explain why your app wants access. The relevant key is "Privacy — Contacts Usage Description" (`NSContactsUsageDescription`). See "Checking for Authorization" on page 899 for a discussion of authorization strategy.

Contact Classes

Here are the chief object types you'll be concerned with when you work with the user's contacts:

CNContactStore
> The contacts database is accessed through an instance of the CNContactStore class. You do not need to keep a reference to an instance of this class. When you want to fetch a contact from the database, or when you want to save a created or modified contact into the database, instantiate CNContactStore, do your fetching

or saving, and let the CNContactStore instance vanish. CNContactStore instance methods for fetching and saving information can take time. Therefore, they should be called on a background thread (see Chapter 25).

CNContact

An individual contact is an instance of the CNContact class. Its properties correspond to the fields displayed in the Contacts app. In addition, it has an identifier which is unique and persistent. A CNContact that comes from the CNContactStore has no connection with the database; it is safe to preserve it and to pass it around between objects and between threads. It is also immutable by default (its properties are read-only). To create your own CNContact, start with its mutable subclass, CNMutableContact; to modify an existing contact, call mutableCopy to make it a CNMutableContact.

The properties of a CNContact are matched by constant key names designating those properties. For instance, a CNContact has a familyName property, and there is also a CNContactFamilyNameKey. This should remind you of MPMedia-Item (Chapter 17), and indeed the purpose is similar: the key names allow you, when you fetch a CNContact from the CNContactStore, to state which properties of the CNContact you want populated. By limiting the properties to be fetched, you fetch more efficiently and quickly.

Most properties of a CNContact have familiar types such as String or an enum. However, the Contacts framework defines a number of specialized types as well; a phone number is a CNPhoneNumber, and a postal address is a CNPostal-Address. Such types tend to be wrapped up in a generic CNLabeledValue, whose purpose I'll explain later. Dates, such as a birthday, are not Date objects but rather DateComponents; this is because they do not necessarily require full date information (I know when someone's birthday is without knowing the year they were born).

CNContactFormatter, CNPostalAddressFormatter

A formatter is an engine for displaying aspects of a CNContact as a string. A CNContactFormatter whose style is .fullName, for instance, assembles the name-related properties of a CNContact into a name string. A formatter will tell you which properties it needs in order to form its string, so that you can easily include them among the contact properties that you fetch initially from the store.

The contacts database can change while your app is running. To detect this, register for the .CNContactStoreDidChange notification. The arrival of this notification means that any contacts-related objects that you are retaining, such as CNContact instances, may be outdated.

Fetching Contact Information

You now know enough to get started! Let's fetch some contacts. When we perform a fetch, there are two parameters to provide in order to limit the information to be returned to us:

A predicate
> An NSPredicate. CNContact provides class methods that will generate the predicates you're allowed to use. You are most likely to call predicateFor-Contacts(matchingName:) or predicateForContacts(withIdentifiers:); there are also predicates for fetching by email address and fetching by phone number.

Keys for properties to be fetched
> An array of objects adopting the CNKeyDescriptor protocol; such an object will be either a string key name, such as CNContactFamilyNameKey, or a descriptor provided by a formatter such as CNContactFormatter.

Fetching a Contact

I'll start by finding the contact that represents me in my contacts database. To do so, I'll fetch all contacts whose name is Matt Neuburg and assume that the first one is me. I'll call the CNContactStore instance method unifiedContacts(matching:keys-ToFetch:) with the matchingName predicate. Lots of combinations will work as the name: "Matt Neuburg", "Neuburg Matt", "Neuburg, Matt", and so on.

To prove that I've found myself, I don't need more than the first name and the last name of those contacts, so those are the keys I'll ask for. There are some parts of the process that I'm not bothering to show: we are using a CNContactStore fetch method, so everything should be done on a background thread, and the fetch should be wrapped in a do...catch construct because it can throw:

```
let pred = CNContact.predicateForContacts(matchingName: "Matt Neuburg")
let matts = try CNContactStore().unifiedContacts(matching: pred,
    keysToFetch: [
        CNContactFamilyNameKey as CNKeyDescriptor,
        CNContactGivenNameKey as CNKeyDescriptor
])
guard let moi = matts.first else {
    print("couldn't find myself")
    return
}
print(moi)
// CNContact: 0x10331dce0: givenName=Matt, familyName=Neuburg, ...
```

Alternatively, I could call enumerateContacts(with:usingBlock:), which hands me contacts one at a time.

One should perhaps regard enumerateContacts(with:usingBlock:) as the *primary* way to fetch contacts. The parameter is a CNContactFetchRequest, a simple value class; in addition to keysToFetch and predicate, it has some powerful properties allowing me to retrieve CNMutableContacts instead of CNContacts, to dictate the sort order, and to suppress the unification of linked contacts (I'll talk later about what that means). I don't need those extra features here, but I'll demonstrate anyway. Again, assume we're in a background thread and inside a do...catch construct:

```
let pred = CNContact.predicateForContacts(matchingName:"Matt Neuburg")
let req = CNContactFetchRequest(keysToFetch: [
    CNContactFamilyNameKey as CNKeyDescriptor,
    CNContactGivenNameKey as CNKeyDescriptor
])
req.predicate = pred
var matt : CNContact? = nil
try CNContactStore().enumerateContacts(with:req) { con, stop in
    matt = con
    stop.pointee = true
}
guard let moi = matt else {
    print("couldn't find myself")
    return
}
```

A commonly asked question is: where's the predicate for fetching information about *all* contacts? There isn't one. Simply call enumerateContacts(with:usingBlock:) without a predicate.

Repopulating a Contact

The contact that I fetched in the preceding examples is only partially populated. That means I can't use it to obtain any further contact property information. To illustrate, let's say that I now want to access my own email addresses. If I were to carry on directly from the preceding code by reading the emailAddresses property of moi, I'd crash because that property isn't populated:

```
let emails = moi.emailAddresses // crash
```

If I'm unsure what properties of a particular contact are populated, I can test for safety beforehand with the isKeyAvailable(_:) method:

```
if moi.isKeyAvailable(CNContactEmailAddressesKey) {
    let emails = moi.emailAddresses
}
```

But even though I'm not crashing any more, I still want those email addresses. One solution, obviously, would have been to plan ahead and include CNContactEmail-AddressesKey in the list of properties to be fetched. Unfortunately, I failed to do that.

Luckily, there's another way; I can go back to the store and *repopulate* this contact, based on its identifier:

```
let moi2 = try CNContactStore().unifiedContact(withIdentifier: moi.identifier,
    keysToFetch: [
        CNContactFamilyNameKey as CNKeyDescriptor,
        CNContactGivenNameKey as CNKeyDescriptor,
        CNContactEmailAddressesKey as CNKeyDescriptor
])
let emails = moi2.emailAddresses
```

Labeled Values

Now let's talk about the structure of the thing I've just obtained — the value of the `emailAddresses` property. It's an array of CNLabeledValue objects.

A CNLabeledValue has a `label` and a `value` (and an `identifier`). This class handles the fact that some contact attributes can have more than one value, each intended for a specific purpose described by the label; for instance, I might have both a home email address and a work email address. This is not a dictionary; the values are not keyed by their labels. That's because the same label can be used with more than one value — I can have *two* work email addresses. The label is just a piece of information paired with the value. You can make up your own labels, or you can use the built-in labels; the latter are very strange-looking strings like `"_$!<Work>!$_"`, but there are also some constants that you can use instead, such as `CNLabelWork`.

Carrying on from the previous example, I'll look for all my work email addresses:

```
let workemails = emails.filter {$0.label == CNLabelWork}.map {$0.value}
```

A phone number is a CNLabeledValue whose value is a CNPhoneNumber object. A postal address is a CNLabeledValue whose value is a CNPostalAddress, which is mostly a value class providing properties such as `street`, `city`, `state`, and `country`.

Contact Formatters

When presenting the user with contact information as a string, you should look to see whether there's a formatter for that information. For a name string, there's CNContactFormatter; for a CNPostalAddress string, there's CNPostalAddress-Formatter.

To illustrate, let's say that I want to present the full name and work email of the `moi` contact to the user, as a string. I should not assume that the full name is to be constructed as `givenName` followed by `familyName`, nor that those are the only two pieces that constitute it. Rather, I should rely on the intelligence of a CNContactFormatter:

```
let full = CNContactFormatterStyle.fullName
let keys = CNContactFormatter.descriptorForRequiredKeys(for:full)
let moi3 = try CNContactStore().unifiedContact(withIdentifier: moi.identifier,
    keysToFetch: [
        keys,
        CNContactEmailAddressesKey as CNKeyDescriptor
])
if let name = CNContactFormatter.string(from: moi3, style: full) {
    print("\(name): \(workemails[0])") // Matt Neuburg: matt@tidbits.com
}
```

CNPostalAddressFormatter turns a CNPostalAddress into a string, nicely lineated and dealing with the numerous international variations.

An intriguing feature of CNPostalAddressFormatter is that it can also provide an *attributed* string, marked with a custom attribute called CNPostalAddressProperty-Attribute (see "Custom Attributes" on page 671). This attribute is applied to each piece of the address, with the attribute's value indicating *which* piece of the address this is. We could use this to present a formatted address to the user, modifying the style of particular semantic stretches. In this example, I'll obtain a contact's postal address, derive the attributed string, learn what range of that string contains the contact's country name, and underline it:

```
let pred = CNContact.predicateForContacts(matchingName:"Charlotte Wilson")
let c = try CNContactStore().unifiedContacts(matching: pred,
    keysToFetch: [CNContactPostalAddressesKey as CNKeyDescriptor])[0]
let addr = c.postalAddresses[0]
let form = CNPostalAddressFormatter()
let attr = form.attributedString(from:addr.value, withDefaultAttributes:[:])
let s = attr.string as NSString
let range = NSRange(location: 0, length: s.length)
let key = NSAttributedString.Key(rawValue:CNPostalAddressPropertyAttribute)
attr.enumerateAttributes(in: range, options: []) { result, r, stop in
    if let val = result[key] as? String {
        if val == "country" {
            // r is the range of the country name; I'll prove it...
            print("country is:", s.substring(with: r)) // New Zealand
            // underline it
            if let mas = attr.mutableCopy() as? NSMutableAttributedString {
                mas.addAttributes([
                    .underlineStyle: NSUnderlineStyle.single.rawValue
                ], range: r)
                // ... do something with the attributed string ...
            }
            stop.pointee = true
        }
    }
}
```

Figure 19-1. A contact created programmatically

Saving Contact Information

All saving of information into the user's contacts database involves a CNSaveRequest object. You describe to this object your proposed changes by calling instance methods such as add(_:toContainerWithIdentifier:), update(_:), and delete(_:). The CNSaveRequest object batches those proposed changes. Then you hand the CNSaveRequest object over to the CNContactStore with execute(_:), and the changes are performed in a single transaction.

In this example, I'll create a contact for Snidely Whiplash with a Home email snidely@villains.com and add him to the contacts database:

```
let snidely = CNMutableContact()
snidely.givenName = "Snidely"
snidely.familyName = "Whiplash"
let email = CNLabeledValue(label: CNLabelHome,
    value: "snidely@villains.com" as NSString)
snidely.emailAddresses.append(email)
snidely.imageData = UIImage(named:"snidely")!.pngData()
let save = CNSaveRequest()
save.add(snidely, toContainerWithIdentifier: nil)
try CNContactStore().execute(save)
```

Sure enough, if we then check the state of the database through the Contacts app, our Snidely contact exists (Figure 19-1).

Contact Sorting, Groups, and Containers

Contacts are naturally sorted either by family name or by given name, and the user can choose between them (in the Settings app) in arranging the list of contacts to be displayed by the Contacts app and other apps that display the same list. The

CNContact class provides a comparator, through the `comparator(forNameSort-Order:)` class method, suitable for use with NSArray methods such as `sorted-Array(comparator:)`. To make sure your CNContact is populated with the properties needed for sorting, call the class method `descriptorForAllComparator-Keys`. Your sort order choices (CNContactSortOrder) are:

- `.givenName`
- `.familyName`
- `.userDefault`

Contacts can belong to groups, and the Contacts application in macOS provides an interface for manipulating contact groups — though the Contacts app on an iOS device does not. A group in the Contacts framework is a CNGroup; its mutable subclass, CNMutableGroup, allows you to create a group and set its name. All manipulation of contacts and groups — creating, renaming, or deleting a group, adding a contact to a group or removing a contact from a group — is performed through CNSaveRequest instance methods.

Contacts come from sources. A contact or group might be on the device or might come from an Exchange server or a CardDAV server. The source really does, in a sense, own the group or contact; a contact can't belong to two sources. A complicating factor, however, is that the same real person might be listed in two different sources as two different contacts; to deal with this, it is possible for multiple contacts to be *linked*, indicating that they are the same person. That's why the methods that fetch contacts from the database describe the resulting contacts as "unified" — the linkage between linked contacts from different sources has already been used to consolidate the information into a single CNContact object. In the rare event that you *don't* want unification of linked contacts across sources as you fetch contacts, call `enumerateContacts(with:usingBlock:)` with a CNContactFetchRequest whose `unifyResults` property is `false`.

In the Contacts framework, a source is a CNContainer. When I called the CNSaveRequest instance method `add(_:toContainerWithIdentifier:)` earlier, I supplied a container identifier of `nil`, signifying the user's default container.

Contacts Interface

The Contacts UI framework endows your app with an interface similar to the Contacts app, where the user can perform common tasks involving the listing, display, and editing of contacts in the database. The framework provides two UIViewController subclasses:

CNContactPickerViewController

> Presents a navigation interface, effectively the same as the Contacts app but without an Edit button: it lists the contacts in the database and allows the user to pick one and view the details.

CNContactViewController

> Presents an interface showing the properties of an individual contact. It comes in three variants:

> *Existing contact*
>> Displays the details, possibly editable, of an existing contact fetched from the database.

> *New contact*
>> Displays editable properties of a new contact, allowing the user to save the edited contact into the database.

> *Unknown contact*
>> Displays a proposed contact with a partial set of properties, for editing and saving or merging into an existing contact in the database.

Some of the Contacts UI framework view controllers allow the user to select (tap) a property of a contact in the interface. Therefore, they need a way to package up the information about that property so as to communicate to your code *what* property this is, such as "Matt Neuburg's work email whose value is `matt@tidbits.com`." For this purpose, the Contacts framework provides the CNContactProperty class. This a value class, consisting of a `key` (effectively the name of the property), a `value`, a `label` (in case the property comes from a CNLabeledValue), a `contact`, and an `identifier`. The `contact` property is a CNContact that arrives fully populated, so we can access all its properties from here without returning to the CNContactStore.

 You do *not* need user authorization to use these view controllers, and in the case of an editable CNContactViewController you *cannot* prevent the user from saving the edited contact into the database.

CNContactPickerViewController

A CNContactPickerViewController is a UINavigationController. With it, the user can see a list of all contacts in the database, and can filter that list by group and by searching.

To use CNContactPickerViewController, instantiate it, assign it a delegate (CNContactPickerDelegate), and present it as a presented view controller:

```
let picker = CNContactPickerViewController()
picker.delegate = self
self.present(picker, animated:true)
```

That code works — the picker appears, and there's a Cancel button so the user can dismiss it. When the user taps a contact, that contact's details are pushed onto the navigation controller. When the user taps a piece of information among the details, some default action is performed: for a postal address, it is displayed in the Maps app; for an email address, it becomes the addressee of a new message in the Mail app; for a phone number, the number is dialed; and so on.

However, we have so far provided no way for any information to travel from the picker *to our app.* For that, we need to implement the delegate method `contact-Picker(_:didSelect:)`. This method comes in two basic forms:

The second parameter is a CNContact
When the user taps a contact name, the contact's details are *not* pushed onto the navigation controller. Instead, the delegate method is called, the tapped contact is passed to us, and the picker is dismissed.

The second parameter is a CNContactProperty
When the user taps a contact name, the contact's details *are* pushed onto the navigation controller. If the user now taps a piece of information among the details, the delegate method is called, the tapped property is passed to us, and the picker is dismissed.

(If we implement both forms of this method, it is as if we had implemented only the first form. However, it's possible to change that, using the `predicateForSelectionOf-Contact` property, as I'm about to explain.)

You can perform additional configuration of what information appears in the picker and what happens when it is tapped, by setting properties of the picker before you present it. These properties are all NSPredicates:

`predicateForEnablingContact`
The predicate describes the contact. A contact will be enabled in the picker only if the predicate evaluates to `true`. A disabled contact cannot be tapped, so it can't be selected and its details can't be displayed.

`predicateForSelectionOfContact`
The predicate describes the contact. If the predicate evaluates to `true`, tapping the contact calls the *first* delegate method (the parameter is the contact). Otherwise, tapping the contact displays the contact details.

`predicateForSelectionOfProperty`
The predicate describes the property (in the detail view). If the predicate evaluates to `true`, tapping the property calls the *second* delegate method (the parameter is a CNContactProperty). Otherwise, tapping the property performs the default action.

You can also determine *what* properties appear in the detail view, by setting the `displayedPropertyKeys` property.

Let's say we want the user to pass us an email address, and that's the only reason we're displaying the picker. Then a reasonable configuration would be:

```
picker.displayedPropertyKeys =
    [CNContactEmailAddressesKey]
picker.predicateForEnablingContact =
    NSPredicate(format: "emailAddresses.@count > 0")
```

We would then implement only the second form of the delegate method (the parameter is a CNContactProperty). Our code then effectively says: "Only enable contacts that have email addresses. When the user taps an enabled contact, show the details. In the details view, show only email addresses. When the user taps an email address, report it to the delegate method and dismiss the picker."

It is also possible to enable multiple selection. To do so, we implement a different pair of delegate methods:

`contactPicker(_:didSelect:)`
> The second parameter is an array of CNContact.

`contactPicker(_:didSelectContactProperties:)`
> The second parameter is an array of CNContactProperty.

This causes a Done button to appear in the interface, and our delegate method is called when the user taps it.

But the interface for letting the user select multiple properties, if incorrectly configured, can be clumsy and confusing, and can even send your app into limbo. Experiment carefully before deciding to use it.

 I regard the implementation of the CNContactPickerViewController as a massive security hole. In the example I gave a moment ago, the user is led to believe that what's being chosen and communicated to the app is an email address. But in fact, because a CNContactProperty contains the fully populated CNContact, the app now knows things about this contact, such as phone numbers and addresses, that the user never intended.

CNContactViewController

A CNContactViewController is a UIViewController. It comes, as I've already said, in three flavors, depending on how you instantiate it:

- Existing contact: `init(for:)`
- New contact: `init(forNewContact:)`
- Unknown contact: `init(forUnknownContact:)`

The first and third flavors display a contact initially, with an option to show a secondary editing interface. The second flavor consists *solely* of the editing interface.

You can configure the initial display of the contact in the first and third flavors, by means of these properties:

allowsActions
> Refers to extra buttons that can appear in the interface if it is `true` — things like Share Contact, Add to Favorites, and Share My Location. Exactly what buttons appear depends on what categories of information are displayed.

displayedPropertyKeys
> Limits the properties shown for this contact.

message
> A string displayed beneath the contact's name.

There are two delegate methods (CNContactViewControllerDelegate):

contactViewController(_:shouldPerformDefaultActionFor:)
> Used by the first and third flavors, in the initial display of the contact. This is like a live version of the picker `predicateForSelectionOfProperty`, except that the meaning is reversed: returning `true` means that the tapped property should proceed to trigger the Mail app or the Maps app or whatever is appropriate. This includes the message and mail buttons at the top of the interface. You are handed the CNContactProperty, so you know what was tapped and can take action yourself if you return `false`.

contactViewController(_:didCompleteWith:)
> Used by all three flavors. Called when the user dismisses the editing interface. If the user taps Done in the editing interface, you receive the edited contact, *which has already been saved into the database*. (If the user cancels out of the editing interface, then if this delegate method is called, the received contact will be `nil`.)

Existing contact

To display an existing contact in a CNContactViewController, call `init(for:)` with a CNContact that has *already* been populated with all the information needed to display it in this view controller. For this purpose, CNContactViewController supplies a class method `descriptorForRequiredKeys`, and you will want to call it to set the keys when you fetch your contact from the store, prior to using it with a CNContactViewController. Here's an example:

```
let pred = CNContact.predicateForContacts(matchingName: "Snidely Whiplash")
let keys = CNContactViewController.descriptorForRequiredKeys()
let snides = try CNContactStore().unifiedContacts(matching: pred,
    keysToFetch: [keys])
```

```
guard let snide = snides.first else {
    print("no snidely")
    return
}
```

We now have a sufficiently populated contact, snide, and can use it in a subsequent call to CNContactViewController's init(for:).

 Handing an insufficiently populated contact to CNContactViewController's init(for:) will crash your app.

Having instantiated CNContactViewController, you set its delegate (CNContactViewControllerDelegate) and *push* the view controller onto an existing UINavigationController's stack.

An Edit button appears at the top right, and the user can tap it to edit this contact in a presented view controller — unless you have set the view controller's allowsEditing property to false, in which case the Edit button is suppressed.

Here's a minimal working example; I'll display the Snidely Whiplash contact that I obtained earlier. Note that, if we were in a background thread earlier when we fetched snide from the database, we need to be on the main thread now:

```
let vc = CNContactViewController(for:snide)
vc.delegate = self
vc.message = "Nyah ah ahhh"
self.navigationController?.pushViewController(vc, animated: true)
```

New contact

To use a CNContactViewController to allow the user to create a new contact, instantiate it with init(forNewContact:). The parameter can be nil, or it can be a CNMutableContact that you've created and partially populated; but your properties will be only suggestions, because the user is going to be shown the contact editing interface and can change anything you've put.

Having set the view controller's delegate, you then do a little dance: you instantiate a UINavigationController with the CNContactViewController as its root view controller, and *present the navigation controller* as a presented view controller. Here is a minimal implementation:

```
let con = CNMutableContact()
con.givenName = "Dudley"
con.familyName = "Doright"
let npvc = CNContactViewController(forNewContact: con)
npvc.delegate = self
self.present(UINavigationController(rootViewController: npvc),
    animated:true)
```

You must dismiss the presented navigation controller yourself in your implementation of `contactViewController(_:didCompleteWith:)`.

Unknown contact

To use a CNContactViewController to allow the user to edit an unknown contact, instantiate it with `init(forUnknownContact:)`. You must provide a CNContact parameter, which you may have made up from scratch using a CNMutableContact. You must set the view controller's `contactStore` to a CNContactStore instance; if you don't, it's not an error, but the view controller is then useless. You then set a delegate and *push* the view controller onto an existing navigation controller:

```
let con = CNMutableContact()
con.givenName = "Johnny"
con.familyName = "Appleseed"
con.phoneNumbers.append(CNLabeledValue(label: "woods",
    value: CNPhoneNumber(stringValue: "555-123-4567")))
let unkvc = CNContactViewController(forUnknownContact: con)
unkvc.message = "He knows his trees"
unkvc.contactStore = CNContactStore()
unkvc.delegate = self
unkvc.allowsActions = false
self.navigationController?.pushViewController(unkvc, animated: true)
```

The interface contains these two buttons (among others):

Create New Contact
> The editing interface is presented, with a Cancel button and a Done button.

Add to Existing Contact
> The contact picker is presented. The user can tap Cancel or tap an existing contact. If the user taps an existing contact, that contact is presented for editing, with fields from the partial contact merged in, along with a Cancel button and an Update button.

If the framework thinks that this partial contact is the same as an existing contact, there will be a third button offering explicitly to update that particular contact. The result is as if the user had tapped Add to Existing Contact and picked this existing contact. In the editing interface, if the user taps Cancel, you'll never hear about it; `contactViewController(_:didCompleteWith:)` won't even be called.

Calendar

The user's calendar information constitutes a database of calendar events. This database also includes reminders. The user can interact with the calendar events through the Calendar app, and with the reminders through the Reminders app. Your code can access the database through the EventKit framework. You'll need to `import` `Event-Kit`. An interface for allowing the user to interact with the calendar from within your app is also provided, through the EventKit UI framework. You'll need to `import` `EventKitUI`.

The database is accessed as an instance of the EKEventStore class. This instance is expensive to obtain but lightweight to maintain, so your usual strategy will be to instantiate and retain one EKEventStore instance. There is no harm in initializing a property or global as an EKEventStore instance and keeping that reference for the rest of the app's lifetime:

```
let database = EKEventStore()
```

In the examples in this chapter, my EKEventStore instance is called `self.database` throughout.

Access to the database requires user authorization. You'll use the EKEventStore class for this. Although there is one database, access to calendar events and access to reminders are considered two separate forms of access and require separate authorizations. To learn what the current authorization status is, call the class method `authorizationStatus(for:)` with an EKEntityType, either `.event` (for access to calendar events) or `.reminder` (for access to reminders). To ask the system to put up the authorization request alert if the status is `.notDetermined`, call the instance method `requestAccess(to:completion:)`. The *Info.plist* must contain some meaningful text that the system authorization request alert can use to explain why your app wants access. The relevant key is either "Privacy — Calendars Usage Description"

(NSCalendarsUsageDescription) or "Privacy — Reminders Usage Description" (NSRemindersUsageDescription). See "Checking for Authorization" on page 899 for a discussion of authorization strategy.

Calendar Database Contents

Starting with an EKEventStore instance, you can obtain two kinds of object — a calendar or a calendar item.

Calendars

A calendar represents a named (title) collection of calendar items, meaning events or reminders. It is an instance of EKCalendar. But an EKCalendar instance doesn't contain or link to its calendar items; to obtain and create calendar items, you work directly with the EKEventStore itself. A calendar's allowedEntityTypes, despite the plural, will probably return just one entity type; you can't create a calendar that allows both.

Calendars themselves come in various types (type, an EKCalendarType), reflecting the nature of their origin: a calendar can be created and maintained by the user locally (.local), but it might also live remotely on the network (.calDAV, .exchange); the Birthday calendar (.birthday) is generated automatically from information in the contacts database; and so on.

The type is supplemented and embraced by the calendar's source, an EKSource whose sourceType (EKSourceType) can be .local, .exchange, .calDAV (which includes iCloud), and so forth; a source can also have a title, and it has a unique identifier (sourceIdentifier). You can get an array of all sources known to the EKEventStore, or specify a source by its identifier. You'll probably use the source exclusively and ignore the calendar's type property.

There are three ways of requesting a calendar:

All calendars
> Fetch all calendars permitting a particular calendar item type (.event or .reminder), by calling calendars(for:). You can send this message either to the EKEventStore or to an EKSource.

Particular calendar
> Fetch an individual calendar from the EKEventStore by means of a previously obtained calendarIdentifier, by calling calendar(withIdentifier:).

Default calendar
> Fetch the default calendar for a particular calendar item type, by asking for the defaultCalendarForNewEvents or defaultCalendarForNewReminders of the

EKEventStore; this is appropriate particularly if your intention is to create a new calendar item.

You can also create a calendar, by means of the initializer `init(for:eventStore:)`. At that point, you can specify the source to which the calendar belongs. I'll give an example later.

Depending on the source, a calendar will be modifiable in various ways. The calendar's `isSubscribed` might be `true`. If the calendar's `isImmutable` is `true`, you can't delete the calendar or change its attributes; but its `allowsContentModifications` might still be `true`, in which case you can add, remove, and alter its events.

Calendar Items

A calendar item (EKCalendarItem) is either a calendar event (EKEvent) or a reminder (EKReminder). Think of it as a memorandum describing when something happens. As I mentioned a moment ago, you don't get calendar items from a calendar; rather, a calendar item *has* a `calendar`, but you get it from the EKEventStore as a whole. There are two chief ways of getting a calendar item:

By predicate
    Fetch all events or reminders according to a predicate (NSPredicate):

* `events(matching:)`
* `enumerateEvents(matching:using:)`
* `fetchReminders(matching:completion:)`

    EKEventStore methods starting with `predicateFor` supply the needed predicate. I'll give an example later.

By identifier
    Fetch an individual calendar item by means of a previously obtained `calendarItemIdentifier`, by calling `calendarItem(withIdentifier:)`.

Calendar Database Changes

Changes to the database can be atomic. There are two prongs to the implementation of this feature:

* The EKEventStore methods for saving and removing calendar items and calendars have a `commit:` parameter. If you pass `false` as the argument, the changes that you're ordering are batched without performing them; later, you can call `commit` (or `reset` if you change your mind). If you pass `false` and fail to call `commit` later, your changes will never happen.

- An abstract class, EKObject, functions as the superclass for all the other persistent object types, such as EKCalendar, EKCalendarItem, EKSource, and so on. It endows those classes with methods `refresh`, `rollback`, and `reset`, along with read-only properties `isNew` and `hasChanges`.

The database can change while your app is running (the user might sync, or the user might edit with the Calendar app), which can put your information out of date. You can register for a single EKEventStore notification, `.EKEventStoreChanged`; if you receive it, you should assume that any calendar-related instances you're holding are invalid. This situation is made relatively painless by the fact that every calendar-related instance can be refreshed with `refresh`. Keep in mind that `refresh` returns a Boolean; if it returns `false`, this object is *really* invalid and you should stop working with it entirely (it may have been deleted from the database).

Creating Calendars, Events, and Reminders

You now know enough for an example! Let's start by creating an events calendar. We need to assign a source type (EKSourceType); we'll choose `.local`, meaning that the calendar will be created on the device itself. We can't ask the database for the local source directly, so we have to cycle through all sources looking for it. When we find it, we make a new calendar called "CoolCal" (saving into the database can fail, so assume we're running inside a `do...catch` construct):

```
let locals = self.database.sources.filter {$0.sourceType == .local}
guard let src = locals.first else {
    print("failed to find local source")
    return
}
let cal = EKCalendar(for:.event, eventStore:self.database)
cal.source = src
cal.title = "CoolCal"
try self.database.saveCalendar(cal, commit:true)
```

On a device where the calendar is subscribed to a remote source, `.local` calendars are inaccessible. The examples in this chapter use a local calendar, because I don't want to risk damaging your online calendars; to test the examples, you'll need to turn off iCloud for your Calendar app temporarily.

Events

Now let's create an event. EKEvent is a subclass of EKCalendarItem, from which it inherits some of its properties. If you've ever used the Calendar app in iOS or macOS, you already have a sense for how an EKEvent can be configured. It has a `title` and optional `notes`. It is associated with a `calendar`, as I've already said. It can have one or more alarms and one or more recurrence rules; I'll talk about those in a moment. All of that is inherited from EKCalendarItem.

EKEvent itself adds the `startDate` and `endDate` properties; these are Dates and involve both date and time. If the event's `isAllDay` property is `true`, the time aspect of its dates is ignored; the event is associated with a day or a stretch of days as a whole. If the event's `isAllDay` property is `false`, the time aspect of its dates matters; an event will then typically be bounded by two times on the same day.

Making an event is simple, if tedious. You *must* provide a `startDate` and an `endDate`! The simplest way to construct dates, and to do the date math that you'll often need in order to derive one date from another, is with DateComponents. I'll create an event and add it to our new calendar. First, I need a way to locate the new calendar. I'll locate it by its title. I really should be using the `calendarIdentifier`; the title isn't reliable, since the user might change it, and since multiple calendars can have the same title. However, it's only an example:

```
func calendar(name:String) -> EKCalendar? {
    let cals = self.database.calendars(for:.event)
    return cals.first {$0.title == name}
}
```

Now I'll create an event, configure it, and add it to our CoolCal calendar:

```
guard let cal = self.calendar(name:"CoolCal") else {
    print("failed to find calendar")
    return
}
// form the start and end dates
let greg = Calendar(identifier:.gregorian)
var comp = DateComponents(year:2020, month:8, day:10, hour:15)
let d1 = greg.date(from:comp)!
comp.hour = comp.hour! + 1
let d2 = greg.date(from:comp)!
// form the event
let ev = EKEvent(eventStore:self.database)
ev.title = "Take a nap"
ev.notes = "You deserve it!"
ev.calendar = cal
(ev.startDate, ev.endDate) = (d1,d2)
// save it
try self.database.save(ev, span:.thisEvent, commit:true)
```

Alarms

An alarm is an EKAlarm, a very simple class; it can be set to fire either at an absolute date or at a relative offset from the event time. On an iOS device, a calendar alarm fires through a local notification (Chapter 14); if the user turns off local notifications for the Calendar app, there will be no indication that the alarm has fired. We could easily have added an alarm to our event as we were configuring it:

```
let alarm = EKAlarm(relativeOffset:-3600) // one hour before
ev.addAlarm(alarm)
```

Recurrence

Recurrence is embodied in a recurrence rule (EKRecurrenceRule); a calendar item can have multiple recurrence rules, which you manipulate through its `recurrence-Rules` property and `addRecurrenceRule(_:)` and `removeRecurrenceRule(_:)` methods. A simple EKRecurrenceRule is described by three properties:

Frequency

> By day, by week, by month, or by year.

Interval

> Fine-tunes the notion "by" in the frequency. A value of 1 means "every." A value of 2 means "every other." And so on.

End

> Optional, because the event might recur forever. It is an EKRecurrenceEnd instance, describing the limit of the event's recurrence either as an end date or as a maximum number of occurrences.

The options for describing a more complex EKRecurrenceRule are best summarized by its initializer:

```
init(recurrenceWith type: EKRecurrenceFrequency,
                interval: Int,
        daysOfTheWeek: [EKRecurrenceDayOfWeek]?,
        daysOfTheMonth: [NSNumber]?,
      monthsOfTheYear: [NSNumber]?,
       weeksOfTheYear: [NSNumber]?,
        daysOfTheYear: [NSNumber]?,
         setPositions: [NSNumber]?,
                 end: EKRecurrenceEnd?)
```

The meanings of all those parameters are mostly obvious from their names and types. The EKRecurrenceDayOfWeek class allows specification of a week number as well as a day number so that you can say things like "the fourth Thursday of the month." Many of the numeric values can be negative to indicate counting backward from the last one. Numbers are all 1-based, not 0-based. The `setPositions:` parameter is an array of numbers filtering the occurrences defined by the rest of the specification against the interval; for instance, if `daysOfTheWeek` is Sunday, `-1` means the final Sunday.

An EKRecurrenceRule is intended to embody the RRULE event component in the iCalendar standard specification (*http://datatracker.ietf.org/doc/rfc5545*); in fact, the documentation tells you how each EKRecurrenceRule property corresponds to an RRULE attribute, and if you log an EKRecurrenceRule, what you're shown *is* the underlying RRULE. RRULE can describe some amazingly sophisticated recurrence rules, such as this one:

```
RRULE:FREQ=YEARLY;INTERVAL=2;BYMONTH=1;BYDAY=SU
```

That means: "Every Sunday in January, every other year." Let's form this rule. Observe that we should attach it to an event whose startDate and endDate actually obey the rule — that is, the event should fall on a Sunday in January. Fortunately, DateComponents makes that easy:

```
let everySunday = EKRecurrenceDayOfWeek(.sunday)
let january = 1 as NSNumber
let recur = EKRecurrenceRule(
    recurrenceWith:.yearly, // every year
    interval:2, // no, every *two* years
    daysOfTheWeek:[everySunday],
    daysOfTheMonth:nil,
    monthsOfTheYear:[january],
    weeksOfTheYear:nil,
    daysOfTheYear:nil,
    setPositions: nil,
    end:nil)
let ev = EKEvent(eventStore:self.database)
ev.title = "Mysterious biennial Sunday-in-January morning ritual"
ev.addRecurrenceRule(recur)
ev.calendar = cal // assume we have our calendar
// need a start date and end date
let greg = Calendar(identifier:.gregorian)
var comp = DateComponents(year:2020, month:1, hour:10)
comp.weekday = 1 // Sunday
comp.weekdayOrdinal = 1 // *first* Sunday
ev.startDate = greg.date(from:comp)!
comp.hour = 11
ev.endDate = greg.date(from:comp)!
try self.database.save(ev, span:.futureEvents, commit:true)
```

In that code, the event we save into the database is a recurring event. When we save or delete a recurring event, we must specify a span: argument (EKSpan). This is either .thisEvent or .futureEvents, and corresponds to the two buttons the user sees in the Calendar interface when saving or deleting a recurring event (Figure 20-1). The buttons and the span types reflect their meaning exactly: the change affects either this event alone, or this event plus all *future* (not past) recurrences. This choice determines not only how this and future recurrences of the event are affected now, but also how they relate to one another from now on.

Reminders

A reminder (EKReminder) is very similar to an event (EKEvent); the chief difference is that EKReminder was invented some years after EKEvent and so its API is a little more modern. They both inherit from EKCalendarItem, so a reminder has a calendar (which the Reminders app refers to as a "list"), a title, notes, alarms, and recurrence rules.

Figure 20-1. The user specifies a span

A reminder has an `isCompleted` property and a `completionDate`. Setting the `isCompleted` property to `true` sets the `completionDate`, and *vice versa*.

Instead of a start date and an end date, a reminder has a start date (`startDate-Components`) and a due date (`dueDateComponents`). As the names suggest, these are expressed directly as DateComponents, so you can supply any desired degree of detail.

You are free to create a reminder with no date information, and that's a common thing to do:

```
let cal = self.database.defaultCalendarForNewReminders()
let rem = EKReminder(eventStore:self.database)
rem.title = "Get bread"
rem.calendar = cal
try self.database.save(rem, commit:true)
```

Here's how to change that to a reminder for tomorrow:

```
// ... create rem as before ...
let greg = Calendar(identifier:.gregorian)
let tomorrow = greg.date(byAdding: DateComponents(day:1), to: Date())
let comps : Set<Calendar.Component> = [.year, .month, .day]
rem.dueDateComponents = greg.dateComponents(comps, from:tomorrow!)
try self.database.save(rem, commit:true)
```

But although we have set the reminder's due date, this reminder will not actively remind the user of anything! If we want to alert the user when the due date arrives, we must also add an EKAlarm to the reminder.

The reminder's `startDateComponents` are needed only if you attach a recurrence rule to the reminder. You'll typically want the reminding to start immediately. Unlike a recurring calendar event, a recurring reminder doesn't generate multiple reminders stretching out into the future; instead, it generates one reminder that automatically generates the next reminder upon completion.

Proximity Alarms

A proximity alarm is triggered by the user's approaching or leaving a certain location (also known as *geofencing*). This is appropriate particularly for reminders: one might wish to be reminded of some task when approaching the place where that task can be accomplished. To form the location, you'll need to use the CLLocation class (see Chapter 22). Here, I'll attach a proximity alarm to a reminder (rem); the alarm will fire when I'm near my local Trader Joe's:

```
let alarm = EKAlarm()
let loc = EKStructuredLocation(title:"Trader Joe's")
loc.geoLocation = CLLocation(latitude:34.271848, longitude:-119.247714)
loc.radius = 10*1000 // meters
alarm.structuredLocation = loc
alarm.proximity = .enter // "geofence": we alarm when *arriving*
rem.addAlarm(alarm)
```

Use of a proximity alarm requires Location Services authorization, but that's of no concern here, because the app that needs this authorization is not our app but the Reminders app! Now that we've placed a reminder with a proximity alarm into the database, the Reminders app will request authorization, if needed, the next time the user brings it frontmost. If you add a proximity alarm to the event database and the Reminders app can't perform background geofencing, the alarm will not fire (unless the Reminders app is frontmost).

 You can also construct a local notification based on geofencing without involving reminders or the Reminders app. See Chapter 22.

Fetching Events and Reminders

Now let's talk about how to extract an event from the database. One way, as I mentioned earlier, is by its identifier (calendarItemIdentifier). Not only is this identifier a fast and unique way to obtain an event, but also it's just a string, which means that it persists even if the EKEventStore subsequently goes out of existence, whereas an actual EKEvent drawn from the database loses its meaning and its usability if the EKEventStore instance is destroyed.

You can also extract events from the database by matching a predicate (NSPredicate). To form this predicate, you specify a start and end date and an array of eligible calendars, and call this EKEventStore method:

- predicateForEvents(withStart:end:calendars:)

That's the only kind of predicate you can use, so any further filtering of events is then up to you. In this example, I'll look through the events of our CoolCal calendar to find the nap event I created earlier; because I have to specify a date range, I ask for events occurring over a two-year span. Because calling enumerate-Events(matching:using:) can be time-consuming, it's a good idea to run it on a background thread (Chapter 25):

```
let greg = Calendar(identifier:.gregorian)
let d = Date() // today
let d1 = greg.date(byAdding:DateComponents(year:-1), to:d)!
let d2 = greg.date(byAdding:DateComponents(year:2), to:d)!
let pred = self.database.predicateForEvents(withStart:
    d1, end:d2, calendars:[cal]) // assume we have our calendar
DispatchQueue.global(qos:.default).async {
    self.database.enumerateEvents(matching:pred) { ev, stop in
        if ev.title.range(of:"nap") != nil {
            self.napid = ev.calendarItemIdentifier
            stop.pointee = true
        }
    }
}
```

When you fetch events from the database, they are provided in no particular order; the convenience method compareStartDate(with:) is provided as a sort selector to put them in order by start date:

```
events.sort { $0.compareStartDate(with:$1) == .orderedAscending }
```

When you extract events from the database, event recurrences are treated as separate events. Recurrences of the same event will have different start and end dates but the same calendarItemIdentifier. When you fetch an event by identifier, you get the *earliest* event with that identifier. This makes sense, because if you're going to make a change affecting this and future recurrences of the event, you'll want to start with the earliest possible recurrence (so that "future" means "all").

Fetching reminders is similar to fetching events, but simpler. When you call fetch-Reminders(matching:completion:), the possible predicates let you fetch all reminders in given calendars, incomplete reminders, or completed reminders. You don't have to call it on a background thread, because it calls your completion function asynchronously.

Calendar Interface

The EventKit UI framework provides three view controller classes that manage views for letting the user work with events and calendars:

EKEventViewController
Shows the description of a single event, possibly editable.

EKEventEditViewController
Allows the user to create or edit an event.

EKCalendarChooser
    Allows the user to pick a calendar.

These view controllers automatically listen for changes in the database and, if needed, will automatically call refresh on the information being edited, updating their display to match. If a view controller is displaying an event in the database and the event is deleted while the user is viewing it, the delegate will get the same notification as if the user had deleted it.

EKEventViewController

EKEventViewController displays an event in the manner familiar from the Calendar app, listing the event's title, date and time, calendar, alert, and notes. To use EKEventViewController, instantiate it, give it an event from the database, assign it a delegate (EKEventViewDelegate), and *push* it onto an existing navigation controller:

```
let ev = self.database.calendarItem(withIdentifier:self.napid) as! EKEvent
let evc = EKEventViewController()
evc.event = ev
evc.delegate = self
self.navigationController?.pushViewController(evc, animated: true)
```

 Do *not* use EKEventViewController for an event that isn't in the database, or at a time when the database isn't open! It won't function correctly if you do.

If allowsEditing is true, an Edit button appears in the navigation bar, and by tapping this, the user can edit the various aspects of an event in an interface just like the Calendar app, including the Delete button at the bottom. If the user ultimately deletes the event, or edits it and taps Done, the change is saved into the database.

If the user deletes the event, you will be notified in the delegate method, eventView-Controller(_:didCompleteWith:). The second parameter is an EKEventView-Action, which will be .deleted; it is then up to you to pop the navigation controller:

```
func eventViewController(_ controller: EKEventViewController,
    didCompleteWith action: EKEventViewAction) {
        if action == .deleted {
            self.navigationController?.popViewController(animated:true)
        }
}
```

 Even if allowsEditing is false (the default), the user can change what calendar this event belongs to, can change the event's alert firing time, and can delete the event. I regard this as a bug.

EKEventEditViewController

EKEventEditViewController (a UINavigationController) presents the interface for editing an event. To use it, set its `eventStore` and `editViewDelegate` (EKEventEdit-ViewDelegate, *not* `delegate`), and optionally its `event`, and *present* it as a presented view controller. The event can be `nil` for a completely empty new event; it can be an event you've just created (and possibly partially configured) and not stored in the database; or it can be an existing event from the database.

The delegate method `eventEditViewControllerDefaultCalendar(forNewEvents:)` may be implemented to specify what calendar a completely new event should be assigned to. If you're partially constructing a new event, you can assign it a calendar then, and of course an event from the database already has a calendar.

You must implement the delegate method `eventEditViewController(_:did-CompleteWith:)` so that you can dismiss the presented view controller. The second parameter is an EKEventEditViewAction telling you what the user did; possible actions are that the user cancelled (`.canceled`), saved the edited event into the database (`.saved`), or deleted an already existing event from the database (`.deleted`). You can get a reference to the edited event as the view controller's `event`.

EKCalendarChooser

EKCalendarChooser displays a list of calendars, choosable by tapping; a chosen calendar displays a checkmark. To use it, instantiate it with its initializer:

- `init(selectionStyle:displayStyle:entityType:eventStore:)`

The `selectionStyle` dictates whether the user can pick one or multiple calendars; the `displayStyle` states whether all calendars or only writable calendars will be displayed. Now set a `delegate` (adopting the EKCalendarChooserDelegate protocol) and do a little dance: make the EKCalendarChooser the root view controller of a UINavigationController and *present the navigation controller* as a presented view controller (which looks best as a popover on the iPad). Two properties, `showsCancel-Button` and `showsDoneButton`, determine whether these buttons will appear in the navigation bar. You can perform additional customizations through the view controller's `navigationItem`.

There are three delegate methods, the first two being required:

- `calendarChooserDidFinish(_:)` (the user tapped Done)
- `calendarChooserDidCancel(_:)`
- `calendarChooserSelectionDidChange(_:)`

In the `finish` and `cancel` methods, you should dismiss the presented view controller.

In this example, we offer to delete the selected calendar. Because this is potentially destructive, we pass through an alert for confirmation:

```
@IBAction func deleteCalendar (_ sender: Any) {
    let choo = EKCalendarChooser(
        selectionStyle:.single, displayStyle:.allCalendars,
        entityType:.event, eventStore:self.database)
    choo.showsDoneButton = true
    choo.showsCancelButton = true
    choo.delegate = self
    choo.navigationItem.prompt = "Pick a calendar to delete:"
    let nav = UINavigationController(rootViewController: choo)
    self.present(nav, animated: true)
}
func calendarChooserDidCancel(_ choo: EKCalendarChooser) {
    self.dismiss(animated:true)
}
func calendarChooserDidFinish(_ choo: EKCalendarChooser) {
    let cals = choo.selectedCalendars
    guard cals.count > 0 else { self.dismiss(animated:true); return }
    let calsToDelete = cals.map {$0.calendarIdentifier}
    let alert = UIAlertController(title:"Delete selected calendar?",
        message:nil, preferredStyle:.alert)
    alert.addAction(UIAlertAction(title:"Cancel", style:.cancel))
    alert.addAction(UIAlertAction(title:"Delete", style:.destructive) { _ in
        for id in calsToDelete {
            if let cal = self.database.calendar(withIdentifier:id) {
                try? self.database.removeCalendar(cal, commit: true)
            }
        }
        self.dismiss(animated:true) // dismiss *everything*
    })
    choo.present(alert, animated: true)
}
```

Maps

Your app can imitate the Maps app, displaying a map interface and placing annotations and overlays on the map. The relevant classes are provided by the Map Kit framework. You'll need to `import MapKit`. The types that describe locations in terms of latitude and longitude, whose names start with "CL," come from the Core Location framework, but you won't need to import it explicitly if you're already importing the Map Kit framework.

Map Views

A map is displayed through a UIView subclass, an MKMapView. You can instantiate an MKMapView in code like any other view. Alternatively, in the nib editor, the Objects library contains an MKMapView object that you can drag into your interface as you design it; you might need to link to the MapKit framework manually (in the app target's Link Binary With Libraries build phase) to prevent the app from crashing as the nib loads.

A map has a `type`, which is usually one of the following (MKMapType):

- `.standard`
- `.satellite`
- `.hybrid`

(A further MKMapType, `.mutedStandard`, dims the map elements so that your additions to the map view stand out.)

Figure 21-1. A map view

Displaying a Region

The area displayed on the map is its `region`, an MKCoordinateRegion. This is a struct comprising two things:

`center`
> A CLLocationCoordinate2D. The latitude and longitude of the point at the center of the region.

`span`
> An MKCoordinateSpan. The quantity of latitude and longitude embraced by the region (and hence the scale of the map).

In this example, I'll initialize the display of an MKMapView (`self.map`) to show a place where I like to go dirt biking (Figure 21-1):

```
let loc = CLLocationCoordinate2DMake(34.927752,-120.217608)
let span = MKCoordinateSpan(latitudeDelta: 0.015, longitudeDelta: 0.015)
let reg = MKCoordinateRegion(center:loc, span:span)
self.map.region = reg
```

An MKCoordinateSpan is described in degrees of latitude and longitude. It may be, however, that what you know is the region's proposed dimensions in meters. To convert, call this MKCoordinateRegion initializer:

- `init(center:latitudinalMeters:longitudinalMeters:)`

The ability to perform this conversion is important, because an MKMapView shows the world through a Mercator projection, where longitude lines are parallel and equidistant, and scale increases at higher latitudes. I happen to know that the area I want to display is about 1200 meters on a side, so this is another way of displaying roughly the same region:

```
let loc = CLLocationCoordinate2DMake(34.927752,-120.217608)
let reg = MKCoordinateRegion(
    center:loc, latitudinalMeters:1200, longitudinalMeters:1200)
self.map.region = reg
```

Another way of describing a map region is with an MKMapRect, a struct built up from MKMapPoint and MKMapSize. The earth has already been projected onto the map for us, and now we are describing a rectangle of that map, in terms of the units in which the map is drawn. The exact relationship between an MKMapPoint and the corresponding location coordinate is arbitrary and of no interest; what matters is that you can ask for the conversion, along with the ratio of points to meters (which will vary with latitude):

- MKMapPoint(_:) (coerces from CLLocationCoordinate2D)

- coordinate (coerces to CLLocationCoordinate2D)

- distance(to:) (meters between map points)

- MKMetersPerMapPointAtLatitude(_:)

- MKMapPointsPerMeterAtLatitude(_:)

To determine what the map view is showing in MKMapRect terms, use its visible-MapRect property. So this is yet another way of displaying approximately the same region:

```
let loc = CLLocationCoordinate2DMake(34.927752,-120.217608)
let pt = MKMapPoint(loc)
let w = MKMapPointsPerMeterAtLatitude(loc.latitude) * 1200
self.map.visibleMapRect =
    MKMapRect(x:pt.x - w/2.0, y:pt.y - w/2.0, width:w, height:w)
```

In none of those examples did I bother with the question of the actual dimensions of the map view itself. I simply threw a proposed region at the map view, and it decided how best to portray the corresponding area. Values you assign to the map view's region and visibleMapRect are unlikely to be the exact values it adopts, because the map view will optimize for display without distorting the map's scale. You can perform this same optimization in code by calling these methods:

- regionThatFits(_:)

- mapRectThatFits(_:)

- mapRectThatFits(_:edgePadding:)

Scrolling and Zooming

By default, the user can zoom and scroll the map with the usual gestures; you can turn this off by setting the map view's isZoomEnabled and isScrollEnabled to false. Usually you will set them both to `true` or both to `false`. Starting in iOS 13, you can limit how far the user can zoom and scroll, using these properties:

cameraZoomRange

An MKMapView.CameraZoomRange. How far the "camera" (the eye through which the map view is looking at the earth) is permitted to be from the center of the region displayed. The initializer takes a maximum distance, a minimum distance, or both (in meters).

cameraBoundary

An MKMapView.CameraBoundary. The maximum region of the earth that the map view can display; the map view cannot be scrolled so as to reveal anything outside this region. Can be expressed as an MKCoordinateRegion or as an MKMapRect, just like the visible region of the map view.

Here, I'll modify my map view to restrict how far the user can zoom and scroll from the initial display:

```
self.map.cameraBoundary = MKMapView.CameraBoundary(
    coordinateRegion: MKCoordinateRegion(
        center: loc, span: MKCoordinateSpan(
            latitudeDelta: 0.6, longitudeDelta: 0.6)))
self.map.cameraZoomRange = MKMapView.CameraZoomRange(
    maxCenterCoordinateDistance: 130_000)
```

You can change programmatically the region displayed, optionally with animation, by calling these methods:

- `setRegion(_:animated:)`
- `setCenter(_:animated:)`
- `setVisibleMapRect(_:animated:)`
- `setVisibleMapRect(_:edgePadding:animated:)`

Even programmatically, you cannot violate the limits set by the map view's `camera-ZoomRange` and `cameraBoundary`.

The map view's delegate (MKMapViewDelegate) is notified as the map loads and as the region changes (including changes triggered programmatically):

- `mapViewWillStartLoadingMap(_:)`
- `mapViewDidFinishLoadingMap(_:)`
- `mapViewDidFailLoadingMap(_:withError:)`
- `mapViewDidChangeVisibleRegion(_:)`
- `mapView(_:regionWillChangeAnimated:)`
- `mapView(_:regionDidChangeAnimated:)`

Other Map View Customizations

An MKMapView has Bool properties such as showsCompass, showsScale, and shows-Traffic; set these to dictate whether those elements of the map should be displayed. Starting in iOS 11, the compass and the scale legend can be displayed as independent views, an MKCompassButton and an MKScaleView; if you use these, you'll probably want to set the corresponding Bool property to false so as not to get two compasses or scales. Both views are initialized with the map view as parameter, so that their display will reflect the rotation and zoom of the map. The MKCompassButton, like the internal compass, is a button; if the user taps it, the map is reoriented with north at the top. The visibility of these views is governed by properties (compassVisibility and scaleVisibility) whose value is one of these (MKFeatureVisibility):

- .hidden
- .visible
- .adaptive

The .adaptive behavior (the default) is that the compass is visible only if the map is rotated, and the scale legend is visible only if the map is zoomed.

Starting in iOS 13, you can dictate what sorts of POI (point of interest) are displayed on the map. In iOS 12 and before, your only choices were to show or suppress points of interest as a whole (showsPointsOfInterest). In iOS 13 and later, the MKPointOf-InterestCategory class consists of static properties (representing strings) that draw fine-grained distinctions, such as .bakery and .brewery. Use these to initialize an MKPointOfInterestFilter with init(excluding:) or init(including:), and assign the filter to the map view's pointOfInterestFilter.

You can also enable 3D viewing of the map (pitchEnabled), and there's a large and powerful API putting control of 3D viewing in your hands. Discussion of 3D map viewing is beyond the scope of this chapter; an excellent WWDC 2013 video surveys the topic. There are 3D flyover map types .satelliteFlyover and .hybridFlyover; a WWDC 2015 video explains about these.

Map Images

To capture a map display as an image, use an MKMapSnapshotter. This is useful when you want to display a mere picture of a map (that is, a noninteractive map). The result is an MKMapSnapshotter.Snapshot whose image is the screenshot. The screenshot captures a runtime-generated map, not *your* map view; therefore, your map view's annotations and overlays are not included. Use the snapshotter's options (MKMapSnapshotter.Options) to configure the region displayed:

```
let opts = MKMapSnapshotter.Options()
opts.region = self.map.region
let snap = MKMapSnapshotter(options: opts)
snap.start { shot, err in
    if let shot = shot {
        let im = shot.image
        // ...
    }
}
```

Starting in iOS 13, you can configure the types of POI shown in the snapshot by setting the options object's `pointOfInterestFilter`.

An MKMapSnapohotter will portray a light mode map or a dark mode map, according to the `traitCollection` you assign to its `options`. But the resulting image, unlike a real map view, does not magically change later on just because the user changes modes; so arranging to change images when the mode changes is up to you.

Annotations

An *annotation* is a marker associated with a location on a map. To make an annotation appear on a map, two objects are needed:

The object attached to the MKMapView

The annotation itself is attached to the MKMapView. It is an instance of any class that adopts the MKAnnotation protocol, which specifies a `coordinate`, a `title`, and a `subtitle` for the annotation. You might have reason to define your own class to handle this task, or you can use the simple built-in MKPoint-Annotation class. The annotation's coordinate is crucial; it says where on earth the annotation should be drawn. The title and subtitle are optional.

The object that draws the annotation

An annotation is drawn by an MKAnnotationView, a UIView subclass. This can be extremely simple. In fact, even a `nil` MKAnnotationView might be perfectly satisfactory, because the runtime will then automatically supply a view for you. In iOS 10 and before, this automatic view was a realistic rendering of a physical pin, red by default but configurable to any color, supplied by the built-in MKPin-AnnotationView class. Starting in iOS 11, it is an MKMarkerAnnotationView, by default portraying a pin schematically in a circular red "balloon."

Not only does an annotation require two distinct objects, but in fact those two objects do not initially exist together. An annotation object has no pointer to the annotation view object that will draw it. Rather, it is up to you to supply the annotation view object in real time, on demand. This architecture may sound confusing, but in fact it's a clever way of reducing the amount of resources needed at any given moment. An annotation itself is merely a lightweight object that a map can always possess; the

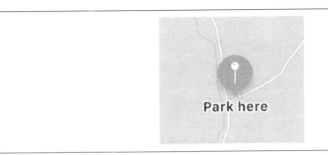

Figure 21-2. A simple annotation

corresponding annotation view is a heavyweight object that is needed only so long as that annotation's coordinates are within the visible portion of the map.

Let's add the simplest possible annotation to our map. The point where the annotation is to go has been stored in an instance property (self.annloc):

```
let annloc = CLLocationCoordinate2DMake(34.923964,-120.219558)
```

We create the annotation, configure it, and add it to the MKMapView:

```
let ann = MKPointAnnotation()
ann.coordinate = self.annloc
ann.title = "Park here"
ann.subtitle = "Fun awaits down the road!"
self.map.addAnnotation(ann)
```

That code is sufficient to produce Figure 21-2. I didn't take any steps to supply an MKAnnotationView, so the MKAnnotationView is nil. But a nil MKAnnotation-View, as I've already said, means an MKMarkerAnnotationView that produces a drawing of a pin in a red balloon.

By default, an MKMarkerAnnotationView displays its title below the annotation. This differs markedly from an MKPinAnnotationView, whose title and subtitle are displayed in a separate *callout* view that appears above the annotation view only when the annotation is *selected* (because the user taps it, or because you set the MKAnnotationView's isSelected to true). A selected MKMarkerAnnotationView is drawn larger and displays the subtitle in addition to the title.

Customizing an MKMarkerAnnotationView

MKMarkerAnnotationView has many customizable properties affecting its display:

markerTintColor
    The balloon color.

`glyphTintColor`
> The color used to tint the glyph portrayed inside the balloon. Has no effect on the default pin image.

`glyphText`
> One or two characters, portrayed as the image in the middle of the balloon.

`glyphImage`
> Replaces the `glyphText`; a 40×40 image, which will be sized down automatically to 20×20 when the view is not selected. Alternatively, supply both a larger and a smaller image, the `selectedGlyphImage` and `glyphImage` respectively. A symbol image works fine here as well. The image is treated as a template image; setting the rendering mode to `.alwaysOriginal` has no effect.

`titleVisibility`
`subtitleVisibility`
> The visibility of the title and subtitle. These are MKFeatureVisibility enums, where `.adaptive` is the default behavior that I've already described. The `subtitleVisibility` has no effect unless you also set the `titleVisibility`.

Doubtless you are now thinking: that's all very well, but *what* MKMarkerAnnotation-View are we talking about? No such view appears in our code, so there is no object whose properties we can set!

One way to access the annotation view is to give the map view a `delegate` and implement the MKMapViewDelegate method `mapView(_:viewFor:)`. The second parameter is the MKAnnotation for which we are to supply a view. In our implementation of this method, we can *dequeue* an annotation view from the map view, passing in a string reuse identifier:

`dequeueReusableAnnotationView(withIdentifier:for:)`
> In the minimal case, pass as the `identifier:` the constant `MKMapViewDefault-AnnotationViewReuseIdentifier`. The second argument should be the annotation that arrived as the second parameter of the delegate method.

If we have taken no steps to the contrary, this will give us the default view, which in this case is an MKMarkerAnnotationView. Having obtained an annotation view, our `mapView(_:viewFor:)` can configure it; ultimately, it will return the annotation view.

The notion of view reuse here is similar to the reuse of table view cells (Chapter 8). The map may have a huge number of annotations, but it needs to display annotation views only for the annotations within its current `region`. So annotation views that have been scrolled out of view can be reused, and are held for us by the map view in a cache for exactly this purpose.

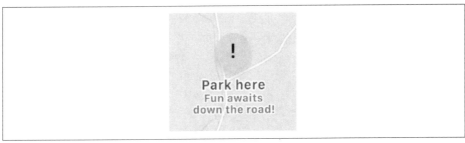

Figure 21-3. Customizing a marker annotation view

In this example, I check to see that my MKAnnotationView is indeed an MKMarkerAnnotationView, as expected. I also attempt to distinguish this particular annotation by looking at its title; that's not a very good way to distinguish annotation types, but I'll postpone further discussion of the matter until later:

```
func mapView(_ mapView: MKMapView,
    viewFor annotation: MKAnnotation) -> MKAnnotationView? {
        let id = MKMapViewDefaultAnnotationViewReuseIdentifier
        if let v = mapView.dequeueReusableAnnotationView(
            withIdentifier: id, for: annotation) as? MKMarkerAnnotationView {
                if let t = annotation.title, t == "Park here" {
                    v.titleVisibility = .visible
                    v.subtitleVisibility = .visible
                    v.markerTintColor = .green
                    v.glyphText = "!"
                    v.glyphTintColor = .black
                    return v
                }
        }
        return nil
}
```

The result is shown in Figure 21-3.

Changing the Annotation View Class

Instead of accepting the default MKMarkerAnnotationView as the class of our annotation view, we can substitute a different MKAnnotationView subclass. This might be our own MKMarkerAnnotationView subclass, or some other MKAnnotationView subclass, or MKAnnotationView itself. The way to do that is to *register* our class with the map view, associating it with the reuse identifier, by calling this method beforehand:

- `register(_:forAnnotationViewWithReuseIdentifier:)`

To illustrate, I'll use MKAnnotationView itself as our annotation view class. We won't get the default drawing of a balloon and a pin, because we're not using MKMarkerAnnotationView any longer; instead, I'll set the MKAnnotationView's

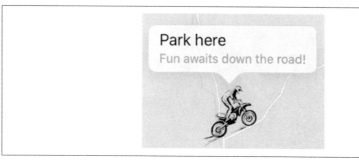

Figure 21-4. A custom annotation image

`image` property directly. We also won't get the title and subtitle drawn beneath the image; instead, I'll set the annotation view's `canShowCallout` to `true`, and the title and subtitle will appear in the callout when the annotation view is selected.

So, assume that I have an identifier declared as an instance property:

```
let bikeid = "bike"
```

And assume that I've registered MKAnnotationView as the class that goes with that identifier:

```
self.map.register(MKAnnotationView.self,
    forAnnotationViewWithReuseIdentifier: self.bikeid)
```

Then my implementation of `mapView(_:viewFor:)` might look like this:

```
func mapView(_ mapView: MKMapView,
    viewFor annotation: MKAnnotation) -> MKAnnotationView? {
        let v = mapView.dequeueReusableAnnotationView(
            withIdentifier: self.bikeid, for: annotation)
        if let t = annotation.title, t == "Park here" {
            v.image = UIImage(named:"clipartdirtbike.gif")
            v.bounds.size.height /= 3.0
            v.bounds.size.width /= 3.0
            v.centerOffset = CGPoint(0,-20)
            v.canShowCallout = true
            return v
        }
        return nil
}
```

The dirt bike image is too large, so I shrink the view's bounds before returning it; I also move the view up a bit, so that the bottom of the image is at the coordinates on the map. The result is shown in Figure 21-4.

Custom Annotation View Class

A better way to write the preceding example might be for us to create our own MKAnnotationView subclass and endow it with the ability to draw itself. This will allow us to move the code that configures the image and the callout out of the delegate method and into the subclass itself, where it more properly belongs.

A minimal implementation of an MKAnnotationView subclass should override the annotation property with a setter observer, so that every time the view is reused and a new annotation value is assigned, the view is reconfigured. It might also override the designated initializer, init(annotation:reuseIdentifier:), and possibly declare some additional instance variables. For purposes of this example, I'll simply set the image in my annotation setter observer, and I'll move the rest of what I was doing in mapView(_:viewFor:) into a didMoveToSuperview override:

```
class MyBikeAnnotationView : MKAnnotationView {
    override var annotation: MKAnnotation? {
        willSet {
            self.image = UIImage(named:"clipartdirtbike.gif")
        }
    }
    override func didMoveToSuperview() {
        super.didMoveToSuperview()
        self.bounds.size.height /= 3.0
        self.bounds.size.width /= 3.0
        self.centerOffset = CGPoint(0,-20)
        self.canShowCallout = true
    }
}
```

We register our custom annotation view class to associate it with our identifier:

```
self.map.register(MyBikeAnnotationView.self,
    forAnnotationViewWithReuseIdentifier: self.bikeid)
```

Our implementation of mapView(_:viewFor:) now has much less work to do:

```
func mapView(_ mapView: MKMapView,
    viewFor annotation: MKAnnotation) -> MKAnnotationView? {
        let v = mapView.dequeueReusableAnnotationView(
            withIdentifier: self.bikeid, for: annotation)
        if let t = annotation.title, t == "Park here" {
            // nothing else to do!
            return v
        }
        return nil
}
```

If, in fact, MyBikeAnnotationView is the *only* annotation view type we will ever use, we can go even further: we can register MyBikeAnnotationView *as the default*:

```
self.map.register(MyBikeAnnotationView.self,
    forAnnotationViewWithReuseIdentifier:
        MKMapViewDefaultAnnotationViewReuseIdentifier)
```

At that point, we can delete our implementation of mapView(_:viewFor:) entirely! It has no work to do, because it has no choices to make; our MKBikeAnnotationView, which configures itself, will be the annotation view class *automatically*.

Custom Annotation Class

Let's suppose precisely the opposite of what I just said — namely, that our implementation of mapView(_:viewFor:) *does* have choices to make. Depending on the nature of the annotation, it must configure our annotation view class differently, or even pick a different annotation view class. Some annotations might show a dirt bike, but other annotations might show a different image.

This difference will need to be expressed somehow as part of *the annotation itself*. Different annotation types must therefore be somehow distinguishable from one another. So far, I've been avoiding that issue entirely by having my mapView(_:view-For:) implementation examine the incoming annotation's title; but that is obviously a fragile and inappropriate solution. The proper way is to use one or more *custom annotation classes* that allow the desired distinction to be drawn.

A minimal custom annotation class will look like this:

```
class MyBikeAnnotation : NSObject, MKAnnotation {
    dynamic var coordinate : CLLocationCoordinate2D
    var title: String?
    var subtitle: String?
    init(location coord:CLLocationCoordinate2D) {
        self.coordinate = coord
        super.init()
    }
}
```

When we create our annotation and add it to the map, our code looks like this:

```
let ann = MyBikeAnnotation(location:self.annloc)
ann.title = "Park here"
ann.subtitle = "Fun awaits down the road!"
self.map.addAnnotation(ann)
```

In mapView(_:viewFor:), we can decide what to do just by looking at the class of the incoming annotation:

```
if annotation is MyBikeAnnotation {
    let v = mapView.dequeueReusableAnnotationView(
        withIdentifier: self.bikeid, for: annotation)
    // ...
    return v
}
return nil
```

You can readily see how this architecture gives our implementation room to grow. At the moment, every MyBikeAnnotation is drawn the same way, but we could now add another property to MyBikeAnnotation that tells us what drawing to use. We could also give MyBikeAnnotation further properties saying such things as which way the bike should face, what angle it should be drawn at, and so on. Each MyBikeAnnotationView instance will end up with a reference to a MyBikeAnnotation instance (as its `annotation` property), so it will be able to read those properties and configure the drawing of its own image appropriately.

Annotation View Hiding and Clustering

Annotation views don't change size as the map is zoomed in and out, so if there are several annotations and they are brought close together by the user zooming out, the display can become crowded. Moreover, if too many annotation views are being drawn simultaneously in a map view, scroll and zoom performance can degrade.

Before iOS 11, the only way to prevent this was to respond to changes in the map's visible region — typically in the delegate method `mapView(_:regionDidChange-Animated:)` — by removing and adding annotations dynamically. MKMapView has extensive support for adding and removing annotations, and its `annotations(in:)` method efficiently lists the annotations within a given MKMapRect. Also, given a bunch of annotations, you can ask your MKMapView to zoom in such a way that all of them are showing (`showAnnotations(_:animated:)`). Nevertheless, deciding which annotations to eliminate or restore, and when, was left up to you, and was decidedly a tricky problem.

In iOS 11 and later, annotation views can *automatically* show and hide themselves as the display becomes crowded. And the built-in solution goes even further: if annotations are hidden, they can be replaced by a special *cluster annotation* so that the user *knows* there are hidden annotations. MKAnnotationView has properties that allow you to customize what happens:

`displayPriority` *(hiding)*
    An MKFeatureDisplayPriority struct, which works rather like a layout constraint priority: a value of `.required`, corresponding to 1000, means that the view shouldn't be hidden, and values `defaultHigh` and `defaultLow`, corresponding to 750 and 250, give some alternative priorities, but you can set any value you like through the struct's `init(rawValue:)` initializer. If all your annotation views

have a `displayPriority` of `.required` (the default), your map view will not participate at all in automatic annotation view hiding.

`clusteringIdentifier` *(clustering)*
A string. The idea is that birds of a feather should flock together: if two annotation views have the same clustering identifier, then the same cluster annotation can be used to represent them when they are hidden. This will in fact happen only if the runtime judges that they are sufficiently close to one another when they are hidden. If you don't set an annotation view's `clusteringIdentifier`, it won't participate in clustering. Giving all annotation views the same `clusteringIdentifier` gives the runtime permission to cluster them however it sees fit.

`collisionMode` *(clustering)*
An MKAnnotationView.CollisionMode. Two annotation views with the same `clusteringIdentifier` will be replaced by a cluster annotation if the map is zoomed out so far that they collide. But what constitutes a collision between two annotation views? To know that, we need a collision edge. It might be:

`.rectangle`
The edge is the view's frame.

`.circle`
The edge is the largest circle inscribable in and centered within the view's frame.

`.none`
(New in iOS 14.) The view is exempted from collisions.

If you need to offset or resize the boundary of the rectangle or circle that describes the collision edge, use the annotation view's `alignmentRectInsets`.

To make your annotation views opt in to both hiding and clustering, a minimal approach would be to set the `displayPriority` of all your annotation views to `.defaultHigh` and the `clusteringIdentifier` of all your annotation views to some single string.

New in iOS 14, you can also regulate the layering order when your MKAnnotation-Views overlap, with these properties:

`zPriority`
`selectedZPriority`
The relative front-to-back layering order of the annotation view, when the view is unselected and selected, respectively. A Float between `0` and `1000` inclusive, wrapped in an MKAnnotationViewZPriority struct, with convenience constants `.max` (1000), `.min` (0), `.defaultSelected` (1000), and `.default-Unselected` (500).

A cluster annotation is a real annotation — an MKClusterAnnotation. Its `member-Annotations` are the annotations whose views have been hidden and subsumed into this cluster. It has a `title` and `subtitle`; by default, these are based on the `member-Annotations`, but you can customize them.

A cluster annotation's view is a real annotation view. It has, itself, a `displayPriority` and a `collisionMode`. (The `displayPriority` is, by default, the highest `display-Priority` among the annotation views it replaces.) If an annotation view has been hidden and replaced by a cluster annotation view, its `cluster` property points to the cluster annotation view. The default cluster annotation view corresponds to a reuse identifier `MKMapViewDefaultClusterAnnotationViewReuseIdentifier`.

You can customize a cluster annotation view as you would any other annotation view. You can substitute your own MKAnnotationView subclass by registering or dequeuing it, exactly as in the earlier examples. Your `mapView(_:viewFor:)` will know that this annotation is a cluster annotation because it will be an MKCluster-Annotation. Or you can register your custom cluster annotation view as the class for `MKMapViewDefaultClusterAnnotationViewReuseIdentifier`, in which case you might not need an implementation of `mapView(_:viewFor:)` at all.

Other Annotation Features

When an MKPinAnnotationView initially appears on the map, if its `animatesDrop` property is `true`, it drops into place from above. When an MKMarkerAnnotation-View initially appears on the map, if its `animatesWhenAdded` property is `true`, it grows slightly into place.

In like fashion, we can add our own animation to an annotation view as it initially appears on the map. To do so, we implement the map view delegate method `map-View(_:didAdd:)`, which hands us an array of MKAnnotationViews. When this method is called, the annotation views have been added but the redraw moment has not yet arrived (Chapter 4); so if we animate a view, that animation will be performed as the view appears onscreen. Here, I'll animate the opacity of our annotation view so that it fades in, while growing the view from a point to its full size; I identify the view type through its `reuseIdentifier`:

```
func mapView(_ mapView: MKMapView, didAdd views: [MKAnnotationView]) {
    for aView in views {
        if aView.reuseIdentifier == self.bikeid {
            aView.transform = CGAffineTransform(scaleX: 0, y: 0)
            aView.alpha = 0
            UIView.animate(withDuration: 0.8) {
                aView.alpha = 1
                aView.transform = .identity
```

```
                }
            }
        }
    }
```

Certain annotation properties and annotation view properties are automatically animatable through view animation, provided you've implemented them in a KVO compliant way. In MyBikeAnnotation, the `coordinate` property *is* KVO compliant
(because we declared it `dynamic`); therefore, we are able to animate shifting the annotation's position:

```
self.map.addAnnotation(ann)
// ...
UIView.animate(withDuration: 0.25) {
    var loc = ann.coordinate
    loc.latitude = loc.latitude + 0.0005
    loc.longitude = loc.longitude + 0.001
    ann.coordinate = loc
}
```

MKMapView has methods allowing annotations to be selected or deselected programmatically, doing in code the same thing that happens when the user taps. The
delegate has methods notifying you when the user selects or deselects an annotation,
and you are free to override your custom MKAnnotationView's `set-`
`Selected(_:animated:)` if you want to change what happens when the user taps an
annotation. You could show and hide a custom view instead of, or in addition to, the
built-in callout.

A callout can contain left and right accessory views; these are the MKAnnotation-
View's `leftCalloutAccessoryView` and `rightCalloutAccessoryView`. They are
UIViews, and should be small (less than 32 pixels in height). There is also a `detail-`
`CalloutAccessoryView` which replaces the subtitle; you could supply a multiline label
with smaller text. You can respond to taps on these views as you would any view or
control. The map view's `tintColor` (see Chapter 13) affects such accessory view elements as template images and button titles.

An MKAnnotationView can optionally be draggable by the user; set its `draggable`
property to `true`. If you're using a custom annotation class, its `coordinate` property
must also be settable. In our custom annotation class, MyBikeAnnotation, the
`coordinate` property *is* settable; it is explicitly declared as a read-write property
(`var`), as opposed to the `coordinate` property in the MKAnnotation protocol which
is read-only. You can also customize changes to the appearance of the view as it is
dragged, by implementing your annotation view class's `setDragState(_:animated:)`
method.

Overlays

An *overlay* differs from an annotation in being drawn entirely with respect to points on the surface of the earth. Whereas an annotation's size is always the same, an overlay's size is tied to the zoom of the map view.

Overlays are implemented much like annotations. You provide an object that adopts the MKOverlay protocol (which itself conforms to the MKAnnotation protocol) and add it to the map view. When the map view delegate method `mapView(_:renderer-For:)` is called, you provide an MKOverlayRenderer and hand it the overlay object; the overlay renderer then draws the overlay on demand. As with annotations, this architecture means that the overlay itself is a lightweight object, and the overlay is drawn only if the part of the earth that the overlay covers is actually being displayed in the map view. An MKOverlayRenderer has no reuse identifier; it isn't a view, but rather a drawing engine that draws into a graphics context supplied by the map view.

Some built-in MKShape subclasses adopt the MKOverlay protocol: MKCircle, MKPolygon, and MKPolyline (and its subclass MKGeodesicPolyline). In parallel to those, MKOverlayRenderer has built-in subclasses ready to draw the corresponding shapes: MKCircleRenderer, MKPolygonRenderer, and MKPolylineRenderer (and its subclass MKGradientPolylineRenderer, new in iOS 14). Starting in iOS 13, multiple polygons or polylines can be combined into an MKMultiPolygon or MKMultiPolyline and drawn by an MKMultiPolygonRenderer or MKMultiPolylineRenderer; this can be useful because renderers, even though they are not views, do involve overhead, so one would like as few separate overlays as possible on the screen simultaneously.

As with annotations, you can base your overlay entirely on the power of existing classes. In this example, I'll use MKPolygonRenderer to draw an overlay triangle pointing up the road from the parking place annotated in our earlier examples (Figure 21-5). We add the MKPolygon as an overlay to our map view, and supply its corresponding MKPolygonRenderer in our implementation of `mapView(_:renderer-For:)`. First, the MKPolygon overlay:

```
let lat = self.annloc.latitude
let metersPerPoint = MKMetersPerMapPointAtLatitude(lat)
var c = MKMapPoint(self.annloc)
c.x += 150/metersPerPoint
c.y -= 50/metersPerPoint
var p1 = MKMapPoint(x:c.x, y:c.y)
p1.y -= 100/metersPerPoint
var p2 = MKMapPoint(x:c.x, y:c.y)
p2.x += 100/metersPerPoint
var p3 = MKMapPoint(x:c.x, y:c.y)
p3.x += 300/metersPerPoint
```

Figure 21-5. An overlay

```
p3.y -= 400/metersPerPoint
var points = [p1, p2, p3]
let tri = MKPolygon(points:&points, count:3)
self.map.addOverlay(tri)
```

Second, the delegate method, where we provide the MKPolygonRenderer:

```
func mapView(_ mapView: MKMapView,
    rendererFor overlay: MKOverlay) -> MKOverlayRenderer {
        if let overlay = overlay as? MKPolygon {
            let r = MKPolygonRenderer(polygon:overlay)
            r.fillColor = UIColor.red.withAlphaComponent(0.1)
            r.strokeColor = UIColor.red.withAlphaComponent(0.8)
            r.lineWidth = 2
            return r
        }
        return MKOverlayRenderer()
}
```

Custom Overlay Class

The triangle in Figure 21-5 is rather crude; I could draw a better arrow shape using a CGPath (Chapter 2). The built-in MKOverlayRenderer subclass that lets me do that is MKOverlayPathRenderer. To structure things similarly to the preceding example, I'd like to supply the CGPath when I add the overlay instance to the map view. No built-in class lets me do that, so I'll use a custom class, MyPathOverlay, that adopts the MKOverlay protocol.

A minimal overlay class looks like this:

```
class MyPathOverlay : NSObject, MKOverlay {
    var coordinate : CLLocationCoordinate2D {
        get {
            let pt = MKMapPoint(
                x:self.boundingMapRect.midX,
                y:self.boundingMapRect.midY)
            return pt.coordinate
```

```
        }
    }
    var boundingMapRect : MKMapRect
    init(rect:MKMapRect) {
        self.boundingMapRect = rect
        super.init()
    }
}
```

Our actual MyPathOverlay class will also have a `path` property; this will be a UIBezierPath that holds our CGPath and supplies it to the MKOverlayPathRenderer.

Just as the `coordinate` property of an annotation tells the map view where on earth the annotation is to be drawn, the `boundingMapRect` property of an overlay tells the map view where on earth the overlay is to be drawn. Whenever any part of the `boundingMapRect` is displayed within the map view's bounds, the map view will have to concern itself with drawing the overlay. With MKPolygon, we supplied the points of the polygon in earth coordinates and the `boundingMapRect` was calculated for us. With our custom overlay class, we must supply or calculate it ourselves.

At first it may appear that there is a typological impedance mismatch: the `bounding-MapRect` is an MKMapRect, whereas a CGPath is defined by CGPoints. However, it turns out that these units are interchangeable: the CGPoints of our CGPath will be translated for us directly into MKMapPoints on the same scale — that is, the *distance* between any two CGPoints will be the distance between the two corresponding MKMapPoints. However, the *origins* are different: the CGPath must be described relative to the top-left corner of the `boundingMapRect`. To put it another way, the `boundingMapRect` is described in earth coordinates, but the top-left corner of the `boundingMapRect` is `.zero` as far as the CGPath is concerned. (You might think of this difference as analogous to the difference between a UIView's frame and its bounds.)

To make life simple, I'll think in meters; actually, I'll think in chunks of 75 meters, because this turns out to be a good unit for positioning and laying out this particular arrow. A line one unit long would in fact be 75 meters long if I were to arrive at this actual spot on the earth and discover the overlay literally drawn on the ground. Having derived this chunk (unit), I use it to lay out the `boundingMapRect`, four units on a side and positioned slightly east and north of the annotation point (because that's where the road is). Then I simply construct the arrow shape within the 4×4-unit square, rotating it so that it points in roughly the same direction as the road:

```
// start with our position and derive a nice unit for drawing
let lat = self.annloc.latitude
let metersPerPoint = MKMetersPerMapPointAtLatitude(lat)
let c = MKMapPoint(self.annloc)
let unit = CGFloat(75.0/metersPerPoint)
// size and position the overlay bounds on the earth
```

```
let sz = CGSize(4*unit, 4*unit)
let mr = MKMapRect(
    x:c.x + 2*Double(unit), y:c.y - 4.5*Double(unit),
    width:Double(sz.width), height:Double(sz.height))
// describe the arrow as a CGPath
let p = CGMutablePath()
let start = CGPoint(0, unit*1.5)
let p1 = CGPoint(start.x+2*unit, start.y)
let p2 = CGPoint(p1.x, p1.y-unit)
let p3 = CGPoint(p2.x+unit*2, p2.y+unit*1.5)
let p4 = CGPoint(p2.x, p2.y+unit*3)
let p5 = CGPoint(p4.x, p4.y-unit)
let p6 = CGPoint(p5.x-2*unit, p5.y)
let points = [start, p1, p2, p3, p4, p5, p6]
// rotate the arrow around its center
let t1 = CGAffineTransform(translationX: unit*2, y: unit*2)
let t2 = t1.rotated(by:-.pi/3.5)
let t3 = t2.translatedBy(x: -unit*2, y: -unit*2)
p.addLines(between: points, transform: t3)
p.closeSubpath()
// create the overlay and give it the path
let over = MyPathOverlay(rect:mr)
over.path = UIBezierPath(cgPath:p)
// add the overlay to the map
self.map.addOverlay(over)
```

The delegate method, where we provide the MKOverlayPathRenderer, is simple. We pull the CGPath out of the MyPathOverlay instance; we hand the CGPath to the MKOverlayPathRenderer; and we tell the MKOverlayPathRenderer how to stroke and fill that path:

```
func mapView(_ mapView: MKMapView,
    rendererFor overlay: MKOverlay) -> MKOverlayRenderer {
        if let overlay = overlay as? MyPathOverlay {
            let r = MKOverlayPathRenderer(overlay:overlay)
            r.path = overlay.path.cgPath
            r.fillColor = UIColor.red.withAlphaComponent(0.2)
            r.strokeColor = .black
            con.setLineWidth(2)
            return r
        }
        return MKOverlayRenderer()
}
```

The result is a much nicer arrow (Figure 21-6), and of course this technique can be generalized to draw an overlay from any CGPath we like.

Custom Overlay Renderer

For full generality, you could define your own MKOverlayRenderer subclass; your subclass must override and implement draw(_:zoomScale:in:). The first parameter

Figure 21-6. A nicer overlay

is an MKMapRect describing a tile of the visible map (not the size and position of the overlay); the third parameter is the CGContext into which you are to draw. Your implementation may be called several times simultaneously on different background threads, one for each tile, so be sure to draw in a thread-safe way. The overlay itself is available through the inherited `overlay` property, and MKOverlayRenderer instance methods such as `rect(for:)` are provided for converting between the map's MKMapRect coordinates and the overlay renderer's graphics context coordinates. The graphics context arrives already configured such that our drawing will be clipped to the current tile. (All this should remind you of CATiledLayer, Chapter 7.)

In our example, we can move the entire functionality for drawing the arrow into an MKOverlayRenderer subclass, which I'll call MyPathOverlayRenderer. Its initializer takes an `angle:` parameter, with which I'll set its `angle` property; now our arrow can point in any direction. Another nice benefit of this architectural change is that we can use the `zoomScale:` parameter to determine the stroke width. For simplicity, my implementation of `draw(_:zoomScale:in:)` ignores the incoming MKMapRect value and just draws the entire arrow every time it is called:

```
var angle : CGFloat = 0
init(overlay:MKOverlay, angle:CGFloat) {
    self.angle = angle
    super.init(overlay:overlay)
}
override func draw(_ mapRect: MKMapRect,
    zoomScale: MKZoomScale, in con: CGContext) {
        con.setStrokeColor(UIColor.black.cgColor)
        con.setFillColor(UIColor.red.withAlphaComponent(0.2).cgColor)
        let scale = UIScreen.main.scale
        con.setLineWidth(2/(zoomScale/scale))
        let unit =
            CGFloat(self.overlay.boundingMapRect.width/4.0)
        let p = CGMutablePath()
        let start = CGPoint(0, unit*1.5)
        let p1 = CGPoint(start.x+2*unit, start.y)
        let p2 = CGPoint(p1.x, p1.y-unit)
        let p3 = CGPoint(p2.x+unit*2, p2.y+unit*1.5)
        let p4 = CGPoint(p2.x, p2.y+unit*3)
```

```
        let p5 = CGPoint(p4.x, p4.y-unit)
        let p6 = CGPoint(p5.x-2*unit, p5.y)
        let points = [start, p1, p2, p3, p4, p5, p6]
        let t1 = CGAffineTransform(translationX: unit*2, y: unit*2)
        let t2 = t1.rotated(by:self.angle)
        let t3 = t2.translatedBy(x: -unit*2, y: -unit*2)
        p.addLines(between: points, transform: t3)
        p.closeSubpath()
        con.addPath(p)
        con.drawPath(using: .fillStroke)
    }
```

To add the overlay to our map, we still must determine its MKMapRect:

```
let lat = self.annloc.latitude
let metersPerPoint = MKMetersPerMapPointAtLatitude(lat)
let c = MKMapPoint(self.annloc)
let unit = 75.0/metersPerPoint
// size and position the overlay bounds on the earth
let sz = CGSize(4*CGFloat(unit), 4*CGFloat(unit))
let mr = MKMapRect(
    x:c.x + 2*unit, y:c.y - 4.5*unit,
    width:Double(sz.width), height:Double(sz.height))
let over = MyPathOverlay(rect:mr)
self.map.addOverlay(over, level:.aboveRoads)
```

The delegate method, providing the overlay renderer, now has very little work to do; in our implementation, it merely supplies an angle for the arrow:

```
func mapView(_ mapView: MKMapView,
    rendererFor overlay: MKOverlay) -> MKOverlayRenderer {
        if overlay is MyPathOverlay {
            let r = MyPathOverlayRenderer(overlay:overlay, angle: -.pi/3.5)
            return r
        }
        return MKOverlayRenderer()
}
```

Other Overlay Features

Our MyPathOverlay class, adopting the MKOverlay protocol, implements the coordinate property by means of a getter method to return the center of the boundingMapRect. This is crude, but it's a good minimal implementation. The purpose of this property is to specify the position where you would add an annotation describing the overlay:

```
// ... create overlay and assign it a path as before ...
self.map.addOverlay(over, level:.aboveRoads)
let annot = MKPointAnnotation()
annot.coordinate = over.coordinate
annot.title = "This way!"
self.map.addAnnotation(annot)
```

The MKOverlay protocol also lets you provide an implementation of `intersects(_:)` to refine your overlay's definition of what constitutes an intersection with itself; the default is to use the `boundingMapRect`, but if your overlay is drawn in some nonrectangular shape, you might want to use its actual shape as the basis for determining intersection.

Overlays are maintained by the map view as an array and are drawn from back to front starting at the beginning of the array. MKMapView has extensive support for adding and removing overlays, and for managing their layering order. When you add the overlay to the map, you can say where you want it drawn among the map view's sublayers. This is also why methods for adding and inserting overlays have a `level:` parameter. The levels are (MKOverlayLevel):

- `.aboveRoads` (and below labels)
- `.aboveLabels`

Perhaps you have your own topo map or your own transit map, and you want to use this as the *content* of the map view. The MKTileOverlay class, adopting the MKOverlay protocol, lets you supplement or replace Apple's map content with your own custom map drawing. You provide a set of tiles at multiple sizes to match multiple zoom levels, and the map view fetches and draws the tiles needed for the current `region` and degree of zoom. It takes a lot of tiles to draw an area of any size, so the MKTileOverlay class is initialized with a URL, which can be a remote URL for tiles to be fetched across the internet as needed.

Map Kit and Current Location

A device may have sensors that can report its current location. Map Kit provides integration with these facilities. Keep in mind that the user can turn off these sensors or can refuse your app access to them (in the Settings app, under Privacy → Location Services), so trying to use these features may fail. Also, determining the device's location can take time.

The real work here is being done by a CLLocationManager instance, which needs to be created and retained; the usual thing is to initialize a view controller instance property by assigning a new CLLocationManager instance to it:

```
let locman = CLLocationManager()
```

Moreover, you must obtain user authorization, and your *Info.plist* must state the reason why you want it (as I'll explain in more detail in Chapter 22):

```
self.locman.requestWhenInUseAuthorization()
```

You can then ask an MKMapView in your app to display the device's location just by setting its `showsUserLocation` property to `true`; the map will automatically put an annotation at that location. This will be an MKUserLocation, adopting the MKAnnotation protocol. The map view's `userLocation` property will also point to this annotation. If your map view delegate's implementation of `mapView(_:viewFor:)` returns `nil` for this annotation, or if there is no such implementation, you'll get the default user location annotation view; you are free to substitute your own annotation view.

An MKUserLocation has a `location` property, a CLLocation, whose `coordinate` is a CLLocationCoordinate2D; if the map view's `showsUserLocation` is `true` and the map view has actually worked out the user's location, the `coordinate` describes that location. It also has `title` and `subtitle` properties, which appear in a callout if the annotation view is selected; plus you can check whether it currently `isUpdating`.

MKMapViewDelegate methods keep you informed of the map's attempts to locate the user:

- `mapViewWillStartLocatingUser(_:)`
- `mapViewDidStopLocatingUser(_:)`
- `mapView(_:didUpdate:)` (provides the new MKUserLocation)
- `mapView(_:didFailToLocateUserWithError:)`

In this cheeky example, I use `mapView(_:viewFor:)` to substitute my own title. Instead of returning `nil`, which would result in the default blue dot, I substitute the pin in a red balloon:

```
func mapView(_ mapView: MKMapView,
    viewFor annotation: MKAnnotation) -> MKAnnotationView? {
        if let annotation = annotation as? MKUserLocation {
            annotation.title = "You are here, stupid!"
            let id = MKMapViewDefaultAnnotationViewReuseIdentifier
            let v = mapView.dequeueReusableAnnotationView(
                withIdentifier: id, for: annotation)
            return v
        }
        return nil
}
```

You can ask the map view whether the user's location, if known, is in the visible region of the map (`isUserLocationVisible`). But what if it isn't? Assigning an appropriate value to the map's `region` — that is, actually *showing* the part of the world where the user is located — is a separate task. The simplest way is to take advantage of the MKMapView's `userTrackingMode` property, which determines how the user's real-world location should be tracked *automatically* by the map display; your options are (MKUserTrackingMode):

`.none`

> If `showsUserLocation` is `true`, the map gets an annotation at the user's location, but that's all; the map's `region` is unchanged. You could set it manually in `mapView(_:didUpdate:)`.

`.follow`

> Setting this mode sets `showsUserLocation` to `true`. The map automatically centers the user's location, and scales itself appropriately. When the map is in this mode, you should *not* set the map's `region`, as you'll be struggling against the tracking mode's attempts to do the same thing.

`.followWithHeading`

> Like `.follow`, but the map is also rotated so that the direction the user is facing is up. In this case, the `userLocation` annotation also has a `heading` property, a CLHeading; I'll talk more about headings in Chapter 22.

This code, then, turns out to be sufficient to start displaying the user's location:

```
self.map.userTrackingMode = .follow
```

When the `userTrackingMode` is one of the `.follow` modes, if the user is left free to zoom and scroll the map, the `userTrackingMode` may be automatically changed back to `.none` (and the user location annotation may be removed). You'll probably want to provide a way to let the user turn tracking back on again, or to toggle among the three tracking modes.

One way to do that is with an MKUserTrackingBarButtonItem, a UIBarButtonItem subclass. You initialize MKUserTrackingBarButtonItem with a map view, and its behavior is automatic from then on: when the user taps it, it switches the map view to the next tracking mode, and its icon reflects the current tracking mode. A map view delegate method tells you when the MKUserTrackingMode changes:

- `mapView(_:didChange:animated:)`

Alternatively, you can use an MKUserTrackingButton; like an MKScaleView or MKCompassButton, it has the advantage that it can be used anywhere (not just in a toolbar or navigation bar).

Communicating with the Maps App

Your app can communicate with the Maps app. Instead of displaying a point of interest in a map view in our own app, we can ask the Maps app to display it. The user could then bookmark or share the location. The channel of communication between your app and the Maps app is the MKMapItem class; you'll call `openInMaps(launchOptions:from:completionHandler:)`. (The `from:` parameter, a UIScene, and the completion handler were introduced in iOS 13.2.)

Figure 21-7. The Maps app displays our point of interest

Here, I'll ask the Maps app to display the same point marked by the annotation in our earlier examples, on a standard map portraying the same region of the earth that our map view is currently displaying (Figure 21-7):

```
let p = MKPlacemark(coordinate:self.annloc, addressDictionary:nil)
let mi = MKMapItem(placemark: p)
mi.name = "A Great Place to Dirt Bike" // label to appear in Maps app
let coord = self.map.region.center
let span = self.map.region.span
let opts : [String:Any] = [
    MKLaunchOptionsMapTypeKey: MKMapType.standard.rawValue,
    MKLaunchOptionsMapCenterKey: coord,
    MKLaunchOptionsMapSpanKey: span
]
let scene = self.view.window?.windowScene
mi.openInMaps(launchOptions: opts, from: scene) { ok in
    // if ok is true, succeeded
}
```

If you start with an MKMapItem returned by the `forCurrentLocation` class method, you're asking the Maps app to display the device's current location. This call doesn't attempt to determine the device's location, nor does it contain any location information; it merely generates an MKMapItem which, when sent to the Maps app, will cause *it* to attempt to determine (and display) the device's location:

```
let mi = MKMapItem.forCurrentLocation()
let opts : [String:Any] = [
    MKLaunchOptionsMapTypeKey: MKMapType.standard.rawValue
]
mi.openInMaps(launchOptions: opts, from: scene) { ok in
    // if ok is true, succeeded
}
```

Geocoding, Searching, and Directions

Map Kit provides your app with three services that involve performing queries over the network:

Geocoding
> Translation of a street address to a coordinate and *vice versa*. What address am I at right now? Or conversely, what are the coordinates of this address?

Searching
> Lookup of possible matches for a natural language search. What are some Thai restaurants near me?

Directions
> Lookup of turn-by-turn instructions and route mapping from a source location to a destination location. How do I get to that Thai restaurant from here?

These services take time and might not succeed at all, as they depend upon network and server availability; moreover, results may be more or less uncertain. Therefore, they involve a completion function that is called back *asynchronously* on the main thread (see Appendix C). The completion function is called with a single response object plus an Error, each wrapped in an Optional. If the response object is nil, the Error tells you what the problem was.

Geocoding

Geocoding functionality is encapsulated in the CLGeocoder class. You call one of these methods:

- geocodeAddressString(_:completionHandler:)

- geocodePostalAddress(_:completionHandler:)

The second method takes a CNPostalAddress, from the Contacts framework, so you'll need to import Contacts (see Chapter 19).

The response, if things went well, is an array of CLPlacemark objects, a series of guesses from best to worst; if things went *really* well, the array will contain exactly one CLPlacemark. A CLPlacemark can be used to initialize an MKPlacemark, a

CLPlacemark subclass that adopts the MKAnnotation protocol, and is therefore suitable to be handed directly over to an MKMapView for display.

Here is a simplified example that allows the user to enter an address in a UISearchBar (Chapter 13) to be displayed in an MKMapView:

```
guard let s = searchBar.text else { return }
let geo = CLGeocoder()
geo.geocodeAddressString(s) { placemarks, error in
    guard let placemarks = placemarks else { return }
    let p = placemarks[0]
    let mp = MKPlacemark(placemark:p)
    self.map.addAnnotation(mp)
    self.map.setRegion(
        MKCoordinateRegion(center:mp.coordinate,
            latitudinalMeters:1000, longitudinalMeters:1000),
        animated: true)
}
```

By default, the resulting annotation's title contains a nicely formatted string describing the address.

The converse operation is *reverse* geocoding: you start with a coordinate — actually a CLLocation, which you'll obtain from elsewhere, or construct from a coordinate using init(latitude:longitude:) — and then, in order to obtain the corresponding address, you call this method:

- reverseGeocodeLocation(_:completionHandler:)

The address is expressed through the CLPlacemark postalAddress property; this is a CNPostalAddress, so you'll need to import Contacts. Recall that you can ask the CNPostalAddress for its street, city, state, and other properties, and that you can use a CNPostalAddressFormatter to format the address nicely. Alternatively, you can consult directly such CLPlacemark properties as subthoroughfare (a house number), thoroughfare (a street name), locality (a town), and administrativeArea (a state).

In this example of reverse geocoding, we have an MKMapView that is already tracking the user, and so we have the user's location as the map's userLocation; we ask for the corresponding address:

```
guard let loc = self.map.userLocation.location else { return }
let geo = CLGeocoder()
geo.reverseGeocodeLocation(loc) { placemarks, error in
    guard let ps = placemarks, ps.count > 0 else {return}
    let p = ps[0]
    if let addy = p.postalAddress {
        let f = CNPostalAddressFormatter()
        print(f.string(from: addy))
    }
}
```

Searching

The MKLocalSearch class, along with MKLocalSearch.Request and MKLocal-Search.Response, lets you ask the server to perform a natural language search for you. This is less formal than forward geocoding, described in the previous section; instead of searching for an address, you can search for a point of interest by name or description. It can be useful, for some types of search, to constrain the area of interest by setting the request's `region`. Starting in iOS 13, you can characterize a request's result types as `.address` or `.pointOfInterest` (or both), and you can assign an MKPointOf-InterestFilter to the request's `pointOfInterestFilter` to limit the applicable categories of POI result.

In this example, I'll do a natural language search for a Thai restaurant near the user location currently displayed in the map (illustrating POI filtering), and I'll display the first (and probably closest) result as an annotation in our map view:

```
guard let loc = self.map.userLocation.location else { return }
let req = MKLocalSearch.Request()
req.naturalLanguageQuery = "Thai"
req.region = MKCoordinateRegion(center: loc.coordinate,
    span: MKCoordinateSpan(latitudeDelta:1, longitudeDelta:1))
req.resultTypes = .pointOfInterest
let filter = MKPointOfInterestFilter(including: [.restaurant])
req.pointOfInterestFilter = filter
let search = MKLocalSearch(request:req)
search.start { response, error in
    guard let response = response else { print(error); return }
    self.map.showsUserLocation = false
    let mi = response.mapItems[0] // I'm feeling lucky
    let place = mi.placemark
    let loc = place.location!.coordinate
    let reg = MKCoordinateRegion(center:loc,
        latitudinalMeters:1200, longitudinalMeters:1200)
    self.map.setRegion(reg, animated:true)
    let ann = MKPointAnnotation()
    ann.title = mi.name
    ann.subtitle = mi.phoneNumber
    ann.coordinate = loc
    self.map.addAnnotation(ann)
}
```

New in iOS 14, you can create an MKLocalSearch consisting of *just* points of interest. To do so, call `init(request:)`. The parameter is an MKLocalPointsOfInterest-Request, a value class specifying a region and POI filter. In this way you could, for example, ask for a list of restaurants in a given area:

```
let req = MKLocalPointsOfInterestRequest(
    coordinateRegion: self.map.region)
req.pointOfInterestFilter =
    MKPointOfInterestFilter(including: [.restaurant])
```

```
let search = MKLocalSearch(request: req)
search.start { response, error in
    // ...
}
```

MKLocalSearchCompleter lets you use the MKLocalSearch remote database to suggest completions as the user types a search query. In effect, you are performing the search after every character that the user types; most likely you'll use a UISearchController (Chapter 8). Initialize and configure the MKLocalSearchCompleter object and give it a delegate (MKLocalSearchCompleterDelegate); starting in iOS 13, an MKPointOfInterestFilter can be applied to the completer. Each time the search bar text changes, set the completer's queryFragment with the current contents of the search field. When the delegate method completerDidUpdateResults(_:) is called, grab the completer's results, which is an array of MKLocalSearchCompletion objects. These have string properties title and subtitle suitable for display in a table view; you'll probably set your table view data source model object to the completer's results and tell the table to reload.

Directions

The MKDirections class, along with MKDirections.Request, looks up walking or driving directions between two locations expressed as MKMapItem objects. The resulting MKDirections.Response includes an array of MKRoute objects; each MKRoute includes an MKPolyline suitable for display as an overlay in your map, as well as an array of MKRoute.Step objects, each of which provides its own MKPolyline plus instructions and distances. The response also has its own source and destination MKMapItems, which may be different from what we started with.

To illustrate, I'll continue from the Thai food example in the previous section, starting at the point where we obtained the Thai restaurant's MKMapItem:

```
// ... same as before up to this point ...
let mi = response.mapItems[0] // I'm still feeling lucky
let req = MKDirectionsRequest()
req.source = MKMapItem.forCurrentLocation()
req.destination = mi
let dir = MKDirections(request:req)
dir.calculate { response, error in
    guard let response = response else { print(error); return }
    let route = response.routes[0] // I'm feeling insanely lucky
    let poly = route.polyline
    self.map.addOverlay(poly)
    for step in route.steps {
        print("After \(step.distance) meters: \(step.instructions)")
    }
}
```

The step-by-step instructions appear in the console; in real life, of course, we would presumably display these in our app's interface. The route is drawn in our map view, provided we have an appropriate implementation of `mapView(_:rendererFor:)`, such as this:

```
func mapView(_ mapView: MKMapView,
    rendererFor overlay: MKOverlay) -> MKOverlayRenderer {
        if let overlay = overlay as? MKPolyline {
            let r = MKPolylineRenderer(polyline:overlay)
            r.strokeColor = UIColor.blue.withAlphaComponent(0.8)
            r.lineWidth = 2
            return r
        }
        return MKOverlayRenderer()
}
```

You can also ask MKDirections to estimate the time of arrival, by calling `calculate-ETA(completionHandler:)`, and there is arrival time estimation for some public transit systems (and you can tell the Maps app to display a transit directions map).

Sensors

A device may contain hardware for sensing the world around itself — where it is located, how it is oriented, how it is moving.

Information about the device's current location and how that location is changing over time using its WiFi, cellular networking, and GPS capabilities, along with information about the device's orientation relative to north using its magnetometer, is provided through the Core Location framework.

Information about the device's change in speed and attitude using its accelerometer is provided through the UIEvent class (for device shake) and the Core Motion framework, which provides increased accuracy by incorporating the device's gyroscope, if it has one, as well as the magnetometer. In addition, the device may have an extra chip that analyzes and records the user's activity, such as walking or running, and even a barometer that reports changes in altitude; the Core Motion framework provides access to this information as well.

A challenge associated with writing code that takes advantage of the sensors is that different devices have different hardware. If you don't want to impose stringent restrictions on what devices your app will run on in the first place (`UIRequired-DeviceCapabilities` in the *Info.plist*), your code must be prepared to fail gracefully, perhaps providing a subset of your app's full capabilities, when it turns out that the current device lacks certain features.

Even on a device that has the necessary hardware, certain sensors may be switched off or may experience momentary inadequacy; for instance, Core Location might not be able to get a fix on the device's position because it can't see cell towers, GPS satellites, or both. And some sensors take time to "warm up," so that the values you'll get from them initially will be invalid. You'll want to respond nimbly to such changes in the external circumstances, in order to give the user a decent experience of your application regardless.

One final consideration: all sensor usage means battery usage, to a lesser or greater degree — sometimes to a *considerably* greater degree. There's a compromise to be made here: you want to please the user with your app's convenience and usefulness, without disagreeably surprising and annoying the user through rapid depletion of the device's battery charge.

Core Location

The Core Location framework (`import CoreLocation`) provides facilities for the device to determine and report its location (*location services*). It takes advantage of three sensors:

WiFi
> The device, if WiFi is turned on, may scan for nearby WiFi networks and compare these against an online database.

Cell
> The device, if it has cell capabilities and they are not turned off, may detect nearby telephone cell towers and compare them against an online database.

GPS
> The device's GPS, if it has one, may be able to obtain a position fix from GPS satellites. The GPS is obviously the most accurate location sensor, but it takes the longest to get a fix, and in some situations it will fail, such as when the user is indoors or among tall buildings where the device can't "see" enough of the sky.

Core Location will automatically use whatever facilities the device has available; all *you* have to do is ask for the device's location. Core Location allows you to specify how accurate a position fix you want; trying to get a more accurate fix may require more time.

To help you test code that depends on where the device is, Xcode lets you pretend that the device is at a particular location on earth. In the Simulator, the Features → Location menu lets you enter a location; in Xcode, in the Scheme editor, the Run action (under Options) lets you set a Default Location; and when running on a real device, the Simulate Location pop-up menu in the debug bar, or the Debug → Simulate Location menu, lets you switch among locations. You can set a built-in location or supply a standard GPX file containing a waypoint. You can also set the location to None; it's important to test for what happens when no location information is available.

Location Manager and Delegate

Use of Core Location requires a *location manager* object, an instance of CLLocation-Manager. This object needs to be created on the main thread and retained thereafter. A standard strategy is to pick an instance that persists throughout the life of your app — such as your app delegate, or your root view controller — and initialize an instance property with a location manager:

```
let locman = CLLocationManager()
```

Your location manager will generally be useless without a *delegate* (CLLocation-ManagerDelegate). You don't want to change a location manager's delegate, so you'll set it once, early in the life of the location manager. This delegate will need to be an instance that persists together with the location manager. If locman is, say, a constant property of our root view controller, then we can set the root view controller as its delegate. It's a good idea to do this as early as possible; the root view controller's initializer is a good place:

```
required init?(coder: NSCoder) {
    super.init(coder:coder)
    self.locman.delegate = self
}
```

Location Services Authorization

You must explicitly request authorization from the user when you first start tracking the device's location. There are two types of authorization:

When In Use authorization
> When In Use authorization allows your app to use Core Location when the app is running. "Running" here means in the foreground or running (not suspended) in the background.

Always authorization
> Always authorization permits your app to configure the system to perform certain Core Location activities on your behalf even when your app is *not* running. I'll describe later what those activities are.

The user can turn off location services as a whole. The CLLocationManager class method locationServicesEnabled reports whether location services are switched off. If location services are off, don't bother with authorization.

However, even if location services are off, you might like to try to use Core Location anyway. The reason is that this may cause the runtime to put up an alert on your behalf offering to switch to the Settings app so that the user can turn location services on (Figure 22-1). The attempt to learn the device's location will fail, but this failure may also cause the user to see the system alert:

Figure 22-1. Location services are turned off

```
if !CLLocationManager.locationServicesEnabled() {
    self.lacman startUpdatingLocation()
    return
}
```

The user might see the alert, tap Settings, and turn on Core Location. The user just might even find your app's listing in Settings and grant it authorization then and there. But don't count on any of that.

Once location services are enabled, you'll fetch the CLLocationManager's authorizationStatus property to learn your app's actual authorization status. (This instance property is new in iOS 14; previously, it was a class method.) There are two types of authorization, so there are two status cases reporting that you have authorization: .authorizedWhenInUse and .authorizedAlways. If the status is .notDetermined, you can request that the system put up the authorization request alert on your behalf by calling one of two instance methods, either requestWhenInUse-Authorization or requestAlwaysAuthorization. You must also have a corresponding meaningful entry in your app's *Info.plist* providing the body of the authorization request alert; these are "Privacy — Location When In Use Description" (NSLocation-WhenInUseUsageDescription) and "Privacy — Location Always and When In Use Usage Description" (NSLocationAlwaysAndWhenInUseUsageDescription) — and if you're planning to call requestAlwaysAuthorization, you will need both of them.

Temporary When In Use authorization

Because location tracking is both battery-intensive and a potential invasion of privacy, Apple wants the user to feel confident that secret or inadvertent location tracking is not taking place. At the same time, Apple wants to give your app a chance to demonstrate to the user its use of Core Location, in order to encourage the user to give your app the authorization it needs. Therefore, starting in iOS 13, the alert that the user sees when you request When In Use authorization includes an Allow Once option (Figure 22-2).

The idea is to give the user an opportunity to let your app use location services on a temporary basis. If the user taps Allow Once, your app will get When In Use authorization, just as if the user had tapped Allow While Using App — but the next time

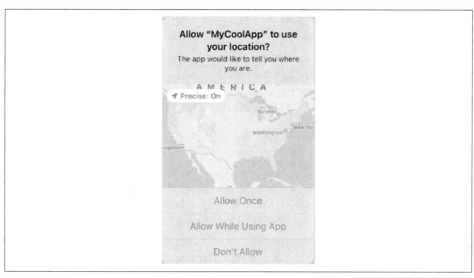

Figure 22-2. Authorization alert for When In Use authorization

your app goes into the background and is suspended, your authorization will be revoked. Then the next time your app runs, you'll discover that your authorization status is .notDetermined, and you can ask for authorization again (and the Figure 22-2 alert will appear again).

The user can also change your app's authorization at any time. The Settings app lets the user turn on and off location access for your app. There are four possibilities: Never, Ask Next Time, While Using the App, and Always. The last option, Always, might not appear unless your app has actually requested Always authorization. The second option, Ask Next Time (introduced in iOS 13), returns your authorization status to .notDetermined; when your app needs to use location services, it will discover this and can ask for authorization again (and the alert will appear again).

Proceeding after authorization

Oddly, the request methods do not take a completion function. Your code just continues blithely on. If you call requestWhenInUseAuthorization and then attempt to track the device's location by calling startUpdatingLocation, you might succeed if the user grants authorization, but you might fail because the user denies it. The Core Location API provides no simple way for you to proceed only after you know the outcome of the authorization request.

On the other hand, whenever the user changes your authorization status, in the authorization request alert or the Settings app, your location manager delegate's locationManagerDidChangeAuthorization(_:) is called. So if you *store* whatever action you want to perform *before* obtaining authorization, then you can *perform* that action *after* obtaining authorization.

Here's a strategy for doing that. Instead of making our CLLocationManager a property of the root view controller, we have a utility class, ManagerHolder, encapsulating ownership and authorization of the location manager. It creates and retains the location manager, asks for authorization if needed, and stores the function we want to call when we have authorization:

```
class ManagerHolder {
    let locman = CLLocationManager()
    var doThisWhenAuthorized : (() -> ())?
    func checkForLocationAccess(always: Bool=false, andThen f: (()->())?=nil) {
        guard CLLocationManager.locationServicesEnabled() else {
            self.locman.startUpdatingLocation()
            return
        }
        let status = self.locman.authorizationStatus
        switch status {
        case .authorizedWhenInUse:
            if always { // try to step up
                self.doThisWhenAuthorized = f
                self.locman.requestAlwaysAuthorization()
            } else {
                f?()
            }
        case .authorizedAlways:
            f?()
        case .notDetermined:
            self.doThisWhenAuthorized = f
            if always {
                self.locman.requestAlwaysAuthorization()
            } else {
                self.locman.requestWhenInUseAuthorization()
            }
        case .restricted: break
        case .denied: break
        default: fatalError()
        }
    }
}
```

I'll attach a ManagerHolder instance to the root view controller. The root view controller initializer creates and stores the ManagerHolder instance as an instance property, bringing the location manager to life as early as possible. For convenience, I'll give the root view controller a locman property, but this will be a computed property that bounces to the ManagerHolder's location manager instance:

```
class ViewController: UIViewController, CLLocationManagerDelegate {
    let managerHolder = ManagerHolder()
    var locman : CLLocationManager {
        return self.managerHolder.locman
    }
    required init?(coder: NSCoder) {
        super.init(coder:coder)
        self.locman.delegate = self
    }
    // ...
}
```

Acting as the location manager delegate, the root view controller can implement `locationManagerDidChangeAuthorizationStatus(_:)` to call the function stored in the ManagerHolder:

```
func locationManagerDidChangeAuthorization(_ manager: CLLocationManager) {
    let status = manager.authorizationStatus
    if status == .authorizedAlways || status == .authorizedWhenInUse {
        self.managerHolder.doThisWhenAuthorized?()
    }
    self.managerHolder.doThisWhenAuthorized = nil
}
```

If we now call our ManagerHolder's `checkForLocationAccess` before tracking location, everything will work correctly. If we pass a completion function in our call to `checkForLocationAccess`, then if we already have authorization, that function will be called immediately; if our status is `.notDetermined` and the authorization request alert is presented, that function will be called as soon as the user authorizes us.

 The delegate method `locationManagerDidChangeAuthorization(_:)` is new in iOS 14, replacing `locationManager(_:didChangeAuthorization:)` from iOS 13 and before. For backward compatibility, implement both; in iOS 14, only the newer method will be called.

Reduced accuracy

New in iOS 14, the user can authorize your app to learn the device's location while reducing the accuracy of the location readings. The idea is that your app might be content to know the general area containing the device, such as a town.

This option appears when the user is shown the dialog offering to grant your app location authorization (Figure 22-2). There's a button: "Precise: On." If the user toggles this to "Precise: Off" and grants authorization, your CLAccuracyAuthorization will be `.reducedAccuracy`. The user can also toggle this setting at any time in the Settings app, where it appears as a Precise Location switch (if the location access setting is not Never).

To learn whether the user has opted out of precise location, get the location manager's accuracyAuthorization; it is a CLAccuracyAuthorization enum, either .fullAccuracy or .reducedAccuracy.

With .reducedAccuracy, the reported location will not be exactly where the user is. Think of it as a proxy for the user's real location. Some intelligence is used in the determination of this proxy, so that it constitutes a natural way of describing a place. In my own experiments from home, my reduced accuracy location is reported as pretty much the exact center of the downtown area in the village where I live. So an app that uses reduced accuracy would know the village I'm in; and that's a good way of describing where I am in general terms. And it could be a useful thing to know! If we're looking for restaurants near me, for instance, we can still get a reasonable answer.

If possible, then, you should rest content with reduced accuracy if that's the user's choice. If your app offers functionality that absolutely requires full accuracy, such as mapping the user's route, then if the user asks for that functionality, you can have the system up a dialog requesting full accuracy, by calling the location manager's requestTemporaryFullAccuracyAuthorization(withPurposeKey:completion:) method.

The purposeKey: is a string identifier that must be matched by an entry in your *Info.plist.* Add the key "Privacy - Location Temporary Usage Description Dictionary" (NSLocationTemporaryUsageDescriptionDictionary). It's a dictionary; give it key-value pairs, where the key is a purpose key and the value is text that will appear in the dialog, explaining to the user why full accuracy is needed. The completion: function receives an Optional Error; if it is nil, full accuracy has been granted. This grant, as the method name implies, is temporary; it will persist as long as the user is actively using the app, in the same sense as the temporary When In Use authorization that I discussed earlier.

At the other extreme, it may be that your app actually *wants* reduced accuracy. In that case, add to the *Info.plist* the key "Privacy - Location Default Accuracy Reduced" (NSLocationDefaultAccuracyReduced); make it a Boolean and set it to YES. The result is that in the authorization dialog, the "Precise: On" button is missing, and you'll get .reducedAccuracy by default.

Location Tracking

The primary use of a location manager is to track the user's location. Make sure the location manager has a delegate, configure the location manager further as needed (I'll go into more detail in a moment), and then tell the location manager to startUpdatingLocation.

The location manager will begin calling the delegate's locationManager(_:didUpdateLocations:) method repeatedly. The delegate should deal with each such call as it arrives. In this way, you will be kept more or less continuously informed of where the device is. This will go on until you call stopUpdatingLocation; don't forget to call it when you no longer need location tracking! Your delegate should also implement locationManager(_:didFailWithError:) to receive error messages.

That pattern is common to virtually *all* uses of the location manager. The location manager can do various kinds of tracking, but they all work the same way: you'll tell it to start, a corresponding delegate method will be called repeatedly (or you'll receive an error), and ultimately you'll tell the location manager to stop.

Here are some location manager configuration properties that are useful to set *before* you start location tracking:

desiredAccuracy
> Your choices are:
>
> - kCLLocationAccuracyBestForNavigation
> - kCLLocationAccuracyBest
> - kCLLocationAccuracyNearestTenMeters
> - kCLLocationAccuracyHundredMeters
> - kCLLocationAccuracyKilometer
> - kCLLocationAccuracyThreeKilometers
> - kCLLocationAccuracyReduced (new in iOS 14)
>
> It might be sufficient for your purposes to know quickly but roughly the device's location; in that case, use kCLLocationAccuracyKilometer or kCLLocation-AccuracyThreeKilometers. At the other end of the scale, highest accuracy may cause the highest battery drain; indeed, kCLLocationAccuracyBestFor-Navigation is supposed to be used only when the device is connected to external power. The accuracy setting is not a filter: the location manager will send you whatever location information it has, even if it isn't as accurate as you asked for, and checking a location's horizontalAccuracy to see if it's good enough is up to you.

distanceFilter
> Perhaps you don't need a location report unless the device has moved a certain distance since the previous report. This property can help keep you from being bombarded with events you don't need. The distance is measured in meters. To turn off the distance filter entirely, set this property to kCLDistanceFilterNone (the default).

`pausesLocationUpdatesAutomatically`
> A Bool. The default, `true`, means that your setting for the location manager's `activityType` is significant. Your `activityType` choices are (CLActivityType):
>
> - `.fitness` (workout)
> - `.automotiveNavigation` (tracking on roads)
> - `.otherNavigation` (tracking, not necessarily on roads)
> - `.airborne` (taxiing or flying; introduced in iOS 12)
> - `.other` (the default)
>
> Think of these as an autopause setting, based on the movement of the device; if we don't seem to be moving sufficiently to warrant updates based on the activity type, updates can pause and we'll conserve power.
>
> The idea here is that the user may have stopped working out, driving, or whatever, but has forgotten to turn off your app's location tracking. A paused location manager does *not* automatically resume updates; it's up to you to implement the delegate method `locationManagerDidPauseLocationUpdates(_:)` and configure updates to resume when appropriate. Apple suggests that, as an alternative, you might save power by setting `pausesLocationUpdatesAutomatically` to `false` but accepting the broadest `desiredAccuracy` (namely `kCLLocationAccuracyThreeKilometers`), which will probably mean that the GPS isn't used.

Here's a basic example, taking advantage of the authorization strategy described in the previous section. Presume that we want to get a very accurate location as soon as possible and keep tracking the user's location until we say to stop:

```
self.managerHolder.checkForLocationAccess {
    self.locman.desiredAccuracy = kCLLocationAccuracyBest
    self.locman.distanceFilter = kCLDistanceFilterNone
    self.locman.activityType = .other
    self.locman.pausesLocationUpdatesAutomatically = false
    self.locman.startUpdatingLocation()
}
```

In that code, we have requested authorization if needed, and if we have or can get authorization, we have configured the location manager and started tracking location. Now we must sit back and wait for our implementation of `locationManager(_:didUpdateLocations:)` to be called. The second parameter is an array of CLLocation, a value class that encapsulates the notion of a location. Its properties include:

`coordinate`
> A CLLocationCoordinate2D, a struct consisting of two Doubles representing latitude and longitude.

---

altitude
> A CLLocationDistance, which is a Double representing a number of meters.

speed
> A CLLocationSpeed, which is a Double representing meters per second.

course
> A CLLocationDirection, which is a Double representing degrees (*not* radians) clockwise from north.

horizontalAccuracy
> A CLLocationAccuracy, which is a Double representing meters.

timestamp
> A Date.

In this situation, the array that we receive is likely to contain just one CLLocation — and even if it contains more than one, the *last* CLLocation in the array is guaranteed to be the newest. So it suffices for our `locationManager(_:didUpdateLocations:)` implementation to extract the last element of the array:

```
let REQ_ACC : CLLocationAccuracy = 10
func locationManager(_ manager: CLLocationManager,
    didUpdateLocations locations: [CLLocation]) {
        let loc = locations.last!
        let acc = loc.horizontalAccuracy
        print(acc)
        if acc < 0 || acc > REQ_ACC {
            return // wait for the next one
        }
        let coord = loc.coordinate
        print("You are at \(coord.latitude) \(coord.longitude)")
}
```

It's instructive to see, from the console logs, how the accuracy improves as the sensors warm up and the GPS obtains a fix:

```
1285.19869645162
1285.19869645172
1285.19869645173
65.0
65.0
30.0
30.0
30.0
10.0
You are at ...
```

In iOS 14, the accuracy authorization might be `.reducedAccuracy`. In that case, calls to `locationManager(_:didUpdateLocations:)` will be sparse — about four per hour!

— and the horizontalAccuracy will be large (8970 on my device). So your strategy will be completely different. You are not expecting accuracy to improve! Instead, just accept the location that you get and use it.

Where Am I?

Rather than tracking location continuously, you might like to get *one* good location *once*. A common beginner mistake is to call startUpdatingLocation and implement locationManager(_:didUpdateLocations:) to stop updating as soon as it is called:

```
func locationManager(_ manager: CLLocationManager,
    didUpdateLocations locations: [CLLocation]) {
        let loc = locations.last!
        let coord = loc.coordinate
        print("You are at \(coord.latitude) \(coord.longitude)")
        manager.stopUpdatingLocation() // this won't work!
}
```

That won't work; as I demonstrated in the preceding section, the sensors take time to warm up, and many calls to locationManager(_:didUpdateLocations:) may be needed before a reasonably accurate CLLocation arrives. The correct strategy would be to do just what I did in the preceding section, and then call stopUpdating-Location at the very end, when a sufficiently accurate location has in fact been received.

But that's a lot of work to get just one reading, and there's a simpler way. Instead of calling startUpdatingLocation, call requestLocation:

```
self.locman.desiredAccuracy = kCLLocationAccuracyBest
self.locman.requestLocation()
```

Your locationManager(_:didUpdateLocations:) will be called once with the best location available, aiming at the desiredAccuracy you've already set:

```
func locationManager(manager: CLLocationManager,
    didUpdateLocations locations: [CLLocation]) {
        let loc = locations.last!
        let coord = loc.coordinate
        print("You are at \(coord.latitude) \(coord.longitude)")
}
```

Calling requestLocation will *not* magically cause an accurate location to arrive any faster! It's a great convenience that locationManager(_:didUpdateLocations:) will be called just once, but some considerable time may elapse before that call arrives. You do not have to call stopUpdatingLocation, though you can do so if you change your mind and decide before the location arrives that it is no longer needed.

(If you call requestLocation soon after calling it previously, you may get a cached value rather than a new position fix.)

Continuous Background Location

Continuous background location is an extension of basic location tracking. You tell the location manager to startUpdatingLocation, and then your app keeps running and keeps receiving location updates even after it goes into the background. (This works even if the accuracyAuthorization is .reducedAccuracy — but the locations you'll receive will still be proxies, and you'll still get only about four updates per hour.)

Use of Core Location to perform continuous background updates is parallel to production of sound in the background (Chapter 15). In your app's *Info.plist*, the "Required background modes" key (UIBackgroundModes) should include location; you can set this up easily by adding the Background Modes capability in the Signing & Capabilities tab when editing the target, and checking "Location updates."

You must also set your location manager's allowsBackgroundLocationUpdates to true. You should do this only at moments when you actually need to start getting background location updates — ideally, just as you go into the background (see Appendix A). You should set it back to false as soon as you no longer need background updates.

 You cannot *start* tracking locations when your app is *already* in the background (well, you can try, but in all probability your app will be suspended and location tracking will cease).

How the device lets the user know that you're tracking location in the background depends on what sort of authorization you have:

Your app has only When In Use authorization
The device will make the user aware that your app is doing background location tracking by displaying a blue symbol in the status bar. (On an iPhone, the whole status bar turns blue.) The user can tap this to summon your app to the front. (If you see the blue *momentarily* as your app goes into the background, that's because you didn't do what I said a moment ago: set allowsBackgroundLocation-Updates to true only when you really are going to track location in the background.)

Your app has Always authorization
The blue status bar doesn't appear by default, because the user has already agreed to let you use location services always. But Apple recommends that you set the location manager's showsBackgroundLocationIndicator to true, so that the blue status bar appears anyway.

Background use of location services can cause a power drain, but if you want your app to function as a positional data logger, it may be the only way. You can help conserve power by making judicious choices, such as:

- By setting a coarse `distanceFilter` value.
- By not requiring overly high accuracy.
- By being correct about the `activityType` and allowing updates to pause.

Location Monitoring

Location monitoring is not something your app does; it's something the system does on your behalf. It *doesn't* require your app to run continuously in the background; in fact, your app doesn't need to be running at all! You do *not* have to set the `UIBackgroundModes` of your *Info.plist*.

Your app still requires a location manager with a delegate, and it needs appropriate user authorization. Even if your app has only When In Use authorization, it can receive delegate messages from location monitoring any time it is running, including running in the background to receive location updates (starting in iOS 13). But in general, if you want the system to perform location monitoring when your app is not actively running, you will need Always authorization.

Always authorization

When you want the system to do location monitoring for you, if you don't already have Always authorization, you'll call `requestAlwaysAuthorization`. There are two possibilities for what happens next:

The authorization status is `.authorizedWhenInUse`
> An alert appears (Figure 22-3), offering to promote your app's authorization level to Always Allow. (This behavior is new starting in iOS 13.4. In earlier versions of iOS 13, no alert appears in this situation.)

The authorization status is `.notDetermined`
> The alert that appears to the user is the same as Figure 22-2. The user's choices are Allow While Using App and Allow Once.

The second case is the interesting one. The user who grants authorization at this point *seems* to have granted When In Use authorization. But in reality your app now has Always authorization! You've been authorized *provisionally*. After your app has made use of its Always powers to initiate location monitoring in the background, the user will be shown the alert (Figure 22-3) offering to promote your authorization to *real* Always authorization. It's unclear just when this will happen; the user needn't be using your app. In my experience it's usually just after coming back from the lock screen. If the user declines, your authorization reverts to `.authorizedWhenInUse`.

Your app, on the other hand, knows nothing of the fact that its Always authorization may be provisional — and it doesn't need to know. If your app finds that the authorization status is `.authorizedAlways`, it can proceed to request location monitoring.

Figure 22-3. The Always authorization alert

Forms of location monitoring

There are four distinct forms of location monitoring:

Significant location change monitoring
Check this class method:

- `significantLocationChangeMonitoringAvailable`

If it returns `true`, you can call this method:

- `startMonitoringSignificantLocationChanges`

Implement this delegate method:

`locationManager(_:didUpdateLocations:)`
Called whenever the device's location has changed significantly.

Visit monitoring
By tracking significant changes in your location along with the *pauses* between those changes, the system decides that the user is visiting a spot. Visit monitoring is basically a form of significant location change monitoring, but requires even less power and notifies you less often, because locations that don't involve pauses are filtered out.

Check this class method:

- `significantLocationChangeMonitoringAvailable`

If it returns `true`, you can call this method:

- `startMonitoringVisits`

Implement this delegate method:

```
locationManager(_:didVisit:)
```
Called whenever the user's location pauses in a way that suggests a visit is beginning, and again whenever a visit ends. The second parameter is a CLVisit, a simple value class wrapping visit data; in addition to `coordinate` and `horizontalAccuracy`, you get an `arrivalDate` and `departureDate`. If this is an arrival, the `departureDate` will be `Date.distantFuture`. If this is a departure and we were not monitoring visits when the user arrived, the `arrivalDate` will be `Date.distantPast`.

Region monitoring

Region monitoring depends upon your defining one or more *regions*. A region is a CLRegion, which basically expresses a *geofence*, an area that triggers an event when the user enters or leaves it (or both). This class is divided into two subclasses, CLBeaconRegion and CLCircularRegion. CLBeaconRegion is used in connection with iBeacon monitoring; I'm not going to discuss iBeacon in this book, so that leaves us with only CLCircularRegion. Its initializer is `init(center:radius:identifier:)`; the `center:` parameter is a CLLocationCoordinate2D, and the `identifier:` serves as a unique key. The region's `notifyOnEntry` and `notifyOnExit` properties are both `true` by default; set one to `false` if you're interested only in the other type of event.

Check this class method:

- `isMonitoringAvailable(for:CLCircularRegion.self)`

If it returns `true`, then you can call this method:

- `startMonitoring(for:)`

Call that method for each region in which you are interested. Regions being monitored are maintained as a set, which is the location manager's `monitoredRegions`. A region's `identifier` serves as a unique key, so that if you start monitoring for a region whose identifier matches that of a region already in the `monitoredRegions` set, the latter will be ejected from the set. Implement these delegate methods:

- `locationManager(_:didEnterRegion:)`
- `locationManager(_:didExitRegion:)`
- `locationManager(_:monitoringDidFailFor:withError:)`

Geofenced local notifications

This is a special case of region monitoring where everything is handled through the local notification mechanism (Chapter 14); therefore, you only need When In Use authorization, you don't start monitoring or stop monitoring, and you don't implement any delegate methods.

You configure a local notification request (UNNotificationRequest) whose trigger is a UNLocationNotificationTrigger. Create the trigger by calling its initializer, `init(region:repeats:)`, supplying a CLRegion. If `repeats:` is `true`, the notification won't be unscheduled after it fires; rather, it will fire again whenever the user crosses the region boundary in the specified direction again (depending on the CLRegion's `notifyOnEntry` and `notifyOnExit` settings).

Region monitoring is impossible without an `accuracyAuthorization` of `.fullAccuracy`; so if your app needs to do region monitoring and you discover that it has `.reducedAccuracy`, you'll need to beg the user to change it. Significant location monitoring and visit monitoring, however, are possible even if the `accuracyAuthorization` is `.reducedAccuracy`; the times will be accurate based on where the user actually went, even though you won't be *told* where the user actually went.

Delegate method calls when your app isn't running

If your app isn't in the foreground at the time the system wants to send your location manager delegate a location monitoring event, there are two possible states in which your app might find itself:

Your app is suspended in the background
Your app is woken up (remaining in the background) long enough to receive the delegate event and do something with it.

Your app is not running at all
Your app is relaunched (remaining in the background), and your app delegate will be sent `application(_:didFinishLaunchingWithOptions:)` with the `options:` dictionary containing the `.location` key, allowing you to discern the special nature of the situation. As soon as possible, you need to make sure you have a location manager with a delegate so that you can receive the appropriate delegate events. (This is another reason why you should create a location manager and assign it a delegate *early* in the lifetime of the app.)

Location monitoring best practices

Location monitoring is less battery-intensive than full-fledged location tracking. That's because it relies on cell tower positions to estimate the device's location. Since the cell is probably operating anyway — if the device is a phone, the cell is usually on and concerned with what cell towers are available — little or no additional power is required. Apple says that the system will also take advantage of other clues requiring no extra battery drain to decide that there may have been a change in location: for instance, the device may observe a change in the available WiFi networks, strongly suggesting that the device has moved.

Nevertheless, location monitoring does use the battery, and over the course of time the user will notice this. Therefore, you should use it only during periods when you need it. Every startMonitoring method has a corresponding stopMonitoring method. Don't forget to call that method when location monitoring is no longer needed! The system is performing this work on your behalf, and it will continue to do so until you tell it not to.

 It is *crucial* that you remember to stop location monitoring. A failure to do this will eventually drain the battery significantly. The user can figure out, by looking at the Battery screen in Settings, that your app is responsible, and if you have provided no other way to turn location monitoring off, the user will have no choice but to delete your app.

Heading

For appropriately equipped devices, Core Location supports use of the magnetometer to determine which way the device is facing (its *heading*). Although this information is accessed through a location manager, you do *not* need location services merely to use the magnetometer to report the device's orientation with respect to *magnetic* north; you *do* need location services to report *true* north, as this depends on the device's location.

As with location, you'll first check that the desired feature is available (heading-Available); then you'll configure the location manager, and call startUpdating-Heading. The delegate will be sent locationManager(_:didUpdateHeading:) repeatedly until you call stopUpdatingHeading (or else locationManager(_:didFail-WithError:) will be called).

A heading object is a CLHeading instance; its magneticHeading and trueHeading properties are CLLocationDirection values, which report degrees (*not* radians) measured clockwise from the reference direction (magnetic or true north, respectively). If the trueHeading is not available, it will be reported as -1. The trueHeading will *not* be available unless both of the following are true in the Settings app:

- Location services are turned on (Privacy → Location Services).
- Compass calibration is turned on (Privacy → Location Services → System Services).

Beyond that, explicit user authorization is *not* needed in order to get the device's heading with respect to true north.

If you want the system's compass calibration alert to be permitted to appear if needed, implement this delegate method to return true:

- locationManagerShouldDisplayHeadingCalibration(_:)

In this example, I'll use the device as a compass. The `headingFilter` setting is to pre-vent us from being bombarded constantly with readings. For best results, the device should probably be held level (like a tabletop, or a compass); we are setting the `headingOrientation` so that the reported heading will be the direction in which the top of the device (the end away from the Home button) is pointing:

```
guard CLLocationManager.headingAvailable() else {return} // no hardware
self.locman.headingFilter = 5
self.locman.headingOrientation = .portrait
self.locman.startUpdatingHeading()
```

In the delegate, I'll display our heading as a rough cardinal direction in a label in the interface (`self.lab`). If we have a `trueHeading`, I'll use it; otherwise I'll use the `magneticHeading`:

```
func locationManager(_ manager: CLLocationManager,
    didUpdateHeading newHeading: CLHeading) {
        var h = newHeading.magneticHeading
        let h2 = newHeading.trueHeading // -1 if no location info
        if h2 >= 0 {
            h = h2
        }
        let cards = ["N", "NE", "E", "SE", "S", "SW", "W", "NW"]
        func degToName(_ d:Double) -> String {
            let divCount = cards.count
            let angularRange = 360.0 / Double(divCount)
            let bucket = Int((d + angularRange/2.0)/angularRange)
            return cards[bucket % divCount]
        }
        let dir = degToName(h)
        if self.lab.text != dir {
            self.lab.text = dir
        }
        if self.lab.text != dir {
            self.lab.text = dir
        }
}
```

Heading is not the same as course. A boat may be *facing* north (its heading) but *moving* northeast (its course). There are times, however, when what you are interested in really is course. In a moving automobile, how the user is holding the device is usually unimportant to you: what you want to know is which way the car is moving. If the runtime concludes, from the nature of the device's motion, that when you ask for heading you probably mean course, it will provide the course as the heading.

If that's not what you want, then instead of using Core Location to determine head-ing, you can use Core Motion (discussed in the next section) to obtain the device's orientation in space as a CMDeviceMotion object's `heading` property.

Acceleration, Attitude, and Activity

Acceleration results from the application of a force to the device, and is detected through the device's accelerometer, supplemented by the gyroscope if the device has one. Gravity is a force, so the accelerometer always has something to measure, even if the user isn't applying a force to the device, and the device can use acceleration detection to report its attitude relative to the vertical.

Acceleration information can arrive in two ways:

As a prepackaged UIEvent
> You can receive a UIEvent notifying you of a predefined gesture performed by accelerating the device. At present, the only such gesture is the user shaking the device.

With the Core Motion framework
> You instantiate CMMotionManager and then obtain information of a desired type. You can ask for accelerometer, gyroscope, or device motion information; device motion combines the gyroscope data with data from other sensors to give you the best possible description of the device's attitude in space, along with magnetometer and heading information.

Shake Events

A shake event is a UIEvent (Chapter 5). Receiving shake events involves the notion of the first responder. To receive shake events, your app must contain a UIResponder which:

- Returns `true` from `canBecomeFirstResponder`.
- Is in fact first responder.

This responder, or a UIResponder further up the responder chain, should implement some or all of these methods:

`motionBegan(_:with:)`
> Something has started to happen that might or might not turn out to be a shake.

`motionEnded(_:with:)`
> The motion reported in `motionBegan` is over and has turned out to be a shake.

`motionCancelled(_:with:)`
> The motion reported in `motionBegan` wasn't a shake after all.

It might be sufficient to implement `motionEnded(_:with:)`, because this arrives if and only if the user performs a shake gesture. The first parameter will be the event subtype, but this is guaranteed to be `.motionShake`, so testing it is pointless.

The view controller in charge of the current view is a good candidate to receive shake events. A minimal implementation might look like this:

```
override var canBecomeFirstResponder : Bool {
    return true
}
override func viewDidAppear(_ animated: Bool) {
    super.viewDidAppear(animated)
    self.becomeFirstResponder()
}
override func motionEnded(_ motion: UIEvent.EventSubtype, with e: UIEvent?) {
    print("hey, you shook me!")
}
```

Suppose some other object is first responder and is of a type that supports undo, such as a UITextField. Then (assuming you have not set the shared UIApplication's applicationSupportsShakeToEdit property to false) a shake event that percolates all the way to the top of the responder chain will be handled by the runtime: it will display an Undo or Redo alert, and will perform undo or redo on that object. Your view controller might not want to rob any responders in its view of this capability. A simple way to avoid doing so is to test whether the view controller is itself the first responder; if it isn't, we call super to pass the event on up the responder chain:

```
override func motionEnded(_ motion: UIEvent.EventSubtype, with e: UIEvent?) {
    if self.isFirstResponder {
        print("hey, you shook me!")
    } else {
        super.motionEnded(motion, with: e)
    }
}
```

 Starting in iOS 13, double tap or left swipe with three fingers signifies Undo, and shake gestures will probably diminish in importance.

Using Core Motion

The standard pattern for using the Core Motion framework (import CoreMotion) is reminiscent of how you use Core Location:

1. You start by instantiating CMMotionManager; retain the instance somewhere, typically as an instance property. There is no reason not to initialize the property directly:

    ```
    let motman = CMMotionManager()
    ```

2. Confirm that the desired hardware is available by checking the appropriate instance property, such as isAccelerometerAvailable.

3. Set the interval at which you wish the motion manager to update itself with new sensor readings by setting the appropriate property, such as `accelerometer-UpdateInterval`.

4. Call the appropriate `start` method, such as `startAccelerometerUpdates`.

5. You probably expect me to say now that the motion manager will call into a delegate. Surprise! A motion manager has no delegate. You have two choices:

   Pull

   > Poll the motion manager whenever you want data, asking for the appropriate `data` property. The polling interval doesn't have to be the same as the motion manager's update interval, when you poll, you'll obtain the motion manager's *current* data — that is, the data generated by its most recent update, whenever that was.

   Push

   > If your purpose is to collect *all* the data, then instead of calling a simple `start` method, you can call a related method that takes a function that will be called back, preferably on a background thread managed by an OperationQueue (Chapter 25). The name of this method will have the form `start...Updates(to:withHandler:)`. For example, for accelerometer updates, instead of `startAccelerometerUpdates`, you would call `start-AccelerometerUpdates(to:withHandler:)`.

6. Don't forget to call the corresponding `stop` method, such as `stopAccelerometer-Updates`, when you no longer need data.

So there are two ways to get motion manager data — pull and push. Which approach should you use? It depends on what you're trying to accomplish. Polling (pull) is a good way to learn the device's instantaneous state at some significant moment. A stream of callbacks (push) is a good way to detect a gesture, typically by recording the most recent data into a circular buffer for subsequent analysis. It's perfectly possible to use *both* methods; having configured push, you can perform an occasional pull.

Raw Acceleration

If the device has an accelerometer but no gyroscope, you can learn about the forces being applied to it, but some compromises will be necessary. The chief problem is that, even if the device is completely motionless, its acceleration values will constitute a normalized vector pointing toward the center of the earth, popularly known as *gravity*. The accelerometer is constantly reporting a combination of gravity and user-induced acceleration. This is good and bad. It's good because it means that, with certain restrictions, you can use the accelerometer to detect the device's attitude in space. It's bad because gravity values and user-induced acceleration values are mixed together. Fortunately, there are ways to separate them mathematically:

With a low-pass filter

A low-pass filter will damp out user acceleration so as to report gravity only.

With a high-pass filter

A high-pass filter will damp out the effect of gravity so as to detect user acceleration only, reporting a motionless device as having zero acceleration.

In some situations, it is desirable to apply both a low-pass filter and a high-pass filter, so as to learn both the gravity values and the user acceleration values. A common additional technique is to run the output of the high-pass filter itself through a low-pass filter to reduce noise and small twitches. Apple provides some nice sample code for implementing a low-pass or a high-pass filter; see especially the Accelerometer-Graph example, which is also helpful for exploring how the accelerometer behaves.

The technique of applying filters to the accelerometer output has some serious downsides, which are inevitable in a device that lacks a gyroscope:

- It's up to you to apply the filters; you have to implement boilerplate code and hope that you don't make a mistake.

- Filters mean *latency*. Your response to the accelerometer values will lag behind what the device is actually doing; this lag may be noticeable.

Gravity and attitude

In this example, I will simply report whether the device is lying flat on its back. I start by configuring my motion manager; then I launch a repeating timer to trigger polling:

```
guard self.motman.isAccelerometerAvailable else { return }
self.motman.accelerometerUpdateInterval = 1.0 / 30.0
self.motman.startAccelerometerUpdates()
self.timer = Timer.scheduledTimer(
    timeInterval:self.motman.accelerometerUpdateInterval,
    target: self, selector: #selector(pollAccel),
    userInfo: nil, repeats: true)
```

My pollAccel method is now being called repeatedly. In it, I ask the motion manager for its accelerometer data. This arrives as a CMAccelerometerData object, which is a timestamp plus a CMAcceleration; a CMAcceleration is simply a struct of three values, one for each axis of the device, measured in Gs:

- The positive x-axis points to the right of the device.

- The positive y-axis points toward the top of the device.

- The positive z-axis points out the front of the screen.

The two axes orthogonal to gravity, which are the x- and y-axes when the device is lying more or less on its back, are much more accurate and sensitive to small variation than the axis pointing toward or away from gravity. So our approach is to ask first whether the x and y values are close to zero; only then do we use the z value to learn whether the device is on its back or on its face. To keep from updating our interface constantly, we implement a crude state machine; the state property (self.state) starts out at .unknown, and then switches between .lyingDown (device on its back) and .notLyingDown (device not on its back), and we update the interface only when there is a state change:

```
guard let data = self.motman.accelerometerData else {return}
let acc = data.acceleration
let x = acc.x
let y = acc.y
let z = acc.z
let accu = 0.08
if abs(x) < accu && abs(y) < accu && z < -0.5 {
    if self.state == .unknown || self.state == .notLyingDown {
        self.state = .lyingDown
        self.label.text = "I'm lying on my back... ahhh..."
    }
} else {
    if self.state == .unknown || self.state == .lyingDown {
        self.state = .notLyingDown
        self.label.text = "Hey, put me back down on the table!"
    }
}
```

That works, but it's sensitive to small motions of the device on the table. To damp this sensitivity, we can run our input through a low-pass filter. The low-pass filter code comes straight from Apple's own examples, and involves maintaining the previously filtered reading as a set of properties:

```
func add(acceleration accel:CMAcceleration) {
    let alpha = 0.1
    self.oldX = accel.x * alpha + self.oldX * (1.0 - alpha)
    self.oldY = accel.y * alpha + self.oldY * (1.0 - alpha)
    self.oldZ = accel.z * alpha + self.oldZ * (1.0 - alpha)
}
```

Our polling code now starts out by passing the data through the filter:

```
guard let data = self.motman.accelerometerData else {return}
self.add(acceleration: data.acceleration)
let x = self.oldX
let y = self.oldY
let z = self.oldZ
// ... and the rest is as before ...
```

As I mentioned earlier, instead of polling (pull), you can receive callbacks to a function (push). This approach is useful particularly if your goal is to collect updates or to receive updates on a background thread (or both). To illustrate, I'll rewrite the previous example to use this technique; to keep things simple, I'll ask for my callbacks on the main thread (the documentation advises against this, but Apple's own sample code does it). We now start our accelerometer updates like this:

```
self.motman.startAccelerometerUpdates(to: .main) { data, err in
    guard let data = data else {
        print(err)
        self.stopAccelerometer()
        return
    }
    self.receive(acceleration:data)
}
```

`receive(acceleration:)` is just like our earlier `pollAccel`, except that we already have the accelerometer data:

```
func receive(acceleration data:CMAccelerometerData) {
    self.add(acceleration: data.acceleration)
    let x = self.oldX
    let y = self.oldY
    let z = self.oldZ
    // ... and the rest is as before ...
}
```

Force applied by the user

In this next example, the user is allowed to slap the side of the device into an open hand — perhaps as a way of telling it to go to the next or previous image or whatever it is we're displaying. We pass the acceleration input through a high-pass filter to eliminate gravity (again, the filter code comes straight from Apple's examples):

```
func add(acceleration accel:CMAcceleration) {
    let alpha = 0.1
    self.oldX = accel.x - ((accel.x * alpha) + (self.oldX * (1.0 - alpha)))
    self.oldY = accel.y - ((accel.y * alpha) + (self.oldY * (1.0 - alpha)))
    self.oldZ = accel.z - ((accel.z * alpha) + (self.oldZ * (1.0 - alpha)))
}
```

What we're looking for, in our polling routine, is a high positive or negative x value. A single slap is likely to consist of several consecutive readings above our threshold, but we want to report each slap only once, so we take advantage of the timestamp attached to a CMAccelerometerData, maintaining the timestamp of our previous high reading as a property and ignoring readings that are too close to one another in time. Another problem is that a sudden jerk involves both an acceleration (as the user starts the device moving) and a deceleration (as the device stops moving); a left slap might be preceded by a high value in the opposite direction, which we might interpret wrongly as a right slap. We can compensate crudely, at the expense of some latency, with delayed performance:

```
@objc func pollAccel(_: Any) {
    guard let data = self.motman.accelerometerData else {return}
    self.add(acceleration: data.acceleration)
    let x = self.oldX
    let thresh = 1.0
    if x < -thresh {
        if data.timestamp - self.oldTime > 0.5 || self.lastSlap == .right {
            self.oldTime = data.timestamp
            self.lastSlap = .left
            self.canceltimer?.invalidate()
            self.canceltimer = .scheduledTimer(
                withTimeInterval:0.5, repeats: false) { _ in
                    print("left")
            ]
        }
    } else if x > thresh {
        if data.timestamp - self.oldTime > 0.5 || self.lastSlap == .left {
            self.oldTime = data.timestamp
            self.lastSlap = .right
            self.canceltimer?.invalidate()
            self.canceltimer = .scheduledTimer(
                withTimeInterval:0.5, repeats: false) { _ in
                    print("right")
        }
    }
    }
}
```

The gesture we're detecting is a little tricky to make: the user must slap the device into an open hand *and hold it there*; if the device jumps out of the open hand, that movement may be detected as the last in the series, resulting in the wrong report (left instead of right, or *vice versa*). And the latency of our gesture detection is very high.

Of course we might try tweaking some of the magic numbers in this code to improve accuracy and performance, but a more sophisticated analysis would probably involve storing a stream of all the most recent CMAccelerometerData objects in a circular buffer and studying the buffer contents to work out the overall trend.

Gyroscope

The inclusion of an electronic gyroscope in the panoply of onboard hardware in some devices makes a huge difference in the accuracy and speed of gravity and attitude reporting. A gyroscope has the property that its attitude in space remains constant, so it can detect any change in the attitude of the containing device. This has two important consequences for accelerometer measurements:

- The accelerometer can be supplemented by the gyroscope to detect quickly the difference between gravity and user-induced acceleration.

- The gyroscope can observe pure rotation, where little or no acceleration is involved and so the accelerometer would not have been helpful. The extreme case is constant attitudinal rotation around the gravity axis, which the accelerometer alone would be unable to detect (because there is no user-induced force, and gravity remains constant).

It is possible to track the raw gyroscope data: make sure the device has a gyroscope (isGyroAvailable), and then call startGyroUpdates. What we get from the motion manager is a CMGyroData object, which combines a timestamp with a CMRotationRate that reports the *rate of rotation* around each axis, measured in radians per second, where a positive value is *counterclockwise* as seen by someone whose eye is pointed to by the positive axis. (This is the opposite of the direction graphed in Figure 1-11.)

But there's a problem: the gyroscope values are *scaled* and *biased*. This means that the values are based on an arbitrary scale and are gradually increasing (or decreasing) over time at a roughly constant rate. So in real life you are unlikely to want raw gyroscope data. Instead, you'll use device motion.

Device motion

The most reliable way to obtain the device's attitude is through a combination of at least the gyroscope and the accelerometer. The mathematics required to combine the data from these sensors can be daunting. Fortunately, there's no need to know anything about that! Core Motion will happily package up the calculated combination of data as a device motion instance (CMDeviceMotion), with the effects of the sensors' internal bias and scaling already factored out.

CMDeviceMotion consists of the following properties, all of which provide a triple of values corresponding to the device's natural 3D frame (x increasing to the right, y increasing to the top, z increasing out the front):

gravity
 A CMAcceleration expressing a vector with value 1 pointing to the center of the earth, measured in Gs.

userAcceleration
 A CMAcceleration describing user-induced acceleration, with no gravity component, measured in Gs.

rotationRate
 A CMRotationRate describing how the device is rotating around its own center. This is essentially the CMGyroData rotationRate with scale and bias already accounted for.

`magneticField`

A CMCalibratedMagneticField describing (in its `field`, a CMMagneticField) the magnetic forces acting on the device, measured in microteslas. The sensor's internal bias has already been factored out. The `accuracy` is one of the following (CMMagneticFieldCalibrationAccuracy):

- `.uncalibrated`

- `.low`

- `.medium`

- `.high`

`attitude`

A CMAttitude, descriptive of the device's instantaneous attitude in space. The attitude is measured against a reference frame (CMAttitudeReferenceFrame) which you specify when you ask the motion manager to start generating updates, having first called the class method `availableAttitudeReferenceFrames` to ascertain that the desired reference frame is available on this device. In every case, the negative z-axis points at the center of the earth; what varies between reference frames is where the x-axis is (and the y-axis is then orthogonal to the other two):

`.xArbitraryZVertical`

The x-axis could be pointing anywhere.

`.xArbitraryCorrectedZVertical`

The same as the previous option, but the magnetometer is used to maintain accuracy (preventing drift of the reference frame over time).

`.xMagneticNorthZVertical`

The x-axis points toward magnetic north.

`.xTrueNorthZVertical`

The x-axis points toward true north. This value will be inaccurate unless you are also using Core Location to obtain the device's location.

The `attitude` value's numbers can be accessed through various CMAttitude properties corresponding to three different systems, each being convenient for a different purpose:

`pitch, roll, yaw`

The device's angle of offset from the reference frame, in radians, around the device's natural x-axis, y-axis, and z-axis respectively (also known as Euler angles).

rotationMatrix

> A CMRotationMatrix struct embodying a 3×3 matrix expressing a rotation in the reference frame.

quaternion

> A CMQuaternion describing an attitude. (Quaternions are commonly used in 3D contexts such as SceneKit and Metal.)

heading

> A Double giving the device's orientation as a number of degrees (*not* radians) clockwise from north, in accordance with the reference frame which must be .xMagneticNorthZVertical or .xTrueNorthZVertical (otherwise, you'll get a value of -1). Unlike a Core Location CLHeading, it is a pure orientation reading, without the course folded into it. Not only the magnetometer but also the accelerometer and gyroscope are used, helping to eliminate errors caused by local magnetic anomalies.

Absolute attitude

In this example, we turn the device into a simple compass/clinometer, merely by asking for its attitude with reference to magnetic north and taking its pitch, roll, and yaw. We begin by making the usual preparations; notice the use of the showsDevice-MovementDisplay property, intended to allow the runtime to prompt the user if the magnetometer needs calibration:

```
guard self.motman.isDeviceMotionAvailable else { return }
let r = CMAttitudeReferenceFrame.xMagneticNorthZVertical
guard CMMotionManager.availableAttitudeReferenceFrames().contains(r) else {
    return
}
self.motman.showsDeviceMovementDisplay = true
self.motman.deviceMotionUpdateInterval = 1.0 / 30.0
self.motman.startDeviceMotionUpdates(using: r)
let t = self.motman.deviceMotionUpdateInterval * 10
self.timer = Timer.scheduledTimer(timeInterval:t,
    target:self, selector:#selector(pollAttitude),
    userInfo:nil, repeats:true)
```

In pollAttitude, we wait until the magnetometer is ready, and then we start taking attitude readings (converted to degrees):

```
guard let mot = self.motman.deviceMotion else {return}
let acc = mot.magneticField.accuracy.rawValue
if acc <= CMMagneticFieldCalibrationAccuracy.low.rawValue {
    return // not ready yet
}
let att = mot.attitude
let to_deg = 180.0 / .pi
print("\(att.pitch * to_deg), \(att.roll * to_deg), \(att.yaw * to_deg)")
```

The values are all close to zero when the device is level (flat on its back) with its x-axis (right edge) pointing to magnetic north, and each value increases as the device is rotated *counterclockwise* with respect to an eye that has the corresponding positive axis pointing at it. A device held upright (top pointing at the sky) has a `pitch` approaching 90; a device lying on its right edge has a `roll` approaching 90; and a device lying on its back with its top pointing north has a `yaw` approaching -90.

There are some quirks in the way Euler angles operate mathematically:

- `roll` and `yaw` increase with counterclockwise rotation from 0 to π (180 degrees) and then jump to -π (-180 degrees) and continue to increase to 0 as the rotation completes a circle; but `pitch` increases to π/2 (90 degrees) and then decreases to 0, then decreases to -π/2 (-90 degrees) and increases to 0. This means that `attitude` alone, if we are exploring it through `pitch`, `roll`, and `yaw`, is insufficient to describe the device's attitude, since a `pitch` value of, say, π/4 (45 degrees) could mean two different things. To distinguish those two things, we can supplement `attitude` with the z-component of `gravity`:

  ```
  let g = mot.gravity
  let whichway = g.z > 0 ? "forward" : "back"
  print("pitch is tilted \(whichway)")
  ```

- Values become inaccurate in certain orientations. In particular, when `pitch` approaches ±90 degrees (the device is upright or inverted), `roll` and `yaw` become erratic. (You may see this effect referred to as "the singularity" or "gimbal lock.") I believe that, depending on what you are trying to accomplish, you can solve this by using a different expression of the attitude, such as the `rotationMatrix`, which does not suffer from this limitation.

Relative attitude

This next example illustrates a use of CMAttitude's `rotationMatrix` property. Our goal is to make a CALayer rotate in response to the current attitude of the device. We start as before, except that our reference frame is `.xArbitraryZVertical`; we are interested in how the device moves from its initial attitude, without reference to any particular fixed external direction such as magnetic north. In `pollAttitude`, our first step is to store the device's current attitude in a CMAttitude property, `self.ref`:

```
guard let mot = self.motman.deviceMotion else {return}
let att = mot.attitude
if self.ref == nil {
    self.ref = att
    return
}
```

That code works correctly because on the first few polls, as the attitude-detection hardware warms up, att is `nil`, so we don't get past the `return` call until we have a valid initial attitude. Our next step is highly characteristic of how CMAttitude is used: we call the CMAttitude instance method `multiply(byInverseOf:)`, which transforms our attitude so that it is relative *to the stored initial attitude*:

```
att.multiply(byInverseOf: self.ref)
```

Finally, we apply the attitude's rotation matrix directly to a layer in our interface as a transform. Well, not quite directly: a rotation matrix is a 3×3 matrix, whereas a CATransform3D, which is what we need in order to set a layer's `transform`, is a 4×4 matrix. However, it happens that the top left nine entries in a CATransform3D matrix constitute its rotation component, so we start with an identity matrix and set those entries directly:

```
let r = att.rotationMatrix
var t = CATransform3DIdentity
t.m11 = CGFloat(r.m11)
t.m12 = CGFloat(r.m12)
t.m13 = CGFloat(r.m13)
t.m21 = CGFloat(r.m21)
t.m22 = CGFloat(r.m22)
t.m23 = CGFloat(r.m23)
t.m31 = CGFloat(r.m31)
t.m32 = CGFloat(r.m32)
t.m33 = CGFloat(r.m33)
let lay = // whatever
CATransaction.setAnimationDuration(1.0/10.0)
lay.transform = t
```

The result is that the layer apparently tries to hold itself still as the device rotates. The example is rather crude because we aren't drawing a three-dimensional object, but it illustrates the principle well enough.

There is a quirk to be aware of in this case as well: over time, the transform has a tendency to drift. Even if we leave the device stationary, the layer will gradually rotate. That is the sort of effect that `.xArbitraryCorrectedZVertical` is designed to help mitigate, at the expense of some CPU and battery usage, by bringing the magnetometer into play.

Core Motion best practices

Here are some additional considerations to be aware of when using Core Motion:

- Your app should create only one CMMotionManager instance.
- Core Motion requires that various sensors be turned on, such as the magnetometer and the gyroscope. This can result in some increased battery drain, so try not to use any sensors you don't have to, and remember to stop generating updates as soon as you no longer need them.

- Use of Core Motion is legal while your app is running in the background. To take advantage of this, your app would need to be running in the background for some *other* reason; there is no Core Motion `UIBackgroundModes` setting in an *Info.plist*. You might run in the background because you're using Core Location, and take advantage of this to employ Core Motion as well.

- If your app will *not* be running in the background, then you should tell the motion manager explicitly to stop generating updates when your app goes into the background.

Other Core Motion Data

In addition to CMDeviceMotion, the Core Motion framework lets you obtain four other types of data:

CMMotionActivityManager
Some devices have a motion coprocessor chip with the ability to detect, analyze, and keep a record of device motion even while the device is asleep and with very little drain on power. This is *not* a form of location determination; it is an analysis of the device's physical motion and attitude in order to draw conclusions about what the user has been doing while carrying or wearing the device. You can learn that the user is walking, or walked for an hour, but not *where* the user was walking.

Start by maintaining a CMMotionActivityManager instance, typically as an instance property. To find out whether the device has a motion coprocessor, call the CMMotionActivityManager class method `isActivityAvailable`. There are two ways to query the motion activity manager:

Real-time updates
This is similar to getting motion manager updates with a callback function. You call this method:

- `startActivityUpdates(to:withHandler:)`

Your callback function is called periodically. When you no longer need updates, call `stopActivityUpdates`.

Historical data
The motion coprocessor stores about a week's-worth of the most recent data. You ask for a chunk of that recorded data by calling this method:

- `queryActivityStarting(from:to:to:withHandler:)`

It's fine to query the historical data while the motion activity manager is already delivering updates.

CMPedometer

The pedometer is a step counter, deducing steps from the back and forth motion of the device; it can also be used to receive events alerting you that the user has started or stopped activity. The pedometer may work reliably under circumstances where Core Location doesn't.

Start by maintaining a CMPedometer instance, typically as an instance property. Before using the pedometer, check the `isStepCountingAvailable` class method. Different devices add further capabilities. Some devices can deduce the size of the user's stride and compute distance (`isDistanceAvailable`); some devices can use barometric data to estimate whether the user mounted a flight of stairs (`isFloorCountingAvailable`). You can also ask for instantaneous cadence (`isCadenceAvailable`) and pace (`isPaceAvailable`).

Pedometer data is queried just like motion activity data:

Real-time updates

You can ask for constant updates with this method:

- `startUpdates(from:withHandler:)`

Historical data

You can ask for the stored history with this method:

- `queryPedometerData(from:to:withHandler:)`

Each bit of data arrives as a CMPedometerData object.

To be notified of changes in the user's motion, call `startEventUpdates(handler:)`; the `handler:` function receives a CMPedometerEvent whose `type` (CMPedometerEventType) is `.pause` or `.resume`.

CMAltimeter

Some devices have an altimeter — in essence, a barometer. The idea here is not so much to tell you the user's absolute altitude, since atmospheric pressure can vary considerably at a fixed altitude, but to alert you to changes in the user's relative altitude during activity.

Start by maintaining a CMAltimeter instance, typically as an instance property. Before using the altimeter, check the `isRelativeAltitudeAvailable` class method. Then call `startRelativeAltitudeUpdates(to:withHandler:)` to start delivery of CMAltitudeData objects; the key metric is the `relativeAltitude` property, an NSNumber wrapping a Double representing meters. It starts life at 0, and subsequent CMAltitudeData objects provide a measurement relative to that initial base.

CMSensorRecorder

Some devices can record the output of the accelerometer over time in the background. Before using the recorder, check the `isAccelerometerRecording-Available`. Then instantiate CMSensorRecorder (you do *not* need to retain the instance) and call `recordAccelerometer(forDuration:)`. Recording is done by the system, 50 times per second, on your behalf, regardless of whether your app is in the foreground or even whether it is running, and stops automatically when the `duration` is over.

To retrieve the data, instantiate CMSensorRecorder again, and call `accelerometerData(from:to:)`. You are given a CMSensorDataList, which unfortunately is rather tricky to deal with. First, you'll need to make CMSensor-DataList conform to Sequence by means of an extension:

```
extension CMSensorDataList: Sequence {
    public typealias Iterator = NSFastEnumerationIterator
    public func makeIterator() -> NSFastEnumerationIterator {
        return NSFastEnumerationIterator(self)
    }
}
```

Now you can iterate over CMSensorDataList to get CMRecordedAccelerometer-Data instances, each consisting of a `timestamp` and an `acceleration`; the latter is a CMAcceleration, discussed earlier in this chapter:

```
let rec = CMSensorRecorder() // and d1 and d2 are Dates
if let list = rec.accelerometerData(from: d1, to: d2) {
    for datum in list {
        if let accdatum = datum as? CMRecordedAccelerometerData {
            let accel = accdatum.acceleration
            let t = accdatum.timestamp
            // do something with data here
        }
    }
}
```

All four types of data have in common that you need user authorization to obtain them (and even if you obtain such authorization, the user can later use the Settings app to withdraw it). Your *Info.plist* must contain an entry under the "Privacy — Motion Usage Description" key (`NSMotionUsageDescription`) explaining your purpose. Oddly, there is no `requestAuthorization` method. In the past, there wasn't even any easy way to learn in advance whether we had authorization; the technique was to "tickle" the appropriate class by trying to query it for data and see if you got an error. In this example, I have a Bool property, `self.authorized`, which I set based on the outcome of trying to query the motion activity manager:

```
guard CMMotionActivityManager.isActivityAvailable() else { return }
let now = Date()
self.actman.queryActivityStarting(from:now, to:now, to:.main) { arr, err in
    let notauth = Int(CMErrorMotionActivityNotAuthorized.rawValue)
    if err != nil && (err! as NSError).code == notauth {
        self.isAuthorized = false
    } else {
        self.isAuthorized = true
    }
}
```

On the first run of that code, the system puts up the authorization request alert if necessary. The completion function is not called until the user deals with the alert, so the outcome tells you what the user decided. On subsequent runs, that same code reports the current authorization status.

Starting in iOS 11, there's an easier way: you can ask the class in question for its authorizationStatus. This returns a status enum with the usual four cases. You *still* need to "tickle" the class to summon the authorization alert if the status is .not-Determined. This allows us to use a strategy similar to the one devised earlier ("Checking for Authorization" on page 899). I assume here that self.actman is a CMMotionActivityManager instance:

```
func checkAuthorization(andThen f:(()->())? = nil) {
    let status = CMMotionActivityManager.authorizationStatus()
    switch status {
    case .notDetermined: // bring up alert
        let now = Date()
        self.actman.queryActivityStarting(from: now, to:now, to:.main) {
            _,err in
            print("asked for authorization")
            if err == nil {
                f?()
            }
        }
    case .authorized: f?()
    case .restricted: break // do nothing
    case .denied: break // could beg for authorization here
    @unknown default: fatalError()
    }
}
```

I'll illustrate querying for historical motion activity manager data by fetching the data for the past 24 hours. I have prepared an OperationQueue property, self.queue:

```
let now = Date()
let yester = now - (60*60*24)
self.actman.queryActivityStarting(
    from: yester, to: now, to: self.queue) { arr, err in
        guard var acts = arr else {return}
        // ...
}
```

We now have an array of CMMotionActivity objects representing every *change* in the device's activity status. This is a value class. It has a `startDate`, a `confidence` (a CMMotionActivityConfidence, `.low`, `.medium`, or `.high`) ranking the activity manager's faith in its own categorization of what the user was doing, and a bunch of Bool properties actually categorizing the activity:

- `stationary`

- `walking`

- `running`

- `automotive`

- `cycling`

- `unknown`

A common first response to the flood of data is to pare it down (sometimes referred to as *smoothing* or *decimating*). To help with this, I've extended CMMotionActivity with a utility method that summarizes its Bool properties as a string:

```
extension CMMotionActivity {
    private func tf(_ b:Bool) -> String {
        return b ? "t" : "f"
    }
    func overallAct() -> String {
        let s = tf(self.stationary)
        let w = tf(self.walking)
        let r = tf(self.running)
        let a = tf(self.automotive)
        let c = tf(self.cycling)
        let u = tf(self.unknown)
        return "\(s) \(w) \(r) \(a) \(c) \(u)"
    }
}
```

As a straightforward way of paring down the data, I remove every CMMotionActivity with no definite activity, or with a low degree of confidence, or with an activity that is the same as its predecessor. Then I set an instance property with my data, ready for use:

```
let blank = "f f f f f f"
acts = acts.filter {act in act.overallAct() != blank}
acts = acts.filter {act in act.confidence == .high}
for i in (1..<acts.count).reversed() {
    if acts[i].overallAct() == acts[i-1].overallAct() {
        acts.remove(at:i)
    }
}
DispatchQueue.main.async {
    self.data = acts
}
```

Final Topics

This part of the book is a miscellany of topics:

- Chapter 23 is about files and how your app can store data persistently. It also discusses sharing files with the user and with other apps, plus the document architecture and iCloud, and surveys some common file formats.

- Chapter 24 introduces networking, with an emphasis on downloading of data, along with some specialized forms of networking such as universal links, on-demand resources, and in-app purchases.

- Chapter 25 is about making your code multithreaded.

- Chapter 26 describes how to support undo in your app.

- Appendix A discusses the lifetime event messages sent to your app.

- Appendix B is a catalog of some useful Swift utility functions that I've written.

- Appendix C is an excursus on asynchronous code execution.

Persistent Storage

Your app can save data into files that persist on the device when your app isn't running or the device is powered down. This chapter is about how and where files are saved and retrieved. It also talks about some of the additional ways in which files can be manipulated, such as how apps can share documents with one another and with the cloud. The chapter also explains how user preferences are maintained in User-Defaults, and describes some specialized file formats and ways of working with their data, such as XML, JSON, SQLite, Core Data, PDF, and images.

The Sandbox

The device's file contents as a whole are not open to your app's view. Instead, a limited region of the device's persistent storage is dedicated to each app: this is the app's *sandbox*. The idea is that every app, seeing only its own sandbox, is hindered from impinging on the files belonging to other apps, and in turn is protected from having its own files impinged on by other apps. Your sandbox, and hence your data, will be deleted if the user deletes your app; otherwise, it should reliably persist.

Standard Directories

The preferred way to refer to a file or directory is with a *file URL*, a URL instance. The other possible way is with a file path, or *pathname*, which is a string; if necessary, you can convert from a file URL to a file path by asking for the URL's path, or from a pathname to a file URL with the URL initializer init(fileURLWithPath:). But on the whole, you should try to stick with URL objects.

The sandbox contains some standard directories, and there are built-in methods for referring to them. You can obtain a URL for a standard directory by starting with a

FileManager instance, which will usually be `FileManager.default`, and calling `url(for:in:appropriateFor:create:)`, like this:

```
do {
    let fm = FileManager.default
    let docsurl = try fm.url(for:.documentDirectory,
        in: .userDomainMask, appropriateFor: nil, create: false)
    // use docsurl here
} catch {
    // deal with error here
}
```

A question that will immediately occur to you is: where should I put files and folders that I want to save now and read later? The Documents directory can be a good place. But if your app supports file sharing (discussed later in this chapter), the user can see and modify your app's Documents directory, so you might not want to put things there that the user isn't supposed to see and change. A good alternative is the Application Support directory. In iOS, each app gets a private Application Support directory in its own sandbox, so you can safely put files directly into it. This directory may not exist initially, but you can obtain it and create it at the same time:

```
do {
    let fm = FileManager.default
    let suppurl = try fm.url(for:.applicationSupportDirectory,
        in: .userDomainMask, appropriateFor: nil, create: true)
    // use suppurl here
} catch {
    // deal with error here
}
```

Temporary files whose loss you are willing to accept (because their contents can be recreated) can be written into the Caches directory (`.cachesDirectory`) or the Temporary directory (the FileManager's `temporaryDirectory`). You can write temporary files elsewhere, but by default this might mean that they can be backed up by the user on a desktop computer or through iCloud; to prevent that, you can exclude an individual file from backup:

```
var rv = URLResourceValues()
rv.isExcludedFromBackup = true
try myFileURL.setResourceValues(rv)
```

Inspecting the Sandbox

While developing your app, you might like to peek inside its sandbox for debugging purposes, to make sure your files are being saved as you expect. The Simulator's sandbox for your app is a folder on your Mac that you can, with some cunning, inspect visually. In your app's code, print to the Xcode console the `path` of your app's Documents directory. Copy that value from the console, switch to the Finder, choose Go → Go to Folder, paste the path into the dialog that appears, and click Go. Now

Figure 23-1. An app's sandbox in the Simulator

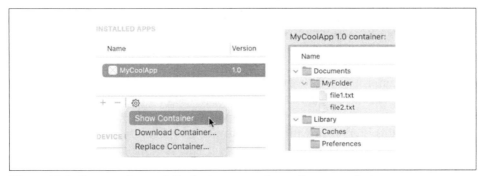

Figure 23-2. Summoning and displaying an app's sandbox on a device

you're looking at your app's Documents directory in the Finder; to see more of the sandbox, press Command-Up.

Figure 23-1 displays my app's sandbox. The Documents folder contains a folder and a couple of files that I've created programmatically (the code that created them will appear later in this chapter).

You can also view the file structure of your app's sandbox on a device. When the device is connected, choose Window → Devices and Simulators, and switch to the Devices tab. Select your device on the left; on the right, under Installed Apps, select your app. Click the Gear icon and choose Show Container; after an extremely long delay, your app's sandbox hierarchy is displayed in a modal sheet (Figure 23-2). Alternatively, choose Download Container to copy your app's sandbox to your computer; the sandbox arrives on your computer as an *.xcappdata* package, and you can open it in the Finder with Show Package Contents.

Basic File Operations

Let's say we intend to create a folder *MyFolder* inside the Documents directory. We already know how to use a FileManager instance to get a URL pointing at the Documents directory; from this, we can generate a reference to the *MyFolder* folder. Using that reference, we can ask the FileManager to create the folder if it doesn't exist already:

```
let foldername = "MyFolder"
let fm = FileManager.default
let docsurl = try fm.url(for:.documentDirectory,
    in: .userDomainMask, appropriateFor: nil, create: false)
let myfolder = docsurl.appendingPathComponent(foldername)
try fm.createDirectory(at:myfolder, withIntermediateDirectories: true)
```

To learn what files and folders exist within a directory, you can ask for an array of the directory's contents:

```
let fm = FileManager.default
let docsurl = try fm.url(for:.documentDirectory,
    in: .userDomainMask, appropriateFor: nil, create: false)
let arr = try fm.contentsOfDirectory(at:docsurl,
    includingPropertiesForKeys: nil)
arr.forEach { print($0.lastPathComponent) } // MyFolder
```

The array resulting from `contentsOfDirectory` lists full URLs of the directory's immediate contents; it is *shallow*. For a *deep* traversal of a directory's contents, you can enumerate it by means of a directory enumerator (FileManager.Directory-Enumerator); this is efficient with regards to memory, because you are handed just one file reference at a time. In this example, *MyFolder* is in the Documents directory, and I am looking for two *.txt* files that I have saved into *MyFolder* (as explained in the next section); I find them by doing a deep traversal of the Documents directory:

```
let fm = FileManager.default
let docsurl = try fm.url(for:.documentDirectory,
    in: .userDomainMask, appropriateFor: nil, create: false)
let dir = fm.enumerator(at:docsurl, includingPropertiesForKeys: nil)!
for case let f as URL in dir where f.pathExtension == "txt" {
    print(f.lastPathComponent) // file1.txt, file2.txt
}
```

A directory enumerator also permits you to decline to dive into a particular subdirectory (`skipDescendants`), so you can make your traversal even more efficient.

Consult the FileManager class documentation for more about what you can do with files, and see also Apple's *File System Programming Guide* in the documentation archive.

Saving and Reading Files

Four Cocoa classes provide a `write` instance method that saves an instance *to* a file, and an initializer that creates an instance by reading *from* a file. The file is represented by its file URL:

NSString and NSData
    NSString and NSData objects map directly between their own contents and the contents of a file. Here, I'll generate a text file in *MyFolder* directly from a string:

```
    try "howdy".write(to: myfolder.appendingPathComponent("file1.txt"),
        atomically: true, encoding:.utf8)
```

NSArray and NSDictionary

NSArray and NSDictionary objects are written to a file as a *property list*. This means that all the contents of the array or dictionary must be *property list types*, which are:

- NSString

- NSData

- NSDate

- NSNumber

- NSArray

- NSDictionary

If you have an array or dictionary containing only those types (or Swift types that are bridged to them), you can write it out directly to a file with write(to:). Here, I create an array of strings and write it out as a property list file:

```
    let arr = ["Manny", "Moe", "Jack"]
    let temp = FileManager.default.temporaryDirectory
    let f = temp.appendingPathComponent("pep.plist")
    try (arr as NSArray).write(to: f)
```

But how do you save an object of some *other* type to a file? The strategy is to *serialize* it to an NSData object (Swift Data). This, as we already know, can be saved directly to a file, or can be part of an array or dictionary to be saved to a file — and so the problem is solved.

Serializing means that we describe the object in terms of the values of its properties. There are two approaches to serializing an object as Data — the older Cocoa way (NSCoding) and the newer Swift way (Codable).

NSCoding

The NSCoding protocol is defined in Cocoa's Foundation framework. If an object's class adopts NSCoding, that object can be converted to NSData and back again by way of the NSCoder subclasses NSKeyedArchiver and NSKeyedUnarchiver. To conform to NSCoding, the class implements encode(with:) to archive the object and init(coder:) to unarchive the object.

Many built-in Cocoa classes adopt NSCoding — and you can make your own class adopt NSCoding as well. An object can refer (through a property) to another object, which may also adopt NSCoding, and you can end up saving an entire graph of interconnected objects. I'll confine myself to illustrating a simple case (and for more, see

Apple's *Archives and Serializations Programming Guide,* in the documentation archive).

Let's say that we have a simple Person class with a firstName property and a last-Name property. We'll declare that it adopts the NSCoding protocol. For this to work, the properties must themselves adopt NSCoding. We can declare them as Swift Strings because String is toll-free bridged to NSString, which adopts NSCoding. Starting in iOS 12, Apple encourages us to step up our game to NSSecureCoding, a protocol that adopts NSCoding; to do so, we implement the static supportsSecureCoding property to return true:

```
class Person: NSObject, NSSecureCoding {
    static var supportsSecureCoding: Bool { return true }
    var firstName : String
    var lastName : String
    override var description : String {
        return self.firstName + " " + self.lastName
    }
    init(firstName:String, lastName:String) {
        self.firstName = firstName
        self.lastName = lastName
        super.init()
    }
    // ...
}
```

In encode(with:), we must first call super if the superclass adopts NSCoding — in this case, it doesn't — and then call the encode method for each property we want preserved:

```
func encode(with coder: NSCoder) {
    // do not call super in this case
    coder.encode(self.lastName, forKey: "last")
    coder.encode(self.firstName, forKey: "first")
}
```

In init(coder:), we call a secure decode method for each property stored earlier, restoring the state of our object. We must also call super, using either init(coder:) if the superclass adopts NSCoding or the designated initializer if not:

```
required init(coder: NSCoder) {
    self.lastName = coder.decodeObject(
        of: NSString.self, forKey:"last")! as String
    self.firstName = coder.decodeObject(
        of: NSString.self, forKey:"first")! as String
    // do not call super init(coder:) in this case
    super.init()
}
```

We can test our code by creating, configuring, and saving a Person instance as a file:

```
let fm = FileManager.default
let docsurl = try fm.url(for:.documentDirectory,
    in: .userDomainMask, appropriateFor: nil, create: false)
let moi = Person(firstName: "Matt", lastName: "Neuburg")
let moidata = try NSKeyedArchiver.archivedData(
    withRootObject: moi, requiringSecureCoding: true)
let moifile = docsurl.appendingPathComponent("moi.txt")
try moidata.write(to: moifile, options: .atomic)
```

We can retrieve the saved Person at a later time:

```
let fm = FileManager.default
let docsurl = try fm.url(for:.documentDirectory,
    in: .userDomainMask, appropriateFor: nil, create: false)
let moifile = docsurl.appendingPathComponent("moi.txt")
let persondata = try Data(contentsOf: moifile)
let person = try NSKeyedUnarchiver.unarchivedObject(
    ofClass: Person.self, from: persondata)!
print(person) // "Matt Neuburg"
```

Even though Person now adopts NSCoding, an NSArray containing a Person object still cannot be written to a file using NSArray's write(to:), because Person is still not a property list type. But the array can be archived with NSKeyedArchiver and the resulting Data object *can* be written to a file. That's because NSArray conforms to NSCoding and, if its elements are Person objects, all its elements conform to NSCoding as well.

Codable

The Codable protocol was introduced in Swift 4; it is a combination of two other protocols, Encodable and Decodable. An object can be serialized (archived) as long as its type conforms to Encodable, and can be restored from serial form (unarchived) as long as its type conforms to Decodable. When the goal is to save to disk, the type will usually conform to both, and this will be expressed by having it adopt Codable. There are three modes of serialization:

Property list
- Use PropertyListEncoder encode(_:) to encode.
- Use PropertyListDecoder decode(_:from:) to decode.

JSON
- Use JSONEncoder encode(_:) to encode.
- Use JSONDecoder decode(_:from:) to decode.

NSCoder
- Use NSKeyedArchiver encodeEncodable(_:forKey:) to encode.
- Use NSKeyedUnarchiver decodeDecodable(_:forKey:) to decode.

You'll probably prefer to use Swift Codable rather than Cocoa NSCoding wherever possible. A class instance, a struct instance, or even a RawRepresentable enum instance can be encoded, and most built-in Swift types are Codable right out of the box. Moreover, in most cases, *your* object type will be Codable right out of the box! There are encode(to:) and init(from:) methods, similar to NSCoding encode(with:) and init(coder:), but you usually won't need to implement them because the default methods, which are synthesized for you, will suffice.

To illustrate, I'll rewrite my Person class to adopt Codable instead of NSCoding:

```
class Person: NSObject, Codable {
    var firstName : String
    var lastName · String
    override var description : String {
        return self.firstName + " " + self.lastName
    }
    init(firstName:String, lastName:String) {
        self.firstName = firstName
        self.lastName = lastName
        super.init()
    }
}
```

That's all! Person conforms to Codable with no further effort on our part. The primary reason is that our properties are Strings, and String is itself Codable. To save a Person to a file, we just have to pick an encoding format. I recommend using a property list unless there is some reason not to; it is simplest, and is closest to what NSKeyedArchiver does under the hood:

```
let fm = FileManager.default
let docsurl = try fm.url(for:.documentDirectory,
    in: .userDomainMask, appropriateFor: nil, create: false)
let moi = Person(firstName: "Matt", lastName: "Neuburg")
let moidata = try PropertyListEncoder().encode(moi)
let moifile = docsurl.appendingPathComponent("moi.txt")
try moidata.write(to: moifile, options: .atomic)
```

And here's how to retrieve our saved Person later:

```
let fm = FileManager.default
let docsurl = try fm.url(for:.documentDirectory,
    in: .userDomainMask, appropriateFor: nil, create: false)
let moifile = docsurl.appendingPathComponent("moi.txt")
let persondata = try Data(contentsOf: moifile)
let person = try PropertyListDecoder().decode(Person.self, from: persondata)
print(person) // "Matt Neuburg"
```

To save an array of Codable Person objects, do exactly the same thing. Array conforms to Codable, so use PropertyListEncoder to encode the array into a Data object and call write(to:options:), precisely as we did for a single Person object. To

Don't Store Absolute File URLs!

The absolute URLs of the sandbox directories, though they will persist during a single run of your app, are volatile over the long term; they may be different during different runs of your app. This means that you must not store your app's absolute file URLs or path strings into any form of persistent storage, as they will be incorrect the next time your app launches. (This is a common beginner mistake.)

Suppose we are about to create a folder in the Documents directory. We generate its URL as a variable `myfolder`:

```
let foldername = // whatever
let fm = FileManager.default
let docsurl = try fm.url(for:.documentDirectory,
    in: .userDomainMask, appropriateFor: nil, create: false)
let myfolder = docsurl.appendingPathComponent(foldername)
```

After that code, do *not* store the URL `myfolder` into persistent storage! If you must store information about files and folders, store their *names*, or *relative* URLs, or *partial* paths, along with some knowledge of what sandbox directory they are in.

Later, you can reconstruct the URL any time you need it, by running again the code that generated it in the first place. In this example, you would obtain the Documents directory URL from the file manager *again,* and derive the folder URL from that. In this way, your URL keeps working even though the Documents directory URL keeps changing.

---

retrieve the array, read the data from the file as a Data object and use a PropertyList-Decoder to call `decode([Person].self, from:data)`.

When your goal is to serialize your own object type to a file, there usually won't be any more to it than that. Your Codable implementation may be more elaborate when the format of the encoded data is out of your hands, such as when you are communicating through a JSON API dictated by a server. I'll illustrate later in this chapter.

The existence of Codable does not mean that you'll never need to use NSCoding. Cocoa is written in Objective-C; its encodable object types adopt NSCoding, not Codable. And the vast majority of your objects will be Cocoa objects. If you want to turn a UIColor into a Data object, you'll use an NSKeyedArchiver, not a PropertyList-Encoder; UIColor adopts NSCoding, not Codable. You can combine Swift Codable with Cocoa NSCoding, thanks to the NSCoder subclass methods `encode-Encodable(_:forKey:)` and `decodeDecodable(_:forKey:)`.

File Coordinators

In spite of sandboxing, a file can be exposed to more than one app. For example, you might permit the Files app to see into your Documents directory, as I'll explain later in this chapter. This raises the danger of simultaneous access. The low-level way to deal with that danger is to read and write through an NSFileCoordinator. Instantiate NSFileCoordinator along with an NSFileAccessIntent appropriate for reading or writing, to which you have handed the URL of your target file. Then call a coordinate method.

I'll demonstrate the use of `coordinate(with:queue:byAccessor:)` The accessor is a function where you do your actual reading or writing in the normal way, except that the URL for reading or writing now comes from the NSFileAccessIntent object. Here, I write a Person's data (moidata) out to a file (moifile) under the auspices of an NSFileCoordinator:

```
let fc = NSFileCoordinator()
let intent = NSFileAccessIntent.writingIntent(with:moifile)
fc.coordinate(with:[intent], queue: .main) { err in
    do {
        try moidata.write(to: intent.url, options: .atomic)
    } catch {
        print(error)
    }
}
```

And later I'll read that Person's data back from the same file:

```
let fc = NSFileCoordinator()
let intent = NSFileAccessIntent.readingIntent(with: moifile)
fc.coordinate(with: [intent], queue: .main) { err in
    do {
        let persondata = try Data(contentsOf: intent.url)
        // do something with data
    } catch {
        print(error)
    }
}
```

File Wrappers

A file needn't be a simple block of data. It can be a *file wrapper*, essentially a folder disguised as a file. On the desktop, a TextEdit *.rtfd* file, used when a styled TextEdit file contains images, is a file wrapper.

A file wrapper will usually contain multiple files along with some sort of file *manifest* reporting what the files are. The format of the manifest is up to you; it's a note to yourself that you configure when you save into the file wrapper, so that you can retrieve files from the file wrapper later.

In this simple example, I'll save the data for three UIImages into a file wrapper (at the file URL `fwurl`). The manifest will be a simple property list representation of an array of the names of the image files:

```
let d = FileWrapper(directoryWithFileWrappers: [:])
let imnames = ["manny.jpg", "moe.jpg", "jack.jpg"]
for imname in imnames {
    d.addRegularFile(
        withContents:
            UIImage(named:imname)!.jpegData(compressionQuality: 1)!,
        preferredFilename: imname)
}
let list = try PropertyListEncoder().encode(imnames)
d.addRegularFile(withContents: list, preferredFilename: "list")
try d.write(to: fwurl, originalContentsURL: nil)
```

The resulting file wrapper now contains four file wrappers, which can be accessed by name through its `fileWrappers` property. So here's how to extract the images later:

```
let d = try FileWrapper(url: fwurl)
if let list = d.fileWrappers?["list"]?.regularFileContents {
    let imnames = try PropertyListDecoder().decode([String].self, from:list)
    for imname in imnames {
        if let imdata = d.fileWrappers?[imname]?.regularFileContents {
            // do something with the image data
        }
    }
}
```

User Defaults

The UserDefaults class acts a gateway to persistent storage of the user's preferences. User defaults are little more, really, than a special case of an NSDictionary property list file. You talk to the UserDefaults `standard` object much as if it were a dictionary; it has keys and values, and you set and fetch values by their keys. The dictionary is saved for you automatically as a property list file; you don't know where or when, and you don't care.

 Actual saving of the dictionary to disk might not take place until several seconds after you make a change. When testing, be sure to allow sufficient time to elapse between runs of your app.

Because user defaults is actually a property list file, the only legal values that can be stored in it are property list values. Therefore, everything I said in the preceding section about saving objects applies. If an object type is not a property list type, you'll have to archive it to a Data object if you want to store it in user defaults. If the object type is a class that belongs to Cocoa and adopts NSCoding, you'll archive it through an NSKeyedArchiver. If the object type belongs to you, you might prefer to make it adopt Codable and archive it through a PropertyListEncoder.

To provide the value for a key before the user has had a chance to do so — the default default, as it were — call `register(defaults:)`. What you're supplying here is a transient dictionary whose key–value pairs will be held in memory but not saved; a pair will be used only if there is no pair with the same key already stored in the user defaults dictionary. Here's an example from one of my apps:

```
UserDefaults.standard.register(defaults: [
    Default.hazyStripy : HazyStripy.hazy.rawValue,
    Default.cardMatrixRows : 4,
    Default.cardMatrixColumns : 3,
    Default.color1 : try! NSKeyedArchiver.archivedData(
        withRootObject: UIColor.blue, requiringSecureCoding:true),
    Default.color2 : try! NSKeyedArchiver.archivedData(
        withRootObject: UIColor.red, requiringSecureCoding:true),
    Default.color3 : try! NSKeyedArchiver.archivedData(
        withRootObject: UIColor.green, requiringSecureCoding:true),
])
```

The idea is that we call `register(defaults:)` extremely early as the app launches. Either the app has run at some time previously and the user has set these preferences, in which case this call has no effect and does no harm, or not, in which case we now have initial values for these preferences with which to get started. In the game app from which that code comes, we start out with a hazy fill, a 4×3 game layout, and the three card colors blue, red, and green; but the user can change this at any time.

You will probably want to offer your user a way to interact explicitly with the defaults. One possibility is that your app provides some kind of preferences interface. The game app from which the previous code comes has a tab bar interface; in the second tab, the user explicitly sets the preferences whose default values are configured in that code (Figure 23-3).

Alternatively, you can provide a *settings bundle*, consisting mostly of one or more property list files describing an interface and the corresponding user defaults keys and their initial values; the Settings app is then responsible for translating your instructions into an actual interface, and for presenting it to the user. Writing a settings bundle is described in Apple's *Preferences and Settings Programming Guide* in the documentation archive.

Using a settings bundle means that the user has to leave your app to access preferences, and you don't get the kind of control over the interface that you have within your own app. Also, the user can set your preferences while your app is backgrounded or not running; you'll need to register for `UserDefaults.didChangeNotification` in order to hear about this.

Figure 23-3. An app's preferences interface

Still, a settings bundle has some clear advantages. Keeping the preferences interface out of your app can make your app's own interface cleaner and simpler. You don't have to write any of the "glue" code that coordinates the preferences interface with the user defaults values. And it may be appropriate for the user to be able to set at least some preferences for your app when your app isn't running.

Moreover, you can transport your user directly from your app to your app's preferences in the Settings app (and a Back button then appears in the status bar, making it easy for the user to return from Settings to your app):

```
let url = URL(string:UIApplication.openSettingsURLString)!
UIApplication.shared.open(url)
```

Every method in your app can access the UserDefaults `standard` object, so it often serves as a global "drop" where one instance can deposit a piece of information for another instance to pick up later, when those two instances might not have ready communication with one another or might not even exist simultaneously. (Starting in iOS 13, the scene session's `userInfo` might be a more appropriate choice.)

UserDefaults is also often used for general data storage. My Zotz! app (Figure 23-3), in addition to using the user defaults to store the user's explicit preferences, also records the state of the game board and the card deck into user defaults every time these change, so that if the app is terminated and then launched again later, we can restore the game as it was when the user left off. One might argue that the contents of the card deck are not a user preference, so I am misusing the user defaults to store state data. However, while purists may grumble, it's a very small amount of data and I don't think the distinction is terribly significant in this case.

Yet another use of UserDefaults is to communicate data between your app and an extension provided by your app. For more information, see the "Handling Common Scenarios" chapter of Apple's *App Extension Programming Guide*.

Simple Sharing and Previewing of Files

iOS provides basic passageways by which a file can pass safely in and out of your sandbox. File sharing lets the user manipulate the contents of your app's Documents directory. UIDocumentInteractionController allows the user to tell another app to hand a copy of a document to your app, or to tell your app to hand a copy of a document to another app; it also permits previewing a document, provided it is compatible with Quick Look.

File Sharing

File sharing means that an app's Documents directory becomes accessible to the user. The user connects the device to a computer and opens iTunes (or, starting in macOS Catalina, a Finder window) to see a list of apps on the device that support file sharing. The user can copy files and folders between the app's Documents directory and the computer, and can delete items from the app's Documents directory.

It could be appropriate for your app to support file sharing if it works with common types of file that the user might obtain elsewhere, such as PDFs or JPEGs. To support file sharing, set the *Info.plist* key "Application supports iTunes file sharing" (UIFile-SharingEnabled) to YES.

Once your entire Documents directory is exposed to the user this way, you are unlikely to use the Documents directory to store private files. As I mentioned earlier, I like to use the Application Support directory instead.

Your app doesn't get any automatic notification when the user has altered the contents of the Documents directory. Noticing that the situation has changed and responding appropriately is entirely up to you; Apple's DocInteraction sample code demonstrates an approach using the kernel-level kqueue mechanism.

Document Types and Receiving a Document

Your app can declare itself willing to open documents of a certain type. In this way, if another app obtains a document of this type, it can propose to hand a copy of the document over to your app. The user might download the document with Mobile Safari, or receive it in a mail message with the Mail app; now we need a way to get it from Safari or Mail to you.

To let the system know that your app is a candidate for receiving a certain kind of document, you will configure the "Document types" (CFBundleDocumentTypes) key

Document Types (2)

PDF

Name PDF   Types com.adobe.pdf
                                      Handler Rank Default

Additional document type properties (1)

Key   Type   Value
> CFBundleTypeIconFiles   Array   (0 items)

TEXT

Name TEXT   Types public.plain-text
                                      Handler Rank Default

Additional document type properties (1)

Key   Type   Value
> CFBundleTypeIconFiles   Array   (0 items)

+

Figure 23-4. Creating a document type

in your *Info.plist*. This is an array, where each entry will be a dictionary specifying a document type by using keys such as "Document Content Type UTIs" (`LSItem-ContentTypes`), "Document Type Name" (`CFBundleTypeName`), `CFBundleTypeIcon-Files`, and `LSHandlerRank`.

The simplest way to configure the *Info.plist* is through the interface available in the Info tab when you edit the target. Suppose I want to declare that my app opens PDFs and text files. In my target's Info tab in Xcode, I would edit the Document Types section to look like Figure 23-4.

(The values in the Types fields in Figure 23-4 are *UTIs* — uniform type identifiers. PDFs and text files are common types, so they have standard UTIs. To find out the standard UTI for a common file type, look in Apple's *Uniform Type Identifiers Reference* in the documentation archive.)

Now suppose the user receives a PDF in an email message. The Mail app can display this PDF, but the user can also tap Share to bring up an activity view offering, among other things, to copy the file to some other app. The interface will resemble Figure 23-5; various apps that can deal with a PDF are listed here, and my app (MyCoolApp) is among them.

So far, so good. But what if the user actually *taps* our icon to send the PDF over to my app? Then, for an app with window scene support, the scene delegate's `scene(_:open-URLContexts:)` will be called. Our job is to open the document whose URL has

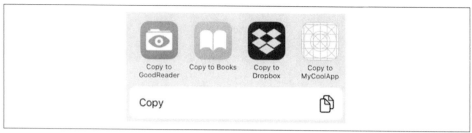

Figure 23-5. The Mail app offers to hand off a PDF

arrived in the second parameter. The system has already copied the document into temporary storage, and now we can copy it to wherever we like, such as the Documents directory, within our sandbox.

In this simple example, my app has just one view controller, which has an outlet to a web view where we will display any PDFs that arrive in this fashion. So my scene delegate contains this code:

```
func scene(_ scene: UIScene,
    openURLContexts URLContexts: Set<UIOpenURLContext>) {
    let cons = URLContexts.first!.url as NSURL
    if let vc = self.window?.rootViewController as? ViewController,
        let url = URLContexts.first?.url {
            do {
                let fm = FileManager.default
                let docsurl = try fm.url(
                    for: .documentDirectory, in: .userDomainMask,
                    appropriateFor: nil, create: false)
                let dest =
                    docsurl.appendingPathComponent(url.lastPathComponent)
                try fm.copyItem(at: url, to: dest)
                vc.displayDoc(url: dest)
            } catch {
                print(error)
            }
        }
}
```

And my view controller contains this code (`self.wv` is the web view):

```
func displayDoc (url:URL) {
    let req = URLRequest(url: url)
    self.wv.loadRequest(req)
}
```

In real life, things might be more complicated. We might check to see whether this really *is* a PDF. Also, our app might be in the middle of something else, possibly displaying a completely different view controller's view; we may have to be prepared to drop whatever we were doing and display the incoming document instead.

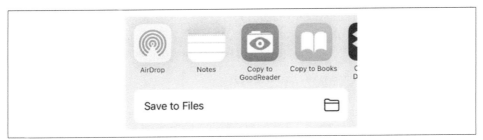

Figure 23-6. The document Open In activity view

What happens if our app is launched from scratch by the arrival of this URL? For an app with window scenes, `scene(_:openURLContexts:)` will *not* be called! Instead, you need to implement `scene(_:willConnectTo:options:)` to check the `options:` parameter for its `urlContexts` property. If this isn't empty, you've got an incoming URL to deal with, which you'll do in much the same way as in `scene(_:open-URLContexts:)`. The chief difference is that you might need to create the view controller hierarchy so that you have a view controller to which you can hand the document.

The example I've been discussing assumes that the UTI for the document type is standard and well-known. It is also possible that your app will operate on a new document type, that is, a type of document that the app itself defines. In that case, you'll also want to add this UTI to your app's list of exported type identifiers in the *Info.plist*. I'll give an example later in this chapter.

Handing Over a Document

The converse of the situation in the previous section is that your app has somehow acquired a document and wants to let the user hand over a copy of it to some other app. This is done through the UIDocumentInteractionController class.

Assume we have a file URL `url` pointing to a stored document file. Presenting the interface for handing the document over to some other application could be as simple as this (`sender` is a button that the user has just tapped):

```
let dic = UIDocumentInteractionController(url: url)
let v = sender as! UIView
dic.presentOpenInMenu(from:v.bounds, in: v, animated: true)
```

The interface is an activity view (Figure 23-6; see Chapter 14). There are actually two activity views available, each of which is summoned by either of two methods (the first method of each pair expects a CGRect and a UIView, while the second expects a UIBarButtonItem):

```
presentOpenInMenu(from:in:animated:)
presentOpenInMenu(from:animated:)
```
Presents an activity view listing apps to which the document can be copied.

```
presentOptionsMenu(from:in:animated:)
presentOptionsMenu(from:animated:)
```
Presents an activity view listing apps to which the document can be copied, along with other possible actions, such as Message, Mail, Copy, and Print.

Previewing a Document

A UIDocumentInteractionController can be used for an entirely different purpose: it can present a preview of the document, if the document is of a type for which preview is enabled, by calling presentPreview(animated:). You must give the UIDocument-InteractionController a delegate (UIDocumentInteractionControllerDelegate), and the delegate must implement documentInteractionControllerViewControllerFor-Preview(_:), returning an existing view controller that will contain the preview's view controller. So, here we ask for the preview:

```
let dic = UIDocumentInteractionController(url: url)
dic.delegate = self
dic.presentPreview(animated:true)
```

In the delegate, we supply the view controller; it happens that, in my code, this delegate *is* a view controller, so it simply returns self:

```
func documentInteractionControllerViewControllerForPreview(
    _ controller: UIDocumentInteractionController) -> UIViewController {
        return self
}
```

If the view controller returned were a UINavigationController, the preview's view controller would be pushed onto it; in this case it isn't, so the preview's view controller is a presented view controller with a Done button. The preview interface also contains a Share button that lets the user summon the Options activity view.

There is another way for the user to reach this interface. If you call presentOptions-Menu on your UIDocumentInteractionController, and if its delegate implements documentInteractionControllerViewControllerForPreview(_:), then the activity view will contain a Quick Look icon that the user can tap to summon the preview interface.

Additional delegate methods allow you to track what's happening in the interface presented by the UIDocumentInteractionController. Probably most important are those that inform you that key stages of the interaction are ending:

- documentInteractionControllerDidDismissOptionsMenu(_:)

- documentInteractionControllerDidDismissOpenInMenu(_:)
- documentInteractionControllerDidEndPreview(_:)
- documentInteractionController(_:didEndSendingToApplication:)

Quick Look Previews

Previews are actually provided through the Quick Look framework. You can skip the UIDocumentInteractionController and present the preview yourself through a QLPreviewController; you'll need to import QuickLook. It's a view controller, so to display the preview you show it as a presented view controller or push it onto a navigation controller's stack, just as UIDocumentInteractionController would have done.

A nice feature of QLPreviewController is that you can give it more than one document to preview; the user can move between these, within the preview, by paging sideways or using a table of contents summoned by a button at the bottom of the interface. Apart from this, the interface looks like the interface presented by the UIDocumentInteractionController.

In this example, I may have somewhere in my Documents directory one or more PDF or text documents. I acquire a list of their URLs and present a preview for them (self.exts has been initialized to a set consisting of ["pdf", "txt"]):

```
self.docs = [URL]()
do {
    let fm = FileManager.default
    let docsurl = try fm.url(for: .documentDirectory,
        in: .userDomainMask, appropriateFor: nil, create: false)
    let dir = fm.enumerator(at: docsurl, includingPropertiesForKeys: nil)!
    for case let f as URL in dir {
        if self.exts.contains(f.pathExtension) {
            if QLPreviewController.canPreview(f as QLPreviewItem) {
                self.docs.append(f)
            }
        }
    }
    guard self.docs.count > 0 else { return }
    let preview = QLPreviewController()
    preview.dataSource = self
    preview.currentPreviewItemIndex = 0
    self.present(preview, animated: true)
} catch {
    print(error)
}
```

You'll notice that I haven't told the QLPreviewController what documents to preview. That is the job of QLPreviewController's data source. In my code, I (self) am also the data source. I simply fetch the requested information from the list of URLs, which I previously saved into self.docs:

```
func numberOfPreviewItems(in controller: QLPreviewController) -> Int {
    return self.docs.count
}
func previewController(_ controller: QLPreviewController,
    previewItemAt index: Int) -> QLPreviewItem {
        return self.docs[index] as QLPreviewItem
}
```

The second data source method requires us to return an object that adopts the QLPreviewItem protocol. By a wildly improbable coincidence, URL *does* adopt this protocol, so the example works.

By giving your QLPreviewController a delegate (QLPreviewControllerDelegate), you can cause a presented QLPreviewController to appear by zooming from a view in your interface. You'll implement these delegate methods:

- `previewController(_:frameFor:inSourceView:)`

- `previewController(_:transitionImageFor:contentRect:)`

- `previewController(_:transitionViewFor:)`

Starting in iOS 13, a QLPreviewController can permit the user to apply Markup to images and PDFs, and to trim and rotate videos. Implement these delegate methods:

- `previewController(_:editingModeFor:)` (return `.disabled`, `.updateContents`, or `.createCopy`)

- `previewController(_:didUpdateContentsOf:)`

- `previewController(_:didSaveEditedCopyOf:at:)`

For document types that you own, you can supply your own Quick Look preview. I'll discuss that later in this chapter.

Document Architecture

A *document* is a file of a specific type. If your app's basic operation depends on opening, saving, maintaining, and possibly creating documents of a certain type, you may want to take advantage of the *document architecture*. At its simplest, this architecture revolves around the UIDocument class. Think of a UIDocument instance as managing the relationship between your app's internal model data and a document file that stores that data.

Interacting with a stored document file involves a number of pesky issues. The good news is that UIDocument handles all of them seamlessly:

- Reading or writing your data might take some time, so UIDocument does those things on a background thread.

- Your document data needs to be synchronized to the document file. UIDocument provides autosaving behavior, so that your data is written out automatically whenever it changes.

- A document owned by your app may be exposed to reading and writing by other apps, so your app must read and write to that document coherently without interference from other apps. The solution is to use an NSFileCoordinator. UIDocument does that for you.

- Information about a document can become stale while the document is open. To prevent this, the NSFilePresenter protocol notifies editors that a document has changed. UIDocument participates in this system.

- Your app might be able to open a document stored in another app's sandbox. To do so, you need special permission, which you obtain by treating the document's URL as a security scoped URL. UIDocument does that automatically.

- With iCloud, your app's documents on one of the user's devices can automatically be mirrored onto another of the user's devices. UIDocument can act as a gateway for allowing your documents to participate in iCloud.

Getting started with UIDocument is not difficult. You'll declare a UIDocument subclass, and you'll override two methods:

`load(fromContents:ofType:)`
: Called when it's time to open a document from its file. You are expected to convert the `contents` value into a model object that your app can use, and to store that model object, probably in an instance property.

`contents(forType:)`
: Called when it's time to save a document to its file. You are expected to convert the app's model object into a Data instance (or, if your document is a package, a FileWrapper) and return it.

To instantiate a UIDocument, call its designated initializer, `init(fileURL:)`. This sets the UIDocument's `fileURL` property, and associates the UIDocument with the file at this URL; typically, this association will remain constant for the rest of the UIDocument's lifetime. You will then probably store the UIDocument instance in an instance property, and use it to create (if necessary), open, save, and close the document file:

Make a new document
: Having initialized the UIDocument with a file URL pointing to a nonexistent file, send it `save(to:for:completionHandler:)`; the first argument will be the document's own `fileURL`, and the second argument (a UIDocument.SaveOperation) will be `.forCreating`. This, in turn, causes `contents(forType:)` to be called, and the contents of an empty document will be saved out to a file. Your UIDocument

subclass will need to supply some default value representing the model data when there is no data.

Open an existing document

Send the UIDocument instance `open(completionHandler:)`. This, in turn, causes `load(fromContents:ofType:)` to be called.

Save an existing document

There are two approaches to saving an existing document:

> *Autosave*
>
> Usually, you'll simply mark the document as "dirty" by calling `updateChangeCount(_:)`. From time to time, the UIDocument will notice this situation and will save the document to its file for you, calling `contents(forType:)` as it does so.

> *Manual save*
>
> On certain occasions, waiting for autosave won't be appropriate. We've already seen one such occasion — when the document file needs to be created on the spot. Another case is that the app is going into the background; we will want to preserve our document there and then, in case the app is terminated. To force the document to be saved right now, call `save(to:for:completionHandler:)`; the second argument will be `.forOverwriting`.

Close an existing document

If you know you're finished with a document — perhaps the interface displaying the document is about to be torn down — you can call `close(completionHandler:)`. The document is saved before closing.

The open, save, and close methods take a `completionHandler:` function. This is UIDocument's solution to the fact that reading and saving may take time. The file operations take place on a background thread; your completion function is then called on the main thread.

A Basic Document Example

We now know enough for an example! I'll reuse my Person class from earlier in this chapter. Imagine a document effectively consisting of multiple Person instances; I'll call each such document a *people group*. Our app, People Groups, will list all people group documents in the user's Documents folder; the user can then select any people group document and our app will open that document and display its contents, allowing the user to create a new Person and to edit any existing Person's `firstName` or `lastName` (Figure 23-7).

Figure 23-7. The People Groups interface

My first step is to edit the app target and use the Info tab (Figure 23-8) to configure the *Info.plist.* I define two things (in reverse order):

- A custom type identifier, associating a file type `com.neuburg.pplgrp` with a file extension `"pplgrp"`. This type identifier is nonstandard (my app creates it), so I configure it to be exported.

- A corresponding document type, declaring that my app is the origin of this type (`Owner`) and that it is able to open and save documents (`Editor`).

In Figure 23-8, when I export my UTI, the entries under "Conforms To" are of particular importance:

Inheritance
I give this UTI a place in the UTI hierarchy. It inherits from no existing type, so it conforms to `public.content`, the base type.

File type
I declare that this UTI represents a simple flat file (`public.data`) as opposed to a package.

Now let's write our UIDocument subclass, which I'll call PeopleDocument. A document consists of multiple Persons, so a natural model implementation is a Person array. PeopleDocument has a public `people` property, initialized to an empty Person array; this will not only hold the model data when we have it, but will also give us something to save into a new empty document. Since Person implements Codable, a Person array can be archived directly into a Data object, and our implementation of the loading and saving methods is straightforward:

Figure 23-8. Defining a custom UTI

```swift
class PeopleDocument: UIDocument {
    var people = [Person]()
    override func load(fromContents contents: Any,
        ofType typeName: String?) throws {
            if let contents = contents as? Data {
                if let arr = try? PropertyListDecoder().decode(
                    [Person].self, from: contents) {
                        self.people = arr
                        return
                }
            }
            // if we get here, there was some kind of problem
            throw NSError(domain: "NoDataDomain", code: -1, userInfo: nil)
    }
    override func contents(forType typeName: String) throws -> Any {
        if let data = try? PropertyListEncoder().encode(self.people) {
            return data
        }
        // if we get here, there was some kind of problem
        throw NSError(domain: "NoDataDomain", code: -2, userInfo: nil)
    }
}
```

The first view controller, GroupLister, is a master table view (its view appears on the left in Figure 23-7). It merely looks in the Documents directory for people group documents and lists them by name; it also provides an interface for letting the user create a new people group. None of that is challenging, so I won't discuss it further.

The second view controller, PeopleLister, is the detail view; it too is a table view (its view appears on the right in Figure 23-7). It displays the first and last names of the people in the currently open people group document. This is the only place where we actually work with PeopleDocument, so let's focus our attention on that.

PeopleLister's designated initializer demands a `fileURL:` parameter pointing to a people group document, and uses it to set its own `fileURL` property. From this, it instantiates a PeopleDocument, keeping a reference to it in its doc property. People-Lister also has a `people` property, acting as the data model for its table view; this is nothing but a pointer to the PeopleDocument's `people` property.

As PeopleLister comes into existence, the document file pointed to by `self.fileURL` might not yet exist. If it doesn't, we create it; if it does, we open it. In both cases, our `people` data are now ready for display, so the completion function reloads the table view:

```swift
let fileURL : URL
var doc : PeopleDocument!
var people : [Person] { // point to the document's model object
    get { return self.doc.people }
    set { self.doc.people = newValue }
}
init(fileURL:URL) {
    self.fileURL = fileURL
    super.init(nibName: "PeopleLister", bundle: nil)
}
required init(coder: NSCoder) {
    fatalError("NSCoding not supported")
}
override func viewDidLoad() {
    super.viewDidLoad()
    self.title =
        (self.fileURL.lastPathComponent as NSString).deletingPathExtension
    // ... interface configuration goes here ...
    let fm = FileManager.default
    self.doc = PeopleDocument(fileURL:self.fileURL)
    func listPeople(_ success:Bool) {
        if success {
            self.tableView.reloadData()
        }
    }
    if let _ = try? self.fileURL.checkResourceIsReachable() {
        self.doc.open(completionHandler: listPeople)
    } else {
        self.doc.save(to:self.doc.fileURL,
            for: .forCreating, completionHandler: listPeople)
    }
}
```

Displaying people, creating a new person, and allowing the user to edit a person's first and last names, are all trivial uses of a table view (Chapter 8). Let's proceed to the only other aspect of PeopleLister that involves working with PeopleDocument, namely saving.

When the user performs a significant editing maneuver, such as creating a person or editing a person's first or last name, PeopleLister updates the model (`self.people`) and the table view, and then tells its PeopleDocument that the document is dirty, allowing autosaving to take it from there:

```
self.doc.updateChangeCount(.done)
```

When the app is about to go into the background, or when PeopleLister's own view is disappearing, PeopleLister forces PeopleDocument to save immediately:

```
func forceSave(_: Any?) {
    self.tableView.endEditing(true)
    self.doc.save(to:self.doc.fileURL, for:.forOverwriting)
}
```

That's all it takes! Adding UIDocument support to your app is easy, because UIDocument is merely acting as a supplier and preserver of your app's data model object. The UIDocument class documentation may give the impression that this is a large and complex class, but that's chiefly because it is so heavily customizable both at high and low levels; for the most part, you won't need any customization. You might work with your UIDocument's undo manager to give it a more sophisticated understanding of what constitutes a significant change in your data; I'll talk about undo managers in Chapter 26. For further details, see Apple's *Document-based App Programming Guide for iOS* in the document archive.

If your app's *Info.plist* key "Application supports iTunes file sharing" (`UIFileSharingEnabled`) is set to `YES` (because your app supports file sharing), and if the *Info.plist* key "Supports opening documents in place" (`LSSupportsOpeningDocumentsInPlace`) is also set to `YES`, then files in your app's Documents directory will be visible in the Files app, and the user can tap a people group file to call your app delegate's `application(_:open:options:)` or your scene delegate's `scene(_:openURLContexts:)`, as described earlier in this chapter. That's safe only if your app accesses files by way of NSFilePresenter and NSFileCoordinator — and because you're using UIDocument, it does.

iCloud

Once your app is operating through UIDocument, basic iCloud compatibility effectively falls right into your lap. You have just two steps to perform:

Figure 23-9. Turning on iCloud support

Entitlements in the project

Edit the target and, in the Signing & Capabilities tab, add the iCloud capability and check iCloud Documents (Figure 23-9). You may also need to create a ubiquity container; click the Plus button to make a container and give it a name. Names should be of the form `"iCloud.com.yourDomain.yourAppID"`. Check the checkbox to make your container the default container.

Ubiquity container in the code

Early in your app's lifetime, call FileManager's `url(forUbiquityContainer-Identifier:)` on a background thread, passing `nil` to get the ubiquity container you checked in the iCloud Documents capability configuration. This gives you the URL of the cloud-shared directory. Any documents your app puts here by way of your UIDocument subclass will be shared into the cloud automatically.

With my entitlements file in hand, I can make my People Groups app iCloud-compatible with just two code changes. In the app delegate, as my app launches, I step out to a background thread (Chapter 25), obtain the cloud-shared directory's URL, and then step back to the main thread and retain the URL through a property, `self.ubiq`:

```
DispatchQueue.global(qos:.default).async {
    let fm = FileManager.default
    let ubiq = fm.url(forUbiquityContainerIdentifier:nil)
    DispatchQueue.main.async {
        self.ubiq = ubiq
    }
}
```

When I determine where to seek and save people groups, I specify `ubiq` — unless it is `nil`, implying that iCloud is not enabled, in which case I specify the user's Documents folder:

```
var docsurl : URL {
    let del = UIApplication.shared.delegate
    if let ubiq = (del as! AppDelegate).ubiq {
        return ubiq
    } else {
        do {
            let fm = FileManager.default
            return try fm.url(for:.documentDirectory, in: .userDomainMask,
```

```
                     appropriateFor: nil, create: false)
        } catch {
            print(error)
        }
    }
    return NSURL() as URL // shouldn't happen
}
```

To test, iCloud Drive must be turned on under iCloud in my device's Settings. I run the app and create a people group with some people in it. I then switch to a different device and run the app there, and tap the Refresh button. This is a very crude implementation, purely for testing purposes; we look through the docsurl directory for pplgrp files and download any cloud-based files:

```
do {
    let fm = FileManager.default
    self.files = try fm.contentsOfDirectory(at: self.docsurl,
        includingPropertiesForKeys: nil).filter {
            if fm.isUbiquitousItem(at:$0) {
                try fm.startDownloadingUbiquitousItem(at:$0)
            }
            return $0.pathExtension == "pplgrp"
        }
    self.tableView.reloadData()
} catch {
    print(error)
}
```

Presto, the app on this device now displays my people group documents created on a different device! It's quite thrilling.

My Refresh button approach, although it works (possibly after a couple of tries), is decidedly crude. My UIDocument works with iCloud, but my app is not a good iCloud citizen. The truth is that I should not be using FileManager like this; instead, I should be running an NSMetadataQuery. The usual strategy is:

1. Instantiate NSMetadataQuery and retain the instance.

2. Configure the search. This means giving the metadata query a search scope of NSMetadataQueryUbiquitousDocumentsScope and supplying a serial queue for it to run on (OperationQueue, see Chapter 25).

3. Register for notifications such as .NSMetadataQueryDidFinishGathering and .NSMetadataQueryDidUpdate.

4. Start the search by calling start. The NSMetadataQuery instance then remains in place, with the search continuing to run more or less constantly, for the entire lifetime of the app.

5. When a notification arrives, check the NSMetadataQuery's `results`. These will be NSMetadataItem objects, whose `value(forAttribute:NSMetadataItem-URLKey)` is the document file URL.

Similarly, in my earlier code I called `checkResourceIsReachable`, but for a cloud item I should be calling `checkPromisedItemIsReachable` instead.

Another problem with our app is that, by turning on iCloud support in this way, we have turned *off* the ability of the Files app to see our files (because they are now cloud-based and not in the Documents directory). I'll give a solution in the next section.

Further iCloud details are outside the scope of this discussion; see Apple's *iCloud Design Guide* in the documentation archive. Getting started is easy; making your app a good iCloud citizen, capable of dealing with the complexities that iCloud may entail, is not. What if the currently open document changes because someone edited it on another device? What if that change is in conflict with changes I've made on *this* device? What if the availability of iCloud changes while the app is open — for example, if the user switches iCloud itself on or off? Apple's own sample code habitually skirts these knotty issues.

Document Browser

The document browser (UIDocumentBrowserViewController), introduced in iOS 11, can improve a document-based app in several ways:

- An iOS device has no universal file browser parallel to the Mac desktop's Finder. So if your app maintains document files, it must also implement for itself the nitty-gritty details of user file management, listing your documents and letting the user delete them, rename them, move them, and so forth. That sounds daunting! The document browser solves the problem; it injects into your app a standard file management interface similar to the Files app.

- The Files app (and document browsers in other apps) will be able to see your app's documents.

- We can ignore everything I said in the preceding section about how to make our app participate in iCloud; with UIDocumentBrowserViewController, our app participates in iCloud *automatically*, with no need for any entitlements or added cloud management code, because iCloud Drive becomes just another place to save and retrieve documents.

Let's convert our People Groups app to use the document browser. The easiest way to get started is from the template provided by Apple; choose File → New → Project and iOS → Application → Document App. The template provides three features:

Info.plist configuration

The template gives us a start on the configuration of our *Info.plist*. In particular, it includes the "Supports Document Browser" key (UISupportsDocument-Browser) with its value set to YES.

Classes and storyboard

The template provides a basic set of classes:

- A UIDocumentBrowserViewController subclass (DocumentBrowserView-Controller)

- A UIDocument subclass (Document)

- A view controller (DocumentViewController) intended for display of documents of that class

The template puts instances of the two view controllers into the storyboard.

Structure

The template's storyboard makes the UIDocumentBrowserViewController instance our app's root view controller. The remainder of our app's interface, where the user views the contents of a document, must be displayed through a fullscreen presented view controller, and the template's code enforces this.

In adapting People Groups to this architecture, we can eliminate the GroupLister view controller class that has been acting as a master view controller to list our documents (left side in Figure 23-7), because the document browser will now fill that role; Document and DocumentViewController, meanwhile, are parallel to, and can be replaced by, our PeopleDocument and PeopleLister classes.

We begin by customizing DocumentBrowserViewController. The template gets us started, setting this class as its own delegate (UIDocumentBrowserViewController-Delegate) and configuring the document browser's capabilities:

```
override func viewDidLoad() {
    super.viewDidLoad()
    self.delegate = self
    self.allowsDocumentCreation = true
    self.allowsPickingMultipleItems = false
}
```

The template also implements delegate methods for when the user selects an existing document or copies a document from elsewhere; both call a custom method, present-Document(at:), for which the template provides a stub implementation:

```
func documentBrowser(_ controller: UIDocumentBrowserViewController,
    didPickDocumentURLs documentURLs: [URL]) {
        guard let sourceURL = documentURLs.first else { return }
        self.presentDocument(at: sourceURL)
}
```

```
func documentBrowser(_ controller: UIDocumentBrowserViewController,
    didImportDocumentAt sourceURL: URL,
    toDestinationURL destinationURL: URL) {
        self.presentDocument(at: destinationURL)
}
```

Providing a real implementation of `presentDocument(at:)` is up to us. We are no longer in a navigation interface, but PeopleLister expects one; so when I instantiate PeopleLister, I wrap it in a navigation controller before presenting it:

```
func presentDocument(at documentURL: URL) {
    let lister = PeopleLister(fileURL: documentURL)
    let nav = UINavigationController(rootViewController: lister)
    nav.modalPresentationStyle = .fullScreen
    self.present(nav, animated: true)
}
```

Finally, we come to the really interesting case: the user asks the document browser to create a People Groups document. This causes the delegate's `document-Browser(_:didRequestDocumentCreationWithHandler:)` to be called. Our job is to provide the URL of *an existing empty document file* and call the `handler:` function with that URL. But where are we going to get a document file? Well, we already know how to create an empty document; we proved that in our earlier example. So I'll create that document in the Temporary directory and feed its URL to the `handler:` function. That is exactly the strategy advised by the documentation on this delegate method, and my code is adapted directly from the example code there.

I'm a little uncertain, though, about what we're intended to do about the *name* of the new file. In the past, Apple's advice was not to worry about this — any unique name would do — but that was before the user could *see* file names in a standard interface. My solution is to present a UIAlertController where the user can enter the new document's name, creating the new document in the OK button's action function. Observe that I call the `importHandler` function under every circumstance:

```
func documentBrowser(_ controller: UIDocumentBrowserViewController,
    didRequestDocumentCreationWithHandler importHandler:
    @escaping (URL?, UIDocumentBrowserViewController.ImportMode) -> Void) {
        var docname = "People"
        let alert = UIAlertController(
            title: "Name for new people group:",
            message: nil, preferredStyle: .alert)
        alert.addTextField { tf in
            tf.autocapitalizationType = .words
        }
        alert.addAction(UIAlertAction(title: "Cancel", style: .cancel) { _ in
            importHandler(nil, .none)
        })
        alert.addAction(UIAlertAction(title: "OK", style: .default) { _ in
            if let proposal = alert.textFields?[0].text {
                if !proposal.trimmingCharacters(in: .whitespaces).isEmpty {
```

```
                    docname = proposal
                }
            }
            let fm = FileManager.default
            let temp = fm.temporaryDirectory
            let fileURL = temp.appendingPathComponent(docname + ".pplgrp2")
            let newdoc = PeopleDocument(fileURL: fileURL)
            newdoc.save(to: fileURL, for: .forOverwriting) { ok in
                guard ok else { importHandler(nil, .none); return }
                newdoc.close() { ok in
                    guard ok else { importHandler(nil, .none); return }
                    importHandler(fileURL, .move)
                }
            }
        ]
    })
    self.present(alert, animated: true)
}
```

If the user cancels or if something else goes wrong, I call importHandler with a nil URL. Just one path of execution calls importHandler with an actual file URL. If that happens, our delegate method documentBrowser(_:didImportDocumentAt:to-DestinationURL:) is called — and so our PeopleLister view controller is presented, displaying the new empty document.

Custom Thumbnails

Now that the user can see our document files represented in the file browser, we will probably want to give some attention to their icons. A document icon is called its *thumbnail*. A straightforward approach is to have our UIDocument subclass write a thumbnail into the file when saving:

```
override func fileAttributesToWrite(to url: URL,
    for saveOperation: UIDocument.SaveOperation)
    throws -> [AnyHashable : Any] {
        let icon = UIImage(named:"smiley")!
        let sz = CGSize(1024,1024)
        let im = UIGraphicsImageRenderer(
            size:sz, format:icon.imageRendererFormat).image { _ in
                icon.draw(in: CGRect(origin:.zero, size:CGSize(1024,1024)))
        }
        var d = try super.fileAttributesToWrite(to: url, for: saveOperation)
        let key1 = URLResourceKey.thumbnailDictionaryKey
        let key2 = URLThumbnailDictionaryItem.NSThumbnail1024x1024SizeKey
        d[key1] = [key2:im]
        return d
}
```

NSExtension		Dictionary	(3 items)
NSExtensionAttributes		Dictionary	(2 items)
QLSupportedContentTypes		Array	(1 item)
Item 0		String	com.neuburg.pplgrp
QLSupportsSearchableItems		Boolean	0
NSExtensionMainStoryboard		String	MainInterface
NSExtensionPointIdentifier		String	com.apple.quicklook.preview

Figure 23-10. Defining a preview extension's document type

 An alternative approach, introduced in iOS 11, is to provide a *thumbnail extension* that is consulted *in real time* whenever a document browser wants to portray one of our documents. But I have not been able to get this to work in iOS 13 and later.

Custom Previews

There are lots of places in the interface where the user can be shown a Quick Look preview of a file. I talked about UIDocumentInteractionController and QLPreviewController earlier in this chapter. In places such as the Files app or a mail message with an attachment, the user can long press a file and ask for a Quick Look preview. All of that works for a standard document type such as a PDF or text file, but not for our custom People Group document type. Let's fix that.

To do so, we can add a *Quick Look preview extension* to our People Groups app. Quick Look preview extensions, introduced in iOS 11, allow your app to supply a Quick Look preview for a custom document type that it exports.

Let's try it! Add a target; choose iOS → Application Extension → Quick Look Preview Extension. The template provides a view controller class, PreviewViewController, and a storyboard containing a PreviewViewController instance and its main view. When the user tries to preview a document of our custom type, this view controller will be instantiated and its main view will be displayed in the Quick Look preview interface.

For this to work, our extension's *Info.plist* must declare, in the QLSupportedContent-Types array, the UTI of the document type for which it provides a preview (Figure 23-10). I've also turned off the QLSupportsSearchableItems setting (it's for Spotlight searches, with which we're not concerned here).

We must now implement preparePreviewOfFile(at:completionHandler:) in our PreviewViewController. We are handed a file URL pointing to a document file. Our job is to examine that file, configure our view controller and its view, and call the completionHandler: function with a parameter of nil (or with an Error object if there was an error).

I'll configure PreviewViewController as a reduced version of PeopleLister. Similar to the right side of Figure 23-7, it will be a UITableViewController whose table shows the first and last names of the people in this group. However, the text fields will be disabled — we don't want the user trying to edit a preview! — and there is no need to implement document saving, or even to maintain a reference to a PeopleDocument. Instead, our PeopleDocument will serve only as a temporary conduit to construct the people array from the document file; it stores the array in an instance property so that our table view data source methods can access it:

```
func preparePreviewOfFile(at url: URL,
    completionHandler handler: @escaping (Error?) -> Void) {
        let doc = PeopleDocument(fileURL:url)
        doc.open { ok in
            if ok {
                self.people = doc.people
                self.tableView.register(
                    UINib(nibName: "PersonCell", bundle: nil),
                    forCellReuseIdentifier: "Person")
                self.tableView.reloadData()
                handler(nil)
            } else {
                handler(NSError(domain: "NoDataDomain",
                    code: -1, userInfo: nil))
            }
        }
    }
```

Document Picker

The document picker (UIDocumentPickerViewController) is a simple way to let the user view a list of document files and choose one (or several). You can open the file directly (probably in conjunction with UIDocument) or copy it into your app's sandbox temporarily. The document picker can also be configured to let the user pick a place to copy a document to.

The document picker can see into the same places as the document browser and the Files app, and its interface looks a lot like theirs, but it's a lightweight momentary dialog. You can use it without declaring any document types, without making your app participate in iCloud in any other way, and without changing your app's architecture. You just present the picker; the user chooses a file or cancels, and the picker is dismissed automatically.

In this example, I'll assume that the user has somehow saved an *.mp3* file into iCloud Drive. We'll permit the user to locate and play this file. In response to a button tap, we instantiate the UIDocumentPickerViewController. New in iOS 14, *how* we instantiate the picker reflects what action the picker is to perform:

```
init(forExporting:)
init(forExporting:asCopy:)
```
The first parameter is an array of URLs for files in our sandbox. The user is specifying a place to put the files. In the first form, a file is to be moved out of our sandbox; in the second form, with `asCopy` set to `true`, the file is to be copied.

```
init(forOpeningContentTypes:)
init(forOpeningContentTypes:asCopy:)
```
The first parameter is an array of UTTypes. The user is choosing files of the specified types. In the first form, a file is to be accessed in place; in the second form, with `asCopy` set to `true`, the file is to be copied into our sandbox.

(Those initializers supersede the architecture in iOS 13 and before, where you had to specify a UIDocumentPickerMode stating what was to be done with the file.)

We are letting the user choose a file outside our sandbox, and we want it copied into our sandbox so that we can play the copy easily; so we will use `init(forOpening-ContentTypes:asCopy:)`.

We make ourselves the document picker's `delegate` (UIDocumentPickerDelegate) and present the picker. If the user chooses an *.mp3* file, the delegate method is called, and we present an AVPlayerViewController to play it:

```
@IBAction func doButton(_ sender: Any) {
    let picker = UIDocumentPickerViewController(
        forOpeningContentTypes: [UTType.mp3], asCopy: true)
    picker.delegate = self
    self.present(picker, animated: true)
}
func documentPicker(_ controller: UIDocumentPickerViewController,
    didPickDocumentsAt urls: [URL]) {
        guard urls.count == 1 else {return}
        guard let vals =
            try? urls[0].resourceValues(forKeys: [.typeIdentifierKey]),
            vals.typeIdentifier == UTType.mp3.identifier
            else {return}
        let vc = AVPlayerViewController()
        vc.player = AVPlayer(url: urls[0])
        self.present(vc, animated: true) { vc.player?.play() }
}
```

The document has been copied into temporary storage in our sandbox, and we can play it from there. If we wanted long-term access to the document, however, we might prefer to move it into permanent storage, such as our Documents directory. On the other hand, if we want to play the *.mp3* directly, in place, *without* copying it, we can; but then it is security scoped, and we must access it accordingly:

```
@IBAction func doButton(_ sender: Any) {
    let picker = UIDocumentPickerViewController(
        forOpeningContentTypes: [UTType.mp3]) // don't copy!
    picker.delegate = self
    self.present(picker, animated: true)
}
func documentPicker(_ controller: UIDocumentPickerViewController,
    didPickDocumentsAt urls: [URL]) {
        guard urls.count == 1 else {return}
        guard urls[0].startAccessingSecurityScopedResource() // *
            else { return }
        guard let vals =
            try? urls[0].resourceValues(forKeys: [.typeIdentifierKey]),
            vals.typeIdentifier == UTType.mp3.identifier
            else {return}
        let vc = AVPlayerViewController()
        vc.player = AVPlayer(url: urls[0])
        self.present(vc, animated: true) { vc.player?.play() }
        urls[0].stopAccessingSecurityScopedResource() // *
}
```

A document picker has a few properties for customizing it. Starting in iOS 11, `allows-MultipleSelection` permits the user to choose more than one file. Starting in iOS 13, `directoryURL` sets the folder whose contents the picker will initially display. Also the document type can *be* a folder, allowing the user to choose an entire folder of files; to deal with the files inside it, call `startAccessingSecurityScopedResource` and use an NSFileCoordinator.

XML

XML is a flexible and widely used general-purpose text file format for storage and retrieval of structured data. You might use it yourself to store data that you'll need to retrieve later, or you could encounter it when obtaining information from elsewhere, such as the internet.

On macOS, Cocoa provides a set of classes (XMLDocument and so forth) for reading, parsing, maintaining, searching, and modifying XML data in a completely general way; but iOS does *not* include these. I think the reason must be that their tree-based approach is too memory-intensive. Instead, iOS provides XMLParser.

XMLParser is a relatively simple class that walks through an XML document, sending delegate messages as it encounters elements. With it, you can parse an XML document once, but what you do with the pieces as you encounter them is up to you. The general assumption here is that you know in advance the structure of the particular XML data you intend to read, and that you have provided classes for representation of the same data in object form, with some way of transforming the XML pieces into that representation.

To illustrate, let's return once more to our Person class with a `firstName` and a `last-Name` property. Imagine that, as our app starts up, we would like to populate it with Person objects, and that we've stored the data describing these objects as an XML file in our app bundle, like this:

```
<?xml version="1.0" encoding="utf-8"?>
<people>
    <person>
        <firstName>Matt</firstName>
        <lastName>Neuburg</lastName>
    </person>
    <person>
        <firstName>Snidely</firstName>
        <lastName>Whiplash</lastName>
    </person>
    <person>
        <firstName>Dudley</firstName>
        <lastName>Doright</lastName>
    </person>
</people>
```

This data could be mapped to an array of Person objects, each with its `firstName` and `lastName` properties appropriately set. Let's consider how we might do that. (This is a deliberately easy example, of course; not all XML is so readily expressed as objects.)

Using XMLParser is not difficult in theory. You create the XMLParser, handing it the URL of a local XML file (or a Data object, perhaps downloaded from the internet), set its delegate, and tell it to `parse`. The delegate starts receiving delegate messages. For simple XML like ours, there are only three delegate messages of interest:

`parser(_:didStartElement:namespaceURI:qualifiedName:attributes:)`
The parser has encountered an opening element tag. In our document this would be `<people>`, `<person>`, `<firstName>`, or `<lastName>`.

`parser(_:didEndElement:namespaceURI:qualifiedName:)`
The parser has encountered the corresponding closing element tag. In our document this would be `</people>`, `</person>`, `</firstName>`, or `</lastName>`.

`parser(_:foundCharacters:)`
The parser has encountered some text between the starting and closing tags for the current element. In our document this would be `"Matt"` or `"Neuburg"` and so on.

In practice, responding to these delegate messages poses challenges of maintaining state. If there is just one delegate, it will have to bear in mind at every moment what element it is currently encountering; this could make for a lot of properties and a lot of if-statements in the implementation of the delegate methods. To aggravate the issue, `parser(_:foundCharacters:)` can arrive multiple times for a single stretch of text; that is, the text may arrive in pieces, which we must accumulate into a property.

An elegant way to meet these challenges is by resetting the XMLParser's delegate to *different delegate objects* at different stages of the parsing process. We make each delegate responsible for parsing one type of element; when a child of that element is encountered, the delegate object makes a new child element delegate object and repoints the XMLParser's `delegate` property at it. The child element delegate is then responsible for making the parent the delegate once again when it finishes parsing its own element. This is slightly counterintuitive because it means `parser(_:didStart-Element:...)` and `parser(_:didEndElement:...)` for the same element are arriving at *two different objects*.

To see what I mean, think about how we could implement this in our example. We are going to need a PeopleParser that handles the `<people>` element, and a Person-Parser that handles the `<person>` elements. Now imagine how PeopleParser will operate when it is the XMLParser's delegate:

1. When `parser(_:didStartElement:...)` arrives, the PeopleParser looks to see if this is a `<person>`. If so, it creates a PersonParser, handing to it (the Person-Parser) a parent reference to itself (the PeopleParser) — and makes the Person-Parser the XMLParser's delegate.

2. Delegate messages now arrive at this newly created PersonParser. We can assume that `<firstName>` and `<lastName>` are simple enough that the PersonParser can maintain state as it encounters them; when text is encountered, `parser(_:found-Characters:)` will be called, and the text must be accumulated into a corresponding property.

3. Eventually, `parser(_:didEndElement:...)` arrives. The PersonParser now uses its parent reference to make the PeopleParser the XMLParser's delegate once again. The PeopleParser, having received from the PersonParser any data it may have collected, is now ready in case another `<person>` element is encountered (and the old PersonParser might now go quietly out of existence).

This approach may seem like a lot of work to configure, but in fact it is neatly object-oriented, with parser delegate classes corresponding to the elements of the XML. Moreover, those delegate classes have a great deal in common, which can readily be factored out and encapsulated into a delegate superclass from which they all inherit.

JSON

JSON (*http://www.json.org*) is often used as a universal lightweight structured data format for server communication. Typically, you'll send an HTTP request to a server

---

using a URL constructed according to prescribed rules, and the reply will come back as JSON that you'll have to parse.

To illustrate, I'll send a request to a server that dispenses quotations; the actual network communication will be explained in Chapter 24:

```
let sess : URLSession = {
    let config = URLSessionConfiguration.ephemeral
    let s = URLSession(configuration: config)
    return s
}()
@IBAction func doGo(_ sender: Any) {
    var comp = URLComponents()
    comp.scheme = "https"
    comp.host = "quotesondesign.com"
    comp.path = "/wp-json/wp/v2/posts"
    var qi = [URLQueryItem]()
    qi.append(URLQueryItem(name: "orderby", value: "rand"))
    qi.append(URLQueryItem(name: "per_page", value: "1"))
    comp.queryItems = qi
    if let url = comp.url {
        let d = self.sess.dataTask(with: url) { data,_,_ in
            if let data = data {
                DispatchQueue.main.async {
                    self.parse(data) // now what?
                }
            }
        }
        d.resume()
    }
}
```

The request returns a Data object representing a JSON string that looks something like this (I've edited and truncated the string for clarity):

```
[{
    "id": 2237,
    "date": "2014-03-28T09:01:07",
    "title": {
        "rendered": "Wim Hovens"
    },
    "content": {
        "rendered":
            "<p>Good design is in all the things you notice.
            Great design is in all the things you don&#8217;t.<\/p>\n",
        "protected": false
    },
    // ...
}]
```

We are calling our `parse` method with that Data object, and we want to parse it. How? Well, we know in advance the expected format of the JSON response, so we have prepared by declaring a nest of structs matching that format and adopting the Decodable protocol (discussed earlier in this chapter). Now we can instantiate JSON-Decoder and call decode(_:from:). In this example, our goal is to extract just the "title" and "content" entries, so those are the only properties our struct needs:

```
struct Item : Decodable {
    let rendered : String
}
struct Quote : Decodable {
    let title : Item
    let content : Item
}
```

Our Quote struct matches the JSON's inner dictionary, but the JSON itself is an array containing that dictionary as an element. Therefore, our call to decode the JSON looks like this:

```
func parse(_ data:Data) {
    if let arr = try? JSONDecoder().decode([Quote].self, from: data) {
        let quote = arr.first!
        // ...
    }
}
```

The JSON is now parsed into a Quote instance, and we can refer to the author and the quotation as quote.title.rendered and quote.content.rendered. Now we can do whatever we like with those values, such as displaying them in our app's interface.

The JSONDecoder class also comes with properties that allow you to specify the handling of certain specially formatted values, such as dates and floating-point numbers (though we didn't need to use any of those properties in our example).

Coding Keys

When we are receiving JSON structured data, the structure is defined by the server, right down to the names of the keys. The JSON dictionary that we are receiving has keys "title" and "content", so we are forced to name our Quote struct's properties title and content. This seems unfair. But there's a workaround: declare a nested enum called CodingKeys with a String raw value and conforming to the CodingKey protocol. Now you can give your struct properties any names you like, using the enum cases and their string raw values to map the JSON dictionary key names to the struct property names:

```
struct Item : Decodable {
    let value : String
    enum CodingKeys : String, CodingKey {
        case value = "rendered"
    }
}
```

```
struct Quote : Decodable {
    let author : Item
    let quotation : Item
    enum CodingKeys : String, CodingKey {
        case author = "title"
        case quotation = "content"
    }
}
```

The outcome is that we can extract the author and quotation as `quote.author.value` and `quote.quotation.value`, which reads more clearly than `quote.title.rendered` and `quote.content.rendered`.

Custom Decoding

We have changed the names of our struct properties, but the overall layout of our structs is *still* being dictated to us by the server. For instance, in the JSON we're receiving, a dictionary's `title` value is itself a dictionary with a `rendered` key. I'm using two structs with an extra level of nesting because the JSON has an extra level of nesting. My Quote struct's `author` and `quotation` properties are Item objects, and to fetch the value I really want, I have to drop down an extra level: I've been saying `quote.author.value` and `quote.quotation.value` even though the only thing I'm *ever* going to be interested in is the `value`. I don't want to have to talk like this. I want my `author` and `quotation` properties to be strings, not Items. I don't want them to *lead* to the Item's `"rendered"` value; I want them to *be* the Item's `"rendered"` value.

The solution is to supply an implementation of `init(from:)`. This initializer is required by the Decodable protocol; but so far, instead of writing it, we have been allowing it to be synthesized for us. Instead, we can write it ourselves — and then we are free to parse the JSON into our object's properties in any way we like.

When you write an implementation of `init(from:)`, the parameter is a Decoder object. Start by extracting an appropriate container. For a JSON dictionary, this will be a KeyedDecodingContainer, obtained by calling `container(keyedBy:)`; we still need a CodingKey adopter to serve as the source of key names. You can then call `decode(_:forKey:)` to get the value for a key. Now you are free to manipulate values and assign the results to your properties. The only requirement is that, as with any initializer, you must initialize all your properties.

So here's my rewrite of Quote, with `author` and `quotation` declared as String, and an explicit `init(from:)` implementation. I have kept the Item struct purely as a way of extracting the `"rendered"` value, but I've made it a private nested type that the caller is unaware of:

```
struct Quote : Decodable {
    let author : String
    let quotation : String
    enum CodingKeys : String, CodingKey {
        case author = "title"
        case quotation = "content"
    }
    private struct Item : Decodable {
        let value : String
        enum CodingKeys : String, CodingKey {
            case value = "rendered"
        }
    }
    init(from decoder: Decoder) throws {
        let con = try decoder.container(keyedBy: CodingKeys.self)
        let author = try con.decode(Item.self, forKey: .author)
        self.author = author.value
        let quotation = try con.decode(Item.self, forKey: .quotation)
        self.quotation = quotation.value
    }
}
```

Now my `quote.author` and `quote.quotation` are strings, and I can display them in the interface directly.

Another common reason for writing a custom `init(from:)` implementation is that there is something indeterminate about the structure of the JSON you're receiving from the server. A typical situation is that there are dictionary keys whose names you don't know in advance. To deal with this, you need a special "mop-up" CodingKey adopter:

```
struct AnyCodingKey : CodingKey {
    var stringValue: String
    var intValue: Int?
    init(_ codingKey: CodingKey) {
        self.stringValue = codingKey.stringValue
        self.intValue = codingKey.intValue
    }
    init(stringValue: String) {
        self.stringValue = stringValue
        self.intValue = nil
    }
    init(intValue: Int) {
        self.stringValue = String(intValue)
        self.intValue = intValue
    }
}
```

(I owe that formulation to Hamish Knight.) When you call `container(keyedBy: Any-CodingKey.self)`, the resulting container can be sent the `allKeys` message to obtain a list of all keys in this dictionary, and you can use any of those keys to fetch the corresponding value.

Yet another common problem is that a value's type may vary. A typical situation is that the same key yields sometimes a String, sometimes an Int. The way to cope with that is to declare a *union* — that is, a Decodable enum with two cases, one with an associated String value, the other with an associated Int value. Your custom `init(from:)` just tries each of them in turn. A widely used formulation runs something like this:

```
enum IntOrString: Decodable {
    case int(Int)
    case string(String)
    init(from decoder: Decoder) throws {
        let container = try decoder.singleValueContainer()
        if let int = try? container.decode(Int.self) {
            self = .int(int)
        } else if let string = try? container.decode(String.self) {
            self = .string(string)
        } else {
            throw DecodingError.typeMismatch(
                IntOrString.self,
                DecodingError.Context(
                    codingPath: decoder.codingPath,
                    debugDescription: "Neither String nor Int"))
        }
    }
}
```

SQLite

SQLite (*http://www.sqlite.org/docs.html*) is a lightweight, full-featured relational database that you can talk to using SQL, the universal language of databases. This can be an appropriate storage format when your data comes in rows and columns (records and fields) and needs to be rapidly searchable. Also, the database as a whole is never loaded into memory; the data is accessed only as needed. This is valuable in an environment like an iOS device, where memory is at a premium.

To use SQLite, say `import SQLite3`. Talking to SQLite involves an elaborate C interface which may prove annoying; fortunately, there are a number of lightweight front ends. In my example, I'll use `fmdb` (*https://github.com/ccgus/fmdb*); it's Swift-friendly, but it's written in Objective-C, so we'll need a bridging header in which we `#import` `"FMDB.h"`.

To illustrate, I'll create a database and add a `people` table consisting of `lastname` and `firstname` columns:

```
let db = FMDatabase(path:self.dbpath)
db.open()
do {
    db.beginTransaction()
    try db.executeUpdate(
        "create table people (lastname text, firstname text)",
        values:nil)
    try db.executeUpdate(
        "insert into people (firstname, lastname) values (?,?)",
        values:["Matt", "Neuburg"])
    try db.executeUpdate(
        "insert into people (firstname, lastname) values (?,?)",
        values:["Snidely", "Whiplash"])
    try db.executeUpdate(
        "insert into people (firstname, lastname) values (?,?)",
        values:["Dudley", "Doright"])
    db.commit()
} catch {
    db.rollback()
}
```

At some later time, I come along and read the data from that database:

```
let db = FMDatabase(path:self.dbpath)
db.open()
if let rs = try? db.executeQuery("select * from people", values:nil) {
    while rs.next() {
        if let firstname = rs["firstname"], let lastname = rs["lastname"] {
            print(firstname, lastname)
        }
    }
}
db.close()
/*
Matt Neuburg
Snidely Whiplash
Dudley Doright
*/
```

You can include a previously constructed SQLite file in your app bundle, but you can't write to it there; the solution is to copy it from your app bundle into another location, such as the Documents directory, before you start working with it.

Core Data

The Core Data framework (import CoreData) provides a generalized way of expressing objects and properties that form a relational graph; moreover, it has built-in facilities for maintaining those objects in persistent storage — typically using SQLite as a file format — and reading them from storage only when they are needed, making efficient use of memory. A person might have not only multiple addresses but also multiple friends who are also persons; expressing persons and addresses as explicit object types, working out how to link them and how to translate between objects in memory and data in storage, and tracking the effects of changes, such as when a person is deleted, can be tedious. Core Data can help.

Core Data is *not* a beginner-level technology. It is difficult to use and extremely difficult to debug. It expresses itself in a verbose, rigid, arcane way. It has its own peculiar way of doing things — everything you already know about how to create, access, alter, or delete an object within an object collection becomes completely irrelevant! — and trying to bend it to your particular needs can be tricky and can have unintended side effects. Nor should Core Data be seen as a substitute for a true relational database.

A full explanation of Core Data would require an entire book; indeed, such books exist, and if Core Data interests you, you should read some of them. See also Apple's *Core Data Programming Guide* in the documentation archive, and the other resources referred to there. Here, I'll just illustrate what it's like to work with Core Data.

I will rewrite the People Groups example from earlier in this chapter as a Core Data app. This will still be a master–detail interface consisting of a navigation controller and two table view controllers, GroupLister and PeopleLister, just as in Figure 23-7. But we will no longer have multiple documents, each representing a single group of people; instead, we will now have a single document, maintained for us by Core Data, containing all of our groups and all of their people.

To construct a Core Data project from scratch, start with the iOS App template and check Use Core Data in the second screen. This gives you template code in the app delegate class for constructing the Core Data *persistence stack*, a set of objects that work together to fetch and save your data; in most cases there will no reason to alter this template code significantly.

The persistence stack consists of three objects:

- A *managed object model* (NSManagedObjectModel) describing the structure of the data
- A *managed object context* (NSManagedObjectContext) for communicating with the data
- A *persistent store coordinator* (NSPersistentStoreCoordinator) for dealing with actual storage of the data as a file

Starting in iOS 10, the entire stack is created for us by an NSPersistentContainer object. The template code provides a lazy initializer for this object, along these lines:

```
lazy var persistentContainer: NSPersistentContainer = {
    let con = NSPersistentContainer(name: "PeopleGroupsCoreData")
    con.loadPersistentStores { desc, err in
        if let err = err {
```

```
                fatalError("Unresolved error \(err)")
            }
        }
        return con
    }()
```

The managed object context is the persistent container's `viewContext`. This will be our point of contact with Core Data. The managed object context is the world in which your data objects live and move and have their being: to obtain an object, you fetch it from the managed object context; to create an object, you insert it into the managed object context; to save your data, you save the managed object context. The template provides a method for saving:

```
func saveContext() {
    let context = self.persistentContainer.viewContext
    if context.hasChanges {
        try? context.save()
    }
}
```

The template also implements the scene delegate's `sceneDidEnterBackground(_:)` to call the app delegate's `saveContext`:

```
func sceneDidEnterBackground(_ scene: UIScene) {
    (UIApplication.shared.delegate as? AppDelegate)?.saveContext()
}
```

To describe the structure and relationships of the objects constituting your data model (the managed object model), you design an object graph in a data model document. Our object graph is very simple: a Group can have multiple Persons (Figure 23-11). The attributes, analogous to object properties, are all strings, except for the timestamps which are dates, and the Group UUID which is a UUID. The timestamps will be used for determining the sort order in which groups and people will be displayed in the interface; this is needed because object collections are stored as sets (which have no order), not as arrays.

Group and Person are not classes; they are *entity* names. And their attributes, such as `name` and `firstName`, are not properties. All Core Data model objects are instances of NSManagedObject, and make themselves dynamically KVC-compliant for attribute names. Core Data knows, thanks to our object graph, that a Person entity is to have a `firstName` attribute, so if an NSManagedObject represents a Person entity, you can set its `firstName` attribute by calling `setValue(_:forKey:)` with a key `"firstName"`, and you can retrieve its `firstName` attribute by calling `value(forKey:)` with a key `"firstName"`.

If that sounds maddening, that's because it *is* maddening. Fortunately, there's a simple solution: you configure your entities, in the Data Model inspector, to perform *code generation* of class definitions (Figure 23-12). Code generation allows us to treat

Figure 23-11. The Core Data model for the People Groups app

entity types as classes, and managed objects as instances of those classes. When we compile our project, class files will be created for our entities (here, Group and Person) as NSManagedObject subclasses endowed with properties corresponding to the entity attributes. So now Person *is* a class, and it *does* have a firstName property.

These generated classes are essentially façades. The properties (representing attributes) generated for our classes (representing entities) are marked @NSManaged. This means that they are basically computed properties whose implementations will be injected at runtime by Cocoa. Those implementations will in fact use KVC to access the actual attributes of the actual entities, just as we would have had to do if we were writing this all out by hand. But thanks to this trick, we don't have to!

Now let's talk about the master view controller, GroupLister. GroupLister's job is to list groups and to allow the user to create a new group (Figure 23-7, on the left). How will GroupLister get a list of groups? The way you ask Core Data for a model object is with a fetch request; and when Core Data model objects are the model data for a table view, fetch requests are conveniently managed through an NSFetchedResults-Controller.

Figure 23-12. Configuring code generation

The standard approach is to start with a fetched results controller stored in an instance property, ready to perform the fetch request and to supply our table view's data source with the actual data:

```
lazy var frc: NSFetchedResultsController<Group> = {
    let req: NSFetchRequest<Group> = Group.fetchRequest()
    req.fetchBatchSize = 20
    let sortDescriptor = NSSortDescriptor(key:"timestamp", ascending:true)
    req.sortDescriptors = [sortDescriptor]
    let del = UIApplication.shared.delegate as! AppDelegate
    let moc = del.persistentContainer.viewContext
    let frc = NSFetchedResultsController(
        fetchRequest:req,
        managedObjectContext:moc,
        sectionNameKeyPath:nil, cacheName:nil)
    frc.delegate = self
    do {
        try frc.performFetch()
    } catch {
        fatalError("Aborting with unresolved error")
    }
    return frc
}()
```

(The first two lines of that code demonstrate not only that Group is now a class with a `fetchRequest` method, but also that both NSFetchedResultsController and NSFetchRequest are generics.)

Now we need to hook our table view's data source to the NSFetchedResultsController somehow. With a diffable data source, this is particularly easy, because the fetched results controller vends an NSDiffableDataSourceSnapshotReference wrapping a snapshot with generic types String and NSManagedObjectID. So we'll declare a diffable data source with those types:

```
lazy var ds : UITableViewDiffableDataSource<String,NSManagedObjectID> = {
    UITableViewDiffableDataSource(tableView: self.tableView) { tv,ip,id in
        let cell = tv.dequeueReusableCell(
            withIdentifier: self.cellID, for: ip)
```

```
        cell.accessoryType = .disclosureIndicator
        let group = self.frc.object(at: ip)
        cell.textLabel!.text = group.name
        return cell
    }
}()
```

But we still have not configured a way of populating the diffable data source. The first step is to "tickle" our lazy instance properties by referring to self.frc in our view-DidLoad implementation:

```
override func viewDidLoad() {
    super.viewDidLoad()
    _ = self.frc // "tickle" the lazy vars
    // ...
}
```

Next, acting as the fetched results controller's delegate (NSFetchedResultsController-Delegate), we implement controller(_:didChangeContentWith:). This method provides a snapshot wrapped up in a snapshot reference (which is just a sort of type eraser). We cast this down to its actual generic snapshot type, and apply it to our diffable data source:

```
func controller(_ con: NSFetchedResultsController<NSFetchRequestResult>,
    didChangeContentWith snapshot: NSDiffableDataSourceSnapshotReference) {
    let snapshot =
        snapshot as NSDiffableDataSourceSnapshot<String,NSManagedObjectID>
    self.ds.apply(snapshot, animatingDifferences: false)
}
```

GroupLister's table now automatically reflects the contents of the fetch results controller. It is initially empty because our app starts life with no data. When the user asks to create a group, I put up an alert asking for the name of the new group. In the handler: function for its OK button, I create a new Group object in the managed object context and navigate to the detail view, PeopleLister:

```
let context = self.frc.managedObjectContext
let group = Group(context: context)
group.name = av.textFields![0].text!
group.uuid = UUID()
group.timestamp = Date()
let pl = PeopleLister(group: group)
self.navigationController!.pushViewController(pl, animated: true)
```

The detail view controller class is PeopleLister (Figure 23-7, on the right). It lists all the people in a particular Group, so I don't want PeopleLister to be instantiated without a Group; therefore, its designated initializer is init(group:). As the preceding code shows, when I want to navigate from the GroupLister view to the People-Lister view, I instantiate PeopleLister and push it onto the navigation controller's stack. I do the same sort of thing when the user taps an existing Group name in the GroupLister table view:

```
override func tableView(_ tableView: UITableView,
    didSelectRowAt indexPath: IndexPath) {
        let pl = PeopleLister(group: self.frc.object(at:indexPath))
        self.navigationController!.pushViewController(pl, animated: true)
}
```

PeopleLister, too, has an `frc` property that's an NSFetchedResultsController. However, a PeopleLister instance should list only the People belonging to *one particular group*, which has been stored as its `group` property. So PeopleLister's implementation of the `frc` initializer contains these lines (`req` is the fetch request we're configuring):

```
let pred = NSPredicate(format:"group = %@", self.group)
req.predicate = pred
```

The PeopleLister interface consists of a table of text fields. Populating the table is just like what GroupLister did; I can use a Person's `firstName` and `lastName` to set the text of the text fields.

When the user edits a text field to change the first or last name of a Person, I hear about it as the text field's delegate, and I update the data model (for `next(ofType:)`, see Appendix B):

```
func textFieldDidEndEditing(_ textField: UITextField) {
    guard let cell = textField.next(ofType: UITableViewCell.self) else {
        return
    }
    let ip = self.tableView.indexPath(for:cell)!
    let object = self.frc.object(at:ip)
    object.setValue(textField.text!, forKey: (
        (textField.tag == 1) ? "firstName" : "lastName"))
}
```

When the user asks to make a new Person, I create a new Person object in the managed object context and configure its attributes with an empty first name and last name:

```
@objc func doAdd(_:AnyObject) {
    self.tableView.endEditing(true)
    let context = self.frc.managedObjectContext
    let person = Person(context:context)
    person.group = self.group
    person.lastName = ""
    person.firstName = ""
    person.timestamp = Date()
}
```

The outcome is that the delegate method `controller(_:didChangeContentWith:)` is called. There, as I've already shown, I obtain the snapshot and apply it to the diffable data source — and so the new empty person is displayed in the table view, waiting for the user to type into its text fields.

We are already saving the managed object context when the scene goes into the background. Let's also do it when a view controller disappears:

```
override func viewWillDisappear(_ animated: Bool) {
    super.viewWillDisappear(animated)
    (UIApplication.shared.delegate as? AppDelegate)?.saveContext()
}
```

Core Data files are not suitable for use as iCloud documents. If you want to reflect structured data into the cloud, a better alternative is the CloudKit framework. In effect, this allows you to maintain a database online, and to synchronize changed data up to and down from that database. You might use Core Data as a form of *local* storage, but you'd still use CloudKit as an intermediary, to communicate the data between different devices. Starting in iOS 13, NSPersistentCloudKitContainer provides automatic linkage between Core Data and CloudKit. See the Core Data framework documentation for more information.

PDFs

Up to this point, I have displayed the contents of a PDF file by means of a web view or in a Quick Look preview. Starting in iOS 11, PDF Kit (`import PDFKit`), brought over from macOS, provides a native UIView subclass, PDFView, whose job is to display a PDF nicely.

Basic use of a PDFView is simple. Initialize a PDFDocument, either from data or from a file URL, and assign it as the PDFView's document:

```
let v = PDFView(frame:self.view.bounds)
self.view.addSubview(v)
let url = Bundle.main.url(forResource: "notes", withExtension: "pdf")!
let doc = PDFDocument(url: url)
v.document = doc
```

There are many other configurable aspects of a PDFView. A particularly nice touch is that a PDFView can embed a UIPageViewController for layout and navigation of the PDF's individual pages:

```
v.usePageViewController(true)
```

A PDFDocument consists of pages, represented by PDFPage objects. You can manipulate those pages, adding and removing pages from the document. You can even draw a PDFPage's contents yourself, meaning that you can create a PDF document from scratch.

As a demonstration, I'll create a PDF document consisting of one page with the words "Hello, world" in the center. I start with a PDFPage subclass, MyPage, where I override the `draw(with:to:)` method. The parameters are a PDFDisplayBox that tells me the page size, along with a CGContext to draw into. There's just one thing to watch out for: a PDF graphics context is flipped with respect to the normal iOS coordinate system. So I apply a transform to the context before I draw into it:

```
override func draw(with box: PDFDisplayBox, to context: CGContext) {
    UIGraphicsPushContext(context)
    context.saveGState()
    let r = self.bounds(for: box)
    let s = NSAttributedString(string: "Hello, world", attributes: [
        .font : UIFont(name: "Georgia", size: 80)!
    ])
    let sz = s.boundingRect(with: CGSize(10000,10000),
        options: .usesLineFragmentOrigin, context: nil)
    context.translateBy(x: 0, y: r.height)
    context.scaleBy(x: 1, y: -1)
    s.draw(at: CGPoint(
        (r.maxX - r.minX) / 2 - sz.width / 2,
        (r.maxY - r.minY) / 2 - sz.height / 2
    ))
    context.restoreGState()
    UIGraphicsPopContext()
}
```

To create and display my PDFPage in a PDFView (v) is simple:

```
let doc = PDFDocument()
v.document = doc
doc.insert(MyPage(), at: 0)
```

If my document consisted of more than one MyPage, they would now all draw the same thing. If that's not what I want, my `draw(with:to:)` code can ask what page of the document this is:

```
let pagenum = self.document?.index(for: self)
```

In addition, a host of ancillary PDF Kit classes allow you to manipulate page thumbnails, selection, annotations, and more.

Image Files

The Image I/O framework provides a way to open image files, to save image files, to convert between image file formats, and to read metadata from standard image file formats, including EXIF and GPS information from a digital camera. You'll need to `import ImageIO`. The Image I/O API is written in C, not Objective-C, and it uses CFTypeRefs, not objects. Unlike Core Graphics, there is no Swift "renamification" overlay that represents the API as object-oriented; you have to call the framework's global C functions directly, casting between the CFTypeRefs and their Foundation counterparts. But that's not hard to do.

Use of the Image I/O framework starts with the notion of an *image source* (CGImage-Source). This can be created from the URL of a file (actually CFURL, to which URL is toll-free bridged) or from a Data object (actually CFData, to which Data is toll-free bridged).

Here we obtain the metadata from a photo file in our app bundle:

```
let url = Bundle.main.url(forResource:"colson", withExtension: "jpg")!
let opts : [AnyHashable:Any] = [kCGImageSourceShouldCache : false]
let src = CGImageSourceCreateWithURL(url as CFURL, opts as CFDictionary)!
let d = CGImageSourceCopyPropertiesAtIndex(src, 0, opts as CFDictionary)
    as! [AnyHashable:Any]
```

Without having opened the image file as an image, we now have a dictionary full of information about it, including its pixel dimensions (keys kCGImagePropertyPixel-Width and kCGImagePropertyPixelHeight), its resolution, color model, color depth, and orientation — plus, because this picture comes originally from a digital camera, the EXIF data such as the aperture and exposure at which it was taken, and the make and model of the camera.

To obtain the image as a CGImage, we can call CGImageSourceCreateImageAtIndex. Alternatively, we can request a *thumbnail* of the image. This is a very useful thing to do, and the name "thumbnail" doesn't really do justice to its importance. If your purpose is to display this image in your interface, you don't care about the original image data; a thumbnail is *precisely* what you want, especially because you can specify any size for this "thumbnail" all the way up to the original size of the image! This is splendid, because to assign a large image to a small image view wastes all the memory reflected by the size difference.

To generate a thumbnail at a given size, you start with a dictionary specifying the size along with other instructions, and pass that, together with the image source, to CGImageSourceCreateThumbnailAtIndex. The only pitfall is that, because we are working with a CGImage and specifying actual pixels, we must remember to take account of the scale of our device's screen. Let's say we want to scale our image so that its largest dimension is no larger than the width of the UIImageView (self.iv) into which we intend to place it:

```
let url = Bundle.main.url(forResource:"colson", withExtension: "jpg")!
var opts : [AnyHashable:Any] = [kCGImageSourceShouldCache : false]
let src = CGImageSourceCreateWithURL(url as CFURL, opts as CFDictionary)!
let scale = UIScreen.main.scale
let w = self.iv.bounds.width * scale
opts = [
    kCGImageSourceShouldAllowFloat : true,
    kCGImageSourceCreateThumbnailWithTransform : true,
    kCGImageSourceCreateThumbnailFromImageAlways : true,
    kCGImageSourceShouldCacheImmediately : true,
    kCGImageSourceThumbnailMaxPixelSize : w
```

```
]
let imref =
    CGImageSourceCreateThumbnailAtIndex(src, 0, opts as CFDictionary)!
let im = UIImage(cgImage: imref, scale: scale, orientation: .up)
self.iv.image = im
```

To save an image using a specified file format, we need an *image destination*. I'll show how to save our image as a TIFF. We never open the image as an image! We save directly from the image source to the image destination:

```
let url = Bundle.main.url(forResource:"colson", withExtension: "jpg")!
let opts : [AnyHashable:Any] = [kCGImageSourceShouldCache : false]
let src = CGImageSourceCreateWithURL(url as CFURL, opts as CFDictionary)!
let fm = FileManager.default
let suppurl = try! fm.url(for:.applicationSupportDirectory,
    in: .userDomainMask, appropriateFor: nil, create: true)
let tiff = suppurl.appendingPathComponent("mytiff.tiff")
let dest = CGImageDestinationCreateWithURL(
    tiff as CFURL, UTType.tiff.identifier as CFString, 1, nil)!
CGImageDestinationAddImageFromSource(dest, src, 0, nil)
let ok = CGImageDestinationFinalize(dest)
```

Basic Networking

Networking is difficult and complicated, not least because it's ultimately out of your control. You can ask for a resource from across the network, but at that point anything can happen. The resource might not be found; it might take a while to arrive; it might *never* arrive. The server or the network might be unavailable, or even worse, might vanish after the resource has partially arrived. There are numerous technicalities to deal with, not to mention the need for extensive background threading so that nothing interferes with the operation of your app's interface. Fortunately, iOS handles all of that behind the scenes, and makes basic networking easy.

Earlier chapters have described interface and frameworks that network for you automatically. Put a web view in your interface (Chapter 12) and poof, you're networking; the web view does all the grunt work, and it does it a lot better than you'd be likely to do it from scratch. The same is true of AVPlayer (Chapter 16), MKMapView (Chapter 21), and so on. Think of that as implicit networking. This chapter discusses explicit networking.

A device used for development has a Network Link Conditioner switch in Settings (under Developer). Use it to simulate different networking situations to stress-test your networking code.

HTTP Requests

An HTTP request is made through a URLSession object. A URLSession is a kind of grand overarching environment in which network-related tasks are to take place.

Obtaining a Session

There are three chief ways to obtain a URLSession:

The shared session

The URLSession class vends a singleton shared session object through its `shared` class property. This object is supplied and configured by the runtime; it is good for very simple, occasional use, where you don't need configuration, authentication, dedicated cookie storage, and so forth. You can't interact with the session while it's performing a networking task for you, because you have no delegate. All you can do is order some task to be performed and then stand back and wait for it to finish, at which point you will be called back.

Session configured without a delegate

You create the URLSession by calling `init(configuration:)`. This means that the session is yours, not shared. You'll hand the session a URLSessionConfiguration object describing the desired environment. This means that you can configure the URLSession. But you still can't interact with the session while it's performing a networking task for you, because you still have no delegate. Again, you'll just be called back when the task finishes.

Session configured with a delegate

You create the URLSession by calling `init(configuration:delegate:delegate-Queue:)`. Like the preceding initializer, you'll hand the session a URLSessionConfiguration object. Now the session is yours and you can configure it — and you also have a delegate that can receive various callbacks during the course of a networking task (and you even get to say whether those callbacks should occur on the main thread or in the background). Clearly this is the most powerful approach; it is also more complicated than the others, but that complexity can be worthwhile.

The shared session is owned by the runtime, so there's no need to retain it; you simply access it and tell it what you want it to do. But if you create a URLSession with a configuration, you'll probably want it to persist. Your app will typically need to create only one URLSession object; it is reasonable to store it in a global variable, or in an instance property of some object that will persist throughout your app's lifetime, such as the app delegate or the root view controller.

Session Configuration

To initialize a URLSession, you'll start by creating a URLSessionConfiguration and setting its properties. The configuration object dictates various options to be applied to the session. (A legitimate reason for creating multiple URLSession objects might be that you need them to have different configurations.)

There are three URLSessionConfiguration class members that you can use to obtain a URLSessionConfiguration instance:

App Transport Security

Since iOS 9, App Transport Security has been enforced, meaning that HTTP requests, by default, must be HTTPS requests, and that the server must be using TLS 1.2 or higher.

To tweak the behavior of App Transport Security, you must make an entry in your app's *Info.plist*, in the "App Transport Security Settings" dictionary (`NSAppTransport-Security`). To allow HTTP requests in general, the dictionary's "Allow Arbitrary Loads" key (`NSAllowsArbitraryLoads`) must be `YES`.

See the "App Transport Security" section in Apple's *Information Property List Key Reference* in the documentation archive.

`default`

> A basic vanilla URLSessionConfiguration. This is what you'll use most of the time.

`ephemeral`

> Configures a URLSession whose cookies and caches are maintained in memory only; they are never saved. You can actually configure a `default` URLSession-Configuration to give the same behavior, so this is purely a convenience.

`background(withIdentifier:)`

> Configures a URLSession that will proceed with its networking tasks independently of your app at some future time. I'll discuss background sessions later.

Here are some of the basic URLSessionConfiguration properties:

`allowsExpensiveNetworkAccess`

> Effectively supersedes `allowsCellularAccess`. The notion "expensive" currently embraces both cellular and device hotspots. If you set this property to `false` and the network is "expensive," attempting to network will get you a URLError whose `networkUnavailableReason` is `.expensive`. (Introduced in iOS 13.)

`allowsConstrainedNetworkAccess`

> The notion of "constrained" network access corresponds to Low Data Mode in Settings (under Cellular and WiFi). The idea is that the user can mark a route as low-bandwidth; the system will respond by turning off background app refresh and so forth, and your app should respond by reducing its network activity and not fetching large resources if a smaller resource (or no resource) will do. If you set this property to `false` and the network is "constrained," attempting to network will get you a URLError whose `networkUnavailableReason` is `.constrained`. (Introduced in iOS 13.)

`waitsForConnectivity`

If `true`, the session will try again later if the network is unavailable initially. Apple says that it is better to use this property, and let the URLSession do the work, than to try to determine reachability for yourself (by using SCNetwork-Reachability or similar).

`httpMaximumConnectionsPerHost`

The maximum number of simultaneous connections to the remote server.

Timeout values

There are two of them:

`timeoutIntervalForRequest`

The maximum time you're willing to wait *between* pieces of data. The timer starts when the connection succeeds, and then starts over each time a piece of data is received. A timeout means that things have stalled in the middle. If this is not a background session, the timeout will trigger failure of the download. The default is one minute.

`timeoutIntervalForResource`

The maximum time for the *entire* download to arrive. The timer starts when the networking task is told to start, and just keeps ticking until completion. This is appropriate for limiting the request's overall time-to-live. Failure to complete in the required time will always trigger failure of the download. The default is seven days.

There are also numerous cookie, caching, credential, proxy, and protocol properties.

Session Tasks

To use a URLSession to perform a networking task, you need a URLSessionTask object, representing a single communication exchange. You do not instantiate a task yourself; rather, you ask the URLSession for a task of the desired type, which will be an appropriate subclass of URLSessionTask:

URLSessionDataTask

You ask for a resource and the data is provided incrementally to your app as it arrives across the network. You should not use a data task for a large hunk of data, because the data is accumulating in memory throughout the download.

URLSessionUploadTask

A URLSessionDataTask subclass. You can provide a file to be uploaded and stand back, though you can also hear about the upload progress if you wish.

URLSessionDownloadTask

You ask for a resource, but the data never passes through your app's memory; instead, it is accumulated into a file, and the saved file URL is handed to you at the end of the process. The file is outside your sandbox and will be destroyed, so preserving it (or its contents) is up to you.

URLSessionStreamTask

This type of task makes it possible to deal conveniently with streams.

URLSessionWebSocketTask

A web socket is a persistent two-way connection between client and server (a "bidirectional stream"). (Introduced in iOS 13.)

URLSessionTask itself is an abstract superclass, embodying various properties common to all types of task, such as:

- A `taskDescription` and `taskIdentifier`; the former is up to you, while the latter is a unique identifier within the URLSession.

- The `originalRequest` and `currentRequest` (the request can change because there might be a redirect).

- The `priority`; a Float between 0 and 1, used as a hint to help rank the relative importance of your tasks. For convenience, URLSessionTask vends three constants:

  - `URLSessionTask.lowPriority` (0.25)

  - `URLSessionTask.defaultPriority` (0.5)

  - `URLSessionTask.highPriority` (0.75)

- An initial `response` from the server.

- Various `countOfBytes...` properties allowing you to track progress.

- A `progress` property that vends a Progress object; this is probably a better way to track progress than the `countOfBytes...` properties.

- A `state`, which might be:

  - `.running`

  - `.suspended`

  - `.canceling`

  - `.completed`

- An `error` if the task failed.

You can tell a task to `resume`, `suspend`, or `cancel`. A task is *born suspended*; it does *not* start until it is told to `resume` for the first time. (Forgetting to `resume` the task to start it is a common beginner error.) Typically you'll obtain the task, configure it, and then tell it to resume to start it. The Progress object vended by a task's progress property is a second gateway to these methods; telling the Progress object to resume, pause, or cancel is the same as telling the task to resume, suspend, or cancel respectively.

Once you've obtained a new session task from the URLSession, the session retains it; you can keep a reference to the task if you wish, but you don't have to. The session will provide you with a list of its tasks in progress; call getAllTasks(completion-Handler:) to receive the existing tasks in the completion function. The session releases a task after the task is cancelled or completed; a URLSession with no running or suspended tasks has no tasks at all.

There are two ways to ask your URLSession for a new session task. Which one you use depends on how you obtained the URLSession; in turn, they entail two different ways of working with the task:

With a completion function
> Take this approach if you are using the shared session or a session configured without a delegate. You'll call a convenience method that takes a completion-Handler: parameter, such as downloadTask(with:completionHandler:). You supply a completion function, typically an anonymous function, to be called when the task ends.

Without a completion function
> Take this approach if you gave the URLSession a delegate when you created it. You'll call a method *without* a completionHandler: parameter, such as download-Task(with:). The delegate is called back at various stages of the task's progress.

For a data task or a download task, the with: parameter can be either a URL or a URLRequest. A URL is simpler, but a URLRequest allows you more power to perform additional configurations.

 Apple says that it is reasonable to call resume on a background queue. By specifying the queue's quality of service (qos), you can rank the priority of this task. See Chapter 25.

Session Delegate

If you create a session by calling init(configuration:delegate:delegateQueue:), you'll specify a delegate, along with the queue (roughly, the thread — see Chapter 25) on which the delegate methods are to be called. For each type of session task, there's a delegate protocol, which may inherit from other protocols:

Data delegate

For a data task, we would want a data delegate — an object conforming to the URLSessionDataDelegate protocol, which itself conforms to the URLSessionTask-Delegate protocol, which in turn conforms to the URLSessionDelegate protocol, resulting in about a dozen delegate methods we could implement, though only a few are crucial:

URLSession(_:dataTask:didReceive:)

Some data has arrived, as a Data object (the third parameter). The data will arrive piecemeal, so this method may be called many times during the download process, supplying new data each time. Our job is to accumulate all those chunks of data; this involves maintaining state between calls.

URLSession(_:task:didCompleteWithError:)

If there is an error, we'll find out about it here. If there's no error, this is our signal that the download is over; we can now do something with the accumulated data.

Download delegate

For a download task, we would want a download delegate, conforming to the URLSessionDownloadDelegate protocol, which conforms to the URLSession-TaskDelegate protocol, which conforms to the URLSessionDelegate protocol. Here are some useful download delegate methods:

URLSession(_:downloadTask:didResumeAtOffset:expectedTotalBytes:)

This method is of interest only in the case of a resumable download that has been paused and resumed.

URLSession(_:downloadTask:didWriteData:totalBytesWritten:totalBytes-ExpectedToWrite:)

Called periodically, to keep us apprised of the download's progress. It might be more convenient to keep a reference to the task's Progress object.

URLSession(_:downloadTask:didFinishDownloadingTo:)

Called at the end of the process. The last parameter is a file URL; we must grab the downloaded file immediately from there, as it will be destroyed.

URLSession(_:task:didCompleteWithError:)

Unlike with a data task, this delegate method is not crucial for a download task. Still, if there was a communication problem, this is where you'd hear about it.

Some delegate methods provide a completionHandler: parameter. These are delegate methods that require a response from you. In the case of a data task, URLSession(_:dataTask:didReceive:completionHandler:) arrives when we first connect to the server. The third parameter is the response (URLResponse), and we could now check its status code. We must also return a response of our own, saying whether or not to proceed (or whether to convert the data task to a download task, which could certainly come in handy). But because of the multithreaded, asynchronous nature of networking (see Appendix C), we do this, not by returning a value directly, but by *calling the completion function* and passing our response into it.

The various delegate protocols also inherit this method from the URLSessionTask-Delegate protocol:

urlSession(_:taskIsWaitingForConnectivity:)
> Called only if the session configuration has its waitsForConnectivity set to true. The task has tried to start and has failed; instead of giving up with an error (as it would have done if waitsForConnectivity were false), it will wait and try again later. You might respond by updating your interface somehow.

HTTP Request with Task Completion Function

At long last, we are ready for some examples! I'll start by illustrating the utmost in simplicity. This is the absolute minimum approach to downloading a file:

- We use the shared URLSession, which takes no configuration.
- We obtain a download task, handing it a remote URL and a completion function. When the download is complete, the completion function will be called with a file URL; we retrieve the data from that URL and do something with it.

Having obtained the session and the task, don't forget to call resume to start the download! Our overall code looks like this:

```
let url = // whatever
let session = URLSession.shared
let task = session.downloadTask(with:url) { loc, resp, err in
    // ... completion function body goes here ...
}
task.resume()
```

All that remains is to write the body of the completion function. The downloaded data (here, an image file) is stored temporarily; if we want to do something with it, we must retrieve it right now. We must make no assumptions about what thread the completion function will be called on; indeed, unless we take steps to the contrary, it will be a background thread. In this particular example, the URL points to an image that I intend to display in my interface; therefore, I step out to the main thread (Chapter 25) in order to talk to the interface:

```
let task = session.downloadTask(with:url) { fileURL, resp, err in
    if let url = fileURL, let d = try? Data(contentsOf:url) {
        let im = UIImage(data:d)
        DispatchQueue.main.async {
```

```
        self.iv.image = im
    }
  }
}
```

That's all there is to it! If there's an error or a negative response from the server (such as "File not found"), url will be nil and we'll do nothing. Optionally, you might like to have the completion function report those conditions:

```
guard err == nil else { print(err); return }
let status = (resp as? HTTPURLResponse)?.statusCode
guard status == 200 else { print(status as Any); return }
```

A data task is similar, except that the data itself arrives as the first parameter of the completion function:

```
let task = session.dataTask(with:url) { data, resp, err in
    if let d = data {
        let im = UIImage(data:d) // ... and so on
```

A session task vends a Progress object (starting in iOS 11). This means that we can track the progress of our task even without a session delegate. If we have a UIProgressView (self.prog) in our interface, displaying the task's progress to the user could be as simple as this:

```
self.prog.observedProgress = task.progress
```

Recall, too, that one Progress object can act as the parent of other Progress objects (Chapter 13). If we are going to perform multiple tasks simultaneously, our UIProgressView's observedProgress can be configured to show the *overall* progress of those tasks.

The Combine framework, in iOS 13 and later, endows a URLSession with a data task *publisher*. To obtain it, call dataTaskPublisher(for:) with a URL or URLRequest. This provides a publish-and-subscribe alternative to a completion function, and you can encapsulate analysis and processing of the response within the pipeline. In this example, self.pipeline is an instance property typed as an Optional AnyCancellable (and you'll need to import Combine):

```
let url = // whatever
let session = URLSession.shared
let pipeline = session.dataTaskPublisher(for: url)
    .tryMap { data, response -> UIImage? in
        if (response as? HTTPURLResponse)?.statusCode != 200 {
            throw NSError(domain: "wrong status", code: 0)
        }
        return UIImage(data:data)
    }.receive(on: DispatchQueue.main)
    .sink { comp in
        if case let .failure(err) = comp {
            print(err)
```

```
        }
    } receiveValue: { im in
        self.iv.image = im
    }
    self.pipeline = pipeline
```

HTTP Request with Session Delegate

Now let's go to the other extreme and be very formal and complete:

- We'll start by creating and configuring a URLSessionConfiguration object.
- We'll create and retain our own URLSession.
- We'll give the session a delegate, implementing delegate methods to deal with the session task as it proceeds.
- When we request our session task, instead of a mere URL, we'll start with a URL-Request.

We are now creating our own URLSession, rather than borrowing the system's shared session. Since one URLSession can perform multiple tasks, there will typically be just one URLSession; so I'll make a lazy initializer that creates and configures it, supplying a URLSessionConfiguration and setting the delegate:

```
lazy var session : URLSession = {
    let config = URLSessionConfiguration.ephemeral
    config.allowsExpensiveNetworkAccess = false
    let session = URLSession(configuration: config, delegate: self,
        delegateQueue: .main)
    return session
}()
```

I've specified, for purposes of the example, that no caching is to take place and that data downloading via cell is forbidden; you could configure things much more heavily and meaningfully, of course. I have specified self as the delegate, and I have requested delegate callbacks on the main thread.

When I ask for the session task, I'll supply a URLRequest instead of a URL:

```
let url = URL(string:s)!
let req = URLRequest(url:url)
// ... ask for the task ...
```

In my examples in this chapter, there is very little merit in using a URLRequest instead of a URL to form our task. Still, a URLRequest can come in handy, and an upload task requires one; this is where you configure such things as the HTTP request method, body, and header fields.

Do *not* use the URLRequest to configure properties of the request that are configurable through the URLSessionConfiguration. There is no point setting the URLRequest's `timeoutInterval`, for instance, as it is the URLSessionConfiguration's timeout properties that are significant.

Download task

To demonstrate the use of a session delegate, I'll recast the image file download task from the previous example. I blank out the image view, to make the progress of the task more obvious for test purposes, and I create and start the download task:

```
self.iv.image = nil
let url = // whatever
let req = URLRequest(url:url)
let task = self.session.downloadTask(with:req)
task.resume()
```

Here are some delegate methods for responding to the download:

```
func urlSession(_ session: URLSession,
    downloadTask: URLSessionDownloadTask,
    didWriteData bytesWritten: Int64,
    totalBytesWritten writ: Int64,
    totalBytesExpectedToWrite exp: Int64) {
        print("downloaded \(100*writ/exp)%")
}
func urlSession(_ session: URLSession,
    task: URLSessionTask,
    didCompleteWithError error: Error?) {
        print("completed: error: \(error)")
}
func urlSession(_ session: URLSession,
    downloadTask: URLSessionDownloadTask,
    didFinishDownloadingTo fileURL: URL) {
        if let d = try? Data(contentsOf:fileURL) {
            let im = UIImage(data:d)
            DispatchQueue.main.async {
                self.iv.image = im
            }
        }
}
}
/*
downloaded 23%
downloaded 47%
downloaded 71%
downloaded 100%
completed: error: nil
*/
```

Instead of implementing URLSession(_:downloadTask:didWriteData:totalBytes-Written:totalBytesExpectedToWrite:) to track the progress of the download, we could use the task's `progress` object. We would configure that when we obtain the download task:

```
self.ob = task.progress.observe(\.fractionCompleted) { prog, change in
    print("downloaded \(Int(100*prog.fractionCompleted))%")
}
```

Data task

A data task is a little more work than a download task, because the data task leaves it up to you to accumulate the data as it arrives in chunks. You'll want to keep a mutable Data object on hand; I'll use an instance property:

```
var data = Data()
```

To get started, I prepare `self.data` by giving it a zero `count`, and then I create and start the data task:

```
self.iv.image = nil
self.data.count = 0 // *
let url = // whatever
let req = URLRequest(url:url)
let task = self.session.dataTask(with:req) // *
task.resume()
```

As the chunks of data arrive, I keep appending them to `self.data`. When all the data has arrived, it is ready for use:

```
func urlSession(_ session: URLSession,
    dataTask: URLSessionDataTask,
    didReceive data: Data) {
        self.data.append(data)
}
func urlSession(_ session: URLSession,
    task: URLSessionTask,
    didCompleteWithError error: Error?) {
        if error == nil {
            DispatchQueue.main.async {
                self.iv.image = UIImage(data:self.data)
            }
        }
}
```

One Session, One Delegate

The URLSession delegate architecture dictates that the delegate belongs to the *session as a whole*, not to each task individually. Because of this architecture, the preceding data task code is actually broken! To see why, ask yourself: What happens if our session is asked to perform another data task while this data task is still in progress? Our one session delegate is accumulating the chunks of data into a single Data property, `self.data`, without regard to what data task this chunk of data comes from. Clearly this is a potential train wreck: we're going to interleave the data from two different tasks, ending up with nonsense.

Let's revise the data task code to fix the problem. We need a way to *separate* the data streams belonging to the different tasks. Fortunately, a session task has a unique identifier — its `taskIdentifier`, which is an Int. So instead of a single Data property, we can maintain a dictionary keyed by each data task's `taskIdentifier`, where the corresponding value is a Data object:

```
var data = [Int:Data]()
```

Our code for obtaining and starting a new data task now adds an entry to the `data` dictionary, like this:

```
let task = self.session.dataTask(with:req)
self.data[task.taskIdentifier] = Data() // *
task.resume()
```

As a chunk of data arrives, we append it to the correct entry in the dictionary:

```
func urlSession(_ session: URLSession,
    dataTask: URLSessionDataTask,
    didReceive data: Data) {
        self.data[dataTask.taskIdentifier]!.append(data)
}
```

When a task's data has fully arrived, we pluck it out of the dictionary and remove that dictionary entry (so that data from stale tasks doesn't accumulate), and proceed to use the data:

```
func urlSession(_ session: URLSession,
    task: URLSessionTask,
    didCompleteWithError error: Error?) {
        let d = self.data[task.taskIdentifier]!
        self.data[task.taskIdentifier] = nil
        if error == nil {
            DispatchQueue.main.async {
                self.iv.image = UIImage(data:d)
            }
        }
}
```

Delegate Memory Management

A URLSession does an unusual thing: it *retains its delegate*. This is understandable, as it would be disastrous if the delegate could simply vanish in the middle of an asynchronous time-consuming process; but it means that all the preceding delegate examples are broken in yet another way: we have a retain cycle! Our view controllers are leaking. That's because the view controller has a URLSession instance property `self.session`, but the URLSession is retaining the view controller (`self`) as its delegate.

The way to break the cycle is to *invalidate* the URLSession at some appropriate moment. There are two ways to do this:

`finishTasksAndInvalidate`
> Allows any existing tasks to run to completion. Afterward, the URLSession *releases* the delegate and cannot be used for anything further.

`invalidateAndCancel`
> Interrupts any existing tasks immediately. The URLSession *releases* the delegate and cannot be used for anything further.

If the delegate caught in this retain cycle is a view controller, then `viewWillDisappear(_:)` could be a good place to invalidate the URLSession; we cannot use `deinit`, because `deinit` won't be called unless we have *already* invalidated the URLSession (that's what it means to have a retain cycle):

```
override func viewWillDisappear(_ animated: Bool) {
    super.viewWillDisappear(animated)
    self.session.finishTasksAndInvalidate()
}
```

Session and Delegate Encapsulation

The solution in the preceding section works, but it is not very satisfying. We are still creating a retain cycle between the session and its delegate, the view controller; to break it, we must remember to invalidate the session. It is not easy to find a place to do that; `viewWillDisappear` can be called many times in the life of a view controller, and invalidating the session there might not be appropriate. It would be much better if we could invalidate the session automatically when the view controller goes out of existence. And it would be even better if there were never any retain cycle to start with!

We can achieve that goal by encapsulating the session and its delegate:

- Start with an instance of some *separate* class whose job is to hold the URLSession in a property.
- Make the URLSession's delegate an instance of yet *another* class — an instance that is not retained by any object other than the URLSession.

Now our memory management problems are over. The URLSession retains its delegate, so there is no need for any *other* object to retain it. The delegate does not retain the session or the instance that holds the session, so there is no retain cycle. And there is no entanglement with the memory management of a view controller. Our URLSession-holding instance can live anywhere — and if it is being retained by a view controller, then it will go out of existence in good order when the view controller goes out of existence.

To illustrate, I'll design a Downloader class that holds a URLSession and creates its delegate. I imagine that our view controller will create and maintain an instance of Downloader early in its lifetime, as an instance property:

```
let downloader : Downloader = {
    // ...
    return Downloader( /* ... */ )
}()
```

In that code, I omitted the initialization of Downloader. How should this work? The Downloader object will create its own URLSession, but I think the client should be allowed to configure the session. So let's posit that Downloader's initializer takes a URLSessionConfiguration parameter:

```
let downloader : Downloader = {
    let config = URLSessionConfiguration.ephemeral
    config.allowsExpensiveNetworkAccess = false
    return Downloader(configuration:config)
}()
```

Now let's design Downloader itself. It creates and retains the URLSession, and makes its delegate an instance of a private class, DownloaderDelegate — an instance that only the URLSession itself will retain. Since there is no retain cycle, Downloader can cancel its own session *automatically* when it goes out of existence:

```
class Downloader: NSObject {
    let config : URLSessionConfiguration
    lazy var session : URLSession = {
        return URLSession(configuration:self.config,
            delegate:DownloaderDelegate(), delegateQueue:.main)
    }()
    init(configuration config:URLSessionConfiguration) {
        self.config = config
        super.init()
    }
    // ...
    deinit {
        self.session.invalidateAndCancel()
    }
}
```

Suppose the client is a view controller with a downloader property, as I suggested earlier. There is no retain cycle, so the view controller can go out of existence in good order when the view controller hierarchy is through with it. And when that happens, its downloader will go out of existence too, taking the URLSession and its delegate with it.

Next, let's decide how a client will communicate with a Downloader object. The client will hand a URL to the Downloader instance; the Downloader will obtain the URLSessionDownloadTask and start it. The DownloaderDelegate will be told when the download is over. At that point, the DownloaderDelegate has a file URL for the downloaded object, which it needs to hand back to the client immediately.

One way to arrange this is that the client, when it hands the Downloader a URL to initiate a download, should also supply a *completion function* (see Appendix C) to be called when the download is over. In that way, we deal with the asynchronous nature of networking, as well as keeping Downloader independent and agnostic about who the caller is. To return the file URL at the end of a download, the DownloaderDelegate *calls* the completion function, passing it the file URL as a parameter. I can even define a type alias naming my completion function type:

```
typealias DownloaderCH = (URL?) -> ()
```

From the client's point of view, then, the process will look something like this:

```
let url = // whatever
self.downloader.download(url:url) { url in
    if let url = url, let d = try? Data(contentsOf: url) {
        let im = UIImage(data:d)
        self.iv.image = im // assume we're called back on main thread
    }
}
```

Now let's implement this architecture within Downloader. We have posited a method download(url:completionHandler:). When that method is called, Downloader stores the completion function; it then asks for a new download task and sets it going:

```
@discardableResult
func download(url:URL,
    completionHandler ch : @escaping DownloaderCH) -> URLSessionTask {
        let task = self.session.downloadTask(with:url)
        // ... store the completion function somehow ...
        task.resume()
        return task
}
```

(We're returning a reference to the task, so that the client can subsequently cancel the task if need be.)

When the download finishes, the DownloaderDelegate calls the completion function:

```
func urlSession(_ session: URLSession,
    downloadTask: URLSessionDownloadTask,
    didFinishDownloadingTo url: URL) {
        let ch = // ... retrieve the completion function somehow ...
        ch(url)
}
```

In my carefree speculative coding design, I have left a blank — the storage and retrieval of the completion function corresponding to each download task. Let's use the same technique I used earlier for accumulating the data of multiple data tasks, namely a dictionary keyed by the task's `taskIdentifier`. This will be a private property of DownloaderDelegate, along with a public method:

```
private var handlers = [Int:DownloaderCH]()
func appendHandler(_ ch:@escaping DownloaderCH, task:URLSessionTask {
    self.handlers[task.taskIdentifier] = ch
}
```

We are now ready to fill in the blank in Downloader's `download(url:completion-Handler:)` method. By the time this method is called by the client, the delegate has already been created and handed to the session, and only the session has a reference to it; so we obtain the delegate from the session and call the `append-Handler(_:task:)` method that we gave it for this purpose:

```
func download(url:URL,
    completionHandler ch : @escaping DownloaderCH) -> URLSessionTask {
        let task = self.session.downloadTask(with:url)
        let del = self.session.delegate as! DownloaderDelegate
        del.appendHandler(ch, task: task)
        task.resume()
        return task
}
```

All that remains is to write the delegate methods for DownloaderDelegate. There are two of them that we need to implement. When the download arrives, we find the completion function corresponding to this download task and call it, handing it the file URL where the downloaded data has been stored:

```
func urlSession(_ session: URLSession,
    downloadTask: URLSessionDownloadTask,
    didFinishDownloadingTo url: URL) {
        let ch = self.handlers[downloadTask.taskIdentifier]
        ch?(url)
}
```

When the task completes, we purge the completion function from the dictionary — and, if there was an error, we pass `nil` to the completion function, guaranteeing that the completion function will be called under all circumstances:

```
func urlSession(_ session: URLSession,
    task: URLSessionTask,
    didCompleteWithError error: Error?) {
        let ch = self.handlers[task.taskIdentifier]
        self.handlers[task.taskIdentifier] = nil
        if let error = error {
            ch?(nil)
        }
}
```

As written, DownloaderDelegate's delegate methods are being called on the main thread. That's not necessarily a bad thing, but it may be preferable to run that code on a background thread. I'll describe in Chapter 25 how to do that.

Downloading Table View Data

To exercise Downloader, I'll tackle a pesky problem that arises quite often in real life: we have a UITableView where each cell displays text and an image, and the image needs to be downloaded from the internet.

What will our implementation of `tableView(_:cellForRowAt:)` do? It must *not* try to network synchronously — that is, it mustn't wait around for the image to arrive before returning the cell. We must not gum up the works; this method needs to return a cell *immediately*. The correct strategy, if we don't have the image yet, is to put a placeholder (or no image at all) in the cell, return the cell, and *then* see about downloading the image. When we have the image, *then* we can insert it into the cell.

The model object for a table row will be an instance of a dedicated Model class, which is nothing but a bundle of properties:

```
class Model {
    init(text: String, picurl: URL) {
        self.text = text
        self.picurl = picurl
    }
    var text : String // text for the cell's text label
    var picurl : URL // url for downloading the image
    var im : UIImage? // image for the cell's image view; initially nil
    var task : URLSessionTask? // current download task, if any
}
```

Presume, for simplicity, that we have only one section, and our table view model is an array of Model. When the table turns to the data source for a cell in `table-View(_:cellForRowAt:)`, the data source will turn to the model and consult the Model object corresponding to the requested row, asking for its `im` property, which is supposed to be its image. Initially, this will be `nil`. In that case, the data source will display no image in this cell, and will immediately return a cell without an image.

We also want to request that the image be downloaded from this Model object's `picurl`. When we get the image, we'll store it in the Model object's `im` property. At that point we can *reload* the row, and this time `tableView(_:cellForRowAt:)` will find that image and display it in the cell.

This is an opportunity to exercise a feature of UITableView (and UICollectionView) that I didn't mention in Chapter 8 — *prefetching*. We assign to our table view's `prefetchDataSource` property some object adopting the UITableViewDataSource-Prefetching protocol. The runtime will then call that object's delegate method `tableView(_:prefetchRowsAt:)` before calling `tableView(_:cellForRowAt:)` — not only when the user *is* scrolling a cell onto the screen, but also when the user *might* scroll a cell onto the screen.

This architecture allows us to separate provision of the data from provision of the cell. Let's say that initially the first 12 rows of the table are displayed. Then the runtime will call `tableView(_:prefetchRowsAt:)` for the *next* 12 rows — because if the user scrolls at all, those are the rows that will come into view.

Presume, then, that we (`self`, the view controller) adopt UITableViewDataSource-Prefetching, and that we have configured the table view accordingly in our `viewDidLoad`:

```
override func viewDidLoad() {
    super.viewDidLoad()
    self.tableView.prefetchDataSource = self // turn on prefetching
}
```

Our implementation of `tableView(_:cellForRowAt:)` is trivial, just as it should be; everything we need to know is right there in the Model object for this row. The image displayed in the image view will be a downloaded UIImage or `nil`, depending on whether the Model has acquired the image for this row:

```
override func tableView(_ tableView: UITableView,
    cellForRowAt indexPath: IndexPath) -> UITableViewCell {
        let cell = tableView.dequeueReusableCell(
            withIdentifier: self.cellID, for: indexPath)
        let m = self.model[indexPath.row]
        cell.textLabel?.text = m.text
        cell.imageView?.image = m.im // image or nil
        return cell
}
```

Meanwhile, the runtime is busy calling `tableView(_:prefetchRowsAt:)` for us. Here we deal directly with the model data. We examine the Model for the given row; if it already has an image, obviously the image was already downloaded, so there's nothing more to do. We also examine the Model's `task`; if it is not `nil`, that's a marker that this image is currently being downloaded, so there's nothing more to do. Otherwise, we start the download, storing a reference to the download task in the Model's `task` as a sign that the download for this row has been requested:

```
func tableView(_ tableView: UITableView,
    prefetchRowsAt indexPaths: [IndexPath]) {
        for ip in indexPaths {
            let m = self.model[ip.row]
            guard m.im == nil else { continue } // we have an image already
            guard m.task == nil else { continue } // already downloading
            m.task = self.downloader.download(url:m.picurl) { url in
```

```
            // ... this is the completion function! ...
        }
    }
}
```

When the download finishes, our completion function is called. In my usual speculative coding style, I left it empty; now I'll fill it in. We reset the Model's `task` to `nil`,
because we are no longer downloading. If the image data has been successfully downloaded, we store it in the Model. Now we call `reloadRows` for this row. There's no
telling when this will happen; remember, the completion function is being called
asynchronously. But that doesn't matter. If the row is visible on the screen, `table-
View(_:cellForRowAt:)` will be called for this row, and the image will be displayed
now; if the row is no longer visible on the screen, there are no ill effects, and the
image is still stored, ready for the next time the row becomes visible:

```
m.task = self.downloader.download(url:url) { url in
    m.task = nil
    if let url = url, let data = try? Data(contentsOf: url) {
        m.im = UIImage(data:data)
        tableView.reloadRows(at:[ip], with: .none)
    }
}
```

That completes our implementation of `tableView(_:prefetchRowsAt:)`.

But there's still a problem: when the table view initially appears, the images are all
missing from the visible rows. That's because the runtime calls `table-
View(_:prefetchRowsAt:)` for *future* table rows, but not for the rows that are initially
visible! (I regard that as a bug in the table view architecture.) However, it's easy to
deal with that; at the end of `tableView(_:cellForRowAt:)`, I can call `table-
View(_:prefetchRowsAt:)` myself:

```
// ... same as before ...
cell.imageView!.image = m.im // image or nil
if m.task == nil && m.im == nil {
    self.tableView(tableView, prefetchRowsAt:[indexPath])
}
return cell
```

Our table view is now working perfectly!

If these are large images, we could end up retaining many large images in the model
array, which might cause us to run out of memory. There are lots of ways to deal with
that. We might start by reducing each image, as it arrives, to the size needed for display (preferably on a serial background thread). If that's still too much memory, we
can implement `tableView(_:didEndDisplaying:forRowAt:)` to expunge each image
from its Model (by setting the Model object's `im` to `nil`) when the cell scrolls out of
sight; if the cell comes back into view, we would then automatically download the
image again. Or, as we expunge the image from the Model, we might save it to disk

and substitute the file URL as its `picurl` (with appropriate adjustments in the rest of the code).

Background Session

If your app goes into the background while in the middle of a big networking task, the task might not be completed. You can ask for extra time to complete an operation in case the app goes into the background (and I'll talk in Chapter 25 about how to do that); but if it isn't crucial to perform this task right now, it might be nice to defer it so that it can be performed at a better time. The way to do that is to make the URL-Session a *background session* by assigning it a URLSessionConfiguration created with the class method `background(withIdentifier:)`. The task should be an upload or download task.

A background session hands the work of uploading or downloading over to the system. Your app can be suspended or terminated and the download will still be taken care of. As with location monitoring (Chapter 22), your app does not formally run in the background just because you have a background session with tasks, so you do not have to set the `UIBackgroundModes` of your *Info.plist*. But the session still serves as a gateway for putting your app in touch with the networking task as it proceeds; in particular, you need to provide the URLSession with a delegate so that you can receive messages informing you of how things are going.

The argument that you pass to `background(withIdentifier:)` is an arbitrary string identifier intended to distinguish your background session. It should be unique within your app, and a good approach is to use your app's bundle ID as its basis.

For large data, you may want to set the URLSessionConfiguration's `isDiscretionary` to `true`. This will permit the system to postpone network communications to some moment that will conserve bandwidth and battery — when WiFi is available and the device is plugged into a power socket. Of course, that might be days from now! But this is part of the beauty of background downloads.

A background session task scheduled while your app is in the background is always treated as discretionary. But if your configuration's `isDiscretionary` is `false`, and if you scheduled this session task while your app was in the foreground, and if you then go into the background, the system will try very hard to perform the session task for you as soon as possible.

There is no need to set a background session's `waitsForConnectivity`; it is `true` automatically, and cannot be changed. Similarly, a task does not fail if a background session's `timeoutIntervalForRequest` arrives; the background session will simply try again. However, a task is abandoned if the `timeoutIntervalForResource` arrives.

You can also set your URLSessionTask's `earliestBeginDate`. This is a date in the future; the start of the networking task is delayed until after that date. In addition, you might implement this delegate method:

`urlSession(_:task:willBeginDelayedRequest:completionHandler:)`
> Called only if your URLSessionTask's `earliestBeginDate` was set. The begin date has arrived, and the system is thinking of starting the networking task. Your app can now change its mind about this task, possibly cancelling it or even substituting a different request. The completion function takes two parameters; your job is to call it, passing as its first argument a URLSession.DelayedRequestDisposition stating your decision:
>
> * `.cancel`
> * `.continueLoading`
> * `.useNewRequest`
>
> The second completion function argument will be `nil`, unless the first argument is `.useNewRequest`, which case it will be the new URLRequest.

Once the background session is configured and the task is told to `resume`, the system will need to get back in touch with your code when it has a delegate message to send you. How it does this depends on what state your app is in at that moment:

Your app is frontmost and still running
> Your app may have gone into the background one or more times, but it was never terminated, and it is frontmost now. In that case, your background URLSession still exists and is still hooked to its delegate, and the delegate messages are simply sent as usual.

Your app is not frontmost or was terminated
> Your app is in the background, or it is not running, or it is frontmost but it was terminated since the time you told your task to `resume`. Now the system needs to perform a handshake with your URLSession in order to get in touch with it. To make that handshake possible, you must implement these two methods:

`application(_:handleEventsForBackgroundURLSession:completionHandler:)`
> This message is sent *to the app delegate*. The `session:` parameter is the string identifier you handed earlier to the configuration object; you might use this to identify the session, or to create and configure the session if you haven't done so already. You do *not* call the completion function now! Instead, you must *store* it, because it will be needed later.

`urlSessionDidFinishEvents(forBackgroundURLSession:)`

> This message is sent *to the session delegate*. This is the moment when you must *call* the previously stored completion function. When you receive the first delegate message, if you create the background session, you should give it a delegate, in order to receive *this* delegate message (and any other delegate messages that may arrive).

By default, when the system wants to send you a delegate message, if your app is not frontmost, your app is *awakened* in the background, and if it is not running, it is *launched* in the background. If you don't need that, but are willing to wait until the next time the *user* brings your app frontmost or launches it, set the URLSessionConfiguration's `sessionSendsLaunchEvents` to `false`.

This is all much easier if the app delegate and the session delegate are one and the same object. In this example, the app delegate holds the URLSession property, which is created lazily; it also provides storage for the completion function:

```
lazy var session : URLSession = {
    let id = "com.neuburg.matt.backgroundDownload"
    let config = URLSessionConfiguration.background(withIdentifier: id)
    config.allowsExpensiveNetworkAccess = false
    // could set config.isDiscretionary here
    let sess = URLSession(
        configuration: config, delegate: self, delegateQueue: .main)
    return sess
}()
var ch : (() -> ())!
```

The URLSessionDownloadDelegate methods are as before, plus we have the two required handshake methods in case the system needs to get back in touch with us:

```
func application(_ application: UIApplication,
    handleEventsForBackgroundURLSession identifier: String,
    completionHandler: @escaping () -> ()) {
        self.ch = completionHandler
        _ = self.session // *
}
func urlSessionDidFinishEvents(forBackgroundURLSession session: URLSession) {
    self.ch?()
}
```

The starred line will "tickle" the `session` lazy initializer and bring the background session to life if needed.

If the user kills your app in the background by way of the app switcher interface, pending background downloads will *not* be completed. The system assumes that the user doesn't want your app coming magically back to life in the background. Also, in a WWDC 2020 video, Apple appears to be saying that if the user has switched off Background App Refresh (in Settings, under General), discretionary background session tasks will not take place.

Universal Links

When a URL is passed to the system, the system decides what to do with it and responds accordingly. There are many ways in which this can happen. As we've already seen, an app's code can call the UIApplication instance method open(_:options:completionHandler:) to pass a URL directly to the system. In addition, the *user* can cause a URL to be passed to the system — typically, by tapping a link. For instance:

- Tappable links can appear in a web page displayed by Mobile Safari or a WKWebView.

- Thanks to attributed strings, text in a UITextView can be a tappable link (Chapter 11).

- The user might encounter a tappable link in a Mail message or in Notes.

When the user taps the link, the underlying URL is passed to the system.

A link that your app receives in this way is essentially a form of user interface. By endowing particular URLs with particular meaning, you can effectively treat the arrival of a URL from the system as a command — and obey it.

 Your app cannot send a link to itself. The URL must be passed to the system by some other process.

One way to arrange for your app to receive certain classes of URL is by having your app declare a *custom URL scheme;* when a URL with that scheme is passed to the system, it is forwarded to your app. But Apple would prefer that you use *universal links* instead.

The remarkable thing about a universal link is that it does *not* use a custom URL scheme — it's an ordinary https: URL. That means it can point to a real web page as well as to your app. If the user doesn't have your app, the link leads to your website. If the user *does* have your app, the link leads to your app.

How on earth is that even possible? Well, you have to *have* a website; and at the root of that website there has to be a special file. When an iOS device's system goes to your website, the first thing it does is look for that special file. If it finds it, it looks inside to learn what URLs should be routed to your app, and if this URL is one of those, and if your app is on the device, the system *does* route the URL to your app.

The special file must be called *apple-app-site-association* (with no file name extension), and it must live in the *.well-known* directory at the root level of your website. The file must consist of some JSON. The rules for structuring this JSON can be quite elaborate, but here's a minimal example:

```
{
    "applinks": {
        "details": [
            {
                "appID": "W3LHX5RTV3.com.neuburg.matt.UniversalLinksTest",
                "components": [
                    {
                        "/": "/testing/*"
                    }
                ]
            }
        ]
    }
}
```

The key name "/" means "the URL's overall path after the domain," and its value is a simple wildcard pattern where the asterisk means "any number of characters." So this file says that if the URL's overall path after the domain starts with "/testing/", then if the user has the app whose bundle identifier is "com.neuburg.matt.Universal-LinksTest", the URL should be routed to that app. The "appID" is actually the app's bundle ID preceded by the *app ID prefix*, which you can find out by examining the app's registration at *https://developer.apple.com/account/* under Identifiers in the Certificates, IDs & Profiles section.

So let's say I've placed that file in my website, which has the domain *www.apeth.com*. The file is in the *.well-known* directory, and is called *apple-app-site-association*.

Now let's talk about the app itself. It must have a special entitlement — the Associated Domains entitlement. Edit the app target, go to the Signing & Capabilities pane, and add the Associated Domains capability. Its value is an array of domains, which are strings. The value of each string should be `applinks:` followed directly by the domain of the website where the *apple-app-site-association* file is located. So I'll have one string in my array, like this:

```
applinks:www.apeth.com
```

We have now established a *two-way handshake:*

In the app

My app has the correct app ID prefix (`W3LHX5RTV3`) and the correct bundle ID (`com.neuburg.matt.UniversalLinksTest`), and its Associated Domains entitlement says: "Look in the domain *www.apeth.com.*"

In the website

At the domain *www.apeth.com,* in the correct location and with the correct name, is a file that says: "Look in the app with app ID prefix `W3LHX5RTV3` and bundle ID `com.neuburg.matt.UniversalLinksTest`."

Those two things point at one another! Therefore the system will obey the instructions in the *apple-app-site-association* file: it will route *http://www.apeth.com* URLs matching the `"/testing/*"` pattern to this app.

New in iOS 14, when you're developing your app, you can append `?mode=developer` to the `applinks:` domain, like this:

```
applinks:www.apeth.com?mode=developer`
```

The reason for doing that is that normally Apple will maintain a cached version of your *apple-app-site-association* file; the developer mode declaration causes the system not to look at that cached version, but always to look directly at your website to get the file. So you can change the file and the system will pick up those changes the next time you test a universal link.

We have established that when a URL that starts *http://www.apeth.com/testing/* is passed to the device's system, that URL will be routed to our app. Then what? In order to receive the URL, we must implement two methods in the scene delegate. If the app is *launched* by the arrival of the URL, this method will be called:

```
func scene(_ scene: UIScene, willConnectTo session: UISceneSession,
    options connectionOptions: UIScene.ConnectionOptions) {
        if let url = connectionOptions.userActivities.first?.webpageURL {
            // got a URL!
        }
}
```

If the app is *already running* when the URL arrives, this method will be called:

```
func scene(_ scene: UIScene, continue userActivity: NSUserActivity) {
    if let url = userActivity.webpageURL {
        // got a URL!
    }
}
```

In both cases, you are receiving an NSUserActivity containing the actual URL.

How will you test that your universal links are working? One way is to run the app in a simulator and use the Terminal to throw a URL at the system. To do so, give a command like this:

App Clips

An *app clip,* new in iOS 14, is a small, temporary version of your app; if the user doesn't have the app itself, the app clip can be downloaded on demand and launched in order to perform a single piece of your app's functionality.

App clips are closely related to universal links. You configure a two-way handshake in your website's *apple-app-site-association* file and in your app clip's Associated Domains entitlement. A URL passed to the system causes the app clip to be downloaded and launched, and the app clip receives an NSUserActivity containing the URL.

For many apps, an app clip may prove to be a convenient way for the user to get a free, lightweight experience of part of the app. As part of WWDC 2020, Apple has provided four twenty-minute videos that constitute an excellent introduction.

```
% xcrun simctl openurl booted "https://www.apeth.com/testing/1"
```

Observe that that URL matches the pattern that we have asked to be routed to our app. And sure enough, our app's second method, scene(_:continue:), is called with that URL!

Testing what happens at launch time is not so easy. If our app isn't running and we throw the link at the system, our app launches in response, but we are not debugging it in Xcode, because we didn't run it from Xcode to begin with. We can use os_log (or the new Logger class) to print to the Console application, but we are still not stopping at breakpoints. Here's how to solve that problem:

1. Edit the scheme, and in the Run action, under Info, where it says Launch, click the second radio button: "Wait for the executable to be launched."

2. Now build and run the app to a Simulator destination. Nothing happens! That's because Xcode is *waiting* for the app to launch in some *other* way.

3. Throw the link at the system on the Simulator, to launch the app. Sure enough, our scene(_:willConnectTo:options:) is called. At the same time, Xcode hooks into the running app, and we can debug normally, pausing at breakpoints. In this mode, log messages from our code still don't appear in the Xcode console, but breakpoints configured to log a message, or to emit the debugger po command, *do* print to the Xcode console (and of course we can still use Logger to print to the Console application).

What should you do in response to the arrival of a universal link URL? That's entirely up to you; it depends on what you intend this URL to mean. You might run some code; you might change your app's data; you might navigate to a particular view controller; you might do all of those things! A URL can be long and elaborate, with many

Figure 24-1. An on-demand resource

path components and many key-value pairs expressed as query items, you can pack a lot of meaning into a single URL.

On-Demand Resources

Your app can store resources, such as images and sound files, on Apple's server instead of including them in the app bundle that the user initially installs on the device. Your app can then download those resources as needed when the app runs. Such resources are *on-demand resources*.

To mark something as an on-demand resource in Xcode, you assign it one or more *tags* (arbitrary strings); you can do this in many places in the Xcode interface. A tag may be assigned to an individual resource or to a folder. Any resources to which you have assigned tags are *not* copied into the app when you build it; they will have to be downloaded to the user's device as on-demand resources.

Your on-demand resource configuration is summarized and managed in the Resource Tags tab of the target editor. Figure 24-1 shows the Resource Tags tab displaying the `"pix"` tag, which has been attached to a folder called *images* in my app bundle.

How do you obtain an on-demand resource? In your code, you instantiate an NSBundleResourceRequest, handing it the tags of the resources you want to use. Let's call this the *request object*. You will likely want to retain the request object, typically in an instance property (I'll talk more about that in a moment). You then toggle access to the resources associated with those tags by sending the request object these messages:

`beginAccessingResources(completionHandler:)`

   Your completion function is called when the resources are available (which could be immediately if they have already been downloaded). *Do not assume that the completion function runs on the main thread.* The parameter is an Optional Error. If it is `nil`, you can now use the resources.

`endAccessingResources`

> Lets the runtime know that you are no longer actively using these resources. After this call, you can no longer access the resources; that doesn't mean they will be deleted, but they might be. You should now abandon use of this NSBundle-ResourceRequest instance! Its life cycle is finished. If you need to access the same resources again, start over by creating a new NSBundleResourceRequest and calling `beginAccessingResources` again.

If your app is terminated before you call `endAccessingResources`, then on relaunch you obviously have no NSBundleResourceRequest instance. But that doesn't matter, because you just keep following the same rules about how to access the resources. When you need access to them, you create an NSBundleResourceRequest and call `beginAccessingResources`; your resources might still be present, in which case you will get access immediately.

If your call to `beginAccessingResources` causes the resources to start downloading, you can track the download progress using the NSBundleResourceRequest's `progress` property, which is a Progress object. This might be desirable if the download causes a perceptible delay in your app's action and you need to let the user know what's happening. (The `progress.fractionCompleted` of an NSBundleResourceRequest that is not actively downloading may be either 0 or 1; it can be 0 after completion because you said `beginAccessing` at a time when the resource was already present.) Optimally, you might use a more proactive strategy to prefetch the resources so that they are present by the time the user needs them.

I mentioned earlier that you'll want your request object to persist, most likely as an instance property of a view controller. That's because if a resource request object goes out of existence, the runtime will assume that you no longer need those resources. Because an individual NSBundleResourceRequest instance is tied to a specific set of tags, and hence to a specific bunch of resources, you might need to keep multiple request objects stored simultaneously. One reasonable strategy might be to declare each instance property as an Optional of type `NSBundleResourceRequest?`. That way, you can set the property to `nil` when you're done with that request instance, so that you won't accidentally use it again. A more sophisticated approach might be to maintain a single mutable dictionary of type `[Set<String>:NSBundleResourceRequest]`, keyed by the request object's `tags`.

Your code that actually accesses on-demand resources does so in the normal way:

- If the resource is an image, you can access it using UIImage's `init(named:)`.
- If it's a data set in the asset catalog, you can access it using NSDataAsset's `init(name:)`.

- If it is a resource at the top level of the main bundle, you can get its URL by calling url(forResource:withExtension:) on the bundle.

And so forth. An attempt to access an on-demand resource in this way *will fail in good order* — you'll get nil — until you have successfully called beginAccessing-Resources. After a call to beginAccessingResources and a signal of success in its completion function, the resources spring to life and you can access them. After calling endAccessingResources, any attempt to access the resources will yield nil again (even if they have not actually been deleted).

How on earth does this architecture work? Is it a violation of the rule that your app bundle can't be modified? No; it's all an ingenious illusion. Your on-demand resources are stored *outside* the app bundle, in your app's *OnDemandResources* directory, but the methods that access resources are rejiggered so as to point to them, or to return nil, as appropriate.

There are two special categories of on-demand resource tags (visible in Figure 24-1) — *initial install* tags and *prefetch* tags:

Initial install tags

Resources with initial install tags are downloaded *at the same time* the app is installed; in effect, they appear to be part of the app.

Prefetch tags

Resources with prefetch tags are downloaded automatically by the system *after* the app is installed.

Neither of these special categories relieves you of the responsibility to call begin-Accessing before you actually use a tagged resource, nor does it prevent the resources from being deleted if you are not accessing them. The difference is that the desired resources will probably be already present when you call beginAccessing early in the lifetime of the app.

 Amazingly, you can test on-demand resources directly by running your app from Xcode. Also, you can check the status of your on-demand resources in the Disk gauge of the Debug navigator.

In-App Purchases

An in-app purchase is a specialized form of network communication: your app communicates with the App Store to permit the user to buy something there, or to confirm that something has already been bought there. This is a way to make your app itself inexpensive or free to download, while providing an optional increased price in exchange for increased functionality later. In-app purchases are made possible through the Store Kit framework; you'll need to import StoreKit.

Figure 24-2. Interface for an in-app purchase

There are various kinds of in-app purchase — consumables, nonconsumables, and subscriptions. You'll want to examine Apple's *In-App Purchase Programming Guide* in the documentation archive and the "Offer In-App Purchases" section of the *App Store Connect Help*.

To make an in-app purchase available to beta testers and App Store users, you will use App Store Connect to describe, in connection with your app, whatever it is that the user can purchase; this is easiest to do if your app is already available through the App Store. For a simple nonconsumable purchase, you are associating your app's bundle ID with a name and arbitrary product ID representing your in-app purchase, along with a price.

Here's an example from an actual game app of mine, which offers a single nonconsumable purchase: it unlocks functionality allowing users to involve their own photos in the game. When the user taps the Choose button, if the in-app purchase has *not* been made, the functionality permitting the user to browse the photo library to pick a photo is missing; instead, a pair of dialogs will appear, offering and describing the purchase (Figure 24-2).

For a nonconsumable in-app purchase, the app must provide the following interface (all of which is visible in Figure 24-2):

- The description of the in-app purchase. You do not hard-code this description into your app; rather, it is downloaded in real time from the App Store, using the Display Name and Description (and price) that you entered at App Store Connect.

- A button that launches the purchase process.

- A button that *restores* an existing purchase. The idea here is that the user has performed the purchase, but is now on a different device or has deleted and reinstalled your app, so that the persistent flag signaling that the purchase has been performed is missing. The user needs to be able to contact the App Store to get your app to recognize that the purchase has been performed and turn on the purchased functionality.

In my app, the purchase process proceeds in two stages. In my first view controller, if the user taps the Learn More button (on the left in Figure 24-2), I first confirm that the user has not been restricted from making purchases; then I create an SKProducts-Request, which will attempt to download an SKProductsResponse object embodying the details about the in-app purchase corresponding to my single product ID:

```
if !SKPaymentQueue.canMakePayments() {
    // ... put up alert saying we can't do it ...
    return
}
let req = SKProductsRequest(productIdentifiers: ["DiabelliChoose"])
req.delegate = self
req.start()
```

This kicks off some network activity, and eventually the delegate of this SKProducts-Request, namely self (conforming to SKProductsRequestDelegate), is called back with one of two delegate messages. If we get request(_:didFailWithError:), I put up an apologetic alert (unless the error code is .paymentCancelled), and that's the end. But if we get productsRequest(_:didReceive:), the request has succeeded, and we can proceed to the second stage.

In productsRequest(_:didReceive:), the response from the App Store arrives as the second parameter. It is an SKProductsResponse object containing an SKProduct representing the proposed purchase. I get on to the main thread (Chapter 25), create my second view controller, give it a reference to the SKProduct, and present it (on the right in Figure 24-2):

```
func productsRequest(_ request: SKProductsRequest,
    didReceive response: SKProductsResponse) {
        let p = response.products[0]
        DispatchQueue.main.async {
            let s = StoreViewController2(product:p)
            if let presenter = self.presentingViewController {
                self.dismiss(animated: true} {
                    presenter.present(s, animated: true)
                }
            }
        }
}
```

My second view controller has a product property that was set in its initializer. In its viewDidLoad, it populates its interface based on the information that the product contains (for my lend utility, see Appendix B):

```
self.titleLabel.text = self.product.localizedTitle
self.descriptionLabel.text = self.product.localizedDescription
self.priceLabel.text = lend { (nf : NumberFormatter) in
    nf.formatterBehavior = .behavior10_4
    nf.numberStyle = .currency
    nf.locale = self.product.priceLocale
}.string(from: self.product.price)
```

If the user taps the Purchase button, I dismiss the presented view controller, load the SKProduct into the default SKPaymentQueue, and stand back:

```
self.dismiss(animated: true) {
    let p = SKPayment(product:self.product)
    let q = SKPaymentQueue.default()
    q.add(p)
}
```

The system is now in charge of presenting a sequence of dialogs, confirming the purchase, asking for the user's App Store credentials, and so forth. My app knows nothing about that. If the user *performs* the purchase, the runtime will call paymentQueue(_:updatedTransactions:) on my *transaction observer*. This is an object adopting the SKPaymentTransactionObserver protocol, whose job it will be to receive messages from the payment queue. But how does the runtime know what object that is? When my app launches, it must *register* the transaction observer:

```
func application(application: UIApplication,
    didFinishLaunchingWithOptions launchOptions:
    [UIApplication.LaunchOptionsKey : Any]?) -> Bool {
        SKPaymentQueue.default().add(
            self.window!.rootViewController
                as! SKPaymentTransactionObserver)
        return true
}
```

As you can see, I've made my root view controller the transaction observer. It adopts the SKPaymentTransactionObserver protocol. There is only one required method — paymentQueue(_:updatedTransactions:). It is called with a reference to the payment queue and an array of SKPaymentTransaction objects. My job is to cycle through these transactions and, for each one, do whatever it requires, and then, if there was an actual transaction (or an error), send finishTransaction(_:) to the payment queue, to clear the queue.

My implementation is extremely simple, because I have only one purchasable product, and because I'm not maintaining any separate record of receipts. For each transaction, I check its transactionState (SKPaymentTransactionState). If its state is .purchased, I pull out its payment, confirm that the payment's productIdentifier is my product identifier (it had darned well better be, since I have only the one product), and, if so, I get onto the main thread and set the UserDefaults flag that indicates to my app that the user has performed the purchase:

```
func paymentQueue(_ queue: SKPaymentQueue,
    updatedTransactions transactions: [SKPaymentTransaction]) {
        for t in transactions {
            switch t.transactionState {
            case .purchasing, .deferred: break // do nothing
            case .purchased, .restored:
                let p = t.payment
                if p.productIdentifier == "DiabelliChoose" {
                    DispatchQueue.main.async {
                        UserDefaults.standard.set(true, forKey: self.CHOOSE)
                        // ... put up an alert thanking the user ...
                    }
                }
                queue.finishTransaction(t)
            case .failed:
                queue.finishTransaction(t)
            }
        }
    }
```

Finally, let's talk about what to do when the user taps the Restore button (on the left in Figure 24-2). It's very simple; I just tell the default SKPaymentQueue to restore any existing purchases:

```
self.dismiss(animated: true) {
    SKPaymentQueue.default().restoreCompletedTransactions()
}
```

Again, what happens now in the interface is out of my hands; the system will present the necessary dialogs. If the purchase is restored, my transaction observer will be sent paymentQueue(_:updatedTransactions:) with a transactionState of .restored. We pass through exactly the same case in my switch as if the user had freshly purchased the app; as before, I set the UserDefaults flag indicating that the user has performed the purchase.

There remains one piece of the puzzle: what if the user taps the Restore button and the purchase is *not* restored? This might happen because the user is lying or mistaken about having previously made this purchase. In that case, paymentQueue(_:updated-Transactions:) is *not* called. (I regard this as a bug in the store architecture; in my opinion, we should be called with a .failed transaction state.)

As a workaround, we can implement the SKPaymentTransactionObserver method paymentQueueRestoreCompletedTransactionsFinished(_:). It is called after any restoration attempt where communication with the store was successful. This method still gives us no way to learn definitively what happened; but if payment-Queue(_:updatedTransactions:) is called, it is called first, so if we find in payment-QueueRestoreCompletedTransactionsFinished(_:) that the UserDefaults flag has not been set, we can guess that restoration failed because the user has never made the purchase in the first place.

Before releasing your app to the general public, you'll want to test your app's in-app purchase interface and functionality. New in Xcode 14, you can do that without doing any networking and without even having configured things at App Store Connect:

1. Choose File → New → File and Other → StoreKit Configuration File.

2. In the editor, click the Plus button to add and configure an in-app purchase or subscription.

3. Edit the scheme. In the Run action, under Options, choose your configuration file from the StoreKit Configuration pop-up menu.

You can now run your app and exercise its Store Kit–related functionality. You won't see any dialogs asking you to sign in or authenticate, because you're not doing any networking. Moreover, you can manipulate the simulated App Store, to test different aspects of your app's behavior. There are two places where you can do that:

The Transactions window
Choose from the Debug → StoreKit menu (or the Manage StoreKit Transactions pop-up menu in the debug bar) to bring up the Transactions window. You can leave the Transactions window open, but it will display transactions only while the app is running from Xcode.

The configuration file
Edit the StoreKit configuration file and look in the Editor menu.

You can enact various test scenarios. Here are some of them:

- In your app, perform a purchase. Your purchase dialog gets its product information from the configuration file. In the Transactions window, you'll see the purchase registered as a transaction.

- In the configuration file's Editor menu, enable interrupted transactions to make the next purchase fail temporarily; when it does, switch to the Transactions window and make it succeed.

- In the configuration file's Editor menu, make future transactions emit a server error; now perform a purchase and see how your app behaves.

- If the in-app purchase is a subscription, use the configuration file's Editor menu to set the rate at which time passes, so that you can see what happens when the subscription expires.

Moreover, the StoreKitTest framework contains special test classes that mock the store, letting you perform unit tests and UI tests as if your app really were talking to the store. When you're done testing locally, don't forget to change the scheme's StoreKit Configuration back to None! For more information, see "Setting Up Store-Kit Testing in Xcode" in the help documentation.

To test with real networking, you create a special Apple ID, called a *sandbox* ID, for testing purposes. Sandbox IDs are created and managed in the Users and Roles section of App Store Connect. You then configure your device (in the Settings app, under App Store → Sandbox Account) to use the sandbox ID when testing. When you build your app onto your device and run it, if you make an in-app purchase, your sandbox ID is used and you are not charged for the purchase. (A downside of this approach is that you have to remember your sandbox account password.)

A simpler approach is to upload your app to App Store Connect and make it available through TestFlight. When a TestFlight tester uses your app's in-app purchase feature, the tester's normal account and password are used, but no actual charge is made.

Unfortunately, in neither scenario are the alerts that the system displays identical to those that a real user would see while making the in-app purchase. As a result, testing in-app purchase functionality remains something of a gamble.

Threads

A *thread* is a subprocess of your app that can execute even while other subprocesses are also executing. Such simultaneous execution is called *concurrency*. The iOS frameworks use threads all the time; if they didn't, your app would be less responsive to the user — perhaps completely unresponsive. For the most part, the iOS frameworks use threads behind the scenes on your behalf; you don't have to worry about threads because the frameworks are worrying about them for you.

Suppose your app is downloading something from the network (Chapter 24). This download doesn't happen all by itself; somewhere, someone is running code that interacts with the network and obtains data. Yet none of that interferes with your code, or prevents the user from tapping and swiping things in your interface. The networking code runs "in the background." That's concurrency in action.

This chapter discusses concurrency that involves *your* code in the use of background threads. It would have been nice to dispense with this topic altogether. Background threads can be tricky and are always potentially dangerous, and should be avoided if possible. But sometimes you *can't* avoid them. So this chapter introduces threads. But beware: background threads entail complications and subtle pitfalls, and can make your code hard to debug. There is much more to threads, and especially to making your threaded code safe, than this chapter can possibly touch on. For detailed information about the topics introduced in this chapter, read Apple's *Concurrency Programming Guide* and *Threading Programming Guide* in the documentation archive.

Main Thread

Distinguish between the *main* thread and all other threads. There is only one main thread; other threads are background threads.

Figure 25-1. The Main Thread Checker is watching you

All your code must run on some thread, but you are not usually conscious of this fact, because that thread is usually the main thread. Why! Well, the only reason your code *ever* runs is that Cocoa calls it — and Cocoa usually calls your code from the main thread.

The main thread is the interface thread. This means that the main thread is the meeting-place between you and your user. When the user interacts with the interface, those interactions are reported as events *on the main thread.* When your code interacts with the interface, it must do so *on the main thread.* Of course that will usually happen automatically, because your code normally runs on the main thread. But when you are involved with background threads, you must be careful.

So pretend now that I'm banging the table and shouting: If your code touches the interface, it *must* do so *on the main thread.* Don't *fetch* any interface-related values on a background thread. Don't *set* any interface-related values on a background thread. Whenever you use background threads, there is a chance you might touch the interface on a background thread. *Don't!*

Touching the interface on a background thread is a very common beginner mistake. A typical sign of trouble is an unaccountable delay of several seconds. In some cases, the console may help with a warning. Also, Xcode's Main Thread Checker will automatically report runtime violations; it's a diagnostic in your scheme's Run and Test actions (Figure 25-1), and is turned on by default.

Since you and the user are both using the main thread, the main thread is a very busy place. Imagine how things proceed in your app:

1. An event arrives — on the main thread. If the user has tapped a button, this is reported to your app as a UIEvent, which passes to the button through the touch delivery mechanism (Chapter 5) — on the main thread.

2. The button emits a control event (Chapter 13) that causes your code (the button's action method) to be called — on the main thread. Your code now runs — on the main thread. *While your code runs, nothing else can happen on the main thread.* Your code might perform some changes in the interface; this is safe, because your code is running — where? — on the main thread.

3. Your code finishes. The main thread's run loop is now free to report more events, and the user is free to interact with the interface once again.

The bottleneck here is the running of your code. Your code runs on the main thread. That means the main thread can't do anything else while your code is running. No events can arrive while your code is running. The user can't interact with the interface while your code is running. Two things can't happen on the main thread at the same time, so main thread code *blocks* the main thread and therefore *blocks* the interface. But this is usually no problem, because:

Your code is fast

Your code executes really fast. It's true that the user can't interact with the interface while your code runs, but this is such a tiny interval of time that the user will probably never notice.

Blocking briefly is good

Your code, as it runs, blocks the user from interacting with the interface. As long as your code finishes quickly, that's actually a good thing! Your code, in response to what the user does, might update the interface; it would be insane if the user could do something else in the interface while you're in the middle of updating it.

Background Threads

The iOS frameworks frequently operate on background threads. This usually doesn't affect you, because the frameworks usually talk to *your* code on the *main* thread:

- During an animation (Chapter 4), the interface remains responsive to the user, and it is possible for your code to run. The Core Animation framework is running the animation and updating the presentation layer on a background thread. But your delegate methods and completion functions are called on the main thread.

- A web view's fetching and loading of its content is asynchronous (Chapter 12); that means the work is done in a background thread. But your delegate methods are called on the main thread.

- Sounds are played asynchronously (Chapters 15 and 17). Loading, preparation, and playing of movies happens asynchronously (Chapter 16). But your delegate methods are called on the main thread.

- Saving a movie file takes time (Chapters 16 and 18). So the saving takes place on a background thread. UIDocument saves and reads on a background thread (Chapter 23). But your delegate methods and completion functions are called on the main thread.

You can (and should) usually ignore the existence of background threads and just keep plugging away on the main thread. Nevertheless, there are two kinds of situation in which your code will need to be explicitly aware of background threads:

Your code is called back, but not on the main thread

Some frameworks explicitly inform you in their documentation that callbacks are not guaranteed to take place on the main thread. The documentation on CATiledLayer (Chapter 7) warns that `draw(_:in:)` is called on a background thread. By implication, our `draw(_:)` code, triggered by CATiledLayer to update tiles, is running on a background thread. (Fortunately, drawing into the current graphics context is thread-safe.)

Similarly, the documentation on AV Foundation (Chapters 16 and 18) warns that its completion functions and notifications can arrive on a background thread. So if you intend to update the user interface, or use a value that might also be used by your main thread code, you'll need to switch explicitly to the main thread.

Your code takes significant time

If your code takes significant time to run, you might need to run that code on a background thread, rather than letting it block the main thread and prevent anything else from happening there:

During launch and other app state transitions

In Chapter 23, we called `URL(forUbiquityContainerIdentifier:)` during app launch. The documentation told us to call this method on a background thread, because it can take some time to return; we don't want to block the main thread waiting for it, because the app is trying to launch on the main thread, and the user won't see our interface until the launch process is over.

Similarly, when the app is in the process of being suspended into the background, or resumed from the background, our code should not occupy the main thread; it must act quickly and get out of the way.

When the user can see or interact with the app

In Chapter 20, we called `enumerateEvents(matching:using:)` on a background thread, because it can take some time to run. If we were to call this method on the main thread, then when the user taps the button that triggers this call, the button might stay highlighted for a significant amount of time, during which the interface would be completely frozen. We would be perceptibly blocking the main thread.

Similarly, in a table view data source (Chapter 8), `tableView(_:cellForRowAt:)` needs to be fast. Otherwise, the user won't be able to scroll the table view; we'll be freezing the interface because we are blocking the main thread.

Moving time-consuming code off the main thread, so that the main thread is not blocked, isn't just a matter of aesthetics or politeness: the system "watchdog" will summarily *kill the app* if it discovers that the main thread is blocked for too long.

Why Threading Is Hard

The one certain thing about computer code is that it just clunks along the path of execution, one statement at a time. Successive lines of code are performed in the order in which they appear, and nothing else happens between them. With threading, that certainty goes right out the window.

If you have code that can be performed on a background thread, then *you don't know* when your code will be performed. Your code is now *concurrent*. This means that any line of your background-thread code could be *interleaved* between any two lines of your main-thread code. Indeed, under certain circumstances, your background-thread code can be called multiple times on multiple background threads, meaning that any line of your background-thread code could be interleaved between any two lines of *itself*.

The reason this can be problematic is because of *shared data*. There are variables in your app, such as instance properties, that persist and can be accessed from multiple places. Background threads mean that such variables can be accessed at unexpected moments. That is a really scary thought. Suppose, while one thread is in the middle of using a variable, another thread changes it. Who knows what horrors might result?

You can't work around this issue by mere logic. Suppose you try to make access to a variable safe with a condition, as in this pseudocode:

```
if no other thread is touching this variable {
    ... do something to the variable ...
}
```

Such logic is specious. Suppose the condition succeeds: no other thread is touching this variable. But between the time when that condition is evaluated and the time when the next line executes and you start to do something to the variable, another thread can still come along and start touching the variable!

It is possible to request assistance at a deeper level to ensure that a section of code is not run by two threads simultaneously. For example, you can implement a *lock* around a section of code. But locks generate an entirely new level of potential pitfalls. In general, a lock is an invitation to forget to use the lock, or to forget to remove the lock after you've set it. And threads can end up contending for a lock in a way that permits neither thread to proceed.

Another problem has to do with thread *lifetimes*. The lifetime of a thread is independent of the lifetimes of other objects in your app. When an object is about to go out of existence and its `deinit` has been called and executed, you are supposed to be guaranteed that none of your code in that object will ever run again. But a thread might still be running, and might try to talk to your object, even after your object has supposedly gone out of existence. This can result in a crash, if you're lucky; if you're not lucky, your object might become a kind of zombie.

Not only is threaded code hard to get right; it's also hard to test and hard to debug. It introduces indeterminacy, so you can easily make a mistake that never appears in your testing, but that does appear for some user. The real danger is that the user's experience will consist only of distant consequences of your mistake, long after the point where you made it, making the true cause of the problem extraordinarily difficult to track down.

Perhaps you think I'm trying to scare you away from using threads. You're right! For an excellent (and suitably frightening) account of some of the dangers and considerations that threading involves, see Apple's technical note "Simple and Reliable Threading with NSOperation" in the documentation archive. If terms like *race condition* and *deadlock* don't strike fear into your veins, look them up on Wikipedia.

Naturally, Xcode provides lots of aids to assist you in studying your app's use of threads:

- The Debug navigator distinguishes threads; you can even see pending calls and learn when a call was enqueued.
- When you call `NSLog` or `os_log` (or the new Logger class), the output in the console displays a number identifying the thread on which it was called.
- In Instruments, the Time Profiler records activity on different threads.
- The Thread Sanitizer (visible in Figure 25-1) can help catch possible race conditions and other issues (look up "Thread Sanitizer" in the documentation).

Blocking the Main Thread

To illustrate making your code multithreaded, I need some code that is worth making multithreaded. I'll use as my example a simple app that draws the Mandelbrot set in black and white. (This code is adapted from a small open source project found on the internet.) That's a sufficiently elaborate calculation to introduce a significant delay, depending on the speed of the device and the number of iterations. The idea is to see how we can safely get that delay off the main thread.

The app contains a UIView subclass, MyMandelbrotView, which has one property, a CGContext called `bitmapContext`. Here's MyMandelbrotView:

```
let MANDELBROT_STEPS = 100 // determines how long the calculation takes
var bitmapContext: CGContext!
// jumping-off point: draw the Mandelbrot set
func drawThatPuppy () {
    self.makeBitmapContext(size: self.bounds.size)
    let center = self.bounds.center
    self.draw(center: center, bounds: self.bounds, zoom: 1)
    self.setNeedsDisplay()
}
// create bitmap context
func makeBitmapContext(size:CGSize) {
    var bitmapBytesPerRow = Int(size.width * 4)
    bitmapBytesPerRow += (16 - (bitmapBytesPerRow % 16)) % 16
    let colorSpace = CGColorSpaceCreateDeviceRGB()
    let prem = CGImageAlphaInfo.premultipliedLast.rawValue
    let context = CGContext(data: nil,
        width: Int(size.width), height: Int(size.height),
        bitsPerComponent: 8, bytesPerRow: bitmapBytesPerRow,
        space: colorSpace, bitmapInfo: prem)
    self.bitmapContext = context
}
// draw pixels of bitmap context
func draw(center:CGPoint, bounds:CGRect, zoom:CGFloat) {
    func isInMandelbrotSet(_ re:Float, _ im:Float) -> Bool {
        var fl = true
        var (x, y, nx, ny) : (Float, Float, Float, Float) = (0,0,0,0)
        for _ in 0 ..< MANDELBROT_STEPS {
            nx = x*x - y*y + re
            ny = 2*x*y + im
            if nx*nx + ny*ny > 4 {
                fl = false
                break
            }
            x = nx
            y = ny
        }
        return fl
    }
    self.bitmapContext.setAllowsAntialiasing(false)
    self.bitmapContext.setFillColor(red: 0, green: 0, blue: 0, alpha: 1)
    var re : CGFloat
    var im : CGFloat
    let maxi = Int(bounds.size.width)
    let maxj = Int(bounds.size.height)
    for i in 0 ..< maxi {
        for j in 0 ..< maxj {
            re = (CGFloat(i) - 1.33 * center.x) / 160
            im = (CGFloat(j) - 1.0 * center.y) / 160
            re /= zoom
            im /= zoom
            if (isInMandelbrotSet(Float(re), Float(im))) {
                self.bitmapContext.fill(
```

```
                CGRect(CGFloat(i), CGFloat(j), 1.0, 1.0))
            }
        }
    }
}
// turn pixels of bitmap context into CGImage, draw into ourselves
override func draw(_ rect: CGRect) {
    if self.bitmapContext != nil {
        let context = UIGraphicsGetCurrentContext()!
        let im = self.bitmapContext.makeImage()
        context.draw(im!, in: self.bounds)
    }
}
```

The draw(center:bounds:zoom:) method, which calculates the pixels of self.bitmapContext, is time-consuming, and we can see this by running the app on a device. If the entire process is kicked off by tapping a button whose action method calls drawThatPuppy, there is a significant delay before the Mandelbrot graphic appears in the interface, during which time the button remains highlighted and the interface is frozen. This is a sure sign that we are blocking the main thread.

We need to move the calculation-intensive part of this code onto a background thread, so that the main thread is not blocked by the calculation. In doing so, we have two chief concerns:

Synchronization of threads

> The button is tapped, and drawThatPuppy is called, on the main thread. And set-NeedsDisplay, and therefore draw(_:), are also called on the main thread — rightly, since they affect the interface. In between, the calculation-intensive draw(center:bounds:zoom:) is to be called on a background thread. Yet these methods must still run *in order*: drawThatPuppy on the main thread, then draw(center:bounds:zoom:) on a background thread, then setNeedsDisplay and draw(_:) on the main thread. But background threads are concurrent, so how will we ensure this?

Shared data

> The property self.bitmapContext is referred to in three different methods — in makeBitmapContext(size:), and in draw(center:bounds:zoom:), and in draw(_:). But we have just said that those three methods involve two different threads; they must not be permitted to touch the same property in a way that might conflict or clash. Indeed, because draw(center:bounds:zoom:) runs on a background thread, it might run on multiple background threads simultaneously; the access to self.bitmapContext by draw(center:bounds:zoom:) must not be permitted to conflict or clash *with itself*. How will we ensure this?

Manual Threading

A naïve way of dealing with our time-consuming code would involve spawning off a background thread as we reach the calculation-intensive part of the procedure, by calling `performSelector(inBackground:with:)`. This is a very bad idea, and you should *not* imitate the code in this section. I'm showing it to you only to demonstrate how horrible it is.

Adapting your code to use `performSelector(inBackground:with:)` is not at all simple. There is additional work to do:

Pack the arguments

> The method designated by the selector in `performSelector(inBackground:with:)` can take only one parameter, whose value you supply as the second argument. So if you want to pass more than one piece of information into the thread, you'll need to pack it into a single object. Typically, this will be a dictionary.

Set up an autorelease pool

> Background threads don't participate in the global autorelease pool. So the first thing you must do in your threaded code is to wrap everything in an autorelease pool. Otherwise, you'll probably leak memory as autoreleased objects are created behind the scenes and are never released.

We'll rewrite MyMandelbrotView to use manual threading. Because our `draw(center:bounds:zoom:)` method takes three parameters, the argument that we pass into the thread will have to pack that information into a dictionary. Once inside the thread, we'll set up our autorelease pool and unpack the dictionary. This will all be much easier if we interpose a trampoline method between `drawThatPuppy` and `draw(center:bounds:zoom:)`. So our implementation now starts like this:

```
func drawThatPuppy () {
    self.makeBitmapContext(size:self.bounds.size)
    let center = self.bounds.center
    let d : [AnyHashable:Any] =
        ["center":center, "bounds":self.bounds, "zoom":CGFloat(1)]
    self.performSelector(inBackground: #selector(reallyDraw), with: d)
}
// trampoline, background thread entry point
@objc func reallyDraw(_ d: [AnyHashable:Any]) {
    autoreleasepool {
        self.draw(center: d["center"] as! CGPoint,
            bounds: d["bounds"] as! CGRect,
            zoom: d["zoom"] as! CGFloat)
        // ...
    }
}
```

In the trampoline method reallyDraw(_:), the comment with the ellipsis indicates a missing piece of functionality: we have yet to call setNeedsDisplay, which will cause the actual drawing to take place. This call used to be in drawThatPuppy, but that is now too soon; the call to performSelector(inBackground:with:) launches the thread and returns immediately, so our bitmapContext property isn't ready yet. Clearly, we need to call setNeedsDisplay *after* draw(center:bounds:zoom:) has finished generating the pixels of the graphics context.

But reallyDraw(_:) runs in a background thread. Because setNeedsDisplay is a form of communication with the interface, we should call it on the main thread, with performSelector(onMainThread:with:waitUntilDone:). It will probably be best to implement a second trampoline method:

```
// trampoline, background thread entry point
func reallyDraw(_ d: [AnyHashable:Any]) {
    autoreleasepool {
        self.draw(center: d["center"] as! CGPoint,
            bounds: d["bounds"] as! CGRect,
            zoom: d["zoom"] as! CGFloat)
        self.performSelector(onMainThread: #selector(allDone), with: nil,
            waitUntilDone: false)
    }
}
// called on main thread! background thread exit point
@objc func allDone() {
    self.setNeedsDisplay()
}
```

This works, in the sense that when we tap the button, it is highlighted momentarily and then immediately unhighlighted; the time-consuming calculation is taking place on a background thread. But the seeds of nightmare are already sown:

- We now have a single object, MyMandelbrotView, some of whose methods are to be called on the main thread and some on a background thread; this invites us to become confused at some later time.

- The main thread and the background thread are constantly sharing a piece of data, the instance property self.bitmapContext; this is messy and fragile. And what's to stop some other code from coming along and triggering draw(_:) while draw(center:bounds:zoom:) is in the middle of manipulating the bitmap context that draw(_:) draws?

To solve these problems, we might need to use locks, and we would probably have to manage the thread more explicitly. Such code can become quite elaborate and difficult to understand; guaranteeing its integrity is even more difficult. There are much better ways, and I will now demonstrate two of them.

Operation

An excellent strategy is to turn to the Operation and OperationQueue classes. The essence of Operation is that it encapsulates a *task*, not a thread. You don't concern yourself with threads directly; the threading is determined for you by an Operation-Queue. You describe the task as an Operation, and you add that Operation to an OperationQueue to set it going. You can arrange to be notified when the task ends, typically by the Operation posting a notification. (You can also safely query both the queue and its operations from outside with regard to their state.)

We'll rewrite MyMandelbrotView to use Operation and OperationQueue. We need an OperationQueue object. I'll make this an instance property (`self.queue`), and I'll create the queue and configure it in the property's initializer:

```
let queue : OperationQueue = {
    let q = OperationQueue()
    // ... further configurations can go here ...
    return q
}()
```

We also have a new class, MyMandelbrotOperation, an Operation subclass. (It is possible to take advantage of a built-in Operation subclass such as BlockOperation, but I'm deliberately illustrating the more general case by subclassing Operation itself.) Our implementation of `drawThatPuppy` creates an instance of MyMandelbrot-Operation, configures it, registers for its notification, and adds it to the queue:

```
func drawThatPuppy () {
    let center = self.bounds.center
    let op = MyMandelbrotOperation(
        center: center, bounds: self.bounds, zoom: 1)
    NotificationCenter.default.addObserver(self,
        selector: #selector(operationFinished),
        name: MyMandelbrotOperation.mandelOpFinished, object: op)
    self.queue.addOperation(op)
}
```

Our time-consuming calculations will be performed by MyMandelbrotOperation. An Operation subclass, such as MyMandelbrotOperation, will typically have at least two methods:

A designated initializer

The Operation may need some configuration data. Once the Operation is added to a queue, it's too late to talk to it, so you'll usually hand it this configuration data as you create it, in its designated initializer.

A `main` method

This method will be called automatically by the OperationQueue when it's time for the Operation to start.

MyMandelbrotOperation has three private properties center, bounds, and zoom, to be set in its initializer; it must be told MyMandelbrotView's geometry explicitly because it is completely separate from MyMandelbrotView. MyMandelbrotOperation also has its own CGContext property, bitmapContext; it must be publicly gettable so that MyMandelbrotView can retrieve the finished graphics context. Note that this is different from MyMandelbrotView's bitmapContext, helping to solve the problem of sharing data promiscuously between threads:

```
static let mandelOpFinished = Notification.Name("mandelOpFinished")
private let center : CGPoint
private let bounds : CGRect
private let zoom : CGFloat
private(set) var bitmapContext : CGContext! = nil
init(center c:CGPoint, bounds b:CGRect, zoom z:CGFloat) {
    self.center = c
    self.bounds = b
    self.zoom = z
    super.init()
}
```

makeBitmapContext(size:) and draw(center:bounds:zoom:), the methods that perform the time-consuming calculation, can be transferred from MyMandelbrotView to MyMandelbrotOperation unchanged; the only difference is that when these methods refer to self.bitmapContext, that now means MyMandelbrotOperation's bitmapContext property:

```
let MANDELBROT_STEPS = 100
func makeBitmapContext(size:CGSize) {
    // ... same as before
}
func draw(center:CGPoint, bounds:CGRect, zoom:CGFloat) {
    // ... same as before
}
```

Finally we come to MyMandelbrotOperation's main method. First we check the Operation isCancelled property to make sure we haven't been cancelled while sitting in the queue; this is good practice. Then we do exactly what drawThatPuppy used to do, initializing our graphics context and drawing into its pixels.

At that point, the calculation is over and it's time for MyMandelbrotView to come and fetch our data. There are two ways in which MyMandelbrotView can learn this; either main can post a notification through the NotificationCenter, or MyMandelbrotView can use key–value observing to be notified when our isFinished property changes. We've chosen the former approach; observe that we check one more time to make sure we haven't been cancelled:

```
override func main() {
    guard !self.isCancelled else {return}
    self.makeBitmapContext(size: self.bounds.size)
    self.draw(center: self.center, bounds: self.bounds, zoom: self.zoom)
    if !self.isCancelled {
        NotificationCenter.default.post(
            name: MyMandelbrotOperation.mandelOpFinished, object: self)
    }
}
```

Now we are back in MyMandelbrotView, hearing through the notification that MyMandelbrotOperation has finished. We must immediately pick up any required data, because the OperationQueue is about to release this Operation. However, we must be careful: the notification may have been posted on a background thread, in which case our method for responding to it will also be called on a background thread. We are about to set our own graphics context and tell ourselves to redraw; those are things we want to do on the main thread. So we immediately step out to the main thread (using Grand Central Dispatch, described more fully in the next section). We remove ourselves as notification observer for this operation instance, copy the operation's `bitmapContext` into our own `bitmapContext`, and we're ready to redraw:

```
// warning! called on background thread
@objc func operationFinished(_ n:Notification) {
    if let op = n.object as? MyMandelbrotOperation {
        DispatchQueue.main.async {
            NotificationCenter.default.removeObserver(self,
                name: MyMandelbrotOperation.mandelOpFinished, object: op)
            self.bitmapContext = op.bitmapContext
            self.setNeedsDisplay()
        }
    }
}
```

Adapting our code to use Operation has involved some work, but the result has many advantages that help to ensure that our use of multiple threads is coherent and safe:

The background task is encapsulated

Because MyMandelbrotOperation is an object, we've been able to move all the code having to do with drawing the pixels of the Mandelbrot set into it. The *only* MyMandelbrotView method that can be called in the background is operation-Finished(_:), and that's a method we'd never call explicitly ourselves, so we won't misuse it accidentally — and it immediately steps out to the main thread in any case.

The data sharing is rationalized

Because MyMandelbrotOperation is an object, it has its own `bitmapContext` property. The only moment of data sharing comes in operationFinished(_:), when we must set MyMandelbrotView's `bitmapContext` to MyMandelbrot-Operation's `bitmapContext` — and that happens on the main thread, so there's no danger. Even if multiple MyMandelbrotOperation objects are added to the queue, they are separate objects with separate `bitmapContext` properties, which MyMandelbrotView retrieves only on the main thread, so there is no conflict.

The threads are synchronized

The calculation-intensive MyMandelbrotOperation doesn't start until MyMandelbrotView calls `self.queue.addOperation(op)` to enqueue it. After that, MyMandelbrotView takes its hands off the steering wheel and makes *no* attempt to draw itself. If `draw(_:)` is unexpectedly called by the runtime, `self.bitmapContext` will be nil or will contain the results of an earlier calculation operation, and no harm done. Nothing else happens until the operation ends and the notification arrives (`operationFinished(_:)`); then and only then does MyMandelbrotView update the interface — on the main thread.

If we are concerned with the possibility that more than one instance of MyMandelbrotOperation might be added to the queue and executed concurrently, we have a further line of defense — we can set the OperationQueue's maximum concurrency level to 1:

```
let q = OperationQueue()
q.maxConcurrentOperationCount = 1
```

This turns the OperationQueue into a *serial* queue: every operation on the queue must be completely executed before the next can begin. This might cause an operation added to the queue to take longer to execute, if it must wait for another operation to finish before it can even get started; however, this delay might not be important. What *is* important is that by executing the operations on this queue separately from one another, we guarantee that only one operation at a time can do any data sharing. A serial queue is therefore implicitly a safe and reliable form of data locking.

Because MyMandelbrotView can be destroyed (if its view controller is destroyed), there is a risk that it will create an operation that will outlive it. So a MyMandelbrotOperation might try to access a MyMandelbrotView that no longer exists. We can reduce that risk by cancelling all operations in our queue as MyMandelbrotView goes out of existence:

```
deinit {
    self.queue.cancelAllOperations()
}
```

There is more to know about Operation; it's a powerful tool. One Operation can have another Operation as a *dependency*, meaning that the former cannot start until the latter has finished, even if they are in different OperationQueues. Moreover, the behavior of an Operation can be customized; for instance, an Operation subclass can override built in state instance properties such as isReady and isFinished, as well as the start and main methods, so as to control when it is capable of execution. Using these features, operations can be combined to express your app's logic, guaranteeing the order in which things happen (cogently argued in a brilliant WWDC 2015 video).

Grand Central Dispatch

Grand Central Dispatch, or *GCD*, is a sort of low-level analogue to Operation and OperationQueue; in fact, OperationQueue uses GCD under the hood. When I say GCD is low-level, I'm not kidding; it is effectively baked into the operating system kernel. It can be used by any code whatsoever and is tremendously efficient.

GCD is like OperationQueue in that it uses queues: you express a task and add it to a queue, and the task is executed on a thread as needed. A GCD queue is represented by a *dispatch queue* (DispatchQueue), a lightweight opaque pseudo-object consisting essentially of a list of functions to be executed. You can use a built-in system queue or you can make your own; if you make your own, your queue by default is a *serial* queue, with each task on that queue finishing before the next is started — which, as I've already said, is a form of data locking.

We'll rewrite MyMandelbrotView to use GCD. We start by creating a queue; I'll store it in an instance property:

```
let MANDELBROT_STEPS = 100
var bitmapContext: CGContext!
let draw_queue = DispatchQueue(label: "com.neuburg.mandeldraw")
```

Our goal is to eliminate data sharing, so our makeBitmapContext(size:) method now returns a graphics context rather than setting a property directly:

```
func makeBitmapContext(size:CGSize) -> CGContext {
    // ... as before ...
    let context = CGContext(data: nil,
        width: Int(size.width), height: Int(size.height),
        bitsPerComponent: 8, bytesPerRow: bitmapBytesPerRow,
        space: colorSpace, bitmapInfo: prem)
    return context!
}
```

For the same reason, our draw(center:bounds:zoom:) method now takes an additional context: parameter — the graphics context to draw into — and operates on that context without ever referring to self.bitmapContext:

```
func draw(center:CGPoint, bounds:CGRect, zoom:CGFloat, context:CGContext) {
    // ... as before, but we refer to local context, not self.bitmapContext
}
```

Now for the implementation of drawThatPuppy. This is where all the action is:

```
func drawThatPuppy () {
    let center = self.bounds.center
    let bounds = self.bounds ❶
    self.draw_queue.async { ❷
        let bitmap = self.makeBitmapContext(size: bounds.size) ❸
        self.draw(center: center, bounds: bounds, zoom: 1, context: bitmap)
        DispatchQueue.main.async { ❹
            self.bitmapContext = bitmap ❺
            self.setNeedsDisplay()
        }
    }
}
```

That's all there is to it: *all* our app's multithreading is concentrated in those few lines! There are no notifications; there is no sharing of data between threads; and the synchronization of our threads is expressed directly through the sequential order of the code.

Our code makes two calls to the DispatchQueue `async` method, which takes as its parameter a function — usually, an anonymous function — expressing what we want done asynchronously on this queue. This is the GCD method you'll use most, because asynchronous execution will be your primary reason for using GCD in the first place.

Our two calls to `async` are *nested* — the first call takes an anonymous function, which contains the second call, which takes another anonymous function. This nesting is crucial, because trailing anonymous functions are closures that can see the higher surrounding scope. As a result, we don't need to pass any parameters from an outer scope to an inner scope. The local variables `center` and `bounds` simply "fall" into the anonymous function of the first call to `async`, and the local variable `bitmap` simply "falls" into the anonymous function of the second call to `async`. There is no data sharing, because values *cascade* from one scope into the next, in sequence.

Here's how `drawThatPuppy` works:

❶ We begin by calculating our `center` and `bounds` (on the main thread). These local variables will be visible within the subsequent anonymous functions, because a function body's code can see its surrounding context and capture it.

❷ Now comes the task to be performed in a separate background thread on our queue, `self.draw_queue`. We specify this task with the `async` method. We describe what we want to do on the background thread in an anonymous function.

❸ In the anonymous function, we begin by declaring `bitmap` as a *local* variable. This is our graphics context. We call `makeBitmapContext(size:)` to create it, and then call `draw(center:bounds:zoom:context:)` to set its pixels. Those calls are made on a *background* thread, because `self.draw_queue` is a background queue.

❹ Now we need to step back out to the *main* thread. How do we do that? With the `async` method again! This time, we specify the main queue (which is effectively the main thread), whose name is `DispatchQueue.main`. We describe what we want to do on the main queue in *another* anonymous function.

❺ Here we are in the second anonymous function. Because the first function is part of the second function's surrounding context, the second function can see the first function's local `bitmap` variable. Using it, we set our `bitmapContext` property and call `setNeedsDisplay` — on the main thread! — and we're done.

The benefits of GCD as a form of concurrency management are stunning:

No data sharing
> The only time we ever refer to a property of `self` is at the start (`self.bounds`) and at the end (`self.bitmapContext`), when we are *on the main thread*. The bitmap context where all the drawing action takes place is a *local* variable, `bitmap`, confined to each individual call to `drawThatPuppy`. Moreover, that drawing action is performed on a serial queue, so no two drawing actions can ever overlap.

Transparent synchronization of threads
> The threads are correctly synchronized, and this is *obvious*, because the nested anonymous functions are executed *in succession*, so any instance of `bitmap` must be completely filled with pixels before being used to set the `bitmapContext` property.

Maintainability and readability
> Our code is easy to maintain, because the entire task on all threads is expressed within the single `drawThatPuppy` method; indeed, the code is modified only very slightly from the original nonthreaded version. The code is also easy to read and understand, because the path of execution passes sequentially from the first line of `drawThatPuppy` to the last line — the very thing we were worried might *not* happen when we adopted background threading in the first place.

You might object that we still have the methods `makeBitmapContext(size:)` and `draw(center:bounds:zoom:context:)` hanging around MyMandelbrotView, and that we must therefore still be careful not to call them on the main thread, or indeed from anywhere except from within `drawThatPuppy`. If that were true, we could at this point destroy both methods and move their functionality completely into `drawThatPuppy`. But we don't have to, because these methods are now *thread-safe*: they are self-contained utilities that touch no properties or persistent objects, so it doesn't matter what thread they are called on. Still, I'll demonstrate later how we can intercept an accidental attempt to call a method on the wrong thread.

Commonly Used GCD Methods

The most important DispatchQueue methods are:

`async(execute:)`
> Pushes a function onto the end of a queue for later execution; the queue will determine when the function will execute, and meanwhile we *proceed immediately* with the next line of our own code without waiting for that to happen (see Appendix C). Commonly, there is *no* next line of our own code; an async call is usually the last statement in its scope. Use this method to execute code in a background thread, or from *within* a background thread to step back onto the main thread.

`asyncAfter(deadline:execute:)`
> Similar to async, but the enqueued function runs only after a certain amount of time has been permitted to elapse following the call (*delayed performance*). Many examples in this book have made use of this method (through my delay utility function; see Appendix B).

`sync(execute:)`
> Pushes a function onto the end of a queue for later execution, and *waits* until the function has executed before proceeding with our own code. You should use this method only in special circumstances, typically where you need the queue as a lock (mediating access to a shared resource) but you also need to *use a result* that the function is to provide.

Synchronous Execution

The use of `sync(execute:)` is sufficiently unusual that it deserves an example. Let's say we'd like to revise the Downloader class from Chapter 24 so that the delegate methods are run on a background thread, taking some strain off the main thread (and hence the user interface) while these messages are flying around behind the scenes. This is reasonable and safe, because the URLSession and its delegate are packaged inside the Downloader object, isolated from our view controller.

To begin with, we'll need our own background OperationQueue, which we can maintain as an instance property of Downloader:

```
let queue = OperationQueue()
```

Our session is now configured and created using this background queue:

```
lazy var session : URLSession = {
    return URLSession(configuration:self.config,
        delegate:DownloaderDelegate(), delegateQueue:self.queue)
}()
```

This means that `urlSession(_:downloadTask:didFinishDownloadingTo:)` will be called on our background queue. So what will happen when we call back into the client through the completion function that the client handed us at the outset? To avoid involving the client in threading issues, we'll step out to the main thread as we call the completion function. But we cannot do this by calling `async`:

```
let ch = self.handlers[downloadTask.taskIdentifier]
DispatchQueue.main.async { // bad idea!
    ch?(url)
}
```

The reason is that the downloaded file is slated to be *destroyed* as soon as we return from `urlSession(_:downloadTask:didFinishDownloadingTo:)` — and if we call `async`, we will return *immediately*, the downloaded file *will* be destroyed, and `url` will end up pointing at nothing by the time the client receives it! The solution is to use `sync` instead:

```
let ch = self.handlers[downloadTask.taskIdentifier]
DispatchQueue.main.sync {
    ch?(url)
}
```

That code steps out to the main thread and also postpones returning from `url-Session(_:downloadTask:didFinishDownloadingTo:)` until the client has had an opportunity to do something with the file pointed to by `url`. In this way we lock down the shared data (the downloaded file). We are blocking our background OperationQueue, but this is legal, and in any case we're blocking very briefly and in a coherent manner. (This is effectively identical to, and used for the same purpose as, the `DispatchQueue.main.sync` code in Chapter 18.)

 Do not call `DispatchQueue.main.sync` if you are already *on* the main queue! That's an instant deadlock and your code will grind to a complete halt.

Dispatch Groups

A dispatch group effectively combines independent tasks into a single task; we proceed only when *all* of them have completed. Its usage is structured as in Example 25-1.

Example 25-1. Dispatch group usage

```
let group = DispatchGroup()
// here we go...
group.enter()
queue1.async {
    // ... do task here ...
    group.leave()
}
group.enter()
queue2.async {
    // ... do task here ...
    group.leave()
}
group.enter()
queue3.async {
    // ... do task here ...
    group.leave()
}
// ... more as needed ...
group.notify(queue: DispatchQueue.main) {
    // finished!
}
```

In Example 25-1, each task to be performed asynchronously is preceded by a call to our dispatch group's enter, all on the same queue. And each call to enter is followed by a call to our dispatch group's leave, on its own queue, at the end of an asynchronous task. (The queues on which the asynchronous tasks are performed do not have to be different queues; the point is that it doesn't matter if they are.)

Finally, after all the enter calls, still on the same queue, is the call to notify; its full form is notify(qos:flags:queue:execute:). Only when every enter has been balanced by a leave will the notify completion function be called (on the specified queue). So this is effectively a way of *waiting* until *all* the asynchronous tasks have completed independently, before proceeding with whatever the notify completion function says to do.

Another useful DispatchGroup method is wait. It does just what you think: it pauses the current queue until every preceding enter is balanced by a leave. You can use it on its own or together with notify. (Just don't call it on the main queue, because if you do, you'll be blocking the main queue.)

wait is useful particularly when you're looping with a DispatchGroup and you want to ensure that the iterations of the loop execute in order. Here's a toy example that demonstrates:

```
let outerQueue = DispatchQueue(label: "outer")
let innerQueue = DispatchQueue(label: "inner")
let group = DispatchGroup()
outerQueue.async {
    let series = "123456789"
    for c in series {
        group.enter()
        innerQueue.asyncAfter(
            deadline:.now() + .milliseconds(Int.random(in: 1...1000))) {
                print(c, terminator:"")
                group.leave()
        }
    }
    group.notify(queue: DispatchQueue.main) {
        print("\ndone")
    }
}
```

The idea of that code is to use the DispatchGroup to wait until all the iterations of the for loop have completed, asynchronously, before proceeding. And that's just what happens. But the iterations are executed *in random order*, depending on how long each takes to complete. Typical output would be:

```
489531267
done
```

So what if you want the iterations of the loop to complete *in the same order* as whatever you're looping through? In effect, we need to run each loop sequentially, even though each loop is itself asynchronous. (I call this *serializing asynchronicity*.) The solution is to insert a single line, group.wait(), at the end of the iteration:

```
for c in series {
    group.enter()
    innerQueue.asyncAfter(
        deadline: .now() + .milliseconds(Int.random(in: 1...1000))) {
            print(c, terminator:"")
            group.leave()
    }
    group.wait() // *
}
```

That takes longer, of course, but the output appears in order:

```
123456789
done
```

One-Time Execution

Sometimes you need a way of ensuring that code is run only once; this is often used to help vend a singleton. In Objective-C, you'd use dispatch_once, which is part of GCD; in Swift, however, dispatch_once is unavailable (apparently because it can't be implemented in a thread-safe way). The Swift workaround is *not* to use GCD, but rather to take advantage of lazy initialization.

Suppose you have a true global variable like this:

```
let globalOnce : Void = {
    print("once in a lifetime") // once, at most
}()
```

Then any of your code anywhere can say globalOnce, but only the *first* time the expression globalOnce is used will the phrase "once in a lifetime" be printed in the console. The global is initialized just once in the lifetime of the app, and its initializer runs some code, so that code runs only once.

You can do something similar at the level of an instance. Here, we need an instance property; an instance property is not naturally lazy, but we can declare it lazy:

```
class ViewController: UIViewController {
    private lazy var instanceOnce : Void = {
        print("once in an instance") // once per instance, at most
    }()
    // ...
}
```

Code elsewhere in this view controller can refer to self.instanceOnce, but only the *first* time it does so will the phrase "once in an instance" be printed in the console:

```
@IBAction func doOnceInAViewController(_ sender: Any) {
    _ = self.instanceOnce
}
```

The assignment to nothing "tickles" the lazy variable and causes it to be initialized. We cannot merely mention the variable, as we did the global, or we'll get a compile error because we are referring to a property without using it.

Concurrent Queues

Besides serial dispatch queues, there are also *concurrent* dispatch queues. A concurrent queue's functions are started in the order in which they were submitted to the queue, but a function is allowed to start while another function is still executing. Obviously, you wouldn't want to submit to a concurrent queue a task that touches a shared resource! The advantage of concurrent queues is a possible speed boost when you don't care about the order in which multiple tasks are finished, as when you want to do something with regard to every element of an array.

The built-in global queues, available by calling DispatchQueue.global(qos:), are concurrent. qos is an acronym for "quality of service." You specify *which* built-in global queue you want by means of the qos: argument, which can be (DispatchQoS.QoSClass):

- .userInteractive
- .userInitiated
- .default
- .utility
- .background

You can also create a concurrent queue yourself by calling the DispatchQueue initializer init(label:attributes:) with a .concurrent attribute.

Here's a toy example, just to demonstrate the difference that a concurrent queue makes. I'll need some genuinely time-consuming code (not just an asynchronous delay), so I'll use the Mandelbrot calculation to impose a pause:

```
let queue = DispatchQueue(label: "queue")
outerQueue.async {
    for k in 1...10 {
        queue.async {
            for i in 1...Int.random(in: 1000...2000) {
                for j in 1...Int.random(in: 1000...2000) {
                    _ = isInMandelbrotSet(Float(i), Float(j))
                }
            }
            print(k)
        }
    }
}
```

The outer loop (iterating with k) completes immediately, scheduling ten tasks onto the queue. The numbers 1 through 10 are printed in order, because the queue is serial: each task must be completed before the next is allowed to start. But now let's change the declaration of queue to make it concurrent:

```
let queue = DispatchQueue(label: "queue", attributes: .concurrent)
```

Now the numbers print in random order, because (to the extent that the system can grant us threads) all the scheduled tasks are permitted to start simultaneously, and after that the order in which they finish is a matter of chance.

Checking the Queue

A question that sometimes arises is how to make certain that a method is called only on the correct queue. You can check in a thread-safe way whether we are on the main queue or a background queue with Thread.isMainThread. But sometimes the question is whether we are on a *particular* background queue.

Recall that in our Mandelbrot drawing example, we may be concerned that a method such as makeBitmapContext(size:) might be called on some other queue than the background queue that we created for this purpose. This sort of problem can be solved quite elegantly by calling the dispatchPrecondition(condition:) global function. It takes a DispatchPredicate enum, whose cases are:

- .onQueue
- .onQueueAsBarrier
- .notOnQueue

These cases each take an associated value which is a DispatchQueue. (I told you it was elegant!) To assert that we are on our draw_queue queue, we would say:

```
dispatchPrecondition(condition: .onQueue(self.draw_queue))
```

The outcome is similar to Swift's native precondition function: if our assertion is false, we'll crash.

App Backgrounding

A problem arises if your app is backgrounded and suspended (Appendix A) while your code is running. The system doesn't want to stop your code while it's executing; on the other hand, some other app may need to be given the bulk of the device's resources now. So as your app goes into the background, the system waits a very short time (less than 5 seconds) for your app to finish doing whatever it may be doing, and it then suspends your app.

This shouldn't be a problem from your main thread's point of view, because your app shouldn't have any time-consuming code on the main thread in the first place; you now know that you can avoid this by using a background thread. On the other hand, it could be a problem for lengthy background tasks, including asynchronous tasks performed by the frameworks.

What we'd like to do in this situation is *protect* a lengthy background task against interruption, requesting extra time for completion just in case the app is backgrounded. There's a way to do that:

1. You call UIApplication's beginBackgroundTask(expirationHandler:) to announce that a lengthy task is beginning; it returns an identification number. This tells the system that if your app is backgrounded, you'd like to be granted some extra time to complete this task. (My experience is that the time granted is usually about 30 seconds.)

2. At the end of your lengthy task, you call UIApplication's endBackgroundTask(_:), passing in the *same identification number* that you got from your call to beginBackgroundTask(expirationHandler:). This tells the system that your lengthy task is over and that there is no need to grant you any more background time.

The function that you pass as the argument to `beginBackgroundTask(expiration-Handler:)` is the *expiration function*. It does *not* express the lengthy task! It expresses what you will do *if your extra time expires* before you finish your lengthy task. This is a chance for you to clean up. At the very least, your expiration function *must* call `endBackgroundTask(_:)`! Otherwise, the runtime won't know that you've run your expiration function, and your app may be killed as a punishment for trying to use too much background time. If your expiration function *is* called, you should make no assumptions about what thread it is running on.

There are two routes by which `endBackgroundTask(_:)` might be called: either our lengthy operation was cancelled because we ran out of time, or it ran to completion. So we end up with a pattern like this:

```
var bti : UIBackgroundTaskIdentifier = .invalid
bti = UIApplication.shared.beginBackgroundTask {
    // ... we didn't finish! do any cleanup ...
    UIApplication.shared.endBackgroundTask(bti) // cancellation
}
// ... do lengthy operation ...
UIApplication.shared.endBackgroundTask(bti) // completion
```

That pattern is so common in my code that it makes sense to encapsulate it. To do so, I've created an Operation subclass, which I call BackgroundTaskOperation:

```
class BackgroundTaskOperation: Operation {
    var whatToDo : (() -> ())?
    var cleanup : (() -> ())?
    override func main() {
        guard !self.isCancelled else { return }
        var bti : UIBackgroundTaskIdentifier = .invalid
        bti = UIApplication.shared.beginBackgroundTask {
            self.cleanup?()
            self.cancel()
            UIApplication.shared.endBackgroundTask(bti) // cancellation
        }
        guard bti != .invalid else { return }
        whatToDo?()
        guard !self.isCancelled else { return }
        UIApplication.shared.endBackgroundTask(bti) // completion
    }
}
```

Let's use MyMandelbrotView as an example. Suppose that if `drawThatPuppy` is started, we'd like it to be allowed to finish, even if the app is suspended in the middle of it, so that our `bitmapContext` property is updated as requested. We have created a global serial background operation queue:

```
let backgroundTaskQueue : OperationQueue = {
    let q = OperationQueue()
    q.maxConcurrentOperationCount = 1
    return q
}()
```

When we call our lengthy self.draw(center:bounds:zoom:context:), we embed it
in a BackgroundTaskOperation:

```
let center = self.bounds.center
let bounds = self.bounds
let bitmap = self.makeBitmapContext(size: bounds.size)
let task = BackgroundTaskOperation()
task.whatToDo = {
    self.draw(center: center, bounds: bounds, zoom. 1, context: bitmap)
    DispatchQueue.main.async {
        self.bitmapContext = bitmap
        self.setNeedsDisplay()
    }
}
backgroundTaskQueue.addOperation(task)
```

There are three possibilities here:

The app doesn't go into the background

> If the app doesn't go into the background while the lengthy background task is
> running, then our use of beginBackgroundTask and endBackgroundTask makes
> no difference. These calls are asking for extra time *if* we go into the background.
> We didn't. self.draw(center:bounds:zoom:context:) is performed on a back-
> ground queue because backgroundTaskQueue is a background queue, and all is as
> it was before.

We finish in the background

> If the app goes into the background and we finish the lengthy background task
> before time runs out, the whole operation is performed in good order. If the user
> subsequently brings the app back to the foreground (and assuming that the app
> has not been terminated in the background), there's MyMandelbrotView dis-
> playing the result.

We run out of time

> If the app goes into the background and we *don't* finish the lengthy background
> task before time runs out, we call endBackgroundTask and the app is suspended
> in good order. If the user subsequently brings the app back to the foreground
> (and assuming that the app has not been terminated in the background), our
> code *resumes* and finishes the drawing.

> If the app *is* terminated in the background, our code has been interrupted in the
> middle and will never complete. This is a tricky situation. Since we don't know,
> when we run out of time, whether we will ever be able to continue, it is best to

assume that the operation might *never* finish and clean up immediately. In the whatToDo function, I usually get a weak reference to task and use it to check task.isCancelled often so that I can stop quickly at a good spot if we run out of time.

Background Processing

Starting in iOS 13, instead of continuing a current task a bit longer in case the app goes into the background, you can request that a task be performed *only* while the app is in the background. The idea is that this would be some lengthy calculation or operation that isn't crucial to perform while the user is looking at the app, but would be nice to do at some future time when the device is more or less idle (such as cleaning up your data). This is called *background processing:*

- Background processing is a background mode, so you'll need to add the Background Modes capability in the Signing & Capabilities tab of the target editor and check "Background processing."

- Background processing uses the Background Tasks framework, so in your code, you'll need to import BackgroundTasks.

- In the *Info.plist,* you *must* add entries under the "Permitted background task schedule identifiers" key (BTTaskSchedulerPermittedIdentifiers); these are arbitrary strings (typically using reverse domain notation) identifying your tasks.

There are two classes involved:

BGProcessingTaskRequest
> A value class describing your background task. You initialize it with an identifier, which must match one of your *Info.plist* background task schedule identifiers; you can also set three properties:

> requiresExternalPower
>> The task should be performed when the device is being charged. The default is false.

> requiresNetworkConnectivity
>> The task should be performed when networking is available. The default is false.

> earliestBeginDate
>> A date in the future. Apple recommends a time somewhere between fifteen minutes from now and a week from now. The default is nil.

BGTaskScheduler

Your gateway for communicating with the runtime about background processing tasks. You'll talk to the shared instance. In your app delegate's `application(_:didFinishLaunchingWithOptions:)`, you *must* call this method:

`register(forTaskWithIdentifier:using:launchHandler:)`

The `identifier:` parameter must match one of your *Info.plist* background task schedule identifiers. The `using:` parameter is a dispatch queue. The last parameter is a function that will be called on that queue. This function is the task! It takes one parameter, a BGTask object. In the function, you have two responsibilities with regard to this object:

- You *must* immediately set the BGTask's `expirationHandler` to a function that will be called if your background time expires.

- You *must* call `setTaskCompleted` with a Bool parameter indicating whether your task finished. At a minimum, in your `expirationHandler` function you'll call `setTaskCompleted(false)`, and at the end of your task function you'll call `setTaskCompleted(true)`. This should remind you of how we implemented `beginBackgroundTask` and `endBackgroundTask` in the previous section.

When you go into the background and you want to ask for your task to be performed, you'll talk to the shared BGTaskScheduler again: you'll call `submit(_:)` with a BGProcessingTaskRequest.

Here's an artificial example, using MyMandelbrotView to provide us with a lengthy task:

```
let taskid = "com.neuburg.matt.lengthy"
func application(_ application: UIApplication,
    didFinishLaunchingWithOptions launchOptions:
    [UIApplication.LaunchOptionsKey : Any]?) -> Bool {
        let v = MyMandelbrotView(frame:CGRect(0,0,500,500))
        let ok = BGTaskScheduler.shared.register(
            forTaskWithIdentifier: taskid,
            using: DispatchQueue.global(qos: .background)) { task in
                task.expirationHandler = {
                    task.setTaskCompleted(success: false)
                }
                let context = v.makeBitmapContext(size: CGSize(500,500))
                v.draw(center: CGPoint(250,250),
                    bounds: CGRect(0,0,500,500),
                    zoom: 1, context: context)
                task.setTaskCompleted(success: true)
        }
        // might check `ok` here
        return true
}
```

```
func applicationDidEnterBackground(_ application: UIApplication) {
    // might check to see whether it's time to submit this request
    let req = BGProcessingTaskRequest(identifier: self.taskid)
    try? BGTaskScheduler.shared.submit(req)
}
```

To help you test, there's a secret dance that lets you trigger your background task artificially. Here's how I would do the dance for my test app:

1. Pepper the registered task function with `print` statements or breakpoints.

2. Run the app on a device from Xcode.

3. On the device, send the app into the background; then bring it back to the foreground.

4. In Xcode, pause the running app.

5. In the console, give the following mysterious command (all on one line, using your actual task identifier):

   ```
   (lldb) e -l objc -- (void)[[BGTaskScheduler sharedScheduler]
       _simulateLaunchForTaskWithIdentifier:@"com.neuburg.matt.lengthy"]
   ```

   The console replies: "Simulating launch for task with identifier…"

6. Still in the console, say `continue`. The task function runs, printing its `print` statements and pausing at its breakpoints.

7. When we get to `task.setTaskCompleted(success: true)`, the console reports "Marking simulated task complete," and the experiment is over.

You can also test whether your expiration function is called in good order. To do that, perform the first six steps and pause again inside the task function at a point after the expiration handler has been set. Now say this in the console:

```
(lldb) e -l objc -- (void)[[BGTaskScheduler sharedScheduler]
    _simulateExpirationForTaskWithIdentifier:@"com.neuburg.matt.lengthy"]
```

Then say `continue`, and if all goes well, the console will reply "Expiring simulated task" and then "Marking simulated task complete."

A second type of background task request, BGAppRefreshTaskRequest, supersedes the use of methods like `application(_:performFetchWithCompletionHandler:)` to implement background app refresh. I don't discuss background app refresh in this book, but if you've been using it, you should switch to the Background Tasks framework.

 In a WWDC 2020 video, Apple appears to be saying that if the user has switched off Background App Refresh (in Settings, under General), background processing tasks will not take place.

Undo

The idea of undo is that the user can reverse a recently performed action. Behind the scenes, the app maintains an internal stack of undoable actions; undoing reverses the action at the top of the stack, and also makes that action available for redo through a secondary stack.

A pervasive undo capability is characteristic primarily of desktop macOS applications, but some iOS apps may also benefit from a limited undo facility, and certain built-in views — in particular, those that involve text entry (Chapter 11) — implement it already. UIDocument (see Chapter 23) integrates with your undo facility to update the document's "dirty" state automatically.

Undo operates through an *undo manager* — an instance of UndoManager. Every time the user performs an action that is to be undoable, you *register* that action with the undo manager. When the user asks to undo, you send undo to the undo manager; when the user asks to redo, you send redo to the undo manager. In both cases, the undo manager performs the registered action and adjusts its internal undo and redo stacks appropriately.

I'll introduce the UndoManager class with a simple example; for more information, read Apple's *Undo Architecture* in the documentation archive, along with the class documentation.

Target–Action Undo

I'll illustrate an UndoManager for a simple app that has just one kind of undoable action. In my example, the user can drag a small square around the screen. Our goal is to make the drag undoable.

We'll start with an instance of a UIView subclass, MyView, to which has been attached a UIPanGestureRecognizer to make it draggable; the gesture recognizer's action target is the MyView instance itself, which implements the typical drag action function described in Chapter 5:

```
@objc func dragging (_ p : UIPanGestureRecognizer) {
    switch p.state {
    case .began, .changed:
        let delta = p.translation(in:self.superview!)
        var c = self.center
        c.x += delta.x; c.y += delta.y
        self.center = c
        p.setTranslation(.zero, in: self.superview!)
    default:break
    }
}
```

We will need an UndoManager instance. Let's store it in a property of MyView itself, self.undoer:

```
let undoer = UndoManager()
```

To test my app's undo capability, the interface also contains two buttons: an Undo button that sends undo to the view's undo manager, and a Redo button that sends redo to the view's undo manager.

We need to tell the undo manager to *register* the drag action as undoable. There are two main ways of doing that. One way is to call this UndoManager method:

• registerUndo(withTarget:selector:object:)

This method uses a target–action architecture: you provide a target, a selector for an action method that takes one parameter, and a value that will *be* that parameter. Later, if the UndoManager is sent the undo or redo message, it calls the action method on that target with the object as argument. The job of the action method is to undo whatever it is that needs undoing.

Let's use registerUndo(withTarget:selector:object:) to configure undo in our app. How? Well, what we want to undo here is the setting of our center property:

```
var c = self.center
c.x += delta.x; c.y += delta.y
self.center = c // *
```

We need to express this as a method taking one parameter, so that the undo manager can call it as the selector: action method. So, in our dragging(_:) method, instead of setting self.center to c directly, we now call a secondary method:

```
var c = self.center
c.x += delta.x; c.y += delta.y
self.setCenterUndoably(c) // *
```

We have posited a method `setCenterUndoably(_:)` that doesn't exist. Let's write it. What should it do? At a minimum, it should do the job that setting `self.center` used to do! At the same time, we want the undo manager to be able to call this method. The undo manager doesn't know the *type* of the parameter that it will be passing to us, so its `object:` parameter is typed as Any. Therefore, the parameter of this method also needs to be typed as Any:

```
func setCenterUndoably (_ newCenter : Any) {
    self.center = newCenter as! CGPoint
}
```

This works, in the sense that the view is draggable exactly as before; but we have not yet made this action undoable — because we have not called `registerUndo(with-Target:selector:object:)`. To do so, we must ask ourselves what message the UndoManager would need to send in order to undo the action we are about to perform. Clearly, we would want the UndoManager to set `self.center` back to the value it has *now*. And what method would the UndoManager call in order to do that? It would call `setCenterUndoably(_:)`, the very method we are implementing! So now we have this:

```
@objc func setCenterUndoably (_ newCenter : Any) {
    self.undoer.registerUndo(withTarget: self,
        selector: #selector(setCenterUndoably),
        object: self.center)
    self.center = newCenter as! CGPoint
}
```

That code works; it makes our action undoable!

Not only is our action now undoable; it is redoable as well. How can this be? Well, it turns out that UndoManager has an internal state, and responds differently to `registerUndo(withTarget:selector:object:)` depending on that state. If the UndoManager is sent `registerUndo(withTarget:selector:object:)` *while it is undoing*, it puts the target–action information on the redo stack instead of the undo stack (because redo *is* the undo of an undo, if you see what I mean).

Confused? Here's how our code works to undo and then redo an action:

1. We set `self.center` by way of `setCenterUndoably(_:)`, which calls `register-Undo(withTarget:selector:object:)` with the *old* value of `self.center`. The UndoManager adds this to its *undo* stack.

2. Now suppose we want to undo that action. We send `undo` to the UndoManager.

3. The UndoManager calls `setCenterUndoably(_:)` with the *old* value that we passed it in step 1. So we are going to set the center back to that old value. But before we do that, we send `registerUndo(withTarget:selector:object:)` to the UndoManager with the *current* value of `self.center`. The UndoManager

knows that it is currently undoing, so it understands this registration as something to be added to its *redo* stack.

4. Now suppose we want to redo that undo. We send `redo` to the UndoManager, and sure enough, the UndoManager calls `setCenterUndoably(_:)` with the value that we previously undid! And, once again, we call `registerUndo(withTarget:selector:object:)` with an action that goes onto the UndoManager's *undo* stack — and we're back to step 1.

Undo Grouping

So far, so good. But our implementation of undo is very annoying, because we are adding a new object to the undo stack every time `dragging(_:)` is called — and it is called many times during the course of a single drag! This means that undoing once merely undoes the tiny increment corresponding to one individual `dragging(_:)` call. What we'd like is for undoing to undo an *entire* dragging gesture. We can implement this through *undo grouping*. As the gesture begins, we start a group; when the gesture ends, we end the group:

```
@objc func dragging (_ p : UIPanGestureRecognizer) {
    switch p.state {
    case .began:
        self.undoer.beginUndoGrouping() // *
        fallthrough
    case .changed:
        let delta = p.translation(in:self.superview!)
        var c = self.center
        c.x += delta.x; c.y += delta.y
        self.setCenterUndoably(c)
        p.setTranslation(.zero, in: self.superview!)
    case .ended, .cancelled:
        self.undoer.endUndoGrouping() // *
    default:break
    }
}
```

This works: each complete drag gesture, from the time the user's finger first touches the view and drags it to the time the user's finger is lifted, is now undoable (and redoable) as a single unit.

A further refinement would be to animate the "drag" that the UndoManager performs when it undoes or redoes a user drag gesture. To do so, we take advantage of the fact that we can examine the UndoManager's state by way of its `isUndoing` and `isRedoing` properties; we animate the `center` change when the UndoManager is "dragging," but not when the user is dragging:

```
@objc func setCenterUndoably (_ newCenter : Any) {
    self.undoer.registerUndo(withTarget: self,
        selector: #selector(setCenterUndoably),
        object: self.center)
    if self.undoer.isUndoing || self.undoer.isRedoing {
        UIView.animate(withDuration:0.4, delay: 0.1) {
            self.center = newCenter as! CGPoint
        }
    } else { // just do it
        self.center = newCenter as! CGPoint
    }
}
```

Functional Undo

I said earlier that there are two main ways of registering an action as undoable with the undo manager. The second way is to call this UndoManager method:

- `registerUndo(withTarget:handler:)`

The handler: is a function that will be called when we call undo or redo. It must take one parameter, which will be whatever you pass here as the target: argument. This is a more modern idiom than the target–action architecture for expressing the registration of an action. If we adopt this approach, then our setCenterUndoably(_:) no longer needs to take an Any as its parameter; it can take a CGPoint:

```
func setCenterUndoably (_ newCenter : CGPoint) {
    self.undoer.registerUndo(withTarget: self) {
        [oldCenter = self.center] myself in
        myself.setCenterUndoably(oldCenter)
    }
    if self.undoer.isUndoing || self.undoer.isRedoing {
        UIView.animate(withDuration: 0.4, delay: 0.1) {
            self.center = newCenter
        }
    } else { // just do it
        self.center = newCenter
    }
}
```

Let's look more closely at my call to registerUndo(withTarget:handler:) and the anonymous handler: function that accompanies it:

```
self.undoer.registerUndo(withTarget: self) {
    [oldCenter = self.center] myself in
    myself.setCenterUndoably(oldCenter)
}
```

The example shows what the target: parameter is for — it's to avoid retain cycles. By passing self as the target: argument, I can retrieve it as the parameter in the handler: function (I've called the parameter myself). In the body of the handler: function, I never have to refer to self and there is no retain cycle.

I've also taken advantage of a little-known feature of Swift anonymous function capture lists, allowing me to get the value of self.center as it is *now* and capture it in a local reference (oldCenter) inside the anonymous function. The reason is that if the anonymous function were to call setCenterUndoably(myself.center), we'd be using the value that myself.center will have *at undo time*, and would be pointlessly setting the center to itself.

Our code works perfectly, but we can go further. We are failing to take full advantage of the fact that we now have the ability to register with the undo manager a full-fledged function body rather than a mere function call. That fact means that the handler: function can contain *everything* that should happen when undoing, including the animation:

```
self.undoer.registerUndo(withTarget: self) {
    [oldCenter = self.center] myself in
    UIView.animate(withDuration: 0.4, delay: 0.1) {
        myself.center = oldCenter
    }
    myself.setCenterUndoably(oldCenter)
}
```

But we can go further still. Let's ask ourselves: Why are we setting self.center here at all? We can do it back in the gesture recognizer's dragging(_:) action method, just as we were doing before we added undo to this app. And in that case, we no longer need a separate setCenterUndoably method! True, we still need some function that calls registerUndo with a call to itself, because that's how we get redo registration during undo; but this can be a local function inside the dragging(_:) method. Our dragging(_:) method can provide a complete undo implementation internally, resulting in a far more legible and encapsulated architecture:

```
@objc func dragging (_ p : UIPanGestureRecognizer) {
    switch p.state {
    case .began:
        self.undoer.beginUndoGrouping()
        fallthrough
    case .began, .changed:
        let delta = p.translation(in:self.superview!)
        var c = self.center
        c.x += delta.x; c.y += delta.y
        func registerForUndo() {
            self.undoer.registerUndo(withTarget: self) {
                [oldCenter = self.center] myself in
                UIView.animate(withDuration: 0.4, delay: 0.1) {
                    myself.center = oldCenter
                }
                registerForUndo()
```

```
            }
        }
        registerForUndo() // *
        self.center = c // *
        p.setTranslation(.zero, in: self.superview!)
    case .ended, .cancelled:
        self.undoer.endUndoGrouping()
    default: break
    }
}
```

Undo Interface

We must also decide how to let the user request undo and redo. While I was developing the code from the preceding section, I used an Undo button and a Redo button. This can be a perfectly reasonable interface, but let's talk about some others.

Shake-To-Edit

By default, your app supports *shake-to-edit*. This means that the user can shake the device to bring up an undo/redo interface. We discussed this briefly in Chapter 22. If you don't turn off this feature by setting the shared UIApplication's application-SupportsShakeToEdit property to false, and if the user doesn't turn it off in Settings, then when the user shakes the device, the runtime walks up the responder chain, starting with the first responder, looking for a responder whose inherited undo-Manager property returns an actual UndoManager instance. If it finds one, it puts up an alert with an Undo button, a Redo button, or both; if the user taps a button, the runtime communicates directly with that UndoManager, calling its undo or redo method for us.

You will recall what it takes for a UIResponder to be first responder in this sense: it must return true from canBecomeFirstResponder, and it must actually be made first responder through a call to becomeFirstResponder. Let's have MyView satisfy those requirements. We might call becomeFirstResponder at the end of dragging(_:), like this:

```
override var canBecomeFirstResponder : Bool {
    return true
}
@objc func dragging (_ p : UIPanGestureRecognizer) {
    switch p.state {
    // ... the rest as before ...
    case .ended, .cancelled:
        self.undoer.endUndoGrouping()
        self.becomeFirstResponder()
    default: break
    }
}
```

Figure 26-1. The shake-to-edit undo/redo alert

Then, to implement undo through shake-to-edit, we have only to provide a getter for the undoManager property that returns our undo manager, self.undoer:

```
let undoer = UndoManager()
override var undoManager : UndoManager? {
    return self.undoer
}
```

This works: shaking the device now brings up the undo/redo alert, and its buttons work correctly. However, I don't like the way the buttons are labeled; they just say Undo and Redo. To make this interface more expressive, we should provide the undo manager with a string describing each undoable action. We do that by calling set-ActionName(_:); we can call it at the same time that we register our undo action:

```
self.undoer.setActionName("Move")
```

Now the undo/redo alert has more informative labels, as shown in Figure 26-1.

Built-In Gestures

Starting in iOS 13, three gestures are interpreted as asking for undo and redo:

- Double tap with three fingers means undo.
- Swipe left with three fingers means undo.
- Swift right with three fingers means redo.

The idea is probably to make shake-to-edit obsolete, as it is rather violent and somewhat unreliable.

The response when the user makes one of these gestures is comparable to shake-to-edit: the runtime walks up the responder chain looking for a responder with an UndoManager in its undoManager property. Unlike shake-to-edit, when it finds this responder it doesn't put up an alert; it simply sends the undo manager undo or redo directly. It also puts up a little caption at the top of the screen explaining what's happening (Figure 26-2).

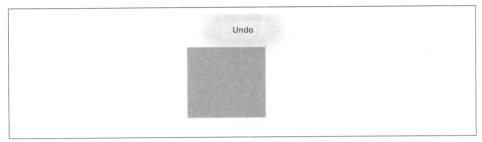

Figure 26-2. The Undo caption

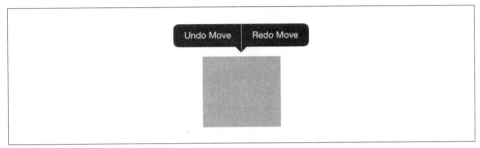

Figure 26-3. The shared menu as an undo/redo interface

The caption is not a button, nor is the user offered a choice; the gesture is obeyed, and when the caption appears, the undo or redo has already been performed. The caption text does not consult the undo manager's action name; it merely reads Undo or Redo. I regard this as unfortunate.

Undo Menu

Another possible undo/redo interface is through a menu (Figure 26-3). We can show the same menu used by a UITextField or UITextView for displaying menu items such as Select, Select All, Copy, and Paste ("Text Field Menu" on page 689). The requirements for summoning this menu are effectively the same as those for shake-to-edit: we need a responder chain with a first responder at the bottom of it. So the code we've just supplied for making MyView first responder remains applicable.

Let's cause the menu to appear in response to a long press on our MyView instance. We'll attach another gesture recognizer to MyView. This will be a UILongPress-GestureRecognizer, whose action method is called `longPress(_:)`.

To configure the menu, we get the singleton global UIMenuController object and specify an array of custom UIMenuItems as its `menuItems` property. To make the menu appear, we send the UIMenuController the `showMenu(from:rect:)` message.

A particular menu item will actually appear in the menu only if we also return `true` from `canPerformAction(_:withSender:)` for that menu item's action. Delightfully, the UndoManager's canUndo and canRedo properties tell us what value canPerform-Action(_:withSender:) should return. We can also get the titles for our custom menu items from the UndoManager itself, through its undoMenuItemTitle and redo-MenuItemTitle properties:

```
@objc func longPress (_ g : UIGestureRecognizer) {
    if g.state == .began {
        let m = UIMenuController.shared
        let mi1 = UIMenuItem(title: self.undoer.undoMenuItemTitle,
            action: #selector(undo))
        let mi2 = UIMenuItem(title: self.undoer.redoMenuItemTitle,
            action: #selector(redo))
        m.menuItems = [mi1, mi2]
        m.showMenu(from: self, rect: self.bounds)
    }
}
override func canPerformAction(_ action: Selector,
    withSender sender: Any?) -> Bool {
        if action == #selector(undo) {
            return self.undoer.canUndo
        }
        if action == #selector(redo) {
            return self.undoer.canRedo
        }
        return super.canPerformAction(action, withSender: sender)
}
@objc func undo(_: Any?) {
    self.undoer.undo()
}
@objc func redo(_: Any?) {
    self.undoer.redo()
}
```

Lifetime Events

The fundamental events that notify you of stages in the lifetime of your app as a whole, giving your code an opportunity to run in response, are extraordinarily important. This appendix is devoted to a survey of them, along with some typical scenarios in which they will arrive.

Application States

In the very early days of iOS — before iOS 4 — the lifetime of an app was extremely simple: either it was running or it wasn't. The user tapped your app's icon in the home screen, and your app was launched and began to run. The user used your app for a while. Eventually, the user clicked the Home button and your app was terminated — it was no longer running. The user had *quit* your app. Launch, run, quit: that was the entire life cycle of an app. If the user decided to use your app again, the whole cycle started over.

The reason for this simplicity was that an iOS device, with its slow processor and its almost brutal paucity of memory and other resources, compensated for its own shortcomings by a simple rule: it could run *only one app at a time*. While your app was running, it occupied not only the entire screen but the vast majority of the device's resources, leaving room only for the system and some hidden built-in processes; it had, in effect, sole and complete control of the device.

Starting in iOS 4, that changed. Apple devised an ingenious architecture whereby, despite the device's limited resources, more than one app could run simultaneously — sort of. The Home button changed its meaning and its effect upon your app. In iOS 4 and later, when the user clicks the Home button to leave your app, your app does not die; technically, the Home button does not terminate your app. Instead, when your app occupies the screen, it is *in the foreground* (or *frontmost*); then, when some other app occupies the screen, your app is *backgrounded and suspended*.

Suspension means that your app is essentially freeze-dried; its process still exists, but it isn't actively running, and it isn't getting any events — though notifications can be stored by the system for later delivery in case your app comes to the front once again. And because it isn't running, it isn't using so much of the device's precious resources. In particular, it's not using the CPU, and some memory may be freed up by clearing the backing store of layers. Later, when the user returns to your app after having left it to use some other app for a while, your app is found in the *very same state* as when the user left it. The app was not terminated; it simply stopped and froze, and waited in suspended animation. Returning to your app no longer means that your app is *launched*, but merely that it is *resumed*.

All of this is not to say, however, that your app can't be terminated. It can be — though not by the user clicking the Home button. The user might switch off the device; that will certainly terminate your app. And a savvy user might force-terminate your app from the app switcher. The most common scenario, however, is that the system quietly *kills* your app while it is suspended. This undermines the app's ability to resume; when the user returns to your app, it will have to launch from scratch, just as in the pre–iOS 4 days. The death of your app under these circumstances is rather like that of the scientists killed by HAL 9000 in *2001: A Space Odyssey* — they went to sleep expecting to wake up later, but instead their life-support systems were turned off while they slept. The iOS system's reasons for killing your app are not quite as paranoid as HAL's, but they do have a certain Darwinian ruthlessness: your app, while suspended, continues to occupy a chunk of the device's memory, and the system needs to reclaim that memory so some other app can use it. This forcible ejection of your suspended app from the land of the living is technically known as *jetsam*.

(I'm simplifying, of course. The reasons why the system kills your app are more complicated than just the amount of memory it uses. An interesting WWDC 2020 video called "Why is my app getting killed?" goes into more detail. Its most important message is that jetsam is *not a bug*. You should do all you can to make your app a good background citizen, and the video makes some suggestions about that, but even after you've done all you can, being killed in the background because the system needs memory is normal and you should expect and plan for it.)

Over time, successive iOS systems have complicated the picture:

- Some apps can be backgrounded *without* being suspended. This is a special privilege, accorded in order that your app may perform a limited range of highly focused activities. An app that is playing music or tracking the device's location when it goes into the background may be permitted to continue doing so in the background. (See Chapters 15 and 22.)

- An app that has been suspended can be woken briefly, *remaining in the background*, in order to receive and respond to a message — in order to be told, for instance, that the user has crossed a geofence, or that a background download has completed. (See Chapters 22 and 24.)

- There is also an intermediate state in which your app can find itself, where it is neither frontmost nor backgrounded. This happens, for instance, when the user summons the control center or notification center in front of your app. In such situations, your app may be *inactive* without actually being backgrounded.

- A modern iPad that does iPad multitasking (Chapter 10) is capable of running two apps at once: they are *both* active (in the foreground) at the same time.

So your app's code can be running even though the app is not frontmost. If your code needs to know the app's state in this regard, it can ask the shared UIApplication object for its `applicationState` (UIApplication.State), which will be one of these:

- `.active`

- `.inactive`

- `.background`

With scene support, things are more complicated if your app supports multiple windows on the iPad. One window can go into the background while another window remains active in the foreground. To describe these possibilities, UIScene has an `activationState` (UIScene.ActivationState), which will be one of these:

- `.unattached`

- `.foregroundActive`

- `.foregroundInactive`

- `.background`

The app's own state is then considered to be the *highest* state of any of its scenes. If any of its scenes is in the `.foregroundActive` state, the app is in the `.active` state. If all of its scenes are in the `.background` state, the app is in the `.background` state. Just as an app can be killed in the background to save memory, a window scene can be disconnected and disposed of in the background to save memory, leaving only its session as a placeholder (see Chapter 10).

Delegate Events

When your app launches, the `UIApplicationMain` function creates its one and only UIApplication instance as the `shared` application object, along with the app delegate, which adopts the UIApplicationDelegate protocol. With the addition of scene support, `UIApplicationMain` also creates a scene and a scene delegate, which adopts the UIWindowSceneDelegate protocol. (See "How an App Launches" on page 6.) The runtime then proceeds to report lifetime events to these delegates through calls to the methods declared in those protocols. Other objects can also register to receive some of these events as notifications.

If your app has scene support, some of the app delegate lifetime events, such as `applicationDidBecomeActive(_:)` and `applicationDidEnterBackground(_:)`, are suppressed. Corresponding messages are sent to the scene delegate instead. In this discussion, I'll assume that you've compiled your app against iOS 14 and that it *does* have scene support. If you want to know what the app delegate messages are when there is *no* scene support, consult an earlier edition of this book.

 App delegate methods start with the word `application`; scene delegate methods start with the word `scene`.

The suite of basic lifetime events that may be sent to your app delegate and scene delegate is surprisingly limited and considerably less informative than one might have hoped:

`application(_:didFinishLaunchingWithOptions:)`
> The app has started up from scratch. You'll typically perform initializations here. But in an app with scene support, these initializations should not involve views or view controllers; that's the job of the scene delegate.

`scene(_:willConnectTo:options:)`
> The scene is being created or reconnected. Perhaps the app has started up from scratch; perhaps a new window has been created in a multiple window app; perhaps this scene was disconnected from its session and is being connected again. Regardless, this is the place to prepare your window's root view controller if needed. If an app doesn't have a main storyboard, or is ignoring the main storyboard at launch time, this is the place to ensure that the scene has a window, to set the window's root view controller, and to show the window ("App Without a Storyboard" on page 7). If the app is launching because of an incoming quick action or URL, this is your chance to respond to it (Chapters 14, 23, and 24).

`sceneWillEnterForeground(_:)`
> The scene is coming to the front. This message is sent both when the scene was previously in the background and when the app is launched from scratch. That's interesting, because in an app without scene support, `applicationWillEnter-Foreground(_:)` is *not* sent on launch to the app delegate. Always followed by `sceneDidBecomeActive(_:)`.

`sceneDidBecomeActive(_:)`

The scene is now well and truly frontmost. Received after `sceneWillEnter-Foreground(_:)`. Also received after the end of any situation that caused the scene delegate to receive `sceneWillResignActive(_:)`.

`sceneWillResignActive(_:)`

The scene is entering a situation where it is neither frontmost nor backgrounded; it will be *inactive*. Perhaps something has blocked the interface — the user has summoned the notification center, or a system alert has appeared, or there's an incoming phone call. Whatever the cause, the scene delegate will receive `scene-DidBecomeActive(_:)` when this situation ends.

Alternatively, the scene may be about to go into the background (and will then probably be suspended); in that case, this event was purely transient, and `scene-DidEnterBackground(_:)` will follow almost immediately.

`sceneDidEnterBackground(_:)`

The scene has been backgrounded. Always preceded by `sceneWillResign-Active(_:)`. Your app itself may now be backgrounded, in which case it will probably be suspended; before that happens, you have a little time to finish up last-minute tasks, such as relinquishing unneeded memory (see Chapter 6), and if you need more time for a lengthy task, you can ask for it (see Chapter 25).

`applicationWillTerminate(_:)`

The application is about to be killed dead. Surprisingly, even though every running app will eventually be terminated, it is quite unlikely that your app will *ever* receive this event! The reason is that, by the time your app is terminated by the system, it is usually already suspended and incapable of receiving events. (I mentioned an exceptional case in Chapter 15, and I'll mention some more in the next section.)

Lifetime Scenarios

A glance at some typical scenarios will demonstrate the chief ways in which your delegates will receive lifetime events. I find it helpful to group these scenarios according to the general behavior of the events.

Major State Changes

During very significant state changes, such as launching, being backgrounded, or coming back to the front, the app and scene delegates receive a sequence of events:

The app launches from scratch
Your delegates receive these messages:

- `application(_:didFinishLaunchingWithOptions:)`
- `scene(_:willConnectTo:options:)`
- `sceneWillEnterForeground(_:)`
- `sceneDidBecomeActive(_:)`

The user clicks the Home button
> If your scene was frontmost, the scene delegate receives these messages:

- `sceneWillResignActive(_:)`
- `sceneDidEnterBackground(_:)`

The user summons your backgrounded scene to the front
> The scene delegate receives these messages:

- `sceneWillEnterForeground(_:)`
- `sceneDidBecomeActive(_:)`

The screen is locked
> If your scene is frontmost, the scene delegate receives these messages:

- `sceneWillResignActive(_:)`
- `sceneDidEnterBackground(_:)`

The screen is unlocked
> If your scene was frontmost, the scene delegate receives these messages:

- `sceneWillEnterForeground(_:)`
- `sceneDidBecomeActive(_:)`

Paused Inactivity

Certain user actions effectively pause the foreground-to-background sequence in the middle, leaving the scene inactive and capable of being either backgrounded or foregrounded, depending on what the user does next. When the scene becomes active again, it might or might not be coming from a backgrounded state:

The user enters the app switcher
> If your scene is frontmost, the scene delegate receives this message:

- `sceneWillResignActive(_:)`

The user, in the app switcher, chooses another app
> If your scene was frontmost, the scene delegate receives this message:

- `sceneDidEnterBackground(_:)`

The user, in the app switcher, chooses your scene
If this scene was frontmost, then it was never backgrounded, so the scene delegate receives just this message:

- `sceneDidBecomeActive(_:)`

The user summons the control center or notification center
If your scene is frontmost, the scene delegate receives this message:

- `sceneWillResignActive(_:)`

Actually, we get `willResignActive` as the user *starts* to pull down the notification center, and then if the user pulls it all the way down, we get `didBecomeActive` and `willResignActive` in quick succession. I regard this as unfortunate.

The user dismisses the control center or notification center
If your scene was frontmost, the scene delegate receives this message:

- `sceneDidBecomeActive(_:)`

But if the user has summoned the notification center, there's another possibility: the user might tap a notification alert to switch to that app. In that case, the scene will continue on to the background, and the scene delegate will receive this message:

- `sceneDidEnterBackground(_:)`

The user holds down the screen-lock button
The device offers to shut itself off. If your scene is frontmost, the scene delegate receives this message:

- `sceneWillResignActive(_:)`

The user, as the device offers to shut itself off, cancels
If your scene was frontmost, the scene delegate receives this message:

- `sceneDidBecomeActive(_:)`

The user, as the device offers to shut itself off, accepts
If your scene was frontmost, the app delegate receives this message:

- `applicationWillTerminate(_:)`

Transient Inactivity on the iPad

There are certain circumstances where your scene may become inactive and then active again in quick succession. These have mostly to do with multitasking on the iPad. If this happens, the scene delegate may receive these messages:

- sceneWillResignActive(_:)

- sceneDidBecomeActive(_:)

The chief case in point is when the user toggles between split sizes. When the scene is resized, it undergoes transient inactivity. If your view controller is notified of a change of size and possibly trait collection, this will happen *during* the period of transient inactivity, while the scene's activation state is .foregroundInactive (and the app's application state will probably be .inactive as well).

Multiple Windows

Here are some special cases that arise in a multiple window app on iPad, when your app manipulates the windows directly:

Your app creates a window
> If your app creates a window by calling requestSceneSessionActivation, your scene delegate receives these messages:
>
> - scene(_:willConnectTo:options:)
>
> - sceneWillEnterForeground(_:)
>
> - sceneDidBecomeActive(_:)

Your app closes a window
> If your app closes a window by calling requestSceneSessionDestruction, then assuming this is not the last window, your delegates receive these messages:
>
> - sceneDidEnterBackground(_:)
>
> - sceneDidDisconnect(_:)
>
> - application(_:didDiscardSceneSessions:)

Scene Death in the App Switcher

The case where the user enters the app switcher and swipes your scene up to remove it is extraordinarily confusing. What happens seems to depend on the device type and the app architecture:

On an iPhone
> If the scene was frontmost, you get these delegate messages:
>
> - sceneDidEnterBackground
>
> - applicationWillTerminate(_:)

On an iPad, if the app does not support multiple windows
> If the scene was frontmost, you get these delegate messages:

- `sceneDidDisconnect(_:)`
- `application(_:didDiscardSceneSessions:)`
- `applicationWillTerminate(_:)`

(The lack of a `sceneDidEnterBackground` call here is surprising.)

On an iPad, if the app does support multiple windows
If the scene was frontmost, you get these delegate messages:

- `sceneDidEnterBackground`
- `applicationWillTerminate(_:)`

But if there's another window still in existence, then the app might not terminate and you won't get `applicationWillTerminate(_:)`. In that case, you might get `sceneDidDisconnect(_:)` and possibly `application(_:didDiscardScene-Sessions:)` later.

If the scene that the user swipes up was *not* frontmost, you'll get nothing; this scene already received `sceneDidEnterBackground`, and you won't get `applicationWill-Terminate(_:)` now, because the app isn't running.

Lifetime Event Timing

The delegate lifetime messages may be interwoven with the lifetime events received by other objects. View controllers ("View Controller Lifetime Events" on page 407) are the primary case in point. There are circumstances where the root view controller may receive its initial lifetime events, such as `viewDidLoad` and `viewWillAppear(_:)`, before `application(_:didFinishLaunchingWithOptions:)` (or, with scene support, `scene(_:willConnectTo:options:)`) has even finished running. That may come as a surprise.

Different systems can also introduce changes in timing. When I started programming iOS, back in the days of iOS 3.2, I noted the opening sequence of events involving the app delegate and the root view controller; they arrived in this order:

1. `application(_:didFinishLaunchingWithOptions:)`
2. `viewDidLoad`
3. `viewWillAppear(_:)`
4. `applicationDidBecomeActive(_:)`
5. `viewDidAppear(_:)`

Relying on that order, I typically used the root view controller's `viewDidAppear(_:)` to register for `UIApplication.didBecomeActiveNotification` in order to be notified of *subsequent* activations of the app.

That worked fine for some years. But iOS 8 brought with it a momentous change: the app delegate now received `applicationDidBecomeActive(_:)` *after* the root view controller received `viewDidAppear(_:)`, like this:

1. `application(_:didFinishLaunchingWithOptions:)`
2. `viewDidLoad`
3. `viewWillAppear(_:)`
4. `viewDidAppear(_:)`
5. `applicationDidBecomeActive(_:)`

This was a disaster for many of my apps, because the notification I had just registered for in `viewDidAppear(_:)` arrived *immediately*.

Then, in iOS 9, the order returned to what it was in iOS 7 and before — knocking my apps into confusion once again. Then, in iOS 11, the order reverted back to what it was in iOS 8!

In iOS 13, with window scene support, the sequence is like this:

1. `application(_:didFinishLaunchingWithOptions:)`
2. `scene(_:willConnectTo:options:)`
3. `sceneWillEnterForeground(_:)`
4. `viewDidLoad`
5. `viewWillAppear(_:)`
6. `sceneDidBecomeActive(_:)`
7. `viewDidAppear(_:)`

But in iOS 14 it changes once again:

1. `application(_:didFinishLaunchingWithOptions:)`
2. `scene(_:willConnectTo:options:)`
3. `sceneWillEnterForeground(_:)`
4. `sceneDidBecomeActive(_:)`
5. `viewDidLoad`
6. `viewWillAppear(_:)`
7. `viewDidAppear(_:)`

Such changes from one system version to the next are likely to pose challenges for the longevity and backward compatibility of your app. The moral is that you should not, as I did, rely upon the timing relationship between lifetime events of different objects.

Some Useful Utility Functions

As you work with iOS and Swift, you'll develop a personal library of frequently used convenience functions. Here are some of mine. Each of them has come in handy in my own life; I keep them available in Xcode's Snippets library, so that I can use them in any project. Many of them have been mentioned earlier in this book.

Core Graphics Initializers

The Core Graphics `CGRectMake` function needs no argument labels when you call it. But Swift cuts off access to this function; instead, you're forced to use various CGRect initializers that *do* need argument labels. I don't like that. Calls with labels take longer to enter into your code, and the labels are superfluous because we know what each argument signifies. My solution is a CGRect initializer *without* labels (Chapter 1):

```
extension CGRect {
    init(_ x:CGFloat, _ y:CGFloat, _ w:CGFloat, _ h:CGFloat) {
        self.init(x:x, y:y, width:w, height:h)
    }
}
```

As long as we're doing that, we may as well supply label-free initializers for the other common Core Graphics structs:

```
extension CGSize {
    init(_ width:CGFloat, _ height:CGFloat) {
        self.init(width:width, height:height)
    }
}
extension CGPoint {
    init(_ x:CGFloat, _ y:CGFloat) {
        self.init(x:x, y:y)
    }
}
```

```
extension CGVector {
    init (_ dx:CGFloat, _ dy:CGFloat) {
        self.init(dx:dx, dy:dy)
    }
}
```

The examples throughout this book, including the rest of this appendix, rely on those extensions.

Center of a CGRect

One frequently wants the center point of a CGRect; it's easy to get it by saying CGPoint(rect.midX, rect.midY), but that becomes tedious. A center property would be nicer:

```
extension CGRect {
    var center : CGPoint {
        return CGPoint(self.midX, self.midY)
    }
}
```

A related value that I often need is a CGRect centered at the center point of my CGRect:

```
extension CGRect {
    func centeredRectOfSize(_ sz:CGSize) -> CGRect {
        let c = self.center
        let x = c.x - sz.width/2.0
        let y = c.y - sz.height/2.0
        return CGRect(x, y, sz.width, sz.height)
    }
}
```

Adjust a CGSize

There's a CGRect method insetBy(dx:dy:), but there's no comparable method for changing an existing CGSize by a width delta and a height delta. Let's make one:

```
extension CGSize {
    func withDelta(dw:CGFloat, dh:CGFloat) -> CGSize {
        return CGSize(self.width + dw, self.height + dh)
    }
}
```

Delayed Performance

Delayed performance is of paramount importance in iOS programming, where we often need to finish the current run loop and commit the current CATransaction, allowing the interface to settle down, before we proceed to the next command. It isn't difficult to call `asyncAfter` (Chapter 25), but we can simplify even more with a utility function:

```
func delay(_ delay:Double, closure: @escaping ()->()) {
    let when = DispatchTime.now() + delay
    DispatchQueue.main.asyncAfter(deadline: when, execute: closure)
}
```

Call it like this:

```
delay(0.4) {
    // do something here
}
```

Dictionary of Views

When you generate constraints from a visual format string by calling NSLayout-Constraint's `constraints(withVisualFormat:options:metrics:views:)`, you need a dictionary of string names and view references as the last argument (Chapter 1). Forming this dictionary is tedious. Let's make it easier.

There are no Swift macros (because there's no Swift preprocessor), so you can't write the equivalent of Objective-C's `NSDictionaryOfVariableBindings`, which forms the dictionary from a literal list of view names. You can, however, generate a dictionary with *fixed* string names, like this:

```
extension Array where Element:UIView {
    func dictionaryOfNames() -> [String:UIView] {
        var d = [String:UIView]()
        for (ix,v) in self.enumerated() {
            d["v\(ix+1)"] = v
        }
        return d
    }
}
```

That method starts with a list of views and simply makes up string names for them, of the form "v1", "v2", and so on, in order. Knowing the rule by which the string names are generated, you then use those string names in your visual format string.

Constraint Debugging

These are UIView methods aimed at helping to detect and analyze constraint issues (referred to in Chapter 1).

The built-in method `constraintsAffectingLayout(for:)` is helpful, but it doesn't tell you what view the constraints belong to, and it returns the constraints for just one axis (`.horizontal` or `.vertical`), so if you want to know all the constraints, you have to call it twice. This utility method *does* call it twice, and also lets you recurse up or

down the view hierarchy, printing each view as well as the constraints that affect it. If
`filtering` is `true`, constraints that don't directly involve the current view are eliminated from the output:

```
@objc extension UIView {
    func listConstraints(recursing:Bool = true, up:Bool = false,
        filtering:Bool = false) {
            let arr1 = self.constraintsAffectingLayout(for:.horizontal)
            let arr2 = self.constraintsAffectingLayout(for:.vertical)
            var arr = arr1 + arr2
            if filtering {
                arr = arr.filter {
                    $0.firstItem as? UIView == self ||
                        $0.secondItem as? UIView == self }
            }
            if !arr.isEmpty {
                print(self); arr.forEach { print($0) }; print()
            }
            guard recursing else { return }
            if !up { // down
                for sub in self.subviews {
                    sub.listConstraints(up:up, filtering:filtering)
                }
            } else { // up
                self.superview?.listConstraints(up:up, filtering:filtering)
            }
    }
}
```

This method calls `hasAmbiguousLayout` and recurses down the view hierarchy,
reporting in the console whether the target view or any of its subviews has ambiguous
layout. If `filtering` is `true`, only views with ambiguous layout are printed:

```
@objc extension UIView {
    func reportAmbiguity(filtering:Bool = false) {
        let has = self.hasAmbiguousLayout
        if has || !filtering {
            print(self, has)
        }
        for sub in self.subviews {
            sub.reportAmbiguity(filtering:filtering)
        }
    }
}
```

You can call those methods during development; be sure to remove the calls before
deployment. Another possibility is to call them while paused in the debugger:

```
(lldb) e self.view.reportAmbiguity(filtering:true)
```

(That's why the extensions are marked `@objc`; otherwise, the injected methods aren't
visible in the debugger.)

Another useful device, assuming you've been assigning an `identifier` to your constraints, is to have a way to retrieve a constraint by its identifier. This utility method recurses up the view hierarchy:

```
extension UIView {
    func constraint(withIdentifier id: String) -> NSLayoutConstraint? {
        return self.constraints.first { $0.identifier == id } ??
            self.superview?.constraint(withIdentifier: id)
    }
}
```

Named Views

Giving a view a string identifier helps with debugging and can even come in handy in code. One approach is to inject a `name` property into all views. That's easy to do because every view has a layer, and CALayer has a `name` property that generally isn't used for anything. While we're up, we may as well make this property settable from the nib editor:

```
extension UIView {
    @IBInspectable var name : String? {
        get { return self.layer.name }
        set { self.layer.name = newValue }
    }
}
```

Walk the Responder Chain

It is often useful to walk up the responder chain looking for a responder of a given type. Similarly, you might want to walk up the view hierarchy looking for a superview of a given type; that's actually the same thing, because the responder chain embraces the view hierarchy. Here's a UIResponder extension to let us do that:

```
extension UIResponder {
    func next<T:UIResponder>(ofType: T.Type) -> T? {
        let r = self.next
        if let r = r as? T ?? r?.next(ofType: T.self) {
            return r
        } else {
            return nil
        }
    }
}
```

Subviews of Given Class

One often needs to find all subviews that belong to a certain class. For example, I might need to find all the UIButtons within my view. Here's a utility function:

```
extension UIView {
    func subviews<T:UIView>(ofType WhatType:T.Type,
        recursing:Bool = true) -> [T] {
            var result = self.subviews.compactMap {$0 as? T}
            guard recursing else { return result }
            for sub in self.subviews {
                result.append(contentsOf: sub.subviews(ofType:WhatType))
            }
            return result
    }
}
```

Attach an Action Handler to a Control

New in iOS 14, an action handler for a control event can be attached directly to a UIControl. But the method provided for doing this, addAction(_:for:), takes a UIAction as the first parameter. The resulting syntax is clumsy; either the UIAction must be formed beforehand, or else it must be initialized inline, with the action handler function defined in the middle of the call.

The natural order, in Swift, is to define the function at the *end* of the call, using trailing closure syntax. Here's a UIControl extension allowing us to talk that way; the UIAction will usually have no title or other properties, so it is sufficient to pass just the handler function:

```
extension UIControl {
    func addAction(for event: UIControl.Event,
        handler: @escaping UIActionHandler) {
            self.addAction(UIAction(handler:handler), for:event)
    }
}
```

Inline Value Class Creation and Configuration

A recurring pattern in Cocoa is that a value class instance is created and configured beforehand for one-time use:

```
let para = NSMutableParagraphStyle()
para.headIndent = 10
para.firstLineHeadIndent = 10
para.tailIndent = -10
para.lineBreakMode = .byWordWrapping
para.alignment = .center
para.paragraphSpacing = 15
content.addAttribute(
    .paragraphStyle,
    value: para,
    range: NSMakeRange(0,1))
```

First we create the NSMutableParagraphStyle; then we set its properties; then we use it once; then we throw it away. That feels clunky, procedural, and wasteful. It would be clearer and more functional, as well as reflecting the natural order of thought, if the creation and configuration of para could happen inline, at the actual moment when we *need* this object, namely when we supply the value: argument. Here's a generic function that permits us to do that:

```
func lend<T> (_ closure: (T)->()) -> T where T:NSObject {
    let orig = T()
    closure(orig)
    return orig
}
```

Now we can express ourselves like this:

```
content.addAttribute(
    .paragraphStyle,
    value: lend { (para:NSMutableParagraphStyle) in
        para.headIndent = 10
        para.firstLineHeadIndent = 10
        para.tailIndent = -10
        para.lineBreakMode = .byWordWrapping
        para.alignment = .center
        para.paragraphSpacing = 15
    },
    range: NSMakeRange(0,1))
```

Downsize a UIImage

It's a waste of memory to hand a UIImageView an image larger than actually needed for display (Chapter 2). A frequent need in iOS programming, therefore, is to downscale a UIImage. Here's a general utility that does that:

```
extension UIImage {
    func scaledDown(into size:CGSize) -> UIImage {
        var (targetWidth, targetHeight) = (self.size.width, self.size.height)
        var (scaleW, scaleH) = (1 as CGFloat, 1 as CGFloat)
        if targetWidth > size.width {
            scaleW = size.width/targetWidth
        }
        if targetHeight > size.height {
            scaleH = size.height/targetHeight
        }
        let scale = min(scaleW,scaleH)
        targetWidth *= scale; targetHeight *= scale
        let sz = CGSize(targetWidth, targetHeight)
        return UIGraphicsImageRenderer(size:sz).image { _ in
            self.draw(in:CGRect(origin:.zero, size:sz))
        }
    }
}
```

How Asynchronous Works

Beginners sometimes don't quite understand what it means for their code to run *asynchronously*. But quite a bit of your code when you're programming iOS *is* asynchronous, and it's important to be clear on what this implies:

- An NSItemProvider hands you its data asynchronously.
- The result of requesting authorization arrives asynchronously.
- AV Foundation properties are set asynchronously, and videos are exported asynchronously.
- Most interactions with the photo library are asynchronous.
- Networking is asynchronous.

And so on.

Asynchronous Code Runs Out of Order

Asynchronous code runs at an indefinite time. More important, it runs *after* the surrounding code. The most important thing to understand about asynchronous code is that *the order in which your code appears is not the order in which it will run.*

Consider the following (and see Chapter 24):

```
func doSomeNetworking() {
    // ... prepare url ...
    let session = URLSession.shared ❶
    let task = session.downloadTask(with:url) { loc, resp, err in ❷
        // ... completion function body goes here ... ❹
    }
    task.resume() ❸
}
```

The method `downloadTask(with:completionHandler:)` calls its completion function asynchronously. It calls it when the networking finishes — and networking takes time. So the order in which the chunks of code run is the numerical order of the numbered lines:

❶ The code before the call.

❷ The call itself.

❸ The code after the call, including the return from the surrounding function `doSomeNetworking`. Your code has now come to a complete stop!

❹ The code inside the completion function. This is the asynchronous code. It runs *later* — possibly much later, and certainly after the surrounding function `doSome-Networking` has returned.

Asynchronous Code Cannot Return a Value

Asynchronous means that your code runs out of order. And that, in turn, means that the surrounding function terminates before the asynchronous code even runs. Therefore, the surrounding function *cannot return a value* from the asynchronous code.

Beginners sometimes try to write this sort thing:

```
func doSomeNetworking() -> UIImage? { // vain attempt to return an image
    // ... prepare url ...
    var image : UIImage? = nil
    let session = URLSession.shared
    let task = session.downloadTask(with:url) { loc, resp, err in
        if let loc = loc, let d = try? Data(contentsOf:loc) {
            let im = UIImage(data:d)
            image = im // too late!
        }
    }
    task.resume()
    return image // can only be nil!
}
```

The author of that code hopes that the image will be downloaded and returned from the surrounding function `doSomeNetworking`. But that can never work, because we return the image (`return image`) *before* the download task ever has a chance to set its value (`image = im`). Therefore, the returned UIImage will always be `nil`.

Beginners might then think: So maybe I can wait until my asynchronous code has finished. Maybe you can, but that's usually the wrong thing to do. Instead, when you obtain a value in some asynchronous code and you want to do something with that value, do it *in* the asynchronous code.

Suppose our goal is to update the interface with the downloaded image. Then we update the interface in the asynchronous code, after the image has been downloaded (remembering, of course, to step out to the main thread to touch the interface, as I explained in Chapter 25):

```
func doSomeNetworking() {
    // ... prepare url ...
    let session = URLSession.shared
    let task = session.downloadTask(with:url) { loc, resp, err in
        if let loc = loc, let d = try? Data(contentsOf:loc) {
            let im = UIImage(data:d)
            DispatchQueue.main.async {
                self.iv.image = im // update the interface _here_
            }
        }
    }
    task.resume()
}
```

Completion Handlers

Now let's say you really do want, somehow, to hand back a value from the asynchronous code to whoever called the surrounding function in the first place, leaving it up to the caller what to do with it. We've already established that you can't return the value. But you can *call back* to whoever called the surrounding function in order to hand them the value.

A typical architecture is that you allow the caller to hand you a *completion function* as one of the parameters of your method (usually the last parameter). Inside your asynchronous code, you then call the caller's completion function, like this:

```
func doSomeNetworking(callBackWithImage: @escaping (UIImage?) -> ()) {
    let s = "https://www.apeth.net/matt/images/phoenixnewest.jpg"
    let url = URL(string:s)!
    let session = URLSession.shared
    let task = session.downloadTask(with:url) { loc, resp, err in
        if let loc = loc, let d = try? Data(contentsOf:loc) {
            let im = UIImage(data:d)
            callBackWithImage(im) // call the caller's completion function
        }
    }
    task.resume()
}
```

Let's look at that example from the caller's point of view. The caller of doSome-Networking(callBackWithImage:) passes in a completion function that does whatever the caller ultimately wants done. Here, once again, our goal is to update the interface with the downloaded image:

```
doSomeNetworking { im in
    // this is the completion function!
    DispatchQueue.main.async {
        self.iv.image = im
    }
}
```

That works perfectly. But there is one further thing to be aware of. That completion function, too, is asynchronous! The caller here doesn't know when or whether this completion function will be called back, and perhaps not even what thread it will be called on. The caller knows only this: when and if the completion function is called back, the image will arrive as its parameter — and now the caller can dispose of it as desired.

Use of a completion handler, then, *propagates asynchronousness*. That is the pattern used throughout Cocoa. You should understand this pattern, become comfortable with it, and implement it in your own code.

Index

current graphics context, 97

D

dark mode (see mode, light or dark)
data
    caching, 414, 1048
    detectors, 701
    downloading, 1109, 1112
    lazy loading, 413
    memory-mapped, 415
    persistent, 1047
    shared, 1141
    table view, 472
date
    calculation, 967
    constructing, 965
    picker, 759
DateComponents, 761, 965, 967
Debug menu of Simulator, 159, 450
debugger, view, 63, 75
Decodable (see Codable)
decoding, 1053
deep links, 1124
delay, 1191
delayed performance, 1154
delegation, 335
detail (see master–detail interface)
detail view controller, 600
device
    attitude, 1032
    heading, 1024, 1035
    location, 997, 1014
    motion, 1028
    shake to undo, 1027, 1173
    user acceleration, 1031
dialogs, modal (see modal dialogs)
dictionaryOfNames, 1191
diffable data source, 516, 559
    changing, 521
    Core Data, 1094
    populating, 518
    pros and cons, 522
    snapshot, 517
        section, 564
    subclassing, 520
dimming background views, 370
dimming tint color, 793
directions, 1004
directories (see folders)

dismissing a view controller, 326
    dragging, 330
    popover, 595
dispatch table, 260, 750
DispatchGroup, 1155
DispatchQueue, 1151
documents (see files)
Documents folder, 1048
double tap vs. single tap, 257, 267
downloading, 1106, 1108
    background, 1121
drag and drop, 618-637
    animation, 629
    flocking, 630
    iPhone, 636
    item provider, 622
    local, 636
    preview, 627
    spring loading, 635
    table views, 630
    text field, 691
    window creation, 647
drag to dismiss, 330
drawing, 81-131
    caching, 134
    efficiently, 15, 159, 449
    hit-testing, 278
    image, 96, 100
    path, 117
    PDF, 1098
    rotated, 126
    text, 672
        Text Kit, 713
    view, 98, 113
    when actually happens, 164, 197
dynamic, 223
    color, 13, 29, 87, 123
    type, 651
dynamics, UIKit, 232, 584

E

EKAlarm, 965
EKCalendarChooser, 972
EKEventEditViewController, 972
EKEventViewController, 971
EKRecurrenceRule, 966
EKReminder, 967
ellipsis, 675, 678
embed segue, 401

About the Author

Matt Neuburg started programming computers in 1968, when he was 14 years old, as a member of a literally underground high school club that met once a week to do timesharing on a bank of PDP-10s by way of primitive teletype machines. He also occasionally used Princeton University's IBM-360/67, but gave it up in frustration when one day he dropped his punch cards. He majored in Greek at Swarthmore College, and received his PhD from Cornell University in 1981, writing his doctoral dissertation (about Aeschylus) on a mainframe. He proceeded to teach Classical languages, literature, and culture at many well-known institutions of higher learning, most of which now disavow knowledge of his existence, and to publish numerous scholarly articles unlikely to interest anyone. Meanwhile he obtained an Apple IIc and became hopelessly hooked on computers again, migrating to a Macintosh in 1990. He wrote some educational and utility freeware, became an early regular contributor to the online journal *TidBITS*, and in 1995 left academe to edit *MacTech* magazine. In August 1996 he became a freelancer, which means he has been looking for work ever since. He is the author of *Frontier: The Definitive Guide*, *REALbasic: The Definitive Guide*, and *AppleScript: The Definitive Guide*.

Colophon

The animal on the cover of *Programming iOS 14* is a kingbird, one of the 13 species of North American songbirds making up the genus *Tyrannus*. A group of kingbirds is called a "coronation," a "court," or a "tyranny."

Kingbirds eat insects, which they often catch in flight, swooping from a perch to grab the insect midair. They may also supplement their diets with berries and fruits. They have long, pointed wings, and males perform elaborate aerial courtship displays.

Both the genus name (meaning "tyrant" or "despot") and the common name ("kingbird") refer to these birds' aggressive defense of their territories, breeding areas, and mates. They have been documented attacking red-tailed hawks (which are more than 20 times their size), knocking bluejays out of trees, and driving away crows and ravens. (For its habit of standing up to much larger birds, the gray kingbird has been adopted as a Puerto Rican nationalist symbol.)

"Kingbird" most often refers to the Eastern kingbird (*T. tyrannus*), an average-size kingbird (7.5–9 inches long, wingspan 13–15 inches) found all across North America. This common and widespread bird has a dark head and back, with a white throat, chest, and belly. Its red crown patch is rarely seen. Its high-pitched, buzzing, stuttering sounds have been described as resembling "sparks jumping between wires" or an electric fence.